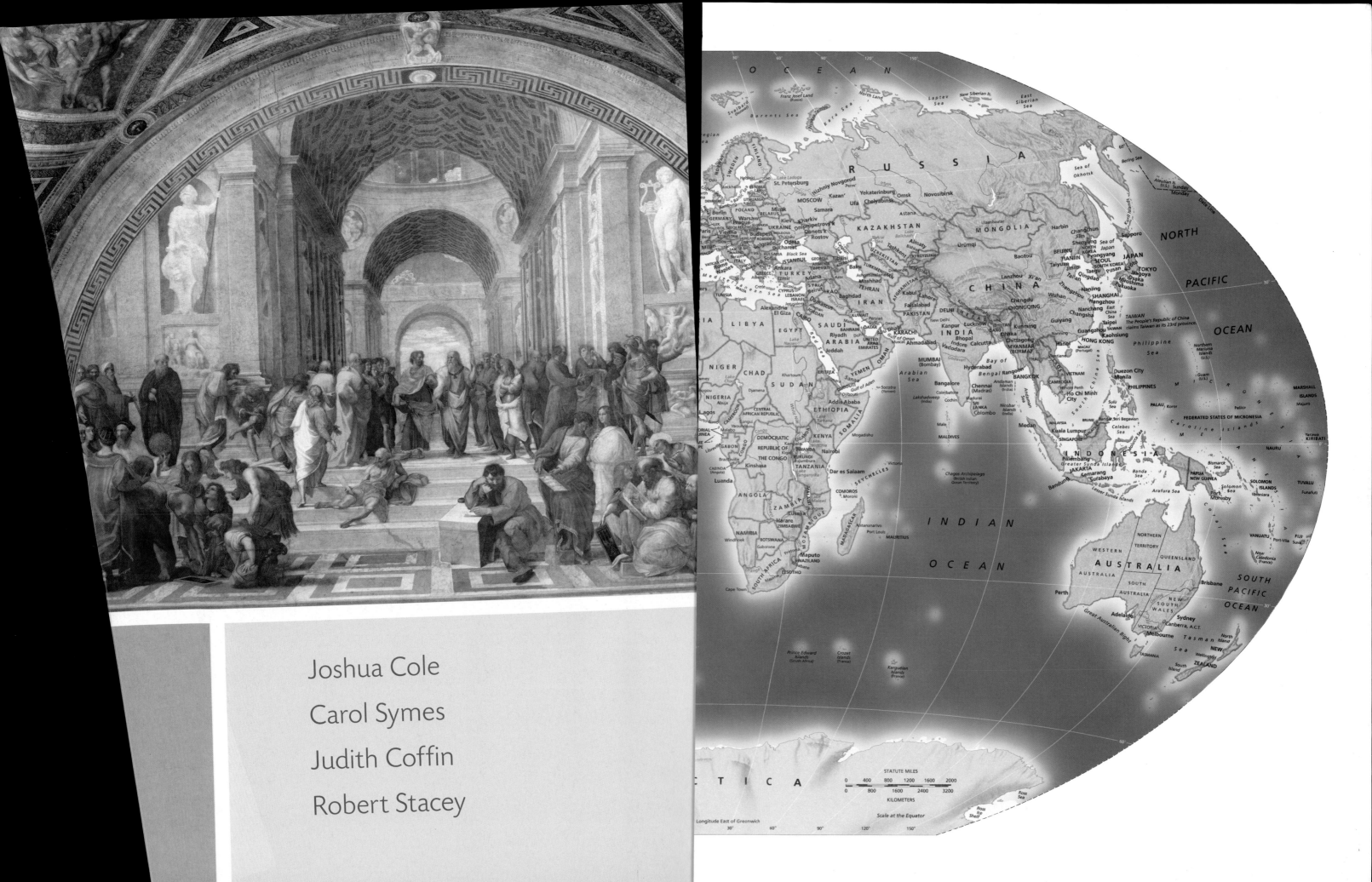

Joshua Cole

Carol Symes

Judith Coffin

Robert Stacey

This registration code provides access to

documents and other sources available at the

Western Civilizations, Brief Third Edition StudySpace site:

wwnorton.com/studyspace

SSAN-IFMU

Western Civilizations

*Their History &
Their Culture*

Brief Third Edition

Western Civilizations

Their History & Their Culture

BRIEF THIRD EDITION

W. W. NORTON & COMPANY ■ NEW YORK ■ LONDON

W. W. Norton & Company has been independent since its founding in 1923, when William Warder Norton and Mary D. Herter Norton first published lectures delivered at the People's Institute, the adult education division of New York City's Cooper Union. The firm soon expanded its program beyond the Institute, publishing books by celebrated academics from America and abroad. By midcentury, the two major pillars of Norton's publishing program—trade books and college texts—were firmly established. In the 1950s, the Norton family transferred control of the company to its employees, and today—with a staff of four hundred and a comparable number of trade, college, and professional titles published each year—W. W. Norton & Company stands as the largest and oldest publishing house owned wholly by its employees.

Editor: Jon Durbin
Editorial assistants: Jason Spears, Justin Cahill
Project editor: Kathleen Feighery
Copyeditor: Michael Fleming
E-media editor: Steve Hoge
Ancillary editor: Lorraine Klimowich
Photo editor: Junenoire Mitchell
Photo research: Donna Ranieri
Senior production manager, College: Benjamin Reynolds
Design director: Rubina Yeh
Book designer: Judith Abbate / Abbate Design
Composition: TexTech, Inc.—Brattleboro, VT
Cartographer: Mapping Specialists—Madison, WI
Manufacturing: R. R. Donnelley & Sons—Jefferson City, MO

Library of Congress Cataloging-in-Publication Data

Western civilizations : their history & their culture / Joshua Cole ... [et al.]. — 3rd brief ed.
    p. cm.
Rev. ed. of: Western civilizations : their history & their culture / Judith G. Coffin, Robert C. Stacey. 2nd brief ed. New York
W. W. Norton & Co., c2009.
Includes bibliographical references and index.

ISBN 978-0-393-93487-8 (pbk.)
  1. Civilization, Western—Textbooks. 2. Europe—Civilization—Textbooks. I. Cole, Joshua, 1961– II. Coffin, Judith G., 1952–
Western civilizations.
  CB245.W4845 2012
  909'.09821—dc23

                                                                   2011026190

W. W. Norton & Company, Inc., 500 Fifth Avenue, New York, N. Y. 10110
wwnorton.com

W. W. Norton & Company Ltd., Castle House, 75/76 Wells Street, London W1T 3QT

2 3 4 5 6 7 8 9 0

To our families:

Kate Tremel, Lucas and Ruby Cole
Tom, Erin, and Connor Wilson
Willy, Zoe, and Aaron Forbath
Robin, Will, and Anna Stacey

with love and gratitude for their support.
And to all our students, who have also been
our teachers.

About the Authors

JOSHUA COLE (Ph.D. University of California, Berkeley) is Associate Professor of History at the University of Michigan at Ann Arbor. His publications include work on gender and the history of the population sciences, colonial violence, and the politics of memory in 19th and 20th century France, Germany, and Algeria. His first book was *The Power of Large Numbers: Population, Politics and Gender in Nineteenth-Century France* (Ithaca, NY: Cornell University Press, 2000).

CAROL SYMES (Ph.D. Harvard University) is Associate Professor of history and Director of Undergraduate Studies in the history department at the University of Illinois, Urbana-Champaign, where she has won the top teaching award in the College of Liberal Arts and Sciences. Her main areas of study include medieval Europe, the history of information media and communication technologies, and the history of theatre. Her first book was *A Common Stage: Theater and Public Life in Medieval Arras* (Ithaca: Cornell University Press, 2007).

JUDITH COFFIN (Ph.D. Yale University) is an associate professor at the University of Texas, Austin, where she won University of Texas President's Associates' Award for Teaching Excellence. Previously, she taught at Harvard University and the University of California, Riverside. Her research interests are the social and cultural history of gender, mass culture, slavery, race relations, and colonialism. She is the author of *The Politics of Women's Work: The Paris Garment Trades, 1750–1915.*

ROBERT STACEY (Ph.D. Yale University) is professor of history, Dean of the Humanities, and a member of the Jewish Studies faculty at the University of Washington, Seattle. A long-time teacher of Western civilization and medieval European history, he has received Distinguished Teaching Awards from both the University of Washington and Yale University, where he taught from 1984 to 1988. He has authored and coauthored four books, including a textbook, *The Making of England to 1399.* He holds an M.A. from Oxford University and a Ph.D. from Yale.

Brief Contents

Contents

Chapter 27 ■ THE COLD WAR WORLD: GLOBAL POLITICS, ECONOMIC RECOVERY, AND CULTURAL CHANGE   649

Chapter 28 ■ RED FLAGS AND VELVET REVOLUTIONS: THE END OF THE COLD WAR, 1960s–1990s   673

Chapter 29 ■ A WORLD WITHOUT WALLS: GLOBALIZATION AND THE WEST   697

Maps

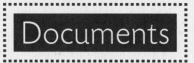

Documents

The motivating principle for the third brief edition of *Western Civilizations* is a relatively simple idea: that history students will be inspired to engage more effectively with the past if they are given a flexible set of tools to use as they approach their readings. *Western Civilizations* has always been known for its clear and vigorous account of Europe's past, and previous editions have been noteworthy for their selection of primary sources and visual images. As the authors of this new brief edition, we have made a special effort to bring greater unity to the pedagogical elements that accompany each chapter, so that students will be able to work more productively with the textbook in mastering this rich history. This pedagogical structure is designed to empower the students to analyze and interpret the historical evidence on their own, and thus to become participants in the work of history. We have also worked hard to create a coherent narrative, since this is one of the major shortcomings of all brief editions. Here we used our new pedagogical tools as guides, particularly the Story Lines, Chronologies, and Core Objectives, to ensure that the chapter themes and core content remained fully present. Moreover, we cut the narrative by 25 percent, rather than the more traditional 40 percent, which again provides a more coherent reading experience.

Of course, students can only find a textbook useful if they read it, and they can only read it if they purchase it. As the demand for concise, affordable texts grows with each passing year, publishers have responded by offering either bare-bones, brief editions or "value" editions of their textbooks—typically smaller-format, black-and-white editions with far fewer and smaller pictures and maps. Both types are far from being highly valuable teaching tools. Fortunately, W. W. Norton, our publisher, decided to take a different approach. Our new edition is full size and full color, includes innovative pedagogical tools, provides a rich support package, and is priced competitively with the most inexpensive brief books and value editions on the market. We hope that you will see this as the best solution for your course and students when you are considering texts.

Undergraduates today have more choices in introductory history courses than they did only twenty or thirty years ago. As public awareness of the importance of global connections grew in the late twentieth century, many colleges and universities enriched their programs by adding courses in world history as well as introductory surveys in Latin American, African, and Asian history alongside the traditional offerings in the history of the United States and Europe. These developments can only be seen as enormously positive, but they do not in any way diminish the need for a broad-based history of European society and culture such as that represented in *Western Civilizations*. The wide chronological scope of this work offers an unusual opportunity to trace the development of central human themes—population movements, economic development, politics and state-building, changing religious beliefs, and the role of the arts and technology—in a dynamic and complex part of the world whose cultural diversity has been constantly invigorated and renewed by its interactions with peoples living in other places. As in previous editions, we have attempted to balance the coverage of political, social, economic, and cultural phenomena, and the chapters also include extensive coverage of material culture, daily life, gender, sexuality, art, and technology. And following the path laid out by the book's previous authors, Judith Coffin and Robert Stacey, we have insisted that the history of European peoples can be best understood through their interactions with people in other parts of the world. The portrait of European society that emerges from this text is thus both rich and dynamic, attentive to the latest developments in historical scholarship and fully aware of the ways that the teaching of European history has changed in the past decades.

Given the general consensus about the importance of seeing human history in its broadest—and if possible, global—context, Europeanists who teach the histories of ancient, medieval, and modern societies have been mindful of the need to rethink the ways that this history should be taught. For good reasons, few historians at the dawn of the twenty-first century uphold a monolithic vision of a single and enduring "Western civilization" whose inevitable march through history can be traced chapter by chapter through time. This idea, strongly associated with the curriculum of early twentieth-century American colleges and universities, no longer conforms to what we know about the human past. Neither the "West" nor "Europe" can be seen as distinct, unified entities in space or time; the meanings attributed to these geographical expressions have changed in significant ways. Most historians now agree that a linear notion of "civilization" persisting over the centuries was made coherent only by leaving out the intense conflicts, extraordinary ruptures, and dynamic processes of change at the heart of the societies that are the subject of this book. Smoothing out the rough edges of the past does students no favors—even an introductory text such as this one should present the past as it appears to the historians who study it—that is, as an ever-changing panorama of human effort and creation, filled with possibility, but also fraught with discord, uncertainty, accident, and tragedy.

New Pedagogical Features

Our goals as the new authors of this dynamic text are to provide a book that students will read, that reinforces your course objectives, that helps your students master core content, and that provides tools for your students to use in thinking critically about our human past. In order to achieve these primary goals, the traditional strengths of the book have been augmented by several exciting new features. The most revolutionary is the new pedagogical framework that supports each chapter. Many students in introductory survey courses find the sheer quantity of information to be a challenge, and so we have created these new pedagogical features to help them approach their reading in a more systematic way. At the outset of every chapter, a **Before You Read This Chapter** box offers three preliminary windows onto the material to be covered: *Story Lines*, *Chronology*, and *Core Objectives*. The *Story Lines* allow the student to become familiar with the primary narrative threads that tie the chapter's elements together, and the *Chronology* grounds these *Story Lines* in the period under study. The *Core Objectives* provide a checklist to ensure that the student is aware of the primary teaching points in the chapter. The student is then reminded of these teaching points on completing the chapter, in the **After You Read This Chapter** section, which prompts the student to revisit the chapter in three ways. The

first, *Reviewing the Core Objectives*, asks the reader to reconsider core objectives by answering a pointed question about each one. The second, *People, Ideas, and Events in Context*, summarizes some of the particulars that students should retain from their reading, through questions that allow them to relate individual terms to the major objectives and story lines. Finally, questions about long-term *Consequences* allow for more open-ended reflection on the significance of the chapter's material, drawing students' attention to issues that connect the chapter to previous chapters and giving them insight into what comes next. As a package, the pedagogical features at the beginning and end of each chapter work together to empower the student, by breaking down the process of reading and learning into manageable tasks.

A second package of pedagogical features is designed to help students think about history and its underlying issues more critically. For us as teachers, good pedagogy and critical thinking begin with good narrative writing. Each chapter starts with an opening vignette that showcases a particular person or event representative of the era as a whole. Within each chapter, an expanded program of illustrations and maps has been enhanced by the addition of **Guiding Questions** that challenge the reader to explore the historical contexts and significance of the maps and illustrations in a more critical way. The historical value of images, artifacts, and material culture is further emphasized in a new feature, **Interpreting Visual Evidence**. We anticipate that this section will provide discussion leaders with a provocative departure point for conversations about the key issues raised by visual sources, which students often find more approachable than texts. Once this conversation has begun, students will further be able to develop the tools they need to read the primary texts. In this new edition, the selection of primary source texts, **Analyzing Primary Sources**, has been carefully revised and many new questions have been added to frame the readings. The dynamism and diversity of Western civilizations is also illuminated through a look at **Competing Viewpoints** in each chapter, in which specific debates are presented through paired primary source texts. Finally, the bibliographical **For Further Reading** section has been edited and brought up to date and is now located at the end of the book.

REVISED CHAPTER TOURS

There are significant changes to each chapter of the book, as well. In Chapter 1, the challenges of locating and interpreting historical evidence drawn from nontextual sources (archaeological, environmental, anthropological, mythic) is a special focus. Chapter 2 further underscores the degree to which recent archeological discoveries and new historical techniques have revolutionized our understanding of ancient history, and have also corroborated ancient peoples' own understandings of their past. Chapter 3 offers expanded coverage of the diverse polities that emerged in ancient Greece, and of Athens' closely related political, documentary, artistic, and intellectual achievements. Chapter 4's exploration of the Hellenistic world is more wide-ranging than before, and it includes an entirely new discussion of the scientific revolution powered by this first cosmopolitan civilization.

With Chapter 5, the unique values and institutions of the Roman Republic are the focus of a new segment, while the account of the Republic's expansion and transformation under the Principate has been sharpened and clarified. Chapter 6's treatment of early Christianity has been deepened and expanded, and more attention has been paid to the fundamental ways in which this fledgling religion itself transformed as a result of its changing status within the Roman Empire. This chapter also draws on cutting-edge scholarship that has significantly revised our understanding of the so-called "Crisis of the Third Century" and the question of Rome's fragmentation and "fall."

Beginning with this chapter, the chronological structure of Volume 1 has been adjusted in order to make the periodization of the Middle Ages more conceptually manageable and the material easier to teach. Chapter 6 therefore ends with the reign of Theodoric in the West and the consolidation of Christian and pagan cultures in the fifth century. Chapter 7 now begins with the reign of Justinian; and while it still examines Rome's three distinctive successor civilizations, it no longer attempts to encapsulate all of Byzantine and Islamic history down to the fifteenth century. Instead, these interlocking histories and that of northwestern Europe are carried forward to about 950 C.E. in this chapter, and continue to intersect in subsequent chapters. And whereas Chapters 8 and 9 used to cover the period 1000–1300 from two different angles (political, social, and economic *versus* religious and intellectual), the new structure interweaves these forces, with Chapter 8 covering the period 950–1100 and Chapter 9 extending from 1100 to 1300.

Chapters 10–12 all assess the transition from medieval to nearly modern. Chapter 10 looks at Europe in the years 1300 to 1500, the centuries of "Crisis, Unrest, and Opportunity." Chapter 11 explores the simultaneous expansion of Europe through "Commerce, Conquest, and Colonization" between 1300 and 1600. And Chapter 12 examines the "Renaissance Ideals and Realities" that stemmed from, and contributed to, these same events. All three chapters have been revised and expanded for this edition.

Thereafter, Chapter 13 characterizes the sixteenth century as "The Age of Dissent and Division," while Chapter 14 surveys the religious, political, and military struggles that arose in the era of confessional difference, contested sovereignty, and military escalation between 1540 and 1660.

Chapters 15–17 cover the history of early modern Europe between the sixteenth and eighteenth centuries, a time that saw powerful absolutist regimes emerge on the continent; the establishment of wealthy European trading empires in Asia, Africa, and the Americas; and successive periods of intense intellectual and philosophical discussion during the Scientific Revolution and the Enlightenment. Chapter 15 has been reorganized to better relate the emergence of absolutist regimes on the continent with the alternatives to absolutism that developed in England, and to clarify the differences between the colonial empires of France, Britain, and Spain. Chapter 16 emphasizes the many facets of scientific inquiry during the Scientific Revolution and introduces a new section on women scientists. Meanwhile, Chapter 17 adds new emphasis to the ways that Enlightenment figures dealt with cultures and peoples in the parts of the world that Europeans confronted in building their empires.

Chapters 18–19 cover the political and economic revolutions of the late eighteenth and early nineteenth centuries. Chapter 18 covers the French Revolution and the Napoleonic empires in depth, while also drawing attention to the way that these central episodes were rooted in a larger pattern of revolutionary political change that engulfed the Atlantic world. Chapter 19 emphasizes both the economic growth and the technological innovations that were a part of the Industrial Revolution, while also exploring the social and cultural consequences of industrialization for men and women in Europe's new industrial societies. The *Interpreting Visual Evidence* box in Chapter 19 allows students to explore the ways that industrialization created new perceptions of the global economy in Europe, changing the way people thought of their place in the world.

Chapters 20–21 explore the successive struggles between conservative reaction and revolutionaries in Europe, as the revolutionary forces of nationalism unleashed by the French Revolution redrew the map of Europe and threatened the dynastic regimes that had ruled for centuries. In all of these chapters, new images have been added to focus students' attention on the many ways that "the people" were represented by liberals, conservatives, and revolutionaries, and the consequences of these contesting representations.

Chapter 22 takes on the history of nineteenth-century colonialism, exploring both its political and economic origins and its consequences for the peoples of Africa and Asia. The chapter gives new emphasis to the significance of colonial conquest for European culture, as colonial power became increasingly associated with national greatness, both in conservative monarchies and in more democratic regimes. Meanwhile, Chapter 23 brings the narrative back to the heart of Europe, covering the long-term consequences of industrialization and the consolidation of a conservative form of nationalism in many European nations even as the electorate was being expanded. The chapter emphasizes the varied nature of the new forms of political dissent, from the feminists who claimed the right to vote to the newly organized socialist movements that proved so enduring in many European countries.

Chapters 24 and 25 bring new vividness to the history of the First World War and the intense conflicts of the interwar period, while Chapter 26 uses the history of the Second World War as a hinge for understanding European and global developments in the second half of the twentieth century. The *Interpreting Visual Evidence* box in Chapter 24 allows for a special focus on the role of propaganda among the belligerent nations in 1914–1918, and the chapter's section on the diplomatic crisis that preceded the First World War has been streamlined to allow students to more easily comprehend the essential issues at the heart of the conflict. In Chapter 25 the *Interpreting Visual Evidence* box continues to explore the theme touched on in earlier chapters, political representations of "the people," this time in the context of fascist spectacles in Germany and Italy in the 1930s. These visual sources help students to understand the vulnerability of Europe's democratic regimes during these years as they faced the dual assault from fascists on the right and Bolsheviks on the left.

Chapters 27–29 bring the volumes to a close in a thorough exploration of the Cold War, decolonization, the collapse of the Soviet Union and the Eastern Bloc in 1989–1991, and the roots of the multifaceted global conflicts that beset the world in the first decade of the twenty-first century. Chapter 27 juxtaposes the Cold War with decolonization, showing how this combination sharply diminished the ability of European nations to control events in the international arena, even as they succeeded in rebuilding their economies at home. Chapter 28 explores the vibrancy of European culture in the crucial period of the 1960s to the early 1990s, bringing new attention to the significance of 1989 as a turning point in European history. Finally, a completely new set of primary documents and questions accompanies Chapter 29, which covers the benefits and tensions of a a newly globalized world. The chapter's conclusion now covers the financial crisis of 2008 and the subsequent election of Barack Obama, as well as recent debates within Islam about Muslims living as minorities in non-Muslim nations.

A Few Words of Thanks

Our first year as members of *Western Civilizations*' authorial team has been a challenging and rewarding one. We are honored to be the partners of two historians whose work we have long admired, and who have been formative influences on us in our careers as students, scholars, and teachers of history. We would also like to thank a number of our colleagues around the country who provided in-depth critiques of large sections of the book: Paul Freedman (Yale University), Sheryl Kroen (University of Florida), Michael Kulikowski (Pennsylvania State University), Harry Liebersohn (University of Illinois, Urbana-Champaign), and Helmut Smith (Vanderbilt University). We are very grateful for the expert assistance and support of the Norton team, especially that of our editor, Jon Durbin. Kate Feighery, our fabulous project editor, has driven the book beautifully through the manuscript process. Jason Spears and Justin Cahill have skillfully dealt with a myriad of issues pertaining to the preparation of the text. Junenoire Mitchell and Donna Ranieri did an excellent job finding many of the exact images we specified. Lorraine Klimowich did an expert job developing the print ancillaries. Ben Reynolds has efficiently marched us through the production process. Steve Hoge has done a great job developing the book's fantastic emedia, particularly the new Author Insight Podcasts and Euro History Tours powered by Google Earth. Michael Fleming and Bob Byrne were terrific in skillfully guiding the manuscript through the copyediting and proofreading stages. Finally, we want to thank Tamara McNeill for spearheading the marketing campaign for the new edition. We are also indebted to the numerous expert readers who commented on various chapters and who thereby strengthened the book as a whole. We are thankful to our families, for their patience and advice, and to our students, whose questions and comments over the years have been essential to the framing of this book. And we extend a special thanks to, and hope to hear from, all the teachers and students we may never meet—their engagement with this book will frame new understandings of our shared past and its bearing on our future.

NEW EDITION REVIEWERS

Donna Allen, Glendale Community College
Marjon Ames, Appalachian State University
Eirlys Barker, Thomas Nelson Community College
Matthew Barlow, John Abbott College
Ken Bartlett, University of Toronto

Volker Benkert, Arizona State University
Dean Bennett, Schenectady City Community College
Patrick Brennan, Gulf Coast Community College
Neil Brooks, Community College of Baltimore County, Essex
James Brophy, University of Delaware
Kevin Caldwell, Blue Ridge Community College
Keith Chu, Bergen Community College
Alex D'erizans, Borough of Manhattan Community College, CUNY
Michael Dusik, College of DuPage
Hilary Earl, Nipissing University
Karin Enloe, Arizona State University
Kirk Ford, Mississippi College
Michael Gattis, Gulf Coast Community College
David M. Gallo, College of Mount Saint Vincent
Jamie Gruring, Arizona State University
Tim Hack, Salem Community College
Bernard Hagerty, University of Pittsburgh
Tony Heideman, Front Range Community College
Paul T. Hietter, Mesa Community College
Paul Hughes, Sussex County Community College
Lacey Hunter, Caldwell College
Kyle Irvin, Jefferson State Community College
Lloyd Johnson, Campbell University
Llana Krug, York College of Pennsylvania
Guy Lalande, St. Francis Xavier University
Chris Laney, Berkshire Community College
Charles Levine, Mesa Community College
Heidi MacDonald, University of Lethbridge
Steven Marks, Clemson University
James Martin, Campbell University
Michael Mckeown, Daytona State University
David Mock, Tallahassee Community College
Dan Puckett, Troy State University
Dan Robinson, Troy State University
Craig Saucier, Southeastern Louisiana University
Aletia Seaborn, Southern Union State College
Nicholas Steneck, Florida Southern College
Victoria Thompson, Arizona State University
Donna Trembinski, St. Francis Xavier University
Pamela West, Jefferson State Community College
Scott White, Scottsdale Community College
Aaron Wilson, Creighton University
Julianna Wilson, Pima Community College

PREVIOUS EDITION REVIEWERS

Eric Ash, Wayne State University
Sacha Auerbach, Virginia Commonwealth University
Ken Bartlett, University of Toronto

Benita Blessing, Ohio University
Chuck Boening, Shelton State Community College
John Bohstedt, University of Tennessee, Knoxville
Dan Brown, Moorpark College
Kevin Caldwell, Blue Ridge Community College
Jodi Campbell, Texas Christian University
Annette Chamberlain, Virginia Western Community College
Jason Coy, College of Charleston
Benjamin Ehlers, University of Georgia
Maryann Farkas, Dawson College
Gloria Fitzgibbon, Wake Forest University
Tina Gaddis, Onondaga Community College
Alex Garman, Eastern New Mexico State University
Norman Goda, Ohio University
Andrew Goldman, Gonzaga University
Robert Grasso, Monmouth University
Sylvia Gray, Portland Community College
Susan Grayzel, University of Mississippi
Timothy Hack, University of Delaware
Hazel Hahn, Seattle University
Derek Hastings, Oakland University
Dawn Hayes, Montclair State University
John Houston, Fordham University
Michael Hughes, Wake Forest University
Bruce Hunt, University of Texas, Austin
Ahmed Ibrahim, Southwest Missouri State University
Kevin James, University of Guelph
Lars Jones, Florida Institute of Technology
John Kearney, Cy Fair Community College
Roman Laba, Hudson Valley Community College
Elizabeth Lehfeldt, Cleveland State University
Thomas Maulucci, State University of New York, Fredonia
Amy McCandless, College of Charleston
John McGrath, Boston University
Nicholas Murray, Adirondack College
Charles Odahl, Boise State University
Bill Olejniczak, College of Charleston
Jeffrey Plaks, University of Central Oklahoma
Peter Pozesky, College of Wooster
Rebecca Schloss, Texas A&M University
James Shedel, Georgetown University
Rebecca Spang, Indiana University, Bloomington
Patrick Speelman, College of Charleston
Robert Taylor, Florida Institute of Technology
Paul Teverow, Missouri Southern State University
James Vanstone, John Abbott College
Kirk Willis, University of Georgia
Ian Worthington, University of Missouri, Columbia

Western Civilizations

*Their History &
Their Culture*

Brief Third Edition

Before You Read This Chapter

Early Civilizations

There was a time, the story goes, when all the peoples of the earth shared a common language and could accomplish great things. They developed new technologies, made bricks, and aspired to build a fortified city with a tower reaching to the sky. But their god was troubled by this, so he destroyed their civilization by making it hard for them to understand one another's speech.

We know this as the legend of Babel. It's a story that probably circulated among peoples of the ancient world for thousands of years before it became part of the Hebrew book we call by its Greek name, Genesis, "the beginning." This story lets us glimpse some of the conditions in which the first civilizations arose, and it also reminds us of the ruptures that make studying them hard. We no longer speak the same languages as those ancient peoples, just as we no longer have direct access to their experiences or their beliefs.

Such foundational stories are usually called *myths*, but they are really an early form of history. For the people who told them, these stories helped to make sense of the present by explaining the past. The fate of Babel conveyed a crucial message: human

3

beings are powerful when they share a common goal, and what enables human interaction is civilization. To the peoples of the ancient world, the characteristic benefits of civilization—stability and safety, government, art, literature, science—were always products of city life. The very word "civilization" derives from the Latin word *civis*, "city." Cities, however, became possible only as a result of innovations that began around the end of the last Ice Age, about 13,000 years ago, and that came to fruition in Mesopotamia 8,000 years later. The history of civilization is therefore a short one. Within the study of humanity, which reaches back to the genus *Homo* in Africa, some 1.7 million years ago, it is merely a blip on the radar screen. Even within the history of *Homo sapiens sapiens*, the species to which we belong and which evolved about 50,000 years ago, civilization is a very recent development.

The study of early civilizations is both fascinating and challenging. Historians still do not understand why the first cities should have developed in the region between the Tigris and the Euphrates rivers, in what is now Iraq. Once developed, however, the basic patterns of urban life quickly spread to other parts of the Near East, both by imitation and by conquest. A network of trading connections linked these early cities, but intense competition for resources made alliances among them fragile. Then, around the middle of the second millennium B.C.E. (that is, "Before the Common Era," equivalent to the Christian dating system B.C., "Before Christ"), emerging powers began to shape these fiercely independent cities into empires. How this happened—and how we know that it happened—is the subject of Chapter 1.

BEFORE CIVILIZATION

More than 9,000 years ago, a town began to develop at Çatalhöyük (*sha-tal-HOO-yuk*) in what is now south-central Turkey. Over the next 2,000 years, it grew to cover an area of thirty-three acres, within which some 8,000 inhabitants lived in more than 2,000 separate houses. If this seems small, consider that Çatalhöyük's population density was actually twice that of today's most populous city, Mumbai (India). It was so tightly packed that there were hardly any streets. Instead, each house was built immediately next to its neighbor, and generally on top of a previous house.

The people of Çatalhöyük developed a highly organized and advanced society. They wove wool cloth; they made kiln-fired pottery; they painted elaborate hunting scenes on the plaster-covered walls of their houses; they made weapons and tools from razor-sharp obsidian imported from the nearby Cappadocian mountains. They honored their ancestors with religious rites and buried their dead beneath the floors of their houses. Settled agriculturalists, they grew grains, peas, and lentils and tended herds of domesticated sheep and goats. But they also hunted and gathered fruits and nuts, like their nomadic ancestors, and their society was egalitarian, another feature common to nomadic societies: both men and women did the same kinds of work. But despite their relatively diverse and abundant food supply, their life spans were very short. Men died, on average, at the age of thirty-four. Women, who bore the additional risks of childbirth, died at around age thirty.

The basic features of life in Çatalhöyük are common to all subsequent human civilizations. But how, when, and why did such settlements emerge? And how do we have access to information about this distant past? The era before the appearance of written records, which begin to proliferate around 3100 B.C.E., is of far greater duration than the subsequent eras we are able to document—and no less important. But it requires special ingenuity to identify, collect, and interpret the evidence of the distant past. In fact, historians have just begun to explore the ways that climatology, neuroscience, and evolutionary biology can further illuminate this period, augmenting the older findings of paleontology, archeology, and historical anthropology.

Societies of the Stone Age

Primates with human characteristics originated in Africa 4 to 5 million years ago, and tool-making hominids—species belonging to the genus *Homo*, our distant ancestors—evolved approximately 2 million years ago. Because these early hominids made most of their tools out of stone, they are designated as belonging to the Stone Age. This vast expanse of time is divided into the Paleolithic ("Old Stone") and the Neolithic ("New Stone") Eras, with the break between them falling around 11,000 B.C.E.

Hominids in Africa were kindling and controlling fire as early as 164,000 years ago, using it to make tools. The Neanderthals, a hominid species that flourished about 200,000 years ago, made jewelry, painted on the walls of caves, and buried their dead in distinctive graves with meaningful objects such as horns (blown to make music) and, in one case, flowers. Could these hominids speak? Did they have a language? At present, there is no way that archeology can answer such questions.

CAVE PAINTINGS FROM LASCAUX. These paintings, which date to between 10,000 and 15,000 B.C.E., show several of the different species of animals that were hunted by people of the Ice Age. The largest animal depicted here, a species of long-horned cattle known as the *auroch*, is now extinct.

However, archeology has shown that in the last phase of the Paleolithic Era, around 40,000 B.C.E., the pace of human development began to accelerate dramatically. Human populations in Africa expanded, suggesting that people were better nourished, perhaps as a result of new technologies. In Europe, *Homo sapiens sapiens* began to produce finely crafted and more-effective tools such as fishhooks, arrowheads, and sewing needles made from wood, antler, and bone. The most astonishing evidence of this change was produced by these new tools: cave paintings like those at Lascaux (France), discovered in 1940. These amazing scenes were purposefully painted in recesses where acoustic resonance is greatest, and were probably intended to be experienced as part of multimedia musical ceremonies. This is almost certain evidence for the development of language.

Despite these changes, the basic patterns of human life altered very little. Virtually all human societies consisted of bands of a few dozen people who moved incessantly in search of food. As a result, these groups have left no continuous archeological record. Their lifestyle also had social, economic, and political limitations which help to explain the differences—both positive and negative—between these subsistence societies and those that can be called "civilizations." Early humans had no domestic animals to transport goods, so they could have no significant material possessions aside from basic tools. And because they could not accumulate goods over time, the distinctions of rank and status created by disparities in wealth could not develop. Hierarchical structures were therefore uncommon. When conflicts arose or resources became scarce, the solution was probably to divide and separate. And al-

though scholars once assumed that men did the hunting and women the gathering, it is more likely that all members of a band (except for the very young and very old) engaged in the basic activity of acquiring food.

THE BUILDING BLOCKS OF CIVILIZATION

What changes allowed some hunter-gatherer societies to settle and build civilizations? The historical divide between the Paleolithic ("Old Stone") Age and Neolithic ("New Stone") Age, around 11,000 B.C.E., reflects very evident developments brought about by changes in the climate, which led to the development of managed food production, which in turn fostered settlements that could trade with one another, both locally and over long distances. For the first time, it became possible for individuals and communities to accumulate and store wealth on a large scale. The results were far-reaching. Communities became more stable, and human interactions more complex. Specialization developed, along with distinctions of status and rank. Both the rapidity and the radical implications of these changes have given this era its name: the Neolithic Revolution.

The Neolithic Revolution

The artists who executed the cave paintings at Lascaux were able to survive in harsh climatic conditions. Between 40,000 and 11,000 B.C.E., daytime temperatures in the Mediterranean basin averaged about 60° F (16° C) in the summer and about 30° F (–1° C) in the winter. These are very low compared to today's temperatures in the city of Marseilles, not far from Lascaux, which average about 86° F (30° C) in summer and 52° F (11° C) in winter. Cold-loving reindeer, elk, wild boar, bison, and mountain goats abounded in regions now famous for their beaches and vineyards. But as the glaciers receded northward with the warming climate, these species retreated with them, all the way to Scandinavia. Some humans moved north with the game, but others stayed behind to create a very different world.

Within a few thousand years after the end of the Ice Age, peoples living in the eastern Mediterranean and some other regions of the world accomplished the most

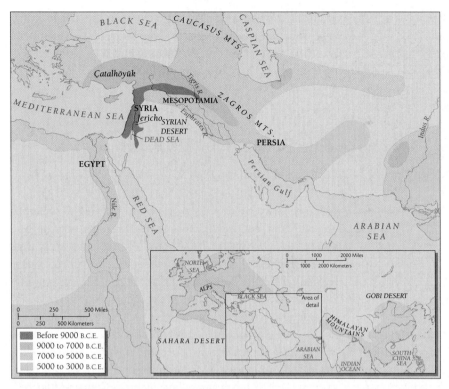

THE GROWTH OF AGRICULTURE. Examine the chronology of agriculture's development in this region. ■ *What areas began cultivating crops first, and why?* ■ *How might rivers have played a crucial role in the spread of farming technologies?*

food supply. They therefore had to increase the food-growing capacity of the land and to devise ways of preserving and storing grain between harvests. Some peoples had learned how to preserve wild grain in storage pits as early as 11,500 B.C.E., and eventually they discovered that they could use this seed to produce even more grain the following year. The importance of this latter discovery cannot be overstated: deliberate cultivation could support larger populations and could also compensate for disasters (such as flooding) that might inhibit natural reseeding. Even more important, intensified seeding and storage provided humans with the stable and predictable surpluses needed to support domestic animals. This brought a host of additional benefits, not only guaranteeing a more reliable supply of meat, milk, leather, wool, bone, and horn, but also providing animal power to pull carts and plows and to power mills.

momentous transformation in human history: a switch from food-gathering for subsistence to food production. The warmer, wetter climate allowed wild grains to flourish, geometrically increasing the food supply. People began to domesticate animals and cultivate plants. Stable settlements grew into cities. This process took several thousand years, but it still deserves to be called "revolutionary." In a relatively short time, people altered patterns of existence that were millions of years old.

This revolution produced new challenges and inequalities. Well-nourished women in sedentary communities can bear more children than women in hunter-gatherer groups, and so the women of this era became increasingly sequestered from their male counterparts, who in turn gave up an equal role in child care. The rapid increase in population was countered by the rapid spread of infectious diseases, while dependence on carbohydrates resulted in earlier deaths than were typical among hunter-gatherers.

But eventually, increased fertility and birthrates outweighed these limiting factors, and by about 8000 B.C.E. human populations were beginning to exceed the wild

The Emergence of Towns and Villages

The accelerating changes of the Neolithic Revolution are exemplified by towns like Çatalhöyük and by the simultaneous rise of trade and warfare—sure signs of increased specialization and competition. Hundreds, and probably thousands, of settlements grew up in the Near East between 7500 and 3500 B.C.E. Some of these can even be classified as cities: centers of administration and commerce with a large and diverse population, often protected by walls. Among the earliest of these was Jericho, in the territory lying between modern Israel and Jordan. Jericho emerged as a seasonal, grain-producing settlement, and by 6800 B.C.E. its inhabitants were undertaking a spectacular building program. Many new dwellings were built on stone foundations, and a massive dressed stone wall was constructed around the western edge of the settlement. It included a circular tower whose excavated remains still reach to a height of thirty feet, a powerful expression of its builders' wealth, technical prowess, and political ambitions.

Jericho covered at least eight acres and supported 3,000 people, so it was even more densely settled than

Çatalhöyük. It was sustained by intensive cultivation, made possible by irrigation, of recently domesticated strains of wheat and barley. Jericho's inhabitants also produced some of the earliest-known pottery, which allowed them to store grain, wine, and oils more effectively. Pottery's most important benefits, however, were in cooking. For the first time, it was possible to produce nourishing stews, porridges, and ales. (The capacity to produce beer is a sure sign of civilization.) Pottery production was not only vital to ancient civilizations, it is vital to those who study them. As the techniques for making pottery spread throughout the Near East and Asia, identifiable regional styles also developed. By studying the different varieties, archeologists can construct a reasonably accurate chronology and can also trace the movements of goods and people.

Jericho and Çatalhöyük illustrate the impact that stored agricultural surpluses have on human relations. For the first time, significant differences began to arise in the amount of wealth individuals could stockpile for themselves and their heirs. Dependence on agriculture also made it more difficult for individuals to split off from the community when disputes and inequities arose. The result was the emergence of a much more stratified society, with more opportunities for a few powerful people to become dominant. The new reliance on agriculture also meant a new dependence on the land, the seasons, and the weather, which led to new speculations about the supernatural. Different life forces were believed to require special services and gifts, and the regular practice of ritual and sacrifice ultimately produced a priestly caste of individuals or families who seemed able to communicate with these forces. Such spiritual leadership was allied to more worldly forms of power, including the capacity to lead war bands, to exact tribute from other settlements, to construct defenses, and to resolve disputes.

Trade was another important element in the development of early settlements. Local trading networks were already established around 9000 B.C.E., and by 5000 long-distance routes linked settlements throughout the Near East. Long-distance trade accelerated the exchange of ideas and information throughout the Fertile Crescent, and it further increased social stratification. Because status was enhanced by access to exotic goods from afar, local elites sought to monopolize trade by organizing and controlling the production of commodities within their own communities and by regulating their export. Certain people could now devote at least a portion of their labor to pursuits other than agriculture: making pottery or cloth, manufacturing weapons or tools, building houses and fortifications, or facilitating trade. Thus the elites who fostered and exploited the labor of others eventually became specialized themselves, with the leisure and resources to engage in intellectual, artistic, and political pursuits. The building blocks of civilization had been laid.

URBAN DEVELOPMENT IN MESOPOTAMIA

The Greeks called it Mesopotamia, the "Land between Rivers." It was a land that received only about eight inches (20 cm) of rainfall per year. Its soils are sandy and summer temperatures exceed 110° F (44° C). The two rivers supplying water—the Tigris and Euphrates—are noted for their violence and unpredictability. Both are prone to flooding, and the Tigris was liable to change its course from year to year. It was in this challenging environment that the first urban society, the civilization of Sumer, flourished.

THE WHITE TEMPLE AT URUK, c. 3400 B.C.E. This temple may have been dedicated to the sky god, An, or designed to provide all the region's gods with a mountaintop home in a part of the world known for its level plains.

The Ubaid Culture

The earliest cities of Mesopotamia were founded by the Ubaid peoples, so called because of their settlement at al-Ubaid (now in Iraq), which dates to around 5900 B.C.E. In this era, the headwaters of the Persian Gulf extended at least 100 miles farther inland than they do today, so some Ubaid settlements bordered on fertile marshlands, which enabled them to develop irrigation systems. Although these began as relatively simple channels and collection pools, Ubaid farmers quickly learned to build more sophisticated canals and to line some pools with stone. They also constructed dikes and levees to control the seasonal flooding of the rivers and to direct the excess water into irrigation canals. Despite the hostility of the environment, Ubaid communities were soon producing surpluses sufficient to support specialists in construction, weaving, pottery making, metalwork, and trade: the typical attributes of Neolithic village life.

Yet there is also early evidence of something quite new: central structures that served religious, economic, and administrative functions, something not found in Çatalhöyük. Starting out as shrines, these structures soon became impressive temples built of dried mud brick, like the bricks described in the story of Babel—and unlike the plentiful stone used at Jericho; the scarcity of stone meant that builders in this region had to be more resourceful. Each large settlement had such a temple, from which a priestly class acted as managers of the community's stored wealth and of the complex irrigation systems that would make the civilization of Sumer possible.

Urbanism in Uruk, 4300–2900 B.C.E.

After about 4300 B.C.E., Ubaid settlements developed into larger, more prosperous, and more highly organized communities. The most famous of these sites, Uruk, became the first Sumerian city-state. Its sophistication and scale is exemplified by the White Temple, built between 3500 and 3300 B.C.E. Its massive sloping platform looms nearly forty feet above the surrounding flatlands, and its four corners are oriented toward the cardinal points of the compass. Atop the platform stands the temple proper, dressed in brick and originally painted a brilliant white.

Such temples were eventually constructed in every Sumerian city, reflecting the central role that worship played in civic life. Uruk in particular seems to have owed its rapid growth to its importance as a religious center. By 3100 B.C.E. it encompassed several hundred acres, enclosing a population of 40,000 people within its massive brick walls. The larger villages of Sumer were also growing rapidly, attracting immigrants just as the great cities did. Grain and cloth production grew tenfold. Trade routes expanded dramatically. And to manage this increasingly complex economy, the Sumerians invented the technology on which most historians rely: writing.

CUNEIFORM WRITING. The image on the left shows a Sumerian clay tablet from about 3000 B.C.E. Here, standardized pictures are beginning to represent abstractions: notice the symbol *ninda* (food) near the top. On the right, carvings on limestone from about 2600 B.C.E. reveal the evolution of cuneiform. ■ *Why would such standardized pictograms have been easier to reproduce quickly?*

The Development of Writing

In 4000 B.C.E., the peoples of the Near East were already using clay tokens to keep inventories. Within a few centuries, they developed a practice of placing tokens inside hollow clay balls and inscribing, on the outside of each ball, the shapes of all the tokens it contained. By 3300 B.C.E., scribes had replaced these balls with flat clay tablets on which they inscribed the symbols representing tokens. These tablets made keeping the tokens themselves unnecessary, and they could also be archived for future reference or sent to other settlements as receipts or requests for goods.

Writing thus evolved as a practical recording technology to support economic pursuits. Because it existed to represent real things, its system of symbols—called pictograms—was also realistic: each pictogram resembled the thing it represented. Over time, however, a pictogram might be used not only to symbolize a physical object but to evoke an idea associated with that object. For example, the symbol for a bowl of food, *ninda*, might be used to express something more abstract, such as "nourishment." Pictograms also came to be associated with particular spoken sounds, or *phonemes*. Thus when a Sumerian scribe needed to employ the sound *ninda*, even as part of another word, he would use the symbol for a bowl of food to represent that phoneme. Later, special marks were added so that a reader could tell whether the writer meant it to represent the object itself, a larger concept, or a sound used in a context that might have nothing to do with food.

By 3100 B.C.E., Sumerian scribes also developed a specialized tool suited to the task of writing, a stylus made of reed. Because this stylus leaves an impression shaped like a wedge (in Latin, *cuneus*), this script is called *cuneiform* (*kyoo-NAY-i-form*). Cuneiform symbols could now be impressed more quickly into clay. And because the new stylus was not suited to drawing pictograms that accurately represented things, the symbols became even more abstract. Meanwhile, symbols were invented for every possible phonetic combination in the Sumerian language, reducing the number of nec-essary pictograms from about 1,200 to 600. But whereas the earliest pictograms could have been written and read by anyone, writing and reading now became specialized, powerful skills accessible only to a small and influential minority who were taught in special scribal schools.

THE CULTURE OF SUMER

The great centers of Sumerian civilization shared a common culture and a common language. They also shared a set of beliefs. However, this common religion did not produce peace. The residents of each city considered themselves to be the servants of a particular god, whom they sought to glorify by exalting their own city above others. The result was intense competition that frequently escalated into warfare. There was also an economic dimension to this conflict, since water rights and access to arable land and trade routes were often at stake.

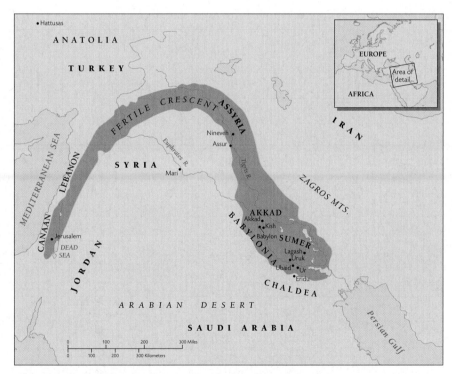

THE FERTILE CRESCENT. Notice the proximity of Sumerian cities to rivers; consider the vital role played by the Tigris and Euphrates in shaping Mesopotamian civilizations. ■ *How many Sumerian city-states can you count on the map?* ■ *Why would Sumerian city-states have been clustered so closely together?* ■ *What challenges and opportunities would this present?*

The Flood: Two Accounts

> One of the oldest stories in the world tells of a great flood that decimated the lands and peoples of the earth, an event that can be traced to the warming of the earth's climate at the end of the last Ice Age. Many ancient cultures told versions of this story, and two of these are excerpted below. The first, included in the Epic of Gilgamesh, was written down during the first half of the third millennium B.C.E., making it at least 1,500 years older than the similar account in the Hebrew Bible. But both are probably the products of much older storytelling traditions. The hero of the Sumerian story is Utnapishtim. The Hebrew story's hero is Noah.

The Epic of Gilgamesh

Utnapishtim spoke to Gilgamesh, saying: "I will reveal to you, Gilgamesh . . . a secret of the gods. . . . The hearts of the Great Gods moved them to inflict the Flood. Their Father Anu uttered the oath (of secrecy). . . . [But the god] Ea . . . repeated their talk [to me, saying]: 'O man of Shuruppak, son of Ubartutu: Tear down the house and build a boat! . . . Spurn possessions and keep alive living beings! Make all living beings go up into the boat. The boat which you are to build, its dimensions must measure equal to each other: its length must correspond to its width. Roof it over like the Apsu.' I understood and spoke to my lord, Ea: 'My lord, thus is the command which you have uttered. I will heed and will do it.' . . . On the fifth day I laid out her exterior. It was a field in area, its walls were each 10 times 12 cubits in height. . . . I provided it with six decks, thus dividing it into seven (levels). . . . Whatever I had I loaded on it. . . . All the living beings that I had I loaded on it. I had all my kith and kin go up into the boat, all the beasts and animals of the field and the draftsmen I had go up.

"I watched the appearance of the weather—the weather was frightful to behold! I went into the boat and sealed the entry. . . . All day long the South Wind blew . . . , submerging the mountain in water, overwhelming the people like an attack. . . . Six days and seven nights came the wind and flood, the storm flattening the land. When the seventh day arrived . . . [t]he sea calmed, fell still, the whirlwind and flood stopped up. . . . When a seventh day arrived, I sent forth a dove and released it. The dove went off, but came back to me, no perch was visible so it circled back to me. I sent forth a swallow and released it. The swallow went off, but came back to me, no perch was visible so it circled back to me. I sent forth a raven and released it. The raven went off, and saw the waters slither back. It eats, it scratches, it bobs, but does not circle back to me. Then I sent out everything in all directions and sacrificed (a sheep). I offered incense in front of the mountain-ziggurat. . . .

"The gods smelled the savor . . . and collected like flies over a sacrifice. . . . Just then Enlil arrived. He saw the boat and became furious. . . . 'Where did a living being escape? No man was to survive the annihilation!' Ea spoke to Valiant Enlil, saying . . . 'How, how could you bring about a Flood without consideration? Charge the violation to the viola-

Much of the economic production of a city passed through the great temple warehouses, where priests redistributed the city's produce. During the third millennium, these great temples began to control the production of textiles, employing thousands of servile women and children. Temple elites also played a key role in long-distance trade, as both buyers and sellers of goods. So for any city-state to surrender its independence would not only offend the conquered city's god, it would jeopardize its entire economy and the power of its ruling class.

Each Sumerian city had its own aristocracy, the group from which priests were drawn. As much as half tor, charge the offense to the offender, but be compassionate lest (mankind) be cut off, be patient lest they be killed.' Enlil went up inside the boat and, grasp- ing my hand, made me go up. He had my wife go up and kneel by my side. He touched our forehead and, standing between us, he blessed us. . . ."

Source: Maureen Gallery Kovacs, trans., *The Epic of Gilgamesh*, Tablet XI (Stanford, CA: 1985, 1989), pp. 97–103.

The Book of Genesis

The Lord saw that the wickedness of humankind was great in the earth and . . . said, "I will blot out from the earth the human beings I have created . . . for I am sorry I have made them." But Noah found favor in the sight of the Lord. . . . God saw that the earth was corrupt and . . . said to Noah, "I have determined to make an end to all flesh. . . . Make yourself an ark of cypress wood, make rooms in the ark, and cover it inside and out with pitch. . . . Make a roof for the ark, and put the door of the ark in its side. . . . For my part I am going to bring a flood on the earth, to destroy from under heaven all flesh. . . . But I will establish a covenant with you, and you shall come into the ark, you, your sons, your wife, and your sons' wives with you. And of every living thing you shall bring two of every kind into the ark, to keep them alive with you. . . . Also take with you every kind of food that is eaten." . . . All the foun- tains of the great deep burst forth, and the windows of the heavens were opened. . . . The waters gradually receded from the earth. . . . At the end of forty days, Noah opened a window of the ark . . . and sent out the raven, and it went to and fro until the waters were dried up from the earth. Then he sent out the dove from him, to see if the waters had subsided from the face of the ground, but the dove found no place to set its foot, and it returned. . . . He waited another seven days, and again sent out the dove [which] came back to him . . . and there in its beak was a freshly plucked olive leaf, so Noah knew the waters had subsided from the earth. Then he . . . sent out the dove, and it did not return to him anymore. . . . Noah built an altar to the Lord . . . and offered burnt offerings. And when the Lord smelled the pleasing odor, the Lord said in his heart, "I will never again curse the ground because of humankind . . . nor will I ever again destroy every living creature as I have done." . . . God blessed Noah and his sons.

Source: Genesis 6:5–9:1, *The New Oxford Annotated Bible* (Oxford: 1994).

Questions for Analysis

1. What are the similarities and differences between these two accounts?

2. What do these differences or similarities reveal about the two societies that told these stories? Does one seem to derive from the other? Why or why not?

3. How is the geography and climate of Mesopotamia reflected in the Sumerian version of the story?

the population consisted of free persons who held parcels of land sufficient to sustain themselves, but the rest were dependents of the temple who worked as artisans or as agricultural laborers, and many of these dependents were slaves. Most of these slaves were prisoners of war from other Sumerian city-states whose bondage was limited to three years, after which time a slave had to be released. But non-Sumerians could be held indefinitely, although a few might manage to buy their freedom. In either case, slaves were the property of their owners. They could be beaten, branded, bought, and sold like any other form of merchandise. Perhaps the only positive thing to say about slavery in antiquity is that it was egalitarian: anyone could become a slave. It was not until the beginning of the modern era that slavery became linked to race (see Chapter 11).

The Early Dynastic Period, 2900–2500 B.C.E.

Around 2900 B.C.E., conflicts among the growing Sumerian city-states became more acute. Competition for resources intensified and warfare became more frequent and destructive. A new type of military leadership began to emerge and eventually evolved into a form of kingship. Historians refer to this phase as the Early Dynastic Period because it was dominated by family dynasties, each headed by a war leader whose prestige earned him the title *lugal*: "big man." Unlike the priestly rulers of the Uruk Period, lugals did not see themselves as humble servants of the city's god. Rather, they believed that success in battle had earned them the right to exploit the city's wealth for their own glory.

The most striking expression of this development is the *Epic of Gilgamesh*, a series of stories recited over many generations and eventually written down on cuneiform tablets: the first literary monument in world history. It recounts the exploits of a lugal named Gilgamesh, who probably lived in Uruk sometime around 2700 B.C.E. Gilgamesh earns his legendary reputation through military conquest and personal heroism, particularly in campaigns against uncivilized—that is, nonurban—tribes. But he becomes so powerful that he ignores his own society's code of conduct; he disrespects the priesthood and commits acts of sacrilege. So the people of Uruk pray to the gods for retribution, and the gods fashion a wild man named Enkidu to challenge Gilgamesh.

The confrontation between Gilgamesh and Enkidu reveals the core values of Sumerian society. Gilgamesh is a creature of the city; Enkidu is a creature of the past, a hunter-gatherer. But then Enkidu has a sexual encounter with a beguiling woman and is unable to return to the wilderness: his urban initiation has civilized him and allowed him to befriend the lord of Uruk. Together they have many adventures. But Enkidu is eventually killed by the goddess Inanna, who punishes the friends for mocking her powers. Gilgamesh, distraught with grief, attempts to find a magical plant that will revive his friend. He finds it at the bottom of a deep pool, only to have it stolen from him by a water snake. In the end, he is forced to confront the futility of all human effort. He becomes "The One Who Looked into the Depths," the name by which his story was known to Sumerians. The larger message seems to be that not even civilization can shield humans from the forces of nature and the inevitability of death.

Sumerian Religion

In the Uruk Period, the Sumerians identified their gods with the capricious forces of the natural world. In the Early Dynastic Period, however, they came to imagine their gods as resembling the powerful lugals who now ruled the city-states as kings. Like them, the gods desired to live in the finest palaces and temples, to wear the costliest clothing and jewels, and to consume the tastiest foods. According to this new theology, which clearly reflects changes in Sumerian society, humans exist merely to provide for their gods. This was, indeed, why the gods had created people in the first place. There was thus a reciprocal relationship between humanity and divinity. The gods depended on their human servants to honor and sustain them; and in return, the gods occasionally bestowed gifts and favors.

As the gods' representatives on earth, kings bore special responsibilities and also enjoyed special privileges. Kings were thus set apart from all other men, including priests. But kings were also obliged to honor the gods through offerings, sacrifices, festivals, and massive building projects. Kings who neglected these duties, or who exalted themselves at the expense of the gods, were likely to bring disaster on themselves and their people. And even kings could not evade death.

Science, Technology, and Trade

The Sumerians' worldview was colored by their adversarial relationship with the environment. Precisely because neither their gods nor their environment were trustworthy, Sumerians cultivated a high degree of self-reliance and ingenuity. These qualities made them the most technologically innovative people of the ancient world.

For example, despite the fact that their land had no mineral deposits, the Sumerians became skilled metallurgists. By 6000 B.C.E., a number of cultures throughout the Near East and Europe had learned how to produce weapons and tools using copper. By the Uruk Period (4300–2900 B.C.E.), trade routes were bringing this raw element into Sumer, where it was processed into weapons and tools. Shortly before 3000 B.C.E., people further discovered that

SUMERIAN WAR CHARIOTS. The earliest known representation of the wheel, dating from about 2600 B.C.E., shows how wheels were fashioned from slabs of wood. (For a later Mesopotamian wheel with spokes, see the illustration on page 50.)

copper could be alloyed with arsenic (or later, tin) to produce bronze. Bronze is almost as malleable as copper, and it pours more easily into molds; but when cooled, it maintains its rigidity and shape even better than copper. For almost two thousand years, until about 1200 B.C.E. and the development of techniques for smelting iron, bronze was the strongest metal known to man—the most useful and, in war, the most deadly. Following the Greeks (see Chapter 3), we call this period the Bronze Age.

Alongside writing and the making of bronze, the invention of the wheel was the fundamental technological achievement of the era. The Sumerians were using potter's wheels by the middle of the fourth millennium B.C.E. and could produce high-quality clay vessels in greater quantity than ever before. By around 3200 B.C.E., the Sumerians were also using two- and four-wheeled chariots and carts drawn by donkeys. (Horses were unknown in the Near East until sometime between 2000 and 1700 B.C.E.). Chariots were another new and deadly military technology, giving warriors a tremendous advantage over armies on foot: the earliest depiction of their use, dating from 2600 B.C.E., shows one trampling an enemy. At the same time, wheeled carts dramatically increased the productivity of the Sumerian workforce.

Other inventions derived from the study of mathematics. In order to construct their elaborate irrigation systems, the Sumerians had to develop sophisticated measuring and surveying techniques as well as the art of map making. Agricultural needs may also lie behind the lunar calendar they invented, which consisted of twelve months, six lasting 30 days and six lasting 29 days. Since this produced a year of only 354 days, the Sumerians eventually began to add a month to their calendars every few years in order to predict the recurrence of the seasons with suffi-

cient accuracy. The Sumerian practice of dividing time into multiples of sixty has lasted to the present day, not only in our notion of the 30-day month but also in our division of the hour into sixty minutes, each comprised of sixty seconds. Mathematics also contributed to Sumerian architecture, allowing them to build domes and arches thousands of years before the Romans would adopt and spread these architectural forms throughout the West.

Sumerian technology depended not only on ingenuity but also the spread of information and raw materials through trade. Sumerian pioneers traced routes up and down the rivers and into the hinterlands of Mesopotamia, following the tributaries of the Tigris and Euphrates. They blazed trails across the deserts toward the west, where they interacted with and influenced the Egyptians. By sea, they traded with the peoples of the Persian Gulf and, directly or indirectly, with the civilizations of the Indus Valley (modern Pakistan and India). And, along with merchandise, they carried ideas: stories, art, the use of writing, and the whole cultural complex that arose from their way of life. The elements of civilization, which had fused in their urban crucible, would thus come together in many other places.

THE FIRST EMPIRES

Evidence shows that competition among Sumerian city-states reached a new level around 2500 B.C.E., as ambitious lugals vied to magnify themselves and their kingdoms. Still, it seems that no Sumerian lugal ever attempted to create an empire by imposing centralized rule on the cities he conquered. As a result, Sumer remained a collection of interdependent but mutually hostile states whose rulers were unable to forge any lasting structures of authority. This pattern would ultimately make the people of Sumer vulnerable to a new style of imperial rulership imposed on them from the north, in the person of Sargon the Akkadian.

Sargon and the Akkadian Empire, 2350–2160 B.C.E.

The Akkadians were the predominant people of central Mesopotamia. Their Sumerian neighbors to the south had greatly influenced them, and they had adopted cuneiform script along with many other elements of Sumerian culture. Yet the Akkadians preserved their own Semitic language, part of the linguistic family that includes Hebrew and Arabic. Sumerians tended to regard them as uncivilized, but in the case of the lugal whom the Akkadians called "great king," this probably meant not being bound by the conventions of Sumerian warfare. For Sargon initiated a systematic program of conquest designed to subject all the neighboring regions to his authority. By 2350 B.C.E., he had conquered the cities of Sumer and then moved to establish direct control over all of Mesopotamia.

From his capital at Akkad, Sargon installed Akkadian-speaking governors to rule the cities of Sumer, ordering them to pull down existing fortifications, collect taxes, and impose his will. Sargon thus transformed the independent city-states of Sumer and Akkad into a much larger political unit: the first known empire, a word derived from the Latin *imperium*, "command." This enabled him to manage and exploit the network of trade routes crisscrossing the Near East. So although his political influence was felt only in Mesopotamia, his economic influence stretched from Ethiopia to India. Sargon's capital became the most splendid city in the world, and he exercised unprecedented power for a remarkable fifty-six years. Sargon's imperialism had a marked effect on Sumerian religion. To unite the two halves of his empire, Sargon merged Akkadian and Sumerian divinities. He also tried to lessen the rivalry of Sumerian cities by appointing a single Akkadian high priest or priestess, often a member of his own family, to preside over several temples.

Sargon's successor, his grandson Naram-Sin, extended Akkadian conquests and consolidated trade, helping to stimulate the growth of cities throughout the Near East and binding them more closely together. By 2200 B.C.E., most people in central and southern Mesopotamia would have been able to converse in the language of either the Sumerians or the Akkadians. Indeed, the two civilizations became virtually indistinguishable except for these different languages.

The Dynasty of Ur and the Amorites, 2100–1800 B.C.E.

After Naram-Sin's death, Akkadian rule faltered. Around 2100 B.C.E., however, a new dynasty came to power in Ur under its first king, Ur-Nammu, and his son Shulgi. Ur-Nammu was responsible for the construction of the great ziggurat at Ur, a massive temple complex that originally rose seventy feet above the surrounding plain. Shulgi continued his father's work, subduing the lands up to the

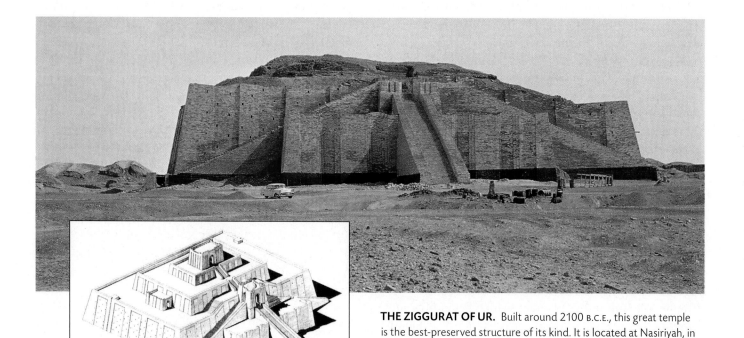

THE ZIGGURAT OF UR. Built around 2100 B.C.E., this great temple is the best-preserved structure of its kind. It is located at Nasiriyah, in what is now Iraq. Archeological investigations (see diagram) reveal that its central shrine, the most sacred part of the temple, was reached by climbing four sets of stairs and passing through a massive portal.

Zagros Mountains northeast of Ur and demanding massive tribute payments from them; one collection site accounted for 350,000 sheep per year, and Shulgi built state-run textile-production facilities to process the wool. He promulgated a code of law, calling for fair weights and measures, the protection of widows and orphans, and limitations on the death penalty for crimes. He also pursued military conquests, the centralization of government, commercial expansion and consolidation, and the patronage of art and literature. Shulgi thus established a pattern of rule that influenced the region for centuries to come.

The Empire of Hammurabi

In 1792 B.C.E., a young Amorite chieftain named Hammurabi (*hah-muh-RAH-bee*) became the ruler of Babylon, an insignificant city in central Mesopotamia. The Amorites, like the Akkadians, were a Semitic people. Until this period they had largely been nomads and warriors, but now they came to control the ancient cities of Mesopotamia.

Hammurabi may have been the first ruler in history to understand that power need not be based on force. He recognized that military intelligence, diplomacy, and strategic planning might accomplish what his small army could not. For Hammurabi used writing itself as a weapon. He did not try to confront his mightier neighbors directly. Rather, through letters and embassies, double-dealing and cunning, he induced his stronger counterparts to fight each other. While other Amorite kings exhausted their resources in costly wars, Hammurabi fanned their mutual hatred and skillfully portrayed himself as a friend and ally to all sides. Meanwhile, he quietly strengthened his kingdom, built up his army, and, when the time was right, fell on his depleted neighbors. By such policies, he transformed his small state into what historians call the Old Babylonian Empire.

Under Hammurabi's rule, Mesopotamia achieved an unprecedented degree of political integration. Ultimately, his empire stretched from the Persian Gulf into Assyria. To help unify these territories, Hammurabi introduced another innovation, promoting the worship of the little-known patron god of Babylon, Marduk, and making him the ruler-god of his entire empire. Although he also paid homage to the ancient gods of Sumer and Akkad, Hammurabi made it clear that all his subjects now owed allegiance to Marduk.

The idea that political power derives from divine approval was nothing new, but Hammurabi's genius was to use Marduk's supremacy over all other gods to legitimate his own claim to rule in Marduk's name, because he was king of Marduk's home city. Hammurabi thus became the first known ruler to launch wars of aggression justified in the name of his primary god. This set a precedent for colonial expansion that would become a characteristic feature of Near Eastern politics, as we will see in Chapter 2, and that lies behind nearly all imperial ventures down to the present day.

Yet Hammurabi did not rely solely on religion to bind his empire together. Building on the precedents of past rulers, he also issued a collection of laws, copies of which were inscribed on stone and set up in public places throughout his realm. The example that survives (see page 17) is an eight-foot-tall *stele* (*STEE-lee*) made of gleaming black basalt, originally erected in a central marketplace. The upper portion shows Hammurabi consulting with the god of justice. The phallic form on which the laws were inscribed would have been immediately recognizable as a potent symbol of Hammurabi's authority, obvious even to those who could not read the laws themselves. (It still makes a strong impression on visitors to the Louvre museum in Paris.)

It is impossible to overemphasize the importance of Hammurabi's decision to become a lawgiver. By collecting and codifying legal precedents, like those of Shulgi, Hammurabi declared himself to be (as he stated in the code's preamble) "the shepherd of the people, the capable king"— not a lugal ruling through fear and caprice. This was setting a new standard of kingship, and expressing a new vision of empire as a union of peoples subject to the same laws.

Law and Society Under Hammurabi

The code of Hammurabi reveals a great deal about the structure and values of Babylonian society. Its 282 pronouncements begin with legislation against false testimony (fraud or lying under oath) and theft; followed by laws regulating business deals; laws regulating the use of public resources, especially water; laws relating to taverns and brothels, many of which appear to have been run by women; laws relating to debt and slavery; many laws dealing with marriage, inheritance, divorce, and widows' rights; and finally laws punishing murder, violent assault, and even medical malpractice. What emerges is a fascinating picture of a complex urban culture that required more formal legislation than the accumulated customs of previous generations.

The division among classes in Babylonian society was marked. As Hammurabi's code indicates, an offense

The Code of Hammurabi

The laws of Hammurabi, published on the authority of this powerful king and set up in central places throughout the Old Babylonian Empire, were influenced both by the needs of an urban society and by older ideas of justice and punishment common among Semitic peoples. In its entirety, the code comprises 282 laws, beginning and ending with statements of Hammurabi's devotion to the gods, his peace-keeping mission, and his sense of his duties as king. The following excerpts are numbered so as to show the order in which these provisions appear on the stele that publicizes them.

When the god Marduk commanded me to provide just ways for the people of the land in order to attain appropriate behavior, I established truth and justice as the declaration of the land. I enhanced the well-being of the people.

* * *

1. If a man accuses another man and charges him with homicide but cannot bring proof against him, his accuser shall be killed.

2. If a man charges another man with practicing witchcraft but cannot bring proof against him, he who is charged with witchcraft shall go to the divine River Ordeal, he shall indeed submit to the divine River Ordeal; if the divine River Ordeal should overwhelm him, his accuser shall take full legal possession of his estate; if the divine River Ordeal should clear that man and should he survive, he who made the charge of witchcraft against him shall be killed; he who submitted to the divine River Ordeal shall take full legal possession of his accuser's estate.

If a man comes forward to give false testimony in a case but cannot bring evidence for his accusation, if that case involves a capital offense, that man shall be killed.

* * *

6. If a man steals valuables belonging to the god or to the palace, that man shall be killed, and also he who received the stolen goods from him shall be killed.

7. If a man should purchase silver, gold, a slave, a slave woman, an ox, a sheep, a donkey, or anything else whatsoever, from a son of a man or from a slave of a man without witnesses or a contract—or if he accepts the goods for safekeeping—that man is a thief, he shall be killed.

8. If a man steals an ox, a sheep, a donkey, a pig, or a boat—if it belongs either to the god or to the palace, he shall give thirtyfold; if it belongs to a commoner, he shall replace it tenfold; if the thief does not have anything to give, he shall be killed.

* * *

15. If a man should enable a palace slave, a palace slave woman, a commoner's slave, or a commoner's slave woman to leave through the main city-gate, he shall be killed.

* * *

committed against a nobleman carried a far more severe penalty than did the same crime committed against a social equal, or against a dependent or slave; nobles were also punished more severely than were commoners for crimes they committed against other nobles. Hammurabi's code also provides evidence as to the status of women in Babylonian society, and shows that they enjoyed certain important protections under the law, including the right to divorce abusive or indigent husbands. If a husband divorced a wife "without cause," he was obliged to provide financial support for her and their children. However, a wife who went around the city defaming her spouse was subject to severe punishment, and she would risk death (as would her lover) if she were caught in adultery. The sexual promiscuity of husbands, by contrast, was protected under the law.

Hammurabi died around 1750 B.C.E., but his administrative efforts had created a durable state in Mesopotamia. For another two centuries, the Old Babylonian Empire played a significant role in the Near East, until invaders from the north sacked the capital and occupied it. But even for another thousand years thereafter, Babylon remained the region's most famous city.

53. If a man neglects to reinforce the embankment of the irrigation canal of his field and then a breach opens and allows the water to carry away the common irrigated area, the man in whose embankment the breach opened shall replace the grain whose loss he caused.

* * *

104. If a merchant gives a trading agent grain, wool, oil, or any other commodity for local transactions, the trading agent shall collect a sealed receipt for each payment in silver that he gives to the merchant.

* * *

128. If a man marries a wife but does not draw up a formal contract for her, she is not a wife.

129. If a man's wife should be seized lying with another male, they shall bind them and throw them into the water; if the wife's master allows his wife to live, then the king shall allow his subject (i.e., the other male) to live.

* * *

142. If a woman repudiates her husband, and declares, "You will not have marital relations with me"—her circumstances shall be investigated by the authorities of her city quarter, and if she is circumspect and without fault, but her husband is wayward and disparages her greatly, that woman will not be subject to any penalty; she shall take her dowry and she shall depart for her father's house.

Source: Martha T. Roth, ed., *Law Collections from Ancient Mesopotamia and Asia Minor* (Atlanta, GA: 1995), pp. 76–135 (excerpted).

Questions for Analysis

1. Based on these excerpts, what conclusions can you draw about the values of Old Babylonian society? For example, what types of crimes are punishable by death, and why?

2. In what ways does the code of Hammurabi exhibit the influences of the urban civilization for which these laws were issued? What are some characteristics and consequences of urbanization? What, for example, do we learn about economic developments?

The Code of Hammurabi. The laws of Hammurabi survive on an eight-foot column made of basalt. The top quarter of the column depicts the Babylonian king (standing, at left) being vested with authority by Shamash, the god of justice. Directly below, one can make out the cuneiform inscriptions that are the law code's text. How would the very format of these laws send a powerful message about Hammurabi's kingship?

THE DEVELOPMENT OF CIVILIZATION IN EGYPT

At about the same time that Sumerian civilization was transforming Mesopotamia, another civilization was taking shape in a very different part of the world and in very different ways. Unlike the Sumerians, the Egyptians did not have to wrest survival from a hostile and unpredictable environment. Instead, their land was renewed every year by the flooding of the Nile River. The fertile black soil left behind every summer made theirs the richest agricultural region in the entire Mediterranean world.

The distinctiveness of Egyptian civilization rests on this fundamental ecological fact. It also explains why ancient Egypt was a narrow, elongated kingdom, running along the Nile north from the First Cataract toward the Mediteranean Sea for a distance of more than 600 miles (1,100 km). Outside this narrow band of territory—which ranged from a few hundred yards to no more than 14 miles (23 km)—lay uninhabitable desert. This contrast, between the fertile Black Land along the Nile and the dessicated Red

Land beyond, deeply influenced the Egyptian worldview, in which the Nile itself was the center of the cosmos and the lands beyond were hostile.

Ancient Egyptian civilization enjoyed a remarkable continuity. Its roots date back to (at least) 5000 B.C.E. From about 3000 B.C.E. the defining element of this civilization would be the pervasive influence of a powerful, centralized, bureaucratic state headed by pharaohs who were regarded as living gods. No other civilization in world history has ever been governed so steadily, for so long, as ancient Egypt.

For convenience, historians have traditionally divided ancient Egyptian history into distinctive "kingdoms" and "periods." Following ancient Egyptian chroniclers, modern historians have also tended to portray these Old, Middle, and New Kingdoms as characterized by unity and prosperity, punctuated by chaotic interludes when central authority broke down: the so-called Intermediate Periods. Like all attempts at periodization, these divisions do not capture the complexities of human experience or even the real pace of historical development.

Predynastic Egypt, c. 10,000–3100 B.C.E.

The phrase "Predynastic Egypt" refers to the period before the emergence of the pharaohs and their royal dynasties—an era for which archeological evidence is difficult to find and interpret. The first-known permanent settlement in Egypt, situated at the southwestern edge of the Nile Delta near the modern town of Merimde Beni Salama, dates to approximately 4750 B.C.E. It was a farming community that may have numbered as many as 16,000 residents, and this number suggests that some Egyptian communities were much larger than those of a comparable period in Mesopotamia. Many other Neolithic farming centers have also been discovered in or near the Nile Delta, where a degree of cultural cohesiveness was already developing, fostered by shared interests and trade. In later centuries, this northern area would be known as Lower Egypt, so called because it was downstream.

Although towns in Lower Egypt were numerous, it was in Upper Egypt that the first Egyptian cities developed. By 3200 B.C.E. (when the Sumerian city of Uruk had been thriving for a thousand years), important communities such as Nekhen, This, and Abydos had all developed high degrees of occupational and social specialization. They had encircled themselves with sophisticated fortifications and had begun to build elaborate shrines to honor their gods. Indeed, the establishment of permanent sites of public worship may be key to explaining the growth of these towns into cities. As in Mesopotamia, a city's role as the center of a prominent religious cult attracted travelers and encouraged the growth of industries. And travel in Upper Egypt was relatively easy compared to Mesopotamia. The Nile bound cities together, and almost all Egyptians lived within sight of it.

It was due to the Nile, therefore, that the region south of the delta was able to forge a cultural and eventually a political unity, despite its enormous length. The Nile fed Egypt and was a conduit for people, goods, and ideas. Centralizing rulers could project their power quickly and effectively up and down its course. Within a remarkably short time, just a century or two after the first cities' appearance in Upper Egypt, they had banded together in a confederacy under the leadership of This. The pressure exerted by this confederacy in turn forced the towns of Lower Egypt to adopt their own form of political organization. By 3100 B.C.E., the rivalry between these competing regions had given rise to the two nascent kingdoms of Upper and Lower Egypt.

The Power of the Pharaoh, c. 3100–c. 2686 B.C.E.

With the rise of powerful rulers in these two kingdoms, Egyptian history enters a new phase, one that can be chronicled with unusual precision. The system for numbering the ruling dynasties that emerged in this era—known as the Archaic Period—was actually devised nearly three thousand years later by an historian named Manetho (mahn-EH-thoh), who wrote in the third century B.C.E. By and large, Manetho's work has withstood the scrutiny of modern historians and archeologists, although recent research has added a "Zero Dynasty" of early kings who were instrumental in bringing about the initial unification of Egypt.

Manetho did not record these rulers because he didn't know about them; we know them almost exclusively from archeological evidence. Among them was an Upper Egyptian warlord known to us as King Scorpion, because the image of a scorpion accompanies engravings that assert his authority. Another warlord, King Narmer, appears to have ruled both Upper and Lower Egypt. His exploits, too, come down to us in powerful pictures (see **Interpreting Visual Evidence**). Both of these kings probably came from Abydos in Upper Egypt, where they were buried. Their administrative capital, however, was at Memphis, the capital city of Lower Egypt and an important center for trade with the Sinai Peninsula and the Near East.

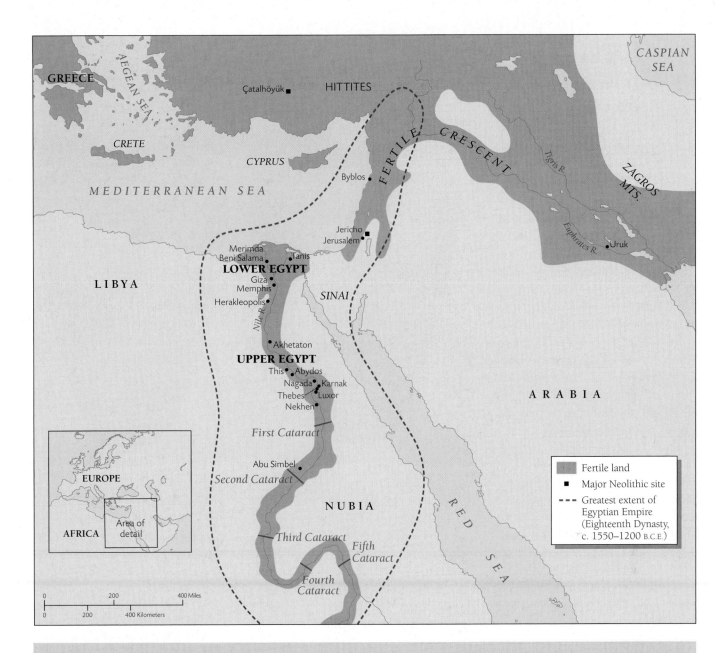

ANCIENT EGYPT AND THE NEAR EAST. Notice the peculiar geography of ancient Egypt and the role played by the Nile River. Identify the Nile on the map. ▪ *In what direction does the Nile flow?* ▪ *How did the lands on either side help to isolate Egyptian culture from outside influences?* ▪ *Consider how the Nile helped forge Egypt into a unitary state under a powerful centralized government. Yet how might Egypt's relationship to the Nile be potentially hazardous, as well as beneficial?*

Following the political unification of Upper and Lower Egypt, the basic features of Egypt's distinctive centralized kingship took shape along lines that would persist for the next 3,000 years. The title used to describe this kingship was *pharaoh*, a word that actually means "great household" and thus refers not to an individual king but to the whole apparatus that sustains his rule. This fact, in turn, helps to explain the extraordinary stability and longevity of Egyptian civilization, which could survive even a dynastic takeover by

Macedonian Greeks in the century before Manetho wrote his chronicle. Indeed, it is comparable to some modern forms of government—none of which has yet lasted so long. As we have seen, kingship in Mesopotamia tended to be a form of personal rule, dependent on the charisma of a particular individual. But in Egypt, the office of the pharaoh was durable enough to survive the deaths of many individual successors, facilitating the peaceful transition of power to new rulers and withstanding the incompetence of many.

The Narmer Palette

The Narmer Palette (c. 3100 B.C.E.) is a double-sided carving made of green silt-stone. Palettes were used to grind pigments for the making of cosmetics, but the large size (63 cm, over 2 feet) of this one is unusual. It was discovered in 1897 by archeologists excavating a temple dedicated to the god Horus at Nekhen, the capital of Upper Egypt. Found nearby were other artifacts, including the so-called Narmer Macehead, thought to depict the marriage of Narmer, king of Upper Egypt, to a princess of Lower Egypt.

On the left, dominating the central panel, Narmer wears the White Crown of Upper Egypt (image A). He wields a mace and seizes the hair of a captive kneeling at his feet. Above the captive's head is a cluster of lotus leaves (a symbol of Lower Egypt) and a falcon representing the god Horus, who may be drawing the captive's life force (*ka*) from his body. The figure behind Narmer is carrying the king's sandals; he is depicted as smaller because he is an inferior. The two men in the lower panel are either running or sprawling on the ground, and the symbols above them indicate the name of a defeated town. On the right, the other side of the palette shows Narmer as the chief figure in a procession (image B). He now wears the Red Crown of Lower

A. Narmer wearing the White Crown of Egypt.

B. Narmer wearing the Red Crown of Egypt.

Egypt and holds a mace and a flail, symbols of conquest. Behind him is the same servant carrying his sandals, and in front of him are a man with long hair and four standard-bearers. There are also ten headless corpses. Below, the entwined necks of two mythical creatures (serpopards, leopards with serpents' heads) are tethered to leashes held by two men. In the lowest section, a bull tramples the body of a man whose city he is destroying.

Questions for Analysis

1. This artifact has been called "the first historical document in the world," but scholars are still debating its meanings.

For example, does it represent something that actually happened, or is it political propaganda? In your view, is this proof that Narmer has united two kingdoms? Why or why not?

2. Do the two sides of the palette tell a coherent story and, if so, on which side does that story begin?

3. What might be significant about the site where the palette was found? Should the palette be interpreted as belonging with the mace found nearby? If so, how might that influence your interpretation of the palette's significance?

This was accomplished, as we shall see, by the efficiency of palace bureaucracy, but it was also a function of the pharaoh's close identification with the divine forces credited with renewing Egypt every year. Like the seasons, the pharaoh died only to be born again, renewed and empowered.

Egyptian rulers thus laid claim to a sacred nature quite different—and much more benign—than that governing Sumeria. And they were more powerful than any Sumerian lugal, who was never more than a mortal who enjoyed (an all too temporary) divine favor.

How the earliest kings of Egypt came to be distinguished as pharaohs and to establish their claims to divinity is still not well understood. We do know, however, that legitimating their rule over all Egypt was difficult. Local civic and religious loyalties remained strong, and for centuries Lower Egyptians would continue to see themselves as distinct from their neighbors to the south. Indeed, it seems probable that the centralization of government in the person of the pharaoh and his association with divinity were related approaches to solving the problem of political unity. And together, these measures had astonishing success. By the end of the Second Dynasty, which coincides with the end of the Archaic Period (2686 B.C.E.), the pharaoh was not just the ruler of Egypt, he *was* Egypt: a personification of the land, the people, and their gods.

The Old Kingdom, C. 2686–2160 B.C.E.

Because so few written sources from the Old Kingdom survive (see below), historians have to rely on funerary texts from the tombs of the elite. These sources are hardly representative, and they have tended to convey the impression that Egyptians were obsessed with death; they also tell us little about the lives of ordinary people. Further complicating the historian's task is the early Egyptians' own belief in the unchanging, cyclical nature of the universe. This makes it difficult for us to reconstruct their history in detail.

However, the surviving inscriptions, papyri, and art of the Third Dynasty (c. 2686–2613 B.C.E.) do tell us a great deal about the workings of the "great household" that undergirded individual rulers' power. This power was vast because the pharaoh was considered to be the intermediary between the land, its people, and their gods, so all the resources of Egypt belonged to him. Long-distance trade was entirely controlled by the pharaoh, as were systems for imposing taxation and conscripting labor. To administer these, the pharaohs installed provincial governors, known to the Greeks as *nomarchs*, many of whom were members of the pharaoh's own family.

Old Kingdom pharaohs kept tight control over the nomarchs and their armies of lesser officials in order to prevent them from establishing local roots in the territories they administered. Writing was therefore critical to internal communication and the management and exploitation of Egypt's vast wealth. This gave rise to a whole class of scribal administrators who enjoyed the power, influence, and status that went along with literacy, a skill few people could command—especially in Egypt, since few could master the

THE ROSETTA STONE. This famous stone, carved in 196 B.C.E., preserves three translations of a single decree in three different forms of writing: hieroglyphs (top), demotic Egyptian (middle), and classical Greek (bottom). ■ *Why would scholars be able to use the classical Greek text to decipher the hieroglyphic and demotic scripts?*

intricacies of hieroglyphic reading or writing. Even a child just beginning his scribal education was considered worthy of great respect because the training was so difficult. But it carried great rewards. Indeed, the scribal author of a document from the Middle Kingdom called "The Satire of the Trades" exhorted the beginning student to persevere by reminding him how much better off he would be than everyone else.

The Power of Writing

Among the many facets of Egyptian culture that have fascinated generations of scholars is the Egyptian system of pictographic writing. Called *hieroglyphs* (HI-eroh-glifs) or "sacred carvings" by the Greeks, these strange and elaborate symbols remained completely impenetrable (and thus all the more mysterious) until the nineteenth century, when a French scholar named Jean François Champollion deciphered them with the help of history's most famous decoding device, the Rosetta Stone. This *stele* preserves three versions of the same decree issued in 196 B.C.E., written in ancient Greek, demotic (a later Egyptian script), and hieroglyphics—still in use after more than 3,000 years. Because he could read the text in Greek, Champollion was eventually able to translate the demotic and hieroglyphic texts as well. From this beginning, generations of scholars have added to and refined the knowledge of ancient Egyptian language.

The development of hieroglyphic writing in Egypt dates to around 3200 B.C.E., when pictograms begin to appear in Mesopotamia. But the uses of writing for government and administration developed far more quickly in Egypt than in Sumer. And unlike Sumerian cuneiform, Egyptian hieroglyphics never evolved into a system of phonograms. Instead, the Egyptians developed a faster, cursive script for representing hieroglyphics called *hieratic*, which they employed for the everyday business of government and commerce. They also developed a shorthand version that scribes could use for rapid note-taking. Little of this hieratic script remains, however, due to the perishable nature of the medium on which it was usually written, papyrus. Produced by hammering, drying, and processing river reeds, papyrus was much lighter, easier to write on, and more transportable than the clay tablets used by the Sumerians. When sewn together into scrolls, papyrus also made it possible to record and store large quantities of information in very small packages. Production of this versatile writing material remained one of Egypt's most important industries and exports throughout antiquity and into the Middle Ages. Yet even in the arid environment of Egypt, which has preserved so many ancient artifacts, papyrus is fragile and subject to decay. Compared to the huge volume of papryrus documents that would have been produced, therefore, the quantity that survives is small, and this significantly limits our understanding of Old Kingdom Egypt.

The origins of the ancient Egyptian language in which these texts were written has long been a matter of debate, and it can be plausibly linked to both the Semitic languages of the Near East and a number of African language groups. Whatever its origins, the Egyptian language has enjoyed a long history. Eventually, it became the tongue known as Coptic, which is still used today in the liturgy of the Coptic Christian church in Ethiopia.

Imhotep and the Step Pyramid

One of the greatest administrative officials in the history of Egypt exemplifies both the skills and the possibilities for advancement that the consummate scribe could command.

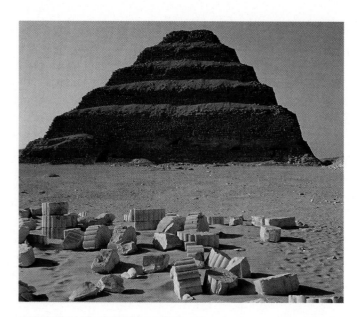

STEP PYRAMID OF KING DJOSER. This monument to the pharoah's power and divinity was designed by the palace official Imhotep around 2650 B.C.E. It served as a prototype for the pyramids constructed at Giza in the following century.

Imhotep (*im-HO-tep*) rose through the ranks of the pharaoh's administration to become a sort of prime minister, the right-hand man to Djoser (*ZOH-ser*), a pharaoh of the Third Dynasty (c. 2686–2613 B.C.E.). Imhotep's learning included medicine, astronomy, theology, and mathematics, but above all he was an architect. Earlier pharaohs had already devoted enormous resources to their burial arrangements at Abydos. It was Imhotep, however, who designed the Step Pyramid, the first building in history constructed entirely of dressed stone. It was not only to be the final resting place of Djoser but an expression of his transcendent power as the pharaoh.

Built west of the administrative capital at Memphis, the Step Pyramid towers over the desert to a height of 200 feet. Surrounding this structure was a huge temple and mortuary complex, perhaps modeled after Djoser's palace. These buildings served two purposes. First and foremost, they would provide Djoser's *ka*, his spirit, with a habitation and sustenance in the afterlife. Second, the design of the buildings, with their labyrinthine passageways, would (it was hoped) thwart tomb robbers, a chronic problem as pharaonic burials became more and more tempting to thieves.

Imhotep set a precedent to which all other Old Kingdom pharaohs would aspire. The pyramids on the plain of Giza, built during the Fourth Dynasty (2613–2494 B.C.E.), are a case in point. The Great Pyramid itself, built for the pharaoh Khufu (*KOO-foo*, called Cheops by the Greeks), was originally 481 feet high and 756 feet along each side of its base, constructed from more than 2.3 million limestone blocks and enclosing a volume of about 91 million cubic feet. In ancient times, the entire pyramid was encased in gleaming white limestone and topped by a gilded capstone, as were the two massive but slightly smaller pyramids built for Khufu's successors. During the Middle Ages, the Muslim rulers of nearby Cairo had their builders strip off the pyramid's casing stones and used them to construct and fortify their new city. (The gold capstones had probably disappeared already.) But in antiquity these pyramids would have glistened brilliantly by day and glowed by night, making them visible for miles in all directions. The Greek historian Herodotus (*heh-RAH-duh-tuhs*), who toured Egypt more than 2,000 years after the pyramids were built, estimated that it must have taken 100,000 laborers 20 years to build the Great Pyramid. This is probably an exaggeration, but it is a measure of the impression these monuments made.

Once thought to have been the work of slaves, the pyramids were in fact raised by tens of thousands of peasant workers, who labored most intensively on the pyramids while their fields were under water during the Nile's annual flood. Still, the investment of human and material resources required to build the great pyramids put grave strains on Egyptian society. Control over the lives of individual Egyptians increased and the number of administrative officials employed by the state grew ever larger. So too did the contrast between the lifestyle of the pharaoh's splendid court at Memphis and that of Egyptian society as a whole.

The End of the Old Kingdom

For reasons that are not entirely clear, the Fifth and Sixth Dynasties of the Old Kingdom (2494–2181 B.C.E.) witnessed the slow erosion of pharaonic power. Although pyramid construction continued, the monuments of this period are less impressive in design, craftsmanship, and size, perhaps mirroring the diminishing prestige of the pharaohs who ordered them built. Instead, the priesthood of Ra at Nekhen, which was the center of worship for the god Horus and the place where Narmer's unification of Egypt was memorialized, began to assert its own authority over that of the pharaoh. Ultimately, it declared that the pharaoh was not an incarnation of Horus or Ra, but merely the god's earthly son. This was a blow to the heart of Egyptian political theology. More practically threatening was the growing power of the pharaoh's nomarchs, whose increased authority in the provinces allowed them to become a hereditary local nobility: precisely what the vigorous kings of earlier dynasties had refused to permit.

PYRAMIDS AT GIZA. The Great Pyramid of Khufu (Cheops) is in the center, and was completed c. 2560 B.C.E. The pyramids are not only monuments to pharaonic power, they exemplify the enormous wealth and human resources of Egyptian society.

Scholars are uncertain as to how certain priests and local officials were able to take power away from the pharaonic center. It may be that the costly building efforts of the Fourth Dynasty had overstrained the economy, while the continued channeling of resources to the royal capital at Memphis increased shortages and resentments in the provinces. Other evidence points to changing climatic conditions that may have disrupted the regular inundations of the Nile, leading to famine in the countryside. Meanwhile, small states were beginning to form to the south in Nubia. With better organization and equipment, the Nubians may have restricted Egyptian access to precious metal deposits, further crippling the Egyptian economy.

As a result, the pharaoh's power diminished accordingly. Local governors and religious authorities began to emerge as the only effective guarantors of stability and order. By 2160 B.C.E., which marks the beginning of what historians call the First Intermediate Period, Egypt had effectively ceased to exist as a united entity. The central authority of the pharaoh in Memphis collapsed, and a more ancient distribution of power reemerged: a northern center of influence based at Herakleopolis (*her-ah-clay-OH-polis*) was opposed by a southern regime headquartered at Thebes, with families from each region claiming to be the legitimate pharaohs of all Egypt.

Compared to the centralized authority of the Old Kingdom, this looks like chaos. But redistribution of power always leads to some important developments in any society. In Egypt, wealth became much more widely and evenly diffused than it had been, as did access to education, the opportunities for the creation of art, and the possibilities for personal advancement. Resources that the pharaoh's court at Memphis had once monopolized now remained in the provinces, enabling local elites to emerge as both protectors of society and as patrons of local artisans. Many arts and luxuries—including elaborate rites for the dead—had been developed originally at the pharaoh's court, and limited to it. Now, however, they became available to Egyptian society as a whole.

EGYPTIAN SOCIETY AND CULTURE

Given the powerful impression conveyed by their monumental architecture, it may seem surprising that the ancient Egyptians lagged far behind the Sumerians and Akkadians in science and mathematics, as well as in the application of new technologies. Only in the calculation of time did the Egyptians make notable advances, since their close observation of the sun for religious and agricultural reasons led them to develop a solar calendar that was far more accurate than the Mesopotamian lunar calendar. Whereas the Sumerians have bequeathed to us their means of dividing and measuring the day, the Egyptian calendar is the direct ancestor of the Julian Calendar adopted for Rome by Julius Caesar in 45 B.C.E. (see Chapter 5) and later corrected by Pope Gregory XIII in 1582 C.E.: this is the calendar we use today.

The social pyramid of Old Kingdom Egypt was extremely steep. At its apex stood the pharaoh and his extended family, whose prestige and power set them entirely apart from all other Egyptians. Below them was a class of nobles, whose primary role was to serve as priests and officials of the pharaoh's government; scribes were usually recruited and trained from among the sons of these families. All of these Egyptian elites lived in considerable luxury. They owned extensive estates, exotic possessions, and fine furniture. They kept dogs and cats and monkeys as pets, and hunted and fished for sport.

Beneath this tiny minority was everyone else. Most Egyptians lived in crowded conditions in simple mud-brick dwellings. During a period of prosperity, master craftsmen— jewelers, goldsmiths, and the like—could improve their own conditions and those of their families by fulfilling the needs of the wealthy, but they did not constitute anything like a middle class. Other skilled professionals—potters, weavers, masons, bricklayers, brewers, merchants, and schoolteachers— also enjoyed some measure of respect as well as a higher standard of living. The vast majority of Egyptians, however, were laborers who provided the brute force necessary for agriculture and construction. Beneath them were slaves, typically captives from foreign wars rather than native Egyptians.

The Egyptians of this era apparently had no need for written laws beyond what was customary in their communities, or what was proclaimed as law by their pharaoh. Yet despite the enormous demands the pharaohs placed on Egypt's wealth, their rule does not appear to have been perceived as particularly oppressive. Commoners' belief in the pharaoh's divinity made them willing subjects, as did the material benefits of living in a stable, well-governed society. Even slaves had certain legal rights, including the ability to own, sell, and bequeath personal property.

Women in the Old Kingdom

Egyptian women also enjoyed unusual freedoms by the standards of the ancient world. Female commoners were recognized as persons in their own right and were allowed to initiate complaints (including suits for divorce), to defend themselves and act as witnesses, to possess property of their own, and to dispose of it: all without the sanction of a male guardian or representative, as was typically required in other ancient societies—and in most modern ones until the twentieth century. Women were not allowed to undergo formal scribal training, but surviving personal notes exchanged between high-born ladies suggest at least some degree of female literacy.

Women were also barred from holding high office, apart from that of priestess and also, importantly, queen. Queens are often represented as the partners of their royal husbands and were certainly instrumental in ruling alongside them. And occasionally, a woman from the royal family might assume pharaonic authority for a time, as did Queen Khasekhemwy (kah-sehk-KEM-wee, d. 2686 B.C.E.) on behalf of her son Djoser before he came of age. Some may even have ruled in their own right; this was certainly the case under the New Kingdom (see Chapter 2).

Gender divisions were less clearly defined among the peasantry. The limitations of our sources, however, means that we can only glimpse the lives of peasants through the eyes of their social superiors. Whatever their status, it seems that women did not enjoy sexual equality. While most Egyptians practiced monogamy, wealthy men could and did keep a number of lesser wives, concubines, and female slaves; and any Egyptian man, married or not, enjoyed freedoms that were denied to women, who would be subject to severe punishments under the law if they were viewed as guilty of any misconduct.

Egyptian Religion and Worldview

As noted above, the environment of Egypt and the special benefits it conferred on its inhabitants were construed as peculiar divine gifts, renewed each year through the mediation of the pharoah, who was god on earth. Although the Egyptians told a variety of stories that dealt with the creation of their world, these were not greatly concerned with how humanity came to exist. Rather, what mattered was the means by which all life was created and re-created in an endless cycle of renewal. At the heart of Egyptian religion lay the myth of Osiris and Isis, two of the gods most fundamental to Egyptian belief. Osiris was, in a sense, the first pharaoh: the first god to hold kingship on earth. But his brother, Seth, wanted the throne for himself. So Seth betrayed and killed Osiris, sealing his body in a coffin. Then his loyal sister Isis retrieved the corpse and managed to revive it long enough to conceive her brother's child, the god Horus. Enraged by this, Seth seized Osiris' body and hacked it to pieces, spreading the remains all over Egypt. Still undeterred, Isis sought the help of Anubis, the god of the afterlife. Together, they found, reassembled, and preserved the scattered portions of Osiris' body, thus inventing the practice of mummification. Afterward, Horus, with the help of his mother, managed to defeat Seth. Osiris was avenged and revived as god of the underworld, and the cycle of his death, dismemberment, and resurrection was reflected in the yearly renewal of Egypt itself.

Life and Death in Ancient Egypt

In addition to embodying Egypt's continual regeneration, Osiris exemplified the Egyptian attitude toward death, which was very different from the Sumerians' bleak view. For the Egyptians, death was a rite of passage, a journey to be endured on the way to an afterlife that was more or less like one's earthly existence, only better. To be sure, the journey was full of dangers. After death, the individual body's *ka*, or life force, would have to roam the Duat, the underworld, searching for the House of Judgment. There, Osiris and forty-two other judges would decide the ka's fate. Demons and evil spirits might try to frustrate the ka's quest to reach the House of Judgment, and the journey might take some time. But if successful and judged worthy, the deceased would enjoy immortality as an aspect of Osiris.

Egyptian funerary rites aimed to emulate the example set by Isis and Anubis, who had carefully preserved the parts of Osiris' body and enabled his afterlife. This is why the Egyptians developed their sophisticated techniques of embalming, whereby all of the body's vital organs were removed and then treated with chemicals—except for the heart, which played a key role in the ka's final judgment. A portrait mask was then placed on the mummy before burial, so that the deceased would be recognizable despite being wrapped in hundreds of yards of linen. To sustain the ka on his or her journey, food, clothing, utensils, weapons, and other items of vital importance would be placed in the grave along with the body.

"Coffin texts," or books of the dead, also accompanied the body and were designed to speed the ka's journey. They contained special instructions that would help the ka travel through the underworld and prepare it for the final test. They also described the "negative confession" the ka would make before the court of Osiris, a formal denial of offenses commited in life. The god Anubis would then weigh the deceased's heart against the principle of *ma'at*: truth, order, justice. Because ma'at was often envisioned as a goddess wearing a plumed headdress, a feather from this headdress would be placed in the scales opposite the heart; only if the heart was light (empty of wrongdoing) and in perfect balance with the feather would the ka achieve immortality.

This manner of confronting death has often led to the erroneous assumption that the ancient Egyptians were pessimistic, but in actuality their practices and beliefs were inherently life affirming, bolstered by confidence in the renewal of creation. Binding together this endless cycle was ma'at, the serene order of the universe, and embodying ma'at on earth was the pharaoh. But when that order broke down, so too did their confidence in the pharaoh's power.

The Widening Horizons of the Middle Kingdom (2055–c. 1650 B.C.E.)

After the disruption of Old Kingdom authority around 2160 B.C.E., warfare between competing pharaonic dynasties would continue for over a century. Then, in 2055 B.C.E., the Theban king Mentuhotep II conquered the northerners and declared himself the ruler of a united Egypt. His reign marks the beginning of Egypt's Middle Kingdom and the reestablishment of a unified government, but this time centered in Thebes rather than Memphis. The architect of this new government was Mentuhotep's chief supporter, Amenemhet (*ah-meh-NEHM-het*), who seized power after the king's death and established himself and his descendants as Egypt's Twelfth Dynasty.

This succession of remarkable pharaohs remained in power for nearly 200 years, and under them the Egyptians began to exploit more thoroughly the potential for trade to the south. They secured their border with Nubia and began to send mounted expeditions to the land they called Punt, probably the coast of Somalia. By the middle of the nineteenth century B.C.E., Nubia was firmly under Egypt's control. Meanwhile, diplomatic relations with the smaller states and principalities of Palestine and Syria led to decisive Egyptian political and economic influence in this region. These lands were not incorporated into Egypt; instead, Amenemhet constructed the Walls of the Prince in Sinai to guard against incursions from the Near East.

These huge fortifications built along Egypt's new frontier demonstrate the great resourcefulness of the Twelfth Dynasty, and their very different ways of allocating resources and expressing ambition. As such, they also display a marked shift in the Egyptian outlook on the world. Gone was the placid serenity epitomized by ma'at and the shared devotion to the pharaoh that had built the pyramids. Egyptians could no longer be dismissive of outsiders or disregard the world beyond their borders. Egypt was not yet an imperial power; the pharaohs of the Middle Kingdom made no attempt to absorb conquests into their kingdom. But unlike their Old Kingdom counterparts, the Egyptians of the Middle Kingdom were not turned in on themselves. Their attitude to the pharaoh also changed. Although they continued to enjoy special position as divine representatives, the pharaohs of the Middle Kingdom represented themselves as what they were expected to be—good shepherds, tenders of their flock. Only by diligently protecting Egypt from a hostile outside world could a pharaoh provide the peace, prosperity, and security desired by his subjects; his alignment with ma'at was now conditional, and it had to be earned.

The literature of the Middle Kingdom expresses the general change in attitude. Among the most popular literary forms were manuals ostensibly written by or for kings, detailing the duties and perils of high office and offering advice for dealing with difficult situations. These include *The Instruction of Ptah-Hotep*, an example of Egyptian "wisdom literature" attributed to a court official of the Old Kingdom, which achieved a wider readership in this new

After You Read This Chapter

Visit StudySpace for quizzes, additional review materials, and multi-media documents. **wwnorton.com/studyspace**

REVIEWING THE OBJECTIVES

- The study of the distant past is challenging because written sources are rare. What other sources of information do historians use?
- All civilizations require the same basic things and share certain characteristics. What are they?
- The cities of Mesopotamia remained largely independent from one another, yet shared a common culture. Why was this the case?
- Hammurabi's empire created a new precedent for governance in Mesopotamia. How did he achieve this?
- The civilizations of ancient Mesopotamia and Egypt differ in profound ways. What were the major causes of their differences?

era. Ptah-Hotep's teaching is upbeat and practical; by contrast, the examples of this genre produced under the Middle Kingdom are bleakly pragmatic. Reading between the lines, we discern that Egyptians' sense of their own superiority—a product of their isolation and their comparatively benign environment—had been shattered. They saw themselves being drawn into a much wider world, and in the course of the next millennium, they would become more fully a part of it.

CONCLUSION

While the story of Babel records the legendary loss of communication, this chapter shows that people of the distant past can still speak to us. The marks they have left on the landscape, the remains of their daily lives, their written records, and their very bodies make it possible for historians to piece together the evidence and to make sense of it. And every year new sources come to light, meaning that we have to be ready to revise, constantly, our understanding of what happened in the past.

Although this chapter has emphasized the differences between the early civilizations of Mesopotamia and Egypt, it is worth noting some significant similarities. Both developed the fundamental technologies of writing at about the same time, and this facilitated political alliances, long-distance trade, and the transmission of vital information to posterity. During the third millennium, both underwent a process of political consolidation, an elaboration of religious ritual, and a melding of spiritual and political leadership. Both engaged in massive building and irrigation projects, and both commanded material and human resources on an enormous scale. At the same time, each of these civilizations cultivated an inward focus. Although they had some contact with each other, and some transfers of information and technology probably took place, there were few significant political or cultural interactions. For all intents and purposes, they inhabited separate worlds. This relative isolation was about to change, however. The next millennium would see the emergence of large-scale, land-based empires that would transform life in Mesopotamia, Egypt, and the lands that lay between them. These are the developments we examine in Chapter 2.

PEOPLE, IDEAS, AND EVENTS IN CONTEXT

- What fundamental changes associated with the **NEOLITHIC REVOLUTION** made early civilizations possible?
- What new technologies allowed the **SUMERIANS** to master the environment of **MESOPOTAMIA**, and how did these technologies contribute to the development of a new, urbanized society?
- By contrast, why did the Nile River foster a very different civilization and enable the centralized authority of the **PHARAOH**?
- How do the differences between **CUNEIFORM** and **HIEROGLYPHS** reflect the different circumstances in which they were invented and the different uses to which they were put?
- In what ways are the **EPIC OF GILGAMESH** and the **CODE OF HAMMURABI** rich sources of information about the civilizations of Sumer and **BABYLON**?
- How do the **ZIGGURATS** of Mesopotamia and the **PYRAMIDS** of Egypt exemplify different forms of power, different ideas about the gods, and different beliefs about the afterlife?
- Why was the worldview of ancient Egyptians, which was strongly reflected in the concept of **MA'AT** during the **OLD KINGDOM**, altered in significant ways by the time of the **MIDDLE KINGDOM**?

CONSEQUENCES

- How do the surviving sources of any period limit the kinds of questions that we can ask and answer about the distant past? In your view, are there sources for this early era that have been undervalued? For example, if writing had not been developed in Mesopotamia and Egypt, what would we still be able to know about the civilizations of these two regions?
- What features of ancient civilizations do modern civilizations share? What might be the implications of these shared ideas, social structures, and technologies?

Before You Read This Chapter

Peoples, Gods, and Empires, 1700–500 B.C.E.

According to Hesiod, a Greek poet who flourished during the eighth century B.C.E., all of human history falls into five ages. The dawn of time was a golden age, when men lived like gods. Everything was good then, food was plentiful, and work was easy. The next age was silver, when men took gods for granted, killed one another, and lived in dishonor. So the gods destroyed them, sending a mighty flood that spared only the family of Deucalion, who built an ark. Then came the age of bronze, when everything was made of bronze—houses and armor and weapons and tools—and giants fought incessantly from huge strongholds, causing destruction so great that no man's name survives. The time following was short but bright, a heroic age, the time of men who ventured with Theseus and fought beside Achilles and sailed with Odysseus, men whose names will live forever. But Hesiod's own age was iron: a dull age, a time of tedium and strife and bickering and petty feuds.`

Hesiod's periodization captures an understanding of history that had evolved with humanity itself and reflects actual developments. The stories he knew told of a time before cities.

They recalled a time when the harmony between gods and men broke down, and the human race was saved by one man's ingenuity: Utnapishtim-Noah-Deucalion. They chronicled the wars of the age we still call Bronze, when the enormous abandoned palaces visible in Hesiod's day were built. And they remembered the race of heroes whose glory was measured by their abiding fame, and who bequeathed a further round of stories. Thanks to new archeological finds, new linguistic discoveries, and new efforts at decoding the historical record, we can both confirm and correct Hesiod's perspective on the past.

In the second millennium B.C.E., the ancient Near East was transformed by the arrival of new peoples and by the emergence of extensive land-based empires built up through systematic military conquest. These migrations and conquests caused upheaval, but they also led to cultural contact and economic integration. By the thirteenth century B.C.E., nations from the southern Balkans in Europe to the western fringes of Iran in the Ancient Near East had been drawn into a wide-ranging web of relationships.

But this extraordinary system proved more fragile than its participants could have imagined. Around 1200 B.C.E., a wave of mysterious invasions led to the destruction of nearly every Bronze Age civilization. As a result, around the turn of the first millennium B.C.E. we enter a new world organized along profoundly different lines. In this new age, iron would slowly replace bronze as the primary component of tools and weapons. New and more brutal empires would come to power, while new ideas about the divine and its relationship to humanity would emerge. Two of the Western world's most enduring religious traditions—Judaism and Zoroastrianism (zoh-roh-AHS-tree-anism)—were born, fundamentally altering conceptions of ethics, politics, and the natural world. This Iron Age would prove a fateful historical crossroads, as elements both old and new combined to reconfigure the ancient world.

INDO-EUROPEAN LANGUAGES AND PEOPLES

In 1786, a British judge serving in India made a discovery that transformed the understanding of history. Turning his spare time to the study of Sanskrit, the ancient language of South Asia, Sir William Jones discovered that it shares the same grammar and vocabulary as ancient Greek and Latin—to an extent inexplicable by sheer coincidence. He then examined the early Germanic and Celtic languages of Europe and the Old Persian language of the Near East, and found that they also exhibit marked similarities. He concluded that all of these languages must have evolved from a common source. Within another generation, the ancient language whose existence Jones had hypothesized, and the later languages derived from it, would be labeled Indo-European, reflecting their wide distribution from India to Ireland. The Biblical story of mankind's shared language, the story of Babel, turns out to be partly true.

Since then, scholars have greatly enlarged our understanding of Indo-European languages and their speakers. Yet much remains controversial. It is certain that Indo-European linguistic forms begin to appear in the Near East and eastern Mediterranean shortly after 2000 B.C.E. Around this same time, a group of Indo-European speakers also moved into the Aegean basin, where the resulting language became an early form of Greek. Other Indo-European speakers went east; some may have reached western China.

These were not the only new peoples moving into the Near East. As we noted in Chapter 1, Semitic-speaking peoples were also making their mark, beginning with the Akkadians and the Amorites, from whose ranks Hammurabi came. The Assyrians, the Phoenicians, and the Canaanites would also become prominent. These newcomers did not wipe out existing cultures; rather, they built on established patterns of urban life and organization. But their collective impact was enormous.

New Settlers in Anatolia

By 1900 B.C.E., the nomadic Assyrians had become caravan merchants whose extensive trade networks stretched across Anatolia and Mesopotamia. They relied on the protection of local rulers and, in turn, they made these rulers rich. They also served as advisers and officials, and married into important urban families. In the process, they carried Mesopotamian civilization and its trappings into far-flung regions.

In their wake, new population groups were attracted to Anatolia, northern Syria, and Mesopotamia. The most formidable of these were the Hittites, an Indo-European-speaking people who arrived around 2000 B.C.E. In contrast to the Assyrians, the Hittites were conquerors and colonists who imposed themselves and their language on the peoples they vanquished. By 1700 B.C.E., they had integrated many city-states into a larger kingdom.

The Hittites' warrior aristocracy fielded the most fearsome army of the Bronze Age. They were quick to adopt the latest technologies, including the chariot and (eventually) the use of iron for weaponry. But the Hittites also adopted the more peaceful practices of those they conquered, using cuneiform to record their own language and laws. And they sought to control trade routes, particularly the overland trade in copper and arsenic, the raw materials for making bronze. By 1595 B.C.E., they had captured Babylon.

A century later, the Kassites, another new people, moved into that devastated city. For the next 500 years, they presided over a largely prosperous Babylonian realm. The Hittites, however, continued to destabilize the region, until they were themselves checked by the arrival of a people known as the Mitannians, whose initial advantage was their use of horses, hitherto unknown outside the steppes of Asia. Their light, horse-drawn chariots became terrifying death-machines, transporting archers rapidly around the battlefield. The Mitannians also pioneered cavalry tactics. Eventually, however, their opponents borrowed these same technologies, and the Hittites once again achieved the advantage and turned their attention to Egypt.

THE NEW KINGDOM OF EGYPT

As we have seen, Egypt's Middle Kingdom had been formed by the many internal changes of the First Intermediate Period, chiefly the redistribution of wealth and power. Now it was further transformed by external forces, through the dynamic movement of new peoples. Some of these came to Egypt as immigrants; others were hired as mercenaries. And for a while, a strategy of accommodation preserved Egypt from large-scale armed attack and fostered commercial exchange with neighboring regions. But around 1700 B.C.E., Egypt was invaded for the first time since the unification of the Upper and Lower Kingdoms. These invaders' origins and identity remain mysterious; the Egyptians called them simply Hyksos (*HIHK-sohs*), "rulers of foreign lands." The Hyksos began to project their authority over most of Lower Egypt.

With this conquest, the central authority of the pharaoh once again dissolved and Egypt entered what scholars call the Second Intermediate Period (c. 1650–1550 B.C.E.). Significantly, however, the Hyksos took over the machinery of pharaonic government in Lower Egypt and took steps to legitimize their rule. In Upper Egypt, by contrast, Hyksos power was weak. Here, a native pharaonic regime maintained a tenuous independence at the traditional capital of Thebes.

Although the Hyksos established Lower Egypt as the most significant power in the Near East, their conquest also weakened the dominion of Upper Egypt over the Nubians, who eventually founded an independent kingdom called Kush. This Nubian kingdom posed a much greater threat to the native dynasty at Thebes than to the Hyksos in Lower Egypt—but it also provided additional incentive to southern pharaohs determined to oust the Hyksos. By the end of the sixteenth century B.C.E., the pharaoh Ahmose had driven them out, establishing the Eighteenth Dynasty and the New Kingdom of Egypt.

The Pharaohs of the Eighteenth Dynasty

Under the Eighteenth Dynasty, Egyptian civilization reached the height of its magnificence and power. Although many Egyptian traditions were renewed and strengthened, the dynamism of the New Kingdom—particularly its new focus on imperial expansion—changed the very fabric of Egyptian life, which had never before looked beyond the narrow world of the Nile Valley. Among the striking developments that took place during this period was the rise of a new aristocracy whose wealth was acquired through warfare and the winning of lands (with slaves to work them) which they received from the pharaoh as rewards for service. The Eighteenth Dynasty itself was forged in battle. Ahmose, the man who expelled the Hyksos, had been reared by the warrior queen Ahhotep. His eventual successor, Thutmose I (r. 1504–1492 B.C.E.), was the son of an unknown warrior who married Ahmose's daughter.

Under Thutmose's leadership, the Egyptians subdued the Nubians to the south, seizing control of their gold mines. They also penetrated beyond their northeastern frontier, driving deep into Palestine and Syria. By the time of his death, Thutmose could claim to rule the land from beyond the Nile's Fourth Cataract to the banks of the Euphrates. Never had Egypt so clearly declared its imperial ambitions. Nor was this success fleeting. The Egyptians would sustain a strong military presence in the Near East for the next 400 years.

The Legacy of Hatshepsut

The early death of Thutmose's son and successor could have resulted in a crisis for the Eighteenth Dynasty. Instead, it led to one of the most remarkable reigns in Egypt's history,

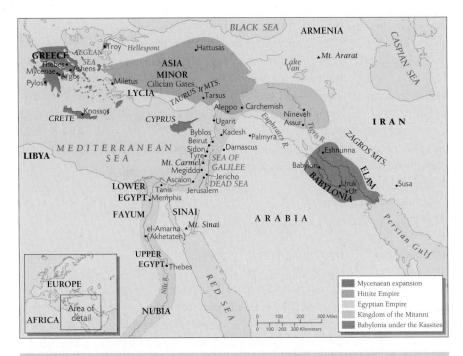

EGYPT AND ITS NEIGHBORS, C. 1400 B.C.E. ▪ *What factors appear to shape patterns of conquest and settlement in the Mediterranean?* ▪ *What political developments dominate this map?* ▪ *What developments would have enabled trade to flourish during this period?*

and extended trade. The arts also flourished, setting standards that would be emulated for a thousand years. Indeed, Hatshepsut was one of the most ambitious builders in Egyptian history, which is saying something. Her own mortuary temple was probably the first tomb constructed in the Valley of the Kings, the New Kingdom's answer to the pyramids.

Yet after Hatshepsut's death in 1458 B.C.E. her legacy was called into question. At some point late in her nephew's reign, attempts were made to remove her name from inscriptions and to destroy her images (see **Interpreting Visual Evidence** on page 34). Scholars used to assume that Thutmose himself was responsible for this, because he resented his stepmother/aunt's power over him. But more recent research has suggested that the culprit was his son, Amenhotep II (r. 1427–1400 B.C.E.), who was thereby blocking the claims of royal rivals, possibly Hatshepsut's daughter, Neferure.

for Thutmose II (r. 1492–1479 B.C.E.) passed the power of pharaoh to his sister, wife, and co-ruler Hatshepsut (*haht-SHEHP-soot*, r. 1479–1458 B.C.E.). Such brother-sister unions were common in the Egyptian royal family, although they do not appear to have been the routine way to produce royal children: pharaohs customarily kept a harem of subsidiary wives and concubines for this purpose. However, Thutmose II and Hatshepsut did conceive at least one child together, Neferure; in fact, she may have been their designated heir. For 21 years, Hatshepsut ruled as pharaoh in her own right, while her daughter took on the usual duties of queen.

Like her great-grandmother, Ahhotep, Hatshepsut was a warrior. Moroever, she was routinely protrayed on monuments and in statuary with the masculine figure and ceremonial beard characteristic of pharaohs. She did not pretend to be a man: inscriptions almost always indicate her gender, and she herself claimed to be the most beautiful woman in the world. But it was important to Egyptians that she use the conventional iconography of power to locate herself firmly within a long history of male dynastic rule.

Hatshepsut's statecraft proved crucial to the continuing success of Egypt. With her stepson/nephew, Thutmose III, she launched several successful military campaigns

The Power of the Priesthood

The great conquests of the Eighteenth Dynasty brought mind-boggling riches to Egypt. Much of this wealth went to the glorification of the pharaoh in the form of grand temples, tombs, and other monuments, including the thousands of steles that provide us with so much information about this era. Another significant portion of the plunder went to the military aristocracy that made such conquests possible. But the lion's share went to the gods as offerings of thanks. As the temples became wealthy and powerful, so too did their priests. But no temple complex was so well endowed as that of Amon at Thebes.

Thebes was not only the capital of New Kingdom Egypt, it was also the place most sacred to Amon (or Amun), the god of creation, who played an important role in the dynasty's self-image. Amon had come into prominence when the political center of gravity shifted to Thebes during the Middle Kingdom, and his cult had steadily increased in status and popularity. By 1550 B.C.E. he had become identified as another manifestation of the sun god Ra, and was believed to be the divine force behind the Eighteenth Dynasty's triumph over the Hyksos. This accounts for the favor shown to his priests at Thebes, who became a formidable political force. Eventually, they surpassed even the military aristocracy in importance and influence.

The Reign of Akhenaten (1352–1336 B.C.E.)

All of these factors are important when we consider the reign of Amenhotep IV, who inherited the vast, well-governed kingdom assembled by his predecessors. This young pharaoh showed an early inclination toward the worship of the sun, but not as an aspect of Amon. Instead, Amenhotep (whose dynastic name means "Amon Is Pleased") exalted Ra as a discrete divinity and laid aside the traditional iconography of this god as a falcon (or a falcon-headed man), replacing it with the symbol *Aten*, the hieroglyph representing the sun's rays. He then went farther, changing his own name to Akhenaten (*AH-keh-NAH-ton*), "He Who Is Profitable to the Aten," and building a new capital to honor the god. Located halfway between Memphis and Thebes, it was called Akhetaten ("The Horizon of the Aten").

Although the priesthood of Amon exalted Amon-Ra, it also recognized all the other gods of Egypt. Akhenaten's theology, by contrast, was closer to monotheism. And unlike traditional Egyptian deities, the Aten could not be imagined as taking on human or animal form. Akhenaten also celebrated his new religion by representing himself in a very unconventional way. In a complete departure from the divine virility of his ancestors—which even his ancestor Hatshepsut had emulated—Akhenaten had himself pictured as a family man enjoying the company of his wife, Nefertiti, and their children. This emphasis on his own humanity might have been an extension of his theology, which honored the life force within every being. But it was also dangerous to the ideology of royal power. The pharaoh was not supposed to be a man with quirky personality. He was supposed to be a god on earth.

Akhenaten's spiritual revolution therefore had enormous political implications. Not surprisingly, the priesthood of Amon also put up strenuous resistance. To make matters worse, Akhenaten did not balance his theological enthusiasm with attention to Egypt's interests abroad. This cost him the support of his nobility and may even have led to his deposition. He was ultimately succeeded by one of his younger sons, Tutankhaten ("Living Image of Aten"), a child of nine whose name was quickly changed to reflect the restoration of the god Amon and his priesthood. He became Tutankhamun (r. 1333–1324 B.C.E.), the boy king whose sumptuous tomb was discovered in

AKHENATEN, HIS WIFE NEFERTITI, AND THEIR CHILDREN. The Aten is depicted here as a sun disk, raining down power on the royal family. ▪ *What messages might this image have conveyed to contemporary Egyptians?* ▪ *How does this depiction of the pharaoh differ from earlier precedents?*

1922. After his early death, he was succeeded by a general called Horemheb, who reigned as the last pharaoh of the Eighteenth Dynasty. When he died, he passed his office to another general. This was Ramses, the founder of the Nineteenth Dynasty, who would restore Egypt to glory in the Near East.

TRANSNATIONAL NETWORKS OF THE LATE BRONZE AGE

Bronze Age history must be understood within the context of what we might call international relations. Yet it is more accurate to call the political and economic networks of this period *transnational*, because this web of alliances and relationships transcended any idea of national identity.

Transnational Diplomacy

The Late Bronze Age was an age of superpowers. The great pharaohs of the Eighteenth Dynasty had transformed Egypt into a conquering state, and the Hittites had created an empire out of the disparate city-states and kingdoms of Anatolia. The Assyrians controlled Near Eastern trade, and

Remembering Hatshepsut

The pharaohs of Egypt's New Kingdom carefully controlled their public images. The visual language they used was highly symbolic, an iconography (vocabulary of images) intended to make each successive pharaoh look as much like his royal predecessors as possible: godlike, steadfast, virile, authoritative—even when the pharaoh was a woman, Hatshepsut (r. 1479–1458 B.C.E., images A and B). So many statues and portraits of her survive that nearly every major museum in the world has at least one (the Metropolitan Museum of Art in New York has a whole room set aside for them). But many of these images show signs of having been defaced during the reign of her successor, Thutmose III, who was also her nephew and stepson. Until very recently, scholars assumed that Hatshepsut must have usurped his powers, and that this was his revenge. Yet the evidence clearly shows that Hatshepsut was Egypt's legitimate ruler. Why, then, would Thutmose III or his heirs have tried to efface her memory?

The two unblemished steles shown here depict Hatshepsut and Thutmose III. In the stele on the left (image C), Hatshepsut is placed in the center of the frame, wearing a royal helmet; she is offering wine to the god Amun. Behind her stands Thutmose III, wearing the crown of Upper Egypt. In the stele on the right (image D), Thutmose III wears the warrior's crown, while Hatshepsut wears the double crown of Upper and Lower Egypt and wields a mace.

A. Defaced head of Hatshepsut.

B. Undefaced statue of Hatshepsut.

the Kassite kingdom of Babylonia remained a significant force in economic and military relationships. In addition to these imperial entities, numerous smaller states also flourished and extended their influence.

Although warfare remained the fundamental mode of interaction, a balance of power among the larger empires gradually helped to stabilize the region. By the fourteenth century B.C.E., a wide-ranging correspondence was binding leaders together and promoting a set of mutual goals and understandings. Surviving letters show that the most powerful rulers address one another as "brother," while lesser princes and chieftains show their deference to the pharaoh, the Hittite king, and other sovereigns by using the term "father." Rulers of this period also exchanged lavish gifts and entered into marriage alliances with each other. Professional envoys journeyed back and forth, conveying gifts and handling politically sensitive missions. Some of these emissaries were also merchants, sent to explore the possibility of trading opportunities as well as to cement alliances.

Questions for Analysis

1. Bearing in mind that few Egyptians could read the hieroglyphs accompanying these images, how might they have "read" the relationship between these two royal relatives? Does this evidence support the hypothesis that Thutmose was slighted by Hatshepsut?

2. What can these images tell us about gender roles? What else would we need to know before making a judgment about masculine and feminine characteristics in ancient Egypt?

3. Given that Hatshepsut was Egypt's legitimate pharaoh, what might have motivated either Thutmose III or his son Amenhotep II to deface her image many years after her death?

C. Stele of Hatshepsut and Thutmose.

D. Stele of Thutmos and Hatshepsut, from the Red Chapel at Karnak.

Transnational Trade

Indeed, it was trade that allowed smaller communities to become integral parts of this transnational network. Seaside centers such as Ugarit and Byblos became centers for the exchange of dazzling commodities. A single vessel's cargo might contain scores of distinct items originating anywhere from the interior of Africa to the Baltic Sea, as demonstrated by the contents of a merchant ship discovered at Uluburun off the Turkish coast in 1982. The region was also supplied with goods brought in overland, via contacts reaching into India and the Far East.

Trade was not only the basis for a new economy, but the conduit for art, ideas, and technology. In the past, such influences spread slowly and unevenly; now, the societies of the late Bronze Age could keep abreast of all the latest developments. This trend was particularly marked in large coastal towns. At Ugarit, on the coast of modern-day Syria, the swirl of commerce and the multiplicity of languages spoken by traders even propelled the development of a simpler form of writing than the cuneiform still current throughout most of the Near East. The Ugaritic alphabet consisted of about thirty symbols representing the sounds of consonants. (Vowels had to be inferred.) This system was far more easily mastered and more flexible than cuneiform, and it would become the model for the development of all modern alphabets.

The search for markets, resources, and trade routes also promoted greater understanding among cultures. After a great battle between Egyptians and Hittites near Kadesh (c. 1275 B.C.E.), the pharaoh Ramses II realized that more was to be gained through peaceful relations with his northern neighbors than through warfare. The treaty he established with the Hittites fostered stability and allowed further economic exchanges to flourish. But greater integration also meant greater mutual dependence. If one economy suffered, the effects of that decline were sure to be felt elsewhere. And the farther this transnational system spread, the more vulnerable it became. Many of the new markets depended on emerging societies in regions far less stable, where civilization was also new.

AEGEAN CIVILIZATION: MINOAN CRETE, MYCENAEAN GREECE

Greek poets like Hesiod described a heroic age when great men mingled with gods and powerful kingdoms contended for wealth and glory. For a long time, modern scholars dismissed these stories as fables. Tales of Theseus and the Minotaur, the Trojan War, and the wanderings of Odysseus were regarded as reflecting no historical reality. Greek history was assumed to begin in 776 B.C.E., when the first recorded Olympic Games occurred. Greece in the Bronze Age was considered a primitive backwater that played no significant role in the Mediterranean world or in the later, glorious history of classical Greece.

But in the late nineteenth century, an amateur archeologist named Heinrich Schliemann became convinced that these myths were really historical accounts. Using the epic poems of Homer as his guide, he found the site of Ilium (Troy) near the coast of northwest Anatolia. He also identified a number of once-powerful citadels on the Greek mainland, including the home of the legendary king Agamemnon at Mycenae (*MY-seh-nee*). Soon afterward, the British archeologist Sir Arthur Evans took credit for discovering the remains of a great palace at Knossos on the island of Crete that predated any of the major citadels

on the Greek mainland. He dubbed this magnificent culture—which no modern person had known to exist—"Minoan," after King Minos, the powerful ruler whom the ancient Greeks described as dominating the Aegean, and the man for whom the engineer Daedalus had designed the Labyrinth. Although some of their conclusions have proven false, the discoveries of Schliemann and Evans forced scholars to revise, entirely, the history of Western civilizations. It is now clear that Bronze Age Greece—or, as it is often termed, Mycenaean Greece—was an important and integrated part of the Mediterranean world during the second millennium B.C.E.

The Minoan Thalassocracy

In the fifth century B.C.E., the Athenian historian Thucydides wrote that King Minos of Crete had ruled a *thalassocracy*, an empire of the sea. We now know that he was correct, that a very wealthy civilization began to flourish on the island of Crete around 2500 B.C.E. Thereafter, for about a millennium, the Minoans controlled shipping around the central Mediterranean and the Aegean, and may have exacted tribute from many smaller islands. At its height between 1900 and 1500 B.C.E., Minoan civilization was the contemporary of Egypt's Middle Kingdom and the Hittite kingdom. And unlike them, it was virtually unassailable by outside forces, protected by the surrounding sea.

Thanks to its strategic position, Crete was not only a safe haven but also a nexus of vibrant economic exchange. Like its counterparts in the Near East, it acted as a magnet for the collection of resources which were then redistributed by its rulers and their emissaries. Knossos was also a production center for textiles, pottery, and metalwork. Minoan merchants traded these with Egypt, southwest Anatolia, and Cyprus for a range of exotic goods. Artistic influences also traveled along these routes; among much else, Minoan-style paintings from this period appear regularly in the Nile Delta and the Levant.

Traces of the bright colors and graceful lines of these paintings are still evident on the ruined walls of the palace at Knossos. Endowed with indoor plumbing, among other luxuries, it covered several acres and comprised hundreds of rooms joined by an intricate network of winding hallways that inspired the famous story of the Labyrinth. The Minoans probably worshiped a god in the form of a bull or bull-man, and they appear to have devised an elaborate ritual sport known as bull-leaping, similar to bull-fighting but

MINOAN FRESCO, C. 1500 B.C.E. A stylized representation of bull-leaping, painted into the plaster of a wall at Knossos. ▪ *Is this likely to represent real practices?* ▪ *Why or why not?*

involving an element of athletic dance. There is also some evidence that they practiced human sacrifice (possibly facilitated by the dangers of bull-dancing) as a religious rite.

Despite all these fascinating remains, Minoan culture remains mysterious because its language has yet to be decoded. Its script is called Linear A, to distinguish it from Linear B, used in Mycenaean Greece, a script that *has* been deciphered. Although Linear A and Linear B represent different languages, the formal relationship between them reflects the fact that Minoan commercial activity engaged the mainland of Greece. The presence of a wide variety of Minoan objects on the Greek mainland corroborates this.

Yet the dynamics of the relationship between Minoans and Mycenaeans remains debatable. Before 1600 B.C.E., the Minoans were clearly much more sophisticated and may have dominated their Greek neighbors. One story told of Theseus describes how the hero was sent to Crete as a hostage, intending to free Athens from the heavy tribute imposed by King Minos. Given what we have already learned about the close relationship between myth and history, it is probable that this story preserves ancient memory, just as

the story of Daedalus is an attempt to explain the technological marvels of the palace at Knossos.

Mycenaean Greece

When Linear B was deciphered in the early 1950s, the texts written in this script spurred scholars to reconsider the history of ancient Greece. Since then, new research shows that the Indo-Europeans whose language became Greek entered the region in several waves after the turn of the second millennium, dominating and displacing the indigenous inhabitants. By 1500 B.C.E., huge citadels dotted the Greek landscape, ruled by warriors whose epitaphs boast of their martial prowess and who were buried with their weapons. The power of these rulers was based on their leadership and their ability to reward followers with plunder. The most successful of them gained control of strategic sites from which they could exploit major trade routes, engaging in both trade and piracy.

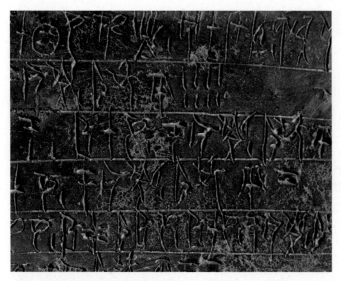

LINEAR B TABLET FROM KNOSSOS. Unlike cuneiform, whose characters are formed using the wedge-shaped tip of a reed, the scripts of Linear A and B used a sharp stylus that incised fine lines in clay or soft stone.

Over time, and perhaps under the influence of Minoan culture, the Mycenaean citadels developed into much more complex societies. They served as both centers of government and warehouses for storage. By the thirteenth century B.C.E., some rulers had carved out territorial kingdoms with as many as 100,000 inhabitants, dwarfing the city-states of the later classical age; Hesiod would imagine their citadels to have been built by giants. These palace centers were adapted from Near Eastern models and their massive size was not ideally suited to the Greek landscape. In war also, Mycenaean imitation of Near Eastern examples had its limits. For example, Mycenaean kings cherished the chariots used by their contemporaries on the plains of Anatolia, yet such chariots were highly impractical on rocky terrain.

Despite these and other differences from their Mediterranean neighbors, the Mycenaean Greeks played an important role in Bronze Age networks. By about 1400 B.C.E., they had subjugated Crete, taking over Knossos and using it as a Mycenaean center. In western Anatolia, not far from Troy, at least one Mycenaean king exercised enough influence for a Hittite ruler to address him as "my brother." This evidence suggests that the Mycenaeans earned prestige as warriors and mercenaries, as the Greeks' heroic poems attest.

The basic political and commercial unit of the Mycenaean world—a powerful king and war leader, a warrior aristocracy, a palace bureaucracy, a complex economy, large territorial kingdoms—differs markedly from the Greek city-state of the classical age (Chapter 3). However,

we can trace some features of this later civilization back to the Mycenaeans, including the Greek language. Linear B tablets speak of a social group with considerable economic and political rights, the *damos*; this may be the precursor of the *demos*, the urban population that sought political empowerment in many Greek cities. The tablets also preserve the names of several gods familiar from the later period, such as Zeus, Poseidon, and Dionysos. And later Greeks believed themselves to be descended from these legendary forebears, whom they credited with superhuman achievements. Although they knew little about their Mycenaean ancestors in fact, the impact of what they imagined about them was considerable.

The Sea Peoples and the End of the Bronze Age

The civilization of Mycenaean Greece seems to have collapsed around the end of the thirteenth century B.C.E. What triggered this cannot be determined with any certainty, but the consequences of the collapse are clear. Because Mycenaean Greece was an integrated part of a transnational network, the effects of its demise were felt throughout the Near East. Thereafter, a wave of devastation swept from north to south, caused by a group of people so thoroughly destructive that they obliterated everything in their path. We might know nothing about them were it not for a narrow victory by the pharaoh Ramses III around 1176 B.C.E.

In the stele set up to commemorate his triumph, Ramses III referred to these invaders as "Sea Peoples" and named several groups as part of a coalition. Some were familiar to the Egyptians, and it seems that many were from the Aegean. Most notable were the Philistines who, after their defeat, withdrew to populate the coast of the region named after them: Palestine.

Because the Sea Peoples' arc of annihilation started in the north, it may have been one of the factors contributing to the collapse of Mycenaean Greece. Disruption of northern commercial networks would have devastated the Mycenaean kingdoms, which could not support their enormous populations without trade. Suddenly faced with an apocalyptic combination of overpopulation, famine, and violence, bands of desperate refugees would have fled the Aegean basin. Meanwhile, the damage to commerce devastated the economy of the Hittites, whose ancient kingdom rapidly disintegrated. Along the Mediterranean coast we find other clues. The king of Ugarit wrote a letter to a "brother" king on the

MYCENAEAN GREECE. ■ *What are the main geographical features of Greece?* ■ *How might this dry, mountainous country surrounded by the sea determine the nature of Greek civilization and economic interests?* ■ *Why was Mycenaean culture able to spread so widely?*

had to fight for their very existence. In Babylon, the peaceful and prosperous rule of the Kassites withered. In the vacuum left behind, new political configurations took shape and a new metallurgical technology began to supplant the use of bronze. Out of the ashes arose the culture of the Iron Age.

THE STATES OF THE EARLY IRON AGE

With the destruction of transnational networks, the geopolitical map of the Near East changed significantly. In Anatolia, a patchwork of small kingdoms grew up within the territories once controlled by the Hittites. Similar developments took place in the Levant, the eastern Mediterranean coastline that today comprises Israel, Lebanon, and parts of Syria. For centuries, this region had been controlled either by the Egyptians or the Hittites. With the collapse of these empires, new states began to emerge here, too. They were small, but they had a huge impact on the history of Western civilizations.

The Phoenicians

The most influential civilization of this period was that of a people whom the Greeks called Phoenicians. They are also known as Canaanites, and were speakers of a Semitic language closely related to Hebrew. During the Late Bronze Age, most Phoenician cities had been controlled by Egypt. But the erosion of Egyptian imperial power after 1200 B.C.E. gave these cities the opportunity to forge a new independence and to capitalize on their commercial advantages. One Phoenician city, Gubla, was a clearing house for papyrus, the highly prized Egyptian writing material. This explains why the Greek name for this city, Byblos, became the basis for the Greek word *biblion*, meaning "book." (The Bible is so called from the plural *biblia*, "the books.") Another valuable commodity came to be the name by which the Phoenicians themselves were known: a rare purple dye derived from the shells of snails culled from seabeds off the

island of Cyprus, begging for immediate aid because he had sent all his own warriors to help the Hittites. Poignantly, however, we have his letter only because the clay tablet on which it was written baked hard in the fire that destroyed his palace. The letter was never sent.

In the end, the Sea Peoples destroyed the civilizations that had flourished in the Near East and Mediterranean for over two thousand years. The devastation was not total; not all cities disappeared, and trade did not cease entirely. But the Hittite Empire was gone, leaving behind it many weak, short-lived principalities. The great cosmopolitan cities of the eastern Mediterranean lay in ruins, and new groups— sometimes contingents of Sea Peoples like the Philistines— populated the coast. The citadels of Mycenaean Greece were depopulated by as much as 90 percent over the next century, and Greece entered into a period of cultural and economic isolation that would last for 250 years.

The victorious Egyptians survived, but with their major trading partners diminished or dead their civilization suffered. The Assyrians, the original architects of the networks that had undergirded the transnational system,

The Diplomacy of the Mycenaeans and the Hittites

Around 1260 B.C.E., the powerful Hittite king Hattusilis III sent the following letter to a "King of Ahhiyawa," identifiable as a leader of the Mycenaean Greeks, who often called themselves Akhaiwoi, Achaeans. This fascinating document exemplifies the tangle of close ties that bound powerful men together within the transnational system of the Late Bronze Age, as well as the problems and misunderstandings that could arise from the misbehavior of men under their command. The events referenced here all occur in western Anatolia (Turkey), a region controlled partly by the Hittites and partly by the Greeks, the same region in which Troy (Ilium) was located. (See the map on page 39.)

have to complain of the insolent and treacherous conduct of one Tawagalawas [*tah-wah-GAH-la-wahs*]. We came into contact in the land of Lycia, and he offered to become a vassal of the Hittite Empire. I agreed, and sent an officer of most exalted rank to conduct him to my presence. He had the audacity to complain that the officer's rank was not exalted enough; he insulted my ambassador in public, and demanded that he be declared vassal-king there and then, without the formality of an interview. Very well: I order him, if he desires to become a vassal of mine, to make sure that no troops of his are found in Iyalanda when I arrive there. And what do I find when I arrive in Iyalanda?—the troops of Tawagalawas, fighting on the side of my enemies. I defeat them, take many prisoners . . . scrupulously leaving the fortress of Atriya intact out of respect for my treaty with you. Now a Hittite subject, Piyamaradus [*pie-yah-ma-RA-dus*] by name, steals my 7,000 prisoners, and makes off to your city of Miletus. I command him to return to me: he disobeys. I write to you: you send a surly message unaccompanied by gift or greeting, to say that you have ordered

your representative in Miletus, a certain Atpas, to deliver up Piyamaradus. Nothing happens, so I go fetch him. I enter your city of Miletus, for I have something to say to Piyamaradus, and it would be well that your subjects there should hear me say it. But my visit is not a success. I ask for Tawagalawas: he is not at home. I should like to see Piyamaradus: he has gone to sea. You refer me to your representative Atpas: I find that both he and his brother are married to daughters of Piyamaradus; they are not likely to give me satisfaction or to give you an unbiased account of these transactions. . . . Are you aware, and is it with your blessing, that Piyamaradus is going round saying that he intends to leave his wife and family, and incidentally my 7,000 prisoners, under your protection while he makes continual inroads on my dominion? . . . Do not let him use Achaea [in Greece] as a base for operations against me. You and I are friends. There has been no quarrel between us since we came to terms in the matter of Ilios [the territory of Troy]: the trouble there was my fault, and I promise it will not happen again. As for my military occupation of Miletus, please regard it as a friendly visit. . . . [As for the problems between us], I suggest that the fault may not lie

with ourselves but with our messengers; let us bring them to trial, cut off their heads, mutilate their bodies, and live henceforth in perfect friendship.

Source: Adapted from Denys Page, *History and the Homeric Iliad* (Berkeley, CA: 1959), pp. 11–12.

Questions for Analysis

1. Reconstruct the relationship between Hattusilis III and the Achaean king, based on the references to people and places in this letter. What picture emerges of their interactions, and of the connections between the Hittite Empire and Mycenaean Greece?

2. Why is Hattusilis so concerned about the disrespect shown to him by the Achaeans? Reading between the lines, what do you think he wanted to accomplish by sending this letter?

3. Based on this letter, what can you deduce about the standards of behavior expected of civilized participants in the transnational system of the Late Bronze Age? Within this code of conduct, what sanctions or penalties could be imposed on individuals or their nations?

Levantine coast. So as far as the Greeks were concerned, those who suppled this dye were *phoinikeoi*, "purple people." The Phoenicians also became expert metalworkers, ivory carvers, and shipbuilders.

Phoenician Colonies and Cultural Influence

The Phoenicians were also aggressive colonists. By the end of the tenth century B.C.E., they had planted settlements from one end of the Mediterranean to the other and had begun to venture out into the Atlantic Ocean.

The widespread colonial and mercantile efforts of the Phoenicians meant that they impacted cultures across the Mediterranean. Among their early overseas trading partners were the Greeks, and the Phoenicians may have played an important role in reintroducing urban life to Greece after the collapse of the Mycenaean citadels. While each city of the Phoenician mainland had its own hereditary royal government, in the Phoenicians' overseas colonies, a new type of political system emerged in which power was shared among a handful of elite families. This aristocratic form of government would become a model for many other Western societies, including those of Greece and Rome.

Without question, however, the most important contribution of the Phoenicians was their alphabet. As we noted earlier, a thirty-character alphabet had evolved at Ugarit by the end of the Bronze Age. Around 1100 B.C.E., the Phoenicians refined this writing system to twenty-two characters. This simpler system further facilitated trade and accounting, and the Phoenicians may have wanted to encourage similar practices among their partners, to safeguard their own interests. The Greeks certainly remained aware of their debt to the Phoenicians: their legends ascribe

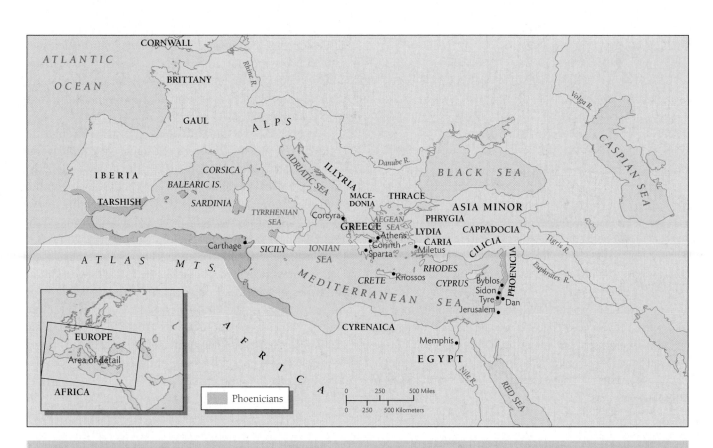

PHOENICIAN COLONIZATION. Compare this map to the more detailed one of Palestine on page 44. ▪ *What part of the Mediterranean serves as the homeland for the Phoenician city-states, and where did Phoenicians establish colonies?* ▪ *Why would overseas colonization be of such crucial importance to Phoenician city-states?* ▪ *What does their westward colonization imply about the Phoenicians' aims and about the different opportunities available in the West, as compared with the East?*

Phoenician	Hebrew	Classical Greek	Modern Alphabetic
✶	א	A	A
⅃	ב	B	B
∧	ג	Γ	G
◢	ד	Δ	D
∃	ה	E	E
Y	ו	Y	V
I	ז	Z	Z
⊟	ח	H	H
⊗	ט	Θ	TH
ใ	י	I	Y
✗	כ	K	K
⎿	ל	Λ	L
⋎	מ	M	M
⤆	נ	N	N
⟊	ס	Ξ	S
O	ע	O	O
⌐	פ	Π	P
⩔	צ		TZ
φ	ק		Q
⅂	ר	P	R
W	ש	Σ	S
✕	ת	T	T

THE EVOLUTION OF THE ALPHABET. This table shows how the shapes of letters changed as the Phoenician alphabet was adapted by the Hebrews, the Greeks, and eventually the Romans (from whom our modern alphabet derives).

the invention of the alphabet to Cadmus, a Phoenician who settled in Greece. Their debt is also clear in the close relationship between the names of letters in Greek (alpha, beta, gamma, delta . . .) and Phoenician letter names (aleph, bayt, gimel, dalet . . .), and from the obvious similarities in letter shapes.

The Philistines

Southward along the Levantine coast from Phoenicia lay the land of the Philistines, descendants of the Sea Peoples defeated by Ramses III. Their bad reputation is the result of their dominance over their neighbors, the herdsmen known as the Hebrews, who used writing as an effective weapon. The Philistines are accordingly the great villains of the Hebrew scriptures, and the word *philistine* has accordingly come to mean a boorish, uncultured person. Unfortunately, the Philistines do not appear to have made use of the same powerful technology to record their own outlook on the world, and almost everything we know about them comes from the work of archeologists, or has to be sifted through the bad press of their detractors. We know little about their language, but their material culture, behavior, and organization exhibit close affinities with Mycenaean Greece.

Philistine power was based on five great strongholds, the so-called Pentapolis (Greek for "five cities"): Gaza, Ashkelon, and Ashdod on the coast, and the inland cities of Ekron and Gath. Again, these citadels are strikingly similar to the fortified palaces of Mycenaean civilization, and they appear to have served many of the same functions. From these strongholds, the Philistines dominated the surrounding countryside by organizing agricultural production and controlling trade routes. An independent lord ruled over each citadel, and no doubt tensions and rivalries existed among them. But much like the heroes of Greek epic, the Philistines could set aside differences when facing a common enemy.

Because we see the Philistines primarily through the eyes of their Hebrew enemies, we must be careful about drawing conclusions about them from the stories of Goliath's brutality or Delilah's sexual treachery. Yet the Hebrews had good reason to fear the Philistines, whose pressure on the Hebrew hill country was constant and who threatened the Hebrews' holy sanctuary at Shiloh, where the sacred Ark of the Covenant was said to contain the original tablets of the law given to Moses on Mount Sinai. In Hebrew tradition, the tribes of Israel had once carried the Ark before them into battle against the Philistines, only to lose it in the fray and to witness thereafter the destruction of Shiloh. The Philistines then established garrisons throughout the land of the Hebrews, exacted tribute, and denied them access to weapons.

The Hebrews and Their Scriptures

The central feature of Hebrew culture, their conception of and relationship to their god, will be discussed at greater length toward the end of this chapter. In this section, we focus our attention on the development of Hebrew society—

while acknowledging that religion is always related to politics, as well as to economic conditions and the concerns of everyday life. Indeed the Hebrews, like all ancient peoples, could not have distinguished among these phenomena.

In reconstructing the early history of the Hebrews, we are indebted to an unusual textual source: a series of scriptures (literally "writings") that comprise mythology, laws and ritual practices, genealogical records, books of prophecy, proverbs, poetry, and royal chronicles. These are collectively known as the Hebrew Bible or (among Christians) as the Old Testament. The books of the Bible were assembled over many centuries, mostly by unknown authors, copyists, and editors. Like other sources, they have to be treated as artifacts produced by particular historical circumstances, which also governed the way that certain texts were preserved and put together.

The first five books of the Hebrew Bible are traditionally attributed to Moses, but most of the materials in these books were borrowed from other Near Eastern cultures, including the stories of creation and the flood, which parallel those of Sumer (as we saw in Chapter 1). The story of Moses' childhood draws on a legend told about the Akkadian king Sargon the Great. And the story of the exodus from Egypt is fraught with problems. Although the later Book of Joshua claims that the Hebrews who returned from Egypt conquered and expelled the native Canaanites, archeological and linguistic evidence suggests that the Hebrews were essentially Canaanites themselves. They may have merged with scattered refugees from Egypt in the aftermath of the Sea Peoples' invasions, but for the most part they had been continuously resident in Canaan for centuries. In other words, the first five books of the Bible constitute a retrospective history whose purpose was to justify Hebrew traditions and claims to territory.

Among the other writings included in the Hebrew Bible are a group of texts which record events of the more recent past, those of the period we are considering now. These books are more straightforwardly verifiable, even if many details are difficult to confirm. According to the Book of Judges, the Hebrews were wandering herdsmen who had just begun to establish permanent settlements around the time of the Philistines' arrival in the Levant. They had organized themselves into twelve tribes—extended clan units whose families owed one another mutual aid and protection in times of war, but who frequently fought over cattle and grazing rights. Each tribe was ruled by a patriarch known as a judge, who exercised the typical functions of authority in a clan-based society: war leadership, high priesthood, and dispute settlement. By the middle of the twelfth century B.C.E., these tribes occupied two major territories, with those settled in the south calling themselves the tribes of Judah, and those in the north the tribes of Israel.

The Struggle for Hebrew Identity

The Hebrew tribes of this period had little experience of organized activity. This made them highly vulnerable, especially when the Philistines conquered the Levantine coast around 1050 B.C.E. To counter the Philistine threat effectively, they needed a leader. Accordingly, around 1025 B.C.E., an influential tribal judge called Samuel selected a king to lead the Hebrew resistance against the Philistines. His name was Saul. However, Saul proved to be an ineffective war-leader. So Samuel withdrew his support from Saul and threw it behind a young warrior in Saul's entourage, Saul's son-in-law David. Waging his own independent military campaigns, David achieved one triumph after another over the Philistines—that is, according to those chroniclers of the Bible who wrote their accounts under David's patronage.

These same books reveal that David was a man on the make; and when Saul finally drove him from his court, he became an outlaw on the fringes of Hebrew society and then a mercenary in Philistine service. It was as a Philistine mercenary that David fought against Saul in the climactic battle in which Saul was killed. Soon thereafter, David himself became king, first over the tribes of Judah, his home territory, and later over Saul's territory of Israel as well.

The Consolidation of the Hebrew Kingdom

After David's victory around 1000 B.C.E., he took advantage of the opportunity afforded by Egypt's decline to expand his control southward, eventually confining the Philistines to an inconsequential strip of coastal land. By the time of his death in 973 B.C.E., David's kingdom stretched from the middle Euphrates in the north to the Gulf of Aqaba in the south, and from the Mediterranean coast eastward into the Syrian deserts.

As David's power and prestige grew, he was able to impose on his subjects a highly unpopular system of taxation and forced labor. His goal was to build a glorious capital at Jerusalem, a Canaanite settlement that he designated as the central city of his realm. It was a shrewd choice. As a newly

The Reign of King Solomon (r. 973–937 B.C.E.)

Continuing his father's policies, but on a much grander scale, David's son Solomon built a great temple complex at Jerusalem to house the Ark. Such visible support of Yahweh's cult was approved by the historians whose works are included in the Bible, and who portray Solomon's reign as a golden age. However, Solomon was a ruthless and often brutal ruler whose promotion of Yahweh coincided with a program of despotism. To finance his expensive tastes and programs, Solomon instituted oppressive taxation and imposed customs duties on the lucrative caravan trade that passed through his country. With the help of the Phoenician king of Tyre, Solomon constructed a commercial fleet whose ships plied the waters of the Red Sea and beyond, trading—among other commodities—the gold and copper mined by Solomon's slaves.

Solomon also maintained a large standing army of conscripts from his own people. To undertake his ambitious building projects, Solomon required many of his subjects to perform forced labor four months out of every year. This level of oppression was too much for many Israelites, and the north seethed with rebellion against the royal capital. Within a decade or so of Solomon's death, in fact, the fragile monarchy split in two. The dynasty descended from David continued to rule the southern kingdom of Judah with its capital at Jerusalem, but the ten northern tribes banded together as the kingdom of Israel, with their capital at Shechem. In the meantime, the changing political situation of the Near East made the Hebrew kingdoms increasingly vulnerable.

THE HEBREW KINGDOM, C. 900 B.C.E. Notice the scale of the map and consider the comparatively small size of the Hebrews' world. ▪ *What advantages did the Philistines and Phoenicians possess, geographically and otherwise?* ▪ *Why did they present such a challenge to the Hebrews?* ▪ *What political and religious consequences might have resulted from the division of the kingdom after the death of King Solomon, given the location of Jerusalem?*

conquered city, Jerusalem had no previous affiliation with any of Israel's twelve tribes and so stood outside the ancient rivalries that divided them. Geographically too, Jerusalem was a strategic choice, lying between the southern tribes of Judah (David's people) and the northern tribes of Israel. David also took steps to exalt the city by making Jerusalem the resting place of the sacred Ark and reorganizing the priesthood of the Hebrew god, Yahweh. By these measures, he sought to forge a new collective identity centered on his own family and its connections to Yahweh. To this end, he also encouraged the writing of histories and prophecies that would affirm this identity and his central role in forging it.

THE REVIVAL OF THE ASSYRIAN EMPIRE

The Assyrians had long played an important role in spreading trade and promoting urban settlements. But like the other great powers of the Near East, their civilization had been devastated by the Sea Peoples. For several centuries afterward they struggled for survival. Then, in the ninth century B.C.E., a brilliant but brutal ruler laid the foundations of what historians call the Neo-Assyrian Empire. Under the leadership of Assurnasirpal II (*ah-sur-NAH-sur-PAHL*, r. 883–859 B.C.E.), these "new" Assyrians began to conduct aggressive military campaigns against their neighbors. Those whom they defeated either had to pay tribute or face the full onslaught of the Assyrian war machine, which under Assurnasirpal acquired a deserved reputation for savagery.

Despite their military successes, Assurnasirpal and his successors inspired stiff resistance. The northern kingdom of Israel formed an alliance with other small states to halt Assyrian expansion. This coalition ultimately forced the Assyrians to settle for smaller victories against the Armenians to the northwest and the Medes to the northeast. Thereafter, a cycle of violent oppression and rebellion continued until the reign of a military commander who took the name Sargon II (r. 722–705 B.C.E.). He claimed to be the direct successor of Sargon of Akkad, the first great king in Mesopotamian history, nearly 1,500 years earlier (Chapter 1).

Like the Hebrews, Sargon and his heirs skillfully deployed history as a political tool. And eventually, they extended the frontiers of the Neo-Assyrian Empire from western Iran to the shores of the Mediterranean. Briefly, they even subjugated parts of Egypt. Sargon himself put an end to the kingdom of Israel in 722 B.C.E., enslaving and deporting most of the population, and he terrified the southern kingdom of Judah into remaining a quiet vassal. By the seventh century B.C.E., Assyria was the unrivaled power of the ancient Near East.

ASSYRIAN ATROCITIES. Judean captives whose city has fallen to the Assyrian king Sennacherib (704–681 B.C.E.) are shown being impaled on stakes. This triumphal carving comes from the walls of Sennacherib's palace at Nineveh. ▪ *What would be the purpose of advertising these captives' fates?*

Neo-Assyrian Government and Administration

The Neo-Assyrian Empire was built on the ability of its army to oppress both enemies and subjects alike. At its head was a hereditary monarch regarded as the earthly representative of the Assyrians' patron god, Assur. Supporting the empire's centralized authority was an extensive bureaucracy of governors, high priests, and military commanders—professions by no means mutually exclusive. These administrators exercised local authority on behalf of the king. They maintained lines of transport and communication and they oversaw construction of an extensive network of roads across the Near East. The Assyrians also deployed a system of spies and messengers to report on the activities of subjects and provincial governors.

Not surprising for a people so mindful of historical precedent, the Assyrians modeled their laws on the code of Hammurabi, though many of their penalties were more severe. Assyrian law was also rigidly patriarchal, which entailed substantial revision of Hammurabi's code: now only husbands had the power of divorce, and they were legally permitted to inflict a variety of penalties on their wives, ranging from corporal punishment to mutilation and death.

The Assyrian Military-Religious Ethos

The Assyrians' religious, political, and military ideology took shape during the long centuries when they fought for survival. Its two fundamental tenets were the waging of holy war and the exaction of tribute through terror.

Rather than defeating their foes once and imposing formal obligations, the Assyrians raided even their vanquished foes each year. This strategy kept the Assyrian military machine primed for battle, but it did little to inspire loyalty among subject peoples. Assyrian battle tactics were notoriously savage—even by the standards of ancient warfare, which regarded the mutilation of prisoners, systematic rape, and mass deportations as commonplace. Moreover, the Assyrian army was not a seasonal army of part-time conscripts or peasants, but a massive standing force of more than 100,000 soldiers. And because the Assyrians mastered iron-smelting techniques on a large scale, they could equip their fighting men with high-quality steel weapons that overwhelmed opponents still reliant on bronze.

The organization of this army also contributed to its success. At its core were heavily armed and armored shock troops, the main force for crushing enemy infantry in the field and for routing the inhabitants of an enemy city once inside. To harass enemy infantry, the Assyrians deployed light skirmishers with slings and javelins, combined archery and chariotry, and also developed the first true cavalry force in the West. They even trained a highly skilled corps of combat engineers to undermine city walls and to build catapults, siege engines, battering rams, and battle towers.

The Assyrians were convinced that their god demanded the constant expansion of his worship through military conquest. Ritual humiliation of a defeated city's gods was therefore a regular feature of Assyrian conquests. Statues of conquered gods would be carried off to the Assyrian capital, where they would remain as hostages. Meanwhile, an image of Assur himself—usually represented as a sun disk with the head and shoulders of an archer—would be installed in the defeated city, and the conquered people would be required to worship him. Although subject peoples did not have to abandon their previous gods altogether, they were made to feel their gods' inferiority. The Assyrians were therefore strict henotheists, meaning that they acknowledged the existence of other gods but believed that one god should be the supreme deity of all peoples.

The Legacy of Assyrian Power

The successors of Sargon II continued Assyrian military policies while devoting great energy to promoting an Assyrian cultural legacy. Sargon's immediate successor Sennacherib (sen-AH-sher-ib, r. 704–681 B.C.E.) rebuilt the ancient Assyrian city of Nineveh, fortifying it with a double wall for a circuit of nine miles. He constructed an enormous palace there, and he ordered the construction of a massive irrigation system, including an aqueduct that carried fresh water to the city from thirty miles away. His son rebuilt the conquered city of Babylon along similar lines. His grandson Assurbanipal (ah-sur-BAHN-uh-pahl, r. 669–627 B.C.E.) was perhaps the greatest of all the Assyrian kings. For a time, he ruled the entire delta region of northern Egypt. He also enacted a series of internal reforms, seeking ways to govern his empire more peacefully.

By Assyrian standards, Assurbanipal was an enlightened ruler, and one to whom all students of history owe a tremendous debt. Like his grandfather Sargon II, he had a strong sense of the rich traditions of Mesopotamian history and laid claim to them. But he did this much more systematically: he ordered the construction of a magnificent library at Nineveh, where all the cultural monuments of Mesopotamian literature were to be copied and preserved. This library also served as an archive for the correspondence and official acts of the king. Fortunately, this trove of documentation has survived. Our knowledge of history, not to mention all modern editions of the *Epic of Gilgamesh*, derive from the library at Nineveh.

When Assurbanipal died in 627 B.C.E., the Assyrian Empire appeared to be at its zenith. Its kings had adorned their capitals with magnificent artwork, and the hanging gardens of Babylon were already famous: these were artificial slopes whose cascading flowers and trees were fed by irrigation systems that pumped water uphill, an amazing marriage of engineering and horticulture. The end of Assyria is therefore all the more dramatic for its suddenness. Within fifteen years of Assurbanipal's reign, Nineveh lay in ruins. An alliance had formed between the Indo-European Medes of Iran and the Chaldeans, a Semitic people who controlled the southern half of Babylonia. By 605 B.C.E., the Chaldeans occupied Babylon itself and had become the predominant imperial power in Mesopotamia and the Levant. In 586 B.C.E. they captured Jerusalem, destroyed the Temple, and deported the population of Judea to Babylon. Meanwhile, the Medes retired to the Iranian Plateau to extend their dominion there.

THE RISE OF THE PERSIANS

The Persian Empire emerged as the successor state to the Assyrians, after the region was ruled for a few decades by the Chaldeans and Medes. On these foundations, the Persians would construct the largest empire known to humanity up until that time.

The Persian Empire of Cyrus the Great

The Persians emerge from obscurity rather suddenly, under an extraordinary prince named Cyrus who succeeded to the rule of a single Persian tribe in 559 B.C.E. Shortly thereafter, Cyrus made himself ruler of all the Persians and then, around 549 B.C.E., threw off the lordship of the Medes and began to claim dominion over lands stretching from the Persian Gulf to the Halys River in Asia Minor.

This brought the Persians into close contact with the kingdom of Lydia. The Lydians had attained great prosperity as producers of gold and silver and as intermediaries for overland commerce between Mesopotamia and the Aegean. Most important, they were the first people in the ancient Near East to use precious-metal coinage as a medium of exchange for goods and services. When Cyrus came to power, their king was Croesus (*CREE-suhs*), a man whose reputation as the possessor of untold riches survives in the expression "rich as Croesus." Distrusting his new neighbor, Croesus decided to launch a preemptive strike against the Persians to preserve his own kingdom from conquest. According to the Greek historian Herodotus, he took the precaution of asking the oracle of Apollo at Delphi whether this strategy was a good one, and was told that he would destroy a great nation if he pursued it. The oracle's pronouncement was both ambiguous and true: but the nation

Croesus destroyed was his own. Cyrus defeated his forces in 546 B.C.E.

Cyrus then invaded Mesopotamia in 539 B.C.E., striking so quickly that he took Babylon without a fight. Once in Babylon, the entire Chaldean Empire was his, and his imperial policies proved very different from those of his predecessors in that region. Cyrus freed the Hebrews who had been held captive in Babylon since 586 B.C.E. and sent them back to Jerusalem, helping them to rebuild their temple and allowing them to set up a semi-independent vassal state. Cyrus also allowed other conquered peoples considerable self-determination, especially with respect to cultural and religious practices, a marked reversal of Assyrian and Chaldean policies. Two hundred years later, a young Macedonian king, Alexander, would emulate many of his exploits and build an empire sustained by many of the same strategies (see Chapter 4).

The Consolidation of Persia

When Cyrus died in battle in 530 B.C.E., Persian expansion continued, and his son conquered Egypt in 525 B.C.E. But although Cambyses was a warrior king like his father, he left the Persian Empire a poorly organized collection of rapid conquests. After a short period of civil war, the aristocratic inner circle that had served both Cyrus and his son settled on a collateral member of the royal family as the new king. This was Darius, whose long reign of 35 years (r. 521–486 B.C.E.) consolidated his predecessors' military gains by improving the administration of the Persian state. Darius divided the empire into provinces, each of which was administered by an official called a *satrap*. Satraps enjoyed extensive powers and considerable political latitude, yet they owed absolute loyalty to the central government, as did vassal states such as the technically autonomous Hebrew kingdom.

Adhering to the tolerant policy of Cyrus, Darius allowed the various peoples of the empire to retain most of their local institutions while enforcing a standardized currency and a system of weights and measures. Beyond this, he had little interest in imposing onerous

THE PERSIAN EMPIRE UNDER DARIUS I, 521–486 B.C.E. Consider the location of the Persian heartland and the four administrative centers of Persepolis, Susa, Ecbatana, and Sardis. ▪ *What older kingdoms and empires did the Persian Empire contain?* ▪ *Why is the Royal Road especially noted on this map?* ▪ *How did Darius I successfully rule such a large and complex empire?*

Competing Viewpoints

Two Perspectives on Imperial Rule

These two inscriptions exemplify two very different attitudes toward imperial power and two very different methods of achieving it. The first glorifies the victories of the Assyrian king Esarhaddon in Syria, and is one of the most important records of his reign (r. 681–669 B.C.E.). The second commemorates the taking of Babylon by the Persian king Cyrus the Great (r. 559–530 B.C.E.), whose empire came to encompass and surpass that of the Assyrians.

The Stele of King Esarhaddon at Senjirli, c. 680 B.C.E.

To Assur, father of the gods, lover of my priesthood, Anu mighty and preeminent, who called me by name, Ba'al, the exalted lord, establisher of my dynasty, Ea, the wise, all-knowing . . . Ishtar, lady of battle and combat, who goes at my side . . . all of them who determine my destiny, who grant to the king, their favorite, power and might . . . [I am] the king, the offering of whose sacrifices the great gods love . . . [he] who has brought all the lands in submission at his feet, who has imposed tribute and tax upon them; conqueror of his foes, destroyer of his enemies, the king, who as to his walk is a storm, and as to his deeds, a raging wolf; . . . The onset of his battle is powerful, he is a consuming flame, a fire that does not sink: son of Sennacherib, king of the universe, king of Assyria, grandson of Sargon, king of the universe, king of Assyria, viceroy of Babylon, king of Sumer and Akkad. . . . I am powerful, I am all-powerful, I am a hero, I am gigantic, I am colossal, I am honored, I am magnified, I am without an equal among all kings, the chosen one of Assur . . . the great lord [who], in order to show to the peoples the immensity of my mighty deeds, made powerful my kingship over the four regions of the world and made my name great.

. . . Of Tirhakah, king of Egypt and Kush, the accursed . . . without cessation I slew multitudes of his men, and him I smote five times with the point of my javelin, with wounds, no recovery. Memphis, his royal city, in half a day . . . I besieged, I captured, I destroyed, I devastated, I burned with fire. . . . The root of Kush I tore up out of Egypt and not one therein escaped to submit to me.

Source: Daniel David Luckenbill, ed., *Ancient Records of Assyria and Babylonia,* Vol. 2 (Chicago: 1926–27), pp. 224–27.

Inscription Honoring Cyrus, c. 539 B.C.E.

He [the god Marduk] scanned and looked (through) all the countries, searching for a righteous ruler who would lead him. (Then) he pronounced the name of Cyrus, king of Anshan [Persia], declared him to be the leader of the world. . . . And he (Cyrus) did always endeavor to treat according to justice the black-headed

taxes, martial law, or hegemonic religious practices. After centuries of Assyrian and Chaldean tyranny, the light hand of Persian rule was welcomed throughout the Near East.

Darius was also a great builder. He erected a new royal residence and ceremonial capital which the Greeks called Persepolis ("Persia City"). He ordered a canal dug from the Nile to the Red Sea to facilitate trade with the Egyptian interior, and directed the installation of irrigation systems on the Persian plateau and the fringe of the Syrian desert to increase agricultural production. Darius also expanded the existing Assyrian road system to enhance trade and communications throughout his huge realm. The most famous artery was the Royal Road, stretching 1,600 miles from Susa, near the Persian Gulf, to Sardis (the old Lydian capital) near the Aegean. Government couriers along this road constituted the first postal system, carrying messages and goods in relay stages from one post to another. Each post was a day's horseback ride from the next, where a fresh horse and rider would be ready to carry the dispatches brought by the postman before him. An extensive imperial [people] whom he (Marduk) made him conquer. Marduk, the great lord, a protector of his people/worshipers, beheld with pleasure his good deeds and his upright mind, (and therefore) ordered him to march against his city Babylon. He made him set out on the road to Babylon, going at his side like a real friend. His widespread troops—their number, like the water of a river, could not be established—strolled along, their weapons packed away. Without any battle, he made them enter his town Babylon, sparing Babylon any calamity. He delivered into his hands Nabonidus, the king who did not worship him. All the inhabitants of Babylon as well as of the entire country of Sumer and Akkad, princes and governors (included), bowed to him and kissed his feet, jubilant that he (had received) the kingship, and with shining faces. Happily they greeted him as a master through whose help they had come (again) to life from death (and) had all been spared damage and disaster, and they worshiped his name.

I am Cyrus, king of the world, great king, legitimate king, king of Babylon, king of Sumer and Akkad, king of the four rims (of the earth), son of Cambyses, great king, king of Anshan, grandson of Cyrus, great king, king of Anshan, descendent of Teipes, great king, king of Anshan, of a family (which) always (exercised) kingship; whose rule Bel and Nebo love, whom they want as king to please their hearts.

When I entered Babylon as a friend and (when) I established the seat of the government in the palace of the ruler under jubilation and rejoicing. . . . My numerous troops walked around Babylon in peace, I did not allow anybody to terrorize (any place) of the (country of Sumer) and Akkad. I strove for peace in Babylon and in all his (other) sacred cities. . . . I abolished the . . . [yoke] which was against their (social) standing, I brought relief to their dilapidated housing, putting (thus) an end to their (main) complaints. . . . All the kings of the entire world from the Upper to the Lower Sea, those who are seated in throne rooms, (those who) live in other (types of buildings as well as) all the kings of the West living in tents, brought their heavy tributes and kissed my feet in Babylon.

Source: Excerpted from James B. Pritchard, ed. *Ancient Near Eastern Texts Relating to the Old Testament*, 3rd ed. (Princeton, NJ: 1969), pp. 315–16.

Questions for Analysis

1. Both of these inscriptions constitute propaganda, but of different kinds. How do they differ? What audience(s) are they addressing? What function(s) does each inscription serve?

2. Each of these rulers claims to have a close relationship with the divine. How do those relationships differ, and what do those differences reveal about their attitudes to kingship and its sources of power?

3. Both of these kings boast of their royal lineage and their connections to past rulers. How different or similar are these perspectives? What do they reveal about these kings' awareness of history?

spy network also used this postal system, famed throughout Persia as "the eyes and ears of the king."

Clearly, Darius was a gifted administrator. But as a military strategist he made an enormous mistake when he attempted to extend Persian rule into Greece. Cyrus's conquest of Lydia had made the Persian king the overlord of some long-established Greek-speaking cities on the western coast of Asia Minor, a region called Ionia. But these cities resisted even the easy terms of Persian rule, desiring instead to model themselves on the self-governing city-states across the Aegean. Consequently, between 499 and 494 B.C.E., the Greeks of Asia waged a war for independence and briefly gained the support of troops from Athens. Darius quelled this uprising, and then decided to send a force to punish Athens and serve notice of Persian dominion over all Greek states. But at the battle of Marathon in 490 B.C.E., the Athenians dealt Darius the only major setback of his reign. And when his son and successor, Xerxes (ZEHRK-zees), attempted to avenge this humiliation in 480 B.C.E., a resistance led by both Athens

A CYLINDRICAL SEAL OF DARIUS THE GREAT (522–486 B.C.E.). Seals were used in place of signatures to authenticate documents and correspondence. The cylindrical matrix (right) was rolled in soft wax to create an impression. This finely wrought example shows the king in a chariot, hunting lions with a bow. A winged representation of the god Ahura-Mazda rises above the scene.

and Sparta forced him to retreat and abandon his plans a year later. (We will discuss these events at greater length in Chapter 3.)

The Persians were thus compelled to recognize that they had reached the limits of their expansion. Thereafter, they concentrated on their Asian possessions and used money and diplomacy to keep the Greeks in check. This was not difficult, because the Greeks' hasty union in the face of Persian hegemony was short-lived, and they were too embroiled in wars with one another to pose any real threat to Persia.

The richness of their culture and the general tolerance they exhibited served the Persians well in maintaining their enormous empire. Unlike the Assyrians or Chaldeans, the Persians could count on the loyalty and even the affection of their subjects. In fact, their imperial model—the accommodation of local institutions and practices, consistent administration through a trained bureaucracy, and rapid communications between center and periphery—would be the one adopted by the great and lasting empires of the near and distant future.

The Legacy of Zoroastrianism

Persia's political and cultural achievements were paralleled by a spiritual one, Zoroastrianism. This important religion was one of the three major universal faiths known to the world before Christianity and Islam, along with Buddhism and Judaism (see below). Its founder was Zarathustra, known to the Greeks as Zoroaster, a Persian who probably lived shortly before 600 B.C.E. Zarathustra sought to reform the traditional customs of the Persian tribes by eradicating

polytheism, animal sacrifice, and magic. That is, he wanted to redefine religion as an ethical practice common to all, rather than as a set of rituals and superstitions that caused divisions among people.

Zoroastrianism teaches that there is one supreme god in the universe, whom Zarathustra called Ahura-Mazda, "Wise Lord." Ahura-Mazda is the essence of light, truth, and righteousness; there is nothing wrathful or wicked about him, and his goodness extends to everyone, not just to one people or tribe. How, then, can there be evil and suffering in the world? Because, Zarathustra posited, there is a counter deity, Ahriman, who rules the forces of darkness. Yet he also posited that Ahura-Mazda must be vastly stronger than Ahriman.

Later teachers and priests of Zoroastrianism, the magi, placed greater emphasis on the dualism of these divine forces. They insisted that Ahura-Mazda and Ahriman are evenly matched, engaged in a desperate and eternal struggle for supremacy. Accordingly, light will not triumph over darkness until the Last Day, when the forces of Ahura-Mazda vanquish those of Ahriman forever. This vision of the universe would prove enormously influential, later informing the developing theologies of Christianity and Islam—not to mention the plots of much modern science fiction, fantasy literature, and film.

The devotion of the Persian imperial dynasty to Zarathustra's teachings made Zoroastrianism important to the conduct of Persian government, and also helps to explain the moderation of Persian rule. Unlike the Assyrians, the Chaldeans, or even the Egyptians, Persian kings saw themselves as presiding over an assemblage of different nations whose customs and beliefs they were prepared to tolerate. Whereas Mesopotamian potentates characteristically called themselves "true king," Persian rulers took the title "king of kings" or "great king," implying that they recognized the legitimacy of other kings who ruled under their canopy.

Unlike other ancient religions, then, Zoroastrianism did not exalt the power of a godlike ruler or support any particular regime. It was a personal religion, making private, spiritual demands as opposed to public, ritual ones. Its Wise Lord supported neither tribes nor states, but only individuals who serve the cause of truth and justice. According to its tenets, individuals possess free will and can choose to sin or not to sin; they are not compelled by an array of conflicting gods to act in particular ways. Zoroastrianism thus urges its adherents to choose good over evil, to be truthful, to love and help one another to the best of their powers, to aid the poor, and to practice generous hospitality. Those who do so will be rewarded in an afterlife, when the dead are resurrected on Judgment Day and consigned either to a realm of joy or to the flames of despair. In the scriptures of the Zoroastrian faith, known as the Avesta (compiled, like the Bible, over the course of many centuries), the rewards for righteousness are great, but not immediate. They are spiritual, not material.

THE DEVELOPMENT OF HEBREW MONOTHEISM

Of all the important trends that we have traced in our study of the Iron Age Near East, perhaps none is of greater significance to the civilizations of the West than monotheism: the belief in a single god, the creator and ruler of all things. This development is traditionally associated with the Hebrews, but even the Hebrews were not always monotheists. Those who argued for the exclusive worship of Yahweh were a minority within Hebrew society, albeit a vocal and assertive one. How the Hebrews came to regard Yahweh as the only divine being in the universe, and to root their identity in such an exclusive religious outlook, is therefore a phenomenon that can only be understood within its historical context.

From Monolatry to Monotheism

For those who later advocated the exclusive worship of Yahweh, the early history of the Hebrews was full of embarrassments. Even the Hebrew scriptures reveal their propensity for the worship of many gods. Yahweh himself, in commanding that his people "have no other gods before me," acknowledged the existence of those gods. The older, polytheistic Hebrew religion honored nature spirits such as Azazel and the Canaanite deity El, whose name is an important element in many Hebrew place-names (for example, Bethel) and soon became a synonym for "God." The temple built by Solomon at Jerusalem even included altars to Ba'al and his wife Asherah, a fertility goddess. Later Hebrew kings continued such practices, overriding the protests of religious purists devoted to Yahweh.

By the beginning of the first millennium, however, the Hebrews living under the rule of David began to practice monolatry, meaning that they worshiped one god exclusively without denying the existence of others. Although the legendary prophet Moses is often credited as the first promoter of Yahweh's cult, sometime around the middle

THE GODDESS ASHERAH. The Canaanite fertility goddess, Asherah, was the wife of the god Ba'al (or his father, El), but she also figures in some inscriptions as the wife of the Hebrew god Yahweh. One Hebrew king even placed an image of her in the temple of Yahweh at Jerusalem. ■ *Why would this be viewed as controversial?*

of the second millennium B.C.E., the ascendancy of Yahweh took place much later under the influence of the Levites, a tribe who claimed unique priestly authority and sought to enhance their own power and prestige by discrediting other gods.

The success of their campaign rested on the Levites' access to writing. The written word was especially potent in the ancient world because the skills necessary for its mastery were rare. In an age of constant threats to Hebrew religious and political sovereignty, the literacy of the Levites helped to preserve and promote Yahweh's worship. So did the political supremacy of the House of David, which bolstered its own legitimacy by allying itself with the Levites. The result was a centralized cult situated in the new royal capital of Jerusalem, which linked the political and the

RECONSTRUCTION OF THE ISHTAR GATE. This is a reconstruction of one of the fifty-foot-high entrance gates built into the walls of Babylon by King Nebuchadnezzar around 575 B.C.E. About half of this reconstruction is original.

religious identity of the Hebrews to the worship of Yahweh as the supreme god.

Nevertheless, the worship of other gods actually increased in the eighth and seventh centuries B.C.E., perhaps in reaction to the austere morality demanded and imposed by the Yahwists. Thus religious figures like Jeremiah (c. 637–587 B.C.E.) railed against "foreign" cults and warned of the disastrous consequences that would arise if Yahweh's people did not remain faithful to him. Moreover, Yahweh remained a somewhat conventional god, even in the eyes of his promoters. He was conceived as possessing a physical body and was often capricious and irascible. Further, he was not omnipotent; his power was largely confined to the territory occupied by the Hebrews.

Still, some of the Hebrews' most important contributions to subsequent Western religions crystallized by the middle of the eighth century B.C.E. One was their theology of Yahweh's transcendence: the teaching that God is not part of nature but exists outside of it. God can therefore be understood in purely intellectual or abstract terms, as entirely separate from the operations of the natural world. Complementing this principle was the belief that Yahweh had appointed humans to be the rulers of nature by divine mandate. When Yahweh orders Adam and Eve to "replenish the earth and subdue it, and have dominion over . . . every living thing," his injunction stands in striking contrast to other accounts of creation in which humans are made to serve the gods. Finally, Hebrew religious thought was moving in this period toward the articulation of universal ethics—a universal theory of justice and righteousness. According to the Babylonian flood story, for example, a particularly petulant god destroys humanity because their noise deprives him of sleep. In Genesis, Yahweh sends a flood in punishment for human wickedness but saves Noah and his family because "Noah was a just man."

The Hebrews honored Yahweh during this period by subscribing to certain moral precepts and taboos. The Ten Commandments in the exact form as they now appear in Exodus 20:3–17 may not have existed, but they certainly reflect earlier ethical injunctions against murder, adultery, lying, and greed. In addition, the Hebrews observed an array of ritual practices unusual in the ancient world, such as infant circumcision, adherence to strict dietary laws, and refraining from labor on the seventh day of the week.

Yet the moral standards imposed by Yahweh on the Hebrew community were not binding when the Hebrews dealt with outsiders. Lending at interest, for example, was not acceptable among Hebrews, but was quite acceptable between a Hebrew and a non-Hebrew. Such distinctions applied also to more serious issues, such as the killing of civilians in battle. When the Hebrews conquered territories in Canaan, they took "all the spoil of the cities, and every man they smote with the sword . . . until they had destroyed them." Far from having any doubts about such a brutal policy, the Hebrews believed that Yahweh had inspired the Canaanites to resist so that the Hebrews could slaughter them: "For it was the Lord's doing to harden their hearts that they should come against Israel in battle, in order that they should be utterly destroyed, and should receive no mercy but be exterminated" (Joshua 11:20).

With the political fragmentation of the Hebrew kingdoms after Solomon's death, important regional distinctions arose within Yahweh's cult. As we noted above, the rulers of the northern kingdom discouraged their citizens from participating in ritual activities at Jerusalem, thereby earning the disapproval of the Jerusalem-based Yahwists who shaped the biblical tradition. The erosion of a cohesive Hebrew identity was further accelerated by the Assyrians, who under Sargon II absorbed the northern kingdom as a province and enslaved nearly 28,000 Hebrews. The southern kingdom of Judah survived, but political collaboration with the Assyrians meant acceptance of the god Assur.

This was the whetstone on which the Yahwist prophets sharpened their demands for an exclusive monotheism that went beyond monolatry. Hebrew prophets were practical political leaders as well as religious figures, and most of them understood that military resistance to the Assyrians was futile. So if the Hebrews were to survive as a people, they had to emphasize the one thing that separated them from everyone else in the known world: the worship of Yahweh and the denial of all other gods. The prophets' insistence that Yahweh alone should be exalted was thus an aggressive reaction to the equally aggressive promotion of Assur by the Assyrians.

The foremost Hebrew prophets of this era were Amos and Hosea, who preached in the kingdom of Israel before it fell to the Assyrians in 722 B.C.E.; Isaiah and Jeremiah, who prophesied in Judah before its fall in 586 B.C.E.; and Ezekiel and the "second Isaiah" (the Book of Isaiah had at least two different authors), who continued to preach "by the waters of Babylon" during the exile there. Despite some differences in emphasis, these prophets' messages consistently emphasize three core doctrines.

1. **Yahweh is the ruler of the universe.** He even makes use of peoples other than the Hebrews to accomplish his purposes. The gods of other nations are false gods. There has never been and never will be more than this one god.
2. **Yahweh is exclusively a god of righteousness.** He wills only the good, and evil in the world comes from humanity, not from him.
3. **Because Yahweh is righteous, he demands ethical behavior from his people.** Over and above ritual and sacrifice, he requires that his followers "seek justice, relieve the oppressed, protect the fatherless, and plead for the widow."

Judaism Takes Shape

Through their insistence on monotheism as the cornerstone of Hebrew identity, the Yahwists made it possible for the Hebrews to survive under Assyrian domination. And as the Assyrian threat receded in the late seventh century B.C.E., so the Yahwists triumphed religiously and politically. The king of Judah during the waning years of the Assyrian Empire, Josiah (r. 621–609 B.C.E.), was a committed monotheist whose court employed prominent prophets, including Jeremiah. With Assyrian power crumbling, Josiah found himself in a position to pursue significant reforms. He presided over the redrafting and revision of the "Law of Moses" to bring it into line with current policies, and it was during his reign that the Book of Deuteronomy was "discovered" and hailed as Moses' "Second Law." Deuteronomy is the most stridently monotheistic book of the Hebrew Bible, and it lent weight to this new political program.

But within a generation of King Josiah's death, the Chaldeans under Nebuchadnezzar conquered Jerusalem, destroyed the Temple, and carried thousands of Hebrews off to Babylon in 587/586 B.C.E. This Babylonian Captivity brought many challenges, paramount among them the maintenance of the Hebrews' identity. The leading voices in defining that identity continued to be the patriotic Yahwists, the same people who would later spearhead the return to Palestine after Cyrus captured Babylon and liberated the Hebrews two generations later. Among the Yahwists, the prophet Ezekiel stressed that salvation could be found only through religious purity, which meant ignoring all foreign gods and acknowledging only Yahweh. Kingdoms and states and empires came to nothing in the long run, Ezekiel said. What mattered for those living in exile was the creature God had made in his image—man—and the relationship between God and his creation.

The period of captivity was therefore decisive in forging a universal religion that transcended politics. Just as Yahweh existed outside creation, so the people who worshiped him could exist outside of a Hebrew kingdom. In Babylon, the worship of Yahweh therefore became something different: it became Judaism, a religion that was not tied to any particular political system or territory, for after 586 B.C.E. there was neither a Hebrew ruling class nor a Hebrew state. Outside of Judah, Judaism flourished. This was an unparalleled achievement in the ancient world: the survival of a religion that had no political power to back it and no holy place to ground it.

After 538 B.C.E., when Cyrus permitted the Hebrews of Babylon to return to their lands and to rebuild the Temple, Jerusalem became once again the central holy place of Hebrew religious life. But the new developments that had fashioned Judaism during captivity would prove lasting, despite the religious conflicts that soon erupted. These conflicts led to ever more specific assertions about the nature of Judaism, and to religious teachings that focused on ethical conduct as an obligation owed by all human beings toward their creator, independent of place or political identity. The observance of ritual requirements and religious taboos would continue, but not as the essence of religious life; rather, they would be symbolic of the special relationship binding Yahweh to the Hebrews. Eventually, the transcendental monotheism that emerged from these historical processes would become common to the worldview of all Western civilizations.

CONCLUSION

The centuries between 1700 and 500 B.C.E. were an epoch of empires. While the two great powers of the second millennium were New Kingdom Egypt and the Hittite Empire in Anatolia, a host of lesser empires also coalesced during this period, including Minoan Crete, Mycenaean Greece, and the trading empire of the Assyrians. All were sustained by a sophisticated network of trade and diplomacy. But between 1200 and 1000 B.C.E. the devastation wrought by the Sea Peoples brought this integrated civilization to an end. These invasions cleared the way for many new, small states, including those of the Phoenicians, the Philistines, the Lydians, and the Hebrews. Many crucial cultural and economic developments were fostered by these small states, including alphabetic writing, coinage, mercantile colonization, and monotheism. But the dominant states of the Iron Age continued to be the great land empires centered in western Asia: first the Neo-Assyrians, then briefly the Chaldeans, and finally the Persians.

The empires of the early Iron Age were quite different from those that had dominated the Near East a thousand years before. These new empires were much more highly unified. They had capital cities, centrally managed systems of communication, sophisticated administrative structures, and ideologies that justified their aggressive imperialism as a religious obligation imposed on them by a single, all-powerful god. They commanded armies of unprecedented size, and they demanded from their subjects a degree of

After You Read This Chapter

Visit StudySpace for quizzes, additional review materials, and multi-media documents. **wwnorton.com/studyspace**

REVIEWING THE OBJECTIVES

- The settlement of Indo-European peoples in the Near East had marked effects on the older civilizations there. What were some major consequences?
- Egypt's New Kingdom differed profoundly from the Old and Middle Kingdoms that preceded it. Why was this the case?
- The civilizations of the late Bronze Age were bound together by transnational networks. What were the strengths and fragilities of these relationships?
- What kingdoms and empires emerged in the Near East after the devastation caused by the Sea Peoples?
- Monotheism was a significant historical development of the first millennium B.C.E. Why is it so important?

obedience impossible for any previous Bronze Age emperor to imagine or enforce. Their rulers declared themselves the chosen instruments of their god's divine will.

At the same time, we can trace the emergence of more personalized religions. Zoroastrian dualism and Hebrew monotheism added an important new emphasis on ethical conduct, and both pioneered the development of authoritative written scriptures that advanced religious teachings. Zoroastrianism, despite its radical re-imagining of the cosmos, proved fully compatible with imperialism and became the driving spiritual force behind the Persian Empire.

Judaism, by contrast, was forged in the struggle to resist the imperialism of the Assyrians and Chaldeans. Both systems of belief would exercise enormous influence on future civilizations. In particular, they would provide the models on which Christianity and Islam would ultimately erect their own traditions, just as the models of imperial governance forged in this period would become the template for future empires. In Chapter 3, we will look at the ways in which the city-states of ancient Greece both built on and departed from these models.

PEOPLE, IDEAS, AND EVENTS IN CONTEXT

- How did the Hittite Empire integrate the cultures of **INDO-EUROPEAN PEOPLES** with the older civilizations of this region?
- What do the reigns of **HATSHEPSUT** and **AKHENATEN** tell us about the continuities and limitations of pharaonic power?
- What factors produced the transnational networks of the Late **BRONZE AGE**?
- How did the civilizations of **MINOAN CRETE** and **MYCENAEAN GREECE** differ from one another, and from the neighboring civilizations of the Near East?
- In what ways do the **PHOENICIANS**, the **PHILISTINES**, and the **HEBREWS** exemplify three different approaches to state-building at the beginning of the first millennium B.C.E.?
- What was new about the **NEO-ASSYRIAN EMPIRE**? How do its methods of conquest and its military-religious ethos compare to the **PERSIAN EMPIRE** that followed it?
- How and why did monotheism develop in the Hebrew kingdoms? In what ways might **JUDAISM** have been influenced by **ZOROASTRIANISM**?

CONSEQUENCES

- In the religions of Akhenaten, the Persians, and the Hebrews we see a rejection of polytheism. What cultural factors may have contributed to this? What would you consider to be the long-term effects of monotheism as a motivating force in history?
- What patterns of success or failure appear to be emerging when we consider the empires that flourished in the Iron Age, particularly those of the Assyrians and the Persians? Are similar patterns visible in other periods of history, including our own?

Before
You
Read
This
Chapter

CORE OBJECTIVES

- **DESCRIBE** the factors that led to the emergence of the Greek polis.

- **DEFINE** hoplite warfare and its effects on democracy.

- **EXPLAIN** the key differences among the poleis of Athens, Sparta, and Miletus.

- **IDENTIFY** the ways in which Athenian culture, philosophy, and art reflect democratic ideals.

- **UNDERSTAND** the impact of the Persian and Peloponnesian Wars.

The Civilization of Greece, 1000–400 B.C.E.

n the fifth century B.C.E., a Greek-speaking subject of the Persian Empire began to write a book. He had been to Egypt and along the African coast, to the Greek colonies of Italy, the cities of Persia, the wilds of Thrace and Macedonia, and all over the Aegean. He had collected stories about peoples and places even farther afield: Ethiopia, India, the Black Sea. We have already met this intrepid traveler, Herodotus (c. 484–c. 425 B.C.E.), who marveled at the pyramids of Giza (Chapter 1) and who told how the king of Lydia lost his power to the Persians (Chapter 2). His reason for compiling this information was timely: he wanted to write a history of recent events. As he put it, "Herodotus of Halicarnassus here sets forth the results of his research, with the aim of preserving the remembrance of what men have done, and of preventing the great and wonderful deeds of both Greeks and barbarians from losing their glory; and in particular to examine the causes that made them fight one another."

Herodotus' fascination with the Persians, Phoenicians, and Egyptians underscores the extent to which all Greek-speakers regarded themselves as different from other peoples. In fact, they had responded very differently to the Bronze Age collapse.

THE ACROPOLIS OF ATHENS AND THE PARTHENON. Many Greek cities were built upon mountain strongholds, but the most famous of these is the Acropolis of Athens. First settled in the Neolithic Period, during the Bronze Age it became a fortified palace—allegedly that of the hero Theseus—and then a precinct sacred to the goddess Athena, for whom the city was named. The Parthenon, its most important surviving structure, was built on the site of an older temple after the Athenian victory over the Persians at Marathon in 490 B.C.E., and then rebuilt after the Persians sacked Athens ten years later. Most of the damage it sustained thereafter occurred during modern wars. ▪ *Why was this site the focal point of so much activity?* ▪ *What do these successive events tell us about the relationship between place and identity?*

off from trade and communication. The use of writing declined to such an extent that knowledge of Linear B disappeared. Archeological evidence suggests a world in stasis, isolated from the centers of civilization that were re-emerging in the Near East.

The material realities of life in this era profoundly shaped the civilization that emerged from it. This civilization would emphasize political equality and modest display, principles that formed the basis of early democracies. At the same time, the hardships of daily life, which contrasted sharply with stories of a heroic and opulent past, made the Greeks suspicious of their gods. They came to rely far more on the power of individual human beings than on divine intervention in human affairs. They also developed an awareness that excessive pride in one's own accomplishments could be dangerous. While the gods favored those who showed initiative and daring, they would punish the *hubris* of those who failed to acknowledge their own limitations.

While they struggled to cooperate politically, they were able to unite around a common language and culture, and their shared values were distinct from those of the people they called *barbarians*: peoples whose speech, to Greek ears, sounded like gibberish ("bar-bar-bar"). They cherished individual liberty, participatory government, artistic innovation, scientific investigation, and the creative powers of the human mind. Although the practical implementation of these ideals would prove problematic—and continues to be so—our own civilization would be unimaginable without the political experiments and cultural achievements of ancient Greece.

FROM CHAOS TO POLIS

By the end of the twelfth century B.C.E., Mycenaean civilization had vanished. Except at Athens, the great citadels that had crowned the heights of mainland kingdoms were destroyed. Settlements shrank in size and moved inland, away from vulnerable coastlines, thus cutting themselves

Homer and the Heroic Tradition

Around the year 1000 B.C.E., the chaotic conditions that had contributed to the isolation of Greece were alleviated by a period of relative peace. The standard of living improved, artisans developed their crafts, and increased contact among individual settlements fostered trade. Greek pottery, in particular, became a sophisticated and sought-after commodity, which Greek merchants could exchange for luxury goods from abroad.

As trade became an increasingly important feature of the new economy, the personal fortunes of those who engaged in trade increased accordingly, leading to a new kind of social stratification based on wealth. The men who controlled that wealth were aware that their status was not founded on warfare or noble birth, as had been the case in the past. Instead, they began to justify their preeminence as a reflection of their own superior qualities as "best men" (*aristoi*). Wealth was one sign of this superiority, but it was not sufficient in itself as a claim to aristocracy, which literally means "the rule of the best." Those who aspired to this status were therefore expected to emulate, as far as possible, the heroes of old, whose stories lived in the prodigious memories and agile voices of the singers of tales.

These singers, the guardians of a rich oral history that had never been written down, were part poets in their own right and part *rhapsodes*, "weavers of songs." The most famous is Homer, the poet credited with having woven together the mesh of stories that we know as the *Iliad* and the *Odyssey*, which crystallized around 800 B.C.E. The epics ascribed to Homer are vast encyclopedias of lore set at the end of the Bronze Age, the time his contemporary Hesiod called "the Age of Heroes" (Chapter 2): the age of Achilles and his Trojan rival, Hector; the age of Odysseus.

But these stories were not fixed in that time. Over centuries of retelling, the social and political relationships portrayed in the poems changed to reflect the assumptions and agendas of later ages. Treating these epics as historical sources, therefore, requires the historian to peel back layers of meaning. For example, Homer depicts a world in which competition and status are of paramount importance to the warrior elite, just as they were of vital concern to the aristocrats of his own day. Through the exchange of expensive gifts and hospitality, men aspiring to positions of power sought to create strong ties of guest friendship (*xenía*, *zeh-NEE-ah*) with one another, and thus to construct networks of influence that would support their economic, social, and political ambitions. This suggests that aristocrats in the Greek world conceived of themselves as having more in common with each other than they did with the local societies they dominated, something that is also reflected in the essential similarity of Trojans and Greeks in the *Iliad*.

However, the shared sense of a common culture among aristocratic households did not lessen the competition among them. Indeed, it led to competition over the epic past, as fledgling aristocratic clans vied to claim descent from one or another legendary hero. A hero cult might begin when an important family claimed an impressive Mycenaean tomb as that of their own famous ancestor, someone named in the *Iliad* said to have come from that place. They would then develop a pious tradition of devotion that would extend to their followers and dependents; eventually, an entire community might come to identify itself with the famous local hero. The heroic ideal thus became a deeply ingrained feature of Greek society, as did the stories that the epics preserved and propagated.

The Rise of the Polis

In the ninth century B.C.E., contacts between Greeks and Phoenicians intensified. Most crucially, the Greeks adopted the Phoenician alphabet, which replaced the long-disused Linear B. The Phoenicians also pointed the way to the revival of another lost art among the Greeks: seafaring. After the devastation of the late Bronze Age, Greek vessels hugged the shoreline and traveled only short distances. By the tenth century, however, Greeks were copying Phoenician designs for merchant vessels, which allowed them to set out on trading ventures of their own. As commercial activity increased, significant numbers of Greeks began to move to the shores of the mainland, to outlying islands, and to the coast of Anatolia.

These economic and cultural developments were accompanied by dramatic growth in the Greek population, which placed heavy demands on the resources of a mountainous country with limited agricultural land. Soon, some degree of economic, political, and social cooperation among the inhabitants of rival communities became necessary. But the values that had developed during centuries of isolation did not make such cooperation easy. Each local community treasured its autonomy and independence, celebrated its own rituals, and honored its own heroes. On what basis could such communities unite?

The Greek solution to this challenge was the *polis*, the root from which we derive the words *politics* and *political*. Yet the Greeks considered the polis to be a social collectivity, first and foremost—not a place. For this reason, our sources speak of groups of people—"the Athenians," "the Spartans"—rather than individual cities (Athens, Sparta). *Poleis* (the plural of *polis*) came to be considered so essential to Greek identity that Aristotle would later define man as "a political animal," someone who participates in the life of the polis and who cannot survive outside it.

In practice, poleis combined both formal institutions and informal structures that could differ widely. Most poleis were organized around a social center known as the *agora*, where markets and important meetings were held. Surrounding the whole urban settlement, the *asty*, was the *khora*, "land." The khora of a large polis might support several other towns or smaller poleis, as well as numerous villages. The Greeks described this early process of community building as the "bringing together of dwellings" (*synoikismos*, synoecism).

Polis formation could also come about through the conquest of one settlement by another and/or through the gradual alliance of neighboring communities. Some poleis took shape around fortified hilltops, such as the Athenian acropolis. Other communities may have borrowed a Near Eastern (and particularly Phoenician) practice of orienting the urban center around a temple precinct. In many Greek cities, however, temple building may have been a consequence of polis formation rather than a cause, as elites competed with one another to exalt their poleis and glorify themselves.

THE CULTURE OF ARCHAIC GREECE, 800–500 B.C.E.

Scholars date the Archaic Period of Greek history to the emergence of the polis and the return of writing, which the Greeks would put to a wide variety of uses. The Athenians, in particular, used writing to establish their cultural dominance over other Greek poleis, controlling the inscription of the Homeric canon, promoting the work of contemporary poets, and fostering the writing of prose histories, which allowed them to pass on to posterity a narrative of history in which they played the central role. It is therefore important to bear in mind that much of what we know about this early period derives from the work of later authors who wrote from this Athenian perspective: these include the Ionian-born Herodotus, who spent much of his later life in Athens; the historians Thucydides (c. 460–c. 395 B.C.E.) and Xenophon (430–354); and the philosophers Plato (c. 428–348) and his pupil Aristotle (384–322).

Colonization and Panhellenism

In the eighth and seventh centuries B.C.E., small-scale Greek trading ventures and settlements had developed into a full-fledged colonial enterprise that followed the example of the Phoenicians. Many larger poleis competed with one another to establish colonies, with Athens and Corinth being particularly successful in such ventures.

Although each of these colonies was an independent foundation, it sustained familial and affective ties to its mother polis; so it was often called upon to support the polis and could become entangled in the political and military affairs of the mainland. At the same time, these individual Greek colonies celebrated their shared language and heritage, which was exported to far-flung reaches of the known world, creating a Panhellenic ("all-Greek") culture that eventually stretched from the Black Sea to the Mediterranean coastline of modern France and Spain.

Greek colonization permanently altered the cultural geography of the Mediterranean world. The western shores of Anatolia would remain a stronghold of Greek culture for the next two thousand years. So many Greeks settled in southern Italy that later Romans called the region Magna Graecia, "Greater Greece"; Greek-speaking enclaves would survive there into the twentieth century of our era. By the fourth century B.C.E., more Greeks lived in Magna Graecia than in Greece itself.

Motives for colonization varied. Some poleis, such as Corinth, were blessed by their strategic location on the land bridge between Attica and the Peloponnesus (*pel-oh-poh-NEE-suss*; the large peninsula of mainland Greece), but cursed by the poverty of their land. Trade therefore became the lifeblood of this polis and of the ruling aristocracy who bankrolled the ambitious planting of colonies. Other poleis, confronted by the pressures of growing populations and political unrest, sponsored new colonies as outlets for undesirable elements or unwanted multitudes. These colonial projects parallel, in many ways, those of modern nation-states.

Colonial expansion also intensified Greek contacts with other cultures. Phoenician pottery brought new artistic motifs, while Egypt profoundly influenced early Greek sculptural representations of the human form (see **Interpreting Visual Evidence**). However, intensified contact with other cultures simultaneously sharpened Greeks' awareness of their own identity as Hellenes (the Greeks' name for themselves). Such self-conscious Hellenism did not lead to greater political cooperation, but it did encourage the establishment of Panhellenic festivals, such as the Olympic Games, and of holy sites.

The most important of these was the temple of Apollo at Delphi, home to the oracle of the sun god. Suppliants who sought to have their questions answered would offer gifts to the shrine and then wait while the god spoke through his priestess, whose mysterious answers would be translated into enigmatic Greek verse by an attending priest. The resulting advice was essentially a riddle that called for further interpretation on the part of the recipient—who often misconstrued it: as we noted in Chapter 2, Croesus of Lydia thought that he was following the advice of the oracle when he attacked the Persians, but the great nation he destroyed turned out to be his own.

At the Olympic Games, Greeks honored the king of the gods, Zeus, near the giant temple dedicated to him at Olympia. The Greeks took great pride in these athletic competitions, and only Hellenes were permitted to participate in them. Like colonization, these games did little to alleviate rivalry among the poleis; in fact, they often increased it. But they further strengthened the Greeks' awareness of their common culture, an awareness that could be harnessed when they faced a common threat.

Hoplite Warfare

In the centuries immediately following the calamities of the late Bronze Age, the defense of surviving Greek communities rested with the few elite warriors who had the resources to invest in armor, chariots, and weaponry. This monopoly on military prowess gave the aristocracy tremendous political and social leverage. As a result, aristocrats dominated political offices and priesthoods in the poleis, as well as economic life.

But during the Archaic Period, a revolution in military tactics brought aristocratic military dominance to an end. Increasingly, the effective defense of a polis required that it be able to call on a standing militia. Accordingly, able-bodied citizens began to equip themselves for battle and to train alongside one another. These citizen-soldiers became known as *hoplites*, from the large round shield (*hoplon*) carried by each. In battle, hoplites stood shoulder to shoulder in a close formation called a *phalanx*, several columns across and several rows deep, with each hoplite carrying his shield on the left arm to protect the unshielded right side of the man next to him. In his right hand, each hoplite carried a spear or sword, so that an approaching phalanx presented a nearly impenetrable wall of armor and weaponry to its opponents. If a man in the front rank fell, the one behind him stepped up to take his place; as a result, the weight of the entire phalanx was literally behind the front line, with each soldier leaning with his shield into the man in front of him.

This tight formation required only one shared skill: the ability to stay together. As long as the phalanx remained intact, it was nearly unbeatable. But like the polis itself, it could fall apart if its men did not share a common goal. The hoplite revolution was therefore bound up with a parallel revolution in politics. As a polis came increasingly to draw upon the resources of more and more citizens, it was forced to offer them a larger part in the exercise of political power. By the seventh century B.C.E., these citizen-soldiers formed a hoplite class that could demand a say in decision-making and thereby challenge the hegemony of old elites.

Aristocracy, Tyranny, and Democracy

For the better part of the seventh and sixth centuries B.C.E., aristocrats continued to dominate the Greek poleis. Struggles for influence among competing families were

GREEK COLONIZATION, C. 550 B.C.E. Compare this map with that on page 41. ▪ *How do you account for the differences in Greek and Phoenician patterns of colonization?* ▪ *Were Greek colonies likely to compete with Phoenician colonies?* ▪ *Where were such conflicts most likely to erupt?*

commonplace, and these differences affected polis government at every level, not least because aristocrats were the only members of society who could afford to hold unpaid and time-consuming political offices.

The aristocrats of this period pursued not only wealth, power, and fame; they also cultivated a distinctive lifestyle. Participating in politics and holding office was part of this lifestyle. So too was the *symposium*, a "drinking party" at which elite men would enjoy wine, poetry and poetic competition, performances by trained dancers and acrobats, and the company of *hetaeras* (courtesans) who provided witty conversation, music, and the promise of sex. Respectable women were excluded from such meetings, as they were from nearly all other aspects of social and political life (see below). So too were non-aristocratic men. The symposium was thus an arena for the display of aristocratic masculinity.

The glorification of male sexuality was another important aspect of this homosocial aristocratic culture. Typically, a man in his late twenties to late thirties, who had just begun to make his career in political life, would take as his lover and protégé an aristocratic youth in his early to mid-teens. The two would form an intimate bond in which sexual intercourse played an important role. This benefited

The Ideal of Male Beauty

he Greek word *kouros* ("young man" or "youth") is now applied to a whole series of life-sized statues from the Archaic Period. The one shown here comes from Anavyssos in Attica, and was made between 540 and 515 B.C.E. (It is now in the National Archeological Museum of Athens.) Although scholars used to believe that such statues were meant to represent the god Apollo, further research has shown that most were made to commemorate the dead, especially young warriors who had fallen in battle. This one appears to be walking forward, smiling, but his eyes are closed. The accompanying inscription reads: "Stop and show your pity here for Kroisos, now dead, who once fighting in the foremost ranks of battle was destroyed by raging Ares."

Questions for Analysis

1. What aspects of the body does the kouros emphasize? If this is intended to be a model of Greek manhood, what values would it convey to contemporary youths?

2. Is this a representation of the young man as he was when living, or in death? How do your conclusions about the ideal of male beauty change if this is a glorification of death?

3. Compare this image to the values expressed in the verses by Tyrtaeus of Sparta on "The Beautiful and the Good" (page 65). How do these two perspectives complement one another?

---

both partners and their familes, and allowed the younger partner to learn the workings of politics while making valuable social connections. Many later philosophers, including Plato, argued that true love could exist only between such lovers, because only within such a relationship could a man find a partner worthy of his affections.

A whole complex of values, ideas, practices, and assumptions thus shaped aristocratic identity. As a result, it was impossible for those outside this elite world to participate fully in the public life of the polis. By the middle of the Archaic Period, moreover, the circle of the aristocratic elite tightened even further, as smaller and smaller groups came to dominate higher offices. Many aristocrats found themselves on the outside of their own culture, looking in.

For these men, one remedy lay close at hand: an alliance with the rising class of hoplites. And occasionally, a single aristocrat with the backing of the hoplites would succeed in setting up an alternative form of government, a *tyranny*. The word *tyrannos* had been borrowed from the Lydians, and it signified someone who ruled outside the traditional framework of the polis.

A tyrant in Archaic Greece was not necessarily an abusive ruler. Indeed, tyranny often led the way to wider political enfranchisement because anyone who sought the support of the hoplite class would have to appease that class by extending further rights of political participation, while all the time striving to keep the reins of power in his own hands. But this was an inherently unstable state of affairs,

HOPLITE INFANTRY ADVANCING INTO COMBAT. This Corinthian vase, dating from around 650 B.C.E., displays the earliest-known depiction of hoplites fighting in a phalanx formation.

because the continuance of tyranny became an obstacle to even greater power for the hoplite class. For this reason, tyrannies rarely lasted for more than two generations and could serve as a stepping-stone from aristocracy to a more broadly participatory form of government: democracy.

It is important to stress that our notion of democracy is quite different from that of the Greeks. In fact, Aristotle denegrated this form of government as "mob rule," because it gave too much power to the *demos*, a word meaning "neighborhood" or "affinity group." He saw it as a system too easily controlled by a particular faction. Our ideal of democracy is closer to what Aristotle would have called a polity, governance by the polis as a whole.

The Power of Poetry

The aristocracy of the Archaic Period were deeply invested in the heroic ideal enshrined in the Homeric epics. But they also strove to express their unique culture in newer poetic forms. The most characteristic of these is the lyric, a series of rhythmic verses sung to the music of the lyre. Because these songs would have been composed orally, even improvised, relatively few survive. But those that do are valuable historical sources. Because they were the focus of entertainment at gatherings, they are often politically charged, sexually explicit, or daringly subversive of accepted norms. For

example, the poet Archilochus of Paros (c. 680–640 B.C.E.) flouts the conventions of epic poetry by mocking his own failures on the battlefield: "Some barbarian waves my shield, since I had to abandon it / . . . but I escaped, so it scarcely matters / . . . I can get another just as good." So much for the heroic ideal of returning either with one's shield, or on it! In another lyric, Archilochus castigates his faithless (female) lover and his even more faithless (male) lover with whom she has run off.

Given the male domination of Greek culture, it is paradoxical that the most famous lyric poet of this age was not a man. Rather, it was Sappho (*SAF-foh*, c. 620–550 B.C.E.), who lived in the polis of Mytilene on the island of Lesbos. Revered by her contemporaries as the Tenth Muse, Sappho composed songs for a wide array of occasions and a range of moods: songs of courtship and marriage, longing and desire, loss, old age, and death. Often, they are passionately dedicated to women: both the women whom Sappho loved and the historical women who occupy the margins of masculine epic. Frequently, they take some image or incident from that inherited tradition and give it a distinctive spin. In one song, Sappho compares herself to Agamemnon, who was only able to return from Troy after he prayed to Hera, a goddess worshiped at Lesbos; Sappho now prays that her beloved will arrive safely with the goddess's help. In another, she imagines a scene not included in the *Iliad*, the joyous wedding of the Trojan Hector and his bride,

Andromache. The intimacy of lyric thus reveals something that few sources from antiquity are able to convey: the feelings and desires of individuals who were often at odds with the dominant culture of their time.

PORTRAITS OF THREE POLEIS

The poleis of the Archaic Period developed in very different ways. To illustrate this diversity, we will examine three particularly well-documented examples: Athens, Sparta, and the Ionian city of Miletus. None of these, however, can be considered typical. There were approximately one thousand poleis in Greece, and about most of them we know almost nothing. But at least we can survey some of the features that, with variations, made each polis unique—and yet comparable, in some ways, to its neighbors.

Athens

The Athenians liked to boast that their city had been a great metropolis since the Bronze Age: a claim integral to their identity and their sense of self-importance within the larger Greek world. But although Attica had long been a populous and prosperous region, Athens itself was of no great significance during the Mycenaean Era. When Athenians first came together to form a polis, theirs was a distinctly agricultural economy. Whatever profits aristocrats acquired through trade, they reinvested in land on the Attic Peninsula. Indeed, Athenian elites came to regard commerce as a disreputable means of earning a living, a mentality that persisted even when the city's excellent harbors made Athens famous as a mercantile polis.

In the Archaic Period, aristocratic dominance over this polis rested on the monopolization of elected offices and control of the city's council, the Areopagus (*ah-ree-OP-ah-guhs*). By the early seventh century B.C.E., an even smaller group of aristocratic officials wielded executive authority in Athens: the *archons* or "first men." Ultimately, nine archons presided over the entire governance of the polis. Although each served for only one year, all became lifetime members of the Areopagus. And because the Areopagus appointed the archons, it could therefore control its own future membership.

As power was consolidated by this small group, deep economic and social divisions developed. A significant proportion of the population fell into slavery through debt, while struggles among aristocratic families destabilized the government and fomented cycles of revenge killings.

Finally, this situation inspired Athens' first attempt to promulgate a set of written laws. In 621 B.C.E., an aristocrat named Drakon sought to control civic violence through harsh punishments: hence our use of the term "draconian" to describe any severe penalty, policy, or regime. This attempt failed, but ultimately led both aristocrats and hoplites to an agreement. In 594 B.C.E., they elected one man, the poet Solon, as the sole archon for one year, and they gave him sweeping powers. Solon was an aristocrat, but he had made his fortune as a merchant and did not hold that vocation in contempt; this meant that he was not allied with any single interest.

Solon's political and economic reforms laid the foundations for the later development of Athenian democracy. He forbade the practice of debt slavery and set up a fund to buy back Athenian slaves who had been sold abroad. He encouraged the cultivation of olives and grapes, thus spurring cash-crop farming and urban industries such as oil and wine production, and the manufacture of pottery storage jars and decorative drinking cups. He also broadened rights of political participation and set up courts in which a range of citizens served as jurors and to which any Athenian might appeal. He based eligibility for political office on property qualifications, not birth, thus making it possible for someone not born into the aristocracy to gain access to power. Moreover, he convened an Athenian assembly, the *ekklesia* (*eh-KLAY-see-a*), and gave it the right to elect archons. Now all free-born Athenian men over the age of eighteen could participate in government.

Yet Solon's reforms were not widely accepted. The aristocracy thought them too radical; the people of the demos, not radical enough. In the resulting generation of turmoil, an aristocrat named Peisistratos (*pi-SIS-trah-tohs*) succeeded in establishing himself as tyrant in 546 B.C.E. Somewhat ironically, Peisistratos then proceeded to institute Solon's reforms. But the apparent mildness of his rule was undergirded by the quiet, persistent intimidation of Athenians by his fellow foreign mercenaries and the ruthlessness with which he crushed any dissent. Still, by enforcing Solon's laws, he strengthened the political role of the demos and remained a popular ruler until his death. His sons, however, were less able to control the various factions that threatened their rule: one was assassinated and the other ousted with the help of the Spartans in 510 B.C.E.

But the following period of Spartan-sponsored oligarchy ("rule of the few") was brief. Two generations of increasing access to power had left the Athenian demos with a taste for self-government. For the first time in recorded history, a group of commoners can be credited with the overthrow of a regime. They rallied behind Cleisthenes (*CLIE-sthen-ees*), an aristocrat who had championed the

"The Beautiful and The Good"

The poet known as Tyrtaeus of Sparta flourished during the middle of the sixth century B.C.E. He may originally have come from Athens, but whatever his origins he expressed ideas of honor, beauty, and virtue that were universal among the hoplite warriors of the new poleis. The key terms he uses in the following verses cannot be adequately translated into English, since these short Greek adjectives are freighted with ancient meanings: kalos *(beautiful, honorable),* agathos *(good, brave, manly). They stand in opposition to the term* aischros *(shameful, ugly, mean).*

alos it is for an *agathos* warrior to die, fallen among the foremost fighters, in battle for his native land; but to leave his polis and rich fields and beg—that is most painful of all, as he wanders with his dear mother and aged father, his small children and his wedded wife. Detested he will be in the eyes of all those to whom he comes, constrained by need and hateful poverty. He shames his birth and belies his glorious appearance; dishonor and misery are his companions.

If no account is taken of a warrior who is a wanderer, if there is no respect for him or his family in the future, then let us fight with all our hearts for this land and die for our children, no longer hesitating to risk our lives. Young men, stand firm beside each other and fight.

Do not begin shameful flight or fear. Rather, create a mighty, valorous spirit in your breasts, and show no love for your lives when you are fighting. Do not flee, abandoning the older men, whose knees are no longer nimble.

For *aischros* it is for an older warrior to fall among the foremost fighters and lie out ahead of the young men—a man whose hair is already white and his beard grey—as he breathes out his valorous spirit in the dust, holding his bloody guts in his own hands, his body laid bare. *Aischros* is this to the eyes, and a cause of resentment to look upon.

But to the young men all is seemly, while the glorious flower of lovely youth is theirs. To men the young man is admirable to look upon, and to women lovable while he lives and *kalos* when he lies among the foremost fighters. So let a man take a firm stance and stand fast, with both feet planted upon the ground, biting his lip with his teeth.

Source: Excerpted and modified from *The Greek Polis*, eds. W. H. Adkins and Peter White (Chicago: 1986), pp. 23–24.

Questions for Analysis

1. How does Tyrtaeus characterize defeat? How does this poem exemplify the values and tactics of hoplite warfare?

2. Why is so much emphasis placed on physical beauty and youth? What other qualities are associated with the word *kalos*? Why is old age potentially *aischros*?

3. How does this ideal of male beauty compare with that made visible in the kouros of Anavyssos (page 62)?

---

cause of the demos after the fall of the Peisistratids. Once voted in as archon in 508/7 B.C.E., Cleisthenes took steps to limit aristocratic power. By reorganizing the Athenian population into ten voting districts, he suppressed traditional aristocratic loyalties. He also introduced the practice of ostracism, whereby Athenians could decide each year whether they wanted to banish someone for a decade and, if so, whom. With this power, Cleisthenes hoped that the demos could prevent the return of a tyrant and quell factional strife.

By 500 B.C.E., these struggles had given Athens a far more populist government than any other Greek polis, and had strengthened its political institutions. In the mean-time, Athens had become the principal exporter of olive oil, wine, and pottery in the Greek world. It was poised to assume the role it would claim for itself during the fifth century B.C.E. as the exemplar of Greek culture and the proponent of democracy.

Sparta

Located in the southern part of the Peloponnesus, Sparta took shape when four villages (and ultimately a fifth) combined to form a single polis. Perhaps as a relic of this unification process, Sparta retained a dual monarchy throughout its history, with two royal families and two lines of succession: a situation that often led to political in-fighting among their respective supporters.

According to local tradition, Spartan hegemony in the surrounding region of Laconia began with the conquest of Messenia, one of the mainland's few agriculturally viable territories. Around 720 B.C.E., the Spartans subjugated and enslaved the indigenous people there, the *helots*, who were forced to work under Spartan lordship. Around 650 B.C.E., however, the helots revolted, briefly threatening Sparta with annihilation. Eventually, Sparta triumphed; but the shock of this rebellion brought about a permanent transformation.

Determined to prevent another uprising, Sparta became the most militarized polis in Greece. By 600 B.C.E. everything was oriented to the maintenance of its hoplite army, a force so superior that Spartans confidently left their city unfortified. At a time when Athenian society was becoming more democratic and when citizens spent more time legislating than fighting, Spartan society was becoming increasingly devoted to an older aristocratic ideal of perpetual warfare.

The Spartan system made every male citizen a professional soldier of the phalanx. At birth, every Spartiate child was examined by officials who determined whether it was healthy enough to raise; if not, the infant was abandoned in the mountains. This was a custom observed elsewhere in the ancient world, but only in Sparta was it institutionalized. If deemed worthy of upbringing, the child was placed at age seven in the polis-run educational system. Boys and girls trained together until age twelve, participating in exercise, gymnastics, and other physical drills and competitions. Boys then went to live in barracks, where their military training would commence in earnest. Girls continued their training until they became the mates of eligible Spartiate males. No such thing as "marriage" was possible under the Spartiate system, or even desirable, for it would merely create a new set of loyalties and interests that would compete with the Spartan state.

Barracks life was designed to accustom youths to physical hardship. At age eighteen, the young man who survived this training would try for membership in a brotherhood whose sworn comrades lived and fought together. Failure to gain acceptance would mean that the young man would lose his rights as a citizen. If accepted, however, he remained with his brotherhood until he was thirty years of age. He was also expected to mate with a Spartiate woman, but occasions for this were few, a fact that partially accounts for the low birthrate among Spartan citizens. After age thirty, a Spartiate male could opt to live with his family, but he was still required to remain on active military duty until he was sixty.

All Spartiate males over the age of thirty were members of the citizens' assembly, the *apella*, which voted on matters proposed to it by the two kings and twenty-eight elders. This *gerousia* (gher-oo-SEE-ah, "council of elders") was the main policymaking body of the polis and also its primary court. Its members were elected for life, but had to be over the age of sixty before they could stand for office. Meanwhile, five *ephors* (overseers), elected annually, supervised the educational system and acted as guardians of Spartan tradition. In the latter role, ephors could even depose an errant king from command of the army while on campaign. The ephors also supervised the Spartan secret service, the *krypteia*. Agents spied on citizens, but their main job was to infiltrate the helot population and identify potential troublemakers.

Spartan policy hinged on the precarious relationship between the Spartiates and the helots, who outnumbered the Spartiates ten to one. Helots accompanied the Spartiates on campaign as shield bearers, spear bearers, and baggage handlers. At home, however, the helots were a constant security concern. Every year the Spartans ritually declared war on them as a reminder that they would not tolerate dissent. Moreover, the threat of unrest meant that the polis was notoriously reluctant to send its army abroad.

Helot slavery therefore made the Spartan system possible, but Sparta's reliance on a hostile population of slaves was also a serious limitation. This system also limited Spartans' contact with the outside world in other respects. Spartiates were forbidden to engage in commerce, because wealth might distract them from the pursuit of martial glory. Nor did Spartiates farm their own lands, as Athenians did. economic activity fell either to the helots or to the free residents of other Peloponnesian cities, who were known as *perioikoi* (pair-ee-OY-koy), "those dwelling round about." The perioikoi enjoyed certain rights and protections within Spartan society, but unlike the residents of Attica, the perioikoi exercised no political rights.

The Spartans also self-consciously rejected innovation, styling themselves as the protectors of the "traditional customs" of Greece. In this role, Sparta tried to prevent the establishment of tyrannies in neighboring states and tried to overthrow them when they arose: hence their willing intervention in the affairs of Athens under the Peisistratids. Indeed, Sparta's stern defense of tradition made it an object of admiration throughout the Greek world, even though few Greeks had any desire to live as the Spartans did.

The fatal flaw in the Spartan system was demographic. There were many ways to fall from the status of Spartiate,

Songs of Sappho

> Although Sappho of Lesbos (c. 620–550 B.C.E.) was a prolific poet and skilled musician, we know very little about her life and only a few examples of her extraordinary verse survive. Of the nine books collected in the third century B.C.E., we now have just one complete lyric and a series of fragments, some consisting of only two or three words, often preserved because they were quoted admiringly by other authors. Astonishingly, though, a papyrus scroll containing a previously unknown part of a poem was identified as recently as 2004.

Fragment 16

Some say thronging cavalry, some say
    foot soldiers,
others call a fleet the most beautiful of
sights the dark earth offers, but I say it's
    whatever you love best.

And it's easy to make this understood by
everyone, for she who surpassed all
    human
kind in beauty, Helen, abandoning her
    husband—that best of
men—went sailing off to the shores of
    Troy and
never spent a thought on her child or
    loving
parents: when the goddess seduced her
    wits and left her to wander,
she forgot them all, she could not
    remember
anything but longing, and lightly straying
aside, lost her way. But that reminds me
    now: Anactória,

she's not here, and I'd rather see her lovely
step, her sparkling glance and her face
    than gaze on
all the troops in Lydia in their chariots
    and glittering armor.

Source: Translated by Jim Powell, *The Poetry of Sappho* (New York: 2007), pp. 6–7.

The New Fragment (2004)

Live for the gifts the fragrant-breasted
    Muses
send, for the clear, the singing, lyre, my
    children.
Old age freezes my body, once so lithe,
rinses the darkness from my hair, now
    white.
My heart's heavy, my knees no longer
    keep me
up through the dance they used to
    prance like fawns in.
Oh, I grumble about it, but for what?
Nothing can stop a person's growing old.

They say that Tithonus was swept away
in Dawn's passionate, rose-flushed arms
    to live
forever, but he lost his looks, his youth,
failing husband of an immortal bride.

Source: Translated by Lachlan Mackinnon, *Times Literary Supplement*, July 15, 2005.

Questions for Analysis

1. How does Sappho use stories from the older tradition she has inherited to address her own concerns? How does the perspective of the female poet transform masculine ideas about heroism, beauty, warfare, aging?

2. What are the challenges of working with such fragmentary sources as these? If these were the only pieces of evidence to survive from Archaic Greece, what conclusions could you draw about the society and its values?

---

but the only way to become one was by birth—and the Spartan birthrate simply could not keep pace with the demand for trained warriors. As a result, the number of full Spartiates declined from perhaps as many as 10,000 in the seventh century to only about 1,000 by the middle of the fourth century B.C.E. Another flaw is historical: because the Spartans placed little value on written records, almost everything we know about them (including the summary offered here) must be gleaned from archeological investigations or the propaganda of their enemies, notably the Athenians.

Miletus and the Ionian Revolution in Thought

Across the Aegean from the Greek mainland lay the Greek cities of Ionia on the central part of the Anatolian coast. Here, Miletus was the foremost commercial and cultural power. Long a part of the Greek world (see **Analyzing Primary Sources** in Chapter 2, page 40), it had also been shaped by Mesopotamian and Egyptian influences, and Milesian intellectuals were well aware of Near Eastern literature and learning. Some even echoed the vaunting rhetoric of Persian imperial decrees ("thus speaks Darius the Great King. . . .") to make their own, quite different observations ("thus speaks Hecataeus of Miletus: the sayings of the Greeks are many and foolish").

The relationship between the Ionians of the coast and the interior kingdom of Lydia was close but difficult. It was through the Ionians that the Lydian invention of coinage was introduced to the Greek world, where it revolutionized trade, made wealth portable for the first time, and introduced a host of new philosophical and ethical problems. The Ionians, in turn, played a crucial role in Hellenizing Asia Minor while at the same time insisting on their independence. The major cities of Ionia ultimately banded together to form the Ionian League, a political and religious confederation of poleis pledged to support each other. This was the first such organization in the Greek world.

The Milesians founded many colonies, especially in and around the Black Sea. They were also active in Egypt. These colonial efforts, combined with its advantageous position for trade, brought Miletus extraordinary wealth. At the same time, it became a center for what the Greeks called *philosophia*, "the love of wisdom." Beginning in the sixth century B.C.E., a series of intellectuals now known as the pre-Socratics (because they came before Socrates) raised new and vital questions about the relationship between the natural world (the *kosmos*), the gods, and men. Often, their explanations moved the direct influence of the gods to the margins or removed it altogether, something that other Greeks regarded as blasphemous. For example, Milesian philosophers sought physical explanations for the movements of the heavens, and did not presume that heavenly bodies were divine. By making human observations the starting point for their knowledge, they began to formulate scientific explanations for the working of the universe.

Stimulated by the cultural diversity of their city, Milesian philosophers also began to rethink humans' place in the cosmos. When Hecataeus (heck-ah-TAY-us) remarked that "the sayings of the Greeks are many and foolish," he was deriding his contemporaries' unquestioning acceptance of a narrow worldview. He set out to expand their horizons by traveling extensively and studying the customs and beliefs of other cultures. Xenophanes (zee-NOFF-uh-nees) further posited that all human knowledge is relative and conditioned by experience: he observed that the Thracians (a people living north of Greece) believed that the gods had blue eyes and red hair as the Thracians themselves did, whereas Ethiopians portrayed the gods as dark skinned and curly haired, as they themselves were. He concluded that human beings make gods in their own image, not the other way around. If oxen could pray, Xenophanes declared, they would pray to gods who looked like oxen.

Such theories would become a distinctive strand in later Greek philosophy, yet they would continue to be regarded as disturbing and dangerous—dangerous enough to warrant the execution of Socrates in Athens a hundred years later (see below). By that time, the Persian conquest of Lydia had made Miletus and its sister cities subject to that great empire. Ultimately, those poleis' resistance to Persian rule would trigger the greatest clash the Greek world had yet known.

THE CHALLENGE OF THE PERSIAN WARS

The two major wars fought between the Greeks and the Persians were construed as defining events by those who witnessed and looked back on them. From the first, the contest was unequal. Persia was the largest and most efficient state the world had ever seen, capable of mustering over a million armed men. The Greeks, by contrast, remained a collection of disparate communities, fiercely competitive and suspicious of one another. An exceptionally large polis, such as Athens or Sparta, might put 10,000 hoplites in the field; but the vast majority of Greek states could only provide a few hundred each. So the threat of Persian conquest loomed large on the Greek horizon.

The Ionian Revolt (499–494 B.C.E.)

For the first time in the history of Western civilizations, we can follow the unfolding of events through the narrative of a contemporary historian: Herodotus, the first person who self-consciously set out to write an account of his own times in careful, unambiguous prose, rather than in the form of heroic poetry or the boastful language of victorious inscriptions. And luckily for us, Herodotus was uniquely qualified to probe the long-term and more immediate causes of the Persian Wars. Raised in the Ionian polis of Halicarnassus, he regarded both the Greeks and the Persians as great peoples. Yet, as a Greek himself—albeit one born within the Persian dominion—he was not impartial. Indeed, his surviving account reflects the intellectual currents of Athens, where he spent the better part of his career, as well as many Athenian prejudices. This is something we must be bear in mind when reading his work.

Herodotus was careful to show that the war between the Persians and Greeks had ancient roots, but his narrative also shows that the catalyst was a political conflict in Miletus. In 501 B.C.E., the city was governed by Aristagoras, a tyrant who owed his power to the backing of the Persian emperor, Darius. But apparently Aristagoras came to believe that his days as the emperor's favorite were numbered. So he turned abruptly from puppet to patriot, rousing the Milesians and the rest of Ionia to revolt against Persian rule. As a safeguard, he also sought military support from sympathetic poleis on the Greek mainland. The Spartans refused to send their army abroad, but Athens and Eretria, on the island of Euboea, agreed to send twenty-five ships and crews. This small force managed to capture the old Lydian capital of Sardis (by then a Persian administrative center) and burn it to the ground. Then the Athenians and Eretrians went home, leaving the Ionians to their own devices. In 494 B.C.E., the rebellious poleis were finally overwhelmed by the vastly superior might of Persia.

A MODERN REPLICA OF AN ATHENIAN TRIREME. These versatile warships were much more powerful than the old fifty-oared pentakonters that had been in use for centuries. As the name suggests, a trireme featured three banks of oars on each side, 170 oars in total. These were manned by citizen rowers seated on benches at three different levels in the vessel's hold. In battle, rowers could help power a ship forward, turn it, and keep it on course in a chase, even when sailing into the wind. In favorable winds, sails could be used to add speed. ▪ *How does this new military technology build on some of the same strategies as hoplite warfare?*

Darius realized, however, that so long as his Greek subjects in Asia Minor could cast a hopeful eye to their neighbors across the Aegean, they would forge alliances. He therefore decided to launch a preemptive strike against Athens and Eretria, to teach these upstart poleis a lesson. In the summer of 490 B.C.E., a punitive expedition of 20,000 soldiers crossed the Aegean. Their forces sacked and burned Eretria to the ground, sending its population into captivity in Persia. They then crossed the narrow strait to Attica, landing on the plain of Marathon, approximately 26 miles from Athens.

Marathon and Its Aftermath

In this emergency, the Athenians sought help from the only polis that could conceivably help them forestall annihilation: Sparta. But the Spartans responded that they were unable to assist—they were celebrating a religious festival. Only the small, nearby polis of Plataea offered the Athenians aid. Heavily outnumbered and without effective cavalry to counter that of the Persians, the Athenian hoplites took a position between two hills blocking the main road to the

polis. After a standoff of several days, the Athenian general Miltiades (*mil-TIE-uh-dees*) received word that the Persians were watering their horses, and that the Persian infantry was vulnerable. Miltiades led a charge that smashed the Persian force and resulted in crippling losses. Almost unbelievably, the Athenians had defeated the world's major imperial power, and they had done it without Spartan help. It was a vindication of hoplite tactics and a tremendous boost to Athenian confidence.

Yet the Athenian politician Themistocles (*theh-MIS-toh-klees*) warned that the Persians would retaliate with an even larger force. So when the Athenians discovered a rich vein of silver ore in the Attic countryside a few years later, they used the windfall to finance a fleet of 200 triremes, state-of-the-art warships.

Xerxes' Invasion

Darius the Great was succeeded by his son Xerxes (*ZERK-sees*), who almost immediately began preparing a massive invasion of Greece to avenge his father's shame. Supported by a fleet of 600 ships, this grand army set out in 480 B.C.E.,

THE PERSIAN WARS WITH GREECE. Imagine that you are the Persian emperor Xerxes, planning the conquest of Greece in 480 B.C.E.
▪ *What are the two possible routes that you could take to attack Greece?* ▪ *What geographical considerations would dictate your military strategy?* ▪ *Bearing in mind that Xerxes' attempt failed, what would you have done differently?*

crossing the narrow strait separating Europe from Asia. But unlike his father, who had dispatched talented generals to lead the earlier attack on Athens, Xerxes led this campaign himself.

Many Greek poleis capitulated immediately. But Athens, Sparta, Corinth, and some thirty others hastily formed a Hellenic League: an unprecedented alliance in the face of an unprecedented threat. In August of 480, a major Persian offensive was held at bay when the outnumbered Greek allies, under the military leadership of Sparta, confronted Xerxes at the mountain pass of Thermopylae (*ther-MO-pih-lie*). For three days, they valiantly held off the Persian multitude. Meanwhile, a Greek fleet led by Athens engaged a Persian flotilla. The Spartans' defense of Thermopylae ultimately failed, but their sacrifice of some 300 warriors allowed the new Athenian warships to inflict heavy losses on the Persians.

However, these engagements left Athens without any men to defend their city. Themistocles therefore persuaded the entire population to abandon Athens for the island of Salamis. From there, the Athenians watched the Persians torch their city. Time, however, was on their side. Xerxes' massive army depended on his damaged fleet for supplies, and the Persians' military tactics—which included a heavy

GREEK FORCES DEFEAT PERSIANS. This detail from a bowl commemorating the defeat of Xerxes' army depicts an Athenian hoplite poised to strike a death-blow to his Persian opponent. The artist has carefully delineated the differences between the enemies' dress and weaponry. To the Greeks, the Persian preference for trousers over short tunics seemed particularly barbaric and effeminate.

reliance on cavalry and chariots—were not adapted for the rocky terrain of Greece.

In late September, the numerically superior Persian fleet sailed into the straits of Salamis. So confident was Xerxes that he had a throne placed above the bay, where he would have a good view of his victory. Instead, he watched as the Athenian triremes demolished the Persian fleet. This was the turning point of the war. When the allied Greek army met the Persians on favorable terrain the next spring—an open plain near Plataea—the Greeks prevailed. Against all odds, the small, fractious poleis had defeated the mightiest army of the known world.

THE GOLDEN AGE OF CLASSICAL GREECE

In the half century after the Persian Wars, Athens enjoyed a meteoric rise in power and prestige, becoming the premier naval power of the eastern Mediterranean. Athens also emerged as leader of the Delian League, a group of poleis whose representatives met on the sacred island of Delos

and pledged to continue the war against Persia. The fifth century B.C.E. also witnessed the greatest achievements in Athenian culture and politics.

Periclean Athens

The reforms of the decades before the Persian Wars continued to encourage further experiments in democracy, including the selection of major officeholders by lot. Only one key position was now filled by traditional voting: the office of *strategos*, or general. This office became the career goal of Athens' most ambitious figures.

Meanwhile, new voices were demanding a greater role in government. Most prominent were the *thetes* (*THAY-tees*), the lowest class of free men that provided the triremes' rowers, the backbone of the all-important Athenian fleet. Like the hoplites of the Archaic Period, who had achieved citizenship because they were indispensible to the defense of the poleis, thetes wanted higher status and equal representation. The man who emerged to champion their cause was Pericles (*PEHR-eh-klees*), an aristocrat from one of Athens' most prestigious families.

Pericles also advocated a foreign policy that was oriented away from cooperation with Sparta. In 462–461 B.C.E. he was elected strategos and immediately used his position to push through reforms that gave every Athenian citizen the right to propose and amend legislation, not just to vote yes or no in the citizens' assembly. And by paying an average day's wage for attendance, he made it easier for poorer citizens to participate in the assembly and in courts of justice. Through such measures, the thetes and other free men of modest means became a dominant force in politics—and loyal to the man who had made that dominance possible.

Athenian Literature and Drama

Pericles also glorified Athens with an ambitious scheme of public building and lavish festivals honoring the gods. The most important of these was the Dionysia, a great spring feast devoted to the god Dionysius, which became a forum for the presentation of drama. From the beginning, therefore, Greek theater was closely connected to the political and religious life of the state that sponsored it. Indeed, the very format of classical tragedy replicates the tensions of democracy, showcasing the conflict among opposing perspectives. This format was perfected under the great tragedian Aeschylus (*EYE-skihl-uhs*, 525–456 B.C.E.) and his

THE THEATER AT EPIDAUROS. Greek dramas were invariably presented in the open air, usually at dawn. Since these were civic spectacles, theaters had to be large enough to accommodate all citizens. Most, like this one at Epidauros (right), took advantage of the natural slope of a hill. The plan for the theater is shown above (left). The acting area would have been backed by a high wall, the *skene*, which housed stage machinery and enhanced the acoustics. A trained actor standing in the circular *orchestra* would have been audible even to those seated in the top tier. ▪ *How would the size and setting of such a theater enhance the political character of the plays performed within it?*

younger contemporary, Sophocles (496–406 B.C.E.). Their dramas made use of two and eventually three professional actors (each of whom could play numerous roles) and a chorus of Athenian citizens, which represented collective opinion and could comment on the action.

Tragedies were almost always set in the distant or mythical past, yet were intended to address the cutting-edge issues of their day. Indeed, the very earliest of all surviving tragedies, Aeschylus' *The Persians*, represents events of the playwright's own lifetime; and we know for certain that he fought at Marathon, because he had this fact proudly recorded on his tomb. Performed for the first time in 472, it tells the story of the great Athenian victory at Salamis, but through the eyes of the defeated Xerxes, who thus becomes its tragic hero.

But even when its subject matter was derived from the epics of Homer, the fundamental themes of tragedy—the conflicting demands of personal desire and public duty, the unforeseen consequences of human actions, the brutalizing effects of power—addressed problems of immediate concern to Athenians. For example, *Oedipus at Colonus*, one of Sophocles' later tragedies, used a story of the mythical king of Thebes to comment bitterly on Athens' disastrous war with Sparta (see below). Similarly, the *Trojan Women* of Euripides (485–406 B.C.E.), presented in 415, marks the tragic turning point in the Athenians' march toward defeat in this war. By looking back at the capture, rape, and enslavement of Troy's defeated women, Athenians were forced

to look ahead to the consequences of their own imperial policies.

Comedy was even more obviously a genre of political commentary, and could deal openly with the absurdities and atrocities of current events. Indeed comedy—then as now—could be effectively deployed to deal with issues that were too hot to handle in any other form: sexual scandals, political corruption, moral hypocrisy, intellectual pretension, popular fads. Aristophanes (*EHR-ih-STOFF-ah-nees*, c. 446–386 B.C.E.), the greatest of the Athenian comic playwrights, lampooned everything from the philosophy of Socrates to the tragedies of his contemporary Euripides, and was an especially outspoken critic of Athenian warmongers and their imperialist aims. He was repeatedly dragged into court to defend himself against the demagogues he attacked, but the power and popularity of comic theater was such that politicians never dared to shut it down for long.

Periclean Athens was also fertile ground for the development of new literary forms. Even though the Greeks were becoming more dependent on writing for legal and commercial transactions, intellectuals had long been used to expressing themselves through poetry, which was always intended to be sung and enjoyed in performance, not to be read. Now, though, the rise of functional literacy in Athens encouraged the emergence of prose as a distinct literary form. Herodotus found a ready market for his histories in Athens. His younger contemporary Thucydides (*thu-SID-ih-dees*) followed suit, using his time in exile to write a masterful—and scathingly critical—history of the war between his polis and Sparta.

Between them, these two historians developed a new approach to the study of the past, emphasizing the need to collect and interpret multiple sources and focusing on human agency as the driving force of history (rather than divine intervention). Both conceived the historian's role as distinct from that of a storyteller. The word *historia* would continue to mean both "story" and "history" in Greek, but for Herodotus and Thucydides the historian's task was to investigate and critically reflect on the events of his own time, as well as to illuminate those of the past. These methods and goals would increasingly come to inform other prose genres, including the philosophical writings of Plato and Aristotle (see Chapter 4).

Art and Architecture

The artists of fifth-century B.C.E. Athens revealed the same range of talents in the visual arts as poets did in their dramas. Perhaps the most striking development was the new attention paid to the crafting of naturalistic figures, both clothed and nude. Nothing like it had ever been seen before, although it is a trend already discernible in the figure of the *kouros* examined above (page 62). What hastened the acceptance of naturalism is a matter of intense debate,

APOLLO OF TENEA, APOLLO OF PIOMBINO, AND THE CRITIAN BOY. These three statues, dating from about 560, 500, and 480 B.C.E., respectively, display the development of Greek statuary art. The first rather stiff and symmetrical statue (left) is imitative of Egyptian sculpture. Roughly half a century later, the second representation (middle) of Apollo begins to display motion, not unlike the kouros on page 62. The last figure (right), showing a boy standing in a relaxed posture with his weight resting on one leg, displays even greater naturalism.

but scholars have long wanted to link this innovation to the triumphant victories over the Persians. Greeks tended to regard the Persian male's modesty of dress, preference for trousers, fondness for jewelry, and luxurious long hair as proofs of effeminacy (see the vase painting on page 71), whereas Greek men took pride in exercising, sculpting their physiques, and participating in athletic contests in the nude. A Greek might have said that only barbarians covered their shameful bodies in constricting clothes; free men celebrate their individuality in the care of the body and its representation.

The Athenians also made exceptional contributions to architecture in this period. All Greek temples sought to create an impression of harmony, but the Parthenon of Athens, built between 447 and 438 B.C.E., is generally considered the finest example of this (see page 58). Construction of this expensive and structurally ambitious building was urged on the Athenians by Pericles as a tribute to their patron goddess, Athena Parthenos ("Athena the Virgin"), and as a symbol of their own power, confidence, and genius.

Women and Men in the Daily Life of Athens

Toward the end of his famous funeral oration, which Thucydides included in his history, Pericles addresses only a few brief remarks to the women of Athens who mourn their fallen fathers, husbands, and sons in the first year of the disastrous war with Sparta (430 B.C.E.). He urges them to do three things: rear more children for the support of Athens, show no more weakness than is "natural to their sex," and attract no attention to themselves. His remarks reveal widely held attitudes toward women in classical Greece, especially in Athens.

The growth of democracy did not lead to greater equality between the sexes; in fact, it had the opposite result. In Mycenaean Greece, women had been viewed as possessing extraordinary funds of courage and wisdom. They were prized for their shrewd advice on political and military matters, and they played an active role in the world. Sometimes they ruled kingdoms in their own right. But as aristocratic ideals gave way to more democratic ones, Greek women increasingly spent their lives in the shadows.

The importance of the hoplite infantry and its spirit of shared purpose encouraged men to train together and to develop close relationships. At the same time, that spirit of equality discouraged displays of wealth, especially by women. Instead, the rearing of children to supply the infantry became the female imperative. Public spaces were restricted to male activities, while domestic, private spaces were reserved for female endeavors such as child care and weaving. Respectable women lived in seclusion, rarely (if ever) venturing forth from their homes.

In Athens, girls could be married at age fourteen—to husbands more than twice their age. A girl's father arranged her marriage and provided a dowry that her husband could use for her support. Legally, wives became the property of their husbands. And shortly after a wife entered her new home, a regular schedule of childbirth would begin. The average young wife would bear between four and six children before she died, usually around the age of thirty-five. Her place might then be taken by another, younger woman. Available evidence even suggests that husbands were not encouraged to form emotional attachments to their wives, although some obviously did. In a revealing passage, Herodotus reports of a certain Lydian king that he "fell in love with his own wife, a fancy that had strange consequences." By contrast, an Athenian orator remarked that "we have prostitutes for pleasure, concubines for daily physical attendance, and wives to bear us legitimate children and be our faithful housekeepers."

Because respectable women seldom went out of doors, since it was thought immodest for them to be seen by men outside their immediate families, slaves did whatever shopping or marketing the household required. Even at home, women were expected to withdraw into private rooms if visitors arrived. But they were not supposed to sit around idly, and their main occupation was spinning and weaving. This was true of all women, from royalty to slaves. And since women's work was basically menial, men looked down on them for it, even though their own livelihoods and comfort depended on it.

In addition to depending on the faithful labor and fertility of its "free" women, Athenians were as reliant on slaves as Spartans were on helots. Without slavery, none of the Athenian accomplishments in politics, philosophy, or art would have been possible. The Athenian ideal of dividing and rotating governmental duties among all free men depended on slaves who worked in fields, businesses, and homes. In fact, the Athenian democratic system began to function fully only with the expansion of Athenian commerce around 500 B.C.E., which enabled the Athenians to buy slaves in larger numbers. Freedom and slavery were thus inescapably, and paradoxically, linked in this democracy—much as they would be many centuries later in the United States.

Although widespread, Athenian slavery was modest in scale. Slaves did not ordinarily work in teams or in factories; the only exceptions were the state-owned silver mines, where large numbers of slaves toiled in miserable conditions. Most slaves were owned in small numbers by a wide range of Athenian families, including the relatively poor. As domestic servants and farm laborers, slaves might even be considered trusted members of the household, although their masters were legally empowered to beat them or abuse them; concubines were often drawn from among this class of slaves. Yet slaves could never be entirely dehumanized, as they were in modern slaveholding societies: the misfortune of becoming a slave through debt was a reality of Athens' recent past, and the real possibility of being enslaved in war would become a widespread consequence of Athens' overreaching ambitions.

"THE GREATEST WAR IN HISTORY" AND ITS CONSEQUENCES

And ultimately, Athens' foreign policy and imperial ambitions undermined its civic and cultural achievements. Since the 470s, Athens had begun crushing those allies who attempted to break from its control. By the early 440s, its only rival for supremacy in the Greek world was Sparta. Rather than attempting to maintain a balance of power, however, Pericles determined on a more aggressive policy. In order to ensure that military resources would be directed toward any Spartan opposition, he concluded a formal peace with Persia. Yet the sole purpose of the Delian League had been the defense of Greece against Persian aggression, so Athens now had no justification for compelling its members to maintain their allegiance. Many remained loyal nonetheless, enjoying the economic benefits of warm relations with Athens. Others, however, did not, and Athens found itself increasingly having to force its allies back into line, often installing Athenian garrisons and planting Athenian colonists—who retained their Athenian citizenship—to ensure future loyalty.

In the context of recent history and longstanding Greek values, such behavior was disturbing. The Persian wars had been fought to preserve Greek independence. Now Athens itself was becoming an oppressive, imperial power. Foremost among its accusers were the Corinthians, whose own economic standing was threatened by Athenian dominance. The Corinthians were close allies of the Spartans, who were in turn the dominant power in what historians call the Peloponnesian League. (The Greeks called it simply the "Spartans and their allies.") When war finally erupted between Athens and Sparta, Thucydides—himself an Athenian—ascribed it to the growing power of Athens and the anxiety this inspired in other poleis. No modern historian has improved on Thucydides' thesis. Yet for the

Athenians and their leaders, there could be no question of relinquishing their empire, or the dream of dominating the Mediterranean world. For Sparta and its allies, meanwhile, the prospect of relinquishing their independence was equally unthinkable. Two very different ideas of Greek superiority were about to fight to the death.

The Peloponnesian War Begins

When the Athenians and Spartans found themselves at war with one another in 431 B.C.E., both sides believed a conclusion would come quickly—a delusion common to many of history's pivotal contests. Instead, the war dragged on for twenty-seven years. Thucydides, writing about it in exile, recalled that he knew from the time of its outbreak that it was going to be "the greatest war in history," amounting to the first world war, because by the time it was over it would involve the entire Mediterranean. He also meant that it was the worst, so devastating to both sides that it destroyed the proud heritage of freedom the Greeks had treasured. By the time Athens was forced to concede defeat, all the poleis were weakened to such an extent that they would never again be able to withstand outside threats.

From the beginning, Athens knew that it could not defeat Sparta on land; and neither Sparta nor its allies had a fleet capable of facing the Athenians at sea. Pericles therefore developed a bold strategy: he would pull the entire population of Attica within the walls of Athens and not attempt to defend the countryside against Sparta. For sustenance, Athens would rely on supplies shipped in by its fleet, which would also be deployed to ravage the coasts of the Peloponnesus.

The Spartans duly plundered the farms and pastures of Attica, frustrated that the Athenians would not engage them in battle. Meanwhile, the Athenians inflicted significant destruction on Spartan territory in a series of raids and by successfully encouraging rebellion among the helots. Time appeared to be on Athens' side. But in 429 B.C.E. the crowded conditions of the besieged city gave rise to a typhus epidemic that killed over a third of the population, including the aged Pericles.

Pericles' death revealed that he had been the only man capable of managing the political forces he had unleashed. His successors were mostly demagogues, ambitious men who played to the worst instincts of the demos. The most successful of these was Cleon, who refused a Spartan offer of peace in 425 B.C.E. and continued the war until his own death in battle four years later. It was under Cleon that Thucydides was given the impossible task of liberating a city under Spartan control; his failure in 423 led to his exile.

THE PELOPONNESIAN WAR. This map shows the patchwork of colonies and alliances that bound together the supporters of Sparta and Athens at the outbreak of the Peloponnesian War in 431 B.C.E. ▪ *Which side had the geographical advantage?* ▪ *Which neutral powers might have been able to tip the balance by entering the war on one side or the other?* ▪ *What strategic and military choices did geography impose on the two combatants and their allies?*

After the death of Cleon, a truce with Sparta was negotiated by an able Athenian leader named Nicias (*NICK-ee-ahs*). But Athenians continued to pursue a "dirty war" by preying on poleis that it feared might support the Spartans. This led to atrocities like the destruction of the entire city of Melos, an island colonized by the Spartans that had maintained its neutrality since the beginning of the war. When the inhabitants of Melos refused to compromise this position by accepting Athenian rule, Athens had the entire male population slaughtered and every woman and child sold into slavery.

Thereafter, Athens' policy of preemptive warfare proved destructive to itself. In 415 B.C.E., a charismatic young aristocrat named Alcibiades (*al-ki-BY-uh-dees*) convinced the Athenians to attack the powerful Greek city of Syracuse in Sicily, which was allegedly harrying Athenian allies in the western Mediterranean. The expedition ended disastrously, with the death or enslavement of thousands of Athenian warriors.

News of the Syracusan disaster shattered the Athenians. Many political leaders were driven from the polis as scapegoats, and in 411 B.C.E. a hastily convened assembly of citizens voted the democracy out of existence, replacing it with an oligarchy of 400 men, many of whom had been present at this vote. The remains of the Athenian fleet, then stationed in Samos on the Ionian coast, responded by declaring a democratic government in exile under the leadership of none other than Alcibiades. The oligarchy proved to be brief, and democracy was restored to Athens by 409. But a pattern of self-destruction had been established, making it difficult for anyone in Athens or outside it to believe in the possibility of restored greatness.

THE FAILURE OF ATHENIAN DEMOCRACY

The Spartans too despaired of bringing the war to an end. Even in its weakened condition, the Athenian fleet was still invincible. Finally, Sparta turned to the Persians, who were glad to avenge themselves on Athens and agreed to supply the gold and expertise necessary to train an effective Spartan navy. Meanwhile, Athenians were turning against each other and making the Spartans' task easier. In 406 B.C.E., a rare Athenian naval victory ended in a sudden storm that prevented Athenian commanders from rescuing the sailors whose ships had been wrecked. A firestorm of protest was fanned by demagogues who insisted on making an example of those generals brave enough to return to Athens. One of these was Pericles' son Pericles, who died a victim of his father's policies. Through such measures, the Athenians killed or exiled the last of their able commanders.

The poorly led Athenian fleet was destroyed in 404 B.C.E. Without ships, the Athenians could neither feed themselves nor defend their city. The Spartans sailed the Aegean unopposed, installing pro-Spartan oligarchies. Finally, they besieged Athens, which surrendered. Corinth and Thebes, remembering the ruthless treatment of Melos, called for Athens' destruction. The Spartans refused, but imposed harsh terms: the dismantling of Athens' defensive walls, the scrapping of its fleet, and the acceptance of an oligarchy under Spartan supervision. These so-called Thirty Tyrants confiscated private property and murdered their political opponents. Their excesses drove committed democrats to plan a desperate coup, a bloodbath averted only through the intervention of the Spartan king.

By the end of 401 B.C.E., Athens had restored a semblance of democratic governance, but it was never more than a shadow of its former self. Meanwhile, Sparta succeeded Athens as the arbiter of the Greek world. But this was a thankless job, made worse by the losses the Spartans had suffered during the war and by the fact that they were even more aggressive in their control than the Athenians had been. In fact, the Spartans found themselves in a position they had avoided throughout their history, because their far-flung interests now sapped their manpower and

undermined their control over the helots. They also faced a reinvigorated Persian Empire, which increased its naval presence in the Aegean.

These were the circumstances in which the Athenian philosopher Socrates (469–399 B.C.E.) attempted to reform his city's ethical and political traditions. To understand something of his accomplishments, and to assess the reasons for his tragic death, we must trace briefly the history of philosophical speculation in the half century before his birth.

The Pythagoreans and the Sophists

After the Persian conquest of Ionia, many Milesian philosophers fled to southern Italy. Philosophical speculation thus continued in the Greek "far west." A major figure here was Pythagoras (*pith-AG-or-us*), who founded a philosophical community. Pythagoras and his followers regarded the speculative life as the highest good, and believed that one must be purified of fleshly desires in order to achieve this. Just as the essence of life lay in the mind, they believed that the essence of the universe was to be found not in the natural world but in the study of abstractions. The Pythagoreans established the key properties of odd and even numbers and also proved an old Babylonian hypothesis in geometry,

SOCRATES. According to Plato, Socrates looked like a goatman but spoke like a god.

Competing Viewpoints

Two Views of Socrates

Socrates as a Sophist

Most people regard Socrates as the sage thinker who challenged the prevailing prejudices of his day. During his own time, however, he was not so universally admired. In Aristophanes' comedy The Clouds, *the protagonist, Strepsiades (strep-SIGH-uh-dees), goes to Socrates and his "Thought Shop" to ask that Socrates make him and his son, Pheidippides (phi-DIP-pid-ees), orators capable of winning lawsuits and growing rich. Aristophanes implies throughout that Socrates is a charlatan who teaches word games and tricks for hire.*

STREPSIADES: See that he [Pheidippides] learns your two Arguments, whatever you call them—oh yes, Right and Wrong—the one that takes a bad case and defeats Right with it. If he can't manage both, then at least Wrong—that will do—but that he must have.

SOCRATES: Well, I'll go and send the Arguments here in person, and they'll teach him themselves.

STREPSIADES: Don't forget, he's got to be able to argue against any kind of justified claim at all.

RIGHT: This way. Let the audience see you. . . .

WRONG: Sure, go wherever you like. The more of an audience we have, the more soundly I'll trounce you.

RIGHT: What sort of trick will you use?

WRONG: Oh, just a few new ideas.

RIGHT: Yes, they're in fashion now, aren't they, [*to the audience*] thanks to you idiots. . . . [*to Pheiddipides*] You don't want to be the sort of chap who's always in the agora telling stories about other people's sex lives, or in the courts arguing about some petty, filthy little dispute. . . .

WRONG: People here at the Thought Shop call me Wrong, because I was the one who invented ways of proving anything wrong, laws, prosecutors, anything. Isn't that worth millions—to have a really bad case and yet win? . . . Suppose you fall in love with a married woman—have a bit of fun—and get caught in the act. As you are now, without a tongue in your head, you're done for. But if you come and learn from me, then you can do whatever you like and get away with it . . . and supposing you do get caught with someone's wife, you can say to him. . . . "What have I done wrong? Look at Zeus; wasn't he always a slave of his sexual passions? And do you expect a mere mortal like me to do any better than a god?" . . .

STREPSIADES [*to Socrates*]: I wonder if you'd accept a token of my appreciation? But my son, has he learned that Argument we were listening to a moment ago?

SOCRATES: Yes, he has.

STREPSIADES: Holy Fraud, how wonderful!

SOCRATES: Yes, you'll now be able to win any case at all.

Source: Aristophanes, *The Clouds*, trans. Alan H. Sommerstein (New York: 1973), pp. 148–50, 154, 159–60 (slightly revised).

Socrates and the Laws of Athens

According to his pupil Plato, Socrates spent the last days of his life in conversation with his friends and followers, some of whom urged him to escape from captivity and live in exile. In the dialogue Crito, *a young aristocrat of that name argues that the very laws that have condemned Socrates are unjust, and that by choosing to obey them Socrates is giving them a legitimacy they do not deserve. Halfway through the debate, Socrates turns the tables on him.*

SOCRATES: I should like you to consider whether we are still satisfied on this point: that the really important thing is not to live, but to live well.

CRITO: Why, yes.

SOCRATES: And that to live well means the same thing as to live honorably, or rightly?

CRITO: Yes.

SOCRATES: Then in light of this agreement we must consider whether or not it is right for me to try to get away without an official pardon. If it turns out to be right, we must make the attempt; if not, we must let it drop. . . .

CRITO: I agree with what you say, Socrates. . . .

SOCRATES: Well, here is my next point, or rather question. Ought one to fulfill all one's agreements, provided they are right, or break them?

CRITO: One ought to fulfill them.

SOCRATES: Then consider the logical consequence. If we leave this place without first persuading the polis to let us go . . . are we or are we not abiding by our just agreements?

CRITO: I can't answer your question, Socrates. I am not clear in my mind.

SOCRATES: Look at it this way. Suppose that while we were preparing to run away (or however one should describe it), the Laws of Athens were to come and confront us with this question: "Now, Socrates, what are you proposing to do? Can you deny that by this act which you are contemplating you intend, so far as you have the power, to destroy us, the Laws, and the whole polis as well? Do you imagine that a city can continue to exist and not be turned upside down, if the legal judgments which are pronounced in it have no force but are nullified and destroyed by private persons?"—How shall we answer this question, Crito, and others of the same kind? . . . Shall we say, "Yes, I do intend to destroy the Laws, because the polis has wronged me by passing a faulty judgment at my trial"? Is this to be our answer, or what?

CRITO: What you have just said, by all means, Socrates.

SOCRATES: Then supposing the Laws say, "Was there provision for this in the agreement between you and us, Socrates? Or did you pledge to abide by whatever judgments the polis pronounced? . . . [I]f you cannot persuade your country you must do whatever it orders, and patiently submit to any punishment it imposes, whether it be flogging or imprisonment. And if it leads you out to war, you must comply, and it is right that you should do so; you must not give way or retreat or abandon your position. Both in war and in the law courts you must do whatever your city and your country commands."

Source: Plato, *Crito*, excerpted (with modifications) from *The Last Days of Socrates*, trans. Hugh Tredennick (New York: 1969), pp. 87–91.

Questions for Analysis

1. Socrates actually refused to teach the art of "making the weaker argument defeat the stronger." But in *The Clouds*, Aristophanes shows him teaching how "to win any case at all." Why were the powers of persuasion considered potentially dangerous in democratic Athens? Why might Aristophanes choose to represent Socrates in this way?

2. How do the arguments of Plato's Socrates compare to those of Aristophanes' character?

3. How does Socrates' sense of honor and his duty toward the polis compare to that of Tyrtaeus of Sparta (page 65)?

known today as the Pythagorean theorem. Even though they shunned the material world, they still exhibited the characteristic Greek quest for regularity and predictability in that world.

Meanwhile, philosophy as it developed in mainland Greece was more attuned to questions of ethics and politics. The increasing power of individual citizens begged the question of how a man should conduct himself, in public and private life, so as to embrace "the beautiful and the good"—or at least to advance himself by the use of his wits. To answer this latter need were a new group of teachers known as Sophists, a term meaning "wise men." Unlike the Milesian philosophers or the Pythagoreans, however, the Sophists made their living from selling their knowledge. Their teachings are best exemplified by Protagoras (*pro-TAB-or-us*), an older contemporary of Socrates. His famous dictum, "man is the measure of all things," means that goodness, truth, and justice are relative concepts, adaptable to the needs and interests of human beings. They are not moral absolutes, established by the gods. Indeed, Protagoras declared that no one could know whether the gods existed or, if they did, what they wanted. He thus concluded that there could be no absolute standards of right and wrong. Empirical facts, established by the perception of the senses, were the only source of knowledge. And because each man experienced the world in a different way, there could be only particular truths valid for the individual knower.

Such teachings struck many Athenians as dangerous. Sophists like Protagoras made everyday life a subject for philosophical discussion, but their relativism could too easily degenerate into a conviction that the wise man (or the wise polis) is the one best able to manipulate others. Both individually and collectively, this conviction could rationalize monstrous acts of brutality—like those committed by Athens in the case of Melos. Indeed, the lessons of the Peloponnesian War went a long way toward demonstrating the disastrous consequences of this self-serving logic: if justice is merely relative, then neither personal morality nor society can survive. This conviction led to the growth of a new philosophical movement grounded on the theory that absolute standards do exist, and that human beings can determine what these are, through the exercise of reason. The initiator of this trend was Socrates.

The Life and Thought of Socrates

Socrates was not a professional teacher, like the Sophists. He may have trained as a stonemason, and he certainly had some sort of livelihood that enabled him to maintain his status as a citizen and hoplite. Having fought in three campaigns as part of the Athenian infantry during the war with Sparta, he was both an ardent patriot and a sincere critic of Athenian policy. His method of instruction was conversation: through dialogue with passers-by, he submitted every presumed truth to examination in order to establish a firm foundation for further inquiry. Everything we know about Socrates' teachings comes from the writings of younger men who considered themselves his pupils, and who participated in these conversations. The most important of these followers was Plato.

According to Plato, Socrates sought to show that all supposed certainties are merely unexamined prejudices inherited from others. Socrates always said that he himself knew nothing, because this was a more secure place from which to begin the learning process. He sought to base his speculations on sound definitions of key concepts—justice, virtue, beauty, love—which he and his pupils could arrive at only by investigating their own assumptions. And he focused his attention on practical ethics rather than the study of the physical world (like the Milesians did) or abstractions (like the Pythagoreans). He urged his listeners to reflect on the principles of proper conduct, both for their own sakes and for that of society as a whole. One should consider the meaning and consequences of one's actions at all times, he taught, and be prepared to take responsibility for them. According to one of his most memorable sayings, "the unexamined life is not worth living."

It is bitterly ironic that such a man, the product of Athenian democracy, should have been put to death by democratic processes. Shortly after the end of the Peloponnesian War in 399 B.C.E., when Athens was reeling from the shock of defeat and from violent internal upheavals, a democratic faction decided that Socrates was a threat to the state. A democratic court agreed, condemning him to death for denying the gods, disloyalty to the polis, and "corrupting the youth." Although his friends made arrangements for him to flee the city and thus evade punishment, Socrates insisted on abiding by the laws, proving himself true to his own principles and setting an example for future citizens. He died calmly by the prescribed method, self-administered poison.

According to Socrates, the goal of philosophy is to help human beings understand and apply standards of absolute good, rather than to master a series of mental tricks that facilitate personal gain at the expense of others. The

After You Read This Chapter

Visit StudySpace for quizzes, additional review materials, and multi-media documents. **wwnorton.com/studyspace**

REVIEWING THE OBJECTIVES

- The Greek polis was a unique form of government. What factors led to its emergence?
- Hoplite warfare had a direct effect on the shaping of early democracy. Why?
- Poleis could develop in very different ways. What are some of the reasons for this?
- In what ways did Athenian culture, philosophy, and art reflect democratic ideals?
- The Persian and Peloponnesian Wars affected Greek civilization in profound ways. Describe some of the consequences of Athens' victory in the former and its defeat in the latter.

circumstances of his death, however, show that it is difficult to translate this philosophy into principles that can be widely accepted. This would be the task of Plato, who would lay the groundwork for all subsequent Western philosophy (see Chapter 4).

CONCLUSION

There are many striking similarities between the civilization of ancient Greece and our own—and many stark differences. Perhaps the most salient example of both is the concept of democracy, which in ancient Greece was defined as rule by a class of propertied male citizens supported by slavery. In theory and in practice, this amounted to only a small percentage of the population in Athens, whereas in Sparta the vast majority were subject to the rule of an even smaller class of Spartiates. At the same time, the growth of Athenian democracy meant, increasingly, the exploitation of other poleis and the spread of imperialism, a ruinous policy of preemptive warfare, and increased intolerance and paranoia. (Socrates was not the only man put to death for expressing his opinions.) Finally, the status of women in this "golden age" was lower than it had been in earlier periods of Greek history, and women had fewer personal rights than in any of the ancient societies we have studied so far.

The profound significance of Greek experiments with new forms of governance, and new ideas about the world, is undeniable. This can be seen with particular clarity if we compare the Greek poleis with the empires and kingdoms of Mesopotamia and ancient Egypt. The typical political regime of the ancient Near Eastern world was, as we have seen, that of a monarch supported by a powerful priesthood. In this context, cultural achievements were mainly instruments to enhance the prestige of rulers, and economic life was controlled by palaces and temples. By contrast, the core values of the Greeks were the primacy of the human male and the principles of competition, individual achievement, responsibility, and human freedom. (The very word for freedom—*eleutheria*—cannot be translated into any ancient Near Eastern language, not even Hebrew.) In his history, Herodotus records a conversation between a Greek (in this case a Spartan) and a Persian, who expresses surprise that the Greeks should raise spears against the supposedly benign rule of his emperor. The Spartan retorts, "You understand how to be a slave, but you know nothing of freedom. Had you tasted it, you would advise us to fight not only with spears but with axes." The story of how the Greeks came to turn those spears on one another within a few generations of their united victory is worthy of one of their own tragedies.

Another way of appreciating the enduring importance of Greek civilization is to recall the essential vocabulary we have inherited from it: not only the word *democracy* but *politics*, *philosophy*, *theater*, *history*. The very notion of humanity comes to us from the Greeks. For them, the fullest development of one's potential should be the aim of existence: every free man is the sculptor of his own monument. This work of growing from childishness to personhood is what the Greeks called *paideia* (*pie-DAY-ah*); the Romans called it *humanitas*. How this and other ideas came to be disseminated beyond Greece, to be adopted by the peoples and places of a much wider world, is the subject of Chapter 4.

PEOPLE, IDEAS, AND EVENTS IN CONTEXT

- How did the epics of **HOMER** transmit the values of the Bronze Age to the **ARISTOCRACY** of the new Greek **POLEIS**?
- How did the spread of **GREEK CULTURE** transform the Mediterranean, even as the adoption of **HOPLITE** military tactics transformed Greek politics?
- Compare and contrast the historical circumstances that led to the development of **ATHENS**, **SPARTA**, and **MILETUS**. What were the main differences among them?
- What were the different motives for the invasions of **DARIUS** and **XERXES**? By what methods did the Greek poleis manage to emerge victorious from the **PERSIAN WARS**?
- What were the triumphs and limitations of **DEMOCRACY** in **PERICLEAN ATHENS**?
- How did the **PELOPONNESIAN WAR** transform Athens and affect the balance of power in the Mediterranean?

CONSEQUENCES

- The trial and execution of Socrates can be seen as a referendum on the relationship between the individual and the state. What does this incident reveal about the limitations of personal power and individual rights? To what degree was this incident a product of Athenian losses during the Peloponnesian War? To what extent does it reflect long-term trends in the Greek world?
- We like to think that we can trace our democratic ideals and institutions back to Athens, but does this mean that the failings of Athenian democracy also mirror those of our own? What parallels can you draw between ancient Athens and today's United States? What are some key differences?

Before You Read This Chapter

The Greek World Expands, 400–150 B.C.E.

CORE OBJECTIVES

- **EXPLAIN** Macedonia's rise to power and its triumph over the Greek poleis.

- **DESCRIBE** Alexander's methods of conquest, colonization, and governance.

- **IDENTIFY** the three main Hellenistic kingdoms and their essential differences.

- **DEFINE** the main characteristics of the Hellenistic world.

- **UNDERSTAND** how new philosophies and artistic movements reflect historical changes.

When the young Alexander of Macedonia set out for Persia in 334 B.C.E, he brought along two favorite books. The first was a copy of the *Iliad*, which his teacher Aristotle had given him. The second was the *Anabasis*, "The Inland Expedition," by an Athenian called Xenophon (ZEN-oh-fon, 430–354 B.C.E). Both choices are significant. The *Iliad* recounts the story of a much earlier Greek assault on Asia, and its protagonist is the hero Achilles—a figure with whom Alexander identified: consummate warrior, favorite of the gods, a man who inspired passionate loyalty. It is also full of information useful to someone planning a long campaign in foreign lands against a formidable enemy, with a fractious army drawn from all parts of Greece and little prospect of bringing them home safely or soon. The *Anabasis* was an even more practical choice. Its author had been one of 10,000 Greek mercenaries hired by a Persian prince to overthrow his older brother, the Great King. The attempted coup failed, but Xenophon's book made the prince, Cyrus, another role model for Alexander. It also told, in detail, how Persians fought, how they lived, how they were governed, and what the terrain of their vast empire

83

was like. Moreover, it showed what a dedicated army of hoplites could accomplish on Persian soil. This book would be Alexander's bible for the next ten years.

By the time of Alexander the Great's early death, a united Greek and Macedonian army had extended Greek culture and Greek governance from Egypt to the frontiers of India. This personal empire, the empire of Alexander, could not last. But the cultural empire built upon it did. This Hellenistic ("Greek-like") civilization joined disparate lands and peoples, forming the basis of the Roman Empire and mirroring the cosmopolitan world of our own time. How this happened is the subject of Chapter 4.

THE DOWNFALL OF THE GREEK POLIS

The Peloponnesian War had left Sparta the dominant power in the Greek world. But by 395, a significant number of poleis were aligned against Sparta in the so-called Corinthian War (395–387 B.C.E.). To quell this rebellion, the Spartans turned once again to Persia, as they had done in the final stages of the Peloponnesian War. This pattern of violence, temporarily halted by the intervention of Persia, would be repeated time and again over the next fifty years.

The Struggle for Hegemony

After the Corinthian War, the Spartans punished the most dangerous of their rivals, Thebes, by occupying the city for four years. But when the Thebans regained their autonomy they elected as their leader a fierce patriot who was also a military genius, Epaminondas (*eh-pa-min-OHN-das*, c. 410–362 B.C.E.). In imitation of the Spartan system, he formed an elite hoplite unit known as the Theban Sacred Band, made up of 150 couples: sworn lovers who pledged to fight to the death for their polis and for each other's honor.

When the Theban and Spartan armies met at Leuctra in 371 B.C.E., the Sacred Band helped carry the Thebans to victory. Epaminondas then marched through the Spartan territory of Messenia and freed the helots. Spartan power—and the unique social system that had supported it—was thereby brought to an end. But as Theban power grew, so did the animosity of the other Greek poleis. In 362, when Epaminondas fell in battle, Athens attempted—and failed—to fill the vacuum by establishing a naval confederacy. Greece thus remained a constellation of petty warring states.

Social and Economic Crises

Meanwhile, the poleis were also riven by internal turmoil. Incessant warfare and political struggles profoundly affected their economic and social infrastructures. Many people were driven from their homes or reduced to slavery. Country towns had been ravaged, as had farmlands throughout Greece. Prices rose while standards of living declined. Taxes increased.

Unemployment was also widespread, and many men turned to mercenary service. Cyrus, brother of the Persian emperor Artaxerxes II, even hired a Greek mercenary force of 10,000 men in an attempt to seize the throne in 401 B.C.E. But when Cyrus was killed in battle, the army—marooned in a hostile country—had to fight its way out under elected leaders. One of these was Xenophon, a former pupil of Socrates, and it was his account of this expedition that would become Alexander the Great's guidebook.

RE-IMAGINING THE POLIS: THE ARTISTIC AND INTELLECTUAL RESPONSE

399 B.C.E., the year of Socrates' execution, marks the end of an era—that of the polis. This basic engine of Greek life had continued to drive innovation and cultural production even during the Peloponnesian War. But now, the failure of democracy had a profound impact on the arts, philosophy, and especially political thought.

The Arts of the Fourth Century

As we observed in Chapter 3, the painters and sculptors of the fifth century B.C.E. were already working to achieve a heightened appearance of realism in their works. This experimentation continued in the fourth century, especially in the relatively new art of portraiture. Artists also grew bolder in their use of tricky techniques, like the casting of full-size statues in bronze. This was a medium in which the era's most famous sculptor, Praxiteles, excelled. Praxiteles was bold, too, in his choice of subjects, and is widely regarded as the first artist to create full-size female nudes (see **Interpreting Visual Evidence**).

In contrast to the visual arts, the forms and functions of drama changed considerably. Tragedy and comedy were no longer mounted as part of publicly funded festivals, but were instead financed by private individuals who could exercise greater control over the content of performances.

Xenophon Describes an Ideal Leader

In his history of "The Inland Expedition" undertaken by the Ten Thousand, Xenophon (430–354 B.C.E.) mourns the death of Cyrus the Younger, whom he believes would have made a better Great King of Persia than the brother he challenged, Artaxerxes II. The following description of the prince's character and leadership became very famous in its time, often circulating as a separate booklet. It is likely to have influenced the young Alexander.

hus then died Cyrus, a man who, of all the Persians since Cyrus the elder [the Great], was the most princely and the most worthy of rule, as is agreed by all who appear to have had personal knowledge of him. In the first place, while he was yet a boy, and when he was receiving his education with his brother and other youths, he was thought to surpass them all in everything. For all the sons of the Persian nobles are educated at the gates of the king, where they may learn many a lesson of virtuous conduct, but can see or hear nothing disgraceful. Here the boys see some honored by the king, and others disgraced, and hear of them, so that in their very childhood they learn to govern and to obey.

Here Cyrus, first of all, showed himself most remarkable for modesty among those of his own age, and for paying more ready obedience to his elders than even those who were inferior to him in station; and next, he was noted for his fondness for horses, and for managing them in a superior manner. They found him, too, very desirous of learning, and most assiduous in practicing, the warlike exercises of archery and hurling the javelin. When it suited his age, he grew extremely fond of the chase and of braving dangers in encounters with wild beasts. On one occasion he did not shrink from a she-bear that attacked him, but, in grappling with her, was dragged from off his horse, and received some wounds, the scars of which were visible on his body, but at last killed her. The person who first came to his assistance he made a happy man in the eyes of many.

When he was sent down by his father, as satrap of Lydia and Great Phrygia and Cappadocia, and was also appointed commander of all the troops whose duty it is to muster in the plain of Castolus, he soon showed that if he made a league or compact with anyone, or gave a promise, he deemed it of the utmost importance not to break his word. Accordingly the states that were committed to his charge, as well as individuals, had the greatest confidence in him; and if anyone had been his enemy, he felt secure that if Cyrus entered into a treaty with him, he should suffer no infraction of the stipulations. When, therefore, he waged war against Tissaphernes, all the cities, of their own accord, chose to adhere to Cyrus in preference to Tissaphernes, except the Milesians; but they feared him, because he would not abandon the cause of the exiles; for he both showed by his deeds and declared in words that he would never desert them, since he had once become a friend to them, not even though they should grow still fewer in number, and be in a worse condition than they were.

Whenever anyone did him a kindness or an injury, he showed himself anxious to go beyond him in those respects; and some used to mention a wish of his that he desired to live long enough to outdo both those who had done him good, and those who had done him ill, in the requital that he should make. Accordingly to him alone of the men of our days were so great a number of people desirous of committing the disposal of their property, their cities, and their own persons.

Source: Excerpted from Xenophon, *Anabasis*, ed. M. I. Finley in *The Portable Greek Historians* (New York: 1959), pp. 383–84.

Questions for Analysis

1. According to Xenophon, what are the attributes of a great leader? How would Alexander have applied these to his own situation?

2. What seems to be Xenophon's attitude toward the Persians? How might his portrayal of them have been influenced by his travels among them? How might it have been colored by his attitude toward his own countrymen?

3. In what ways does Cyrus the Younger appear to have followed the example of his ancestor, Cyrus the Great (Chapter 2, page 47)?

As a result, fourth-century playwrights did not have the freedom to use drama as a vehicle for political and social critique, as earlier dramatists had done. Instead, the "New Comedy" of this era relied more and more on mistaken identities, tangled familial relationships, and breaches of etiquette. Similar trends toward escapism are also apparent in a new literary genre: the prose novel. These pleasant fictions targeted an increasingly literate audience, including (as with many modern romance novels) an audience of women.

Philosophy after Socrates: The Schools of Plato and Aristotle

The intellectual and political legacy of Socrates was carried forward by Plato (429–349 B.C.E.), who as a young man witnessed the trial and death of his mentor. Plato strove to vindicate Socrates by constructing a philosophical system based on his precepts. He did this by founding an informal school called the Academy and by writing a series of dialogues that feature Socrates as the central character.

The longest and most famous of these dialogues is now known by its Latin title, the *Republic*. In it, Plato argues that social harmony and order are more important than individual liberty or equality. He imagines an ideal polis governed by a superior group of "guardians" chosen in their youth for natural attributes of intelligence and character. Those found to be the wisest would ultimately become "philosopher-kings." This imaginary system is clearly a response to the failures of Athenian democracy. But whether Plato himself believed in it is open to question. For such a system presumes that properly educated rulers will never be corrupted by power, a proposition that has yet to be sustained in practice.

The practical application of philosophy would be the preoccupation of Plato's own student, Aristotle (384–322 B.C.E.). The son of a physician, Aristotle learned from

PLATO AND ARISTOTLE. Although many artistic representations of Plato and Aristotle were made in antiquity, the image that best captures the essential difference between their philosophies is this one, the focal point of a fresco by the Renaissance painter Raphael Sanzio (1483–1520 C.E., to be discussed further in Chapter 12). Plato is the older central figure to the viewer's left, who points with his right hand to the heavens; Aristotle is the younger man beside him, gesturing with an open palm to the earth. ■ *How does this double portrait reflect these philosophers' teachings and perspectives?*

Reconstructing an Ideal of Female Beauty

The lost statue known as the Aphrodite of Knidos was considered the most beautiful in the ancient world, but we can only study it by looking at later copies. It was the work of the fourth century's most renowned sculptor, Praxiteles (*prak-SIT-el-eez*), who was reputed to have modeled it after the Athenian courtesan known as Phryne, a renowned beauty who inspired several contemporary artists and many apocryphal stories. The most reliable of these concerns the riches she accrued: apparently she became so wealthy that she offered to finance the rebuilding of Thebes in

336—on the condition that the slogan "destroyed by Alexander, restored by Phryne the Courtesan" be prominently displayed on the new walls. (Her offer was rejected.)

Praxiteles' original statue is thought to have been the first monumental female nude fashioned in antiquity. According to one authority, he had initially received a commission from the island of Kos, for which he made both clothed and naked versions of Aphrodite. Apparently, the scandalized citizens approved only the draped version and refused to pay for the nude. It was purchased instead by the city of Knidos on Cyprus, where it was displayed in an open-air

temple so that it could be seen from all sides. It quickly became a tourist attraction and was widely copied and emulated. Two of the more faithful replicas, made by artists working in Rome, are pictured here.

Questions for Analysis

1. As we have seen, the male nude was a favorite subject of Greek artists from the Archaic Period onward. Based on your knowledge of contemporary Greek culture and society, why was it only in the fourth century B.C.E. that a life-size female nude could be publicly displayed? Are there any precedents for statues like this?

2. Compare and contrast the ideal of female beauty suggested by the Knidian Aphrodite with the male ideals discussed in Chapter 3. What can you conclude about the relationship between these ideals and the different expectations of male and female behavior in Greek society? Why, for example, would ancient sources insist that the model for the original statue was a courtesan?

3. Among the Romans, a statue like the Knidian Aphrodite was called a *Venus pudica*, a "modest Venus" (image A). Yet the citizens of Kos were allegedly shocked by its indecency, while old photographs of the copy in the Vatican Museum (image B) show that it was displayed until 1932 with additional draperies made of tin. How do you account for these very different standards of decency? To what degree do they suggest that concepts of "beauty" or "modesty" are historically constructed?

A. Roman copy of the Aphrodite of Knidos.

B. Second century C.E. copy of the Aphrodite of Knidos.

his father the importance of observing natural phenomena. His own philosophical system was geared toward understanding the workings of the world through empirical knowledge—that is, information gained through sensory experience. In contrast to Plato, who taught that everything we see and touch is an untrustworthy reflection of some intangible ideal, Aristotle advocated the rigorous investigation of real phenomena. His method of instruction was also different. Unlike Socrates and Plato, whose dialogues were witty and often playful, Aristotle delivered lectures on which his students took detailed notes, and which eventually became the basis of treatises on politics, ethics, logic, metaphysics, and poetics.

Aristotle taught that the highest good consists in the harmonious functioning of the individual human mind and body. Good conduct is therefore rational conduct, and consists in acting moderately. And whereas Plato conceived of politics as a means to an end which could never be achieved in this life, Aristotle thought of politics as an end in itself: the collective exercise of moderation.

Aristotle also took it for granted that some people—like barbarians—are not fully human, and so are intended by nature to be slaves. He also believed that women are not endowed with a full measure of humanity. So when Aristotle asserted that "man is by nature a political animal" (or, to be more faithful to the Greek, "a creature of the polis"), he meant only Greek males of privileged status. Nor did he believe that the best form of government is a democracy. Like Plato, he saw that as a "debased" form of government.

Men of Thought, Men of Action

Despite these philosophical breakthroughs, Plato and Aristotle offered few prescriptions for reforming their own societies. But there were other intellectuals who were considering more radical alternatives. The Athenian Xenophon, a veteran of the Ten Thousand and another product of the Socratic tradition, spent much of his adult life in Sparta, and it is thanks to his admiring account that we know anything about the Spartiate system described in Chapter 3. He intended his description to be a rebuke to democratic Athens and a model for a different kind of ideal society.

The Athenian orator Isocrates (436–338 B.C.E.) was another direct contemporary of Plato. But rather than imagining an ideal polis, he proposed instead that the Greeks stage a massive invasion of Persia. This assault, he prophesied, should be led by a man of vision and ability who could unite the Greek world behind his cause. Isocrates spent most of his life casting about to find such a leader.

Finally, he began to think that the man for the job was someone most Greeks considered no Greek at all: the king of Macedonia, Philip II.

THE RISE OF MACEDONIA

Until the fourth century, Macedonia (or Macedon) had been a weak kingdom, regarded by most Greeks as a throwback to the "dark ages" before the emergence of enlightened poleis. As recently as the 360s, it had nearly succumbed to the even smaller kingdoms and predatory tribes that surrounded it. No one knows whether the ancient Macedonians were Greek-speaking during this period, but the royal family and nobility would at least have spoken Greek as a second language. Still, they were definitely outsiders. So when a young and energetic king consolidated the southern Balkans under his rule, many Greeks saw it as an alarming development.

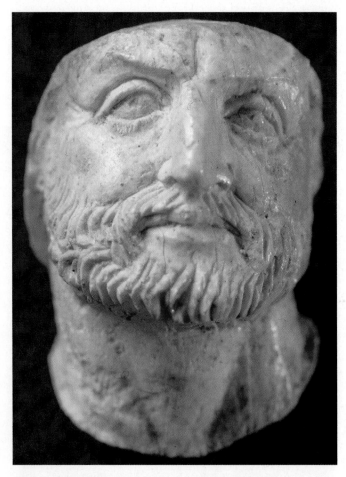

PHILIP II OF MACEDONIA. This tiny ivory head was discovered in a royal tomb at Vergina and is almost certainly a bust of the king himself. Contemporary sources report that Philip the Great had his right eye blinded by a catapult bolt, a deformity visible here—and testimony to the unflinching realism of Greek portraiture in the fourth century B.C.E.

MACEDONIAN PHALANX. Philip of Macedonia's hoplite infantry—the model for Alexander's—was armed with two-handed pikes of graduated lengths, from 13 to 21 feet, and was massed in squares sixteen rows deep and wide. Members of the phalanx were trained to wheel quickly in step formation and to double the width of their front rank as needed, by filing off in rows of eight. The reach of their spears, called *sarissas*, extended the phalanx's fighting range.

The Reign of Philip II (359–336 B.C.E.)

Philip II of Macedonia was not supposed to be its ruler. Born in 382, he was the third and youngest son of King Amyntas III, and was considered so dispensable that he was sent to Thebes as hostage when he was fourteen. This turns out to have been the making of him: he become the protégé of the brilliant Epaminondas and may even have trained in the Theban Sacred Band. By the time he returned to the Macedonian capital of Pella, he had received a more thorough education than any Macedonian before him. He was also ambitious. So when both of his older brothers died in battle, Philip was not content with the role of regent for an infant nephew. By 356, he was reigning as king, the same year that his queen, Olympias, bore him an heir. The boy was given the dynastic name Alexandros, "leader of men."

The first problem of Philip's reign was the fragility of Macedonia's northern borders. Through a combination of warfare and diplomacy, he subdued the tribes of the southern Balkans and incorporated their territory into his kingdom. His success had much to do with his reorganization of Macedonian warriors into a hoplite infantry along Theban lines, as well as access to mineral resources that he used to pay and equip a standing professional army. Philip also organized an elite cavalry squad—the Companions—who fought with and beside the king, perhaps in emulation of the Sacred Band. These young men were drawn exclusively from the nobility, and Philip thereby gained valuable young hostages to ensure the good conduct of fractious men. Their sons were now being brought up alongside Alexander and sharing his lessons with Aristotle, who had arrived at the Macedonian court in 343 B.C.E.

Isocrates saw in Philip a potential savior of Greece, but many Athenians believed that his ultimate aim was to conquer them. In actuality, he was probably trying to forge an alliance with Athens, whose fleet could facilitate an invasion of Persia by sea; in return, Philip promised to support Athens' old claim to hegemony over Greece.

But the Athenians refused to cooperate. This miscalculation ultimately led to war, which sent the Athenians scrambling to ally with Thebes. At the battle of Chaeronea in 338 B.C.E., an army led jointly by Philip and Alexander (aged 18) won a narrow victory, decimating the Athenian forces and destroying the Theban Sacred Band. In the aftermath, Philip called delegates from around mainland Greece to Corinth, where he established a new league whose main purpose was to provide forces for the planned invasion of Persia and maintain peace among the rival poleis.

But Philip never realized his dream of Persian conquest. Two years later, in 336 B.C.E., he was assassinated during a festival at Pella. The kingship now fell to Alexander. Among the Greeks, he would be known as Alexander, the Sacker of Cities. To the Romans, he was Alexander the Great.

THE CONQUESTS OF ALEXANDER, 336–323 B.C.E.

By the time of Alexander's early death at the age of 32, a monumental legend had already built up around him. This makes it all the more ironic that no contemporary account of his life and achievements survives. The great library assembled in his capital of Alexandria in Egypt—the repository of all Greek learning and literature—was destroyed centuries later, and with it a great portion of assembled knowledge. So when we try to reconstruct the history of Alexander, we are depending on the writings of men who lived and worked under the Roman Empire, notably Plutarch (46–120 C.E.) and Arrian (c. 86–160 C.E.), both of whom were separated from their subject by a distance of four hundred years. Luckily, they were basing their histories on sources derived from two first-hand accounts, one written by Alexander's general (and purported half-brother) Ptolemy (c. 367–c. 284 B.C.E.), who founded a new dynasty of Egyptian pharaohs, and another by Æschines Socraticus (c. 387–322 B.C.E.), an Athenian statesman.

It is a salutary reminder of how fragile the historical record of antiquity is, that the sources for the life of the era's most famous man are so hard to come by.

The Conquest of Persia

When Alexander succeeded his father in 336 B.C.E, he had to put down the revolts that erupted immediately after Philip's death—notably at Thebes, which he punished by destroying its famous walls. Two years later, he was crossing the Hellespont to challenge the Great King of Persia, Darius III.

Darius was a minor member of the royal family who had been placed on the throne after a palace coup, at the relatively old age of 45—in the same year that Alexander himself became king at 20. Darius and his advisors failed to take the Macedonian threat seriously, despite the Persians' past history of defeat at the hands of Greek armies. Perhaps they assumed that the enormous forces they could rally in defense of their empire would easily overwhelm a comparatively small army of 42,000; perhaps they misunderstood Alexander's aims.

In any event, Alexander soon achieved a series of extraordinary victories, beginning in northwest Anatolia, near the site of the epic field of Troy, and continuing down the Ionian coastline. A year later, in 333 B.C.E. Darius was persuaded to engage Alexander personally. But the chosen site, on the banks of a river near Issus, favored Alexander's fast-moving infantry, not the heavy cavalry and chariots of the Persians. No warrior himself, Darius disgraced himself by fleeing the battlefield, abandoning not only his army but his entire household, which included his wife and his mother. (They were captured by Alexander and treated with great respect.) Darius spent the remainder of his life running from Alexander's advancing forces, until his decisive defeat at Gaugamela (near Mosul in modern Iraq) in 331, when he was killed by a local chieftain who hoped to win Alexander's favor. Instead, Alexander—acting as the new Great King—had the chieftain executed for treason. The next spring, Alexander destroyed the royal capital of Persepolis, lest it serve as a rallying point for Persian resistance.

Meanwhile, in the two years that had passed since Darius' humiliation at Issus, Alexander had completed his conquest of Asia Minor. One by one, the cities of Syria and Palestine surrendered. Following the example of Cyrus the Great, Alexander had developed a policy of offering amnesty to cities that submitted peacefully—but dealing mercilessly with those that resisted. The fortified city of Gaza, the last Persian stronghold on the Egyptian border, provides an example: when the fortress was finally taken, Alexander's troops slew all the adult males and enslaved the women and children. According to a later Roman historian, Alexander also dragged the body of the commander around the city's walls behind his chariot, imitating Achilles' legendary treatment of Hector.

ALEXANDER'S WORLD. This view of the world, modeled on maps made in antiquity, represents what intellectuals of Alexander's own time knew about geography. ▪ *Comparing it to the map of Alexander's campaigns on page 91, how do you think this worldview affected the planning of his route?* ▪ *Based on available knowledge, why would he have traveled down the Indus river (near the marking India) and traveled overland to Susa?* ▪ *What similarities and differences do you find generally, comparing this ancient map with the other maps that appear in this book?*

Alexander in Egypt

After this, Alexander marched into Egypt unopposed. In fact, he was welcomed as a liberator: Egypt had been governed as a Persian satrapy since 525 B.C.E. Now Alexander himself was hailed as pharaoh and given the double crown of Upper and Lower Egypt, becoming the latest in a succession of rulers reaching back three thousand years to the time of King Narmer (Chapter 1). The "barbarian" chieftain of a backwater kingdom had become pharaoh of the oldest civilization on earth and heir to its immense riches and extraordinary history.

While the Persians had long been the Greeks' traditional enemies, the Egyptians had always been too far away to pose a threat; indeed, they were an object of awe. This may help to explain Alexander's response to the oracle of Ammon, the name the Greeks gave to the Egyptian sun god Amun-Ra, whom they identified with Zeus. At the oracle's desert oasis of Siwa, Alexander was reportedly told that he was "son of Ammon" and a god himself. Ever mindful of historical precedent, Alexander seems to have decided at this point that Egypt should be the capital of his new empire: it was in Egypt that he would build his shining new

THE CAMPAIGNS OF ALEXANDER. The conquests of Alexander the Great brought Greek culture to the vast expanse of the former Persian Empire, as far east as the Indus River. Trace Alexander's route with your finger. ▪ *Where did he start and end?* ▪ *What was the farthest point east that he traveled on his conquests?* ▪ *Why might Alexander have chosen to found so many cities named after him, and what can you conclude about the purposes of these cities, based on their locations?*

city of Alexandria. In the end, he just had time to lay out a plan for the streets. When he finally returned, he was in his sarcophagus.

Alexander's Final Campaigns

Over the ensuing five years, Alexander campaigned in the far reaches of the Persian Empire, in the mountainous regions that had been only loosely yoked with the more settled lands of Mesopotamia. This is the region encompassed today by Afghanistan, and a terrain famous for defeating every attempt at conquest. Here, Alexander and his army experienced the hardest fighting of their long campaign. Indeed, they never succeeded in getting more than a tenuous hold on the territory, despite Alexander's marriage to Roxane, daughter of a local chieftain. Thereafter, Alexander moved down through what is now Pakistan to the Indus Valley, meeting stiff resistance from its warlords

but eventually defeating their leader, Porus, at the Battle of Hydaspes in 326 B.C.E.

This was to be the last major battle of his career, and the one in which his famous warhorse, Bucephalus, was killed. And it was here that Alexander's exhausted army refused to go on, thousands of miles and eight years from home. He was forced to turn back, and rather than attempting to recross the mountains, he pressed southward to the shores of the Arabian Sea—what was then the end of the world. The ensuing march through the Gedrosian Desert, combined with a decade of continuous fighting, weakened him and his army considerably.

When Alexander reached the royal palace of Susa he took steps that indicate how he would have tried to combine his Greco-Macedonian Empire with that of Persia, had he lived. He announced that he would begin training Persian youths to fight alongside Greeks and Macedonians in hoplite formation. He arranged a mass marriage between hundreds of his officers and a corresponding number of Persian

MARBLE HEAD OF ALEXANDER. Alexander the Great is reported to have been very striking in appearance, although sources vary in their assessment. This portrait bust was made in 180 B.C.E., about 150 years after his death. ▪ *Given the trends in sculpture during that period (see page 102), is this likely to have been an accurate portrait?*

on further conquests, perhaps in Arabia, perhaps toward "Greater Greece"—Italy and Sicily. But in late May of 323 B.C.E., he began to show signs of what may have been malarial fever. Some ancient sources even suggest that he was poisoned; his closest companion, Hephaistion, had died the year before at Ecbatana, leaving Alexander without his most vigilant bodyguard. In any case, Alexander ignored the advice of his doctors. His condition worsened, and he died on June 10 or 11, 323 B.C.E., in the palace built by the Chaldean king Nebuchadnezzar in Babylon, the ancient capital of Hammurabi. He was not yet thirty-three years old.

THE HELLENISTIC KINGDOMS

According to one account—by a later Roman historian—Alexander's officers gathered around his bed as he lay dying and asked to whom he wished to leave his empire. He had replied, "To the strongest." According to other sources, he was actually incapable of speech. According to still other sources, he silently gave his signet ring to a Macedonian called Perdiccas, the leader of his cavalry.

It was certainly Perdiccas who attempted to arrange a settlement among all the possible claimants for power, albeit unsuccessfully. It was eventually decided that the infant Alexander IV, his son by Roxane, should rule jointly with Alexander's half-brother, Philip, the son of Philip II by one of his lesser wives. But this solution was never put into effect, because both the child and his uncle were soon murdered, as was Perdiccas. Meanwhile, the satrapies that had been alloted to various leaders of Alexander's armies became the bases from which these men attempted to seize control.

The turmoil lasted for two generations. By about 275 B.C.E., however, three separate axes of military and political power had emerged, each headed by a Greco-Macedonian ruling class but with a distinctive character. Indeed, a striking feature of this period is the renewal of ancient political patterns within the common culture that continued to unite Alexander's fragmented empire. This is why the world created by his conquests is called Hellenistic, "Greek-like."

noblewomen. Most controversially, he showed respect for his Persian subjects by adopting Persian dress—considered by Greeks to be effeminate and barbaric—and by encouraging those around him to perform the ritual of *proskynesis* (*pros-kin-EE-sis*). This was a gesture of bodily submission performed by those of lesser social standing when they met their superiors, and by all Persians—even those of royal rank—to honor the Great King. The person paying homage would bow deeply, in some cases prostrating himself entirely. To the Greeks, this practice suggested that the Persians worshiped their king as a god. To Alexander and his close advisors, it was more likely intended to level cultural differences. In any case, it was not a success, and it fueled a mutiny among the Macedonians, which Alexander himself had to quell.

Alexander's Death

Apart from these attempts to create cohesion, Alexander took no realistic steps to create an administration for his vast empire. He seems to have fixed his sights more clearly

Ptolemaic Egypt

By far the most stable of these three Hellenistic states was Egypt, thanks in large part to the canny governance of Alexander's former general Ptolemy (*TOHL-eh-mee*), who was possibly an illegitimate son of Philip II. Ptolemy decided to

Analyzing Primary Sources

Alexander Puts Down a Mutiny

The following account comes from the history of Alexander's campaigns by the Greek-speaking Roman historian Arrian (c. 86–160 C.E.), who lived in the Roman province of Bythinia in northern Anatolia. This is the closest thing we have to a primary source, since histories written by Alexander's own contemporaries have not survived. The following passage describes Alexander's response to a mutiny among his troops after his return from India in 324 B.C.E.

My countrymen, you are sick for home—so be it! I shall make no attempt to check your longing to return. Go wherever you will; I shall not hinder you. But if go you must, there is one thing I would have you understand—what I have done for you, and in what coin you have repaid me. . . .

"[M]arching out from a country too poor to maintain you decently, [I] laid open for you at a blow, and in spite of Persia's naval supremacy, the gates of the Hellespont. My cavalry crushed the satraps of Darius, and I added all Ionia and Aeolia, the two Phrygias and Lydia to your empire. . . . I took them and gave them to you for your profit and enjoyment. The wealth of Egypt and Cyrene, which I shed no blood to win, now flows in your hands; Palestine and the plains of Syria and Mesopotamia are now your property; Babylon and Bactria and Susa are yours; you are the masters of the gold of Lydia, the treasures of Persia, the wealth of India—yes, and the seas beyond India, too. You are my captains, my generals, my governors of provinces.

"From all this that I have labored to win for you, what is left for me myself except the purple and the crown? I keep nothing for my own. . . . Perhaps you will say that, in my position as your commander, I had none of the labors and distress which you had to endure to win me what I have won. . . . Come now—if you are wounded, strip and show your wounds, and I will show mine. There is no part of my body but my back which does not have a scar; not a weapon a man may grasp or fling, the mark of which I do not carry on me . . . and all for your sakes: for your glory and your gain. Over every land and sea, across river, mountain, and plain, I led you to the world's end, a victorious army. I marry as you marry, and many of you will have children related by blood to my own. . . . But you all wish to leave me. Go then! And when you reach home, tell them that Alexander your king, who vanquished the Persians and Medes and Bactrians . . . tell them, I say, that you deserted him and left him to the mercy of barbarian men, whom you yourselves conquered. . . ."

On the Macedonians, the immediate effect of Alexander's speech was profound. . . . But when they were told [three days later that] . . . command was being given to Persian officers, foreign troops drafted into Macedonian units, a Persian corps of Guards called by a Macedonian name, Persian infantry units given the coveted title of Companions, . . . every man of them hurried to the palace . . . and [they] swore they would not stir from the spot until Alexander took pity on them.

Source: Arrian, *The Campaigns of Alexander,* trans. Aubrey de Selincourt (New York: 1958), pp. 360–65 (slightly modified).

Questions for Analysis

1. What qualities of leadership does Alexander display in this speech? How do these qualities compare to those of Cyrus the Younger, in Xenophon's description of him (page 85)?

2. Given the circumstances that precipitated this mutiny, why does Alexander use the term *barbarians* to describe the Persians and other conquered peoples? What does he hope to convey by using this word, and then by reorganizing his forces to replace Macedonians with Persians?

3. Histories written well into the nineteenth century of our era feature speeches that were allegedly spoken by historical characters on momentous occasions. How closely do you think Arrian's reconstruction of this speech reflects historical reality? How might you go about arguing that it is, in fact, an accurate reflection of what Alexander actually said?

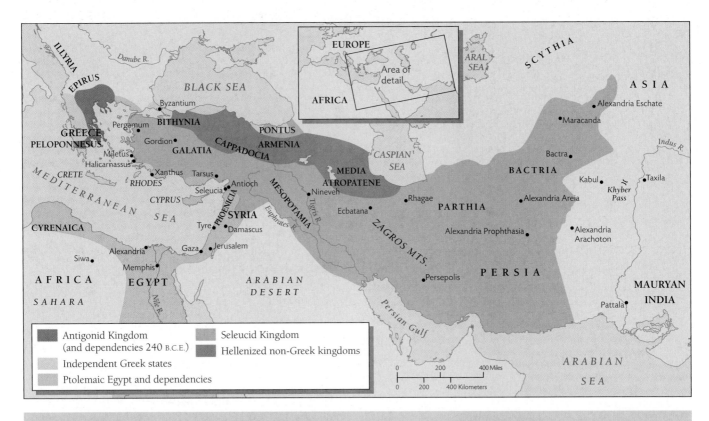

THE HELLENISTIC WORLD. Each of the three successor kingdoms to Alexander's empire was based in one of the three major civilizations we have studied so far: Egyptian, Mesopotamian, and Greek. ▪ *Based on the map above, what were the names of the three main successor states and where were they located?* ▪ *What might the division of Alexander's empire along such lines suggest about the lasting cultural differences among these regions?* ▪ *What might it suggest about the likelihood of forging a united empire, had he lived?*

withdraw from the contest over the larger empire and asked only to be given Egypt as his satrapy. Clearly, he recognized Egypt's virtual invulnerability to attack. He also seems to have appreciated, as had Alexander, its historical cachet. And he may already have been planning to make Egypt an independent monarchy and a shrine to Alexander's memory. It was thanks to Ptolemy, in fact, that Alexander's embalmed body was brought to Egypt in 323 B.C.E. It was supposed to have gone to the royal burial ground in Macedonia, but Ptolemy hijacked the funeral cortege and brought it to Memphis. Later, his son Ptolemy II moved the sarcophagus to a tomb in Alexandria, where it became a pilgrimage site and an object of veneration.

The Ptolemies ruled for 300 years, until Egypt became a Roman province in 30 B.C.E. (see Chapter 5). This dynasty, the thirty-second since the fourth millennium B.C.E., would be the last. The male heirs of the line all took the name Ptolemy (hence the term "Ptolemaic Egypt"). Many of their sisters were called Cleopatra, the name of Alexander's own sister and a dynastic name among Macedonian royal women. Beginning in the reign of Ptolemy II Philadelphus ("sibling-lover"), the Ptolemies even began to follow ancient Egyptian custom by marrying their sisters. And in many

other ways, they showed reverence for the culture of their kingdom while bringing it within the ambit of the wider Hellenistic world.

They achieved this, in part, by ruling from the new city of Alexandria on the Mediterranean coast. In Alexandria, they acted as Macedonian kings toward their Greek and Macedonian citizens; outside of Alexandria, they played the role of pharaohs, surrounding themselves with the trappings and symbols of Egypt's heritage. But until the last Ptolemaic ruler, Cleopatra VII (69–30 B.C.E.), none of them bothered to learn the Egyptian language—although, as the Rosetta Stone attests (Chapter 1), they surrounded themselves with able administrators who could communicate effectively with their multilingual and multicultural subjects.

For the Ptolemies, as for the ancient pharaohs, all of Egypt was land to be exploited for the benefit of the royal house. Supporting this tradition was the Macedonian idea that conquered land was plunder, to be used for personal enrichment and glorification. Accordingly, the Ptolemies exploited the wealth of the Egyptian countryside to the fullest. Most of this wealth ended up in Alexandria, which became the brilliant hub of the Hellenistic world. But there was little interest in improving the lives of the Egyptian

TWO PORTRAITS OF PTOLEMY I OF EGYPT. The Ptolemaic rulers of Egypt represented themselves as pharaohs to their Egyptian subjects (as in this bust) and as Greeks to their Macedonian and Greek subjects (as on this gold coin). ■ *Why would it have been important to project these two very different images?*

peasantry, whose bread-winning labors made their rulers rich. So although the third century was a prosperous and relatively peaceful one in Egypt, future pharoahs would face regular and dangerous revolts.

Nevertheless, Ptolemaic Egypt was the most succesful of the Hellenistic kingdoms. It was also the most influential, because of its key role in preserving and transmitting the accumulated heritage of the civilizations that had preceded it: Egyptian, Mesopotamian, and Greek. The Ptolemies used much of their wealth to patronize science and the arts, and they established a great Museum ("home of the Muses") and library which attracted the greatest minds of the Hellenistic world. Many breakthroughs in astronomy, mechanical engineering, and physics occurred in Alexandria. In particular, the study of medicine advanced greatly: freed from the taboos of their homeland, Greek researchers were permitted to perform autopsies, making it possible for anatomy to become a scientific discipline in its own right. It was also in Alexandria that the texts of Greek poetry, drama, history, and philosophy were copied and preserved in the forms in which we know them, and here that the Hebrew scriptures were translated into Greek for a wider audience. Any history of western civilizations would be impossible without these initiatives.

Seleucid Asia

The vast possessions that Alexander had accumulated in Asia—both within the Persian Empire and outside of it—eventually fell to another Macedonian, Seleucus (*seh-LOO-kus*). Seleucus had navigated the turmoil after Alexander's death successfully and exploited the connections he made

through his Persian wife. At his death in 281 B.C.E., his half-Persian son Antiochus inherited an expansive realm whose capital was the city named after him, Antioch.

Throughout its history, the dynasty founded by Seleucus (known as the Seleucids) struggled with the problem of holding the disparate parts of this realm together. Seleucus himself solved part of this problem by ceding much of the Indus Valley to the great warrior-king Chandragupta in exchange for a squad of war elephants. By the middle of the third century B.C.E., the Seleucids had also lost control of Bactria, where a series of Indo-Greek states were emerging with a uniquely complex culture of their own. The Seleucid heartland now became northern Syria, parts of Anatolia, Mesopotamia, and the western half of Persia: still a great, wealthy kingdom, but far less than what Alexander had left.

Like the Ptolemies, the Seleucids presented two faces to their subjects, one looking to ancient Mesopotamian tradition, another looking to Greece. In his proclamations, Antiochus used terms reminiscent of Sargon, Hammurabi, and Cyrus: "I am Antiochus, Great King, legitimate king . . . king of Babylon, king of all countries." But on his coins, he wore his hair short in the fashion of the Greeks and styled himself *basileus*, the Greek word for "king." Although the Seleucids' bureaucracy was less organized than that of the Ptolemies, even haphazard tax collection could reap huge rewards in an empire of 30 million inhabitants. They had more than enough cash to defend their borders through the third century, a period of regular warfare with Egypt. It was not until the second century, when Antiochus III lost a costly war with the Romans, that he had to plunder temples and private wealth to pay off the indemnity imposed on him.

Antigonid Macedon and Greece

The Macedonian homeland did not possess the vast wealth of the new kingdoms carved from Alexander's conquests. It also remained highly unstable from the time of Alexander's death until 276 B.C.E., when a general named Antigonus finally established his own dynasty (known as the Antigonids). Thereafter, Macedonia drew its strength from its considerable natural resources and from its influence over Aegean trade, as well as its status as overlord of Greece. Moreover, the Macedonians continued to field the most effective army in the Hellenistic world.

Antigonus himself was influenced by a philosophical outlook called Stoicism (discussed later in this chapter) and viewed kingship as a form of noble servitude, to be endured rather than enjoyed. This perspective, combined with his modest resources, convinced him not to compete with the Seleucids and Ptolemies for dominance. Instead, Antigonid policy was to keep these other two powers at war with one another and away from the Macedonian sphere of influence. Antigonus and his successors thus pursued a strategy more reminiscent of Philip II than of his son. They secured the northern frontiers, maintained a strong, standing army, and kept the fractious Greeks at heel.

The Greeks, however, were restive under the Antigonids, and two emergent powers served as rallying points for those who resented "barbarian" rule. These two forces, the Aetolian League and the Achaean League, were a departure in Greek political organization. Unlike the defensive alliances of the classical period, each represented a real political unification, with some centralization of governance. Citizens of the leagues' member poleis participated in councils of state that dealt with foreign policy and military affairs. New members were admitted on an equal footing with existing members, and all citizens of the various poleis enjoyed joint citizenship throughout the league. The same laws, weights and measures, coinage, and judicial procedures also applied throughout each federation. So effective was this mode of cooperation that James Madison, John Jay, and Alexander Hamilton employed it as one of their models for federalism in the United States.

FROM POLIS TO COSMOPOLIS

So what became of the polis, that building-block of classical Greece? As we have seen, the changes of the fourth century B.C.E. were already disrupting patterns of social and political life. Alexander's conquests hastened this process of transformation, and they also opened up a wider world—a world that came to admire all things Greek. By 300 B.C.E., a common Hellenistic culture was transcending political and geographical boundaries. It was fueled by the hundreds of thousands of adventurers who joined the Greek *diaspora* ("dispersion"), and whose emigration reduced the population of the Greek mainland by as much as fifty percent in the century after 325 B.C.E.

This exciting, urbane world was made up of interconnected cities whose scale dwarfed anything imaginable in Periclean Athens. In the fifth century B.C.E., direct participation in government had meant that every male citizen had some share in his society, its institutions, its gods, its army, and its cultural life. In the huge and cosmopolitan Hellenistic city, by contrast, all these ways of defining oneself were no longer relevant. The individual male's intimate connection with the state was broken, as was his nexus of social relationships. An average Greek in one of the Hellenistic kingdoms might have only his immediate family to rely on, if that. Very often, he was alone. What resulted was a traumatic disjunction between the traditional values and assumptions of Greek life and these new realities—and a host of entirely new opportunities.

Commerce and Urbanization

The Hellenistic world was prosperous. Alexander's conquests had opened up a vast trading area stretching from Egypt to the Persian Gulf, dominated by Greek-speaking rulers and well-established merchant communities. These conquests also stimulated the economy by putting into circulation hoards of Persian gold and silver coins, jewelry, and other commodities acquired through plunder. Industries benefited too, because autocratic rulers found manufacturing to be a further means of increasing their revenues.

Every facility was provided by the Ptolemies and the Seleucids for the encouragement of commerce. Harbors were improved, warships were sent out to police the seas, roads and canals were built. The Ptolemies even employed geographers to discover new routes to distant lands. As a result of such methods, Egypt developed a flourishing commerce in the widest variety of products obtainable. Into the port of Alexandria came spices from Arabia, gold from Ethiopia and India, tin from Britain, elephants and ivory from Nubia, silver from Spain, fine carpets from Asia Minor, and even silk from China.

The rapid growth of cities had both political and economic ramifications. Greek rulers imported Greek officials and especially Greek soldiers to maintain their control over non-Greek populations, making many new settlements necessary. Alexander himself had founded some 70 cities as outposts of domination; in the next two centuries, his successors founded about 200 more. Urbanization also increased due to the expansion of commerce and industry, but the most significant factors were the Greek diaspora and the migration of workers from rural areas. Population growth in some centers was explosive. At Antioch, the population quadrupled during a single century. Seleucia on the Tigris grew from nothing to a metropolis of several hundred thousand in less than two centuries. Alexandria in Egypt had half a million inhabitants; only imperial Rome would have surpassed it in size, and it would not be until the eighteenth century of our era that European cities like London and Paris were as large. Alexandria was not only populous, it was magnificent and spacious—which Rome never was. Its wide streets were paved and laid out in an orderly grid. It had splendid public buildings and parks, the great

Museum, and the famous library containing half a million books. It was the storehouse and showcase of Greek culture.

Not everyone enjoyed prosperity. Agriculture remained the major occupation, and small farmers in particular suffered severely from exploitative taxation. Although industrial production increased, it continued to be based on manual labor by individual artisans, most of whom lived in poverty. Among the teeming populations of Hellenistic cities, unemployment was a constant concern. Even those who prospered in the new economy were subject to drastic fluctuations in their fortunes, owing to the precarious nature of mercantile endeavors. Merchants were also vulnerable to the boom-and-bust syndrome: an investor, thinking he could make a fortune during an upward price spiral, might go into debt to take advantage of the trend, only to find that supply exceeded demand, leaving him nothing with which to pay his creditors. The economic landscape of the Hellenistic world was therefore one of contrasting extremes. In many ways, this was also the case with respect to its culture.

HELLENISTIC WORLDVIEWS

Life in the Hellenistic boomtowns produced new world-views and new philosophies that differed significantly from those of Plato and Aristotle. Another major departure was the separation of philosophy from scientific inquiry, which now became its own field of study. Despite these differences, however, scientists, philosophers, and religious teachers were all motivated by the same thing: the need to make human existence meaningful in a new age that lacked traditional civic structures and social values.

Two Paths to Tranquility: Stoicism and Epicureanism

The two strains of philosophy that dominated the Hellenistic world both originated in Athens around 300 B.C.E.: Stoicism and Epicureanism. Their teachings had several features in common. Both were concerned with the well-being of the individual, not with the welfare of society as a whole. Both were firmly rooted in the material world; even the soul was considered to be part of the mortal body. Both responded to the new cosmpolitan age by promoting universal values: they taught that people are the same the world over, and recognized no distinctions between Greeks and the peoples hitherto known as "barbarians."

But in other ways the two systems were radically different. The Stoics who followed Zeno of Citium (c. 335–

c. 263 B.C.E.)—they took their name from the *stoa* ("colonnade") in which he regularly taught—believed that the cosmos is an ordered whole in which all contradictions are resolved for ultimate good. Evil is only relative; the particular misfortunes that befall human beings are merely incidents that will lead to the final perfection of the universe. Everything that happens is therefore predetermined. People are free only in the sense that they can accept fate or rebel against it. By freely submitting to the workings of the universe, and by acknowledging that whatever happens must be for the best, one can attain true happiness: tranquility of mind.

The Stoics' theory of ethics and social responsibility grew out of this personal philosophy. Believing that the highest good is serenity of mind, they emphasized self-discipline and the fulfillment of one's duties. They taught tolerance and forgiveness, and they also urged participation in public affairs as a special responsibility for those with able minds. They condemned slavery and violence, although they took no real actions against these evils because they saw them as inevitable—and because extreme social change might be worse.

With some some later modifications, Stoic philosophy became the driving force behind the values of the Roman Republic and of early Christianity, and can be considered one of the most important products of the Hellenistic world. Even those who do not embrace its tenets or its perspective may recognize that they have been influenced by it.

The teachings of Epicurus (341–270 B.C.E.) were based on the atomic theory of an earlier Greek philosopher called Democritus, who lived in the latter part of the fifth century B.C.E. According to his central thesis, the universe is made up entirely of atoms, and every individual object or organism is therefore the product of a combination of atoms. Studying Democritus' writings, Epicurus reached a conclusion exactly opposite to that of the Stoics: he interpreted the atomic theory to mean that there is no ultimate purpose in the workings of the universe. So the highest good cannot come of submitting oneself stoically to the endurance of hardship, because suffering is not part of a larger plan: it is merely the chance by-product of random atomic actions. The highest good, then, must be pleasure: the moderate satisfaction of bodily appetites, the intellectual pleasure of contemplating excellence and remembering past enjoyments, and serenity in the face of death. Indeed, an individual who understands that the soul itself is material, that the universe operates at random, and that no gods intervene in human affairs will have no fear of death or any other supernatural phenomena.

The Epicureans thus came by a very different route to the same general conclusion as the Stoics: nothing is better than tranquility of mind. In contrast to the Stoics, however,

Competing Viewpoints

Debating the Education and Role of Women

> The drastic political, social, and economic changes of the fourth century led philosophers to re-imagine the traditional structures of the polis, and to debate the proper role of women within these structures. Meanwhile, the cosmopolitan culture of the expanding Hellenistic world made it increasingly difficult to limit women's access to public spaces. The following excerpts represent two philosophical responses to these problems. The first comes from Plato's treatise on "Polis-matters" (Politeía), known to us as The Republic, the longest of his philosophical dialogues and the most influential work of political thought in history. Its conceptual narrator and protagonist is Socrates, who engages in a series of debates with his pupils. The second excerpt is taken from a philosophical treatise attributed to a female follower of Pythagoras (see Chapter 3), but it was really written around 200 B.C.E. in Hellenistic Italy, and by a man.

Plato, *The Republic*, c. 380 B.C.E.

SOCRATES: For men born and educated like our citizens, the only way, in my opinion, of arriving at a right conclusion about the possession and use of women and children is to follow the path on which we originally started, when we said that the men were to be the guardians and watchdogs of the herd.

GLAUCON: True.

SOCRATES: Let us further suppose the birth and education of our women to be subject to similar or nearly similar regulations; then we shall see whether the result accords with our design.

GLAUCON: What do you mean?

SOCRATES: . . . The education which was assigned to the men was music and gymnastic[s].

GLAUCON: Yes.

SOCRATES: Then women must be taught music and gymnastic[s] and also the art of war, which they must practice like the men?

GLAUCON: That is the inference, I suppose.

SOCRATES: I should rather expect . . . that several of our proposals, if they are carried out, being unusual, may appear ridiculous.

GLAUCON: No doubt of it.

SOCRATES: Yes, and the most ridiculous thing of all will be the sight of women naked in the palaestra, exercising with the men, especially when they are no longer young; they certainly will not be a vision of beauty, any more than the enthusiastic old men who in spite of wrinkles and ugliness continue to frequent the gymnasia. . . . [Yet] not long ago, as we shall remind them, the Hellenes were of the opinion, which is still generally received among the barbarians, that the sight of a naked man was ridiculous and improper; and when first the Cretans and then the Lacedaemonians [Spartans] introduced the custom, the wits of that day might equally have ridiculed the innovation.

GLAUCON: No doubt . . .

SOCRATES: First, then, whether the question is to be put in jest or in earnest, let us come to an understanding about the nature of woman: Is she capable of sharing either wholly or partially in the actions of men, or not at all? And is the art of war one of those arts in which she can or cannot share? That will be the best way of commencing the enquiry, and will probably lead to the fairest conclusion. . . .

GLAUCON: I suppose so. . . .

SOCRATES: And if . . . the male and female sex appear to differ in their fitness for any art or pursuit, we should say that such pursuit or art ought to be assigned to one or the other of them; but if the difference consists only in women bearing and men begetting children, this does not amount to a proof that a woman differs from a man in respect of the sort of education she should receive; and we shall therefore continue to maintain that our guardians and their wives ought to have the same pursuits.

GLAUCON: Very true.

SOCRATES: Next, we shall ask . . . how, in reference to any of the pursuits or arts of civic life, the nature of a woman differs from that of a man? . . .

GLAUCON: By all means.

SOCRATES: . . . [W]hen you spoke of a nature gifted or not gifted in any respect, did you mean to say that one man will acquire a thing easily, another with difficulty; a little learning will lead the one to discover a great deal; whereas the other, after much study and application, no sooner learns than he forgets? Or again, did you mean, that the one has a body which is a good servant to his mind, while the body of the other is a hindrance to him? Would not these be the sort of differences which distinguish the man gifted by nature from the one who is ungifted?

GLAUCON: No one will deny that.

SOCRATES: And can you mention any pursuit of mankind in which the male sex has not all these gifts and qualities in a higher degree than the female? Need I waste time in speaking of the art of weaving, and the management of pan- cakes and preserves, in which woman- kind does really appear to be great, and in which for her to be beaten by a man is of all things the most absurd?

GLAUCON: You are quite right ... in maintaining the general inferiority of the female sex: although many women are in many things superior to many men, yet on the whole what you say is true.

Source: Excerpted from Plato, *The Republic*, Book V, trans. Benjamin Jowett (New York: 1982), pp. 170–76.

Treatise Attributed to Phintys, Third/Second Century B.C.E.

Now some people think that it is not appropriate for a woman to be a philosopher, just as a wom- an should not be a cavalry officer or a politician.... I agree that men should be generals and city officials and politicians, and women should keep house and stay inside and receive and take care of their husbands. But I believe that courage, justice, and intelligence are qualities that men and women have in common.... Courage and intelligence are more ap- propriately male qualities because of the strength of men's bodies and the power of their minds. Chastity is more appro- priately female.

Accordingly, a woman must learn about chastity and realize what she must do quantitatively and qualitatively to be able to obtain this womanly virtue. I believe that there are five qualifications: (1) the sancitity of her marriage bed, (2) the cleanliness of her body, (3) the manner in which she chooses to leave her house, (4) her refusal to participate in secret cults ..., (5) her readiness and moderation in sacrificing to the gods.

Of these, the most important quality for chastity is to be pure in respect of the marriage bed, and for her not to have af- fairs with men from other households. If she breaks the law in this way she wrongs the gods of her family and provides her family and home not with its own off- spring but with bastards.... She should also consider the following: that there is no means of atoning for this sin; no way she can approach the shrines or the altars of the gods as a pure woman.... The greatest glory a freeborn woman can have—her foremost honor—is the witness her own children will give to her chastity toward her husband, the stamp of the likeness they bear to the father whose seed produced them....

As far as adornment of her body is concerned ... [h]er clothes should not be transparent or ornate. She should not put on silken material, but moderate, white- colored clothes. In this way, she will avoid being overdressed or luxurious or made- up, and not give other women cause to be uncomfortably envious.... She should not apply imported or artificial coloring to her face—with her own natural color- ing, by washing only with water, she can ornament herself with modesty....

Women of importance leave the house to sacrifice to the leading divin- ity of the community on behalf of their husbands and their households. They do not leave home at night nor in the evening, but at midday, to attend a reli- gious festival or to make some purchase, accompanied by a single female servant or decorously escorted by two servants at most.... They keep away from secret cults ... particularly because these forms of worship encourage drunkenness and ecstasy. The mistress of the house and head of the household should be chaste and untouched in all respects.

Source: From Mary R. Lefkowitz and Maureen B. Fant, eds., *Women's Life in Greece & Rome: A Source Book in Translation*, 2nd ed. (Baltimore, MD: 1992), pp. 163–64.

Questions for Analysis

1. Follow the steps of the argument made by Socrates. How does he go about proving that women and men are different, and should have differ- ent roles in society? Are there flaws in this argument? What are they?

2. How does the author of the trea- tise seem to define "chastity," and why does "she" (actually he) say that it corresponds to more masculine qualities of courage and intelligence? Why would this author have wanted to attribute these reflections to female members of the community founded by the philosopher Pythagoras (c.570– c. 495), three centuries earlier? How might this treatise be responding to the changes brought about by the expansion of the Greek world in the fourth and third centuries B.C.E?

3. What are main points on which these two perspectives agree? How might ideas like those expressed here have influenced contemporary ideas of fe- male beauty and modesty (see ***Inter- preting Visual Evidence***, page 87)?

they did not insist on virtue as an end in itself, or on the fulfillment of one's duties. For an Epicurean, the only duty a person has is to the self, and the only reason to act virtuously is to increase one's own happiness. Similarly, Epicureans denied that there is any such thing as justice; laws and political institutions are "just" only insofar as they contribute to the welfare of the individual. Yes, certain rules have been found necessary for the maintenance of order, but these rules should be obeyed solely because that is to one's advantage. The state is, at best, a mere convenience, and the wise man should take no active part in politics. Instead, he should withdraw to study philosophy and enjoy the fellowship of a few congenial friends. Modern libertarian and anarchic movements share many characteristics with Epicureanism.

Extreme Doubt: Skepticism

The most pessimistic philosophy generated by the Hellenistic era was propounded by the Skeptics, whose name means "those on the lookout" or "the spies." Skepticism reached the zenith of its popularity in the second century under the influence of Carneades (*car-ne-AH-dehs*, c. 214–129 B.C.E.), a man born in the Greek city of Cyrene, in North Africa, who spent his youth in Athens. His chief teaching (filtered through Aristotle) was that all knowledge is based on sense perception and is therefore limited and relative. From this, the Skeptics concluded that no one can prove anything. Moreover, because our senses can deceive us, we cannot even be certain about the truth we think we have gained by observation of the world. All we can say is that things *appear* to be such and such; we do not *know* that they really *are* that way. It follows, furthermore, that we can have no definite knowledge of the supernatural, of the meaning of life, or of right and wrong.

The only sensible course for the Skeptic is therefore to suspend judgment. If we abandon the fruitless quest for truth and cease to worry about good conduct and the existence of evil, we can at least attain a certain peace of mind, the highest satisfaction that an uncertain life affords. Needless to say, the Skeptics were even less concerned than the Epicureans with political and social problems, from which they felt wholly alienated. Their ideal was one of escape from an incomprehensible world. In some key respects they anticipated modern existentialism and nihilism.

Varieties of Religion

Like Epicureanism and Skepticism, Hellenistic religion tended to offer vehicles of escape from political commitments. When we think back to how close was the link between Greek selfhood and politics down to the middle of the fourth century B.C.E.—"man is a creature of the polis"—we can begin to appreciate what a radical change had occurred in just a few generations. In all the societies we have studied so far, religion was wholly interconnected with politics. Divine worship centered on the gods who protected a community and furthered its interests. Hence, the most serious of the charges brought against Socrates was that he had "denied the gods of the polis" and thus committed treason. Religious crimes were political crimes, and piety was the same as patriotism.

Although this sense of a vital connection between a place and its gods persisted to a certain extent during the Hellenistic period, civic-oriented worship was compromised by rootless multiculturalism. In its place, some elite members of society gravitated toward one of the philosophies discussed above. Ordinary people, though, were more likely to embrace religious cults that offered emotional gratification or the diversion of colorful rituals, as well as some assurance of an afterlife.

Cults that stressed extreme methods of atonement, mystical union with the divine, or contact with supernatural forces accordingly attracted many followers. Among these so-called mystery religions was the cult of Dionysus, which celebrated the cyclical death and resurrection of that Greek god. The Egyptian cult of Isis (Chapter 1) also revolved around rituals of death and rebirth. So too did Zoroastrianism (Chapter 2), which became increasingly dualistic: its magi now taught that the material world was entirely evil and urged believers to adopt ascetic practices that would purify their souls and prepare them for ethereal joy in the afterlife.

Like the peoples who worshiped them, the gods of the Hellenistic world were often immigrants from other lands. Temples to Greek gods and goddesses were dedicated throughout the Near East and Egypt; conversely, temples to Near Eastern divinities were constructed in the cities of the Greek homeland. In Alexandria, scholars of religion collected Egyptian and Near Eastern mythologies, which were recorded and reformulated for Greek-speaking audiences.

Even among the Jews of Palestine, who resisted assimilation and the adoption of foreign customs, Hellenistic culture put down deep roots. This was especially true among elite Jews living outside Palestine, who outnumbered the Palestinian population by a considerable margin. To meet the needs of these Greek-speaking Jews, and to satisfy the curiosity of Gentiles interested in Jewish beliefs, scholars working in Alexandria produced a Greek version of the Hebrew scriptures. It is known as the Septuagint (*sep-TOO-ah-gint*), from the Greek word meaning "the seventy": legend has it that seventy scribes, each working independently, produced individual translations from Hebrew to Greek that were identical in every respect. This meant that the Septuagint could be regarded as no less a product of divine inspiration than the original books that made up the Hebrew Bible, and could be treated as an authoritative text in its own right. For Jews concerned about their social and cultural standing vis-à-vis their Greek neighbors, the Septuagint was proof of their Hellenistic values—although, ironically, some of the very portions of scripture that were now written in Greek disapproved strongly of those values.

worked directly for royal or civic patrons. In the Hellenistic world, art became commodified. Sometimes a work would be made expressly for a particular patron, but many works of art were fashioned for the open market. They were also designed to suit the tastes and lifestyles of those merchant classes who had disposable income and wanted to increase their social standing through conspicuous consumption. This was as true of literature as of sculpture or the decorative arts: we know the names of over a thousand Hellenistic authors. Indeed, the number of texts and *objets d'art* that exist from this period is huge when compared to earlier eras.

THE SCIENTIFIC REVOLUTION OF ANTIQUITY

The Hellenistic period was the most brilliant age in the history of science before the seventeenth century of our era. There are three major reasons for this. First, there was the stimulus to intellectual inquiry caused by the fusion of Mesopotamian and Egyptian science with the philosophical methods of the Greeks. Second, as in the more famous scientific revolution, the use of a common language (in the seventeenth century it was Latin) and the ease of communication facilitated by affordable travel made the circulation of knowledge and sharing of ideas easier (in the seventeenth century, communication was increased by the printing press). Finally, as in the seventeenth century, the competition among patrons of science was intense: every autocrat wanted to be thought enlightened and to be associated with new discoveries. Even purely theoretical advances were so much admired that a Hellenistic prince who had bankrolled such a breakthrough would share the glory of it. It was especially profitable to subsidize research that led to the development of new technologies, because they might have military applications.

The arts were also transformed by the economic and political conditions of the Hellenistic world. Artists working in various media strove to demonstrate their mastery of difficult techniques and so to attract the notice of potential patrons. New markets for art also changed *what* was being made, how, and for whom. In all of the civilizations we have studied so far, artists

Measuring and Mapping: Astronomy, Geography, and Mathematics

Hellenistic scientists took a major interest in measurements and mapmaking, whether of the heavens (astronomy), the earth (geography), or the forms occuring in nature (geometry). The most renowned—and most wronged—of the Hellenistic astronomers was Aristarchus of Samos (310–230 B.C.E.), whose major discovery anticipated that of Copernicus by 1,700 years: he deduced that the earth and other planets revolve around the sun. Unfortunately,

THE CITADEL OF PERGAMON. An artist's reconstruction of Pergamon in the second century B.C.E., based on the work of nineteenth-century German archeologists. High atop the hill is the massive altar of Zeus (now in the Pergamon Museum in Berlin) and below it slope the tiers of the theater. Other features include fortifications, terraces, and artificial landscaping for public gardens. ▪ *How does this complex of buildings compare to that of another citadel, the Acropolis of Athens (see Chapter 3, page 58)?*

however, this view was not accepted by many of his contemporaries or successors because it conflicted with the teachings of Aristotle, which in turn reflected the Greek conviction that humanity, and therefore the earth, must be at the center of the universe. The sad fate of his discovery was sealed in the second century C.E., when the Alexandrian scholar Claudius Ptolemaeus (known as Ptolemy) unequivocally argued that Aristotle was correct, and that all heavenly bodies revolve around the earth. This misinformative view would not be overturned until the much later scientific revolution occurred (see Chapter 16).

Closely allied with astronomy were geography and mathematics. The most influential Hellenistic mathematician was Euclid, whose *Elements of Geometry* (c. 300 B.C.E.) remained the basic textbook of that subject until the twentieth century of our era. In the field of geography—and in a host of other pursuits, too—the most original thinker was Eratosthenes of Alexandria (*air-ah-TOS-then-ees*, c. 276–c. 196 B.C.E.). Not only did he accurately calculate the circumference of the earth (within a tiny margin of error, less than 200 miles), he was the first to suggest the possibility of reaching eastern Asia by sailing west. In addition, he founded the science of chronology by attempting to establish the dates of major events reaching back to the siege of Troy. Students of history are forever in his debt.

Medicine and Mechanics: The Sciences of Physiology and Physics

Before the third century B.C.E., physics had been a branch of philosophy. Now it became a separate, experimental science thanks to the genius of one man, Archimedes of Syracuse (c. 287–212 B.C.E.). It was he who discovered the law of floating bodies, or specific gravity, now known as "Archimedes' principle." According to legend, the idea came to him when he was in his bath, and the stunning insight so excited him that he lept from the water and dashed out naked into the street, shouting "*Eureka!*" ("I have found it!"). Archimedes also established the principles of the lever, the pulley, and the screw, and he invented both a compound pulley and a propeller. All of these discoveries had numerous practical uses in the construction of buildings, ships, and military machinery.

Other extraordinary advances were made in the field of medicine. Especially significant was the work of Herophilus of Chalcedon (c. 335–c. 280 B.C.E.), the greatest anatomist of antiquity and probably the first to practice human dissection. Herophilus' achievements included a detailed description of the brain, which allowed him to prove that it was the engine of human intellect (Aristotle thought that it was

the heart), as well as the discovery that the arteries contain blood alone (not a mixture of blood and air, as Aristotle had taught), and that their function is to carry blood from the heart to all parts of the body. His colleague Erasistratus (*air-ah-sis-STRAH-tus*) made allied discoveries, establishing that the heart was a pump and not an organ of emotion. Erasistratus also rejected the widely held theory of the physician Hippocrates (c. 460–c. 370), who had posited that the body consists of four "humors" which need to be kept in balance through bloodletting and other invasive practices. Unfortunately, this discovery went the way of the heliocentric universe posited by Aristarchus: another encyclopedist of the second century C.E., Galen, preferred the erroneous theory of Hippocrates. The practice of bloodletting thus persisted into the nineteenth century of our era.

Urban Architecture and Sculpture

Hellenistic architecture drew on Greek models, but it was also influenced by tastes more characteristic of Egypt and Persia. The best surviving example comes from Pergamon, a city on the coast of Anatolia that became the capital of a new kingdom wrested from the control of the Seleucids in

DYING GAUL. The original (now lost) statue on which this Roman copy was based was sculpted in Pergamon around 220 B.C.E. The sculptor clearly wished to exhibit skill in depicting an unusual subject: the Gauls were a Celtic people about whom very little was known in this era. ▪ *How does this sympathetic representation of a "barbarian" express the new values of Hellenistic philosophy?*

the second century B.C.E. It boasted an enormous altar dedicated to Zeus that crowned the heights of the city, below which an open-air theater was built into the steep slope of the hill. In Ephesus, not far away, the streets were not only paved, they were paved with marble.

But the most influential of all Hellenistic arts was sculpture, which placed even more emphasis on realism than the fourth-century sculptures discussed earlier in this chapter. And because awkward human postures offered the greatest technical challenges, sculptors often preferred to show people stretching themselves or balancing on one leg or performing other unusual feats. It is clear that the goal was to create something unique in both conception and craftsmanship—something a collector could show off as the only one of its type. It is not surprising, therefore, that complexity came to be admired for its own sake, and extreme naturalism sometimes teetered on the brink of absurdity. Yet to our eyes, such works appear familiar because of the influence they exerted on later sculptors like

Michelangelo (see Chapter 12) and Auguste Rodin. Three of the most famous examples are pictured here, each exhibiting different aesthetic qualities and artistic techniques: the *Dying Gaul*, made in Pergamon around 220 B.C.E.; the *Winged Victory of Samothrace*, dating from around 200 B.C.E.; and the *Laocoön* group, from the first century B.C.E.

Literary Fantasy and Historical Reality

In the sixth century B.C.E. it was the lyric, in the fifth century it was tragedy, and in the fourth century it was the novel; but in the Hellenistic era, the new literary genre was pastoral verse. These poems tapped into a strong vein of nostalgia for rural pastimes and simple pleasures, a make-believe world of shepherds and wood nymphs. The most important pastoral poet of the age was Theocritus, who flourished around 270 B.C.E. in the big-city environment of Alexandria. In the midst of urban bustle and within sight

THE WINGED VICTORY OF SAMOTHRACE (left). This marble sculpture of the goddess Nike (Victory) may originally have been displayed on the prow of a monumental ship. It formed part of a temple complex on the island of Samothrace in the northern Aegean, and dates to around the year 200 B.C.E. It is now in the Louvre Museum, Paris. **LAOCOÖN AND HIS SONS (right).** In sharp contrast to the serene and confident *Winged Victory* is this famous sculpture group from the first century B.C.E. According to legend, Laocoön warned the Trojans not to accept the wooden horse sent by the Greeks and was accordingly punished by the sea-god Poseidon, who sent two serpents to kill him and his sons. The intense physicality of this work was an important influence on Michelangelo, a millennium and a half later.

of overcrowded slums, he celebrated the charms of country life and lazy summer afternoons. He thereby founded an enduring tradition that would be taken up by poets from the Roman Virgil to the Englishman (and classical scholar) A. E. Houseman, which has provided a wealth of themes for the visual arts. Even composers like Beethoven and Debussy owe a debt to Theocritus.

By contrast, Hellenistic prose literature was dominated by historians who modeled their work on earlier pioneers, especially Thucydides. By far the most important was Polybius (c. 203–120 B.C.E.), a well-born Greek whose father was a prominent politician in the Achaean League. Polybius himself was trained as a cavalry officer at a time when the Achaean League was trying to position itself favorably in ongoing wars between the rising republic of Rome and the various kingdoms of northern Greece. In 168 B.C.E., the Romans became suspicious of the Achaeans' declared neutrality and demanded that a thousand noble hostages be sent to Rome as a guarantee of the League's good behavior. Polybius was one of those hostages, and he spent the next seventeen years living in Rome, where he became a fervent admirer of its unique form of government (see Chapter 5).

The result was a series of histories that glorified the achievements of Rome and its political system. Polybius also attempted to account for the patterns that he discerned in the history of Greece since the Peloponnesian War. He argued that historical developments follow regular cycles, and that nations pass inevitably through stages of growth and decay. Hence, it should be possible to predict exactly where a given state is heading if one knows what has happened to it in the past. Yet Polybius also argued that the special character of Rome's constitution would allow it to break the cycle, because it combined all of the different forms of government that Aristotle had outlined in his *Politics*. This view of history galvanized the framers of the United States Constitution, directly influencing their conception of our own political institutions.

CONCLUSION

Judged from the perspective of classical Greece, Hellenistic civilization seems strange. The autocratic governments of the age that followed Alexander's conquests would probably appear repugnant to a staunch proponent of Athenian democracy, and the Hellenistic love of extravagance can contrast strikingly with the tastes of the fifth century B.C.E.

After You Read This Chapter

Visit StudySpace for quizzes, additional review materials, and multi-media documents. **wwnorton.com/studyspace**

REVIEWING THE OBJECTIVES

- Macedonia's successful conquest of the Greek poleis can be attributed to several factors. What are they?
- Alexander the Great's imperial policies were influenced by his own upbringing, the different cultures he encountered, and some key historical precedents. Give at least one example of each type of influence.
- Explain how the three Hellenistic kingdoms reflect the differences among the three main civilizations we have studied so far.
- Why is the Hellenistic world described as "cosmopolitan"? How did this urban culture differ from that of the Greek poleis?
- The philosophies of Plato and Aristotle both derive from the teachings of Socrates, but they diverge in some important ways. What are those main differences?

Yet Hellenistic civilization had its own achievements that the classical age could not match. Most Hellenistic cities offered a greater range of public facilities than any Greek cities of the previous period, and the numerous advances in science and technology are astonishing when compared to anything that came before, or even after.

But the most important contribution of the Hellenistic era to subsequent historical developments was its role as intermediary between the nascent empire of Rome and the older civilizations of Mesopotamia, Egypt, and Greece. The economic and political infrastuctures that were put in place after Alexander's conquests would form the framework of Roman imperial government. The Romans would also take advantage of the common language and cultural expectations that bound the far reaches of the Greek-speaking world together. Their own Latin language would never supplant Greek as the preeminent language of scholarship and administration in the eastern portions of their empire.

The Hellenistic era must also be recognized as the bridge that connects us to the earlier ages of antiquity: most of what is contained in the first four chapters of this book is known to us because older texts and artifacts were copied and collected by the scholars of Alexandria and other Hellenistic cities. And it was Hellenistic art and architecture, Hellenistic city planning and civic culture, that the Romans strove to emulate—not those of Periclean Athens. The same can be said of drama and poetry.

For us, two further aspects of Hellenistic culture deserve special mention: its cosmopolitanism and its modernity. The word *cosmopolitan* means "universal city," and it was the Hellenistic period that came closest to turning this ideal of globalization into reality. Around 250 B.C.E. a Greek tourist could have traveled from Sicily to the borders of India—the two ends of the earth—and never have found himself among people who did not speak his language or share his basic outlook. Nor would this tourist have identified himself in ethnic or nationalist terms, or felt any exclusive loyalty to a city-state or kingdom. He would have considered himself a citizen of the world. He would also have considered himself a modern man, not bound by the old prejudices and superstitions of the past. It is for these reasons that Hellenistic civilization seems so closely related to our own. It was a world of stark contrasts and infinite possibilities, where economic instability, extremism, and authoritarian regimes existed side by side with unprecedented prosperity, rational inquiry, and extraodinary freedoms. In Chapter 5, we will see how this world adapted itself to the dominion of a single Italian city.

PEOPLE, IDEAS, EVENTS IN CONTEXT

- In what ways were the military strategies of **PHILIP II OF MACEDON** variations on older forms of hoplite warfare? How did the rise of mercenary armies and of **THEBES** further change military strategies in the fourth century?
- How did the philosophies of **PLATO** and **ARISTOTLE** respond to the crisis of the polis?
- To what degree did the conquests of **ALEXANDER THE GREAT** unite Mesopotamia, Egypt, and Greece?
- Why and how did the three **HELLENISTIC KINGDOMS** emerge? How were the **AETOLIAN AND ACHAEAN LEAGUES** new models for governance and cooperation in Greece?
- In what ways were **STOICISM, EPICUREANISM**, and other new philosophies a response to **COSMOPOLITANISM** and the breakdown of traditional societies and values?
- What were the driving forces behind the **SCIENTIFIC REVOLUTION OF ANTIQUITY**? What were its main achievements?
- What are some essential characteristics of **HELLENISTIC ART**? In what ways did it differ from that of the fifth century B.C.E. (Chapter 3)?

CONSEQUENCES

- "The history of the world is but the biography of great men"—so the Scottish historian Thomas Carlyle (1795–1881) summarized the impact of figures like Alexander the Great. How would you construct an argument in support of this proposition, using what you've learned in this chapter? How would you refute it?
- In what ways do Alexander's actions demonstrate his own knowledge of history, as well as a capacity to apply that knowledge to his own circumstances? Can you identify leaders of our own day who have mobilized their understanding of history in similar ways?
- In your view, which civilization more resembles our own: classical Athens or the Hellenistic world? Why? What characteristics make an era seem "modern"?

STORY LINES

- Romans were proud of their unique history, especially the legend that they had overthrown their kings. They clung to this story even when individual men came to wield kingly powers.

- Roman identity, religion, and politics were intimately bound up in the worship of ancestors, especially male ancestors. As a result, fathers (living and dead) wielded extraordinary power in early Rome.

- Roman women enjoyed more freedoms than the women of ancient Greece, but they were still subject to the authority of their male relatives.

- The Roman army had unprecedented strength and importance in this civilization, but the army's relationship to Roman politics and society changed drastically as Rome's empire grew.

- Paradoxically, the Romans celebrated their farming heritage even as they built a highly urbanized society. At the same time, they regarded Greek culture as both superior and dangerous.

Before
You
Read
This
Chapter

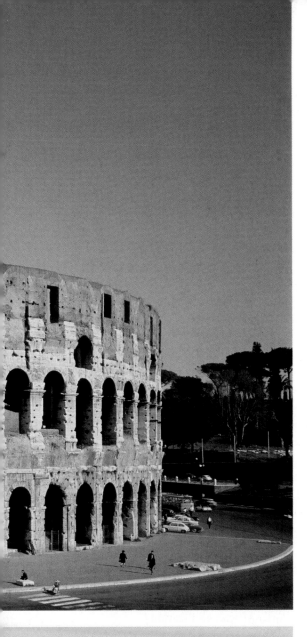

The Civilization of Ancient Rome

CORE OBJECTIVES

- **IDENTIFY** the factors that influenced the formation of the Roman Republic.

- **UNDERSTAND** the basic elements of Roman identity.

- **DEFINE** the classes of people who struggled for power in Rome.

- **DESCRIBE** the impact of territorial expansion on Roman society.

- **TRACE** the events leading up to the establishment of the Principate.

C ould anyone be so indifferent or slow-witted as not to care how, and under what system of government, the Romans managed to bring nearly the whole inhabited world under their rule? Can anything be more important than understanding this?" So the Greek soldier Polybius (c. 203–120 B.C.E.) addresses Greek readers in a history celebrating the achievements of the Roman Republic. Polybius had witnessed some of these firsthand: on the battlefield, in Rome itself as a hostage and guest, and on a visit to newly conquered Carthage. What better testament could there be to the success of a small Italian city than the admiration of a cultivated Greek aristocrat who, having been subjected to Roman authority, wholeheartedly embraced it? None, unless we cite the equally enthusiastic endorsement of the same Jews who had rebelled against Greek influence in 164 B.C.E. They, too, could not say enough in praise of the Romans, and they willingly placed themselves under Roman protection.

Those whom they wish to help and to make kings, they make kings, and those whom they wish they depose; and they have been greatly exalted. Yet for all

107

that, not one of them has put on a crown or worn purple as a mark of pride, but they have built for themselves a senate chamber and every day three hundred and twenty senators constantly deliberate concerning the people, to govern them well. (1 Maccabees 8:12–15)

The only people who could say more in praise of Rome were the Romans themselves. To them, the enormous success of their empire meant that they were divinely chosen to colonize the world. This was the message conveyed by the poet Virgil (70–19 B.C.E.), commissioned by the Emperor Augustus to tell the story of Rome's rise to glory in a manner imitating the epics of Homer. In one key passage, the father of Aeneas, Virgil's epic hero, "foretells" the future and addresses posterity: "Remember, Roman, you whose power rules / all peoples, that these are your arts: plant peace, / make law, spare subjects, and put down the proud" (*Aeneid*, Book VI, lines 851–3).

While the Greeks struggled against the Persians and against each other, a new civilization emerged beyond the northern fringes of the Greek world, on the banks of the river Tiber in central Italy. By 300 B.C.E. Rome was the dominant power on the Italian peninsula. Two centuries later, it had conquered Greece itself. For the next three centuries after that—an unprecedented period of sustained expansion—its power steadily increased. In the first century of our era, it ruled the Hellenistic world as well as a vast region that Greek culture had never touched: northwestern Europe. Eventually, Rome's empire united the entire Mediterranean and most of Asia Minor, while at the same time embracing provinces that are now parts of France, Spain, Portugal, Britain, Belgium, Germany, Switzerland, and the Balkans. Rome thus built a historical arch that enabled Europe to share in a rich heritage reaching back to ancient Mesopotamia and Egypt. Without Rome, European culture as we know it would not exist, and neither would the political and legal institutions that formed the United States. To echo Polybius: "Can anything be more important than understanding this?"

THE TIME OF THE KINGS

Romans looked back uneasily on their early history, for this was the time when they were ruled by kings. It may have been necessary in those days: Romans had never been peaceful settlers, and their land did not yield an easy living. Although Italy had much more fertile land than Greece, its extensive coastline boasts only a few good harbors, and most of these are on the western side, away from the com-

mercial hubs of Greece and the Near East. Nor does the length of this coastline offer secure natural defenses. So the Romans were a warlike people from the first, continually forced to defend their own conquests against other invaders.

Early Influences

When the Romans arrived in Italy, the dominant inhabitants of the peninsula were the Etruscans, a people who remain mysterious despite the rich archeological record they left behind. This is because their language (not a branch of Indo-European) has never been fully deciphered, even though the Etruscans used an alphabet borrowed from the Greeks. By the sixth century B.C.E., the Etruscans had established a confederation of independent city-states in north-central Italy. They were skilled metalworkers, artists, and architects, from whom the Romans later took their knowledge of the arch and the vault, among much else, including the bloody sport of gladiatorial combat.

The two most important foundation myths told by the Romans were also derived from Etruscan tradition: the story of Aeneas' escape from Troy, which became the basis of Virgil's *Aeneid*, and also the story of the infant twins Romulus and Remus, abandoned at birth and then raised by a maternal wolf, afterward founding a fledgling city. Both legends would be mined by Rome's historians for their metaphorical significance, and further details would be added to increase their relevance for a changing audience. For example, the story of Aeneas' seduction and abandonment of Dido, queen of Carthage, reflected Rome's defeat of that powerful North African civilization.

In marked contrast to Greek society, Etruscan women enjoyed a very high status and played important roles in public life. Etruscan wives even ate meals with their husbands, another departure from both Greek and Roman custom. After death, devoted couples were buried together in the same mortuary vaults, and their tombstones and sarcophagi often emphasize mutual affection. Some of these practices certainly affected the Romans, whose women were less sequestered than their Greek counterparts. Yet Rome's women did not enjoy the same freedoms as Etruscan women until very late in Roman history, and by then such freedoms were condemned as signs of decadence (see below).

The Romans also borrowed ideas from the Greek settlers who had begun to colonize southern Italy and Sicily during the eighth century B.C.E. From them, Romans derived their alphabet, many of their religious beliefs, and much of their art. But the Romans downplayed Greek influence in their founding mythology, preferring to emphasize their alleged descent from the Trojans and also from an

AN ETRUSCAN COUPLE. This sarcophagus lid dates from middle of the fourth century B.C.E. and depicts a deceased couple as they lie together naked, emphasizing by their embrace the closeness of their marital bond.

Italic people called the Sabines, from whom (according to legend) Romulus and his men had forcibly abducted their wives. This was a practice Romans would continue, as the legions who planted new colonies intermarried with indigenous populations from the Persian Gulf to the lowlands of Scotland.

The Founding of Rome

The real founders of Rome were a tribe called the Latins, descendents of Indo-European-speaking peoples who crossed the Alps into Italy and settled on the banks of the Tiber by the tenth century B.C.E. This location was advantageous. Trading ships (but not large war fleets) could navigate the river as far as the city, yet no farther; Rome could thus serve as a commercial port and was not threatened by attack from the sea. Rome also sat astride the first good ford across the Tiber, making it a major crossroads. There were also strategic advantages to the seven hills among which Rome was nestled. Eventually, its central markeplace—the *forum* or "open space"—would become the beating heart of the world's most populous and powerful city, with approximately a million people crowded into an area of five square miles.

At an early date, the Romans negotiated a series of agreements with their neighbors which were collectively known as the Latin Right: a trading pact called the *commercium*, provisions for intermarriage called the *connubium*, and the *migratio*, which allowed a Latin resident of one settlement to emigrate to another and, after a year's residence, to have the full rights of a citizen there. These privileges contrast strongly with the mutual suspicion that divided the cities of Sumer or Greece. Indeed, the Romans' later willingness to extend the Latin Right far beyond Latium was a key factor in the success of their empire.

According to their own legends, the Romans' early government mirrored the structure of Roman households, with a patriarchal king whose power was checked only by a council of elders, the Senate (from the Latin *senex*, "old man"). Seven kings, including Romulus, are said to have ruled in succession. The last, Tarquinus Superbus (Tarquin the Arrogant), is reputed to have been an Etruscan who paved the way for Rome's imperial expansion by dominating the agriculturally wealthy district of Campania to the south. But his power came at the price of Roman freedom and dignity, as was made clear when Tarquin's son raped a virtuous Roman wife, Lucretia, around 510 B.C.E. When she commited suicide to avoid dishonor, the Romans—led by Lucretia's kinsman, Lucius Junius Brutus—rose up in rebellion, overthrowing not only the Etruscan dynasty but rejecting the very idea of monarchy as a legitimate form of government. Henceforth, any claim to royal authority in Rome was considered anathema, and the very word "king" (*rex*) was a term of insult. The Brutus who would be instrumental in the assassination of Julius Caesar nearly five centuries later was a descendant of that same Brutus who had driven out the Tarquin kings—something he and his contemporaries never forgot.

THE TRIUMPH OF THE EARLY REPUBLIC

The story of Lucretia was both a patriotic myth and a potent statement of Roman attitudes toward female chastity and family honor. And it signalled a radical change in Roman governance. This change was so radical, in fact, that it did not match any of Aristotle's political categories (see Chapter 4), but instead combined elements of them all. The Romans themselves didn't know what to call their political system: they spoke of it merely as *res publica*, "the public thing."

The early Republic was marked by almost constant warfare aimed at stitching together a patchwork of valuable territories that could support Rome's growing population. Gradually, Romans came to control the valuable port of Ostia at the mouth of the Tiber, about twenty miles from their city. They also pushed northward into Etruscan territory, and southward to Naples, another good port. By 300 B.C.E., Rome had absorbed or allied itself with all of central Italy and began to look even farther south, to the wealthy Greek colonies of Sicily. Their rapid success is remarkable when compared to the patterns familiar to us from our study of classical Greece. What was the secret of it? For one thing, the Romans did not impose heavy burdens of taxation and tribute on the settlements they conquered. More often, they demanded that they contribute only soldiers to the Roman army. Rome also extended the Latin Right to many of these conquered territories, giving them a further stake in its political and military expansion.

Rome thus gained for itself nearly inexhaustible reserves of fighting men. By the middle of the third century B.C.E, its army may have numbered as many as 300,000—a huge force even by modern standards. As we have seen, the Greeks had eventually turned to paid soldiering out of economic necessity, but they fought in smaller numbers; Xenophon's army was 10,000 and Alexander's 100,000. The Great King of Persia could claim to muster a million men, but these were private or tribal armies commanded by his satraps, not a standing army loyal to him.

The Romans also devoted themselves to the discipline of warfare in ways the Greeks (except for the Spartans) and the Persians did not. Although they originally used the phalanx formation, they quickly replaced it with smaller, more flexible divisions that could adjust to the hilly conditions of central Italy. While the major unit of the Roman army was always the legion (5,000 men), the combat unit was the *maniple* ("handful"), a group of 120 infantrymen who trained together and who often performed specialized tasks or used special weaponry. The Greek Polybius could not say enough in praise of this system, which made the army adaptable to climate, terrain, and new military techniques.

The Republic's early history reinforced not only the military character of the Roman nation but its commitment to agriculture as the only proper peacetime employment for a Roman. The acquisition of new lands made it possible for citizens to maintain themselves as farmers. As a result,

Romans developed an interest in commerce fairly late when compared with the Greeks or Phoenicians. And they would continue—even at the height of their empire—to valorize rural life over that of the city.

The paragon of Roman heroism in this era was Lucius Quinctius Cincinnatus (519–c. 430 B.C.E.), a stout-hearted citizen-farmer who reluctantly accepted political office when Rome was threatened by attack. According to legend, he was found plowing his fields when a delegation of senators arrived to bring him to Rome, where he found that he had been named *dictator* ["decider"]. This was a position of power to which the Romans elected one man during times of crisis that required decisive leadership. As legend has it, Cincinnatus dutifully performed this role, led Rome in wars with hostile neighbors—and then went back to his plow. If Lucretia was the Roman ideal of female fortitude, Cincinnatus was the paradigm of manly virtue. George Washington was frequently compared to him, to his own satisfaction.

The Constitution of the Early Republic

During this period of expansion, Rome's political system evolved accordingly. Initially, the overthrow of the monarchy had resulted in only moderate changes; instead of a king, the Republic was headed by two elected officers called *consuls*. Although the consuls of the infant republic were supposedly chosen by all citizens, they were inevitably members of aristocratic families, known in Rome as *patricians* because they traced descent from a famous ancestor or "father" (*pater*). During his term of office, which lasted for one year, each consul exercised essentially the same power as a king: dealing justice, making law, and commanding the army. The only limit on power was the right of each consul to veto the actions of the other, which often led to stalemate or violent conflict. In times of grave emergency, such as that resulting in Cincinnatus' election, a dictator might be appointed for a term not longer than six months.

By the early fifth century, within a generation after the establishment of the Republic, patrician dominance of the government began to be challenged by the *plebs* ("people"). This was the first stage in a centuries-long contest known as the Struggle of the Orders. The plebeian classes made up nearly 98 percent of the Roman population. Some had grown wealthy through trade, but most were smallholding farmers, artisans, or the urban poor. Their causes for grievance were numerous. Although they were forced to serve in the army, they were nevertheless excluded from holding office. They were also the victims of discriminatory decisions in judicial trials, which were judged by patricians. They did not even know what their legal rights were, because Rome had as yet no established laws: there were only unwritten customs whose meaning was interpreted by the patricians to their own advantage. The plebians were also, like the poorer citizens of Greek poleis, threatened with debt slavery.

These wrongs prompted a rebellion in the early fifth century B.C.E., when plebeians refused to join in the defense of Rome and instead seceded from the city, camping out on the Aventine hill (see the map of Rome on page 128). This general strike of military labor forced the patricians to allow the people to elect of their own officers, who were known as *tribunes* (tribal leaders). The job of each tribune was to protect his constituents from patrician injustice. Moreover, the plebeians guaranteed the safety of these officers by vowing to kill any person who hindered the exercise of their powers.

The plebs' victory led to the codification of the Law of the Twelve Tables, issued around 450 B.C.E. and inscribed on wooden tablets (hence "tables"). Although it was really a perpetuation of ancient custom, the fact that the law was now *defined* made it a significant improvement. Plebeians were made eligible to hold elected offices and they gradually gained access to the Senate. A further victory came in 287 B.C.E., when they succeeded in passing a law that made decisions enacted in their own assembly binding on the Roman government—whether the Senate approved them or not. It was at this time that the phrase *Senatus Populusque Romanum* came into regular use, abbreviated *SPQR* and designating any decree or decision made by "the Roman Senate and People." Visitors to Rome will still find *SPQR* emblazoned on everything from public buildings to the manhole covers of Rome's sewers.

These reforms had several important consequences. Successful plebeians could now work their way into the upper reaches of Roman society, which loosened the hold of patrician families. At the same time, laws prevented senators from engaging directly in commerce. This restriction had the effect of creating a new social order, that of the equestrians ("horsemen" or knights): men whose wealth made it possible for them to own and equip warhorses, and thus to provide Rome's cavalry. But the equestrians and the senators were never wholly distinct. Often, some members of a wealthy family would underwrite the political careers of their brothers and cousins. Those families who managed to win election by such means, generation after generation, became increasingly influential. Meanwhile, patricians who chose politics over wealth became impoverished and resentful. By the first century B.C.E., many were

tempted to pursue their political agendas by styling themselves champions of the people (see below).

Later Roman patriots would regard this as a golden age of shared government, but Rome was never a democracy. A republic differs from a monarchy only because power is exercised by officers whose offices are not (at least in theory) hereditary. It is essentially a system for reserving power to an oligarchy or privileged group. The constitution that emerged in these key centuries therefore broadened and stabilized oligarchy by the balance it struck between competing institutions: the assembly, the Senate, and executive officeholders. Thanks to this distribution of powers, no single individual or clique could become overwhelmingly strong; but neither could direct expressions of the popular will affect Roman policy.

For the Greek historian Polybius, this was an ideal system, combining elements of the monarchy (executive officeholders, the consuls), the aristocracy (the Senate), and the polity (the people's assembly and the tribunes). For the framers of the United States Constitution, it was a model for the three branches of a new government designed to *prevent* the vast majority of Americans from participating directly in politics, while allowing some citizens (white men with sufficient property) a say in choosing their representatives. Polybius prophesied that such a system would break the political cycle that had destroyed the Greek poleis—that it could last forever. He was wrong.

THE ESSENCE OF ROMAN IDENTITY

Romans accepted new things reluctantly but then preserved them fiercely. The prevailing force was the *mos maiorum*, "the custom of the ancestors" or even—to use a word derived from the Latin *mos*—"morality." This unwritten code was essential to Roman identity. It accounts for the remarkable coherence of Roman culture, religion, and law, all of which rested on ancestor worship. The Latin word *pietas* ("piety") meant reverence for family traditions and for one's fathers—living and dead. What made the legendary Aeneas "pious Aeneas" was his devotion to his father, Anchises, whom he carried to safety while Troy burned. Metaphorically, this meant that Aeneas was the carrier of tradition, a man willing to shoulder the burdens of his ancestors and carry them forever.

This helps to explain why the Romans, in the ensuing centuries of their world domination, continued to identify so strongly with their homeland and its customs: to a Roman, "going native" in a foreign place was a terrible betrayal of the *mos maiorum*. It also explains the maxim of *patria potestas* ("fatherly power") upheld by the Twelve Tables. A Roman father, no matter what his social class, had absolute authority within his household. If he was too poor to raise a child, he could expose it (leaving it to perish or to charity) or sell it into slavery. If his wife or child dishonored him, he could kill with impunity. We begin to understand why Lucretia killed herself: otherwise, her father would have killed her with his own hands.

These values set the Romans apart. The Greeks, for example, never condoned anything like *patria potestas*. When fathers kill their children in Greek mythology, they are inevitably killed in revenge by another family member or by the gods. And while pride in one's ancestry is a very human attribute, the Romans' contemporaries were awed by their extreme devotion to these principles.

While Roman religion resembled that of the Greeks in some respects, the Roman equation of religion with family meant that all gods were essentially family gods of the Roman state. The Republic was like a giant, timeless household run by "elders" (senators) and "father figures" (patricians), some of whom traced their ancestry back to these gods: the mother of Aeneas was Venus. Like a Roman household, then, the Roman state could flourish only if the ancestral gods lent their continuing and active support. Committees of priests therefore functioned as branches of the government; and in stark contrast to other ancient societies, these priests were not full-time professionals who formed a special caste, but prominent men who rotated in and out of office while serving as leaders of the Senate. Their dual roles made Roman religion even more integral to political life than it had been in Greece (Chapter 3), similar in some ways to the integration of religion and politics in ancient Mesopotamia (Chapter 1).

The all-important devotion to ancestors is further reflected in Roman naming practices, another custom that separated them from other cultures. Most free men in antiquity were known by a given name and their father's name only: Alexander was "son of Philip." A free-born Roman, by contrast, had at least two names. The name that mattered was the name of his earliest ancestor. Gaius Julius Caesar, to take a famous example, would have entered public life as Julius, a member of the family of the Julii, who claimed ancestry from Iulus, the son of Aeneas. His forename, Gaius (*GUY-us*), was the most common name in Rome, the equivalent of "Joe" or "John," and he would never be addressed by this name in public, except perhaps by very intimate friends. His third name, Caesar, was a nickname he acquired in the course of his career: "hairy head." And because it was the most distinctive of his names, it became the name by which he was universally known. The same

A ROMAN PATRICIAN OF THE FIRST CENTURY B.C.E. This man, who wears the toga of an aristocrat, displays his piety by holding the busts of his ancestors. Busts, like the funerary masks described by Polybius (see page 113), commemorated the dead and served as the focus for family worship in household shrines. ▪ *How does the Roman attitude toward age and death differ from that of the Greeks (see the image on page 102)?* ▪ *What do these differences suggest about the broader values of these two societies?*

Analyzing Primary Sources

Polybius Describes the Romans' Worship of Their Ancestors

The Law of the Twelve Tables forbade excessive display at funerals, especially displays of wealth and grief on the part of women. Instead, funerals were supposed to be occasions for the display of family piety. In the following passage, the Greek historian Polybius—who had spent a formative fourteen years of his life in Rome—describes Roman burial customs and these rites' relationship to the strength of republican ideals.

quote just one example to illustrate the pains taken by the Roman state to produce men who will endure anything to win a reputation for valor in their country. Whenever one of their celebrated men dies . . . his body is carried with every kind of honor into the Forum . . . sometimes in an upright position so as to be conspicuous, or else, more rarely, recumbent. The whole mass of the people stand round to watch, and his son, if he has one of adult age who can be present, or if not some other relative, then . . . delivers an address which recounts the virtues and successes achieved by the dead man during his lifetime. By these means the whole populace . . . are involved in the ceremony, so that when the facts of the dead man's career are recalled . . . their sympathies are so deeply engaged that the loss seems . . . to be a public one which affects the whole people. Then, after the burial of the body and the performance of the customary rites, they place the image of the dead man in the most conspicuous position in the house, where it is enclosed in a wooden shrine. This image consists of a mask which is fashioned with extraordinary fidelity . . . to represent the features of these dead men. On occasions when public sacrifices are offered, these masks are displayed and decorated with great care. And when any distinguished member of the family dies, the masks are taken to the funeral, and are worn by men who are considered to bear the closest resemblance to the original, both in height and their general appearance and bearing. . . .

It would be hard to imagine a more impressive scene for a young man who aspires to win fame and practice virtue. For who could remain unmoved at the sight of the images of all these men who have won renown in their time, now gathered together as if alive and breathing? What spectacle could be more glorious than this?

Source: Polybius, *The Rise of the Roman Empire*, trans. Ian Scott-Kilvert (New York: 1979), pp. 346–47.

Questions for Analysis

1. Why does Polybius place so high a premium on the Romans' conduct of funerals? How can such rites be related to republican ideals?

2. Compare this analysis of Roman funerary rites to the image of a Roman patrician and his ancestors on page 112. How do they complement one another?

---

goes for Marcus Tullius Cicero (Cicero means "chickpea"). The illustrious Cincinnatus was actually "Curly."

What's in a name? Everything, if you were a Roman man. And nothing, at least nothing of personal significance, if you were a Roman woman. Lucretia's name was not her own, but her father's—or forefathers': the feminine version of Lucretius. If she had a sister, they would both be called Lucretia, differentiated only as Major and Minor ("big/elder" and "little/younger") Lucretia. If there were two more girls, they would be Tertia and Quarta ("Third" and "Fourth") Lucretia, and so on. The only people in Rome who had personal names were slaves (who were named by their masters, like pets) or very low-born Romans and immigrants who had no lineage that mattered.

FROM REPUBLIC TO EMPIRE

For more than two centuries after the founding of the Republic, warfare and agriculture remained the chief occupations of most Romans. The fact that Rome had no standard system of coinage until 289 B.C.E suggests strongly that commerce was an insignificant component of its economy. Apparently, Romans didn't need portable wealth; when they weren't fighting, they wanted to be home on the farm, not gadding about the world. If they had money, they put it into real estate: land or slaves.

All of this changed rapidly when Romans began to look beyond Italy. In 265 B.C.E., they controlled most of the peninsula. A year later, they were already embroiled in a war overseas. For a home-loving people with ample resources, this seems paradoxical. Indeed, historians still argue about the motives for Roman expansion. Did Rome constantly extend its rule as a matter of policy, to feed a collective appetite for warfare and plunder? Or was it an accidental empire, built up in a series of reactions to changing pressures and threats—real and imagined? No definitive answer is possible, but it is in this crucial period that the Roman Republic began to transform Western civilizations, and to transform itself into the Roman Empire.

The Punic Wars, 264–146 B.C.E.

In 265 B.C.E., Roman territory extended to the tip of Italy's "boot," but there it ended. Just off its coast, the large islands of Corsica and Sardinia and the western half of Sicily were part of another state, much older and far wealthier. This was the great maritime empire of Carthage, which stretched along the northern coast of Africa from modern-day Tunisia through the Straits of Gibraltar and into modern Spain. Carthage itself had been founded around 800 B.C.E. as a Phoenician colony (see Chapter 2). It had the largest and most effective navy of its day, and it commanded the vast resources of commercial networks that reached as far north as Britain and deep into Egypt and the Near East. In every respect but one it was far superior to Rome. Yet that one factor was decisive: Carthage had no standing army. It relied on mercenaries bankrolled by the enormous profits of its merchants.

The epic struggle between Rome and Carthage lasted well over a century. It crystallized in three periods of concentrated warfare known as the Punic Wars (because the Romans called their enemies Poeni, "Phoenicians"). The first of these wars began in 264 B.C.E. Twenty-three years of bitter fighting were protracted because the Carthaginians only needed to suffer one defeat in a land battle before resolving to engage the Romans solely at sea. There, they had the advantage—until the Romans built their own navy. Eventually, in 241 B.C.E., Carthage was forced to cede all of her Sicilian lands to Rome and to pay a large indemnity.

Thereafter, the Romans were determined not to let Carthage revive its maritime power. So when Carthage attempted to expand its presence in Spain, Rome interpreted this as a threat and declared a new war that lasted for sixteen years: the Second Punic War. This time, Rome was thrown entirely off its guard by the brilliant exploits of the Carthaginian commander Hannibal (247–183 B.C.E), who very nearly defeated the Romans at their own game. Daringly, Hannibal raised an army in Spain and equipped it with dozens of war elephants and siege engines. He then led this entire force across the Pyrenees into Gaul (now southern France), and then over the Alps into Italy. There, he harried Roman forces in their home territories for nearly sixteen years, from 218 to 202 B.C.E.

Hannibal was challenged more by the difficulty of supplying his army than by the Romans themselves. He also seems to have counted on winning the support of the Italian provinces that Rome had conquered, but Rome's generous treatment of its Latin allies kept them loyal. As a result, Rome could call on vast resources while Hannibal had only his exhausted army and no reserves forthcoming. Nevertheless, he won several amazing victories in Italy before retreating—technically undefeated—in 203. He also won the admiration of the Romans themselves, whose own histories frankly acknowledge his genius.

This phase of warfare ended only when a Roman general, Publius Cornelius Scipio [*SKIP-ee-oh*], took a leaf out of Hannibal's book. After campaigning successfully in Spain, he crossed into Africa and met Hannibal at Zama, near Carthage, in 201 B.C.E. His victory ended the Second Punic War and won him a new name, "Africanus," in honor of his conquest.

Carthage was now compelled to abandon all of its possessions except the city itself and its immediate hinterlands, and to pay an indemnity three times greater than the already crippling reparations demanded after the First Punic War. Yet Roman suspicion remained obsessive, and by the middle of the second century, some warmongers were urging a preemptive strike. Among the most vocal was an elderly patrician called Marcus Porcius Cato, who ended every speech he gave—no matter what the topic—with the words: "And furthermore, I strongly advise that Carthage be destroyed." This won him the nickname Cato the Censor, from the Latin verb "to advise."

In 149 B.C.E., the Senate seized on a minor pretext to demand that the Carthaginians abandon their city and settle at least ten miles from the sea. Of course, this absurd mandate amounted to a death sentence for a city dependent on maritime commerce, and it was refused—as the Romans knew it would be. The result was the Third Punic War and the siege of Carthage, which ended in 146 B.C.E. Those who survived the ensuing massacre were sold into slavery, and their once-magnificent city was razed to the ground.

The legend that the Romans sowed the land with salt (to make it infertile) is a myth, but a vivid way of describing the successful eradication of an entire civilization. It would stand as a warning to Rome's other potential enemies.

Roman Control of the Hellenistic World

Rome's victories over Carthage led to the creation of new colonial provinces in Sicily, North Africa, and Hispania (Spain). This not only brought Rome great new wealth, it was also the beginning of the westward expansion that became Rome's defining influence on the history of Western civilizations.

At the same time, Rome's expansion brought it into conflict with eastern Mediterranean powers. During the Second Punic War, for example, Philip V of Macedonia had entered into an alliance with Carthage. Rome sent an army to stop him, and later foiled the plans of the Achaean League (see Chapter 4). This was when Polybius was sent to Rome as a hostage, and became a guest-friend in the family of Scipio Africanus, later witnessing the destruction of Carthage. Rome also thwarted similar efforts by the Seleucid monarch Antiochus III. In neither of these cases did Rome set out to conquer the eastern Mediterranean. By 146 B.C.E., however, both Greece and Macedonia had become Roman provinces, Seleucid Asia had lost most of its territories, and Ptolemaic Egypt had largely become a pawn of Roman interests.

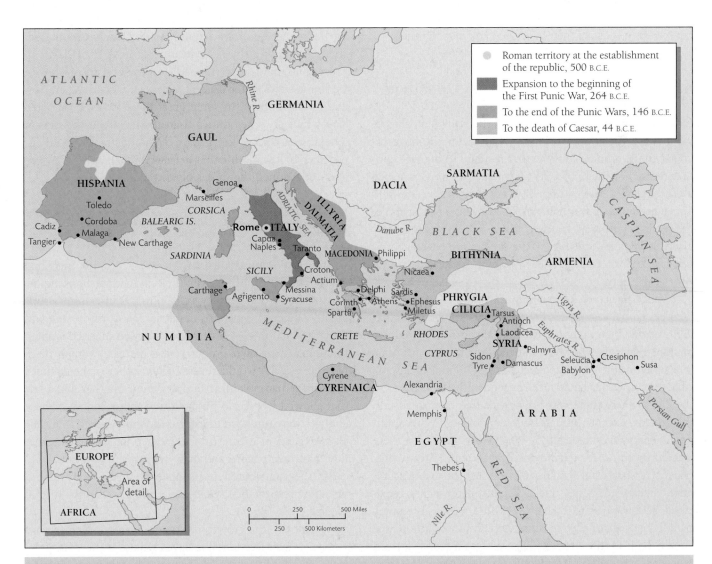

THE EXPANSION OF ROME, 264–44 B.C.E. The rapid increase of Rome's territories opened up new opportunities and challenges.
■ *Looking at the phases of expansion on this map, in what directions did Roman dominion move?* ■ *Why was this the case?* ■ *What particular problems might have been created by the eventual extension of Roman rule into Gaul, well beyond the "Roman lake" of the Mediterranean?*

THE CONSEQUENCES OF IMPERIALISM

Rome's inadvertent conquest of Greece and Asia Minor transformed the Republic. New wealth poured in, increasing the inequalities within Roman society and challenging traditional values. Small farmers left the land and swelled the impoverished urban population, unable to compete with huge plantations worked by gangs of slaves. Slaves also played an increasing role in Roman cities as artisans, merchants, and household servants.

Roman rule over the Hellenistic world had a particularly pervasive impact—so much so that many Romans considered themselves to have been "conquered" by Greece. Hitherto self-assured and self-satisfied, they now felt their own language and customs to be uncouth and barbaric compared to those of their cultivated colonial subjects.

Economic Change and Social Upheaval

Like all peoples of the ancient world, Romans took slavery for granted. But they were not prepared for the huge increase in the number of slaves that resulted from these conquests. In 146 B.C.E., 55,000 Carthaginians were enslaved after the destruction of their city; not long before, 150,000 Greek prisoners of war had met the same fate. By the end of the second century B.C.E., there were a million slaves in Italy alone. Rome's became one of the most slave-based economies in history, rivaling ancient Egypt or the antebellum American South.

The majority of Roman slaves worked as agricultural laborers on the vast (and growing) estates known as *latifundia*, created when Roman aristocrats absorbed the holdings of citizen-farmers who were now required to serve for years at a time on foreign campaigns and often found it impossible to maintain their farms. Consequently, they moved to the city—where there was no way for free men to sustain themselves, except through trade or violence. With abundant, cheap slaves to do all the rough work, moreover, there was no incentive for technological innovation. Meanwhile, expensive slaves did the specialized jobs: they were secretaries, bookkeepers, personal assistants, playwrights, musicians, sculptors, artists. There was little reason to employ paid labor at all, or even to train oneself in these arts, as the Greeks had. By the first century B.C.E., as a result, a third of Rome's one million inhabitants were receiving free grain from the state, partly to keep them alive and partly to keep them quiet. The poet Juvenal would later satirize the plebs as needing only "bread and circuses."

The ready availability of slaves made Roman slavery a far more impersonal and brutal institution than it had been in other ancient civilizations. The standard policy of slave owners was to get as much work out of their human possessions as possible, until they died of exhaustion or were "freed" in old age to fend for themselves. The same irascible Cato the Censor who had demanded the destruction of Carthage even wrote a "how-to" book on this subject. Of course, there were exceptions. Some domestic slaves were treated as trusted family members, and slave secretaries vital to the business of Roman governance and literature could even win fame or earn enough to buy their freedoms. Some slave artisans were permitted to run their own businesses, keeping some of the profits.

But the general lot of slaves was horrendous. Some businessmen owned slaves whom they trained as gladiators, to be mauled by wild animals or by other gladiators for the amusement of a paying public. The luxurious lifestyles of the wealthy also meant that dozens of slaves in every household were trapped in a cycle of menial tasks, as doorkeepers, litter-bearers, couriers, valets, wet-nurses, and child-minders. In some great households, designated slaves had no other duties than to rub down the master after his bath or to keep track of the mistress's social engagements. It was a life that debased both slave and owner, and undermined the values of the republic.

New Money, New Values

In the early Republic, as we have seen, Roman men had nearly absolute powers over their individual households. During the second century B.C.E., however, two innovations greatly altered this pattern of patriarchal control. One was the introduction of new laws that allowed married women to control their own property; if a married woman died, her possessions would revert to her father or her father's heirs if she had no children of her own. Another was a law that allowed women to initiate divorce proceedings. These changes were intended to safeguard family wealth, but they also resulted in greater independence for women. A wife now had much more authority within the household because she contributed to its upkeep. If her husband did not show respect, she could leave him and deprive him of income.

Ironically, the growth of Rome's slave system also gave women greater freedom, for slaves took over the traditional work of child rearing, household maintenance, and the endless tasks of spinning and weaving. Women from well-to-do families now began to engage in a range of social, intellectual, and artistic activities. Indeed, women were among the chief consumers of the new Hellenistic fashions, commodities, and ideas available in Rome.

In earlier centuries, Romans had taken pride in the simplicity of their lives. Now, however, elite Romans began to indulge in creature comforts and to cultivate Hellenistic habits. Bilingualism became increasingly common, and Greek literature became the standard against which Roman authors measured themselves. For Latin was not yet a literary language. It was fine for politics or farming, but if one wanted to express lofty or beautiful thoughts one did so in Greek, which was far more flexible and sophisticated. Well-educated Greek slaves were therefore at a premium, to lend social cachet, to write letters, and to tutor Roman children.

But many Romans regarded these foreign influences with disgust. For them, the good old ways of paternal authority and stern discipline were giving way to effeminacy and soft living. Increasingly, hard-line conservatives passed laws to restore "family values" and regulate the conspicuous consumption of luxuries, especially by women. These measures were ineffectual. Rome was being irreversibly transformed into a complex metropolitan empire reliant on foreign slaves, foreign grain, and foreign luxuries, in which a vast gulf was widening between rich and poor, and where traditional behavioral constraints were giving way to new freedoms for both men and women.

Spirituality and Philosophy in the Late Republic

The religious practices of Rome changed markedly in this era. The most pronounced innovation was the spread of Eastern mystery cults, which satisfied a need for more emotionally intense spiritual experiences—especially for women, who were largely excluded from the rites of the patriarchal state religion. From Egypt came the cults of Isis and Osiris, while from Asia came the worship of the Great Mother, all emphasizing the power of female sexuality and reproduction. Despite the attractions of these new cults, Romans continued to honor their traditional gods alongside these new, exotic deities. Roman polytheism could absorb them all, so long as the ancestor gods of the household and the city were paid due reverence.

The Hellenistic philosophies of Epicureanism and Stoicism both found strong adherents in Rome (Chapter 4), but more congenial to Roman values was Stoicism. Its most influential proponent was Cicero (106–43 B.C.E.), famous in his day as an orator, statesman, and staunch defender of republican virtues. Cicero based his ethical teachings on the Stoic premise that tranquility of mind is the highest good: the ideal man is rational, indifferent to sorrow and pain. Yet Cicero diverged from the Stoics in his approval of the active, political life. He became an advocate for the revival of Roman tradition through service to the state. His elegant prose style also advanced the use of Latin as a language of eloquence and became the standard model for literary composition. Students learning Latin today still begin with Cicero.

"RESTORING THE REPUBLIC": THE STRUGGLE FOR POWER

Politically, the century after the Third Punic War was one of turbulence. Bloody competitions among rival dictators and insurrections were common occurrences. Slave uprisings added to the general disorder. The most threatening revolt of all was led by Spartacus, a Thracian captive who was being trained as a gladiator. He and a band of 200 fellow slaves escaped from a gladiatorial training camp at Capua [KAH-poo-ah] (near Naples), heavily armed, to the slopes of Mount Vesuvius, where their cause attracted a huge host of other fugitives. From 73 to 71 B.C.E. this desperate army defeated Roman forces of as many as 10,000 men before Spartacus himself was killed. The Senate, terrified of the precedent, ordered 6,000 of the captured slaves to be crucified along the length of the road from Capua to Rome—about 150 miles—as a warning to future insurgents. Crucifixion was a form of punishment reserved for slaves and non-Roman rebels, and it meant a slow, terrible, and public death from gradual suffocation and exposure.

The Reforming Efforts of the Gracchi

These waves of rebellion were mirrored by urban unrest in various forms, and the poorer classes were finding new champions among some progressive patricians. In 133 B.C.E., a grandson of Scipio Africanus, Tiberius Gracchus [GRAH-cus], was elected a tribune of the people. He proposed to alleviate social and economic stress by instituting major reforms, chiefly the redistribution of property. As we have noted, small farmers had been losing their lands to those whose new wealth allowed them to amass giant estates, the latifundia. To counter this, Tiberius Gracchus invoked old laws that had, under the early republic, limited the amount of land that could be held by a single person. His motives were not entirely populist. There was now a grave manpower shortage in the Roman army, which had been forced to expand its presence in the far reaches of the world and had left Rome itself prey to uprisings like that of Spartacus. Since a man had to meet certain property qualifications to serve in the Roman army, the available pool of citizen soldiers was contracting. So Tiberius Gracchus aimed to refresh the reserves by creating new citizens.

With the support of his brother Gaius, Tiberius Gracchus proposed a law that would restrict estates to a maximum of 300 acres per citizen, plus 150 acres for each child in his family, with the excess land to be divided among poor settlers. Not surprisingly, most senators stood to lose from this legislation, and so engineered its veto by Gracchus's fellow tribunes. Gracchus retaliated, arguing that tribunes who opposed the people's interests were betraying their offices, and he announced plans to stand for reelection. A conservative faction in the Senate then alleged that Gracchus had his sights set on a dictatorship, and with this excuse they attacked and murdered him and his supporters on the day of the elections.

Ten years later, Gaius Gracchus renewed his older brother's struggle after being elected to the same office. Although a version of Tiberius's land reforms had finally been enacted, Gaius believed that the campaign had to go further. In 123 B.C.E. he enacted several laws for the benefit of the poor. He also imposed controls on provincial governors suspected of exploiting their subjects for personal gain. Most controversially, Gaius proposed to extend full Roman citizenship to all the allied states of Italy, a move that would have kept the army well supplied with new soldiers, but which would alter the political landscape of Rome to the detriment of the existing elite. Accordingly, the Senate proclaimed Gaius Gracchus an outlaw. In the ensuing conflict, Gaius and about 3,000 of his followers became the victims of a purge.

Rivalry among Rome's Generals

Although the reforms of the Gracchi were ultimately unsuccesful, they exposed the weakness of the Senate and increased the power of the plebs, whose favor was now courted by a succession of ambitious men. Most were professional soldiers who controlled one or more legions of the Roman army and who traded on military victories abroad to win the confidence of the people. The first of these was Gaius Marius, who had fought a successful campaign against King Jugurtha of Numidia, a small kingdom in North Africa. In 107 B.C.E. Marius's popularity catapulted him to the consulship, despite the protests of the Senate's aristocracy, and he would be elected to that office six more times.

Marius set a powerful precedent by demonstrating how easily an army command could be an alternative path to political power. He also changed the course of Rome's history by reorganizing and expanding the army. Desperate for more men to fight in Africa and in Gaul, Marius abolished the property qualification that had hitherto limited military service; the potential pool of soldiers now included the urban poor and landless peasants. As a result, a career as a Roman legionnaire became an end in itself, and a soldier's loyalty was directed toward his commander—whose success would win rewards for his men—rather than to an abstract ideal of patriotism. This change also meant that factional fighting could lead to full-blown civil war, as legions loyal to one general were pitted against those of another.

This happened in Marius's own lifetime. The aristocratic general Lucius Cornelius Sulla [SUH-la] had fought with distinction in the so-called Social War of 91–88 B.C.E., a conflict between Rome and her Italian allies that resulted in the extension of Roman citizenship throughout the peninsula. Therafter, Sulla seemed the likely person to lead Rome's army to war in Asia Minor. Marius, however, forced the Senate to deny Sulla's claim. Sulla's response was to rally the five victorious legions that had just fought under his command and, with a Roman army at his back, to march on Rome.

Strong taboos had long prevented any armed force from entering the city limits, but Sulla argued that his actions were in keeping with the *mos maiorum*, which Marius and the Senate had betrayed. He was then given the coveted command in Asia Minor, after which Marius again seized control of the city. When Marius died soon afterward, a conservative backlash led the aristocracy to appoint Sulla to the office of dictator—and not for the traditional six months. Instead, Sulla's term had no limits, and he used this time to exterminate his opponents. He packed the Senate with men loyal to himself and curtailed the authority of the peoples' tribunes. Then, after three years of rule, he retired to a life of luxury on his country estate.

Caesar's Triumph—and His Downfall

The effect of Sulla's dictatorship was to empower the aristocracy and weaken the power of the plebs. Soon, however, new leaders emerged to espouse the people's cause, once again using the army as their tool of influence. The most prominent of these military men were Gnaeus Pompeius Magnus (106–48 B.C.E.) and Gaius Julius Caesar (100–44 B.C.E.). Initially, they cooperated in a plot to "restore the republic" by forming an alliance with a third general, Marcus Junius Crassus, the man credited with finally defeating Spartacus. This alliance was known as a *triumvirate*, meaning "rule of three men," but it soon dissolved into open rivalry. Pompey (as generations of English-speaking historians have called him) had won fame as the conqueror of Syria and Palestine, while Caesar had campaigned in Gaul, adding the territories of modern France,

Belgium, and western Germany to the Roman Empire, and extending its northern border the length of the Rhine.

It had become accepted that the best general should be the leader of Rome, and the example of Sulla had made it possible for that leader to be a dictator for life, a king in all but name. But it was Pompey, not Caesar, who was actually in Rome and in a position to influence the Senate directly. So in the face of tremendous popular protest and even some opposition from the aristocracy, Pompey had himself elected sole consul. Essentially, this meant that he could act as dictator. Using this authority, he declared that Caesar, who was still stationed in Gaul, was an enemy of the republic, and that his ambition was to make himself king.

The result was a pervasive and deadly civil war. In 49 B.C.E., Caesar crossed the Rubicon River, the northern boundary of Rome's Italian territories, thereby signalling his intention to take Rome by force. Pompey fled to the east in the hope of gathering an army large enough to confront Ceasar's legions. Caesar pursued him, and in 48 B.C.E. the two Roman armies met at Pharsalus in Greece. Pompey was defeated and fled to Alexandria, where he was murdered by a Roman officer attached to the court of Ptolemy XIII (62/61–47? B.C.E.). Ptolemy was then about fourteen years old and engaged in a civil war of his own—with his elder sister and co-ruler, Cleopatra VII (69–30 B.C.E.). Caesar threw his support on the side of the twenty-one-year old queen. The two must have become lovers soon after their first meeting, because their son Caesarion ("Little Ceasar") was born nine months later.

After that, Caesar returned to Rome in triumph—literally. A *triumph* was a spectacular honor awarded to a victorious Roman general by the Senate, and was the only legal occasion on which (unarmed) soldiers were allowed to parade in the streets of Rome. Triumphs had been celebrated since the earliest days of the republic and featured columns of prisoners and spoils of war, chained captives (often enemy kings) led in humiliation to their public executions, floats commemorating the achievements of the triumphant man, and thousands of cheering Romans who received extra rations of grain and gathered up coins thrown by the handful. Through it all, Caesar would have ridden in a chariot with a golden wreath held above his head, while a slave stood behind him, murmuring in his ear the words *Memento mori*: "Remember: you will die." A triumph was so glorious and—under the republic—so rarely granted that those thus honored might forget their own mortality.

Caesar's power seemed absolute. In 46 B.C.E. he was named dictator for ten years; two years later, this was changed to a lifetime appointment. In addition, he assumed nearly every other title that could augment his power. He even governed the reckoning of time: in imitation of the Egyptian calendar, he revised the Roman calendar so as to make a 365-day year with an extra day added every fourth year. This Julian calendar (as adjusted by Pope Gregory XIII

CLEOPATRA VII AS EGYPTIAN PHARAOH AND HELLENISTIC RULER. Like her ancestor, Ptolemy I, Cleopatra represented herself as both enlightened Greek monarch and as Pharaoh. It was perhaps due to her example that Julius Caesar was the first Roman leader to issue coins impressed with his own image. ■ *How does Cleopatra's self-representation compare to that of Hatshepsut (see Chapter 2) or Ptolemy (Chapter 4)?*

in 1582) is still observed, and the seventh month is still named after Julius.

Caesar also took important steps toward eliminating the distinction between Italians and provincials within the empire by conferring citizenship on the residents of Hispania (Spain) and the newly annexed provinces in Gaul. By settling many of his army veterans in these lands, moreover, he furthered colonization. By incorporating Gaul into the Roman world he brought in a much-needed source of food and natural resources and created a new outlet for the spread of Roman influence.

In the eyes of many contemporaries, however, Caesar's achievements were further signs that he intended to make himself king: a hateful thought to those who still glorified the early days of the republic. Indeed, it was around a descendant of Lucretia's avenger, Brutus, that a faction of the Senate crystallized into conspiracy. On the Ides of March in 44 B.C.E.—the midpoint of the month, according to his own calendar—Caesar was attacked on the floor of the Senate's chamber and stabbed to death by a group of men. His body would later be autopsied, the first such examination in recorded history. It was found that he had received 23 wounds.

THE PRINCIPATE AND THE PAX ROMANA, 27 B.C.E.–180 C.E.

In his will, Caesar had adopted his grandnephew Gaius Octavius (or Octavian, 63 B.C.E.–14 C.E.), then a young man of eighteen. On learning of Caesar's death, Octavian hastened to claim his inheritance and to avenge his slain "father," whose name he took: he was now Gaius Julius Caesar the younger. But he soon found that he had rivals among those supporters of Caesar who had not been implicated in the plot to kill him, most notably Marcus Antonius (or Mark Antony, 83–30 B.C.E.), who had served under Caesar in Gaul and was determined to make himself governor of that whole province.

Octavian engineered his own election to the office of consul (though he was far too young for this honor) and used his powers to have Caesar's assassins declared outlaws. He then pursued Antony to Gaul, at the head of an army. Antony's forces were overwhelmed, and in 43 B.C.E. he and Octavian reconciled and formed an alliance, bringing in a third man, a senator called Marcus Aemilius Lepidus, to make up a second triumvirate. They then set about crushing the faction responsible for Caesar's murder.

Their methods were brutal: prominent conspirators were hunted down and their property confiscated. The most

OCTAVIAN. Caesar's adopted heir was later granted the title "Augustus" by the Senate, and was also known as *princeps*, "first man." Eventually, he would be worshiped as a god in Rome's provinces, and idealized statues like this one would be erected in temples and public places throughout the empire.

notable of these victims was Cicero. Meanwhile, the masterminds behind the assasination, Brutus and Gaius Cassius, fled Rome and raised an army of legions from Greece and Asia Minor. But they were defeated by the united forces of Antony and Octavian on a battlefield near the Macedonian town of Philippi (founded by Alexander's father) in 42 B.C.E. Both Brutus and Cassius committed suicide.

Analyzing Primary Sources

Antony and Cleopatra

In his Parallel Lives, *the Greek intellectual Plutarch (c. 46–120 C.E.) paired the biographies of famous Greeks with those of famous Romans, always to the disadvantage of the latter; for example, Julius Caesar suffers in comparison to Alexander the Great, as Romulus does when set up against Theseus. The following excerpt is from Plutarch's* Life of Mark Antony, *in which the Hellenistic ruler of Egypt, Cleopatra, plays a starring role.*

Caesar and Pompey knew Cleopatra when she was] still a girl, and ignorant of the world, but it was a different matter in the case of Antony, because she was ready to meet him when she had reached the time of life when women are most beautiful and have full understanding. So she prepared for him many gifts and money and adornment, of a magnitude appropriate to her great wealth and prosperous kingdom, but she put most of her hopes in her own magical arts and charms. . . . For (as they say), it was not because her beauty in itself was so striking that it stunned the onlooker, but the inescapable impression produced by daily contact with her: the attractiveness in the persuasiveness of her talk, and the character that surrounded her conversation was stimulating. It was a pleasure to hear the sound of her voice, and she tuned her tongue like a many-stringed instrument expertly to whatever language she chose, and only used interpreters to talk to a few foreigners. . . . She is said to have learned the languages of many peoples, although her predecessors on the throne did not bother to learn Egyptian, and some had even forgotten how to speak the Macedonian dialect.

She took such a hold over Antony that, while his wife Fulvia was carrying on the war in Rome against Octavian on his behalf, and the Parthian army . . . was about to invade Syria, Antony was carried off by Cleopatra to Alexandria, and amused himself there with the pastimes of a boy . . . Whether Antony was in a serious or a playful mood, she could always produce some new pleasure or charm, and she kept watch on him by night and day and never let him out of her sight. She played dice with him and hunted with him and watched him exercising with his weapons and she roamed around and wandered about with him at night when he stood at people's doors and windows and made fun of people inside, dressed in a slave-woman's outfit; for he also attempted to dress up like a slave. He returned from these expeditions having been mocked in return, and often beaten, although most people suspected who he was. But the Alexandrians got pleasure from his irreverence . . . enjoying his humor and saying that he showed his tragic face to the Romans and his comic one to them.

Source: Plutarch, *Life of Marcus Antonius,* cc. 25–29, excerpted in *Women's Life in Greece & Rome: A Sourcebook in Translation,* eds. Mary R. Lefkowitz and Maureen B. Fant (Baltimore, MD: 1992), pp. 147–49.

Questions for Analysis

1. How do Cleopatra's behavior and accomplishments, in Plutarch's description of her, compare to those of Roman women?

2. Given what you have learned about the values of the Roman Republic, how would a Roman reader respond to this description of Antony's behavior under the influence of the Egyptian queen? What do you think were Plutarch's motives in portraying him in this light?

With the opposition destroyed, tensions mounted between Antony and Octavian. Antony went to the East and made an alliance with Cleopatra. Octavian, meanwhile, reestablished himself in Rome, where he skillfully portrayed Antony as having been seduced and emasculated by the Egyptian queen. For ten years, Antony played the king in Egypt, fathering three of Cleopatra's children and making big plans for annexing Rome's eastern provinces. Eventually, Octavian had him declared a traitor while the Senate declared war on Cleopatra.

In 31 B.C.E. Octavian's superior forces defeated those of Antony and Cleopatra in the naval battle of Actium, off the coast of Greece. Soon afterward, both Antony and Cleopatra committed suicide. Their children were taken back to Rome, and although their lives were spared they

Two Views of Augustus's Rule

Augustus Speaks for Himself

The emperor Augustus was a master propagandist with an unrivaled capacity for presenting his own actions in the best possible light. This list of his own deeds was written by Augustus himself and was displayed on two bronze pillars set up in the Roman forum.

Below is a copy of the accomplishments of the deified Augustus by which he brought the whole world under the empire of the Roman people, and of the moneys expended by him on the state and the Roman people....

1. At the age of nineteen, on my own initiative and at my own expense, I raised an army by means of which I liberated the republic, which was oppressed by the tyranny of a faction.

2. Those who assassinated my father I drove into exile, avenging their crime by due process of law.

3. I waged many wars throughout the whole world by land and by sea, both civil and foreign....

5. The dictatorship offered to me ... by the people and by the Senate ... I refused to accept.... The consulship, too, which was offered to me ... as an annual office for life, I refused to accept.

6. [T]hough the Roman Senate and people together agreed that I should be elected sole guardian of the laws and morals with supreme authority, I refused to accept any office offered me which was contrary to the traditions of our ancestors.

7. I have been ranking senator for forty years.... I have been *pontifex maximus*, augur, member of the college of fifteen for performing sacrifices, member of the college of seven for conducting religious banquets, member of the Arval Brotherhood, one of the *Titii sodales*, and a *fetial* [all priestly offices].

9. The Senate decreed that vows for my health should be offered up every fifth year by the consuls and priests.... [T]he whole citizen body, with one accord, ... prayed continuously for my health at all the shrines.

17. Four times I came to the assistance of the treasury with my own money ... providing bonuses for soldiers who had completed twenty or more years of service.

20. I repaired the Capitol and the theater of Pompey with enormous expenditures on both works, without having my name inscribed on them. I repaired ... the aqueducts which were falling into ruin in many places ... I repaired eighty-two temples.... I reconstructed the Flaminian Way....

34. [H]aving attained supreme power by universal consent, I transferred the state from my own power to the control of the Roman Senate and people.... After that time I excelled all in authority, but I possessed no more power than the others who were my colleagues in each magistracy.

35. At the time I wrote this document I was in my seventy-sixth year.

Source: "Res Gestae Divi Augusti," in *Roman Civilization, Sourcebook II: The Empire,* eds. Naphtali Lewis and Meyer Reinhold (New York: 1966), pp. 9–19.

were paraded through the streets as captives. This marked the end of Egypt's independence: Cleopatra had been its last pharaoh. After more than three thousand years of self-rule, Egypt was now another province in Rome's empire. Octavian's power was consolidated.

The Principate of Augustus

The victory at Actium ushered in a new period of Roman history. The new Gaius Julius Caesar was now the only man left standing, with no rivals for power. For the first time in

The Historian Tacitus Evaluates Augustus's Reign

Writing in the first decades of the second century C.E., the senatorial historian Tacitus (c. 56–117) began his chronicle of imperial rule, the Annals, *with the death of Augustus a century earlier.*

ntelligent people praised or criticized Augustus in varying terms. One opinion was as follows. Filial duty and a national emergency, in which there was no place for law-abiding conduct, had driven him to civil war—and this can be neither initiated nor maintained by decent methods. He had made many concessions to Antony and to Lepidus for the sake of vengeance on his father's murderers. When Lepidus grew old and lazy, and Antony's self-indulgence got the better of him, the only possible cure for the distracted country had been government by one man. However, Augustus had put the State in order not by making himself king or dictator but by creating the Principate. The empire's frontiers were on the ocean, or on distant rivers. Armies, provinces, fleets, the whole system was interrelated. Roman citizens were protected by the law. Provincials were decently treated. Rome itself had been lavishly beautified. Force had been sparingly used—merely to preserve peace for the majority.

The opposite view went like this. Filial duty and national crisis had been merely pretexts. In actual fact, the motive of Octavian, the future Augustus, was lust for power. Inspired by that, he had mobilized ex-army settlers by gifts of money, raised an army—while he was only a half-grown boy without any official status—won over a consul's brigade by bribery, pretended to support Sextus Pompeius [the son of Pompey], and by senatorial decree usurped the status and rank of a praetor. Soon both consuls . . . had met their deaths—by enemy action; or perhaps in the one case by the deliberate poisoning of his wound, and in the other at the hand of his own troops, instigated by Octavian. In any case, it was he who took over both their armies. Then he had forced the reluctant Senate to make him consul. But the forces given him to deal with Antony he used against the State. His judicial murders and land distributions were distasteful even to those who carried them out. True, Cassius and Brutus died because he had inherited a feud against them; nevertheless, personal enmities ought to be sacrificed to the public interest. Next he had cheated Sextus Pompeius by a spurious peace treaty, Lepidus by spurious friendship. Then Antony, enticed by treaties and his marriage with Octavian's sister, had paid the penalty of that delusive relationship with his life. After that, there had certainly been peace, but it was a bloodstained peace. . . . And gossip did not spare his personal affairs—how he had abducted [Livia] the wife of Tiberius Claudius Nero, and asked the priests the farcical question whether it was in order for her to marry while pregnant. Then there was the debauchery of his friend Publius Vedius Pollio. But Livia was a real catastrophe, to the nation, as a mother and to the house of the Caesars as a stepmother.

Source: Tacitus, *Annals* i.9–10. Based on *Tacitus: The Annals of Imperial Rome*, trans. Michael Grant (New York: 1989), pp. 37–39.

Questions for Analysis

1. How does Augustus organize his list, and why? What does he leave out and what does he choose to emphasize?

2. Tacitus presents two contrasting views of Augustus's motives. Which does he himself seem to believe? How does his account complement or undermine that of Augustus himself?

3. Could you write a new account of Augustus's life making use of both sources? How would you strike a balance between them? What would your own conclusion be?

---

nearly a century, Rome was not embroiled in civil war. But it was no longer a republic, even though Octavian maintained the fiction that he was governing as a mere citizen. For four years he ruled as sole consul, until he accepted the titles of *imperator* (emperor) and *augustus*. Although these honorifics had been in use under the republic—*imperator* meant "victorious general" and *augustus* meant "worthy of honor"—they now became attached to the person of the sole ruler. Rome had long been an empire, but it was only now that it had a single emperor. To avoid confusion, historians therefore refer to this phase of Rome's history as the Principate, from the title Augustus himself preferred: *princeps*, or "first man."

Because Augustus was determined not to be regarded as a tyrant or (worse) a king, he left most of Rome's republican institutions in place—but emptied them of their power. In theory, the emperor served at the will of "the Roman Senate and People." In practice, though, he controlled the army, which meant that he also controlled the workings of government. Fortunately, Augustus was an able ruler. He introduced a range of public services, including a police force and fire brigade; he reorganized the army; and he allowed cities and provinces more substantial rights of self-government than they had enjoyed before. He instituted a new system of coinage throughout the empire, and he abolished the old, corrupt system of taxation, whereby tax collectors were compensated by being allowed to keep a portion of what they collected. Instead, Augustus appointed his own representatives, paid them regular salaries, and kept them under strict supervision. He also conducted a census of the empire's population, and it was during one of these "enrollments" that the birth of Jesus is said to have taken place, according to the gospel of Luke (see Chapter 6). Augustus also established new colonies in the provinces, encouraging the emigration of Rome's urban and rural poor, thereby removing a major source of social tension and promoting the integration of the Roman heartland with its far-flung hinterland.

Although his rule had definitively ended the republic, Augustus represented himself as a stern defender of the *mos maiorum* and traditional Roman virtues. He rebuilt many of the city's ancient temples and prohibited the worship of foreign gods. In an attempt to increase the birthrate of Rome's citizens, he penalized men who failed to marry, required widows to remarry within two years of their husbands' deaths, and rewarded women who gave birth to more than two children. He also introduced laws punishing adultery and making divorces more difficult to obtain. To hammer the message home, Augustan propaganda portrayed the imperial family as a model of domestic virtue and propriety, despite the emperor's own notorious extramarital affairs and the well-known fact that the sexual promiscuity of his daughter Julia finally forced Augustus to have her exiled.

More land was gained for Rome in the lifetime of Augustus than in that of any other ruler. His generals advanced into central Europe, conquering the modern-day territories of Switzerland, Austria, and Bulgaria. Only in Germania did Roman troops meet defeat, when three legions were slaughtered in 9 C.E., a setback that convinced Augustus to hold the Roman borders at the Rhine and Danube rivers. Subsequently, though, the Emperor Claudius would begin the conquest of Britain in 43 C.E., while the Emperor Trajan (91–117 C.E.) would push beyond the Danube to add Dacia (now Romania) to the empire. Trajan also conquered territories in the heartland of Mesopotamia, but in so doing aroused the enmity of the Parthians, who now ruled in Persia. His successor, Hadrian (117–138 C.E.), accordingly halted Rome's expansion and embarked on a defensive policy epitomized by the construction of Hadrian's Wall in northern Britain. The empire had now reached its greatest extent; in the third century, as we shall see (Chapter 6), the tide would turn and these limits would recede.

When Octavian died in 14 C.E. he was not only Caesar, Imperator, and Augustus; he was *pontifex maximus* (high priest) and "father of the fatherland" (*pater patriae*). He was even deified by the Senate. These titles would be passed on to his successors, as would the system of government he had devised. And even those who mourned the passing of the republic and loathed these displays of imperial *hubris* had to admit that the system worked. Rome enjoyed nearly two centuries of peace, prosperity, and stability because of it. For the true test of any political institution is its capacity to survive incompetent officeholders. Aside from one brief period of civil war in 68 C.E., the transition of power between emperors was generally peaceful and the growing imperial bureaucracy could manage affairs competently even when individual emperors proved vicious and ineffectual, as did Caligula (37–41 C.E.). Nevertheless, the fact that

HADRIAN'S WALL. Stretching 73.5 miles across northern England, this fortification (begun in 122 C.E.) marked the frontier of Britain as established by the emperor Hadrian. (A later wall, built farther north by Antoninus Pius in 142, was quickly abandoned.) Long stretches of the wall still exist, as do many of the forts built along it. The tree in this photograph stands on the site of a "mile castle," one of the smaller watchtowers built at intervals of a Roman mile and garrisoned by sentries.

Rome had become an autocratic state became harder and harder to conceal.

The height of the Augustan system is generally considered to be the era between 96 and 180 C.E., often known as the reign of the "Five Good Emperors": Nerva (96–98 C.E.), Trajan (98–117 C.E.), Hadrian (117–138 C.E.), Antoninus Pius (138–161 C.E.), and Marcus Aurelius (161–180 C.E.). All were capable politicians, and since none but the last had a son that survived him, each adopted a worthy successor—a policy that avoided the messy family dysfunctions that absorbed Augustus and his immediate heirs. They also benefited from the fact that Rome had few external enemies left. The Mediterranean was under the control of a single power for the first time in history. On land, Roman officials ruled from Britain to Persia. Now was the *Pax Romana*, the time of Roman Peace.

SPOILS FROM JERUSALEM. A bas-relief inside the triumphal Arch of Titus in the Roman forum shows plundered treasures from the Temple at Jerusalem, including the Menorah, being carried in triumph through Rome.

MAKING THE WORLD ROMAN

Occasionally, the Roman Peace was broken. In Britannia, Roman legions had to put down a rebellion led by the Celtic warrior queen Boudica ([*BOO-di-kah*] d. 60/61 C.E.), a war that ended in a massacre of the island's inhabitants. Another rebellion was violently quashed in Judea, the most restive of all Roman provinces, leading to the destruction of the Temple at Jerusalem in 70 C.E. In 135 C.E., a second rebellion completed the destruction of the city. Although Jerusalem was later refounded by Hadrian as Aelia Capitolina, a colony for veterans of Rome's army, Jews were forbidden to settle there.

Such rebellions were not the norm, however. Although the Roman Empire had been gradually achieved by conquest, it was not maintained by force. Instead, Rome controlled its territories by offering incentives to assimiliation. Local elites were encouraged to adopt Roman modes of behavior and dress in order to gain entrance to political office. Local gods became Roman gods and were adopted into the Roman pantheon. Cities were constructed on a set model of urban planning, and the amenities of urban life were introduced: baths, temples, amphitheaters, aqueducts, and paved roads (see **Interpreting Visual Evidence** on page 128). Rights of citizenship were extended, and able provincials could rise far in the imperial government. Some, like the emperors Trajan and Hadrian—both raised in Hispania—came to control it. Meanwhile, tens of thousands of army veterans were settled in the provinces, marrying local women and putting down local roots. It was common for soldiers born in Syria to end their days peacefully in northern Gaul. In Camulodunum (now Colchester, England), the gravestone of a legionnaire called Longinus sketches a typical career: born in Serdica (modern Sofia, in Bulgaria) to a local man named Szdapezematygus, he rose through the ranks to become sergeant of the First Thracian Cavalry under the emperor Claudius and one of the first Roman colonists of Britannia.

Even the outer fringes of the empire need to be understood as part of Rome's orbit. Although historians speak of the empire's "borders" for the sake of convenience, these were in fact permeable zones of intensive interaction. Roman influence reached far beyond these zones, into the heartland of Germania and lands farther to the east. By the middle of the third century C.E., when some frontier garrisons were withdrawn to take part in civil wars within the empire, many of these peoples moved southward, too, sometimes as plunderers but more often as aspiring Romans (see Chapter 6).

The Entertainments of Empire

The cultural and intellectual developments of the late Republic came to fruition during the Principate, and are richly reflected in its literature. For the first time, Latin began to replace Greek as a language of learning and poetry— much of it, not surprisingly, propagandistic: its purpose was to advertise and justify Rome's achievements. The poetry of Publius Virgilius Maro (Virgil, 70–19 B.C.E.) is typical, and we have already noted his strategic use of "prophecy" in the story of Aeneas (see page 108). Other major poets of the Augustan age were Quintus Horatius Flaccus (Horace, 65–8 B.C.E.) and Publius Ovidius Naso (Ovid, 43 B.C.E.–17 C.E.): the former a master of the lovely short lyric and the latter our major source for Greek mythology, which he retold in a long poem called the *Metamorphoses* ("Transformations").

After Augustus's death, Roman authors had more license and became important cultural critics. The tales of Petronius and Apuleius describe the more bizarre and sometimes sordid aspects of Roman life, and the satirist Juvenal (60?–140 C.E.) wrote with savage wit about the moral degeneracy he saw in his contemporaries. A similar attitude toward Roman society characterizes the writings of Tacitus (55?–117? C.E.), an aristocratic historian who describes the events and people of his age largely for the purpose of passing judgment on them. His *Annals* offer a subtle but devastating portrait of the political system constructed by Augustus and ruled by his heirs; his *Germania* contrasts the manly virtues of northern barbarians with the effeminate vices of the decadent Romans.

To many people today, the most fascinating (and repellant) aspect of Roman culture during the Principate was its spectacular cruelty. Gladiatorial contests were not new, but they were now presented in ampitheaters built to hold tens of thousands. Everyone, even emperors, attended these events, and they became increasingly bloody and brutal as people demanded more and more innovative violence. Individual gladiators fought to the death with swords or the exotic weapons of their homelands. Teams of gladiators fought pitched battles, often simulating historic Roman victories. Occasionally, a wealthy entrepreneur would fill an arena with water and stage a naval battle. Hundreds of men would die in these organized slaughters. On other occasions, hundreds of half-starved animals imported from Africa, India, or the forests of Germania would tear one another—

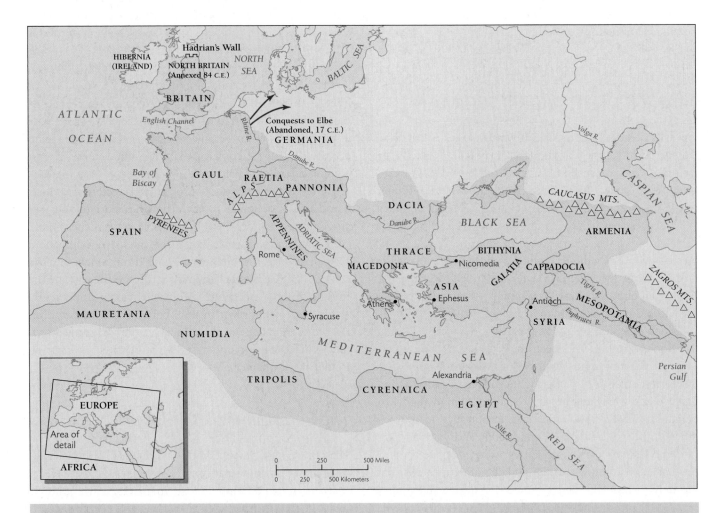

THE ROMAN EMPIRE AT ITS GREATEST EXTENT, 97–117 C.E. ▪ *How much farther north and west does the empire now reach compared to its earlier extent (see map on page 115)?* ▪ *How did geography influence the process of expansion?* ▪ *How did it dictate its limits?* ▪ *For example, what role do major river systems seem to play?*

or their human victims—apart. When a fighter went down with a disabling wound, the crowd would be asked to decide whether to spare his life or to kill him. If the arena floor became too slippery with blood, a fresh layer of sand would be spread over the gore so that the performance could continue.

Roman Art, Architecture, and Engineering

Like Latin literature, Roman art assumed its distinctive character during the Principate. Before this time, most artworks displayed in Roman homes were imported from the Hellenistic east. As demand for such works increased, hundreds of copies were made by Roman artisans. In many cases, these copies proved more durable than their originals: in Chapter 4, for example, we were able to examine the lost Aphrodite of Knidos, courtesy of Roman sculptors.

Encouraged by the patronage of Augustus and his successors, artists began to experiment with more distinctively Roman styles and subjects. The relief sculpture of this period is particularly notable for its delicacy and naturalism, and sculptors also became adept at portraiture. Painting, however, was the Romans' most original and most intimate art. Romans loved intense colors, and those who could afford it surrounded themselves with brilliant wall paintings and mosaics made of tiny fragments of glass and stone, which were often set into the floors of houses or which formed the centerpieces of gardens. Lavish mosaics have been found in the remains of Roman villas in all the

ROMAN AQUEDUCT IN SOUTHERN GAUL (FRANCE). Aqueducts conveyed water from mountains and lakes to the larger cities of the Roman Empire. The massive arches shown here were originally part of a 31-mile-long complex that supplied water to the city of Nemausus (Nîmes). It is now known as the Pont du Gard (Bridge of the Gardon), reflecting the use to which it was put after the aqueduct ceased to function, some eight centuries after its construction in the first century C.E. Many Roman aqueducts remained operational into the modern era: the one at Segovia, Spain was still in use at the end of the twentieth century. ■ *What does the magnitude and longevity of such projects tell us about Roman power and technology?*

territories of the empire, and similar design features indicate that many were mosaic "kits" that could be ordered from a manufacturer, who would ship out all the necessary components, along with a team of workmen to assemble them.

Augustus liked to boast that he had found Rome a city of clay and left it a city of marble. But in reality, marble was too precious to be used in common construction. Instead, marble panels or ornaments were added to the facings of buildings that were otherwise made of concrete. For the Roman had discovered how to make a mixture of quick-lime, volcanic ash, and pumice, and it was this—along with superior engineering skills—that allowed them to build massive structures like the Colosseum, which could accommodate 50,000 spectators at gladiatorial combats.

Roman engineers also excelled in the building of roads and bridges, many of which were constructed by Rome's armies as they moved into new territories. Like the Persian Royal Road of the sixth century B.C.E. or the German Autobahn of the 1930s and the interstate highways of the United States begun in the 1950s, roads have always been, first and foremost, a device for moving armies and then, secondarily, for moving goods and people. Many of these Roman roads still survive, or form the basis for modern European highways. In Britain, for example, the only major thoroughfares before the building of high-speed motorways were based on Roman roads, to which the motorways now run parallel.

THE COLOSSEUM. Constructed between 75 and 80 C.E., this was the first ampitheater in Rome purposely built to showcase gladiatorial combats. Prior to this, gladiators would often fight in improvised arenas in the Forum or in other public places. ■ *How does this fact change your perception of Roman history?*

Roman Urban Planning

Prior to Roman imperial expansion, most cities in the ancient world were not planned cities—with the exception of the new settlements established by Alexander the Great, notably Alexandria in Egypt. Rome itself was not carefully planned, but grew up over many centuries, expanding outward and up the slopes of its seven hills from the nucleus of the Forum. By the time of Augustus, it was a haphazard jumble of buildings and narrow streets. Outside of Rome, however, the efficiency of Roman government was in large part due to the uniformity of imperial urban planning. As their colonial reach expanded, Romans sought to ensure that travelers moving within their vast domain would encounter the same amenities in every major city. They also wanted to convey, through the organization of the urban landscape, the ubiquity of Roman authority and majesty.

A. Imperial Rome

B. Roman settlement in Aelia Capitolina (Jerusalem) after 135 C.E.

The inhabitants of Roman cities also enjoyed the benefits of a public water supply. By the early decades of the second century C.E., eleven aqueducts brought water into Rome from the nearby hills for drinking and bathing and for flushing a well-designed sewage system. These amenities were common in cities throughout the empire, and the homes of the wealthy even had indoor plumbing and central heating. Water was also funneled into the homes of the rich for private gardens, fountains, and pools. The emperor Nero (54–68 C.E.) built a famous Golden House with special pipes that sprinkled his guests with perfume, baths supplied with medicinal waters, and a pond "like a sea." "At last," said Nero on moving day, "I can live like a human being."

The Reach of Roman Law

Roman architecture and engineering are impressive, but the most durable and useful of this civilization's legacies was its legal system. Over the course of several centuries,

Questions for Analysis

1. Looking closely at the map of Rome (map A), how have topographical features—like the river Tiber and the seven hills—determined the shape and layout of the city? What are the major buildings and public areas? What were the functions of these spaces,

and what do they reveal about Roman society and values?

2. Compare the plan of Rome to those of Roman London (map C) and Jerusalem (map B). What features do all three have in common, and why? What features are unique to each place, and what might this reveal

about the different regions of the empire and the needs of the different cities' inhabitants?

3. Given that all Roman cities share certain features, what message(s) were Roman authorities trying to convey to inhabitants and travelers through urban planning? Why, for example, would they have insisted on rebuilding Jerusalem as a Roman city—Aelia Capitolina—after the rebellion of 135 C.E.?

C. London under the Romans, c. 200 C.E.

the primitive code of the Twelve Tables was largely replaced by a series of new laws that reflect the changing needs of Rome's diverse and ever-growing population.

The most sweeping legal changes occurred during the Principate. This was partly because the reach of Roman law had to match the reach of the empire. But the major reason for the rapid development of Roman legal thinking during these years was the fact that Augustus and his successors appointed a small number of eminent jurists to deliver opinions on the issues raised by cases under

trial in the courts. The five most prominent of these experts flourished in the second century C.E.: Gaius (only this most common of his names is known), Domitius Ulpianus (Ulpian), Modestinus, Aemelianus Papinianus (Papinian), and Paulus. Taken together, their legal opinions constitute the first philosophy of law and the foundation for all subsequent jurisprudence, a word derived from the Latin phrase meaning "legal wisdom."

As it was developed by the jurists, Roman law comprised three great branches: civil law, the law of nations, and natural law. Civil law was the law of Rome and its citizens, both written and unwritten. It included the statutes of the Senate, the decrees of the emperor, the edicts of magistrates, and ancient customs that had the force of law (like the *mos maiorum*). The law of nations was not specific to Rome but extended to all people of the world regardless of their origins and ethnicity: it is the precursor of international law. This law authorized slavery; protected the private ownership of property; and defined the mechanisms of purchase and sale, partnership, and contract. It supplemented civil law and applied especially to those inhabitants of the empire who were not citizens, as well as to foreigners.

The most interesting (and in many ways the most important) branch of Roman law was natural law, a product not of judicial practice but of legal philosophy. Roman Stoics, following in the footsteps of Cicero, posited that nature itself is rationally ordered, and that careful study will reveal the laws by which the natural world operates, including the nature of justice. They affirmed that all men are by nature equal, and that they are entitled to certain basic rights that governments have no authority to transgress. Accordingly, no person or institution has the authority to infringe on this law, repeal it, or ignore it. This law supersedes any state or ruler; a ruler who transgresses it is a tyrant.

Although the practical law applied in local Roman courts often bore little resemblance to the law of nature, the development of a concept of abstract justice as a fundamental principle was one of the noblest achievements of Roman civilization. It has given us the doctrine of human rights, even if it has not resulted in ending abuses of those rights.

CONCLUSION

The resemblances between Rome's history and that of Great Britain and the United States have often been noted. Like the British Empire, the Roman Empire was founded on conquest and overseas colonization intended to benefit both the homeland and its colonial subjects, who were seen as the beneficiaries of a "civilizing mission." Like America's, the Roman economy evolved from agrarianism to a complex system of domestic and foreign markets, problems of unemployment, gross disparities of wealth, and vulnerability to financial crisis. And like both the British and the American

After You Read This Chapter

Visit StudySpace for quizzes, additional review materials, and multi-media documents. **wwnorton.com/studyspace**

REVIEWING THE OBJECTIVES

- The founding of the Roman Republic was both a cherished myth and a series of events. What factors contributed to this unique system of government?
- The shared identity and values of the Roman people differed in many ways from those of other ancient civilizations. What were some of these major differences?
- Rome's population was divided among classes of people who often struggled with one another for power. Identify these classes and their points of contention.
- The expansion of Rome's empire had a profound impact on Roman society. Why?
- The establishment of the Principate ushered in a new era in the history of Rome. What events led to this?

empires, the Roman Empire justified itself by celebrating the peace its conquests allegedly brought to the world.

Ultimately, however, such parallels break down when we remember that Rome's civilization differed profoundly from any society of the modern world. It was not an industrialized society. Its government never pretended to be representative of all its citizens. Roman class divisions are not directly comparable to ours. The Roman economy rested on slavery to a degree unmatched in any modern state. As a result, technological advances were not encouraged, social stratification was extreme, and gender relations were profoundly unequal. Religious practice and political life were inseparable.

Nevertheless, the civilization of ancient Rome continues to structure our everyday lives in ways so profound that they often go unnoticed. Our days are mapped onto the Roman calendar. The constitution of the United States is largely modeled on that of the Republic, and Roman architecture survives in the design of our public buildings. Roman law forms the basis of most European legal codes, and American judges still cite Gaius and Ulpian. Virtually all modern sculpture is inspired by Roman sculpture, and Roman au-

thors continue to set the standards for prose composition in many Western countries. Indeed, most European languages are either derived from Latin—Romance languages are so called because they are "Roman-like"—or have borrowed Latin grammatical structures or vocabulary. As we shall see in the following chapters, the organization of the modern Roman Catholic Church can be traced back to the structure of the Roman state: even today, the pope bears the title of Rome's high priest, *pontifex maximus*.

But perhaps the most important of all Rome's contributions was its role as mediator between Europe and the civilizations of the ancient Near East and Mediterranean. Had Rome's empire not come to encompass much of Europe, there would be no such thing as the concept of Western civilization and no shared ideas and heritage to link us to those distant places and times. Although we shall pursue the history of Rome's fragmentation and witness the emergence of three different civilizations in the territories once united by its empire, we shall see that they all shared a common cultural inheritance. In this sense, the Roman Empire did not collapse. But it was transformed, and the factors driving that transformation will be the subject of Chapter 6.

PEOPLE, IDEAS, AND EVENTS IN CONTEXT

- In what ways were the early Romans influenced by their **ETRUSCAN** neighbors and by their location in central **ITALY**?
- What were the components of the **REPUBLIC'S CONSTITUTION**? What was the relationship between **ROMAN CITIZENSHIP** and the **ROMAN ARMY** in this era?
- How do the stories of **AENEAS**, **LUCRETIA**, and **CINCINNATUS** reflect core Roman values? How did those values, summarized in the phrase *MOS MAIORUM*, set the Romans apart from the other civilizations we have studied?
- Why did the Romans come into conflict with **CARTHAGE**? How did the **PUNIC WARS** and Rome's other conquests change the balance of power in the Mediterranean?
- How did **IMPERIALISM** and contact with **HELLENISTIC CULTURE** affect the core values of Roman society, its economy, and its political system? What role did **SLAVERY** play in this civilization?
- What were the major crises of the late republic, and what were the means by which ambitious men achieved power? How did **JULIUS CAESAR** emerge triumphant, and why was he assassinated?
- In what ways did the **PRINCIPATE** differ from the **REPUBLIC**? What were the new powers of the **EMPEROR**, and how did **AUGUSTUS** exemplify these?
- How did the Romans consolidate their **EMPIRE** during the *PAX ROMANA*? By what means did they spread Roman culture?

CONSEQUENCES

- Polybius believed that the Roman Republic would last forever, because it fused together aspects of monarchy, aristocracy, and polity. What were the chief factors that led to its demise in the first century B.C.E.? Could these have been avoided—and if so, how?
- In what ways does the Roman Empire share the characteristics of earlier empires, especially that of Alexander? In what ways does it differ from them?
- The Roman Empire could be said to resemble our own civilization in different ways. What features does today's United States share with the Republic? With the Principate? What lessons can we draw from this?

CONSTANTINVS MINOR IMPERATOR
HERACLII ET TIRERII IMPERATOR

AR COP VS

PRIVILEGIA

Before You Read This Chapter

The Transformation of Rome

CORE OBJECTIVES

- **IDENTIFY** the historical factors that shaped early Christianity.

- **DESCRIBE** the crises that faced Roman imperial administration during the third century.

- **TRACE** the ways that Christianity changed after it became a legal religion.

- **EXPLAIN** how the mass migrations of the fourth century affected the empire.

- **UNDERSTAND** the difference between the traditional Roman and Christian worldviews.

n the year 203 C.E., a young woman called Vivia Perpetua was brought before the Roman governor at Carthage. She was twenty-two years old, well educated, from a respectable family. At the time of her arrest she had an infant child who was still nursing. She also had two brothers (one of whom was arrested with her) and a father who doted on her. She must, one presumes, have had a husband, but he is conspicuously absent from the firsthand account of her experiences. Perpetua herself says nothing about him, though she says a great deal about her father's grief and the efforts he made to intercede on her behalf. Not only did he beg the judge for mercy, he begged his daughter to confess so that her life could be spared. He admitted to having loved her more than her brothers and blamed himself for the liberal education he had given her. Clearly, he had failed as a Roman father. For Perpetua's crime was terrible. It was not only treason against the Roman state but an act of gross impiety toward her family and her ancestors. Worse, it was punishable by a death so debasing that it was reserved for slaves, barbarian prisoners, and hardened criminals. No respectable Roman matron would allow herself to be stripped

133

naked before a holiday crowd and mauled by wild beasts in the arena of her own city. Yet that was the death Perpetua died. Perpetua was a Christian.

Early Christianity posed a challenge to the Roman Empire and its core values at almost every level. To be a Christian was to be, by definition, an enemy of Rome, because Christians refused to worship the emperor as the embodiment of Rome's gods; denying his divinity meant denying his authority. Moreover, the Christ whom Christians worshiped had himself been declared a criminal, a political insurgent, and had been duly tried and put to death by the Roman state. How, then, did a Roman emperor become a Christian just a few centuries after Christ's death—and just a century or so after Perpetua's? What changes did both Rome and Christianity have to undergo in order for this to happen?

The Rome in which Perpetua was raised stretched from central Asia to the British Isles, from the Rhine to her own province of North Africa. But as we shall see, the governance of this enormous state and its diverse population was straining the bureaucracy that had been built on the foundations of the old Republic. By the end of the third century, it was increasingly obvious that Rome's western and eastern provinces could not be controlled by a single centralized authority. In the fourth century, Rome itself ceased to be the capital and hub of the empire; it now shared prestige with the new city of Constantinople, named by the Christian emperor who founded it. At the same time, Rome's settled provinces were coming under increased pressure from groups of people who had long lived beyond its borders, but who were now moving from the periphery to the center. These peoples, too, would challenge what it meant to be Roman, and would contribute to the transformation of the Roman world.

THE CHALLENGE OF CHRISTIANITY

All faiths have histories. Like the Hebrew monotheism that undergirds Judaism or the central tenets of Zoroastrianism (Chapter 2), Christianity was (and is) the product of historical processes. It began with the teachings of Jesus, who lived and worked among his fellow Jews in rural Judea and Galilee around the year 30 c.e. It took root, however, in the Hellenistic world we studied in Chapter 4: the cosmopolitan, Greek-speaking cities around the eastern Mediterranean, which had now been absorbed into the Roman Empire.

The Career of Jesus

Yeshua bar Yosef (Joshua, son of Joseph), known to the Greeks as Jesus, is one of the few figures of the ancient world—certainly one of the few commoners—about whose life we know a great deal. The earliest writings that mention Jesus specifically are the letters of his follower, Paul of Tarsus, a Hellenized Jew and Roman citizen who was active during the 50s and 60s c.e. These are closely followed by many different narratives of Jesus's life and teachings, most written between 70 and 100 c.e. Four such accounts were eventually included in the New Testament, a collection of Christian writings appended to the Greek text of the Hebrew Bible around the third century c.e. In their original Greek, these accounts were called *evangelia* ("good messages"); we know them as *gospels*, an Old English word that means the same thing.

Jesus was born around the year 4 b.c.e., a generation or so after Augustus came to power in Rome. (He was not born precisely in the first year of the Common Era as we now reckon it. When the monk Dionysius Exiguus first calculated time "in the year of Our Lord" during the sixth century, he made some mistakes.) When Jesus was around thirty years old, he was endorsed by a Jewish preacher of moral reform, John the Baptist, whom some considered to be a prophet. Thereafter, Jesus began preaching and displaying unusual healing powers. He accumulated a number of disciples, some of whom had political ambitions.

Around the year 30 c.e., Jesus staged an entry into Jerusalem during Passover, a major religious holiday. This move was interpreted as a bid for political power by both the Roman colonial government and the high-ranking Jews of the Temple. Three gospel accounts say that Jesus also drew attention to himself by physically attacking merchants and moneychangers associated with the Temple. The city's religious leaders therefore arrested him and turned him over to the Roman governor, Pontius Pilate, for sentencing.

Pilate's main concern was to preserve peace during a volatile religious festival. He knew that his authority depended on maintaining good relations with local Jewish elites and with Herod, who ruled the province of Galilee as a client king of the empire. Because Jesus was a resident of Galilee, not a citizen of Roman Judea, Pilate sent Jesus to Herod for sentencing. But Herod sent him back to Pilate, politely indicating that dealing with Jesus fell under Roman jurisdiction. So Pilate chose to make an example of Jesus by condemning him to death by crucifixion, the standard criminal penalty for those judged guilty of sedition. It had been rumored that Jesus planned to lead a rebellion, and something similar had happened in the second century B.C.E., when the Maccabees overthrew Seleucid rule. Indeed, Roman occupation of this region had only begun in 67 B.C.E. and was still resented by many Jews. Pilate would have been mindful of all this.

That might have been the end of the story. But soon after Jesus's execution, his followers began to assert that he had risen from the dead before being taken up into Heaven. Moreover, they said that Jesus had promised to return again at the end of time. Meanwhile, he had promised spiritual support to his followers. His entire career now had to be rethought and reinterpreted. The evidence of this reinterpretation has come down to us in the letters of Paul and in the gospel narratives.

Jesus and Second Temple Judaism

In 1947, an extraordinary cache of scrolls was discovered in a cave near Qumran, on the shores of the Dead Sea. Over the course of the next decade, eleven more caves were found to house similar texts, all dating from the first century C.E. Written in Hebrew, Greek, and Aramaic at various times between 100 B.C.E and 70 C.E., the Dead Sea Scrolls have revolutionized our understanding of Judaism in the lifetime of Jesus, a period known as Second Temple Judaism. What these documents show, overwhelmingly, is the diversity of religious practice in this period, and the intense competition among groups of believers.

When Jesus was born, Roman rule was still inspiring extreme responses among Jews. Many were content to live under Rome's protection—especially the urban elite, who reaped the rewards of participation in the Roman economy. But those disadvantaged by Roman rule hoped for a messiah, a leader who would establish a new Jewish kingdom. The most extreme of these were the Zealots, whose activities eventually led to two disastrous revolts. The first, between 66 and 70 C.E., ended in the Romans' destruction of the Temple that had been rebuilt when Cyrus the Great released the Jews from captivity in Babylon (Chapter 2). The second, in 132–35 C.E., caused the destruction of Jerusalem itself and prompted the Romans to expel the entire Jewish population. Whereas the first exile of the Jews had ended after fifty years, this new diaspora would not be reversed until the controversial establishment of the modern state of Israel in 1948. For over 500 years, Jerusalem even ceased to exist; on its ruins the Romans built the colony of Aelia Capitolina (Chapter 5). It was only in 638, when the Islamic Caliphate established Arab rule in the region and restored Jerusalem as a holy site, that Jews were allowed to settle there (see Chapter 7).

This political context is essential to understanding the circumstances of Jesus's death and the many different interpretations of his words and actions. The Dead Sea Scrolls reveal that significant divisions had arisen among Jewish communities, and that Jesus would have participated in several key debates. The hereditary Temple priesthood was controlled by a group known as the Sadducees, who collaborated closely with Rome; the high priest of the Temple was even appointed by the Roman Senate. The Sadducees' chief rivals were the Pharisees, preachers of religious doctrine who were heirs to the prophetic tradition of the First Temple period. In contrast to the Sadducees, who claimed the right to control the interpretation of the Torah (the five books attributed to Moses) the Pharisees argued that Yahweh had given Moses a Torah as well as a written one, a tradition which they now claimed as their special inheritance.

The Pharisees were accordingly quite flexible in the practical application of religious law. They also believed in a life after death, a day of judgment, and the damnation or reward of individual souls. They actively sought out converts through preaching, and looked forward to the imminent arrival of the messiah whom God (through the prophets) had long promised. In all these respects they differed significantly from the Sadducees, who interpreted the Torah more strictly, who considered Judaism closed to anyone who had not been born a Jew, and who had a vested interest in maintaining the political *status quo*. Even more radical than the Pharisees was a faction known as the Essenes, a quasi-monastic group that hoped for spiritual deliverance through repentance, asceticism, and sectarian separation from their fellow Jews.

Although some scholars see Essene influence behind the career of Jesus, his contemporaries probably saw him as some sort of Pharisee. Jesus's emphasis on the ethical requirements of the law rather than its literal interpretation is reflected in many of his teachings. Jesus's apparent belief in life after death and the imminent coming of "the kingdom of God" also fits within a Pharisaic framework, as does his willingness to reach out to people beyond the Jewish community. Yet he seems to have carried these principles considerably further than did the Pharisees.

For most Jews at this time, Judaism consisted of going up to the Temple on holy days; paying the annual Temple tax; reciting the morning and evening prayers; and observing certain fundamental laws, such as circumcision (for men), ritual purity (especially for women), and prohibitions on the consumption of certain foods. Jesus de-emphasized such observances, and it may have seemed to some that he wished to abolish them. But what made him most controversial was his followers' claim that he was the messiah sent to deliver Israel from its enemies.

After Jesus's death, such claims grew more assertive, yet they never persuaded more than a small minority of Jews.

But when Jesus's followers began to preach to non-Jewish audiences, they found many willing listeners. They began to represent Jesus in terms that made sense to the Greek-speaking communities of the Hellenistic world. Jesus, his followers now proclaimed, was not merely a messiah for the Jews. He was the "anointed one" (in Greek, *Christos*), who had suffered and died for the sins of all humanity. He had risen from the dead and ascended into Heaven, and he would return to judge all the world's inhabitants at the end of time.

Christianity in the Hellenistic World

The key figure to develop this new understanding of Jesus's divinity was his younger contemporary, Paul of Tarsus (c. 10–c. 67 C.E.). Named Saul when he was born in the capital city of the Roman province of Cilicia (now south-central Turkey), he was the son of a Pharisee and staunchly sympathetic to that cause. The *Acts of the Apostles*, the continuation of Luke's gospel and a major source for Saul's early life, says that he was dedicated to stamping out the cult that had grown up around the crucified Jesus. But at some point in his mid-twenties—a few years after Jesus's death—he underwent a dramatic conversion experience, changed his name to Paul, and devoted the rest of his life to spreading the new faith to Greek-speaking, mainly non-Jewish communities.

Unlike Peter and the other early disciples, Paul had never met Jesus. Instead, he claimed to have received a direct revelation of his teachings. This led to a number of major disputes. For example, Peter and his companions believed that followers of Jesus had to be Jews or converts to Judaism. Paul declared that Jewish religious law was now irrelevant: Jesus had made a new covenant possible between God and humanity, and the old covenant between God and the Jews no longer applied. This position was vehemently opposed by the Jewish Christians of Jerusalem, a group led by Jesus's brother, James. But after a series of difficult debates that took place around 49 C.E., Paul's position triumphed. Although some early Christians would continue to obey Jewish law, most of the converts who swelled the movement were Gentiles. Paul began to call this new community of believers an *ekklesia*, the Greek word for a legislative assembly. The Latinized form of this word is translated as "church."

These earliest converts to Christianity were attracted for a variety of reasons. Some were Hellenized Jews like Paul himself. Some were non-Jews known as "God-fearers," who gathered around Greek-speaking Jewish communities. God-fearers did not follow all the precepts of Jewish law, but they admired the Jews for their loyalty to ancestral tradition and their high ethical standards. Christianity was also attractive to ordinary cosmopolitan Greeks. Some saw Jesus as living by Stoic principles or as the embodiment of Ahura-Mazda, the good god of Zoroastrianism. Others were already devotees of mystery religions, like the very old cult of the Egyptian goddess Isis or the newer worship of the warrior-god Mithras, popular among Rome's soldiers. Both of these religions also revolved around stories of sacrifice, death, and regeneration. Indeed, it was largely for the benefit of these converts that Christians began to practice elaborate initiation ceremonies such as baptism, a ritual purification common to many ancient religions and exemplified among Jews in the ministry of John the Baptist.

At the same time, there were significant differences between Christianity and these other religions. Most mystery cults stressed the rebirth of the *individual* through spiritual transformation, but Christianity emphasized the importance of community. By the middle of the second century, the Christian church at Rome even had a recognizable structure, headed by a bishop (in Greek, *episcopos* or "overseer") and lesser officeholders, including priests, deacons, confessors, and exorcists. Women were extremely prominent in these churches, not only as benefactors but as officeholders. This was unusual: in other ancient religions, women could be priests only in cults open solely to women; they never took precedence over men. Many cults denied them access entirely. The fact that Christianity drew its adherents from a broad range of social classes also distinguished it from other cults, which were accessible mainly to those with money and leisure. In time, these unusual features were distorted by Christianity's detractors, who alleged that Christians were political insurgents like the Jesus they worshiped, that they engaged in illicit acts during their "love feasts," and even that they practiced human sacrifice and cannibalism.

As both Christianity and Judaism redefined themselves during the second and third centuries, they grew further apart. Judaism was adapting to the destruction of the Temple and the mass exile of Jews from Jerusalem and surrounding provinces. By and large, the scholars who reshaped it during these difficult years ignored Christianity. It simply did not matter to them. Christians, however, could not ignore Judaism. Their religion rested on the belief that Jesus was the savior promised by God to Israel in the Hebrew Bible. The fact that so few Jews accepted this claim threatened to undermine the credibility of the Christian message.

More Christians could have responded as did Marcion, a second-century Christian scholar who declared that the entire Hebrew Bible could be ignored. Most Christians, however, refused to abandon their religion's Jewish foundation. For them, the heroes of Jewish scripture prefigured Jesus, while the major events of Hebrew history could be read, allegorically, as Christian paradigms. Christ was the

PAUL'S MISSIONARY JOURNEYS. Quite apart from its theological importance, Paul's career offers fascinating glimpses into the life of a Roman citizen from one of the empire's eastern provinces. ▪ *What were the main phases of Paul's travels in the eastern Mediterranean?* ▪ *How were his itineraries probably shaped by geography and by various modes of transport?* ▪ *What conclusions about his mission can you draw from the extent of his travels and his major destinations?*

new Adam, reversing man's original sin. Christ, like Abel, had died at the hands of a brother and his blood continued to cry out from the ground. Christ was the new Noah, saving creation from its sins. Christ was prefigured in Isaac, in Joseph, in Moses. All the words of the Hebrew prophets point to Jesus, as do the Psalms and the Proverbs.

In short, Christian theologians argued that the Christian church is the true Israel, and that when the Jews rejected Jesus, God rejected the Jews and made Christians his new chosen people. The Hebrew Bible was henceforth the Old Testament, vital to understanding Christianity but superceded by the New Testament. At the end of time, the Jews would see the error of their ways and convert. Until then, their own impiety had caused their exile from the Holy Land and would continue to bring suffering down on their descendants.

Christianity and the Roman State

So long as Christianity remained a minority religion within the Roman Empire, such attitudes had no effect on the position of Jews under Roman rule. Judaism remained a legally recognized religion and many Jews were further protected by their Roman citizenship. Because of this, Paul could not be summarily put to death (as the noncitizen Jesus had been) when brought up on charges of treason. Instead, the *Acts of the Apostles* follows his progress through the Roman judicial system, until he was finally brought to trial at Rome and executed (by beheading) under Nero. Even the Jews of the diaspora were allowed to maintain the special status they had always had under Roman rule and were not required, as other subject peoples were, to offer sacrifices to the emperor as a god.

The Prosecution of a Roman Citizen

The Acts of the Apostles *was written by the same author as Luke's gospel, and was intended as a continuation of that book. It recounts the adventures and ministry of Jesus's original disciples and also follows the career of Paul, a Hellenized Jew who became apostle to Gentiles throughout the Roman world. It offers fascinating glimpses into the workings of the Roman legal system because Paul, as a Roman citizen, had special rights under Roman law (as Jesus had not). In this passage, Paul has been accused of treason against the emperor by a group of Pharisees and has been sent to Felix, the governor of Judea. These events took place between 57 and 59 C.E.*

So the soldiers, according to their instructions, took Paul and brought him by night to Antipatris. The next day, they let the horsemen go on with him, while they returned to the barracks. When they came to Caesarea and delivered the letter to the governor, they presented Paul also before him. On reading the letter, he asked what province he belonged to, and when he learned that he was from Cilicia he said, "I will give you a hearing when your accusers arrive." Then he ordered that he be kept under guard in Herod's headquarters.

Five days later the high priest Ananias came down with some elders and an attorney, a certain Tertullus, and they reported their case against Paul to the governor. When Paul had been summoned, Tertullus began to accuse him, saying: "Your Excellency, because of you we have long enjoyed peace, and reforms have been made for this people because of your foresight. We welcome this in every way and everywhere with utmost gratitude. But, to detain you no further, I beg you to hear us briefly with your customary graciousness. We have, in fact, found this man a pestilent fellow, an agitator among all the Jews throughout the world, and a ringleader of the sect of the Nazarenes. He even tried to profane the temple, and so we seized

him. By examining him yourself you will be able to learn from him concerning everything of which we accuse him." The Jews also joined in the charge by asserting that all this was true.

When the governor motioned to him to speak, Paul replied: "I cheerfully make my defense, knowing that for many years you have been a judge over this nation. As you can find out, it is not more than twelve days since I went up to worship in Jerusalem. They did not find me disputing with anyone in the temple or stirring up a crowd either in synagogues or throughout the city. Neither can they prove to you the charge that they now bring against me. But this I admit to you, that according to the Way, which they call a sect, I worship the God of our ancestors, believing everything laid down according to the law or written in the prophets. I have hope in God—a hope that they themselves also accept—that there will be a resurrection of both the righteous and the unrighteous. Therefore I do my best always to have a clear conscience toward God and all people. . . ."

But Felix, who was rather well informed about the Way [i.e. Paul's approach to Jesus], adjourned the hearing with the comment, "When Lysias the tribune comes down, I will decide your case." Then he ordered the centurion to keep him in custody, but to let him have

some liberty and not to prevent any of his friends from taking care of his needs.

When some days Felix later came with his wife Drusilla, who was Jewish, he sent for Paul and heard him speak concerning faith in Christ Jesus. And as he discussed justice and self-control and future judgment, Felix was alarmed and said, "Go away for the present; when I have an opportunity I will summon you." At the same time he hoped that money would be given him by Paul. So he sent for him often and conversed with him. But when two years had elapsed, Felix was succeeded by Porcius Festus; and desiring to do the Jews a favor, Felix left Paul in prison.

Source: *Acts of the Apostles* 23:31–24:27, in *The New Oxford Annotated Bible*, New Revised Standard Version, eds. Bruce M. Metzger and Roland E. Murphy (New York: 1994).

Questions for Analysis

1. Based on this account, what legal procedures are in place for dealing with any Roman citizen accused of a crime?

2. What seems to be the relationship between the Jewish elite of Judea and the Roman governor? What is the role of their spokesman, Tertullus?

3. What is the nature of the accusation against Paul, and how does he defend himself?

A CHRISTIAN LOVE FEAST. This fresco, an image from the catacombs of Rome, shows Christians celebrating a feast. The inscription above reads, "I join with you in love." ▪ *How might a Roman viewer interpret this scene?* ▪ *How might this interpretation differ from that of a Christian?*

Christianity, by contrast, raised suspicions on many levels: it encouraged women and slaves to hold office and therefore to rise above their proper stations; it revolved around the worship of a criminal condemned by the Roman state; its secret meetings could be breeding grounds for illegal activities. Nevertheless, the official attitude of the Roman state toward Christians was largely one of indifference. There were not enough of them to matter, and few of them had any political power. During the first and second centuries C.E., therefore, Christians were tolerated by Roman officials, except when local magistrates chose to make an example of someone who flagrantly flouted authority.

THE CHALLENGE OF IMPERIAL EXPANSION

The emergence of Christianity coincided with the Roman Empire's most dramatic period of growth and with a growing variety of challenges. For a long time, emperors and administrators had clung to the methods of governance put in place under Augustus, which were based on a single centralized authority. The reality, however, was that Rome's empire was no longer centered on Rome, or even on Italy. It embraced ecosystems, ethnicities, economies, and political systems of vastly different kinds. More and more people could claim to be Roman citizens, and more and more people wanted a share of Rome's power. This placed enormous stress on the imperial administration, as the centrifugal forces of Rome's own making constantly pulled

resources into her far-flung provinces. The fact that the empire had no defensible borders was another problem. Hadrian had attempted to establish one after 122, by building a wall between Roman settlements in southern Britannia and the badlands of northern tribes (Chapter 5); but this act was more symbolic than defensive.

For much of the second century, these stresses were masked by the peaceful transfer of power among the aforementioned "Five Good Emperors": Nerva, Trajan, Hadrian, Antoninus Pius, and Marcus Aurelius (Chapter 5). Because none of these first four rulers had a surviving male heir, and so a custom developed whereby each adopted a young man of a good family and trained his successor in the craft of government. But this sensible practice changed with the death of Marcus Aurelius in 180 C.E.

Although he was the closest Roman equivalent to Plato's ideal of the philosopher-king, Marcus was not wise enough to recognize that his own son, Commodus, lacked the capacity to rule effectively. After his father's death, Commodus alienated the army by withdrawing from costly wars along the Danube. This move was also unpopular with the Senate, as were Commodus's violent tendencies and his scorn for the traditional norms of aristocratic conduct, including his appearance as a gladiator in the Colosseum. In 192, a conspiracy was hatched inside his own palace, where he was strangled by his wrestling coach.

The Empire of the Severan Dynasty

Because Commodus had no obvious successor, the armies stationed in various provinces of the empire raised their own candidates. Civil war ensued, as it had during the crises of the late republic and in 68 C.E., when three men had struggled for imperial power. In this case, there were five major contenders. The eventual victor was a North African general called Septimius Severus (r. 193–211 C.E.).

Under Severus and his successors, the administration of Rome's empire changed to a greater extent than it had since the time of Augustus. In many respects, these changes were long overdue. Even the "Five Good Emperors" had been somewhat insulated from the realities of colonial rule. Many of them were able commanders, but they were not professional soldiers as Severus was. Another major difference was that fact that Severus had been born and raised in the North African town of Leptis Magna (now in Libya) and identified strongly with his father's Punic ancestors. Unlike Trajan and Hadrian, who had also grown up in the provinces, Severus did not regard Rome as the center of the universe, and the time he spent in the imperial capital as a

Competing Viewpoints

The Development of an Imperial Policy toward Christians

It was not until the third century that the Roman imperial government began to initiate full-scale investigations into the activities of Christians. Instead, the official position was akin to a policy of "don't ask, don't tell." Local administrators handled only occasional cases, and they were often unsure as to whether the behavior of Christians was illegal. The following letter was sent to the Emperor Trajan by Gaius Plinius Caecilius Secundus (Pliny the Younger), the governor of Bithynia-Pontus (Asia Minor), around 112 C.E. Pliny was anxious to follow proper procedures in dealing with the new sect and wanted advice about this. His letter indicates what Romans did and didn't know about early Christian beliefs and practices.

From Pliny to Trajan

It is my regular custom, my lord, to refer to you all questions which cause me doubt, for who can better guide my hesitant steps or instruct my ignorance? I have never attended hearings concerning Christians, so I am unaware what is usually punished or investigated, and to what extent. . . . In the meantime, this is the procedure I have followed in the cases of those brought before me as Christians. I asked them whether they were Christians. If they admitted it, I asked them a second and a third time, threatening them with execution. Those who remained obdurate I ordered to be executed, for I was in no doubt . . . that their obstinacy and inflexible stubbornness should at any rate be punished. Others similarly lunatic were Roman citizens, so I registered them to be sent back to Rome.

Later in the course of the hearings, as usually happens, the charge rippled outwards, and more examples appeared. An anonymous document was published containing the names of many. Those who denied that they were or had been Christians and called upon the gods after me, and with incense and wine made obeisance to your statue . . . and who moreover cursed Christ . . . I ordered to be acquitted.

Others, who were named by an informer, stated that they were Christians and then denied it. They said that they had been, but had abandoned their

young man seems to have convinced him that little could be accomplished there.

In fact, Severus represents the degree to which the Roman Empire had succeeded in making the world Roman—succeeded so well that Rome itself was becoming irrelevant. One could be as much a Roman in Britannia or Africa as in central Italy. Severus's second wife, Julia Domna, exemplifies this trend in a different way. Descended from the Aramaic aristocracy who ruled the Roman client kingdom of Emesa (Syria), her father was the high priest of its sun-god Ba'al. She was highly educated and proved an effective governer during her husband's almost perpetual absence on campaign.

Severus largely ignored the politics of the Senate and slighted what remained of its powers. He preferred to rule through the army, which he reorganized and expanded. Two of his reforms had long-term consequences. The first

was a drastic raise in army pay, perhaps as much as 100 percent, which had the effect of securing the soldiers' absolute loyalty and diminishing their need to augment their wages through plunder. The other was a relaxation of the long-standing rule forbidding soldiers to marry while still in service. This encouraged men to put down roots in local communities, but it also made them reluctant to move when their legion was called up. On the one hand, this domesticated the army (hitherto a highly mobile fighting machine) and may have made it less effective. On the other, it gave the army a stake in the peaceful governance of Rome's colonies and further contributed to the decentralization of power.

Severus died at Eboracum (York, England) in 211, after conducting a series of successful negotiations with Pictish tribes north of Hadrian's Wall. He is reported to have said to his sons, "Get along together, you two, keep the soldiers allegiance some years previously.... They maintained, however, that all that their guilt or error involved was that they were accustomed to assemble at dawn on a fixed day, to sing a hymn antiphonally to Christ as God, and to bind themselves by an oath ... to avoid acts of theft, brigandage, and adultery.... When these rites were completed, it was their custom to depart, and then reassemble again to take food, which was, however, common and harmless. They had ceased, they said, to do this following my edict, by which in accordance with your instructions I had outlawed the existence of secret brotherhoods. So I thought it all the more necessary to ascertain the truth from two maidservants [i.e., slaves], who were called deaconnesses, even by employing torture. I found nothing other than a debased and boundless superstition....

From Trajan to Pliny

Y**ou** have followed the appropriate procedures, my Secundus.... [N]o general rule can be laid down which would establish a definite routine. Christians are not to be sought out. If brought before you and found guilty, they must be punished, but in such a way that a person who denies that he is a Christian, and demonstrates this by his action ... may obtain pardon for his repentance, even if his previous record is suspect. Documents published anonymously must play no role in any accusation, for they give the worst example, and are foreign to our age.

Source: Exerpted from *Pliny the Younger: The Complete Letters*, trans. P. G. Walsh (Oxford: 2006), pp. 278–79 (X.96–97).

Questions for Analysis

1. How does Pliny's treatment of Christians differ according to their social class? How does it differ from Felix's treatment of Paul (above)?

2. Why would Trajan insist that anonymous accusations, like those discussed by Pliny, should not be used as evidence? Why is this "foreign to our age"?

3. What do you conclude from this exchange about the relationship between religion and politics under the Roman Empire?

rich, and don't bother about anyone else." His elder son, Caracalla, didn't heed the first of these injunctions for long: by the end of the year, he had assassinated his brother. The second of his father's orders he did obey, by extending the rights of Roman citizenship to everyone in the empire, including the entire army. This was beneficial in some respects, but it may also have cheapened Roman citizenship, which was no longer a prize to be won through service or the adoption of Roman values and manners. His father's final piece of advice helped to shorten Caracalla's reign significantly, since it exacerbated his already pronounced tendency to alienate everyone who disagreed with him. He was assassinated in 217.

Caracalla's true successor was his mother's sister, Julia Maesa, who ruled through his heir and cousin, her adolescent grandson. This youth was known as Heliogabalus (or Elagabalus, r. 218–22) because of his devotion to the Syrian sun-god Ba'al. But when Heliogabalus caused controversy by attempting to replace Jupiter, Rome's patron god, with a Latinized version of this Eastern deity, Sol Invictus ("Invincible Sun"), his own grandmother engineered his assassination. Another of her grandsons, Alexander Severus (r. 222–35 C.E.), took his place. Alexander, in turn, was ruled by his mother, Julia Mamea—the third in a succession of strong women behind the Severan dynasty—who even traveled with her son on military campaigns. This eventually proved fatal. The new prominence of the army made Rome's legions engines of political advancement even more so than under the dictators of the late Republic. In 235 Alexander and his mother were murdered in Germania when the army of the region turned against them. The Pax Romana was over.

The End of the Roman Peace

From 235 to 284 C.E. there were no fewer than twenty-six "barracks emperors": military commanders who, backed by a few loyal legions, struggled with one another. This period is sometimes called the "Third-Century Crisis" and interpreted as the time when the Roman Empire was nearly destroyed. It is more accurately interpreted as a time when the consequences of Roman imperialism made themselves acutely felt. Those aspects of the empire that were strong survived. Those that had always been fragile gave way.

In particular, the disruptions of the mid-third century exposed weaknesses in economic and administrative infrastructures. Inflation, caused by the devaluation of currency under Severus, nearly drained Roman coinage of its value. Meanwhile, aspiring emperors levied exorbitant taxes on civilians in their provinces, as warfare among rival claimants and their armies destroyed crops and interrupted trade, causing food shortages. Poverty and famine led to a new form of slavery in Italy, as free artisans, local businessmen, and small farmers were forced to labor on the estates of large landholders in exchange for protection and food.

In 251, a terrible plague, probably smallpox, swept through the empire's territories and recurred in some areas for almost two decades. A similar plague had ravaged Rome a century earlier, but its effects had been mitigated by sound governance. Now, with an estimated 5,000 people dying every day in the crowded city, people sought local scapegoats. Christians were among those targeted. Beginning in the short reign of Decius (r. 249–51), all Roman citizens were required to swear a public oath affirming their loyalty to Rome, which meant worshipping Rome's gods. Large numbers of Christians were implicated when this edict was put into effect. The enlightened policies of earlier emperors were abandoned.

The Reorganized Empire of Diocletian

As it happens, the most zealous persecutor of Christians was also responsible for reining in these destructive forces. Diocletian (r. 284–305) was a cavalry officer from the Roman province of Dalmatia (modern Croatia) who had risen through the ranks. He could have been another "barracks emperor." Instead, he embraced the reality of Rome as a multicultural entity that could not be governed from one place by one person with one centralized bureaucracy. He appointed a fellow officer, Maximian, as co-emperor, putting him in charge of the western half of the empire and retaining the wealthier eastern half for himself. In 293, he delegated new authority to two junior emperors or "caesars," Galerius and Constantius. The result was a tetrarchy, a "rule of four," with each man governing a quarter of the empire, further subdivided into administrative units called *dioceses*. This system not only responded to the challenges of imperial administration, it was designed to secure a peaceful transfer of power, since the two young "caesars" were being groomed to take the place of the two senior "augusti."

Diocletian recognized that disputes over succession had been a fatal flaw of the Augustan system. Also unlike Augustus, who had cloaked the reality of power in the trappings of the Republic, Diocletian presented himself as an undisguised autocrat. His title was not *princeps* ("first man"), but *dominus* ("lord"). In fact, his style of imperial rule borrowed more from the Persian model than it did from the Roman. Gone were the days of republican simplicity and the scorn of kingly pomp. Diocletian wore a diadem and a purple gown of silk interwoven with gold, and he introduced Persian-style ceremonies at his court. Those lucky enough to gain an audience with him had to prostrate themselves, while a privileged few could kiss his robe. Too much familiarity with their soldiers had bred contempt for the "barracks emperors;" as a soldier-turned-emperor himself, Diocletian was able to avoid this mistake.

Although Diocletian retained close personal control over the army, he took steps to separate military from civilian chains of command: never again would Roman armies make and unmake emperors. To control the devastatingly high rates of inflation that were undermining the economy, Diocletian

THE TETRARCHY: DIOCLETIAN AND HIS COLLEAGUES. This grouping, carved from a valuable purple stone called porphyry, shows the two augusti, Diocletian and Maximian, embracing their younger ceasars, Galerius and Constantius. ▪ *Why do you think that these rulers are portrayed with identical facial features and military regalia?* ▪ *What message does this convey?*

stabilized the currency and attempted to fix prices and wages. He reformed the tax system. He even moved the administrative capital of the empire away from Italy to Nicomedia, in the Roman province of Bithynia (modern Turkey). Rome remained the symbolic capital of the empire, not least because the Senate continued to meet there. But Diocletian had little need for the Senate's advice. The real power lay elsewhere.

THE CONVERSION OF CHRISTIANITY

By the beginning of the fourth century, the number of Christians living within the jurisdiction of Rome was statistically insignificant, probably no more than 5 percent of the total population in the West and possibly 10 percent of the Greek-speaking East. Still, Christians were making an impact, and one of Diocletian's methods for promoting unity within the empire was to take a proactive stance against any group perceived as subversive. Those who could not show proof of their loyalty to Rome's gods were stripped of their rights as citizens. Christians who had been serving in the army or in government offices were dismissed. So were Manicheans, followers of the Persian prophet Mani (c. 216–276), whose teachings paralleled Zoroastrianism. Indeed, Christianity and Manichaeism must have seemed very similar to outsiders, and both were implicated in a full-scale purge of religious dissidents in 303. This was the Great Persecution, a time when many became martyrs—a Greek word meaning "witnesses"—to their faith.

Christianity and Neoplatonism

Ironically, the very crises that prompted Diocletian's Great Persecution were contributing to a growing interest in Christianity. Its message of social justice and equality before God was attractive to those suffering from the breakdown of political, economic, and social structures. It also appealed to followers of a new and influential philosophical system called Neoplatonism ("New Platonism"), which drew upon the more mystical aspects of Plato's thought. Its founder was Plotinus (204–270 C.E.), a Hellenistic philosopher from Egypt.

Plotinus taught that everything has its source in a single supreme being. The material world is part of this creation, but it is merely the residue of the divine, from which all spirituality has been drained. Human beings are thus composed of matter (bodies) and emanations of the divine (souls). This means that the individual soul is separated from its divine source by the fact of its embodiment.

The highest goal of life is therefore to attain spiritual reunion with God through acts of self-denial that will help to liberate the soul from its earthly bondage. Asceticism (from the Greek word meaning "exercise" or "training") was therefore a major focus: Plotinus believed that the body could be tamed by fasting and other forms of self-denial, and thus made a more fitting vessel for the soul.

Neoplatonism became so popular in Rome that it almost supplanted Stoicism. Neoplatonism also struck a blow at traditional Roman precepts, including the worship of ancestors and the devotion to the empire's gods. It was thus a natural ally of Christianity, and many important Christian theologians would be influenced by it, while many educated Romans found their way to Christianity because of it. This was not, however, the path by which Christianity's first imperial convert reached it.

Constantine's Vision

In 305 Diocletian built a palace near his hometown of Split and retired there to raise cabbages—the first time a Roman ruler had voluntarily removed himself from power since Sulla had resigned his dictatorship, nearly four hundred years earlier (Chapter 5). Diocletian obliged his fellow augustus Maximian to retire at the same time, and the two caesars Galerius and Constantius moved up the ladder of succession. But the transfer of power was not as orderly as Diocletian had intended. One of the candidates to fill the now vacant post of ceasar was Constantius's son, Constantine, who was being trained at Galerius's court. But when he was mysteriously passed over, Constantine left Nicomedia and joined his father in Gaul. From there, father and son went to Britannia and campaigned on the northern borders until 306, when Constantius died and named Constantine as his successor. This infuriated Galerius, but with Constantine in control of a large army he was forced to concede.

Meanwhile, war broke out among several other claimants to imperial authority, reducing Diocletian's tetrarchy to chaos. Constantine remained aloof from this struggle, waged mostly in Italy, and concentrated on securing his quarter of the empire. Beginning around 310, he also began to promote himself as a devotee of the sun-god Sol Invictus, whose cult had been revived and was associated not only with the Roman gods of light and war, Apollo and Mars, but also with Mithras, the cult popular with soldiers. It was increasingly popular in Rome as well, where the feast long dedicated to the sky-god Saturn, the Saturnalia, was now being celebrated as the rebirth of the sun after the winter solstice, on December 25.

From the worship of the "Invincible Sun" to the worship of Christ was, at least for Constantine, a small step (see *Interpreting Visual Evidence* on page 145). In 312, Constantine decided to march on Italy, which was now in the hands of a man called Maxentius, who had declared himself emperor and was trying to build up a coalition of supporters. Among them was the Christian community of Rome. It may have been this that gave Constantine the idea of currying favor in the same way, or it may have been divine inspiration that led him to emblazon Christian symbols on his banners and on the shields of his soldiers the night before a major battle north of Rome, at the Milvian Bridge over the Tiber. According to later legend, Constantine had seen a vision of two intertwined letters inscribed on the sky, the first two letters in the name of Christ, and was told that "In this sign, you will conquer." He did.

In gratitude for his victory, Constantine showered benefits on the Christian clergy of Rome and patronized the construction of churches throughout the empire. He also forced Licinius, the augustus of the East, to join him in promoting religious tolerance when they met at Milan in 313. Their Edict of Milan guaranteed freedom of worship to all Rome's citizens, Christian and non-Christian. But it soon became apparent that Christianity was the pathway for anyone with political ambitions. Almost overnight, Christians ceased to be members of an illegal cult and became affiliates of a prestigious religion. The entire basis of Christianity's appeal had changed.

From Illegal Sect to Imperial Institution

In his letters, Paul of Tarsus had addressed small Christian assemblies that he called churches. But it is doubtful that Paul could have imagined a day when representatives of an official Church could meet openly, or a time when his letters to separate churches would be gathered together in a single book.

Early Christianity had grown organically; it had not been designed as a religious system. It had no absolute teachings, apart from the words of Jesus reported in the gospels—which do not always agree on those teachings. And not all Christian communities had access to the same scriptures. Some churches had a few of Paul's letters, some had none. Some had bishops, priests, deacons, and other officeholders; some had only a handful of believers. Some counted women as their leaders; others disapproved of women in authority. Some had come under the influence of Neoplatonism or Manichaeism; others considered Neoplatonism and Manichaeism to be perversions.

In every respect, then, the Christianity that emerged after Constantine's conversion had to reinvent itself. Members of this new official Church needed to agree on a shared set of beliefs. They needed a shared set of scriptures. They needed a chain of command. All of these fundamentals had to be hammered out in a painful process that never quite managed to forge a common understanding. For the varieties of Christianity had been too separate for too long, and were products of the same diversity that made the Roman Empire hard to govern. Indeed,

DIOCLETIAN'S DIVISION OF THE EMPIRE, c. 304 C.E. ▪ *What areas did each of the four divisions of the empire cover?* ▪ *What seems to be the strategy behind the location of the four major capitals, both within their respective quarters and in relation to one another?* ▪ *What is the status of Rome itself, according to this map?*

Interpreting Visual Evidence

The Power of the Invincible Sun

Roman emperors often linked their power with those of Rome's traditional gods, and they were also worshipped as gods in their own right. Look carefully at the following images and consider the visual language of power that came to be associated with Sol Invictus, "the Invincible Sun," and eventually with Jesus Christ.

Questions for Analysis

1. How did Constantine use the iconography of Sol Invictus (image A)? What messages did this convey?

2. How might Constantine's use of this imagery have been interpreted by Christians? How might it have been interpreted by followers of Rome's other religions? Do you think it was designed to be ambiguous?

3. The mosaic shown at right was found beneath St. Peter's Basilica (image B). Is it likely that this is a representation of Jesus as Sol Invictus? How would you explain the later association of this pagan deity with the Christian God?

A. This gold medallion was issued by Constantine in 313, a year after his victory at the Battle of the Milvian Bridge. The legend calls him "Invincible Constantine."

B. This mosaic comes from a necropolis (cemetery) found beneath St. Peter's Basilica in Rome. Its precise dating is in dispute, but it was made sometime between the mid-third and mid-fourth century.

---

the degree to which Christians of the fourth century were able to agree on so many things is remarkable, given these challenges.

The Hierarchy of the Church

When it came to organization, Rome's imperial administration provided practical models. Because the empire's basic unit of governance was the city, the city became the basic unit of ecclesiastical administration, too. Each major city now had a bishop who oversaw all the churches and rural areas of his diocese. Bishops of the empire's largest cities were called *metropolitans*, and those who ruled the most

prestigious Christian communities were called *patriarchs*. These patriarchal cities also jockeyed for preeminence: among the main contenders were Rome, Alexandria, and Constantinople, the new city founded by Constantine on the Hellespont between Europe and Asia. Which of these Roman cities should be the capital of the Roman Church?

The patriarch of Rome's claim rested on several foundations. Rome had long been venerated as the place where both Peter and Paul were martyred. And according to one of the gospels (Matthew 16:18–19), Jesus had designated Peter as his representative on earth. Peter's successors, the subsequent bishops of Rome, thus claimed to exercise the same powers. But so far as Rome's eastern bishops were concerned, the patriarch of Constantinople should exercise control over the entire Church. In time, this difference of opinion would lead to a very real division within Christianity, one that has never been resolved.

Orthodoxy, Heresy, and Imperial Authority

While followers of Jesus had disagreed about his teachings since the time of his death, these disagreements were of little political consequence so long as Christianity remained an illegal movement. Under Constantine, however, doctrinal disputes had the potential to ignite riots and to undermine the credibility of the emperor. It was imperative, therefore, that these disputes be resolved.

The most divisive theological issue concerned the nature of God. Jesus had taught his followers that he was the Son of God, and that after his death he would leave behind him a comforting Spirit that would also be an emanation of God. Accordingly, many Christians believed that God encompassed a Trinity of equal persons: Father, Son, and Holy Spirit. But some Christians, influenced by Neoplatonism, rejected the idea that Jesus could be equal with God. Instead, they maintained that Jesus was part of God's creation and therefore not equal to God. This latter school of thought was called Arianism, after the Christian teacher Arius. (It should not be confused with Aryanism, a modern racial concept.) After protracted struggles, Arianism was condemned as a heresy, a word that comes from the Greek verb meaning "to choose for oneself" and which became the Church's term for false beliefs punished with damnation.

This new emphasis on orthodoxy (Greek for "correct teaching") was another major consequence of Christianity's conversion. Before Christianity became a legal religion, doctrinal disputes could only be addressed informally, by small local councils that had no power to enforce their decisions. In the fourth century, however, doctrinal disputes had real political consequences. At the same time, Christian intellectuals had to demonstrate that their beliefs could withstand intense scrutiny, and that they were in fact superior to pagan philosophy.

As a result of these trends, the Roman state became increasingly enmeshed in the governance of the Church. In 325 C.E., in recognition of this, Constantine summoned Christian representatives to the first ecumenical ("worldwide") meeting of the Christian community, the Council of Nicea, where Arianism was condemned and discrepancies over the canon of the Christian Bible were largely resolved. His successors carried this intervention much further, claiming to preside over Church councils as Christ's representatives on earth.

Essentially, these imperial interventions were an extension of Augustan policies, which had made the emperor *pontifex maximus*, Rome's high priest. It began to look as though this tradition would continue, and that secular and spritual authority would be combined in the person of the emperor.

New Attitudes toward Women and the Body

Even though they had long been deacons and may even have performed priestly duties, women were now firmly and completely excluded from any position of power within the Church. This was an enormous change. Jesus had included many women among his close followers, and one of the early gospels (now rejected from the biblical canon) was ascribed to Mary Magdalene. Paul had relied on women to organize and preside over churches, and had declared in one letter (Galatians 3:28) that there should be no distinctions of gender, rank, or ethnicity among Christians. Women like Perpetua were prominent among the martyrs, and were often regarded as prophets.

What acounts for this drastic reversal? Three factors can be clearly identified. When Christianity was absorbed into the staunch patriarchy of Rome, it could no longer promote the authority of women. The Church now replicated the structures of governance that had been the province of men since the founding of the Republic. It thus had the capacity to censor writings that represented women as the companions of Jesus and as founders of the religion based on his teachings. These efforts were so successful that it was not until the Dead Sea Scrolls were discovered that the gospel attributed to Mary Magdalene (among other writings) was known to exist.

The second factor was the growing identification of Christianity with Roman cults that emphasized masculinity, particularly the worship of Sol Invictus and the soldier-god Mithras. This was a deliberate strategy. It is easier to convert people to a new religion if that religion embraces elements of other religions. In common with these two cults, Christianity emphasized the heroic suffering and death of a male god and his eventual victory over death itself. Christ was increasingly identified with Sol Invictus and his birthday came to be celebrated on December 25, which marked the passing of the winter solstice.

The third factor contributing to women's exclusion from power was the new emphasis on asceticism. As we noted above, Neoplatonism taught that the goal of life was to liberate the soul from the tyranny of bodily desires. None of this was emphasized in the teachings of Christ. Quite the contrary: Christ celebrated the body, and had encouraged feasting, touching, bathing, and marriage. His followers insisted that he had been bodily resurrected, and that the bodies of all the faithful would be resurrected, too. Although early Christians had to be willing to sacrifice their lives for their faith, if need be, they were not required to renounce pleasures.

After Christianity became legal, however, there were few opportunities to "bear witness" through martyrdom. Instead, some Christians began to practice asceticism as an alternative path to sanctity. This meant renunciation of the flesh, especially sex and eating: activities both associated with women, who were in charge of any household's food supply and who were (obviously) sexual partners. A new spiritual movement called monasticism also took hold, providing an alternative lifestyle for men who wanted to reject the world entirely; the word for this movement and its followers comes from the Greek word *monos*, "alone." Early monks lived as hermits and practiced extraordinary feats of self-denial and self-abasement. Some penned themselves in small cages, while others hung heavy weights around their necks. A monk named Simeon "the Stylite" lived on top of a high pillar for thirty-seven years while crowds gathered below to marvel.

SAINT SIMEON THE STYLITE. This gold plaque dating from the sixth century depicts the exertions of the ascetic saint who defied the devil (shown as a huge snake) by abusing his own body. Admirers wishing to speak to the saint could climb the ladder shown on the left. ▪ *What do you make of the relationship between the luxurious medium of this image (gold) and the austere message it conveys?*

This extreme denial of the body was a departure not only from previous Christian practices but from the practices of nearly all civilizations up to this point. All ancient religions celebrated sexuality as a delight, as well as a necessity. Moreover, marriage was so important a marker of social respectability in the ancient world that unmarried men were objects of deep suspicion. Furthermore, Romans had regarded citizens' bodies as being at the service of the state: men as soldiers and fathers, women as mothers and wives. Now, however, some Christians were asserting that to serve God fully meant no longer serving the state—or posterity—by bearing children.

This was a revolutionary shift. Celibacy for both men and women began to be preached as the highest spiritual standard. Marriage remained acceptable for average people, the laity, but was often represented as a second-best option. Moreover, because pseudo-scientific theories stemming back to Aristotle posited that women were inherently more lustful than men, the denigration of sexuality had a disproportionately negative effect on attitudes toward women.

Christians and Pagans

The urban focus of Christianity is reflected in the Latin word referring to a non-Christian: *paganus*, meaning someone who lives in the countryside. The implication is that only a rustic would cling to the old Roman religion and so spoil his chances of advancement. For as Christians came to occupy positions of power, men with political ambitions were increasingly forced to convert—or at least to conform.

Constantine had retained both pagan and Christian officials in his court, but his successors were less inclined to tolerate competing faiths. (The sole exception was Julian "the Apostate" [r. 360–63], Constantine's nephew, who attempted to revive traditional Roman piety.) By 391, the emperor Theodosius (r. 379–95) had prohibited pagan worship. Within three generations, Christianity had gone from being a persecuted faith to a persecuting religion. Theodosius even removed the altar to the goddess Victory from the Senate house, prompting pagan loyalists to prophecy the end of the empire. Fifteen years later, Rome fell to a barbarian army.

SHIFTING CENTERS AND MOVING FRONTIERS

In 324, Constantine broke ground for the capital city he named after himself. It was built on the site of a settlement called Byzantium, chosen for its strategic location at the mouth of the Black Sea and the crossroads between Europe and Asia. It would remain the political and economic center of the Roman Empire until 1453, when it was conquered by the Ottoman Turks and became the capital of a new empire (see Chapters 11 and 12).

East and West

The founding of Constantinople epitomizes the shift in Rome's center of gravity from west to east. It also signalled Constantine's intention to abandon the institution of the tetrarchy. Instead, imperial succession became hereditary—the very form of dynastic monarchy that Romans had rejected 800 years earlier. Even more ominously, Constantine divided the empire among his three sons. Civil war ensued, made more bitter because each son represented a different faction within the Church. As a result, the empire became ever more fragmented. The last ruler who could claim to govern a united Rome was the same Theodosius who outlawed its venerable religion. Then he, too, divided the empire between his sons.

As we have seen, there had always been linguistic and cultural differences between the Greek- and Latin-speaking peoples under Roman rule. Now these differences were heightened. The Greek East was becoming more prosperous and more central to imperial policy; the Latin West was becoming poorer and more peripheral. Rome itself, which had been demoted to provincial status under Diocletian, now lost even its symbolic position: the Italian city of Ravenna on the Adriatic coast became the new stopping-place for emperors and ambassadors traveling to the administrative centers of Milan and Trier. Thereafter, only two of Constantine's successors ever visited Rome, and none of them lived there.

Internal and External Pressures

The shifting center of the empire and the widening gap between East and West were not the only fault lines emerging in this period. There were also secessionist movements among residents of Britannia, Gaul, Hispania, and Germania. The residents of Egypt were particularly affected by high levels of taxation, which targeted their rich agricultural lands. Meanwhile, North Africans and other citizens living in the empire's interior regions were increasingly ignored by authorities. Italians especially resented their status as provincial subjects of Constantinople. The fourth-century empire was slowly dissolving into its constituent parts.

It was also coming under renewed pressure from its borders. Since the third century, the growing power of a new Persian dynasty, the Sassanids, had shifted Roman military weight to the eastern frontier, reducing the number of troops stationed elsewhere. Partly as a result of this, the western empire suffered a devastating series of raids along the porous frontier of Germania. Relations between Romans and their non-Roman neighbors had been generally peaceful. But now, starting in the early fifth century, a new wave of settlers moved into the empire's oldest provinces, permanently altering their histories and cultures.

From the Periphery to the Center

The tribes that lived along the empire's northern frontiers were barbarians in the pure sense of that (Greek) term: they did not speak either of the empire's civilized languages and they did not live in cities. But in no sense were they a savage people. They were settled agriculturalists and sophisticated metalworkers who had enjoyed trading relationships with the Roman world for centuries. In some frontier areas, entire tribes had become Roman *foederati*: allied troops who reinforced Roman garrisons or even took their places when legions were withdrawn. By the end of the fourth century, many of these tribes had even adopted the form of Christianity preached by disciples of Arius. Although this made them heretics from the perspective of the institutional Church, it also tied them more closely to Roman civilization.

What altered this relatively peaceful coexistence? Our study of many previous civilizations has prepared us to answer this question: the arrival of new peoples, and the subsequent struggle for land and resources. During the mid-fourth century, a group of nomadic herdsmen known as the Huns began to migrate westward from central Asia, into the region north and east of the Black Sea. Around 370, their arrival forced a number of other groups, notably the Goths, to migrate south and west—and in a hurry. Within a few years, they had reached the Roman frontier along the Danube River. Although the Goths had been clients of the Roman state for several centuries, they were now refugees, and too numerous and too desperate to repel by force. The Romans therefore permitted them to cross the Danube and settle within the empire. In return for food and other supplies, they were to guard the region against other migrant groups.

Local officials, however, failed to uphold their end of the bargain. Instead, they forced the starving Goths to sell themselves and their children into slavery in return for food. So in 378, the Goths revolted and the Roman army sent to suppress them was defeated at Adrianople. Peace was restored by accommodating the Goths' demands for goods and farmland and by enrolling them in the Roman army under their own military leaders.

A Senator Defends the Traditional Religion of Rome

In 382 the emperor Theodosius ordered the removal of the ancient altar dedicated to the goddess of Victory from the Senate chamber in Rome, as part of his efforts to make Christianity the dominant religion in the empire. This controversial move sparked heated debate and strong protests from Rome's senatorial elites. The following statement of their case was made by Quintus Aurelius Symmachus (c. 345–402), at that time prefect of the city of Rome.

o what is it more suitable that we defend the institutions of our ancestors, and the rights and destiny of our country . . . than to the glory of these times, which is all the greater when you understand that you may not do anything contrary to the custom of your ancestors? We demand then the restoration of that condition of religious affairs which was so long advantageous to the state. . . .

For who is so friendly with the barbarians as not to require an Altar of Victory? . . . But even if the avoidance of such an omen were not sufficient, it would at least have been seemly to abstain from injuring the ornaments of the Senate House. Allow us, we beseech you, as old men to leave to posterity what we received as boys. The love of custom is great. . . . Where shall we swear to obey your laws and commands? By what religious sanction shall the false mind be terrified, so as not to lie in bearing witness? All things are indeed filled with God, and no place is safe for the perjured, but to be urged in the very presence of religious forms has great power in producing a fear of sinning. That altar preserves the concord of all, that altar appeals to the good faith of each, and nothing gives more authority to our decrees than that the whole of our order issues every decree as it were under the sanction of an oath. . . .

Let us now suppose that Rome is present and addresses you in these words: "Excellent princes, fathers of your country, respect my years to which pious rites have brought me. Let me use the ancestral ceremonies, for I do not repent of them. Let me live after my own fashion, for I am free. This worship subdued the world to my laws, these sacred rites repelled Hannibal from the walls, and the Senones [Gauls] from the capitol. Have I been reserved for this, that in my old age I should be blamed? I will consider what it is thought should be set in order, but tardy and discreditable is the reformation of old age."

We ask, then, for peace for the gods of our fathers and of our country. It is just that all worship should be considered as one. We look on the same stars, the sky is common, the same world surrounds us. What difference does it make by what pains each seeks the truth? We cannot attain to so great a secret by one road; but this discussion is rather for persons at ease, we offer now prayers, not conflict.

Source: Excerpted from *A Select Library of the Nicene and Post-Nicene Fathers*, 2nd Series, Vol. X, (New York: 1896), pp. 411–14.

Questions for Analysis

1. How does Symmachus's defense exemplify the traditional values of the Roman Republic?

2. How does Symmachus justify the coexistence of Christianity and Rome's state religion? How would a Christian refute his position?

3. Less than a decade after the altar's removal, Theodosius outlawed all religions but Christianity. Based on your reading of this letter, how would that edict have affected Romans like Symmachus?

But when Theodosius divided the empire between his two young sons, their military advisors constantly undermined one another. This provided an opening for Alaric, a young leader of the Goths. Targeting the wealthier East, he led his army into Greece, looting or capturing many ancient cities, including Athens. In a desperate attempt to halt these incursions, Alaric was offered a Roman military command and encouraged to move into Italy. Meanwhile, the Huns had arrived in the region corresponding to modern-day Hungary, forcing several other peoples westward toward the Rhine. In 406, a people known as the Vandals invaded Gaul but were repulsed by Alaric and his Goths.

THE MIGRATIONS OF ROME'S FRONTIER PEOPLES. ▪ *What do the routes followed by these different peoples suggest about their identities and motives?* ▪ *Why did so many converge on Rome, even though the city was no longer the capital of the Roman Empire?* ▪ *Why did the Romans refer to these peoples as "barbarians"?*

Alaric seems to have wanted to win a permanent place for himself in the imperial hierarchy. Yet he did not understand how to use violence as a means toward that end, as many aspiring emperors had before him. In 410, after a protracted siege, his army even sacked the city of Rome. By now, though, Rome had little to offer in the way of spoils. So many of the Goths moved on, eventually settling in southern Gaul and Hispania, where they established what came to be known as the Visigothic ("West Gothic") kingdom. Others, known as the Ostrogoths ("East Goths") remained in Italy. The Vandals, meanwhile, crossed the Strait of Gibraltar to settle in North Africa. Other tribes, including the Franks and the Burgundians, followed the Vandals across the Rhine into Gaul and established kingdoms of their own.

A generation later, the Huns—whose migrations had set all of these gears in motion—themselves invaded Roman territory under the leadership of their warlord, Attila. Britannia, meanwhile, had been abandoned when its remaining legions were hastily withdrawn in 410. Eventually, its mixed population of Romans and Celts were overcome by invaders from northwestern Germania and Scandinavia: Angles, Saxons, and Jutes. These conquering tribes were so efficient that they dominated all but the western-most and northern portions of the island within a few generations. Many Celts accordingly settled in the regions where Celtic languages are still spoken today, including Wales and Scotland. The rest of Britain became Angle-land: England (see Chapter 7).

The last Roman emperor in the West was an ineffectual usurper derisively known as Romulus Augustulus ("Little Augustus"), who was deposed in 476 by a mixed band of barbarians and disgruntled Romans. Viewed from the perspective of Constantinople, this event was decisive; the only way Rome's imperial agenda could be carried forward in the West was through a strong barbarian ruler. Luckily, the emperor Zeno (r. 474–91) knew just the man: Theodoric, the son of an Ostrogothic king who had been sent to Constantinople as a hostage and raised in the civilized surroundings of the imperial court. After a decade of fierce fighting, Theodoric and his imperially equipped Gothic army managed to establish an Ostrogothic kingdom based in Ravenna, which he ruled (with imperial support from Constantinople) until his death in 526.

The Impact of the Fifth-Century Migrations

The migrations of the fifth century exposed the fragility of the empire's northern boundaries and penetrated to its core western provinces. Yet the groups that moved through these territories were never more than war-bands. So why couldn't long-established imperial cities sustain themselves?

By the beginning of the fifth century, many Roman legions in the West had been withdrawn to protect the richer East. Those that remained tended to be integrated into local populations, making it difficult to move troops even in an emergency. And even if the citizens of Rome's western provinces had been able to maintain a fighting force on the frontier, there was little reason to think that such expenditure was necessary. Many of their barbarian neighbors were so Romanized that cultural differences are difficult to trace.

THEODORIC THE OSTROGOTH. This coin shows the king in Roman dress but with the long hair characteristic of a barbarian chieftain. The inscription reads *Rex Theodericvs pivs princis,* "King Theodoric, pious prince." ▪ *How does this image compare to that of Constantine (see page 145)?*

In the East, by contrast, a thriving economy made it easier to equip and maintain a strong fighting force. Moreover, potential invaders could be bought off or bribed to direct their attention elsewhere—as Alaric had been. For all these reasons, the eastern empire prospered while the western empire floundered.

After the fifth-century migrations, these differences were exacerbated. Ten years after the Goths sacked Rome, the area was capable of producing only 15 percent of the revenues it had generated in 407. And as barbarian newcomers began to set up their own kingdoms in the West, these areas ceased to pay any taxes at all to imperial authorities.

The consequences of these structural changes were far-reaching. Although regional and local systems of exchange continued after 500, long-distance trade in bulk goods could be sustained only in the East. As markets disappeared in the West, skilled artisans had to find other ways to make a living, or had to emigrate. Standards of living there declined, and so did the overall population. It is likely that the population of western Europe did not return to its fourth-century levels for a thousand years, until just before the Black Death (see Chapter 10).

Other aspects of Roman life in the West changed, too, but more gradually. Roman bureaucracies often survived, although the proceeds from taxes now went to the new barbarian rulers or Christian bishops. Roman agricultural patterns, too, continued in most areas, while Roman aristocrats continued to dominate civic life and Roman cities continued to dominate their surrounding regions. Nor did the influx of new peoples bring an end to Roman culture or to the influence of Roman values. As King Theodoric was fond of remarking: "An able Goth wishes to be like a Roman; but only a poor Roman would want to be like a Goth."

THE SHAPING OF A NEW WORLDVIEW

Throughout these upheavals, Christian intellectuals were formulating a new outlook on the world that would remain dominant until the sixteenth century. As the empire succumbed to attack, it seemed clearer than ever that a new age was beginning. Christ had promised to come again at the end of time, when all human souls would be judged. How, then, should Christians prepare for that imminent event?

The men who forged answers to this question were contemporaries who knew and influenced one another, though they did not always agree. They are now regarded as saints and "fathers" of the Church: Jerome (c. 340–420), who came from the northeastern edge of Italy; Ambrose (c. 340–397), who grew up in Trier (Germany) and was eventually named bishop of Milan; and Augustine (354–430), born and raised in North Africa, where he became a bishop in later life.

Jerome: Translating the Christian Message

Jerome's signal contribution was his translation of the Bible from Hebrew and Greek into Latin. Known as the Vulgate or "common" version, Jerome's translation is vigorous, colloquial, and clear; its powerful prose and poetry would influence Latin authors for a thousand years. Jerome was also an influential commentator on the Bible's interpretation, encouraging readings that emphasized a passage's symbolic or allegorical significance, as well as its literal or historical meaning.

Jerome was among the first to argue that pagan learning could and should be adapted to Christian aims. Yet Jerome himself never succeeded in subordinating his love of classical authors to his love for God. He liked to tell a story about a dream he'd experienced, in which he arrived at the gates of Heaven and was asked by God if he were a Christian. When he replied that he was, God retorted, "You're not a Christian; you're a Ciceronian." Perhaps in an effort to compensate for this, Jerome became a rigorous ascetic and promoter of monasticism. He also held a narrow view of women's roles that exercised a strong influence on later Christian teachers.

Ambrose and the Authority of the Church

While Jerome was primarily a scholar, Ambrose was a man of the world who helped to define the relationship between the sacred authority of the Church and the secular authority of rulers. As patriarch of the administrative capital at Milan, for example, he fearlessly rebuked the pious emperor Theodosius for massacring innocent civilians in one of his periodic purges of pagan communities: until he did penance for his sins, Ambrose refused to admit him into his church. On matters of faith, Ambrose declared, "The emperor is within the Church, not above the Church."

Like Jerome, Ambrose was an admirer of Cicero—but because of Cicero's Stoicism, not his prose. He wrote an ethics handbook, *On the Duties of Ministers*, that drew heavily on Cicero's treatise *On Duties*, written nearly four centuries earlier for the senatorial elite of the Roman Republic. Unlike Cicero, however, Ambrose argued that the motive and goal of human conduct should be reverence for God, not social or political advancement. Ambrose also argued that God assists all Christians by sharing with them the power of divine grace, but extends more grace to some Christians than to others. This view would be refined and amplified by his disciple, Augustine.

The Salvation of Saint Augustine

Apart from Jesus, Augustine is often considered the greatest of all Christianity's founders. His theology is essential to the doctrine of the medieval Church and thus to modern Catholicism, and it also had a profound effect on Martin Luther and the development of Protestant Christianities (see Chapter 13). Many Christian philosophers describe themselves as neo-Augustinians.

Augustine's Christianity was the result of a long process of self-discovery which he described in a remarkable book: the *Confessions*, a series of autobiographical reflections addressed to God. For Augustine was not, as Jerome and Ambrose were, a confident Christian from the cradle. His father was a pagan, and although his mother was a Christian he scorned her influence and refused baptism. Full of ambition, he left North Africa for Italy when he was still a young man, winning early fame as a teacher and charismatic orator. All the while, he gravitated from one philosophical system to another without finding intellectual or spiritual satisfaction. He regarded Christianity as a religion for fools, and only his increasing doubts and the appeal of Ambrose's teachings drove him to enquire further. After a spiritual epiph-

any, Augustine decided at the age of thirty-three to embrace Christianity. His skills as a preacher and commentator led to his rapid advancement in the Church hierarchy, and he returned to North Africa as the bishop of Hippo Regis in 395.

Although he led an extremely active life—when he died in 430, he was defending Hippo against the Vandals—Augustine found time to write more than a hundred profound and powerful treatises analyzing the problems of Christian belief. All of these grapple with a basic question: if humanity is the creation of an omnipotent God whose nature is entirely good, why are human beings so profoundly wicked? He adduced himself as a supreme example. In the *Confessions*, he remembers that he and a few other boys once stole some pears from a neighbor's garden, simply for the sake of doing something bad. He also recounted his many sexual adventures as a young man, when rather than asking God's help in suppressing his desires he had prayed, "O God, give me chastity—but not right now!" In short, he argued that the human inclination toward evil is innate. But how, if we are the creatures of a good God?

Augustine traced the origin of evil back to the Garden of Eden, where God had given Adam and Eve the freedom to follow either his will or their own. All the evils that plague the world are thus the result of the human propensity to place our own desires ahead of God's. This fact alone would justify God's condemnation of all mankind. But because God is merciful, he chose instead to save some human beings through the sacrifice of his son, Jesus.

Why only some? Because human beings are inherently sinful, Augustine reasoned, they cannot achieve salvation on their own; they need to be led to accept Jesus by an act of God's grace. (Hence the power of Augustine's own transformative experience, which led him to embrace Christianity *against his own will*, but in accordance with God's.) By granting grace to some and not to others, God predestines a portion of the human race to salvation and sentences the rest to be damned. If this seems unfair, Augustine would answer that strict fairness would condemn everyone to Hell. Moreover, he would say that the basis for God's choice is a mystery far beyond the realm of human comprehension.

Defending the City of God

Augustine's audience consisted of converted Christians and intelligent skeptics, like he himself had been. And after the sack of Rome in 410, he knew that some Romans blamed Christianity for it. In response, Augustine wrote one of his most famous works, *On the City of God*, a new interpretation of human history. He argued that mankind has always been divided into two opposing societies: those who live for the world and those who seek eternal life. The former belong to the City of Man and their rewards are the riches, fame, and power they may win on earth—all of which are tainted by sin. Only those predestined to salvation, members of the City of God, will be saved on Judgment Day.

Augustine knew that many biblical texts are obscure and that a certain amount of education is needed to understand them. In consequence, he approved of some Christians acquiring a classical education, so long as they directed their learning toward its proper end. Along with Jerome, Augustine thus formulated the rationale for Christianity's preservation of the pagan past.

CLASSICAL LEARNING AND THE CHRISTIAN LIFE

Jerome, Ambrose, and Augustine were members of the first generation to grow up in a world where Christianity was legal, even normal. For three centuries there had been no such thing as a Roman Christian: this was a contradiction in terms. Now, many Romans *were* Christians. How could these identities be reconciled? As we have seen, none of these influential teachers wanted to discard the heritage of the past. But for all of them it posed serious challenges. Since the time of Socrates, philosophy had been characterized by its capacity to absorb and blend many competing ideas. Christian intellectuals wanted to be regarded as philosophers, but they also wanted to replace the doctrines of pagan philosophy with the doctrine of Christ. To do this, they needed to make classical learning applicable to a Christian way of life.

Preserving and Recycling the Classics

Reinterpreting pagan culture for a Christian audience involved careful selection, something made easier by the fact that a gradual winnowing of Greek texts had already occurred in Alexandria centuries before and had continued in Rome. Those Roman authors whose works were most immediately useful to Christians, like Cicero and Virgil, enjoyed continued celebrity. So did the major classics of Latin poetry, as well as the histories that recorded the errors of Rome's pagan past. But texts that could not be readily adapted were subjected to careful editing. One of the men who undertook this task was Anicius Manlius Severinus Boethius (*boh-EE-thee-us*, c. 480–524), an aristocrat attached to the court of Theodoric. His goal was to preserve the best aspects of ancient learning in a series of handbooks

and anthologies that packaged and explained classical texts in ways appropriate for Christian readers.

Boethius devoted special attention to logic, translating several of Aristotle's treatises from Greek into Latin. Because Roman philosophers had never been much interested in logic, Boethius thus forged a crucial link between classical Greek thought and the new intellectual culture of Christianity. This is also evident in *The Consolation of Philosophy*, which he wrote in prison after Theodoric condemned him to death for treason. (The justice of the charge is unclear.) In this treatise, Boethius concludes that happiness is not found in earthly rewards such as riches or fame but in the "highest good," which is God. Yet he comes to this realization not through any reference to Christian revelation but through a series of imaginary conversations with "Lady Philosophy," the embodiment of wisdom. For the next millennium, Boethius's *Consolation* was one of the most read and imitated books in the West: the ultimate example of classical philosophy's absorption into the Christian worldview.

Monastic Education

The vital work of preserving selected classics was increasingly done by monks, whose way of life had undergone some significant changes during the fourth century. Leaders of

CASSIODORUS. This frontispiece from a Bible depicts Cassiodorus as a copyist and keeper of books. Monasteries were instrumental in changing the form of the book from the ancient scroll to the modern codex. Because their parchment pages were heavy, codices were customarily stored in cupboards, lying flat, as we see them here.

the monastic movement recognized that few men were capable of ascetic feats, and some disapproved of such showmanship. Rather, they advocated a more moderate approach and emphasized the benefits of communal life. In the East, the most important figure in this new monasticism was Basil of Caesarea (c. 330–379). Basil's guidelines prohibited monks from engaging in prolonged fasts or extreme self-discipline. Instead, he encouraged useful work and silent meditation.

In the West, the most influential proponent of the monastic movement was a contemporary of Boethius, Benedict of Nursia (c. 480–c. 547), the son of a Roman nobleman. Benedict founded a monastery at Monte Cassino, southeast of Rome, where he urged his followers to adopt "a simple rule for beginners." Benedict's *Rule* is notable for its brevity and practicality. It established a carefully defined cycle of daily prayers, lessons, and communal worship. It laid down guidelines for what monks should eat and how the work of the monastery should be performed. Physical labor was encouraged, but there was also time for private study and contemplation. In all such matters, Benedict left much to the discretion of the monastery's abbot (from the Syriac word *abba*, "father").

Cassiodorus and the Classical Canon

Benedict believed that monks must study the Bible in order to participate fully in a life of worship. This meant they had to be educated along the lines prescribed by Augustine.

And because many monks entered religious life as children, the monastery would need to provide schooling. Through this somewhat roundabout path, classical learning entered the monastic curriculum.

The man largely responsible for this was Flavius Magnus Aurelius Cassiodorus Senator (c. 490–c. 583), a younger contemporary of Benedict. Like Boethius, Cassiodorus was attached to Theodoric's court, and was for many years the secretary in charge of the king's correspondence. He also wrote a *History of the Goths*, which depicted Theodoric's people as part of Rome's history. After Theodoric's death, Cassiodorus founded an important monastery at Vivarium in southern Italy. There he composed his most influential work, the *Institutes*. The *Institutes* is essentially a syllabus, a list of readings arranged so that a monk could begin with simpler, straightfoward works of pagan literature before moving on to more difficult works and finally to the demanding study of theology. Cassiodorus thereby defined a classical canon that formed the basis of Christian education in the West for a thousand years.

In order to ensure that monks had access to the necessary readings, Cassiodorus encouraged the copying of books. Monasteries thus became engines for the collection, preservation, and transmission of knowledge. Nearly all the Greek and Latin texts on which we rely for our study of Western civilizations survive because they were copied in monasteries. Monks also developed an important new information technology: the codex. For millennia, the book

After You Read This Chapter

REVIEWING THE OBJECTIVES

- A number of historical factors shaped the way that Jesus's teachings were received. Describe the most important of these.
- The expansion of Rome and the strain on its central government posed significant challenges in the third century. How did Roman emperors respond?
- Christianity's acceptance as a legal religion changed it in profound ways. Why was this?
- In the fourth and fifth centuries, a new wave of migrations penetrated to the very heart of the empire. What made this possible?
- The differences between traditional Roman and Christian cultures were gradually reconciled through the efforts of Christian intellectuals. Why was this considered necessary?

had been a scroll, a clumsy format that made searching for a particular passage difficult and confined the reader to one passage at a time. By contrast, the codex facilitates indexing (from the Latin word for "finger"), because a reader can flip back and forth among various pages and keep a finger in one place while looking at another. Codices also store information more safely and efficiently, because they compress many hundreds of pages within protective bindings. They are less wasteful, too, because texts can be copied on both sides of a page. They even make finding a given book easier, since titles can be written on the codex's spine. It's arguable, in fact, that the invention of the codex was more revolutionary than the invention of printing a thousand years later. Your copy of *Western Civilizations* is a codex—unless you are reading an e-book!

CONCLUSION

Since the English historian Edward Gibbon published the first volume of *The Decline and Fall of the Roman Empire* in 1776—a year when Britain's own empire suffered a setback—more has been written about "the fall of Rome" than the passing of any other civilization. Gibbon himself blamed Christianity, depicting it as a debilitating disease that sapped the empire's strength. Others have accused the barbarian peoples whose movements put pressure on Rome's frontiers. But even in the time of Augustus, Roman moralists had declared that Rome was already in decline. Indeed, any self-respecting republican would say that Rome fell when Augustus came to power.

More recent scholarship has stressed that this period should really be understood as one of transformation. No civilization is static and unchanging; civilizations, like human beings, are living organisms. Moreover, any evidence of Rome's decline can also be read as evidence of its adaptability. The imperial policies of Septimius Severus and Diocletian responded to the realities of Rome's size and diversity. The settlement of frontier peoples in Rome's western provinces gave rise to hybrid polities that found new uses for Roman buildings, political offices, and laws. Through Christianity, the language, adminstrative structures, and culture of ancient Rome were preserved and extended. The flexibility of the Roman political system made this possible, because it was inclusive to a degree no modern empire has ever matched.

This transformation changed what it meant to be Roman, to the extent that historians now call this period "late antiquity" to distinguish it from the classical world that preceded it. By the seventh century, indeed, so much had changed that the contours of three distinctive civilizations can be discerned, each one exhibiting different aspects of Roman influence and crystallizing around different regions of the former empire. We will explore each of these civilizations in Chapter 7.

PEOPLE, IDEAS, AND EVENTS IN CONTEXT

- What were the main differences between **JESUS** and other Jewish leaders of his day?
- How did **PAUL OF TARSUS** reach out to peoples of the **HELLENISTIC WORLD**? How did his teachings influence the development of early Christianity?
- In what ways did **DIOCLETIAN**'s division of the empire and his institution of the **TETRARCHY** respond to longstanding problems?
- How and why was Christianity changed under **CONSTANTINE**? What effects did this have on attitudes toward women and their role in the Church?
- How did the relocation of the imperial capital to **CONSTANTINOPLE** contribute to the growing divide between the **GREEK EAST** and the **LATIN WEST**? How did the mass migrations of frontier peoples further transform the West?
- What were the key contributions of **JEROME**, **AMBROSE**, and **AUGUSTINE** to the development of a specifically Christian outlook toward the end of the fourth century?
- How did **BOETHIUS**, **BENEDICT**, and **CASSIODORUS** reshape classical culture in the fifth century?

CONSEQUENCES

- In your opinion, which phenomenon had a more profound impact on Rome: the overextension of imperial power or the mass migration of peoples from Rome's frontier? Why?
- Few historians would now agree with the judgment of Edward Gibbon, who posited that Christianity destroyed the Roman Empire. But to what extent did Christianity alter the traditional values and infrastructure of the Roman state? Were these alterations inevitable?

Before You Read This Chapter

Rome's Three Heirs, 500–950

Around the year 600, Anglo-Saxon tribes on the island of Britain were approached by missionaries sent from Rome. These Latin-speaking Christians faced an enormous challenge: they had to find a way to translate the central ideas of their faith into languages and concepts that made sense in a new cultural context. They also needed to look for ways to meld Roman practices with Anglo-Saxon ones, building churches on sacred sites and gradually turning the worship of pagan gods into the rituals of Christianity. An account of these negotiations comes down to us in *The History of the English Church and People*, written by a monk named Bede (c. 672–735) several generations later. Bede describes how Celtic and Anglo-Saxon peoples came to adopt Latin as a language of learning and worship. At the same time, he shows how Roman ideals were changed and adapted to meet new needs.

This is but one of the ways in which the legacy of Rome was transmitted and transformed during the pivotal period known as the Middle Ages. This term is an unfortunate one. In fact, "The Middle Ages" is a modern invention: in the seventeenth century, intellectuals began to argue that an intermediate, "medieval period" (*medium ævum*) separated their own "modern age" from the empire of ancient Rome, which many European states were trying to emulate by establishing empires of their own. But in fact, it is arguable that the period between 500 and 1500 was the beginning of that "modern age." In this era, the foundations of modern political institutions were laid. In this era, the relationships among Judaism, Christianity, and Islam were first articulated. In this era, three new civilizations became heirs of the Western civilizations formerly encompassed by the Roman Empire: the New Rome of Byzantium, the new empire of Islam, and the western European territories that looked increasingly to the Roman Church for leadership. Each civilization preserved and modified different aspects of their shared inheritance, and our world is still being shaped by the interactions among them.

JUSTINIAN'S IMPERIAL AMBITIONS

As we observed in Chapter 6, the eastern and western portions of Rome's empire were divided along linguistic, cultural, and economic lines. By the end of the fourth cen-

tury, this division also became political. The Ostrogothic conquest of Italy under Theodoric (r. 493–526)—which was supported by the imperial government—briefly placed Constantinople in a position to influence affairs in the old Roman heartland. But in 535 this Ostrogothic kingdom was overthrown in an attempt reunify the Roman Empire.

The man responsible for this was Justinian (r. 527–65), the most ambitious emperor since Constantine. Although his efforts to reconstruct the empire ultimately failed, they had a lasting influence on the entire Mediterranean world.

The Codification of Roman Law

Justinian's most positive and lasting accomplishment was his codification of Roman law. This was a necessary project, and long overdue: since the time of the third-century jurists (Chapter 5), the number of statutes and legal decisions had multiplied, while social and political conditions had changed so radically that many legal principles could no longer be applied. To carry out this work, Justinian appointed a team of lawyers under the supervision of a jurist called Tribonian. Within two years, this commission published the Code, a systematic compilation of imperial statutes which was later supplemented by the Novels (*Novellae*, "new laws").The commission also completed the Digest, a summary of the writings of Rome's great legal authorities. Its final product was the Institutes, a textbook of legal principles. Together, these four volumes constitute the *Corpus Juris Civilis*, or the "body of civil law." Eventually it would influence the legal systems of many European nations.

The *Corpus* also had a profound impact on political philosophy. Starting from the maxim that "what pleases the prince has the force of law," it granted unlimited powers to the emperor and was therefore adopted by early modern rulers as a foundation for absolutism (see Chapter 15). But the *Corpus* also provided support for constitutional forms of government, because it maintained that a sovereign's powers are delegated to him by the people, and that what is mandated by the people can also be taken away by them. Equally important is the fundamental principle that the state is a corporate body, not the extension of an

THE MEDITERRANEAN WORLD UNDER JUSTINIAN, 527–65. Compare this map with the one on page 144. (Here, the green shading represents those regions controlled by Justinian.) ▪ *What was the geographical extent of Justinian's empire?* ▪ *Which areas of the former Roman Empire did Justinian not attempt to reconquer?* ▪ *What may have been the strategy behind this decision?*

individual's private property. The modern conception of the state as a public entity derives from the legal maxims of the *Corpus*.

Justinian's Attempted Reconquest

Justinian's initial efforts to reunite the Roman Empire seemed successful. In 533, his general Belisarius conquered the Vandal kingdom of northwest Africa, thereby facilitating campaigns in Ostrogothic Italy and Visigothic Spain. By 536, he appeared poised to occupy Rome's old homeland. But these early victories were illusory. When Justinian died in 565, the human and financial costs of these campaigns had drastically strained imperial resources. The Roman army in Italy was overextended, and Justinian's need to levy soldiers had led to oppressive taxes which undermined support for his imperial project.

Justinian's campaigns also distracted attention from dangers closer to Constantinople: in particular, the developing strength of Persia under the Sassanid dynasty. His successors were eventually forced to withdraw their troops from Italy and North Africa. This left both regions dangerously exposed to further invasions and still failed to protect the eastern frontier.

Justinian's Impact on the West

Justinian's wars proved more devastating to Italy than the previous incursions of barbarian peoples. Around Rome, the vital supply lines of the aqueducts were cut and the elaborate system of conduits, drainage ditches, and reservoirs was destroyed. In 568 a new people, the Lombards, took advantage of the chaos to conquer the northern third of the peninsula. Thereafter, Italy would be divided between Lombard territories in the north and imperial territories in the southeast, with Rome and its region precariously sandwiched between them. The controlling forces within these territories would change over time, but this tripartite division remained the essential political configuration of Italy until the nineteenth century. It divides Italian politics to this day.

Meanwhile Constantinople's control over North Africa lasted only a few generations longer. Weakened by religious conflict and heavy taxation, this area fell easily to invading Muslims in the seventh century, along with Egypt and the rest of Roman Africa (see below). Meanwhile, tensions between Arian Visigoths and their Latin subjects in Hispania continued even after after the Visigothic king officially submitted to the Roman church in 587. This mutual hostility would subsist until the Visigothic kingdom, too, was largely absorbed by Islam. By the end of the eighth century, Christian rulers controlled only the northernmost parts of the Iberian peninsula, and Al-Andalus (Muslim Spain) became part of a new Islamic world.

THE ROMAN EMPIRE OF BYZANTIUM

With the failure of Justinian's imperial project, the history of the Eastern Roman Empire can be said to enter a new phase. Indeed, many historians regard it as a new empire,

JUSTINIAN AND THEODORA. These sixth-century mosaics from the Church of San Vitale, in the imperial capital of Ravenna, show the emperor and empress processing toward the main altar of the church carrying the holy vessels used for the consecration of bread and wine. ▪ *What do these images convey about the sacred and secular powers of both figures?*

the Byzantine Empire, from the name of the ancient port where Constantinople was situated. Byzantium thus became *one* of Rome's three heirs, not the sole heir of Roman authority, as Justinian had claimed. But according to its inhabitants, it never ceased to be Rome, and they were never anything but Romans.

As a result of Justinian's policies, however, this Rome was struggling for survival. By 610, the Greek-speaking dynasty that began with Heraclius (r. 610–41) was unable to extend its influence farther west than the Adriatic. Meanwhile, the Persians had conquered almost all of the empire's eastern and southern territories in Syria and Palestine. They had even plundered Jerusalem. With an enormous effort, Heraclius rallied his remaining military powers and routed the Persians, recapturing Jerusalem in 627.

But these gains were short-lived. Arab armies, inspired by the new religion of Islam, soon occupied the newly reconquered Byzantine territories and claimed Jerusalem as a holy site for Muslims. They also absorbed the entire Persian Empire and rapidly made their way westward to North Africa. They then took to the sea, and in 677 attempted a naval conquest of Constantinople. Repulsed, they made another attempt in 717. This new threat was countered by the emperor Leo III (r. 717–41). Deploying keen strategy and a secret incendiary mixture now known as "Greek fire" (of course, the Byzantines called it "Roman fire"), Leo's forces were able to defeat the Arabs. Over the next few decades, moreover, Byzantium reconquered most of Asia Minor, which remained the imperial heartland for the next 300 years.

Sources of Stability

In many ways, the internal politics of the Byzantine Empire were as tumultuous as the history of its changing neighborhood. Because all power was concentrated in the imperial court at Constantinople, opposition usually took the form of intrigue, treason, and violence. Indeed, Byzantine politics is now so famous for its cloak-and-dagger complexity that the word *byzantine* denotes devious or elaborate systems of courtship and bureaucracy. Yet many able rulers in Byzantium wielded their powers very effectively, while a centralized government continued to function even in times of upheaval. No polity in western Europe had anything like it until a much later period.

Strong, self-perpetuating political institutions thus constituted a major source of stability in Byzantium and offer an explanation for the extraordinary longevity of the empire's core provinces: nearly a thousand years. The imperial bureaucracy in Constantinople regulated prices and wages, maintained systems of licensing, and controlled exports and trade. Its highly educated officials also supervised many aspects of social and cultural life, overseeing schools, the organization of the Orthodox Church, and the observance of religious rites and holidays. Established bureaucracies also regulated the army and navy, the courts, and the diplomatic service.

Another source of stability was Byzantium's well-managed economy, which was far superior to that of western Europe. Commerce and cities continued to flourish as they had done in late antiquity. Constantinople became a central emporium for Far Eastern luxury goods and western raw materials. The empire also nurtured and protected its own industries, most notably the manufacture and weaving of silk; and it was renowned for its stable gold and silver coinage, which undergirded the entire economy. Nor was Constantinople the only great urban center of Byzantium. The Hellenistic capital Antioch and the bustling cities of Thessalonica and Trebizond each dwarfed any western European city. Constantinople may have had a population of close to a million when Paris was still a village and Rome may have had only a few thousand people living among the ruins.

Orthodoxy, Iconoclasm, and Identity

Law, strong governance, and a thriving economy: viewed from our perspective, these seem to be the basis of Byzantine civilization. Yet the inhabitants of Byzantium seem to have cared more about religion. In old Rome, the *mos maiorum* had undergirded Roman pride and superiority (Chapter 5); in New Rome, Orthodox Christianity occupied the same fundamental place. Intense preoccupation with questions of religious doctrine could thus be a catalyst for political and social dissension, but it was also essential to Byzantine identity and endowed the empire's inhabitants with a sense of shared purpose.

The most contentious issue resulted in a violent clash over the meaning and use of religious images, known as the Iconoclast ("image-breaking") Controversy. Christians had long been accustomed to expressing their devotion to Christ and the saints through the making and veneration of images. At the same time, however, there was an awareness that any representation of a holy person came close to being a form of idolatry, something that Jewish tradition strongly condemned. Although Christians insisted that images were only *aids* to worship, not *objects* of worship, the line between the two was always fine.

In Byzantium, where the veneration of icons was an especially potent part of daily devotion, any suggestion that such images should be suppressed or destroyed was bound to be divisive. Yet iconoclasts argued that honoring images was blasphemous, and that Christ's divinity could not be represented artistically. Traditionalists, known as iconodules, responded that images themselves were never objects of worship; rather, icons were windows through which a glimpse of Heaven might be granted to human beings.

The Iconoclast movement was initiated by the same Emperor Leo III who had saved Constantinople from invasion by Muslims, and it is even possible that the iconoclasm so central to Islamic belief played an influential role in his thinking: in other words, it may have been his attempt to answer one of Islam's greatest criticisms of Christianity. The emperor may also have intended to reassert control over the Orthodox Church and thus to combat the growing strength of monasteries, which were major producers of

DEVOTIONAL IMAGE—OR DANGEROUS IDOL? This icon of *Christos Pantokrator* ("Christ the Almighty") was painted in the sixth century and is preserved at the Orthodox monastery of St. Catherine on Mount Sinai (Egypt). ▪ *According to the proponents of iconoclasm, why would such an image be considered blasphemous?*

icons, as well as books. So when the monasteries rallied to the cause of images, Leo's successors took this opportunity to confiscate much of their wealth.

The Iconoclast Controversy was resolved toward the end of the eighth century, and in favor of the iconodules, the promoters of religious imagery. But it had some long-lasting effects. One was that much of the art produced or preserved in Byzantium was destroyed by imperial edict. A second consequence was the opening of another religious and political breach between the Greek East and the Latin West. Prior to Emperor Leo's iconoclastic initiatives, the patriarch of Rome—known familiarly as "papa" in Latin slang—had often been a close ally of Byzantium's rulers. But iconoclasm called into question not only the veneration of images but the cult of the saints, and by extension the claims of papal primacy that were based on the Roman patriarch's claim to be Saint Peter's successor.

The ultimate defeat of iconoclasm also crystallized some characteristics of Byzantine identity. One was a renewed emphasis on the Orthodox faith of the empire as the key to political unity and military success. This emphasis on tradition helped orthodoxy gain new adherents in the ninth and tenth centuries, but it also reinforced the hegemony of Constantinople's own Christian traditions, marginalizing those of Syria and Armenia. Fear of heresy tended to inhibit freedom of thought, too. Although the Byzantine emperors eventually founded a university in Constantinople, its students and faculty were never permitted to express dissenting opinions or to engage in any significant degree of intellectual speculation—in marked contrast to the freewheeling intellectual atmosphere cultivated by the universities of western Europe (see Chapters 8 and 9).

Tradition and Innovation

Although religion was central to the identity of Romans in Byzantium, so was their direct link with the Hellenistic past. Byzantine schools based their instruction on classical Greek literature to a degree that might seem surprising given the more tentative attitude toward classical learning in western Europe (Chapter 6). Educated people around the Byzantine court who quoted only a single line of Homer could expect their listeners to recognize the entire passage from which it came. In the English-speaking world, only the King James Bible has ever achieved the same degree of cultural saturation.

Byzantine scholars also studied the philosophy of Plato and the historical prose of Thucydides intensively. By contrast, Aristotle's works were less well known. Meanwhile,

Competing Viewpoints

Debating the Power of Icons

> The Iconoclast Controversy of the eighth century divided Byzantine society and was a factor in the growing division between the Latin Church of Rome and the Eastern Orthodox Church. The excerpts below are representative of the two main arguments voiced at the time. The first is from a treatise by John of Damascus (c. 675–749), a Christian in the service of the Muslim Umayyad caliphs. The second is an official report issuing from the synod convened by the emperor Constantine V (r. 741–75) in 754. Constantine was carrying forward the iconoclastic policies of his father, Leo III.

John of Damascus on Holy Images

Now adversaries say: God's commands to Moses the law-giver were, "Thou shalt adore the Lord thy God, and thou shalt worship him alone, and thou shalt not make to thyself a graven thing that is in heaven above, or in the earth beneath." . . .

These injunctions were given to the Jews on account of their proneness to idolatry. Now we, on the contrary, are no longer in leading strings. . . . We have passed the stage of infancy, and reached the perfection of manhood . . . and we know what may be imaged and what may not. . . . An image is a likeness of the original with a certain difference, for it is not an exact reproduction of the original. Thus, the Son is the living, substantial, unchangeable Image of the invisible God, bearing in Himself the whole Father, being in all things equal to Him, differing only in being begotten by the Father. . . . That which is divine is immutable; there is no change in Him, nor shadow of change. . . . God has noted and settled all that He would do, the unchanging future events before they came to pass. In the same way, a man who wished to build a house, would first make and think out a plan. Again, visible things are images of invisible and intangible things, on which they throw a faint light. Holy Scripture clothes in figure God and the angels. . . . If, therefore, Holy Scripture, providing for our need, ever putting before us what is intangible, clothes it in flesh, does it not make an image of what is thus invested with our nature, and brought to the level of our desires, yet invisible? . . . For the invisible things of God since the creation of the world are made visible through images. We see images in creation which remind us faintly of God, as when, for instance, we speak of the holy and adorable Trinity, imaged by the sun, or light, or burning rays, or by a running fountain, or a full river, or by the mind, speech, or the spirit within us, or by a rose tree, or a sprouting flower, or a sweet fragrance. . . .

Source: Excerpted from *St. John Damascene on Holy Images*, trans. Mary H. Allies (London: 1898), pp. 6–12.

the living philosophical traditions of the pagan past were deemed dangerous to orthodox belief. Even Justinian, who had presided over the codification of ancient Roman (and thus pagan) law, registered his distrust of philosophy by shutting down the Athenian Academy founded by Plato. Eventually, the emperor Alexius Comnenus (d. 1118) would ban the teaching of Aristotelian logic. The traditions of Greek scientific inquiry and the advances of Hellenistic science were also neglected. Tradition was more highly prized than originality, as was preservation over innovation. The benefit of this, for posterity, is that Byzantium rescued Greek and Hellenistic writings for later ages. The vast majority of ancient Greek texts known today survive because they were copied by Byzantine scribes.

Also in contrast to the West, as we shall see, Byzantine classicism and learning were the products of an educational system that extended to the laity and was open to women as well as to men. This commitment to the formal education of women was especially unusual. Although most girls from aristocratic or prosperous families were educated at home by private tutors, they nevertheless mingled freely with their male counterparts at court or on social occasions, and many

Canons of the Synod of 754

I t is the unanimous doctrine of all the holy Fathers and of the six Ecumenical Synods, that no one may imagine any kind of separation or mingling in opposition to the unsearchable, unspeakable, and incomprehensible union of the two natures in the one hypostasis or person. What avails, then, the folly of the painter, who from sinful love of gain depicts that which should not be depicted—that is, with his polluted hands he tries to fashion that which should only be believed in the heart and confessed with the mouth? He makes an image and calls it Christ. The name *Christ* signifies *God and man.* Consequently it is an image of God and man, and consequently he has in his foolish mind, in his representation of the created flesh, depicted the Godhead which cannot be represented, and thus mingled what should not be mingled. Thus he is guilty of a double blasphemy—the one in making an image of the Godhead, and the other by mingling the Godhead and manhood . . .

like the Monophysites, or he represents the body of Christ as not made divine and separate and as a person apart, like the Nestorians.

The only admissible figure of the humanity of Christ, however, is bread and wine in the holy Supper. This and no other form, this and no other type, has he chosen to represent his incarnation. Bread he ordered to be brought, but not a representation of the human form, so that idolatry might not arise. And as the body of Christ is made divine, so also this figure of the body of Christ, the bread, is made divine by the descent of the Holy Spirit; it becomes the divine body of Christ by the mediation of the priest who, separating the oblation from that which is common, sanctifies it. . . .

Source: Excerpted from *The Seven Ecumenical Councils of the Undivided Church*, trans. H. R. Percival, in *Nicene and Post-Nicene Fathers,* 2d Series, ed. P. Schaff and H. Wace (repr. Grand Rapids, MI: 1955), pp. 543–44.

Questions for Analysis

1. To what other phenomena does John of Damascus compare the making of images? How do these comparisons help him to make his argument in favor of them?

2. To what phenomena do the theologians of the synod compare the making of images? Why do they declare the bread and wine of the Eucharist to be the only legitimate representations of Christ?

3. What is the significance of the fact that John of Damascus did not fall under the jurisdiction of the emperor of Byzantium, but that of the Muslim Umayyad caliph? What conclusions can you draw about the relative religious freedoms in these two realms?

learned women were praised for being able to discourse on Plato or Pythagoras. There were also female physicians in the Byzantine Empire, another extraordinary departure both from ancient tradition and from the practices of western Europe until the latter part of the nineteenth century.

Byzantine achievements in the realms of architecture and art are also remarkable. The finest example of both may be the church of Hagia Sophia (Greek for "Holy Wisdom") in Constantinople, constructed at enormous cost under the patronage of Justinian. Its purpose was not to express pride in human accomplishment, but rather to

symbolize the mysteries of the holy knowledge imparted by Christ to the soul of the believer. For this reason, the architects paid little attention to the external appearance of the building. The interior, however, was decorated with richly colored mosaics, gold leaf, colored marble columns, and bits of tinted glass set on edge to refract rays of sunlight like sparkling gems. Light appeared to be generated from within. The magnificent dome over its central square represented an unprecedented engineering feat, and was upheld by four great arches springing from pillars at the four corners of the square. Its effect is heightened by the many windows placed around the dome's rim, which convey the impression that it floats in midair.

Many aspects of Byzantine arts and learning exerted strong influence on the craftsmen and scholars of western Europe through New Rome's continued economic and cultural contact with portions of Italy. The basilica of San Marco in Venice (c. 1063) reflects this influence, as do medieval mosaics in such cities as Ravenna and Palermo. Greek-speaking monasteries in southeastern Italy also maintained close ties with their counterparts in the eastern empire, and many were allowed to practice the rituals of the Orthodox Church. But much of the heritage of Western civilizations that was cultivated in Byzantium was largely inaccessible elsewhere in Europe, as the knowledge of Greek became increasingly rare.

MUHAMMAD AND THE TEACHINGS OF ISLAM

In many ways, the civilization that formed around the religion of Islam mirrors the Roman Empire in its global reach and longevity. Islam (Arabic for "submission") also resembles the early Republic of Rome in that it demands from its followers not just adherence to common forms of worship but also to certain social and cultural norms. But whereas the Roman Empire undergirded Christianity and helped to advance it, the Islamic faith was itself the engine of imperial expansion. Indeed, Islam is unique among the major religions in the way that it *created* empires rather than relying on them.

The Revelations of Muhammad

Islam had its beginnings in Arabia, a desert land considered so forbidding that neither the Romans nor the Persians sought to conquer it. Arabian society was tribal, and did not revolve around urban settlements. But like the Hittites in the second millennium B.C.E. (Chapter 2), the Arabs' mobility, ingenuity, and pioneering spirit made them excellent explorers and long-distance traders. In the second half of the sixth century, they quickly established themselves as guides, couriers, and guardians of transit routes between Africa and Asia.

As part of this process, towns began to emerge. The most prominent of these was Mecca, a sacred site that lay at the crossroads of major caravan routes. Mecca was home to the Kaaba, a shrine housing the Black Stone worshiped by

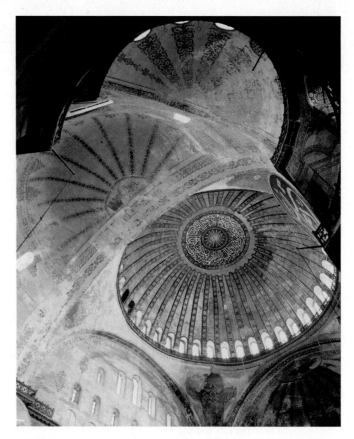

INTERIOR OF HAGIA SOPHIA. The revolutionary structure of the church, shown here, made it appear as if the enormous dome floated on light and air.

many Arabian tribes. The tribe that controlled this shrine, the Quraish (*kur-AYSH*), thus came to control the economic and spiritual life of the whole region.

Muhammad, the founder of Islam, was a member of this tribe. He was born in Mecca about 570. Until middle age he probably lived as a prosperous trader, little different from his fellow townsmen. At this time, the Arabs worshipped many gods. Yet like the ancient Hebrews they also acknowledged one god as more powerful. For the Hebrews, God was Yahweh; for the Arabs, Allah. But whereas the Hebrews' embrace of monotheism was a long and gradual process, Muhammad's dedication to Allah alone was a sudden spiritual epiphany experienced around 610.

At first, Muhammad was not very successful in gaining converts to this new faith, perhaps because tribal leaders feared that his teachings would diminish the importance of the Kaaba, and thus of Mecca. So Muhammad and a few loyal friends moved north to the settlement of Yathrib in 622. This migration—in Arabic, the Hijrah (*HIJ-ruh*)—marks the beginning of Muhammad's wider influence. Just as Christians date all events according to the birth of Jesus, so Muslims begin their dating system with the Hijrah.

Analyzing Primary Sources

A Sura from the Qu'ran

The Qu'ran preserves the teachings of Muhammad in a series of suras, *or chapters. Composed in verse forms that draw on much older traditions of Arabic poetry, they are meant to be sung or chanted. Indeed, the word* Qu'ran *means "recitations," referring both to Muhammad's method of revealing divine truths and to the Muslim practice of memorizing and repeating portions of this sacred scripture.*

Sura 81: The Overturning

In the Name of God the Compassionate
the Caring

When the sun is overturned
When the stars fall away
When the mountains are moved
When the ten-month pregnant
    camels are abandoned
When the beasts of the wild
    are herded together   5
When the seas are boiled over
When the souls are coupled
When the girl-child buried alive
is asked what she did to deserve
    murder
When the pages are folded out   10
When the sky is flayed open
When Jahím [the Day of Reckoning]
    is set ablaze

When the garden is brought near
Then a soul will know what it
    has prepared
I swear by the stars that slide,   15
stars streaming, stars that sweep
    along the sky
By the night as it slips away
By the morning when the fragrant
    air breathes
This is the word of a messenger
    ennobled,
empowered, ordained before
    the lord of the throne,   20
holding sway there, keeping trust
Your friend [Muhammad] has
    not gone mad
He saw him on the horizon clear
He does not hoard for himself
    the unseen
This is not the word of a satan
    struck with stones   25

Where are you going?
This is a reminder to all beings
For those who wish to walk straight
Your only will is the will of God lord
    of all beings

Source: From *Approaching the Qu'ran: The Early Revelations*, trans. Michael Sells (Ashland, OR: 1999), pp. 48–50.

Questions for Analysis

1. What impressions of Arab culture emerge from this *sura*? What does the litany of unlikely or mystical events reveal about the values of Muhammad's contemporaries?

2. How does Muhammad speak of himself and his role in society?

Muhammad changed the name of Yathrib to Medina ("City of the Prophet") and established himself as its ruler. Yet he did not abandon his desire to exercise political and prophetic authority among his own people, the Quraish. Accordingly, he and his followers began raiding Quraish caravans traveling beyond Mecca. The Quraish could not continue to operate an extensive commercial enterprise in the face of such threats, and by 630 they submitted themselves to Muhammad's authority. Muhammad, for his part, ensured that the Kaaba was established as Islam's holy shrine, a status it maintains today. And because Mecca had long been a pilgrimage site and gathering place for tribes throughout Arabia, many people were exposed to

Muhammad's teachings. At the time of his death in 632, Islam had become an established faith.

Muhammad and the Qu'ran

As its name indicates, the faith of Islam calls for absolute submission to Allah, the same God worshiped by Jews and Christians. The Muslim saying "there is no god but Allah" is more accurately translated as "there is no divinity but God." For Muslims, the history and prophecies of the Hebrews are therefore important components of their religion, as are the teachings of Jesus, who is venerated as a great prophet. But they consider Muhammad to be the last and greatest prophet, and the closest to God.

Muhammad's teachings are preserved in the sacred scripture of Islam, the Qu'ran (*kuhr-AHN*), an Arabic word meaning "recitations." This is because Muhammad recited his revelations to his listeners, and these were eventually gathered together and transcribed, a process that continued after Muhammad's death. Unlike the Christian gospels, which offer different perspectives on Jesus' ministry and which were recorded a generation or two after his crucifixion, the Qu'ran is considered a direct link with Muhammad. It is also unlike most books of the Bible because it takes the form of poetry, drawing on ancient genres of Arabic song.

Like Christianity, Islam teaches that a day of judgment is coming—and soon. On this day, the righteous will be granted eternal life in a paradise of delights, but wrongdoers will be damned to a realm of eternal fire. Every person is therefore offered a fundamental choice: to begin a new life of divine service or to follow their own path. If they choose to follow God, they will be blessed; if they do not, God will turn away from them. Thus the only sure means of achieving salvation is observance of the Five Pillars of the faith: submission to God's will as described in the teachings of Muhammad, frequent prayer, ritual fasting, the giving of alms, and an annual pilgrimage to Mecca (the Hajj).

Unlike Christianity, Islam is a religion without sacraments or priests. It more closely resembles Judaism as it developed after the Diaspora, when Jews no longer had access to the Temple but instead gathered around a master teacher (*rabbi*). Similarly, Muslims often rely on a community leader (*imam*) or scholar qualified to comment on matters of faith, who may also act as a judge in disputes. Like Judaism, Islam emphasizes the inextricable connection between religious observance and daily life, between spirituality and politics. There is no opposition of sacred and secular authority, as in Christianity. But in marked contrast to Judaism, Islam is a religion that aspires to unite the world in a shared faith. This means that Muslims, like Christians, consider it their duty to engage in the work of conversion. This further means that there will inevitably be competition between the followers of Christianity and Islam, as both try to carry out this mission.

THE WIDENING ISLAMIC WORLD

As we have frequently observed, the death of any charismatic leader precipitates a series of crises. Muhammad and Alexander the Great represent different types of leadership, but both created communities whose very survival seemed to depend on that leadership. Neither designated his own successor, and both left behind a number of close followers who disagreed as to the proper uses of the power they had inherited.

Arab Conquests

Muhammad's closest followers were his father-in-law, Abu-Bakr (*ah-BOO-BAK-uhr*), and an early convert named Umar. After Muhammad's death, Abu-Bakr took the title *caliph*, a word meaning "deputy" or "representative." In this capacity, he began a campaign to subdue various tribes unwilling to accept his authority as Muhammad's successor. In the course of this, Abu-Bakr's forces began to move northward beyond the borders of Arabia, where they met only minimal resistance from Byzantine and Persian armies.

When Abu-Bakr died two year later, he was succeeded as caliph by Umar, who continued to direct his growing warrior bands against Byzantium and Persia. In 636 they routed a Byzantine army in Syria and then occupied the cities of Antioch, Damascus, and Jerusalem. In 637 they took the Persian capital of Ctesiphon. By 651, the Muslim conquest of the entire Persian Empire was complete.

Islamic forces now turned westward, capturing Byzantine Egypt and extending their control throughout the rest of North Africa. Attempts to capture Constantinople were not successful, as we noted earlier, but in 711 Muslims crossed from North Africa into Visigothic Spain and quickly absorbed most of that territory, too. Within less than a century, they had conquered the ancient Near East and much of the Roman Mediterranean.

How can we explain this prodigious achievement? On a basic level, what motivated the Arabs had motivated the Sumerians, the Neo-Assyrians, the Greeks, the Macedonians, and the Romans: the search for richer territory and new wealth. There is little evidence that Arab Muslims attempted to convert subject peoples to the faith of Islam at this time. Instead, they aimed to establish themselves as a superior ruling class. Yet religious enthusiasm certainly played a crucial role in forging a shared identity among tribes hitherto at war with one another. This identity and sense of superiority must have been further strengthenend by the absence of any serious opposition. Indeed, many of the local populations living within the Persian and Byzantine empires were restive and exhausted by the demands of these far-reaching imperial bureaucracies. To them, conquest brought deliverance. The Arabs did not demand that Jews or Christians convert to Islam, and because they exacted fewer taxes, they were often preferred to the old rulers. For all these reasons, Islam quickly spread over the territory between Egypt and Iran, and has been rooted there ever since.

The Shi'ite–Sunni Schism

As Arab conquests widened the reach of Islam, disputes continued to divide the Muslims of Mecca. When the caliph Umar died in 644, he was replaced by a member of the Umayyad (*oo-MY-yad*) family, a wealthy clan that had originally resisted Muhammad's authority. Opponents of this new caliph, Uthman, rallied instead around Muhammad's cousin and son-in-law, Ali, whose family ties to Muhammad made him seem a more appropriate choice. When Uthman was murdered in 656, Ali's supporters declared him the new caliph. But Uthman's powerful family refused to accept this. Ali was murdered and another member of the Umayyad family replaced him. From 661 to 750, this Umayyad dynasty ruled the Islamic world, establishing its capital at Damascus in Syria.

Ali's followers, however, did not accept defeat. They formed a separate group known as the Shi'ites (from *shi'a*, the Arabic word for "faction"). The Shi'ites insisted that only descendants of Ali and his wife, Muhammad's daughter Fatimah, could legitimately rule the Muslim community. Moreover, the Shi'ites did not accept the customary religious practices (*sunna*) that had developed under the first two caliphs who succeeded Muhammad. Hence those Muslims who supported the Umayyad family and who *did* regard these customs as binding were called Sunnis. This division between Shi'ites and Sunnis has lasted until the present day. Often persecuted by the Sunni majority as heretics, Shi'ites consider themselves the only true exponents of Islam. Today, Shi'ites predominate in Iran and are the largest single Muslim group in Iraq, yet they constitute only one-tenth of the world's Muslims.

The Umayyad and Abbasid Dynasties

The political triumph of the Umayyads in 661 created a strong state centered on Damascus, formerly an administrative center of the Roman Empire. And in many ways, the Umayyad caliphate functioned as a Roman successor state; it even continued to employ Greek-speaking bureaucrats trained in the techniques of Byzantine governance. But the failure of its attacks on Constantinople checked Umayyad power, which was also being challenged by a rival dynasty, the Abbasids. In 750, the Abbasids led a successful rebellion with the help of the Persians, forcing the Umayyads to retreat to their territories in Al-Andalus (Spain).

In contrast with the Umayyads, the Abbasid caliphate stressed Persian elements over Roman ones. Symbolic of this change was its relocation from Damascus to Baghdad, the old Persian capital. The Abbasid caliphs also modeled their behavior on that of Persian princes, presiding over an extravagantly luxurious court. This is the world described in the *1001 Nights* whose dominating presence is Harun al-Rashid, the caliph who ruled from 786 to 809. His reign marked the height of Abbasid power.

Meanwhile, the Umayyad dynasty continued to claim that it was the only legitimate sucessor of Muhammad. Relations between the Umayyads of Al-Andalus and Abbasids of Persia were therefore very cold; but because their realms were far apart, the hostility between them rarely erupted into war. Instead, the two courts competed for preeminence through literary and cultural patronage, much as the Hellenistic kingdoms had done (Chapter 4). Philosophers, artists, and especially poets flocked to both. The *1001 Nights* was one

THE EXPANSION OF ISLAM TO 750. This map shows the spread of Islam from the time of Muhammad to the middle of the eighth century. ▪ *What was the geographical extent of Islam in 750?* ▪ *What role did the Byzantine Empire play in the expansion of Islam?* ▪ *What conclusions can you draw regarding the period of especially rapid expansion in the generation after Muhammad's death?*

ARABIC CALLIGRAPHY. Muslim artists experimented with the art of calligraphy to make complex designs, sometimes abstract but often representing natural forms. This ink drawing on paper dates from the seventh century, and also represents the Muslim mastery of papermaking.

product of this rivalry in Baghdad. Not to be outdone, the caliphs at the Umayyad capital of Córdoba amassed a library of more than 400,000 volumes—at a time when a European monastery that possessed 100 books qualified as a major center of learning.

Islamic Commerce and Industry

Alongside its political and military triumphs, the transformation of tiny settlements into thriving metropolitan commercial centers was one of Islam's most remarkable achievements. Conversion to Islam actually increased the reach of this economic infrastructure, as trading contacts grew in tandem with the growth of the Islamic world. By the tenth century, Muslim merchants had penetrated into southern Russia and equatorial Africa and had become masters of the caravan routes that led eastward to India and China. Ships from the Muslim world established new trade routes across the Indian Ocean, the Persian Gulf, and the Caspian Sea, and for a time dominated the Mediterranean as well.

The growth of Muslim commerce was also sustained by a number of important new industries. Mosul, in Iraq, was a center for the manufacture of cotton cloth; Baghdad specialized in glassware, jewelry, pottery, and silks; Damascus was famous for its fine steel and for its woven-figured silk known as "damask"; Morocco and Al-Andalus were both noted for leatherworking; Toledo produced excellent swords. These and other products were carried throughout the Mediterranean world by Muslim merchants. They were also carried into central Asia, along the road to China that came to be known as the Silk Road. With them went the Islamic faith, which took root among some peoples of modern India, Pakistan, and Afghanistan.

One commodity in particular deserves special mention: paper. Muslims learned papermaking from the Chinese and became became masters of the art in their own right. Paper was cheaper to produce, easier to store, and far easier to use than papyrus or parchment. As a result, paper replaced papyrus in the Islamic world by the early eleventh century—even in Egypt, the heartland of papyrus production for almost 4,000 years.

The ready availability of paper brought about a revolution in the Islamic world. Many of the characteristic features of Islamic civilization—record keeping, high levels of literacy, even the standard form of Arabic script—would have been impossible without it. Only in the thirteenth century would western Europeans begin papermaking, and they would continue to rely on the more durable parchment for the copying of most books and documents. It was not until the advent of print that paper began to replace parchment as the reading and writing material of western Europe.

Mobility, Opportunity, and Status

As the reach of Islam extended, the preeminence of trade and ease of travel increased geographical and social mobility. Muhammad's teachings, too, stressed the equality of all Muslim men. At the courts of Baghdad and Córdoba, in consequence, careers were open to men of talent, regardless of birth or wealth. And because literacy was remarkably widespread, many could rise through education and achieve top offices through enterprise and skill.

For those men wishing instead to embrace the religious life, Islam offered two main alternatives. One was that of the *ulama*, a learned man whose studies qualified him to offer advice on aspects of religious law and practice. Complementary to *ulamas* were the Sufis, mystics who stressed individual contemplation and the cultivation of spiritual ecstasy. Sufis were usually organized into brotherhoods and eventually made many succesful efforts to convert the peoples of Africa and India to Islam. Sufism also provided a channel for the most intense religious impulses. The ability of the *ulama* and the Sufis to coexist is testimony to the cultural pluralism of the Islamic world.

The absence of comparable careers for religious women, even comparable to those available to Christian nuns (see below), is a reminder of the limits often imposed by gender. There are significant exceptions, of course. Muhammad's favored wife, Aisha (*ah-EE-sha*, d. 678), played an important role in the creation and circulation of *hadith* (Arabic for "narrative"): stories and sayings that shed light on the Prophet's life and teachings. But in general, women did not benefit from Muslim egalitarianism and opportunity. They were valuable mostly as indicators of a man's wealth and status. Because the Qu'ran allowed any Muslim man to marry as many as four wives, the number of women available for marriage was often far smaller than the number of men who desired to marry. This made for intense competition, and those men who had wives and daughters needed to ensure that their prized assets were safeguarded. So women were usually kept from the sight of men who were not members of the family or trusted friends, and were housed in a segregated part of the residence called the *haram* ("forbidden place"). Within these enclaves, women vied with one another for precedence and worked to advance the fortunes of their children. But this was often the only power they could exercise.

Islam's Neighbors

For the inhabitants of Byzantium, the triumph of the Abbasid caliphate in the eighth century released the Mediterranean from the pressures of Umayyad expansion. Farther west, the Franks of Gaul also benefited. Because an Umayyad dynasty still controlled Al-Andalus, the great Frankish ruler Charlemagne (*SHAHR-leh-mayn*, r. 768–814) could counter their power by maintaining strong relations with the Abbasid caliphate. The most famous symbol of this connection was an elephant called Abul Abbas, a gift from Harun al-Rashid to Charlemagne. More important, however, was the flow of silver that found its way from the Abbasid Empire north through Russia and the Baltic into the Rhineland, where it was exchanged for Frankish exports, especially slaves: western Europeans who were captured and sold for profit by other western Europeans. Jewels, silks, spices, and other luxury goods from India and the Far East also flowed north and west into Frankish territory. These links with the Abbasid world helped to fuel the extraordinary achievements of Charlemagne's own empire, which had a lasting effect on the culture and politics of Europe.

THE CONVERSION OF NORTHWESTERN EUROPE

At the end of the sixth century, the Frankish chronicler Gregory of Tours (c. 538–594) considered himself a Roman, living in a Roman world. Gregory took it for granted that he and his male relatives should rule, by right of birth and status, over their cities and the surrounding countryside. Like others of his senatorial class, Gregory still spoke and wrote Latin—a rather different Latin from the polished prose of Cicero, but a Latin that would certainly have been comprehensible to the Romans of the Republic. And although Gregory was aware that the western territories of the Roman Empire were now ruled by Frankish, Visigothic, and Lombard kings, he regarded at least some of these kings as Roman successors because they ruled in accordance with Roman models.

Two hundred years later, this sense of direct continuity with the earlier Roman world was no longer tenable. Instead, intellectuals at Charlemagne's court would set out to revive a Roman Empire from which they felt estranged. They sought a *renovatio Romanorum imperii*, "a renewal of the empire of the Romans." This awareness of a break with the Roman past, which developed during the seventh century, was the consequence of profound changes.

Economic and Political Instability

Even though the economy of the Roman Empire had become increasingly regionalized during the third century (Chapter 6), the Mediterranean remained an effective nexus of trade and communication. By about 650, however, this Mediterranean world disintegrated. This was partly a result of Justinian's failed efforts to reconquer the Western empire, but imperial overtaxation of Egypt and North Africa also played a role. So did the temporary disruptions caused by Muslim raiders—temporary, because the merchants and rulers of Islam would soon do much to reconstruct and encourage patterns of commerce.

The most significant causes of economic instability in northwestern Europe were therefore internal. The cities of Italy, Gaul, and Hispania could no longer maintain their walls, their public buildings, and their urban infrastructures. Although bishops and their aristocratic kinsmen still governed from these cities and continued to provide a market for certain kinds of luxury goods, barbarian kings and their nobles were moving to the countryside during the seventh century, living as much as possible from the produce of their own estates rather than purchasing their supplies in the marketplace. At the same time, much agricultural land was passing out of cultivation. This is because the slaves or servile peasants who had farmed the large plantations for hundreds of years had no state to enforce their obedience; they were able to become more independent—yet they were also less effective. Productivity declined, as did revenues.

The coinage systems of western Europe were also breaking down, which meant that wealth ceased to be portable, hindering long-distance exchange. And in any case, gold coins were now too valuable to be useful in a local market economy. By the 660s, those western European rulers who were still in a position to mint coins and guarantee their value had shifted from a gold to a silver coinage. Indeed, Europe would remain a silver-based economy for the next thousand years, until the supply of gold from European conquests in Africa and America once again made a gold standard viable (see Chapter 11).

As a result of these processes, western Europe came to rely on a two-tier economy of a kind that had not been necessary in any Western civilization since the Lydians introduced a standardized currency in the sixth century B.C.E. (Chapter 3). Gold, silver, and luxury goods circulated among the very wealthy, but most people relied on barter and various substitute currencies to facilitate transactions. Lords collected rents from their peasants in food or labor, but then found it difficult to convert these in-kind payments into the weapons, jewelry, and silks that brought prestige. This was problematic not only for social reasons but for political ones: the power of lords depended on their ability to bestow such gifts on their followers (see **Interpreting Visual Evidence**). When they could not acquire these items through trade, they had to win them through plunder and extortion. Either way, the process led to violence.

The successful chieftains of this era therefore tended to be those whose areas of influence adjoined wealthy but poorly defended territories that could be easily attacked or blackmailed. Such "soft frontiers" provided land and booty which could then be distributed to followers. So long as more conquests were made, the process of amassing power and wealth would continue. But power acquired through plunder and conquest was inherently unreliable. A few defeats might speedily reverse the fortunes of lords reliant on it, leaving their followers to seek plunder elsewhere.

Another factor contributing to the instability of power in this world was the difficulty of ensuring its peaceful transfer. Most of the rulers who established themselves during the mass migrations of the fifth and sixth centuries did not come from the traditional royal families of their peoples, and thus faced constant opposition. Moreover, the groups who took possession of territories were usually made up of many different tribes, including a sizable number of displaced Romans. Such unity as they possessed was largely the creation of the charismatic chieftain who led them, and this charisma was not easily passed on.

The Merovingian Kingdom of the Franks

Of all the groups that set up kingdoms in western Europe during the fifth and sixth centuries, only the Franks succeeded in establishing a single dynasty from which leaders would be drawn for the next 250 years. This dynasty reached back to Clovis (r. c. 481–511), a warrior-king who established an alliance with powerful bishops in Gaul by converting to Roman Christianity—emulating the example of Constantine on many levels. Clovis's family came to be known as the Merovingians, after his legendary grandfather Merovech. Clovis's own name proved even more long-lasting. As the language of the Franks merged with the Latin of Gaul to become French, the name "Clovis" lost its hard "C" and the pronunciation of the "V" was softened. It became "Louis," the name borne by kings up to the time of the French Revolution over 1,200 years later (see Chapter 18).

The power of the Merovingians was due, in part, to their capacity to transfer it from one generation to another. In medieval Europe, as in other times and places, the right of inheritance was not limited to the eldest male of a family. When it came to property or power, all the sons of a king—and frequently all his male cousins and nephews, and even his daughters—could consider themselves rightful heirs. So even when the hegemony of any family was not threatened by outsiders, the transfer of power was almost always bloody. The Merovingians managed to contain this bloodshed through various means.

Under the Merovingian kings, many elements of late Roman local administration survived. Latin literacy, fostered by a network of monasteries linked to the Frankish court, remained an important element in this administration, providing a foundation on which Charlemagne would later build. Indeed, these monasteries became the engines that made Merovingian Gaul wealthier and more stable than other regions of northwestern Europe. Approximately 550 of them were thriving by the year 700, more than 300 of which had been established in the preceding century. The cities of Frankish bishops also prospered, amassing landed possessions from which their successors would continue to profit until the French Revolution.

This redistribution of wealth reflected a fundamental shift in the economic gravity of the region. In the year 600, the wealth of Gaul was still concentrated in the south, where it had been since the Roman conquest of the area under Julius Caesar. By the year 750, however, the economic center of the kingdom lay north of the Loire, in territories that extended from the Rhineland westward to the North Sea. It was here that most of the new monastic foundations of the seventh century were established.

Behind this shift in prosperity lay a long and successful effort to bring the rich, heavy soils of northern Europe under cultivation. This effort was largely engineered by the new monasteries, which harnessed the peasant workforce and pioneered agricultural technologies adapted to the climate and terrain. The most important were heavy, wheeled plows capable of cutting and turning soils very different from those of the Mediterranean. Gradually warming weather also improved the fertility of the wet northern soils, lengthening the growing season and making possible more efficient crop-rotation systems. As food became more plentiful, the population began to expand. Although much of Frankish Gaul remained a land of scattered settlements separated by dense forests, it was far more populous by 750 than it had been in the time of Clovis. All of these developments would continue during the reign of Charlemagne and beyond.

The Power of Monasticism

As we just noted, the seventh century witnessed a rapid increase in the foundation of monastic houses all over northwestern Europe. Although monasteries had existed since the fourth century, most were located in highly Romanized areas. But beginning in the fifth century, a powerful monastic movement began in Ireland, as well, and eventually spread to the Celtic regions of Britain and from there to the Continent. Important monasteries were also established on the island of Iona, off the western coast of what is now Scotland, and at Lindisfarne, off Britain's northeastern coast. In all of these cases, close ties were forged between monks and local tribal leaders or powerful families, much to the political and economic gain of all parties.

Indeed, the material advantages of monastic innovation were a powerful incentive toward conversion. Prosperity in turn was a powerful advertisement for authority, and a chieftain who had the support of a monastery and its beneficent Christian God would be regarded as worthy of loyalty. Because monasteries played such a key role in economic development and political order, lords often granted them special privileges, freeing them from the control of local bishops and giving them jurisdiction over their own lands. Thus, monasteries became politically and economically powerful not only because they had been founded by powerful men, but because they were lordships in their own right.

Frequently, these new foundations were double monasteries that accommodated women as well as men. Some were established for women only. In either case, they were often ruled by abbesses drawn from noble or royal families. Monasticism thus became a road to political power for women. It also gave women—commoners as well as queens—freedoms they did not have elsewhere, or at any other time in history up to this point. Within the monastery, women had more control over their own minds and bodies. Outside it, they could wield enormous influence, promoting their families' diplomatic and dynastic interests without the dangers and uncertainties of pregnancy. Moreover, the prayers of holy women were regarded as particularly effective in securing divine support or retribution. This further enriched convents through donations of land and wealth, although it could not always safeguard them from violence.

THE LINDISFARNE GOSPELS. This page from one of the astonishing illuminated ("light-filled") books produced by the monastery at Lindisfarne shows the opening of the gospel of John. ▪ *Why would monastic scribes have devoted so much time, energy, and skill to the decoration of a text?* ▪ *How do these artistic motifs compare to those featured on the metalwork found at Sutton Hoo (pages 172 and 173)?* ▪ *What conclusions can you draw from these similarities?*

The Ship Burial of Sutton Hoo

The most impressive finds in the history of British archeology have been made by amateurs. The most recent, in the summer of 2009, was the largest hoard of worked gold and silver ever found in one place (more than 5 kilograms of gold and 2.5 kilograms of silver: image A). It was discovered by a man in Staffordshire who was walking over a neighbor's farm with a metal detector. The hoard's extraordinary value—and its historical implications—can only be guessed at now; even the dating is inconclusive.

Another amateur find, made in 1939, was a royal gravesite dating from the seventh century (image B). Many scholars believe it to be the tomb of King Redwald of East Anglia, described by Bede as a baptized Christian who refused to give up the worship of his ancestral gods. The king's body was placed in a wooden structure in the middle of a 90-foot-long ship that had been dragged to the top of a bluff (a *hoo*), eleven miles from the English Channel. The ladder in the photograph of the original excavation reaches into the burial chamber.

The contents of the grave included:

- a lamp and a bronze bucket, once suspended from a chain

- a ceremonial helmet (image C), modeled on those worn by Roman cavalry

A. The Staffordshire Hoard, found in 2009.

B. The original excavation of the Burial Chamber at Sutton Hoo, 1939.

Convents and monasteries also served the interests of men, which is why kings and lords supported them. They were dynamic repositories of prayer, which could further the ambitions of their male benefactors and protect them from harm. They provided a dignified place of retirement for inconvenient but powerful women, such as the sisters and daughters of rivals or the widow of a previous ruler. And by limiting the number of powerful women who could reproduce, convents helped reduce the number of male claimants to power. Establishing aristocratic and royal women in convents was thus an important way of controlling successions and managing political disputes.

officers just before the withdrawal of the legions from Britain in 410—but decorated like helmets found in eastern Sweden

- a sword and a large, circular shield, resembling those found in Swedish burial sites

- exquisitely crafted belt buckles and shoulder clasps (image D), made of gold and garnet

- a pair of silver spoons with long handles, possibly crafted in Byzantium, inscribed in Greek with the names PAULOS and SAULOS (Paul and Saul)

- a large silver dish made in Byzantium between 491 and 518

- a bronze bowl from the eastern Mediterranean

- a six-stringed lyre in a bag made of beaver skin, similar to lyres found in Germany

- a purse containing 37 gold coins, each from a different Merovingian mint, the most recent datable to the 620s

- heaps of armor, blankets, cloaks, and other gear.

Questions for Analysis

1. What do these artifacts, and the context in which they were found, reveal about the extent of Anglo-Saxon contact with the rest of the world? Which regions are represented, and why?

2. Based on this evidence, what conclusions can you draw about Anglo-Saxon culture and values?

3. Do any of these grave-goods indicate that the occupant was a Christian king? Why or why not?

C. Sutton Hoo helmet.

D. Sutton Hoo buckles.

Monasticism played an important role in missionary activity, too. The work of Irish monks was crucial to the spread of Christianity in areas of northern Europe virtually untouched by the Roman Empire. Missionaries were also sponsored by the fledgling papacy in tandem with the Merovingian royal family—especially its women. The best example of this is the conversion of Britain's Anglo-Saxon tribes, which we glimpsed in the opening paragraph of this chapter. In 597, a group of Benedictine monks was sent by Pope Gregory I (r. 590–604) to the southeastern kingdom of Kent, where their efforts were assisted by the fact that the king, Æthelbehrt, had married a Frankish princess who was already a Christian. This pattern of influence repeated itself all over southern and eastern Britain. Writing a hundred years later in the monastery of Monkwearmouth in Northumbria, the historian Bede could claim that the tribes of England were now united in their shared allegiance to the Roman Church and its English archbishop, whose seat was the cathedral in Æthelbehrt's capital at Canterbury. Bede credited the Roman pope for initiating this remarkable feat, and the monastic rule under which he himself lived for bringing it to fruition.

The Papacy of Gregory the Great

Pope Gregory I, also known as Gregory the Great, was the first bishop of Rome to envision a new role for the papacy in northwestern Europe. We have seen that the Roman "papa" frequently asserted his superiority over other patriarchs; but in reality, he was subordinate to the emperors in Constantinople and to the greater prestige of bishops in the Christian East. As Byzantine power in Italy declined, however, Gregory sought to create a more autonomous Latin Church. An influential theologian, he is considered the successor of Jerome, Ambrose, and Augustine (Chapter 6) because he greatly extended the applicability of their teachings. Among his doctrinal contributions were an emphasis on the necessity of penance for the forgiveness of sins and the concept of Purgatory as a place where the soul could be purified before it was admitted into Heaven—instead of being sent immediately to perpetual damnation. Alongside this emphasis on penance, Gregory especially emphasized the importance of pastoral care: the proper instruction and encouragement of the laity. He even sought to increase the affective power of Christian worship by promoting the performance of music, to such a degree that the very style of singing that emerged in this period is known as "Gregorian chant."

Gregory was also a statesman and leader in the model of his Roman forebears. Within Italy, he ensured the survival of the papacy in the face of Lombard invaders by clever diplomacy and expert management of papal estates and revenues. He maintained good relations with Byzantium while asserting his authority over other bishops of the Latin Church. Yet Gregory's influence was not always benign. He was among the first to articulate the Church's official policy toward the Jews, which became increasingly negative. Building on Gregory's example, later popes would insist that the Jews' alleged role in Christ's crucifixion had deprived them of their rights in a Christian world.

THE EMPIRE OF CHARLEMAGNE

Toward the end of the seventh century, tensions among Frankish noble families were increasing. Those in the border region of Austrasia had profited from their steady push into the "soft frontier" east of the Rhine, acquiring wealth and military power in the process. In the Merovingians' heartland of Neustria, by contrast, a considerable portion of their land had been given to monasteries, which decreased their wealth and their capacity to attract followers. A succession of short-lived kings then opened the door to a series of civil wars, and finally to a decisive challenge to the Merovingian dynasty.

Kings and King-Makers

In 687, an Austrasian nobleman called Pepin (635/45–714) succeeded in forcing his way into power by making himself the king's right-hand man. He took the title *maior domus*, "big man of the house," and began to exercise royal authority while maintaining the fiction that he was merely a royal servant. He did this effectively for more than twenty-five years. After his death, his illegitimate son Charles Martel ("the Hammer," 688–741) further consolidated control over royal administration. In 733 or 734 he also repelled a Muslim force that had ventured into Frankish territory, meeting them at Tours, some 150 miles from the Merovingian capital at Paris. Although the Muslim contingent was a raiding party rather than a full-scale army, Charles' victory won him great prestige.

At the same time, Charles developed an alliance with Benedictine missionaries from England, who were attempting to convert the Low Countries and central Germany to Christianity. Charles' family had long been active in the drive to conquer and settle these areas, and he understood that missionary work and Frankish expansion could go hand in hand. Charles assisted these conversion efforts. In return, the leader of the English Benedictines, Boniface (c. 672–754), brought him into contact with the papacy.

Although Charles never sought to become king himself, he was so clearly the effective ruler of the Franks that they did not bother to choose a new king when the reigning Merovingian died in 737. But then Charles himself died in 741, and his sons Carloman and Pepin were forced to allow the election of a new king while they continued to exercise power behind the scenes. This compromise did not last long, however. In 750, Pepin decided to seize the throne for himself.

Analyzing Primary Sources

An Anglo-Saxon Slave Girl and Frankish Queen

The Anglo-Saxon Saint Balthild became the wife of the Merovingian king Clovis II (r. 639–57), but she began life as a slave. After the king's death, she was left in a precarious position at the Frankish court as regent for her son, Clothar III, and was eventually forced to enter the convent she had founded at Chelles, near Paris. The following excerpt from her Latin vita ("life") describes her rise to a position of power. It was probably written by a nun of Chelles.

[P]raise should first be sung of Him Who made the humble great and raised the pauper from the dunghill and seated him among the princes of his people. Such a one is the woman present to our minds, the venerable and great lady Balthild the queen. Divine Providence called her from across the seas. She, who came here as God's most precious and lofty pearl, was sold at a cheap price. Erchinoald, a Frankish magnate and most illustrious man, acquired her and in his service the girl behaved most honorably.... For she was kind-hearted and sober and prudent in all her ways, careful and plotting evil for none.... And since she was of the Saxon race, she was graceful in form with refined features, a most seemly woman with a smiling face and serious gait. And she so showed herself just as she ought in all things, that she pleased her master and found favor in his eyes. So he determined that she should set out the drinking cup for him in his chamber and, honored above all others as his housekeeper, stand at his side always ready to serve him.... She gained such happy fame that, when the said lord Erchinoald's wife died, he hoped to unite himself to Balthild, that faultless virgin, in a matronal bed....

[But] when she was called to the master's chamber she hid herself secretly in a corner and threw some vile rags over herself so that no one could guess that anyone might be concealed there.... She hoped that she might avoid a human marriage bed and thus merit a spiritual and heavenly spouse.... Thereafter it happened, with God's approval, that Balthild, the maid who escaped marriage with a lord, came to be espoused to Clovis, son of the former king, Dagobert. Thus by virtue of her humility she was raised to a higher rank....

Source: Excerpted from *Sainted Women of the Dark Ages,* ed. and trans. John E. Halborg, Jo Ann McNamara, and E. Gordon Whatley (Chapel Hill, NC: 1992), pp. 268–70.

Questions for Analysis

1. Based on what you have learned about the prevalence of the slave trade in early medieval Europe, what might you speculate about Balthild's actual role in Erchinoald's household?

2. Balthild would have been a contemporary of the king buried at Sutton Hoo. Is it likely that she would have been a Christian when she was sold into slavery in England? Why or why not?

3. In light of Balthild's later status as a queen and regent for her son, why would her biographer stress that she was "careful and plotting evil for none"? To what allegations or incidents might the author of this life be responding?

This turned out to be harder than he may have expected. Even though the reigning king was ineffectual, Frankish identity was bound up with loyalty to Clovis's descendants; and though tribal leaders had the power to elect a new king, they were reluctant to do so. Pepin therefore turned to the pope, trading on his father's support of the Benedictines. The pope, for his part, saw that a powerful leader of the Franks could be a potential ally in his political struggle with the Byzantine emperors over iconoclasm (which the papacy opposed) and in his military struggle against the Lombard kings for control of central Italy.

So Boniface, acting as papal emissary, anointed Pepin king of the Franks in 751. This was a new ritual, but it had a powerful biblical precedent: the ceremony by which the prophet Samuel had made Saul the first king of Israel, by anointing him with holy oil (Chapter 2). Indeed, the significance of the Old Testament association would grow under Pepin's son Charlemagne (associated with David) and his grandson Louis the Pious (associated with Solomon). To contemporary observers, however, the novelty of these proceedings underscored the uncertainty of the process by which a legitimate king had been deposed and a new king created. And as we will see, this king-making process was the first stage in the development of a principle that would ultimately limit the power of later medieval kings and modern rulers alike: the principle that kingship is an office and can be occupied, at least theoretically, by anyone. By extension, this means that if a king is ineffectual or tyrannical, he can be deposed and replaced.

The Reign of Charlemagne

Pepin's position as king was a tenuous one, and when he died it seemed likely that the Frankish kingdom would break up into mutually hostile regions: Austrasia, Neustria, and Aquitaine. That it did not was the work of Pepin's son, Charles, known to the French as Charlemagne and to the Germans as Karl der Grosse—"Charles the Great." It is from him, as well as from his grandfather Charles Martel, that this new Frankish dynasty takes the name "Carolingian" (from *Carolus*, the Latin form of "Charles").

When Charlemagne came to power in 768, he managed to unite the Franks by the tried and true method of attacking a common external enemy. In a series of campaigns, the Franks succeeded in annexing the Lombard kingdom of northern Italy, most of what is now Germany, portions of central Europe, and Catalonia. These conquests provided the victorious Franks with the spoils of war and vast new lands that enabled Charlemagne to reward his closest followers. Many of the peoples whom Charlemagne conquered were already Christians. In Saxony, however, Charlemagne's armies fought for twenty years before subduing the inhabitants and forcing their conversion. This

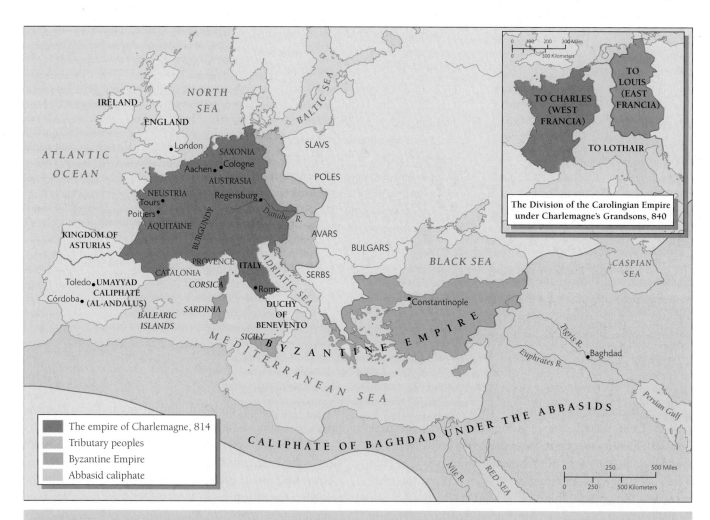

THE EMPIRE OF CHARLEMAGNE IN 814. When Charlemagne died in 814, he had created an empire that embraced a large portion of the lands formerly united under the Western Roman Empire. ▪ *What were the geographical limits of his power?* ▪ *How were these limits dictated by the historical forces we have been studying?* ▪ *Along what lines was Charlemagne's empire divided after his death?*

created a precedent with momentous consequences: in time, the assumption that the subjugation of a vanquished people should be accompanied by their (often unwilling) conversion would become ingrained in the ideology and practice of most Western civilizations.

To rule his vast new empire, Charlemagne enlisted the help of the Frankish warriors he had enriched. These counts (in Latin, *comites*, "followers") supervised local governance within their territories. Charlemagne also established a network of other officials who convened courts, established tolls, administered royal lands, and collected taxes. To facilitate transactions and trade, he created a new coinage system based on a division of the silver pound into units of twenty shillings, each worth twelve pennies; this system would last in parts of Europe and in Britain until the 1970s. As we noted above, much of the silver for this new coinage originated in the Abbasid caliphate and was payment for furs, cloth, and slaves captured in Charlemagne's wars.

Like Carolingian administration generally, this new monetary system depended on the regular use of written records, which means that the sources supporting historical research on Charlemagne's empire are numerous. But Charlemagne did not rely on the written word alone to make his will felt. Periodically, his court sent special messengers, known as *missi*, on tours through the countryside to relay his instructions and report back on the conduct of local administrators. This was the most thorough system of governance known in Europe since the height of the Roman Empire, reaching many parts of the Continent that the Romans had never occupied. It set the standard for royal administration in Europe for centuries.

Christianity and Kingship

Charlemagne took his responsibilities as a Christian king seriously. As his empire expanded, moreover, he came to see himself as the leader of a unified Christian society, Christendom, which he was obliged to defend. Like his contemporaries in Byzantium and Islam—as well as his Roman predecessors—he recognized no distinction between religion and politics. Religious reforms were therefore no less central to proper kingship than were justice and defense. In some ways, indeed, a king's responsibilities for his kingdom's spiritual welfare were more important than his other, secular responsibilities.

These ideas were not new in the late eighth century, but they took on a new importance because of the extraordinary power Charlemagne wielded. Like other rulers of this period, Charlemagne was able to appoint and depose bishops and abbots, just as he did his counts and other offi-

CHARLEMAGNE'S IMAGE OF AUTHORITY. A silver penny struck between 804 and 814 in Mainz (as indicated by the letter *M* at the bottom) represents Charlemagne in a highly stylized fashion, as a Roman emperor with a military cloak and laurel wreath. The inscription reads *KAROLVS IMP AVG* (Charles, Emperor, Augustus). Charlemagne's portrait is closely modeled on both Hellenistic and Roman coins.

cials. But he also changed the liturgy of Frankish churches, declared changes in basic statements of Christian belief, prohibited pagan practices, and imposed basic Christian observances on the conquered peoples of Saxony. As the dominant political power in central Italy, Charlemagne was also the protector of the papacy. Although he acknowledged the pope as spiritual leader of western Christendom, Charlemagne dealt with the bishop of Rome much as he did with other bishops in his empire. He supervised and approved papal elections, and he also protected the pope from his many enemies. To Charlemagne, such measures were clearly required if God's new chosen people, the Franks, were to avoid the fate that befell biblical Israel whenever its people turned away from their obedience to God.

The Carolingian Renaissance

Similar ideals lay behind the Carolingian Renaissance, a cultural and intellectual flowering that took place around the Carolingian court. Like their biblical exemplars David and Solomon, Charlemagne and his son Louis the Pious considered it a crucial part of their role to be patrons of learning and the arts. In so doing, they created a paradigm of the court as an intellectual and cultural center that would profoundly influence western European cultural life until the First World War (Chapter 24).

Behind the Carolingians' support for scholarship was the conviction that learning was essential to salvation.

Charlemagne therefore recruited intellectuals from all over Europe, chief among them the Anglo-Saxon monk Alcuin, whose command of classical Latin established him as the leader of the court. Under Alcuin's direction, scholars produced original Latin poetry and an impressive number of theological and pastoral tracts. But their primary efforts were devoted to recopying classical Latin texts and correcting the text of the Latin Bible, which had accumulated many generations of copyists' mistakes. Alcuin and his associates also developed a new style of handwriting with simplified letter forms and spaces inserted between words, in an effort to guard against new mistakes and making reading easier. Literacy was further facilitated by the addition of punctuation. This new style of handwriting, known as Carolingian miniscule, is the foundation for the typefaces of most modern books—including this one.

The Revival of the Western Roman Empire

On Christmas Day in the year 800, Charlemagne was crowned emperor by Pope Leo III. Centuries later, popes would cite this epochal event as precedent for the political superiority they claimed over the "Holy Roman Empire," as it came to be called (see Chapter 9). In the year 800, however, Pope Leo was entirely under Charlemagne's thumb. And Charlemagne's biographer, Einhard, would later claim that the coronation was planned without the emperor's knowledge. For one thing, it was certain to anger the true Roman emperor in Byzantium, with whom Charlemagne had strained relations. Nor did the imperial title add much to Charlemagne's position; he was already a de facto emperor in his own right. Why, then, did he accept the title and later transfer it to his son Louis?

Historians are still debating this question. What is clear, in any case, is the symbolic significance of the action. Although the Romans of Byzantium no longer influenced western Europe directly, they continued to regard it (somewhat vaguely) as an outlying province of their empire. Moreover, the emperor in Constantinople claimed to be the political successor of Caesar Augustus. Charlemagne's assumption of the imperial title was a clear slap in the face, and it deepened Byzantium's suspicion of his cordial relationship with Byzantium's enemy, Harun al-Rashid, the Abbasid caliph in Baghdad. But for Charlemagne's followers—and for all the medieval rulers who came after him—it was a declaration of independence and superiority. With only occasional interruptions, western Europeans would continue to crown Roman emperors until the nine-teenth century, while territorial claims and concepts of national sovereignty continued to rest on Carolingian precedent. Whatever his own motives may have been, Charlemagne's revival of the Western Roman Empire was crucial to the developing self-consciousness of western Europe.

DISPUTED LEGACIES AND NEW ALLIANCES

When Charlemagne died in 814, his empire descended intact to his only surviving son, Louis the Pious. Under Louis, however, the empire disintegrated, and it was divided among his three sons in 840. Western Francia (the core of modern France) went to Charles the Bald; Eastern Francia (which became the principalities of Germany) went to Louis the German; and a third kingdom (stretching from the Rhineland to Rome) went to Lothair, along with the imperial title. But when Lothair's line died out in 856, this fragile compromise dissolved into open warfare, as the East and West Franks fought over Lothair's former territories and the imperial power that went with them. The heartland of this disputed domain, known to the Germans as Lotharingia and to the French as Alsace-Lorraine, would continue to be a site of bitter contention until the end of the Second World War (see Chapter 26).

The Collapse of the Carolingian Empire

Louis faced an impossible situation of a kind we have studied many times before: the task of holding together an artificial constellation of territories united by someone else. By 814, moreover, Charlemagne had pushed the borders of his empire beyond the practical limits of his administration. To the southwest, he now faced the Umayyad rulers of Al-Andalus; to the north, the pagan inhabitants of Scandinavia; and in the east, his armies were too preoccupied to secure the Slavic lands that lay beyond Saxony. Meanwhile, the pressures that had driven these conquests—the need for land and plunder—had become ever more pronounced as a result of their very success. The number of counts had tripled, from approximately 100 to 300, and each of them wanted more wealth and power.

Frustrated by their new emperor's inability to reward them, the Frankish aristocracy turned against Louis and on each other. As centralized authority broke down, the vast majority of the empire's free inhabitants found themselves increasingly dominated by local lords who treated them as if they were unfree serfs. At the same time, troubles in the Abbasid Empire caused a breakdown in the commercial system through which Scandinavian traders brought Abbasid silver into Carolingian domains. Deprived of their livelihood, these traders turned to raiding, which is what the Norse word "Viking" means. Under these combined pressures, a new map of Europe began to emerge.

The Impact of the Viking Invasions

Scandinavian traders were already familiar figures in the North Sea and Baltic ports of Europe when Charlemagne came to power. They had begun to establish strategic settlements in what is now Russia, from which they navigated down the rivers to Byzantium (through the Black Sea) and the Abbasid caliphate (through the Caspian Sea). But when the power of the Abbasids declined, they turned to plunder, ransom, tribute collection, and slaving. At first, these were small-scale operations. But soon, some Viking attacks involved organized armies numbering in the thousands. The small tribal kingdoms of the Anglo-Saxons and Celts made the British Isles easy targets, as were the kingdoms of the divided Franks.

By the tenth century, the Vikings controlled independent principalities in eastern England, Ireland, the islands of Scotland, and the region of France that is still called "Norseman-land," Normandy. A Viking people known as the Rus' established the beginnings of a kingdom that would become Russia. At the end of the tenth century, Vikings ventured farther west and colonized Iceland, Greenland, and a distant territory they called Vinland (Newfoundland, Canada). In 1016 a Viking army placed a Danish king on the English throne.

The threat of Viking attacks began to lessen with Scandinavia's conversion to Christianity, from the late tenth century onward. It was also mitigated by the fact that Viking populations quickly assimilated into the world of northwestern Europe. By 1066, when the "Norsemen" of Normandy conquered England, the English—many descended from Vikings themselves—perceived these Normans to be French.

In this era, many of the monasteries of Frankish, Anglo-Saxon, and Celtic lands were destroyed—along with countless precious books and historical artifacts. Yet the Vikings were not the only source of disorder. The local political rivalries that had replaced the centralized states of Charlemagne and the Islamic caliphates contributed mightily to the chaos and made the Vikings' successes easily won. Nor were the Vikings a source of disorder alone. In Ireland and eastern England, Vikings founded a series of new towns. As long-distance traders, Vikings transported large quantities of silver into western Europe, fueling the European economy.

In those few regions where people did succeed in fending off Viking attacks, the unifying force of victory was strong. The best example of this phenomenon is England, which had never been part of Charlemagne's empire and which had remained divided into small kingdoms at war with one other. But as a direct response to the Viking threat, a loosely consolidated kingdom emerged for the first time under Alfred the Great (r. 871–99). His success in defending his own West Saxon kingdom from Viking attacks, combined with the destruction of every other competing royal dynasty, allowed Alfred and his heirs to assemble effective armed forces, institute mechanisms of local government, found new towns, and codify English laws. In addition, Alfred established a court school

PATTERNS OF VIKING ACTIVITY AND SETTLEMENT, c. 800–1100. The Vikings were instrumental in maintaining commercial contacts among northern Europe, Byzantium, and Islam until the eighth century, when changing historical forces turned them into raiders and colonists. ▪ *What area was the original homeland of the Vikings?* ▪ *What geographic region did the Vikings first conquer, and why?* ▪ *The areas marked in green show territories that were later targeted by pillagers. Why would the Vikings have avoided settlement in these areas?*

in imitation of Charlemagne, and fostered a distinctive Anglo-Saxon literary culture. While the Anglo-Saxon vernacular had been a written language since the time of the Roman missions, it now came to rival Latin as a language of administration, history, scholarship, and spirituality. Moreover, oral traditions of poetic composition and storytelling were preserved and extended, as exemplified by the epic *Beowulf*. Until the the eleventh century, Anglo-Saxon was the only European vernacular used for regular written communication.

The Disintegration of the Islamic World

As we noted above, the declining power of the Abbasid caliphate contributed to the escalation of Viking raids. A major cause of this decline was the gradual impoverishment of the ancient Tigris-Euphrates basin, which resulted from ecological crises and a devastating revolt by the enslaved African workforce there. Tax revenues were also declining, as provincial rulers in North Africa, Egypt, and Syria retained larger and larger portions of those revenues for themselves. As their sources of income became depleted, the Abbasids were unable to support either their large civil service or the mercenary army on which they relied for de-

fense. Massively expensive building projects, including the construction of the new Abbasid capital at Baghdad, further exacerbated the crisis.

Behind the Abbasid collapse lay two fundamental developments of great significance for the future of the Islamic world: the growing power of regional rulers and the sharpening religious divisions between Sunnis and Shi'ites, and among the Shi'ites themselves. In 909, regional and religious hostilities came together when a local Shi'ite dynasty known as the Fatimids seized control of the Abbasid province of North Africa. In 969, the Fatimids succeeded in conquering Egypt also. Meanwhile, another Shi'ite group attacked Baghdad in 927 and Mecca in 930, seizing the Kaaba. Although an Abbasid caliphate continued to exist in Baghdad until 1258 (when invading Mongol armies dispatched it), its empire had effectively disappeared by the 930s.

In Al-Andalus, disputes over succession within the Umayyad dynasty were matched by new external pressures. Beginning in the mid-ninth century, the small Christian kingdoms of northern and eastern Iberia began to encroach on Muslim territory. By the opening years of the eleventh century, the caliphate had dissolved, to be replaced by a host of smaller kingdoms, some of which paid tribute to the Christian rulers of the north.

The fractured political basis of the Islamic world deepened the divisions that had always existed among Muslim

After You Read This Chapter

Visit StudySpace for quizzes, additional review materials, and multi-media documents. **wwnorton.com/studyspace**

REVIEWING THE OBJECTIVES

- Justinian's attempted reunification of the Roman Empire proved destructive. What were its effects in the East? In the West?
- Byzantine culture was distinctive in many ways. What are some of its important features?
- The rapid expansion of Islam can be explained with reference to several historical factors. What were they?
- What accounts for the close relationship between monasticism and secular power in early medieval Europe?
- What was the Carolingian Empire, and why is it important?

groups. While Islamic rulers were extremely tolerant of religious and cultural differences when dealing with Jews and Christians, dissent within Islam itself was another matter. Under the strong rule of the caliphates, some different groups had learned to coexist; but with the disappearance of these centralized states it would be increasingly difficult to reconcile the ideal of Muslim universality with the realities of regional and ethnic differences.

CONCLUSION

The three civilizations that emerged as Rome's heirs each exhibit aspects of Roman civilization, which was itself a product of older civilizations. Which was Rome's true successor? It depends on the criteria used to make this evaluation. If imperial Rome's most fundamental characteristics were the maintenance of legal and political institutions, the answer is Byzantium. If its strength lay in combining the rich legacies of the Near East, Egypt, and the Hellenistic world, the answer is the Muslim caliphates, which also emulated Rome in promoting commerce and cultural exchange. If one associates Rome chiefly with the city itself and the Latin language of the first Romans, the answer is northwestern Europe.

There are many connections to be drawn among these three successors. All took on their defining characteristics in the sixth and seventh centuries and, by the eighth century, had developed unique strengths and weaknesses. Moreover, they had fruitful—if uneasy—relationships with one another, and many mutual dependencies. Italian traders were active in Constantinople, and Muslim traders were common in the ports of southern Italy and Gaul. Anglo-Saxon merchants were regular visitors to the Mediterranean, and Jewish merchants in the Rhineland were carrying on an active trade with the communities of Muslim Egypt, while Viking traders had opened trade routes from the Baltic through Russia to the Black Sea and were busily founding cities from Novgorod to Dublin.

But the crises of the ninth and tenth centuries disrupted these networks and created new centers of power. Western Europeans began to share a sense of common identity: within the vast territory that extended from the Baltic to the Mediterranean, and from the Pyrenees to Poland, every ruler was (or would soon be) looking to the Roman Church for spiritual guidance and to his fellow rulers for aid and alliance. At the same time, western Europe became a society mobilized for war to a degree unmatched in either Byzantium or the Islamic world. In the centuries to come, this militarization was to prove a decisive factor in the shifting relationship among Rome's heirs, not only because it led to conquest but because it spurred innovation.

PEOPLE, IDEAS, AND EVENTS IN CONTEXT

- In what ways do **JUSTINIAN'S CODE OF ROMAN LAW** and the building of **HAGIA SOPHIA** reflect his desire to revive the glories of ancient Rome?

- What were **BYZANTIUM'S** sources of stability, and of dissent? What effect did the **ICONOCLAST CONTROVERSY** have on Byzantine society?

- What factors contributed to **MUHAMMAD'S** rise to power? What are the **FIVE PILLARS** of ISLAM and what is the role of the **QU'RAN**?

- To what extent were the **UMAYYAD** and **ABBASID CALIPHATES** heirs of Rome? What made Islamic culture of this period distinctive?

- How did the **MEROVINGIAN** kings of the Franks acquire and hold power? How did **BENEDICTINE MONASTICISM** contribute to the economy of western Europe and how was it linked to politics?

- How did **CHARLEMAGNE** build an empire, and how did the **CAROLINGIAN RENAISSANCE** revive and extend **CLASSICAL LEARNING**?

- How did the **VIKING INVASIONS** contribute to the disorder of the ninth and tenth centuries?

CONSEQUENCES

- Arguably, each of the three civilizations that emerged in this era could claim the mantle of the Roman Empire. In your view, which one is most successful in carrying forward the legacies of the classical past?

- How do the historical circumstances in which Islam emerged compare to those that shaped early Christianity (Chapter 6)? What are some key similarities and differences?

Before
You
Read
This
Chapter

The Expansion
of Europe,
950–1100

CORE OBJECTIVES

- **EXPLAIN** the reasons for the fragmentation of political power throughout most of Europe in the ninth and tenth centuries.

- **IDENTIFY** the most important outcomes of the medieval agricultural revolution.

- **DESCRIBE** the effects of the reforming movement with the Church.

- **UNDERSTAND** the motives behind the Crusades.

- **TRACE** the political, economic, social, religious, and cultural effects of the Crusades.

In the version of history popularized by medieval minstrels, Charlemagne and his knights defeat a Muslim army on Spanish soil. They then face only one remaining obstacle: the castle of a Muslim king whose stalwart courage commands the Christians' respect. So when ambassadors from the king promise his conversion in exchange for the safety of his people, Charlemagne readily agrees. One of his men must now negotiate the terms of surrender. Roland, Charlemagne's noblest knight, suggests that his stepfather Ganelon be the chosen messenger. But Ganelon is furious, certain that the mission will end in his death. Secretly, he resolves to betray his stepson and his liege lord: he convinces the Muslim king that Charlemagne only intends to trick him into converting, and thus incites the king to attack the Christian warriors as they travel homeward through the mountain pass. Because Roland is the bravest knight, Ganelon knows that he will volunteer to command the rear guard.

And so it happens. Roland's men are ambushed and his sworn companion, Olivier, urges him to call for help. But Roland refuses; he will never endanger his lord by any such dishonorable deed. Instead, he will fight to the death and, with his last ounce of strength, break his sword. For it would never do to have this sacred gift of Charlemagne—made holier still by the relic in its pommel—fall into the hands of heathens. As Roland reminds Olivier, "We must not be the theme of mocking songs." The worst thing imaginable is shame; the best, to become the hero of just such an epic.

Like the *Iliad*, *The Song of Roland* is the product of an oral storytelling tradition that took shape over hundreds of years. Written down around the year 1100, it reflects the many ways in which the world had changed since the time of Charlemagne. Its very language exemplifies one such change: the language we call French. In Charlemagne's time, moreover, there was no such thing as knighthood or chivalry, there were no major castles, there was no holy war against Muslims. All of these features were added over time, to mirror a new reality.

In this chapter, we will begin to trace the processes that transformed western Europe from an economic backwater and political patchwork into the premier power among the three successor civilizations of the Roman Empire. With the increased authority and prestige of the Roman Church, European Christendom came to embrace the formerly outlying provinces of Scandinavia, Hungary, Poland, and Bohemia. Christian colonists and missionaries would also push eastward into Prussia, Lithuania, Livonia, and the Balkans. Allied Christian armies would come to dominate Muslim Spain and Constantinople. They would also establish (and eventually lose) a Latin kingdom centered on Jerusalem, and control commerce in the Mediterranean as well as trade routes to Central Asia and China. This expansion would be accompanied by a revolution in agricultural production, significant urbanization, a rising standard of living, and a growing population. It would foster the growth of territorial monarchies, create a wealthy but highly stratified new social order, and spur remarkable intellectual and cultural achievements.

WESTERN EUROPE AROUND THE YEAR 1000

In the aftermath of the Viking invasions, new political entities began to emerge in western Europe. Indeed, the Viking colony of Iceland can claim to be Europe's oldest state and the world's first parliamentary democracy. Its political institutions date back to the year 930, when settlers formed a legislative assembly called the Althing, a Norse word with the same meaning as the Latin *res publica*. In regions where Vikings settled among more established groups—the British Isles, Scandinavia, Russia, and the Low Countries—they both absorbed and affected these cultures. In Normandy, for example, the descendants of Vikings maintained marriage alliances and ties of kinship with the rest of the Norse world, while at the same time intermarrying with the Franks and adopting their language.

The Heirs of Charlemagne

The most powerful monarchs on the Continent in this era were the Saxon kings who modeled themselves on Charlemagne. Just as the Carolingians had built their power on the conquest of Saxony in the eighth century, the Saxon kings now built theirs on the conquests of Slavic lands to the east. They also nurtured their image as guardians of Christendom. In 955, King Otto I of Saxony defeated the pagan Magyars while carrying a sacred lance that had belonged to Charlemagne. This victory established him as Charlemagne's worthy successor. In 962, accordingly, he went to Rome to be crowned emperor by Pope John XII. But Otto then turned the tables on the pope, deposing him for his scandalous lifestyle and selecting a new pope to replace him. Otto thereby laid the foundation for his successors' later claims to imperial autonomy.

Otto also advertised his inheritance of Charlemagne's power through his patronage of arts and learning. He presided over the establishment of cathedral schools and helped the bishops of his domain turn their own courts into cultural centers, too. However, Otto could not control either the papacy or the independent towns of northern Italy unless he maintained a permanent presence there. And if he remained in Italy too long, his authority in Saxony broke down. This was a dilemma that neither he nor his successors were able to solve, and the rift between local elites and the king widened when the imperial crown passed to a new dynasty, the Salians of neighboring Franconia. By the 1070s, when the Salian Henry IV attempted to assert control over Saxony, he touched off a war that was to have momentous repercussions (see below).

Aspects of Charlemagne's legacy also survived in Catalonia, where counts descended from Carolingian appointees continued to administer justice in public courts of law and to draw revenues from tolls and trade. The city of Barcelona grew rapidly as both a long-distance and a regional market under the protection of these counts. In Aquitaine also, the counts of Poitiers and Toulouse continued to rest their authority on Carolingian foundations.

In Charlemagne's own Frankish kingdom, however, Carolingian rule collapsed. In some areas, a few Carolingian institutions survived, but they were used to build up new, autonomous principalities such as Anjou and Flanders. But in the Franks' traditional heartland, Carolingian authority disappeared. The Franks still had a king, but he was no longer a descendant of Charlemagne. Moreover, his domain had been reduced to the tiny region around Paris,

EUROPE, c. 1100. This map shows the patchwork of political power in western Europe after the millennium, although it cannot accurately illustrate the degree of fragmentation within these major territories, especially those of the Holy Roman Empire. ▪ *What factors account for the close relationship between Italy and the German principalities?* ▪ *How are they related to the northwestern regions of the Continent and the British Isles?* ▪ *Which geopolitical entities would you expect to emerge as dominant in the following centuries?*

which the local count, Hugh Capet, had managed to defend against the Vikings in 987 thus earning himself the title of king. Marooned on this Ile de France (literally, "island of France"), the Capetian kings clung to the fiction that they were the heirs of Charlemagne's greatness. Yet it would be another two hundred years before one of them made this fiction a political reality.

AN AGRICULTURAL REVOLUTION

Agricultural innovation tends to occur slowly, yet it is still appropriate to call the profound changes that took place in this period revolutionary. Indeed, it is arguable that this agricultural revolution was more important than that of the modern era (see Chapter 19).

EMPEROR OTTO THE GREAT. In this opening from a deluxe set of Gospels he commissioned for himself, Otto is shown seated on a throne and vested with the regalia of imperial and royal authority, surrounded by clerical and secular counselors, and receiving tribute from a procession of women representing the four regions of his domain: Slavinia, Germania, Gallia, and Roma. ▪ *Compare this image to that of Emperor Justinian on page 159 (Chapter 7).* ▪ *In what ways is Otto making use of similar iconography?* ▪ *What claims to power does he make thereby?*

New Technologies

The driving force behind the agricultural boom of the Middle Ages was technological: the heavy, wheeled plow developed in this era could cut and turn the rich soil of northern Europe far more effectively than traditional Mediterranean plows. Related improvements in collars and harnesses enhanced the efficiency of plow oxen and made it possible for horses to pull heavy loads without choking themselves. The development of iron horseshoes and the tandem harnessing of paired teams also made the use of horses more effective for the transport of agricultural surpluses to new markets.

Labor-saving devices further increased productivity. The wheelbarrow was a crucial invention, as was the harrow, a tool drawn over the field after plowing to level the earth and mix in the seed. Watermills represented another major innovation. The Romans had relied mainly on human- and animal-powered wheels to grind grain into flour, but the lack of such slave labor led medieval engineers—probably monks—to experiment with various ways of harnessing water power. Local lords followed suit, recognizing the mill as a source of economic and political power to which they could control access through the imposition of tolls. Mills

also drove saws for lumber, processed cloth, pressed olive oil, provided power for iron forges, and crushed pulp for manufacturing paper. They would remain the world's only source of mechanical power for manufacturing until the invention of the steam engine (see Chapter 19).

New Conditions for Growth

Climate change also played a role in this agricultural revolution. Starting in the eighth or ninth century, average temperatures in Europe gradually rose by about 1° or 2°C (3.6°F)—the same increment that has led to global warming today. Eventually, these higher temperatures made it possible to raise crops as far north as Greenland and to produce wine in southern England. Moreover, the warming climate benefited northern Europe by lengthening the growing season, while hotter summers and diminishing rainfall hurt Mediterranean agriculture in equal measure.

At the same time, the settlement of Viking and Magyar peoples decreased the disruption of planting cycles and damage to crops. Left in relative peace, monasteries could develop and implement the tools described above. Productivity was also linked to increased population, fundamental changes in patterns of settlement, and the organization of the peasant work force.

Harnessing People

During the early Middle Ages, most farmers lived on individual plots of land worked by themselves and their families. Starting in the ninth century, however, many individual holdings were merged into large, common fields farmed collectively by entire villages. The complex resulting from such collective endeavors is sometimes called a *manor* (from the Latin verb meaning "to dwell"). Common fields increased efficiency and were more productive, allowing villagers to experiment with new crops and to support larger numbers of animals. In time, prosperous peasants might be able to establish a parish church, a communal oven, a blacksmith, a mill, and a tavern. They could also socialize and assist their neighbors. In a difficult and demanding natural environment, these were important considerations.

In many cases, the impetus for the consolidation of manors came from the peasants themselves. In other cases, a manor could be created or co-opted by a local lord. Its greater productivity meant a larger share of the peasants' surplus; it was also easier to control and exploit peasants who lived together in villages and who were bound by ties of kinship and dependence. Over time, some lords were thus able to reduce formerly free peasants to the status of serfs. Like slaves, serfs inherited their servile status; but unlike slaves, they were not supposed to be sold apart from the lands they worked. From a material perspective, there may have been little difference between a serf and and a free peasant. But as we have seen, social mobility is often tied to geographical mobility—and the inability of serfs to move freely would prevent them from achieving the liberties of those who could.

The Conquest of the Land

For centuries, farmers had known that if they sowed the same crop in the same field year after year, they would eventually exhaust the soil. The traditional solution was to divide one's land, planting half in the fall to harvest in the spring, and leaving the other half to lie fallow. In this era, however, farmers of northern Europe slowly discovered that a three-field crop-rotation system could produce a sustainable increase in overall production. One-third of the land would lie fallow or be used as pasture, one-third would be planted with winter wheat or rye to be harvested in the early summer, and one-third would be planted in the spring, with another crop to be harvested in the fall. These fields were then rotated over a three-year cycle.

This system increased the amount of land under cultivation from 50 to 67 percent, while the two separate growing seasons provided some insurance against loss due to natural disasters or inclement weather. The system also produced higher yields per acre, particularly if fodder crops like oats were a regular part of the rotation pattern, because they replaced the nitrogen that wheat and rye leach out of the soil. Both humans and animals could eat oats, and additional fodder supported more and healthier animals, increasing the efficiency of plow beasts and providing an additional source of protein through meat and milk. The new crop-rotation system also spread labor more evenly over the course of the year.

THE GROWTH OF TOWNS AND TRADE

As we observed in Chapter 7, the urban infrastructure of the Western Roman Empire was weakened in the course of the fifth and sixth centuries. In most areas, monasteries replaced cities as the nuclei of civilization in northwestern Europe. Then, under Charlemagne and his imitators, towns came to be planted by royal initiative, as centers for markets and administration. In Anglo-Saxon England, too, King Alfred and his successors established new towns in strategic locations while at the same time reviving older Roman cities.

Fostering Commerce

Although many of these towns were devastated by Viking raids, the agricultural revolution helped to revitalize them. The rapid urbanization of Europe was also fostered by the initiatives of lords who profited by providing safe havens for travelers and trade. This was especially true in the Rhineland, the Low Countries, and the independent counties of Flanders and Champagne. In southwestern Europe, towns also prospered from their status as ports or their location along overland routes connecting the Mediterranean with the Atlantic.

In Italy, which had been decimated by five centuries of warfare and invasion, the growth of towns gave rise to especially dramatic changes. Initially, the most successful cities were situated in Byzantine-controlled areas of the peninsula: Venice in the north and Amalfi, Naples, and Palermo in the south. In the eleventh century, however, Norman invasions of southern Italy disrupted this trade and opened new opportunities for the northern ports of Genoa and Pisa.

1. Cathedral
2. Alt St. Thomas
3. Alt St. Peter
4. Jung St. Peter
5. St. Nikolaus
6. St. Johann
7. St. Wilhelm
8. St. Stephen

0 50 100   200   300m

☐ Roman fortification, the 'city'
▦ Frankish settlement, called 'New City', walled at end of ninth century
▨ Extension of Frankish settlement before 1200 to include Alt St. Peter's parish
▥ Jung St. Peter's parish, walled 1202–1220
▧ St. Nikolaus parish, walled thirteenth and fourteenth centuries
▦ St. Johann Parish, walled 1374–1390
--- St. Wilhelm parish, walled 1387–1441

THE METAMORPHOSIS OF A MEDIEVAL CITY. The city of Strasbourg, on the long-disputed border between modern Germany and France, exemplifies the multilayered dynamics of urban change throughout the Middle Ages. It began as a Roman settlement, which became the nucleus for an episcopal see—hence the cathedral (1) located in the ancient precinct. It was fortified with new walls at the end of the ninth century, as the Carolingian Empire was collapsing and the Vikings were on the move. It then responded to the renewed prosperity of the eleventh and twelfth centuries, far outgrowing its original bounds, and continued to expand for several centuries thereafter. ▪ *Note the scale of the map. What can you conclude from this about the density of settlement in a medieval city?*

From Italy, exotic goods flowed northward to the towns of Flanders and the fairs (international markets convened at certain times of the year) that enriched the county of Champagne. Flemish towns, in turn, kept up a brisk trade with England, processing English wool into the cloth which, alongside wheat and wine, was the staple commodity of medieval Europe.

It would be misleading, however, to overemphasize the role of long-distance trade. Some towns dependent on such commerce, like Venice and Genoa, attracted populations approaching 100,000 by 1300. But others that grew to be as large, including Paris and London, drew primarily on the wealth of their surrounding hinterlands. Towns large and small existed in a symbiotic relationship with the countryside, transforming raw materials into marketable goods through manufacturing.

"Town Air Makes You Free"

To modern eyes, most premodern towns would still have seemed half rural. Streets were often unpaved and animals were everywhere. Sanitary conditions were poor, and disease could spread rapidly. Fire was another omnipresent danger, because wooden and thatched buildings were clustered close together.

But these inconveniences were far outweighed by the advantages of urban life. As a German adage puts it, "Town air makes you free" (*Stadtluft macht Frei*). The citizens of most medieval towns were not subject to the arbitrary jurisdiction of a lord—or if they were, the lord realized that rewarding initiative with further freedoms fostered still more initiative and produced more wealth. Many Catalonian and Flemish towns accordingly received charters of liberty from the counts of these regions, and were given the right to govern themselves. Others seized that right: in 1127, the people of Arras, on the Franco-Flemish border, declared that they were no longer the serfs of the local monastery and banded together to form a commune, a form of representative government. The monastery was forced to free them, and then free to tax them. The arrangement was mutually beneficial: by the end of the century, Arras was the wealthiest town in northern Europe.

Urban areas further expanded through the constant immigration of free peasants and escaped serfs in search of a better life. For once a town had established its independence, newcomers could claim the status of citizens after a year and a day. For this reason, some powerful lords and rulers resisted the efforts of towns to claim independence. Almost inevitably, they paid a high price for this. In Rome, the pope's claim to secular authority over the city led to frequent uprisings. In the French city of Laon, the bishop who attempted to suppress a newly formed commune was murdered in 1112. In 1127, the count of Flanders was assassinated by a powerful family who resented his claims that they were, in fact, his serfs.

Portable Wealth: Money and Credit

The growth of towns and trade depends not only on surplus goods, initiative, and mobility. It also depends on money: it is no accident that the earliest participants in the commercial

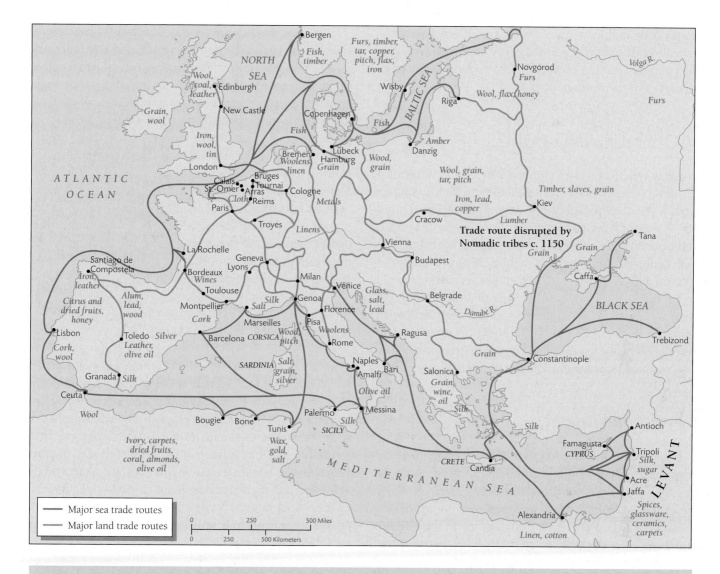

Furs, timber, tar, copper, pitch, flax, iron

Wool, flax, honey

Furs

NORTH SEA

BALTIC SEA

ATLANTIC OCEAN

Wool, coal, leather — Edinburgh

Grain, wool

New Castle

Iron, wool, tin

London

Bremen — Woolens — linen

Hamburg — Lübeck

Copenhagen

Wisby

Riga

Novgorod — Furs

Volga R.

Fish, timber

Bergen

Fish

Danzig — Amber

Wood, grain

Wool, grain, tar, pitch

Iron, lead, copper

Timber, slaves, grain

Tana

Calais — Bruges — Tournai — Arras

St.-Omer

Cloth — Reims

Cologne — Metals

Paris

Troyes

Linens

Cracow

Vienna

Lumber

Trade route disrupted by Nomadic tribes c. 1150

Kiev

Grain

Grain

La Rochelle

Santiago de Compostela

Iron, leather

Bordeaux — Wines

Geneva — Lyons

Milan

Venice — Glass, salt, lead

Budapest

Belgrade

Danube R.

Caffa

BLACK SEA

Toulouse

Alum, lead, wood

Montpellier

Cork

Salt

Genoa

Florence

Woolens

Pisa

Ragusa

Constantinople

Trebizond

Citrus and dried fruits, honey

Marseilles

Lisbon

Cork, wool

Toledo — Silver

Leather, olive oil

Barcelona — CORSICA

Wool, pitch

Rome

Grain

Granada — Silk

SARDINIA — Salt, grain, silver

Naples — Bari

Amalfi

Olive oil

Salonica — Grain, wine, oil

Silk

Ceuta

Wool

Bougie — Bone

Tunis

Palermo

SICILY

Silk

Messina

Silk

Silk

Antioch

Famagusta — CYPRUS

Tripoli — Silk, sugar

LEVANT

Ivory, carpets, dried fruits, coral, almonds, olive oil

Wax, gold, salt

MEDITERRANEAN SEA

CRETE — Candia

Acre

Jaffa

Spices, glassware, ceramics, carpets

Alexandria

Linen, cotton

— Major sea trade routes
— Major land trade routes

0   250   500 Miles
0   250   500 Kilometers

MEDIEVAL TRADE ROUTES. ▪ *What does this map reveal about the relationship between waterways and overland routes during the eleventh and twelfth centuries?* ▪ *Which regions appear to be most extensively interconnected, and why?* ▪ *How does the trade in certain specialized goods create particular commercial patterns?*

revolution of the Middle Ages were cities located in regions whose rulers minted and regulated a strong currency. Yet precisely because there were so many currencies in circulation, the economy also depended on moneychangers and bankers who could extend credit, thus obviating the need for merchants to travel with bags full of cash.

In western Europe, much of this crucial activity was facilitated by bankers situated within the network of close-knit Jewish communities that connected cities like Constantinople, Baghdad, and Córdoba to the burgeoning cities of the north. In many regions, Jews had a virtual monopoly on these activities, because Christians were technically forbidden to lend money at interest. This practice was called *usury* (from the Latin word for "interest"), and Christian theologians cited

various passages from the Old and New Testaments which seemed to condemn it. But in practice, the Church turned a blind eye to such practices. Indeed, many prominent churchmen, including bishops, made fortunes lending money.

Still, the moral stigma attaching to this necessary practice meant that Jews were often targeted at times of crisis, just as they were the people to whom rulers would turn when they needed funds—which helps to explain why many kings, princes, and bishops protected the Jewish communities in their realms and often extended special privileges to them. The unfortunate result of this Christian hypocrisy was the circulation of conspiracy theories harmful to Jews, who were perceived as exercising control over Christians through secret channels of communication and a stranglehold on finance.

Jewish communities' reliance on the protection of powerful men also made them vulnerable when those men withdrew their support or were incapable of controlling the violence unleashed by their own policies.

VIOLENCE AND LORDSHIP

The new wealth of western Europe fostered social mobility, yet it also created a more stratified society. In the Carolingian period, the nobility had comprised a relatively small number of ancient families who counted one another as equals and married among themselves. During the tenth and eleventh centuries, however, new families began to emerge as territorial lords, rivaling and sometimes surpassing the old aristocracy in power and wealth. Some of these new families were descended from lesser officeholders in the Carolingian administration, men who had established independent powers after the empire collapsed. Others were interlopers who sustained war-bands of treasure-hungry young men.

Castles and Knights

The predatory lords who emerged in this period protected their families and followers by building strongholds: castles, from the Latin word *castellum*, "little fortress." These structures, scarcely known in Europe before the Viking invasions, came to dominate the landscape in the eleventh and twelfth centuries. The castle was both defensive and offensive. It rendered its owner more secure from arson and attack—though it was vulnerable to siege—and it enabled him to subdue the surrounding countryside. Indeed, castles often formed the nucleus of a new town by providing protection for those who clustered their dwellings close to its walls. In case of attack, these outliers could move inside.

Most early castles were modest structures built of wood, situated on earthwork mounds surrounded by a ditch or moat. But stone walls and keeps (fortified towers) soon replaced wooden palisades as the level of competitive violence increased. In Italy, rival families even built castles in the middle of towns. Eventually, some castellans ("castle-holders") acquired enough power to challenge more established authorities. These new lords didn't descend from Roman senators or Carolingian counts; instead, they boasted of lineages reaching back to successful warlords like Rollo the Viking, whom the Normans claimed to be their first duke (from the Latin *dux*, "leader").

Both the older aristocracy and these self-made lords needed the help of warriors to enforce their claims to power. Each accordingly maintained a private army of men equipped with the new weaponry and armor that the availability of iron—and new techniques for smelting it—made possible. These men fought on horseback and were therefore called "horsemen": in French, *chevaliers*, and in English, *knights*. Some were the younger sons of lords who sought to increase their chances of winning wealth by attaching themselves to the households of still greater lords. Others were youths recruited from the peasantry, mounted and armed. All that bound them together was the violent prosecution of their lord's interests. Gradually, though, knights also came to regard themselves as belonging to a special military caste with its own rules of conduct. The beginnings of this process are discernible in *The Song of Roland*, and further developments in the twelfth and thirteenth centuries would transform the meaning of chivalry from "horsemanship" to something very different (see Chapter 9).

Kings, Lords, and Vassals

Despite the emergence of self-governing cities and predatory lordships, the Capetian rulers of Paris kept alive the pretence that everyone dwelling in the lands once ruled by more powerful Frankish kings still owed allegiance to them, while the Ottonians claimed to be kings in northern Italy as well as in their own Saxon domain. In practice, however, neither the Ottonians nor the Capetians were able to control the territories they claimed to rule. Effective political and military power lay in the hands of dukes, counts, castellans, and knights. From their castles, these lords (*domini*) constructed dominions: lordships within which they exercised the rights to mint money, judge legal cases, collect taxes, impose tolls, raise troops, and wage war.

YORK CASTLE (ENGLAND). This fortification exemplifies some of the major phases of medieval castle building. The large mound is the remains of an earthwork erected on the orders of William the Conqueror in 1068, when it would have been crowned by a wooden palisade: this most basic type of construction is called a motte-and-bailey castle. York's castle remained a wooden tower until it was destroyed by fire and rebuilt in stone after 1245. It is now known as Clifford's Tower after a rebel leader called Sir Roger Clifford, who was held there prior to his execution in 1322.

The Problem of Feudalism

This highly diffused distribution of power is conventionally known as "feudalism." This is a misleading term, not least because it is a modern invention. As such, it is also confusing, because it has been used by different people to mean different things. For example, scholars influenced by the work of Karl Marx (1818–1883, see Chapter 20) once used "feudalism" to describe a "mode of production" in which wealth is entirely agricultural and cities have not yet formed; but as we have seen, this does not reflect the historical reality of the eleventh and twelfth centuries. For other scholars, "feudalism" is an aristocratic social order in which propertied men are supported by the labor of serfs attached to manors; again, this does not explain the varieties of power wielded in this period. Still others have described "feudalism" as a system in which lesser men hold land from greater men in return for military service of various kinds; but it was not always the greater man who held the most land.

Because all of these definitions are more or less anachronistic, many recent historians have abandoned the term altogether. If, however, we look for a common denominator, we can say that "feudalism" entails the abuse of official privileges for personal gain: the pattern that emerged after the Carolingian Empire had disintegrated. And although people of the time would never have heard the term "feudalism," they would have understood the word at its root: *feudum*, usually translated as "fief" (*FEEF*). A fief is a gift or grant that creates a kind of contractual relationship between the giver and receiver. This gift could be land, but it could also be the revenues from a toll or a mill, or an annual sum of money. In return, the recipient would owe the giver loyalty or services of some kind, and might even be subordinate to the giver, becoming the giver's *vassal* (from a Celtic word meaning "boy").

This relationship was dramatized in an act of *homage*, a powerful ceremony that made the vassal "the man" (in French, *homme*) of his lord. Typically, the vassal would kneel and place his hands together in a gesture of supplication, and the lord would cover the clasped hands with his own. He would then raise up his new "man" and exchange a kiss with him. The symbolic importance of these actions is powerfully clear: the lord (*dominus*) was literally the dominating figure, who could protect and raise up his man— but could also discipline and humiliate him.

In a violent world where no central authority existed, these personal relationships were essential to creating and maintaining order. However, these relationships were not forged or understood in the same ways all over Europe. Nor were they neatly hierarchical. "Feudalism" therefore created no "feudal pyramids," in which knights held fiefs from counts, and counts held fiefs from kings, all in an orderly fashion. Sometimes, kings would insist that the world *should* be structured this way, but they were seldom able to enforce this.

A New Feudal Monarchy: England

The first place where we can begin to observe the efforts of a particular line of kings to establish a monarchy that did operate along these lines is England. In 1066, Duke William of Normandy claimed that he was the rightful successor of the English king, Edward, who had just died. But the English elected a new king, Harold, ignoring William's claim. So William and his army crossed the English Channel to take the kingdom by force, defeating Harold's forces at the Battle of Hastings (see **Interpreting Visual Evidence** on page 192).

Now, however, William had to subjugate all of the other English chieftains who held power, many of whom also aspired to be king. He accomplished this, first, by asserting that he was king by imperial conquest as well as by succession, and that all the land of England consequently belonged to him. Then William rewarded his Norman followers with fiefs: extensive grants of land taken from their English holders, which the Norman lords were allowed to exploit and subdue; in return, William received their homage, loyalty, and a share of their revenues.

The Normans were already accustomed to holding land in return for service in Normandy. But in England, their subordination to the new king was enforced by the effective machinery of the English state and by longstanding English customs that had the force of law. In England, unlike on the Continent, only the king could coin money, collect taxes, supervise justice, and raise an army. William also retained the Anglo-Saxon officers of local government, known as sheriffs, to administer and enforce these rights. William's kingship thus represented a fusion of Carolingian-style traditions of public power with the new type of lordship that had grown up in the tenth and eleventh centuries. It was a feudal monarchy.

The Struggle for Imperial Power

We can contrast the wide-ranging powers of the new Anglo-Norman kings with those of Germany. The German king ruled only a single principality, and his imperial authority over a host of other rulers was only maintained through a close alliance with the Church. Indeed, his chief administrators were archbishops and bishops whom the emperor himself had appointed and installed in their sacred offices, just as Charlemagne had done.

Interpreting Visual Evidence

The Graphic History of the Bayeux Tapestry

One of the most famous historical documents of all time is not a document at all: it is an embroidered strip of linen 231 feet long (originally much longer) and 20 inches wide. It is also not a tapestry, as its name misleadingly implies, but an elaborate exercise in needlepoint. It tells the story of the Norman Conquest of England and the events leading up to it. The circumstances of its making remain mysterious, but it was certainly commissioned by someone close to William the Conqueror (1027–1087), the Norman duke who claimed the throne of England in 1066. Indeed, its purpose was to justify William's invasion of England after Harold Godwinson (c. 1022–1066), was crowned king of England in his place (image B). One likely patron is Queen Edith of England, the widow of the late King Edward (r. 1042–66) and sister of Harold, who became a friend and advisor to William. Edith was noted for her skill in embroidery as well as for her political acumen, and she would have been able to oversee the making of this visual history by the women of her household. Two of its evocative scenes, with translations of accompanying Latin texts, are reproduced here.

A. Here Harold Sails the Sea. In this scene from the first portion of the Tapestry, Harold has been sent on an embassy by King Edward. He feasts with friends in a hall on the English coast before crossing the Channel.

B. Here Is Seated Harold, King of the English. Although Harold may have promised to relinquish his claim to the English throne, the central scene of the tapestry is his coronation. Stigant, the archbishop of Canterbury, stands on his left. Outside the cathedral, the people of London look on curiously. Some appear to be surprised or alarmed.

Questions for Analysis

1. Like a graphic novel or a comic strip, the Bayeux Tapestry tells its story through images; words (in very simple Latin) play a minor role. What do the Tapestry's artists choose to express exclusively through visualization? When do they choose to state something verbally? What might be the motivation behind these choices? What is left out of the story, or left ambiguous? What might be the reason(s) for this?

2. In addition to being a source for political and military historians, the Bayeux Tapestry provides us with fascinating glimpses into the daily life and material culture of the Middle Ages. What, for example, can you conclude about the necessary preparations for a voyage by sea, or about the history of clothing, or weaponry, or animals?

3. If Queen Edith is responsible for making the Tapestry, it would constitute one of the few surviving historical accounts by a woman prior to the twentieth century. Would the fact of the creator's gender change your perception of this artifact, or of these particular scenes? Why or why not?

R*exrogat* Abbatem Mathildim SupplicatAtq̃;

MATILDA OF TUSCANY MEDIATES BETWEEN EMPEROR AND POPE. Matilda was one of the most powerful rulers in eleventh-century Europe, controlling many strategic territories in northern Italy. Fluent in German as well as Latin and Italian, she was a supporter of the reforming movement within the Church. The Latin inscription accompanying this manuscript miniature reads: "The King entreats the Abbot [i.e., the pope] and also humbles himself before Matilda." ▪ *How does this image represent the relationships among these figures?* ▪ *Which appears to be the most powerful, and why?*

But in the latter half of the eleventh century, this close cooperation between sacred and secular authority was fractured. In 1056, the six-year-old Henry IV (1050–1106) succeeded his father as king and emperor, and the German princes of various regions tried to gain control of the royal government at the expense of Henry's regents. When Henry began to rule in his own right, in 1073, these hostilities escalated into a civil war. At the same time, the newly elected pope, Gregory VII (r. 1073–85), began to insist that no laymen—not even kings—should have any influence within the Church.

King Henry, of course, resisted any initiative that would prohibit him from selecting his own bishops, who were the key administrators of his realm. So Pope Gregory allied himself with the rebellious nobility and moved to depose Henry. In order to save his crown, Henry was thus forced to

acknowledge the pope's superiority. Crossing the Alps into Italy in 1077, in the depths of winter, he found Gregory at the castle of Canossa and under the protection of one of Europe's most powerful rulers, Matilda of Tuscany. Encouraged by Matilda, Henry performed an elaborate ritual of penance, standing for three successive days outside the castle, barefoot, stripped of imperial trappings, clad only in sackcloth.

This performance forestalled Henry's deposition but it did not resolve his dispute with the German nobility. And it also reversed the relationship between secular power and religious power. Since the time of Constantine, popes had been dependant on the rulers who protected them. Now an emperor had been bested by the pope.

RELIGIOUS REFORM AND PAPAL POWER

The increased power of the papacy in the eleventh century was a development that would have been hard to foresee at the time of the Charlemagne's death. But the redistribution of power within the former Carolingian Empire meant that no ruler could maintain Charlemagne's hold on the Church. Those parish churches that survived were often regarded as the personal property of some local family. Bishoprics, too, were co-opted by families who regarded Church lands and offices as their private property. Even monasteries underwent a process of privatization, becoming safe havens for aristocratic younger sons and daughters with little inclination for religious life. Meanwhile, the holders of papal office were its worst abusers. Most were incompetent or corrupt, the sons or tools of powerful Roman families. Many fathered sons who themselves succeeded to high ecclesiastical office, including that of pope. By the tenth century, the papacy's credibility had been severely compromised.

The Monastic Reform Movement

The first successful attempts to restore the spiritual authority of the Church can be traced to the founding of a new kind of monastery in Burgundy (now southeastern France). In 910, a Benedictine abbey called Cluny freed itself from any obligation to local families by placing itself under the direct protection of the papacy. Although it had a wealthy benefactor, this lord relinquished control over Cluny's property; instead, he and his family were granted special spiritual privileges, thus guaranteeing their eternal reward in Heaven.

This arrangement would set a new precedent for the relationship between monasteries and powerful families for centuries to come, as Cluny began to sponsor other

Analyzing Primary Sources

A Miraculous Reliquary

Although pilgrimages had been a part of Christian religious practice for centuries, they became more central elements of popular piety from the tenth century on. Pilgrims brought money and spiritual prestige to the monasteries that housed miracle-working relics, and competition among monastic houses sometimes led one house to steal the relics of another. But some critics worried that these newly popular shrines were encouraging idolatry. Bernard of Angers (c. 960–1028) was one such critic. His account of a visit to the shrines of several saints, including that of Sainte Foy ("Saint Faith") at Conques in southern France, reveals the negative impression that ornate reliquaries made on him—and the power of wonder-working relics to correct that impression.

t is an ancient custom in all of Auvergne, Rodez, Toulouse, and the neighboring regions that the local saint has a statue of gold, silver, or some other metal . . . [that] serves as a reliquary for the head of the saint or for a part of his body. The learned might see in this a superstition and a vestige of the cult of demons, and I myself . . . had the same impression the first time I saw the statue of Saint Gerard . . . resplendent with gold and stones, with an expression so human that the simple people . . . pretend that it winks at pilgrims whose prayers it answers. I admit to my shame that turning to my friend Bernerius and laughing I whispered to him in Latin, "What do you think of the idol? Wouldn't Jupiter or Mars be happy with it?" . . .

Three days later we arrived at [the shrine of] St. Faith. . . . We approached [the reliquary] but the crowd was such that we could not prostrate ourselves like so many others already lying on the floor. Unhappy, I remained standing, fixing my view on the image and murmuring this prayer, "St. Faith, you whose relics rest in this sham, come to my assistance on the day of judgment." And this time I looked at my companion . . . because I found it outrageous that all of these rational beings should be praying to a mute and inanimate object. . . .

Later I greatly regretted to have acted so stupidly toward the saint of God.

This was because among other miracles [that] Don Adalgerius, at that time dean and later . . . abbot [of Conques], told me [was] a remarkable account of a cleric named Oldaric. One day when the venerable image had to be taken to another place, . . . he restrained the crowd from bringing offerings and he insulted

The reliquary of Saint Faith, early tenth century.

and belittled the image of the saint. . . . The next night, a lady of imposing severity appeared to him: "You," she said, "how dare you insult my image?" Having said this, she flogged her enemy with a staff. . . . He survived only long enough to tell the vision in the morning.

Thus there is no place left for arguing whether the effigy of St. Faith ought to be venerated, since it is clear that he who reproached the holy martyr nevertheless retracted his reproach. Nor is it a spurious idol where nefarious rites of sacrifice or of divination are conducted, but rather a pious memorial of a holy virgin, before which great numbers of faithful people decently and eloquently implore her efficacious intercession for their sins.

Source: Bernard of Angers, "The Book of the Miracles of St. Faith," in Patrick J. Geary, ed. and trans., *Readings in Medieval History*, 3rd ed. (Peterborough, Ont., Canada: 2003), pp. 333–34 (slightly modified).

Questions for Analysis

1. Why does Bernard initially object to the display of relics in ornate reliquaries? Why would he consider this practice blasphemous? How does he become reconciled to it?

2. Can you think of present-day practices that resemble the medieval fascination with collecting, displaying, and venerating relics? What do such practices reveal about any society?

monasteries on the same model. Indeed, the foundation of daughter houses was another innovation: prior to this, all Benedictine monasteries had been independent of one another, united only by their observance of Benedict's *Rule*. Now Cluny established a network of Cluniac clones across Europe, each one performing the same elaborate round of prayer and worship for which Cluny became famous, and each one entirely free from the control of local lords.

Cluniac influence was strongest in the former Frankish territories and in Italy, where the virtual absence of effective rulers allowed monastic reforms to thrive unchecked. In Germany and Anglo-Saxon England, by contrast, monastic reform emerged as an essential responsibility of Christian kings whose role model was the pious Charlemagne. These kings, too, followed Cluniac example by insisting on the strict observance of poverty, chastity, and obedience within the monastery, and on the performance of liturgical prayer. Yet because these kings were the guarantors of the monasteries' freedom from outside interference, it was they who appointed the abbots, just as they also appointed the bishops of their kingdoms.

These parallel reforming movements made monasticism the dominant spiritual model for Latin Christianity, and monasteries' peaceful, orderly round of daily worship was regarded as mirroring the perfect harmony of Heaven. Monasteries also had an important influence on the piety of ordinary people, because many monastic communities maintained parishes that ministered to the laity. The spiritual practices that had once been unique to monks and nuns in earlier centuries therefore came to influence daily life outside the cloister.

One potent example of this new popular spirituality is the growing devotion to relics. Monasteries were often the repositories of cherished objects associated with saints, such as fragments of bone or pieces of cloth cut from the garments of some holy person. These souvenirs were believed to possess special protective and curative powers. A relic was usually buried beneath the altar of a monastery's church, and relics were also collected and displayed in elaborate reliquaries made of precious metals and studded with jewels. Indeed, the relics themselves were so valuable that monasteries competed with one another for their acquistion and even plotted the "holy theft" of a particularly prized treasure. For instance, the relics of Nicholas, a fourth-century bishop of Myra (in Turkey), were stolen from the saint's tomb during the eleventh century and brought to Bari in southeastern Italy, where Benedictine monks built a magnificent church to house them.

The possession and display of relics thus became a way for monasteries to generate revenue, since those who sought cures or favors at the shrine of a saint would often make a donation to the monastery in the saint's honor. If a saint was especially famous for a particular type of miracle, pilgrims might travel thousands of miles to visit a shrine. Saint Nicholas was famous for increasing the wealth of his suppliants, and for bestowing gifts—hence his later incarnation as Santa Claus. Those of the apostle James at Compostela (northwestern Spain) became the chief destination on a major pilgrimage route, rivaling even the holy sites of Rome and Jerusalem. Pilgrimage was another of the important ways in which the new patterns of Christian piety that developed in monasteries began to spread to the laity.

The Reform of the Papacy

By the eleventh century, the powerful movement toward spiritual renewal began to embrace the sees of bishops. This was a major change: bishops and the priests who served in their dioceses were secular clergy, living in the world (*saeculum* in Latin); it had long been expected that they would share some of the worldly preoccupations and lifestyles of their parishioners. But as their influence grew, the monasteries under the sway of Cluny began to lobby for even larger reforms, amounting to a fundamental dismantling of customs that reached back to the organization of the Church under Constantine, seven centuries earlier. They centered their attacks on simony (*SIGH-mony*), a term describing any use of ecclesiastical office for personal gain, including the purchase or sale of a bishopric or a priest's living (i.e., house, goods, and annual salary).

Even more radical was the reformers' demand that secular clergy share the lifestyles of monks, taking vows of personal poverty and celibacy. Although some early councils of the Church had attempted to regulate the marriage of bishops and priests, none had been successful. There were good reasons for this: the task of ministering to the laity was very different from the monk's task of perpetual prayer and communal life. For a thousand years, it had been conceded that the demands of priestly celibacy were not only unreasonable, they would deprive a priest's parishioners of an additional resource and ministry: that of his wife. As a result, the vast majority of parish priests all across Europe were married, and in the Eastern Orthodox Church they would remain so. Married bishops were rarer, but not unknown. In Brittany, the archbishop of Dol and his wife publicly celebrated the marriages of their daughters, endowing them with lands belonging to the bishopric; in Milan, the archbishops flatly rejected reformers' calls for celibacy, declaring that their patron saint, Ambrose (Chapter 6), had been married, too.

In Rome, the papacy remained resolutely unreformed until 1046, when the German emperor Henry III deposed three rival Roman nobles who claimed to be pope and appointed in their place his own relative, a monk who adopted the name Leo IX (r. 1049–54). Leo and his supporters began to promulgate decrees against simony and clerical marriage. They then took steps to enforce these decrees by traveling throughout the Continent, disciplining clerics deemed guilty of simony or obstinately determined not to "put away" their wives—whom the reformers insisted on calling "concubines" as a way of discrediting these respectable relationships.

Implicit in Leo's reforming efforts was a new vision of the Church as a type of feudal monarchy, with the pope at the apex of a spiritual pyramid. Not surprisingly, therefore, Leo and his successors met with considerable opposition within the Church itself, and they could only enforce their claims in regions where they had the support of secular rulers.

But when Henry III died in 1056, the regents of his child heir Henry IV (whose reign we discussed above) were neither able nor willing to stand behind the reforming movement. The Roman aristocracy seized this opportunity to install one of their own number on the papal throne. By this time, however, the reform movement had gathered momentum; a year later, a new pope had been installed who was determined to counter any interference from either the German or Italian nobility. To this end, Nicholas II (r. 1059–61) created a new legislative body, the College of Cardinals (from the Latin for "collection" of "hinges"). The College became the pivotal force for the creation of papal policy, and it also ensured the continuity of the papal office by overseeing the selection of new popes, a role it still plays today. Most fundamentally, this removed the emperor's power to oversee the process of elections himself.

The Investiture Conflict

A few years after Henry IV began to rule in his own right, the new College of Cardinals selected as pope a zealous reformer called Hildebrand, a Cluniac monk of Tuscan origins who took the name Gregory VII. Initially, pope and emperor treated one another with deference. Henry IV's position in Germany had been weakened by civil wars, and he needed papal backing to restore his authority.

Two years later, however, relations between pope and emperor were riven by a conflict that would permanently alter the relationship between spiritual and temporal rulers in western Europe. Superficially, the issue that divided Gregory and Henry was that of investiture: the right to appoint bishops and to equip them with the trappings of office. Since the time of the Carolingians, this had been the prerogative of the emperor. But to Gregory, this practice smacked of simony, since a lay lord would obviously choose bishops who would be politically useful to him, regardless of their spiritual qualifications.

The real issue, however, was not the political power of bishops; it was control of that power. For paradoxically, the papal reform movement was predicated on liberating the Church from powerful influences in order that the Church itself might become more powerful. This was the principle that lay behind the discouraging of clerical marriage, too: Church offices and Church property had to be protected by the Church for the Church. Allowing priests to marry might encourage the handing down of offices to sons, just as allowing rulers to appoint bishops encouraged bishops to act as the rulers' agents. These practices tainted the austere authority that the pope was trying to cultivate, and it also threatened to alienate property that the papacy wanted to harness for its own purposes.

Gregory took the reform movement to a new level by insisting that adherence to these principles was not just a matter of policy but a matter of religious dogma, defined as "a truth necessary for salvation." When Henry IV defiantly proceeded to invest the new archbishop of Milan, Gregory excommunicated a number of Henry's advisors, including several bishops. Henry thereupon renounced his obedience to Gregory, calling on him to resign. Gregory responded by excommunicating Henry.

In itself, the excommunication of a king was not terribly unusual. Gregory, however, went much further by equating excommunication with deposition: since Henry was no longer a faithful son of the Church, he was no longer the king of Germany and his subjects had a sacred duty to rebel against him. It was this that occasioned Henry's humiliating stand before the castle at Canossa in January of 1077, which we discussed above. But the story does not end there, because Henry eventually used his restored powers to drive Gregory himself from Rome. In 1085, the aged pope died in exile in southern Italy. By then, however, he had established the principles on which papal governance would be based for the remainder of the Middle Ages.

In 1122, the conflict over investiture was ultimately resolved at the Concordat of Worms (VOHRMS) in Germany. Its terms declared that the emperor was forbidden to invest bishops with the *religious* symbols of their office, but was allowed to bestow their rights as *temporal* rulers, in his capacity as their overlord. In practice, then, the rulers of Europe retained a great deal of influence over ecclesiastical appointments. But they also had to acknowledge that bishops were now part of a new hierarchy headed by the pope, loyal to Rome and not to the ruler of the region in which they lived.

CRUSADING CAUSES AND OUTCOMES

Gregory VII's equation of excommunication with deposition had given the pope a powerful new weapon to use against wayward rulers. Indeed, Gregory insisted that the pope has the power to judge all men but cannot himself be judged by any earthly authority. Moreover, he asserted the pope's power to free any man from obligations to his lord, on the grounds that every Christian owes ultimate loyalty to the pope, the sole representative of Christ on earth and the arbiter of eternal life or death. These were big claims. How could they be realized? In the end, it took the appeal of a Byzantine emperor and the preaching of a crusade against Islam to unite western Christendom under the banner of the papacy.

The Expansion and Limitations of Byzantium

As western Europe expanded and grew prosperous, the Eastern Roman Empire was undergoing its own transformations. The decline of the Abbasid caliphate in Baghdad had relieved some of the pressures on the eastern frontier in the course of the ninth century. Yet at the same time, a Muslim fleet captured the Byzantine islands of Sicily and Crete; the migration of pagan Slavs into the Balkans was rapidly undermining Byzantine control of that region; and a formidable enemy had emerged in the north, as the Vikings known as the Rus' established themselves along the river systems that fed into the Black and Caspian Seas. The Rus's most important trading partner was the Abbasid caliphate, with which they exchanged slaves, honey, wax, and furs in return for silver, Indian spices, and Chinese silks. But the Rus' knew their way to Constantinople, too. In 860, while the Byzantine emperor and his army were busy elsewhere, a fleet of Russian Vikings sailed into the Black Sea and attacked the capital.

A century later, Greek-speaking missionaries began converting the Balkan Slavs to Orthodox Christianity, devising for them a written language known as Old Church Slavonic and creating the Cyrillic alphabet still used today in Bulgaria, Serbia, and Russia. Byzantine rulers also established a military and commercial alliance with the Rus' kingdom centered around Kiev. In 911, about 700 Rus' fought with the Byzantine fleet in an attack on Muslim Crete. In 957, a Kievan Christian princess named Olga was lavishly entertained on a state visit to Constantinople. And in 989, the emperor Basil II turned to Vladimir, prince of Kiev, for the troops he needed to win a civil war against an imperial rival. In return

for Vladimir's help, Basil married him to his sister Anna; and Vladimir, along with his people, accepted baptism into the Orthodox Church. Russia has remained strongly Orthodox to this day, despite Soviet efforts to dismantle the Russian Orthodox Church in the twentieth century.

At the same time, the Byzantines launched a series of successful campaigns against the Abbasids, reconquering territories that had been lost since the seventh century. Most peoples of this region had remained Christian through three centuries of benign Islamic rule, but the Armenians and the Syrians in particular had their own distinctive Christian traditions that were at odds, both doctrinally and linguistically, with the Greek-speaking church at Constantinople. Reincorporating these "heretics" into the empire thus strained the limits of Byzantine orthodoxy to a considerable degree, and it also created centers of power that lay outside the imperial capital at Constantinople. Accordingly, rivalries divided the eastern nobility and the imperial court, eventually erupting into warfare after one aristocratic family attempted a coup.

Meanwhile, these projects of reconquest and expansion were overextending the Byzantine military and its treasury. In an effort to raise cash, some emperors in the mid-eleventh century began to debase the gold coinage that had kept the empire competitive with the Muslim caliphates, thus undermining Byzantine commerce at the very moment when Venice, Genoa, and Pisa were consolidating their control in the eastern Mediterranean and taking over the lucrative trade between Muslim North Africa (including Egypt) and western Europe.

The failing economy, ongoing civil war, a divided army, and unrest in the Balkans had therefore already weakened Byzantine sovereignty when the empire was confronted with yet another threat. The Seljuqs, a powerful dynasty of Sunni Muslims who were building their own empire based in Persia, began to move westward. In 1071, they captured Armenia and moved swiftly into the Byzantine heartland of Anatolia (Turkey), where they destroyed the army sent to deflect them. In the same year, the Seljuqs captured Jerusalem, which had been part of the Shi'ite caliphate based in Egypt, ruled by the Fatimids (Chapter 7). By 1081, when the eastern nobility of Byzantium finally emerged triumphant in its ongoing bid for the imperial throne, the new emperor Alexius Comnenus (r. 1081–1118) found himself at the head of a crippled state.

The Call for a Crusade

In the first decade of his rule, Alexius managed to shore up the failing economy and to secure his hold over the Balkans. He then began to plan a campaign against the Seljuqs. But with what forces? The Byzantine army barely

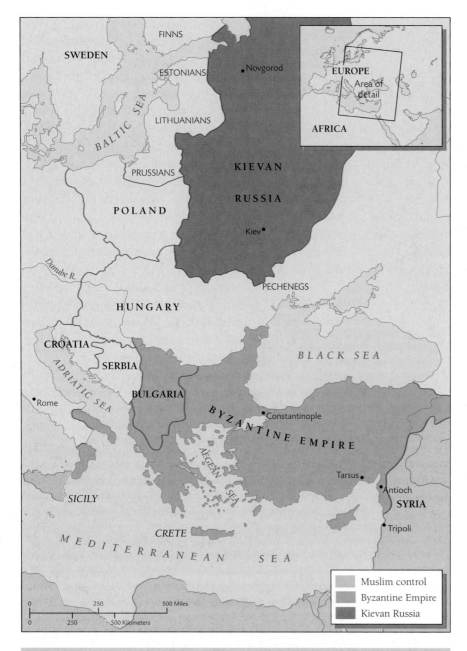

THE BYZANTINE EMPIRE, c. 1025. ▪ *According to this map, what political challenges faced the Byzantine Empire in the eleventh century?* ▪ *How was the long-standing influence of Muslims in the Near East likely to affect the character of Byzantine culture?* ▪ *How did the domain of Kievan Russia potentially create additional economic and military pressure on Byzantium, directly as well as indirectly?*

would be successful if pitted against the lightly armored Seljuqs.

It was in the hopes of recruiting a mercenary force, therefore, that Alexius approached Pope Urban II (r. 1088–99). This was a move that played into the hands of the papacy. Urban was trying hard to realize some of the powerful claims that Gregory VII had made on behalf of papal authority, and this seemed like a golden opportunity. By coming to the aid of Byzantium, he would show the restive princes of western Europe that the papacy was a force to be reckoned with. At the same time, he hoped to show that Western military and spiritual might was greater than that of the weakened East, thereby realizing a centuries-old dream of a universal Christian Church based in Rome, with the pope himself at its head. In addition, Urban would show support for another reforming effort that had gained momentum in recent years: a peace movement that was attempting to quell the endemic violence unleashed by competitive bands of knights and their rapacious lords. What better way to defuse the situation than to ship those violent energies overseas, deploying them against a common enemy?

So Alexius got far more than he had bargained for. He had needed a modest contingent of a few thousand troops, to help him reconquer Anatolia. What he got was a vast army of 100,000 men, charged by Urban II to retake the holy city of Jerusalem for Christendom. For Urban decided to interpret Alexius's request loosely. Speaking before an assembled crowd at Clermont (in France) in 1095, he announced that any knights who wished to fight, pillage, and wreak havoc could do so for a just and Christian cause by liber-

existed, having been decimated in Greece by a far superior cavalry of Norman knights in 1085. For by this time, the Normans had established independent principalities in southern Italy and Sicily, taking advantage of the perpetual power vacuum in those regions and showcasing the effective tactics of chivalry. This encounter between the Byzantine emperor and western Europe's best warriors was fateful: it convinced Alexius that heavily armed horsemen

ating the Holy Land from its Muslim captors. Here at home, he said they were riffraff and marauders, destined for hellfire and damnation; abroad, they would be crusaders, which meant that anyone fighting or dying in the service of Christ would win absolution for his sins. By taking up the cross (*crux*, hence "crusade"), a warrior stood to win glory, booty, and salvation.

The ultimate response to Urban's call exceeded all expectations. Indeed, his message was amplified by other

ROLAND AS A CRUSADING KNIGHT. The association between knighthood and crusading helped to raise the social status of knights and contributed to the refinement of a chivalric ethos. Here, a crusading knight, dressed head to foot in expensive chain mail, is shown kneeling in homage to his lord, God.

their vows, the vast majority went home. So why did they go in the first place? The risks of dying on such a journey were high; the costs of embarking were enormous. By any rational assessment, the Crusade was a fool's errand.

Hence the importance of reckoning with the reality of the crusaders' piety. Crusading was the ultimate pilgrimage. If one could receive special blessings by traveling to Compostela, Conques, or Bari, how much more blessed would one be if one fought through to the Holy Land itself! Urban II made this point explicit at Clermont, and some preachers went even further, promising that crusaders would be entirely freed from otherworldly punishments for all sins committed up to that point in their lives, and that the souls of those who died on crusade would go straight to Heaven.

Crusade preaching also emphasized the vengeance that Christ's soldiers should exact on the Church's enemies in the East. But to some crusaders, it seemed absurd to wait until they arrived in Jerusalem to undertake this aspect of their mission. Muslims might hold Jesus's property at Jerusalem, but Christian theology held Jews responsible for the death of Jesus himself. Assaults against Jewish communities therefore began in the spring of 1096 and quickly spread eastward with the crusaders. Hundreds of Jews were killed in the German towns of Mainz, Worms, Speyer, and Cologne, and hundreds more were forcibly baptized as the price for escaping death at the hands of crusading knights. Many individual churchmen attempted to prevent these attacks, among them the bishops in whose dioceses Jews lived. But the Church's own negative propaganda thwarted these efforts, and pogroms against Europe's Jews would remain a regular and terrible feature of Christian crusading.

The Christian Conquest of Jerusalem

Surprised by the scale of the response to his appeal, Emperor Alexius did his best to move the crusaders quickly through Constantinople and into Asia Minor. But differences in outlook between the crusaders and the emperor quickly became apparent. Alexius had little interest in an expedition to Jerusalem, and insisted that the crusaders promise to restore any territory they captured to him. To the crusaders—whose view of their mission had been shaped by Urban's policies (not those of Alexius)—this seemed like treachery. The crusaders, furthermore, did not understand the Byzantine emperor's willingness to make alliances with some Muslim rulers (the Shi'ite Fatimids of Egypt and the Abassids of Baghdad) against other Muslim rulers (the Sunni Seljuqs), and they ignorantly concluded that the Byzantines were working to undermine the crusading effort.

preachers, including a zealous priest called Peter the Hermit, who alleged that the Seljuqs had prevented him from visiting the Holy Land. Within a year, tens of thousands of warriors and a large number of women and children were on the move toward Constantinople. As with any large enterprise, the participants' motives must have varied. A few might have hoped to win principalities for themselves in the wild East. Many were the dependents of other men, and had no choice but to accompany their lords; some hoped to free themselves from dependence by fighting. Most had no idea how long the journey would be, or knew anything about the places for which they were destined.

But except for a few of the greatest lords—mostly Normans from southern Italy—the prospect of winning new lands in the East was both unlikely and undesired. Indeed, one of the greatest challenges facing the Christian kingdom established in Jerusalem after 1099 was the fact that crusaders so rarely wanted to stay there. After fulfilling

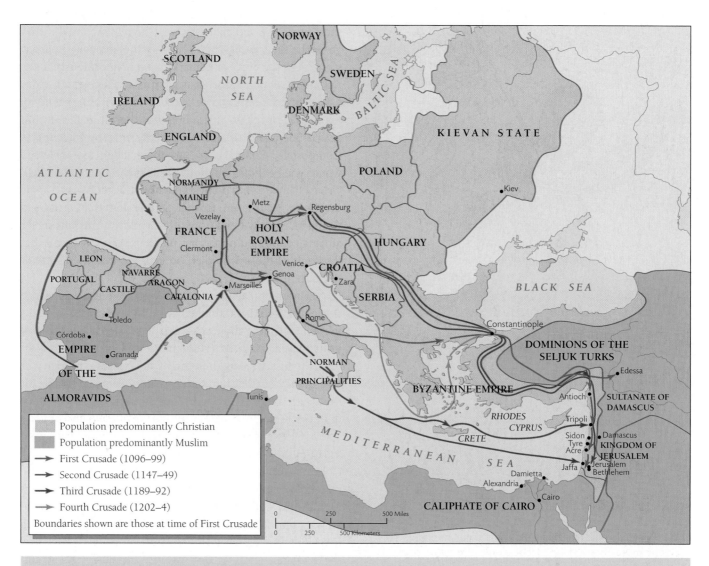

THE ROUTES OF THE CRUSADERS, 1096–1204. Compare the routes followed by participants in the first three Crusades. ▪ *What were the three main routes followed by crusaders?* ▪ *What geographical and political factors appear to be determining these trajectories?* ▪ *Why was the Fourth Crusade's route so different?*

Viewed from the perspective of Alexius, the Crusade was a disaster. But from that of the papacy, it was a triumph. In 1098, crusaders captured the old Hellenistic city of Antioch and with it most of the Syrian coast. At the end of 1099, they took Jerusalem, indiscriminately slaughtering its Muslim, Jewish, and Christian inhabitants. Their quick success stemmed mainly from the fact that their Muslim opponents were at that moment divided amongst themselves: the Fatimids had in fact recaptured Jerusalem just months before the crusaders arrived, and the defeated Seljuqs were at war with one other. Western military tactics, in particular the dominance of heavily armored knights, also played an important role in the crusaders' success. Equally critical was the naval support offered by Genoa

and Pisa, whose merchant adventurers hoped to control the Indian spice trade that passed through the Red Sea and on to Alexandria. The Crusade thereby contributed to the decline of Byzantine sovereignty and decisively altered the balance of power between Byzantium and western Europe.

The Consequences of the Crusades

For Byzantium, the consequences of the crusading movement were clearly tragic. On the Islamic world, by contrast, the impact was much more modest. The crusader kingdoms were never more than a sparsely settled cluster of colonies along the coastline of Syria and Palestine. Because the crusaders never did control the Red Sea, Muslim commerce with India and the Far East was unaffected. In any case, the crusaders did not *want* to interfere with the caravan routes that wound through their new territories. Trade between Islam and the West therefore continued despite periodic interruptions. The greatest economic gains went to the Italian maritime republics of Venice and Genoa, and to Islamic merchants who came to depend on Western markets for their goods. Both sides also gained in military terms: Westerners learned new techniques of fortification, and Muslims learned new methods of siege warfare and new respect for the uses of heavy cavalry.

But the most long-lasting consequence of the Crusades has also proved the most deadly in the long run: the development of both Christian and Islamic doctrines of holy war, the ideologies of crusade and *jihad* that continue to be so destructive in the twenty-first century. By 1144, most of the crusader principalities in Syria had been recaptured. Not long afterward, Syria and Egypt were united under the great Muslim leader Salah ad-Din (Saladin), who decisively recaptured Jerusalem in 1187. Further Crusades were launched in response, none of them successful and all of them putting renewed pressure on Byzantium. The only Latin kingdom that survived was Acre (Akko in northern Israel), and its fall in 1291 marked the end of any viable western European presence in the region—until the short-lived conquests of Napolean at the end of the eighteenth century (see Chapter 18).

Despite the movement's ultimate failure, then, crusading continued to dictate the terms of western Europeans' attitudes toward the wider world and even toward one another, as we shall see in the following chapters. It fostered a new political and religious ethos that would spur the "reconquest" of the Iberian peninsula by the Christian rulers of Spain and lead to the massacre or forced conversion of Muslims and Jews. Crusading also provided the rhetoric underlying English wars against the Welsh and the Scots, and the language that justified the massacre and dispossession of "heretics" in southern France by northern French colonists. It motivated voyages of discovery from the fifteenth century onward and the subsequent conquest of the Americas and the colonization of Asia, Africa, and Australia (Chapter 11). And it has continued to exacerbate Western relations with Islam to this day.

THE CULTURE OF THE MUSLIM WEST

It would be misleading to assert that all the consequences of the Crusades were negative. Increased intellectual and cultural contact between the Latin West and the Islamic world had an enormous impact on European learning, literature, music, and art. The study and practical applications of mathematics were revolutionized when Europeans adopted Arabic numerals and the concept of zero—first promoted in western Europe, not surprisingly, by the son of a Pisan merchant who grew up in Muslim Algeria, Leonardo Fibonacci (c. 1170–c. 1250).

Even Christian theology was transformed by contact with Islam. Muslim scholars had inherited, preserved, and developed not only Hellenistic medicine and science but the philosophy of Aristotle, which would form the basis of a new Christian philosophy in the twelfth and thirteenth centuries (see Chapter 9). Up to now, Europeans had been almost entirely ignorant of Muslim beliefs, assuming that Muslims were pagans who worshiped a god called Mahomet or Mahoun. But in 1143, a scholar called Robert of Ketton (c. 1100–c. 1160), originally from a small town in England, completed a Latin translation of the Qu'ran, working in Spain with the encouragement of the abbot of Cluny. For back in the 1130s, he and a friend, Hermann of Carinthia (in Slovenia), had traveled to the crusader kingdoms, to become students of Arabic. They exemplify the world of possibilities that had been opened up to northwestern Europeans as a result of new contacts with Islam.

Muslim Philosophy, Science, and Medicine

The scholars of Byzantium had long taken a conservative approach to Greek philosophy, in every sense of the word (Chapter 7). The dialogues of Plato and some works of Aristotle were copied and studied, but the latter's ideas were so hard to reconcile with Orthodox theology that Emperor Alexius Comnenus eventually banned the teaching of Aristotelian logic. Ironically, then, the cultures that provided the most direct access to Greek learning were Arabic-speaking, and it was through Arabic translations that western European intellectuals became acquainted with these ideas, thanks to the pioneering labors of Arabists like Robert and Hermann.

Many of these Arabic translations had been sponsored by the Abbasid court at Baghdad, which established a special school for this purpose known as the House of Wisdom. By the end of the tenth century, as a result, Arabic translations of Plato, Aristotle, Plotinus, and other Greek authors were widely available and intensively studied throughout the Muslim world. Even in the remote Persian city of Bukhara, the great Muslim philosopher and physician Avicenna (Ibn Sīnā, 980–1037) was able to read all of Aristotle's surviving works before he reached the age of eighteen.

Competing Viewpoints

Preaching the First Crusade: Two Accounts

> We owe the following account of Urban II's call for a crusade to Fulcher of Chartres, a priest who was present at the Council of Clermont in 1095 and who later served as chaplain to the first Norman king of Jerusalem, Baldwin. It forms part of Fulcher's contemporary chronicle of the First Crusade. The second account of the motives behind the crusade come from a biography of the Byzantine emperor Alexius Comnenus, written by his daughter Anna (1083–1153), who also lived through these events.

Pope Urban II's Call at Clermont, November 1195

Most beloved brethren: Urged by necessity, I, Urban, by the permission of God chief bishop and prelate over the whole world, have come into these parts as an ambassador with a divine admonition to you, the servants of God. . . .

Although, O sons of God, you have promised more firmly than ever to keep the peace among yourselves and to preserve the rights of the Church, there remains still an important work for you to do. Freshly quickened by the divine correction, you must apply the strength of your righteousness to another matter which concerns you as well as God. For your brethren who live in the East are in urgent need of your help, and you must hasten to give them the aid which has often been promised them. For, as most of you have heard, the Turks and Arabs have attacked them and have conquered the territory of Romania [the Byzantine Empire] as far west as the shore of the Mediterranean and the Hellespont. . . . They have occupied more and more of the lands of those Christians, and have overcome them in seven battles. They have killed and captured many, and have destroyed the churches and devastated the empire.

If you permit them to continue thus for a while with impunity, the faithful of God will be much more widely attacked by them. On this account I, or rather the Lord, beseech you as Christ's heralds to publish this everywhere and to persuade all people of whatever rank, footsoldiers and knights, poor and rich, to carry aid promptly to those Christians and to destroy that vile race from the lands of our friends. I say this to those who are present, but it is meant also for those who are absent. Moreover, Christ commands it.

All who die by the way, whether by land or by sea, or in battle against the pagans, shall have immediate remission of sins. This I grant them through the power of God with which I am invested. O what a disgrace, if such a despised and base race, which worships demons, should conquer a people which has the faith of omnipotent God and is made glorious with the name of Christ! With what reproaches will the Lord overwhelm us if you do not aid those who, with us, profess the Christian religion!

Let those who have been accustomed to wage unjust private warfare against the faithful now go against the infidels and end with victory this war which should have been begun long ago. Let those who for a long time have been robbers now become knights. Let those who have been fighting against their brothers and relatives now fight in a proper way against the barbarians. Let those who have been serving as mercenaries for small pay now obtain the eternal reward. Let those who have been wearing themselves out in both body

---

Like their counterparts in Byzantium, Muslim philosophers strove to reconcile Greek and Hellenistic philosophical traditions with each other and with the tenets of Islamic theology. Reconciling Aristotelianism and Neoplatonism was the easier task. Many of the translations and commentaries from which Muslim philosophers worked had already been filtered through the philosophical traditions of Alexandria and Rome. Moreover, Aristotle and the Neoplatonists shared a number of common assumptions, including the eternity of the world and the capacity of the human mind to understand the rational principles that govern the world's workings. Both traditions also stressed and soul now work for a double honor. Behold! On this side will be the sorrowful and poor, on that, the rich; on this side, the enemies of the Lord, on that, his friends. Let those who go not put off the journey, but rent their lands and collect money for their expenses; and as soon as winter is over and spring comes, let them eagerly set out on the way with God as their guide.

Source: S. J. Allen and Emilie Amt, eds., *The Crusades: A Reader* (Peterborough, Ont., Canada: 2003), pp. 39–40.

Anna Comnena Describes the Beginnings of the First Crusade

[Alexius] had no time to relax before he heard a rumour that countless Frankish armies were approaching. He dreaded their arrival, knowing as he did their uncontrollable passion, their erratic character and their irresolution, not to mention . . . their greed for money. . . . So far from despairing, however, he made every effort to prepare for war if need arose. What actually happened was more far-reaching and terrible than rumour suggested, for the whole of the West and all the barbarians who lived between the Adriatic and the Straits of Gibraltar migrated in a body to Asia, marching across Europe country by country with all their households. The reason for this mass movement is to be found more or less in the following events. A certain Kelt, called Peter [the Hermit] . . . left to worship at the Holy Sepulchre and after suffering much ill-treatment at the hands of the Turks and Saracens who were plundering the whole of Asia, he returned home with

difficulty. Unable to admit defeat, . . . he worked out a clever scheme. He decided to preach in all the Latin countries. A divine voice, he said, commanded him to proclaim to all the counts in France that all should depart from their homes, set out to worship at the Holy Shrine, and . . . strive to liberate Jerusalem. . . . Surprisingly, he was successful. . . . Full of enthusiasm and ardour they thronged every highway, and with these warriors came a host of civilians, outnumbering the sand of the seashore or the stars of heaven, carrying palms and bearing crosses on their shoulders. There were women and children, too, who had left their own countries. . . .

The upheaval that ensued as men *and* women took to the road was unprecedented within living memory. The simpler folk were in very truth led on by a desire to worship at Our Lord's tomb and visit the holy places, but the more villainous characters . . . had an ulterior purpose, for they hoped on their

journey to seize the capital [Jerusalem] itself, looking upon its capture as a natural consequence of the expedition. . . .

Source: Excerpted from Anna Comnena, *The Alexiad*, trans. E. R. A. Sewter (New York: 1969), pp. 308–11.

Questions for Analysis

1. Given Urban II's explanation of the problems confronting the Byzantine Empire, how do you account for the fact that the Crusades were directed toward the Holy Land, and not to the relief of Byzantium?

2. How does Anna Comnena represent the motives of Peter the Hermit and the crusaders? What distinctions does she make among the various participants?

3. Are there points of comparison between these two accounts? On what do they agree? How would you explain the differences between them?

the freedom of individual humans to choose between good and evil.

Reconciling Greek philosophy with Islamic theology was more difficult. Like Judaism and Christianity, Islam holds that a single omnipotent God created the world as an act of pure will, and that the world can exist only so long as

God continues to will it. This runs counter to the Greek view of the world as eternal. Moreover, both Christian and Islamic theologies rest on the immortality of the individual human soul, another doctrine in conflict with Aristotelian and Neoplatonic thought. There were also conflicts over the concept of free will, and again Muslims and Christians had more

An Arab Aristocrat Encounters the Crusaders

Usama ibn Munqidh (1095–1188) was an Arab Muslim from Syria, whose family maintained a prominent place in the local administration even after the conquests of the Seljuqs and the Christian crusaders. He traveled widely and worked in various cities as a diplomat and scholar. He ended his life in the service of Salah ad-Din (Saladin), the great Muslim leader who reconquered Jerusalem the year before Usama's death. The following excerpt is from Usama's memoir, which he called The Book of Contemplation. *The Templars mentioned in the account are the Christian military order of the Knights of the Temple, who dedicated themselves to protecting pilgrims in Jerusalem and guarding the holy sites. Their headquarters were in the main mosque of the city, which stood on the Temple Mount.*

 nyone who is recently arrived from the Frankish lands is rougher in character than those who have become acclimated and have frequented the company of Muslims. Here is an instance of their rough character (may God abominate them!):

Whenever I went to visit the holy sites in Jerusalem, I would go in and make my way up to the al-Aqsa Mosque, beside which stood a small mosque that the Franks had converted into a church. When I went into the al-Aqsa Mosque—where the Templars, who are my friends, were—they would clear out that little mosque so that I could pray in it. One day, I went into the little mosque, recited the opening formula 'God is great!' and

stood up in prayer. At this, one of the Franks rushed at me and grabbed me and turned my face towards the east, saying, 'Pray like *this*!'

A group of Templars hurried towards him, took hold of the Frank and took him away from me. I then returned to my prayers. The Frank, that very same one, took advantage of their inattention and returned, rushing upon me and turning my face to the east, saying, 'Pray like *this*!'

So the Templars came in again, grabbed him and threw him out. They apologized to me, saying, 'This man is a stranger, just arrived from the Frankish lands sometime in the past few days. He has never before seen anyone who did not pray towards the east.'

'I think I've prayed quite enough,' I said and left. I used to marvel at that

devil, the change of his expression, the way he trembled and what he must have made of seeing someone praying towards Mecca.

Source: Usama ibn Munqidh, *The Book of Contemplation: Islam and the Crusades,* trans. Paul M. Cobb (New York: 2008), p. 147.

Questions for Analysis

1. What does Usama's account reveal about the variety of relationships among Christians and Muslims in the crusader kingdom of Jerusalem?

2. Who is the true outsider in this scenario? What does Usama's treatment by the Templars suggest about the policy of Christian leaders toward the city's Muslim residents?

---

in common with one another than with ancient Greek tradition. Although medieval theologians emphasized the individual responsibility of believers to choose between good and evil, virtually all Muslims—like most Christians—believed that nothing good can occur unless God actively wills it.

By adopting an array of different intellectual tactics to deal with these challenges, Islamic philosophers therefore laid the groundwork for the Christian theologians who relied on them. The most influential of these was Averroès (*ah-VER-oh-ayz*; Ibn Rushd, 1126–1198), an amazingly gifted scholar born in Córdoba and active as a judge and physician in Seville. Averroès single-handedly advanced the

study of Aristotelian logic by publishing a series of careful commentaries that sought to purge the Greek philosopher's works of all later (and confusing) Neoplatonic influences, and thus to allow for their proper analysis and interpretation. Soon translated from Arabic into Latin, these commentaries influenced the way all subsequent Christian scholars read and understood Aristotle, and they earned Averroès the admiration of poets and artists as well as scholars. His prestige was so great that Christian intellectuals called him simply "The Commentator," as if there were no others. Sadly, his learning did not impress the new Muslim dynasty that came to power in his lifetime, the Almohads,

ARISTOTLE TEACHING ARAB ASTRONOMERS. In this Arabic manuscript from the thirteenth century, Aristotle is represented as a contemporary of the astronomers he is instructing.
▪ *What does this suggest about Muslims' attitude toward Greek philosophy?*

tion, diagnose cancer of the stomach, prescribe antidotes in cases of poisoning, and make notable progress in treating eye diseases. They even recognized the infectious character of bubonic plague, pointing out that it could be transmitted by clothing. Muslim physicians were also pioneers in organizing hospitals and licensing medical practitioners. At least thirty-four great hospitals were located in the principal cities of Persia, Syria, and Egypt, each with separate wards for particular illnesses, a dispensary for giving out medicine, and a library. Chief physicians and surgeons lectured to students and interns, examined them, and issued licenses to practice medicine. Even the owners of leeches (used for bloodletting, a standard medical practice) had to submit their medicinal worms for inspection at regular intervals.

Islamic scientists also made important advances in optics and chemistry, as well as mathematics. Using what Westerners know as Arabic numerals—which Muslim scholars actually adopted from the Hindus—mathematicians developed a decimal arithmetic based on place values and hinged on the concept of the zero. Their work enabled

who demanded that all philosophical inquiry be subordinated to orthodox Muslim belief. After burning several of Averroës' works, they exiled him to Morocco, where he died in 1198. Thereafter, Islamic philosophy may have had more impact on Europe than on some Islamic kingdoms.

Many Muslim philosophers were also distinguished physicians and scientists. While the study of philosophy could bring a man renown (or censure) but few tangible rewards, successful physicians and astrologers might rise to positions of wealth and power. Both astrology and medicine were applied sciences that relied on careful, accurate observation of natural phenomena. Muslim observations of the heavens were so accurate, indeed, that some astronomers corroborated the findings of Hellenistic scientists (see Chapter 4), that the earth must revolve around the sun. But because these theories conflicted with the (mistaken) assumptions of Aristotle, they were not generally accepted in the Islamic world or in Europe. Yet they may have influenced Nicolaus Copernicus (1473–1543), who is usually credited as the first to suggest that the earth orbited the sun (see Chapter 16).

Islamic accomplishments in medicine were equally remarkable. Avicenna discovered the contagious nature of tuberculosis, described pleurisy and several varieties of nervous ailments, and noted that diseases could spread through contaminated water and soil. His *Canon of Medicine* would remain an authoritative textbook in the Muslim world and in western Europe until the seventeenth century. Later Muslim physicians would learn the value of cauteriza-

IVORY PYXIS FROM AL-ANDALUS. Fashioned in the tenth century, this little round box is made from a segment of elephant tusk and would have had a matching lid (now lost). Such boxes usually held spices or incense. The decorative motifs seen here are echoed on a larger scale in contemporary architecture, reminding us that medieval Islam did not prohibit the representation of natural and fanciful figures, as is often supposed.

fundamental advances in two entirely new areas, both of which bear Arabic names: algebra and algorithms. Building on Greek geometry and their own astronomical observations, they also made great progress in spherical trigonometry. Muslim mathematicians thus brought together and pushed forward all the areas of mathematical knowledge that would later be adopted and developed in western Europe from the sixteenth century on. And they made an indispensible contribution to the burgeoning European economy, since the sophisticated accounting systems that supported commerce would have been impossible if merchants and bankers had continued to use the clumsy system of Roman numerals (try balancing your checking account this way!). Thanks to Arabic mathematics, western Europeans could now add, subtract, divide, and multiply quickly and accurately, with or without the help of another Muslim invention, the abacus.

Islamic Literature and Art

Poetry was integral to Muslim culture and identity, not least because it was the form in which Muhammad expressed the Qu'ran (Chapter 7). Not all poetry was composed in Arabic, however; particularly around the Abbasid court, poets writing in Persian enjoyed great renown. The best known of these is Umar Khayyam (d. 1123), whose *Rubaiyat* was turned into a popular English verse cycle by the Victorian poet Edward Fitzgerald (1809–1883). Although Fitzgerald's translation distorts much, the sensuality of Umar's poetic imagery ("A book of verses underneath the bough—a jug of wine, a loaf of bread—and thou") faithfully reflects themes that were common to much Muslim poetry. Jews also participated in this elite literary world, especially in Al-Andalus, where they wrote similarly sensuous, playful lyrics in both Hebrew and Arabic, praising wine, sexual intimacy, and their own songs.

Indeed, Muslim Spain saw a great flowering of Jewish intellectual life. The greatest Jewish scholar of the period was Moses Maimonides (*my-MAHN-eh-dees*, c. 1137–1204), whose systematic exposition of Jewish law in the *Mishneh Torah* earned him the title "the second Moses." Like Averroès, Maimonides may have been driven into exile by the Almohads; he traveled first to North Africa and then to Egypt, where he became famous as a teacher, jurist, and physician. Like Averroès, too, he exercised great influence on Christian theologians.

Perhaps the most distinctive of Islamic arts are those that created the spaces in which artists and intellectuals interacted with their patrons. Many characteristic elements of Muslim architecture were adapted from Byzantine models, but were then combined with the intricate tracery and ambitious scale of Persian buildings. Muslim artistry was also expressed in the magnificent gardens and fountains that adorned palaces, and in the more portable magnificence of gorgeous carpets, tooled leather, sumptuous brocaded silks and tapestries, inlaid metalwork, enameled glassware, and painted pottery. Their complex designs can

After You Read This Chapter

Visit StudySpace for quizzes, additional review materials, and multi-media documents. **wwnorton.com/studyspace**

REVIEWING THE OBJECTIVES

- The fragmentation of power in the ninth and tenth centuries created a world very different from that of Charlemagne. Describe some of the key changes. What were their causes?
- The agricultural revolution of the Middle Ages had far-reaching economic, social, and political consequences. What were they?
- The reforming movement with the Church changed the relationship between the papacy and the secular rulers of Christendom. Explain why.
- The motives behind the Crusades were political as well as religious. Why was this the case?
- The Crusades had profound effects on western Europe, Byzantium, and Islam, as well as on the relationships among different groups within these societies. In what ways were these three civilizations transformed?

often seem strikingly modern, precisely because they anticipate the abstract forms that were considered new in the twentieth century.

CONCLUSION

The new Europe that emerged in the twelfth century would rely heavily on what it had learned from the Islamic world. This is reflected in the large number of Arabic and Persian words that passed into the European languages still spoken today. Essential words for commerce and trade include *traffic, tariff, alcohol, muslin, orange, lemon, alfalfa, saffron, sugar, syrup,* and *musk,* to name just a few. The word *admiral* also comes from Arabic (from the title *emir*), as do words that tell the story of Europe's reliance on Islamic science and technology: *alchemy, algebra, algorithm, alkali, almanac, amalgam, cipher, soda, magazine, zenith,* and *zero*—not to mention the names of stars, such as Aldebaran and Betelgeuse.

In the year 1000, Europe had been the least powerful, least prosperous, and least sophisticated of the three civilizations that had emerged from the Roman world. A hundred years later, it was a force to be reckoned with. This metamorphosis rested on economic foundations: increasingly efficient agriculture, a growing population, and expanding trade. These changes produced a dynamic, expansionist, self-confident, and mobile society in which individuals cast off old roles and took on new ones with bewildering speed.

No less important, however, were the political and military changes that began to alter the map of Europe in these centuries. By 1100, the heavily armored, mounted knight had emerged as a formidable military weapon, and new conceptions of power—both spiritual and temporal—were being articulated and contested within Europe, and on crusade.

But it was not yet possible for either kings or popes to control the energies of the workers, town-dwellers, merchants, knights, and scholars whose endeavors were transforming their world. Yet a new approach to political organization was developing. Up to this point, the civilizations of the West had rested largely on two types of government: city-states and empires. City-states were more capable of mobilizing the loyalty of their citizens; as a result, they could sometimes win extraordinary victories against more-powerful imperial rivals, as the Greeks did against the Persians. But city-states were frequently divided by internal economic and social rivalries; and in the long run, they were not strong enough to defend themselves against foreign conquerors. Empires, by contrast, could win battles and maintain powerful administrative bureaucracies, but they were generally too far-flung to inspire deep loyalties among their subjects.

Where, then, do the monarchies of medieval Europe fit into this picture? How would the struggle for the control of western Europe's expanding resources be carried forward in the wake of the Crusades? And what cultural, spiritual, social, and intellectual innovations would result? These are the questions we address in Chapter 9.

PEOPLE, IDEAS, AND EVENTS IN CONTEXT

- How was Europe affected by **VIKING** raids and settlements? Which territorial rulers imitated **CAROLINGIAN** models in the wake of these upheavals?
- What new technologies drove the **AGRICULTURAL REVOLUTION** of the Middle Ages? Why did the organization of labor on **MANORS** sometimes lead to **SERFDOM**?
- What conditions led to the growth of medieval **TOWNS** and why did the formation of urban **COMMUNES** foster new types of liberty? How were **MONEY AND CREDIT** essential to medieval commerce?
- Why is **"FEUDALISM"** a problematic concept? How did the ceremony of **HOMAGE** symbolize the relationship between a **VASSAL** and his **LORD**?
- What were the causes of the **INVESTITURE CONFLICT**?
- Why did **EMPEROR ALEXIUS** ask **POPE URBAN II** for assistance? Why did the pope use this as a pretext for urging the **FIRST CRUSADE**?
- How and why did **MUSLIM LEARNING AND CULTURE** exercise a profound influence on western Europeans?

CONSEQUENCES

- In what ways does the Investiture Conflict reflect the unique historical circumstances of the late eleventh century, and in what ways can it be viewed as an extension of longer-term phenomena?
- Based on what we have learned about the relationship between political power and religious power in previous chapters, would you say that the clash between the papal and imperial powers was inevitable?
- Given the many negative aspects of the crusading movement—and its eventual failure—how might you explain the continuing appeal of crusading rhetoric down to the present day?

STORY LINES

- The power of Europe's new monarchies and of the papacy depended on new methods of oversight, administration, and documentation.

- Schools and universities were therefore crucial to the development of these institutions, and they also provided ambitious men with unprecedented intellectual, social, and political opportunities.

- The Church's increased presence in the daily lives of the laity produced vibrant forms of spirituality, yet placed strict limitations on women, religious dissidents, and non-Christians.

- Throughout this era, Europe's princely courts, wealthy towns, universities, and cathedrals fostered new forms of entertainment, art, and architecture.

Before You Read This Chapter

CHRONOLOGY

1079–1142	Lifetime of Peter Abelard
c. 1090–c. 1164	Lifetime of Heloise
1098	Cistercian order established
1098–1179	Lifetime of Hildegard of Bingen
1099	First Crusade ends
1122–1204	Lifetime of Eleanor of Aquitaine
c. 1140	Gratian's *Concordance of Discordant Canons*
1152–1190	Reign of Frederick I Barbarossa
1180–1223	Reign of Philip II Augustus
1192–1194	Alfonso II of Aragon compiles the *Liber feudorum maior*
1194–1250	Lifetime of Frederick II the Great
1198–1216	Reign of Pope Innocent III
1209	Franciscan order established
1215	Magna Carta and the canons of the Fourth Lateran Council are formulated
1216	Dominican order established

The Consolidation of Europe, 1100–1300

CORE OBJECTIVES

- **IDENTIFY** the differences among Europe's emerging monarchies.

- **UNDERSTAND** the connections between new religious movements and the power of the papacy.

- **DEFINE** scholasticism and trace its development.

- **EXPLAIN** the changing meaning of *chivalry*.

- **DESCRIBE** the cultural trends of this era.

A t the turn of the twelfth century, the eldest son of a nobleman did something unusual: he traded lordship for scholarship. His name was Peter Abelard. In his own estimation, he was the smartest man in the world, and the best looking. He was certainly one of the most ambitious. After leaving his father's lands in Brittany and besting all the established teachers in Paris, he was appointed to the position of master in the cathedral school, one of the highest academic posts then available. There he met Heloise, the niece of a priest called Fulbert. Heloise had received an excellent education in a nearby convent, but the normal path of intellectual advancement—Abelard's school—was closed to her. So Fulbert arranged for her to become Abelard's private pupil. But she soon became more than that: his intellectual partner, his lover, and his wife.

This last step was particularly problematic, because marriage was no longer an option for clerics, and would therefore ruin Abelard's chances of a brilliant career in the Church. So it remained a secret, as did Heloise's subsequent pregnancy and the birth of their son. Yet Fulbert eventually found out and took revenge on Abelard, sending some local thugs to castrate him. Heloise and

Abelard lived out the remainder of their lives in isolation from one another, and most of what we know about their relationship comes from letters they exchanged years later, when Heloise was the leader of a new religious community and Abelard was laying the intellectual foundations of the first university.

The developments of the twelfth and thirteenth centuries altered Europe in profound and lasting ways. This period witnessed the emergence of large-scale territorial monarchies and the papacy as dominant forces, while cathedral schools and universities turned out larger and larger cohorts of the professional men needed to run the bureaucracies that supported them. In the wake of the Crusades, both ancient texts and novel ideas generated the intellectual revolution in which Abelard and Heloise participated. New artistic and technological influences were galvanizing forces, too; financed by prelates and kings, princely courts and wealthy towns engaged in an integrated and far-reaching economy. New opportunities for social advancement and new spiritual practices also transformed daily life. Moreover, new literary forms took shape as the spoken vernaculars of Europe became languages of learning, devotion, and entertainment. By 1300, the political institutions and cultural practices that still define Europe today had been formed.

THE MAKING OF MEDIEVAL MONARCHIES

As we learned in Chapter 8, the independent towns and lords of the tenth and eleventh centuries often refused to acknowledge royal authority, while kings no longer wielded the broad powers of Charlemagne. How, then, did some European rulers come to build the foundations of states that still exist today? For crucially, the *idea* of a national state, an idea forged in the twelfth and thirteenth centuries, would endure to become the basis on which the political systems of the modern world were constructed.

Not all attempts were equally successful. Some monarchies would not be consolidated until the nineteenth century (Germany is the best example) and, even then, *political* unification could not hide the continued fact of cultural and linguistic disintegration (as is evident in Italy, Belgium, and Switzerland to this day). Yet it became so vital for modern European states to trace their origins to the medieval past that those states without a medieval pedigree would eventually have to invent one.

England and the Angevin Empire of Henry II

The conquest of England in 1066 allowed the first Norman king, William, to experiment with a new type of kingship. In theory, he commanded the allegiance of every person dwelling in his kingdom. In practice, however, William needed to impose his will on his new subjects. This often took the form of violence, yet it was also expressed through the effective administrative structures of his Anglo-Saxon predecessors. This process was carried forward by his energetic son Henry I (r. 1100–35). Henry strengthened the Anglo-Norman system of local administration and instituted a method of financial accounting carried out by an office known as the Exchequer—so called because clerks moved counters around on a checkered cloth to calculate receipts and expenditures.

ABELARD AND HELOISE. This image from a thirteenth-century manuscript shows Abelard in a scholar's gown and cap and Heloise wearing a nun's habit; their gestures indicate that they are engaged in debate. The story of their passionate and doomed marriage was already famous during their lifetimes, and by the time this manuscript was copied, theirs had become the ultimate example of star-crossed love.

Henry's hands-on approach to governance was both new and unpopular. Then, as now, those opposed to "big government" could react violently, and after Henry's death a civil war lasted throughout the reign of his cousin and successor, Stephen (r. 1135–54)—until the people of England began to long for the effective royal leadership of Henry. They found it in Henry's grandson Henry of Anjou (b. 1133, r. 1154–89), who at the age of twenty-one was already the duke of Normandy and the lord of two other independent counties, Anjou and Maine. He also controlled the Aquitaine, thanks to his recent alliance with its powerful and brilliant ruler, Eleanor (1122–1204), who had annulled her first marriage to the French king Louis VII in order to marry Henry. As a result, England under Henry II found itself integrated into the political and cultural world of the Continent in unprecedented ways, as part of an Angevin empire (from Henry's position as count of Anjou).

In England, Henry II extended the reach of his grandfather's royal administration. He ordered juries (from the Latin *jus*, meaning both "law" and "right") of local men to report every major crime that occurred in their districts, and empowered them to investigate civil cases. Henry II also made it easier for common people to seek justice in royal courts. These innovations are the origin of our modern legal system, and by involving average people in the exercise of government they also generated loyalty to the king.

Yet these measures brought Henry into conflict with the Church, because the extension of royal justice impinged on that of ecclesiastical courts: tribunals overseen by bishops that claimed the exclusive right to try and sentence members of the clergy. Henry declared that clerics convicted of serious crimes should lose their clerical status and be handed over to the royal court for sentencing. Opposition to his plan came from an unexpected source: Thomas Becket, a longtime friend of Henry's who was now the archbishop of Canterbury.

Thomas was a self-made man, the son of immigrants who had benefited from the social mobility of town life (he grew up in London) to obtain an education and thereby rise through the ranks of the Church. He saw the advantages to be gained from maintaining the independence of ecclesiastical procedures, and felt bound by his episcopal office to uphold them. Henry responded to his obstinacy by exiling Thomas for several years. When Thomas returned to England in 1170, he was assassinated in his own cathedral by four of Henry's knights.

Thomas was quickly proclaimed a martyr and a saint, and his tomb at Canterbury became one of the most important pilgrimage sites of the Middle Ages. Henry, for his part, was compelled to ask the saint's forgiveness for his sins against the Church. In the long run, he did not win the

THE MURDER OF THOMAS BECKET. In this illumination from a thirteenth-century prayer book, one of the knights has struck the archbishop so violently that he has broken his sword. ▪ *How might a contemporary viewer have interpreted this?*

right to sentence clerics in royal courts, but he did retain the right to nominate clerics to high office and thereby to exercise a large measure of control over the churches in his realm.

The Meaning of Magna Carta

The most concrete proof of Henry II's success is that his government continued to work efficiently after his death, to the extent that his swashbuckling son Richard "the Lionheart" (r. 1189–99) could rule his father's empire for ten years *in absentia*, spending only about six months in England itself during all that time.

Richard was succeeded by his brother John (r. 1199–1216), an efficient administrator and far less enthusiastic warrior who lacked the means to hold the Angevin Empire

France at the
Death of
Philip Augustus
1223

ATLANTIC OCEAN

Royal domain

Under English rule

Bay of Biscay

Compostela

FRANCE

ENGLAND

Paris

AQUITAINE

LÉON

0 100 200 300 Miles

0 300 Kilometers

SCOTLAND

Edinburgh

Carlisle

Durham

IRELAND

Dublin

York Stamford
Bridge

*NORTH
SEA*

WALES

Hereford

ENGLAND

Ely

Gloucester Cambridge

Oxford London

Runnymede

Southampton Winchester

Canterbury

Calais

Bruges Antwerp

Ypres Lille

FLANDERS Brussels

Arras

HOLY

English Channel

Amiens

Rouen VERMANDOIS

Bayeux Caen Beauvais Rheims Verdun

Mont-St.-Michel NORMANDY St. Denis

ROMAN

BRITTANY Paris CHAMPAGNE LORRAINE

Chartres ISLE

MAINE Brétigny DE Troyes

FRANCE

ANJOU BURGUNDY EMPIRE

Nantes

ATLANTIC TOURAINE

Poitiers Bourges Dijon

OCEAN POITOU Autun

Geneva

*Bay of
Biscay* AQUITAINE Lyon

Bordeaux Angoulême

Périgueux

PROVENCE

GASCONY Albi Avignon

TOULOUSE Aigues-Mortes

NAVARRE Montpellier Marseilles

LANGUEDOC Narbonne

ARAGON

*MEDITERRANEAN
SEA*

CATALONIA

EUROPE

Area of
detail

0 100 200 Miles

0 100 200 Kilometers

AFRICA

ENGLAND AND FRANCE, 1180–1223. ▪ *What areas did Henry II's Angevin Empire control
in 1180?* ▪ *What would have been its effects on the political orientation of England?* ▪ *What
advantages would the king of France have when challenging English control over continental
territories, even though his own power was confined to the "island" (Ile) of France around Paris?*

together. By 1204, John had been forced to
cede nearly all of his father's Continental
possessions to the newly powerful king
of France, Philip II; only the Aquitaine,
the inheritance of his mother Eleanor, remained. This was politically disastrous,
because the most powerful lords of
England lost their ancestral lands when
John lost Normandy. And when John attempted to recover these territories by
raising taxes to equip an army, he only
angered the barons further. In 1215 they
forced John to set his seal to Magna Carta,
a "great charter" that defined their own
rights while limiting those of the king.

Magna Carta established some important general principles that would
continue to shape the laws of England
and, eventually, its colonies: the king
could levy no taxes without the consent
of his subjects, no free man could be
punished until he had been judged guilty
by a jury of his peers, no one could be
arrested and imprisoned without a warrant, and no unqualified person could
hold public office. The charter also provided for the establishment of a council
of barons, which later came to represent the common people of England,
too—Parliament (a word derived from
the French "talking together"). Above
all, Magna Carta expressed the extraordinary idea that a king is bound by the
law of the land. By contrast, the various
powerful lawgivers we have studied so
far held themselves to be above the law.

In sum, Magna Carta normalized
the idea that strong, centralized government was a good thing. When the barons
of England revolted again in the reign
of John's son, Henry III (r. 1216–72),
they did so because Henry's rule was not
effective enough. Henry III's son Edward
(r. 1272–1307) accordingly made Parliament into a legislative body that could
help run the kingdom. Since Magna
Carta had demanded that no taxation
be imposed without common consent,
Edward convened Parliament to secure
such consent. But he also used meetings
of Parliament to take advice, to hear

judicial cases, to hear complaints, and to promulgate new laws. Gradually, England's feudal monarchy was becoming the constitutional monarchy it remains to this day.

Philip Augustus and the Emergence of France

Compared to the Anglo-Norman and Angevin kings of England, the king of the Franks presided over a miniscule kingdom over which he exercised little control. When the empire of Henry II was at its height, the kingdom of Louis VII (r. 1137–80)—who had lost both his wife Eleanor and her lands to that same Henry—was tiny and insignificant.

But in many ways the Capetian kings of this realm were fortunate. Against all biological odds, they managed to produce an unbroken line of able male heirs for over 300 years (from the accession of Hugh Capet in 987 to 1328). On average, each Capetian king ruled for thirty years, and this longevity also contributed greatly to political stability. And this kingdom, though small, was a rich center of agriculture and trade, and was becoming the intellectual capital of Europe, thanks to the new university that had grown around the school of Abelard in Paris.

The king who capitalized on these strengths was Philip II (r. 1180–1223), also called "Augustus" and the first to use the title "king of France"—thereby indicating that he was king of a sovereign state (rather than "king of the Franks," a loose agglomeration of people). Philip came to the throne at the age of eighteen, having witnessed the constant humiliation of his father Louis VII at the hands of Henry II. He understood that he could not win a war against either Henry or his son Richard. John, however—known to his detractors as "Soft Sword"—was another matter. So Philip declared that John owed him homage and allegiance for Normandy and its adjacent territories. When John objected, Philip declared all John's lands forfeit to the French crown and backed this declaration with armies that won decisive victories in 1204 and 1214.

With Normandy and other formerly English territories added to his domain, Philip now had the resources to build an effective system of local administration. He supplemented existing bureaucratic structures by appointing royal overseers who had judicial, administrative, and military authority. Philip drew these men from among the needy knights and lesser nobility of his own domain and rotated them frequently from region to region. This ensured their loyalty to Philip, and also prevented them from developing personal ties to the regions they governed.

Philip's administrative pattern, which recognized regional diversity while promoting centralized royal control, would continue to characterize French government down to the time of the French Revolution (see Chapter 18). Although he and his heirs experimented with representative assemblies similar to the English Parliament, the French Parlement never played a comparable role in French government. There are many reasons for this, but the most fundamental was the French nobility's exemption from taxation, something that would remain a political problem.

Other significant points of contrast between England and France would continue to mark the intertwined history of these two states. England, a far smaller country, was much more tightly unified at a much earlier date. In France, regional separatism remained (and still remains) a significant force, to the extent that ambitious insurgents have long capitalized on regional animosity toward the French government when making bids for power. While English kings could rely on local men to do much of the work of local government without pay, French kings ruled through salaried officers who had little connection to local society and, as a result, lacked effective mechanisms for mobilizing public support. In the eigtheenth century, these features would be the undoing of the French monarchy.

German Kingship and the Holy Roman Empire

The struggles between the German emperor Henry IV and the papacy ultimately led to the weakening of imperial authority (Chapter 8). But in the middle of the twelfth century, a newly elected emperor made an ambitious attempt to free himself from papal control. This was Frederick Barbarossa ("Red Beard," r. 1152–90), who coined the term "Holy Roman Empire" to describe his realm, thereby asserting that its holiness derived from the blessing of God and not from the intervention of the pope.

Frederick forged a close alliance with other German princes by supporting their efforts to control their own territories, in exchange for their support of his wars in northern Italy. Meanwhile, he attempted to bypass the power of the papacy by supporting a series of papal pretenders, or "antipopes." But this move was successfully countered by the reigning pope, Alexander III (r. 1159–81), who drove a shrewd bargain: if Frederick would concede the sovereignty of the pope's rule within Rome and its adjacent territories—lands that came to be known as the Papal States—then Alexander would concede the emperor's sovereignty within his own domains, and even his overlordship of the Church in these domains. Frederick eventually agreed.

When Frederick left for the Holy Land in 1189—joining Richard the Lionheart and Philip Augustus on the (failed)

Third Crusade to reconquer Jerusalem—he accordingly left his realm in a powerful position. Although he died soon after, his son, Henry VI, succeeded to his throne without opposition and enjoyed a huge income from the northern Italian towns; he ultimately became the king of Sicily, too. This strengthened the empire's position even further, for now the Papal States were surrounded by the lands of a single powerful ruler.

Henry VI died in 1197 at the age of thirty-two, leaving a three-year-old son as his heir apparent. This Frederick II is one of the most fascinating of all medieval rulers. Having grown up in Sicily, he spoke Arabic and Italian as well as Latin, German, and French. He was both a patron of learning and a scholar in his own right, the author of an important treatise on falconry that is still considered a model of scientific investigation. He maintained a menagerie of exotic animals, a troop of Muslim archers, and a harem of veiled and secluded women, all of whom traveled with him on his journeys.

But by the time Frederick II came of age, the German princes had become so entirely autonomous that there was little he could do except recognize their privileges in exchange for their loyalty. In Italy, meanwhile, the northern cities banded together in the Lombard League had long since ceased to pay their taxes; and the powerful administrative structure of Sicily had fallen into chaos. Frederick tackled all these problems in turn, and eventually restored control over the disparate territories of his empire.

In 1237, however, he made the mistake of asserting his rule over the northern Italian cities directly, bypassing their own independent governments. The result was a lengthy war which continued until Frederick's death in 1250. The papacy took every advantage of this situation, even excommunicating Frederick and, after his death, denying the rights of his heirs. When Frederick's last legitimate son died in 1254, the prospect of effective imperial rule died with him. For the next six hundred years, until the founding of the modern German state in 1871, political power in the Holy Roman Empire would be divided among several hundred territorial princes.

The "Reconquest" of Spain

Although the Christian kingdoms of the Iberian peninsula were even more distinct from one another than were the principalities of Germany, a unified kingdom of Spain would emerge as the most powerful monarchy in Europe and the wider Atlantic world by the end of

THE "RECONQUEST" OF SPAIN, 900–1250. ▪ *What were the boundaries of the Christian kingdoms in 900? 1150? 1250?* ▪ *What geographical factors might have helped to sustain these small kingdoms?* ▪ *Why might Castile have become the largest of the Christian kingdoms over time?* ▪ *How could Aragon and Catalonia have maintained important positions as wealthy and significant powers?*

the Middle Ages (a process we will continue to trace in future chapters). The key to this extraordinary development lay in the successful alliances forged among Christian rulers and their eventual defeat of Iberia's Muslim kingdoms. This process is somewhat misleadingly termed "the Reconquista," or "the reconquest" of Christian Spain. But in reality, the Roman province of Hispania had been only nominally Christian when the Visigoths settled there in the fifth century (see Chapter 6), and the Visigoths themselves had barely converted to Latin Christianity before the Muslims arrived in 711 (Chapter 7). Reality aside, conceptualizing this struggle as a holy war to "recover" Christian territory allowed Christian propagandists to cast it as another crusade.

By the middle of the twelfth century, there were four major Christian kingdoms in Iberia. In the north and northwest were the states of Navarre and León-Castile, the latter governed as a united kingdom after 1037. Beyond them to the south lay a broad swathe of Muslim territory. To the east was the Crown of Aragon, enlarged in 1137 when the count of Barcelona, who ruled the independent principality of Catalonia, married its queen. Then there was the new western kingdom of Portugal, which had been the first territory gained by Christian conquests in the ninth century and which eventually won independence from León-Castile in 1139.

Like their counterparts elsewhere in Europe, the kings of Iberia struggled to control the power of great lords. Centuries of warfare between Muslims and Christians, and among competing Christian clans, had left the landscape sown with enormous castles, and even those strongholds nominally controlled by kings were in fact the property of castellans who used them as power bases. A ruler seeking to establish sovereignty thus had to use a combination of force and effective administration. This is best exemplified by King Alfonso II of Aragon (r. 1162–96), who was also the count of Barcelona. Alfonso used documentation as the ultimate tool of power, presiding over the compilation of a richly illustrated "big book of fiefs" (*Liber feudorum maior*: see **Interpreting Visual Evidence**). This book recounted property transactions and family lineages dating back centuries, enabling Alfonso to ground his authority on his command of history.

THE DOMINION OF THE CHURCH

Like their secular counterparts, the popes of this era established their authority by building up bureaucratic structures that increased the visibility of papal power and its effects on daily life. Specially commissioned papal legates (legal representatives) were now sent out from Rome to convey and enforce papal commands. For like the kings of England, France, and Aragon, the pope sought to establish a reputation for justice as a means of acquiring power.

The Codification of Canon Law

The growing number of cases heard in the papal court both encouraged and required the development of a systematic body of law by which such cases could be judged. Myriad papal decrees and decisions of Church councils reached back to the second century, forming a body of legal precedents known as canons (from the Greek word meaning "rules" or "supports"). The problem, though, was that these canons often contradicted one another, and so any usable compilation would have to determine which were most authoritative.

The resulting *Concordance of Discordant Canons*, first redacted around 1139 and later known as the *Decretum*, is attributed to a jurist known only as Gratian, who was presumably active in Bologna. Significantly, Gratian was influenced by the *Corpus Juris Civilis* codified under Justinian (see Chapter 7)—because another outcome of the Crusades, and of western Europe's increased contact with Byzantium, was the rediscovery of Roman law and the tradition of legal commentary associated with the great jurists of the later Roman Empire (Chapter 5).

The *Decretum* claimed ecclesiastical jurisdiction for all sorts of cases, including such matters as marriage, inheritance, and bequests. Although these cases were supposed to be heard in local ecclesiastical courts overseen by bishops, popes increasingly insisted that they alone could issue dispensations exempting certain petitioners from established precedents (such as the annulment of Eleanor's marriage to Louis VII) and moreover that the papal court should function as a final court of appeals in all cases touching the Church. Just as kings had to become more skillful administrators, so the popes of this era were almost invariably trained as canon lawyers.

The Reign of Innocent III

One examplar of this new breed of popes was Alexander III, who had dealt so skillfully with Frederick Barbarossa. Another was Innocent III (r. 1198–1216), a highly successful administrator whose chief goal was to unify all Christendom under papal hegemony. But unlike Gregory VII (Chapter 8), Innocent never questioned the right of kings and princes to rule in their own secular spheres. Instead, he saw the

Interpreting Visual Evidence

Picturing Legal Transactions

Between the years 1192 and 1194, King Alfonso II of Aragon (r. 1162–1196) and his court scribes compiled a remarkable book. The codex known today as "the big book of fiefs" (*Liber feudorum maior*) may have been made to assist Alfonso and his descendants in legitimizing their authority over the many areas they controlled, but it was also a way of expressing that authority: its very existence marked a new claim to royal power. In its original form, it consisted of 888 parchment folios (1776 pages) on which 903 separate documents were copied.

This "big book" represents a new trend in Europe. In most places, claims to property were made on the basis of custom and memory, not on documentation. When property changed hands, the chief witnesses were people, and when questions arose it was these people (or their heirs) whose testimony proved ownership. But in Catalonia, the habit of documenting things had a long history, and it was not unusual for individual families to keep archives of documents. At the same time, however, documentation was never sufficient on its own: verbal exchanges of agreement and the public performance of transactions constituted legally binding ceremonies meaningful to the entire community, and the validity of these actions was not dependant on the making of a written record.

With all this in mind, it is striking that 79 of the documents copied into this book are accompanied by images that convey important messages about documentation and its limitations.

On the book's opening frontispiece (image A), King Alfonso consults with his chief archivist, Ramón de Caldes. Ramón discusses one of the charters taken from a large pile at his elbow, while a scribe makes copies behind him—perhaps to aid in the compilation of the "big book." The king is backed by men who look on approvingly.

One of the charters copied into the "big book" is accompanied by the second image (B). It records that the viscount of Nîmes betrothed his daughter, Ermengarde of Carcassone, to the count of Roussillon. Ermengarde, her flowing hair uncovered as a sign of her maidenhood, stands between her bearded father and her seated mother, Cecilia of Provence.

Questions for Analysis

1. Why would a book designed to document property transactions contain images, too? What functions could they have served?

2. Why would the artist of the "big book" have depicted the king consulting his archivist in the very first image? How does he depict the relationship between them? Which seems more powerful? Why does the artist include a group of men as witnesses to their discussion?

3. Women figure prominently in many of the book's images, including the one below. On what basis could you argue that their active presence is crucial to the transactions being described?

A. King Alfonso and Ramón de Caldes.

B. Betrothal of Ermengarde to the Count of Roussillon.

THE JEWISH BADGE. The distinctive apparel that marked Jews as different from their Christian neighbors varied from region to region. In some places it was a pointed hat, like those worn by the Old Testament Jews in this manuscript illumination from a fourteenth-century French vernacular Bible. This hat would later become associated with idiocy or witchcraft, as in the dunce's cap or the witch's peak. In other regions, Jews wore a distinctive patch on their clothing, often colored yellow to make it more visible.

pope's role as regulatory and disciplinary, which meant that when rulers sinned they should be reprimanded or excommunicated by the pope—who could thereby call into question the legitimacy of their rule.

Innocent was even more insistent than his predecessors on the obligation of every Christian to obey the pope, and sought to achieve this goal in many different ways. He made the papacy financially and politically independent by expanding and consolidating papal territories in central Italy; Vatican City is now the last surviving remnant of these territories, and continues to function as an independent state within Rome and Italy. He displayed his power as kingmaker and -breaker by brokering the selection of the Holy Roman Emperor, and he also disciplined both Philip Augustus of France (for marital misconduct) and John of England, who at one point was compelled to grant England itself to the papacy, as a fief.

But the crowning achievement of Innocent's pontificate was the ratification of his agenda at a representative assembly of the entire western church, the Fourth Lateran Council of 1215 (so called because it was held in the Roman palace and church of St. John Lateran). This council redefined the central dogmas of the Christian faith, and made one of them the acknowledgment of papal supremacy. Since a dogma is defined as "a truth necessary for salvation," this meant that all Christians had to acknowledge the pope's ultimate power; those unwilling to do so were, by definition, heretics—and as heretics, they could be prosecuted and punished.

In a further effort to achieve uniformity, the Fourth Lateran Council took an unprecedented interest in the religious education and habits of every Christian. It responded to urbanization by establishing free primary schools (for boys) in all the major cities, required bishops to recruit effective preachers, and outlawed all kinds of misbehavior on the part of the clergy. It also sought to increase the distance between Christians and their Muslim and Jewish neighbors by discouraging social relationships, economic exchanges, and intermarriage. Perhaps most disturbingly, Innocent's Council mandated that "infidels" be visibly distinguished from Christians by the wearing of distinctive clothing, the infamous "Jewish badge."

The Limits of Papal Power

Innocent's reign achieved the height of papal power, but it also sowed some seeds of future dissent. The popes of the thirteenth century continued to centralize the government of the Church, but they also became involved in protracted political struggles that compromised the papacy's credibility. For example, when one of Innocent's successors came into conflict with Frederick II, he not only excommunicated him, as Innocent might have done, he also called for a crusade against him—a cynical admission of crusading's overtly political motives. In 1300, Pope Boniface VIII (r. 1294–1303) even celebrated a papal jubilee in Rome by offering a full crusader's indulgence to every pilgrim: the promise of absolution from all sins. This implied that Rome, not Jerusalem, was henceforth the center of the Christian world.

Just nine years later, Rome had become obsolete and the new capital of Christendom was in France. King Philip IV had challenged Boniface to a political duel, and had exposed the practical limits of papal power. For when Boniface protested against the king's plan to arraign a French bishop on a charge of treason, Philip accused Boniface of heresy and sent a troop of knights to arrest him. Boniface (then in his seventies) was so mistreated by Philip's thugs that he died a month later. Philip then forced the new pope, Clement V, to thank him publically for his zealous defence of the faith and finally, in 1309, he moved the entire papal court to Avignon (*AH-vee-nyon*), a city near the southeastern border of his own realm. It would remain there until 1378 (see Chapter 10).

The papacy's capitulation to the exercise of royal force illustrates the enormous gap that had opened up between rhetoric and reality in the centuries since the Investiture Conflict (Chapter 8). Although Boniface had claimed that kings rule only through the "will and sufferance" of the Church, in fact the Church now exercised its authority only through the will and sufferance of a king. The growth of strong territorial monarchies, combined with the increasing sophistication of royal administration and propaganda, had shifted the balance of power decisively. This trend would continue into the seventeenth century, and would only be halted after a century of religious wars, when the distinction between religious and political authority would be asserted as a fundamental principle (see Chapter 14).

SPIRITUAL AWAKENINGS AND CHALLENGES

As we saw in Chapter 8, the Investiture Conflict had engaged both clergy and laity in debates over the essential meaning of Jesus Christ's life and teachings. In many regions of western Europe, the papacy's claim to jurisdictional supremacy over the whole Church was supported, but in others there was marked resistance to its encroachment on centuries-old local practices and social networks. After all, priests had been married men since the establishment of the first Christian churches, and the wives of priests were not only their husbands' companions and partners, they were also ministers to the communities in which they lived. When the papacy preached against "fornicating priests" and their "concubines," it was attacking relationships that had been socially and spiritually essential for generations.

On the one hand, therefore, the reforms of Pope Gregory VII and his successors gave common people an important role to play, by urging them to reject certain practices and sanctioning retaliation against offenders. Combined with the fervor that had been whipped up by the Crusades, the result was more widespread participation in religious life—as well as increased violence. On the other hand, however, the reforming movement severely limited the ways in which the laity were allowed to express their spirituality or to participate meaningfully in the life of the Church.

The New Monasticism

In the tenth century, the abbey of Cluny had revived the observance of Benedict's *Rule* and, at the same time, had kept Cluny and its daughter houses independent of local lords. As a result, these monasteries became lordships in their own right, acquiring extensive lands and enormous wealth. Those seeking to reject worldliness thus had to look elsewhere for a lifestyle that would foster self-denial and striving toward God. The result, beginning in the late eleventh century, was the founding of new orders such as the Carthusians, whose name derives from the Chartreuse foothills of the French Alps and whose rule requires monks to live in separate cells and to observe a life of strict asceticism.

Another new order, and one that became more widespread, was that founded at the monastery of Cîteaux in 1098. Cistercian monks followed Benedict's *Rule* in the purest and most austere way possible, and they founded new monasteries in remote areas, far from worldly temptations. They also shunned all unnecessary decoration and elaborate liturgical rites. Instead, they practiced contemplation and committed themselves to hard manual labor. Under the charismatic leadership of Bernard of Clairvaux (1090–1153), one of the most influential personalities of his age, the Cistercian order grew exponentially, from five houses in 1115 to 343 by 1153. This astonishing increase meant that many more men and women were becoming professional religious, but it also meant that still more were donating funds and lands to support monasteries and thereby participating indirectly in a life of devotion.

Another manifestation of popular piety was a new focus on the sacrament of the Mass, the liturgical reenactment of Christ's last meal with his disciples. This celebration, the Eucharist, had always been an important part of Christian religious and social practice (Chapter 6). But only in the twelfth century did it become the central act of worship in the western Church. Bernard of Clairvaux was instrumental in making it so, by developing and preaching the doctrine of transubstantiation. According to this doctrine, every Mass is a miraculous event because the priest's blessing transforms the bread and wine on the altar into the body and blood of Christ—hence the term *transubstantiation*, since earthly substances thereby become the substance of Christ's divine body.

THE MYSTERY OF THE MASS. In this manuscript illumination, the visionary Hildegard of Bingen (see below) illustrates the doctrine of transubstantiation. In the lower register, the bread and wine of the Mass have been placed on the altar and are being transformed into the body and blood of the crucified Christ, depicted in the upper register. Paired scenes from Christ's life (his birth and death, his ministry and resurrection) emphasize the fact that earthly substances—bread and wine—participate in a divine cycle of regeneration. Note that Hildegard does not imagine the mediating figure as a priest, but as the (female) Church, represented as a crowned queen and associated with the Virgin Mary. ▪ *What might be the significance of this choice?*

Not incidentally, this new theology of the Eucharist further enhanced the prestige of the priesthood by seeming to endow it with wonder-working powers. Indeed, the Latin words spoken at the consecration of the Host, *Hoc est corpus meum* ("This is my body"), were liable to be (mis)-understood as a magical formula: *Hocus pocus.*

Holy Women, Human and Divine

Popular devotion to the Eucharist was matched by another new and hugely influential religious practice: the veneration of Jesus's mother, Mary. In this development, too, Bernard of Clairvaux played an important role. Under his influence, the Church now taught that Mary had not only given birth to Jesus while still a virgin, but that she remained a virgin even after Jesus' birth—and, more radically, that she herself had been conceived without sin. This made Mary the exact opposite of Eve, the woman whose disobedience had allegedly brought sin into the world for the first time; for Mary had given birth to Christ, a second Adam, whose obedient sacrifice of himself atoned for that original sin. New doctrines also raised Mary from the position of God's humble handmaid to that of heaven's queen, with the power to intercede on behalf of all, even the worst sinners. Her soaring reputation is amply testified by the thousands of devotional images created during this period, the many stories and hymns celebrating her virtues and miracles, and the fact that practically all the magnificent new cathedrals of the age were dedicated to "Our Lady." (Hence the many churches of Notre Dame in France, the Frauenkirchen of Germany, and so on.)

The burgeoning cult of the Blessed Virgin had two contradictory effects. On the one hand, it elevated a female figure to a prominent place in the Roman Church for the first time, and it thereby celebrated virtues associated with femininity: motherhood, healing, nourishment, mercy, kindness. On the other hand, it made Mary an unobtainable model of female perfection. No real woman could begin to emulate her, and thus real women were increasingly compared to Eve and perceived as weak, deceitful, and disobediant. Moroever, the veneration of a single, idealized woman coincided exactly with the suppression of most real women's access to positions of power within the Church. As the cult of the Blessed Virgin grew, so the opportunities for aspiring holy women shrank.

This did not go unremarked at the time. The career of Heloise (c. 1090–1164) exemplifies both the avenues of advancement for women and also the successful blocking of those avenues by new constraints on women's activities. Heloise's exact contemporary, Hildegard of Bingen

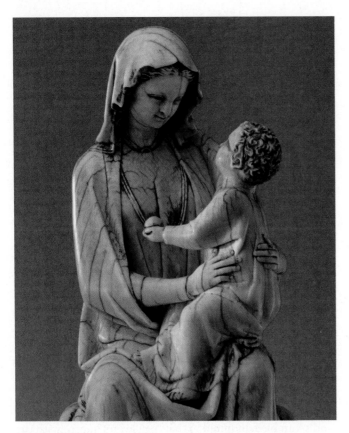

VIRGIN AND CHILD. This exquisite ivory sculpture (just over seven inches high) was carved in Paris in the mid- to late thirteenth century, as an aid to private devotion and prayer. The mother of Jesus, Mary was also regarded as the mother of all humanity, the *alma mater* ("nourishing mother") who could be relied on to protect and heal those who asked for her help.

(1098–1179), was also creative in her efforts to make a place for herself and her female followers, and more outspoken than Heloise in her criticism of attempts to thwart them. Like Heloise, she was an abbess and a highly original thinker. But she was not, like Heloise, a scholar; she was a mystic who claimed to receive regular revelations from God. She also composed hymns and ambitious musical dramas for her nuns—music now widely available on CD and MP3—and prepared treatises on subjects as diverse as cosmology, pharmacology, and medicine. Her advice was frequently sought by religious and secular authorities, including Bernard of Clairvaux and Frederick Barbarossa, and she even received a special papal dispensation that allowed her to preach publicly.

Despite all this, Hildegard had to fight constantly for her rights and those of her nuns during her lifetime, and after her death she was never officially recognized as a saint. Indeed, she was one of the first candidates for whom a new canonization process was instituted in the papal curia, as a way of controlling the popular veneration of charismatic figures whom the Church considered threatening. So while many high-ranking clergy of her own day recognized her holiness, the papal courts of subsequent centuries would not acknowledge it. The standards of acceptable female behavior had become too narrow to contain her.

Heresy or Piety?

Christianity has been successfully transmitted to many different civilizations because it is relatively open-ended and absorbent of new influences. In this era, however, the Church began to lose its capacity to respond inclusively to new challenges, preferring instead to crack down on "heresies" that undermined its power. This trend would eventually lead to a reforming movement so intense that it could not be contained within the Church: the Protestant Reformation (see Chapter 13). For the more the Church claimed the right to control every aspect of belief and practice, the more it made itself vulnerable to those who challenged its enforcment of orthodoxy. This resulted in popular opposition to papal authority, and also to counter-initiatives aimed at harnessing popular piety to that same authority.

The best way to understand this is through Innocent III's very different responses to rather similar religious movements. On the one hand, the pope resolved to crush all disobedience of papal authority; on the other, he wanted to support idealistic groups that could be made to acknowledge papal authority. For example, Innocent labelled as "heretical" a spiritual awakening that began in southern France, that of the Cathars (from the Greek word for "purity"). He accused Cathars of beliefs that resemble Zoroastrianism (Chapter 2) and Manichaeism (Chapter 6), alleging that they held all material creation to be evil, and that they believed the power of God to be opposed by that of a malevolent deity associated with the fallen angel Lucifer. Whatever the truth of these allegations, the fact that many Cathar leaders were women made the movement "heretical" by definition.

Innocent eventually took steps to eradicate the Cathars, who were also known as Albigensians, by authorizing the violent seizure of their lands and property. But this "Albigensian Crusade" was really a war of conquest that enabled the French monarchy to expand into southern lands. Innocent also began the process of instituting inquisitorial procedures that would enable the legal prosecution, torture, and execution of convicted heretics like the Waldensians. Waldensians were lay people who followed the teachings of a merchant called Peter Waldo (or Waldes). They were active in the vernacular translation of the Gospels and

HILDEGARD OF BINGEN'S DIVINE INSPIRATION. This portrait of Hildegard and her male secretary, Volmar, appears in her book *Scivias* ("Know the Ways"). It shows Hildegard as the recipient of a divine vision (represented by tongues of heavenly fire) which she transcribes onto a wax tablet using a stylus, a common method for creating the first draft of a written work. Volmar is placed outside the frame in which her vision occurs, but he is prepared to copy it onto parchment. ▪ *What does this image tell us about medieval ideas of authorship and authority?* ▪ *What does it suggest about the relationship and status of the two figures?*

dedicated to lives of poverty and preaching. For a while, the Church did not interfere with Waldensians' ministry. But when they began to preach without authorization they were condemned as heretics. Many of their leaders, too, were women.

At the same time, Innocent ratified two other popular movements and turned them into two new religious orders, the Dominicans and the Franciscans. Like the Waldensians, the friars ("brothers") of these orders imitated Jesus by preaching and offering assistance to the poor. They also begged for a living—hence their categorization as *mendicants*, from the Latin verb *mendicare*, "to beg." But essentially the only thing that separated them from the Waldensians was their willingness to subject themselves to papal authority.

The first of these orders, formally known as the Order of Preachers, was founded by Dominic of Osma (1170–1221), a Castilian theologian. Approved in 1216, it was particularly dedicated to the prosecution of heretics and to the conversion of Jews and Muslims. At first, the Dominicans hoped to achieve these ends by preaching and public debate, and so many of its members pursued academic careers and contributed to the development of philosophy and theology; indeed, the most influential intellectual of the Middle Ages, Thomas Aquinas (1225–1274), was a Dominican (see below). But the Dominicans soon became associated with the use of other persuasive techniques through the administration of the Inquistition, which became formalized in the thirteenth century. (It is now called the Congregation for the Doctrine of the Faith, and is still staffed by members of the order.)

The Franciscans, formally known as the Order of the Friars Minor ("Little Brothers"), were quite different from the Dominicans, commited less to doctrine and discipline than to the welfare of the poor and the cultivation of personal spirituality. Whereas Dominic and his followers were ordained priests, the founder of the Franciscans was the ne'er-do-well son of an Italian merchant, Francis of Assisi (1182–1226), who eventually rebelled against the materialistic values of his father. Stripping himself (literally) of all his worldly possessions, he put on the tattered garb of a beggar and began to preach and to minister to outcasts in the darkest corners of Italian cities. Unlike Dominic, Francis did all of this without official approval, thereby risking rejection as a heretic. But when he showed himself willing to profess obedience in 1209, Innocent granted Francis and his followers permission to preach.

This was not, however, an approved religious lifestyle for women. Francis's most important female follower, Clare of Assisi (1194–1253), wanted to found an order along the same lines, but members of the Order of Poor Ladies (also known as the Poor Clares) were not allowed to work directly among the poor, as men did, but instead lived in cloistered convents supported by charitable donations. Their counterparts in northern Europe were the Beguines, communities of lay women who ministered to the poor. Their relationship with Church officials was often strained because the Beguines embraced many of the practices associated with "heretics," including the unauthorized translation and study of the Bible. The fact that they were women made them even more suspect.

Two Conversion Experiences

> Peter Waldo, later branded as a heretic, and Francis of Assisi, later canonized as a saint, were both moved to take up lives of preaching and poverty after undergoing a process of conversion. These experiences exhibit some striking similarities, despite the very different fates of these two men. The first account is that of an anonymous chronicler in Peter's home town of Lyons; the second is by Francis's contemporary and hagiographer, Thomas of Celano (c. 1200–c. 1260/70).

The Conversion of Peter Waldo

At about this time, in 1173, there was a citizen of Lyons named Peter Waldo, who had made a great deal of money by the evil means of usury. One Sunday he lingered by a crowd that had gathered round a traveling storyteller, and was much struck by his words. He took him home with him, and listened carefully to his story of how St. Alexis had died a holy death in his father's house. Next morning Waldo hastened to the schools of theology to seek advice about his soul. When he had been told of the many ways of coming to God he asked the master whether any of them was more sure and reliable than the rest. The master quoted to him the words of the Lord, "If thou wilt be perfect go sell what thou hast and give it to the poor and thou shalt have treasure in heaven. And come follow me."

Waldo returned to his wife and gave her the choice between having all his movable wealth or his property in land.... She was very upset at having to do this and chose the property. From his movable wealth he returned what he had acquired wrongly, conferred a large portion on his two daughters, whom he placed in the order of Fontevrault without his wife's knowledge, and gave a still larger amount to the poor.

At this time a terrible famine was raging through Gaul and Germany.... Waldo generously distributed bread, soup and meat to anyone who came to him. On the [Feast of the] Assumption of the Virgin [August 15] he scattered money among the poor in the streets saying, "You cannot serve two masters, God and Mammon." The people around thought he had gone out of his senses. Then he stood up on a piece of high ground and said, "Friends and fellow-citizens, I am not mad as you think.... I know that many of you disapprove of my having acted so publicly. I have done so both for my own sake and for yours: for my sake, because anybody who sees me with money in future will be able to say that I am mad; for your sake, so that you may learn to place your hopes in God and not in wealth."...

In 1177 Waldo, the citizen of Lyons whom we have already mentioned, who had vowed to God that he would possess neither gold nor silver, and take no thought for the morrow, began to make converts to his opinions. Following his example they gave all they had to the poor, and willingly devoted themselves to poverty. Gradually, both in public and in private they began to inveigh against both their own sins and those of others....

In 1178 Pope Alexander III held a council at the Lateran palace.... The council condemned heresy and all those who fostered and defended heretics. The pope embraced Waldo, and applauded the vows of voluntary poverty which he had taken, but forbade him and his companion to assume the office of preaching except at the request of the priests. They obeyed this instruction for a time, but later they disobeyed, and affronted many, bringing ruin on themselves.

Source: Excerpted from *Chronicon universale anonymi Laudunensis*, ed. and trans. Robert I. Moore, *The Birth of Popular Heresy* (London: 1975), pp. 111–13 (slightly modified).

The Conversion of Francis of Assisi

There was a man by the name of Francis, who from his earliest years was brought up by his parents proud of spirit, in accordance with the vanity of the world.... These are the wretched circumstances among which the man whom we venerate today as a saint, for he is truly a saint, lived in his youth; and almost up to the twenty-fifth year of his age, ... he outdid all his contemporaries in vanities and he came to be a promoter of evil and was more abundantly zealous for all kinds of foolishness. . . . And while, not knowing how to restrain himself, he was . . . worn down by a long illness, [and he] began to think of things other than he was used to thinking upon. When he had recovered somewhat and had begun to walk about the house with the support of a cane to speed the recovery of his health, he went outside one day and began to look about at the surrounding landscape with great interest. But the beauty of the fields, the pleasantness of the vineyards, and whatever else was beautiful to look upon, could stir in him no delight. He wondered therefore at the sudden change that had come over him. . . . From that day on, therefore, he began to despise himself. . . .

Now since there was a certain man in the city of Assisi whom he loved more than any other because he was of the same age as the other, and since the great familiarity of their mutual affection led him to share his secrets with him, he often took him to remote places, places well suited for counsel, telling him that he had found a certain precious and great treasure. This one rejoiced and, concerned about what he heard, he willingly accompanied Francis whenever he was asked. There was a certain grotto near the city where they frequently went and talked about this treasure. The man of God, who was already holy by reason of his holy purpose, would enter the grotto, while his companion would wait for him outside; and filled with a new and singular spirit, he would pray to his Father in secret. . . .

One day, however, when he had begged for the mercy of God most earnestly, it was shown to him by God what he was to do. . . . He rose up, therefore,

fortified himself with the sign of the cross, got his horse ready and mounted it, and taking with him some fine cloth to sell, he hastened to the city called Foligno. There, as usual, he sold everything he had with him . . . and, free of all luggage, he started back, wondering with a religious mind what he should do with the money. . . . When, therefore, he neared the city of Assisi, he discovered a certain church . . . built of old in honor of St. Damian but which was now threatening to collapse because it was so old. . . . And when he found there a certain poor priest, he kissed his sacred hands with great faith, and offered him the money he had with him, . . . begging the priest to suffer him to remain with him for the sake of the Lord. . . .

When those who knew him . . . compared what he was now with what he had been . . . they began to revile him miserably. Shouting out that he was mad and demented, they threw the mud of the streets and stones at him. . . . Now . . . the report of these things finally came to his father . . . [who] shut him up mercilessly in a dark place for several days. . . . It happened, however, when Francis's father had left home for a while on business and the man of God remained bound in the basement of the house, his mother, who was alone with him and did not approve of what her husband had done, spoke kindly to her son . . . and loosening his chains, she let him go free. . . .

He [the father] then brought his son before the bishop of the city, so that, renouncing all his possessions into his hands, he might give up everything he had. . . . Indeed, he [Francis] did not wait for any words nor did he speak any, but immediately putting off his clothes and

casting them aside, he gave them back to his father. Moreover, not even retaining his trousers, he stripped himself completely naked before all. The bishop, however, sensing his disposition and admiring greatly his fervor and constancy, arose and drew him within his arms and covered him with the mantle he was wearing. . . .

Source: Excerpted from Thomas of Celano, "The First Life of Saint Francis" in *Saint Francis of Assisi: Writings and Biographies*, ed. Marion A. Habiq (Chicago: 1973), pp. 229–41.

Questions for Analysis

1. How do the conversions of Peter and Francis reflect the social and economic changes of the twelfth century? What new sources of tension and temptation are evident?

2. How do these two accounts describe these new converts' relationship(s) with their families, communities, and Church authorities? What are the similarities and differences, and why would these be important factors in determining the sanctity of either?

3. The story of Peter's conversion is written by an anonymous chronicler of Lyons, that of Francis by his follower and official biographer. How do these different perspectives shape these two accounts? Which is the more reliable, and why?

Christians against Jews

Although violence and exploitation continued to reduce the size and strength of Europe's Jewish communities, the Church's official position held that Jews posed a serious threat to Christians. It never explicitly endorsed the wilder claims made by popular rabble-rousers, but it did little to combat such attitudes either. As a result, many ordinary Christians came to believe that their Jewish neighbors were agents of evil who routinely crucified Christian children, profaned the body of Christ in the Eucharist, and spread disease in Christian communities by poisoning wells. Fanciful stories of Jewish wealth added an economic element to the development of anti-Semitism, as did the fact that the Jews' social and cultural networks facilitated rapid communication. From these, conspiracy theorists inferred the existence of organized Jewish plots to undermine Christian society, which were regularly cited as justifications for pogroms, mass executions, and other atrocities.

The precarious position of Europe's Jews worsened throughout the thirteenth century, as both secular and ecclesiastical authorities devised more systematic mechanisms for controlling and policing undesirable segments of society: not only "heretics" but the indigent poor, prostitutes, "sodomites," and lepers. The canons of the Fourth Lateran Council had mandated that Jews be exposed and marginalized through the wearing of the Jewish badge, and this made them easier targets in times of unrest. Meanwhile, the protections which Europe's rulers had once extended to their Jewish subjects were gradually withdrawn. In Iberia, the "Reconquista" had absorbed many of the Muslim kingdoms in which Jews had enjoyed a measure of tolerance, and they were not easily accommodated within the emerging monarchies of Christian Spain. Starting in the 1280s, rulers elsewhere in Europe began to expel their Jewish subjects from their kingdoms altogether, in most cases because they could no longer repay the enormous sums they had extorted from Jewish moneylenders; this was the case in the kingdoms of Sicily (1288), England (1290), and France (1306). Further expulsions followed during the fourteenth century in the Rhineland, and in 1492 from Spain. By 1500, only northern Italy and various eastern European regions (encompassed today by Poland, Belorus, and Ukraine) were home to sizable Jewish communities. They would survive there until the more efficient persecutions of the Holocaust destroyed them (see Chapter 26).

THE BURNING OF JEWS. This manuscript account, written in the German vernacular, records an incident in which Jews were accused of poisoning the wells in a Christian town—and shows the punishment meted out to them. The wooden enclosure may represent the walls of the Jewish ghetto. As in the image on page 217, the Jews are identified by their distinctive conical hats.

THE INTELLECTUAL REVOLUTION

As we noted above, the Fourth Lateran Council responded to the growing population and urbanization of Europe by mandating the education of the laity and by insisting on more rigorous training for all clergy. But even before 1215, the growth of towns had led to the growth of schools in those towns, for the most part founded by local bishops or monasteries. At the same time, the Crusades had become conduits for the transmission of Muslim learning and, through Muslim mediation, the precepts of ancient Greek philosophy. The infusion of these new ideas created an extraordinary new forum for intellectual endeavor: the university. In much the same way that ease of travel and communication had fostered a scientific revolution in the cities of the Hellenistic world (Chaper 4), so the conditions which gave rise to the university mark the beginning of a revolution in the intellectual history of Europe.

Access to Education

Around 800, Charlemagne had ordered that primary schools be established in every city and monastery of his realm. But it was not until the economic revival of the late eleventh century that such educational opportunities were widely available. By 1179, Pope Alexander III decreed that all cathedrals should set aside income for at least one schoolteacher, whose task would be to accept all comers, rich or poor, without fee. The recently martyred Thomas Becket had been an early beneficiary of such schooling.

At first, cathedral schools existed almost exclusively for the training of priests, but their curriculum was soon broadened as the growth of bureaucracies escalated the demand for men with more sophisticated skills. The most fundamental elements of this curriculum were known as the *trivium*, "the three ways": grammar, logic, and rhetoric. This meant a thorough grounding in Latin through the study of classical Roman authors, such as Cicero and Virgil (Chapter 5), and training in the formulation and expression of sound arguments. Students who mastered the trivium were fit to perform basic clerical tasks, but those who wanted to achieve the reputation and advantages of scholars had to master the remaining branches of learning. These were arithmetic, geometry, astronomy, and music: the *quadrivium* or "four ways." Together, these seven liberal arts—so called because they free the minds and bodies of those who acquire them—were the prerequisites for advanced study in philosophy, theology, law, and medicine.

Until about 1200, most students in urban schools would have belonged to the minor orders of the clergy. This means that they took vows of obedience and were immune from prosecution by secular authorities, but were not re-quired to remain celibate—unlike priests and bishops (who were in major orders). But by the thirteenth century, most boys who entered schools were not members of the clergy and never intended to be. Some were children of wealthy families, who regarded Latin literacy as a practical neces-sity. Others were future notaries, estate managers, and mer-chants who needed to be literate and numerate in order to succeed in these careers. In many cases, Latin ceased to be the language of instruction in these schools and was replaced by the vernacular language of the region.

Formal schooling remained restricted to males. Yet many girls and women became highly educated. Heloise

had an unusual degree of access to the educational milieu of Paris, but she had already received excellent prepara-tory training in the convent at Argentueil before she began her studies with Abelard. Most lay women were taught at home, sometimes by private tutors but more often by other women. In fact, lay women were more likely to be literate than lay men, and it is for this reason that women were often the patrons of poets and the primary readers and owners of books. Significantly, the effigy that Eleanor of Aquitaine commissioned for her own tomb shows her lying awake till Judgment Day, reading.

The Development of Scholasticism

This educational revolution led to the development of new critical methods for framing and resolving complex prob-lems. These methods are collectively known as *scholasti-cism*, meaning that they had their orgins in the pedagogy of medieval schools. Scholastic methods are highly respect-ful of authority, but they also rely on rigorous questioning and argumentation. They therefore place great emphasis on evidence derived from reason. Indeed, scholasticism can be defined as the theory and practice of reconciling various forms of knowledge through logical debate, often called *dialectic*.

The earliest practitioner of the scholastic method is often considered to be Anselm of Canterbury (1033–1109).

THE TOMB OF ELEANOR OF AQUITAINE. Eleanor probably commissioned the effigies representing herself, her husband Henry II, and her son Richard the Lionheart (both of whom died years before she did). She was eventually buried alongside them in the vault of the convent of Fontevrault in Anjou, where she spent the last years of her life.

The central premise of Anselm's teaching was that the human mind can reconcile wisdom gained through education and experience with divine revelation—so long as one has faith in God and careful scholastic training. Building on the writings of Augustine and Boethius (Chapter 6), Anselm developed various rational proofs for the truths of Christian doctrine. The most famous of these is his proof for the existence of God, known as the ontological proof ("proof from the fact of existence") because it reasons that human beings could not have ideas of goodness or truth or justice unless some higher being had instilled these ideas in us. He further reasoned that God, as the essence of all ideals, must be "that than which nothing greater can be conceived" and as such must exist, or else God could not be the greatest thing conceivable.

Anselm's writings were influential, but the philosopher who popularized the scholastic method was Abelard. It was largely thanks to him that Paris became the intellectual capital of Europe and a magnet for ambitious young men who were attracted to Abelard's unorthodox teaching style. We can glimpse it through the audacious treatise called the *Sic et Non* ("Yes and No" or "So and Not So"). In this book, Abelard gathered a collection of seemingly contradictory statements from the Church Fathers, organized around 150 key theological problems. Like his contemporary Gratian, the codifier of canon law, his ultimate ambition was to show that these divergent authorities could be reconciled—in this case, through the skillful use of dialectic.

Yet Abelard did not propose any solutions in the *Sic et Non*, and the work therefore caused grave concern. More inflammatory still were Abelard's meditations on the doctrine of the Trinity, which circulated in a book of lectures that was denounced and burned in 1121. Twenty years later, Bernard of Clairvaux had Abelard brought up on another charge of heresy, and he was condemned a second time. But his very skills as a teacher helped to salvage his reputation, since his many pupils eventually vindicated his teachings. His student Peter Lombard would ask the same fundamental questions, but he took care to resolve the tensions which the *Sic et Non* had left open-ended. His great work, known as the *Sentences*, became the standard theological textbook of the medieval university, on which all aspirants to the doctorate were required to comment.

The Nature of the University

The emergence of the university—a unique public forum for advanced study, the questioning of received ideas, and the resolution of critical problems—was the natural extension of Abelard's teachings. His reputation and that of his students attracted many other intellectuals to Paris, and together they could offer more varied and advanced instruction than anything obtainable in the average cathedral school. By 1200, this loose association of teachers formed a *universitas* ("corporation" in Latin), and the resulting faculty began to collaborate in the higher academic study of the liberal arts, with a special emphasis on theology. At about the same time, students in Bologna came together in a *universitas* whose speciality was law.

Paris and Bologna provided the two basic models on which all medieval universities were based. In southern Europe, the universities of Montpellier, Salamanca, and Naples were patterned after Bologna, where the students themselves constituted the corporation. They hired the teachers, paid their salaries, and fined or discharged them for neglect of duty or poor instruction. The universities of northern Europe, modeled on Paris, were guilds of teachers who governed themselves and established fees for tuition and rules of conduct. By the end of the thirteenth century, the northern universities also expanded to include separate, semi-autonomous colleges, which usually provided housing for poorer students and were often endowed by a private benefactor. Over time, these colleges became centers of instruction as well as residences. The universities of Oxford and Cambridge still retain this pattern of organization.

Most of the academic degrees granted in our modern universities derive from those awarded in the Middle Ages, even though the actual courses of study are very different. Prior to the nineteenth century, no university curriculum included history or vernacular languages, or anything like the social sciences. The medieval student was assumed to know Latin grammar thoroughly before entrance into a university. On admission, he was required to spend about four years studying the basic liberal arts, which meant doing advanced work in Latin rhetoric and mastering the rules of logic. If he passed his examinations, he received the preliminary degree of bachelor of arts (the prototype of our BA). But to ensure himself a place in professional life he had to devote additional years to the pursuit of an advanced degree, the master of arts (MA) or doctor of laws, medicine, or theology. This was accomplished by reading and commenting on standard texts such as Peter Lombard's *Sentences* (theology), Gratian's *Decretum* (law), or Aristotle's *Physics* (medicine). The requirements for the degree of doctor of philosophy (PhD) included more specialized training, and those for the doctorate in theology were particularly arduous, requiring twelve or thirteen years of further study.

Student life in medieval universities was rowdy. Many students began their studies between the ages of twelve

Peter Abelard Critiques Theological Contradictions

In 1120, Abelard published the Sic et Non, *"So and Not So," a pioneering work of dialectic theology and a model for the development of later scholastic methods. In it, he arranged passages from Scripture as well as writings of the Church Fathers that had bearing on important doctrinal issues and that appeared to offer contradictory views. His eventual aim, as the prologue to this work indicates, was to reconcile these differences through the use of critical analysis.*

 here are many seeming contradictions and even obscurities in the innumerable writings of the church fathers. Our respect for their authority should not stand in the way of an effort on our part to come at the truth. The obscurity and contradictions in ancient writings may be explained upon many grounds, and may be discussed without impugning the good faith and insight of the fathers. A writer may use different terms to mean the same thing, in order to avoid a monotonous repetition of the same word. Common, vague words may be employed in order that the common people may understand; and sometimes a writer sacrifices perfect accuracy in the interest of a clear general statement. Poetical, figurative language is often obscure and vague. . . .

Doubtless the fathers might err; even Peter, the prince of the apostles, fell into error; what wonder that the saints do not always show themselves inspired? The fathers did not themselves believe that they, or their companions, were always right. Augustine found himself mistaken in some cases and did not hesitate to retract his errors. He warns his admirers not to look upon his letters as they would upon the Scriptures, but to accept only those things which, upon examination, they find to be true.

All writings belonging to this class are to be read with full freedom to criticise, and with no obligation to accept unquestioningly; otherwise the way would be blocked to all discussion, and posterity be deprived of the excellent intellectual exercise of debating difficult questions of language and presentation. But an explicit exception must be made in the case of the Old and New Testaments. In the Scriptures, when anything strikes us as absurd, we may not say that the writer erred, but that the scribe made a blunder in copying the manuscripts, or that there is an error in interpretation, or that the passage is not understood. The fathers make a very careful distinction between the Scriptures and later works. They advocate a discriminating, not to say suspicious, use of the writings of their own contemporaries.

In view of these considerations, I have ventured to bring together various dicta of the holy fathers, as they came to mind, and to formulate certain questions which were suggested by the seeming contradictions in the statements. These questions ought to serve to excite tender readers to a zealous inquiry into truth and so sharpen their wits. The master key of knowledge is, indeed, a persistent and frequent questioning. Aristotle, the most clear-sighted of all the philosophers, was desirous above all things else to arouse this questioning spirit, for in his *Categories* he exhorts a student as follows: "It may well be difficult to reach a positive conclusion in these matters unless they be frequently discussed. It is by no means fruitless to be doubtful on particular points." By doubting we come to examine, and by examining we reach the truth.

Source: Peter Abelard, prologue to the *Sic et Non*, trans. James Harvey Robinson in *Readings in European History*, 2 vols. (Boston, MA: 1904), vol. 1, pp. 450–51.

Questions for Analysis

1. On what grounds can religious authorities be challenged, according to Abelard? What distinctions does he make between criticism of the Scriptures and of other authorities, and why?

2. Abelard did not attempt, in this work, to resolve the contradictions among his sources. Based on what you have learned, why would his project have seemed threatening to the authority of the Church?

CENTURY UNIVERSITY WAS FOUNDED

- ■ Twelfth century
- ■ Thirteenth century
- □ Fourteenth century
- ▪ Fifteenth century
- — Boundaries c. 1500

THE SPREAD OF UNIVERSITIES. This map shows the geographical distribution of Europe's major universities and indicates the dates of their foundation. ▪ *Where were the first universities founded and why?* ▪ Notice the number and location of the universities founded in the fourteenth and fifteenth centuries. ▪ *What pattern do you see in these later foundations?* ▪ *What might explain this?*

and fifteen, and so were working through all the challenges of adolescence as they worked toward their degrees; this helps to explain the many injunctions against drunkenness, gambling, and other pursuits included among the canons of the Fourth Lateran Council. Moreover, university students generally believed that they constituted an independent and privileged community, apart from the local communities in which they lived. This often led to riots or even pitched battles between "town" and "gown."

That said, the time devoted to actual study was very intensive. Because books were prohibitively expensive, the primary mode of instruction was the lecture (Latin for "reading") in which a master would read an authoritative work aloud to his students and comment on it while the students took notes. As students advanced in their disciplines, they were expected to develop their own skills of analysis and interpretation in formal, public disputations. Advanced disputations could become extremely complex and abstract; sometimes they might last for days. Often they sparked public debates of great magnitude. The ninety-five theses posted by Martin Luther in 1517 were actually a set of debating points organized along these lines (see Chapter 13).

Classical Thought and Christian Theology

The intellectual revolution of the Middle Ages was further advanced by renewed access to classical philosophy and Muslim science, epitomized by the works of Avicenna and Averroès (Chapter 8). Many Greek texts were available in Latin translation after the middle of the twelfth century, and by the middle of the thirteenth nearly all of Aristotle's surviving works and much Arabic scientific knowledge was accessible to western Europeans. Scholars were now faced with the task of reconciling these "new" ideas with a thousand years of doctrinal developments. This was relatively straightforward in the case of the natural sciences, because scholasticism had already established the principles for reconciling reason and observation with faith. But many other aspects of Greek and Arabic learning were not readily compatible and therefore had to be filtered through the dialectical methods pioneered by Abelard and his pupils.

By far the greatest accomplishments in this endeavor were made by Thomas Aquinas (1225–1274), who became the leading theologian at the University of Paris. As a member of the Dominican order, Thomas was committed to the defense of faith through reason. He also believed that the study of the physical world was a legitimate way of gaining knowledge of the divine, because God had created both the world and the many ways of knowing it. Imbued with a deep confidence in the value of human reason, Thomas worked quietly and steadily on his two great summaries of theology, the *Summa contra Gentiles* (a summary of the arguments for refuting non-Christian religions) and the compendious *Summa*

Theologiae. The theology of the modern Roman Catholic Church continues to rest on Thomistic methods, doctrines, and principles.

COURTS, CITIES, AND CATHEDRALS

In the eleventh century, it was still possible to describe European society as divided among "those who worked, those who prayed, and those who fought." By 1200, such a description no longer bore much relationship to reality. New elites had emerged in the burgeoning cities of western Europe. The wealthiest members of society were merchants and bankers, and aristocrats either had to best them (by engaging in trade themselves) or join them through strategic intermarriage. The aristocracy still fought, but so did upwardly mobile knights, urban crossbowmen, longbowmen, citizen militias, and peasant levies. Meanwhile, such lines as existed between town and countryside were easily crossed. Rural people moved to towns and townspeople moved back to the countryside with regularity and ease. And the pupils of the new schools made up a growing professional class that further defied neat categorization. We have noted that careers in the Church or royal bureaucracies were particularly open to self-made, educated men. But medieval courts and cities also provided opportunities for advancement.

From Chevalerie to Chivalry

The ennoblement of chivalry and the emergence of medieval court culture were connected to the growing wealth of Europe, the competition among monarchies, and contemporary developments in military technology. In 1100, a knight could get by with a woolen tunic and leather corselet, a couple of horses, a groom, and a sword. A hundred years later, a knight needed full-body armor made of iron, a visored helmet, a broadsword, a spear, a shield, and warhorses capable of carrying all this gear. By 1250, a knight also had to keep up appearances at tournaments, which meant maintaining a string of horses, sumptuous silk clothing for himself and caparisons for his steeds, and a retinue of liveried squires and servants. As the costs of a warrior's equipment rose, the number of men who could personally afford it declined dramatically, which made knightly display something increasingly prized by the nobility and newly rich merchants alike.

There were still other factors contributing to the prestige of knighthood. As part of a larger effort to control the violent competition for land and wealth, both secular and ecclesiastical rulers had begun to promote a new set of values that would come to redefine chivalry: bravery, loyalty, generosity, and civility. This new chivalry appealed to knights because it distinguished them from all the other "new men" who were emerging as powerful in this period, especially merchants and clerics. It also appealed to the nobility, whose status in this socially mobile world no longer depended on descent from high-born ancestors; families who *did* have such ancestors did not necessarily have the wealth to maintain a noble lifestyle, while many families who lived as "nobility" did not have prestigious ancestors.

What, then, was "nobility"? Was high status a matter of birth or was it the result of individual achievement? The amalgamation of knighthood and nobility offered something to all sides. To the older aristocracy, it was a visible sign of good breeding. To professional warriors, and to the merchants and bureaucrats who adopted its language and customs, chivalry offered a way of legitimizing social positions attained through bravery or skill. As a result, mounted combat—whether on the battlefield, in tournaments, or in the hunt—would remain the defining pastime of European gentlemen until the end of the First World War.

The Culture of the Court

Closely linked to this new ideology of chivalry was a new emphasis on *courtoisie*, "courtliness," the refined behavior appropriate to a court. This stemmed in part from practical necessity. Those great lords who could support a knightly retinue would have households full of randy young men whose appetites had to be controlled. Hence, the emerging code of chivalry encouraged a view of noblewomen as objects of veneration who could only be wooed and won by politesse, poetry, and valiant deeds; they had to be courted. Non-noble women, though, were fair game and could be taken by force if they did not yield willingly to the desires of a knight.

Whole new genres of poetry, song, and storytelling emerged in the twelfth century to celebrate the allied cultures of chivalry and courtliness. These genres stand in marked contrast to the heroic epics that are often the earliest literary artifacts of various vernacular languages: the Anglo-Saxon *Beowulf*, *The Song of Roland*, the Norse sagas, the German *Song of the Nibelungs*, and the Spanish *Poem of the Cid*. These epics portray a virile, violent society. If women are mentioned, often they are prizes to be won in battle. The courtly entertainments introduced in the twelfth century are very different. Many of them were addressed to, and commissioned by, women. In some cases, they were even composed by women, or in close collaboration with a female patron. An example of the former is the collections of *lais* (versified stories) of Marie de France, who was active during the reigns of Henry II and Eleanor of Aquitaine, and who may have been an abbess as well as a member of the Anglo-Norman aristocracy. An example of the latter is one of the Arthurian tales composed by Marie's contemporary, Chrétien de Troyes (*kray-TYAN duh TWAH*, fl. 1165–90),

MAKING A KNIGHTLY APPEARANCE. The costs of maintaining a chivalric lifestyle mounted steeply in the twelfth and thirteenth centuries, not only because a knight needed the most up-to-date equipment but because he was expected to cut a gallant figure at tournaments and to dazzle female spectators. This image is one of many sumptuous full-page illuminations in the Manesse Codex, made in Zurich in the early fourteenth century and preserving the compositions of courtly poets.

who spent some time working under the patronage of Eleanor's daughter (by her first husband, Louis VII), Marie of Champagne.

These new storytelling forms often focused on the exploits of King Arthur and his knights or some other heroic figure of the past, like Alexander the Great. But they were also attuned to the interests and concerns of women: threats to women's independence, enforced or unhappy marriages, disputed inheritances, fashion, fantasies of power. The heroine of one anonymous romance is a woman who dresses as a knight and travels the world performing valiant deeds. Other heroines accompany their husbands on quests, or defend their castles against attack, or have supernatural powers. Following in Chrétien's footsteps, the German poets Wolfram von Eschenbach and Gottfried von Strassburg vied to produce romances that retained the scope and complexity of heroic epics while featuring women in strong, central roles: Wolfram's *Parzival*, the story of the search for the Holy Grail, and Gottfried's *Tristan*, which re-told the Celtic story of the adulterous love between Tristan and Isolde. Both inspired the operatic reconceptions of Richard Wagner (1813–1883).

The poetic tradition initiated by the southern French troubadours and northern French trouvères (terms deriving from the verbs *trobar/trouver*: "to discover, to invent") also contributed to the culture of chivalry. Much troubadour poetry displays sensitivity to feminine beauty and the natural world, and pays eloquent tribute to the political and sexual power of women.

But to what extent do these entertainments reflect real changes in noblewomen's status? Certainly, there were women throughout this period who wielded tremendous power, particularly in Scandinavia and parts of southern Europe, where women could inherit property, rule in their own right, and were treated as lords in fact and in name. For example, Eleanor remained sole ruler of Aquitaine throughout her long life, and she played a crucial role in the government of England at various times. The strong-willed Blanche of Castile (1188–1252), Eleanor's granddaughter, ruled France during the minority of her son Louis IX and again when he went on crusade.

Queens are not typical, of course, but their activities in this period reflect some of the opportunities open to other well-born women—and the freedoms that set most western European women apart from their counterparts in the Byzantine and Muslim worlds. A striking symbol of this is the figure of the queen in the game of chess. In the Muslim courts where the game originated, the equivalent of the queen was a male figure, the king's chief minister, who could move only diagonally, and only one square at a time. In twelfth-century Europe, this piece became the queen. Eventually, she was the only figure powerful enough to move all over the board.

Urban Opportunities and Inequalities

Towns were crucibles of activity, and as such became political powerhouses as well as economic ones. As we noted in Chapter 8, many of the towns that emerged in the twelfth century were governed by associations of citizens who undertook a wide variety of civic responsibilities. But urban governance was also apt to fall into the hands of oligarchs, a trend that became increasingly marked during the thirteenth century when the enormous wealth generated by some forms of commerce led to social inequalities. In Italy, some cities sought to control the resulting violence by turning to an outsider who would rule as a dictator for a (supposedly) limited term. Others cities adopted the model of Venice and became formal oligarchies, casting off all pretence to democracy. Some cities remained republics in principle, like Florence, but became increasingly oligarchical in practice.

But even in places where town governance was controlled by a powerful few, there were many meaningful opportunities for collective activity. Urban manufacturing was regulated by professional associations known as guilds or, in some regions, confraternities ("brotherhoods"). Guilds promoted the interests of their members by trying to preserve monopolies and limit competition. To these ends, terms of employment and membership were strictly regulated. If an apprentice or a journeyman worker (from the French *journée*, meaning "day" and, by extension, "day's work") wished to become a master, he had to produce a "masterpiece" to be judged by the masters of the guild. If the market was considered too weak to support additional master craftsmen, even a masterpiece would not secure a craftsman the coveted right to set up his own shop. Most guilds were closed to Jews and Muslims and they also restricted the opportunities available to women.

Guilds and confraternities were therefore instruments of economic control, but they were also important social, political, and cultural institutions. Most combined the functions of religious association, drinking club, and benevolent society, looking after members and their families in hard times. Guilds also empowered their members in much the same way that unions do today, providing them with political representation and raising their social status. In Arras, there was even a guild of professional entertainers, the confraternity of jongleurs, which became the most powerful organization in the town during the thirteenth century.

The Varieties of Vernacular Entertainment

Like courts, towns fostered new kinds of vernacular entertainment in the twelfth and thirteenth centuries. Even the genres of Latin poetry, song, and drama produced in this period can be considered "vernacular" because they made use of vernacular elements (like rhyme, which had not been a feature of classical Latin poetry), dealt with current events, and were popular with a wide audience.

Perhaps the genre most representative of urban culture is the fabliau, a "fable" or short story with a salacious or satirical twist. Fabliaux drew attention to the absurdities of urban life and lampooned the different types of people who were striving to reinvent themselves in the permissive world of the town: the oafish peasant, the effete aristocrat, the corrupt priest, the sex-starved housewife, the wily student, the greedy merchant, the con man. Gender-bending and reversals of fortune are common themes. In one fabliau, a young noblewoman is forced to marry a buffoonish shopkeeper who thereby gains a knighthood. To shame him, she herself dresses as a knight and beats her husband in a jousting match. The earliest of these fabliaux come from Arras, the prosperous banking center and the entertainment capital of Europe in the thirteenth century. Thanks to Arras's close contacts with England, southern France, and Italy, many of the entertainments developed there traveled far abroad.

It was through these channels that the accomplishments of poets active in French-speaking lands came to inspire the work of Dante Alighieri (1265–1321) of Florence. Dante composed a series of semi-autobiographical songs in what he called the "sweet new style" of poetry in his native tongue, Italian, which was now so different from Latin that it had become a language in its own right. Yet Dante also strove to make his own vernacular an instrument for serious political and social critique. His great work, known in his own day as the *Comedy* (called by later admirers the *Divine Comedy*) was composed during the years he spent in exile from his beloved city, after the political party he supported was ousted from power in 1301.

The *Comedy* describes the poet's imaginary journey through Hell, Purgatory, and Paradise, a journey beginning in a "dark wood," a metaphor for the personal and political crises that threatened his faith. Dante is led out of this forest and through the first two realms by the Roman poet Virgil, who represents the best of classical culture; but Dante can only be guided toward knowledge of the divine by his deceased beloved, Beatrice, who symbolizes Christian wisdom. In the course of this visionary pilgrimage, Dante meets the souls of many historical personages and contemporaries who explain why they met their several fates: this is his ingenious way of commenting on current events and passing judgment on his enemies. In many ways, this monumental poem represents the fusion of classical and Christian cultures, Latin learning and vernacular artistry.

The Medieval Cathedral

The cathedrals constructed in Europe's major cities during this period exemplify the ways in which the cultural communities of the court, the schools, and the town came together. For although any cathedral-building campaign would have been spearheaded by a bishop looking to glorify his episcopal see, it could not be completed without the support of the nobility, the resources of the wealthy, the learning of trained theologians, and the talents of urban craftsmen. And cathedrals were not merely edifices: they were theaters for liturgy, music, drama, and preaching.

Cathedrals were not, in themselves, new: the seat of a bishop had long been known as his *cathedra*, his throne, and the church that housed it was the principal church of the diocese. But the size, splendor, and importance of cathedrals increased exponentially in the twelfth and thirteenth centuries alongside the growing power of the Church, the population of cities, and the wealth and knowledge necessary for their construction. Indeed, the cathedrals of this period are readily distinguishable from their predecessors by their architectural style, which came to be called "Gothic," while the style of earlier buildings is known as "Romanesque." As the term suggests, Romanesque buildings use the basic elements of public architecture under the

Roman Empire: the rounded arch, massive stone walls, and sturdy supporting columns. By contrast, the structural elements of Gothic architecture are the pointed arch, ribbed vaulting, and the flying buttress, an external support that strengthened the much thinner stone walls and supported enormous stained-glass windows whose light illuminated the interior.

CONCLUSION

A century ago, the American medievalist Charles Homer Haskins described the intellectual, religious, and cultural changes of this era as "the Renaissance of the twelfth century." A generation later, his student Joseph Strayer located "the medieval origins of the modern state" in this same period, and with them the modern ideas of national sovereignty and identity. In recent decades, the British medievalists R. I. Moore and Robert Bartlett have also argued that this era marks the beginning of the modern world, but not necessarily in positive ways. Moore sees the growth of strong institutions like the Church and the state as leading to "the formation of a persecuting society" in which bureaucracies are used to identify, control, and punish groups of people deemed threatening to those in power; Bartlett views this era as the key phase in a brutal process of "conquest and colonization" visible in the expansion of the Holy Roman Empire, the Norman conquest of England, the growth of papal power, and the Crusades. Most recently,

ROMANESQUE AND GOTHIC. Some distinguishing features of the Romanesque and Gothic styles are exhibited in these two churches, both dedicated to the Virgin Mary and built within a century of one another. On the left is the west front of the Church of Notre-Dame-la-Grande in Poitiers, the ancestral domain of Eleanor of Aquitaine. Constructed between 1135 and 1145, it featured rounded arches, massive supporting pillars, and small windows. On the right is the cathedral of Notre-Dame at Reims in Champagne, built between 1220 and 1299. The emphasis on stolid, horizontal registers is here replaced by soaring, vertical lines. The gabled portals, pointed arches, and bristling pinnacles all accentuate the height of this structure, while the multitude of stained-glass windows—chiefly the enormous rose window—flood the vast interior with colored light.

Thomas Bisson has argued that the twelfth century was a period of crisis, exposing the need for strong governments that can check the personal ambitions and the violence of rapacious and unscrupulous men.

Common to all of these paradigms is a recognition that European power and influence began to expand around the year 1000 and was consolidated in the twelfth and thirteenth centuries. By 1300, as a result, Europe had taken on the geographic, political, linguistic, and cultural characteristics that continue to define it today. Indeed, many European nations look to these centuries for their origins and for the monuments of their cultural heritage. Magna Carta is still cited as the foundational document of English law and English constitutional monarchy, while the territories united under the rule of Frankish kings still form the nation of France. The doctrines crystallized in

After You Read This Chapter

 Visit StudySpace for quizzes, additional review materials, and multi-media documents. **wwnorton.com/studyspace**

REVIEWING THE OBJECTIVES

- The emerging monarchies of Europe shared certain features but differed from one another in significant ways. What were the major similarities and differences of kingship in England, France, and Christian Spain?
- The growth of papal power made religion an important part of daily life for all Christians in unprecedented ways, but it also limited lay spirituality and the rights of non-Christians. How?
- Scholasticism was the method of teaching and learning fostered by medieval schools but it was also a method of debating and resolving problems. How did scholasticism assist in the reconciliation of classical and Christian thought?
- The meaning of chivalry changed in the twelfth century. Why?
- New literary genres and art forms were fostered by courts, universities, and towns. What are some good examples?

medieval canon law and scholastic theology have become the core doctrines of the modern Roman Catholic Church, and devotion to the Virgin Mary is still central to the piety of millions. The religious orders that emerged to educate and govern a burgeoning medieval population continue their ministries. The daughter houses of medieval monastic orders continue to proliferate in lands unknown to medieval people: Japan, China, Australia, New Zealand, the Americas. Students still pursue the degrees first granted in medieval universities, and those who earn them wear the caps and gowns of medieval scholars. Meanwhile, poets still aspire to the eloquence of Dante, singers record the music of Hildegard, and Hollywood films are based on chivalric romances and the tragic love story of Abelard and Heloise. It is difficult to tell where the Middle Ages end and the modern world begins.

PEOPLE, IDEAS, AND EVENTS IN CONTEXT

- What was **MAGNA CARTA** and why was it made? How did **PHILIP AUGUSTUS** consolidate royal authority in France, and why were the German emperors unable to do so?
- What were the main achievements of **INNOCENT III**? Why did the imperial power of **FREDERICK II** weaken the papacy?
- How do the **CULT OF THE VIRGIN** and the careers of **HILDEGARD OF BINGEN** and **HELOISE** exemplify the ideals and realities of women's roles in the Church?
- Why were **ABELARD**'s teachings condemned by the Church? In what sense can he be considered the founder of the **UNIVERSITY OF PARIS**?
- How did noblewomen like **ELEANOR OF AQUITAINE** contribute to the emergence of a new vernacular culture? What types of entertainment are characteristic of medieval cities?

CONSEQUENCES

- The growth of towns, monarchies, and the Church increased the degree of control that those in power could exercise; but they also increased access to education and new forms of social mobility. Is this a paradox, or are these two phenomena related?
- The U.S. Constitution is based on the legal principles and institutions that emerged in medieval England, but it also drew on Roman models. Which do you consider to be more influential, and why?
- Some historians have argued that the extent and methods of persecution discernible in this era are unprecedented in the history of Western civilizations. How would you support or refute this thesis? For example, does the persecution of Jews in medieval Europe differ from their treatment under the neo-Assyrians and Chaldeans, or under the Roman Empire? Why or why not?

STORY LINES

- The Black Death altered the landscape, economy, and societies of Europe in profound ways.

- Meanwhile, the competing territorial claims of Europe's sovereign powers led to warfare on a large scale, as well as to the emergence of national monarchies that could draw on the loyalty and support of their populations.

- The failure of the papacy to make internal reforms led to the decline of papal power and credibility; at the same time, popular piety flourished, and a number of popular religious movements sought more radical reforms of the Church.

- The new opportunities and challenges of this era are dynamically reflected in its artistic, intellectual, and scientific achievements.

CHRONOLOGY

1240	Mongol Khanate established at Kiev
1309	"Babylonian Captivity" of the papacy in Avignon begins
1315–1322	The Great Famine ravages Europe
c. 1330–1384	Lifetime of John Wyclif
1337	Edward III of England claims the French throne
1347–1350	Spread of the Black Death
1377	The papacy restored to Rome
1378	The Great Schism begins
1414–1418	Council of Constance is convened; Jan Hus burned at the stake
1429–1431	Career of Joan of Arc
1431–1449	Council of Basel fails to curtail papal power
1453	The Hundred Years' War ends; fall of Constantinople
1454–1455	Gutenberg's Bible printed at Mainz
1462–1505	Reign of Ivan the Great in Muscovy
1492	Christian armies of Spain conquer Granada; expulsion of Jews

Before You Read This Chapter

Crisis, Unrest, and Opportunity, 1300–1500

CORE OBJECTIVES

- **EXPLAIN** the economic and social effects of the Black Death.

- **DEFINE** the concept of national monarchy and summarize its implications.

- **IDENTIFY** the factors leading to the rise of Muscovy.

- **UNDERSTAND** the significance of the conciliar movement and its defeat by the papacy.

- **DESCRIBE** the spiritual, cultural, and technological innovations of the later Middle Ages.

n June of 1381, thousands of laborers from the English countryside rose up in rebellion. Most were peasants or village craftsmen, yet the revolt was carefully coordinated. Plans were spread in coded messages circulated by word of mouth and by the followers of a renegade Oxford professor, John Wyclif, who had called for the redistribution of Church property. The rebellion's immediate cause had been a series of exorbitant taxes levied by Parliament for the support of an ongoing war with France, but its more fundamental cause was an epidemic that had occurred thirty years earlier. The Black Death had reduced the entire population of Europe by 30 to 50 percent and had drastically altered the world of the survivors. In this new world, workers were valuable and could rebel against those who paid them poorly or treated them like slaves. In that fateful summer of 1381, the laborers of England even vowed to kill all the representatives of both the Church and the government—as they put it, all the lawyers—and to destroy all the documents that had been used to keep them down. It was a revolution, and it partly succeeded. Although the leaders were eventually captured and executed, the rebellion had made the strength of the common people known to all.

The fourteenth and fifteenth centuries are often seen as a time of crisis. And certainly, this was an age of adversity in both Asia and Europe. Famine and plague cut fearful swaths through the population; war was a brutally recurrent fact of life; and the papacy spent seventy years in continuous exile from Italy, only to see its prestige decline further after its return to Rome. But this period was also a time of opportunity. The exhausted land of Europe recovered from centuries of overfarming while workers gained economic, social, and political power. Popular and intellectual movements sought to reform the Church; and a host of artistic and scientific innovations contributed to all of these phenomena. It was a period of intense creativity that would redefine European civilization.

THE BLACK DEATH AND ITS CONSEQUENCES

By 1300, the European economy was reaching its limits. The population had tripled since 1000, and a sea of grain fields stretched, almost unbroken, from Ireland to Ukraine. Forests were cleared, marshes drained, and still Europe was barely able to feed itself. At the same time, the warming trend that had begun in the late eighth century (Chapter 8) reversed itself. For even a reduction of one or two degrees centigrade is enough to cause substantial changes in rainfall patterns, shorten growing seasons, and so lessen productivity.

The new vulnerability of the European ecosystem was dramatically revealed in the great famine that lasted from 1315 to 1322. In these years, adverse weather conditions were nearly continuous, and the result was starvation on a very large scale. Approximately 10 to 15 percent of the population north of the Alps perished. In the decades following, cold winters and floods threatened southern Europe, and in 1343 a tsunami destroyed ports in southern Italy. Earthquakes and comets seemed like further terrifying portents of disaster.

Tracking the Black Death

The Black Death is the name given to a pandemic that spread from China to Mongolia, northern India, and the Middle East during the 1330s and 1340s. By 1346, the disease had reached the Black Sea. From there, in 1347, Genoese ships inadvertently brought it to Sicily and northern Italy. From Italy it spread westward along trade routes, moving with astonishing rapidity. By 1350 it had reached Scandinavia and northern Russia, then spread southward

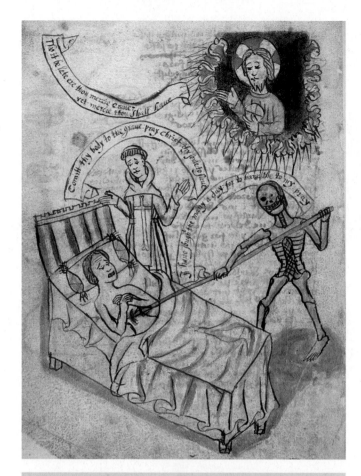

THE PLAGUE CLAIMS A VICTIM. A priest gives last rites to a bedridden plague victim, as a smiling devil pierces him with a spear and Christ looks mercifully down from Heaven. ▪ *What are the possible meanings of this image?* ▪ *What does it reveal about contemporary attitudes toward death?*

again. It continued to erupt in some localities for the next 300 years. The last Europe-wide instance occurred between 1661 and 1669.

The scale of mortality is almost unimaginable: at least a third, and probably half, of Europe's people died between 1347 and 1350. By the following century, the combined effects of plague, famine, and warfare had reduced the total population further, perhaps by as much as two thirds. In Germany, more than 40,000 villages disappeared. Around Paris, more than half the farmland cultivated in 1348 had become pasture by 1450. Elsewhere, abandoned fields reverted to woodland, increasing the forested areas of Europe by as much as one third.

Immediate reactions ran the gamut from panic to resignation. Observers quickly realized that the plague was contagious, but precisely how it spread remained a mystery. Some urged people to flee from stricken areas, which caused the disease to spread even faster. Others looked for scapegoats, and revived old conspiracy theories that implicated Jews in the poisoning of wells. Scores of Jewish communities were attacked and thousands of their inhabitants massacred in the Rhineland, southern France, and Christian Spain. (No such attacks are known to have occurred in the Muslim world.) Another response was the Flagellant movement, so called because of the whips (*flagella* in Latin) with which traveling bands of penitents lashed themselves in order to appease the wrath of God. But the unruly, hysterical mobs that gathered around the flagellants aroused concern, and the movement was suppressed by papal order.

What caused the Black Death? In 2010, scientists confirmed that it was the deadly microbe *Yersinia pestis*, which causes bubonic plague and its even deadlier cousins, pneumonic and septicemic plague. In its bubonic form, humans catch it only if they are bitten by an infected flea or rat. Bubonic

THE PROGRESS OF THE BLACK DEATH, FOURTEENTH CENTURY. ▪ *What trajectories did the Black Death follow once it was introduced into Europe?* ▪ *How might the growth of towns, trade, and travel have contributed to its spread?* ▪ *Would such a rapid advance have been likely during the early Middle Ages or even in the ancient world?*

Responses to the Black Death

> *Many chroniclers, intellectuals, and private individuals have left accounts of the plague and its effects, and many attempted to understand why it had occurred, how it spread, and how communities should respond to it.*

The Spread of the Plague According to Gabriele D'Mussis (d. 1356), a Lawyer in Piacenza (Northern Italy)

Oh God! See how the heathen Tartar races, pouring together from all sides, suddenly invested the city of Caffa [near Constantinople] and besieged the trapped Christians there for almost three years.... But behold, [in 1346] the whole army was affected by a disease which overran the Tartars and killed thousands upon thousands every day. It was as though arrows were raining down from heaven to strike and crush the Tartars' arrogance. All medical advice and attention was useless; the Tartars died as soon as the signs of disease appeared on their bodies: swellings in the armpit or groin caused by coagulating humours, followed by a putrid fever.

The dying Tartars, stunned and stupefied by the immensity of the disaster brought about by the disease, and realising that they had no hope of escape, lost interest in the siege. But they ordered corpses to be placed in catapults and lobbed into the city in the hope that the intolerable stench would kill everyone inside. What seemed like mountains of dead were thrown into the city, and the Christians could not hide or flee or escape from them, although they dumped as many of the bodies as they could in the sea. And soon the rotting corpses tainted the air and poisoned the water supply.... Moreover one infected man could carry the poison to others, and infect people and places with the disease by look alone. No one knew, or could discover, a means of defence.

Thus almost everyone who had been in the East ... fell victim ... through the bitter events of 1346 to 1348—the Chinese, Indians, Persians, Medes, Kurds, Armenians, Cilicians, Georgians, Mesopotamians, Nubians, Ethiopians, Turks, Egyptians, Arabs, Saracens and Greeks....

* * *

As it happened, among those who escaped from Caffa by boat were a few sailors who had been infected with the poisonous disease. Some boats were bound for Genoa, others went to Venice and to other Christian areas. When the sailors reached these places and mixed with the people there, it was as if they had brought evil spirits with them....

* * *

Scarcely one in seven of the Genoese survived. In Venice, where an inquiry was held into the mortality, it was found that more than 70 percent of the people had died.... The rest of Italy, Sicily, and Apulia and the neighbouring regions maintain that they have been virtually emptied of inhabitants.... The Roman Curia at Avignon, the provinces on both sides of the Rhône, Spain, France, and the Empire cry up their griefs....

* * *

Everyone has a responsibility to keep some record of the disease and the

plague attacks the lymphatic system, producing enormous swellings (buboes) of the lymph nodes in the groin, neck, and armpits. Pneumonic plague results when *Y. pestis* infects the lungs, allowing the contagion to spread in the same ways as the common cold. Septicemic plague occurs when an infected flea introduces the microbe directly into the human bloodstream, causing death within hours, often before any symptoms of the disease appear. One of the things that made the Black Death so frightening, therefore, is that it manifested itself in unpredictable ways. Those afflicted by the hideous bubonic plague might actually recover, while others—seemingly untouched—might die suddenly.

deaths, and because I am myself from Piacenza I have been urged to write more about what happened there in 1348....

I don't know where to begin. Cries and laments arise on all sides. Day after day one sees the Cross and the Host being carried about the city, and countless dead being buried.... The living made preparations for their [own] burial, and because there was not enough room for individual graves, pits had to be dug in colonnades and piazzas, where nobody had ever been buried before. It often happened that man and wife, father and son, mother and daughter, and soon the whole household and many neighbours, were buried together in one place....

A Letter from the Town Council of Cologne to the Town Council of Strasbourg (Germany), 12 January 1349

Very dear friends, all sorts of rumours are now flying about against Judaism and the Jews prompted by this unexpected and unparalleled mortality of Christians.... Throughout our city, as in yours, many-winged Fame clamours that this mortality was initially caused, and is still being spread, by the poisoning of springs and wells, and that the Jews must have dropped poisonous substances into them. When it came to our knowledge that serious charges had been made against the Jews in several small towns and villages on the basis of this mortality, we sent numerous letters to you and to other cities and towns to uncover the truth behind these rumours, and set a thorough investigation in train....

If a massacre of the Jews were to be allowed in the major cities (something which we are determined to prevent in our city, if we can, as long as the Jews are found to be innocent of these or similar actions) it could lead to the sort of outrages and disturbances which would whip up a popular revolt among the common people—and such revolts have in the past brought cities to misery and desolation. In any case we are still of the opinion that this mortality and its attendant circumstances are caused by divine vengeance and nothing else. Accordingly we intend to forbid any harassment of the Jews in our city because of these flying rumours, but to defend them faithfully and keep them safe, as our predecessors did—and we are convinced that you ought to do the same....

Source: From Rosemary Horrox, ed. and trans. *The Black Death* (Manchester: 1994), pp. 16–21, 219–20.

Questions for Analysis

1. How does Gabriele d'Mussis initially explain the causes of the plague? How and why does his understanding of it change as he traces its movements from East to West?

2. Why does the Council of Cologne wish to quell violence against the Jews? How does this reasoning complement or challenge what we have learned so far about the treatment of Jews in medieval Europe?

3. In your view, do these two perspectives display a rational approach to the horrors of the Black Death? Why or why not?

The Impact on the Countryside

In the decades following the plague, a new demographic reality permanently altered established social and economic patterns. First and foremost, the drastic decrease in population meant a relative abundance of food. The price of grain fell, which made it more affordable. At the same time, the scarcity of workers made peasant labor valuable: wages rose and work became easily obtainable. With wages high and food prices low, ordinary people could now afford more bread, and could also spend their surplus cash on dairy products, meat, fish, fruits, and wine. As a result, the people of Europe in the later Middle Ages were better nourished than they have ever been—better than many are today. A recent study of fifteenth-century rubbish dumps has concluded that the people of Glasgow (Scotland) ate a healthier diet in 1405 than they did in 2005.

A healthier ecological balance was also reestablished. Forests began to recover and expand. The declining demand for grain allowed many farmers to expand their livestock herds, increasing their profits while improving the fertility of the soil through manuring. Some farmers were even able to enlarge their holdings because so much land had been abandoned.

Most of these innovations were made by small farmers, because great lords—individuals, as well as monasteries—were slower to adjust to the changing circumstances. Some landholders responded to the shortage of workers by forcing their tenants to perform additional unpaid labor. In eastern Europe, many free peasants became serfs for the first time. In Castile, Poland, and Germany, too, lords succeeded in imposing new forms of servitude. In other parts of Iberia and in Italy, actual slavery—which had nearly been eradicated during the economic boom of the twelfth and thirteenth centuries—became common for the first time in centuries.

In France, peasants remained relatively free, although many were forced to pay a variety of fees and taxes to their lords and to the king. In England, by contrast, where peasant bondage had been more common than in France, serfdom ultimately disappeared altogether. In the new world of geographical mobility and economic opportunity, English serfs were able to vote with their feet, either by moving to town or to the lands of a lord who offered more favorable terms: lower rents, fewer work requirements, and greater personal freedoms.

The Urban Impact

Many towns, overcrowded and unsanitary, were particularly vulnerable to plague. Thereafter, they were vulnerable to the effects of violence. In Florence, the population rebounded quickly after the Black Death only to be depleted again by civil unrest: by 1427, it had dropped from around 300,000 to about 100,000. In Toulouse (southern France), the population remained fairly stable until 1430, when it was reduced 75 percent by the Hundred Years' War (see below). In London and Paris, however, large-scale immigration from the countryside reversed the short-term effects of the plague. For although the overall population declined, a far larger percentage of all people were living in towns by 1500: approximately 20 percent, as opposed to 10 or 15 percent prior to the Black Death.

Fueling this urban growth was the increasing specialization of the late-medieval economy. With farmers under less pressure to produce grain in bulk, land could be devoted to livestock, dairy farming, and the production of a more diverse array of fruits and vegetables; and these could now be exchanged efficiently on the open market. Towns with links to extant trading networks benefited accordingly. In northern Germany, a group of cities even formed a coalition to build a new network, the Hanseatic League, whose members controlled commerce from Britain and Scandinavia to the Baltic. In northern Italy, the increased demand for luxury goods—which even some peasants and urban laborers could now afford—brought new wealth to the spice- and silk-trading city of Venice and to the fine-cloth manufacturers of Milan and the jewelers of Florence. Milan's armaments industry also prospered, supplying its warring neighbors and the armies of Europe.

The economic boom also stimulated the development of business practices and accounting techniques. The development of insurance contracts helped to minimize the risks associated with long-distance trading. Double-entry book-keeping, widely used in Italy by the mid-fourteenth century, gave merchants a much clearer picture of their profits and losses than had been possible before. The Medici family of Florence established branches of their bank in each of the major cities of Europe and were careful that the failure of one would no longer bankrupt the entire firm, as previous branch-banking arrangements had done. Banks also experimented with advanced credit techniques borrowed from Muslim and Jewish financiers, allowing their clients to transfer funds between branches without any real money changing hands. Such transfers were carried out by written orders, the ancestors of the modern check.

SOCIAL MOBILITY AND SOCIAL INEQUALITY

The Black Death was ultimately beneficial for many of those who survived it. But European society did not adjust easily to the new world created by the plague. It seemed to many like a world turned upside down.

Revolts and Rebellions

Hundreds of popular rebellions challenged the status quo in many regions of Europe. In 1358, for example, peasants in northeastern France rose up violently against their lords, destroying property and even murdering targeted individuals.

This incident is known as the Jacquerie Rebellion because all French peasants were caricatured by the aristocracy as "Jacques" ("Jack"). In England, as we have already noted, a very different uprising occurred in June of 1381, much more organized and involving a much wider segment of society. Thousands of people marched on London, targeting the bureaucracies of the royal government and the Church, capturing and killing the archbishop of Canterbury, and meeting personally with the fourteen-year-old king, Richard II, to demand an end to serfdom and taxation and the redistribution of property. In Florence, workers in the cloth industry—known as the Ciompi (*chee-OM-pee*)—protested high unemployment and mistreatment by the manufacturers who also ran the Florentine government. They seized control of the city, demanding relief from taxes, full employment, and political representation. They maintained power for a remarkable six weeks before their reforms were revoked.

The local circumstances that lay behind each of these revolts are unique, but they exhibit certain common features. Those who took part in them had actually been empowered by the new economic conditions and wanted to leverage their position in order to enact even larger changes. Some rebellions, like the English Peasants' Revolt, were touched off by resistance to new and higher taxes. Others, like the Jacquerie and the revolt of the Ciompi, took place at moments when unpopular governments were weakened by factionalism. The English revolt was also fueled by widespread corruption within the Church and the royal administration.

Behind this social and political unrest, therefore, lies not poverty and hunger but the growing prosperity and self-confidence of village communities and urban workers. Although the rebels' hopes that they could fundamentally alter the conditions of their lives were frustrated, this tradition of popular rebellion would remain an important feature of Western civilizations.

Aristocratic Life in the Later Middle Ages

Despite these upheavals, the later Middle Ages was hardly a period of crisis for those in power. Quite the contrary: the great noble families of Europe were far wealthier than their ancestors had been. Nor did the plague undermine the dominant position they had established in European society. It did, however, make their world substantially more complex and uncertain.

Across Europe, most noble families continued to derive much of their revenue from vast landholdings. But many lords also tried to increase their sources of income through investment in trading ventures. In Catalonia, Italy, Germany, and England, this became common practice. In France and Castile, however, direct involvement in commerce was regarded as socially demeaning and was, therefore, avoided. Commerce could still be a route to ennoblement in these kingdoms, but once aristocratic rank was achieved one was expected to abandon these employments and adopt an appropriate way of life: maintaining a rural castle or urban palace surrounded by a lavish household, embracing the conventions of chivalry, and serving the prince at court and in war.

Nobility became, as a result, even more difficult to define than it had been during the twelfth and thirteenth centuries. In countries where nobility entailed clearly defined legal privileges—such as the right to be tried only in special courts—proven descent from noble ancestors might be required. But in most cases, nobility was expressed through display and conspicuous consumption, which meant that the lines of social distinction between noble and nonnoble families remained fuzzy. On the battlefield, too, the supremacy of the mounted knight was being threatened by the growing importance of professional soldiers, archers, and artillery experts. There were even radical critiques of

A NOBLE BANQUET. Uncle of the mad king Charles VI, the duke of Berry received enormous subsidies from the royal government, which he spent on sumptuous buildings, festivals, and artworks—including the famous Book of Hours (prayer book) that includes this image. Here, the duke (seated at right, in blue) gives a New Year's Day banquet for his household, who exchange gifts while his hunting dogs dine on scraps from the table. In the background, knights confront one another in a battle or a tournament.

aristocratic claims to innate superiority. As the English rebels put it in 1381: "When Adam dug and Eve spun, Who then was a gentleman?" In other words, all human beings are equal and social distinctions are entirely artificial.

Precisely because nobility was contested, those who claimed the status took elaborate measures to assert its exclusivity. This accounts, in part, for the extraordinary number, variety, and richness of the artifacts and artworks that survive from this period. Aristocrats vied with one another in hosting lavish banquets. They dressed in rich and extravagant clothing. They maintained enormous households: around 1400, the French duke of Berry had 400 matched pairs of hunting dogs and 1,000 servants. They took part in elaborately ritualized tournaments and pageants, in which the participants pretended to be the heroes of chivalric romances. Nobility existed only if it was recognized; and to be recognized, noble status had to be constantly reasserted.

Rulers contributed to this process of noble self-assertion; indeed, they were among its principal supporters. Kings and princes across Europe competed in founding chivalric orders such as the Knights of the Garter in England and the Order of the Star in France. By exalting the nobility as a class, these orders helped cement the links that bound the aristocracy to their kings and princes. So too did the gifts, pensions, offices, and marriage prospects that kings and princes could bestow. Indeed, the alliance that was forged in the fifteenth century between kings and their noble supporters would become one of the most characteristic features of "old regime" (*ancien régime*) Europe. In France, this alliance lasted until the French Revolution of 1789. In Germany, Austria, and Russia, it would last until the outbreak of World War I. In England, it persisted in some respects until World War II.

WARFARE AND NATION-BUILDING

The partnership between royalty and nobility was partly a response to the new world created by the plague. But it was also a product of the unprecedented scale of warfare. Beginning in the fourteenth century and continuing into the twentieth, Europeans were almost constantly at war. To fight these wars, governments claimed new powers to tax their subjects and to control their subjects' lives. Armies became larger, military technology deadlier. Wars became more destructive, society more militarized. As a result of these developments, the most successful European states— the monarchies of Portugal, Spain, and France—were aggressively expansionist. By 1600, their impact would be global (see Chapter 11).

England, France, and the Hundred Years' War

The Hundred Years' War was the largest, longest, and most wide-ranging military conflict in the West since Rome's wars with Carthage in the third and second centuries B.C.E. (Chapter 5). England and France were its principal antagonists, but almost all of Europe became involved at some stage. Active hostilities lasted from 1337 until 1453, interrrupted by truces of varying lengths. The roots of the conflict, however, reached back into the 1290s, when King Edward I of England attempted to conquer the neighboring kingdom of Scotland, thereby provoking the Scots to ally with France. And the threat of war continued until 1558, when Calais, the last English toehold on the Continent, finally passed into French hands.

The most fundamental cause of the war was the fact that the kings of England held the duchy of Gascony as vassals of the French king; this was part of Eleanor of Aquitaine's former domain (Chapter 9). In the twelfth and thirteenth centuries, when the French kings had not yet absorbed this region, this fact had seemed less of an anomaly. But as monarchies began to claim sovereignty within the "natural" boundaries of their domains, the English presence in "French" Gascony became more and more problematic. That England also had close commercial links with Flanders—which consistently resisted French expansion— added fuel to the fire. So did the French alliance with the Scots, who had been resolutely resisting English expansion.

Complicating this situation was the disputed succession of the French crown. In 1328, the last of King Philip IV's three sons died without leaving a son to succeed him: the Capetian dynasty, founded by the Frankish warlord Hugh Capet in 987 (Chapter 8), had finally exhausted itself. A new dynasty, the Valois, came to the throne—but only by insisting that women could neither inherit royal power nor pass it on. For otherwise, the heir to France was Edward III of England, whose mother, Isabella, was Philip IV's only daughter. In 1337, therefore, when the disputes over Gascony and Scotland erupted into war, Edward raised the stakes by claiming to be the rightful king of France.

The hostilities that make up the Hundred Years' War can be divided into three main phases (see the map on page 245). In the first phase, from 1337 until 1360, the English won a series of startling military victories, most famously at Crécy (1346), Calais (1347), and Poitiers (1356). Although France was richer and more populous than England by a factor of at least three to one, the English government was more effective in mobilizing the entire population, for reasons that were discussed in Chapter 9. Moreover, the huge but poorly led armies assembled by the French proved no match for the tactical superiority of these smaller English forces. English armies pillaged the French countryside at will, while civil wars broke out among individual French lords. Meanwhile, mercenary bands of soldiers roamed the countryside, attacking and looting peasant villages still struggling to recover from the Black Death. In 1358, popular frustration boiled over in the rebellion of the Jacquerie (discussed above).

This first phase ended in 1360, when Edward III agreed to renounce his claim to the French throne in return for full sovereignty over a greatly enlarged duchy of Gascony and the promise of a huge ransom for the king of France, whom he held captive. But the terms of the treaty were never honored. Instead, a proxy war developed in which English and French troops, organized into "Free Companies," hired themselves out in the service of warring factions in Castile and northern Italy. By 1376, when hostilities resumed between England and France, the Hundred Years' War had become a Europe-wide phenomenon.

In this second phase of the war, from 1376 to 1429, the tide quickly shifted in favor of France. The new king of France, Charles V (r. 1364–80), imposed a series of national taxes, disbanded the Free Companies, and hired the leader of one as the commander of his army. He thereby created a professional military that could match the English in discipline and tactics. His counterpart, the new king of England, Richard II (r. 1377–99), had no interest in the French war begun by his grandfather. During his minority its conduct was mismanaged by his advisors—one of the issues that had triggered the Peasants' Revolt in 1381. Yet the nobility stood to gain from the war's continuation, and Richard's failure to press his claims turned the barons against him. In 1399, Richard was deposed and eventually murdered. His cousin, Henry of Lancaster, seized the throne.

As a usurper, Henry IV (r. 1399–1413) struggled to maintain his authority in the face of repeated rebellions and was in no position to pursue the French war. When his son Henry V succeeded him in 1413, however, the new king immediately began to prepare for a renewed offensive.

THE PROGRESS OF THE HUNDRED YEARS' WAR. Here we see the changing political geography of France during the Hundred Years' War. ▪ *What areas did England control at the outbreak of war in 1337?* ▪ *How and why were the gains of 1360 (in green) reduced by 1429 (the areas in yellow)?* ▪ *What geographic and strategic advantages did the French monarchy enjoy after 1429 that might help explain its success in recapturing the French kingdom from the English?*

A brilliant diplomat, Henry sealed alliances with both the emperor in Germany and the powerful duke of Burgundy, who was in control of the French royal government. So when he invaded France in 1415, he faced only a partial army representing the anti-Burgundian faction within the royal court. Then, at Agincourt, Henry managed to win a crushing victory over a vastly larger but badly disciplined French force. By 1420, he had conquered most of northern France and had forced the aged and infirm King Charles VI (r. 1380–1422) to give him his daughter in marriage and to recognize him as heir to the throne of France—thus dispossessing the heir apparent, known as the Dauphin ("the dolphin"), the future King Charles VII.

JOAN OF ARC. A contemporary sketch of Joan was drawn in the margin of this register documenting official proceedings at the Parlement of Paris in 1429. Note that she carries a banner bearing Constantine's symbolic IHS (Chapter 6).

Henry V's astonishing success seemed to put the stamp of divine approval on his claim to be the rightful king of France. But Henry's successes also transformed the nature of the war, turning it from a profitable war of conquest into an extended and expensive military occupation. It thereby sowed the seeds of eventual English defeat.

Henry died early in 1422, at the age of 34. Charles VI of France died only a few months later. The new king of England and France, Henry VI (r. 1422–61), was an infant. Meanwhile, the Dauphin's confidence in his right to the throne had been shattered by his own mother's declaration that he was illegitimate. Then, in 1429, a peasant girl from Lorraine (a territory only nominally part of France) made her way to the Dauphin's court and announced that an angel had told her that he, Charles, was the rightful king, and that she, Joan, should drive the English out of France.

The fact that she even got a hearing underscores the hopelessness of the Dauphin's position, as does the extraordinary fact that he gave her a contingent of troops. With this force, Joan liberated the strategic city of Orléans, then under siege, after which a series of victories culminated in

Charles's coronation in the cathedral of Reims, the traditional site for the crowning of French kings. But despite her victories, Joan was an embarrassment whose very charisma made her dangerous: a peasant leading aristocrats, a woman leading men, and a commoner who claimed to have been commissioned by God. When, a few months later, the Burgundians captured her in battle and handed her over to the English, King Charles VII did nothing to save her. Condemned by the theologians of Paris and tried for heresy by an English ecclesiastical court, Joan was burned to death in the market square at Rouen in 1431. She was nineteen years old.

In the war's final phase, from 1429 to 1435, the French forces whom Joan had inspired continued on the offensive. In 1435, the Duke of Burgundy withdrew from his alliance with England, and a series of French military victories brought hostilities to an end with the capture of Bordeaux. English kings would threaten to renew the war for another century, but English control over French territory would be limited to the port of Calais until it, too, fell in 1558.

The Hundred Years' War had challenged the very existence of France, but its outcome had dramatic effects on the English monarchy as well. In France, the nobility had endured the insanity of Charles VI because his government was not powerful enough to threaten them. In England, royal power was so centralized that neither the nobility nor the nation could afford the incompetent kingship of Henry VI. The result was an aristocratic rebellion that led to a full-blown civil war: the Wars of the Roses, so called—by the novelist Sir Walter Scott (1771–1832)—from the emblems of the two competing noble families, Lancaster (red) and York (white), who were both descended from Edward III. It ended only when a Lancastrian claimant, Henry Tudor (r. 1485–1509), resolved the dynastic feud by marrying Elizabeth of York, ruling as Henry VII and establishing a new dynasty whose symbol was a rose with both white and red petals. His son would be Henry VIII (see Chapter 13).

Conflict in the Holy Roman Empire and Italy

The endemic warfare that begins to characterize the history of Europe in the later Middle Ages was usually even more destructive than it proved to be in the struggle between England and France. In the lands of the Holy Roman Empire, armed conflict among territorial princes weakened all the combatants significantly. The dominant trend was toward the continuing dissolution of power, with German princes dividing territories among their heirs while free cities and local lords strove to shake off the princes' rule.

In northern and central Italy, the last half of the fourteenth century was also marked by incessant conflict. With the papacy based in Avignon from 1309 until 1377, the Papal States collapsed and Rome itself was riven by factional violence. Warfare among northern city-states added to the chaos caused by urban rebellions. By around 1400, however, Venice, Milan, and Florence had succeeded in stabilizing their differing forms of government. Venice was now ruled by an oligarchy of merchants; Milan by a family of despots; and Florence was a nominal republic dominated by the influence of the Medici banking family. These three cities then began to expand their territories, subordinating other cities to their rule. By 1454, almost all the towns of northern Italy were allied with one of these powers. An exception was the port of Genoa, which remained an independent shipping and trading hub.

The Emergence of a United Spain

The kingdoms of the Iberian peninsula were also in constant conflict during the fourteenth and fifteenth centuries. In Castile, civil war allowed the Castilian nobility to gain independence from the crown. After 1458, Aragon was also enmeshed in a civil war over a disputed succession, a war in which both France and Castile became involved.

The solution would ultimately lie in the blending of powerful families. In 1469, Prince Ferdinand of Aragon was recognized as the undisputed heir to that throne and, in the same year, married Isabella, the heiress of Castile. Although Castile and Aragon continued to be ruled as separate kingdoms until 1714, the union of Ferdinand and Isabella enabled them to spend their extraordinary resources on the creation of Europe's most powerful army, which was initially employed to conquer Granada, the last remaining Muslim principality in Spain.

The conquest of Granada in 1492 was a turning point. Both Castile and Aragon had been shaped for centuries by their involvement in the "reconquest" of Spain, and the victory earned Ferdinand and Isabella the title of Europe's "Most Catholic" monarchs. It also meant that the crusading ethos now sought outlets elsewhere. Only a few months after the conquest of Granada, Queen Isabella granted three ships to a Genoese adventurer who promised to reach India by sailing westward across the Atlantic. He failed, of course, but he extended the crusading tradition to the New World, with enduring consequences (see Chapter 11).

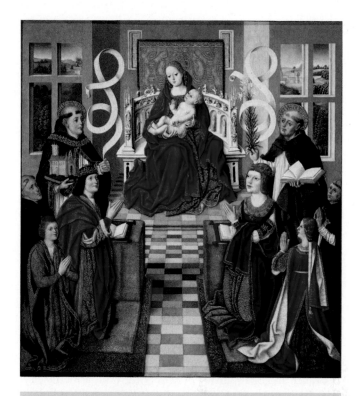

FERDINAND AND ISABELLA HONORING THE VIRGIN. In this contemporary Spanish painting, the royal couple are shown with two of their children and two household chaplains—and in the company of the Blessed Virgin, the Christ Child, and saints from the Dominican order (the Dominicans were instrumental in conducting the affairs of the Spanish Inquisition). ▪ *How clear is the distinction between these holy figures and the royal family?* ▪ *What message is conveyed by their proximity?*

The year 1492 also saw the expulsion of the entire Jewish community from Spain, the culmination of a process that had accelerated in the late thirteenth century (Chapter 9). The Spanish expulsion stands out, however, because of its vast scope and because of the rich cultural legacy fostered by the Jews of this region over a thousand years. The motives for ordering this expulsion are still debated. Tens of thousands of Spanish Jews had converted to Christianity between 1391 and 1420, many as a result of coercion, but for a generation or so it seemed possible that these *conversos* might successfully assimilate. Yet the conflicts that led to the union of Ferdinand and Isabella made the *conversos* targets of discriminatory legislation and fueled popular suspicions that they remained Jews in secret. The "Most Catholic" monarchs may have concluded that they needed to remove the "bad influence" posed by the continuing presence of a Jewish community in Spain. The expulsion of Jews thus enabled the creation of a new and explicitly Christian identity for the hybrid Spanish nation, transcending the many rival regional identities there and attaching that new identity to the crown.

The Growth of National Monarchies

The later Middle Ages saw the emergence of European states more powerful and cohesive than any before. The formative twelfth and thirteenth centuries had made this possible, yet the active construction of a sense of national identity in these territories, and the fusion of that identity with kingship, were new phenomena. Forged by war and fueled by the growing cultural importance of vernacular languages, this fusion produced a new type of political organization: the national monarchy.

The advantages of these national monarchies is most clearly visible when viewed from the perspective of Italy. Until the end of the fifteenth century, the Italian city-states had appeared to be well governed and powerful, and Venice even had a maritime empire of its own. But when the armies of France and Spain invaded, neither the militias of the city-states nor the far-flung resources of Venice were a match for them. Germany and the Low Countries would suffer the same fate only a few generations later, and would remain battlegrounds for competing armies until the mid nineteenth century. But the new national monarchies brought significant disadvantages, too. They guaranteed the continued prevalence of warfare in Europe, and they eventually transported their rivalries to every corner of the globe.

THE RISE OF MUSCOVY, "THE THIRD ROME"

This era also witnessed the consolidation of a state that would become the dominant power in eastern Europe and one of the great powers of the world. Yet Russia developed very differently from the national monarchies of western Europe. It was, instead, the largest multiethnic empire in the pre-modern world. And by 1500, it claimed to be the rightful successor to the Rome of the Caesars, as well as to that of Constantine.

Kievan Rus' and the Mongol Khanate

As we saw in Chapter 8, the Viking people known as Rus' had played a key role in establishing a principality at Kiev (now in Ukraine), which maintained diplomatic and trad-ing relations with western Europe and Byzantium. That dynamic changed with the arrival of the Mongols (whose movements will be discussed more fully in Chapter 11). Commanded by a grandson of the great Chingiz (Genghis) Khan, the Mongols overran Kiev in 1240. Two years later, they created their own state on the lower Volga River, known as the Khanate of the Golden Horde.

Initially, the Mongols ruled their Russian territories directly, even requiring Russian princes to subject themselves to the Great Khan himself, by traveling to Mongolia. Around 1300, however, the Mongols began to tolerate the existence of semi-independent principalities from which they demanded regular tribute. Kiev never recovered its dominant position, but one of the newer principalities would enable the construction of a Russian state: Muscovy, the duchy centered on Moscow.

The Rise of Muscovy and the Expansion of Poland

Moscow was the tribute-collecting center for the Mongol Khanate. Mongol support helped Moscow's dukes to absorb neighboring territories, and because Moscow was far from the Mongol base on the lower Volga, its dukes could further consolidate their strength without attracting too much attention. The location was also advantageous for forging commercial contacts with the Baltic and Black Sea regions. Yet Moscow's ties with western Europe remained undeveloped because it was loyal to the Orthodox Church of Byzantium. And Moscow's sensitivity to threats from European Christianity was further escalated by the growing strength of a Catholic kingdom on its borders.

In the thirteenth century, the small kingdom of Poland had struggled to defend itself from absorption into the Holy Roman Empire. But when the empire's strength waned after the death of Frederick II (Chapter 9), Poland's situation grew more secure. In 1386, its reigning queen, Jadwiga, married Jagiello, the duke of neighboring Lithuania, thus doubling the size of her kingdom. Lithuania had already begun to carve out an extensive territory stretching from the Baltic to modern-day Belarus and Ukraine, and this expansionist momentum increased after its union with Poland. Although many of Lithuania's aristocratic families were Orthodox Christians, the established church in Lithuania was loyal to Rome, as it was in Poland. Thus when the inhabitants of the region around Moscow began to feel threatened by Poland-Lithuania, one way of constructing a shared Muscovite identity was to direct shared hostility toward Latin Christendom.

The Russian Church and the Third Rome

As Byzantium grew weaker, the responsibility for defending Orthodox Christianity devolved onto the Russian Church. Muscovites saw themselves as the natural champions of Constantinople, which was now surrounded by the Muslim empire of the Ottoman Turks (to be discussed further in Chapter 11). But when the patriarch of Constantinople agreed to submit to the authority of Rome in 1438, in the desperate hope that the papacy would rally military support for the besieged city, Russian clergy refused to follow suit. After Constantinople fell to the Turks in 1453—predictably, without any help from Latin Christendom—the Russian Church therefore emerged as the only surviving proponent of Orthodox Christianity and the heir apparent to imperial Rome. To drive the point home, the Muscovite duke began to take the title *tsar*, "caesar." "Two Romes have fallen," said a Muscovite chonicler, "the third is still standing, and a fourth there shall not be."

THE EXPANSION OF MUSCOVITE RUSSIA TO 1505. The grand duchy of Moscow was the heart of what would soon become the Russian Empire. ▪ *With what other empires and polities did the Muscovites have to compete during this period of expansion?* ▪ *How did the relative isolation of Moscow, compared with early Kiev, allow for the growth of Muscovite power on the one hand and Moscow's distinctive orientation on the other?* ▪ *How might the natural direction of the expansion of Muscovite power until 1505 help to encourage attitudes often at odds with those of western European civilization?*

The Reign of Ivan the Great (1462–1505)

Along with the imperial title, the Muscovite rulers borrowed the Byzantine ideology of the ruler's divine election, and this undergirded the sacred position later ascribed to the tsars. But ideology alone could not have built the Russian Empire. Behind its growth lay the steadily increasing power of Moscow's rulers, who achieved effective independence from the Mongols when a rebellious Mongol warlord named Timur the Lame (Tamburlane) destroyed the Khanate of the Golden Horde at the end of the fourteenth century. This allowed the Muscovite grand duke, Ivan III, known as Ivan the Great, to carry forward his own imperial agenda.

Ivan launched a series of conquests that annexed all the independent principalities lying between Moscow and the border of Poland-Lithuania. After invading Lithuania in 1492 and 1501, Ivan even succeeded in bringing parts of that domain under his control. Meanwhile, he married the niece of the last Byzantine emperor and rebuilt his fortified residence, known as the Kremlin, in magnificent Italianate style. He would later adopt, as his imperial insignia, a double-headed eagle representing Rome and its legions. By the time of his death in 1505, the power of the tsar was more absolute than that of any European monarch.

THE TRIALS OF THE ROMAN CHURCH

The later Middle Ages changed the Roman Church in ways that would prove definitive. The papacy endured almost seventy years of exile from Rome, followed by a debilitating forty-year schism. It then faced a protracted battle with reformers who sought to reduce the pope's role in Church governance. Though the papacy won this battle in the short term, the renewed abuse of papal power would, in the long run, bring about the permanent schism caused by the Reformation of the sixteenth century (Chapter 13).

THE PAPAL PALACE AT AVIGNON. This great palace, begun in 1339, symbolizes the apparent permanence of the papal residence in Avignon.

The "Babylonian Captivity" of the Papacy

The subjugation of papal authority to the French crown (Chapter 9) is often called the "Babylonian Captivity" of the Church, recalling the Jews' exile in Babylon during the sixth century B.C.E. (Chapter 2). From 1309 until 1378, the papal court resided at Avignon, a small city in southern France. Avignon soon proved to have a number of advantages over Rome. It was closer to the major centers of power, it was far removed from the tumultuous politics of Rome, and it was safe from the aggressive attentions of the German emperor. And as the papal bureaucracy grew in size, it became more difficult to move. In time, Avignon began to feel like home; in fact it *was* home for all of the popes elected there, who were natives of the region, as were nearly all the cardinals they appointed. This helped to cement their loyalty to the French king.

The papacy never abandoned its claims to the overlordship of Rome and the Papal States, but making good on these claims from a distance took a great deal of money. The Avignon popes accordingly imposed new taxes on the dioceses of France, England, Germany, and Spain. Judicial cases also brought large revenues into the papal coffers. Most controversially, the Avignon popes claimed the right to appoint bishops and priests to vacant offices, bypassing the electoral rights of individual dioceses and collecting huge fees from successful appointees.

By these and other measures, the Avignon popes strengthened their administrative control over the Church but weakened their moral authority. Stories of the court's unseemly luxury circulated widely, especially during the reign of the notoriously corrupt Clement VI (r. 1342–52), whose rule coincided with the Black Death. But in the subsequent decades that were transforming European society in so many other ways, calls for the papacy's return to Rome grew more insistent. The most successful of these was the letter-writing campaign of the nun and mystic Catherine of Siena (1347–1380), whose teasing but pious missives to Gregory XI (r. 1370–78) ultimately persuaded him to make the move back to Rome.

The Great Schism and the Conciliar Movement

The papacy's restoration was short-lived. A year after Gregory's return to Rome, he died. His cardinals—many of them Frenchmen—struggled to interpret the wishes of the volatile Romans and would later claim to have capitulated to the mob when they elected an Italian candidate, Urban VI. When Urban fell out with them soon afterward, the cardinals fled the city and declared his selection invalid. They then elected a new pope, a Frenchman who took the name Clement VII. Urban retaliated by naming a new, entirely Italian, College of Cardinals. The French pope and his cardinals then withdrew ignominiously to Avignon, while the Italian pope remained in Rome. The resulting rift is known as the Great Western Schism. Between 1378 and 1417, the Church was divided between two (and, ultimately, three) competing papacies, each stridently denouncing the heresy of the others.

Not surprisingly, Europe's religious allegiances fractured along the political lines drawn by the ongoing Hundred Years' War: France and her allies Scotland, Castile, Aragon, and Naples recognized the pope in Avignon; while England, Germany, northern Italy, Scandinavia, Bohemia, Poland, and Hungary recognized the Roman pope. Nor was there any obvious way to end this embarrassing state of affairs. In 1409, some cardinals from both camps met at Pisa, where they ceremoniously declared the deposition of both popes and named a new one from among their number. But neither of the popes accepted that decision, so there were now three rival popes excommunicating each other.

This debacle was ultimately addressed between 1414 and 1418 at the Council of Constance, the largest and longest ecclesiastical gathering since the Council of Nicea, over a thousand years before (Chapter 6). Its chief mission was to remove all rival claimants for papal office before agreeing on the election of a new pope: an Italian who took the name

Martin V. But many of the council's delegates had more far-reaching plans for the reform of the Church, ambitions that stemmed from the legal doctrine that gave the council power to depose and elect popes in the first place. This doctrine, known as conciliarism, holds that supreme authority within the Church rests not with the pope, but with a representative general council—and not just the council convened at Constance, but any future council. The delegates at Constance thus decreed that general councils should meet regularly to oversee the governance of the Church and to act as a check on the unbridled use of papal power.

Had conciliarism triumphed, the Reformation of the following century might not have occurred. But, perhaps predictably, Martin V and his successors did everything they could to undermine this doctrine, precisely because it limited their power. When the next general council met at Siena in 1423, Pope Martin duly sent representatives—but they then turned around and immediately went back to Rome. (The Council of Constance had specified that councils must meet frequently, but had not specified how long those meetings should last.) The following year, the delegates to a general council at Basel took steps to ensure that the pope could not dismiss their authority, after which a lengthy struggle for power ensued. Twenty-five years later, in 1449, the Council of Basel dissolved itself, bringing to an end a radical experiment in conciliar government—and dashing the hopes of those who thought it would lead to an internal reformation thorough enough to keep the Roman Church intact.

The Growth of National Churches

The papacy's victory over the conciliarists was a costly one. To win the support of Europe's kings and princes, various popes negotiated a series of treaties which granted rulers extensive authority over churches within their domains. The popes thus secured their own theoretical supremacy by surrendering their real power. For kings now received

THE GREAT SCHISM, 1378–1417. During the Great Schism, the various territories of Europe were divided in their allegiances. ▪ *What common interests would have united the supporters of the Avignon pope, or the Roman pope?* ▪ *Why would areas like Portugal and Austria waver in their support?*

many of the revenues that had previously gone to the papacy. They also acquired new powers to appoint candidates to church offices. It was a reversal of the hard-won reforms of the eleventh and twelfth centuries.

With both papal authority and spiritual prestige in decline, kings and princes became the primary figures to whom both clergy and laity looked for religious and moral guidance. The result was an increasingly close link between national monarchies and national churches, a link that would become even stronger after the Reformation (see Chapter 13). Meanwhile, the popes of the late fifteenth century became even more dependent on their own territories in central Italy, which they had to rule like other Italian princes: leading armies, jockeying for alliances, and undermining their opponents by covert operations, murder, and assassination. Judged by secular standards, these efforts paid off: the Papal States became one of the better-governed and wealthier principalities of Italy. But such methods did nothing to increase the popes' reputation for piety, and disillusionment with the papacy became even more widespread.

Competing Viewpoints

Council or Pope?

> The Great Schism spurred a fundamental and far-reaching debate about the nature of authority within the Church. Arguments for papal supremacy rested on traditional claims that the popes were the successors of Saint Peter, to whom Jesus Christ had delegated his own authority. Arguments for the supremacy of a general council had been advanced by many intellectuals throughout the fourteenth century, but it was only in the circumstances of the schism that these arguments found a wide audience. The following documents trace the history of the controversy, from the declaration of conciliar supremacy at the Council of Constance (Haec Sancta), to the council's efforts to guarantee regular meetings of general councils thereafter (Frequens), to the papal condemnation of appeals to the authority of general councils issued in 1460 (Execrabilis).

Haec Sancta Synodus (1415)

This holy synod of Constance . . . declares that being lawfully assembled in the Holy Spirit, constituting a general council and representing the Catholic Church Militant, it has its power directly from Christ, and that all persons of whatever rank or dignity, even a Pope, are bound to obey it in matters relating to faith and the end of the Schism and the general reformation of the church of God in head and members.

Further, it declares that any person of whatever position, rank, or dignity, even a Pope, who contumaciously refuses to obey the mandates, statutes, ordinances, or regulations enacted or to be enacted by this holy synod, or by any other general council lawfully assembled, relating to the matters aforesaid or to other matters involved with them, shall, unless he repents, be . . . duly punished. . . .

Source: R. L. Loomis, ed. and trans., *The Council of Constance* (New York: 1961), p. 229

Frequens (1417)

The frequent holding of general councils is the best method of cultivating the field of the Lord, for they root out the briars, thorns, and thistles of heresies, errors, and schisms, correct abuses, make crooked things straight, and prepare the Lord's vineyard for fruitfulness and rich fertility. Neglect of general councils sows the seeds of these evils and encourages their growth. This truth is borne in upon us as we recall times past and survey the present.

Therefore by perpetual edict we . . . ordain that henceforth general councils shall be held as follows: the first within the five years immediately following the end of the present council, the second within seven years from the end of the council next after this, and subsequently every ten years forever. . . . Thus there will always be a certain continuity. Either

THE PURSUIT OF HOLINESS

Despite the travails of the institutional Church, religious devotion among the laity was more widespread and intense during the later Middle Ages than it had ever been. Some of these devotional paths led believers in directions the Church declared heretical. But for the vast majority of Christians, extreme forms of dissent held no appeal. The local parish church, and especially the sacraments performed by the parish priest, were the center of religious life.

Sacrament and Ritual

Innocent III's insistence that all Christians should have direct access to sound religious instruction (Chapter 9) ensured that nearly all of Europe was covered by a network of local parish churches by the time of the Black Death. In these churches, parish priests administered the sacraments ("holy rites") that conveyed the grace of God to individual Christians and that marked significant moments in the lifecycle of every person. There were seven sacraments:

a council will be in session or one will be expected at the end of a fixed period. . . .

Source: R. L. Loomis, ed. and trans., *The Council of Constance* (New York: 1961), pp. 246–47.

Execrabilis (1460)

An execrable abuse, unheard of in earlier times, has sprung up in our period. Some men, imbued with a spirit of rebellion and moved not by a desire for sound decisions but rather by a desire to escape the punishment for sin, suppose that they can appeal from the Pope, Vicar of Jesus Christ—from the Pope, to whom in the person of blessed Peter it was said, "Feed my sheep" and "whatever you bind on earth will be bound in heaven"—from this Pope to a future council. How harmful this is to the Christian republic, as well as how contrary to canon law, anyone who is not ignorant of the law can understand. For . . . who would not consider it ridiculous to appeal to something which does not now exist anywhere nor does anyone know when it will exist? The poor are heavily oppressed by the powerful, offenses remain unpunished, rebellion against the Holy See is encouraged, license for sin is granted, and all ecclesiastical discipline and hierarchical ranking of the Church are turned upside down.

Wishing therefore to expel this deadly poison from the Church of Christ, and concerned with the salvation of the sheep committed to us . . . with the counsel and assent of our venerable brothers, the Cardinals of the Holy Roman Church, together with the counsel and assent of all those prelates who have been trained in canon and civil law who follow our Court, and with our own certain knowledge, we condemn appeals of this kind, reject them as erroneous and abominable, and declare them to be completely null and void. And we lay down that from now on, no one should dare . . . to make such an appeal from our decisions, be they legal or theological, or from any commands at all from us or our successors. . . .

Source: Reprinted by permission of the publisher from *Defensorum Obedientiae Apostolicae Et Alia Documenta* by Gabriel Biel, edited and translated by Heiko A. Oberman, Daniel E. Zerfoss, and William J. Courtenay, pp. 224–27, Cambridge, Mass.: The Belknap Press of Harvard University Press, Copyright © 1968 by the President and Fellows of Harvard College.

Questions for Analysis

1. On what grounds does *Haec Sancta* establish the authority of a council? Why would this be considered a threat to papal power?

2. Why was it considered necessary for councils to meet regularly (*Frequens*)? What might have been the logical consequences of such regular meetings?

3. On what grounds does *Execrabilis* condemn the appeals to future councils that have no specified meeting date? Why would it not have condemned the conciliar movement altogether?

baptism, confirmation, confession (penance), marriage, extreme unction, ordination, and communion. Baptism, a ceremony of initiation administered in the early centuries of Christianity to adults (Chapter 6), became in the course of the Middle Ages a sacrament administered to infants as soon as possible after birth. Confirmation of adolescents therefore "confirmed" the promises made on a child's behalf by parents and godparents. Periodic confession of sins to a priest guaranteed forgiveness. Marriage was a relatively new sacrament, increasingly emphasized but very seldom practiced; for in order to be valid, marriage in this period required only that promises be exchanged by a man and a woman, and in many cases the fact of cohabitation was taken as proof of marriage. Extreme unction (or last rites) was administered to a dying person, and ensured the final absolution of all sins and so was essential to the assurance of salvation.

Like baptism, extreme unction could be administered in an emergency by any Christian believer. The other sacraments, however, could be administered only by a

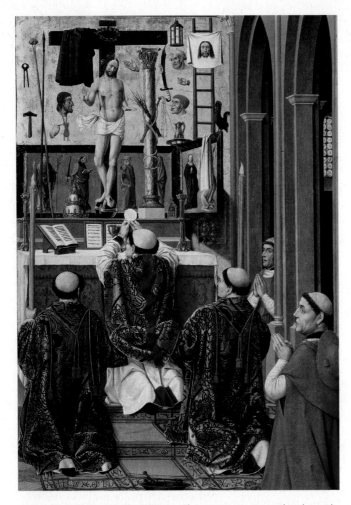

THE REAL PRESENCE OF CHRIST. This painting, executed in the mid-fifteenth century, refers to a popular legend underscoring the doctrine of transubstantiation. According to this legend, Pope Gregory the Great (c. 540–604) was celebrating Mass in his private chapel when he had a vision of the crucified Christ, whose body and blood were rendered visible when Gregory consecrated the bread and wine on the altar. Here, Christ displays his wounds to the astonished onlookers. The instruments of Christ's passion—the people and implements that tortured and killed him—are also displayed.

properly ordained priest—or, in the case of confirmation and ordination, by a bishop. Ordination was therefore the only sacrament reserved for the small percentage of those who became priests, and it conveyed to the priest his special authority to share God's grace through the sacraments: a power that could never be lost, even by a priest who led an immoral life.

This sacramental system was the foundation on which the practices of medieval popular piety rested. Pilgrimages, for example, were a form of penance. Crusading was a kind of extreme pilgrimage. Many other pious acts—saying the prayers of the rosary, for example, or giving alms to the poor—could also serve as penance for sins while constitut-

ing good works that would help the believer in his or her journey toward salvation.

But the sacrament that was most central to the lives of medieval Christians was the communion ceremony of the Mass (or the Eucharist). As we noted in Chapter 9, the ritual power of the Mass was greatly enhanced in the twelfth century, when the Church began promoting the doctrine of transubstantiation. Christians attending Mass understood that when the priest spoke the ritual words "This is my body" and "This is my blood," the substances of bread and wine held in the priest's hands were miraculously transformed into the body and blood of Jesus Christ. To consume one or both of these substances was to ingest holiness; and so powerful was this idea that many Christians only received the sacramental bread once a year, at Easter.

But in order to share in the miracle of the Eucharist one did not have to consume it: one had only to witness the elevation of the Host. So the practice of attending Mass merely to view the Host became a common form of daily devotion, as did the practice of displaying a consecrated wafer in a special reliquary called a monstrance ("showcase"). Believers sometimes attributed astonishing properties to the eucharistic Host, and rushed from church to church to see the consecrated bread as many times as possible in a day. Some of these practices were criticized as superstitious or even heretical. But by and large, these expressions of devotion were encouraged.

Spirituality and the Social Order

The spiritual and social lives of medieval Christians were inextricably intertwined; the parish church stood literally at the center of their lives. Churchyards were communal meeting places, sometimes the sites of markets, and church buildings were a refuge and a gathering place. The church's holidays marked the passage of the year, and the church's bells marked the hours of the day. The church was essential to daily life.

Yet some medieval Christians—many regarded today as saints—were not satisfied with these conventional practices and developed forms of piety that were distinctly controversial during their lifetimes. As Joan of Arc's predicament reveals, medieval women found it particularly challenging to find outlets for their piety that would not earn them the condemnation of the Church. Many therefore internalized those practices or confined them to the domestic sphere—sometimes to the inconvenience of their families and communities. For example, the young Catherine of Siena refused to help with the housework or to support her large working-class family, and instead took over one of the house's two rooms for her own private prayers. The English housewife Margery Kempe (c. 1372– c. 1439), resented the fact that she had a husband, several children, and a household to support, and in later life renounced her duties and devoted her life to performing acts of histrionic piety which alienated many of those who came into contact with her.

The extraordinary devotion of such individuals could be inspiring, but it could also threaten the Church's control and weaken the links that bound individuals to their communities. It could, therefore, be dangerous. Even less radical figures might find themselves treading on treacherous ground, especially if they published their ideas in the vernacular. The preacher Master Eckhart (c. 1260–1327), a German Dominican, taught that there was a "spark" deep within every human soul, and it was in this spark that God lived. This conveyed the message that a layperson might access divinity and attain salvation through her own efforts, without the intervention of a priest. As a result, many of Eckhart's teachings were condemned as heretical. More safely orthodox was the practical mysticism preached by Thomas à Kempis, whose *Imitation of Christ* (c. 1427) taught readers to appreciate aspects of the divine in their everyday lives. Originally written in Latin, the *Imitation* was quickly translated into many vernacular languages and is now more widely read than any other Christian book except the Bible.

Lollards and Hussites

For the most part, the threat of heretical movements was less dangerous to the Church than the corruption of the papacy. But in England and Bohemia, some popular movements did pose serious challenges. The key figure in both cases was John Wyclif (c. 1330–1384), an Oxford theologian and powerful critic of the Church. A survivor of the Black Death, Wyclif concluded that the empty sacraments of a corrupt Church could not save anyone. He therefore urged the English king to confiscate ecclesiastical wealth and to replace corrupt priests and bishops with men who would live according to apostolic standards of poverty and piety. Some of Wyclif's followers, known to their detractors as Lollards (from a word meaning "mumblers" or "beggars"), went even further, dismissing the sacraments as fraudulent attempts to extort money from the faithful. Lollard preachers also promoted an English translation of the Bible attributed to Wyclif himself.

Wyclif's teachings played an important role in the Peasants' Revolt of 1381, and Lollardy gained numerous

adherents in the decades after his death. But after a failed Lollard uprising in 1414, both the movement and its supporters went underground in England.

In Bohemia and eastern Europe, however, Wyclif's ideas lived on and struck even deeper roots. They were adopted by Jan Hus (c. 1373–1415), a charismatic teacher at the royal university in Prague. Hus emphasized the centrality of the Eucharist to Christian piety and demanded that the laity be allowed to receive not only the consecrated bread but also the consecrated wine, usually reserved solely for priests. This demand became a rallying cry for the Hussite movement. Influential nobles also supported Hus,

THE TEACHINGS OF JAN HUS. An eloquent religious reformer, Jan Hus was burned at the stake in 1415 after having been found guilty of heresy at the Council of Constance. This lavishly illustrated booklet of his teachings was published over a century later in his native Bohemia, and includes texts in the Czech vernacular and in Latin. ▪ *What does this later publication suggest about the uses to which Hus's image and theology were put during the Protestant Reformation?*

partly in the hope that the reforms he demanded might restore revenues they had lost to the Church over the previous century. Accordingly, most of Bohemia was behind him when Hus traveled to the Council of Constance to publish his views and to urge the assembled delegates to undertake sweeping reforms.

But rather than giving him a hearing, the other delegates convicted Hus of heresy and had him burned at the stake. Back home, Hus's supporters raised the banner of open revolt, and the aristocracy took advantage of the situation to seize Church property. Between 1420 and 1424, armed bands of fervent Hussites defeated several armies. These victories increased popular fervor, but they also made radical reformers increasingly volatile. In 1434, accordingly, a more conservative arm of the Hussite movement was able to negotiate a settlement with the Bohemian church. By the terms of this settlement, Bohemians could receive both the bread and wine of the Mass, which thus placed them beyond the pale of Latin orthodoxy and effectively separated the Bohemian national church from the Church of Rome.

Lollardy and Hussitism exhibit a number of striking similarities. Both began in universities and then spread to the countryside. Both called for the clergy to live in simplicity and poverty, and both attracted noble support. Both movements were also strongly nationalistic, employing their own vernacular languages (English and Czech) in opposition to a "foreign" Church. They also relied on preaching and social activism. In all these respects, they established patterns that would emerge again in the stronger currents of the Protestant Reformation.

MEDIEVAL CREATIVITY AND INNOVATION

Many of the extraordinary achievements of the later Middle Ages have often been ascribed to the Renaissance, the name given to an intellectual and artistic movement that began concurrently in Italy. We will discuss this movement more fully in Chapter 12. For now, we focus on parallel developments closely tied to the trends discussed above.

Knowledge of the World and of God

In the thirteenth century, Thomas Aquinas had constructed a theological view of the world as rational, organized, and comprehensible to the inquiring human mind (Chapter 9). Confidence in this picture began to wane in the fourteenth century, even before the Black Death posed a new challenge to it. Philosophers such as the English Franciscan William of Ockham (d. 1349) denied that human reason could prove fundamental theological truths such as the existence of God. Instead, he argued that human knowledge of God depends entirely on what God himself has chosen to reveal through scripture. Humans can investigate the natural world, but there is no necessary connection between the observable regularities of nature and the unknowable essence of divinity.

This philosophical position, known as nominalism, has had an enormous impact on modern thought. The nominalists' distinction between the comprehensibility of the natural world and the incomprehensibility of God actually encourages investigation of the natural world without reference to supernatural explanations—one of the most important foundations of the scientific method (see Chapter 16). Nominalism also encourages empirical observation by positing that knowledge should rest on sensory experience rather than abstraction. Late medieval philosophy is thus fundamental to modern science.

Capturing Reality in Writing

The entertainments of the later Middle Ages also exhibit an intense interest in the world as it is. Such naturalism was not new, but authors were now able to reach a far larger and more diverse audience than their predecessors. For increasingly,

CHRISTINE DE PISAN. One of the most prolific authors of the fifteenth century, Christine used her influence to uphold the dignity of women and to celebrate their history and achievements. Here she is seen describing the prowess of an Amazon warrior who could defeat men effortlessly in armed combat.

ideas were published in the vernacular languages of Europe. Behind this phenomenon lay three interrelated developments: the growing identification between vernacular languages and national monarchies, the increasing accessibility of lay education, and the emergence of a substantial reading public for vernacular literature. We can see these influences at work in three of the major authors of this period: Giovanni Boccaccio, Geoffrey Chaucer, and Christine de Pisan.

Boccaccio (*bohk-KAHT-chee-oh*, 1313–1375) is best known for the *Decameron*, a collection of prose tales about sex, adventure, and trickery which he represents as being told over a period of ten days by a sophisticated party of ten young women and men temporarily residing in a country villa outside Florence to escape the Black Death. Boccaccio borrowed the outlines of many of these tales from earlier sources, especially the fabliaux discussed in Chapter 9, but he couched them in a freely colloquial style, in an attempt to capture the relationships and foibles of real human beings.

Similar in many ways to Boccaccio, whose influence on him was profound, is the English poet Geoffrey Chaucer (c. 1340–1400). Chaucer is among the first generation of English authors whose compositions can be understood by modern readers with relatively little effort: by the fourteenth century, the Anglo-Saxon language of England's pre-Conquest inhabitants had mixed with the French spoken by their Norman conquerors, to create the language that is the ancestor of our own. Chaucer's masterpiece is the *Canterbury Tales*. Like the *Decameron*, this is a collection of stories held together by a framing narrative. In this case, the stories are told by an array of people traveling together on a pilgrimage from London to the shrine of Saint Thomas Becket at Canterbury. But there are also significant differences between the *Decameron* and the *Canterbury Tales*. Chaucer's stories are in verse, for the most part, and they are recounted by people of all different social classes—from a high-minded knight to a poor university student to a lusty widow. Each character tells a story that is particularly illustrative of his or her own occupation and outlook, forming a kaleidoscopic human comedy.

The later Middle Ages also saw the emergence of professional authors who made their living by writing. One of the first was a woman, Christine de Pisan (c. 1365–c. 1434). Although born in northern Italy, Christine spent her adult life in France, where her husband was a member of the king's household. When he died, the widowed Christine wrote to support herself and her children. She mastered a wide variety of literary genres, including treatises on chivalry and warfare that she dedicated to her patron, Charles VI of France. She also wrote for a larger and more popular audience. Her imaginative *Book of the City of Ladies* is an extended defense of the character, capacities, and history of women, designed to refute their male detractors. Christine also took part in a vigorous pamphlet campaign that refuted misogynistic claims made by male authors like Boccaccio. This debate was ongoing for several hundred years, and became so famous that it was given a name: the *querelle des femmes*, "the debate over women." Remarkably, Christine also wrote a song in praise of Joan of Arc. Poignantly, she probably lived long enough to learn that this other extraordinary woman had been put to death for behaving in a way that was considered unwomanly.

Visualizing Reality

Just as naturalism was a dominant trait of late medieval philosophy and literature, so it was of later medieval art. The sculptors of the thirteenth century were already paying close attention to the way plants, animals, and human

THE MEETING OF JOACHIM AND ANNA BY GIOTTO. According to legend, Anna and Joachim were an aged and infertile couple who were able to conceive their only child, Mary, through divine intervention. Since Mary was supposed to have been conceived without the taint of sin, theologians taught that she had been miraculously engendered without sexual contact. Hence, this painting may portray the moment of her conception—but it also portrays the affection of husband and wife. ▪ *What values does it convey to the viewer?*

Why a Woman Can Write about Warfare

Christine de Pisan (c. 1365–c. 1434) was one of the West's first professional writers, best known today for her Book of the City of Ladies *and* The Treasure of the City of Ladies, *works which aimed to provide women with an honorable and rich history, and to combat generations of institutionalized misogyny. But in her own time, she was probably best known for the work excerpted here,* The Book of the Deeds of Arms and of Chivalry, *a manual of military strategy and conduct written at the height of the Hundred Years' War, in 1410.*

 s boldness is essential for great undertakings, and without it nothing should be risked, I think it is proper in this present work to set forth my unworthiness to treat such an exalted matter. I should not have dared even to think about it, but although boldness is blameworthy when it is foolhardy, I should state that I have not been inspired by arrogance or foolish presumption, but rather by true affection and a genuine desire for the welfare of noble men engaging in the profession of arms. I am encouraged, in the light of my other writings, to undertake to speak in this book of the most honorable office of arms and chivalry. . . . So to this end I have gathered together facts and subject matter from various books to produce this present volume. But inasmuch as it is fitting for this matter to be discussed factually, diligently, and sensibly . . . and also in consideration of the fact that military and lay experts in the aforesaid art of chivalry are not usually clerks or writers who are expert in language, I intend to treat the matter in the plainest possible language. . . .

As this is unusual for women, who generally are occupied in weaving, spinning, and household duties, I humbly invoke . . . the wise lady Minerva [Athena], born in the land of Greece, whom the ancients esteemed highly for her great wisdom. Likewise the poet Boccaccio praises her in his *Book of Famous Women*, as do other writers praise her art and manner of making trappings of iron and steel, so let it not be held against me if I, as a woman, take it upon myself to treat of military matters. . . .

O Minerva! goddess of arms and of chivalry, who, by understanding beyond that of other women, did find and initiate among the other noble arts and sciences the custom of forging iron and steel armaments and harness both proper and suitable for covering and protecting men's bodies against arrows slung in battle—helmets, shields, and protective covering having come first from you—you instituted and gave directions for drawing up a battle order, how to begin an assault and to engage in proper combat. . . . In the aforementioned country of Greece, you provided the usage of this office, and insofar as it may please you to be favorably disposed, and I in no way appear to be against the nation from which you came, the country beyond the Alps that is now called Apulia and Calabria in Italy, where you were born, let me say that like you I am an Italian woman.

Source: From *The Book of the Deeds of Arms and of Chivalry*, trans. Sumner Willard and ed. Charity Cannon Willard (University Park, PA: 1999), pp. 11–13.

Questions for Analysis

1. Christine very cleverly deflects potential criticism for her "boldness" in writing about warfare. What tactics does she use?

2. The Greco-Roman goddess Athena (Minerva) was the goddess of wisdom, weaving, and warfare. Why does Christine invoke her aid? What parallels does she draw between her own attributes and those of Minerva?

---

beings really looked. Carvings of leaves and flowers are clearly recognizable to modern botanists as distinct species. Statues of humans also became more realistic in their portrayals of facial expressions and bodily proportions.

In the fourteenth and fifteenth centuries, this trend toward naturalism in sculpture was extended to manuscript illumination and painting. (The latter was, to a large extent, a distinctively medieval art.) As we saw in Chapter 1, wall paintings are one of the oldest forms of artistic expression in human history, and throughout antiquity and the Middle Ages artists had decorated the walls of public and private buildings with frescoes (paintings executed on "fresh"—

wet—plaster). But in addition to frescoes, Italian artists in the thirteenth century began to adapt the techniques used by icon painters in Byzantium, making free-standing pictures on pieces of wood or canvas using tempera (pigments mixed with water and natural gums). Around 1400, painting in oils was introduced in the Low Countries, and this technique soon spread southward to Italy and beyond.

These new artistic media created new aesthetic and commercial opportunities. Artists were now able to paint and sell portable altarpieces, devotional images, and portraits. And so long as they could afford the necessary materials, they did not have to wait for a specific commission and had more freedom to put an individual stamp on their work—one of the reasons why we know the names of so many late-medieval artists. One of these, Giotto di Bondone of Florence (c. 1267–1337), painted both walls and portable wooden panels. Giotto (*gee-AHT-toh*) was preeminently an imitator of nature. Not only do his human beings and animals look lifelike, they do natural things. When Christ enters Jerusalem on Palm Sunday, boys climb trees to get a better view; when Saint Francis is laid out in death, someone checks to see whether he has really received the marks of Christ's wounds, the *stigmata*; and when the Virgin's parents, Joachim and Anna, meet after a long separation, they embrace and kiss one another tenderly. This style became the norm by 1400, and it is for this reason that Giotto is often regarded as the first painter of the Renaissance, a movement that is really an outgrowth of the Middle Ages.

In northern Europe, manuscript illumination remained the dominant artistic medium. But oil painting also caught on, especially in Flanders, where artists found a ready market for their works. Practitioners like Rogier van der Weyden (c. 1400–1464) excelled at communicating both deep piety and the minute details of everyday experience (see **Interpreting Visual Evidence**). Just as contemporary spirituality saw divinity in nature, so a Flemish painter could portray the Virgin and Child against a background of contemporary life, with people going about their business or a man urinating against a wall. This was not blasphemous; quite the contrary. It conveyed the message that the events of the Bible are constantly present, here and now.

The same immediacy is also evident in medieval drama. Plays were often devotional exercises that involved the efforts of an entire community. In the English city of York, for example, an annual series of pageants reenacted the entire history of human salvation from the Creation to the Last Judgment in a single summer day, beginning at dawn and ending late at night. Each pageant was produced by a particular craft guild and showcased that guild's special talents: "The Last Supper" was performed by the bakers,

while "The Crucifixion" was performed by the nail-makers. In Italy, confraternities competed to honor the saints with songs and processions. In Spain and Catalonia, there were elaborate dramas celebrating the life and miracles of the Virgin, one of which is still performed every year in the Basque town of Elche—the oldest European play in continuous production. Elsewhere on the Continent there were civic spectacles performed over a period of several days. But not all plays were pious. Some honored visiting kings and princes. Others celebrated the flouting of social conventions, featuring cross-dressing and the reversal of hierarchies.

Technological Advances

As in other places and times, warfare was the engine driving the development of many medieval technologies. Although explosive powder had been invented in China, it was first put to devastating use in the guns of the Hundred Years' War. The earliest cannons were as dangerous to those who fired them as to those who were targeted, but by the middle of the fifteenth century they were reliable enough to revolutionize the nature of warfare. In 1453, heavy artillery played a leading role in the outcomes of two crucial conflicts: the Ottoman Turks breached the defenses of Constantinople (see Chapter 11) and the French captured the city of Bordeaux, thereby ending the Hundred Years' War. Thereafter, cannons made it more difficult for rebellious aristocrats to hole up in their stone castles. Cannons placed aboard ships made Europe's developing navies more effective. A hand-held firearm, the pistol, was also invented, and around 1500 the musket ended forever the dominance of heavily armored cavalry, giving the advantage to foot soldiers.

A FIFTEENTH-CENTURY SIEGE WITH CANNON. Cannons were an essential element in siege warfare during the Hundred Years' War and thereafter.

Realizing Devotion

These two paintings by the Flemish artist Rogier van der Weyden (*FAN-der-VIE-den*, c. 1400–1464) capture some of the most compelling characteristics of late medieval art, particularly the trend toward realistic representations of holy figures and sacred stories. On the left (image A), the artist depicts himself as the evangelist Luke, regarded in Christian tradition as a painter of portraits; he sketches the Virgin nursing the infant Jesus in a town house overlooking a Flemish city. On the right (image B), van der Weyden imagines the entombment of the dead Christ by his followers, including the Virgin (left), Mary Magdalene (kneeling), and the disciple John (right). Here, he makes use of a motif that became increasingly prominent in the later Middle Ages: Christ as the Man of Sorrows, displaying his wounds and inviting the viewer to share in his suffering. In both paintings, van der Weyden emphasizes the humanity of his subjects rather than their iconic status (see Chapter 7), and he places them in the urban and rural landscapes of his own world.

Questions for Analysis

1. How are these paintings different from the sacred images of the earlier Middle Ages (see, for example, pages 161 and 219)? What messages does the artist convey by setting these events in his own immediate present?

2. In what ways do these paintings reflect broad changes in popular piety and medieval devotional practices? Why, for example, would the artist display the dead and wounded body of Christ—rather than depicting him as resurrected and triumphant, or as an all-seeing creator and judge?

3. In general, how would you use these images as evidence of the worldview of the fifteenth century? What do they tell us about people's attitudes, emotions, and values?

A. Saint Luke drawing the portrait of the Virgin.

B. The Deposition.

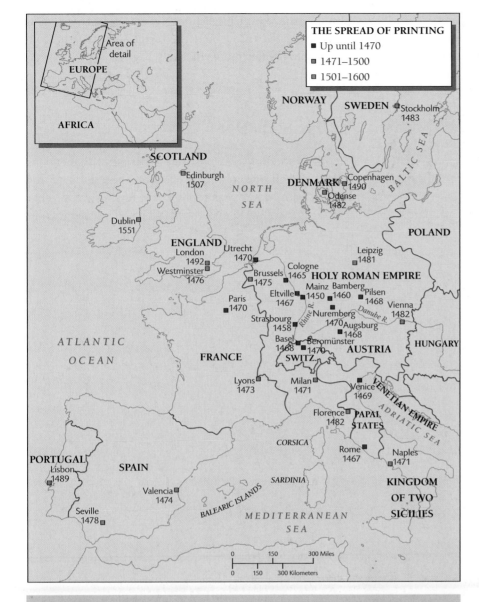

THE SPREAD OF PRINTING. This map shows how quickly the technology of printing spread throughout Europe between 1470 and 1500. ▪ *In what regions were printing presses most heavily concentrated?* ▪ *What factors would have led to their proliferation in the Low Countries, northern Italy, and Germany—as compared to France, Spain, and England?* ▪ *Why would so many have been located along waterways?*

and expensive for private purchase, but towns vied with one another to install them in prominent public buildings. Mechanical timekeeping had two profound effects. One was the further stimulation of interest in complex machinery of all sorts. More significant was the regulation of daily life. Until the advent of clocks, time was flexible. Days had been theoretically divided into hours, minutes, and seconds since the time of the Sumerians (Chapter 1), but there had never been a way of mapping these measurements onto an actual day. Now, clocks relentlessly divided time into exact units and thus gave rise to new expectations about labor and productivity. People were expected to start and end work "on time," and many came to believe that "time is money." This emphasis on timekeeping brought new efficiencies but also created new tensions and obsessions.

The development of printing was even more momentous. A major stimulus was the more widespread availability of paper. Parchment, Europe's chief writing material since the seventh century, was extremely expensive to manufacture and even required special training on the part of scribes—one reason why writing remained a specialized skill for much of the Middle Ages, while the ability to read was common. Paper, made from rags turned into pulp by mills, was both cheaper and far easier to use. Accordingly, reading and writing also became cheaper and easier. Increased literacy led to a growing demand for books, which in turn led to experimentation with different methods of book production. A breakthrough came around 1450, when it was discovered that movable type (letter forms and punctuation marks) could be slotted into iron frames to form lines of words, and whole pages could thus be reproduced by coating those frames with ink and pressing them onto paper or parchment, after which the type could be reused. The most famous early result of this technique is the Bible completed in the workshop of Johann Gutenberg in Mainz, around 1454.

By saving labor and time, the printing press made the cost of printed books about one fifth as expensive and

Other late medieval technologies were more life enhancing. Eyeglasses, first invented in the 1280s, were perfected in the fourteenth century. The use of the magnetic compass helped ships sail farther away from land. Numerous improvements in shipbuilding, mapmaking, and navigational devices enabled Europeans to venture out into the Atlantic. We will discuss the implications of these developments in Chapter 11.

Among the many implements of modern life invented in this era, the most familiar are clocks and printed books. Mechanical clocks came into use shortly before 1300 and proliferated immediately thereafter. They were too large made book culture a more basic part of daily life. Printing thereby facilitated the rapid exchange of information and ideas, and also made it more difficult for those in power to suppress these ideas effectively. Martin Luther could create an immediate and far-flung network of support by employing this new communication technology (Chapter 13); had printing not been available, he might have died ignominiously, as Hus had a century before. The spread of books also standardized national languages. Regional dialects were often so diverse that people living within the same state could not understand each other. Now, each European country began to develop its own linguistic standards. For example, the "King's English," the dialect of London, could be promulgated throughout the realm, allowing the government to operate more efficiently.

CONCLUSION

The later Middle Ages constitute a period of tremendous creativity and revolutionary change. The effects of the Black Death were catastrophic, but the resulting labor shortages encouraged experimentation and opened up new

After You Read This Chapter

Visit StudySpace for quizzes, additional review materials, and multi-media documents. **wwnorton.com/studyspace**

REVIEWING THE OBJECTIVES

- The Black Death had short-term and long-term effects on the economy and societies of Europe. What were some of the most important changes?
- The melding of strong kingship with the promotion of national identity was a new development in the later Middle Ages. What circumstances made this possible? Why is this development significant?
- Several key factors enabled the growth of a Russian state centered on Muscovy. What were they?
- The conciliar movement sought to limit the power of the papacy. How? Why was this movement unsuccessful?
- In what ways do the spiritual, cultural, and technological innovations of the later Middle Ages reflect the political, social, and economic changes brought about by the Black Death?

opportunities. Europe's economy diversified and expanded. Increasing wealth and access to education produced new inventions, ideas, and forms of art. Medieval intellectuals came to see the natural world as operating according to its own laws, which were empirically verifiable: an essential step toward the emergence of a scientific worldview. Women were still excluded from formal schooling, but nevertheless became active—and perhaps dominant—participants in literate culture and religious life. Average men and women also became more active in cultivating their own spiritualities, at a time when the Church provided little inspiring leadership. Meanwhile, incessant warfare prompted more powerful governments to harvest a larger percentage of their subjects' wealth through taxation, which they proceeded to invest in ships, guns, and the standing armies made possible by new technologies and effective administration.

In short, the generations who survived the calamaties of famine, plague, and warfare seized the opportunities their new world presented to them. By 1500, most Europeans lived more secure lives than their ancestors had, and they stood on the verge of an extraordinary period of expansion and conquest that enabled them to dominate the globe.

PEOPLE, IDEAS, AND EVENTS IN CONTEXT

- Compare and contrast the **BLACK DEATH'S** effects on rural and urban areas.
- In what ways do the rebellions of the later fourteenth and fifteenth centuries reflect the changes brought about by the plague? How did the nobility of Europe respond to this changing world?
- What were the main causes and consequences of the **HUNDRED YEARS' WAR**? How did **FERDINAND AND ISABELLA** begin to construct a national monarchy in Spain?
- On what grounds did **MUSCOVY** claim to be "the third Rome"? What is the significance of **IVAN THE GREAT'S** use of the title **TSAR**?
- How did the **COUNCIL OF CONSTANCE** respond to the crisis of the **GREAT SCHISM**?
- How did the teachings of **JOHN WYCLIF** and **JAN HUS** critique religious trends?
- What were the major artistic and technological innovations of the later Middle Ages?

CONSEQUENCES

- In 2000, a group of historians was asked to identify the most significant historical figure of the past millennium; but rather than choosing a person (e.g., Martin Luther, Napoleon, Adolf Hitler) they chose the microbe *Yersinia pestis*. Do you agree with this assessment? Why or why not?
- In your view, which was more crucial to the formation of the modern state: the political and legal developments we surveyed in Chapter 9 or the emergence of national identities in the later Middle Ages? Why?
- Was the conciliar movement doomed to failure, given what we have learned about the history of the Roman Church? How far back in history does one need to go in order to trace the development of disputes over ecclesiastical governance?

Before
You
Read
This
Chapter

Commerce, Conquest, and Colonization, 1300–1600

CORE OBJECTIVES

- **DESCRIBE** the effects of the Mongol conquests.

- **EXPLAIN** the consequences of the Ottoman Empire's dependence on slave labor.

- **IDENTIFY** the factors that drove exploration and colonialism in the fourteenth and fifteenth centuries.

- **DEFINE** the essential difference between modern slavery and that of all previous civilizations.

- **UNDERSTAND** the far-reaching impact of the New World conquests.

When Christopher Columbus set sail from Genoa in 1492, he carried with him two influential travel narratives. One was largely factual and one was fantastic, but it is doubtful that Columbus could tell the difference between them. The first was the *Book of Marvels*, attributed to Jehan de Mandeville, an English adventurer (writing in French) who claimed to have traveled beyond the boundaries of the known world. The second was Marco Polo's account of his journeys in the Far East and of his sojourn at the court of the Great Khan in China. Both of these books shaped the Genoese mariner's expectations of what he would find during his travels, and they also shaped his descriptions of the places and peoples he encountered. As a result, it is difficult to separate fiction from reality when we read his accounts—or those of many other European explorers. What we can know for certain is that the civilizations of the New World and the Old had a profound impact on one another.

In 1352, when Mandeville's *Book of Marvels* began to circulate, Europe had become a politically coherent and culturally unified region. It had also reached its geographical limits;

there was, it seemed, no more room for expansion. With the completed conquest of Muslim territory in 1492, Ferdinand and Isabella eradicated a Muslim presence in western Europe that dated to the seventh century. Yet there was no longer any viable prospect of Latin Christendom's dominion in the Holy Land, North Africa, or any of the other Muslim territories that had been targeted by crusaders. The growing power of the Ottoman Turks was forging a new empire that would soon come to encompass all these regions, as well as the lands of the Eastern Roman Empire in Byzantium. Meanwhile, the rise of Poland-Lithuania and the emergence of Muscovy as a contender for power on

Europe's northeastern frontier arrested German princes' drive to conquer territories in eastern Europe; and their efforts would be halted altogether by the eventual absorption of these territories into the Ottoman Empire.

Europe was also reaching its ecological limits. Indeed, the pressure on its natural resources was eased only by the dramatic population losses that had resulted from the combined effects of famine, plague, and war in the fourteenth and fifteenth centuries. But despite these challenges—or because of them—Europeans did not turn inward. As land-based conquests became less viable, new maritime empires coalesced around chains of colonies that extended from the

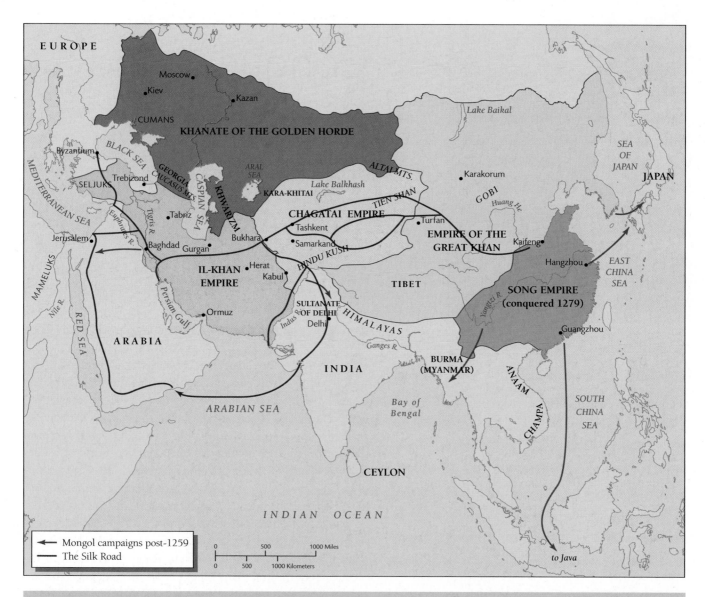

STATES OF THE MONGOL EMPIRE. Like Alexander's, Chingiz Khan's empire was swiftly assembled and encompassed vast portions of Europe and Asia. ▪ *How many separate Mongol empires were there, and how far did they stretch geographically?* ▪ *How might the Mongol occupation of the Muslim world have aided the expansion of European trade?* ▪ *At the same time, why would it have complicated the efforts of crusader armies in the Holy Land?*

Black Sea to the Canary Islands. Trade routes were opened through the Strait of Gibraltar, resulting in greater economic integration between the Mediterranean and Atlantic economies, and increasing Europe's demand for Asian spices and African gold. By the late fifteenth century, Mediterranean mariners and colonists were reaching farther into the Atlantic and pushing down the west coast of Africa. In 1498, one such expedition would make its way to India.

The fifteenth-century expansion of the Mediterranean world into the Atlantic was the essential preliminary to Columbus's voyages, and to European colonization of the Americas. Because these later events seem so familiar, we can easily underestimate both their improbability and their significance for the Western civilizations we have been studying, as well as for the "new world" they encountered. For the indigenous peoples and empires of the Americas, the results were cataclysmic. Within a hundred years of Europeans' arrival, between 50 and 90 percent of the native population had perished from disease, massacre, and enslavement. Moreover, Europeans' capacity to further their imperial ambitions wherever ships could sail and guns could penetrate profoundly destabilized Europe and its neighbors, sharpening the divisions among competing kingdoms and empires. The effects of this process, which reached its apogee in the nineteenth century, are still being felt today.

MONGOLS, EUROPEANS, AND THE FAR EAST

Trade between the Mediterranean world and the Far East dates back to antiquity, but it was not until the late thirteenth century that Europeans were able to establish direct trading connections with India, China, and the so-called Spice Islands of the Indonesian archipelago. These connections would prove profoundly important, as much for their impact on the European imagination as for their economic significance. For the peoples of Asia, however, the appearance of European traders on the fabled Silk Road between Central Asia and China was merely a curiosity. The really consequential event in their world was the rise of the Mongol Empire that made such connections possible.

The Expansion of the Mongol Empire

The Mongols were one of many nomadic peoples inhabiting the steppes of Central Asia. Although closely connected with the Turkic populations with whom they frequently intermarried, the Mongols spoke their own distinctive language and had their own homeland, to the north of the Gobi Desert in present-day Mongolia. Sheep provided them with shelter (sheepskin tents), woolen clothing, milk, and meat. And like many nomadic peoples, the Mongols were highly accomplished horsemen and raiders. In fact, it was in part to control their raiding ventures that the Chinese had built the fortified Great Wall, many centuries before. Primarily, though, China defended itself by attempting to ensure that the Mongols remained internally divided, with their energies turned against each other.

In the late twelfth century, however, a Mongol chief named Temüjin began to unite the various tribes under his rule. He did so by incorporating the warriors of each tribe he defeated into his own army, thus building up a large military force. In 1206 his supremacy was formally acknowledged by all the Mongols, and he took the title Chingiz (Genghis) Khan, or "universal ruler." He now directed his enormous army against his neighbors, and began conquering China one region at a time. In 1279, his grandson

THE HEAD OF TIMUR THE LAME. This bust of the Mongol leader, known in the West as Tamerlane, is based on a forensic reconstruction of his exhumed skull.

Competing Viewpoints

Two Travel Accounts

Two of the books that influenced Columbus and his contemporaries were travel narratives describing the exotic worlds that lay beyond Europe: worlds that may or may not have existed as they are described. The first excerpt below is taken from the account published by Marco Polo of Venice in the early fourteenth century. The young Marco traveled overland from Constantinople to the court of Qubilai Khan in the early 1270s, together with his father and uncle. He proved to be a gifted linguist, and remained at the Mongol court until the early 1290s, when he returned to Europe after a journey through Southeast Asia, Indonesia, and the Indian Ocean. The second excerpt is from the Book of Marvels attributed to Jehan de Mandeville, an almost entirely fictional account of wonders that also became a source for European ideas about South and East Asia. This particular passage concerns a legendary Christian figure called Prester ("Priest") John, who is alleged to have traveled to the East and become a great ruler.

Marco Polo's Description of Java

Departing from Ziamba, and steering between south and southeast, fifteen hundred miles, you reach an island of very great size, named Java. According to the reports of some well-informed navigators, it is the greatest in the world, and has a compass above three thousand miles. It is under the dominion of one king only, nor do the inhabitants pay tribute to any other power. They are worshipers of idols.

The country abounds with rich commodities. Pepper, nutmegs, spikenard, galangal, cubebs, cloves, and all the other valuable spices and drugs, are the produce of the island; which occasion it to be visited by many ships laden with merchandise, that yields to the owners considerable profit.

The quantity of gold collected there exceeds all calculation and belief. From thence it is that . . . merchants . . . have imported, and to this day import, that metal to a great amount, and from thence also is obtained the greatest part of the spices that are distributed throughout the world. That the Great Khan [Qubilai] has not brought the island under subjection to him, must be attributed to the length of the voyage and the dangers of the navigation.

Source: *The Travels of Marco Polo,* rev. and ed. Manuel Komroff (New York: 1926), pp. 267–68.

Mandeville's Description of Prester John

This emperor Prester John has great lands and has many noble cities and good towns in his realm and many great, large islands. For all the country of India is separated into islands by the great floods that come from Paradise, that divide the land into many parts. And also in the sea he has many islands. . . .

This Prester John has under him many kings and many islands and many varied people of various conditions. And this land is full good and rich, but not so rich as is the land of the Great Khan. For the merchants do not come there so commonly to buy merchandise as they do in the land of the Great Khan, for it is too far to travel to. . . .

[Mandeville then goes on to describe the difficulties of reaching Prester John's lands by sea.]

This emperor Prester John always takes as his wife the daughter of the Great Khan, and the Great Khan in the same way takes to wife the daughter of Prester John. For these two are the greatest lords under the heavens.

In the land of Prester John there are many diverse things, and many precious stones so great and so large that men make them into vessels such as platters, dishes, and cups. And there are many other marvels there that it would be too cumbrous and too long to put into the writing of books. But of the principal islands and of his estate and of his law I shall tell you some part.

This emperor Prester John is Christian and a great part of his country is Christian also, although they do not hold to all the articles of our faith as we do. . . .

And he has under him 72 provinces, and in every province there is a king. And these kings have kings under them, and all are tributaries to Prester John.

And he has in his lordships many great marvels. For in his country is the sea that men call the Gravelly Sea, that is all gravel and sand without any drop of water. And it ebbs and flows in great waves as other seas do, and it is never still. . . . And a three-day journey from that sea there are great mountains out of which flows a great flood that comes out of Paradise. And it is full of precious stones without any drop of water. . . .

He dwells usually in the city of Susa [in Persia]. And there is his principal palace, which is so rich and so noble that no one will believe the report unless he has seen it. And above the chief tower of the palace there are two round pommels of gold and in each of them are two great, large rubies that shine full brightly upon the night. And the principal gates of his palace are of a precious stone that men call sardonyxes [a type of onyx], and the frames and the bars are made of ivory. And the windows of the halls and chambers are of crystal. And the tables upon which men eat, some are made of emeralds, some of amethyst, and some of gold full of precious stones. And the legs that hold up the tables are made of the same precious stones. . . .

Source: *Mandeville's Travels*, ed. M. C. Seymour (Oxford: 1967), pp. 195–99 (language modernized from Middle English by R. C. Stacey).

Questions for Analysis

1. What does Marco Polo want his readers to know about Java, and why? What does this suggest about the interests of these intended readers?

2. What does Mandeville want his readers to know about Prester John and his domains? Why are these details so important?

3. Which of these accounts seems more trustworthy, and why? Even if we cannot accept one (or both) at face value, what insight do they give us into the expectations of Columbus and the other European adventurers who relied on these accounts?

Qubilai (Kublai) Khan completed this project, thus reuniting China for the first time in centuries.

At the same time, Chingiz Khan was turning his forces westward, conquering much of Central Asia and incorporating the important commercial cities of Tashkent, Samarkand, and Bukhara into his empire. When he died in 1227, his son and successor, Ögedei (*EHRG-uh-day*), not only completed the conquest of China, he laid plans for a massive invasion of the West. Between 1237 and 1240, the Mongol horde (so called from the Turkish word *ordu*, meaning "tent" or "encampment") conquered southern Russia and then launched a two-pronged assault that pushed them farther west. The smaller of two Mongol armies swept through Poland toward eastern Germany; a larger army went southwest toward Hungary. In April of 1241, the smaller force met a hastily assembled army of Germans and Poles at the battle of Liegnitz, where the two sides fought to a bloody standstill. Two days later, the larger Mongol army annihilated the Hungarian army at the River Sajo.

It is possible that the Mongol armies could have moved even farther west after this important victory, but when the Great Khan died in December of that same year, the leaderless Mongol forces withdrew from eastern Europe. Although Mongol conquests continued in Persia, the Middle East, and China, attacks on Europe never resumed. Yet the descendants of Chingiz Khan continued to rule their enormous empire—the largest land empire in the history of the world—for another half-century. Later, under the leadership of Timur the Lame (known as Tamerlane to Europeans) it looked briefly as if the Mongol Empire might expand again. But Timur died in 1405, and thereafter the various parts of the Mongol Empire fell into the hands of local rulers, including (in Asia Minor) the Ottoman Turks. Mongol influence continued, however, in the Mughal Empire of India, whose rulers were descended from followers of Chingiz Khan.

The Mongols owed their success to the size, speed, and training of their mounted armies; to the intimidating ferocity with which they treated those who resisted them; and to their ability to adapt the traditions of their subjects to their own purposes. For example, they were highly tolerant of the religious beliefs of others—a distinct advantage in governing an empire that comprised an array of Buddhist,

VENETIAN AMBASSADORS TO THE GREAT KHAN. Around 1270, the Venetian merchants Niccolò and Matteo Polo returned to Europe after their first prolonged journey through the empire of the Great Khan, bearing with them an official letter to the Roman pope. This image shows them at the moment of their arrival at the Great Khan's court, to which they have allegedly carried a Christian cross and a Bible. It comes from a manuscript copy of Jehan de Mandeville's *Book of Marvels*, which offered readers an alternative vision of the lands and peoples described by Niccolò's famous son, Marco, who accompanied his father and uncle when they made their second journey to the Great Khan's court several years later. ▪ *Why might many such visual references to the Polo family's adventures have been included in Mandeville's more fanciful travel narrative?*

Christian, and Muslim sects. And for the most part, Mongol governance was directed at securing the steady payment of tribute, which meant that local rulers could retain much of their power. Except in China, where a Mongol dynasty maintained an ancient and complex administrative bureaucracy, Mongol rule was highly decentralized.

A Bridge to the East

The Mongols had a keen eye for the commercial advantages of their empire. They began to control the caravan routes that led from China through Central Asia to the Black Sea. They also encouraged commercial contacts with European traders, especially through the Persian city of Tabriz, from which both land and sea routes led on to China. Until the Mongol conquests, the Silk Road had been closed to most Western merchants and travelers. But almost as soon as the Mongol Empire was established, we find Europeans venturing on its routes.

The first such travelers were Franciscan missionaries like William of Rubruck, sent by King Louis IX of France as ambassador to the Mongol court in 1253. Western merchants quickly followed. The most famous of these were three Venetians: the brothers Niccolò and Matteo Polo, and

Niccolò's son, Marco. Marco Polo's account of his travels, which began when he was seventeen, includes details of his twenty-year sojourn in the service of Qubilai Khan and of his journey home through the Spice Islands, India, and Persia. The book had an enormous effect on the imagination of his contemporaries: for the next two centuries, most of what Europeans knew about the Far East they learned from Marco Polo's *Travels*. Christopher Columbus's copy of this book still survives.

European connections with the western outposts of the Silk Road would continue until the mid-fourteenth century. The Genoese were especially active in this, not least because their rivals, the Venetians, already dominated the Mediterranean trade with Alexandria and Beirut, through which the bulk of Europe's Far Eastern luxury goods continued to pass. Thereafter, however, the Mongols of Persia became more hostile to Westerners, and the Genoese finally abandoned Tabriz after attacks made their position there untenable. Then, in 1346, the Mongols of the Golden Horde besieged the Genoese colony at Caffa on the Black Sea, an event memorable because it became a conduit for the Black Death, which was passed from the Mongol army to the Genoese defenders, who transmitted it to western Europe (see Chapter 10).

The window of opportunity that made Marco Polo's travels possible was thus relatively small. By the middle of the fourteenth century, divisions among the various parts of the Mongol Empire were already making travel along the Silk Road perilous. After 1368, when the last Mongol dynasty in China was overthrown, most Westerners were excluded from the empire now ruled by the new Ming Dynasty. The overland trade routes from China to the Black Sea continued to operate, but Europeans had no easy access to them.

The integrated world that Mongol rule had briefly created continued to exercise a lasting effect on Europe, despite the relatively short time during which Europeans themselves were able to participate directly in it. European memories of the Far East would be preserved, and the dream of reestablishing close connections between Europe and China would survive to influence a new round of European commercial and imperial expansion from the late fifteenth century onward.

THE RISE OF THE OTTOMAN EMPIRE

Like the Mongols, the Turks were initially a nomadic people whose economy depended on raiding. They were already established in northwestern Anatolia when the Mongols arrived there, and were slowly converting to Islam. But unlike the established Muslim powers in the region, whom the Mongols weakened and ultimately destroyed, the Turks were the principal beneficiaries of the Mongol conquest. For when the Mongols toppled the Seljuk sultanate of Anatolia and the Abbasid caliphate of Baghdad, they eliminated the two traditional authorities that had previously kept Turkish border chieftains like the Ottomans in check. Now they were free to raid, unhindered, along the soft frontiers of Byzantium. At the same time, they remained far enough from the centers of Mongol authority to avoid being destroyed themselves.

The Conquest of Constantinople

By the end of the thirteenth century, members of the Ottoman clan had established themselves as leaders among the Turks of the Anatolian frontier. By the mid-fourteenth century, they had guaranteed their preeminence by capturing a number of important cities. These successes brought the Ottomans to the attention of the Byzantine emperor, who hired a contingent of their warriors as mercenaries in 1345. They were extraordinarily successful—so much so that the Eastern Roman Empire could not control their movements. By 1370, the Ottomans had extended their control all the way to the Danube. In 1389, an Ottoman army defeated a powerful coalition of Serbian forces at the battle of Kosovo, enabling them to extend control over Greece, Bulgaria, and the Balkans.

In 1396, the Ottoman army attacked Constantinople itself, but withdrew to repel a Western crusading force that had been sent against it. In 1402, Ottoman forces attacked Constantinople again, but were once more forced to withdraw, this time to confront a Mongolian invasion of Anatolia. Led by Timur the Lame, the Mongols captured the Ottoman sultan and destroyed his army; for the next decade it appeared that Ottoman hegemony over Anatolia might have ended. By 1413, however, Timur was dead and the Ottomans were able to resume their conquests.

Ottoman pressure on Constantinople continued during the 1420s and 1430s, producing a steady stream of Byzantine refugees bound for Italy who brought with them the surviving masterworks of classical Greek literature (see Chapter 12). But it was not until 1451 that the Ottoman sultan, Mehmet II, turned his full attention to the conquest of the imperial city. In 1453, after a brilliantly executed siege, Mehmet succeeded in breaching the walls of Constantinople. The Byzantine emperor was killed in the assault, the city was thoroughly plundered, and its remaining population was sold into slavery. The Ottomans then settled down

SULTAN MEHMET II, "THE CONQUEROR" (r. 1451–81). This portrait, executed by the Ottoman artist Siblizade Ahmed, exhibits features characteristic of both Central Asia and Europe. The sultan's pose—his aesthetic appreciation of the rose, his elegant handkerchief—are indicative of the former, as is the fact that he wears the white turban of a scholar and the thumb ring of an archer. But the subdued coloring and three-quarter profile may reflect the influence of Italian portraiture. ■ *What did the artist achieve through this blending of styles and symbols?* ■ *What messages does this portrait convey?*

to rule their new capital in a style reminiscent of their Byzantine predecessors.

The Ottoman conquest of Constantinople administered a cultural and psychological shock to many European rulers and intellectuals, but its economic impact was minor. Ottoman control over the former Byzantine Empire reduced Europeans' direct access to the Black Sea, but the bulk of the Far Eastern luxury trade with Europe had never passed through Black Sea ports in the first place. Europeans got most of their spices and silks through Venice, which imported them from Alexandria and Beirut, and these two cities did not fall to the Ottomans until the 1520s. So the Ottoman Empire was not necessarily the force that later motivated Portuguese efforts to locate a sea route to India and the Spice Islands. If anything, it was Portuguese access to India, and European attempts to exclude Muslims from the Indian

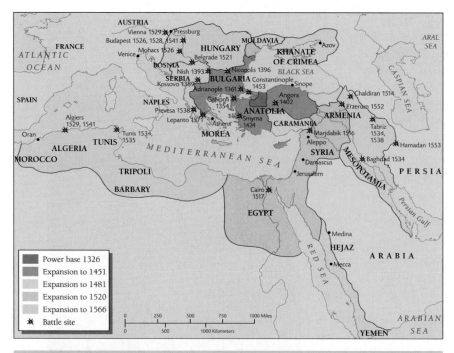

THE GROWTH OF THE OTTOMAN EMPIRE. Consider the patterns of Ottoman expansion. ■ *Where is Constantinople, and how might its capture in 1453 have facilitated further conquests?* ■ *Compare the extent of the Ottoman Empire in 1566 with that of the Byzantine Empire under Justinian (see the map on page 158). How would you account for their similarities?* ■ *How might you explain the fact that the Ottoman Empire did not continue its rapid expansion after 1566?*

spice trade, that helped spur the later Ottoman conquests of Syria, Egypt, and Hungary during the 1520s and 1530s.

But if the practical effects of the Ottoman conquest were modest where western Europe was concerned, the effects on the Turks themselves were transformative. Vast new wealth poured into Anatolia, which the Ottomans increased by carefully tending to the industrial and commercial interests of the city which they called Istanbul—the Turkish pronunciation of the Greek phrase "to/in the city." Trade routes were redirected to feed the capital, and the Ottomans became a naval power in the eastern Mediterranean and the Black Sea. As a result, Constantinople's population grew from fewer than 100,000 in 1453 to more than 500,000 in 1600, making it the largest city in the world outside of China.

War, Slavery, and Social Advancement

Despite the Ottomans' careful attention to commerce, their empire continued to rest on the spoils of conquest until the end of the sixteenth century. In order to manage this continual expansion, the size of the Ottoman army and administration grew exponentially, drawing more and more manpower from the empire. And because the Ottoman army and administration were largely composed of slaves, the demand for more soldiers and administrators could best be met through further conquests that would capture yet more slaves. This in turn required a still larger army and even more extensive bureaucracy—and so the cycle continued. It mirrors, in many respects, the dilemma of the Roman Empire (Chapter 5). Indeed, another way in which the Ottoman Empire resembled that of Rome was in this insatiable demand for slaves.

Not only were slaves the backbone of the Ottoman army and bureaucracy, they were also critical to the lives of the Turkish upper class. One of the important measures of status in Ottoman society was the number of slaves in one's household. After 1453, new wealth permitted some elites to maintain households in the thousands. In the sixteenth century, the sultan alone possessed more than 20,000 slave attendants, not including his bodyguard and elite infantry units, both of which were also composed of slaves.

Where did all of these slaves come from? Many were captured in war. Many others were taken on raiding forays into Poland and Ukraine and shipped to the slave markets of Constantinople. But slaves were also recruited (some willingly, some by coercion) from rural areas of the Ottoman Empire itself. Because the vast majority of slaves were household servants and administrators rather than laborers, some people willingly accepted enslavement, believing that they would be better off as slaves in Constantinople than as impoverished peasants in the countryside. In the Balkans especially, many people were enslaved as children, handed over by their families to pay the "child tax" the Ottomans imposed on rural areas too poor to pay a monetary tribute. Although unquestionably a wrenching experience for families, this practice did open up opportunities for social advancement. Special academies were created at Constantinople to train the most able of the enslaved male children, and some rose to become powerful figures in the Ottoman Empire. Slavery, indeed, carried relatively little social stigma. The sultan himself was most often the son of an enslaved woman.

Analyzing Primary Sources

Ottoman Janissaries

The following account is from a memoir written by Konstantin Mihailovic, a Serbian Christian who was captured as a youth by the army of Sultan Mehmet II. For eight years, he served in the Ottoman janissary ("gate-keeper") corps. In 1463, the fortress he was defending for the Sultan was captured by the Hungarians, after which he recorded his experiences for a Christian audience.

henever the Turks invade foreign lands and capture their people, an imperial scribe follows immediately behind them, and whatever boys there are, he takes them all into the janissaries and gives five gold pieces for each one and sends them across the sea [to Anatolia]. There are about two thousand of these boys. If, however, the number of them from enemy peoples does not suffice, then he takes from the Christians in every village in his land who have boys, having established what is the most every village can give so that the quota will always be full. And the boys whom he takes in his own land are called *cilik*. Each one of them can leave his property to whomever he wants after his death. And those whom he takes among the enemies are called *pendik*. These latter after their deaths can leave nothing; rather, it goes to the emperor, except that if someone comports himself well and is so deserving that he be freed, he may leave it to whomever he wants. And on the boys who are across the sea the emperor spends nothing; rather, those to whom they are entrusted must maintain them and send them where he orders. Then they take those who are suited for it on ships and there they study and train to skirmish in battle. There the emperor already provides for them and gives them a wage. From there he chooses for his own court those who are trained and then raises their wages.

Source: Konstantin Mihailovic, *Memoirs of a Janissary* (Michigan Slavic Translations 3), trans. Benjamin Stolz (Ann Arbor, MI: 1975), pp. 157–59.

Questions for Analysis

1. Why might the Ottoman emperor have established this system for "recruiting" and training janissaries? What are its strengths and weaknesses?

2. Based on your knowledge of Western civilizations, how unusual would you deem this method of raising troops? How does it compare to the strategies of other rulers we have studied?

Because Muslims were not permitted to enslave other Muslims, the vast majority of Ottoman slaves were Christian—although many eventually converted to Islam. And because so many of the elite positions within Ottoman government were held by these slaves, the paradoxical result was that Muslims, including the Turks themselves, were effectively excluded from the main avenues of social and political influence in the Ottoman Empire. Nor was this power limited to the government and the army. Commerce and business also remained largely in the hands of non-Muslims, most frequently Greeks, Syrians, and Jews. Jews in particular found in the Ottoman Empire a welcome refuge from the persecutions and expulsions that had characterized Jewish life in late-medieval Europe. After their expulsion from Spain in 1492, more than 100,000 Spanish (Sephardic) Jews ultimately immigrated to the territories of the Ottoman Empire.

Religious Conflicts

The Ottoman sultans were Sunni Muslims who lent staunch support to the religious and legal pronouncements of the Islamic schools in their realm. When Ottomans captured the cities of Medina and Mecca in 1516, they also became the defenders of the two principal holy sites of Islam. Soon after, they captured Jerusalem and Cairo, too, putting an end to the Mamluk sultanate of Egypt and becoming the keepers of the Holy Land. In 1538, accordingly, the Ottoman ruler formally adopted the title of caliph, thereby declaring himself to be the legitimate successor of Muhammad.

In keeping with Sunni traditions, the Ottomans were tolerant of non-Muslims, especially during the fifteenth and sixteenth centuries. They organized the major religious groups of their empire into legally recognized units

OTTOMAN ORTHODOXY. This genealogical chart is designed to show the descent of Sultan Mehmet III (r. 1595–1603) from his own illustrious ancestors—both warriors and scholars—as well as from Muhammad, whose central image is piously veiled. ▪ *Why was it desirable for the Ottoman sultans to proclaim themselves caliphs, too, and therefore heirs to Muhammad?* ▪ *How might this have increased the hostility between the Sunni Turks and the Shi'ite Muslims of neighboring Persia?*

support from their Orthodox Christian subjects, even during their wars with the Christians of western Europe. The Ottomans' principal religious conflicts were therefore not with their own subjects, but with the Shi'ite Muslim dynasty that ruled neighboring Persia. Time and again during the sixteenth century, Ottoman expeditions into western Europe had to be abandoned when hostilities erupted with the Persians.

The Ottomans and Europe

For a variety of reasons, the contest between the Ottoman Empire and the rulers of western Europe never lived up to the rhetoric of holy war that both sides employed in their propaganda. In Europe, especially, there were internal divisions that frustrated any attempts to mount a unified campaign. By the sixteenth century, as we shall see (Chapters 13 and 14), Catholic and Protestant sects were turning that same crusading rhetoric against one another. But even before that, Christian military initiatives were ineffectual. In 1396, a Western crusader army was annihilated by the Ottomans at the battle of Nicopolis, and Ottoman armies besieged Vienna several times during the following two centuries.

But apart from these few dramatic events, conflicts between the Ottomans and the rulers of western Europe were fought out mainly through pirate raids and naval battles in the Mediterranean. The result was a steady escalation in the scale and cost of navies. In 1571, when a combined Habsburg and Venetian force defeated the Ottoman fleet at Lepanto, more than 400 ships took part, with both sides deploying naval forces ten times larger than they had possessed half a century before. Although undeniably a victory for the Habsburgs and their Venetian allies, the battle of Lepanto was far less decisive than is often suggested. The Ottoman navy was speedily rebuilt; and by no means did Lepanto put an end to Ottoman influence over the eastern Mediterranean Sea.

Moreover, both Ottoman and Habsburg interests soon shifted away from their conflict with each other. The Ottomans embarked on a long and costly war with Persia, while the Spanish Habsburgs turned their attention toward their new empire across the Atlantic. By the mid-seventeenth century, when a new round of conflicts began, the strength of the Ottoman Empire had been sapped by the tensions that arose within the empire itself as it ceased to expand. Although it would last until 1918 (see Chapter 24), it was in no position to rival the global hegemony that European powers were beginning to achieve.

and permitted them considerable rights of self-government. After 1453, when they gained control of Constantinople, the Ottomans were particularly careful to protect and promote the authority of the Greek Orthodox patriarch of Constantinople. As a result, the Ottomans enjoyed staunch

EUROPEAN EXPLORATION AND COLONIALISM

During the fifteenth century, Europeans focused their commercial ambitions more and more on the western Mediterranean and Atlantic. As we noted above, this reorientation can be attributed only partially to the rising power of the Ottoman Empire. It was more significantly the product of two related developments: the growing importance of the African gold trade and the growth of European colonial empires in the western Mediterranean.

The Search for African Gold

The European trade in African gold was not new. It had been going on for centuries, facilitated by Muslim middlemen whose caravans brought it from the Niger River to the North African ports of Algiers and Tunis. In the thirteenth century, Catalan and Genoese merchants established trading colonies in Tunis to expedite this process, exchanging woolen cloth from northern Europe for North African grain and sub-Saharan gold.

But the demand for gold was greatly accelerated during the fourteenth century, when a silver shortage began to affect the entire European economy. Silver production—which enabled the circulation of coinage in Europe—fell markedly as Europeans reached the limits of their technological capacity to extract ore from deep mines. This shortfall was compounded during the fifteenth century by a serious cash-flow problem: more European silver was moving east in the spice trade than could now be replenished from extant sources. Gold therefore represented an obvious alternative currency for large transactions, and in the thirteenth century some European rulers began minting gold coins. But Europe itself had few natural gold reserves. To maintain and expand gold coinages, therefore, new and larger supplies of gold were needed. The most obvious source was Africa.

The Mediterranean Empires of Catalonia, Venice, and Genoa

European interest in the African gold trade coincided with the creation of entrepreneurial empires in the Mediterranean. During the thirteenth century, the Catalans had conquered and colonized a series of western Mediterranean islands, including Majorca, Ibiza, Minorca, Sicily, and Sardinia. Except in Sicily, the pattern of Catalan exploitation was largely the same on all these islands: expulsion or extermination of the existing population, usually Muslim; the extension of economic concessions to attract new settlers; and a heavy reliance on slave labor to produce foodstuffs and raw materials for export.

These new colonial efforts were mainly carried out by private individuals operating under royal charters. They therefore contrast strongly with older patterns of Venetian colonization, which had long been controlled directly by the city's rulers, and which focused mainly on the eastern Mediterranean where the Venetians dominated the trade in spices and silks. The Genoese, to take yet another case, had extensive interests in the western Mediterranean, where they traded bulk goods such as cloth, hides, grain, timber, and sugar. But Genoese colonies tended to be more informal than either Venetian or Catalan colonies, constituting family networks rather than an extension of state sovereignty. The Genoese were also more closely integrated with the societies of North Africa, Spain, and the Black Sea than were their Venetian or Catalan counterparts.

Genoese colonists pioneered the production of sugar and sweet wines in the western Mediterranean and later in the Atlantic islands off the west coast of Africa, particularly

SPANISH GALLEON. The larger, full-bottomed ships that came into use during the fifteenth century would become engines of imperial conquest—and the vessels that brought the riches of those conquests back to Europe. This wooden model was made for the Museo Storico Navale di Venezia (Naval History Museum) in Venice.

Madeira. Meanwhile, they moved away from reliance on the oared galleys favored by the Venetians and began to use larger, fuller-bodied sailing ships that could carry greater volumes of cargo. With further modifications to accommodate the rougher sailing conditions of the Atlantic Ocean, these were the ships that would carry sixteenth-century Europeans around the globe.

From the Mediterranean to the Atlantic

For centuries, European maritime commerce had been divided between a Mediterranean and a northeastern Atlantic world. Starting around 1270, however, Italian merchants began to sail through the Strait of Gibraltar and on up to the wool-producing regions of England and the Netherlands. This was a step toward the extension of Mediterranean patterns of commerce into the Atlantic Ocean. Another step was the discovery (or possibly the rediscovery) of the Atlantic island chains known as the Canaries and the Azores, which Genoese sailors reached in the fourteenth century. Efforts to colonize the Canary Islands, and to convert and enslave their inhabitants, began almost immediately. But an effective conquest of these islands did not really begin until the fifteenth century, when it was undertaken by Portugal and completed by Castile. The Canaries, thereafter, became the base from which further Portuguese voyages down the west coast of Africa proceeded. They were also the jumping-off point from which Christopher Columbus would sail westward across the Atlantic Ocean in the hope of reaching Asia.

Naval Technology and Navigation

These new European empires of the fifteenth and sixteenth centuries rested on a mastery of the oceans and demanded new naval technologies. The Portuguese caravel—the workhorse ship of the fifteenth-century voyages to Africa—was based on designs that had been in use among Portuguese fishermen since the thirteenth century. Starting in the 1440s, however, Portuguese shipwrights began building larger caravels of about 50 tons displacement with two masts, each carrying a triangular (lateen) sail. Columbus's *Niña* was of this design, although it was refitted with two square sails to enable it to sail more efficiently before the wind during an Atlantic crossing. Such ships required much smaller crews than did the multi-oared galleys that were still commonly used in the Mediterranean. By the end of the fifteenth century, even larger caravels of around 200 tons were being constructed, with a third mast and a combination of square and lateen sails.

Europeans were also making significant advances in navigation during the fifteenth and sixteenth centuries. Quadrants, which could calculate latitude in the Northern Hemisphere by the height of the North Star above the horizon, were in widespread use by the 1450s. As sailors approached the equator, however, the quadrant became less and less useful, and navigators instead made use of astrolabes, which reckoned latitude by the height of the sun. Like quadrants, astrolabes had been known in western Europe for centuries. But it was not until the 1480s that the astrolabe became a really useful instrument for seaborne navigation, with the preparation of standard tables sponsored by the Portuguese crown. Compasses, too, were coming into more widespread use during the fifteenth century. Longitude, however, remained impossible to calculate accurately until the eighteenth century, when the invention of the marine chronometer finally made it possible to keep accurate time at sea. In this earlier era, Europeans sailing east or west across the oceans generally had to rely on their skill at dead reckoning to determine where they were on the globe.

European sailors also benefited from a new interest in maps and navigational charts. Especially important to Atlantic sailors were books known as *rutters* or *routiers*. These contained detailed sailing instructions and descriptions of the coastal landmarks a pilot could expect to encounter en route to a variety of destinations. Mediterranean sailors had used similar books since at least the fourteenth century: known as *portolani*, or portolan charts, they mapped the ports along the coastlines, tracked prevailing winds and tides, and warned

PORTOLAN CHART. Maritime maps like this one were crucial navigational aids, and came to be widely used outside the Mediterranean in the fifteenth century. This chart, made by Vesconte Maggiolo in 1541, plainly shows the Mediterranean and Atlantic coastlines of Europe and North Africa.

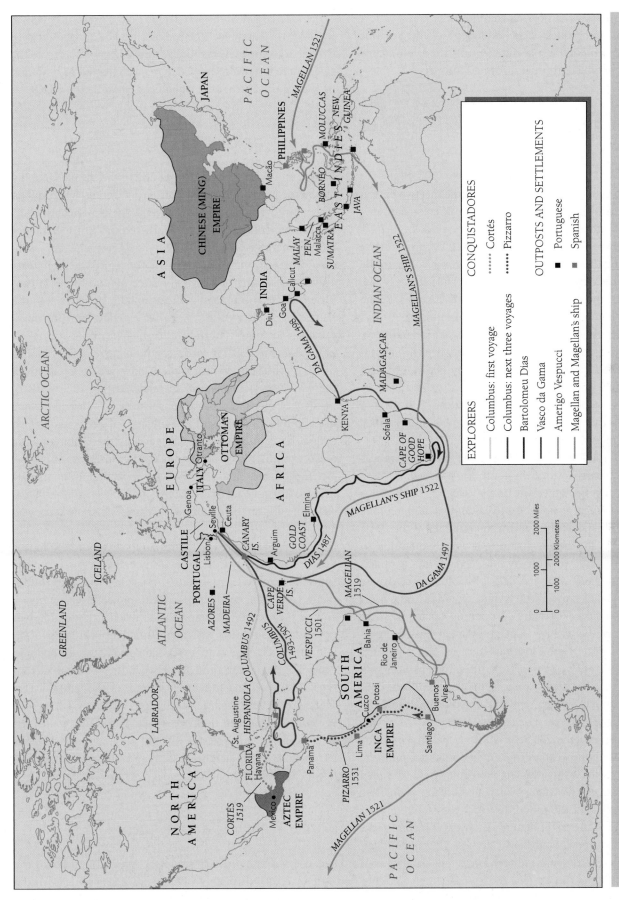

OVERSEAS EXPLORATION IN THE FIFTEENTH AND SIXTEENTH CENTURIES. ■ *What were the major routes taken by European explorers of the fifteenth and sixteenth centuries?* ■ *What were the explorers' main goals?* ■ *How might the establishment of outposts in Africa, America, and the East Indies have radically altered the balance of power in the Old World, and why?*

EXPLORERS

— Columbus: first voyage
— Columbus: next three voyages
— Bartolomeu Dias
— Vasco da Gama
— Amerigo Vespucci
— Magellan and Magellan's ship

CONQUISTADORES

····· Cortés
····· Pizarro

OUTPOSTS AND SETTLEMENTS

■ Portuguese
■ Spanish

of reefs and shallow harbors. In the fifteenth century, these map-making techniques were extended to the Atlantic Ocean; by the end of the sixteenth century, the accumulated knowledge contained in rutters spanned the globe.

Portugal, Africa, and the Sea Route to India

As we have seen, it was among the Portuguese that two critical interests—the African gold trade and Atlantic colonization—first came together. Their successes were rapid. In 1415, a Portuguese expedition captured the North African port of Ceuta. During the 1420s, the Portuguese colonized both the island of Madeira and the Canary Islands. During the 1430s, they extended these colonization efforts to the Azores. By the 1440s, they had reached the Cape Verde Islands off Africa's west coast. In 1444, Portuguese explorers first landed on the West African mainland, in the area between the Senegal and the Gambia river mouths, where they began to collect cargoes of gold and slaves for export back to Portugal. By the 1470s, Portuguese sailors had rounded the West African "bulge" and were exploring the Gulf of Guinea. In 1483, they reached the mouth of the Congo River.

In 1488, the Portuguese captain Bartolomeu Dias was accidentally blown around the southern tip of Africa by a gale, after which he named the point "Cape of Storms." But the king of Portugal, João II (r. 1481–95), took a more optimistic view of Dias's achievement: he renamed it the Cape of Good Hope and began planning a naval expedition to India. In 1497–98, accordingly, Vasco da Gama rounded the cape and then, with the help of a Muslim navigator named Ibn Majid, crossed the Indian Ocean to Calicut on the southwestern coast of India, opening up for the first time a sea route between Europe and the Far Eastern spice trade. Although da Gama lost half his fleet and one-third of his men on this two-year voyage, his cargo of spices was so valuable that his losses were deemed insignificant. His heroism became legendary, and his story became the basis for the Portuguese national epic, the *Lusiads*.

Now masters of the quickest route to riches in the world, the Portuguese swiftly capitalized on da Gama's accomplishment. Portuguese trading fleets sailed regularly to India after 1500. In 1509, the Portuguese defeated an Ottoman fleet and then blockaded the mouth of the Red Sea, attempting to cut off one of the traditional routes by which spices had traveled to Alexandria and Beirut, in order to monopolize trade. By 1510, Portuguese military forces had established a series of forts along the western Indian coastline, including their headquarters at Goa. In 1511, Portuguese ships seized Malacca, a center of the spice trade on the Malay peninsula. By 1515, they had reached the Spice Islands and the coast of China. So completely did the Portuguese now dominate the spice trade that even the Venetians were forced to buy their pepper in the Portuguese capital of Lisbon by the 1520s.

Artillery and Empire

Larger, more maneuverable ships and improved navigational aids made it possible for the Portuguese and other European mariners to reach Africa, Asia, and the Americas by sea. But fundamentally, these sixteenth-century European commercial empires were a military achievement. As such, they reflected what Europeans had learned in their wars against each other during the fourteenth and fifteenth centuries. Perhaps the most critical military advance was the increasing sophistication of artillery, a development made possible not only by gunpowder but by improved metallurgical techniques for casting cannon barrels. By the middle of the fifteenth century, as we observed in Chapter 10, the use of artillery pieces had rendered the stone walls of medieval castles and towns obsolete, a fact brought home in 1453 by the successful French siege of Bordeaux (which ended the Hundred Years' War), and by the Ottoman siege of Constantinople (which ended the Byzantine Empire).

Indeed, the new ship designs were important in part because their larger size made it possible to mount more effective guns on them. European vessels were now conceived as floating artillery platforms, with scores of guns mounted in fixed positions along their sides and swivel guns mounted fore and aft. These guns were vastly expensive, as were the ships that carried them; but for those rulers who could afford them, such ships made it possible to project military power around the world. Just being able to reach a destination was not enough; although Vasco da Gama had been able to sail into the Indian Ocean in 1498, the Portuguese did not gain control of that ocean until 1509, when they defeated a combined Ottoman and Indian naval force at the battle of Div. Thus, Portuguese trading outposts in Africa and Asia also became fortifications, built not so much to guard against the attacks of native peoples as to ward off assaults from other Europeans. Without this essential military component, European maritime empires could not have existed.

Prince Henry the Navigator

Because we know that Portuguese expeditions down the African coast ultimately opened up a sea route to India and the Far East, it is tempting to presume that this was their goal from the beginning. Hence the traditional narrative of these events presents exploration as their mission, India as their goal, and Prince Henry the Navigator (1394–1460) as the guiding genius behind them. But it was only a generation after Henry's death, in the 1480s, that India became the target toward which these voyages were directed. Before this time, Portuguese involvement in Africa was driven instead by much more traditional goals: crusading ambitions against the Muslims of North Africa; the desire to establish direct links with the sources of African gold production south of the Sahara Desert; the desire to colonize the Atlantic islands; the burgeoning market for slaves in Europe and in the Ottoman Empire; and the hope that they might find the kingdom of the legendary Prester John.

Still, Prince Henry remains a central figure in the history of Portuguese exploration. He personally directed eight of the thirty-five Portuguese voyages to Africa that occurred during his lifetime, and he played an important part in organizing the Portuguese colonization of Madeira, the Canary Islands, and the Azores. He also pioneered the Portuguese slave trade, first on the Canaries (whose population was almost entirely eradicated) and then along the Senegambian coast of western Africa. His main motivation was to outflank the cross-Saharan African gold trade by intercepting this trade at its source. This was also his reason for colonizing the Canary Islands, which he saw as a staging ground for expeditions into the African interior. He was therefore a man of his time rather than one ahead of his time: a crusader against Islam, a lord seeking resources to support his followers, and an aspiring merchant who hoped to make a killing in the gold trade but instead found his main profits in slaving.

Atlantic Colonization and Slave Networks

Although slavery had effectively disappeared in much of northwestern Europe by the early twelfth century, slavery continued in Iberia, Italy, and elsewhere in the Mediterranean world. It existed, however, on a small scale; there were no slave-powered factories or large-scale agricultural systems in this period. The major slave markets and slave economies, as we have noted, were in the Ottoman Empire. And, as had been the case since antiquity, no aspect of this slave trade was racially based. Most slaves of this era were European Christians, predominantly Poles, Ukrainians, Greeks, and Bulgarians; in previous eras, they had been Germanic and Celtic peoples.

What was new about slavery in the fifteenth century, then, was its racialization—an aspect of modern slavery that has made an indelible impact on our own society. To Europeans, African slaves were visibly distinctive in ways that other slaves were not, and it became convenient for those who dealt in them to justify the mass deportation of entire populations by alleging their racial inferiority and their "natural" fitness for a life of bondage. This nefarious practice has had long-lasting and tragic consequences.

From as early as the mid-fifteenth century, Lisbon began to emerge as a significant market for enslaved Africans. Something on the order of 15,000 to 20,000 men and women were sold there within a twenty-year period during Prince Henry's lifetime. In the following half century, the numbers amounted to perhaps 150,000. For the most part, the purchasers of these slaves regarded them as status symbols; it became fashionable to have African footmen, page boys, and ladies' maids. In the Atlantic colonies—Madeira, the Canaries, and the Azores—land was worked mainly by European settlers and sharecroppers. Slave labor, if employed at all, was generally used only in sugar mills. On Madeira and the Canaries, where sugar became the predominant cash crop during the last quarter of the fifteenth century, some slaves were therefore introduced. But even sugar production did not lead to the widespread introduction of slavery on these islands.

However, a new kind of slave-based sugar plantation began to emerge in Portugal's Atlantic colonies in the 1460s, starting on the Cape Verde Islands and then extending southward into the Gulf of Guinea. These islands were not populated when the Portuguese began to settle them, and their climate generally discouraged most Europeans from living there. They were ideally located, however, along the routes of slave traders venturing outward from the nearby West African coast. It was this plantation model that would be exported to Brazil by the Portuguese and to the Caribbean islands of the Americas by their Spanish conquerors, with devastating consequences.

NEW WORLD ENCOUNTERS

When King Ferdinand and Queen Isabella of Spain decided to underwrite a voyage of exploration, they were hoping to steal some thunder from the successful Portuguese ventures of the past half century. For it was clear that tiny Portugal would soon dominate the sea-lanes if rival entrepreneurs did not attempt to find alternate routes. Hence the bold—and ill-informed—decision to reach Asia by sailing west. Like his contemporaries, the sailor called Christoffa Corombo (in his own Genoese dialect) understood that the world

Discoveries

Of course, Columbus was not the first European to set foot on the American continents. As we noted in Chapter 7, Viking sailors briefly settled present-day Newfoundland, Labrador, and perhaps even portions of New England around the year 1000. But knowledge of these Viking landings had been forgotten or ignored outside of Iceland for hundreds of years. Moreover, the tiny Scandinavian colonies on Greenland had been abandoned by the fifteenth century, when the cooling of the climate (Chapter 10) destroyed the fragile ecosystems that had barely sustained the lives of Norse settlers there.

Although Columbus brought back no Asian spices to prove that he had found an alternate route on his voyages, he did return with some small samples of gold and a few indigenous people—whose existence gave promise of entire tribes that might be "saved" (by conversion to Christianity) and enslaved by Europeans. This provided sufficient incentive for the Spanish monarchs to finance three more expeditions by Columbus, and many more by others. Soon the mainlands of two hitherto unknown continents were identified, as were clusters of new islands. Gradually, Europeans reached the conclusion that what they had encountered was an entirely "New World," and one that had—shockingly—never been foretold either by the teachings of Christianity or the wisdom of the ancients. Awareness of this fact was most widely publicized by the Italian explorer and geographer Amerigo Vespucci (1454–1512), whose name was soon adapted as a descriptor for the new continents (see **Interpreting Visual Evidence** on page 281).

At first, the realization that this world was not, in fact, an outpost of Asia came as a disappointment to the Spanish: two major land masses and two vast oceans disrupted their plans to beat the Portuguese to the Spice Islands. But this sense of frustration began to lift in 1513, when Vasco Núñez de Balboa first viewed the Pacific Ocean from the Isthmus of Panama. Thereafter, Ferdinand and Isabella's grandson, the Holy Roman Emperor Charles V, renewed their dream: he accepted Ferdinand Magellan's proposal to see whether a route to Asia could be found by sailing around South America.

But Magellan's voyage of 1519 demonstrated beyond question that the globe was simply too large for any such plan to be feasible. Of the five ships that left Spain under his command, only one returned, three years later, having been forced to circumnavigate the globe. Out of a crew of 265 sailors, only eighteen survived. Most had died of scurvy or starvation; Magellan himself had been killed in a skirmish with native peoples in the Philippines.

This fiasco ended all hope of discovering an easy southwest passage to Asia—although the deadly dream of a

THE AZTEC CITY OF TENOCHTITLÁN. The Spanish conquistador Bernal Díaz del Castillo (1492–1585) took part in the conquest of the Aztec Empire and later wrote an account of his adventures. His admiring description of the Aztec capital at Tenochtitlán records that the Spaniards were amazed to see a huge city built in the midst of a vast lake, with gigantic buildings arranged in a meticulous urban plan around a central square, and broad causeways linking the city to the mainland. This hand-colored woodcut was included in an early edition of Hernando Cortés's letters to Emperor Charles V, printed at Nuremberg (Germany) in 1524.

was a sphere. But like them, he also thought it was much smaller than it actually is. (As we saw in Chapter 4, the accurate calculation of the globe's circumference, made in ancient Alexandria, had been suppressed centuries later by the Roman geographer Ptolemy.) Furthermore, it had been accepted since antiquity that there were only three continents: Europe, Asia, and Africa.

What made the scheme seem plausible to Ferdinand and Isabella was, first, the discovery and colonization of the Canary Islands and the Azores, which had reinforced the hypothesis that the Atlantic was dotted with islands all the way to Japan; and second, the Genoese mariner's egregious miscalculation of the earth's size, which convinced him that he could reach Japan and China in about a month's clear sailing after leaving the Canary Islands. The man we know as Christopher Columbus (1451–1506) never realized his mistake. When he reached the Bahamas and the island of Hispaniola in 1492, after only a month's sailing, he returned to Spain and reported that he had reached the outer islands of Asia.

Interpreting Visual Evidence

America as an Object of Desire

Under the influence of Mandeville's *Book of Marvels* and a host of other popular narratives, Columbus and his fellow voyagers were prepared to find the New World full of cannibals. They also assumed that the indigenous peoples' custom of wearing little or no clothing—not to mention their "savagery"—would render their women sexually available. In the letters he sent back to Europe, Columbus recounts one notable encounter with a "cannibal girl" whom he had taken captive in his tent. Her wantonly naked body aroused his desire, yet she resisted his advances so fiercely that he had to tie her up—which of course made it easier for him to "subdue" her. In the end, he cheerfully reports, the girl's sexual performance was so satisfying that she might have been trained, as he put it, in a "school for whores."

The Flemish artist Jan van der Straet (1523–1605) would have heard many such reports of the encounters between (mostly male) Europeans and the peoples of the New World. This engraving, based on one of his drawings, is among the thousands of mass-produced images that circulated widely in Europe, thanks to the invention of printing. It imagines the first encounter between a male "Americus" (like Columbus, or Amerigo Vespucci himself) and the New World, "America," depicted as a voluptuous, available woman. The Latin caption reads: "America rises to meet Americus; and whenever he calls her, she will always be aroused."

Americen Americus retexit, & Semel vocauit inde semper excitam.

Questions for Analysis

1. The New World itself—America—is imagined as female in this image. Why is this? What messages might this—and the suggestive caption—have conveyed to a European viewer?

2. Study the details of this image carefully. What does each symbolize, and how do they work together as an allegory of conquest and colonization?

3. On what stereotypes of indigenous peoples does this image draw? Notice, for example, the cannibalistic campfire of the group in the background, or the enticing posture of "America."

northwest passage survived, and motivated many European explorers of North America into the twentieth century. It has been revived today: in our age of global warming, the retreat of Arctic pack ice has led to the opening of new shipping lanes, and in 2008 the first commercial voyage successfully traversed the Arctic Ocean.

The Spanish Conquest of America

Although the discovery of two continents was initially construed as a setback, it quickly became clear that this New World had great wealth of its own. From the start, Columbus's gold samples, in themselves rather paltry, had nurtured

A Spanish Critique of New World Conquest

Not all Europeans approved of European imperialism or its "civilizing" effects on the peoples of the New World. One of the most influential contemporary critics was Bartolomé de las Casas (1474–1566), who left his home city of Seville at the age of eighteen, joined the Dominican order, and eventually became bishop of Chiapas (in Mexico). Although he was a product of his times—he owned many slaves—he was also prescient in discerning the devastating effects of European settlement in the West Indies and Central America, and he particularly deplored the exploitation and extermination of indigenous populations. The following excerpt is from one of the many eloquent manifestos he published in an attempt to gain the sympathies of the Spanish crown and to reach a wide readership. It was printed in 1542.

God made all the peoples of this area, many and varied as they are, as open and as innocent as can be imagined. The simplest people in the world—unassuming, long-suffering, unassertive, and submissive—they are without malice or guile, and are utterly faithful and obedient both to their own native lords and to the Spaniards in whose service they now find themselves.... They are innocent and pure in mind and have a lively intelligence, all of which makes them particularly receptive to learning and understanding the truths of our Catholic faith and to being instructed in virtue; indeed, God has invested them with fewer impediments in this regard than any other people on earth....

It was upon these gentle lambs ... that from the very first day they clapped eyes on them the Spanish fell like ravening wolves upon the fold, or like tigers and savage lions who have not eaten meat for days. The pattern established at the outset has remained unchanged to this day, and the Spaniards still do nothing save tear the natives to shreds, murder them, and inflict upon them untold misery, suffering, and distress, tormenting, harrying, and persecuting them mercilessly....

When the Spanish first journeyed there, the indigenous population of the island of Hispaniola stood at some three million; today only two hundred survive. The island of Cuba, which extends for a distance almost as great as that separating Valladolid from Rome, is now to all intents and purposes uninhabited; and two other large, beautiful, and fertile islands, Puerto Rico and Jamaica, have been similarly devastated. Not a living soul remains today on any of the islands

hopes that gold might lie piled in ingots somewhere in these vast new lands, ready to enrich any European adventurer who discovered them. Rumor fed rumor, until a few free-lance Spanish soldiers really did strike it rich beyond their most avaricious imaginings. Between 1519 and 1521, the *conquistador* (Spanish for "conqueror") Hernándo Cortés, accompanied by a force of only 600 men, unwittingly contributed to the destruction of the Aztec Empire of Mexico and was accordingly on hand to plunder its rulers' fabulous wealth. Then in 1533, another conquistador, Francisco Pizarro, spearheaded efforts that toppled the highly centralized South American empire of the Incas and seized its great stores of gold and silver. His force numbered only 180. Despite the sophistication and enormous resources of these two extra-

SPANISH CONQUISTADORS IN MEXICO. This sixteenth-century drawing of conquistadors slaughtering the Aztec aristocracy emphasizes the advantages that plate armor and steel weaponry gave to European soldiers.

of the Bahamas . . . even though every single one of the sixty or so islands in the group . . . is more fertile and more beautiful than the Royal Gardens in Seville and the climate is as healthy as anywhere on earth. The native population, which once numbered some five hundred thousand, was wiped out by forcible expatriation to the island of Hispaniola, a policy adopted by the Spaniards in an endeavour to make up losses among the indigenous population of that island. . . .

At a conservative estimate, the despotic and diabolical behaviour of the Christians has, over the last forty years, led to the unjust and totally unwarranted deaths of more than twelve million souls, women and children among them. . . .

The reason the Christians have murdered on such a vast scale and killed anyone and everyone in their way is purely and simply greed. . . . The Spaniards have shown not the slightest consideration for these people, treating them (and I speak from first-hand experience, having been there from the outset) not as brute animals—indeed, I would to God they had done and had shown them the consideration they afford their animals—so much as piles of dung in the middle of the road. They have had as little concern for their souls as for their bodies, all the millions that have perished having gone to their deaths with no knowledge of God and without the benefit of the Sacraments. One fact in all this is widely known and beyond dispute, for even the tyrannical murderers themselves acknowledge the truth of it: the indigenous peoples never did the Europeans any harm whatever. . . .

Source: Bartolomé de la Casas, *A Short Account of the Destruction of the Indies*, trans. Nigel Griffin (Harmondsworth: 1992), pp. 9–12.

Questions for Analysis

1. Given his perspective on the behavior of his countrymen, how might Bartolomé de las Casas have justified his own presence in New Spain (Mexico)? What do you think he may have hoped to achieve by publishing this account?

2. What comparisons does the author make between the New Spain and the Old, and between indigenous peoples and Europeans? What is he trying to convey?

3. Compare this account with the contemporary engraving on page 281. What new light does this excerpt throw on that visual allegory? How might a reader-viewer of the time have reconciled these two very different pictures of European imperialism?

ordinary civilizations—the Aztec capital of Tenochtitlán (*ten-och-tit-LAN*, now Mexico City) rivaled any European city in size and amazed its conquerors by the height and grandeur of its buildings—Cortés and Pizarro had the advantage. They had cannons, firearms, steel swords, armor, and horses: all unknown to the native peoples of the Americas. But a more potent weapon turned out to be their own germs and the indigenous peo-ples' extreme susceptibility to infectious European diseases, which had already weakened these populations as a result of their earlier contacts with explorers and settlers following in the wake of Columbus. Those peoples who survived were promised liberation from the oppressive regimes of the Aztecs and Incas—little knowing how much worse their new oppressors would be.

The Profits of Empire

Cortés and Pizarro captured hoards of gold and silver that had been accumulated for centuries by the indigenous peoples of Mexico and Peru. Almost immediately, however, a search for the sources of these precious metals was launched. The first gold deposits were discovered on Hispaniola, where surface mines were speedily established using native laborers, who died in appalling numbers from disease, brutality, and overwork. Of the approximately 1 million native inhabitants who had welcomed Columbus in 1492, only 100,000 survived by 1510: 90 percent of the population had died within a generation. By 1538, there were fewer than 500 left alive.

With the loss of so many workers, the mines of Hispaniola became uneconomical to operate, and the European colonists turned instead to cattle raising and sugar production. Modeling their sugarcane plantations on those of the Cape Verde Islands and St. Thomas (São Tomé) in the Gulf of Guinea, colonists began to import thousands of African slaves to labor in the new industry. Sugar production was, by its nature, a capital-intensive undertaking. The need to import slave labor added further to its costs, guaranteeing that control over the new industry would fall into the hands of a few extremely wealthy planters and financiers. Meanwhile, cattle ranching on the Mexican mainland had a devastating effect on the fragile ecosystem of Central America.

Yet mining continued to shape the Spanish colonies of Central and South America in fundamental ways. Gold was the lure that had initially drawn the Spanish to the New World, but silver became their most lucrative export. Even before the discovery of vast silver deposits north of Mexico City and at Potosí in Bolivia, between 1543 and 1548, the Spanish crown had taken steps to assume direct control over its new colonies' wealth. It was therefore to the Spanish crown that the profits from these astonishingly productive mines accrued. Potosí quickly became the most important mining town in the world. By 1570, it numbered 120,000 inhabitants, despite being located at an altitude of 15,000 feet, where the temperature never climbs above 59°F. As on Hispaniola, enslaved native laborers died by the tens of thousands in these mines and in the disease-infested boomtowns that surrounded them.

Thereafter, new mining techniques made it possible to produce even greater quantities of silver, though at the cost of still greater mortality among the native laborers. Between 1571 and 1586, silver production at Potosí quadrupled, reaching a peak in the 1590s, when 10 million ounces of silver per year were arriving in Spain from the Americas. (In the 1540s, the corresponding figure was only 1.5 million ounces.) By contrast, the peak years of domestic European silver production yielded only about 3 million ounces of silver per year between 1525 and 1535, and this figure dropped steadily from about 1550 on.

Europe's silver shortage therefore came to an end during the sixteenth century, but the silver that now circulated there came almost entirely from the New World. And this massive infusion of silver into the European economy accelerated an inflation that had already begun in the late fifteenth century. Initially, it had been driven by the renewed growth of the European population, an expanding economy, and a relatively fixed supply of food. From the 1540s on, however, inflation was largely the product of the greatly increased supply of coinage that was now entering the

After You Read This Chapter

Visit StudySpace for quizzes, additional review materials, and multi-media documents. **wwnorton.com/studyspace**

REVIEWING THE OBJECTIVES

- The conquests of the Mongols made a significant impact on Europe. What were some key effects?
- The Ottomans' dependence on slavery had a number of notable consequences. What were they?
- Colonialism and overseas exploration were driven by an array of factors. Identify some of the main economic and technological changes that occurred during the fourteenth and fifteenth centuries.
- In what ways did the practice of slavery and its justification change in the fifteenth century?
- The "discovery" of the New World had profound effects on the Old World, as well as on the indigenous peoples of the Americas. Describe some of these effects.

European economy. The result was a rapid rise in prices. Although the effects of this were felt throughout Europe, Spain was particularly hard hit. Prices doubled between 1500 and 1560, and they doubled again between 1560 and 1600. These price spikes in turn undermined the competitiveness of Spanish industries. Then, when the flow of New World silver slowed dramatically during the 1620s and 1630s, the Spanish economy collapsed.

After 1600, when smaller quantities of New World silver were entering the European economy, prices rose more slowly. But the price of grain still ballooned to five or six times the level of the previous century by 1650, producing social dislocation and widespread misery for many of Europe's poorest inhabitants (see Chapter 14). In England, for example, the period between about 1590 and 1610 was the most desperate the country had experienced since the Great Famine, nearly three hundred years before. As the population rose and wages fell, living standards declined dramatically. Indeed, if we compute living standards by dividing the price of an average basket of food by the average daily wage of a common laborer, then standards of living were lower in England at the beginning of the modern era than they had been at any time during the Middle Ages. It is no wonder, then, that so many Europeans found emigration to the Americas a tempting prospect.

CONCLUSION

By 1600, commerce, colonization, and overseas conquest had profoundly changed both Europe and the wider world. Even though Europeans had little direct contact with China after the fall of the Mongol Empire, the economy of Europe was still closely tied to that of Asia through the trade routes maintained by the Ottoman Empire. At the same time, the emergence of Portugal and Spain as Europe's leading long-distance traders was moving the center of economic gravity away from the Mediterranean toward the Atlantic. Displaced by Ottoman Constantinople from its role as the principal conduit for the spice trade, Venice gradually declined, while the Genoese moved increasingly into the world of finance, backing the commercial ventures of other powers, particularly Spain, whose Atlantic ports bustled with vessels and shone with wealth. By the mid-seventeenth century, however, both Spain and Portugal had become the victims of their own success. They would retain their American colonies until the nineteenth century, but it would be the Dutch, the French, and especially the English who would establish the most successful European empires in North America, Asia, Africa, and Australia. Meanwhile, these and other developments were moving Italy to the center of European affairs for the first time since the fragmentation of the Roman Empire. How this happened is the subject of Chapter 12.

PEOPLE, IDEAS, AND EVENTS IN CONTEXT

- What circumstances enabled **MARCO POLO**'s travels in the East? Why was the period of commercial contact between the **MONGOL EMPIRE** and Europe so brief?

- What forces drove the **OTTOMAN EMPIRE** to expand its reach? Why was the Ottoman caliph more tolerant of Jews and Christians than of dissent within Islam?

- What set the **GENOESE** entrepreneurs apart from other colonial powers in the Mediterranean?

- How does **PRINCE HENRY THE NAVIGATOR** exemplify the motives for pursuing overseas expansion, as well as the mythology that has grown up around these early efforts?

- What were the expectations that launched **COLUMBUS**'s voyage? Why were **FERDINAND AND ISABELLA** of Spain motivated to finance it?

- What advantages did the Spanish **CONQUISTADORS** have over the native peoples of the **AMERICAS**? What were the immediate effects of European conquest?

CONSEQUENCES

- How do the patterns of conquest and colonization discussed in this chapter compare to those of earlier periods, particularly those of antiquity? Which developments seem new? Which are familiar?

- In what ways did the slave trade of the Atlantic world differ from the slave economies of antiquity? How might Europeans have used Greek and Roman justifications of slavery in defense of these new ventures? (See Chapters 4 and 5.)

- How important a role does technology play in the developments we have surveyed in this chapter? In your view, which technological innovation was of the greatest historical significance, and why?

CHRONOLOGY

1304–1374	Lifetime of Petrarch
1377	The papacy returns to Rome
1378–1417	The Great Schism
1434	The Medici family comes to rule Florence
1440	Lorenzo Valla debunks the "Donation of Constantine"
1453	The fall of Constantinople prompts a diaspora of Greek scholars
1455	Invention of the printing press
1492	Columbus's first voyage
1498	Leonardo da Vinci's *The Last Supper*
1511	Raphael's *The School of Athens*
1512	Michelangelo completes the Sistine ceiling
1513	Niccolò Machiavelli's *The Prince*
1514	Albrecht Dürer's *Saint Jerome*
1516	Thomas More publishes *Utopia* Erasmus completes his new translation of the New Testament
1528	Castiglione's *Book of the Courtier*

Before You Read This Chapter

Renaissance Ideals and Realities, c. 1350–1550

CORE OBJECTIVES

- **DEFINE** the movement known as the Renaissance.

- **EXPLAIN** why the Renaissance began in Italy.

- **IDENTIFY** the principle characteristics of Renaissance art.

- **UNDERSTAND** the relationship between Renaissance ideals and political realities.

- **DESCRIBE** the ways in which the Renaissance of northern Europe differed from that of Italy.

Rummaging through some old books in a cathedral library, an Italian bureaucrat attached to the papal curia at Avignon was surprised to find a manuscript of Cicero's letters—letters that no living person had known to exist. They had probably been copied in the time of Charlemagne, and had then been forgotten for hundreds of years. How many other works of this great Roman orator had met the same fate? he wondered. And how many more books might still remain to be discovered? Clearly, thought Francesco Petrarca (1304–1374), he was living in an age of ignorance. A great gulf seemed to open up between his own time and that of the ancients: a middle age that separated him from those well-loved models.

For centuries, Christian intellectuals had regarded "the middle ages" as the time between Adam's expulsion from Eden and the birth of Christ. But now, Petrarca redefined that concept and applied it to his own era. According to him, this "dark age" was not the pagan past but the time that separated him from direct communion with the classics. Yet this did not stop him from trying to bridge the gap. "I would have written to you long ago," he wrote in a Latin letter to the Greek poet Homer (dead for over two thousand years), "had it not been for the fact that we lack a common language."

Petrarca (known to English-speakers as Petrarch) would become famous in his own day as an Italian poet, a Latin stylist, and a tireless advocate for the resuscitation of classical antiquity. The values that he and his contemporaries began to espouse would give rise to a new intellectual and artistic movement in Italy, a movement strongly critical of the present and admiring of a past that had disappeared with the fragmentation of Rome's empire and the end of Italy's greatness. We know this movement as the Renaissance, the French word for "rebirth" that was applied to it in the nineteenth century. It has since become shorthand for the epoch following the Middle Ages, but it is really a parallel phenomenon—as the overlapping chronologies of this chapter and the two previous chapters show. Talking about the Renaissance is therefore a way of talking about some significant changes in education and outlook that transformed the culture of Italy from the late fourteenth to the early sixteenth centuries, and which eventually influenced the rest of Europe in important ways.

MEDIEVAL OR RENAISSANCE?

The term *renaissance* has usually been taken literally, as though the cultural accomplishments of antiquity had ceased to be appreciated and imitated, and therefore needed to be "reborn." Yet we have been tracing the enduring influence of classical civilization throughout the Middle Ages for many chapters, and we have noted the reverence accorded to Aristotle, Virgil, Cicero, and a host of other figures, as well as the persistence of Roman law and Roman institutions. It is also misleading to characterize the Renaissance as rejecting the fervent Christianity of the Middle Ages, and as a return to the pagan past: however much the scholars and artists of this age loved the pagan classics, none saw them as superseding Christianity. Indeed, all discussions of "the Renaissance" must be qualified by the fact that there was no single set of Renaissance ideals, and must recognize that these ideals were constantly reshaped and determined by political, social, and economic realities.

Renaissance Classicism

Renaissance thinkers and artists were enormously diverse in their attitudes, achievements, and approaches. That said, one can certainly find distinguishing traits that make the concept of a "Renaissance" meaningful. With respect to knowledge of the classics, for example, there was a significant quantitative difference between the learning of the Middle Ages and that of the Renaissance. Medieval scholars knew many Roman authors—especially Virgil, Ovid, and Cicero—but the discovery of "new" works by Livy, Tacitus, and Lucretius expanded the classical canon considerably. Equally important was the recovery of Greek literature. In the twelfth and thirteenth centuries, as we have seen (Chapters 8 and 9), Greek scientific and philosophical works became available to western Europeans thanks to increased contact with Islam; but no Greek poems or plays were available in Latin translations, and neither were the major dialogues of Plato. Nor could more than a handful of western Europeans read the language of ancient Greece. But as the Ottoman Turks put increasing pressure on the shrinking borders of the Byzantine Empire (Chapter 11), more and more Greek-speaking intellectuals fled to Italy, bringing their books and their knowledge with them.

Renaissance thinkers not only knew many more classical texts, they used them in new ways. Medieval intellectuals had long regarded ancient sources as complementing and confirming their own assumptions. By contrast, the new reading methods of the Renaissance fostered an increased awareness of the conceptual gap that separated their contemporary world from that of antiquity. At the same time, the structural similarities between ancient Greek poleis and the city-states of Italy encouraged political theorists to use these ancient forms of government as models. This firm determination to learn from antiquity was even more pronounced in the realms of architecture and art, areas in which classical models contributed most strikingly to the creation of a distinctive Renaissance style.

Finally, although Renaissance culture was by no means pagan, it was more overtly materialistic and more commercialized. For one thing, the competition among and within Italian city-states fostered a culture of display and conspicuous consumption. The relative weakness of the Church in Italy also contributed to the growth of secular power and a more worldly outlook. Italian bishoprics were small and relatively powerless compared to those north of the Alps, and Italian universities were much more independent of ecclesiastical supervision than those elsewhere. Even the papacy—restored to Rome after Petrarch's death—was severely limited, not the least because the papacy's role as a political rival in central Italy compromised its moral authority. All these factors fostered the emergence of new aesthetics and aspirations.

Renaissance Humanism

The most basic of Renaissance intellectual ideals is summarized in the term *humanism*. This was a program of study that aimed to replace the scholastic emphasis on logic and metaphysics with the study of language, literature, rhetoric, history, and ethics. The humanists also preferred ancient literature to the writings of more recent authors. Although some wrote in both Latin and the vernacular, most humanists regarded contemporary vernacular literature as a lesser diversion for the uneducated; serious scholarship and praiseworthy poetry could be written only in Latin or Greek. Latin, moreover, had to be the classical Latin of Cicero and Virgil, not the evolving, changing Latin of the universities and the Church.

Renaissance humanists therefore condemned the living Latin of their scholastic contemporaries as a barbarous departure from ancient (and therefore "correct") standards of Latin style. Despite their belief that they were thereby reviving the study of the classics, the humanists actually contributed to Latin's demise. By insisting on ancient standards of grammar, syntax, and diction, they turned Latin into a fossilized language that ceased to have any direct relevance to daily life. They thus hastened, ironically and unwittingly, the ultimate triumph of the various European vernaculars as languages of intellectual and cultural life, while bringing about the death of Latin as a common European language.

Humanists were convinced that their own educational program was the best way to produce virtuous citizens and able public officials. And because women were excluded from Italian political life, the education of women was therefore of little concern to most humanists, although some aristocratic women did acquire humanist training. Here again there are paradoxes: for as more and more Italian city-states fell into the hands of autocratic rulers, the humanist educational curriculum lost its immediate connection to the republican ideals of Italian political life. Nevertheless, humanists never lost their conviction that the study of the "humanities" (as the humanist curriculum came to be known) was the best way to produce political leaders.

THE RENAISSANCE OF ITALY

Although the Renaissance eventually became a Europe-wide intellectual and artistic movement, it developed first and most distinctively in Italy. Understanding why this happened is important not only to explaining the origins of this movement, but also to understanding its essential characteristics.

The most fundamental reason was that, after the Black Death, northern Italy became the most urbanized region of Europe. Moreover, Italian aristocrats customarily lived in urban centers rather than in rural castles, and consequently became more fully involved in urban public affairs than their counterparts north of the Alps. Elsewhere in Europe, moreover, most aristocrats lived on the income from their landed estates, while rich town dwellers gained their living from trade; but in Italy, many town-dwelling aristocrats engaged in banking or mercantile enterprises while many rich mercantile families imitated the manners of the aristocracy. The noted Florentine family the Medici, for example, originally came from the rustic region north of Florence. But they eventually made a fortune in banking and commerce, and were able to assimilate into the aristocracy.

The results of these developments are tied to the history of the new humanist education mentioned above. Not only was there great demand for the skills of reading and accounting necessary to become a successful merchant in Italy, but the richest and most prominent families sought to find teachers who would impart to their sons the knowledge

POPE JULIUS II (r. 1503–13). This portrait of one of the most powerful popes of the Renaissance—it was he who commissioned Michelangelo's paintings in the Sistine Chapel—was executed by Raffaello Sanzio da Urbino, known as Raphael (1483–1520). The acorns atop the posts of the throne are visual puns on the pope's family name, della Rovere ("of the oak"). ■ *What impression of the pope's personality does this portrait convey?*

Competing Viewpoints

The Humanists' Educational Program

These three selections illustrate the confidence placed by humanists in their elite educational program, and their conviction that it would be of supreme value to the state as well as to the individual students who pursued it. Not everyone agreed with the humanists' claims, however, and a good deal of self-promotion lies behind them.

Vergerius on Liberal Studies

We call those studies *liberal* which are worthy of a free man; those studies by which we attain and practice virtue and wisdom; that education which calls forth, trains, and develops those highest gifts of body and of mind which ennoble men, and which are rightly judged to rank next in dignity to virtue only. . . . It is, then, of the highest importance that even from infancy this aim, this effort, should constantly be kept alive in growing minds. For . . . we shall not have attained wisdom in our later years unless in our earliest we have sincerely entered on its search. [P. P. Vergerius (1370–1444), "Concerning Excellent Traits."]

Alberti on the Importance of Literature

Letters are indeed so important that without them one would be considered nothing but a rustic, no matter how much a gentlemen [he may be by birth]. I'd much rather see a young nobleman with a book than with a falcon in his hand. . . .

Be diligent, then, you young people, in your studies. Do all you can to learn about the events of the past that are worthy of memory. Try to understand all the useful things that have been passed on to you. Feed your minds on good maxims. Learn the delights of embellishing your souls with good morals. Strive to be kind and considerate [of others] when conducting civil business. Get to know those things human and divine that have been put at your disposal in books for good reason. Nowhere [else] will you find . . . the elegance of a verse of Homer, or Virgil, or of some other excellent poet. You will find no field so delightful or flowering as in one of the orations of Demosthenes, Cicero, Livy, Xenophon, and other such pleasant and perfect orators. No effort is more fully compensated . . . as the constant reading and rereading of good things. From such reading you will rise rich in good maxims and good arguments, strong in your ability to persuade others and get them to listen to you; among the citizens you will willingly be heard, admired, praised, and loved. [Leon Battista Alberti (1404–1472), "On the Family."]

---

and skills necessary to cutting a figure in society and speaking with authority in public affairs. Consequently, Italy produced a large number of lay educators, many of whom also demonstrated their learning by producing political and ethical treatises and works of literature. Italian schools and tutors accordingly turned out the best-educated urban elites in all of Europe, men who became wealthy, knowledgeable patrons ready to invest in the cultivation of new ideas and new forms of literary and artistic expression.

A second reason why late-medieval Italy was the birthplace of an intellectual and artistic movement has to do with its vexed political situation. Unlike France, England, Spain, and the kingdoms of Scandinavia and eastern Europe, Italy had many competing political institutions, the most important of which—the papacy and the Holy Roman Empire—based their claims on different sources of authority. Italians therefore looked to the classical past for their time of unity and glory, dreaming of a day when Rome

Bruni on the Humanist Curriculum

The foundations of all true learning must be laid in the sound and thorough knowledge of Latin: which implies study marked by a broad spirit, accurate scholarship, and careful attention to details. Unless this solid basis be secured it is useless to attempt to rear an enduring edifice. Without it the great monuments of literature are unintelligible, and the art of composition impossible. To attain this essential knowledge we must never relax our careful attention to the grammar of the language, but perpetually confirm and extend our acquaintance with it until it is thoroughly our own. . . .

But the wider question now confronts us, that of the subject matter of our studies, that which I have already called the realities of fact and principle, as distinct from literary form. . . . First among such studies I place History: a subject which must not on any account be neglected by one who aspires to true cultivation. . . . For the careful study of the past enlarges our foresight in contemporary affairs and affords to citizens and to monarchs lessons . . . in the or-

dering of public policy. From History, also, we draw our store of examples of moral precepts. . . .

The great Orators of antiquity must by all means be included. Nowhere do we find the virtues more warmly extolled, the vices so fiercely decried. From them we may learn, also, how to express consolation, encouragement, dissuasion, or advice. . . .

Familiarity with the great poets of antiquity is essential to any claim to true education. For in their writings we find deep speculations upon Nature, and upon the Causes and Origins of things, which must carry weight with us both from their antiquity and from their authorship. . . .

Proficiency in literary form, not accompanied by broad acquaintance with facts and truths, is a barren attainment; whilst information, however vast, which lacks all grace of expression would seem to be put under a bushel or partly thrown away. . . . Where, however, this double capacity exists—breadth of learning and grace of style—we allow the highest title to distinction and to abiding

fame. . . . [Leonardo Bruni (1369–1444), *"Concerning the Study of Literature."*]

Sources: Vergerius and Bruni: William Harrison Woodward, ed., *Vittorino da Feltre and Other Humanist Educators* (London: 1897), pp. 96–110, 124–29, 132–33. Alberti: Eric Cochrane and Julius Kirshner, eds., *University of Chicago Readings in Western Civilization.* Vol. 5: *The Renaissance* (Chicago: 1986), pp. 81–82.

Questions for Analysis

1. What is the purpose of education, according to these authorities? What elements do their programs share? What are their potential areas of contention?

2. Why did humanists such as Leonardo Bruni consider the study of history essential to education?

would be, again, the center of the world. They boasted that ancient Roman monuments were omnipresent in their landscape, and that classical Latin literature referred to cities and sites they recognized as their own.

Italians were particularly intent on reappropriating their classical heritage because they were seeking to establish an independent cultural identity that could help them oppose the intellectual and political supremacy of France. The removal of the papacy to Avignon for most of the fourteenth

century and the subsequent Great Schism (Chapter 10) had heightened antagonism between the city-states of Italy and the burgeoning nation-states and empires of the Continent. This coincided with a rejection of the scholasticism taught in northern Europe's universities, and the embrace of the intellectual alternatives offered by new readings of classical sources. As Roman literature and learning took hold in the imaginations of Italy's intellectuals, so too did Roman art and architecture, for Roman models could help Italians create an artistic alternative to French Gothic, just as Roman learning offered an intellectual alternative to the scholasticism of Paris.

Finally, the Italian Renaissance could not have occurred without the underpinning of Italian wealth gained through the increasing commercial ventures described in Chapter 11. This meant that talented men seeking employment and patronage were more likely to stay at home than to seek opportunities abroad. Investment in art and learning also arose from an intensification of urban pride and the growing concentration of individual and family wealth in urban areas. Cities themselves became primary patrons of artists and scholars in the fourteenth century. During the fifteenth century, however, when most city-states succumbed to the hereditary rule of powerful dynasties, patronage was monopolized by the princely aristocracy. Among these great princes were the popes in Rome, who controlled the Papal States and for a few decades made Rome the artistic capital of Europe.

LITERARY AND INTELLECTUAL ACTIVITY

We have already encountered the man who strove to leave behind "the middle age" of his own time, and who is therefore considered the founder of the Renaissance movement: Francesco Petrarca (1304–1374). Petrarch was a trained cleric, but he believed that the scholastic theology taught in universities was misguided, because it concentrated on abstract speculation rather than the achievement of virtue and ethical conduct. Instead, he felt that the truly Christian writer must cultivate literary eloquence, and so inspire others to do good through the pursuit of beauty and truth. For him, the best models of eloquence were to be found in the classical texts of Latin literature, which were doubly valuable because they were also filled with ethical wisdom. Petrarch dedicated himself, therefore, to rediscovering such texts and to writing his own poems and moral treatises in a Latin style modeled on that of classical authors. But Petrarch was also a prolific vernacular poet. His Italian sonnets—which spawned a new literary genre—were written in praise of his semi-fictional beloved, Laura, in the chivalrous style of the troubadours. They were widely admired and imitated, inspiring poets in other European vernaculars. William Shakespeare (1564–1616) would later adopt the form.

Petrarch's ultimate ideal for human conduct was a solitary life of contemplation. But subsequent Italian thinkers and scholars, located mainly in Florence, developed a different vision of life's true purpose. For them, the goal of classical education was civic. Humanists such as Leonardo Bruni (c. 1370–1444) and Leon Battista Alberti (1404–1472) agreed with Petrarch on the importance of eloquence and the value of classical literature, but they also taught that man's nature equipped him for action, for usefulness to his family and society, and for serving the state: ideally, a city-state after the Florentine model. In their view, ambition and the quest for glory were noble impulses that ought to be encouraged and channeled toward these political and social ends. They also refused to condemn the accumulation of material possessions, arguing that the history of human progress is inseparable from the human dominion of the earth and its resources.

Many of the humanists' civic ideals are expressed in Alberti's treatise *On the Family* (1443), in which he argued that the nuclear family is the fundamental unit of the city-state and should be governed in such a way as to further the city-state's political, social, and economic goals. Alberti accordingly argued that the family should mirror the city-state's own organization, and he thus consigned women—who, in reality, governed the household—to child-bearing, child-rearing, and subservience to men. He asserted, furthermore, that women should play no role whatsoever in the public sphere. Although such dismissals of women's abilities were fiercely resisted by actual women, the humanism of the Renaissance was characterized by a pervasive denigration of them—a denigration often mirrored in the works of the classical literature these humanists so much admired.

The Emergence of Textual Scholarship

The humanists of Florence also went far beyond Petrarch in their knowledge of classical (especially Greek) literature and philosophy. In this they were aided by a number of Byzantine scholars who had migrated to Italy in the first half of the fifteenth century and who gave instruction in the language. There were also attempts on the part of Italians to acquire Greek masterpieces for themselves, which often involved journeys back to Constantinople. In 1423, for example, one adventurous scholar managed to bring back 238 manuscript books, among them rare works of Sophocles, Euripides, and Thucydides, all of which were quickly paraphrased in Latin and thus made accessible to western Europeans for the first time. By 1500, most of the Greek classics, including the writings of Plato, the dramatists, and the historians, had been translated and were more widely available than they had ever been, even in their own day.

Analyzing Primary Sources

Machiavelli's Patriotism

These passages are from the concluding chapter of Machiavelli's treatise The Prince. *Like the book itself, they are addressed to Lorenzo de' Medici, head of Florence's most powerful family. Here, Machiavelli laments Italy's "barbarian occupation" by foreign powers, by which he means the invading armies of France, Spain, and the Holy Roman Empire. He may also be alluding to the many companies of foreign mercenaries that fought for Italy's various city-states.*

eflecting on the matters set forth above and considering within myself whether the times were propitious in Italy at present to honor a new prince and whether there is at hand the matter suitable for a prudent and virtuous leader to mold in a new form, giving honor to himself and benefit to the citizens of the country, I have arrived at the opinion that all circumstances now favor such a prince, and I cannot think of a time more propitious for him than the present. If, as I said, it was necessary in order to make apparent the virtue of Moses, that the people of Israel should be enslaved in Egypt, and that the Persians should be oppressed by the Medes to provide an opportunity to illustrate the greatness and the spirit of Cyrus, and that the Athenians should be scattered in order to show the excellence of Theseus, thus at the present time, in order to reveal the valor of an Italian spirit, it was essential that Italy should fall to her present low estate, more enslaved than the Hebrews, more servile than the Persians, more disunited than the Athenians,

leaderless and lawless, beaten, despoiled, lacerated, overrun and crushed under every kind of misfortune. . . . So Italy now, left almost lifeless, awaits the coming of one who will heal her wounds, putting an end to the sacking and looting in Lombardy and the spoliation and extortions in the Realm of Naples and Tuscany, and cleanse her sores that have been so long festering. Behold how she prays God to send her someone to redeem her from the cruelty and insolence of the barbarians. See how she is ready and willing to follow any banner so long as there be someone to take it up. Nor has she at present any hope of finding her redeemer save only in your illustrious house [the Medici] which has been so highly exalted both by its own merits and by fortune and which has been favored by God and the church, of which it is now ruler. . . .

This opportunity, therefore, should not be allowed to pass, and Italy, after such a long wait, must be allowed to behold her redeemer. I cannot describe the joy with which he will be received in all these provinces which have suffered so much from the foreign deluge, nor with

what thirst for vengeance, nor with what firm devotion, what solemn delight, what tears! What gates could be closed to him, what people could deny him obedience, what envy could withstand him, what Italian could withhold allegiance from him? THIS BARBARIAN OCCUPATION STINKS IN THE NOSTRILS OF ALL OF US. Let your illustrious house then take up this cause with the spirit and the hope with which one undertakes a truly just enterprise. . . .

Source: Niccolò Machiavelli, *The Prince,* trans. and ed. Thomas G. Bergin (Arlington Heights, IL: 1947), pp. 75–76, 78.

Questions for Analysis

1. Why does Machiavelli argue that Italy needed the type of ruler he described in *The Prince?*

2. According to Machiavelli, what was wrong with the Italy of his own day? What does "patriotism" mean for him?

3. How does Machiavelli use historical precedents and parallels to make his argument?

This influx of new texts spurred a new interest in textual criticism. A pioneer in this activity was Lorenzo Valla (1407–1457). Born in Rome and active primarily as a secretary to the king of Naples and Sicily, Valla had no allegiance to the republican ideals of the Florentine humanists. Instead, he turned his skills to the painstaking analysis of Greek and Latin texts in order to show how the thorough study of language could discredit old assumptions about these texts' meanings, and even unmask some texts as forgeries. For example, papal propagandists argued that the papacy's claim to secular power in Europe derived from rights granted to the bishop of Rome by the emperor Constantine in the fourth century, enshrined in the so-called Donation of Constantine. By analyzing the language

Interpreting Visual Evidence

The Blending of Classical and Christian

The paintings known today as *The Birth of Venus* (image A) and *The Madonna of the Pomegranate* (image B) were both executed by Sandro Botticelli in Florence in the years 1485–87. Separately and together, they exhibit the artist's signature devotion to blending classical and Christian motifs. For example, Neoplatonic philosophers like Ficino taught that all pagan myths prefigure Christian truths—including the story that Aphrodite, goddess of love, was miraculously engendered from the foam of the sea by the god of Time. This helps to explain the visual reference to a pomegranate in the painting of the Virgin

A. *The Birth of Venus.*

of this spurious document, Valla proved that it could not have been written in the time of Constantine because it contained more recent Latin usages and vocabulary. He concluded that it had in fact been the work of a papal supporter active many centuries after Constantine's death.

This demonstration not only discredited the more traditional methods of scholasticism, it introduced the concept of anachronism into all subsequent textual study and historical thought. Indeed, Valla also applied his expert knowledge of Greek to elucidating the meaning of Saint Paul's holding the infant Jesus. In Greek mythology, the pomegranate was the fruit whose seeds were eaten by Persephone, daughter of the goddess of fertility, when she was sent to the Underworld to become the bride of Hades. Because she had eaten six of these seeds, Persephone was allowed to return to her mother Demeter for only part of the year; in the winter months, consequently, the Earth becomes less fertile, because Demeter is in mourning for her child.

Questions for Analysis

1. Some scholars have argued that *The Birth of Venus* can be read as an allegory of Christian love that also prefigures the Blessed Virgin's immaculate conception and sinless nature. How would you go about proving this? What elements in this painting and in the myth of Aphrodite's birth lend themselves to that interpretation?

2. In what ways can the cyclical story of Jesus's death and resurrection, which Christians celebrate each year, be linked to the Greek myth invoked by *The Madonna of the Pomegranate*?

3. Like many artists, Botticelli used the same models for an array of different pictures. Do you recognize the resemblance between the Virgin and Venus? How does the depiction of the same young woman in these two different contexts underscore the relationship between pagan mythology and Christian sacred history?

B. *The Madonna of the Pomegranate.*

letters, which he believed had been obscured by Jerome's Latin translation (Chapter 6). This work was to prove an important link between Italian Renaissance scholarship and the subsequent Christian humanism of the north, which in turn fed into the Reformation (see Chapter 13).

Renaissance Neoplatonism

In the wake of these discoveries, Italian thought became dominated by a new interest in the philosophy of Plato (Chapter 4) and the Neoplatonism of Plotinus (Chapter 6). So many intellectuals were engaged in the study of Plato that scholars used to believe that there was even a "Platonic Academy" in Florence; but in reality, the work of intellectuals like Marsilio Ficino (1433–1499) and Giovanni Pico della Mirandola (1463–1494) was informally fostered by the patronage of the wealthy Cosimo de' Medici.

From the standpoint of posterity, Ficino's greatest achievement was his translation of Plato's works into Latin, which made them widely available to Europeans. Ficino's Platonic philosophy moved away from the ethics of civic humanism. He taught that the individual should look primarily to the salvation of the immortal soul from its "always miserable" mortal body: a very Platonic idea. His disciple

Pico likewise rejected the mundanity of public affairs, arguing that man has the capacity to achieve union with God through the exercise of his unique individual talents, a glory that can be attained in life as well as in death.

The Influence of Machiavelli

The greatness of these humanist scholars lay not in their originality but in their efforts to popularize aspects of ancient thought. And none of them was so influential in this regard as the era's greatest philosophical pragmatist, the Florentine Niccolò Machiavelli (1469–1527). Machiavelli's political writings both reflect the unstable condition of Italy and strive to address it. By the end of the fifteenth century, Italy had become the arena of bloody international struggles. Both France and Spain had invaded the peninsula and were competing for the allegiance of the Italian city-states, which in turn were torn by internal dissension.

In 1498, Machiavelli became a prominent official in the government of the new Florentine Republic, set up four years earlier when the French invasion had led to the expulsion of the Medici. His duties largely involved diplomatic missions to other Italian city-states. While in Rome, he became fascinated with the attempt of Cesare Borgia, son of Pope Alexander VI, to create his own principality in central Italy. He noted with approval Cesare's ruthlessness and his complete subordination of personal ethics to political ends. In 1512, when the Medici returned to overthrow the fledgling republic of Florence, Machiavelli was stripped of his position. Disappointed and embittered, he retired to the country and devoted his energies to the articulation of a new political philosophy that he hoped would earn him a powerful job.

On the surface, Machiavelli's two great works of political analysis appear to contradict each other. In his *Discourses on Livy*, which drew on the works of that Roman historian, he praised the ancient Roman Republic as a model for his own contemporaries, lauding constitutional government, equality among citizens,

THE STATES OF ITALY, c. 1494. This map shows the divisions of Italy on the eve of the French invasion in 1494. Contemporary observers often described Italy as being divided among five great powers: Milan, Venice, Florence, the Papal States, and the Kingdom of the Two Sicilies (based in Naples). ▪ *Which of these powers would have been most capable of expanding their territories?* ▪ *Which neighboring states would have been most threatened by such attempts at expansion?* ▪ *Why would Florence and the Papal States so often find themselves in conflict with each other?*

and the subordination of religion to the service of the state. There is little doubt, in fact, that Machiavelli was a committed believer in the free city-state as the ideal form of human government. But Machiavelli also wrote *The Prince*, "a handbook for tyrants" in the eyes of his critics, and he dedicated this work to Lorenzo, son of Piero de' Medici, whose family had overthrown the Florentine republic that Machiavelli himself had served.

Because *The Prince* has been so much more widely read than the *Discourses*, interpretations of Machiavelli's political thought have often mistaken the former as an endorsement of power for its own sake. Machiavelli's real position was quite different. In the political chaos of early-sixteenth-century Italy, Machiavelli saw the likes of Cesare Borgia as the only hope for revitalizing the spirit of independence among his contemporaries, and so making Italy fit, eventually, for self-governance. However dark his vision of human nature, Machiavelli never ceased to hope that his Italian contemporaries would rise up, expel their French and Spanish conquerors, and restore ancient traditions of liberty and equality. He regarded a period of despotism as a necessary step toward that end, not as a permanent and desirable form of government.

Machiavelli remains a controversial figure. Some modern scholars, like many of his own contemporary readers, see him as disdainful of conventional morality, interested solely in the acquisition and exercise of power as an end in itself. Others see him as an Italian patriot, who viewed princely tyranny as the only way to liberate Italy from its foreign conquerors. Still others see him as influenced by Saint Augustine, who understood that in a fallen world populated by sinful people, a ruler's good intentions do not guarantee that his policies will have good results. Accordingly, Machiavelli insisted that a prince's actions must be judged by their consequences and not by their intrinsic moral quality. He argued that "the necessity of preserving the state will often compel a prince to take actions which are opposed to loyalty, charity, humanity, and religion. . . . So far as he is able, a prince should stick to the path of good. But, if the necessity arises, he should know how to follow evil."

The Ideal of the Courtier

Far more congenial to contemporary tastes than the shockingly frank political theories of Machiavelli were the guidelines for proper aristocratic conduct offered in *The Book of the Courtier* (1528), by the diplomat and nobleman Baldassare Castiglione. This forerunner of modern handbooks of etiquette stands in sharp contrast to earlier treatises on civic humanism. Whereas Bruni and Alberti taught the sober virtues of strenuous service on behalf of the city-state, Castiglione taught how to attain the elegant and seemingly effortless skills necessary for advancement in Italy's princely courts. More than anyone else, Castiglione developed and popularized a set of talents now associated with the "Renaissance man": one accomplished in many different pursuits, witty, canny, and stylish. Castiglione also eschewed the misogyny of the humanists by stressing the ways in which court ladies could rise to influence and prominence through the graceful exercise of their womanly powers. Widely read throughout Europe, Castiglione's *Courtier* set the standard for polite behavior into the nineteenth century.

RENAISSANCE ARTS

Without question, the most enduring legacy of the Italian Renaissance has been the contributions of its artists, particularly those who embraced new techniques and approaches to painting. We have already noted (Chapter 10) the creative and economic opportunities afforded by this medium, which freed artists from having to work on site and on commission: paintings executed on wooden panels are portable—unlike wall paintings—and can be displayed in different settings, reach different markets, and be more widely distributed. To these benefits, the artists of Italy added an important technical ingredient: mastery of a vanishing (one-point) perspective that gave to painting an illusion of three-dimensional space. Fifteenth-century artists also experimented with effects of light and shade, and studied intently the anatomy and proportions of the human body.

Meanwhile, increasing private wealth and the growth of lay patronage opened up new markets and created a huge demand for a diverse array of visual narratives: not only religious images, which were as important as ever, but the depiction of classical subjects. Portraiture also came into its own, as princes and merchants alike sought to glorify themselves and their families. The use of oil paints, a medium that had been pioneered in Flanders, further revolutionized fifteenth-century painting styles. Because oil does not dry as quickly as water-based pigments, a painter can work more carefully, taking time with the more difficult parts of a picture and making corrections as he or she goes along.

Painting in Florence

In the fifteenth century, the majority of the great painters were Florentines. First among them was the precocious Masaccio (1401–1428) who, although he died at the age of twenty-seven, inspired the work of artists for the next

THE IMPACT OF PERSPECTIVE. Masaccio's painting *The Trinity with the Virgin* illustrates the startling sense of depth made possible by observing the rules of perspective.

century. Masaccio's greatness rested on his successful employment of one-point perspective and his use of dramatic lighting effects. Both are evident in his painting of the Trinity, where the body of the crucified Christ appears to be thrust forward by the impassive figure of God the Father, while the Virgin's gaze directly engages the viewer.

Masaccio's best-known successor was Sandro Botticelli (1445–1510), who was equally drawn to classical and Christian subjects. Botticelli excels in depicting graceful motion and the sensuous pleasures of nature. He is most famous today for paintings that evoke classical mythology without any overtly Christian frame of reference. For centuries, indeed, these were taken to be expressions of Renaissance "paganism," but many can be understood as Christian allegories (see *Interpreting Visual Evidence*).

The most technically adventurous and versatile artist of this period was Leonardo da Vinci (1452–1519). Leonardo personifies our ideal of the Renaissance man: he was a painter, architect, musician, mathematician, engineer, and inventor. The illegitimate son of a notary, Leonardo set up an artist's shop in Florence by the time he was twenty-five and gained the patronage of the Medici ruler, Lorenzo the Magnificent. But Leonardo had a weakness: he worked

slowly, and he had difficulty finishing anything. This naturally displeased Lorenzo and other Florentine patrons, who regarded artists as craftsmen who worked on commission, and on their patrons' time—not their own. Leonardo, however, strongly objected to this view; he considered himself to be an inspired, independent innovator. He therefore left Florence in 1482 and went to work for the court of the Sforza dictators in Milan, where he was given freer rein in structuring his time and work (see page 302). He remained there until the French invasion of 1499; he then wandered about, finally accepting the patronage of the French king, Francis I, under whose auspices he lived and worked until his death.

Leonardo's approach to painting was that it should be the most accurate possible imitation of nature. He based his work on his own detailed observations: a blade of grass, the wing of a bird, a waterfall. He obtained human corpses for dissection and reconstructed in drawing the minutest features of anatomy, carrying this knowledge over to his paintings. Indeed, Leonardo was convinced of the essential divinity in all living things. It is not surprising, therefore, that he was a vegetarian and that he went to the marketplace to buy caged birds, which he released to their native habitat. *The Virgin of the Rocks* typifies not only his marvelous technical skill but also his passion for science and his belief in the universe as a well-ordered place. The figures are arranged geometrically, with every stone and plant depicted in accurate detail.

Leonardo's *The Last Supper*, painted on the refectory walls of a monastery in Milan (and now in an advanced state of decay) is a study of human psychology. A serene Christ,

THE VIRGIN OF THE ROCKS. This painting reveals Leonardo's interest in the variety of human faces and facial expressions, and in natural settings.

resigned to his terrible fate, has just announced to his disciples that one of them will betray him. The artist succeeds in portraying the mingled emotions of surprise, horror, and guilt on the faces of the disciples as they gradually perceive the meaning of their master's statement. He also implicated the painting's original viewers in this dramatic scene, since they too dined alongside Christ, in the very same room.

The Venetian and Roman Schools

The innovations of Florentine artists were widely imitated. By the end of the fifteenth century, they had influenced a group of painters active in the wealthy city of Venice, among them Tiziano Vecelli, better known as Titian (c. 1490–1576). Many of Titian's paintings evoke the luxurious, pleasure-loving life of this thriving commercial center. For although they copied Florentine techniques, most Venetian painters showed little of that city's concerns for philosophical issues and religious allegory. Their aim was to appeal to the senses by painting idyllic landscapes and sumptuous portraits of the rich and powerful. In this subordination of form and meaning to color and elegance they may have mirrored the tastes of the men for whom they worked.

Rome, too, became a major artistic center in this era, and a place where the Florentine school exerted a more potent influence. Among its eminent painters was Raffaello Sanzio (1483–1520) or Raphael, a native of Urbino. Although Raphael was influenced by Leonardo, he cultivated a more spiritual and philosophical approach to his subjects, suggestive of Botticelli. As we noted in Chapter 4, his fresco *The School of Athens* depicts both the harmony and the differences of Platonic and Aristotelian thought (see page 86). It also includes a number of Raphael's contemporaries as models. The image of Plato is actually a portrait of Leonardo, while the architect Donato Bramante (c. 1444–1514)

stands in for the geometer Euclid, and Michelangelo for the philosopher Heraclitus.

Michelangelo Buonarroti (1475–1564), who spent many decades in Rome, was actually a native of Florence. If Leonardo was a naturalist, Michelangelo was an idealist, despite the harsh political and material realities of the conditions in which he worked. He was also a polymath: painter, sculptor, architect, poet—and he expressed himself in all these forms with a similar power.

Michelangelo's greatest achievements in painting appear in a single location, the Sistine Chapel of the Vatican palace, yet they are products of two different periods in the artist's life and consequently exemplify two different artistic styles and outlooks on the human condition. More famous are the extraordinary frescoes painted on the ceiling from 1508 to 1512, depicting scenes from the book of Genesis. All the panels in this series, including *The Creation of Adam*, exemplify the young artist's commitment to classical artistic principles. Correspondingly, all affirm the sublimity of the Creation and the heroic qualities of humankind. But a quarter of a century later, when Michelangelo returned to work in the Sistine Chapel, both his style and mood had changed dramatically. In the enormous *Last Judgment*, a fresco done for the Chapel's altar wall in 1536, Michelangelo repudiated classical restraint and substituted a style that communicated the older man's pessimistic conception of humanity. He included himself in it: but unlike Raphael's, his self-portrait is a doomed soul whose flayed skin is all that remains of worldly ambition.

Renaissance Sculpture

Sculpture was not a new medium for artists, the way that oil painting was, but it too was an important area of Renaissance innovation. Statues were not only incorporated into columns or doorways or as effigies on tombs; for the first

THE LAST SUPPER. This fresco on the refectory wall of the monastery of Santa Maria delle Grazie in Milan is a testament to both the powers and limitations of Leonardo's artistry. It skillfully employs the techniques of one-point perspective to create the illusion that Jesus and his disciples are actually dining at the monastery's head table; but because Leonardo had not mastered the techniques of fresco painting, he applied tempera pigments to a dry wall which had been coated with a sealing agent. As a result, the painting's colors began to fade just years after its completion. By the middle of the sixteenth century, it had seriously deteriorated. Large portions of it are now invisible.

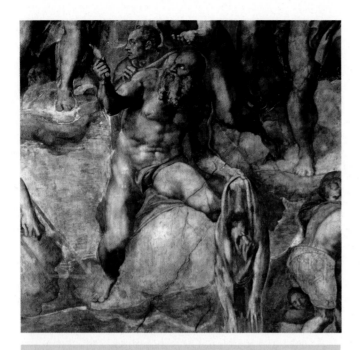

SELF-PORTRAIT OF THE ARTIST AS AN OLD MAN: DETAIL FROM *THE LAST JUDGMENT*. When Michelangelo returned to the Sistine Chapel to paint this fresco on the wall behind the main altar, he emphasized different aspects of humanity: not the youthful heroism of the new-born Adam, but the grotesque weakness of the aging body. Here, St. Bartholomew holds his own flayed skin (tradition held that he had been skinned alive) – but the face is that of Michelangelo himself. ▪ *What is the significance of this change?*

that of Michelangelo—whose *David*, executed in 1501, was a public expression of Florentine ideals, not merely graceful but heroic. Michelangelo regarded sculpture as the most exalted of the arts because it allowed the artist to imitate God most fully in recreating human forms. Furthermore, in Michelangelo's view, the most divinely inspired sculptor disdained slavish naturalism: anyone can make a plaster cast of a human figure, but only an inspired creative genius can endow his sculpted figures with a sense of life. Accordingly, Michelangelo's sculpture subordinated reality to the force of his imagination and sought to express his ideals in ever more astonishing forms. He also insisted on working in marble (the "noblest" sculptural material) and created a figure twice as large as life. By sculpting a serenely confident young man at the peak of physical fitness, Michelangelo celebrated the Florentine republic's own efforts to resist tyrants and uphold ideals of civic justice.

Yet the serenity seen in *David* is no longer prominent in the works of Michelangelo's later life, when (as in his painting) he began to explore the use of anatomical distortion to create effects of emotional intensity. While his statues remained awesome in scale, they also communicate rage, depression, and sorrow. The culmination of this trend is his unfinished but intensely moving *Descent from the Cross*, a depiction of an old man (the sculptor himself) grieving over the distorted, slumping body of the dead Christ.

Renaissance Architecture

To a much greater extent than either sculpture or painting, Renaissance architecture had its roots in the past. The Gothic style pioneered in northern France (Chapter 9) had seldom found a friendly reception in Italy; most of the buildings constructed there during the Middle Ages were Romanesque in style, and the great architects of the Renaissance generally adopted their building plans from these structures—some of which they believed (mistakenly)

time since late antiquity they became figures "in the round." By freeing sculpture from its reliance on architecture, the Renaissance reestablished it as a separate, secular art form.

The first great master of Renaissance sculpture was Donatello (c. 1386–1466). His bronze statue of David, triumphant over the head of the slain Goliath, is the first free-standing nude of the period. Yet this David is clearly an agile adolescent rather than a muscular Greek athlete like

THE CREATION OF ADAM. This is one of a series of frescoes painted on the ceiling of the Sistine Chapel of the Vatican palace in Rome, executed by Michelangelo over a period of many years and in circumstances of extreme physical hardship. It has since become an iconic image. ▪ *How might it be said to capture Renaissance ideals?*

THE POWER AND VULNERABILITY OF THE MALE BODY. Donatello's *David* (left) was the first free-standing nude executed since antiquity. It shows the Hebrew leader as an adolescent youth, and is a little over 5 feet tall. The *David* by Michelangelo (center) stands thirteen feet high, and was placed prominently in front of Florence's city hall to proclaim the city's power and humanistic values. Michelangelo's *Descent from the Cross* (right), which shows Christ's broken body in the arms of the elderly Nicodemus, was made by the sculptor for his own tomb. (The gospels describe Nicodemus as a Pharisee who became a follower of Jesus and who was present at his death.) ▪ *Why would Michelangelo choose this figure to represent himself?* ▪ *How does his representation of David—and the context in which this figure was displayed—compare to that of Donatello?*

to be ancient rather than medieval. They also copied decorative devices from the authentic ruins of ancient Rome.

Renaissance buildings emphasize geometrical proportion. Italian architects of this era, under the influence of Neoplatonism, concluded that certain mathematical ratios reflect the harmony of the universe. For example, the proportions of the human body serve as the basis for the proportions of the quintessential Renaissance building: St. Peter's Basilica in Rome. Designed by some of the most celebrated architects of the time, including Bramante and Michelangelo, it is still one of the largest buildings in the world. Yet it seems smaller than a Gothic cathedral because it is built to human scale. The same artful proportions are evident in smaller-scale buildings, too, as in the aristocratic country houses designed by the northern Italian architect Andrea Palladio (1508–1580), who created secular

miniatures of ancient temples (such as the Roman Pantheon) to glorify the aristocrats who dwelled within them.

The Waning of the Renaissance in Italy

The intensive intellectual and artistic activity that characterizes the Renaissance began to wane toward the end of the fifteenth century. The causes of this decline are varied. The French invasion of 1494 and the incessant warfare that ensued were among the major factors. A second invasion created uninterrupted warfare from 1499 until 1529. Alliances and counteralliances followed each other in bewildering succession, but they managed only to prolong the hostilities. The worst blow came in 1527, when rampaging troops sacked the city of Rome, causing enormous destruction. Only in 1529

Analyzing Primary Sources

Leonardo da Vinci Applies for a Job

Few sources illuminate the tensions between Renaissance ideals and realities better than the résumé of accomplishments submitted by Leonardo da Vinci to a prospective employer, Ludovico Sforza of Milan. In the following letter, Leonardo explains why he deserves to be appointed chief architect and military engineer in the duke's household administration. He got the job, and moved to Milan in 1481.

1. I have the kind of bridges that are extremely light and strong, made to be carried with great ease, and with them you may pursue, and, at any time, flee from the enemy; . . . and also methods of burning and destroying those of the enemy.

2. I know how, when a place is under attack, to eliminate the water from the trenches, and make endless variety of bridges . . . and other machines. . . .

3. . . . I have methods for destroying every rock or other fortress, even if it were built on rock, etc.

4. I also have other kinds of mortars [bombs] that are most convenient and easy to carry. . . .

5. And if it should be a sea battle, I have many kinds of machines that are most efficient for offense and defense. . . .

6. I also have means that are noiseless to reach a designated area by secret and tortuous mines. . . .

7. I will make covered chariots, safe and unattackable, which can penetrate the enemy with their artillery. . . .

8. In case of need I will make big guns, mortars, and light ordnance of fine and useful forms that are out of the ordinary.

9. If the operation of bombardment should fail, I would contrive catapults, mangonels, trabocchi [trebuchets], and other machines of marvelous efficacy and unusualness. In short, I can, according to each case in question, contrive various and endless means of offense and defense.

10. In time of peace I believe I can give perfect satisfaction that is equal to any other in the field of architecture and the construction of buildings. . . . I can execute sculpture in marble, bronze, or clay, and also in painting I do the best that can be done, and as well as any other, whoever he may be.

Having now, most illustrious Lord, sufficiently seen the specimens of all those who consider themselves master craftsmen of instruments of war, and that the invention and operation of such instruments are no different from those in common use, I shall now endeavor . . . to explain myself to your Excellency by revealing to your Lordship my secrets. . . .

Source: Excerpted from Leonardo da Vinci, *The Notebooks,* in *The Italian Renaissance Reader,* eds. Julia Conaway and Mark Mosa (Harmondsworth: 1987), pp. 195–96.

Questions for Analysis

1. Based on the qualifications highlighted by Leonardo in this letter, what can you conclude about the political situation in Milan and the priorities of its duke? What can you conclude about the state of military technologies in this period and the conduct of warfare?

2. What do you make of the fact that Leonardo mentions his artistic endeavors only at the end of the letter? Does this fact alter your opinion or impression of him? Why or why not?

did the papacy's champion, Emperor Charles V, manage to gain control over most of the Italian peninsula, putting an end to the fighting for a time (see Chapter 15).

To these political disasters was added a waning of Italian prosperity. A virtual monopoly of trade with Asia in the fifteenth century had been one of the chief economic underpinnings for Renaissance patronage, but the gradual shifting of trade routes from the Mediterranean to the Atlantic region (Chapter 11), slowly eroded Italy's supremacy as the center of European trade. Warfare also contributed to Italy's economic hardships. As Italian wealth diminished, there was less and less of a surplus to support artistic endeavors. But by this time, Renaissance ideas and techniques were spreading from Italy to the rest of Europe;

ST. PETER'S BASILICA, ROME. This eighteenth-century painting shows the massive interior of the Renaissance building. But were it not for the perspective provided by the tiny human figures, the human eye would be fooled into thinking this a much smaller space.

so even as Italy's political and economic power waned, its cultural and intellectual cachet lent it more prominence than it had enjoyed for centuries.

THE RENAISSANCE NORTH OF THE ALPS

Contacts between Italy and northern Europe ensured that primacy: Italian merchants and financiers were familiar figures at northern courts; students from all over Europe studied at Italian universities such as Bologna or Padua; poets (including Geoffrey Chaucer, Chapter 10) and their works traveled to and from Italy; and northern soldiers were frequent participants in Italian wars. Only at the end of the fifteenth century, however, were the new currents of Italian Renaissance learning exported to Spain and northern Europe.

A variety of explanations have been offered for this delay. Northern European intellectual life in the later Middle Ages was dominated by universities such as Paris, Oxford, and Charles University in Prague, whose curricula focused on the study of philosophical logic and Christian theology. This approach left little room for the study of classical literature. In Italy, by contrast, universities were more often professional schools for law and medicine, and universities themselves exercised much less influence over intellectual life. As a result, a more secular, urban-oriented educational tradition took shape in Italy, within which

Renaissance humanism was able to develop. Even in the sixteenth century, northern scholars influenced by Italian Renaissance ideals usually worked outside the university system, under the patronage of kings and princes.

Before the sixteenth century, northern rulers were less interested in patronizing artists and intellectuals than were the city-states and princes of Italy. In Italy, as we have seen, such patronage was an important arena for competition among political rivals. In northern Europe, however, political units were larger and political rivals were fewer. It was therefore less necessary to use art for political purposes in a kingdom than it was in a city-state. In Florence, a statue erected in a central square would be seen by nearly all the city's residents. In Paris, such a statue would be seen by only a tiny minority of the French king's subjects. But in the sixteenth century, as northern nobles began to spend more time in residence at the royal court, kings could be reasonably certain that their patronage of artists and intellectuals would be noticed by those whom they were trying to impress.

Christian Humanism and the Career of Erasmus

The northern Renaissance was the product of the grafting of certain Italian Renaissance ideals onto preexisting northern traditions. This can be seen very clearly in the case of the most prominent northern Renaissance intellectual movement: Christian humanism. Although they shared the Italian humanists' rejection of scholasticism, northern Christian humanists more often sought ethical guidance from biblical and religious precepts than from Cicero or Virgil. Like their Italian counterparts, then, they sought wisdom from antiquity; but the antiquity they had in mind was Christian rather than classical—the antiquity, that is, of the New Testament and the early Church. Similarly, northern Renaissance artists were inspired by the accomplishments of Italian masters to learn classical techniques. But northern artists depicted classical subject matter far less frequently than did Italians, and almost never portrayed completely nude human figures.

Any discussion of the northern Renaissance must begin with the career of Desiderius Erasmus (c. 1469–1536). The illegitimate son of a priest, Erasmus was born near Rotterdam in the Netherlands. Forced into a monastery against his will when he was a teenager, the young Erasmus found little formal instruction there but plenty of freedom to read what he liked. He devoured all the classics he could get his hands on and the writings of the Church Fathers (Chapter 6). When he was about thirty years old, he obtained permission to leave the monastery and enroll in the University of Paris, where he completed the requirements for the degree of bachelor of divinity.

But Erasmus subsequently rebelled against what he considered the arid learning of Parisian scholasticism. Nor did he ever serve actively as a priest. Instead, he made his living from teaching, writing, and the proceeds of various ecclesiastical offices that required no pastoral duties. Ever on the lookout for new patrons, he traveled often to England, stayed once for three years in Italy, and resided in several different cities in Germany and the Netherlands before settling finally, toward the end of his life, in Basel (Switzerland). By means of a voluminous correspondence that he kept up with learned friends, Erasmus became the leader of a humanist circle. And through the popularity of his numerous publications, he became the arbiter of northern European cultural tastes during his lifetime.

Erasmus's urbane Latin style and humor earned him a wide audience on those grounds alone, yet he intended everything he wrote to promote what he called the "philosophy of Christ." Erasmus believed that the society of his day was caught up in corruption and immorality because

people had lost sight of the simple teachings of the Gospels. Accordingly, he offered his contemporaries three different kinds of publication: clever satires meant to show people the error of their ways, serious moral treatises meant to offer guidance toward proper Christian behavior, and scholarly editions of basic Christian texts.

In the first category belong the works of Erasmus that are still widely read today: *The Praise of Folly* (1509), in which he ridiculed hypocrisy and dogmatism as well as ignorance and gullibility; and the *Colloquies* (from the Latin for "discussions," 1518), in which he held up contemporary religious practices for examination in a more serious but still pervasively ironic tone. In such works, Erasmus let fictional characters do the talking; hence his own views can be determined only by inference from their points of view. But in his second mode, Erasmus did not hesitate to speak clearly in his own voice. The most prominent treatises in this genre are the quietly eloquent *Handbook of the Christian Knight* (1503), which urged the laity to pursue lives of serene inward piety, and the *Complaint of Peace* (1517), which pleaded movingly for Christian pacifism. Erasmus's pacifism was one of his most deeply held values, and he returned to it again and again in his published works.

Despite the success of these varied writings, Erasmus considered textual scholarship his greatest achievement. Revering the authority of Augustine, Jerome, and Ambrose, he brought out reliable editions of all their works. He also used his extraordinary command of Latin and Greek to produce a more accurate edition of the New Testament. After reading Lorenzo Valla's *Notes on the New Testament* in 1504, Erasmus became convinced that nothing was more imperative than divesting these biblical books of the myriad errors in transcription and translation that had piled up in the course of preceding centuries—for no one could be a good Christian without being certain of what Christ's message really was. Hence he spent ten years studying and comparing all the early Greek biblical manuscripts he could find, in order to establish an authoritative text. Erasmus's Greek New Testament, published in 1516 with explanatory notes and his own new Latin translation, became one of the most important scholarly landmarks of all time. In the hands of Martin Luther, it would play a critical role in the early stages of the Reformation (see Chapter 13).

The Influence of Erasmus

One of Erasmus's closest friends, and a close second to him in distinction among Christian humanists, was the Englishman Sir Thomas More (1478–1535). Following a

***ERASMUS* BY HANS HOLBEIN THE YOUNGER.** This is generally regarded as the most evocative portrait of the preeminent Christian humanist.

it is useful," war and monasticism do not exist, and toleration is granted to all who recognize the existence of God and the immortality of the soul. Although More advanced no explicit arguments in favor of Christianity, he probably meant to imply that if the Utopians could manage their society so well without the benefit of Christian revelation, Europeans who knew the Gospels ought to be able to do even better.

Erasmus and More head a long list of energetic and eloquent Christian humanists who made signal contributions to the collective enterprise of revolutionizing the study of early Christianity, and their achievements had a direct influence on Martin Luther and other Protestant reformers. Yet very few of them were willing to join Luther in rejecting the fundamental principles on which the power of the Church was based. Most tried to remain within its fold while still espousing an ideal of inward piety and scholarly inquiry. But as the leaders of the Church grew less and less tolerant of dissent, even mild criticism came to seem like heresy. Erasmus himself died

SIR THOMAS MORE BY HANS HOLBEIN THE YOUNGER. Holbein's skill in rendering the gravity and interiority of his subject is matched by his masterful representation of the sumptuous chain of office, furred mantle, and velvet sleeves that indicate the political and professional status of Henry VIII's chancellor.

successful career as a lawyer and as speaker of the House of Commons, More was appointed lord chancellor of England in 1529. He was not long in this position, however, before he opposed the king's design to establish a national church under royal control, thus denying the supremacy of the pope (see Chapter 13). In 1534, when More refused to take an oath acknowledging Henry as head of the Church of England, he was imprisoned in the Tower of London and executed a year later. He is now revered as a Catholic martyr.

Much earlier, however, in 1516, More published the work for which he is best remembered, *Utopia* ("No-place" in Greek). Purporting to describe an ideal community on an imaginary island, the book is really an Erasmian critique of the glaring abuses of the era—poverty undeserved and wealth unearned, drastic punishments, and the senseless slaughter of war. The inhabitants of Utopia hold all their goods in common, work only six hours a day so that all may have leisure for intellectual pursuits, and practice the natural virtues of wisdom, moderation, fortitude, and justice. Iron is the precious metal "because

SAINT JEROME IN HIS STUDY BY DÜRER. Jerome, the biblical translator of the fourth century (Chapter 6), was a hero to both Dürer and Erasmus: the paragon of inspired Christian scholarship. Note how the scene exudes contentment, even down to the sleeping lion, which seems more like an overgrown tabby cat than a symbol of Christ.

early enough to escape persecution, but several of his less fortunate followers lived on to suffer as victims of the Inquisition.

The Literature of the Northern Renaissance

Although Christian humanism would be severely challenged by the Reformation, the northern artistic Renaissance continued throughout the sixteenth century. Poets in France and England vied with one another to adapt the elegant lyric forms pioneered by Petrarch, particularly the sonnet. Meanwhile, the more satirical side of Renaissance humanism was embraced by the French writer François Rabelais (*RA-beh-lay*, c. 1494–1553). Like Erasmus, whom he greatly admired, Rabelais began his career in the Church, but soon left the cloister to study medicine. A practicing physician, Rabelais interspersed his professional activities with literary endeavors, the most enduring of which is *Gargantua and Pantagruel*, fictional chronicles of the lives and times of giants whose gross appetites serve as vehicles for much lusty humor. Like Erasmus, Rabelais satirized religious ceremonialism, scholasticism, superstition, and bigotry. But unlike Erasmus, who wrote in a highly cultivated Latin style comprehensible only to learned readers, Rabelais chose to address a far wider audience by writing in extremely crude French, and by glorifying every human impulse as natural and healthy.

Northern Architecture and Art

Although many architects in northern Europe continued to build in the flamboyant Gothic style of the later Middle Ages, the classical values of Italian architects can be seen in some of the splendid new castles constructed in France's Loire valley—châteaux too elegant to be defensible—and in the royal palace (now museum) of the Louvre in Paris, which replaced an old twelfth-century fortress. The influence of Renaissance ideals is also visible in the work of the foremost artist of this era, the German Albrecht Dürer (1471–1528). Dürer (*DIRR-er*) who mastered the techniques of proportion and perspective, and who also shared with contemporary Italians a fascination with nature and the human body. But Dürer never really embraced classical allegory, drawing inspiration instead from Christian legends and the Christian humanism of Erasmus. Thus Dürer's serenely radiant engraving of Saint Jerome expresses the scholarly absorption that Erasmus may have enjoyed while working quietly in his study.

Indeed, Dürer aspired to immortalize Erasmus himself in a major portrait, but circumstances prevented him from doing this because the paths of the two men crossed only once. Instead, the accomplishment of capturing Erasmus's spirit in oils was left to another great northern artist, the German Hans Holbein the Younger (1497–1543, see page 304). During a stay in England, Holbein also painted an acute portrait of Erasmus's kindred spirit Sir Thomas More, whom a contemporary called "a man of . . . sad gravity; a

After You Read This Chapter

REVIEWING THE OBJECTIVES

- The Renaissance was an intellectual and cultural movement that coincided with the later Middle Ages but fostered a new outlook on the world. Explain the ways in which this outlook differed from its medieval counterpart.
- The Renaissance began in Italy. Why?
- What was the relationship between Renaissance ideals and Italy's political realities?
- What were the principal features of Renaissance art?
- How were Renaissance ideas adapted in northern Europe?

man for all seasons" (see page 305). These two portraits in and of themselves point to a major difference between medieval and Renaissance culture. Whereas the Middle Ages produced no convincing naturalistic likenesses of any leading intellectual figures, Renaissance culture's glorification of human individuality created the environment in which Holbein was able to make Erasmus and More come to life.

CONCLUSION

The ideals of the Renaissance stand in sharp contrast to the harsh realities alongside which they coexisted, and in which they were rooted. They arose from the devastating events of the fourteenth century, which had a particularly drastic effect on Italy. Ravaged by the Black Death, abandoned by the papacy, reduced to the status of pawn in other powers' rivalries, Italy was exposed as a mere shadow of what it had been under the Roman Empire. It was therefore to the precedents and glories of the past that Italian intellectuals, artists, and statesmen looked for inspirations.

But to which aspects of the past? Some humanists may have wanted to revive the principles of the Roman Republic, but many of them worked for ambitious despots who modeled themselves on Rome's dictators or on the tyrants of ancient Greece. Artists could thrive in the atmosphere of competition and one-upmanship that characterized Italy's warring principalities and city-states, but they

could also find themselves reduced to the status of servants in the households of the wealthy and powerful—or forced to subordinate their artistry to the demands of warfare and espionage. Access to a widening array of classical texts, in Greek as well as Latin, broadened the horizons of Renaissance readers; yet women were largely barred from the humanist education that led men to boast of their proximity to God. New critical tools enabled the study of classical texts, but the insistence on a return to the "pure" language of the Roman Empire eventually succeeded in bringing about the death of Latin as a living medium of communication.

Although the Renaissance began in northern Italy, where it filled a cultural and political vacuum, it did not remain confined there. By the end of the fifteenth century, humanist approaches to education and textual criticism had begun to influence intellectual endeavors all over Europe. The techniques of Renaissance artists melded with the artistry of the later Middle Ages in striking ways, while opportunities for patronage expanded along with the demand for artworks and the prestige they lent to their owners. Eventually, the theories that undergirded Renaissance politics—civic and princely—were being used to legitimize many different kinds of power, including that of the papacy. All of these trends would be carried forward into the sixteenth century, and would have a role to play in the upheaval that shattered Europe's fragile religious unity and tenuous balance of power. It is to this upheaval, the Reformation, that we turn in Chapter 13.

PEOPLE, IDEAS, AND EVENTS IN CONTEXT

- Why was the ancient past so important to the intellectuals and artists of the **RENAISSANCE**? What was **HUMANISM**, and how did it influence education during this era?
- What were the political and economic underpinnings of the Renaissance? How do the **MEDICI** of Florence and the papacy exemplify new trends in patronage?
- What were some major scholarly achievements of the Renaissance? How did **LORENZO VALLA** and **NICCOLÒ MACHIAVELLI** advance new intellectual and political ideas?
- How do the works of **BOTTICELLI**, **LEONARDO**, **RAPHAEL**, and **MICHELANGELO** capture Renaissance ideals? Which is the most paradigmatic Renaissance artist, in your opinion, and why?
- How did Christian humanists like **DESIDERIUS ERASMUS** and **THOMAS MORE** apply Renaissance ideas in new ways? How were these ideas expressed in art?

CONSEQUENCES

- The Renaissance is often described as being the antithesis of the Middle Ages, yet it was actually a simultaneous movement. Can you think of other eras when two or more divergent trends have coexisted?
- To what extent do the ideals of the Renaissance anticipate those we associate with modernity? To what extent are they more faithful to either the Christian or the classical past?
- Phrases like "Renaissance man" and "a Renaissance education" are still part of our common vocabulary. Given what you have learned in this chapter, how has your understanding of such phrases changed? How would you explain their true meaning to others?

Before You Read This Chapter

The Age of Dissent and Division, 1500–1600

n the year 1500, Europe's future seemed bright. After two centuries of economic, social, and political turmoil, its economy was expanding, its cities were growing, and the monarchs of many states were securely established on their thrones. The population was increasing, and governments at every level were extending and deepening their control over people's lives. Europeans had also embarked on a new period of colonial expansion. And although the papacy pursued its territorial wars in Italy, the Church itself had weathered the storms of the Avignon captivity and the Great Schism. Heresies had been suppressed or contained. In the struggle over conciliarism, the papacy had won the support of all major European rulers, which effectively relegated the conciliarists to academic isolation at the University of Paris. Meanwhile, at the local level, the devotion of ordinary Christians was strong and the parish was a crucial site of community identity. To be sure, there were some problems. The educational standards of parish clergy were higher than they had ever been, but reformers noted that too many priests were ignorant or neglectful of their spiritual duties. Monasticism, by and large, seemed to have lost its spiritual fire. Religious enthusiasm sometimes led to superstition. Yet on the whole, the Church's problems were manageable.

No one could have predicted that Europe's religious and political coherence would be irreparably shattered in the course of a generation, or that the next century would witness an appallingly destructive series of wars. Nor could anyone have foreseen that the catalyst for these extraordinary events would be a university professor. For it was Martin Luther (1483–1546), a German monk and teacher of theology, who set off the chain reaction we know as the Reformation. Initially intended as a call for another phase in the Church's long history of internal reforms, Luther's teachings would instead launch a religious revolution that would splinter western Christendom into a variety of Protestant ("dissenting") faiths, while prompting the Church of Rome to re-affirm its status as the only true Catholic ("universal") faith, through a parallel revolution. These movements deepened existing divisions among peoples, rulers, and states, while opening up new divisions and points of contention. The result was a profound transformation of the religious, social, and political landscape that affected the lives of everyone in Europe—and everyone in the new European colonies, then and now.

MARTIN LUTHER'S CHALLENGE

To explain the impact of Martin Luther's ideas, we must answer three central questions:

1. Why did Luther's theology lead him to break with Rome?
2. Why did large numbers of people rally to his cause?
3. Why did so many German princes and towns impose the new religion within their territories?

As we shall see, those who followed Luther found his message appealing for different reasons. Many peasants hoped that the new religion would free them from the oppression of their lords; towns and princes thought it would allow them to consolidate their political independence; political leaders thought it would liberate Germany from the demands of foreign popes bent on feathering their own nest in central Italy.

Despite these differences, what Luther's followers shared was a conviction that their new understanding of Christianity would lead them to Heaven, whereas the traditional religion of Rome would not. For this reason, *reformation* is a misleading term for the movement they initiated. Although Luther himself began as a reformer seeking to change the Church

from within, he quickly developed into an uncompromising opponent of its principles and practices. Many of his followers were even more radical. The movement that began with Luther therefore went beyond "reformation." It was a definitive assault on institutions that had been in place for over a thousand years.

Luther's Quest for Justice

Although Martin Luther would become an inspiration to millions, he was a terrible disappointment to his father. The elder Luther was a Thuringian peasant who had prospered by leasing some mines. Eager to see his clever son rise further, he sent young Luther to the University of Erfurt to study law. In 1505, however, Martin shattered his father's hopes by becoming a monk of the Augustinian order. In some sense, though, Luther remained true to his roots: throughout his life, he lived simply and preferred to express himself in the vigorous, earthy vernacular of the German peasantry. He was, indeed, famous for his coarse (often obscene) language.

Luther arrived at his new understanding of religious truth by a dramatic conversion experience. As a monk, he zealously pursued all the traditional means for achieving his own salvation. Yet, try as he might, Luther could find no spiritual peace because he feared that he could never perform enough good deeds to deserve so great a gift as salvation. Then, in 1513, he hit upon an insight that changed the course of his life.

Luther's insight was a new understanding of God's justice. For years, he had worried that it seemed unfair for God to issue commandments that he knew human beings could not observe, and then to punish them with eternal

MARTIN LUTHER. This late portrait is by Lucas Cranach the Elder (1472–1553), court painter to the electors of Brandenburg and a friend of Luther.

damnation. But Luther's further study of the Bible revealed to him that God's justice has nothing to do with his power to punish, but rather with his mercy in saving sinful mortals through faith. As Luther later wrote, "At last, by the mercy of God, I began to understand the justice of God as that by which God makes *us* just, in his mercy and through faith . . . and at this I felt as though I had been born again, and had gone through open gates into paradise."

After that, everything seemed to fall into place. Lecturing at the University of Wittenberg in the years immediately following, Luther pondered a passage in Saint Paul's Letter to the Romans—"[T]he just shall live by faith" (1:17)—until he reached his central doctrine of "justification by faith alone." Luther concluded that God's justice does not demand endless good works and religious rituals for salvation, because humans can never be saved by their own efforts. Rather, humans are saved by God's grace alone, which God offers as an utterly undeserved gift. Men and women are therefore "justified" (i.e., made worthy of salvation) by faith alone. Those whom God has justified through faith will manifest that fact by performing works of piety and charity, but such works are not what saves them. Piety and charity are merely visible signs of each believer's invisible spiritual state, which is known to God alone.

The essence of this doctrine was not original to Luther. It had been central to the thought of Augustine (see Chapter 6), the patron saint of Luther's own monastic order. During the twelfth and thirteenth centuries, however, theologians such as Peter Lombard and Thomas Aquinas (Chapter 9) had developed a very different understanding of salvation. They emphasized the role that the Church itself (through its sacraments) and the individual believer (through acts of piety and charity) could play in the process of salvation. None of these theologians claimed that a human being could earn his or her way to Heaven by good works alone, but the late medieval Church unwittingly encouraged this misunderstanding by presenting the process of salvation in increasingly quantitative terms—declaring, for example, that by performing a specific action (such as a pilgrimage or a pious donation), a believer could reduce the penance she or he owed to God by a specific number of days.

By the late fifteenth century, popes began to proclaim that the dead could speed their way through Purgatory by means of indulgences: special remissions of penitential obligations. When indulgences were first conceived, in the eleventh and twelfth centuries, they could be earned only through difficult spiritual exercises, such as joining a crusade (see Chapter 8). By the end of the fifteenth century, however, indulgences were for sale.

To many, this looked like simony: the sin of exchanging God's grace for cash. It had been a practice loudly condemned by Wyclif and his followers (Chapter 10), and it was even more widely criticized by reformers like Erasmus (Chapter 12). But Luther's objections to indulgences had much more radical consequences, because they rested on a set of theological presuppositions that, taken to their logical conclusion, resulted in dismantling much of contemporary religious practice, not to mention the authority and sanctity of the Church. Surprisingly, Luther himself does not appear to have realized this at first.

LUTHER'S TRANSLATION OF THE BIBLE. The printing press was instrumental to the rapid dissemination of Luther's messages, as well as those of his supporters and challengers. Also essential was the fact that Luther addressed his audience in plain language, in their native German, and that pamphlets and vernacular Bibles like this one could be rapidly and cheaply mass-produced.

The Scandal of Indulgences

Luther developed his ideas as a university professor in the relative privacy of the classroom. But in 1517 he was provoked into attacking indulgences more publicly. The worldly

SAINT PETER'S BASILICA, ROME. The construction of a new papal palace and monumental church was begun in 1506. This enormous complex replaced a modest basilica built by Constantine on the site of the apostle Peter's tomb. ▪ *How might this building project have been interpreted in different ways, depending on one's attitude toward the papacy?*

prince Albert of Hohenzollern had paid a large sum for papal permission to hold the bishoprics of Magdeburg and Halberstadt concurrently—even though, at twenty-three, he was not old enough to be a bishop at all. Moreover, when the prestigious and lucrative archbishopric of Mainz fell vacant in the next year, Albert bought that, too. Obtaining the necessary funds by taking out loans from a German banking firm, he then struck a bargain with Pope Leo X (r. 1513–21): Leo would authorize the sale of indulgences in Albert's ecclesiastical territories, with the understanding that half of the income would go to Rome for the building of St. Peter's Basilica, the other half going to Albert.

Luther did not know the sordid details of Albert's bargain, but he did know that a Dominican friar named Tetzel was soon hawking indulgences throughout much of the region, and that Tetzel was deliberately giving people the impression that an indulgence was an automatic ticket to Heaven for oneself or one's loved ones in Purgatory. For Luther, this was doubly offensive: not only was Tetzel violating Luther's conviction that people are saved by faith, he was also misleading people into thinking that they no

longer needed to confess their sins to a priest but could instead purchase grace with money. Tetzel was thus putting innocent souls at risk. So on the eve of the feast of All Souls (Halloween night) in 1517, Luther published a list of ninety-five theses that he was prepared to debate, all aimed at dismantling the doctrine of indulgences. According to tradition, he nailed this document to the door of the church—and whether or not he did so in fact, the metaphor is clear.

Luther wrote up these points for debate in Latin, not German, and meant them for academic discussion within the University of Wittenberg. But when some unknown person translated and published them, the hitherto obscure academic suddenly gained widespread notoriety. Tetzel and his allies now demanded that Luther withdraw his theses. Rather than backing down, however, Luther became even bolder in his attacks. In 1519, at a public disputation held before throngs in Leipzig, Luther defiantly maintained that the pope and all clerics were merely fallible men, and that the highest authority for an individual's conscience was the truth of Scripture. Pope Leo X responded by charging Luther with heresy; after that, Luther had no alternative but to break with the Church.

Luther's year of greatest activity came in 1520 when, in the midst of the crisis caused by his defiance, he composed a series of pamphlets setting forth his three primary premises: justification by faith, the authority of Scripture, and "the priesthood of all believers." We have already examined the meaning of the first premise. By the second, Luther meant that the reading of Scripture took precedence over Church traditions—including the teachings of all theologians—and that beliefs (such as Purgatory) or practices (such as prayers to the saints) not explicitly grounded in Scripture could be rejected as human inventions. Luther also declared that Christian believers were spiritually equal before God, which meant denying that priests, monks, and nuns had any special qualities by virtue of their vocations: hence "the priesthood of all believers."

From these premises a host of practical consequences followed. Because works could not lead to salvation, Luther declared fasts, pilgrimages, and the veneration of relics to be spiritually valueless. He also called for the dissolution of all monasteries and convents. He advocated a demystification of religious rites, proposing the substitution of German and other vernacular languages for Latin, and calling for a reduction in the number of sacraments from seven to two. In his view, the only true sacraments were baptism and the Eucharist, both of which had been instituted by Christ. (Initially, he included penance, too.) But although Luther continued to teach that Christ was physically and spiritually present in the consecrated bread and wine of the Eucharist, he insisted that it was only through the faith of each individual believer that this sacrament could lead anyone to God. To further emphasize that clergy had no supernatural authority, he insisted on calling them "ministers" or "pastors" rather than priests, and he proposed to abolish the entire ecclesiastical hierarchy, from popes to bishops on down. Finally, on the principle that no spiritual distinction existed between clergy and laity, Luther argued that ministers could and should marry. In 1525 he himself took a wife, Katharina von Bora, one of a dozen nuns whom he had helped to escape from a Cistercian convent.

The Challenge to Rome

As word of Luther's defiance spread, his pamphlets became a publishing sensation. Whereas the average press run of a printed book before 1520 had been 1,000 copies, the first run of *To the Christian Nobility* (1520) was 4,000—and it sold out in a few days. Many thousands of copies quickly followed. Even more popular were woodcut illustrations mocking the papacy and exalting Luther. These sold in the tens of thousands and could be readily understood even by the illiterate. (See *Interpreting Visual Evidence*.)

Luther's denunciations reflected widespread public dissatisfaction with the conduct and corruption of recent popes. Pope Alexander VI (r. 1492–1503) had bribed cardinals to gain his office, and had then used the money raised from the papal jubilee of 1500 to support the military campaigns of his illegitimate son. He was also suspected of incest with his own daughter, Lucrezia Borgia. Julius II (r. 1503–13) devoted his reign to enlarging the Papal States in a series of wars; a contemporary remarked of him that he would have gained great glory—if only he had been a secular prince. Leo X (r. 1513–21), Luther's opponent, was a member of the Medici family of Florence and held a very different view of the Church and its earthly mission.

In Germany, resentment of the papacy ran especially high because there were no special agreements (concordats) limiting papal authority in its principalities, as there were in Spain, France, and England (see Chapter 10). As a result, German princes complained that papal taxes were so exorbitant that the country was drained of its wealth. Meanwhile, Germans felt that they had almost no influence over papal policy. Frenchmen, Spaniards, and Italians dominated the College of Cardinals and the papal bureaucracy, and the popes were almost always Italian (as they would continue to be until 1978 and the election of John Paul II). As a result, graduates from the rapidly growing German universities almost never found employment in Rome. Instead, many joined the throngs of Luther's supporters to become leaders of the new religious movement.

THE EMPEROR CHARLES V. This portrait by the Venetian painter Titian depicts Europe's most powerful ruler sitting quietly in a chair, dressed in simple clothing of the kind worn by judges or bureaucrats. ▪ *Why might Charles have chosen to represent himself in this way—rather than in the regalia of his many royal, imperial, and princely offices?*

The Condemnation at Worms

In the year 1520, Pope Leo X issued a papal edict condemning Luther's publications, and threatening him with excommunication if he did not recant. This edict was of the most solemn kind, known as a *bulla* or "bull," from the lead seal it bore. Luther's reponse was flagrant: rather than acquiescing to the pope's demand, he staged a public burning of the document. Thereafter, his heresy confirmed, he was formally consigned to punishment by his lay overlord, the elector Frederick "the Wise" of Saxony. Frederick, however, proved a supporter of Luther and a critic of the papacy. Rather than burning Luther at the stake for heresy, Frederick declared that Luther had not yet received a fair hearing. Early in 1521, he brought Luther to the city of Worms to be examined by a select representative assembly known as a "diet."

At Worms, the diet's presiding officer was the newly elected Holy Roman emperor, Charles V. As a member of the Habsburg family, he had been born and bred in his ancestral holding of Flanders, part of the Netherlands. By 1521, through the unpredictable workings of dynastic inheritance, marriage, election, and luck, he had become not only the ruler of the Netherlands, but also king of Bohemia and Hungary, Holy Roman Emperor, duke of Austria, duke of Milan, and ruler of the Franche-Comté. And as the grandson of Ferdinand and Isabella on his mother's side, he was

Interpreting Visual Evidence

Decoding Printed Propaganda

The printing press has been credited with helping to spread the teachings of Martin Luther and so with securing the success of the Protestant Reformation. But even before Luther's critiques were published, reformers were using this new technology to disseminate images that attacked the corruption of the Church. After Luther rose to prominence, both his supporters and detractors vied with one another in disseminating propaganda that appealed, visually, to a lay audience and that could be understood even by those who were unable to read.

The first pair of images below is really a single printed artifact datable to around 1500: an early example of a "pop-up" card. It shows Pope Alexander VI (r. 1492–1503) as stately pontiff (image A) whose true identity is concealed by a flap. When the flap is raised (image B), he is revealed as a devil. The Latin texts read: "Alexander VI, *pontifex maximus*" (image A) and "I am the pope" (image B).

The other two images represent two sides of the debate over Luther's new theology as it had developed by 1530, and both do so with reference to the same image: the seven-headed beast mentioned in the Bible's Book of

A. Alexander as pontiff.

B. Alexander as a devil.

also king of Spain; king of Naples, Sicily, and Sardinia; and ruler of all the Spanish possessions in the New World. Governing such an extraordinary combination of territories posed enormous challenges. Charles's empire had no capital and no centralized administrative institutions; it shared no common language, no common culture, and no geographically contiguous borders. It thus stood completely apart from the growing nationalism of late medieval political life.

Charles recognized the diversity of his enormous empire and tried wherever possible to rule it through local

Revelation. On the left below (image C), a Lutheran engraving shows the papacy as the beast, with seven heads representing seven orders of Catholic clergy. The sign on the cross (referring to the sign hung over the head of the crucified Christ) reads, in German: "For money, a sack full of indulgences." (The Latin words on either side say "Kingdom of the Devil.") On the right (image D), a Catholic engraving produced in Germany shows Luther as Revelation's beast, with seven heads labeled: "Doctor–Martin–Luther–Heretic–Hypocrite–Fanatic–Barabbas," the last alluding to the thief who should have been executed instead of Jesus, according to the Gospels.

Questions for Analysis

1. Given that this attack on Pope Alexander VI precedes Martin Luther's critique of the Church by nearly two decades, what can you conclude about its intended audience? To what extent can it be read as a barometer of popular disapproval? What might have been the reason(s) for the use of the concealing flap?

2. What do you make of the fact that both Catholic and Protestant propagandists were using the same imagery? What do you make of the key differences? For example, note that the seven-headed beast representing the papacy sprouts out of an altar on which a Eucharistic chalice is displayed, while the seven-headed Martin Luther is reading a book.

3. All of these printed images also make use of words. What are some of the different relationships between these two media (words and images)? Would the message of each image be clear without the use of texts? Why or why not?

C. The seven-headed papal beast.

D. The seven-headed Martin Luther.

officials and institutions. But he could not tolerate threats to the two fundamental forces that held his empire together: himself, in his role as emperor, and Catholicism, as the religion of Rome was coming to be called. There was therefore little doubt that the Diet of Worms would condemn Martin Luther for heresy. But when Luther refused to back down, thereby endangering his life, his lord Frederick the Wise once again intervened, this time arranging for Luther to be "kidnapped" and hidden for a year at the elector's castle of the Wartburg, where he was kept out of harm's way.

THE EUROPEAN EMPIRE OF CHARLES V, c. 1550. Charles V ruled a vast variety of widely dispersed territories in Europe and the New World, and as Holy Roman Emperor he was also the titular ruler of Germany. ▪ *What were the main countries and kingdoms under his control?* ▪ *Which regions would have been most threatened by Charles's extraordinary power, and where might the rulers of these regions turn for allies?* ▪ *How might the expansion of the Ottoman Empire have complicated the political and religious struggles within Christian Europe?*

Thereafter, Luther was never again in mortal danger. Although the Diet of Worms proclaimed him an outlaw, this edict was never enforced. Instead, Charles V left Germany in order to conduct a war with France. In 1522, Luther returned in triumph to Wittenberg, to find that the changes he had called for had already been put into practice by his university supporters. When several German princes formally converted to Lutheranism, they brought their territories with them. In a little over a decade, a new form of Christianity had been established.

The German Princes and the Lutheran Church

At this point, the last of our three major questions must be addressed: Why did some German princes, secure in their own powers, nonetheless establish Lutheran religious

practices within their territories? This is a crucial development, because popular support for Luther would not have been enough to ensure the success of his teachings. Indeed, it was only in those territories where rulers formally established Lutheranism that the new religion prevailed. Elsewhere in Germany, Luther's sympathizers were forced to flee, face death, or conform to Catholicism.

The power of individual rulers to determine the religion of their territories reflects developments we noted in Chapter 10. Kings and great lords had long sought to control appointments to Church offices in their own realms, to restrict the flow of money to Rome, and to limit the independence of ecclesiastical courts. In the fifteenth century, the most powerful rulers in western Europe—primarily the kings of France and Spain—had therefore taken advantage of the continuing struggles between the papacy and the conciliarists to extract such concessions from the embattled popes. But in Germany, as noted above, neither the emperor nor individual princes were strong enough to secure special treatment.

This changed as a result of Luther's initiatives. As early as 1520, Luther recognized that he could never hope to institute new religious practices without the strong arms of princes, so he explicitly encouraged them to confiscate the wealth of the Church as an incentive. At first the princes bided their time. But when they realized that Luther had enormous public support, several moved to introduce Lutheranism into their territories. Personal piety surely played a role in individual cases, but political and economic considerations were generally more decisive. Protestant princes could consolidate authority by naming their own pastors, collecting taxes usually sent to Rome, and curtailing the jurisdiction of Church courts. They could also guarantee that the political and religious boundaries of their territories would now coincide. No longer would a rival ecclesiastical prince (such as a bishop or archbishop) be able to use his spiritual position to undermine a secular prince's sovereignty.

Similar considerations also moved a number of free German cities (independent of territorial princes) to adopt Lutheranism. Town councils and guild masters could thus establish themselves as the supreme governing authorities within their towns, cutting out local bishops or powerful monasteries. Given the added fact that monasteries and convents could be shut down and their lands appropriated, the practical advantages of the new faith were overwhelming— quite apart from any considerations of religious zeal.

Once safely ensconced in Wittenberg under princely protection, Luther began to express his own political and social views ever more vehemently. In a treatise of 1523, *On Temporal Authority*, he insisted that "godly" (Protestant) rulers must be obeyed in all things and that even "ungodly" ones should never be actively resisted since tyranny "is not to be resisted but endured." In 1525, when peasants throughout Germany rebelled against their landlords, Luther therefore responded with intense hostility. In his vituperative pamphlet of 1525, *Against the Thievish, Murderous Hordes of Peasants*, he urged readers to hunt down the rebels as though they were mad dogs. After the ruthless suppression of this revolt, which may have cost as many as 100,000 lives, the firm alliance of Lutheranism with state power helped preserve and sanction the existing social order.

As for Luther himself, he concentrated in his last years on debating with younger, more radical religious reformers. Never tiring in his prolific literary activity, he wrote an average of one treatise every two weeks for twenty-five years. Many of these are colored by extreme anti-Semitism, one of Luther's less positive legacies.

THE SPREAD OF PROTESTANTISM

Originating as a term applied to Lutherans who "protested" against an imperial diet convened in 1529, the word *Protestant* was soon applied to a much wider range of dissenting Christianities. Lutheranism itself struck lasting roots only in northern Germany and Scandinavia, where it became the state religion of Denmark, Norway, and Sweden as early as the 1520s. Early Lutheran successes in southern Germany, Poland, and Hungary were eventually rolled back. Elsewhere in Europe, meanwhile, competing forms of Protestantism soon emerged from the seeds that Luther had sown. By the 1550s, Protestantism had become an increasingly diverse and divisive movement.

Protestantism in Switzerland

In the early sixteenth century, Switzerland was ruled neither by kings nor by territorial princes; instead, prosperous Swiss cities were either independent or on the verge of becoming so. Hence, when the leading citizens of a Swiss municipality decided to adopt Protestant reforms, no one could stop them. Although religious arrangements varied from city to city, three main forms of Protestantism emerged in Switzerland between 1520 to 1550: Zwinglianism, Anabaptism, and Calvinism.

Zwinglianism, founded by Ulrich Zwingli (*TSVING-lee*, 1484–1531) in Zürich, was the most theologically moderate form of the three. Zwingli began his career as a Catholic priest, but his humanist-inspired study of the Bible convinced him that Catholic theology conflicted with the Gospels. His biblical

CONFESSIONAL DIFFERENCES, c. 1560. The religious affiliations (confessions) of Europe's territories had become very complicated by the year 1560, roughly a generation after the adoption of Lutheranism in some areas. ▪ *What major countries and kingdoms had embraced Protestantism by 1560?* ▪ *To what extent do these divisions conform to political boundaries, and to what extent would they have complicated the political situation?* ▪ *Why might Lutheranism have spread north, into Scandinavia, rather than south?*

THE ANABAPTISTS' CAGES, THEN AND NOW. After the three Anabaptist leaders of Münster were executed in 1535, their corpses were prominently displayed in cages hung from a tower of the marketplace church. As can be seen from the photo on the right, the bones are gone but the iron cages remain. ▪ *What would be the purpose of keeping these cages on display?*

studies eventually led him to condemn religious images and hierarchical authority, yet he did not speak out publicly until Luther set the precedent. In 1522, Zwingli began attacking the authority of the Church openly. Soon much of northern Switzerland had accepted his religious leadership.

Zwingli's reforms closely resembled those of the Lutherans in Germany. Zwingli differed from Luther, however, as to the theology of the Eucharist: whereas Luther believed in the real presence of Christ's body in the sacrament, for Zwingli the Eucharist conferred no grace at all; it was simply a reminder and communal celebration of Christ's historical sacrifice. This fundamental disagreement prevented Lutherans and Zwinglians from uniting in a common Protestant front. Fighting independently, Zwingli fell in battle against Catholic forces in 1531. Soon thereafter, his movement was absorbed by the more systematic Protestantism of John Calvin (see below).

Before Calvinism prevailed, however, a far more radical form of Protestantism arose in Switzerland and Germany: Anabaptism. The first Anabaptists were members of Zwingli's circle in Zürich, but they broke with him around 1525 on the issue of infant baptism. Anabaptists were convinced that the sacrament of baptism was only effective if administered to willing adults who understood its significance, and they required followers who had been baptized as infants to be baptized again as adults (the term *Anabaptism* means "rebaptism"). This doctrine reflected the Anabaptists' fundamental belief that the true church of Christ was a small community of believers whose members had to make a deliberate, inspired

decision to join it. No other Protestant groups were prepared to go so far in rejecting the traditional view of the Church as a single vast body to which all members of Christian society belonged from birth. Yet in its first few years the movement did gain numerous adherents, above all because it appealed to sincere spiritual values in calling for pacifism, strict personal morality, and extreme simplicity of worship.

This changed when a group of Anabaptist extremists managed to gain control of the German city of Münster in 1534. These zealots combined sectarianism with millenarianism: the belief that God intends to institute a completely new order of justice and spirituality throughout the world before the end of time. Determined to help bring about this goal, the extremists attempted to turn Münster into a new Jerusalem. A former tailor named John of Leyden assumed the title "King of the New Temple" and proclaimed himself the successor of the Hebrew king David. Under his leadership, Anabaptist religious practices were made obligatory, private property was abolished, and even polygamy was permitted on the grounds of Old Testament precedents. Such practices were deeply shocking to Protestants and Catholics alike. Accordingly, Münster was besieged and captured by Catholic forces little more than a year after the Anabaptist takeover; the new "David," together with two of his lieutenants, was put to death by torture and their decaying bodies displayed in cages hung from a church in the marketplace.

Thereafter, Anabaptists throughout Europe were ruthlessly persecuted on all sides. The few who survived banded together in the Mennonite sect, named for its founder, the Dutchman Menno Simons (c. 1496–1561). This sect, dedicated to pacifism and a simple "religion of the heart," has continued to exist to the present day and is particularly strong in the central United States.

John Calvin's Reformed Theology

A year after the events in Münster, a twenty-six-year-old Frenchman named John Calvin (1509–1564), published the first version of his *Institutes of the Christian Religion*, the most influential formulation of Protestant theology ever written. Born in Noyon in northern France, Calvin had originally trained for the law. By 1533 he was studying the Greek and Latin classics while living off the income from a priestly benefice. As he later wrote, although he was "obstinately devoted to the superstitions of popery," at this time in his life he experienced a miraculous conversion. He became a Protestant theologian and propagandist, and evenually fled to the Swiss city of Basel to escape persecution.

Although some aspects of Calvin's early career resemble those of Luther, the two men were very different. Luther was emotionally volatile and a lover of controversy. He responded to theological problems piecemeal as they arose or as the impulse struck him; he never attempted to systematize his beliefs. Calvin, however, was coolly analytical and resolved to set forth all the principles of Protestantism comprehensively, logically, and systematically. As a result, Calvin's *Institutes* became the Protestant equivalent of Thomas Aquinas's *Summa Theologiae* (Chapter 9).

Calvin's austere theology started with the omnipotence of God. For Calvin, the entire universe depends utterly on the will of the Almighty, who created all things for his greater glory. Because of man's original fall from grace, all human beings are sinners by nature, bound to an evil inheritance they cannot escape. Nevertheless, God (for reasons of his own) has predestined some for eternal salvation and damned all the rest to the torments of Hell. Nothing that human beings may do can alter this fate: all souls are stamped with God's blessing or curse before they are born. Nevertheless, Christians cannot be indifferent to their conduct on earth. If they are among the elect, God will implant in them the desire to live according to his laws. Upright conduct is thus a sign, though not an infallible one, that an individual has been chosen to sit at the throne of glory. Membership in the reformed church (as Calvinist churches are more properly known) is another presumptive sign of election to salvation. But most of all, Calvin urged Christians to conceive of themselves as chosen instruments of God, charged to work actively to fulfill God's purposes on earth. Because sin offends God, Christians should do all they can to prevent it, not because their actions will lead to anyone's salvation, but simply because God's glory is diminished if sin is allowed to flourish unchecked.

Calvin always acknowledged a great theological debt to Luther, but his religious teachings diverged in several essentials. First of all, Luther's attitude toward proper Christian conduct in the world was much more passive than Calvin's. For Luther, a Christian should endure the trials of this life through suffering, whereas for Calvin the world was to be actively mastered through unceasing labor for God's sake. Calvin's religion was also more legalistic than Luther's. Luther, for example, insisted that his followers attend church on Sunday, but he did not demand that during the remainder of the day they refrain from all pleasure. Calvin, however, issued stern strictures against worldliness of any sort on the Sabbath and forbade all sorts of minor self-indulgences on other days.

The two men also differed on fundamental matters of church governance and worship. Although Luther broke with the Catholic system of hierarchical church government, Lutheran district superintendents exercised some of the same powers as bishops, including supervision of parish clergy. Luther also retained many features of traditional worship, including altars, music, and ritual. Calvin, however, rejected everything that smacked of "popery." He argued for the elimination of all traces of hierarchy within the church. Instead, each congregation should elect its own ministers, and assemblies of ministers and "elders" (laymen responsible for maintaining proper religious conduct) were to govern the reformed church as a whole. Calvin also insisted on the utmost simplicity in worship, prohibiting (among much else) vestments, processions, instrumental music, and religious images of any sort. He also dispensed with all remaining vestiges of Catholic sacramental theology by making the sermon, rather than the Eucharist, the centerpiece of worship.

Calvinism in Geneva

Calvin was intent on putting his religious teachings into practice. Sensing an opportunity in the French-speaking Swiss city of Geneva—then in the throes of political and religious upheaval—he moved there late in 1536 and immediately began preaching and organizing. In 1538, his activities caused him to be expelled by the city council, but in 1541 he returned and brought the city under his sway.

Under Calvin's guidance, Geneva's government became a theocracy. Supreme authority was vested in a "Consistory" composed of lay elders and pastors, whose weekly meetings Calvin dominated. Aside from passing legislation, the Consistory's main function was to supervise morality, both public and private. To this end, Geneva was divided into districts, and a committee of the Consistory visited every household, without prior warning, to check on the behavior of its members. Dancing, card playing, attending the theater, and working or playing on the Sabbath—all were outlawed as works of the devil. Murder, treason, adultery, witchcraft, blasphemy, and heresy were all capital crimes. Even penalties for lesser crimes were severe. During the first four years after Calvin gained control in Geneva, there were fifty-eight executions in this city with a total population of only 16,000.

As objectionable as this may seem today, Calvin's Geneva was a beacon of light to thousands of Protestants throughout Europe in the mid-sixteenth century. Calvin's disciple John Knox, who brought the reformed church to Scotland, declared Geneva "the most perfect school of Christ that ever was on earth since the days of the Apostles." Converts such as Knox flocked to Geneva for refuge or instruction and then returned home to become ardent proselytizers for the new religion. Geneva thus became the center of an international movement dedicated to spreading reformed religion to the rest of Europe through organized missionary activity and propaganda.

These efforts were remarkably successful. By the end of the sixteenth century, Calvinists were a majority in Scotland (where they were known as Presbyterians) and Holland (where they founded the Dutch Reformed Church). They were also influential in England. Although the Church of England adopted reformed theology but not reformed worship, Calvinists there who sought further reforms in worship were known as Puritans. There were also substantial Calvinist minorities in France (where they were called Huguenots), Germany, Hungary, Lithuania, and Poland.

THE DOMESTICATION OF REFORM

Protestantism was a movement whose radical claims for the spiritual equality of all Christian believers had the potential to undermine the political, social, and even gender hierarchies on which European society rested. Luther himself did not anticipate that his ideas might have such implications, and he was genuinely shocked when the rebellious German peasants and the radical Anabaptists at Münster interpreted his teachings in this way. And Luther was by no means the only staunchly conservative Protestant. Most Protestant reformers depended on the support of existing social and political leaders: territorial princes, but also the ruling elites of towns. As a result, the Reformation movement was speedily "domesticated," in two senses. Its revolutionary potential was muffled, and there was an increasing emphasis on the patriarchal family as the central institution of Protestant life.

Reform and Discipline

As we have seen (Chapter 10), injunctions to lead a more disciplined and godly life had been a frequent message of fifteenth-century religious reform movements. Many of these efforts were actively promoted by princes and town councils, most famously perhaps in Florence, where the Dominican preacher Girolamo Savonarola led the city on an extraordinary but short-lived campaign of puritanism and moral reform between 1494 and 1498. But there are many other examples of rulers legislating against immoral behavior. When Desiderius Erasmus called on secular authorities to think of themselves as abbots and of their territories as giant monasteries, he was sounding an already-familiar theme.

Protestant rulers, however, took the need to enforce godly discipline with particular seriousness, because the depravity of human nature was a fundamental tenet of Protestant belief. Following Saint Augustine (Chapter 6), Protestants believed that people would inevitably turn out

bad unless they were compelled to be good. It was, therefore, the responsibility of secular and religious leaders to control and punish the behavior of their people, because otherwise their evil deeds would anger God and destroy human society.

Protestant godliness began with the discipline of children. Luther himself wrote two catechisms (instructional tracts) designed to teach children the tenets of their faith and the obligations—toward parents, masters, and rulers—that God imposed on them. Luther also insisted that all children, boys and girls alike, should be taught to read the Bible in their own languages. Schooling thus became a characteristically Protestant preoccupation. Even the Protestant family was designated a "school of godliness" in which fathers were expected to instruct and discipline their wives, their children, and their household servants.

Family life in the early sixteenth century left much to be desired in the eyes of Protestant reformers. Drunkenness, domestic violence, illicit sexual relations, lewd dancing, and the blasphemous swearing of oaths were frequent topics of reforming discourse. Various methods of discipline were attempted, including public confessions of wrongdoing, public penances and shamings, exclusion from church services, and even imprisonment. All these efforts met with varying, but generally modest, success. To create godly Protestant families, and to enforce godly discipline on entire communities, was going to require the active cooperation of godly authorities.

Protestantism, Government, and the Family

The domestication of the Reformation in this sense—its embeddedness in daily life—in the free towns of Germany and Switzerland began and from there spread westward to the New World. Protestant attacks on monasticism and clerical celibacy had found a receptive audience among townsmen who resented the immunity of monastic houses from taxation and regarded clerical celibacy as a subterfuge for the seduction of their own wives and daughters. Protestant emphasis on the depravity of the human will and the consequent need for that will to be disciplined by authority also resonated powerfully with guilds and town governments, which were anxious to maintain and increase their control. By eliminating the competing jurisdictional authority of the Catholic Church, Protestantism allowed town governments to consolidate all authority into their own hands.

Meanwhile, Protestantism reinforced the control of individual men over their own households by emphasizing the family as the basic unit of religious education. An all-powerful father figure was now expected to assume responsibility for instructing and disciplining his household. At the same time, Protestantism introduced a new religious ideal for women. No longer was the celibate nun the exemplar of female holiness; in her place now stood the married and obedient "goodwife." To some extent, then, Protestantism resolved the tensions between piety and sexuality that had long characterized Christian teachings, by declaring the holiness of marital sex.

But this did not promote a new view of women's spiritual potential, nor did it elevate their social and political status; quite the contrary. Luther regarded women as more sexually driven than men and less capable of controlling their sexual desires—despite the fact that Luther confessed himself to be utterly incapable of celibacy. His opposition to women's monasteries allegedly rested on his belief that it was impossible for women to remain chaste, so that sequestering them simply made illicit behavior inevitable. To prevent sin, it was therefore necessary that all women should be married, preferably at a young age, and so placed under the governance of a godly husband.

For the most part, Protestant town governments were happy to cooperate in shutting down monasteries for women. The convent's property went to the town, after all. But conflicts still arose between Protestant reformers and town fathers over marriage and sexuality, especially over the reformers' insistence that both men and women should marry young as a restraint on lust. In many German towns, men were traditionally expected to delay marriage until they had achieved the status of a master craftsman. Accordingly, apprentices and journeymen were not supposed to marry. Instead, they were expected to frequent brothels and taverns, a legally sanctioned outlet for extramarital sexuality long viewed as necessary to men's physical well-being—but a practice that Protestant reformers now deemed morally abhorrent.

Towns responded in a variety of ways to these opposing pressures. Some instituted special committees to police public morals, of the sort we have noted in Calvin's Geneva. Some abandoned Protestantism altogether. Others, like Augsburg, alternated back and forth between Protestantism and Catholicism for several decades. Yet regardless of a town's final choice of religious allegiance, a revolution was taking place with respect to attitudes toward public morality. In their competition with each other, neither Catholics nor Protestants wished to be seen as soft on sin. The result, by 1600, was the widespread abolition of publicly licensed brothels, the outlawing of prostitution, and far stricter governmental supervision of many other aspects of private life than had ever been the case in any Western civilization up to this point in time.

The Control of Marriage

Protestantism also increased parents' control over their children's choice of marital partners. Although the medieval Church had defined marriage as a sacrament, it did not require the involvement of a priest: the mutual free consent of two individuals, even if exchanged without witnesses or parental approval, was enough to constitute a legally valid marriage. Opposition to this doctrine came from many quarters, however. Because marriage involved rights of inheritance to property, it was regarded as too important a matter to be left to the choice of adolescents. Instead, parents wanted the power to prevent unsuitable matches and, in some cases, to force their children to accept the marriage arrangements their families might negotiate on their behalf.

Protestantism offered an opportunity to achieve such control. Luther had declared marriage to be a purely secular matter, not a sacrament at all, and one that could be regulated as governing authorities thought best. Calvin largely followed suit, although Calvinist theocracy drew less of a distinction than did Lutheranism between the powers of church and state. Even the Catholic Church was eventually forced to give way; although it never abandoned its insistence that both members of a couple must freely consent, it eventually required formal public notice of intent to marry and insisted on the presence of a priest at the actual wedding ceremony. Both of these measures were supposed to prevent elopements, allowing families time to intervene before an unsuitable marriage was concluded. In somewhat different ways, then, both Protestantism and Catholicism moved to strengthen the control that parents could exercise over their children—and, in the case of Protestantism, that husbands could exercise over their wives.

THE REFORMATION OF ENGLAND

In England, the Reformation took a rather different course than it did in continental Europe. Although a tradition of popular reform had long flourished there, the number of dissidents was usually small and their influence limited. Nor was England particularly oppressed by the papal exactions and abuses that roiled Germany. When the sixteenth century began, English monarchs already exercised close control over Church appointments within their kingdom; they also received the lion's share of the papal taxation collected from England. Why, then, did sixteenth-century England become a Protestant country at all?

Marriage and Celibacy: Two Views

These two selections illustrate strongly contrasting views on the spiritual value of marriage versus celibacy. The first selection is part of Martin Luther's more general attack on monasticism, which emphasizes his contention that marriage is the natural and divinely intended state for all human beings. The second selection, from the decrees of the Council of Trent (1545–63), restates traditional Catholic teaching on the holiness of marriage but also emphasizes the spiritual superiority of virginity and the necessity of clerical celibacy.

Luther's Views on Celibacy

Listen! In all my days I have not heard the confession of a nun, but in the light of Scripture I shall hit upon how matters fare with her and know I shall not be lying. If a girl is not sustained by great and exceptional grace, she can live without a man as little as she can without eating, drinking, sleeping, and other natural necessities.

Nor, on the other hand, can a man dispense with a wife. The reason for this is that procreating children is an urge planted as deeply in human nature as eating and drinking. That is why God has given and put into the body the organs, arteries, fluxes, and everything that serves it. Therefore what is he doing who would check this process and keep nature from running its desired and intended course? He is attempting to keep nature from being nature, fire from burning, water from wetting, and a man from eating, drinking, and sleeping.

Source: E. M. Plass, ed., *What Luther Says*, vol. 2 (St. Louis, MO: 1959), pp. 888–89.

Canons on the Sacrament of Matrimony (1563)

Canon 1. If anyone says that matrimony is not truly and properly one of the seven sacraments . . . instituted by Christ the Lord, but has been devised by men in the Church and does not confer grace, let him be anathema [cursed].

Canon 9. If anyone says that clerics constituted in sacred orders or regulars [monks and nuns] who have made solemn profession of chastity can contract marriage . . . and that all who feel that they have not the gift of chastity, even though they have made such a vow, can contract marriage, let him be anathema, since God does not refuse that gift to those who ask for it rightly, neither does *he suffer us to be tempted above that which we are able.*

Canon 10: If anyone says that the married state excels the state of virginity or celibacy, and that it is better and happier to be united in matrimony than to remain in virginity or celibacy, let him be anathema.

Source: H. J. Schroeder, trans., *Canons and Decrees of the Council of Trent* (St. Louis, MO: 1941), pp. 181–82.

Questions for Analysis

1. On what grounds does Luther attack the practice of celibacy? Do you agree with his basic premise?

2. How do the later canons of the Catholic Church respond to Protestant views like Luther's? What appears to be at stake in this defense of marriage and celibacy?

"The King's Great Matter"

By 1527, King Henry VIII of England had been married for eighteen years to Ferdinand and Isabella's daughter, Catherine of Aragon. Yet all the offspring of this union had been stillborn or died in infancy, with the exception of a daughter, Mary. Because Henry needed a male heir to preserve the peaceful succession to the throne, and because Catherine was now past childbearing age—and had shown no signs of pregnancy for over a decade—Henry had political reasons to propose a change of wife. He also had more personal motives, having become infatuated with a lady-in-waiting named Anne Boleyn.

Henry therefore appealed to Rome to annul his marriage to Catherine, arguing that because she had previously been married to his older brother Arthur (who had died in adolescence), Henry's marriage to Catherine had been invalid from the beginning. As Henry's representatives pointed out, the Bible pronounced it "an unclean thing" for a man to take his brother's wife and cursed such a marriage with childlessness (Leviticus 20:21). Even a papal dispensation—which Henry and Catherine had long before obtained for their marriage—could not exempt them from such a clear prohibition, as the marriage's childlessness appeared to prove.

Henry's suit put Pope Clement VII (r. 1523–34) in an awkward position. Popes in the past had granted annulments to reigning monarchs on far weaker grounds than the ones Henry was alleging. If, however, the pope granted Henry's annulment, he would cast doubt on the validity of all papal dispensations because he would be repealing a previous papal decree. More seriously, he would provoke the wrath of the emperor Charles V, Catherine of Aragon's nephew, whose armies were in firm command of Rome and who at that moment held the pope himself in captivity. Clement was trapped; all he could do was procrastinate and hope that the matter would resolve itself.

Exasperated by the delay, Henry began to increase pressure on the pope. In 1531, he compelled an assembly of English clergy to declare him "protector and only supreme head" of the Church in England. In 1532, he encouraged Parliament to produce an inflammatory list of grievances against the English clergy and used this to force them to concede his right to approve or disapprove all Church legislation. In January of 1533, Henry preemptively married Anne Boleyn (already pregnant) even though his marriage to Queen Catherine had still not been annulled. The new archbishop of Canterbury, Thomas Cranmer, provided the required annulment, acting on his own authority.

In September, Princess Elizabeth was born; her father, disappointed again in his hopes for a son, refused to attend her christening. Nevertheless, Parliament settled the succession to the throne on the children of Henry and Anne, redirected all papal revenues from England into the king's hands, prohibited appeals to the papal court, and formally declared "the King's highness to be Supreme Head of the Church of England." In 1536, Henry executed his former tutor and chancellor Sir Thomas More (Chapter 12) for his refusal to accept the marriage or endorse this declaration of supremacy. He also took the first steps toward dissolving England's monasteries. By the end of 1539, their lands and wealth were confiscated by the king, who distributed them to his supporters.

These measures broke the bonds that linked the English Church to Rome, but they did not make England a truly Protestant country. Although certain traditional practices (such as pilgrimages and the veneration of relics) were prohibited, the English Church remained overwhelmingly Catholic in organization, doctrine, ritual, and language. Oral confession to priests, masses for the dead, and clerical celibacy were all confirmed; the Latin Mass continued; and Catholic Eucharistic doctrine was not only confirmed but its denial made punishable by death. To most English people, only the disappearance of the monasteries and the king's own continuing matrimonial adventures were evidence that their Church was no longer in communion with Rome.

The Reign of Edward VI

For truly committed Protestants, and especially those who had visited Calvin's Geneva, the changes Henry VIII enforced on the English Church did not go nearly far enough. In 1547, the accession of the nine-year-old king Edward VI (Henry's son by his third wife, Jane Seymour) gave them their opportunity to finish the task of reform. Encouraged by the apparent sympathies of the young king, Edward's government moved quickly to reform the creeds and ceremonies of the English Church. Priests were permitted to marry; English services replaced Latin ones; the veneration of images was discouraged, and the images themselves defaced or destroyed; formal prayers for the dead were forbidden, and endowments for such prayers were confiscated; and new articles of belief were drawn up,

HENRY VIII OF ENGLAND. Hans Holbein the Younger executed several portraits of the English king. This one represents him in middle age, confident of his powers.

repuditating all sacraments except baptism and communion and affirming the Protestant doctrine of justification by faith alone. Most radically, a new prayer book was published to define precisely how the new English-language services of the Church were to be conducted. By 1553, when the youthful Edward died, the English Church appeared to have become a distinctly Protestant institution.

Mary Tudor and the Restoration of Catholicism

Edward's successor, however, was his pious and much older half-sister Mary (r. 1553–58), granddaughter of "the most Catholic monarchs" of Spain, Ferdinand and Isabella (see Chapter 11). Mary speedily reversed her brother's religious policies, restoring the Latin Mass and requiring married priests to give up their wives. She even prevailed on Parliament to vote a return to papal allegiance. Hundreds of Protestant leaders fled abroad, many to Geneva; others, including Archbishop Thomas Cranmer, were burned at the stake. News of these martyrdoms spread like wildfire through Protestant Europe. In England, however, Mary's policies sparked relatively little resistance. After two decades of religious upheaval, most English men and women were probably hoping that Mary's reign would bring some stability to their lives.

This, however, Mary could not do. The executions she ordered were insufficient to wipe out religious resistance—instead, Protestant propaganda about "Bloody Mary" caused widespread unease. Nor could Mary do anything to restore monasticism: too many leading families had profited from

QUEEN MARY AND QUEEN ELIZABETH. The two daughters of Henry VIII were the first two queens regnant of England: the first women to rule there in their own right. Despite the similar challenges they faced, they had strikingly different fates and have been treated very differently in popular histories. ■ *How do these two portraits suggest differences in their personalities and their self-representation as rulers?*

Henry VIII's dissolution for this to be reversed. Mary's marriage to her cousin Philip, Charles V's son and heir to the Spanish throne, was another miscalculation. Although the marriage treaty stipulated that Philip could not succeed Mary in the event of her death, some of her English subjects never trusted him. When the queen allowed herself to be drawn into a war with France on Spain's behalf—in which England lost Calais, its last foothold on the European continent—many English people became highly disaffected. Ultimately, however, what doomed Mary's policies was simply the accident of biology: Mary was unable to conceive an heir and, when she died after only five years of rule, her throne passed to her Protestant half-sister.

The Elizabethan Compromise

The daughter of Henry VIII and Anne Boleyn, Elizabeth (r. 1558–1603) was predisposed in favor of Protestantism by the circumstances of her parents' marriage as well as by her upbringing. But Elizabeth was no zealot, and wisely recognized that supporting radical Protestantism in England might provoke bitter sectarian strife. Accordingly, she presided over what is often known as "the Elizabethan settlement." Under Elizabeth, Parliament repealed Mary's Catholic legislation, prohibited foreign religious powers (i.e., the pope) from exercising any authority within England, and declared the queen "supreme governor" of the English church—a more seemly title than Henry VIII's "supreme head," since most Protestants believed that Christ alone was the head of the Church. She also adopted many of the Protestant liturgical reforms instituted under her brother Edward, including a revised version of the prayer book. But she retained vestiges of Catholic practice too, including bishops, church courts, elaborate liturgy, and vestments for the clergy.

On most doctrinal matters, including predestination and free will, Elizabeth's Thirty-Nine Articles of Faith (approved in 1562) struck a decidedly Protestant, even Calvinist, tone. But the prayer book was more moderate, and on the critical issue of the Eucharist was deliberately ambiguous. Indeed, by combining Catholic and Protestant interpretations of the last supper and its commemoration, the prayer book permitted an enormous latitude for competing interpretations of the service by priests and parishioners alike.

Yet religious tensions persisted in Elizabethan England, not only between Protestants and Catholics but also between moderate and more extreme Protestants. The queen's artful fudging of these competing Christianities was by no means a recipe for success. Rather, what preserved "the Elizabethan settlement," and ultimately made England a Protestant country, was the extraordinary length of Queen

Elizabeth's reign combined with the fact that for much of that time Protestant England was at war with Catholic Spain. Under Elizabeth, Protestantism and English nationalism gradually fused together into a potent conviction that God himself had chosen England for greatness. After 1588, when English naval forces won an improbable victory over Spain's "Invincible Armada" (Chapter 11), Protestantism and Englishness became nearly indistinguishable to most of Queen Elizabeth's subjects. Laws against Catholic practices became increasingly severe, and although an English Catholic tradition did survive, its adherents were a persecuted minority. Significant, too, was the situation in Ireland, where the vast majority of the population remained Catholic despite the government's efforts to impose Protestantism on them. By 1603, Irishness was as firmly identified with Catholicism as was Englishness with Protestantism; but it was the Protestants who were in power.

THE REBIRTH OF THE CATHOLIC CHURCH

So far, our emphasis on the spread of Protestantism has cast the spotlight on dissident reformers such as Luther and Calvin. But there was also a powerful internal reform movement within the Church during the sixteenth century, which resulted in the birth (or rebirth) of a Catholic ("universal") faith. For some, this movement is the "Catholic Reformation"; for others, it is the "Counter-Reformation." Those who prefer the former term emphasize that the Church carried forward significant reforming movements that can be traced back to the eleventh century (Chapter 8) and which gained new momentum in the wake of the Great Schism (Chapter 10). Others, however, insist that most Catholic reformers of this period were inspired primarily by the urgent need to resist Protestantism and to strengthen the Church's power to oppose it.

Catholic Reforms

Even before Luther's challenge to the Church, as we have seen, there was a movement for moral and institutional reform within some religious orders. But while these efforts received strong support from several secular rulers, the papacy showed little interest in them. In northern Europe, Christian humanists such as Erasmus and Thomas More played an especially central role, not only by criticizing abuses and editing sacred texts but also by encouraging the laity to lead lives of sincere religious piety (Chapter 12).

As a response to the challenges posed by Protestantism, however, these internal reforms proved entirely inadequate. Starting in the 1530s, therefore, a more aggressive phase of reform began to gather momentum. The leading Counter-Reformation popes—Paul III (r. 1534–49), Paul IV (r. 1555–59), Pius V (r. 1566–72), and Sixtus V (r. 1585–90)—were the most zealous leaders of the Church since the twelfth century. All led upright lives; some, indeed, were so grimly ascetic that contemporaries longed for the bad old days. Yet in confronting Protestantism, an excessively holy pope was vastly preferable to a self-indulgent one. And these Counter-Reformation popes were not merely holy men. They were also accomplished administrators who reorganized papal finances and filled ecclesiastical offices with bishops and abbots no less renowned for austerity and holiness than themselves.

Papal reform efforts intensified at the Council of Trent, a General Catholic Council convoked by Paul III in 1545, which met at intervals thereafter until 1563. The decisions taken at Trent (a provincial capital of the Holy Roman Empire, located in modern-day Italy) provided the foundations on which a new Catholic Church would be erected. Although the council began by debating some form of compromise with Protestantism, it ended by reaffirming all of the traditional tenets challenged by Protestant critics. "Good works" were affirmed as necessary for salvation, and all seven sacraments were declared indispensable means of grace. Transubstantiation, Purgatory, the invocation of saints, and the rule of celibacy for the clergy were all confirmed as dogmas— essential elements—of the Catholic faith. The Bible (even in its imperfect Vulgate form) and the teachings of the Catholic fathers and medieval theologians were held to be of equal authority. Papal supremacy over every bishop and priest was expressly maintained, and the supremacy of the pope over any Church council was taken for granted outright, signalling a final defeat of the conciliar movement (Chapter 10). The Council of Trent even reaffirmed the doctrine of indulgences that had touched off the Lutheran revolt, although it condemned the worst abuses connected with their sale.

The legislation of Trent was not confined to matters of doctrine. To improve pastoral care of the laity, bishops and priests were forbidden to hold more than one spiritual office. To address the problem of an ignorant priesthood, a theological seminary was to be established in every diocese. The council also suppressed a variety of local religious practices and saints' cults, replacing them with new cults authorized and approved by Rome. To prevent heretical ideas from corrupting the faithful, the council further decided to censor or suppress dangerous books. In 1564, a specially appointed commission published the first *Index of Prohibited Books*, an official list of forbidden writings. All of Erasmus's works were immediately placed on the *Index*,

THE INSPIRATION OF SAINT JEROME BY GUIDO RENI. The Council of Trent declared Saint Jerome's Latin translation of the Bible, the Vulgate, to be the official version of the Catholic Church. Since biblical scholars had long known that Saint Jerome's translation contained numerous errors, Catholic defenders of the Vulgate insisted that even his mistakes had been divinely inspired. ■ *How does Guido Reni's painting of 1635 attempt to make this point?*

even though he had been a chosen champion of the Church only forty years before. It was to become symbolic of the doctrinal intolerance that characterized sixteenth-century Christianity, both in its Catholic and Protestant varieties. It was maintained until 1966, when it was abolished after the Second Vatican Council.

Ignatius Loyola and the Society of Jesus

In addition to the independent activities of popes and the legislation of the Council of Trent, a third main force propelling the Counter-Reformation was the foundation of the Society of Jesus (commonly known as the Jesuits) by Ignatius Loyola (1491–1556). In the midst of a career as a mercenary, this young Spanish nobleman had been wounded in battle in 1521, the same year in which Luther defied authority at the Diet of Worms. While recuperating, Ignatius turned from the reading of chivalric romances to a romantic vernacular retelling of the life of Jesus—and on the strength of this, decided to become a spiritual soldier of Christ. For ten months he lived as a hermit in a cave near the town of Manresa, where he experienced ecstatic visions and worked out the principles of his subsequent guidebook, the *Spiritual Exercises*. This manual, completed in 1535 and first published in 1541, offered practical advice on how to master one's will and serve God through a systematic program of meditations. It eventually became a basic handbook for all Jesuits and has been widely studied by Catholic laypeople as well. Indeed, Loyola's *Spiritual Exercises* ranks alongside Calvin's *Institutes* as the most influential religious text of the sixteenth century.

The Jesuit order originated as a small group of six disciples who gathered around Loyola during his belated career as a student in Paris. They vowed to serve God in poverty, chastity, and missionary work, and were formally constituted by Pope Paul III in 1540. By the time of Loyola's death, the Society of Jesus already numbered some 1,500 members. It was by far the most militant of the religious orders fostered by the Catholic reform movements of the sixteenth century: not merely a monastic society, but a company of soldiers sworn to defend the faith with weapons of eloquence, persuasion, and instruction in correct doctrines. Yet the Society also became accomplished in more worldly methods of exerting influence; its organization was patterned after that of a military unit, whose commander in chief enforced iron discipline on all members. Individuality was suppressed, and a soldierlike obedience was required from the rank and file. Indeed, the Jesuit general, sometimes known as the "black pope" (from the color of the order's habit), was elected for life and answered only to the pope in Rome, to whom all senior Jesuits took a special vow of strict obedience. As a result of this vow, all Jesuits were held to be at the pope's disposal at all times.

As missionaries, the early Jesuits preached to non-Christians in India, China, and Spanish America. One of Loyola's closest associates, Francis Xavier (1506–1552), baptized thousands of native people and traveled thousands of miles in South and East Asia. For although Loyola had not at first conceived of his society as a batallion of "shock troops" in the fight against Protestantism, that is what it primarily became. Through preaching and diplomacy—sometimes at the risk of their lives—Jesuits in the second half of the sixteenth century fanned out across the globe. In many places, they were instrumental in keeping rulers and their subjects loyal to Catholicism; in others they met martyrdom; and in some others, notably Poland and parts of Germany and France, they succeeded in regaining territory previously lost to Protestantism. Wherever they were allowed to settle, they set up schools and colleges, based on the conviction that only a vigorous Catholicism nurtured by widespread literacy and education could combat Protestantism.

A New Catholic Christianity

The greatest achievement of these reform movements was the revitalization of the Roman Church. Had it not been for such determined efforts, Catholicism would not have swept

Analyzing Primary Sources

The Demands of Obedience

The necessity of obedience in the spiritual formation of monks and nuns can be traced back to the Rule *of Saint Benedict in the early sixth century (Chapter 6). In keeping with the mission of its founder, Ignatius of Loyola (1491–1556), the Society of Jesus brought a new militancy to this old ideal.*

Rules for Thinking with the Church

1. Always to be ready to obey with mind and heart, setting aside all judgment of one's own, the true spouse of Jesus Christ, our holy mother, our infallible and orthodox mistress, the Catholic Church, whose authority is exercised over us by the hierarchy.

2. To commend the confession of sins to a priest as it is practised in the Church; the reception of the Holy Eucharist once a year, or better still every week, or at least every month, with the necessary preparation. . . .

4. To have a great esteem for the religious orders, and to give the preference to celibacy or virginity over the married state. . . .

6. To praise relics, the veneration and invocation of Saints: also the stations, and pious pilgrimages, indulgences, jubilees, the custom of lighting candles in the churches, and other such aids to piety and devotion. . . .

9. To uphold especially all the precepts of the Church, and not censure them in any manner; but, on the contrary, to defend them promptly, with reasons drawn from all sources, against those who criticize them.

10. To be eager to commend the decrees, mandates, traditions, rites, and customs of the Fathers in the Faith or our superiors. . . .

11. That we may be altogether of the same mind and in conformity with the Church herself, if she shall have defined anything to be black which to our eyes appears to be white, we ought in like manner to pronounce it to be black. For we must undoubtingly believe, that the Spirit of our Lord Jesus Christ, and the Spirit of the Orthodox Church His Spouse, by which Spirit we are governed and directed to salvation, is the same. . . .

From the *Constitutions of the Jesuit Order*

Let us with the utmost pains strain every nerve of our strength to exhibit this virtue of obedience, firstly to the Highest Pontiff, then to the Superiors of the Society; so that in all things . . . we may be most ready to obey his voice, just as if it issued from Christ our Lord . . . leaving any work, even a letter, that we have begun and have not yet finished; by directing to this goal all our strength and intention in the Lord, that holy obedience may be made perfect in us in every respect, in performance, in will, in intellect; by submitting to whatever may be enjoined on us with great readiness, with spiritual joy and perseverance; by persuading ourselves that all things [commanded] are just; by rejecting with a kind of blind obedience all opposing opinion or judgment of our own. . . .

Source: Henry Bettenson, ed., *Documents of the Christian Church*, 2nd ed. (Oxford: 1967), pp. 259–61.

Questions for Analysis

1. How might Loyola's career as a soldier have inspired the language used in his "Rules for Thinking with the Church"?

2. In what ways do these Jesuit principles respond directly to the challenges of Protestant reformers?

---

over the globe during the seventeenth and eighteenth centuries or reemerged in Europe as a vigorous spiritual force. There were some other consequences, as well. One was the advancement of lay literacy in Catholic countries. Another was the growth of intense concern for acts of charity: because Catholicism continued to emphasize good works as well as faith, charitable activities took on an extremely important role.

There was also a renewed emphasis on the role of religious women. Reformed Catholicism did not exalt marriage as a route to holiness to the same degree as did Protestantism, but it did encourage the piety of a female religious elite. For example, it embraced the mysticism of Saint Teresa of Avila (1515–1582) and established new orders of nuns, such as the Ursulines and the Sisters of Charity. Both Protestants and Catholics continued to exclude women from the priesthood or ministry, but Catholic women could pursue religious lives with at least some degree of independence, and the convent continued to be a route toward spiritual and even political advancement in Catholic countries.

The new Catholic Church did not, however, perpetuate the tolerant Christianity of Erasmus. Instead, Christian humanists lost favor with the papacy, and even Catholic scientists such as Galileo were regarded with suspicion (see Chapter 16). Yet contemporary Protestantism was just as intolerant, and even more hostile to the cause of rational thought. Indeed, because Catholic theologians turned for guidance to the scholasticism of Thomas Aquinas (Chapter 9), they tended to be much more committed to the dignity of human reason than were their Protestant counterparts, who emphasized the literal interpretation of the Bible and the importance of unquestioning faith. It is no coincidence that René Descartes, one of the pioneers of rational philosophy ("I think, therefore I am"), was educated by Jesuits.

It would be wrong, therefore, to claim that the Protestantism of this era was more forward-looking or progressive than Catholicism. Both were, in fact, products of their times. Each variety of Protestantism responded to specific historical conditions and the needs of specific peoples in specific places, while carrying forward certain aspects of the Christian tradition considered valuable by those communities. The Catholic Church also responded to new spiritual, political, and social realities—to such an extent that it must be regarded as distinct from either the early Church of the later Roman Empire or even the oft-reformed Church of the Middle Ages. That is why the phrase "Roman Catholic Church" has not been used in this book prior to this chapter, because the Roman Catholic Church as we know it emerged for the first time in the sixteenth century. Like Protestantism, it is a modern phenomenon.

CONCLUSION

The Reformation grew out of the complex historical processes that we have been tracing through the last few chapters. Foremost among these was the increasing power of Europe's sovereign states (Chapter 10). As we have seen, those German princes who embraced Protestantism were moved to do so by the desire for sovereignty. The kings of Denmark, Sweden, and England followed suit for many of the same reasons. Since Protestant leaders preached absolute obedience to godly rulers, and since the state in Protestant countries assumed direct control of its churches, Protestantism bolstered state power. Yet the power of the state had been growing for a long time prior to this, especially in such countries as France and Spain, where Catholic kings already exercised most of the same rights that were seized by Lutheran German princes and by

After You Read This Chapter

Visit StudySpace for quizzes, additional review materials, and multi-media documents. **wwnorton.com/studyspace**

REVIEWING THE OBJECTIVES

- The main premises of Luther's theology had political and social implications, too. What were they?
- A number of different Protestant movements rose in the sixteenth century. What were they, and how did they differ from one another?
- The Reformation had a profound effect on the basic structures of family life and on attitudes toward marriage and morality. Describe these changes.
- The Church of England was established in response to a specific political situation. What was this?
- How did the Catholic Church respond to the challenge of Protestantism?

Henry VIII of England. Those rulers who aligned themselves with Catholicism, then, had the same need to bolster their sovereignty and authority.

Ideas of national identity, too, were already influential and thus available for manipulation by Protestants and Catholics alike. These new religions, in turn, became sources of identity and disunity. Until the sixteenth century, for example, the peoples in the different regions of Germany spoke such different dialects that they had difficulty understanding each other. But Luther's German Bible gained such currency that it eventually became the linguistic standard for all these disparate regions, which eventually began to conceive of themselves as part of a single community. Yet religion alone could not achieve the political unification of Germany, which did not occur for another three hundred years (see Chapter 21); indeed, religion contributed to existing divisions by cementing the opposition of Catholic princes and peoples. Elsewhere in Europe—as in the Netherlands, where Protestants fought successfully against a foreign, Catholic overlord—religion created a shared identity where politics could not. In England, where it is arguable that a sense of nationalism had already been fostered before the Reformation, membership in the Church of England became a new, but not uncontested, attribute of "Englishness."

Ideals characteristic of the Renaissance (Chapter 12) also contributed something to the Reformation and the Catholic responses to it. The criticisms of Christian humanists helped to prepare Europe for the challenges of Lutheranism, and close textual study of the Bible led to the publication of the newer, more accurate editions used by Protestant reformers. For example, Erasmus's improved edition of the Latin New Testament enabled Luther to reach some crucial conclusions and became the foundation for Luther's own translation of the Bible. Yet Erasmus was no supporter of Lutheran principles and most other Christian humanists followed suit, shunning Protestantism as soon as it became clear to them what Luther was actually teaching. Indeed, in certain basic respects, Protestant principles were completely at odds with the principles, politics, and beliefs of most Renaissance humanists, who were staunch supporters of the Catholic Church.

In the New World and Asia, both Protestantism and Catholicism became forces of imperialism and new catalysts for competition. The race to secure colonies and resources now became a race for converts, too. In the process, the confessional divisions of Europe were mapped onto these far-flung territories, often with violent results. And over the course of the ensuing century, newly sovereign nation-states would continue to struggle for hegemony at home and abroad, setting off a series of religious wars that would cause as much destruction as any plague. We will discuss these upheavals and their long-term consequences in Chapter 14.

PEOPLE, IDEAS, AND EVENTS IN CONTEXT

- How did **MARTIN LUTHER**'s attack on **INDULGENCES** tap into more widespread criticism of the papacy? What role did the printing press and the German vernacular play in the dissemination of Luther's ideas?
- Why did many German principalities and cities rally to Luther's cause? Why did his condemnation at the **DIET OF WORMS** not lead to his execution on charges of heresy?
- How did the Protestant teachings of **ULRICH ZWINGLI**, **JOHN CALVIN**, and the **ANABAPTISTS** differ from one another and from those of Luther?
- What factors made some of Europe's territories more receptive to **PROTESTANTISM** than others? Why, for example, did Switzerland, the Netherlands, and the countries of Scandinavia embrace it?
- How did the **REFORMATION** alter the status and lives of women in Europe? Why did it strengthen male authority in the family?
- Why did **HENRY VIII** break with Rome? How did the **CHURCH OF ENGLAND** differ from Protestant churches elsewhere in Europe?
- What decisions were made at the **COUNCIL OF TRENT**? What were the founding principles of **IGNATIUS LOYOLA**'s **SOCIETY OF JESUS**, and what was its role in the **COUNTER-REFORMATION** of the **ROMAN CATHOLIC CHURCH**?

CONSEQUENCES

- Our study of Western civilizations has shown that reforming movements are nothing new: Christianity has been continuously reformed throughout its long history. What made this Reformation so different?
- Was a Protestant break with the Catholic Church inevitable? Why or why not?
- The political, social, and religious structures put in place during the Reformation continue to shape our lives in such profound ways that we scarcely notice them—or we assume them to be inevitable and natural. In your view, what is the most far-reaching consequence of this age of dissent and division, and why? In what ways has it formed your own values and assumptions?

Before You Read This Chapter

Religion, Warfare, and Sovereignty: 1540–1660

CORE OBJECTIVES

- **UNDERSTAND** the ways in which early modern religious and political conflicts were intertwined.

- **TRACE** the main phases of religious warfare on the Continent.

- **IDENTIFY** the causes for Spain's decline and France's rise to power.

- **EXPLAIN** the origins and significance of the English Civil War.

- **DESCRIBE** some of the ways that intellectuals and artists responded to the challenges of this era.

n the early spring of 1592, a new play was mounted at the Rose Theatre, one of the enclosed places of entertainment recently constructed in London's suburbs. It was the prequel to two vastly popular plays that chronicled the dynastic wars that had divided England in the fifteenth century, when English losses in the Hundred Years' War gave way to civil wars at home. The play, *The First Part of Henry VI*, was intended to explore the origins of those wars during the reign of the child-king who had suceeded the heroic Henry V, and it completed a trilogy that launched an ambitious young playwright called Will Shakespeare.

Civil strife was a hot topic in the sixteenth century. Shakespeare's England was much more peaceful and unified than almost any other country in Europe, but that unity was fragile. It had been shattered numerous times because of ongoing religious divisions, and it was only being maintained by a growing sense of national identity. Shakespeare's early plays promoted that identity by celebrating the superiority of the average Englishman over his European neighbors, who were often represented as either ridiculous or villainous. So in this new play, the most interesting and ultimately dangerous character is the French heroine Joan of Arc, whose fervent Catholic faith turns out to be a mask for witchcraft. In Shakespeare's version of her legend, Joan attempts to be released from the tortures of the stake by claiming to be pregnant, and dies calling on her demon familiars to rescue her from the flames.

Shakespeare's plays, like many other products of contemporary popular culture, reveal the profound tensions that fractured the kingdoms and communities of Europe in the century after the Reformation. Martin Luther's call for universal access to the Bible had not resulted in a unified interpretation of the Christian faith; nor did his dream of a "priesthood of all believers" topple the clerical hierarchy of the Roman Church. Instead, Europe's religious divisions multiplied, often crystallizing along political lines. By the time of Luther's death in 1546, a clear pattern had already emerged. With only rare exceptions, Protestantism triumphed in areas where those in power stood to gain by rejecting the Church's hold over them; meanwhile, Catholicism prevailed in territories whose rulers had forged close political alliances with Rome. In both cases, Protestants and Catholics clung to the same belief in the mutual interdependence of religion and politics, an old certainty that had also undergirded the civilization of ancient Rome (Chapter 5) and most other Western civilizations before it.

Ironically, then, Catholics and Protestants were united in one conviction: western Europe had to return to a single religious faith enforced by properly constituted political authorities. What they could not agree on was *which* faith—and which authorities. The result was a brutal series of wars whose reverberations continue to be felt in many regions of Europe and in her former colonies. Vastly expensive and destructive, these wars affected everyone from peasants to princes. Yet it would be misleading to suggest that they were caused by religious differences alone. Regional tensions, dynastic politics, and nascent nationalist tendencies were also potent contributors to the violence. Together, these forces brought into question the very survival of the political institutions that had emerged in the twelfth and thirteenth centuries (Chapter 9). Faced with the prospect of annihilation, those who still held power a century later were forced to embrace, gradually and grudgingly, a notion that had long seemed impossible: religious tolerance as the only way to preserve political, social, and economic order.

SOURCES OF TENSION AND UNREST

The troubles that engulfed Europe during the long, traumatic century between 1540 and 1660 caught contemporaries unaware. Most of Europe had enjoyed steady economic growth since the middle of the fifteenth century, and the colonization of the Americas seemed certain to be the basis of greater prosperity to come. Political trends too seemed auspicious, because most western European governments were becoming more efficient and effective. By the middle of the sixteenth century, however, there were warning signs.

The Price Revolution

The first of these warning signs was economic: an unprecedented inflation in prices that began in the latter half of the sixteenth century. In Flanders, the cost of wheat tripled between 1550 and 1600; grain prices in Paris quadrupled; and the overall cost of living in England more than doubled. The twentieth century would see much more dizzying inflations than this, but in the sixteenth century the skyrocketing of prices was a terrifying novelty, what many historians describe as the "price revolution."

Two developments in particular underlay the soaring prices. The first was demographic. Starting in the later fifteenth century, Europe's population began to grow again after the plague-induced decline of the fourteenth century (Chapter 10); roughly estimated, Europe had about 50 million people around 1450, and 90 million around 1600. Because Europe's food supply remained more or less constant, owing to the lack of any noteworthy breakthroughs in agricultural technology analogous to those of the eleventh century (Chapter 8), food prices were driven sharply higher by greater demand. At the same time, wages stagnated or even declined. As a result, workers around 1600 were paying a higher percentage of their wages to buy food.

Population trends explain much, but other explanations for the great inflation are also necessary. Foremost among these is the enormous influx of bullion from Spanish America. In just four years, from 1556 to 1560, roughly 10 million ducats' worth of silver passed through the Spanish port of Seville. That figure doubled between 1576 and 1580, and between 1591 and 1595 it more than quadrupled. Most of this silver was used by the Spanish crown to pay its foreign creditors and its armies abroad; as a result, this bullion quickly circulated throughout Europe, where much of it was minted into coins. This dramatic increase in the volume of money in circulation fueled the spiral of rising prices. "I learned a proverb here," said a French traveler to Spain in 1603: "everything costs a lot, except silver."

Aggressive entrepreneurs and large-scale farmers profited most from the changed economic circumstances, while the masses of laboring people were hurt the most because wages rose far more slowly than prices. Moreover, because the cost of food staples rose at a sharper rate than the cost of most other items, poor people had to spend an ever-greater percentage of their paltry incomes on necessities. The picture that emerges is one of the rich getting richer and the poor getting poorer.

The price revolution also placed new pressures on the sovereign states of Europe. Since inflation depressed the real value of money, fixed incomes from taxes and tolls yielded less and less income. So governments were forced to raise taxes merely to keep their revenues constant. But to compound this problem, most states needed more real income because they were engaging in more wars; and warfare was becoming increasingly expensive. The only recourse, then, was to raise taxes precipitously. Hence governments faced continuous threats of defiance and even armed resistance from their subjects. A few areas—notably the Netherlands—bucked the trend, and the wealthy were usually able to hold their own, but the lives of the poor in many places deteriorated further as the mid-seventeenth century saw particularly destructive wars in which helpless civilians were plundered by rapacious tax collectors or looting soldiers, sometimes both. The Black Death also returned, wreaking havoc in London and elsewhere during the 1660s.

Political and Religious Instability

Compounding these problems were the disunities inherent within major European monarchies. Most states had grown during the later Middle Ages by absorbing or colonizing smaller, autonomous territories—sometimes by conquest, but more often through marriage alliances or inheritance arrangements among ruling families. At first, some degree of provincial autonomy was usually preserved. But in the period we are now examining, governments began making ever-greater financial claims on all their subjects while trying to enforce religious uniformity. As a result, rulers often rode roughshod over the rights of these traditionally independent provinces.

At the same time, claims to sovereignty—that is, to the unity, autonomy, and authority of a state—were increasingly made on the basis of religious uniformity. Both Catholic and Protestant rulers felt that religious minorities, if allowed to flourish in their realms, would inevitably engage in sedition; nor were they always wrong, since militant Calvinists and Jesuits were indeed dedicated to subverting constituted powers in areas where their parties had not yet triumphed. Thus states tried to extirpate all potential religious resistance and, in the process, sometimes provoked civil wars in which each side tended to assume there could be no victory until the other was exterminated. And of course, civil wars could become international in scope if foreign powers chose to aid their embattled religious allies.

Regionalism, economic grievances, and religious animosities were thus compounded into a volatile and destructive mixture. Nor was that all, since most governments seeking money and/or religious uniformity tried to rule with a firmer hand than before and thus increasingly provoked armed resistance from subjects seeking to preserve traditional liberties. As a result, the long century between 1540 and 1660 was one of the most turbulent in all of European history.

A CENTURY OF RELIGIOUS WARS

The greatest single cause of warfare during this period was religious conflict. These "wars of religion" are usually divided into four phases:

    I. a series of regional wars in Germany from the 1540s to 1555
    II. the French wars of religion from 1562 until 1598
    III. the simultaneous revolts of the (Protestant) Dutch against the (Catholic) Spanish Habsburg Empire between 1566 and 1609
    IV. the Thirty Years' War that devasted German-speaking lands again, between 1618 and 1648.

In addition, as we shall see, the English Civil War resulted in part from religious differences, even though it is not usually considered a war of religion (see below).

Regional Warfare in Germany

Wars between Catholics and Protestant rulers in Germany began in the 1540s, less than a generation after Lutheranism first took hold there. As we have seen, the Holy Roman emperor, Charles V, was also king of Spain and a devout supporter of the Church (Chapter 13). His goal was to reestablish Catholic unity in Germany by launching a military campaign against several German princes who had instituted Lutheran worship in their territories. But despite several notable victories, Charles's efforts failed. In part, this was because he was simultaneously involved in wars against France, but primarily it was because the Catholic princes of Germany also worked against him, fearing that any suppression of Protestant princes might suppress their own independence, too. As a result, the Catholic princes' support for the foreign-born Charles was only lukewarm; at times, they even joined with Protestants in battle against the emperor.

This regional warfare sputtered on and off until a compromise was reached via the Peace of Augsburg in 1555. Its governing principle was *cuius regio, eius religio*: "as the ruler, so the religion." This meant that in those principalities where Lutherans ruled, Lutheranism would be the sole state religion; but where Catholic princes ruled, the people of their territories would also be Catholic. For better and for worse, the Peace of Augsburg was a historical milestone. For the first time since Luther had been excommunicated, Catholic rulers were forced to acknowledge the legality of Protestantism. But the peace set a dangerous precedent because it legitimated the principle that no sovereign state could tolerate religious diversity. Moreover, it excluded Calvinism entirely, and thus spurred German Calvinists to become aggressive opponents of the status quo.

The French Wars of Religion

From the 1560s on, Europe's religious wars became far more brutal, partly because the combatants had become more intransigent and partly because they were aggravated by regional and dynastic animosities. For example, Calvin's Geneva bordered on France; and because Calvin himself was a Frenchman, Calvinist missionaries made considerable headway. But their concentration in the southern part of France reflected long-standing hostilities that reached back to the ravages of northern French "crusaders" against Albigensian "heretics" during the thirteenth century (Chapter 9). Also assisting the Calvinist cause was the conversion of many aristocratic Frenchwomen, who in turn won over their husbands, many of whom maintained large private armies. The foremost example of these was Jeanne d'Albret, queen of Navarre, who converted her husband, the prominent aristocrat Antoine de Bourbon, and her brother-in-law, the prince of Condé.

Within two decades, French Calvinists—known as Huguenots (*YOO-guh-nohs*) for reasons that remain obscure—made up between 10 and 20 percent of the population. Although they lived uneasily alongside their Catholic neighbors, there was no open warfare until 1562, when the reigning king died unexpectedly, leaving a young child

as his heir. This spurred a struggle between two factions which formed along religious lines: the Huguenots, led by the prince of Condé, and the Catholics, led by the duke of Guise. And since both Catholics and Protestants believed that a kingdom could have only one *roi*, *foi*, and *loi* ("king," "faith," and "law"), this political struggle turned into a religious war. Although the Huguenots were not numerous enough to gain a victory, they were too strong to be defeated entirely, especially in their stronghold of southern France. Hence warfare dragged on for a decade until a truce was arranged in 1572. This truce required the young Huguenot leader, Prince Henry of Navarre, to marry the Catholic sister of the reigning French king.

Yet this compromise was placed in jeopardy by the powerful dowager queen of France, Catherine de' Medici, scion of the Florentine family that was closely aligned with the papacy (Chapter 13). Instead of honoring the truce, she plotted with members of the Catholic faction at court to kill all the Huguenot leaders while they were assembled in Paris for her daugher's wedding. In the early morning of St. Bartholomew's Day in 1572 (August 24), most of these leaders were murdered in their beds, while thousands of other Protestants were slaughtered in the streets or drowned in the Seine by Catholic mobs. When word of the Parisian massacre spread to the provinces, some 10,000 more Huguenots were killed. Henry of Navarre escaped, along with his new bride; but now the conflict entered an even more bitter phase.

Catherine's death in 1589 enabled Henry of Navarre to be crowned king as Henry IV, but peace was not restored until he renounced his Protestant faith in order to placate France's Catholic majority. In 1598, however, he offered limited religious freedom to the Huguenots by issuing the Edict of Nantes, which recognized Catholicism as the official religion of the kingdom but allowed Huguenot aristocrats to hold Protestant services privately in their homes, while other Huguenots were allowed to worship in certain specified places at certain times. The Huguenot party was also permitted to fortify some towns, especially in the south and west, for their own military defense. Huguenots were further guaranteed the right to hold public office and to enter universities and hospitals.

The Edict of Nantes did not guarantee absolute freedom of worship, but it was still a major stride in the direction of tolerance. Unfortunately, however, the effect was to divide the kingdom into separate religious enclaves. In southern and western France, Huguenots established their own law courts, staffed by their own judges. They also received substantial powers of self-government. The edict thus represented a concession to the long-standing traditions of

The Devastation of the Thirty Years' War

The author of the following excerpt, Hans Jakob Christoph von Grimmelshausen (1621–1676), barely survived the horrors of the Thirty Years' War. His parents were killed, probably when he was thirteen years old, and he himself was kidnapped the following year and forced into the army. By age fifteen, he was a soldier. His darkly satiric masterpiece, Simplicissimus (The Simpleton), *drew heavily on these experiences. Although technically a fictional memoir, it portrays with brutal accuracy the terrible realities of this era.*

 lthough it was not my intention to take the peaceloving reader with these troopers to my dad's house and farm, seeing that matters will go ill therein, yet the course of my history demands that I should leave to kind posterity an account of what manner of cruelties were now and again practised in this our German war: yes, and moreover testify by my own example that such evils must often have been sent to us by the goodness of Almighty God for our profit. For, gentle reader, who would ever have taught me that there was a God in Heaven if these soldiers had not destroyed my dad's house, and by such a deed driven me out among folk who gave me all fitting instruction thereupon? . . .

The first thing these troopers did was, that they stabled their horses: thereafter each fell to his appointed task: which task was neither more nor less than ruin and destruction. For though some began to slaughter and to boil and to roast so that it looked as if there should be a merry banquet forward, yet others there were who did but storm through the house above and below stairs. Others stowed together great parcels of cloth and apparel and all manner of household stuff, as if they would set up a frippery market. All that they had no mind to take with them they cut in pieces. Some thrust their swords through the hay and straw as if they had not enough sheep and swine to slaughter: and some shook the feathers out of the beds and in their stead stuffed in bacon and other dried meat and provisions as if such were better and softer to sleep upon. Others broke the stove and the windows as if they had a never-ending summer to promise. Houseware of copper and tin they beat flat, and packed such vessels, all bent and spoiled, in with the rest. Bedsteads, tables, chairs, and benches they burned, though there lay many cords of dry wood in the yard. Pots and pipkins must all go to pieces, either because they would eat none but roast flesh, or because their purpose was to make there but a single meal.

Our maid was so handled in the stable that she could not come out, which is a shame to tell of. Our man they laid bound upon the ground, thrust a gag into his mouth, and poured a pailful of filthy water into his body: and by this, which they called a Swedish draught, they forced him to lead a party of them to another place where they captured men and beasts, and brought them back to our farm, in which company were my dad, my mother, and our Ursula.

And now they began: first to take the flints out of their pistols and in place of them to jam the peasants' thumbs in and so to torture the poor rogues as if they had been about the burning of witches: for one of them they had taken they thrust into the baking oven and there lit a fire under him, although he had as yet confessed no crime: as for another, they put a cord round his head and so twisted it tight with a piece of wood that the blood gushed from his mouth and nose and ears. In a word each had his own device to torture the peasants, and each peasant his several tortures.

Source: Hans Jakob Christoph von Grimmelshausen, *Simplicissimus*, trans. S. Goodrich (New York: 1995), pp. 1–3, 8–10, 32–35.

Questions for Analysis

1. The first-person narrator here recounts the atrocities committed "in this our German war," in which both perpetrators and victims are German. How believable is this description? Why does he emphasize this? What lends it credibility?

2. Why might Grimmelshausen have chosen to publish his account as a satirical fiction, rather than as a straightforward historical narrative or autobiography? How would this choice affect a reader's response to scenes such as this?

provincial autonomy within the various regions of France, raising the fear that the kingdom might once again crumble into its constituent parts, as it had during the Hundred Years' War. On its own terms, however, the Edict of Nantes was a success. France began to recover from decades of devastation, and peace was maintained even after Henry IV was assassinated by a Catholic in 1610.

The Revolt of the Netherlands

Bitter warfare also broke out between Catholics and Protestants in the Low Countries. For almost a century, the territories comprising much of the modern-day Netherlands and Belgium had been ruled by the Habsburg family of Holy Roman emperors, who also ruled Spain. The southern Netherlands in particular had prospered greatly from this. Through trade and manufacture, their inhabitants generated the greatest per capita wealth of all Europe, and their metropolis of Antwerp was northern Europe's leading commercial and financial center. Moreover, the half-century rule of Charles V had been successful here. Charles had been born in the Flemish city of Ghent, and had a strong rapport with his Flemish subjects, whom he allowed a large measure of self-government.

But a year after the Peace of Augsburg in 1555, Charles V retired to a monastery and ceded all of his vast territories outside of the Holy Roman Empire and Hungary to his son Philip II (r. 1556–98). Unlike Charles, Philip had been born in Spain and made Spain his residence and the focus of his policy. He viewed the Netherlands primarily as a source of income. So the better to exploit the region's wealth, Philip tried to tighten his control over it, which aroused the resentment of the region's fiercely independent cities. A religious storm was also brewing. French Calvinists were beginning to stream into the southern Netherlands, intent on making converts. Within decades, there were more Calvinists in Antwerp than in Geneva. To Philip, an ardent supporter of the Roman Catholic Church, this was intolerable.

Worried by the growing tensions, a group of Catholic aristocrats petitioned Philip to allow toleration for Calvinists within the Netherlands. They were led by William of Orange, known as "William the Silent" because he was so successful at hiding his religious and political leanings. But before Philip could respond, radical Protestant mobs began ransacking Catholic churches, desecrating altars, smashing statuary, and shattering stained-glass windows. Local troops brought the situation under control, but Philip nonetheless decided to dispatch an army of 10,000 Spanish soliders, led by the duke of Alva, to wipe out Protestantism in the Netherlands. Alva's rule quickly became a reign of terror. Operating under martial law, his "Council of Blood" examined some 12,000 people on charges of heresy or sedition, of whom 9,000 were convicted and thousands executed. William fled the country, and all hope for peace in the Netherlands seemed lost.

Yet the tide turned quickly. The exiled William converted openly to Protestantism and sought help from religious allies in France, Germany, and England; meanwhile, organized bands of Protestant privateers harassed Spanish shipping. In 1572, William was able to seize the northern Netherlands, even though the north had been predominantly Catholic. Thereafter, geography played a major role in determining the outcome of the conflict. Spanish armies were stopped by a combination of impassable rivers and dikes that could be opened to flood out the invaders. Although William was assassinated by a Catholic in 1584, his son continued to lead the resistance until the Spanish crown agreed to recognize the independence of a northern Dutch Republic in 1609. For ironically, the pressures of war and persecution had made the whole north Calvinist, whereas the south—which remained under Spanish control—returned to Catholicism.

England and the Spanish Armada

Religious strife could spark civil war, as in France, or political rebellion, as in the Netherlands. But it could also provoke warfare between sovereign states, as in the struggle between England and Spain. As we noted in Chapter 13, the Catholic queen Mary of England (r. 1553–58), herself the granddaughter of Ferdinand and Isabella, had married her cousin Philip II of Spain in 1554. After her death, Philip appears to have extended a marriage proposal to her half-sister, the Protestant queen Elizabeth (r. 1558–1603)—and to have been rejected. Adding to the animosity created by religious differences and dynastic politics was the fact that English economic interests were directly opposed to those of Spain: English seafarers and traders were steadily making inroads into Spanish naval and commercial networks. The greatest source of antagonism lay in the Atlantic, where English privateers, with the tacit consent of Queen Elizabeth, began attacking Spanish treasure ships. Taking as an excuse the Spanish oppression of Protestants in the Netherlands, English sea captains such as Sir Francis Drake and Sir John Hawkins plundered Spanish vessels on the high seas. In a particularly dramatic exploit lasting from 1577 to 1580, prevailing winds and lust for gold propelled Drake all the way around the world, to return

THE "ARMADA PORTRAIT" OF ELIZABETH. This is one of several portraits that commemorated the defeat of the Spanish Armada in 1588. Through the window on the left (the queen's right hand), an English flotilla sails serenely on sunny seas; on the right, Spanish ships are wrecked by a "Protestant wind." Elizabeth's right hand rests protectively—and commandingly—on the globe. ▪ *How would you "read" this image?*

with stolen Spanish treasure worth twice as much as Queen Elizabeth's annual revenue.

All this might have been sufficient provocation, but Philip resolved to invade the island only after the English openly allied with Dutch rebels in 1585. Even then, Philip moved slowly. Finally, in 1588 he dispatched an enormous fleet, confidently called the "Invincible Armada." However, the smaller English warships, more agile and armed with longer-range guns, outmaneuvered the Spanish fleet, while English fireships set some Spanish galleons ablaze and forced the rest to break formation. A fierce "Protestant wind" did the rest. After a disastrous circumnavigation of the British Isles and Ireland, the shattered Spanish flotilla limped home with almost half its ships lost. Elizabeth quickly took credit for her country's miraculous escape.

The Thirty Years' War

After the Peace of Augsburg in 1555, the balance of powers between Protestant and Catholic territories within the Holy Roman Empire had remained largely undisturbed. In 1618, however, the Catholic Habsburg prince who ruled Poland, Austria, and Hungary was elected king of Protestant Bohemia, prompting a rebellion among the Bohemian aristocracy. When this same prince, Ferdinand, became Holy Roman Emperor a year later, German Catholic forces were sent to crush the rebellion against him. But this military intervention threatened the political autonomy of all German princes, Catholic and Protestant alike. So when the Lutheran king of Sweden, Gustavus Adolphus, championed the Protestant cause in 1630, he was welcomed by several German Catholic princes, too.

To make matters still more complicated, the Swedish king's Protestant army was secretly subsidized by Catholic France, whose policy was then dictated by Cardinal Richelieu (*RIH-shlyuh*, 1585–1642). Richelieu was determined to prevent France from being surrounded by a strong Habsburg alliance on the north, east, and south. But when Gustavus died in battle in 1632, Cardinal Richelieu found himself having to conduct the war on his own. In 1635, France openly declared itself for Sweden, against Austria and Spain. In the middle lay Germany, a helpless battleground.

Germany suffered more from warfare in the terrible years between 1618 and 1648 than than at any time until the twentieth century. Several German cities were besieged and sacked nine or ten times over, and soldiers from all nations, who had to sustain themselves by plunder, gave no quarter to defenseless civilians. With plague and disease adding to the toll of outright butchery, some parts of Germany lost more than half their populations.

The eventual adoption of the Peace of Westphalia in 1648 was a watershed in European history. It marked the emergence of France as the predominant power on the Continent, a position it would hold for the next two centuries. The greatest losers in the conflict (aside from the millions of German victims) were the Austrian Habsburgs, who were forced to surrender all the territory they had gained and to abandon their hopes of using the office of Holy Roman Emperor to dominate central Europe. Spain became increasingly relegated to the margins of Europe, and Germany remained a volatile checkerboard of Protestant and Catholic principalities.

DIVERGENT POLITICAL PATHS: SPAIN AND FRANCE

The long century of war between 1540 and 1648 decisively altered the balance of power among the major kingdoms of western Europe. Germany emerged from the Thirty Years' War a devastated and exhausted land. Spain, too, was crippled by its unremitting military exertions. The French monarchy, by contrast, steadily increased its power. By 1660, France had become the most powerful country on the European mainland. In England, meanwhile, a bloody

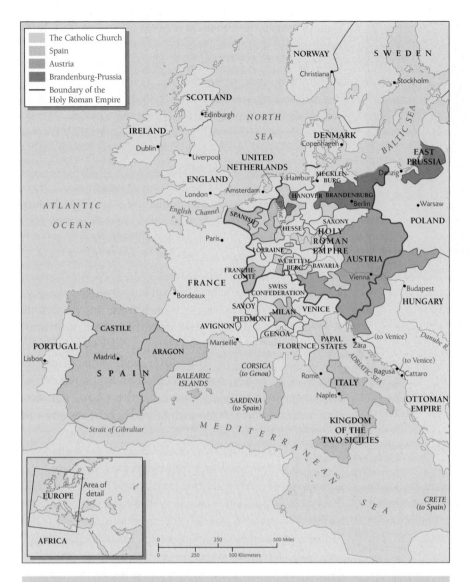

The Catholic Church
Spain
Austria
Brandenburg-Prussia
Boundary of the
Holy Roman Empire

EUROPE AT THE END OF THE THIRTY YEARS' WAR. This map shows the fragile political checkerboard that resulted from the Peace of Westphalia in 1648. ▪ *When you compare this map to the map on page 316 in Chapter 13, what are the most significant territorial changes between 1550 and 1648?* ▪ *Which regions would have been weakened or endangered by this arrangement?* ▪ *Which would be in a strong position to dominate Europe?*

Portugal, which had been annexed by Phillip II in 1580), half of Italy, half of the Netherlands, all of Central and South America, and the Philippine Islands in the Pacific Ocean—was the mightiest power not just in Europe but in the world. Yet only a half century later, this empire was beginning to fall apart.

Spain's greatest underlying weakness was economic. At first this may seem odd, considering that in 1600—as in the three or four previous decades—huge amounts of American silver were being unloaded at the port of Seville. Yet as contemporaries themselves recognized, the New World that Spain had conquered was now conquering Spain. Lacking both agricultural and mineral resources of its own, Spain desperately needed to develop industries and a balanced trading pattern, as some of its Atlantic rivals were doing. But the Spanish nobility prized honor and chivalric ideals over practical business affairs. They used imperial silver to buy manufactured goods from other parts of Europe and, as a result, had no incentive to develop industries and exports of their own. When the river of silver began to abate, Spain was plunged into debt.

Meanwhile, the crown's commitment to supporting the Roman Catholic Church and maintaining Spain's international dominance meant the continuance of costly wars. Even in the relatively peaceful year of 1608, about 4 million ducats—out of a total revenue of 7 million—were spent on military ventures. Spain's involvement in the Thirty Years' War was the last straw. In 1643, French troops inflicted a stunning defeat on the famed Spanish infantry at Rocroi in nothern France, the first time that a Spanish army had been overcome in battle since the end of the "Reconquista" (Chapter 11).

By then, two of Spain's Iberian territories were in open revolt. The governing power of Spain lay entirely in Castile, which had emerged as the dominant power after the marriage of Queen Isabella to Ferdinand of Aragon in 1469. In the absence of any great hardships, semi-autonomous Catalonia had endured Castilian hegemony. But in 1640, when the

civil war had broken out between the king and his critics in Parliament, culminating in an unprecedented event: the legal execution of a reigning monarch by his own parliamentary government.

The Decline of Spain

The story of Spain's fall from grandeur unfolds almost as relentlessly as a Greek tragedy. In 1600, the Spanish Empire—comprising all of the Iberian Peninsula (including

338 | CHAPTER 14 *Religion, Warfare, and Sovereignty: 1540–1660*

strains of warfare induced Castile to limit Catalan liberties and to raise more money and men for combat, Catalonia revolted. When the Portuguese learned of the Catalan uprising, they revolted as well, followed by southern Italians who rose up against Castilian viceroys in Naples and Sicily in 1647. It was only by chance that Spain's greatest external enemies, France and England, could not act in time to take advantage of its plight. This gave the Castilian government time to put down the Italian revolts; by 1652 it had also brought Catalonia to heel. But Portugal retained its independence, while Spain's isolation after the Peace of Westphalia further increased.

The Growth of France

A comparison of the fortunes of Spain and France in the first half of the seventeenth century shows some striking similarities. Both countries were of almost identical size, and both had been created by the same process of accretion and conquest over the course of the previous centuries (Chapters 9 and 10). Just as the Castilian crown had gained Aragon, Catalonia, Granada, and then Portugal, so the kingdom of France had grown by adding such diverse territories as Languedoc, Provence, Burgundy, and Brittany. Since the inhabitants of all these territories cherished traditions of local independence and their own distinct languages and cultures, and since French and Spanish monarchs were determined to govern their provinces ever more firmly—especially when the costs of the Thirty Years' War made ruthless tax collecting an urgent necessity—a direct confrontation between both central governments and their provinces became inevitable in both cases.

The fact that France emerged powerfully from this while Spain did not can be attributed in part to France's greater natural resources and the greater prestige of the French monarchy. Most subjects of the French king, including those from the outlying provinces, were loyal to him. Certainly they had excellent reason to be so during the reign of Henry IV. Having established religious peace by the Edict of Nantes, the affable Henry declared that there should be a chicken in every family's pot each Sunday, and therefore set out to restore the prosperity of a country devastated by civil war. And France had enormous economic resiliency, owing primarily to its extremely rich and varied agricultural productivity. Unlike Spain, which had to import food, France was able to feed itself well; and Henry's finance minister, the duke of Sully, quickly ensured that it did just that. Among other things, Sully distributed free copies of a guide to recommended farming techniques and financed the building or rebuilding of roads, bridges, and canals to facilitate the flow of goods. Henry IV, meanwhile, ordered the construction of royal factories to manufacture luxury goods such as crystal, glass, and tapestries while supporting the growth of silk, linen, and woolen cloth industries in many different parts of the country. Henry's patronage also allowed the explorer Samuel de Champlain to claim parts of Canada as France's first foothold in the New World.

The Reign of Cardinal Richelieu

Henry IV's reign can be counted as one of the most benevolent and effective in France's history. Far less benevolent was that of Henry's de facto successor, Cardinal Richelieu. The real king of France, Henry's son Louis XIII (r. 1610–43), came to the throne at the age of nine. But his reign was dominated by his chief minister of state. It was Richelieu who centralized royal power at home and expanded French influence abroad. For example, when Huguenots rebelled against certain restrictions that had been placed on them by the Edict of Nantes, Richelieu amended the edict to revoke their political and military rights altogether. He then moved to gain more income for the crown by ending the semi-autonomy of Burgundy, the Dauphiné, and Provence so that he could introduce direct royal taxation in all three areas. Later, to make sure taxes were efficiently collected, Richelieu instituted a new system of local government by royal officials who were expressly commissioned to put down provincial resistance. By these and other methods, Richelieu made the French monarchy more powerful and far-reaching than any in Europe and managed to double the crown's income during his rule. He also engaged in ambitious foreign wars against the Habsburgs of Austria and Spain, as we have seen. Yet increased centralization and France's costly involvement in the Thirty Years' War would lead to increased internal pressures in the years after Richelieu's death.

The Fronde

An immediate reaction to French governmental control was the series of uncoordinated revolts known collectively as the *Fronde* (from the French word for "slingshot"), which occured in 1643, a year after Richelieu's death. Louis XIII had just been succeeded by the five-year-old Louis XIV, whose regents were his mother, Anne of Austria, and Cardinal Mazarin, who was rumored to be her lover. Both were foreigners—Anne was a Habsburg and Mazarin was an Italian adventurer named Giulio Mazarini—and many of their subjects, including some extremely powerful nobles, hated them. Popular resentments were greater still because the costs of the ongoing Thirty Years' War were now combined with several consecutive years of bad harvests.

Neither the aristocratic leaders of the Fronde nor the commoners who joined them in revolt claimed to be resisting the young king; their targets were the alleged corruption and mismanagement of Mazarin. Some of the rebels, indeed, insisted that part of Mazarin's fault lay in his pursuit of Richelieu's centralizing, antiprovincial policy. But most aristocrats wanted to become part of this centralizing process. So when Louis XIV began to rule in his own right in 1651, and pretexts for revolt against corrupt ministers no longer existed, the opposition was soon silenced. Yet Louis XIV remembered the turbulence of the Fronde for the rest of his life, and resolved never to let his aristocracy or his provinces get out of hand. Pursuing this policy, he became the most effective absolute monarch in Europe (see Chapter 15).

MONARCHY AND CIVIL WAR IN ENGLAND

The power of Louis XIV in France stands in stark contrast to the challenges faced by his older contemporary, King Charles I of England. Of all the revolts that shook mid-seventeenth-century Europe, the most radical in its consequences was the English Civil War. The causes of this conflict were similar to those that sparked rebellions in Spain and France: hostilities between the component parts of a composite kingdom; religious animosities between Catholics and Protestants and within the ruling camp; struggles for power among competing factions of aristocrats at court; and a fiscal system that could not keep pace with the increasing costs of government, much less those of war. But in England, these conflicts led to the deposition and execution of the king (1649), an eleven-year "interregnum" during which England was ruled as a parliamentary republic (1649–60), and ultimately to the restoration of the monarchy under conditions designed to safeguard Parliament's place in government, an arrangement that has endured up to the present day.

The Origins of the English Civil War

The chain of events leading to war between royalist and Parliamentary forces in 1642 can be traced to the last decades of Queen Elizabeth's reign. During the 1590s, the expenses of war with Spain, together with a rebellion in Ireland, widespread crop failures, and the inadequacies of the antiquated English taxation system, drove the queen's government deeply into debt. Factional disputes around the court also became more bitter as courtiers, anticipating the aging queen's death, jockeyed for position under her presumed successor, the Scottish king James Stuart (James VI). Only on her deathbed, however, did the queen finally confirm that her throne should go to her Scottish cousin. As a result, neither James nor his new English subjects knew very much about each other when he took the throne at the end of 1603, ruling England as James I.

The relationship did not begin well. James's English subjects looked down on the Scots whom he brought with him to London. Although English courtiers were pleased to accept their new king's generosity to themselves, they resented the grants he made to his Scottish supporters. James, meanwhile, saw that to resolve his debts he had to have more revenue. But rather than bargain with parliamentary representatives for increased taxation, he chose to lecture them on the prerogatives of kingship. When this approach failed, James raised what revenues he could without Parliament's approval, by imposing new tolls on trade and selling trading monopolies to favored courtiers. These measures aroused further resentments and so made voluntary grants of taxation from Parliament even less likely.

James was more adept with respect to religious policy. Scotland had been a firmly Calvinist country since the 1560s. England, too, was a Protestant country, but of a very different kind, since the Church of England retained many of the rituals, hierarchies, and doctrines of the medieval Catholic Church (Chapter 13). Although a significant number of English Protestants wanted to bring their church more firmly into line with Calvinist principles, others resisted such efforts and labeled their Calvinist opponents "Puritans." As king, James was compelled to mediate these conflicts. By and large, he did so successfully. In Scotland, he convinced the reformed (Calvinist) church to retain bishops as leaders; in England, he encouraged Calvinist doctrine while resisting any alterations to the religious tenets articulated in the English Prayer Book and the Thirty-Nine Articles of the Faith. Only in Ireland, which remained overwhelmingly Catholic, did James stir up future trouble. By encouraging the "plantation" of more than 8,000 Scottish

Calvinists in the northern province of Ulster, he undermined the property rights of Irish Catholics and created religious animosities that still continues today.

The Reign of Charles Stuart

In 1625, James was succeeded by his surviving son, Charles. Charles almost immediately launched a new war with Spain, exacerbating his financial problems. He then alarmed his Protestant subjects by marrying Henrietta Maria, the Catholic daughter of France's Louis XIII. The situation became truly dangerous, however, when Charles and his archbishop of Canterbury, William Laud, began to favor the most anti-Calvinist elements in the English church, thus threatening the allegiance of the forthrightly Calvinist church in Scotland. The Scots rebelled, and in 1640 a Scottish army marched south into England to demand the withdrawal of Charles's "Catholicizing" reforms.

To meet the Scottish threat, Charles was forced to summon the English Parliament, something he (like his father) had avoided doing. Relations between the king and Parliament had broken down severely in the late 1620s, when Charles responded to Parliament's denial of additional funds by demanding loans from his subjects—and punishing those who refused by forcing them to lodge soldiers in their homes, or throwing them into prison without trial. In response, Parliament compelled the king to accept the Petition of Right in 1628, which declared all taxes not voted by Parliament illegal, condemned the quartering of soldiers in private houses, and prohibited arbitrary imprisonment and martial law in time of peace. Angered rather than chastened by the Petition of Right, Charles resolved to rule England without Parliament, funding his government during the 1630s with a variety of levies and fines imposed without parliamentary consent.

When the Scottish invasion of 1640 finally forced Charles to summon a new Parliament, therefore, its representatives were determined to impose a series of radical reforms on the king's government before they would even consider granting him money to raise an army. Charles initially cooperated with these reforms, even allowing Parliament to execute his chief minister. But it soon became clear that parliamentary leaders had no intention of fighting the Scots, and actually shared with them a common Calvinist outlook. In 1642, Charles attempted to break this stalemate by marching his own guards into the House of Commons and attempting to arrest its leaders. When he failed in this, he withdrew from London to raise an army

CHARLES I. King Charles of England was a connoisseur of the arts and a patron of artists. He was adept at using portraiture to convey the magnificence of his tastes and the grandeur of his conception of kingship. ▪ *How does this portrait by Anthony Van Dyck compare to the engravings of the "martyred" king on page 344 in* **Interpreting Visual Evidence?**

of Royalist supporters. Parliament responded by levying its own armed force and voting the taxation to pay for it. By the end of 1642, open warfare had erupted between the English king and the English government—something inconceivable in France, where the king and the government were inseparable.

Arrayed on the king's side were most of England's aristocrats and largest landowners, who were almost all loyal to the established Church of England, despite their opposition to some of Charles's own religious innovations. The parliamentary forces, by contrast, were made up of smaller landholders, tradesmen, and artisans, many of whom were Puritan sympathizers. The king's royalist supporters were commonly known by the aristocratic name of Cavaliers. Their opponents, who cut their hair short in contempt for the fashionable custom of wearing long curls, were derisively called Roundheads. At first the Cavaliers, having obvious advantages of military experience, won most of the victories.

Competing Viewpoints

Debating the English Civil War

> The English Civil War raised fundamental questions about political rights and responsibilities. Many of these are addressed in the two excerpts below. The first comes from a lengthy debate held within the General Council of Cromwell's army in October of 1647. The second is taken from the speech given by King Charles, moments before his execution in 1649.

The Army Debates, 1647

Colonel Rainsborough: Really, I think that the poorest man that is in England has a life to live as the greatest man, and therefore truly, sir, I think it's clear, that every man that is to live under a government ought first by his own consent to put himself under that government, and I do think that the poorest man in England is not at all bound in a strict sense to that government that he has not had a voice to put himself under . . . insomuch that I should doubt whether I was an Englishman or not, that should doubt of these things.

General Ireton: Give me leave to tell you, that if you make this the rule, I think you must fly for refuge to an absolute natural right, and you must deny all civil right, and I am sure it will come to that in the consequence. . . . For my part, I think it is no right at all. I think that no person has a right to an interest or share in the disposing of the affairs of the kingdom, and in determining or choosing those that shall determine what laws we shall be ruled by here, no person has a right to this that has not a permanent fixed interest in this kingdom, and those persons together are properly the represented of this kingdom who, taken together, and consequently are to make up the representers of this kingdom. . . .

We talk of birthright. Truly, birthright there is. . . . [M]en may justly have by birthright, by their very being born in England, that we should not seclude them out of England. That we should not refuse to give them air and place and ground, and the freedom of the highways and other things, to live amongst us, not any man that is born here, though he in birth or by his birth there come nothing at all that is part of the permanent interest of this kingdom to him. That I think is due to a man by birth. But that by a man's being born here he shall have a share in that power that shall dispose of the lands here, and of all things here, I do not think it is a sufficient ground.

Source: *Divine Right and Democracy: An Anthology of Political Writing in Stuart England*, ed. David Wootton (New York: 1986), pp. 286–87 (language modernized).

In 1644, however, the parliamentary army was effectively reorganized, and afterward the fortunes of battle shifted. The royalist forces were badly beaten, and in 1646 the king was compelled to surrender. Soon thereafter, the episcopal hierarchy of the Church of England was abolished and a Calvinist-style reformed church was mandated throughout England and Wales.

The struggle might have ended here had not a quarrel developed within the parliamentary party. The majority of its members were ready to restore Charles to the throne as a limited monarch, under an arrangement whereby a uniformly Calvinist faith would be imposed on both Scotland and England as the state religion. But a radical minority of Puritans distrusted Charles and insisted on religious tolera-tion for themselves and all other Protestants. Their leader was Oliver Cromwell (1599–1658), who had risen to command the Roundhead army, which he had reconstituted as "the New Model Army." Ultimately, he became the new leader of Parliament, too.

The Fall of Charles Stuart and the Commonwealth

Taking advantage of the dissension within the ranks of his opponents, Charles renewed the war in 1648 but, after a brief campaign, was forced again to surrender. Cromwell

Charles I on the Scaffold, 1649

I think it is my duty, to God first, and to my country, for to clear myself both as an honest man, a good king, and a good Christian.

I shall begin first with my innocence. In truth I think it not very needful for me to insist long upon this, for all the world knows that I never did begin a war with the two Houses of Parliament, and I call God to witness, to whom I must shortly make an account, that I never did intend to incroach upon their privileges. . . .

As for the people—truly I desire their liberty and freedom as much as anybody whatsoever. But I must tell you that their liberty and freedom consists in having of government those laws by which their lives and goods may be most their own. It is not for having share in government. That is nothing pertaining to them.

A subject and a sovereign are clean different things, and therefore, until they do that—I mean that you do put the people in that liberty as I say—certainly they will never enjoy themselves.

Sirs, it was for this that now I am come here. If I would have given way to an arbitrary way, for to have all laws changed according to the power of the sword, I needed not to have come here. And therefore I tell you (and I pray God it be not laid to your charge) that I am the martyr of the people.

Source: Brian Tierney, Donald Kagan, and L. Pearce Williams, eds., *Great Issues in Western Civilization* (New York: 1967), pp. 46–47.

Questions for Analysis

1. What fundamental issues are at stake in both of these excerpts? How do the debaters within the parliamentary army (first excerpt) define "natural" and "civil" rights?

2. How does Charles defend his position? What is his theory of kingship? How does it conflict with the ideas expressed in the army's debate?

3. It is interesting that none of the participants in these debates seem to have recognized the implications of their arguments for the political rights of women. Why would that have been the case?

---

was now resolved to end the life of "that man of blood" and, ejecting all the moderates from Parliament by force, he obliged this "Rump" (remaining) Parliament to put the king on trial and eventually to condemn him to death for treason against his own subjects. Charles Stuart was publicly beheaded on January 30, 1649: the first time in history that a reigning king had been legally deposed and executed by his own government. Europeans reacted to his death with horror, astonishment, or rejoicing, depending on their own political convictions (see **Interpreting Visual Evidence** on page 344).

A short time later, Parliament's hereditary House of Lords was abolished and England was declared a Commonwealth, an English translation of the Latin *res publica*. But

founding a republic was far easier than maintaining one. Technically, the Rump Parliament continued as the legislative body; but Cromwell, with the army at his command, possessed the real power. In 1653, he marched a detachment of troops into the Rump Parliament, which he dissolved in his own favor. The Commonwealth ceased to exist and was replaced by the "Protectorate," a thinly disguised autocracy established under a constitution drafted by officers of the army. Called the Instrument of Government, this text is the nearest approximation to a written constitution England has ever had. Extensive powers were given to Cromwell as Lord Protector, and his office was made hereditary. At first, a new Parliament exercised limited authority to make laws and levy taxes, but in 1655

Interpreting Visual Evidence

The Execution of a King

his allegorical engraving (image A) accompanied a pamphlet called *Eikon Basilike* ("The Kingly Image"), which began to circulate in Britain just weeks after the execution of King Charles I. It purported to be an autobiographical account of the king's last days and a justification of his royal policies. It was intended to arouse widespread sympathy for the king and his exiled heir, Charles II, and it succeeded admirably: the cult of Charles "King and Martyr" became increasingly popular. Here, the Latin inscription on the shaft of light suggests that Charles's piety will beam "brighter through the shadows," while the scrolls at the left proclaim that "virtue grows beneath weight" and "unmoved, triumphant." Charles's earthly crown (on the floor at his side) is "splendid and heavy," while the crown of thorns he grasps is "bitter and light" and the heavenly crown is "blessed and eternal." Even people who could not read these and other Latin mottoes would have known that Charles's last words were: "I shall go from a corruptible to an incorruptible Crown, where no disturbance can be."

At the same time, broadsides showing the moment of execution (image B) circulated in various European countries with explanatory captions. This one was

A. King Charles I as a kingly martyr.

Cromwell abruptly dismissed its members. Thereafter the government became a virtual dictatorship, with Cromwell wielding a sovereignty more absolute than any previous English monarch had ever dreamed of claiming. Indeed, many contemporary intellectuals noted the similarities between these events and those that had given rise to the Principate of Augustus after the death of Julius Caesar (Chapter 5).

The Restoration of the Monarchy

Given the choice between a Puritan military dictatorship and the old royalist regime, most of England opted for the latter. Years of unpopular Calvinist austerities—such as the prohibition of any public recreation on Sundays and the closing of London's theaters—had made people long for the milder Church of England, and for monarchy. So not long after printed in Germany, and there are almost identical versions surviving from the Netherlands. It shows members of the crowd fainting and turning away at the sight of blood spurting from the king's neck, while the executioner holds up the severed head.

B. The execution of Charles I.

Questions for Analysis

1. How would you interpret the message of the first image? How might it have been read differently by Catholics and by Protestants, within Britain and in Europe?

2. What would have been the political motives underlying the publication and display of these images? For example, would you expect the depiction of the king's execution to be intended as supportive of monarchy, or as antiroyalist? Why?

3. Given what you have learned about political and religious divisions in Europe at the time of the king's execution, where do you think the first image would have found the most sympathetic audiences? Why might it be significant that the second image circulated more in Germany and the Netherlands, rather than in France or Spain?

Cromwell's death in 1658, one of his generals seized power and called for the election of a new Parliament, which met in the spring of 1660. Almost overnight, England was a monarchy again and Charles I's exiled son, Charles II, was proclaimed its king and recalled from the court of his cousin, Louis XIV.

Charles II (r. 1660–85) restored bishops to the Church of England but he did not return to the provocative religious policies of his father. Quipping that he did not wish to "resume his travels," Charles agreed to respect Parliament and to observe the Petition of Right that had so enraged his father. He also accepted all the legislation passed by Parliament immediately before the outbreak of civil war in 1642, including the requirement that Parliament be summoned at least once every three years. England thus emerged from its civil war as a limited monarchy, in which power was exercised by "the king in Parliament." It remains a constitutional monarchy to this day.

THE PROBLEM OF DOUBT AND THE QUEST FOR CERTAINTY

Between 1540 and 1660, Europeans were forced to confront a world in which all that they had once taken for granted was suddenly cast into doubt. Vast new continents had been discovered in the Americas, populated by millions of people whose very existence compelled Europeans to rethink some of their most basic ideas about humanity and human nature. Equally disorienting, the religious uniformity of medieval Europe, although never absolute, had been shattered to an unprecedented extent by the Reformation and the religious wars that arose from it. In 1540, it was still possible to imagine that these religious divisions might be temporary. By 1660, it was clear they would be permanent. No longer could Europeans regard revealed religious faith as an adequate foundation for universal philosophical conclusions, for even Christians now disagreed about the fundamental truths of faith. Political allegiances were similarly under threat, as intellectuals and common people alike began to assert a right to resist princes with whom they disagreed. Even morality and custom were beginning to seem arbitrary, detached from the natural ordering of the world.

Europeans responded to this pervasive climate of doubt in a variety of ways, ranging from radical skepticism to authoritarian assertions of ecclesiastical control and political absolutism. What united their responses, however, was a sometimes desperate search for new foundations on which to construct some measure of certainty in the face of enormous change.

Witchcraft and the Power of the State

Adding to Europeans' fears was the conviction of many that witchcraft was a new and increasing threat to their world. Although the belief that certain individuals could heal or harm through the practice of magic had always been widespread, it was not until the late fifteenth century that authorities began to insist that such powers could derive only from some kind of satanic bargain. Once this belief became widely accepted, judicial officers became much more active in seeking out suspected witches for prosecution. In 1484, Pope Innocent VIII had ordered papal inquisitors to use all means at their disposal to detect and eliminate witchcraft, even condoning the torture of suspected witches. Predictably, torture increased the number of accused witches who "confessed" to their alleged crimes;

and as more accused witches "confessed," more and more witches were "discovered," tried, and executed—even in Protestant realms like England and Scotland where torture was not legal and where the Inquisition of the Roman Catholic Church did not operate.

In considering the rash of witchcraft persecutions that swept early modern Europe, then, we need to keep two facts in mind. First of all, witchcraft trials were by no means limited to Catholic countries: Protestant reformers believed in the insidious powers of Satan just as much as Catholics did, if not more so. Second, it was only when religious authorities' efforts to detect witchcraft were backed by the coercive powers of secular governments that the fear of witches could translate into imprisonment, torture, and execution. It was therefore through this fundamental agreement between Catholics and Protestants, and with the complicity of secular states, that a witch craze could claim tens of thousands of victims, of whom the vast majority were women.

The final death toll will never be known, but in the 1620s there were, on average, 100 burnings a year in the German cities of Würzburg and Bamberg; around the same time, it was said that the town square of Wolfenbüttel "looked like a little forest, so crowded were the stakes." When accusations of witchcraft diminished in Europe, they became endemic in some European colonies, such as the English settlement of Salem, Massachusetts.

This witch mania reflects the fears that early modern Europeans held about the adequacy of traditional remedies (such as prayers, relics, and holy water) to combat the evils of their world, another consequence of religious dissent and uncertainty. It also reflects their growing conviction that only the state had the power to protect them. Even in Catholic countries, where witchcraft prosecutions were sometimes begun in ecclesiastical courts, these cases would be transferred to the state's courts for final judgment and punishment, because Church courts were forbidden to impose capital penalties. In most Protestant countries, where ecclesiastical courts had been abolished (only England retained them), the entire process of detecting, prosecuting, and punishing suspected witches was carried out under the supervision of the state. In both Catholic and Protestant countries, the result of these witchcraft trials was thus a considerable increase in the scope of the state's powers to regulate the lives of its subjects.

The Search for a Source of Authority

The crisis of Europe's "iron century"—the name given to this era by some contemporary intellectuals—was fundamentally a crisis of authority, with far-reaching implications.

Attempts to reestablish some foundation for a new authority therefore took many forms. For the French nobleman Michel de Montaigne (1533–1592), who wrote during the height of the French wars of religion, the result was a searching skepticism about the possibilities of any certain knowledge whatsoever. The son of a Catholic father and a Huguenot mother of Jewish ancestry, the well-to-do Montaigne retired from a legal career at the age of thirty-eight to devote himself to a life of reflection. The *Essays* that resulted were a new literary form originally conceived as "experiments" (the French *essai* means "attempt").

Although the range of subjects covered by the *Essays* is wide, two main themes are dominant. One is constant questioning. Making his motto *Que sais-je?* ("What do I know?"), Montaigne decided that he knew very little for certain. According to him, "it is folly to measure truth and error by our own capacities," because our capacities are severely limited. As he maintained in one of his most famous essays, "On Cannibals," what may seem indisputably true and moral to one nation may seem absolutely false to another, because "everyone gives the title of barbarism to everything that is not of his usage." From this, Montaigne's second main principle followed: the need for moderation. Because all people think they know the perfect religion and the perfect government, yet few agree on what that perfection might be, Montaigne concluded that no religion or government is really perfect, and consequently no belief is worth fighting or dying for. Instead, people should accept the teachings of religion on faith, and obey the governments constituted to rule over them, without resorting to fanaticism in either sphere.

Although Montaigne's writings seem modern in many ways—that is, familiar to us today—he was very much a man of his time, and also the product of a long philosophical tradition reaching back to antiquity (Chapters 3 and 4). At heart, he was a Stoic: in a world governed by unpredictable fortune, he believed that the best human strategy was to face the good and the bad with steadfastness and dignity.

Another attempt to resolve the problem of doubt was offered by the French philosopher Blaise Pascal (1623–1662). Pascal began his career as a mathematician and scientist. But at age thirty he abandoned science after a profound conversion experience. This led him to embrace an extreme form of puritanical Catholicism known as Jansenism (after its Flemish founder, Cornelius Jansen). From then until his death, he worked on a highly ambitious philosophical-religious project meant to establish the truth of Christianity by appealing simultaneously to intellect and emotion.

After his premature death, the results of this effort were published as a series of "Thoughts" (*Pensées*). In this collection of intellectual fragments, Pascal argues that faith alone can resolve the contradictions of the world and that "the heart has its reasons of which reason itself knows nothing." Pascal's *Pensées* express the author's own terror, anguish, and awe in the face of evil and uncertainty, but present that awe as evidence for the existence of God. Pascal's hope was that, on this foundation, some measure of confidence in humanity and its capacity for self-knowledge could be rediscovered, thus avoiding both the dogmatism and the extreme skepticism that were so prominent in seventeenth-century society.

Theories of Absolute Government

Montaigne's contemporary, the French lawyer Jean Bodin (1530–1596), took a more active approach to the problem of uncertain authority. He wanted to resolve the disorders of the day by reestablishing the powers of the state on new and more secure foundations. Like Montaigne, Bodin was particularly troubled by the upheavals caused by the religious wars in France; he had witnessed the St. Bartholomew's Day Massacre of 1572. But he was resolved to offer a practical, political solution to such turbulence. In his monumental *Six Books of the Commonwealth* (1576), he developed a theory of absolute state sovereignty.

According to Bodin, the state arises from the needs of collections of families and, once constituted, should brook no opposition to its authority because maintaining order is its paramount duty. For Bodin, sovereignty was "the most high, absolute, and perpetual power over all subjects," which could make and enforce laws without the consent of those governed by the state—precisely what Charles I of England would have argued, and precisely what his rebellious subjects disputed. Although Bodin acknowledged the possibility of government by the aristocracy or even by a democracy, he assumed that the powerful nation-states of his day would have to be ruled by monarchs, and insisted that such monarchs should in no way be limited—whether by legislative and judicial bodies, or even by the laws of their own predecessors. Even if the ruler proved a tyrant, Bodin insisted that his subjects had no right to resist, for any resistance would open the door "to a licentious anarchy which is worse than the harshest tyranny in the world."

Bodin's younger contemporary, Thomas Hobbes (1588–1679) was moved by the turmoil of the English Civil War to advance a new political theory in his treatise *Leviathan* (1651). Yet Hobbes's formulation differs from that of Bodin in several respects. Whereas Bodin assumed that absolute sovereign power should be vested in a monarch, Hobbes argued that any form of government capable of protecting its subjects' lives and property might act as sovereign and hence all-powerful. And whereas Bodin defined his state as "the lawful government of families" and did not believe that the state could abridge private property rights, Hobbes's state exists to rule over individuals, and is thus licensed to trample over both liberty and property if the government's own survival is at stake.

But the most fundamental difference between Bodin and Hobbes lay in the latter's uncompromisingly pessimistic view of human nature. Hobbes posited that the "state of nature" that existed before government was "war of all against all." Because man naturally behaves as "a wolf" toward other men, human life without government is necessarily "solitary, poor, nasty, brutish, and short." To escape such consequences, people must therefore surrender their liberties to a sovereign ruler in exchange for his obligation to keep the peace. Having traded away their liberties, subjects have no right to win them back, and the sovereign may rule as he likes—free to oppress his subjects in any way other than to kill them, an act that would negate the very purpose of his rule, which is to preserve his people's lives.

THE ART OF BEING HUMAN

Doubt and uncertainty were also primary themes in the profusion of literature and art produced in this era. Moved by the ambiguities and ironies of existence and the horrors of war and persecution, writers and artists sought to find redemptive qualities in human suffering and hardship.

The Adventures of Don Quixote

A timeless example of this artistic response is the satirical novel *Don Quixote*, which its author, Miguel de Cervantes (1547–1616), composed largely in prison. It recounts the adventures of an idealistic Spanish gentleman, Don Quixote of La Mancha, who becomes deranged by his constant reading of chivalric romances. His mind filled with all kinds of fantastic adventures, he sets out at the age of fifty on the slippery road of knight-errantry, imagining windmills to be glowering giants and flocks of sheep to be armies of infidels. His distorted worldview also mistakes inns for castles and serving girls for courtly ladies. His sidekick, Sancho Panza, is his exact opposite: a plain, practical man with his feet on the ground, content with modest bodily plea-

sures. Yet Cervantes does not suggest that realism is categorically preferable to "quixotic" idealism. Rather, these two men represent different facets of human nature. On the one hand, *Don Quixote* is a devastating satire of the anachronistic chivalric mentality that was already hastening Spain's decline. On the other, it is a sincere celebration of the human capacity for optimism and goodness.

English Playwrights and Poets

In the late sixteenth century, the emergence of public playhouses made drama an especially effective mass medium for the expression of opinions, the dissemination of ideas, and the articulation of national identies. This was especially so in England during the last two decades of Elizabeth's reign and that of her successor, James. Among the large number of playwrights at work in London during this era, the most noteworthy are Christopher Marlowe (1564–1593), Ben Jonson (c. 1572–1637), and William Shakespeare (1564–1616). Marlowe, who may have been a spy for Elizabeth's government and who was mysteriously murdered in a tavern brawl before he reached the age of thirty, was extremely popular in his own day. In plays such as *Tamburlaine* (1587/8)—about the life of the Mongolian emperor Timur the Lame (Chapter 11)—and *Doctor Faustus* (c. 1589), Marlowe created vibrant heroes who pursue larger-than-life ambitions only to be felled by their own human limitations. In contrast to the heroic tragedies of Marlowe, Ben Jonson wrote dark comedies that expose human vices and foibles. In the particularly bleak *Volpone* (1606), Jonson shows people behaving like deceitful and lustful animals. In the later *Alchemist* (1610), he balances an attack on pseudo-scientific quackery with admiration for resourceful lower-class characters who cleverly take advantage of their supposed betters.

William Shakespeare was born into the family of a tradesman in the provincial town of Stratford-upon-Avon, where he attained a modest education before moving to London around the age of twenty. There he found employment in the theater as an actor and playwright, a "maker of plays." He eventually earned a reputation as a poet, too, but it was his success at the box office that enabled him to retire, rich, to his native Stratford about twenty-five years later. Shakespeare composed or collaborated in the writing of an unknown number of plays, of which some forty survive in whole or in part. They have since become a kind of secular English Bible, and owe their longevity to the author's unrivaled gifts of verbal expression, humor, and psychological insight.

DAVID BY BERNINI (1598–1680). Whereas the earlier conceptions of David by the Renaissance sculptors Donatello and Michelangelo were serene and dignified (see page 301), the Baroque sculptor Bernini chose to portray his young hero at the peak of physical exertion. ▪ *Can you discern the influence of Hellenistic sculpture (Chapter 4, pages 102–3) in this work?* ▪ *What are some shared characteristics?*

Shakespeare's dramas fall thematically into three groups. Those written during the playwright's early years reflect the political, religious, and social upheavals of the late sixteenth century. As we have already seen, these include many history plays which recount episodes from England's medieval past and the struggles that established the Tudor dynasty of Elizabeth's grandfather, Henry VII. They also include the lyrical tragedy *Romeo and Juliet* (1595/6) and a number of comedies, including *A Midsummer Night's Dream* (1595/6), *Much Ado about Nothing* (1598/9), *As You Like It* (1599), and *Twelfth Night* (1601/2). Most explore fundamental problems of identity, honor and ambition, love and friendship.

The plays from Shakespeare's second period are, like other contemporary artworks, characterized by a troubled searching into the mysteries and meaning of human existence. They showcase the perils of indecisive idealism (*Hamlet,*

1600/1) and the abuse of power (*Measure for Measure,* 1604), culminating in the searing tragedies of *King Lear* (1605) and *Macbeth* (1606). Finally, those plays composed at the end of his career emphasize the possibilities of reconciliation and peace, even after years of misunderstanding and sorrow: *Cymbeline* (1609/10), *A Winter's Tale* (1610/11), and *The Tempest* (1611), which is an extended reflection on the paradoxical relationship between the weakness of human nature and the power of the human artist.

Though less versatile than Shakespeare, the Puritan poet John Milton (1608–1674) is considered to be his equal in the grandeur of his artistic vision. The leading publicist of Oliver Cromwell's regime, Milton wrote the official defense of the beheading of Charles I as well as a number of treatises justifying Puritan ideologies. But he loved the Greek and Latin classics at least as much as the Bible. When forced into retirement by the accession of Charles II, Milton (now blind) embarked on a classical epic based on Genesis, *Paradise Lost* (1667). Setting out to "justify the ways of God to man," Milton first plays "devil's advocate" by creating the compelling character of Satan, who defies God with boldness and subtlety. Indeed, the eloquence of his Satan is never quite counterbalanced by the supposed hero, Adam, who learns to accept the human lot of moral responsibility.

The Artistry of Southern Europe

The ironies and tensions inherent in human existence were also explored in the visual arts. In Italy and Spain, many painters of the sixteenth century cultivated a highly dramatic and emotionally compelling style sometimes known as "Mannerism." The most unusual of these artists was El Greco ("the Greek," c. 1541–1614), a pupil of the Venetian master Tintoretto (1518–1594). Born Domenikos Theotokopoulos on the Greek island of Crete, El Greco absorbed some of the stylized elongation characteristic of Byzantine icon painting (Chapter 7) before traveling to Italy. He eventually settled in Spain. Many of his paintings were too strange to be greatly appreciated in his own day and even now appear so *avant garde* as to be almost surreal. His *View of Toledo* (c. 1596–1600), for example, is a transfigured landcape, mysteriously lit from within. Equally amazing are his swirling Biblical scenes and the stunning portraits of gaunt, dignified saints who radiate austerity and spiritual insight.

The dominant artistic style of southern Europe in the seventeenth century was that of the Baroque, a school

***VIEW OF TOLEDO* BY EL GRECO.** This is one of many landscape portraits representing the hilltop city that became the artist's home in later life. Its supple "Mannerist" style almost defies historical periodization.

of self-referentiality. It shows the artist himself at work on a double portrait of the Spanish king and queen, but the scene is dominated by the children and servants of the royal family.

Dutch Painting in the Golden Age

Southern Europe's main rival for artistic laurels was the Netherlands, where many painters explored the theme of man's greatness and wretchedness to the fullest. Pieter Bruegel the Elder (*BROY-ghul*, c. 1525–1569) exulted in portraying the busy, elemental life of the peasantry. Most famous in this respect are his rollicking *Peasant Wedding* and *Peasant Dance* (1568) and his spacious *Harvesters* (1565), whose vistas celebrate the natural rhythms of life. But late in his career, Bruegel became appalled by the intolerance and bloodshed of religious warfare, expressing his criticism in an understated yet searing manner. From a distance, *The Massacre of the Innocents* (c. 1567) looks like a snug scene of Flemish village life; but in fact, soldiers are methodically slaughtering helpless infants, just as Herod's soldiers once did, according to the Gospel account of Jesus's birth.

whose name has become a synonym for elaborate, highly wrought sculpture and architectural details. The Baroque style originated in Rome during the Counter-Reformation and promoted a glorified Catholic worldview. Its most imaginative and influential figure was the architect and sculptor Gianlorenzo Bernini (1598–1680), a frequent employee of the papacy who created the sweeping colonnades leading up to St. Peter's Basilica. Bernini's architecture retained such classical elements as columns and domes but combined them in ways meant to express aggressiveness and power. This was also the aim of Bernini's sculpture, which drew inspiration from the restless motion and artistic bravado of Hellenistic statuary (Chapter 4).

Although the Baroque movement began in Rome and was originally expressed in three dimensions, characteristics of this style can also be found in painting. Many consider its greatest master to be the Spanish artist Diego Velázquez (1599–1660). Unlike Bernini, Velázquez was a court painter in Madrid, not a servant of the Church. And although many of his canvases display a Baroque attention to motion and drama, his most characteristic work is more restrained and conceptually thoughtful. An example is *The Maids of Honor*, completed around 1656 and a masterpiece

***THE MAIDS OF HONOR (LAS MENINAS)* BY DIEGO VELÁZQUEZ.** The artist himself (at left) is shown working at his easel and gazing out at the viewer—or at the subjects of his double portrait, the Spanish king and queen, visible in a distant mirror. But the real focus of the painting is the delicate, impish princess in the center, flanked by two young ladies-in-waiting, a dwarf, and another royal child. Courtiers in the background look on.

THE MASSACRE OF THE INNOCENTS BY BRUEGEL (c. 1525–1569).
This painting shows how effectively art can be used as a means
of political and social commentary. Here, Bruegel depicts the
suffering of the Netherlands at the hands of the Spanish in his own
day, with reference to the Biblical story of Herod's slaughter of Jewish
children after the birth of Jesus—thereby conflating these two historical
incidents.

THE HORRORS OF WAR BY RUBENS (1577–1640). In his old age,
Rubens took a far more critical view of war than he had done for most of
his earlier career. Here, the war-god Mars casts aside his mistress Venus,
goddess of love, and threatens humanity with death and destruction.

SELF-PORTRAITS. Self-portraits became common during the sixteenth and seventeenth centuries, reflecting the intense
introspection of the period. Left: Rembrandt painted more than sixty self-portraits; this one, dating from around 1660, captures
the artist's creativity, theatricality (note the costume), and honesty of self-examination. Right: Judith Leyster (1609–1660) was
a contemporary of Rembrandt who pursued a successful career during her early twenties, before she married. Respected in her
own day, she was all but forgotten for centuries—but is once again the object of much attention.

Vastly different from Bruegel was the Netherlandish painter Peter Paul Rubens (1577–1640) of Antwerp. Since the Baroque was an international movement closely linked to the spread of the Counter-Reformation, it should offer no surprise that Baroque style was extremely well represented in just that part of the Netherlands which, after long warfare, had been retained by Spain and reintroduced to the Catholic faith. Rubens painted literally thousands of robust canvases that glorified resurgent Catholicism or exalted second-rate aristocrats by portraying them as epic heroes. But Rubens was not lacking in subtlety or depth. Although he celebrated martial valor for most of his career, his late *The Horrors of War* (1657/8) movingly portrays what he himself called "the grief of unfortunate Europe."

Living across the border from the Spanish Netherlands in the staunchly Calvinist Dutch Republic, Rembrandt van Rijn (*vahn-REEN*, 1606–1669) belonged to a society that was too austere to tolerate the unbuckled realism of Bruegel or the fleshy excess of Rubens. Yet Rembrandt managed to put both realistic and Baroque traits to new uses. In his early career, he gained fame and fortune as a painter of biblical scenes and as a portrait painter who knew how to flatter his subjects. But his later portraits, including several self-portraits, are highly introspective and suggest that only part of the story is being told. Equally compelling is the frank gaze of Rembrandt's slightly younger contemporary, Judith Leyster (1609–1660), who looks out of her own self-portrait with a refreshingly optimistic and good-humored expression.

After You Read This Chapter

Visit StudySpace for quizzes, additional review materials, and multi-media documents. **wwnorton.com/studyspace**

REVIEWING THE OBJECTIVES

- Religious and political conflicts have always been intertwined, but the combination was especially deadly in the era between 1540 and 1660. Why was this?
- Although the religious warfare of this period seems almost continuous, it took distinctive forms in France, the Netherlands, and Germany. Explain why.
- What factors led to the decline of Spain as Europe's dominant power, and to the rise of France?
- The main causes of the English Civil War can be traced back to the reign of Elizabeth I and her successor, James Stuart of Scotland. What were the main sources of disagreement between the Stuart monarchy and Parliament?
- Intellectuals and artists responded to the challenges of this era in creative ways. Identify some of the major figures and ideas that emerged from this period of crisis.

CONCLUSION

Between 1540 and 1660, Europe was racked by a combination of religious warfare, political rebellion, and economic crisis that undermined confidence in traditional structures of authority. The result was disillusionment, skepticism, and a search for new foundations on which to rebuild strong political and social institutions. For artists and intellectuals, the period proved to be one of the most creative epochs in the history of Western civilizations. But for most common people, the century was one of extraordinary suffering.

By 1660, after a hundred years of destructive efforts to restore the religious unity of Europe through war, a de facto religious toleration among states was beginning to emerge as the only way to preserve political order. But within states, toleration was still very limited. In territories where religious rivalries ran too deep to be overcome, rulers began to discover that loyalty to the state could override even religious divisions among their subjects. The end result of this century of crises was a strengthening of Europeans' reliance on the state's capacity to heal their wounds and right their wrongs, with religion relegated more and more to the private sphere of individual conscience. In the following centuries, this new confidence in the state as an autonomous moral agent acting in accordance with its own "reasons of state" and for its own purposes, would prove a powerful challenge to the traditions of limited consensual government that had emerged from the Middle Ages.

PEOPLE, IDEAS, AND EVENTS IN CONTEXT

- What were the main sources of instability in Europe during the sixteenth century? How did the **PRICE REVOLUTION** exacerbate these?
- How did the **EDICT OF NANTES** challenge the doctrine *CUIUS REGIO, EIUS RELIGIO* ("as the ruler, so the religion") established by the **PEACE OF AUGSBURG**?
- What were the initial causes of the **THIRTY YEARS' WAR**? Why did Sweden and France become involved in it?
- Describe the political configuration of Europe after the **PEACE OF WESTPHALIA**. Why did Spain's power decline while France emerged as dominant? How did the policies of **CARDINAL RICHELIEU** strengthen the power of the French monarchy?
- What factors led to the **ENGLISH CIVIL WAR** and the execution of **CHARLES I**?
- In what ways did the **WITCH CRAZE** of early modern Europe reveal the religious and social tensions of the sixteenth and seventeenth centuries?
- How did **MONTAIGNE** and **PASCAL** respond to the problem of authority? What were the differences between **JEAN BODIN**'s theory of absolute sovereignty and that of **THOMAS HOBBES**?

CONSEQUENCES

- The period between 1540 and 1660 is considered to be one of the most turbulent in Europe's history, but it also has deep roots in the more distant past of Western civilizations. How far back would you trace the origins of this "perfect storm"?
- The execution of King Charles I of England was a watershed event, and yet the English monarchy itself survived this crisis. How would you account for this remarkable fact? In what ways did the concept of English kingship have to change in order for monarchy itself to survive?
- In your view, do the various artistic movements of this era seem especially modern? Or are they better understood as comparable to the movements responding to the crisis of the Black Death (Chapter 10), or to the artistic innovations characteristic of the Renaissance (Chapter 12)? What elements make a work of art seem "modern"?

STORY LINES

- After the devastation caused by the crisis of the seventeenth century, European rulers sought stability in the centralization of government authority and by increasing their own power at the expense of other groups and institutions in society, such as the nobility and the church.

- Population growth, increased agricultural productivity, and innovations in business practices created new wealth and new incentives for economic development and colonial expansion to other continents. All of these processes favored European powers with access to Atlantic trade, especially France and Britain, who opened up profitable trading networks to the Americas and the Caribbean.

- Within Europe, only a few regimes continued to pursue expansionist foreign policies. Others sought stability through treaties that aimed at an international balance of power.

CHRONOLOGY

1500s–1800s	Europeans engage in slave trade from Africa to the Caribbean, Brazil, and North America
1600s	Britain and France establish colonies in North America and the Caribbean and outposts in Africa and India
1643–1715	Louis XIV of France
1685	Revocation of the Edict of Nantes
1688	Glorious Revolution in England
1689–1725	Peter the Great of Russia's reign
1702–1713	War of the Spanish Succession
1713	Treaty of Utrecht
1740–1780	Maria Theresa of Austria's reign
1740–1786	Frederick the Great of Prussia's reign
1756–1763	The Seven Years' War
1762–1796	Catherine the Great of Russia's reign
1772–1795	Partition of Poland
1775–1783	United States War of Independence

Before
You
Read
This
Chapter

Absolutism and Empire, 1660–1789

I n the mountainous region of south-central France known as the Auvergne in the 1660s, the marquis of Canillac had a notorious reputation. His noble title gave him the right to collect minor taxes on special occasions, but he insisted that these small privileges be converted into annual tributes. To collect these payments, he housed in his castle twelve accomplices whom he called his apostles. Their other nicknames—one was known as Break Everything—gave a more accurate sense of their activities in the local villages. The marquis imprisoned those who resisted and forced their families to buy their freedom. In an earlier age, the marquis might have gotten away with this profitable arrangement. In 1662, however, he ran up against the authority of a king, Louis XIV, who was determined to demonstrate that the power of the central monarch was absolute. The marquis was brought up on charges before a special court of judges from Paris. He was found guilty and forced to pay a large fine. The king confiscated his property and had the marquis's castle destroyed.

Louis XIV's special court in the Auvergne heard nearly a thousand civil cases over four months in 1662. It convicted

692 people, and many of them, like the marquis of Canillac, were noble. The verdicts were an extraordinary example of Louis XIV's ability to project his authority into the remote corners of his realm and to do so in a way that diminished the power of other elites. During his long reign (1643–1715), Louis XIV systematically pursued such a policy on many fronts, asserting his power over the nobility, the clergy, and the provincial courts. Increasingly, these elites were forced to look to the crown to guarantee their interests, and their own power became more closely connected with the sacred aura of the monarchy itself. Louis XIV's model of kingship was so successful that it became known as absolute monarchy. In recognition of the success and influence of Louis XIV's political system, the period from around 1660 (when the English monarchy was restored and Louis XIV began his personal rule in France) to 1789 (when the French Revolution erupted) is traditionally known as the age of absolutism. This is a crucial period in the development of the modern, centralized, bureaucratic state.

Absolutism was a political theory that encouraged rulers to claim complete sovereignty within their territories. An absolute monarch could make law, dispense justice, create and direct a bureaucracy, declare war, and levy taxes, without the approval of any other governing body. Assertions of absolute authority were buttressed by claims that rulers governed by divine right with power granted by God. Absolutist theorists frequently compared this authority to the power of fathers in the household. After the chaos of the previous century, many Europeans came to believe that it was only by exalting the sovereignty of absolute rulers that order could be restored to European life.

European monarchs also successfully projected their power abroad during this period. By 1660, the French, Spanish, Portuguese, English, and Dutch had all established important colonies in the Americas and in Asia. These colonies created important trading networks that brought profitable new consumer goods such as sugar, tobacco, and coffee to a wide public in Europe, while also encouraging the spread of slavery to produce these goods. Rivalry among colonial powers to control the trade in slaves and consumer goods was intense. In the eighteenth century, Europe's wars were driven by colonial considerations and imperial conflicts, as global commerce assumed a growing role in the European economy.

Absolutism was not the only political theory used by European governments during this period. England, Scotland, the Dutch Republic, Switzerland, Venice, Sweden, and Poland-Lithuania were all either limited monarchies, or republics. In Russia, an extreme autocracy emerged that gave the tsar a degree of control over his subjects' lives and property far beyond anything imagined by western

European absolutists. Even in Russia, however, absolutism was never unlimited in practice. Even the most absolute monarchs could rule effectively only with the consent of their subjects (particularly the nobility). When serious opposition erupted, even absolutists were forced to back down. In 1789, when an outright political revolution occurred, the entire structure of absolutism came crashing to the ground.

THE APPEAL AND JUSTIFICATION OF ABSOLUTISM

Absolutism's promise of stability was an appealing alternative to the disorder of the "iron century" that preceded it. Louis XIV was profoundly disturbed by an aristocratic revolt that occurred while he was still a child. Louis saw the revolt as a horrid affront not only to his own person but to the majesty of the French state he personified. Such experiences convinced him that he must rule assertively and without limitation if France was to survive as a great European state.

Absolutist monarchs sought control of the state's armed forces and its legal system and demanded the right to collect and spend the state's financial resources at will. To achieve these goals, they also needed to create an efficient, centralized bureaucracy that owed its allegiance directly to the monarch. Creating and sustaining such a bureaucracy was expensive but essential to the larger absolutist goal of weakening the special interests that hindered the free exercise of royal power. The nobility and the clergy, with their traditional legal privileges; the political authority of semi-autonomous regions; and representative assemblies such as parliaments, diets, or estates general were all obstacles—in the eyes of absolutists—to strong, centralized monarchical government. The history of abolutism is a history of attempts by aspiring absolutists to bring such institutions to heel.

In most Protestant countries, the power of the church had already been subordinated to the state when the age of absolutism began. In France, Spain, and Austria, however, where Roman Catholicism remained the state religion, absolutist monarchs now devoted considerable attention to bringing the church and its clergy under royal control.

The most important potential opponents of royal absolutism were not churchmen, however, but nobles. Monarchs dealt with this threat in various ways. Louis XIV deprived the French nobility of political power in the provinces but increased their social prestige by making them live at his lavish court at Versailles. Peter the Great of Russia (r. 1689–1725) forced his nobles into lifelong government service. Later in the century, Catherine II of Russia (r. 1762–96) struck a bargain whereby, in return for vast estates and a variety of privileges (including exemption from taxation), the Russian nobility virtually surrendered the administrative and political power of the state into the empress's hands. In Prussia, the army was staffed by nobles, as was generally the case in Spain, France, and England.

The most effective absolutist monarchies of the eighteenth century continued to trade privileges for allegiance, so that nobles came to see their own interests as tied to those of the crown. For this reason, cooperation and negotiation more often characterized the relations between kings and nobles during the eighteenth-century *ancien régime* ("old regime") than did open conflict.

THE ABSOLUTISM OF LOUIS XIV

In Louis XIV's state portrait, it is almost impossible to discern the human being behind the facade of the absolute monarch, dressed in his coronation robes and surrounded by the symbols of his authority. That facade was artfully constructed by Louis, who recognized more fully than any other early modern ruler the importance of theater to effective kingship. Previous monarchs realized the importance of displays of power and majesty, but Louis and his successors took this to unprecedented levels, staging theatrical demonstrations of their sovereignty to enhance their position as rulers endowed with godlike powers.

Performing Royalty at Versailles

Louis's most elaborate exhibitions of his sovereignty took place at his palace at Versailles (*vair-SY*), the town outside of Paris to which he moved his court. The palace and its grounds became a stage for Louis's performance of his daily rituals and demonstrations of royal power. Inside, tapestries and paintings celebrated French military victories and royal triumphs; mirrors reflected shimmering light throughout the building. In the vast gardens outside, statues of the Greek god Apollo, god of the sun, recalled Louis's claim to be the "Sun King" of France. Noblemen vied to attend him when he arose from bed, ate his meals, strolled in his gardens, or rode to the hunt. France's leading nobles were required to reside with him at Versailles for a portion of the year; the splendor of Louis's court was deliberately calculated to blind them to the possibility of

disobedience while raising their prestige by associating them with himself. At the same time, the almost impossibly detailed rules of etiquette at court left these privileged nobles in constant suspense, forever fearful of offending the king by committing some trivial violation of proper manners.

Of course, the nobility did not surrender their social and political power entirely under the absolutist system. The social order defended by the monarchy was still a hierarchical one, and the nobility retained enormous privileges and rights over local peasants within their jurisdiction. The absolutist system may have forced the nobility to depend on the crown to defend their privileges, but it did not seek to undermine their superior place in society. In this sense, the relationship between Louis XIV and the nobility was more of a negotiated settlement than a complete victory of the king over other powerful elites. In their own way, absolutists depended on the consent of those they ruled.

Administration and Centralization

Louis defined his responsibilities in absolutist terms: to concentrate royal power so as to produce domestic tranquility. While coopting the nobility into his own theater of royalty, he also recruited the upper bourgeoisie as royal administrators and especially as intendants, responsible for administering the thirty-six *généralités* into which France was divided. Louis's administrators devoted much of their time and energy to collecting the taxes necessary to finance the large standing army on which his aggressive foreign policy depended. Absolutism was fundamentally an approach to government by which ambitious monarchs could increase their own power through conquest and display. As such, it was enormously expensive. In addition to the *taille*, or land tax, which increased throughout the seventeenth century, Louis's government introduced a *capitation* (a head tax) and pressed successfully for the collection of indirect taxes on salt (the *gabelle*), wine, tobacco, and other goods. Because the nobility was exempt from the *taille*, its burden fell most heavily on the peasantry, whose local revolts Louis easily crushed.

Regional opposition was curtailed, but not eliminated, during Louis's reign. By removing the provincial nobility to Versailles, Louis cut them off from their local sources of power and influence. To restrict the powers of regional *parlements*, Louis decreed that members of any *parlement* that refused to approve and enforce his laws would be summarily exiled. The Estates-General, the national French representative assembly last summoned in 1614, did not meet at all during Louis's reign. It would not meet again until 1789.

Competing Viewpoints

Absolutism and Patriarchy

> These selections show how two political theorists justified royal absolutism by deriving it from the absolute authority of a father over his household. Bishop Jacques-Benigne Bossuet (1627–1704) was a famous French preacher who served as tutor to the son of King Louis XIV of France before becoming bishop of Meaux. Sir Robert Filmer (1588–1653) was an English political theorist. Filmer's works attracted particular attention in the 1680s, when John Locke directed the first of his Two Treatises of Government to refuting Filmer's views on the patriarchal nature of royal authority.

Bossuet on the Nature of Monarchical Authority

There are four characteristics or qualities essential to royal authority. First, royal authority is sacred; Secondly, it is paternal; Thirdly, it is absolute; Fourthly, it is subject to reason. . . . All power comes from God. . . . Thus princes act as ministers of God and his lieutenants on earth. It is through them that he exercises his empire. . . . In this way . . . the royal throne is not the throne of a man, but the throne of God himself. . . .

We have seen that kings hold the place of God, who is the true Father of the human race. We have also seen that the first idea of power that there was among men, is that of paternal power; and that kings were fashioned on the model of fathers. Moreover, all the world agrees that obedience, which is due to public power, is only found . . . in the precept which obliges one to honor his parents. From all this it appears that the name "king" is a father's name, and that goodness is the most natural quality in kings. . . .

Royal authority is absolute. In order to make this term odious and insupportable, many pretend to confuse absolute government and arbitrary government. But nothing is more distinct, as we shall make clear when we speak of justice. . . . The prince need account to no one for what he ordains. . . . Without this absolute authority, he can neither do good nor suppress evil: his power must be such that no one can hope to escape him. . . . [T]he sole defense of individuals against the public power must be their innocence. . . .

One must, then, obey princes as if they were justice itself, without which there is neither order nor justice in affairs. They are gods, and share in some way in divine independence. . . . It follows from this that he who does not want to obey the prince . . . is condemned irremissibly to death as an enemy of public peace and of human society. . . . The prince can correct himself when he knows that he has done badly; but against his authority there can be no remedy. . . .

Source: Jacques-Benigne Bossuet, *Politics Drawn from the Very Words of Holy Scripture,* trans. Patrick Riley (Cambridge: 1990), pp. 46–69, 81–83.

Louis XIV's Religious Policies

Both for reasons of state and of personal conscience, Louis was determined to impose religious unity on France, regardless of the economic and social costs. Although the vast majority of the French population was Roman Catholic, French Catholics were divided among different groups. Louis supported the Jesuits in their efforts to create a Counter-Reformation Catholic Church in France. Louis's support for the Jesuits upset the traditional Gallican Catholics of France, however, who desired a French church independent of papal, Jesuit, and Spanish influence. As a result of this dissension among Catholics, the religious aura of Louis's kingship diminished during the course of his reign.

Against the Protestant Huguenots, however, Louis waged unrelenting war. Protestant churches and schools were destroyed, and Protestants were banned from many professions, including medicine and printing. In 1685, Louis revoked the Edict of Nantes, the legal foundation of the toleration Huguenots had enjoyed since 1598. Many families converted,

Filmer on the Patriarchal Origins of Royal Authority

The first government in the world was monarchical, in the father of all flesh, Adam, being commanded to multiply, and people the earth, and to subdue it, and having dominion given him over all creatures, was thereby the monarch of the whole world; none of his posterity had any right to possess anything, but by his grant or permission, or by succession from him. . . . Adam was the father, king, and lord over his family: a son, a subject, and a servant or a slave were one and the same thing at first. . . .

I cannot find any one place or text in the Bible where any power . . . is given to a people either to govern themselves, or to choose themselves governors, or to alter the manner of government at their pleasure. The power of government is settled and fixed by the commandment of "honour thy father"; if there were a higher power than the fatherly, then this commandment could not stand and be observed. . . .

All power on earth is either derived or usurped from the fatherly power, there being no other original to be found of any power whatsoever. For if there should be granted two sorts of power without any subordination of one to the other, they would be in perpetual strife which should be the supreme, for two supremes cannot agree. If the fatherly power be supreme, then the power of the people must be subordinate and depend on it. If the power of the people be supreme, then the fatherly power must submit to it, and cannot be exercised without the licence of the people, which must quite destroy the frame and course of nature. Even the power which God himself exercises over mankind is by right of fatherhood: he is both the king and father of us all. As God has exalted the dignity of earthly kings . . . by saying they are gods, so . . . he has been pleased . . . [t]o humble himself by assuming the title of a king to express his power, and not the title of any popular government.

Source: Robert Filmer, "Observations upon Aristotle's Politiques" (1652), in *Divine Right and Democracy: An Anthology of Political Writing in Stuart England,* ed. David Wootton (Harmondsworth: 1986), pp. 110–18.

Questions for Analysis

1. Bossuet's definition of *absolutism* connected the sacred power of kings with the paternal authority of fathers within the household. What consequences does he draw from defining the relationship between king and subjects in this way?

2. What does Filmer mean when he says, "All power on earth is either derived or usurped from the fatherly power"? How many examples does he give of paternal or monarchical power?

3. Bossuet and Filmer make obedience the basis for order and justice in the world. What alternative political systems did they most fear?

---

but 200,000 Protestant refugees fled to England, Holland, Germany, and America, bringing with them their professional and artisanal skills. This was an enormous loss to France.

Colbert and Royal Finance

Louis's drive to unify and centralize France depended on a vast increase in royal revenues engineered by Jean Baptiste Colbert, the king's finance minister from 1664 until his death in 1683. Colbert tightened the process of tax collection and eliminated wherever possible the practice of tax farming (which permitted collection agents to retain for themselves a percentage of the taxes they gathered for the king). When Colbert assumed office, only about 25 percent of the taxes collected throughout the kingdom reached the treasury. By the time he died, that figure had risen to 80 percent. Colbert also tried to increase the nation's income by controlling and regulating foreign trade. As a confirmed mercantilist, Colbert believed that France's wealth

Interpreting Visual Evidence

The Performance and Display of Absolute Power at the Court of Louis XIV

istorians studying the history of absolutism and the court of Louis XIV in particular have emphasized the Sun King's (image B) brilliant use of symbols and display to demonstrate his personal embodiment of sovereignty. Royal portraits, such as that painted by Hyacinthe Rigaud in 1701 (image A), vividly illustrate the degree to which Louis's power was based on a studied performance. His pose, with his exposed and shapely calf, was an important indication of power and virility, necessary elements of legitimacy for a hereditary monarch. In the elaborate rituals of court life at Versailles, Louis often placed his own body at the center of attention, performing in one instance as the god Apollo in a ballet before his assembled courtiers. His movements through the countryside (image C), accompanied by a retinue of soldiers, servants, and aristocrats, were another occasion for highly stylized ritual demonstrations of his quasi-divine status. Finally, of course, the construction of his palace at Versailles (image D), with its symmetrical architecture and its sculpted gardens, was a demonstration that his power extended over the natural world as easily as it did over the lives of his subjects.

Questions for Analysis

1. Who was the intended audience for the king's performance of absolute sovereignty?

2. Who were Louis's primary competitors in this contest for eminence through the performance of power?

3. What possible political dangers might lay in wait for a regime that invested so heavily in the sumptuous display of semi-divine authority?

A. Hyacinthe Rigaud's 1701 portrait of Louis XIV.

B. Louis XIV as the Sun King.

C. *The Royal Procession of Louis XIV* by Adam Franz van der Meulen.

D. *Louis XIV arrives at the Palace of Versailles* by Pierre Patel.

would increase if its imports were reduced and its exports increased. He therefore imposed tariffs on foreign goods imported into France while using state money to promote the domestic manufacture of formerly imported goods, such as silk, lace, tapestries, and glass. He was especially anxious to create domestic industries capable of producing the goods France would need for war.

Despite Colbert's efforts to increase crown revenues, his policies ultimately foundered on the insatiable demands of Louis XIV's wars (see page 364). Colbert himself foresaw this result when he lectured the king in 1680: "Trade is the source of public finance and public finance is the vital nerve of war. . . . I beg your Majesty to permit me only to say to him that in war as in peace he has never consulted the amount of money available in determining his expenditures." Louis, however, paid him no heed. By the end of Louis's reign, his aggressive foreign policy lay in ruins and his country's finances had been shattered by the unsustainable costs of war.

ALTERNATIVES TO ABSOLUTISM

Although absolutism was the dominant model for seventeenth- and eighteenth-century European monarchs, it was by no means the only system by which Europeans governed themselves. A republican oligarchy continued to rule in Venice. In the Netherlands, the territories that had won their independence from Spain during the early seventeenth century combined to form the United Provinces, also a republic. The most significant exception to the trend toward absolutism, however, was the English monarchy.

Limited Monarchy: The Case of England

While the powers of representative assemblies were being undermined across much of Europe, the English Parliament was the longest-surviving such body in Europe. English political theorists had long seen their government as a mixed monarchy, composed of monarchical, noble, and nonnoble elements. During the seventeenth century, these traditions came under threat, first through Charles I's attempts to rule without Parliament and then during Oliver Cromwell's dictatorial Protectorate. The restoration of the monarchy in 1660 resolved the question of whether England would in future be a republic or a monarchy, but the sort of monarchy England would become remained an open question.

THE REIGN OF CHARLES II

Despite the fact that he was the son of the beheaded and much-hated Charles I, Charles II (r. 1660–85) was initially welcomed by most English men and women. He declared limited religious toleration for Protestant "dissenters" (Protestants who were not members of the Church of England). He promised to observe the Magna Carta and the Petition of Right, declaring, with characteristic good humor, that he did not wish to "resume his travels." The unbuttoned moral atmosphere of his court, with its risqué plays, dancing, and sexual licentiousness, reflected a public desire to forget the restraints of the Puritan past.

During the 1670s Charles began openly to model his kingship on the absolutism of Louis XIV. As a result, the great men of England soon came to be publicly divided between Charles's supporters (called "Tories," a popular nick-

CHARLES II OF ENGLAND (r. 1660–85) IN HIS CORONATION ROBES. This full frontal portrait of the monarch, holding the symbols of his rule, seems to confront the viewer personally with the overwhelming authority of the sovereign's gaze. Compare this classic image of the absolutist monarch with the very different portraits of William and Mary, who ruled after the Glorious Revolution of 1688 (page 363). ■ *What had changed between 1660, when Charles II came to the throne, and 1688, when the more popular William and Mary became the rulers of England?*

name for Irish Catholic bandits) and his opponents (known as "Whigs," a nickname for Scottish Presbyterian rebels).

Religion also remained a divisive issue. Charles was sympathetic to Roman Catholicism, even to the point of a deathbed conversion in 1685. During the 1670s, he briefly suspended civil penalties against Catholics and Protestant dissenters by asserting his right as king to ignore Parliamentary legislation. The resulting public outcry compelled him to retreat, but this controversy, together with rising opposition to Charles's ardently Catholic brother James as the heir to the throne, led to a series of Whig electoral victories between 1679 and 1681. Charles died in 1685 with his power enhanced, but he left behind a political and religious legacy that was to be the undoing of his less able successor.

THE REIGN OF JAMES II

James II was the very opposite of his worldly brother. A zealous Catholic convert, he alienated his Tory supporters, who were close to the established Church of England, by suspending the laws preventing Catholics and Protestant dissenters from holding political office. James flaunted his own Roman Catholicism, openly declaring his wish that his subjects convert and publicly parading papal legates through the streets of London. In June 1688, he ordered all Church of England clergymen to read his decree of religious toleration from their pulpits. Seven bishops refused and were promptly imprisoned. At their trial, however, they were declared not guilty of sedition, to the enormous satisfaction of the Protestant English populace.

When James declared in 1688 that his newborn son and heir was to be raised a Catholic, a delegation of Whigs and Tories crossed the channel to Holland to invite Mary Stuart and her Protestant husband, William of Orange, to cross to England with an invading army to preserve Protestantism and English liberties by summoning a new Parliament.

THE GLORIOUS REVOLUTION

James fled the country, and Parliament declared the throne vacant, clearing the way for William and Mary to succeed him. William III and Mary II ruled as joint sovereigns until Mary's death in 1694, and William ruled alone until 1702. The Bill of Rights, passed by Parliament and accepted by the new king and queen in 1689, reaffirmed English civil liberties such as trial by jury, habeas corpus (a guarantee that no one could be imprisoned unless charged with a crime), and the right to petition the monarch through Parliament. The Bill of Rights further declared that the monarchy was sub-

WILLIAM AND MARY. In 1688, William of Orange and his wife, Mary Stuart, became joint Protestant rulers of England in a bloodless coup that took power from her father, the Catholic James II. Compare this contemporary print with the portraits of Louis XIV (page 360) and Charles II (page 362). ▪ *What relationship does it seem to depict between the royal couple and their subjects?* ▪ *What is the significance of the gathered crowd in the public square in the background?* ▪ *How is this different from the spectacle of divine authority projected by Louis XIV or the image of Charles II looking straight at the viewer?*

ject to the law of the land. The Act of Toleration, also passed in 1689, granted Protestant dissenters the right to worship freely, though not to hold political office. And in 1701, the Act of Succession ordained that every future English monarch must be a member of the Church of England.

The English soon referred to the events of 1688 and 1689 as the "Glorious Revolution" because it firmly established England as a mixed monarchy governed by the "king in Parliament." Although William and Mary and their successors continued to exercise a large measure of executive power, after 1688 no English monarch attempted to govern without Parliament, which has met annually from that time on. Parliament, and especially the House of Commons, also strengthened its control over taxation and expenditure.

Yet 1688 was not all glory. It was a revolution that consolidated the position of large property holders, whose control over local government had been threatened by Charles II and James II. It thus restored the status quo on behalf of a wealthy class of magnates that would soon become even wealthier from government patronage and the profits of war. It also brought misery to the Catholic minority in Scotland and to the Catholic majority in Ireland. After 1690, power in Ireland would lie firmly in the hands of a "Protestant Ascendancy," whose dominance over Irish society would last until modern times.

JOHN LOCKE AND THE CONTRACT THEORY OF GOVERNMENT

The Glorious Revolution was the product of unique circumstances, but it also reflected antiabsolutist theories of politics that were taking shape in the late seventeenth century. Chief among these opponents of absolutism was the Englishman John Locke (1632–1704), whose *Two Treatises of Government* were written before the revolution but published for the first time in 1690.

Locke maintained that humans had originally lived in a state of nature characterized by absolute freedom and equality, with no government of any kind. The only law was the law of nature (which Locke equated with the law of reason), by which individuals enforced for themselves their natural rights to life, liberty, and property. Soon, however, humans began to perceive that the inconveniences of the state of nature outweighed its advantages. Accordingly, they agreed first to establish a civil society based on absolute equality and then to set up a government to arbitrate the disputes that might arise within this civil society. But they did not make government's powers absolute. All powers not expressly surrendered to the government were reserved to the people themselves; as a result, governmental authority was both contractual and conditional. If a government exceeded or abused the authority granted to it, society had the right to dissolve it and create another.

Locke condemned absolutism in every form. He denounced absolute monarchy, but he was also critical of claims for the sovereignty of parliaments. Government, he argued, had been instituted to protect life, liberty, and property; no political authority could infringe these natural rights. The law of nature was therefore an automatic and absolute limitation on every branch of government. In the late eighteenth century, Locke's ideas would resurface as part of the intellectual background of both the American and French revolutions.

During the beginning of the eighteenth century, then, both France and Britain had solved the problem of political dissent and social disorder in their own way. The emergence of a stable constitutional monarchy in England after 1688 contrasted vividly with the absolutist system developed by Louis XIV, but both systems worked well enough to contain the immediate threat to royal authority posed by

a powerful class of landed nobles. Domestic stability was no guarantee of international peace, however, and the period from 1661, when Louis XIV assumed personal rule, to his death in 1715, was marked by almost constant warfare.

WAR AND THE BALANCE OF POWER, 1661–1715

Louis XIV's foreign policy reflected his belief that military victories abroad were necessary to reinforce the glory of his realm and the power that he wielded at home. Louis's wars also sought to meet the threat posed by the Habsburg powers in Spain, the Spanish Netherlands, and the Holy Roman Empire. Through a series of conquests in the Low Countries, Louis expanded his territory. In response, William of Orange (r. 1672–1702) organized the League of Augsburg, which over time included Holland, England, Spain, Sweden, several German states, and the Austrian Habsburgs. The resulting Nine Years' War extended from Ireland to India to North America (where it was known as King William's War).

The League of Augsburg reflected the emergence of a new diplomatic goal in western and central Europe: the preservation of a balance of power. This goal would animate European diplomacy for the next two hundred years, until the balance-of-power system collapsed with the outbreak of the First World War. The main proponents of balance of power diplomacy were England, the United Provinces (Holland), Prussia, and Austria. By 1697, the league forced Louis XIV to make peace, because France was exhausted by war and famine. Louis gave back much of his recent gains but kept Strasbourg and the surrounding territory of Alsace. He was nevertheless looking at the real prize: a French claim to succeed to the throne of Spain and so control the Spanish Empire in the Americas, Italy, the Netherlands, and the Philippines.

The War of the Spanish Succession

In the 1690s it became clear that King Charles II of Spain (r. 1665–1700) would soon die without a clear heir, and both Louis XIV of France and Leopold I of Austria (r. 1658–1705) were interested in promoting their own relatives to succeed him. Either solution would have upset the balance of power in Europe, and several schemes to divide the Spanish realm between French and Austrian candidates were discussed. Meanwhile, King Charles II's advisers sought to avoid partition by passing the entire Spanish Empire to a single heir: Louis XIV's grandson, Philip of Anjou. When Charles II died, Philip V (1700–1746) was proclaimed king of Spain, and the War of the Spanish Succession began, with England, the United Provinces, Austria, and Prussia arrayed against France, Bavaria, and Spain. Although William of Orange died in 1702, just as the war was beginning, his generals led an extraordinary march deep into the European Continent, inflicting a devastating defeat on the French and their Bavarian allies at Blenheim (1704). Soon after, the English captured Gibraltar, establishing a commercial foothold in the Mediterranean. By 1709, France was on the verge of defeat, but when they met the British at the battle of Malplaquet in present-day Belgium they inflicted twenty-four thousand casualties before retreating from the field. Meanwhile, the costs of the campaign created a chorus of complaints from English and Dutch merchants, who feared the damage that was being done to trade and commerce. Queen Anne of England (Mary's sister and William's successor) gradually grew disillusioned with the war, and her government sent out peace feelers to France.

The Treaty of Utrecht

In 1713, the war finally came to an end with the Treaty of Utrecht. Its terms were reasonably fair to all sides. Philip V, Louis XIV's grandson, remained on the throne of Spain and retained Spain's colonial empire intact. In return, Louis agreed that France and Spain would never be united under the same ruler. Austria gained territories in the Spanish Netherlands and Italy, including Milan and Naples. The biggest winner by far was Great Britain, as the combined kingdoms of England and Scotland were known after 1707. The British kept Gibraltar and Minorca in the Mediterranean and also acquired substantial French territory in North America and the Caribbean. Even more valuable, however, Britain also extracted from Spain the right to transport and sell African slaves in Spanish America. As a result, the British were now poised to become the principal slave merchants and the dominant colonial and commercial power of the eighteenth-century world.

The Treaty of Utrecht reshaped the balance of power in western Europe in fundamental ways. Spain's collapse was already precipitous; by 1713 it was complete. Holland's decline was more gradual, but by 1713, its greatest days were also over. In the Atlantic world, Britain and France were now the dominant powers. Although they would duel for another half century for control of North America, the balance of colonial power tilted decisively in Britain's favor after Utrecht. Within Europe, the myth of French military

supremacy had been shattered. Britain's navy, not France's army, would rule the new imperial and commercial world of the eighteenth century.

THE REMAKING OF CENTRAL AND EASTERN EUROPE

The decades between 1680 and 1720 were also decisive in reshaping the balance of power in central and eastern Europe. As Ottoman power waned, the Austro-Hungarian Empire of the Habsburgs emerged as the dominant power in central and southeastern Europe. To the north, Brandenburg-Prussia was also a rising power. The most dramatic changes, however, occurred in Russia, which emerged from a long war with Sweden as the dominant power in the Baltic Sea and would soon threaten the combined kingdom of Poland-Lithuania.

The Habsburg Empire

In 1683, the Ottoman Turks launched their last assault on Vienna. Only the arrival of seventy thousand Polish troops saved the Austrian capital from capture. Thereafter, Ottoman power in southeastern Europe declined rapidly. By 1718, Austria had reconquered all of Hungary from the Ottomans, and also Transylvania and Serbia. With Hungary now a buffer state between Austria and the Ottomans, Vienna emerged as one of the great cultural and political capitals of eighteenth-century Europe, and Austria became one of the arbiters of the European balance of power.

Although the Austrian Habsburgs retained their title as Holy Roman Emperors and after 1713 also held lands in the Netherlands and Italy, their real power lay in Austria, Bohemia, Moravia, Galicia, and Hungary. These territories were geographically contiguous, but they were deeply divided by ethnicity, religion, and language. Despite the centralizing efforts of a series of Habsburg rulers, their empire would remain a rather loose confederation of distinct territories.

In Bohemia and Moravia, the Habsburgs encouraged landlords to produce crops for export by forcing peasants to provide three days of unpaid work per week to their lords. In return, the landed elites of these territories permitted the emperors to reduce the political independence of their traditional legislative estates. In Hungary, however, the powerful and independent nobility resisted such compromises, and Hungary remained a semi-autonomous region within the empire whose support the Austrians could never take for granted.

MARIA THERESA OF AUSTRIA AND HER FAMILY. A formidable and capable ruler who fought to maintain Austria's dominance in central Europe against the claims of Frederick the Great of Prussia, Maria Theresa had sixteen children, including Marie Antoinette, later queen of France as wife of Louis XVI. ▪ *Why did she emphasize her role as mother in a royal portrait such as this one, rather than her undeniable political skills?* ▪ *How does this compare to the portraits of William and Mary or of Louis XIV elsewhere in this chapter?*

After 1740, the empress Maria Theresa (r. 1740–80) and her son Joseph II (r. 1765–90; from 1765 until 1780 the two were co-rulers) pioneered a new style of "enlightened absolutism" within their empire: centralizing the administration in Vienna, increasing taxation, creating a professional standing army, and tightening their control over the church while creating a statewide system of primary education, relaxing censorship, and instituting a new, more liberal criminal code. But in practice, Habsburg absolutism, whether enlightened or not, was always limited by the diversity of its imperial territories and by the weakness of its local governmental institutions.

The Rise of Brandenburg-Prussia

After the Ottoman collapse, the main threat to Austria came from the rising power of Brandenburg-Prussia. Like Austria, Prussia was a composite state made up of several geographically divided territories acquired through inheritance by the Hohenzollern family. Their two main holdings were Brandenburg, centered on its capital city, Berlin, and the duchy of East Prussia. Between these two territories lay Swedish Pomerania and a substantial part of the kingdom of Poland. The Hohenzollerns' aim was to unite their state by acquiring these intervening territories. Over the course of more than a century of steady state building, they finally succeeded in doing so. In the process, Brandenburg-Prussia became a dominant military power and a key player in the balance-of-power diplomacy of the mid-eighteenth century.

The foundations for Prussian expansion were laid by Frederick William, the "Great Elector" (r. 1640–88). He obtained East Prussia from Poland in exchange for help in a war against Sweden. Behind the Elector's diplomatic triumphs lay his success in building an army and mobilizing the resources to pay for it. He gave the powerful nobles of his territories (known as *Junkers*) the right to enserf their peasants, and he guaranteed them immunity from taxation. In exchange, they staffed the officer corps of his army and supported his highly autocratic taxation system. Secure in their estates and made increasingly wealthy in the grain trade, the Junkers surrendered management of the Prussian state to the Elector's newly reformed bureaucracy, which set about its main task: increasing the size and strength of the Prussian army.

The Great Elector's son, Frederick I (r. 1688–1713) earned the right to call himself "king in Prussia" from the Austrian emperor and devoted his attention to developing the cultural life of his new royal capital, Berlin. His son, Frederick William I (r. 1713–40) focused, like his grandfather, on building the army. During his reign, the Prussian army became the fourth largest in Europe, after those of France, Austria, and Russia. To support his army, Frederick William I increased taxes and shunned the luxuries of court life.

Frederick William I had made Prussia a strong state. His son Frederick II the Great (r. 1740–86) raised his country to the status of a major power. As soon as he became king in 1740, Frederick mobilized the army his father had never taken into battle and occupied the Austrian province of Silesia. The new Habsburg empress, Maria Theresa, counterattacked; but despite the support of both Britain and Hungary, she was unable to recover Silesia. Emboldened, Frederick spent the rest of his reign consolidating his gains in Silesia and extending his control over the Polish territories that lay between Prussia and Brandenburg. Through relentless diplomacy and frequent war, by 1786 Frederick transformed Prussia into a powerful, contiguous territorial kingdom with the most professional and efficient bureaucracy in Europe, staffed with nobles from the powerful Junker class.

Frederick was an enlightened absolutist. He supervised a series of social reforms, prohibited the judicial torture of accused criminals, abolished the bribing of judges,

THE CITY OF STETTIN UNDER SIEGE BY THE GREAT ELECTOR, FREDERICK WILLIAM, IN THE WINTER OF 1677–78 (c. 1680). This painting depicts the growing sophistication and organization of military operations under the Prussian monarchy. Improvements in artillery and siege tactics forced cities to adopt new defensive strategies, especially the zone of battlements and protective walls that became ubiquitous in central Europe during this period. ▪ *How might these developments have shaped the layout of Europe's growing towns and cities?* ▪ *How might this emphasis on the military and its attendant bureaucracy have affected the relationship between the monarchy and the nobility or between the king and his subjects?*

the next—certainly added to the outsize impression he made on his contemporaries. Peter was not the first tsar to bring his country into contact with western Europe, but his policies were decisive in making Russia a great European power.

The Early Years of Peter's Reign

Since 1613 Russia had been ruled by members of the Romanov Dynasty, who had attempted to restore political stability after the chaotic "time of troubles" that followed the death of Ivan the Terrible in 1584. Like Louis XIV of France, Peter came to the throne as a young boy, and his minority was marked by political dissension and court intrigue. In 1689, however, at the age of seventeen, he overthrew the regency of his half-sister Sophia and assumed personal control of the state. Determined to make Russia into a great military power, the young tsar traveled to Holland and England during the 1690s to study ship-building and to recruit skilled foreign workers to help him build a navy. While he was abroad, however, his elite palace guard (the *streltsy*) rebelled, attempting to restore Sophia to the throne. Peter quickly returned home and crushed the rebellion with striking savagery.

and established a system of elementary schools. Although strongly anti-Semitic, he encouraged religious toleration and declared that he would happily build a mosque in Berlin if he could find enough Muslims to fill it. On his own royal estates he abolished capital punishment, curtailed the forced labor services of his peasantry, and granted them long leases on the land they worked. He encouraged scientific forestry and the cultivation of new crops. He cleared new lands in Silesia and brought in thousands of immigrants to cultivate them. When wars ruined their farms, he supplied his peasants with new livestock and tools. But he never attempted to extend these reforms to the estates of the Prussian nobility. To have done so would have alienated the very group on whom Frederick's rule depended.

AUTOCRACY IN RUSSIA

An even more dramatic transformation took place in Russia under Tsar Peter I (1672–1725). Peter's accomplishments alone would have earned him his title of "Great." But his imposing height—he was six feet eight inches tall—as well as his mercurial personality—jesting one moment, raging

The Transformation of the Tsarist State

Peter is most famous as the tsar who attempted to westernize Russia by imposing a series of social and cultural reforms on the traditional Russian nobility: ordering noblemen to cut off their long beards and flowing sleeves; publishing a book of manners that forbade spitting on the floor and eating with one's fingers; encouraging polite conversation between the sexes; and requiring noblewomen to appear, together with men, in Western garb at weddings, banquets, and other public occasions. Thousands of western European experts were brought to Russia to staff the new schools and academies Peter built; to design the new buildings he constructed; and to serve in the tsar's army, navy, and administration.

These measures were important, but the tsar was not primarily motivated by a desire to modernize or westernize Russia. Peter's policies transformed Russian life in fundamental ways, but his real goal was to make Russia a great military power, not to remake Russian society. His new taxation system (1724), for example, which assessed taxes on individuals rather than on households, rendered many of the traditional divisions of Russian peasant society obsolete. It was created, however, to raise more money for war. His Table of Ranks, imposed in 1722, had a similar

ЦЫРЮЛНІКЪ ХО ÉТЪ РАСКОЛНИКУ БОРОДУ СТРИЧЪ

РАСКОЛНИКЪ ГОВОРИТЪ СЛУШАЙ ШЫРЮЛНІКЪ Я БОРОДЫ СТРИЧЪ НЕ ХОЧУ ВОТ Ь ГЛЕДИ Я НА ТЕБЯ СКОРО КАРУЛ ЗАКРУ

PETER THE GREAT CUTS THE BEARD OF AN OLD BELIEVER.
This woodcut depicts the Russian emperor's enthusiastic policy of westernization, as he pushed everybody in Russia who was not a peasant to adopt Western styles of clothes and grooming. The Old Believer (a member of a religious sect in Russia) protests that he has paid the beard tax and should therefore be exempt.
▪ *Why would an individual's choices about personal appearance be so politically significant in Peter's Russia?* ▪ *What customs were the target of Peter's reforms?*

impact on the nobility. By insisting that all nobles must work their way up from the (lower) landlord class to the (higher) administrative class and to the (highest) military class, Peter reversed the traditional hierarchy of Russian noble society, which had valued landlords by birth above administrators and soldiers who had risen by merit. But he also created a powerful new incentive to lure his nobility into administrative and military service to the tsar.

Peter the Great was the absolute master of his empire to a degree unmatched elsewhere in Europe. After 1649, Russian peasants were legally the property of their landlords; by 1750, half were serfs and the other half were state peasants who lived on lands owned by the tsar himself. State peasants could be conscripted to serve as soldiers in the tsar's army, as workers in his factories (whose productive capacity increased enormously during Peter's reign), or

as forced laborers in his building projects. Serfs could also be taxed by the tsar and summoned for military service, as could their lords. All Russians, of whatever rank, were expected to serve the tsar, and all Russia was considered in some sense to belong to him.

To further consolidate his power, Peter replaced the Duma—the nation's rudimentary national assembly—with a hand-picked senate, a group of nine administrators who supervised military and civilian affairs. In religious matters, he took direct control over the Russian Orthodox Church by appointing an imperial official to manage its affairs. To cope with the demands of war, he also fashioned a new, larger, and more efficient administration, for which he recruited both nobles and nonnobles. One of his principal advisers, Alexander Menshikov, began his career as a cook and finished as a prince. This degree of social mobility would have been impossible in any contemporary western European country. Instead, noble status depended on governmental service, with all nobles expected to participate in Peter's army or administration. The administrative machinery Peter devised furnished Russia with its ruling class for the next two hundred years.

Peter's Foreign Policy

The goal of Peter's foreign policy was to secure year-round ports for Russia on the Black Sea and the Baltic Sea. In the Black Sea, his enemy was the Ottomans, and he had little success. In the north, however, Peter achieved much more. In 1700, he began what would become a twenty-one-year war with Sweden, then the dominant power in the Baltic Sea. By 1703, Peter had secured a foothold on the Gulf of Finland and immediately began to build a new capital city there, which he named St. Petersburg. The centerpiece of the new city was a royal palace designed to imitate and rival Louis XIV's Versailles.

The Great Northern War with Sweden ended in 1721 with the Peace of Nystad. This treaty marks a realignment of power in eastern Europe comparable to that effected by the Treaty of Utrecht in the West. Sweden lost substantial territories to Hanover, Prussia, and Russia, and was now a second-rank power. Poland-Lithuania was also a declining power; by the end of the eighteenth century, the kingdom would disappear altogether, its territories swallowed up by Russia, Austria, and Prussia. The victors at Nystad were the Prussians and the Russians. These two powers secured their position along the Baltic coast, positioning themselves to take advantage of the lucrative eastern European grain trade with western Europe.

Peter's victory came at enormous cost. Direct taxation increased 500 percent during his reign, and his army in the 1720s numbered more than three hundred thousand men. Nevertheless, Peter made Russia a force to be reckoned with on the European scene. A series of ineffective tsars followed, mostly creatures of the palace guard, under whom the resentful nobles reversed many of Peter the Great's reforms. In 1762, however, the crown passed to Catherine the Great, a ruler whose ambitions and determination were equal to those of her great predecessor.

Catherine the Great and the Partition of Poland

Catherine was a German who came to the throne in 1762 on the death of her husband, the weak (and possibly mad) Tsar Peter III, who was deposed and executed in a palace coup that Catherine herself may have helped arrange. Although she cultivated an image of herself as an enlightened ruler, Catherine was determined not to lose the support of the nobility who had placed her on the throne. As a result, her efforts at social reform did not extend much beyond the founding of hospitals and orphanages and the creation of an elementary school system for the children of the provincial nobility. Like her contemporary enlightened absolutists Joseph of Austria and Frederick the Great of Prussia, she too summoned a commission, in 1767, to codify and revise Russian law. But few of its radical proposals (which included the abolition of capital punishment, an end to judicial torture, and prohibitions on the selling of serfs) were ever implemented. When a peasant revolt led by a Cossack named Emelyan Pugachev briefly threatened Moscow in 1773–75, Catherine responded by further centralizing her own government and by tightening aristocratic control over the peasantry.

Catherine's greatest achievements were gained through war and diplomacy. In 1769, she renewed Peter the Great's push to secure a warm-water port on the Black Sea. In the resulting war with the Ottoman Turks (which ended in 1774), Russia won control over the northern coast of the Black Sea, secured the independence of Crimea (which Russia would annex in 1783), and obtained safe passage for Russian ships through the Bosporus and into the Mediterranean Sea. In the course of this campaign, Russia also won control over several Ottoman provinces in the Balkans.

Russia's gains alarmed Austria, however, which now found itself with the powerful Russian Empire on its southern doorstep. Prussia too was threatening to become in-

CATHERINE THE GREAT.

volved in the war as an ally of the Ottomans. Frederick the Great's real interests, however, lay much closer to home. To preserve the peace among Russia, Prussia, and Austria, he proposed instead a partition of Poland. Russia would abandon its Balkan conquests and, in return, would acquire the grain fields of eastern Poland, along with a population of 1 to 2 million Poles. Austria would take Galicia (divided between Poland and Ukraine today), acquiring 2.5 million Poles. Prussia, meanwhile, would take the coastal regions of Poland, including the port of Gdansk (Danzig). As a result of this agreement, finalized in 1772, Poland lost about 30 percent of its territory and about half of its population.

Poland was now paying the price for its political conservatism. Alone among the major central European powers, the Polish nobility had successfully opposed any move toward monarchical centralization as a threat to its liberties, among which was the right of any individual noble to veto any measure proposed in the Polish representative assembly, the Diet. In 1772, King Stanislaus reluctantly accepted the partition of his country because he was too weak to resist it. In 1793 the Russians and Prussians took two more enormous bites out of Poland, and a final swallow by Russia, Austria, and Prussia in 1795 left nothing of Poland at all.

COMMERCE AND CONSUMPTION

Despite the increased military power of Russia, Prussia, and Austria, the balance of power within Europe was shifting steadily toward the West during the eighteenth century. The North Atlantic economies in particular were growing more rapidly than those anywhere else in Europe. As a result, France and Britain were becoming preponderant powers both in Europe and the wider world.

Economic Growth in Eighteenth-Century Europe

The reasons for this rapid economic and demographic growth in northwestern Europe are complex. In Britain and Holland, new, more intensive agricultural systems produced more food per acre. New crops, especially maize and potatoes (both introduced to Europe from the Americas),

POPULATION GROWTH c. 1600. ▪ *Where did the population grow more rapidly?* ▪ *Why were the largest gains in population on the coasts?* ▪ *How did urbanization affect patterns of life and trade?*

370 | CHAPTER 15 *Absolutism and Empire, 1660–1789*

also helped increase the supply of food. Infectious disease continued to kill half of all Europeans before the age of twenty, but plague was ceasing to be a major killer, as a degree of immunity began to emerge within the European population.

Northwestern Europe was also becoming increasingly urbanized. Across Europe as a whole the total number of urban dwellers did not change markedly between 1600 and 1800. What did change was, first, the fact that larger cities were increasingly concentrated in northern and western Europe and, second, the extraordinary growth of the very largest cities. Amsterdam, the hub of early modern international commerce, increased from 30,000 in 1530 to 200,000 by 1800. Naples, the busy Mediterranean port, went from a population of 300,000 in 1600 to nearly half a million by the late eighteenth century. Even more spectacular population growth occurred in the administrative capitals of Europe. London grew from 674,000 in 1700 to 860,000 a century later. Paris went from 180,000 people in 1600 to more than 500,000 in 1800.

The rising prosperity of northwestern Europe depended on developments in trade and manufacturing as well as agriculture. Spurred by improvements in transportation, entrepreneurs began to promote the production of textiles in the countryside. They distributed ("put out") wool and flax to rural workers who would card, spin, and weave it into cloth on a piece-rate basis. The entrepreneur then collected and sold the finished cloth in a market that extended from local towns to international exporters. For country dwellers, this system (sometimes called *protoindustrialization*) provided welcome employment during otherwise slack seasons of the agricultural year. For the merchant-entrepreneurs who administered it, the system allowed them to avoid expensive guild restrictions in the towns and to reduce the overall costs of production. The putting-out system led to increased employment and higher levels of industrial production, not only for textiles but also for iron, metalworking, and even toy and clock making.

The role of cities as manufacturing centers also continued to grow during the eighteenth century. In northern France, a million men and women were employed in the textile trade in Amiens, Lille, and Rheims. The rulers of Prussia made it their policy to develop Berlin as a manufacturing center, taking advantage of an influx of French Protestants to establish a silk-weaving industry there. Most urban manufacturing took place in small shops employing from five to twenty journeymen working under a master. But the scale of such enterprise was growing and becoming more specialized, as workshops began to group together to form a single manufacturing district in which several thousand workers might be employed to produce the same product.

Techniques in some crafts remained much as they had been for centuries. In others, however, inventions changed the pattern of work as well as the nature of the product. Knitting frames, simple devices to speed the manufacture of textile goods, made their appearance in Britain and Holland. Wire-drawing machines and slitting mills, the latter enabling nail makers to convert iron bars into rods, spread from Germany into Britain. Techniques for printing colored designs directly on calico cloth were imported from Asia. New and more efficient printing presses appeared, first in Holland and then elsewhere.

Workers did not readily accept innovations of this kind. Labor-saving machines threw people out of work. Artisans, especially those organized into guilds, were by nature conservative, anxious to protect not only their rights but also the secrets of their trade. Often, therefore, governments would intervene to block the widespread use of machines if they threatened to increase unemployment or in some other way to create unrest. States might also intervene to protect the interests of their powerful commercial and financial backers. Mercantilist doctrines could also impede innovation. In both Paris and Lyons, for example, the use of indigo dyes was banned because they were manufactured abroad. But the pressures for economic innovation were irresistable, because behind them lay an insatiable eighteenth-century appetite for goods.

A World of Goods

In the eighteenth century, for the first time, a mass market for consumer goods emerged in Europe, and especially in northwestern Europe. Houses were now stocked with hitherto uncommon luxuries such as sugar, tobacco, tea, coffee, chocolate, newspapers, books, pictures, clocks, toys, china, glassware, pewter, silver plate, soap, razors, furniture (including beds with mattresses, chairs, and chests of drawers), shoes, cotton cloth, and spare clothing. Demand for such products consistently outstripped the supply, causing prices for these items to rise faster than the price of foodstuffs throughout the century. But the demand for them continued unabated.

The exploding consumer economy of the eighteenth century spurred demand for manufactured goods of all sorts. But it also encouraged the provision of services. In eighteenth-century Britain, the service sector was the fastest-growing part of the economy, outstripping both agriculture and manufacturing. Almost everywhere in urban Europe, the eighteenth century was the golden age of the small shopkeeper. People bought more prepared foods and more ready-made (as opposed to personally tailored) clothing. Advertising became an important part of doing

***TOPSY-TURVY WORLD* BY JAN STEEN**. This Dutch painting depicts a household in the throes of the exploding consumer economy that hit Europe in the eighteenth century. Consumer goods ranging from silver and china to clothing and furniture cluttered the houses of ordinary people as never before.

business, helping create demand for new products and shaping popular taste for changing fashions. Even political allegiances could be expressed through consumption when people purchased plates and glasses commemorating favorite rulers or causes.

The result of all these developments was a European economy vastly more complex, more specialized, more integrated, more commercialized, and more productive than anything the world had seen before.

COLONIZATION AND TRADE IN THE SEVENTEENTH CENTURY

Many of the new consumer goods that propelled the economy of eighteenth-century Europe, including such staples as sugar, tobacco, tea, coffee, chocolate, china, and cotton cloth, were the products of Europe's growing colonial empires in Asia, Africa, and the Americas. The economic history of these empires is part of a broader pattern of accelerating global connection beginning in the late fifteenth century that witnessed an extraordinary exchange of peoples, plants, animals, diseases, goods, and culture between the African and Eurasian land mass on the one hand, and the Americas, Australia, and the Pacific Islands on the other. Historians refer to this as the "Columbian exchange"—a reference to Columbus's voyage in 1492—and many see it as a fundamental turning point in

human history and in the history of the earth's ecology. The exchange brought new agricultural products to Europe—such as cane sugar, tobacco, corn, and the potato—and new domesticated animals to the Americas and Australia, transforming agriculture on both sides of the Atlantic and the Pacific Oceans, and reshaping the landscape itself. The transfer of human populations in the form of settlers, merchants, and slaves accelerated the process of cultural change for many peoples, even as other groups saw their cultures wiped out through violence or forced resettlement. The accompanying transfer of disease agents, meanwhile, had devastating effects—some historians suggest that between 50 and 90 percent of the pre-Columbian population of the Americas died from communicable diseases brought from Europe such as smallpox, cholera, influenza, typhoid, and measles.

Europe's growing colonial empires between the fifteenth and eighteenth centuries were thus a part of a series of fundamental changes that transformed people's lives, and their relation to their environment over the long term in many parts of the world. Europe's growing wealth during this period had complex causes, but it is impossible to imagine the prosperity of the eighteenth century without understanding this history of colonialism.

Spanish Colonialism

After the exploits of the conquistadors, the Spanish established colonial governments in Peru and in Mexico, which they controlled from Madrid. In keeping with the doctrines of mercantilism, the Spanish government allowed only Spanish merchants to trade with their American colonies, requiring all colonial exports and imports to pass through a single Spanish port (first Seville, then later the more navigable port of Cadíz). During the sixteenth century, this system worked reasonably well. The Spanish colonial economy was dominated by mining; the lucrative market for silver in East Asia even made it profitable to establish an outpost in Manila, where Spanish merchants exchanged Asian silk for South American bullion. But Spain also took steps to promote farming and ranching in Central and South America and established settlements in Florida and California.

Throughout this empire, a relatively small number of Spaniards had conquered complex and highly populous Native American societies. To rule these new territories, the Spanish replaced existing elites with Spanish administrators and churchmen. By and large, they did not attempt to uproot or eliminate existing native cultures but focused on controlling and exploiting native labor for their own profit, above all in extracting mineral resources. The native peoples of Spanish America already lived, for the most part, in large, well-organized villages and towns. The Spanish collected tribute from these communities and attempted to convert them to Catholicism but did not attempt to change their basic patterns of life.

The result was widespread cultural assimilation between the Spanish colonizers and the native populations, combined with a relatively high degree of intermarriage between them. Out of this reality emerged a complex and distinctive system of racial and social castes, with Spaniards at the top, peoples of mixed descent (combinations of Spanish, African, and Native American) in the middle, and nontribal American Indians at the bottom. In theory, these racial categories corresponded with class distinctions, but in practice race and class did not always coincide, and race itself was often a social fiction. Individuals of mixed descent who prospered economically often found ways to establish their "pure" Spanish ancestry by adopting the social practices that characterized elite (that is, Spanish) status. Spaniards always remained at the top of the social hierarchy, however, even when they fell into poverty.

The wealth of Spain's colonial trade tempted the merchants of other countries to win a share of the treasure for themselves. Probably the boldest challengers were the English, whose leading buccaneer was Sir Francis Drake. Three times Drake raided the east and west coasts of Spanish America. His career illustrates the mixture of piracy and patriotism that characterized England's early efforts to break into the colonial trade. Until the 1650s, however, the English could only dent the lucrative Spanish trade in bullion, hides, silks, and slaves.

French Colonialism

French colonial policy matured under Louis XIV's mercantilist finance minister, Jean Baptiste Colbert. Realizing the profits to be made in responding to Europe's growing demand for sugar, he encouraged the development of sugar-producing colonies in the West Indies, the largest of which was Saint-Domingue (present-day Haiti). Sugar, virtually unknown in Christian Europe during the Middle Ages, became a popular luxury item in the late fifteenth cen-

tury. It took the slave plantations of the Caribbean to turn sugar into a mass-market product. By 1750, slaves in Saint-Domingue produced 40 percent of the world's sugar and 50 percent of its coffee, exporting more sugar than Jamaica, Cuba, and Brazil combined. France also dominated the interior of the North American continent, where French traders brought furs to the American Indians and missionaries preached Christianity in a vast territory that stretched from Quebec to Louisiana. The financial returns from North America were never large, however, and never matched the profits from the Caribbean sugar colonies or from the trading posts that the French maintained in India.

Like the Spanish colonies, the French colonies were established and administered as direct crown enterprises. The elite of French colonial society were military officers and administrators sent from Paris. Below their ranks were fishermen, fur traders, small farmers, and common soldiers who constituted the bulk of French settlers in North America. Because the fishing and the fur trades relied on cooperative relationships with native peoples, a mutual economic interdependence grew up between the French colonies and the peoples of the surrounding region. Intermarriage, especially between French traders and native women, was common. These North American colonies remained dependent on the wages and supplies sent to them from the mother country. Only rarely did they become truly self-sustaining economic enterprises.

The phenomenally successful sugar plantations of the Caribbean had their own social structure, with slaves at the bottom, people of mixed African and European descent forming a middle layer, and wealthy European plantation

ILLINOIS INDIANS TRADING WITH FRENCH SETTLERS. This engraving from Nicholas De Fer's 1705 map of the Western Hemisphere illustrates the economic interdependence that developed between early French colonies and the native peoples of the surrounding region. ▪ *How did this differ from relations between Native Americans and English agricultural communities on the Atlantic coast?*

owners at the top, controlling the lucrative trade with the outside world. Because the monarchy controlled the prices that colonial plantation owners could charge French merchants for their goods, traders in Europe who bought the goods for resale abroad could also make vast fortunes. Historians estimate that as many as a million of the twenty-five million inhabitants of France in the eighteenth century lived off the money flowing through this colonial trade, making the slave colonies of the Caribbean a powerful force for economic change in France.

English Colonialism

Unlike those of Spain, England's American colonies had no significant mineral wealth. As a result, English colonists sought profits by establishing agricultural settlements in North America and the Caribbean basin. Their first permanent, though ultimately unsuccessful, colony was founded in 1607 at Jamestown, Virginia. Over the next forty years, eighty thousand English emigrants would sail to more than twenty autonomous settlements in the New World. Many of these early settlers were driven by religious motives. The Pilgrims who landed at Plymouth, Massachusetts, in 1620 were one of many dissident groups, both Protestant and Catholic, that sought to escape the English government's religious intolerance by emigrating to North America. Strikingly, however, English colonists showed little interest in trying to convert Native American peoples to Christianity. Missionaries played a much larger role in Spanish efforts to colonize Central and South America and French efforts to penetrate the North American hinterlands.

These English colonies did not begin as crown enterprises as in the Spanish or French empires. Instead they were private ventures, either proprietary (as in Maryland and Pennsylvania) or joint-stock companies (as in Virginia and the Massachusetts Bay colony). Building on their experience in Ireland, English colonists established planned settlements known as plantations, in which they attempted to replicate as many features of English life as possible. Geography also contributed to the English settlement patterns, as the rivers and bays of the northeast Atlantic coast provided the first locations for colonists. Aside from the Hudson, however, there were no great rivers to lead colonists very far inland, and the English colonies clung to the coast and to each other.

Once they realized the profits to be made in colonial trade, however, the governments of both Oliver Cromwell and Charles II began to intervene in their management. Mercantilist-inspired navigation acts, passed in 1651 and 1660, decreed that exports from English colonies to the mother country be carried in English ships and forbade the direct exporting of "enumerated" products, such as sugar and tobacco, directly from the colonies to foreign ports. The English sugar-producing colonies competed directly with the French, and during the eighteenth century, profits from the tiny islands of Jamaica and Barbados were worth more than all British imports from China and India combined. Tobacco, which was first brought to Europe by the Spaniards, became profitable as smoking caught on in Europe in the seventeenth century, popularized by English explorers who learned about it from Native Americans in Virginia. Governments at first joined the church in condemning it, but eventually encouraged its production and consumption, realizing the profits to be made from the trade.

The early English colonies in North America soon grew into agricultural communities populated by small- and medium-scale landholders. In part this reflected the kinds of people recruited by the private colonial enterprises for settlement in North America. But the focus on agriculture also resulted from the demographic catastrophe that struck the native populations of the Atlantic seaboard during the second half of the sixteenth century. European diseases—brought by Spanish armies and by the French, British, and Portuguese fisherman who frequented the rich fishing banks off the New England coast—had already decimated the native peoples of eastern North America even before the first European colonists set foot there. By the early seventeenth century, a great deal of rich agricultural land had been abandoned simply because there were no longer enough native farmers to till it.

Unlike the Spanish, English colonists along the Atlantic seaboard had neither the need nor the opportunity to control a large native labor force. What they wanted, rather, was complete and exclusive control over native lands. To this end, the English colonists soon set out to eliminate, through expulsion and massacre, the indigenous peoples of their colonies. There were exceptions—in the Quaker colony of Pennsylvania, colonists and Native Americans maintained friendly relations for more than half a century. In the Carolinas, on the other hand, there was widespread enslavement of native peoples, either for sale to the West Indies or, from the 1690s, to work on the rice plantations along the coast. Elsewhere, however, attempts to enslave the native peoples of North American failed. When English planters looked for bond laborers, they either recruited indentured servants from England (most of whom would be freed after a specified period of service) or purchased African captives (who would usually be enslaved for life).

In contrast to the Spanish and French colonies, intermarriage between English colonists and native populations was rare. Instead, a rigid racial division emerged that distinguished all Europeans from all Native Americans and

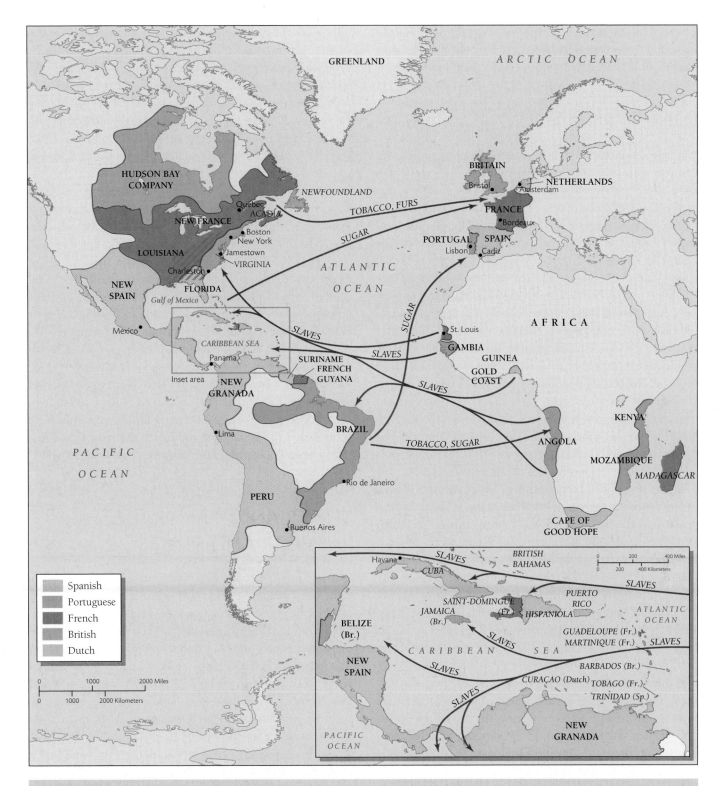

THE ATLANTIC WORLD c. 1700. ▪ *Why were European governments so concerned with closely controlling the means by which certain products traveled from the colonies to European ports?* ▪ *What products did French and British colonies in North America provide to the European market in the eighteenth century?* ▪ *Which colonies were most dependent on slave labor?* ▪ *What products did they produce?*

Africans. Intermarriage between natives and Africans was relatively common, but between the English and the native peoples of the colonies an unbridgeable gulf developed.

Dutch Colonialism

Until the 1670s, the Dutch controlled the most prosperous commercial empire of the seventeenth century. Although some Dutch settlements were established, including one at the Cape of Good Hope in modern-day South Africa, Dutch colonialism generally followed the "fort and factory" model established by the Portuguese in Asia. In Southeast Asia, the Dutch East India Company, founded in 1602, seized control of Sumatra, Borneo, and the Moluccas (Spice Islands), driving Portuguese traders from an area they had previously dominated and establishing a Dutch monopoly within Europe over pepper, cinnamon, nutmeg, mace, and cloves. In the Western Hemisphere, however, their achievements were less spectacular. After a series of trade wars with England, in 1667 they formally surrendered their colony of New Amsterdam (subsequently renamed New York), retaining only Surinam (off the northern coast of South America) and Curaçao and Tobago (in the West Indies). Although the Dutch dominated the seventeenth-century slave trade with Africa, they lost this position to the British after 1713.

The Dutch also pioneered new financial mechanisms for investing in colonial enterprises. One of the most important of these was the joint-stock company, of which the Dutch East India Company was among the first. Such companies raised cash by selling shares in their enterprise to investors. Even though the investors might not take any role in managing the company, they were joint owners of the business and therefore entitled to a share in the profits. Initially, the Dutch East India Company intended to pay off its investors ten years after its founding, but the directors soon recognized the impossibility of this plan. The directors therefore urged investors anxious to realize their profits to sell their shares on the Amsterdam stock exchange to other investors, thereby ensuring the continued operation of their enterprise and, in the process, establishing a method of continuous business financing that would soon spread to elsewhere in Europe.

Colonial Rivalries

The fortunes of these colonial empires changed dramatically in the course of the seventeenth and early eighteenth centuries. Spain proved unable to defend its early monopoly over colonial trade, and in 1650 the Spanish suffered a crippling blow when they were forced to surrender Jamaica and several treasure ships lying off of the Spanish harbor of Cadíz. By 1700, although Spain still possessed a colonial empire, it lay at the mercy of its more dynamic rivals. Portugal, too, found it impossible to prevent foreign penetration of its colonial empire. In 1703, the English signed a treaty with Portugal allowing English merchants to export woolens duty-free into Portugal and allowing Portugal to ship its wines duty-free into England. Access to Portugal also led British merchants to trade with the Portuguese colony of Brazil, an important sugar producer and the largest of all the American markets for African slaves. In the eighteenth century, English merchants would dominate these Brazilian trade routes.

The 1713 Treaty of Utrecht opened a new era of colonial rivalries. The biggest losers were the Dutch, who gained only a guarantee of their own borders, and the Spanish, who were forced to concede to Britain the right to market slaves in the Spanish colonies. The winners were the British (who acquired large chunks of territory in North America) and to a lesser extent, the French, who retained Quebec and other territories in North America, as well as their foothold in India. The eighteenth century would witness a continuing struggle between Britain and France for control over the expanding commerce that now bound the European economy to the Americas and to Asia.

THE TRIANGULAR TRADE IN SUGAR AND SLAVES

During the eighteenth century, European colonial trade came to be dominated by trans-Atlantic routes that developed in response to the increased demand for sugar and tobacco and the corresponding market for slaves to produce these goods on American and Caribbean plantations. In this "triangular" trade, naval superiority gave Britain a decisive advantage over its French, Spanish, Portuguese, and Dutch rivals. Typically, a British ship might begin its voyage from New England with a consignment of rum and sail to Africa, where the rum would be exchanged for a cargo of slaves. From the west coast of Africa the ship would then cross the South Atlantic to the sugar colonies of Jamaica or Barbados, where slaves would be traded for molasses. It would then make the final leg of the journey back to New England, where the molasses would be made into rum. A variant triangle might see cheap manufactured goods move from England to Africa, where they would be traded for slaves. Those slaves would then be shipped to Virginia and exchanged for tobacco, which would be shipped to England and processed there for sale throughout Europe.

The cultivation of New World sugar and tobacco depended on slave labor. As European demand for these products increased, so too did the traffic in enslaved Africans. At the height of the Atlantic slave trade in the eighteenth century, seventy-five to ninety thousand Africans were shipped across the Atlantic yearly: at least six million in the eighteenth century, out of a total of over eleven million for the entire history of the trade. About 35 percent went to English and French Caribbean plantations, 5 percent (roughly five hundred thousand) to North America, and the rest to the Portuguese colony of Brazil and to the Spanish colonies in Central and South America. By the 1780s, there were more than five hundred thousand slaves on the largest French plantation island, Saint-Domingue, and at least two hundred thousand on its English counterpart, Jamaica.

Although run as a monopoly by various governments in the sixteenth and early seventeenth centuries, the slave trade in the eighteenth century was open to private entrepreneurs who operated ports on the West African coast. These traders exchanged Indian cloth, metal goods, rum, and firearms with African slave merchants in return for their human cargo, who would then be packed by the hundreds into the holds of slave ships for the gruesome Middle Passage across the Atlantic (so called to distinguish it from the slave ship's voyage from Europe to Africa, and then from the colonies back to Europe). Shackled belowdecks without sanitary facilities, the captive men, women, and children suffered horribly. The mortality rate, however, remained at about 10 or 11 percent, not much higher than the rate for a normal sea voyage of a hundred days or more. Since traders had to invest as much as £10 per slave in their enterprise, they were generally anxious to ensure that their consignment would reach its destination in good enough condition to be sold for a profit.

The Commercial Rivalry between Britain and France

British dominance of the slave trade gave it decisive advantages in its colonial struggles with France. As one Englishman wrote in 1749, the slave trade had provided

HOW SLAVES WERE STOWED ABOARD SHIP DURING THE MIDDLE PASSAGE. Men were "housed" on the right; women on the left; children in the middle. The human cargo was jammed onto platforms six feet wide without sufficient headroom to permit an adult to sit up. This diagram is from evidence gathered by English abolitionists and depicts conditions on the Liverpool slave ship *Brookes*.

"an unexhastible fund of wealth to this nation." But even apart from the slave trade, the value of colonial commerce was increasing dramatically during the eighteenth century. French colonial trade, valued at 25 million livres in 1716, rose to 263 million livres in 1789. In England, during roughly the same period, foreign trade increased in value from £10 million to £40 million, the latter amount more than twice that for France.

The growing value of colonial commerce tied the interests of governments and transoceanic merchants together in an increasingly tight embrace. Merchants engaged in the colonial trade depended on their governments to protect and defend their overseas investments; but governments depended in turn on merchants and their financial backers to build the ships and sustain the trade on which national power depended. In the eighteenth century, even the ability to wage war rested largely (and increasingly) on a government's ability to borrow the necessary funds from wealthy investors and then to pay back those debts, with interest, over time. As it did in commerce, so too in finance, Britain came to enjoy a decisive advantage in this respect over France. The Bank of England, founded in the 1690s, managed the English national debt with great success, providing the funds required for war by selling shares to investors, then repaying those investors at moderate rates of interest. In contrast, chronic governmental indebtedness forced the French crown to borrow at ruinously high rates of interest, provoking a series of fiscal crises that in 1789 finally led to the collapse of the French monarchy.

The American Declaration of Independence

The Declaration of Independence, issued from Philadelphia on July 4, 1776, is perhaps the most famous single document of American history. But its familiarity does not lessen its interest as a statement of political philosophy. The indebtedness of the document's authors to the ideas of John Locke will be obvious from the selections here. But Locke, in turn, drew many of his ideas about the contractual and conditional nature of human government from the conciliarist thinkers of the fifteenth and early sixteenth centuries. The appeal of absolutism notwithstanding, the declaration shows how vigorous the medieval tradition of contractual, limited government remained at the end of the eighteenth century.

 hen in the course of human events, it becomes necessary for one people to dissolve the political bonds which have connected them with another, and to assume among the powers of the earth the separate and equal station to which the Laws of Nature and of Nature's God entitle them, a decent respect to the opinions of mankind requires that they should declare the causes which impel them to the separation.... We hold these truths to be self-evident, that all men are created equal, that they are endowed by their Creator with certain unalienable rights, that among these are Life, Liberty and the pursuit of Happiness.... That to secure these rights, Governments are instituted among men, deriving their just powers from the consent of the governed.... That whenever any form of Government becomes destructive of these ends, it is the Right of the People to alter or to abolish it, and to institute new Government, laying its foundation upon such principles and organizing its power in such form, as to them shall seem most likely to effect their Safety and Happiness. Prudence, indeed, will dictate that Governments long established should not be changed for light and transient causes; and accordingly all experience has shown, that mankind are more disposed to suffer, while evils are sufferable, than to right themselves by abolishing the forms to which they are accustomed. But when a long train of abuses and usurpations, pursuing invariably the same Object, evinces a design to reduce them under absolute despotism, it is their right, it is their duty, to throw off such Government, and to provide new Guards for their future security.... Such has been the patient sufferance of these Colonies; and such is now the necessity which constrains them to alter their former Systems of Government....

Questions for Analysis

1. Who are "the people" mentioned in the first sentence of this selection? Are the rights of "the people" the same as individual rights? How did the authors of this declaration come to think of themselves as the representatives of such a body?

2. What is the purpose of government, according to this document? Who gets to decide if the government is doing its job?

3. How would Robert Filmer or Bossuet have viewed such a declaration? How might John Locke have defended it?

War and Empire in the Eighteenth-Century World

After 1713, western Europe remained largely at peace for a generation. In 1740, however, that peace was shattered when Frederick the Great of Prussia took advantage of the accession of a woman, the empress Maria Theresa, to the throne of Austria to seize the Austrian province of Silesia (discussed earlier in this chapter). In the resulting War of the Austrian Succession (1740–48), France and Spain sided with Prussia, against Britain, the Dutch Republic, and Austria. This war quickly spread beyond the frontiers of Europe, as the French and the British continued to struggle for dominance in India and North America.

These colonial conflicts reignited when Prussia once again attacked Austria in 1756. This time, however, Prussia allied itself with Great Britain. Austria found support from both France and Russia. In Europe, the Seven Years' War (1756–63) ended in stalemate. In India and North America, however, the war had decisive consequences. In India, mercenary troops employed by the British East India Company joined with native allies to eliminate their French competitors. In North America (where the conflict was known as the French and Indian War), British troops captured both Louisbourg and Quebec and also drove French forces from the Ohio River Valley and the Great Lakes. By the Treaty of Paris in 1763, which brought the Seven Years' War to an end, France formally surrendered both Canada and India to the British. Six years later, the French East India Company was dissolved.

The American Revolution

Along the Atlantic seaboard, however, the rapidly growing British colonies were beginning to chafe at rule from London. To recover some of the costs of the Seven Years' War and to pay for the continuing costs of protecting its colonial subjects, the British Parliament imposed a series of new taxes on its American colonies. These taxes were immediately unpopular. Colonists complained that because they had no representatives in Parliament, they were being taxed without their consent—a fundamental violation of their rights as British subjects. They also complained that British restrictions on colonial trade, particularly the requirement that certain goods pass first through British ports before being shipped to the Continent, were strangling American livelihoods and making it impossible to pay even the king's legitimate taxes.

The British government, led since 1760 by the young and inexperienced George III, responded to these complaints with a badly calculated mixture of vacillation and force. Various taxes were imposed and then withdrawn in the face of colonial resistance. In 1773, however, when East India Company tea was dumped in Boston Harbor by rebellious colonials objecting to the customs duties that had been imposed on it, the British government closed the port of Boston and curtailed the colony's representative institutions. These "Coercive Acts" galvanized the support of the other American colonies for Massachusetts. In 1774, representatives from all the American colonies met at Philadelphia to form the Continental Congress to negotiate with the crown over their grievances. In April 1775, however, local militiamen at Lexington and Concord clashed with regular British troops sent to disarm them. Soon thereafter, the Continental Congress began raising an army, and an outright rebellion erupted against the British government.

THE SEVEN YEARS' WAR, 1756–63. ▪ *What continents were involved in the Seven Years' War?* ▪ *What was the impact of naval power on the outcome of the war?* ▪ *What were the consequences for the colonies involved in the conflict?*

On July 4, 1776, the thirteen colonies formally declared their independence from Great Britain. During the first two years of the war, it seemed unlikely that such independence would ever become a reality. In 1778, however, France, anxious to undermine the colonial hegemony Great Britain had established since 1713, joined the war on the side of the Americans. Spain entered the war in support of France, hoping to recover Gibraltar and Florida (the latter lost in 1763 to Britain). In 1780, Britain also declared war on the Dutch Republic for continuing to trade with the rebellious colonies. Now facing a coalition of its colonial rivals, Great Britain saw the war turn against it. In 1781, combined land and sea operations by French and American troops forced the surrender of the main British army at Yorktown in Virginia. As the defeated British soldiers surrendered their weapons, their band played a song entitled "The World Turned Upside Down."

Negotiations for peace began soon after the defeat at Yorktown but were not concluded until September 1783. The Treaty of Paris left Great Britain in control of Canada and Gibraltar. Spain retained its possessions west of the Mississippi River and recovered Florida. The United States gained its independence; its western border was fixed on the Mississippi River, and it secured valuable fishing rights off the eastern coast of Canada. France gained only the satisfaction of defeating its colonial rival; but even that satisfaction was short lived. Six years later, the massive debts France had incurred in supporting the American Revolution helped bring about another, very different kind of revolution in France that would permanently alter the history of Europe.

CONCLUSION

Seen in this light, the American War of Independence was the final military conflict in a century-long struggle between Great Britain and France for colonial dominance. But the consequences of Britain's defeat in 1783 were far less significant than might have been expected. Even after American independence, Great Britain would remain the most important trading partner for its former American colonies, while elsewhere around the globe, the commercial dominance Britain had already established would continue to grow. The profits of slavery certainly helped fuel the eighteenth-century British economy; by the end of the century, however, British trade and manufacturing had reached such high levels of productivity that even the abolition of the slave trade (in 1808) and of slavery itself (in 1833) did not impede its continuing growth.

The economic prosperity of late-eighteenth-century Britain was mirrored to some degree throughout northwestern Europe. Improved transportation systems, more-reliable

After You Read
This Chapter

Ⓢ Visit StudySpace for quizzes, additional review materials, and multi-media documents. **wwnorton.com/studyspace**

REVIEWING THE OBJECTIVES

- Absolutist rulers claimed a monopoly of power and authority within their realms. What did they do to achieve this goal?
- Monarchies in both western and eastern Europe adopted the absolutist system, but they faced different challenges. How did the absolutist monarchies in eastern Europe differ from their counterparts in western Europe?
- England developed an alternative to absolutism by the end of the seventeenth century. What was it?
- The commercial revolution of the eighteenth century resulted in major changes in the European economy. What were they?
- Colonial expansion in the Atlantic world and the African slave trade connected Africa and the Americas with Europe in new ways. Who profited most from the Atlantic's new political and economic relationships?

food supplies, and growing quantities of consumer goods brought improved standards of living to large numbers of Europeans, even as the overall population of Europe was rising faster after 1750 than it had ever done before. Population growth was especially rapid in the cities, where a new urban middle class was emerging whose tastes drove the market for goods and whose opinions were reshaping the world of ideas.

But the prosperity of late-eighteenth-century Europe remained very unevenly distributed. In the cities, rich and poor lived separate lives in separate neighborhoods. In the countryside, regions bypassed by the developing commercial economy of the period continued to suffer from hunger and famine, just as they had done in the sixteenth and seventeenth centuries. In eastern Europe the contrasts between rich and poor were even more extreme, as many peasants fell into a new style of serfdom that would last until the end of the nineteenth century. War, too, remained a fact of European life, bringing death and destruction to hundreds of thousands of people across the continent and around the world—yet another consequence of the worldwide reach of these European colonial empires.

Political change was more gradual. Throughout Europe, the powers of governments steadily increased. Administrators became more numerous, more efficient, and more demanding, partly to meet the mounting costs of war but also because governments were starting to take on a much wider range of responsibilities for the welfare of their subjects. Despite the increasing scope of government, however, the structure and principles of government changed relatively little. Apart from Great Britain and the Dutch Republic, the great powers of eighteenth-century Europe were still governed by rulers who styled themselves as absolutist monarchs in the mold of Louis XIV. By 1789, however, the European world was a vastly different place than it had been a century before, when the Sun King had dominated European politics. The full extent of those differences was about to be revealed.

PEOPLE, IDEAS, AND EVENTS IN CONTEXT

- What did **LOUIS XIV** of France, **PETER THE GREAT** of Russia, **FREDERICK THE GREAT** of Prussia, and **MARIA THERESA** of Austria have in common? How did they deal with those who resisted their attempts to impose absolutist rule?
- What limits to royal power were recognized in Great Britain as a result of the **GLORIOUS REVOLUTION**?
- What does the **TREATY OF UTRECHT** (1713) tell us about the diminished influence of Spain and the corresponding rise of Britain as a European power?
- How did European monarchies use the economic theory known as **MERCANTILISM** to strengthen the power and wealth of their kingdoms?
- What was the **COLUMBIAN EXCHANGE**? What combination of demographic, cultural, and ecological transformations are contained within this idea?
- How did the **COMMERCIAL REVOLUTION** change social life in Europe?
- What was the **TRIANGULAR TRADE** and how was it related to the growth of commerce in the Atlantic world during this period?
- What debt does the American **DECLARATION OF INDEPENDENCE** owe to the ideas of the English political thinker **JOHN LOCKE**?

CONSEQUENCES

- Was any European monarch's power ever really *absolute*?
- What do you suppose had more effect on the lives of ordinary Europeans: the rise of absolutist regimes or the commercial revolution of the eighteenth century?
- In a world in which a British merchant's fortune depended on the price of molasses in Boston, the demand for African slaves in Jamaica, and the price of rum in Senegal, could one already speak of *globalization*?

Before You Read This Chapter

STORY LINES

- After c. 1550, new sciences in Europe questioned older beliefs about the physical universe. New methods of inquiry led to the development of astronomy, physics, biology, and chemistry, and new institutions that supported scientific research and education.

- The scientific revolution entailed both theoretical breakthroughs in explaining the physical universe as well as advances in the practical knowledge of artisans who built mechanical devices such as telescopes. This combination of scientific inquisitiveness and craft techniques encouraged technological developments that would later be useful in industrialization.

- The new sciences did not mark a clean rupture with older traditions of religious thinking. Most scientists in the 1600s remained essentially religious in their worldview, and in any case, their work was only accessible to a small, literate minority who had access to books.

CHRONOLOGY

1543	Nicolaus Copernicus (1473–1543) publishes *On the Revolutions of the Heavenly Spheres*
1576	Tycho Brahe sets up Uraniborg observatory
1609	Johannes Kepler (1571–1643) publishes *Astronomia Nova*
1610	Galileo Galilei (1564–1642) publishes *Starry Messenger*
1620	Francis Bacon (1561–1626) publishes *Novum Organum*
1632	Galileo publishes *Dialogue Concerning the Two Chief World Systems*
1633	Galileo's trial
1637	René Descartes (1596–1650) publishes *Discourse on Method*
1660	Royal Society of London founded
1666	French Academy of Sciences founded
1687	Isaac Newton (1642–1727) publishes *Principia Mathematica*

The New Science of the Seventeenth Century

Doubt thou the stars are fire,
Doubt that the sun doth move,
Doubt truth to be a liar,
But never doubt I love.

<small>SHAKESPEARE, *HAMLET*, II.2</small>

CORE OBJECTIVES

- **DEFINE** *scientific revolution* and explain what is meant by *science* in this historical context.

- **UNDERSTAND** the older philosophical traditions that were important for the development of new methods of scientific investigation in the seventeenth century.

- **IDENTIFY** the sciences that made important advances during this period and understand what technological innovations encouraged a new spirit of investigation.

- **EXPLAIN** the differences between the Ptolemaic view of the universe and the new vision of the universe proposed by Nicolas Copernicus.

- **UNDERSTAND** the different definitions of scientific method that emerged from the work of Francis Bacon and René Descartes.

oubt thou the stars are fire" and "that the sun doth move." Was Shakespeare alluding to controversial ideas about the cosmos that contradicted the teachings of medieval scholars? *Hamlet* (c. 1600) was written more than fifty years after Copernicus had suggested, in his treatise *On the Revolutions of the Heavenly Spheres* (1543), that the sun did not move and that the earth did, revolving around the sun. Shakespeare probably knew of such theories, although they circulated only among small groups of learned Europeans. As Hamlet's love-torn speech to Ophelia makes clear, they were considered conjecture—or strange mathematical hypotheses. These theories were not exactly new—a heliocentric universe had been proposed as early as the second century B.C.E. by ancient Greak astronomers. But

383

they flatly contradicted the consensus that had set in after Ptolemy proposed an earth-centered universe in the second century c.e., and to Shakespeare's contemporaries, they defied common sense and observation. Learned philosophers, young lovers, shepherds, and sailors alike could watch the sun and the stars move from one horizon to the other each day and night, or so they thought.

Still, a small handful of thinkers did doubt. Shakespeare was born in 1564, the same year as Galileo. By this time the long process of revising knowledge about the universe was under way. A hundred years later, the building blocks of the new view had been put in place. This intellectual transformation brought sweeping changes to European philosophy and to Western views of the natural world and of humans' place in it.

Science entails at least three things: a body of knowledge, a method or system of inquiry, and a community of practitioners and the institutions that support them and their work. The *scientific revolution* of the seventeenth century (usually understood to have begun in the mid-sixteenth century and culminated in 1687 with Newton's *Principia*) involved each of these three realms. The scientific revolution saw the emergence and confirmation of a heliocentric (sun-centered) view of the planetary system, which displaced the earth—and humans—from the center of the universe. Even more fundamental, it brought a new mathematical physics that described and confirmed such a view. Second, the scientific revolution established a method of inquiry for understanding the natural world: a method that emphasized the role of observation, experiment, and the testing of hypotheses. Third, *science* emerged as a distinctive branch of knowledge. During the period covered in this chapter, people referred to the study of matter, motion, optics, or the circulation of blood as natural philosophy (the more theoretical term), experimental philosophy, medicine, and—increasingly—science. The growth of societies and institutions dedicated to what we now commonly call scientific research was central to the changes at issue here. Science required not only brilliant thinkers but patrons, states, and communities of researchers; the scientific revolution was thus embedded in other social, religious, and cultural transformations.

The scientific revolution was not an organized effort. Brilliant theories sometimes led to dead ends, discoveries were often accidental, and artisans grinding lenses for telescopes played a role in the advance of knowledge just as surely as did great abstract thinkers. Educated women also claimed the right to participate in scientific debate, but their efforts were met with opposition or indifference. Old and new worldviews often overlapped as individual thinkers struggled to reconcile their discoveries with their faith

or to make their theories (about the earth's movements, for instance) fit with received wisdom. Science was slow to work its way into popular understanding. It did not necessarily undermine religion, and it certainly did not intend to; figures like Isaac Newton thought their work confirmed and deepened their religious beliefs. In short, change came slowly and fitfully. But as the new scientific method began to produce radical new insights into the workings of nature, it eventually came to be accepted well beyond the small circles of experimenters, theologians, and philosophers with whom it began.

THE INTELLECTUAL ORIGINS OF THE SCIENTIFIC REVOLUTION

The scientific revolution marks a decisive break between the Middle Ages and the modern world, but it was rooted in earlier developments. Medieval artists and intellectuals had been observing and illustrating the natural world with great precision since at least the twelfth century. The link between observation, experiment, and invention was not new to the sixteenth century. The magnetic compass had been known in Europe since the thirteenth century; gunpowder since the early fourteenth; printing, which permeated the intellectual life of the period, since the middle of the fifteenth. "Printing, firearms, and the compass," wrote Francis Bacon, "no empire, sect, or star appears to have exercised a greater power and influence on human affairs than these three mechanical discoveries." A fascination with light, which was a powerful symbol of divine illumination for medieval thinkers, encouraged the study of optics and, in turn, new techniques for grinding lenses. Lens grinders laid the groundwork for the seventeenth-century inventions of the telescope and microscope, creating reading glasses along the way. Astrologers were also active in the later Middle Ages, charting the heavens in the firm belief that the stars controlled the fates of human beings.

Behind these efforts to understand the natural world lay a nearly universal conviction that the natural world had been created by God. Religious belief spurred scientific study. One school of thinkers (the Neoplatonists) argued that nature was a book written by its creator to reveal the ways of God to humanity. Convinced that God's perfection must be reflected in nature, Neoplatonists searched for the ideal and perfect structures they believed must lie behind the "shadows" of the everyday world. Mathematics, particularly geometry, were important tools in this quest.

Renaissance humanism also helped prepare the grounds for the scientific revolution. Humanists revered the authority of the ancients. Yet the energies the humanists poured into recovering, translating, and understanding classical texts (the source of conceptions of the natural world) made many of those important works available for the first time, and to a wider audience. Previously, Arabic sources had provided Europeans with the main route to ancient Greek learning; Greek classics were translated into Arabic and then picked up by late medieval scholars in Spain and Sicily. The humanists' return to the texts themselves encouraged new study and debate. The humanist rediscovery of works by Archimedes—the great Greek mathematician who had proposed that the natural world operated on the basis of mechanical forces, like a great machine, and that these forces could be described mathematically—profoundly impressed important late-sixteenth- and seventeenth-century thinkers, including the Italian scientist Galileo.

The Renaissance also encouraged collaboration between artisans and intellectuals. Twelfth- and thirteenth-century thinkers had observed the natural world, but they rarely tinkered with machines and they had little contact with the artisans who developed expertise in constructing machines for practical use. During the fifteenth century, however, these two worlds began to come together. Renaissance artists such as Leonardo da Vinci were accomplished craftsmen; they investigated the laws of perspective and optics, they worked out geometric methods for supporting the weight of enormous architectural domes, they studied the human body, and they devised new and more effective weapons for war. The Renaissance brought a vogue for alchemy and astrology; wealthy amateurs built observatories and measured the courses of the stars. These social and intellectual developments laid the groundwork for the scientific revolution.

What of the voyages of discovery? Sixteenth-century observers often linked the exploration of the globe to new knowledge of the cosmos. An admirer wrote to Galileo that he had kept the spirit of exploration alive: "The memory of Columbus and Vespucci will be renewed through you, and with even greater nobility, as the sky is more worthy than the earth." The parallel does not work quite so neatly. Columbus had not been driven by an interest in science. The discoveries made the most immediate impact in the field of natural history, which was vastly enriched by travelers' detailed accounts of the flora and fauna of the Americas. Finding new lands and cultures in Africa and Asia and the revelation of the Americas, a world unknown to the ancients and unmentioned in the Bible, also laid bare gaps in Europeans'

inherited body of knowledge. In this sense, the exploration of the New World dealt a blow to the authority of the ancients.

In sum, the late medieval recovery of ancient texts long thought to have been lost, the expansion of print culture and reading, the turmoil in the church and the fierce wars and political maneuvering that followed the Reformation, and the discovery of a new world across the oceans to explore and exploit all shook the authority of older ways of thinking. What we call the scientific revolution was part of the intellectual excitement that surrounded

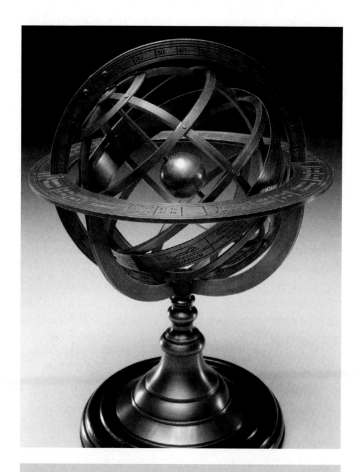

PTOLEMAIC ASTRONOMICAL INSTRUMENTS. This armillary sphere was built in the 1560s to facilitate the observation of planetary positions relative to the earth, in support of Ptolemy's theory of an earth-centered universe. In the sphere, seven concentric rings rotated about different axes. When the outermost ring was set to align with a north–south meridian, and the next was set to align with the celestial pole (the North Star, or the point around which the stars seem to rotate), one could determine the latitude of the place where the instrument was placed. The inner rings were used to track the angular movements of the planets, key measurements in validating the Ptolemaic system. ▪ *What forms of knowledge were necessary to construct such an instrument?* ▪ *How do they relate to the breakthrough that is known as the scientific revolution?*

these challenges, and, in retrospect, the scientific revolution enhanced and confirmed the importance of these other developments.

THE COPERNICAN REVOLUTION

Medieval cosmologists, like their ancient counterparts and their successors during the scientific revolution, wrestled with the contradictions between ancient texts and the evidence of their own observations. Their view of an earth-centered universe was particularly influenced by the teachings of Aristotle (384–322 B.C.E.), especially as they were systematized by Ptolemy of Alexandria (100–178 C.E.). In fact, Ptolemy's vision of an earth-centered universe contradicted an earlier proposal by Aristarchus of Samos (310–230 B.C.E.), who had deduced that the earth and other planets revolve around the sun (see Chapter 4). According to Ptolemy, the heavens orbited the earth in a carefully organized hierarchy of spheres. Earth and the heavens were fundamentally different, made of different matter and subject to different laws of motion. The heavens—first the planets, then the stars—traced perfect circular paths around the stationary earth. The motion of these celestial bodies was produced by a prime mover, whom Christians identified as God. The view fit Aristotelian physics, according to which objects could move only if acted on by an external force, and it fit with a belief that each fundamental element of the universe had a natural place. Moreover, the view both followed from and confirmed belief in the purposefulness of God's universe.

By the late Middle Ages astronomers knew that this cosmology, called the "Ptolemaic system," did not correspond exactly to what many had observed. Orbits did not conform to the Aristotelian ideal of perfect circles. By the early fifteenth century, the efforts to make the observed motions of the planets fit into the model of perfect circles in a geocentric (earth-centered) cosmos had produced astronomical charts that were mazes of complexity. Finally, the Ptolemaic system proved unable to solve serious difficulties with the calendar. That practical crisis precipitated Nicolaus Copernicus's intellectual leap forward.

Realizing that the old Roman calendar was significantly out of alignment with the movement of the heavenly bodies, Catholic authorities consulted mathematicians and astronomers all over Europe. One of these was a Polish church official and astronomer, Nicolaus Copernicus (1473–1543). Educated in Poland and northern Italy, he was a man of diverse talents. He was trained in astronomy, canon law,

and medicine. He read Greek. He was well versed in ancient philosophy. He was also a careful mathematician and a devout Catholic, who did not believe that God's universe could be as messy as the one in Ptolemy's model. His proposed solution, based on mathematical calculations, was simple and radical: Ptolemy was mistaken; the earth was neither stationary nor at the center of the planetary system; the earth rotated on its axis and orbited with the other planets around the sun. Reordering the Ptolemaic system simplified the geometry of astronomy and made the orbits of the planets comprehensible.

Copernicus was in many ways a conservative thinker. He did not consider his work to be a break with either the church or with the authority of ancient texts. He believed, rather, that he had restored a pure understanding of God's design, one that had been lost over the centuries. Still, the

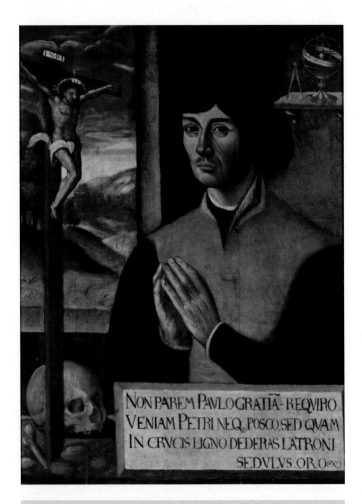

NICOLAUS COPERNICUS. This anonymous portrait of Copernicus characteristically blends his devotion and his scientific achievements. His scholarly work (behind him in the form of an early planetarium) is driven by his faith (as he turns toward the image of Christ triumphant over death). ■ *What relationship between science and religion is evoked by this image?*

tions that developed standards of research. England's Royal Society spawned imitators in Florence and Berlin and later in Russia. The French Royal Academy of Sciences had a particularly direct relationship with the monarchy and the French state. France's statesmen exerted control over the academy and sought to share in the rewards of any discoveries its members made.

New, too, were beliefs about the purpose and methods of science. The practice of breaking a complex problem down into parts made it possible to tackle more and different questions in the physical sciences. Mathematics assumed a more central role in the new science. Finally, rather than simply confirming established truths, the new methods were designed to explore the unknown and provide means to discover new truths. As Kepler wrote to Galileo, "How great a difference there is between theoretical speculation and visual experience, between Ptolemy's discussion of the Antipodes and Columbus's discovery of the New World." Knowledge itself was reconceived. In the older model, to learn was to read: to reason logically, to argue, to compare classical texts, and to absorb a finite body of knowledge. In the newer one, to learn was to discover, and what could be discovered was boundless.

CONCLUSION

The pioneering natural philosophers remained circumspect about their abilities. Some sought to lay bare the workings of the universe; others believed humans could only catalog and describe the regularities observed in nature. By unspoken but seemingly mutual agreement, the question of first causes was left aside. The new science did not say *why*, but *how*. Newton, for one, worked toward explanations that would reveal the logic of creation laid out in mathematics. Yet in the end, he settled for theories explaining motions and relationships that could be observed and tested.

The eighteenth-century heirs to Newton were much more daring. Laboratory science and the work of the scientific societies largely stayed true to the experimenters' rules and limitations. But as we will see in the next chapter, the natural philosophers who began investigating the human sciences cast aside some of their predecessors' caution. Society, technology, government, religion, even the individual human mind seemed to be mechanisms or parts of a larger nature waiting for study. The scientific revolution overturned the natural world as it had been understood for a millennium; it also inspired thinkers more interested in revolutions in society.

PEOPLE, IDEAS, AND EVENTS IN CONTEXT

- How did the traditions of **NEOPLATONISM** and **RENAISSANCE HUMANISM** contribute to a vision of the physical world that encouraged scientific investigation and explanation?
- In what way did the work of **NICOLAS COPERNICUS, TYCHO BRAHE, JOHANNES KEPLER,** and **GALILEO GALILEI** serve to undermine the intellectual foundations of the **PTOLEMAIC SYSTEM?** Why did their work largely take place outside of the traditional centers of learning in Europe, such as universities?
- What differences in scientific practice arose from **FRANCIS BACON'S** emphasis on observation and **RENÉ DESCARTES'** insistence that knowledge could only be derived from unquestionable first principles?
- What were **ISAAC NEWTON'S** major contributions to the scientific revolution? Why have some suggested that Newton's interests and thinking were not all compatible with modern conceptions of scientific understanding?
- What was important about the establishment of institutions such as the British **ROYAL SOCIETY** or the French **ACADEMY OF SCIENCES** for the development of scientific methods and research?
- What prevented women from entering most of Europe's scientific academies? How did educated women such as **LAURA BASSI, MARGARET CAVENDISH, MARIA WINKELMANN,** and **MARIA SYBILLA MERIAN** gain the skills necessary to participate in scientific work?

CONSEQUENCES

- What long-term social and cultural developments since the medieval period may have encouraged the intellectual openness that was necessary for the ideas of the scientific revolution to take root and flourish?
- How revolutionary was the "scientific revolution" really? Can one really point to this as a period of intellectual or cultural rupture?

in Europe. Well connected and a prolific writer, Voltaire took up his pen to clear Calas's name. Calas's case exemplified nearly everything Voltaire opposed in his culture. Intolerance, ignorance, and what Voltaire throughout his life called religious "fanaticism" and "infamy" had made a travesty of justice. Torture demonstrated the power of the courts but could not uncover the truth. Legal procedures that included secret interrogations, trials behind closed doors, summary judgment, and barbaric punishments defied reason, morality, and human dignity. Any criminal, however wretched, "is a man," wrote Voltaire, "and you are accountable for his blood."

Voltaire's comments on the Calas case illustrate the classic concerns of the Enlightenment: the dangers of arbitrary and unchecked authority, the value of religious toleration, and the overriding importance of law, reason, and human dignity in all affairs. He borrowed most of his arguments from others—from his predecessor the Baron de Montesquieu and from the Italian writer Cesare Beccaria, whose *On Crimes and Punishments* appeared in 1764. Voltaire's reputation did not rest on his originality as a philosopher. It came from his effectiveness as a writer and advocate, his desire and ability to reach a wide audience. In this, too, he was representative of the Enlightenment project.

THE FOUNDATIONS OF THE ENLIGHTENMENT

The Enlightenment lasted for most of the eighteenth century. Not every important thinker who lived and worked during these years rallied to the Enlightenment banner. Some opposed almost everything the Enlightenment stood for. Others accepted certain Enlightenment values but sharply rejected others. Patterns of Enlightenment thought varied from country to country, and they changed everywhere over the course of the century. Many eighteenth-century thinkers nonetheless shared the sense of living in an exciting new intellectual environment in which the "party of humanity" would prevail over superstition and traditional thought.

Enlightenment writings shared several basic characteristics. They were marked, first, by a confidence in the powers of human reason. This self-assurance stemmed from the accomplishments of the scientific revolution, which provided a model for scientific inquiry into other phenomena. Nature operated according to laws that could be grasped by study, observation, and thought. The work of the extraordinary Scottish writer David Hume provided the most direct bridge from science to the Enlightenment. Just as Isaac Newton had argued for the precise description of natural phenomena (see Chapter 16), Hume called for the same rigor and skepticism in the study of morality, the mind, and government. Hume criticized the "passion for hypotheses and systems" that dominated much philosophical thinking. Experience and careful observation, he argued, usually did not support the premises on which those systems rested.

Embracing human understanding and the exercise of human reason also required confronting the power of Europe's traditional monarchies and the religious institutions that supported them. "Dare to know!" the German philosopher Immanuel Kant challenged his contemporaries in his classic 1784 essay "What Is Enlightenment?" For Kant, the Enlightenment represented a declaration of intellectual independence. Kant likened the intellectual history of humanity to the growth of a child. Enlightenment, in this view, was an escape from humanity's "self-imposed immaturity" and a long overdue break with humanity's self-imposed parental figure, the Catholic Church. Coming of age meant the "determination and courage to think without the guidance of someone else," as an individual. Reason required autonomy, or freedom from tradition and well-established authorities.

Despite their declarations of independence from the past, Enlightenment thinkers recognized a great debt to their immediate predecessors. Voltaire called Bacon, Newton, and John Locke his "Holy Trinity." Indeed, much of the eighteenth-century Enlightenment consisted of translating, republishing, and thinking through the implications of the great works of the seventeenth century. Enlightenment thinkers drew heavily on Locke's studies of human knowledge, especially his *Essay Concerning Human Understanding* (1690). All knowledge, Locke argued, originates from sense perception. The human mind at birth is a "blank tablet" (in Latin, *tabula rasa*). Only when an infant begins to experience things, to perceive the external world with its senses, does anything register in its mind. Locke's starting point, which became a central premise for those who followed, was the goodness and perfectibility of humanity. Building on Locke, eighteenth-century thinkers made education central to their project, because education promised that social progress could be achieved through individual moral improvement. It is worth noting that Locke's theories had potentially more radical implications: if all humans were capable of reason, education might be able to level hierarchies of status, sex, or race. As we will see, only a few Enlightenment thinkers made such egalitarian arguments. Still, optimism and a belief in universal human progress constituted a second defining feature of nearly all Enlightenment thinking.

Third, Enlightenment thinkers sought nothing less than the organization of all knowledge. The *scientific method*, by

The Enlightenment

CORE OBJECTIVES

- **DEFINE** the term *Enlightenment* as eighteenth-century thinkers used it, and identify the figures most closely associated with this intellectual movement.

- **EXPLAIN** how the ideas associated with the Enlightenment spread internationally and the consequences of this expanded world of public discussion.

- **DESCRIBE** the ways that the Enlightenment was linked to imperial expansion and the growth of commerce, as larger numbers of Europeans became more aware of the globe's diverse cultures and peoples.

- **UNDERSTAND** how Enlightenment thought undermined central tenets of eighteenth-century culture and politics.

- **DESCRIBE** the broader changes in European society, such as increased literacy and the spread of printed material, that made the Enlightenment possible.

I n 1762, the *Parlement* (law court) of Toulouse, in France, convicted Jean Calas of murdering his son. Calas was a Protestant in a region where Catholic–Protestant tensions ran high. Witnesses claimed that the young Calas had wanted to break with his family and convert to Catholicism, and they convinced the magistrates that Calas had killed his son to prevent this conversion. French law stipulated the punishment. Calas was tortured twice: first to force a confession and, next, as a formal part of certain death sentences, to identify his alleged accomplices. His arms and legs were slowly pulled apart, gallons of water were poured down his throat, and his body was publicly broken on the wheel, which meant that each of his limbs was smashed with an iron bar. Then the executioner cut off his head. Throughout the trial, torture, and execution, Calas maintained his innocence. Two years later, the *Parlement* reversed its verdict, declared Calas not guilty, and offered the family a payment in compensation.

François Marie Arouet, also known as Voltaire, was one of those appalled by the verdict and punishment. At the time of the case, Voltaire was the most famous Enlightenment thinker

403

which they meant the empirical observation of particular phenomena to arrive at general laws, offered a way to pursue research in all areas—to study human affairs as well as natural ones. Thus they collected evidence to learn the laws governing the rise and fall of nations, and they compared governmental constitutions to arrive at an ideal and universally applicable political system. They took up a strikingly wide array of subjects in this systematic manner: knowledge and the mind, natural history, economics, government, religious beliefs, customs of indigenous peoples in the New World, human nature, and sexual (or what we would call gender) and racial differences.

Historians have called the Enlightenment a "cultural project," emphasizing Enlightenment thinkers' interest in practical, applied knowledge and their determination to spread knowledge and to promote free public discussion. Although they shared many of their predecessors' theoretical concerns, they wrote in a very different style and for a much larger audience. Hobbes and Locke had published treatises for small groups of learned seventeenth-century readers. Voltaire, in contrast, wrote plays, essays, and letters; Rousseau composed music, published his *Confessions*, and wrote novels that moved his readers to tears. A British aristocrat or a governor in the North American colonies would have read Locke. But a middle-class woman might have read Rousseau's fiction, and shopkeepers and artisans could become familiar with popular Enlightenment-inspired pamphlets. Among the elite, newly formed "academies" sponsored prize essay contests, and well-to-do women and men discussed affairs of state in salons. In other words, the intellectual achievements of the Enlightenment were absorbed by a much broader portion of European society in the course of the eighteenth century. This was possible because of cultural developments that included the expansion of literacy, growing markets for printed material, new networks of readers, and new forms of intellectual exchange. Taken together, these developments marked the emergence of what some historians call the first "public sphere."

THE WORLD OF
THE *PHILOSOPHES*

Enlightenment thought was European in a broad sense, including southern and eastern Europe as well as Europe's colonies in the New World. British thinkers played a—perhaps *the*—key role. France, however, provided the stage for some of the most widely read Enlightenment books and the most closely watched battles. For this reason, Enlightenment thinkers, regardless of where they lived, are often called by the French word *philosophes*. *Philosophe*, in French, simply meant "a free thinker," a person whose reflections were unhampered by the constraints of religion or dogma in any form.

Voltaire

At the time, the best known of the *philosophes* was Voltaire, born François Marie Arouet (1694–1778). Voltaire virtually personified the Enlightenment, commenting on an enormous range of subjects in a wide variety of literary forms. Educated by the Jesuits, he emerged quite young as a gifted and sharp-tongued writer. His gusto for provocation landed him in prison for libel and soon afterward in temporary exile in England. In his three years there, Voltaire became an admirer of British political institutions, British culture, and British science; above all, he became an extremely persuasive convert to the ideas of Newton, Bacon, and Locke. His single greatest accomplishment may have been popularizing Newton's work in France and more generally championing the cause of British empiricism and the scientific method against the more Cartesian French.

Voltaire's themes were religious and political liberty, and his weapons were comparisons. His admiration for British culture and politics became a stinging critique of France—and other absolutist countries on the Continent. He praised British open-mindedness and empiricism: the country's respect for scientists and its support for research. He considered the relative weakness of the British aristocracy a sign of Britain's political health. Unlike the French, the British respected commerce and people who engage in it, Voltaire wrote. The British tax system was rational, free of the complicated exemptions for the privileged that were ruining French finances. The British House of Commons represented the middle classes and, in contrast with French absolutism, brought balance to British government and checked arbitrary power. Of all Britain's reputed virtues, religious toleration loomed largest of all. Britain, Voltaire argued, brought together citizens of different religions in a harmonious and productive culture. In this and other instances, Voltaire oversimplified: British Catholics, Dissenters, and Jews did not have equal civil rights. Yet the British policy of "toleration" did contrast with Louis XIV's intolerance of Protestants. Revoking the Edict of Nantes (1685) had stripped French Protestants of civil rights and had helped create the atmosphere in which Jean Calas—and others—were persecuted.

Of all forms of intolerance Voltaire opposed religious bigotry most, and with real passion he denounced religious fraud, faith in miracles, and superstition. His most famous battle cry was *"Écrasez l'infâme!"* (Crush this infamous thing), by which he meant all forms of repression, fanaticism, and bigotry. "The less superstition, the less fanaticism; and the less fanaticism, the less misery." He did not oppose religion per se; rather he sought to rescue morality, which he believed came from God, from dogma—elaborate ritual, dietary laws, formulaic prayers—and from a powerful church bureaucracy. He argued for common sense and simplicity, persuaded that these would bring out the goodness in humanity and establish stable authority.

Voltaire relished his position as a critic, and it never stopped him from being successful. He was regularly exiled from France and other countries, his books banned and burned. As long as his plays attracted large audiences, however, the French king felt he had to tolerate their author. Voltaire had an attentive international public, including Frederick of Prussia, who invited him to his court at Berlin, and Catherine of Russia, with whom he corresponded about reforms she might introduce in Russia. When he died in 1778, a few months after a triumphant return to Paris, he was possibly the best-known writer in Europe.

Montesquieu

The Baron de Montesquieu (*mahn-tuhs-KYOO*, 1689–1755) was a very different kind of Enlightenment figure. Montesquieu was born to a noble family. He was not a stylist or a provocateur like Voltaire but a relatively cautious jurist, though he did write a satirical novel, *The Persian Letters* (1721), published anonymously (to protect his reputation). The novel was composed as letters from two Persian visitors to France. The visitors detailed the odd religious superstitions they witnessed, compared manners at the French court with those in Turkish harems, and likened French absolutism to their own brands of *despotism*, or the abuse of government authority. *The Persian Letters* was an immediate best seller that inspired many imitators as other authors used the formula of a foreign observer to criticize contemporary French society.

Montesquieu's serious treatise *The Spirit of Laws* (1748) may have been the most influential work of the Enlightenment. It was a groundbreaking study and very Newtonian in its careful, empirical approach. Montesquieu suggested that there were three forms of government: republics, monarchies, and despotisms. A republic was governed by many—either an elite aristocracy or the people as a whole. The soul of a republic was virtue, which allowed individual citizens to transcend their particular interests and rule in accordance with the common good. In a monar-

chy, on the other hand, one person ruled in accordance with the law. The soul of a monarchy, wrote Montesquieu, was honor, which gave individuals an incentive to behave with loyalty toward their sovereign. The third form of government, despotism, was rule by a single person unchecked by law or other powers. The soul of despotism was fear, since no citizen could feel secure and punishment took the place of education. Montesquieu devoted two chapters to the French monarchy, in which he spelled out what he saw as a dangerous drift toward despotism in his own land. Like other Enlightenment thinkers, Montesquieu admired the British system and its separate and balanced powers—executive, legislative, and judicial—which guaranteed liberty in the sense of freedom from the absolute power of any single governing individual or group. His idealization of "checks and balances" had formative influence on Enlightenment political theorists and members of the governing elites, particularly those who wrote the United States Constitution in 1787.

Diderot and the Encyclopedia

Voltaire's and Montesquieu's writings represent the themes and style of the French Enlightenment. But the most remarkable French publication of the century was a collective one: the *Encyclopedia*. The *Encyclopedia* claimed to summarize all the most advanced contemporary philosophical, scientific, and technical knowledge, making it available to any reader. In terms of sheer scope, this was the grandest statement of the *philosophes'* goals. It demonstrated how scientific analysis could be applied in nearly all realms of thought. The guiding spirit behind the venture was Denis Diderot. Diderot was helped by other leading men of letters, including mathematician Jean Le Rond d'Alembert, Voltaire, and Montesquieu. The *Encyclopedia* was published between 1751 and 1772; by the time it was completed, it ran to twenty-eight volumes and contained over seventy-one thousand articles. A collaborative project, it helped create the *philosophes'* image as the "party of humanity."

Diderot commissioned articles on machines and technology to demonstrate how the everyday applications of science could promote progress and alleviate all forms of human misery. Diderot turned the same methods to matters of politics and the foundations of the social order, including articles on economics, taxes, and the slave trade. Censorship made it difficult to write openly antireligious articles. Diderot, therefore, thumbed his nose at religion in oblique ways; at the entry on the Eucharist, the reader found a terse cross-reference: "See *cannibalism*." Gibes like this aroused storms of controversy when the early volumes of the *Encyclopedia* appeared. The French government revoked the publishing permit for the *Encyclopedia*, declaring in 1759 that the encyclopedists were trying to "propagate materialism" (by which they meant atheism) "to destroy Religion, to inspire a spirit of independence, and to nourish the corruption of morals." The volumes sold remarkably well despite such bans and their hefty price. Purchasers belonged to the elite: aristocrats, government officials, prosperous merchants, and a scattering of members of the higher clergy. That elite, though, stretched across Europe, including its overseas colonies.

Although the French *philosophes* sparred with the state and the church, they sought political stability and reform. Montesquieu, not surprising in light of his birth and position, hoped that an enlightened aristocracy would press for reforms and defend liberty against a despotic king. Voltaire, persuaded that aristocrats would represent only their particular narrow interests, looked to an enlightened monarch for leadership. Neither was a democrat, and neither conceived of reform being spurred from below. Still, their widely read writings were subversive. Their satires of absolutism and, more broadly, arbitrary power, stung. By the 1760s the French critique of despotism provided the language in which many people across Europe articulated their opposition to existing regimes.

INSTRUMENTS OF TORTURE. A man being stretched on the rack (left) and a thumbscrew (right), both from an official Austrian government handbook. By 1800, Beccaria's influence had helped phase out the use of such instruments.

INTERNATIONALIZATION OF ENLIGHTENMENT THEMES: HUMANITARIANISM AND TOLERATION

The party of humanity was international. French became the lingua franca of much Enlightenment discussion, but "French" books were often published in Switzerland, Germany, and Russia. As we have seen, Enlightenment thinkers admired British institutions and British scholarship, and Great Britain also produced important Enlight-

enment thinkers: the historian Edward Gibbon and the Scottish philosophers David Hume and Adam Smith. The *philosophes* considered Thomas Jefferson and Benjamin Franklin part of their group. Despite stiffer resistance from religious authorities, stricter state censors, and smaller networks of educated elites, the Enlightenment flourished across central and southern Europe. Frederick II of Prussia housed Voltaire during one of his exiles from France, though the *philosophe* quickly wore out his welcome. Frederick also patronized a small but unusually productive group of Enlightenment thinkers. Northern Italy was an important center of Enlightenment thought. Enlightenment thinkers across Europe raised similar themes: humanitarianism, or the dignity and worth of all individuals; religious toleration; and liberty.

Among the most influential writers of the entire Enlightenment was the Italian (Milanese) jurist Cesare Beccaria (1738–1794). Beccaria's *On Crimes and Punishments* (1764) sounded the same general themes as did the French *philosophes*—a critique of arbitrary power and respect for reason and human dignity—and it provided Voltaire with most of his arguments in the Calas case. Beccaria also proposed concrete legal reforms. He attacked the prevalent view that punishments should represent society's vengeance on the criminal. The only legitimate rationale for punishment was to maintain social order and to prevent other crimes.

Beccaria argued for the greatest possible leniency compatible with deterrence; respect for individual dignity dictated that humans should punish other humans no more than is absolutely necessary. Above all, Beccaria's book eloquently opposed torture and the death penalty. The spectacle of public execution, which sought to dramatize the power of the state and the horrors of hell, dehumanized the victim, judge, and spectators. *On Crimes and Punishments* was translated into a dozen languages. Owing primarily to its influence, most European countries by around 1800 abolished torture, branding, whipping, and mutilation, and they reserved the death penalty for only the gravest crimes.

Humanitarianism and reason also counseled religious toleration. Enlightenment thinkers spoke almost

LESSING AND MENDELSSOHN. This painting of a meeting between the *philosophe* Gotthold Lessing (standing) and his friend Moses Mendelssohn (seated right) emphasizes the personal nature of their intellectual relationship, which transcended their different religious backgrounds (Christian and Jewish, respectively). The Enlightenment's atmosphere of earnest discussion is invoked both by the open book before them and the shelf of reading material behind Lessing. Compare this image of masculine discussion (note the role of the one woman in the painting) with the image of the aristocratic salon on page 417 and the coffeehouse on page 420. ▪ *What similarities and differences might one point to in these various illustrations of the Enlightenment public sphere?*

as one on the need to end religious warfare and the persecution of heretics and religious minorities. It is important, though, to differentiate between the church as an institution and dogma, against which many Enlightenment thinkers rebelled, and as religious belief, which most accepted. Only a few Enlightenment thinkers, notably Paul Henri d'Holbach (1723–1789), were atheists, and only a slightly greater number were avowed agnostics. Many (Voltaire, for instance) were deists, holding a religious outlook that saw God as a "divine clockmaker" who, at the beginning of time, constructed a perfect timepiece and then left it to run with predictable regularity. Enlightenment inquiry proved compatible with very different stances on religion.

Enlightenment support for toleration was limited. Most Christians saw Jews as heretics and Christ killers. And although Enlightenment thinkers deplored persecution, they commonly viewed Judaism and Islam as backward religions, mired in superstition and obscurantist ritual. One of the few Enlightenment figures to treat Jews sympathetically was the German *philosophe* Gotthold Lessing (1729–1781). Lessing's extraordinary play *Nathan the Wise* (1779) takes place in Jerusalem during the Fourth Crusade and begins with a pogrom—or violent, orchestrated attack—in which the wife and children of Nathan, a Jewish merchant, are murdered. Nathan survives to become a sympathetic and wise father figure. He adopts a Christian-born daughter and raises her with three religions: Christianity, Islam, and Judaism. At several points, authorities ask him to choose the single true religion. Nathan shows none exists. The three great monotheistic religions are three versions of the truth. Religion is authentic, or true, only insofar as it makes the believer virtuous.

Lessing modeled his hero on his friend Moses Mendelssohn (1729–1786), a self-educated rabbi and bookkeeper (and the grandfather of the composer Felix Mendelssohn). Moses Mendelssohn moved—though with some difficulty—between the Enlightenment circles of Frederick II and the Jewish community of Berlin. Mendelssohn unsuccessfully tried to avoid religion as a subject. Repeatedly attacked and invited to convert to Christianity, he finally took up the question of Jewish identity. In a series of writings, the best-known of which is *On the Religious Authority of Judaism* (1783), he defended Jewish communities against anti-Semitic policies and Jewish religion against Enlightenment criticism. At the same time, he also promoted reform within the Jewish community, arguing that his community had special reason to embrace the broad Enlightenment project: religious faith should be voluntary, states should promote tolerance, humanitarianism would bring progress to all.

Economics, Government, and Administration

Enlightenment ideas had a very real influence over affairs of state. The *philosophes* defended reason and knowledge for humanitarian reasons. But they also promised to make nations stronger, more efficient, and more prosperous. In other words, the Enlightenment spoke to individuals but also to states. The *philosophes* addressed issues of liberty and rights but also took up matters of administration, tax collection, and economic policy.

The rising fiscal demands of eighteenth-century states and empires made these issues newly urgent. Which economic resources were most valuable to states? Enlightenment economic thinkers argued that long-standing mercantilist policies were misguided. By the eighteenth century, *mercantilism* had become a term for a very wide range of policies based on government regulation of trade (see Chapter 15). Many Enlightenment thinkers advocated simplifying the tax system and following a policy of laissez-faire, which comes from the French expression *laissez faire la nature* ("let nature take its course"), letting wealth and goods circulate without government interference.

The now-classic expression of laissez-faire economics came from the Scottish economist Adam Smith (1723–1790), and especially from Smith's landmark treatise *An Inquiry into the Nature and Causes of the Wealth of Nations* (1776). For Smith, the central issues were the productivity of labor and how labor was used in different sectors of the economy. Mercantile restrictions—such as high taxes on imported goods, one of the grievances of colonists throughout the American empires—did not encourage the productive deployment of labor and thus did not create real economic health. For Smith, general prosperity could best be obtained by allowing individuals to pursue their own interests without interference from state-chartered monopolies or legal restraints. As Smith wrote in his earlier *Theory of Moral Sentiments* (1759), self-interested individuals could be "led by an invisible hand . . . without knowing it, without intending it, [to] advance the interest of the society."

The Wealth of Nations owed much to Newton and to the Enlightenment's idealization of both nature and human nature. Smith wanted to follow what he called, in classic Enlightenment terms, the "obvious and simple system of natural liberty." Smith thought of himself as the champion of justice against state-sponsored economic privilege and monopolies. He was also a theorist of human feelings as well as of market forces. Smith emerged as the most influential of the new eighteenth-century economic thinkers. In the following century, ironically, his work and his followers became the target of reformers and critics of the new economic world.

EMPIRE AND ENLIGHTENMENT

Smith's *Wealth of Nations* formed part of a debate about the economics of empire: *philosophes* and statesmen alike asked how the colonies could be profitable, and to whom. The colonial world loomed large in Enlightenment thinking in several other ways. Enlightenment thinkers saw the Americas through a highly idealized vision, as an uncorrupted territory where humanity's natural simplicity was expressed in the lives of native peoples. In comparison, Europe and Europeans appeared decadent or corrupt. Second, Europeans' colonial activities—especially, by the eighteenth century, the slave trade—could not help but raise pressing issues about humanitarianism, individual rights, and natural law. The effects of colonialism on Europe were a central Enlightenment theme.

Smith wrote in *The Wealth of Nations* that the "discovery of America, and that of a passage to the East Indies by the Cape of Good Hope are the two greatest and most important events recorded in the history of mankind. What benefits, or what misfortunes to mankind may hereafter result from those great events," he continued, "no human wisdom can foresee." Smith's language was nearly identical to that of a Frenchman, the Abbé Guillaume Thomas François Raynal. Raynal's massive *Philosophical and Political History of European Settlements and Trade in the Two Indies* (1770), a co-authored work like the *Encyclopedia*, was one of the most widely read works of the Enlightenment, going through twenty printings and at least forty pirated editions. Raynal drew his inspiration from the *Encyclopedia* and aimed at nothing less than a total history of colonization: customs and civilizations of indigenous peoples, natural history, exploration, and commerce in the Atlantic world and India.

Raynal also asked whether colonization had made humanity happier, more peaceful, or better. The question was fully in the spirit of the Enlightenment. So was the answer: Raynal believed that industry and trade brought improvement and progress. Like other Enlightenment writers, however, he and his co-authors considered natural simplicity an antidote to the corruptions of their culture. They sought out and idealized what they considered examples of "natural" humanity, many of them in the New World. In the colonies, they argued, Europeans found themselves with virtually unlimited power, which encouraged them to be arrogant, cruel, and despotic. In a later edition, after the outbreak of the American Revolution, the book went even further, drawing parallels between exploitation in the colonial world and inequality at home: "We are mad in the way we act with our colonies, and inhuman and mad in our conduct toward our peasants," asserted one author. Eighteenth-century radicals repeatedly warned that over-extended empires sowed seeds of decadence and corruption at home.

Slavery and the Atlantic World

Discussing Europe's colonies and economies inevitably raised the issue of slavery. The sugar islands of the Caribbean were among the most valued possessions of the colonial world and the sugar trade one of the leading sectors of the Western economy. The Atlantic slave trade reached its peak in the eighteenth century. European slave traders sent at least one million Africans into New World slavery in the late seventeenth century, and at least six million in the eighteenth century. On this topic, however, even thinkers as radical as Raynal and Diderot hesitated, and their hesitations are revealing about the tensions in Enlightenment thought. Enlightenment thinking began with the premise that individuals could reason and govern themselves. Individual moral freedom lay at the heart of what the Enlightenment considered to be a just, stable, and harmonious society. Slavery defied natural law and natural freedom. Nearly all Enlightenment thinkers condemned slavery in the metaphorical sense. That the "mind should break free of its chains" and that "despotism enslaved the king's subjects" were phrases that echoed through much eighteenth-century writing. Writers dealt more gingerly, however, with the actual enslavement and slave labor of Africans.

Some Enlightenment thinkers skirted the issue of slavery. Others reconciled principle and practice in different ways. Smith condemned slavery as uneconomical. Voltaire, quick to expose his contemporaries' hypocrisy, wondered whether Europeans would look away if Europeans—rather than Africans—were enslaved. Voltaire, however, did not question his belief that Africans were inferior peoples. Montesquieu (who came from Bordeaux, one of the central ports for the Atlantic trade) believed that slavery debased master and slave alike. But he also argued that all societies balanced their systems of labor in accordance with their different needs, and slave labor was one such system. Finally, like many Enlightenment thinkers, Montesquieu defended property rights, including those of slaveholders.

The *Encyclopedia*'s article on the slave trade did condemn the slave trade, in the clearest possible terms, as a violation of self-government. Humanitarian antislavery movements, which emerged in the 1760s, advanced similar arguments. From deploring slavery to imagining freedom for slaves, however, proved a very long step, and one that few were willing to take. In the end, the Enlightenment's environmental determinism—the belief that environment shaped character—provided a common way of postponing the entire issue. Slavery corrupted its victims, destroyed their natural virtue, and crushed their natural love of liberty. Enslaved people, by this logic, were not ready for freedom. It was characteristic for Warville de Brissot's Society of the Friends of Blacks to call for abolition of the slave trade and to invite Thomas Jefferson, a slaveholder, to join the organization. Only a very few advocated abolishing slavery, and they insisted that emancipation be gradual. The debate about slavery demonstrated that different currents in Enlightenment thought could lead to very different conclusions.

Exploration and the Pacific World

The Pacific world also figured prominently in Enlightenment thinking. Systematically mapping new sections of the Pacific was among the crucial developments of the age, and one with a tremendous impact on the public imagination. These explorations were also scientific missions, sponsored as part of the Enlightenment project of expanding scientific knowledge. In 1767 the French government sent Louis-Anne de Bougainville (1729–1811) to the South Pacific in search of a new route to China, new lands suitable for colonization, and new spices for the ever-lucrative trade. They sent along scientists and artists to record his findings. His travel accounts—above all his fabulously lush descriptions of the earthly paradise of Nouvelle-Cythère, or Tahiti—captured the attention and imaginations of many at home. The British captain James Cook (1728–1779), who followed Bougainville, made two trips into the South Pacific (1768–71 and 1772–75), with impressive results. He charted the coasts of New Zealand and added the New Hebrides and Hawaii to European maps. He explored the coast of the Antarctic continent, the shores of the Bering Sea, and the Arctic Ocean. The artists and scientists who accompanied Cook and Bougainville vastly expanded the boundaries of European botany, zoology, and geology. Their drawings—such as Sydney Parkinson's extraordinary portraits of the Maori and William Hodge's portraits of Tahitians—appealed to a wide public. So did the accounts of dangers overcome and peoples encountered. A misguided attempt to communicate with South Pacific islanders, perhaps with the intention of conveying them to Europe, ended in the grisly deaths of Cook and four royal marines on Hawaii in late January 1779, which only added to European readers' fascination with his travels. Large numbers of people in Europe avidly read travel accounts of these

The Impact of the New World on Enlightenment Thinkers

The Abbé Guillaume Thomas François Raynal (1713–1796) was a clergyman and intellectual who moved in the inner circles of the Enlightenment. As a senior cleric he had access to the royal court; as a writer and intellectual he worked with the encyclopedists and other authors who criticized France's institutions, including the Catholic Church of which Raynal himself was a part. Here he tries to offer a perspective on the profound effects of the discovery of the Americas, and he ends by asking whether particular historical developments and institutions lead to the betterment of society.

here has never been any event which has had more impact on the human race in general and for Europeans in particular, than that of the discovery of the New World, and the passage to the Indies around the Cape of Good Hope. It was then that a commercial revolution began, a revolution in the balance of power, and in the customs, the industries, and the government of every nation. It was through this event that men in the most distant lands were linked by new relationships and new needs. The produce of equatorial regions were consumed in polar climes. The industrial products of the north were transported to the south; the textiles of the Orient became the luxuries of Westerners; and everywhere men mutually exchanged their opinions, their laws, their customs, their illnesses, and their medicines, their virtues and their vices. Everything changed, and will go on changing. But will the changes of the past and those that are to come be useful to humanity? Will they give man one day more peace, more happiness, or more pleasure? Will his condition be better, or will it be simply one of constant change?

Source: Abbé Guillaume Thomas François Raynal, *Philosophical and Political History of European Settlements and Trade in the Two Indies* (1770), as cited in Dourinda Outram, *The Enlightenment* (Cambridge: 1995), p. 73.

Questions for Analysis

1. Why does Raynal attribute such significance to the voyages of exploration that connected Europe to the Americas and to Africa and Asia? Which peoples were changed by these voyages?

2. Why is Raynal concerned with people's conduct and happiness, rather than, say, the wealth of states?

3. Is Raynal clear about whether the changes he enumerates represent a gain or a loss for humanity?

---

voyages, and they served as inspiration to later scientist-travelers such as Alexander von Humboldt and Charles Darwin.

THE IMPACT OF THE SCIENTIFIC MISSIONS

Enlightenment thinkers drew freely on reports of scientific missions. Since they were already committed to understanding human nature and the origins of society and to studying the effects of the environment on character and culture, stories of new peoples and cultures were immediately fascinating. In 1772 Diderot published his own reflections on the cultural significance of those accounts, the *Supplément au Voyage de Bougainville*. For Diderot, the Tahitians were the original human beings and, unlike the inhabitants of the New World, were virtually free of European influence. They represented humanity in its natural state, Diderot believed, uninhibited about sexuality and free of religious dogma. Their simplicity exposed the hypocrisy and rigidity of overcivilized Europeans. Such views said more about Europe and European utopias than about indigenous cultures in the Pacific. Enlightenment thinkers found it impossible to see other peoples as anything other than primitive versions of Europeans. Even these views, however, marked a change from former times. In earlier periods Europeans had understood the world as divided between Christendom and heathen others. In sum, during the eighteenth century a religious understanding of Western identity was giving way to more secular and historical conceptions.

The Europeans Encounter the Peoples of the Pacific in the Eighteenth Century

When European explorers set out to map the Pacific, they brought with them artists to paint the landscapes and peoples they encountered. Later, other artists produced engravings of the original paintings and these engravings were made available to a wider public. In this way, even people of modest means or only limited literacy could learn something about the different cultures and peoples elsewhere in the world that were now in more regular contact with European commerce.

These artists documented what they saw, but their vision was also shaped by the ideas that they brought with them and by the classical European styles of portraiture and landscape painting that they had been trained to produce. On the one hand, their images sometimes emphasized the exotic or essentially different quality of life in the Pacific. At the same time, the use of conventional poses in the portraiture or in the depiction of human forms suggested hints of a developing understanding of the extent to which Europeans and people elsewhere in the world shared essential

A. *Portrait of Omai* by Joshua Reynolds (c. 1774).

B. "Omiah [*sic*] the Indian from Otaheite, presented to their Majesties at Kew," 1774.

Thus Europeans who looked outward did so for a variety of reasons and reached very different conclusions. For some Enlightenment thinkers and rulers, scientific reports from overseas fitted into a broad inquiry about civilization and human nature. That inquiry at times encouraged self-criticism and at others simply shored up Europeans' sense of their superiority. These themes reemerged during the nineteenth century, when new empires were built and the West's place in the world was reassessed.

THE RADICAL ENLIGHTENMENT

How revolutionary was the Enlightenment? Enlightenment thought did undermine central tenets of eighteenth-century culture and politics. It had wide resonance, well beyond a small group of intellectuals. Yet Enlightenment thinkers did not hold to any single political position. Even the most radical among them disagreed on the implications of their thought. Jean-Jacques Rousseau and Mary Wollstonecraft provide good examples of such radical thinkers.

C. *View of the Inside of a House in the Island of Ulietea, with the Representation of a Dance to the Music of the Country*, engraving after Sydney Parkinson, 1773.

human characteristics. This ambiguity was typical of Enlightenment political and social thought, which sought to uncover universal human truths, while at the same time remaining deeply interested and invested in exploring the differences they observed in peoples from various parts of the globe.

The first two images here depict a Tahitian named Omai, who came to Britain as a crew member on a naval vessel in July 1774. Taken three days later to meet King George III and Queen Charlotte at Kew (image B), he became a celebrity in England and had his portrait drawn by Joshua Reynolds, a famous painter of the period (image A). The third image is an engraving by two Florentine artists after a drawing by Sydney Parkinson, who was with James Cook on his first voyage to the Pacific in 1768 (image C). The two artists had never visited the South Pacific, and their image is noteworthy for the way that the bodies of the islanders were rendered according to the classical styles of European art.

Questions for Analysis

1. Does the Reynolds portrait, in its choice of posture and expression, imply that Europeans and the peoples of the Pacific might share essential traits? What uses might Enlightenment thinkers have made of such a universalist implication?

2. How might a contemporary person in Britain have reacted to the portrait of Omai kneeling before the king?

3. Do you think image C is an accurate representation of life in the South Pacific? What purpose did such imaginary and idyllic scenes serve for their audience in Europe?

The World of Rousseau

Jean-Jacques Rousseau (*roo-SOH*, 1712–1778) was an "outsider" who quarreled with the other *philosophes* and contradicted many of their assumptions. He shared the *philosophes*' search for intellectual and political freedom, attacked inherited privilege, and believed in the good of humanity and the possibility of creating a just society. Yet he introduced other strains into Enlightenment thought, especially morality and what was then called "sensibility," or the cult of feeling. Rousseau's interest in emotions led him to develop a more complicated portrait of human psychology than that of Enlightenment writers, who emphasized reason as the most important attribute of human beings. He was also considerably more radical than his counterparts, one of the first to talk about popular sovereignty and democracy. He was surely the most utopian, which made his work popular at the time and has opened it to different interpretations since. In the late eighteenth century he was the most influential and most often cited of the *philosophes*, the thinker who brought the Enlightenment to a larger audience.

Rousseau's milestone and difficult treatise on politics, *The Social Contract*, began with a now famous paradox: "Man was born free, and everywhere he is in chains." Rousseau argued that in the state of nature, all men had been equal. (On women, men, and nature, see pages 418–419.) Social inequality, he observed, was anchored in private property and it profoundly corrupted "the social contract," or the formation of government. Under conditions of inequality, governments and laws represented only the rich and privileged. Legitimate governments could be formed, Rousseau argued. "The problem is to find a form of association . . . in which each, while uniting himself with all, may still obey himself alone, and remain as free as before." Freedom did not mean the absence of restraint, it meant that equal citizens obeyed laws they had made themselves. Rousseau hardly imagined any social leveling, and by *equality* he meant only that no one would be "rich enough to buy another, nor poor enough to have to sell oneself."

Rousseau believed that legitimate authority arose from the people alone. His argument has three parts. First, sovereignty belonged to the people alone. This meant sovereignty should not be divided among different branches of government (as suggested by Montesquieu), and it emphatically could not be usurped by a king. Second, exercising sovereignty transformed the nation. Rousseau argued that when individual citizens formed a "body politic," that body became more than just the sum of its parts. He offered what was to many an appealing image of a regenerated and more powerful nation in which citizens were bound by mutual obligation rather than coercive laws, and united in equality rather than divided and weakened by privilege. Third, the national community would be united by what Rousseau called the "general will." This term is notoriously difficult. Rousseau proposed it as a way to understand the common interest, which rose above particular individual demands. The general will favored equality; that made it general, and in principle at least equality guaranteed that citizens' common interests would be represented in the whole.

Rousseau's lack of concern for balancing private interests against the general will leads some political theorists to consider him authoritarian, coercive, or moralistic. Others interpret the general will as one expression of his utopianism. In the eighteenth century, *The Social Contract* was the least understood of Rousseau's works. Yet it provided influential radical arguments and, more important, extraordinarily powerful images and phrases, which were widely cited during the French Revolution.

Rousseau was better known for his writing on education and moral virtue. His widely read novel *Emile* (1762) tells the story of a young man who learns virtue and moral autonomy in the school of nature rather than in the academy. Rousseau disagreed with other *philosophes'* emphasis on reason, insisting instead that "the first impulses of nature are always right." Children should not be forced to reason early in life. Books, which "teach us only to talk about things we do not know," should not be central to learning until adolescence. Emile's tutor thus walked him through the woods, studying nature and its simple precepts, cultivating his conscience and, above all, his sense of independence. "Nourished in the most absolute liberty, the greatest evil he can imagine is servitude."

Rousseau argued that women should have very different educations. "All education of women must be relative to men, pleasing them, being useful to them, raising them when they are young and caring for them when they are old, advising them, consoling them, making their lives pleasant and agreeable; these have been the duties of women since time began." Women were to be useful socially as mothers and wives. In *Emile,* Rousseau laid out just such an education for Emile's wife-to-be, Sophie. At times, Rousseau seemed convinced that women "naturally" sought out such a role: "Dependence is a natural state for women; girls feel themselves made to obey." At other moments he insisted that girls needed to be disciplined and weaned from their "natural" vices.

Rousseau's conflicting views on female nature provide a good example of the shifting meaning of *nature*, a concept central to Enlightenment thought. Enlightenment thinkers used nature as a yardstick against which to measure society's shortcomings. "Natural" was better, simpler, uncorrupted. What, though, was nature? It could refer to the physical world. It could refer to allegedly primitive societies. Often, it was a useful invention.

How did Rousseau's ideas fit into Enlightenment views on gender? As we have seen, Enlightenment thinkers considered education key to human progress. Many lamented the poor education of women, especially because, as mothers, governesses, and teachers, many women were charged with raising and teaching children. What kind of education, however, should girls receive? Here, again, Enlightenment thinkers sought to follow the guidance of nature, and they produced scores of essays and books in philosophy, history, literature, and medicine, discussing the nature or character of the sexes. Were men and women different? Were those differences natural, or had they been created by custom and tradition? Diderot wrote essays on the nature of the sexes; scientific travel literature reported on the family structures of indigenous peoples in the Americas, the South Pacific, and China. Histories of civilization by Adam Smith among many others commented on family and gender roles at different stages of history. Montesquieu's *The Spirit of Laws* included an analysis of how the different stages of government affected women. To speculate on the subject, as Rousseau did, was a common Enlightenment exercise.

Some disagreed with his conclusions. Diderot, Voltaire, and the German thinker Theodor Von Hippel, among many others, deplored legal restrictions on women. Rousseau's prescriptions for women's education drew especially sharp criticism. The English writer and historian Catherine Macaulay set out to refute his points. The Marquis de Condorcet argued on the eve of the French Revolution that the Enlightenment promise of progress could not be fulfilled unless women were educated—and Condorcet was virtually alone in asserting that women should be granted political rights.

The World of Wollstonecraft

Rousseau's sharpest critic was the British writer Mary Wollstonecraft (1759–1797). Wollstonecraft published her best known work, *A Vindication of the Rights of Woman*, in 1792, during the French Revolution. Her argument, however, was anchored in the debates of the Enlightenment. Wollstonecraft shared Rousseau's political views and like Rousseau, Wollstonecraft was a republican, opposed to monarchy. She spoke even more forcefully than Rousseau against inequality and the artificial distinctions of rank, birth, or wealth, arguing that equality laid the basis for virtue. Most radically, she argued that (1) women had the same innate capacity for reason and self-government as men, (2) *virtue* should mean the same thing for men and women, and (3) relations between the sexes should be based on equality.

Wollstonecraft did what few of her contemporaries even imagined. She applied the radical Enlightenment critique of monarchy and inequality to the family. The legal inequalities of marriage law, which among other things deprived married women of property rights, gave husbands "despotic" power over their wives. Just as kings cultivated their subjects' deference, so culture, she argued, cultivated women's weakness. "Civilized women are . . . so weakened by false refinement, that, respecting morals, their condition is much below what it would be were they left in a state nearer to nature." Middle-class girls learned manners, grace, and seductiveness to win a husband; they were trained to be dependent creatures. A culture that encouraged feminine weakness produced women who were childish, cunning, cruel—and vulnerable. To Rousseau's specific prescriptions for female education, which included teaching women timidity, chastity, and modesty, Wollstonecraft replied that Rousseau wanted women to use their reason to "burnish their chains rather than to snap them." Instead, education for women had to promote liberty and self-reliance.

MARY WOLLSTONECRAFT. The British writer and radical suggested that Enlightenment critiques of monarchy could also be applied to the power of fathers within the family.

Wollstonecraft was a woman of her time. She argued for the common humanity of men and women but believed that they had different duties and that women's foremost responsibility was mothering and educating children. Like many of her fellow Enlightenment thinkers, Wollstonecraft believed that a natural division of labor existed and that it would ensure social harmony. "Let there be no coercion *established* in society, and the common law of gravity prevailing, the sexes will fall into their proper places." Like others, she wrote about middle-class women, for whom education and property were issues. She was considered scandalously radical for merely hinting that women might have political rights.

The Enlightenment as a whole left a mixed legacy on gender, closely parallel to its legacy on slavery. Enlightenment writers developed and popularized arguments about natural rights. They also elevated natural differences to a higher plane by suggesting that nature should dictate different, and quite possibly unequal, social roles. Mary Wollstonecraft and Jean-Jacques Rousseau shared a radical opposition to despotism and slavery, a moralist's view of a corrupt society, and a concern with virtue and community. Their divergence on gender is characteristic of Enlightenment disagreements about nature and its imperatives and a good example of different directions in which the logic of Enlightenment thinking could lead.

THE ENLIGHTENMENT AND EIGHTEENTH-CENTURY CULTURE

The Book Trade

What about the social structures that produced these debates and received these ideas? To begin with, the Enlightenment was bound up in a much larger expansion of printing and print culture. From the early eighteenth century on, book publishing and selling flourished, especially in Britain, France, the Netherlands, and Switzerland. National borders, though, mattered very little. Much of the book trade was both international and clandestine. Readers bought books from stores, by subscription, and by special mail order from book distributors abroad. Cheaper printing and better distribution also helped multiply the numbers of journals, some specializing in literary or scientific topics and others quite general. They helped bring daily newspapers, which first appeared in London in 1702, to Moscow, Rome, and cities and towns throughout Europe. By 1780, Britons could read 150 different magazines, and 37 English towns had local newspapers. These changes have been called a "revolution in communication," and they form a crucial part of the larger picture of the Enlightenment.

Governments did little to check this revolutionary transformation. In most countries, laws required publishers to apply in advance for the license or privilege (in the sense of "private right") to print and sell any given work. Some regimes granted more permissions than others. In Britain, the press had few restrictions. The French government alternately banned and tolerated different volumes of the *Encyclopedia*. In practice, publishers frequently printed books without advance permission, hoping that the regime would not notice, but bracing themselves for fines, having their books banned, or finding their privileges temporarily revoked. Russian, Prussian, and Austrian censors tolerated much less dissent; but those governments also sought to stimulate publishing and, to a certain degree, permitted public discussion. That governments were patrons as well as censors of new scholarship illustrates the complex relationship between the age of absolutism and the Enlightenment.

As one historian puts it, censorship only made banned books expensive, keeping them out of the hands of the poor. Clandestine booksellers, most near the French border in Switzerland and the Rhineland, smuggled thousands of books across the border to bookstores, distributors, and private customers. What did readers want, and what does this tell us about the reception of the Enlightenment? Many clandestine dealers specialized in what they called "philo-sophical books," which meant subversive literature of all kinds: stories of languishing in prison, gossipy memoirs of life at the court, pornographic fantasies (often about religious and political figures), and tales of crime and criminals. Much of this flourishing eighteenth-century "literary underground," as the historian Robert Darnton calls it, echoed the radical Enlightenment's themes, especially the corruption of the aristocracy and the monarchy's degeneration into despotism. Less explicitly political writings, however, such as Raynal's *History*, Rousseau's novels, travel accounts, biographies, and futuristic fantasies such as Louis Sebastien Mercier's *The Year 2440* proved equally popular. Even expensive volumes like the *Encyclopedia* sold remarkably well, testifying to a keen public interest. It is worth underscoring that Enlightenment work circulated in popular form, and that Rousseau's novels sold as well as his political theory.

High Culture, New Elites, and the Public Sphere

The Enlightenment was not simply embodied in books; it was produced in networks of readers and new forms of sociability and discussion. Eighteenth-century elite or "high" culture was small in scale but cosmopolitan and very literate, and it took discussion seriously. Among the institutions that produced this new elite were learned societies: the American Philosophical Society of Philadelphia, British literary and philosophical societies, and the Select Society of Edinburgh. Such groups organized intellectual life outside of the universities, and they provided libraries, meeting places for discussion, and journals that published members' papers or organized debates. Elites also met in "academies," financed by governments to advance knowledge, whether through research into the natural sciences (the Royal Society of London, and the French Academy of Science, both founded in 1660). Many academies flourished as centers of Enlightenment thinking. The academies' journals published members' papers every year for a European audience. In France, provincial academies played much the same role. Works such as Rousseau's *Discourse on the Origins of Inequality* were entered in academy-sponsored essay contests.

SALONS

Salons did the same but operated informally. Usually they were organized by well-connected and learned aristocratic women. The prominent role of women distinguished the salons from the academies and universities. Salons brought

A READING IN THE SALON OF MADAME GEOFFRIN, 1755. Enlightenment salons encouraged a spirit of intellectual inquiry and civil debate, at least among educated elites. Such salon discussions were notable for the extent to which women helped organize and participate in the conversations. This fact led Rousseau to attack the salons for encouraging unseemly posturing and promiscuity between the sexes, which he believed were the antithesis of rational pursuits. In this painting, Madame Geoffrin, a famed hostess (at left in gray), presides over a discussion of a learned work. Note in the background the bust of Voltaire, the patron saint of rationalist discourse. ■ *What developments were required for this notion of free public discussion among elites to become more general in society?* ■ *Would Enlightenment thinkers favor such developments? (Compare with images on pages 408 and 420).*

together men and women of letters with members of the aristocracy for conversation, debate, drink, and food. Rousseau loathed this kind of ritual and viewed salons as a sign of superficiality and vacuity in a privileged and overcivilized world. Some of the salons reveled in parlor games. Others lay quite close to the halls of power and served as testing grounds for new policy ideas. Madame Marie-Thérèse Geoffrin, another celebrated French *salonière*, became an important patron of the *Encyclopedia* and exercised influence in placing scholars in academies. Salons in London, Vienna, Rome, and Berlin worked the same way; and like academies, they promoted among their participants a sense of belonging to an active, learned elite.

Scores of similar societies emerged in the eighteenth century. Masonic lodges, organizations with elaborate secret rituals whose members pledged themselves to the regeneration of society, attracted a remarkable array of aristocrats and middle-class men. Mozart, Frederick II, and Montesquieu were Masons. Behind their closed doors, the lodges were egalitarian. They pledged themselves to a common project of rational thought and benevolent action, and to banishing religion and social distinction—at least from their ranks.

Other networks of sociability were less exclusive. Coffeehouses multiplied with the colonial trade in sugar, coffee, and tea, and they occupied a central spot in the circulation of ideas. A group of merchants gathering to discuss trade, for instance, could turn to politics; and the many newspapers lying about the café tables provided a ready-to-hand link between their smaller discussions and news and debates elsewhere.

The philosopher Immanuel Kant remarked that a sharper public consciousness seemed one of the hallmarks of his time. "If we attend to the course of conversation in mixed companies consisting not merely of scholars and subtle reasoners but also of business people or women, we notice that besides storytelling or jesting they have another entertainment, namely, arguing." The ability to think critically and speak freely, without deferring to religion or tradition, was a point of pride, and not simply for intellectuals. Eighteenth-century cultural changes—the expanding networks of sociability, the flourishing book trade, the new genres of literature, and the circulation of Enlightenment ideas—widened the circles of reading and discussion, expanding what some historians and political theorists call the *public sphere*. That, in turn, began to change politics. Informal deliberations, debates about how to regenerate the nation, discussions of civic virtue, and efforts to forge a consensus played a crucial role in moving politics beyond the confines of the court.

The eighteenth century gave birth to the very idea of public opinion. A French observer described the changes this way: "In the last thirty years alone, a great and important revolution has occurred in our ideas. Today, public opinion has a preponderant force in Europe that cannot be resisted." Few thought the "public" involved more than the elite. Yet by the late eighteenth century, European governments recognized the existence of a civic-minded group that stretched from salons to coffeehouses, academies, and circles of government and to which they needed, in some measure, to respond.

Middle-Class Culture and Reading

Enlightenment fare constituted only part of the new cultural interests of the eighteenth-century middle classes. Lower down on the social scale, shopkeepers, small merchants,

Competing Viewpoints

Rousseau and His Readers

> *Jean-Jacques Rousseau's writings provoked very different responses from eighteenth-century readers—women as well as men. Many women readers loved his fiction and found his views about women's character and prescriptions for their education inspiring. Other women disagreed vehemently with his conclusions. In the first excerpt here, from Rousseau's novel* Emile *(1762), the author sets out his views on a woman's education. He argues that her education should fit with what he considers her intellectual capacity and her social role. It should also complement the education and role of a man. The second selection is an admiring response to* Emile *from Anne-Louise-Gennaine Necker, or Madame de Staël (1766–1817), a well-known French writer and literary critic. While she acknowledged that Rousseau sought to keep women from participating in political discussion, she also thought that he had granted women a new role in matters of emotion and domesticity. The third excerpt is from Mary Wollstonecraft, who shared many of Rousseau's philosophical principles but sharply disagreed with his assertion that women and men should have different virtues and values. She believed that women like Madame de Staël were misguided in embracing Rousseau's ideas.*

Rousseau's *Emile*

Researches into abstract and speculative truths, the principles and axioms of sciences—in short, everything which tends to generalize our ideas—is not the proper province of women; their studies should be relative to points of practice; it belongs to them to apply those principles which men have discovered. . . . All the ideas of women, which have not the immediate tendency to points of duty, should be directed to the study of men, and to the attainment of those agreeable accomplishments which have taste for their object; for as to works of genius, they are beyond their capacity; neither have they sufficient precision or power of attention to succeed in sciences which require accuracy; and as to physical knowledge, it belongs to those only who are most active, most inquisitive, who comprehend the greatest variety of objects. . . .

She must have the skill to incline us to do everything which her sex will not enable her to do herself, and which is necessary or agreeable to her; therefore she ought to study the mind of man thoroughly, not the mind of man in general, abstractedly, but the dispositions of those men to whom she is subject either by the laws of her country or by the force of opinion. She should learn to penetrate into the real sentiments from their conversation, their actions, their looks and gestures. She should also have the art, by her own conversation, actions, looks, and gestures, to communicate those sentiments which are agreeable to them without seeming to intend it. Men will argue more philosophically about the human heart; but women will read the heart of men better than they. . . . Women have most wit, men have most genius; women observe, men reason. From the concurrence of both we derive the clearest light and the most perfect knowledge which the human mind is of itself capable of attaining.

Source: Jean-Jacques Rousseau, *Emile* (1762), as cited in Mary Wollstonecraft, *A Vindication of the Rights of Woman* (New York: 1992), pp. 124–25.

lawyers, and professionals read more and more different kinds of books. Instead of owning one well-thumbed Bible to read aloud, a middle-class family would buy and borrow books to read casually, pass on, and discuss. This literature consisted of science, history, biography, travel literature, and fiction. A great deal of it was aimed at middle-class women, among the fastest-growing groups of readers in the eighteenth century. Etiquette books sold very well; so did how-to manuals for the household. Scores of books about the manners, morals, and education of daughters, popular versions of Enlightenment treatises on education and the mind, illustrate close parallels between the intellectual life of the high Enlightenment and everyday middle-class reading matter.

Madame de Staël

Though Rousseau has endeavoured to prevent women from interfering in public affairs, and acting a brilliant part in the theatre of politics; yet in speaking of them, how much has he done it to their satisfaction! If he wished to deprive them of some rights foreign to their sex, how has he forever restored to them all those to which it has a claim! And in attempting to diminish their influence over the deliberations of men, how sacredly has he established the empire they have over their happiness! In aiding them to descend from an usurped throne, he has firmly seated them upon that to which they were destined by nature; and though he be full of indignation against them when they endeavour to resemble men, yet when they come before him with all the *charms*, *weaknesses*, *virtues*, and *errors* of their sex, his respect for their *persons* amounts almost to adoration.

Source: Cited in Mary Wollstonecraft, *A Vindication of the Rights of Woman* (New York: 1992), pp. 203–4.

Mary Wollstonecraft

Rousseau declares that a woman should never, for a moment, feel herself independent, that she should be governed by fear to exercise her *natural* cunning, and made a coquettish slave in order to render her a more alluring object of desire, a *sweeter* companion to man, whenever he chooses to relax himself. He carries the arguments, which he pretends to draw from the indications of nature, still further, and insinuates that truth and fortitude, the corner stones of all human virtue, should be cultivated with certain restrictions, because, with respect to the female character, obedience is the grand lesson which ought to be impressed with unrelenting rigour.

What nonsense! When will a great man arise with sufficient strength of mind to puff away the fumes which pride and sensuality have thus spread over the subject! If women are by nature inferior to men, their virtues must be the same in quality, if not in degree, or virtue is a relative idea; consequently, their conduct should be founded on the same principles, and have the same aim.

Source: Cited in Susan Bell and Karen Offen, eds., *Women, the Family, and Freedom: The Debate in Documents*, Vol. 1, *1750–1880* (Stanford, CA: 1983), p. 58.

Questions for Analysis

1. Why did Rousseau seek to limit the sphere of activities open to women in society? What capacities did he feel they lacked? What areas of social life did he feel women were most suited for?

2. Did Madame de Staël agree with Rousseau that women's social roles were essentially different from men's roles in society?

3. What is the basis for Mary Wollstonecraft's disagreement with Rousseau?

4. Why did gender matter to Enlightenment figures such as Rousseau, de Staël, and Wollstonecraft?

The rise of a middle-class reading public, much of it female, helps account for the soaring popularity and production of novels, especially in Britain. Novels were the single most popular new form of literature in the eighteenth century. A survey of library borrowing in late-eighteenth-century Britain, Germany, and North America showed that 70 percent of books taken out were novels. For centuries, Europeans had read romances such as tales of the knights of the Round Table. Novels, though, did not treat quasimythical subjects, the writing was less ornate, and the setting and situations were literally closer to home. The novel's more recognizable, nonaristocratic characters seemed more relevant to common middle-class experience. Moreover, examining emotion and inner feeling also linked novel writing with a larger eighteenth-century concern with personhood and humanity.

Many historians have noted that women figured prominently among fiction writers. In England, Fanny Burney (1752–1840), Ann Radcliffe (1764–1823), and Maria Edgeworth (1767–1849) all wrote extremely popular novels. The works of Jane Austen (1775–1817), especially *Pride and Prejudice* and *Emma,* are to many readers the height of a novelist's craft. Women writers, however, were not the only ones to write novels, nor were they alone in paying close attention to the domestic or private sphere. Their work took up central eighteenth-century themes of human nature, morality, virtue, and reputation. Their novels, like much of the nonfiction of the period, explored those themes in domestic as in public settings.

Popular Culture: Urban and Rural

How much did books and print culture touch the lives of the common people? Literacy rates varied dramatically by gender, social class, and region, but were generally higher in northern than in southern and eastern Europe. It is not surprising that literacy ran highest in cities and towns—higher, in fact, than we might expect. In early eighteenth-century Paris, 85 percent of men and 60 percent of women could read. Well over half the residents of poorer Parisian neighborhoods, especially small shopkeepers, domestic servants and valets, and artisans, could read and sign their names. Even the illiterate, however, lived in a culture of print. They saw one-page newspapers and broadsides or fly-sheets posted on streets and tavern walls and regularly heard them read aloud. Moreover, visual material—inexpensive woodcuts especially, but also prints, drawings, satirical cartoons—figured as prominently as text in much popular reading material. By many measures, then, the circles of reading and discussion were even larger than literacy rates might suggest, especially in cities.

Neither England nor France required any primary schooling, leaving education to haphazard local initiatives. In central Europe, some regimes made efforts to develop state-sponsored education. Catherine of Russia summoned an Austrian consultant to set up a system of primary schools, but by the end of the eighteenth century only twenty-two thousand of a population of forty million had attended any kind of schools. In the absence of primary schooling, most Europeans were self-taught. The varied texts in the itinerant peddler's cart—whether religious, political propaganda, or entertainment—attest to a widespread and rapidly growing popular interest in books and reading.

Like its middle-class counterpart, popular culture rested on networks of sociability. Guild organizations offered discussion and companionship. Street theater and singers mocking local political figures offered culture to people from different social classes. For historians, the difficulties of deciphering popular culture are considerable. Most testimony comes to us from outsiders who regarded the common people as hopelessly superstitious and ignorant. Still, historical research has begun to reveal new insights. It has shown, first, that popular culture did not exist in isolation. Particularly in the countryside, market days and village festivals brought social classes together, and popular entertainments reached a wide social audience. Folktales and traditional songs resist pigeonholing as either elite, middle-class, or popular culture, for they passed from one cultural world to another, being revised and reinterpreted in the process. Second, oral and literate culture overlapped. In other words, even people who could not read often had a great deal of "book knowledge": they argued seriously about points from books and believed that books conferred authority. The logic and worldview of popular culture needs to be understood on its own terms.

A COFFEEHOUSE IN LONDON, 1798. Coffeehouses served as centers of social networks and hubs of opinion, contributing to a public consciousness that was new to the Enlightenment. This coffeehouse scene illustrates a mixing of classes, lively debate, and a burgeoning culture of reading. Compare this image with that of the aristocratic salon on page 417 and the meeting of Mendelssohn and Lessing on page 408. ▪ *How were coffeehouses different from aristocratic salons or the middle-class drawing room discussion between the two German thinkers?* ▪ *Can they all be seen as expressions of a new kind of "public sphere" in eighteenth-century Europe?*

It remains true that the countryside, especially in less economically developed regions, was desperately poor. Life there was far more isolated than in towns. A yawning chasm separated peasants from the world of the high Enlightenment. The *philosophes*, well established in the summits of European society, looked at popular culture with distrust and ignorance. They saw the common people of Europe much as they did indigenous peoples of other continents. They were humanitarians, critical thinkers, and reformers; they were not democrats. Nonetheless, the Enlightenment, while well entrenched in eighteenth-century elite culture, involved changes that reached well beyond elite society.

Eighteenth-Century Music

European elites sustained other forms of high culture. English gentlemen who read scientific papers aloud in clubs also commissioned architects to design classical revival country houses for the weekends. Royal courts underwrote the academies of painting, which upheld aristocratic taste and aesthetics; Austrian salons that hosted discussions of Voltaire also staged performances of Mozart. We have already noted that the *philosophes*' work crossed genres, from political theory to fiction. Rousseau not only wrote discourses and novels but composed music and wrote an opera. A flourishing musical culture was one of the most important features of the eighteenth century.

BACH AND HANDEL

The early eighteenth century brought the last phase of Baroque music, culminating in the work of Johann Sebastian Bach (1685–1750) and George Frideric Handel (1685–1759). Bach was a deeply pious man, a devout Protestant, whose life was entirely unaffected by the secularism of the Enlightenment. A church musician in Leipzig for most of his adult life, he wrote music for every Sunday and holiday service, music of such intensity that the listener feels the salvation of the world hanging on every note. He also wrote concertos and suites for orchestra as well as subtle and complex fugues for piano and organ.

Handel, in contrast, was a publicity-seeking cosmopolitan who sought out large, secular audiences. Born in Brandenburg-Prussia, he studied composition in Italy and eventually established himself as a celebrity composer in London, known for his oratorios (musical dramas performed in concert, without staging) composed in English. Handel's greatest oratorio, *Messiah*, is still sung widely throughout the English-speaking world every Christmas; its stirring "Hallelujah" chorus remains the most popular choral piece in the classical repertoire.

HAYDN AND MOZART

If Bach and Handel were the last (and the greatest) composers of Baroque music, the Austrians Joseph Haydn (1732–1809) and Wolfgang Amadeus Mozart (1756–1791) were the leading representatives of the Classical style, which transformed musical culture in Europe in the second half of the eighteenth century. Classicism in music sought to organize itself around the principles of order, clarity, and symmetry, and its practitioners developed new forms of composition for pursuing these goals, including the string quartet and, most enduringly, the symphony, sometimes called a novel in music.

Mozart wrote forty-one symphonies, and his last three (especially Symphony no. 41, known as the *Jupiter* Symphony) are often said to be unequaled in their grace, variety, and technical perfection. He was a child prodigy of astounding talents and celebrity who died at thirty-five after a career of extraordinary productivity and financial instability. His inability to secure steady employment from a wealthy patron in spite of his well-known genius illustrated the challenges that faced even the most talented of artists in the eighteenth century. Contrary to myth he was not buried in a pauper's grave, but was buried after a simple and cheap funeral in keeping with his Masonic principles and Enlightenment opposition to Catholic ritual.

Joseph Haydn knew much better than Mozart how to appeal to a patron, and he spent the bulk of his career in the service of a wealthy aristocratic family that maintained its own private orchestra. Only toward the end of his life, in 1791, did Haydn strike out on his own by traveling to London where he supported himself handsomely by writing for a paying public. Eighteenth-century London was one of the rare places with a commercial market for culture—later, entrepreneurial opportunities for musicians would open up elsewhere, and in the nineteenth century serious music would leave the aristocratic salon for urban concert halls all over Europe. Haydn furthered this development with his last twelve symphonies (he wrote over a hundred), performed to great acclaim in London.

OPERA

Opera flourished in the eighteenth century. Developed as a musical form in Italy during the seventeenth century by Baroque composers such as Claudio Monteverdi (1567–1643), opera's combination of theater and music spread rapidly throughout Europe in the space of a single generation.

During the classical period, opera's popularity grew due to the spectacles organized by Christoph Willibald von Gluck. Gluck insisted that the text was as important as the music, and he simplified arias and emphasized dramatic action. The much beloved operas of Mozart—including *The Marriage of Figaro*, *Don Giovanni*, and *The Magic Flute*—remain the most popular operas of the Classical period today.

The Marriage of Figaro, indeed, followed a classic eighteenth-century path to popularity. The author of the play was born Pierre Caron, the son of a watchmaker. Caron rose to become watchmaker to the king, bought a noble office, married well, took the name Pierre Augustin de Beaumarchais, and wrote several comedies in an Enlightenment tone satirizing the French nobility. *Figaro* ran into trouble with French censors, but like so many other banned works, the play sold well. It was translated into Italian, was set to music by Mozart, and played to appreciative elite audiences from Paris to Prague. The play's themes—satire, self-criticism, the criticism of hierarchy, optimism and social mobility—are key to understanding eighteenth-century culture as well as the Enlightenment.

CONCLUSION

The Enlightenment arose from the scientific revolution, from the new sense of power and possibility that rational thinking made possible, and from the rush of enthusiasm for new forms of inquiry. Enlightenment thinkers scrutinized a remarkably wide range of topics: human nature, reason, understanding, religion, belief, law, the origins of government, economics, new forms of technology, and

After You Read This Chapter

Visit StudySpace for quizzes, additional review materials, and multi-media documents. **wwnorton.com/studyspace**

REVIEWING THE OBJECTIVES

- Many eighteenth-century thinkers used the term *Enlightenment* to describe what their work offered to European society. Who were they, and what did they mean by the term?

- Enlightenment ideas spread rapidly throughout Europe and in European colonies. How did this expanded arena for public discussion shape the development of Enlightenment thought?

- Enlightenment debates were shaped by the availability of new information about peoples and cultures in different parts of the globe. How did Enlightenment thinkers incorporate this new information into their thought?

- Enlightenment thinkers were often critical of widely held cultural and political beliefs. What was radical about the Enlightenment?

- The Enlightenment took place in an expanded sphere of public discussion and debate. How broad was the audience for Enlightenment thought, and how important was this audience for our understanding of the period?

social practices—such as marriage, child-rearing, and education. In doing so, they made many of their contemporaries (and sometimes, even themselves) uncomfortable. Ideas with radical or even subversive implications circulated in popular forms from pamphlets and journalism to plays and operas. The intellectual movement that lay behind the Enlightenment thus had broad consequences for the creation of a new kind of elite, based not on birth but on the acquisition of knowledge and the encouragement of open expression and debate. A new sphere of public opinion had come into existence, one that would have profound consequences in the nineteenth and twentieth centuries.

The Atlantic revolutions (the American Revolution of 1776, the French Revolution of 1789, and the Latin American upheavals of the 1830s) were steeped in the language of the Enlightenment. The constitutions of the new nations formed by these revolutions made reference to the fundamental assumptions of Enlightenment liberalism: on the liberty of the individual conscience and the freedom from the constraints imposed by religious or government institutions. Governmental authority could not be arbitrary; equality and freedom were natural; and humans sought happiness, prosperity, and the expansion of their potential. These arguments had been made tentatively earlier, and even after the Atlantic revolutions their aspirations were only partially realized. But when the North American colonists declared their independence from Britain in 1776, they called such ideas "self-evident truths." That bold declaration marked both the distance traveled since the late seventeenth century and the self-confidence that was the Enlightenment's hallmark.

PEOPLE, IDEAS, AND EVENTS IN CONTEXT

- Who were the *PHILOSOPHES*? What gave them such faith in **REASON**?
- What did **DAVID HUME** owe to **ISAAC NEWTON**? What made his work different from that of the famous physicist?
- What did **VOLTAIRE** admire about the work of **FRANCIS BACON** and **JOHN LOCKE**? What irritated Voltaire about French society?
- What was **MONTESQUIEU**'s contribution to theories of government?
- What made **DENIS DIDEROT**'s *ENCYCLOPEDIA* such a definitive statement of the Enlightenment's goals?
- What influence did **CESARE BECCARIA** have over legal practices in Europe?
- What contributions did **ADAM SMITH** make to economic theory?
- What was radical about **JEAN-JACQUES ROUSSEAU**'s views on education and politics?
- What does the expansion of the **PUBLIC SPHERE** in the eighteenth century tell us about the effects of the Enlightenment?

CONSEQUENCES

- If humans were as rational as Enlightenment thinkers said they were, why did they need Enlightenment *philosophes* to tell them how to live? How might a *philosophe* have answered this question?
- Did increases in literacy, the rise of print culture, and the emergence of new forms of intellectual sociability such as salons, reading societies, and coffeehouses really make public opinion more rational?

Before
You
Read
This
Chapter

The French Revolution

W hen a crowd of Parisians attacked the antiquated and nearly empty royal prison known as the Bastille on July 14, 1789, they were doing several things all at once. On the one hand, the revolt was a popular expression of support for the newly created National Assembly. This representative body had only weeks earlier declared an intention to put an end to absolutism in France by writing a constitution that made the nation, rather than the king, the sovereign authority in the land. But the Parisians in the street on July 14 did not express themselves like members of the National Assembly, who spoke the language of the Enlightenment. The actions of the revolutionary crowd were an expression of violent anger at the king's soldiers, who they feared might turn their guns on the city in a royal attempt to restore order by force. When the governor of the Bastille prison opened fire on the attackers, killing as many as a hundred, they responded with redoubled fury. By the end of the day, the prison had fallen, and its governor's battered body was dragged to the square before the city hall, where he was beheaded. Among the first to meet such an end as a consequence of revolution in France, he would not be the last.

This tension between noble political aspirations and cruel violence lies at the heart of the French Revolution.

Other kingdoms were not immune to the same social and political tensions that divided the French. Aristocrats across Europe and the colonies resented monarchical inroads on their ancient freedoms. Members of the middle classes chafed under a system of official privilege that they increasingly saw as unjust and outmoded. Peasants fiercely resented the endless demands of central government on their limited resources. Nor were resentments focused exclusively on absolutist monarchs. Bitter resentments and tensions existed between country and city dwellers, between rich and poor, overprivileged and underprivileged, slave and free. The French Revolution was the most dramatic and tumultuous expression of all of these conflicts.

This age of revolution opened on the other side of the Atlantic ocean. The American Revolution of 1776 was a crisis of the British Empire, linked to a long series of conflicts between England and France over colonial control of North America. It led to a major crisis of the Old Regime in France. Among "enlightened" Europeans, the success with which citizens of the United States had thrown off British rule and formed a republic based on Enlightenment principles was a source of tremendous optimism.

By any measure, the accomplishments of the revolutionary decade were extraordinary: it proved that the residents of an old monarchy in the heart of Europe could come together to constitute themselves as citizens of a new political idea, the nation. Freed from the shackles of tradition, revolutionaries in France posed new questions about the role of women in public life, about the separation of church and state, about the rights of Jews and other minorities. A slave revolt in the French colonies convinced the revolutionaries that the new liberties they defended so ardently also belonged to African slaves, though few had suggested such a thing at the outset. Meanwhile, the European wars precipitated by the revolution marked the first time that entire populations were mobilized as part of a new kind of

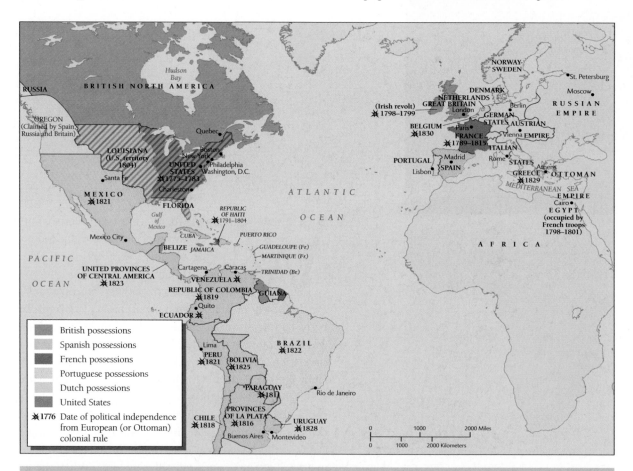

THE ATLANTIC REVOLUTIONS. The Atlantic revolutions shook nations and empires on both sides of the ocean, challenging the legitimacy of Europe's dynastic realms, lending further support to notions of popular sovereignty, and forcing contemporaries to rethink the meanings of citizenship in a context of intense political and economic struggle. ▪ *How many of these struggles took place within Europe?* ▪ *How many appear to have taken place on the periphery of the Atlantic world?* ▪ *What circumstances may have made it more difficult for such revolutionary movements to develop within Europe itself?*

devastating international conflict, the first "total wars." In other words, in spite of the optimism of those who began the revolution in 1789, it quickly became something much more costly, complex, and violent. Its effects were to resonate throughout Europe for the next half century.

THE FRENCH REVOLUTION: AN OVERVIEW

The term *French Revolution* is a shorthand for a complex series of events between 1789 and 1799. Some historians also include the period of Napoleon's rule, 1799–1814. To simplify, the period from 1789–1814 can be divided into four stages. In the first stage, running from 1788 to 1792, the struggle was constitutional and relatively peaceful. An increasingly bold elite articulated its grievances against the king. Like the American revolutionaries, French elites refused taxation without representation; attacked despotism, or arbitrary authority; and offered an Enlightenment-inspired program to rejuvenate the nation. Reforms, many of them breathtakingly wide ranging, were instituted—some accepted or even offered by the king, and others enacted over his objections. This peaceful, constitutional phase did not last.

The threat of dramatic change within one of the most powerful countries in Europe created international tensions. In 1792 these tensions exploded into war, and the crises of war, in turn, spelled the end of the Bourbon monarchy and the beginning of the republic. The second stage of the revolution, which lasted from 1792 to 1794, was one of acute crisis, consolidation, and repression. A ruthlessly centralized government mobilized all the country's resources to fight the foreign enemy as well as counterrevolutionaries at home, to destroy traitors and the vestiges of the Old Regime.

The Terror, as this policy was called, did save the republic, but it exhausted itself in factions and recriminations and collapsed in 1794. In the third phase, from 1794 to 1799, the government drifted. France remained a republic. It continued to fight with Europe. Undermined by corruption and division, the state fell prey to the ambitions of a military leader, Napoleon Bonaparte. Napoleon's rule, punctuated by astonishing victories and catastrophes, stretched from 1799 to 1815, and constitutes the end of the revolution. It began as a republic, became an empire, and ended—after a last hurrah—in the muddy fields outside the Belgian village of Waterloo. After Napoleon's final defeat, the other European monarchs restored the Bourbons to the throne. That restoration, however, would be short lived, and the cycle of revolution and reaction continued into the nineteenth century.

THE COMING OF THE REVOLUTION

What were the long-term causes of the revolution in France? Historians long ago argued that the causes and outcomes should be understood in terms of class conflict. According to this interpretation, a rising bourgeoisie, or middle class, inspired by Enlightenment ideas and by its own self-interest, overthrew what was left of the aristocratic order.

Historians have substantially modified this bold thesis. French society was not simply divided between a bourgeois class and the aristocracy. Instead, it was increasingly dominated by a new elite or social group that brought together aristocrats, officeholders, professionals, and—to a lesser degree—merchants and businessmen. To understand the revolution, we need to understand this new social group and its conflicts with the government of Louis XVI.

French society was divided legally into Three Estates. (An individual's *estate*, or status, determined legal rights, taxes, and so on.) The First Estate comprised all the clergy; the Second Estate, the nobility. The Third Estate, by far the largest, included everyone else, from wealthy lawyers and businessmen to urban laborers and poor peasants. These legal distinctions often seemed artificial. To begin with, the social boundaries between nobles and wealthy commoners were ill-defined. Noble title was accessible to those who could afford to buy an ennobling office. Fifty thousand new nobles were created between 1700 and 1789. The nobility depended on a constant infusion of talent and economic power from the wealthy social groups of the Third Estate.

Most noble wealth was proprietary—that is, tied to land, urban properties, purchased offices, and the like. Yet noble families did not disdain trade or commerce, as historians long thought. In fact, noblemen financed most industry, and they also invested heavily in banking and such enterprises as shipping, the slave trade, mining, and metallurgy. Moreover, the very wealthy members of the Third Estate also preferred to invest in secure, proprietary holdings. Thus, throughout the century, much middle-class wealth was transformed into noble wealth, and a significant number of rich bourgeois became noblemen. Wealthy members of the bourgeoisie themselves did not see themselves as a separate class. They thought of themselves as different from—and often opposed to—the common people, who worked with their hands, and they identified with the values of a nobility to which they frequently aspired.

There were, nonetheless, important social tensions. Less prosperous lawyers—and there were an increasing number of them—were jealous of the privileged position of a favored few in their profession. Over the course of the century the

PREREVOLUTIONARY PROPAGANDA. Political cartoons in late-eighteenth-century France commonly portrayed the Third Estate as bearing the burden of taxation while performing the bulk of the nation's productive work. ■ *Would one expect the nobility or the clergy to defend their status on the basis of their usefulness to society?* ■ *Can one detect the power of certain Enlightenment ideas behind these forms of social critique?* ■ *Which ones?* ■ *How might an opponent of Enlightenment thought have confronted such arguments?*

price of offices rose, making it more difficult to buy one's way into the nobility, and creating tensions between middling members of the Third Estate and the very rich in trade and commerce who, by and large, were the only group able to afford to climb the social ladder. Less wealthy nobles resented the success of rich, upstart commoners whose income allowed them to live in luxury. In sum, several fault lines ran through the elite and the middle classes. All these social groups could nonetheless join in attacking a government and an economy that were not serving their interests.

The Enlightenment had changed public debate (see Chapter 17). Ideas did not cause the revolution, but they played a critical role in articulating grievances. The political theories of Locke, Voltaire, and Montesquieu could appeal to both discontented nobles and members of the middle class. Voltaire was popular because of his attacks on noble privileges; Locke and Montesquieu gained widespread followings because of their defense of private property and limited sovereignty. Montesquieu's ideas appealed to the noble lawyers and officeholders who dominated France's powerful law courts, the *parlements*. They read his doctrine of checks and balances as support for their argument that *parlements* could provide a check to the despotism of the

king's government. When conflicts arose, noble leaders presented themselves as defenders of the nation threatened by the king and his ministers.

The campaign for change was also fueled by economic reformers. The "physiocrats" urged the government to simplify the tax system and free the economy from mercantilist regulations. They advocated an end to price controls in the grain trade, which had been imposed to keep the cost of bread low. Such interventions, they argued, interfered with the natural workings of the market.

In the countryside, peasants were caught in a web of obligations to landlords, church, and state: a tithe, or levy, on farm produce owed to the church; fees for the use of a landlord's mill or wine press; rents to the landlord; and fees when land changed hands. In addition, peasants paid a disproportionate share of both direct and indirect taxes—the most onerous of which was the salt tax—levied by the government. Further grievances stemmed from the requirement to maintain public roads (the *corvée*) and from the hunting privileges that nobles for centuries had regarded as the distinctive badge of their order.

Social and economic conditions deteriorated on the eve of the revolution. A general price increase during much of the eighteenth century, which permitted the French economy to expand by providing capital for investment, created hardship for the peasantry and for urban tradesmen and laborers. Their plight deteriorated further at the end of the 1780s, when poor harvests sent bread prices sharply higher. In 1788 families found themselves spending more than 50 percent of their income on bread, which made up the bulk of their diet. The following year the figure rose to as much as 80 percent. Poor harvests reduced demand for manufactured goods, and contracting markets in turn created unemployment. Many peasants left the countryside for the cities, hoping to find work there—only to discover that urban unemployment was far worse than that in rural areas. Evidence indicates that between 1787 and 1789 the unemployment rate in many parts of urban France was as high as 50 percent.

Failure and Reform

An inefficient tax system further weakened the country's financial position. Taxation was tied to differing social standings and varied from region to region—some areas were subject to a much higher rate than others. The financial system, already burdened by debts incurred under Louis XIV, all but broke down completely under the increased expenses brought on by French participation in the American Revolution.

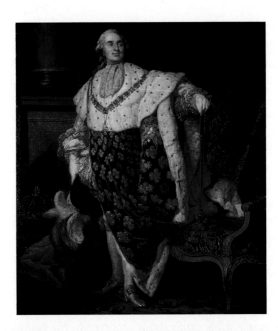

LOUIS XVI. The last prerevolutionary French king, who was to lose his life in the Terror, combined in his person a strong attachment to the monarchy's absolutist doctrine with an inability to find workable solutions to the financial crisis facing his government. His royal portrait mimicked the forms of spectacular display that proved so useful to his ancestor Louis XIV in shoring up the power of the monarchy. ▪ *What made this display so much less potent in the late eighteenth century?* ▪ *What caused the monarchy to lose its aura?*

Problems with the economy reflected weaknesses in France's administrative structure, ultimately the responsibility of the country's absolutist monarch, Louis XVI (r. 1774–92). Louis wished to improve the lot of the poor, abolish torture, and shift the burden of taxation onto the richer classes, but he lacked the ability to accomplish these tasks. When he pressed for new taxes to be paid by the nobility, he was defeated by the provincial *parlements*, who defended the aristocracy's immunity from taxation. By 1788, a weak monarch, together with a chaotic financial situation and severe social tensions, brought absolutist France to the edge of political disaster.

THE DESTRUCTION OF THE OLD REGIME

The fiscal crisis precipitated the revolution. In 1787 and 1788 the king's ministers proposed new taxes to meet the growing deficit, notably a stamp duty and a direct tax on the annual produce of the land.

Hoping to persuade the nobility to agree to these reforms, the king summoned an Assembly of Notables from among the aristocracy and clergy. This group insisted that any new tax scheme must be approved by the Estates General, the representative body of the Three Estates of the realm, and that the king had no legal authority to arrest and imprison arbitrarily. These proposed constitutional changes echoed the English aristocrats of 1688 and the American revolutionaries of 1776.

Faced with economic crisis and financial chaos, Louis XVI summoned the Estates General (which had not met since 1614) to meet in 1789. His action appeared to many as the only solution to France's deepening problems. Long-term grievances and short-term hardships produced bread riots across the country in the spring of 1789. Fear that the forces of law and order were collapsing and that the common people might take matters into their own hands spurred the Estates General. Each of the three orders elected its own deputies—the Third Estate indirectly through local assemblies. These assemblies were charged as well with the responsibility of drawing up lists of grievances (*cahiers des doléances*), further heightening expectations for fundamental reform.

By tradition, each estate met and voted as a body. In the past, this had generally meant that the First Estate (the clergy) had combined with the Second (the nobility) to defeat the Third. The king's finance minister, Jacques Necker, feared that this would place the government at the mercy of the most conservative nobles and so prevent financial reform. Members of the Third Estate, meanwhile, argued that the representatives of the Three Estates should sit together and vote as individuals, and that the Third Estate delegation should be doubled in size, so as to give the commoners an equal voice. Necker convinced the king to go along with this plan in December 1788. When the nobility predictably protested against what they saw as a royal betrayal, a radical priest named Abbé Sieyès penned an incendiary pamphlet, "What Is the Third Estate?" His answer: everything. Comparing the nobility to parasites, he argued that they were not even a part of the body politic.

The king, alarmed by this violent language, backed away from his support of the Third Estate when the Estates General convened in May 1789. Angered by the king's attitude, the Third Estate's representatives took the revolutionary step of leaving the body and declaring themselves the National Assembly. The king tried to prevent the National Assembly from meeting, but when the delegates found themselves locked out of their meeting hall on June 20, the representatives moved to a nearby tennis court, along with a handful of sympathetic nobles and clergymen. Here, under the leadership of the volatile, maverick aristocrat Mirabeau and the radical clergyman Sieyès, they swore an oath not to disband until France had a constitution.

This Tennis Court Oath, sworn on June 20, 1789, can be seen as the beginning of the French Revolution. By claiming the authority to remake the government in the name of the people, the National Assembly was asserting its right to act as the highest sovereign power in the nation. On June 27 the king virtually conceded this right by ordering all the delegates to join the National Assembly.

First Stages of the French Revolution

The first stage of the French Revolution extended from June 1789 to August 1792. In the main, this stage was moderate, its actions dominated by the leadership of liberal nobles and men of the Third Estate. Yet three events in the summer and fall of 1789 furnished evidence that their leadership would be challenged.

POPULAR REVOLTS

From the beginning of the political crisis, the public paid close attention. Many believed that the aristocracy and the king were conspiring to punish the Third Estate by encouraging scarcity and high prices. Rumors circulated in Paris during the latter days of June 1789 that the king's troops were mobilizing to march on the city. The electors of Paris (those who had voted for the Third Estate) feared not only the king but also the Parisian poor, who had been parading through the

streets and threatening violence. The common people would soon be referred to as *sans-culottes* (*sahn koo-LAWTS*). The term, which translates to "without breeches," was an antiaristocratic badge of pride: a man of the people wore full-length trousers rather than aristocratic breeches with stockings and gold-buckled shoes. Led by the electors, the people formed a provisional municipal government and organized a militia of volunteers to maintain order. Determined to obtain arms, they made their way on July 14 to the Bastille, an ancient fortress and symbol of royal authority where guns and ammunition were stored. When crowds demanded arms from its governor, he procrastinated and then, fearing a frontal assault, opened fire, killing ninety-eight of the attackers. The crowd took revenge, capturing the fortress and decapitating the governor. Similar groups took control in other cities across France. The fall of the Bastille was the first instance of the people's role in revolutionary change.

The second popular revolt occurred in the countryside. Peasants, too, feared a counterrevolution. Rumors flew that the king's armies were on their way, that Austrians, Prussians, or "brigands" were invading. Frightened and uncertain, peasants and villagers organized militias; others attacked and burned manor houses, sometimes to look for grain but usually to find and destroy records of manorial dues. This "Great Fear," as historians have labeled it, compounded the confusion in rural areas in July and August 1789. The news, when it reached Paris, convinced deputies at Versailles that the administration of rural France had simply collapsed.

The third instance of popular uprising, the "October Days of 1789," was brought on by economic crisis. This time Parisian women from the market district, angered by the soaring price of bread and fired by rumors of the king's continuing unwillingness to cooperate with the assembly, marched to Versailles on October 5 and demanded to

What Is the Third Estate? (1789)

The Abbé Emmanuel-Joseph Sieyès (1748–1836) was, by virtue of his office in the church, a member of the First Estate of the Estates General. Nevertheless, his political savvy led him to be elected as a representative of the Third Estate from the district of Chartres. Sieyès was a formidable politician as well as a writer. His career during the revolution, which he ended by assisting Napoleon's seizure of power, began with one of the most important radical pamphlets of 1789. In What Is the Third Estate?, *Sieyès posed fundamental questions about the rights of the estate, which represented the great majority of the population and helped provoke its secession from the Estates General.*

he plan of this book is fairly simple. We must ask ourselves three questions.

1. What is the Third Estate? *Everything.*

2. What has it been until now in the political order? *Nothing.*

3. What does it want to be? *Something.*

It suffices to have made the point that the so-called usefulness of a privileged order to the public service is a fallacy; that without help from this order, all the arduous tasks in the service are performed by the Third Estate; that without this order the higher posts could be infinitely better filled; that they ought to be the natural prize and reward of recognized ability and service; and that if the privileged have succeeded in usurping all well-paid and honorific posts, this is both a hateful iniquity towards the generality of citizens and an act of treason to the commonwealth.

Who is bold enough to maintain that the Third Estate does not contain within itself everything needful to constitute a complete nation? It is like a strong and robust man with one arm still in chains. If the privileged order were removed, the nation would not be something less but something more. What then is the Third Estate? All; but an "all" that is fettered and oppressed. What would it be without the privileged order? It would be all; but free and flourishing. Nothing will go well without the Third Estate; everything would go considerably better without the two others.

Source: Emmanuel-Joseph Sieyès, *What Is the Third Estate?*, trans. M. Blondel, ed. S. E. Finer (London: 1964), pp. 53–63.

Questions for Analysis

1. How might contemporaries have viewed Sieyès's argument that the Three Estates should be evaluated according to their usefulness to the "commonwealth"?

2. Was Sieyès's language—accusing the privileged orders of "treason" and arguing for their "removal"—an incitement to violence?

3. What did Sieyès mean by the term *nation*? Could one speak of France as a nation in these terms before 1789?

---

be heard. Not satisfied with its reception by the assembly, the crowd broke through the gates to the palace, calling for the king to return to Paris from Versailles. On the afternoon of the following day the king yielded and returned to Paris, accompanied by the crowd and the National Guard.

Each of these popular uprisings shaped the political events unfolding at Versailles. The storming of the Bastille persuaded the king and nobles to agree to the creation of the National Assembly. The Great Fear compelled the most sweeping changes of the entire revolutionary period. In an effort to quell rural disorder, on the night of August 4 the assembly took a giant step toward abolishing all forms of privilege. It eliminated the church tithe (tax on the harvest), the labor requirement known as the *corvée*, the nobility's hunting privileges, and a wide variety of tax exemptions and monopolies. In effect, these reforms obliterated the remnants of feudalism. One week later, the assembly abolished the sale of offices, thereby sweeping away one of the fundamental institutions of the Old Regime. The king's return to Paris during the October Days of 1789 undercut his ability to resist further changes.

THE NATIONAL ASSEMBLY AND THE RIGHTS OF MAN

The assembly issued its charter of liberties, the Declaration of the Rights of Man and of the Citizen, in August 1789. It declared rights to property, liberty, security, and "resistance to oppression," as well as freedom of speech, religious toleration, and liberty of the press. All (male) citizens were to be treated equally before the law. No one was to be imprisoned or punished without due process of law. Sovereignty resided in the people, who could depose officers of the government if they abused their powers. The Declaration became the preamble to the new constitution, which the assembly finished in 1791.

Whom did the Declaration mean by "man and the citizen"? The constitution distinguished between "passive" citizens, guaranteed rights under law, and "active" citizens, who paid a certain amount in taxes and could thus vote and hold office. About half the adult males in France qualified as active citizens. Even their power was curtailed, because they could vote only for "electors," men whose property ownership qualified them to hold office. Later in the revolution, the more radical republic abolished the distinction between active and passive, and the conservative regimes reinstated it.

Which men could be trusted to participate in politics and on what terms was a hotly contested issue. The revolution gave full civil rights to Protestants and, hesitantly, to Jews. Religious toleration, a central theme of the Enlightenment, meant ending persecution; it did not mean that the regime was prepared to accommodate religious difference. The assembly abolished serfdom and banned slavery in continental France. It remained silent on colonial slavery, however, and the assembly exempted the colonies from the constitution's provisions. Events in the Caribbean, as we will see, later forced the issue.

The rights and roles of women became the focus of sharp debate, as revolutionaries confronted demands that working women participate in guilds or trade organizations, and laws on marriage, divorce, poor relief, and education were reconsidered. Only a handful of thinkers broached the subject of women in politics: among them were the aristocratic Enlightenment thinker the Marquis de Condorcet and Marie Gouze, the self-educated daughter of a butcher. Gouze became an intellectual and playwright and renamed herself Olympe de Gouges. Like many "ordinary" people, she found in the explosion of revolutionary activity an opportunity to address the public by writing speeches, and publishing pamphlets and newspaper articles. She composed her own manifesto, the *Declaration of the Rights of Woman and the Citizen* (1791). Beginning with the proposition that "social distinctions can only be based on the common utility," she declared that women had the same rights as men, including resistance to authority and participation in government. She also insisted that women had unique rights, including naming the fathers of illegitimate children. This last demand offers a glimpse of the shame, isolation, and hardship faced by an unmarried woman.

De Gouges's demand for equal rights was unusual, but many women nevertheless participated in the everyday activities of the revolution, joining clubs, demonstrations, and debates and making their presence known, sometimes forcefully. Women artisans' organizations used the revolution as an opportunity to assert their rights to produce and sell goods. Market women were often central to the circulation of news and spontaneous popular demonstrations (the October Days are a good example). When the revolution became more radical, however, some revolutionaries saw autonomous political activity by women's organizations as a threat to public order, and in 1793 the revolutionaries shut down the women's political clubs. Even so, many ordinary women were able to make use of the revolution's new legislation on marriage (divorce was legalized in 1792) and inheritance to support claims for relief from abusive husbands or absent fathers, claims that would have been impossible under the prerevolutionary Old Regime.

THE NATIONAL ASSEMBLY AND THE CHURCH

In November 1789, the National Assembly decided to confiscate all church lands to use them as collateral for issuing interest-bearing notes known as *assignats*. The assembly hoped that this action would resolve the economy's inflationary crisis, and eventually these notes circulated widely as paper money. In July 1790, the assembly enacted the Civil Constitution of the Clergy, bringing the church under state authority. The new law forced all bishops and priests to swear allegiance to the state, which henceforth paid their salaries. The aim was to make the Catholic Church of France a national institution, free from interference from Rome.

These reforms were bitterly divisive. For centuries the parish church had been a central institution in small towns and villages, providing poor relief and other services, in addition to baptisms and marriages. When the pope threatened to excommunicate priests who signed the Civil Constitution, he raised the stakes: allegiance to the new French state meant damnation. Many people, especially peasants in the deeply Catholic areas of western France, were driven into open revolt.

The National Assembly made a series of economic and governmental changes with lasting effects. To raise money, it sold off church lands, although few of the genuinely needy could afford to buy them. To encourage the growth of economic enterprise, it abolished guilds. To rid the country of local aristocratic power, it reorganized local governments, dividing France into eighty-three equal departments. These measures aimed to defend individual liberty and freedom from customary privilege. Their principal beneficiaries were, for the most part, members of the elite, people on their way up under the previous regime who were able to take advantage of the opportunities that the new one offered. In this realm as elsewhere, the social changes of the revolution endorsed changes already under way in the eighteenth century.

Declaration of the Rights of Man and of the Citizen

One of the first important pronouncements of the National Assembly after the Tennis Court Oath was the Declaration of the Rights of Man and of the Citizen. *The authors drew inspiration from the American Declaration of Independence, but the language is even more heavily influenced by the ideals of French Enlightenment philosophes, particularly Rousseau. Following are the* Declaration's *preamble and some of its most important principles.*

The representatives of the French people, constituted as the National Assembly, considering that ignorance, disregard, or contempt for the rights of man are the sole causes of public misfortunes and the corruption of governments, have resolved to set forth, in a solemn declaration, the natural, inalienable, and sacred rights of man, so that the constant presence of this declaration may ceaselessly remind all members of the social body of their rights and duties; so that the acts of legislative power and those of the executive power may be more respected . . . and so that the demands of the citizens, grounded henceforth on simple and incontestable principles, may always be directed to the maintenance of the constitution and to the welfare of all. . . .

Article 1. Men are born and remain free and equal in rights. Social distinctions can be based only on public utility.

Article 2. The aim of every political association is the preservation of the natural and imprescriptible rights of man. These rights are liberty, property, security, and resistance to oppression.

Article 3. The source of all sovereignty resides essentially in the nation. No body, no individual can exercise authority that does not explicitly proceed from it.

Article 4. Liberty consists in being able to do anything that does not injure another; thus the only limits upon each man's exercise of his natural laws are those that guarantee enjoyment of these same rights to the other members of society.

Article 5. The law has the right to forbid only actions harmful to society. No action may be prevented that is not forbidden by law, and no one may be constrained to do what the law does not order.

Article 6. The law is the expression of the general will. All citizens have the right to participate personally, or through representatives, in its formation. It must be the same for all, whether it protects or punishes. All citizens, being equal in its eyes, are equally admissable to all public dignities, positions, and employments, according to their ability, and on the basis of no other distinction than that of their virtues and talents. . . .

Article 16. A society in which the guarantee of rights is not secured, or the separation of powers is not clearly established, has no constitution.

Source: *Declaration of the Rights of Man and of the Citizen,* as cited in K. M. Baker, ed., *The Old Regime and the French Revolution* (Chicago: 1987), pp. 238–39.

Questions for Analysis

1. Who is the Declaration addressed to? Is it just about the rights of the French or do these ideas apply to all people?

2. What gave a group of deputies elected to advise Louis XVI on constitutional reforms the right to proclaim themselves a National Assembly? What was revolutionary about this claim to represent the French nation?

3. Article 6, which states that "law is the expression of general will," is adapted from Rousseau's *Social Contract.* Does the Declaration give any indication of how the "general will" can be known?

A NEW STAGE: POPULAR REVOLUTION

In the summer of 1792, the revolution's moderate leaders were toppled and replaced by republicans, who repudiated the monarchy and claimed to rule on behalf of a sovereign people. Historians have focused on three factors to explain the revolution's radical turn: changes in popular politics, a crisis of leadership, and international polarization.

First, the revolution politicized the common people, especially in cities. Newspapers filled with political and social commentary multiplied, freed from censorship. From 1789 forward, a wide variety of political clubs became part of daily political life. Some were formal, almost like political parties, gathering members of the elite to debate issues facing the country and influence decisions in the assembly. Other clubs opened their doors to those excluded from formal politics. Members read aloud from newspapers and discussed the options facing the country. Shortages and high prices particularly exasperated the working people of Paris who had eagerly awaited change since their street demonstrations of 1789. Urban demonstrations, often led by women, demanded cheaper bread; political leaders in clubs and newspapers called for the government to control rising inflation.

A second major reason for the revolution's change of course was a lack of effective national leadership. Louis XVI remained a weak monarch. He was forced to support measures personally distasteful to him, and he was sympathetic to the plottings of the queen, who was in contact with her brother Leopold II of Austria. Urged on by Marie Antoinette, Louis agreed to attempt an escape from France in June 1791, hoping to rally foreign support for counterrevolution. The members of the royal family were apprehended near the border at Varennes and brought back to the capital. The constitution of 1791 declared France a monarchy, but after the escape to Varennes, Louis was little more than a prisoner of the assembly.

The Counterrevolution

The third major reason for the dramatic turn of affairs was war. From the outset of the revolution, men and women across Europe had been compelled, by the very intensity of the events in France, to take sides in the conflict. In the years immediately after 1789, the revolution in France won the enthusiastic support of a wide range of thinkers, including the English poet William Wordsworth and the German writer Johann Gottfried von Herder, who declared the revolution the most important historical moment since the Reformation. In Britain, the Low Countries, western Germany, and Italy, "patriots" proclaimed their allegiance to the new revolution.

Others opposed the revolution from the start. Exiled nobles, who fled France for sympathetic royal courts in Germany and elsewhere, did all they could to stir up counterrevolutionary sentiment. In Britain the conservative cause was strengthened by the publication in 1790 of Edmund Burke's *Reflections on the Revolution in France*, which attacked the revolution as a monstrous crime against the social order (see page 436).

The first European states to express public concern about events in revolutionary France were Austria and Prussia, declaring in 1791 that order and the rights of the monarch of France were matters of "common interest to all sovereigns of Europe." The leaders of the French as-

sembly pronounced the declaration an affront to national sovereignty. Nobles who had fled France played into their hands with plots and pronouncements against the new government. Oddly, perhaps, both supporters and opponents of the revolution in France believed war would serve their cause. The National Assembly's leaders expected an aggressive policy to shore up the people's loyalty and bring freedom to the rest of Europe. Counterrevolutionaries hoped the intervention of Austria and Prussia would undo all that had happened since 1789. Radicals, suspicious of aristocratic leaders and the king, believed that war would expose traitors with misgivings about the revolution and flush out those who sympathized with the king and European tyrants. On April 20, 1792, the assembly declared war against Austria and Prussia. Thus began the war that would keep the Continent in arms for a generation.

As the radicals expected, the French forces met serious reverses. By August 1792 the allied armies of Austria and Prussia had crossed the frontier and were threatening to capture Paris. Many, including soldiers, believed that the military disasters were evidence of the king's treason. On August 10, Parisian crowds, organized by their radical leaders, attacked the royal palace. The king was imprisoned and a second and far more radical revolution began.

The French Republic

From this point, the country's leadership passed into the hands of the more egalitarian leaders of the former Third Estate. These new leaders were known as Jacobins, the name of a political club to which many of them belonged. Although their headquarters were in Paris, their membership extended throughout France. Their members included large numbers of professionals, government officeholders, and lawyers; but an increasing number of artisans joined Jacobin clubs as the movement grew, and other, more democratic, clubs expanded as well.

The National Convention, elected by free white men, became the effective governing body of the country for the next three years. It was elected in September 1792, at a time when enemy troops were advancing, spreading panic. Rumors flew that prisoners in Paris were plotting to aid the enemy. They were hauled from their cells, dragged before hastily convened tribunals, and killed. The "September Massacres" killed more than a thousand "enemies of the Revolution" in less than a week. Similar riots engulfed Lyons, Orléans, and other French cities.

The newly elected convention was far more radical than its predecessor, and its leadership was determined to end the monarchy. On September 21, the convention declared

France a republic. In December it placed the king on trial, and in January 1793 he was condemned to death by a narrow margin. The heir to the grand tradition of French absolutism met his end bravely as "citizen Louis Capet," beheaded by the guillotine. Introduced as a swifter and more humane form of execution, the frightful mechanical headsman came to symbolize revolutionary fervor.

The convention took other radical measures. It confiscated the property of enemies of the revolution, and it canceled the policy of compensating nobles for their lost privileges. It repealed primogeniture, so that property would be divided in substantially equal portions among all immediate heirs. It abolished slavery in French colonies (discussed later). It set maximum prices for grain and other necessities. In an astonishing effort to root out Christianity from everyday life, the convention adopted a new calendar. The calendar year began with the birth of the republic (September 22, 1792) and divided months in such a way as to eliminate the Catholic Sunday.

The convention also reorganized its armies, with astonishing success. By February 1793, Britain, Holland, Spain, and Austria were in the field against the French. Britain came into the war for strategic and economic reasons: they feared a French threat to Britain's growing global power. The revolution flung fourteen hastily drafted armies into battle under the leadership of newly promoted, young, and inexperienced officers. What they lacked in training and discipline they made up for in organization, mobility, flexibility, courage, and morale. In 1793–94, the French armies preserved their homeland. In 1794–95, they occupied the Low Countries; the Rhineland; and parts of Spain, Switzerland, and Savoy. In 1796, they invaded and occupied key parts of Italy and broke the coalition that had arrayed itself against them.

The Reign of Terror

In 1793, however, those victories lay in a hard-to-imagine future. France was in crisis. In 1793, the convention drafted a new democratic constitution based on male suffrage. That constitution never took effect—suspended indefinitely by wartime emergency. Instead, the convention delegated its responsibilities to a group of twelve leaders, the Committee of Public Safety. The committee had two purposes: to seize control of the revolution and to prosecute all the revolution's enemies—"to make terror the order of the day." The Terror proper lasted from September 1793–July 1794, but this was only the climax of a two-year period between the summer of 1792 and the summer of 1794 that saw repeated episodes of war and civil conflict. The Terror left a bloody and authoritarian legacy.

THE EXECUTION OF LOUIS XVI. The execution of Louis XVI shocked Europe, and even committed revolutionaries in France debated the necessity of such a dramatic act. The entire National Convention (a body of over seven hundred members) acted as jury, and although the assembly was nearly unanimous in finding the king guilty of treason, a majority of only one approved the final death sentence. Those who voted for Louis XVI's execution were known forever after as "regicides." ▪ *What made this act necessary from the point of view of the most radical of revolutionaries?* ▪ *What made it repugnant from the point of view of the revolution's most heated enemies?*

Perhaps the three best-known leaders of the radical revolution were Jean Paul Marat, Georges Jacques Danton, and Maximilien Robespierre, the latter two members of the Committee of Public Safety. Marat, educated as a physician, opposed nearly all of his moderate colleagues' assumptions. Persecuted by powerful factions in the constituent assembly who feared his radicalism, he was forced to take refuge in unsanitary sewers and dungeons. He persevered as the editor of the popular news sheet *The Friend of the People*. In the summer of 1793, at the height of the crisis of the revolution, he was stabbed in his bath by Charlotte Corday, a young royalist, and thus became a revolutionary martyr.

Danton, like Marat, was a popular political leader, well known in the more plebian clubs of Paris. Elected a member of the Committee of Public Safety in 1793, he had much to do with organizing the Terror. As time went on, however, he wearied of ruthlessness and displayed a tendency to compromise, which gave his opponents in the convention their opportunity. In April 1794, Danton was sent to the guillotine.

The most famous of the radical leaders was Maximilien Robespierre. Robespierre trained in law and quickly became a modestly successful lawyer. His eloquence and his consistent, or ruthless, insistence that leaders respect the "will of the people" eventually won him a following in the Jacobin club. Later, he became president of the National

Debating the French Revolution: Edmund Burke and Thomas Paine

The best known debate in English on the French Revolution set the Irish-born conservative Edmund Burke against the British radical Thomas Paine, who participated in both the American and French revolutions, and became an American citizen. Burke opposed the French Revolution from the beginning, because he believed that "rights" were not natural, but rather the product of specific historical traditions. In Reflections on the Revolution in France *(1970), he argued that the revolutionaries had undermined the fabric of French civilization by attempting to remodel the state without reference to tradition and custom.*

Thomas Paine responded to Burke in The Rights of Man *(1791–92) with a defense of the revolutionary concept of universal and natural rights. In the polarized atmosphere of the revolutionary period in Britain, simply possessing Paine's pamphlet was grounds for imprisonment.*

Edmund Burke

You will observe, that from the Magna Carta to the Declaration of Right, it has been the uniform policy of our constitution to claim and assert our liberties, as an entailed inheritance derived to us from our forefathers. . . . We have an inheritable crown; an inheritable peerage; and a house of commons and a people inheriting privileges, franchises, and liberties, from a long line of ancestors. . . .

You had all these advantages in your ancient states, but you chose to act as if you had never been moulded into civil society, and had every thing to begin anew. You began ill, because you began by despising every thing that belonged to you. . . . If the last generations of your country appeared without much luster in your eyes, you might have passed them by, and derived your claims from a more early race of ancestors. . . . Respecting your forefathers, you would have been taught to respect yourselves. You would not have chosen to consider the French as a people of yesterday, as a nation of low-born servile wretches until the emancipating year of 1789. . . . [Y]ou would not have been content to be represented as a gang of Maroon slaves, suddenly broke loose from the house of bondage, and therefore to be pardoned for your abuse of liberty to which you were not accustomed and ill fitted. . . .

. . . The fresh ruins of France, which shock our feelings wherever we can turn our eyes, are not the devastation of civil war; they are the sad but instructive monuments of rash and ignorant counsel in time of profound peace. They are the display of inconsiderate and presumptuous, because unresisted and irresistible, authority. . . .

Nothing is more certain, than that of our manners, our civilization, and all the good things which are connected with manners, and with civilization, have, in this European world of ours, depended upon two principles; and were indeed the result of both combined; I mean the spirit of a gentleman, and the spirit of religion. The nobility and the clergy, the one by profession, the other by patronage, kept learning in existence, even

---

Convention and a member of the Committee of Public Safety. Though he had little to do with starting the Terror, he was nevertheless responsible for enlarging its scope. "The Incorruptible," he came to represent ruthlessness justified as virtue and as necessary to revolutionary progress.

The two years of the radical Republic (August 1792–July 1794) brought dictatorship, centralization, suspension of any liberties, and war. The committee faced foreign enemies and opposition from both the political right and left at home. In June 1793, responding to an escalating crisis, leaders of the "Mountain," a party of radicals allied with Parisian artisans, purged moderates from the convention. Rebellions broke out in the provincial cities of Lyons, Bordeaux, and Marseilles, mercilessly repressed by the committee and its local representatives. The government also faced counterrevolution in the western region known as the Vendée, where movements enlisted peasants and artisans, who believed their local areas were being invaded and who fought for their local in the midst of arms and confusions.... Learning paid back what it received to nobility and priesthood.... Happy if they had all continued to know their indissoluble union, and their proper place.

Happy if learning, not debauched by ambition, had been satisfied to continue the instructor, and not aspired to be the master! Along with its natural protectors and guardians, learning will be cast into the mire, and trodden down under the hoofs of a swinish multitude.

Source: Edmund Burke, *Reflections on the Revolution in France (1790)* (New York: 1973), pp. 45, 48, 49, 52, 92.

Thomas Paine

Mr. Burke, with his usual outrage, abuses the *Declaration of the Rights of Man*.... Does Mr. Burke mean to deny that man has any rights? If he does, then he must mean that there are no such things as rights any where, and that he has none himself; for who is there in the world but man? But if Mr. Burke means to admit that man has rights, the question will then be, what are those rights, and how came man by them originally?

The error of those who reason by precedents drawn from antiquity, respecting the rights of man, is that they do not go far enough into antiquity. They stop in some of the intermediate stages of an hundred or a thousand years, and produce what was then a rule for the present day. This is no authority at all....

To possess ourselves of a clear idea of what government is, or ought to be, we must trace its origin. In doing this, we shall easily discover that governments must have arisen either *out* of the people, or *over* the people. Mr. Burke has made no distinction....

What were formerly called revolutions, were little more than a change of persons, or an alteration of local circumstances. They rose and fell like things of course, and had nothing in their existence or their fate that could influence beyond the spot that produced them. But what we now see in the world, from the revolutions of America and France, is a renovation of the natural order of things, a system of principles as universal as truth and the existence of man, and combining moral with political happiness and national prosperity.

Source: Thomas Paine, *The Rights of Man* (New York: 1973), pp. 302, 308, 383.

Questions for Analysis

1. How does Burke define *liberty*? Why does he criticize the revolutionaries for representing themselves as slaves freed from bondage?

2. What does Paine criticize about Burke's emphasis on history? According to Paine, what makes the French Revolution different from previous changes of regime in Europe?

3. How do these two authors' attitudes about the origins of human freedoms shape their understandings of the revolution?

---

priest or against the summons from the revolutionaries' conscription boards. Determined to stabilize France, whatever the cost, the committee launched murderous campaigns of pacification—torching villages, farms, and fields and killing all who dared oppose them as well as many who did not.

During the period of the Terror, from September 1793 to July 1794, the most reliable estimates place the number of deaths at close to 40,000—about 16,500 from actual death sentences, with the rest resulting from extrajudicial killings and deaths in prison. Approximately 300,000 were incarcerated between March 1793 and August 1794. These numbers, however, do not include the pacification of the Vendée and rebellious cities in the Rhone Valley, which took more than 100,000 lives. Few victims of the Terror were aristocrats. Many more were peasants or laborers accused of hoarding, treason, or counterrevolutionary activity. Anyone who appeared to threaten the republic, no matter what his or her social or economic position, was at risk.

The Legacy of the Second French Revolution

The "second" French Revolution affected the everyday life of French men, women, and children in a remarkably direct way. Workers' trousers replaced the breeches that had been a badge of the middle classes and the nobility. A red cap, said to symbolize freedom from slavery, became popular headgear, while wigs vanished. Men and women addressed each other as "citizen" or "citizeness." Public life was marked by ceremonies designed to dramatize the break with the Old Regime and celebrate new forms of fraternity. In the early stages of the revolution, these festivals seem to have captured genuine popular enthusiasm. Under the Committee of Public Safety, they became didactic and hollow.

The radical revolution of 1792–93 also dramatically reversed the trend toward decentralization and democracy. The assembly replaced local officials with "deputies on mission," whose task was to conscript troops and generate patriotic fervor. When these deputies appeared too eager to act independently, they were replaced by "national agents," with instructions to report directly to the committee. In another effort to stabilize authority, the assembly closed down all the women's political clubs, decreeing them a political and social danger. Ironically, those who claimed to govern in the name of the people found the popular movement threatening.

Finally, the revolution eroded the strength of those traditional institutions—church, guild, parish—that had for centuries given people a common bond. In their place now stood patriotic organizations and a culture that insisted on loyalty to one national cause. Those organizations had first emerged with the election campaigns, meetings, and pamphlet wars of 1788 and the interest they heightened. They included the political clubs and local assemblies, which at the height of the revolution (1792–93) met every day of the week and offered an apprenticeship in politics. The army of the republic become the premier national institution.

On the one hand, the revolution divided France, mobilizing counterrevolutionaries as well as revolutionaries. At the same time, the revolution, war, and the culture of sacrifice forged new bonds. The sense that the rest of Europe sought to crush the new nation and its citizens unquestionably strengthened French national identity.

FROM THE TERROR TO BONAPARTE: THE DIRECTORY

The Committee of Public Safety might have saved France from enemy armies but could not save itself. Inflation became catastrophic. The long string of military victories convinced growing numbers that the committee's demands for continuing self-sacrifice and Terror were no longer justified. By July 1794, the committee was virtually without allies. On July 27 (9 Thermidor, according to the new calendar), Robespierre was shouted down while attempting to speak on the floor of the convention. The following day, along with twenty-one associates, he met his death by guillotine.

Ending the Terror did not immediately bring moderation. Vigilante groups of royalists hunted down Jacobins. The repeal of price controls, combined with the worst winter in a century, caused widespread misery. Other measures that had constituted the Terror were gradually repealed. In 1795 the National Convention adopted a new and more conservative constitution. It granted suffrage to all adult male citizens who could read and write. Yet it set up indirect elections: citizens voted for electors, who in turn chose the legislative body. Wealthy citizens thus held authority. Eager to avoid personal dictatorship, the new constitution vested executive authority in a board of five men known as the Directory, chosen by the legislative body. The constitution included not only a bill of rights but also a declaration of the duties of the citizen.

The Directory lasted longer than its revolutionary predecessors. It still faced discontent on both the radical left and the conservative right. On the left, the Directory repressed radical movements to abolish private property and parliamentary-style government. Dispatching threats from

THE DEATH OF MARAT. This painting by the French artist David immortalized Marat. The note in the slain leader's hand is from Charlotte Corday, his assassin. ▪ **Why was it important to represent Marat as a martyr?**

PATRIOTIC WOMEN'S CLUB. The members of this patriotic club wear constitutional bonnets to show their support for the revolution and the reforms of the convention. ▪ *What can one conclude about the atmosphere in Paris during the revolution from the existence of such associations?*

the right proved more challenging. In 1797 the first free elections held in France as a republic returned a large number of monarchists to the councils of government, alarming politicians who had voted to execute Louis XVI. Backed by the army, the Directory annulled most of the election results. After two years of more uprisings and purges, and with the country still plagued by severe inflation, the Directors grew desperate. This time they called for help from a brilliant young general named Napoleon Bonaparte.

Bonaparte's first military victory had come in 1793, with the recapture of Toulon from royalist and British forces, and had earned him promotion from captain to brigadier general at the age of twenty-four. After the Terror, he was briefly arrested for his Jacobin associations. But he proved his usefulness to the Directory in October 1795 when he put down an uprising with "a whiff of grapeshot," saving the new regime from its opponents. Promoted, he won a string of victories in Italy, forcing Austria to withdraw (temporarily) from the war. He attempted to defeat Britain by attacking British forces in Egypt and the Near East, a campaign that went well on land but ran into trouble at sea, where the French fleet was defeated by Admiral Horatio Nelson (Aboukir Bay, 1798). Bonaparte found himself trapped in Egypt by the British and unable to win a decisive victory.

It was at this point that the call came from the Directory. Bonaparte slipped away from Egypt and appeared in Paris, already having agreed to participate in a coup d'état with the leading Director, that former revolutionary champion of the Third Estate, the Abbé Sieyès. On November 9, 1799

(18 Brumaire), Bonaparte was declared a "temporary consul." He was the answer to the Directory's prayers: a strong, popular leader who was not a king. Sieyès declared that Bonaparte would provide "confidence from below, authority from above." With those words Sieyès pronounced the end of the revolutionary period.

NAPOLEON AND IMPERIAL FRANCE

Few figures in Western history have compelled the attention of the world as Napoleon Bonaparte did during the fifteen years of his rule in France. Few men have lived on with such persistence as myth, not just in their own countries, but across the West. Why? For the great majority of ordinary Europeans, memories of the French Revolution were dominated by those of the Napoleonic wars, which devastated Europe, convulsed its politics, and traumatized its peoples for a generation.

And yet, Bonaparte's relationship to the revolution was not simple. His regime consolidated some of the revolution's political and social changes but sharply repudiated others. He presented himself as the son of the revolution, but he also borrowed freely from very different regimes, fashioning himself as the heir to Charlemagne or to the Roman Empire. His regime remade revolutionary politics and the French state; offered stunning examples of the new kinds of warfare; and left a legacy of conflict and legends of French glory that lingered in the dreams, or nightmares, of Europe's statesmen and citizens for more than a century.

Consolidating Authority: 1799–1804

Bonaparte owed his career to the revolution. The son of a provincial Corsican nobleman, he would have been unable to rise beyond the rank of major in prerevolutionary France, because he was not wealthy enough to buy a regimental command. The revolution, however, abolished the purchase of military office, and Bonaparte quickly became a general. Here, then, was a man who had risen from obscurity because of his own gifts, which he lent happily to the service of France's revolution.

Once in power, however, Bonaparte showed less respect for revolutionary principles. After the coup of 1799, he assumed the title of "First Consul." A new constitution established universal white male suffrage and set up two legislative bodies. Elections, however, were indirect, and the power of the legislative bodies sharply curbed. "The

Interpreting Visual Evidence

Representing the People during the French Revolution

From the moment the population of Paris came to the assistance of the beleaguered National Assembly in July 1789, representations of "the people" in the French Revolution took on an overwhelming significance. Building a new government that was committed to an idea of popular sovereignty meant that both the revolution's supporters and its opponents were deeply invested in shaping perceptions of the people. And of course, Article III of the Declaration of the Rights of Man ("The principle of sovereignty resides essentially in the na-

tion") meant that any individual, group, or institution that could successfully claim to represent the will of the people could wield tremendous power, so long as others accepted that claim.

Of course, revolutionary crowds did not always conform to the images of them that circulated so widely in prints and paintings during the period 1789–99. Some were spontaneous, and others were organized; some were made up of recognizable social and professional groups with clear political goals, and others were a hodgepodge of conflicting and even inarticulate aspirations. Many were nonviolent; some were exceedingly

threatening and murderous. All politicians sought to use them to support their political programs, and many learned to fear their unpredictable behavior.

These four images give a sense of the competing visions of the people that appeared in the public realm during the French Revolution. The first (image A) shows the killing of Foulon, a royal official who was lynched and beheaded by an enthusiastic crowd barely a week after the fall of the Bastille because he was suspected of conspiring to starve the Parisian population as punishment for their rebellion against the king. The second (image B) shows a more carefully

A. The punishment of Foulon (revolutionary print, 1789).

B. *The Festival of Federation* by Charles Thévenin, 1790.

choreographed representation of the people during the Festival of Federation, organized in July 1790 by the revolutionary government to commemorate the first anniversary of the fall of the Bastille. Finally, the last two documents show contrasting images of the revolutionary *sans-culottes,* the working-class revolutionaries who supported the government during the Terror in 1792–94. The first (image C), a sympathetic portrait of a sans-culottes as a virtuous and self-sacrificing working man, standing with an eye to the future, seems completely incongruous when paired with the British satirist James Gilray's portrait of a cannibalistic sans-culottes family (image D), drawn literally "without pants," feasting on the bodies of their victims after a hard day's work.

Questions for Analysis

1. Image A depicts an event from July 1789—that is, before the August publication of the Declaration of the Rights of Man. How does this image portray the crowd's vengeance on Foulon? What possible political messages are contained in this image?

2. Image B, on the other hand, chooses to display the people celebrating their own birth as a political body, by convening on the anniversary of the fall of the Bastille. What emotions is this painting designed to invoke, and how is it related to more disturbing images such as Image A?

3. How are the positive and negative portrayals of sans-culottes as political actors (Images C and D) constructed? Can one imagine a painting of a worker like Image C being produced before 1789? What does Image D tell us about how the revolution was viewed from Britain?

C. *A Sans-Culotte* by Louis-Léopold Boilly, 1792.

D. A family of sans-culotts [sic] refreshing after the fatigues of the day. (British satirical cartoon by James Gilray, 1793).

government?" said one observer. "There is Bonaparte." Bonaparte instituted what has since become a common authoritarian device, the plebiscite, which put a question directly to popular vote. This allows the head of state to bypass politicians or legislative bodies who might disagree with him—as well as permitting local officials to tamper with ballot boxes. In 1802, flush with victory abroad, he asked the legislature to proclaim him consul for life. When the senate refused to do so, Bonaparte's Council of State stepped in, offered him the title, and had it ratified by plebiscite. Throughout, his regime retained the appearance of consulting with the people, but its most important feature was the centralization of authority.

That authority came from reorganizing the state, and on this score Bonaparte's accomplishments were extraordinary and lasting. Bonaparte's regime confirmed the abolition of privilege, thereby promising "careers open to talent." He also accomplished what no recent French regime had yet achieved: an orderly and generally fair system of taxation. More efficient tax collection and fiscal management also helped halt the inflationary spiral that had crippled the revolutionary governments, although Bonaparte's regime relied heavily on resources from areas he had conquered to fund his military ventures. He replaced elected officials and local self-government with centrally appointed prefects and subprefects, who answered directly to the Council of State in Paris. The prefects were in charge of everything from collecting statistics and reporting on the economy and the population to education, roads, and public works. With more integrated administration, a more professional bureaucracy, and more rational and efficient taxation (though the demands of war strained the system), Napoleon's state marked the transition from Bourbon absolutism to the modern state.

Law, Education, and a New Elite

Napoleon's most significant contribution to modern state building was the promulgation of a new legal code in 1804. The Napoleonic Code, as the civil code came to be called, pivoted on two principles that had remained significant through all the constitutional changes since 1789: uniformity and individualism. It cleared through the thicket of contradictory legal traditions that governed the ancient provinces of France, creating one uniform law. It confirmed the abolition of feudal privileges of all kinds: not only noble and clerical privileges but the special rights of craft guilds, municipalities, and so on. It set the conditions for exercising property rights: the drafting of contracts, leases, and stock companies. The code's provisions on the family, which

Napoleon developed personally, insisted on the importance of paternal authority and the subordination of women and children. In 1793, during the most radical period of the revolution, men and women had been declared "equal in marriage"; now Napoleon's code affirmed the "natural supremacy" of the husband. Married women could not sell property, run a business, or have a profession without their husbands' permission. Fathers had the sole right to control their children's financial affairs, consent to their marriages, and (under the ancient right of correction) to imprison them for up to six months without showing cause. Divorce remained legal, but under unequal conditions; a man could sue for divorce on the grounds of adultery, but a woman could do so only if her husband moved his "concubine" into the family's house. Most important to the common people, the code prohibited paternity suits for illegitimate children.

In all, Napoleon developed seven legal codes covering commercial law, civil law and procedures, crime, and punishment. Like the civil code, the new criminal code consolidated some of the gains of the revolution, treating citizens as equals before the law and outlawing arbitrary arrest and imprisonment. Yet it, too, reinstated brutal measures that the revolutionaries had abolished, such as branding and cutting off the hands of parricides. The Napoleonic legal regime was more egalitarian than law under the Old Regime but no less authoritarian.

Napoleon also rationalized the educational system. He ordered the establishment of *lycées* (high schools) in every major town, and a school in Paris to train teachers. He brought the military and technical schools under state control and founded a national university to supervise the entire system. He built a new military academy and reorganized the premier schools of higher education, to which students would be admitted based on examinations and from which would issue the technical, educational, and political elites of the country. These reforms reinforced measures introduced during the revolution, and were intended to abolish privilege and create "careers open to talent." Napoleon also embraced the social and physical sciences of the Enlightenment. He sponsored the Institute of France, divided into four sections, or academies: fine arts, sciences, humanities, and language (the famous Académie française). These academies, created under the monarchy, acquired under Napoleon the character that they have preserved to this day: centralized, meritocratic, and geared to serving the state.

To win support for these ambitious reforms, Bonaparte made allies without regard for their past political affiliations. He admitted back into the country exiles of all political stripes. His two fellow consuls were a regicide of the Terror and a bureaucrat of the Old Regime. His minister of police had been an extreme radical republican; his minister of foreign affairs was the aristocrat and opportunist Charles Talleyrand. The most remarkable act of political reconciliation came in 1801, with Bonaparte's concordat with the pope, an agreement that put an end to more than a decade of hostility between the French state and the Catholic Church. Although it shocked anticlerical revolutionaries, Napoleon, ever the pragmatist, believed that reconciliation would create domestic harmony and international solidarity. The agreement gave the pope the right to depose French bishops and to discipline the French clergy. In return, the Vatican agreed to forgo any claims to church lands expropriated by the revolution. That property would remain in the hands of its new middle-class rural and urban proprietors. The concordat did not revoke the principle of religious freedom established by the revolution, but it did win Napoleon the support of conservatives who had feared for France's future as a godless state.

Such political balancing acts increased Bonaparte's general popularity. Combined with early military successes (peace with Austria in 1801 and with Britain in 1802), they muffled any opposition to his personal ambitions. He had married Josephine de Beauharnais, a Creole from Martinique who had been the mistress of several revolutionary leaders after the execution of her first husband in the Terror. Josephine had given the Corsican soldier-politician legitimacy and access among the revolutionary elite early

NAPOLEON'S EUROPEAN EMPIRE AT ITS HEIGHT. At the height of his power in 1812, Napoleon controlled most of Europe, ruling either directly or through dependent states and allies. ▪ *By what means did Napoleon expand French control over continental Europe?* ▪ *Which major countries remained outside of French control?* ▪ *Which areas felt the most long-lasting impact of Napoleon's reign?*

in his career. Neither Bonaparte nor his ambitious wife were content to be first among equals, however; and in December of 1804, he finally cast aside any traces of republicanism. In a ceremony that evoked the splendor of medieval kingship and Bourbon absolutism, he crowned himself Emperor Napoleon I in the Cathedral of Notre Dame in Paris. Napoleon did much to create the modern state, but he did not hesitate to proclaim his links to the past.

In Europe as in France: Napoleon's Empire

The nations of Europe had looked on—some in admiration, others in horror, all in astonishment—at the phenomenon that was Napoleon. Austria, Prussia, and Britain led two coalitions against revolutionary France in 1792–95 and in 1798, and both were defeated. After Napoleon came to power in 1799, the alliance split. Russia and Austria withdrew from the fray in 1801, and even the intransigent British were forced to make peace the following year.

By 1805 the Russians, Prussians, Austrians, and Swedes had joined the British in an attempt to contain France. Their efforts were to no avail. Napoleon's military superiority led to defeats, in turn, of all the continental allies. Napoleon

NAPOLEON ON HORSEBACK AT THE ST. BERNARD PASS **BY JACQUES LOUIS DAVID, 1801.** David painted many episodes of the revolution: the Tennis Court Oath, the death of Marat, and the rise and rule of Napoleon. Here Napoleon heroically leads his troops over the Alps into Italy to attack Austrian troops.

was a master of well-timed, well-directed shock attacks on the battlefield: movement, regrouping, and pressing his advantage. He led an army that had transformed European warfare; first raised as a revolutionary militia, it was now a trained conscript army, loyal, well supplied by a nation whose economy was committed to serving the war effort, and led by generals promoted largely on the basis of talent. This new kind of army inflicted crushing defeats on his enemies. The battle of Austerlitz, in December 1805, was a triumph for the French against the combined forces of Austria and Russia and became a symbol of the emperor's apparent invincibility. His subsequent victory against the Russians at Friedland in 1807 only added to his reputation.

Out of these victories Napoleon created his new empire and affiliated states. To the southeast, the empire included Rome and the pope's dominions, Tuscany, and the Dalmatian territories of Austria (now the coastline of Croatia). To the east Napoleon's rule extended over a federation of German states known as the Confederation of the Rhine and a section of Poland. These new states served as a military buffer against renewed expansion by Austria. The empire itself was ringed by the allied kingdoms of Italy, Naples, Spain, and Holland, whose thrones were occupied by Napoleon's brothers, brothers-in-law, and trusted generals.

The empire brought the French Revolution's practical consequences—a powerful, centralizing state and an end to old systems of privilege—to Europe's doorstep, applying to the empire principles that had already transformed France. Administrative modernization, which meant overhauling the procedures, codes, and practices of the state, was the most powerful feature of the changes introduced. The empire changed the terms of government service ("careers open to talent"), handing out new titles and recruiting new men for the civil service and the judiciary. It ended the nobility's monopoly on the officer corps. The new branches of government hired engineers, mapmakers, surveyors, and legal consultants. Public works and education were reorganized. Prefects in the outer reaches of the empire, as in France, built roads, bridges, dikes (in Holland), hospitals, and prisons; they reorganized universities and built observatories. In the empire and some of the satellite kingdoms, tariffs were eliminated, feudal dues abolished, new tax districts formed, and plentiful new taxes collected to support the new state.

In the realm of liberty and law, Napoleon's rule eliminated feudal and church courts and created a single legal system. The Napoleonic Code was often introduced, but not always or entirely. Reforms eliminated many inequalities and legal privileges. In most areas, the empire gave civil rights to Protestants and Jews. In some areas, Catholic monasteries, convents, and other landholdings were broken up and sold, almost always to wealthy buyers. In the empire as in France, and under Napoleon as during the revolution, many who benefited were the elite: people and groups already on their way up and with the resources to take advantage of opportunities.

In government, the regime sought a combination of legal equality (for men) and stronger state authority. The French and local authorities created new electoral districts, expanded suffrage, and wrote constitutions, but newly elected representative bodies were dismissed if they failed to cooperate, few constitutions were ever fully applied, and political freedoms were often fleeting. Napoleon's regime referred to revolutionary principles to anchor its legitimacy, but authority remained its guiding light. All governmental direction emanated from Paris and therefore from Napoleon.

Finally, in the empire as in France, Napoleon displayed his signature passions. The first of these was an Enlightenment zeal for accumulating useful knowledge. The empire gathered statistics as never before, for it was important to know the resources—including population—that a state had at its disposal. Napoleon's second passion was cultivating his relationship to imperial glories of the past. He poured time and energy into (literally) cementing his image for posterity. The Arc de Triomphe in Paris, designed to imitate the Arch of Constantine in Rome, is the best example; but Napoleon also ordered work to be undertaken to restore ruins in Rome, to make the Prado Palace in Madrid a museum, and to renovate and preserve the Alhambra in Granada.

Such were Napoleon's visions of his legacy and himself. How did others see him? Europe offered no single reaction. Some countries and social groups collaborated enthusiastically, some negotiated, some resisted. Napoleon's image as a military hero genuinely inspired young men from the elite, raised in a culture that prized military honor. Yet the Napoleonic presence proved a mixed blessing. Vassal states contributed heavily to the maintenance of the emperor's military power. The French levied taxes, drafted men, and required states to support occupying armies. In Italy, the policy was called "liberty and requisitions"; and the Italians, Germans, and Dutch paid an especially high price for reforms—in terms of economic cost and numbers of men recruited. From the point of view of the common people, the local lord and priest had been replaced by the French tax collector and army recruiting board.

THE RETURN TO WAR AND NAPOLEON'S DEFEAT: 1806–15

Napoleon's boldest attempt at consolidation, a policy banning British goods from the Continent, was a dangerous failure. Britain had bitterly opposed each of France's revolutionary regimes since the death of Louis XVI; now it tried to rally Europe against Napoleon with promises of generous financial loans and trade. Napoleon's Continental System, established in 1806, sought to starve Britain's trade and force its surrender. The system failed for several reasons. Throughout the war Britain retained control of the seas, and the British naval blockade of the Continent, begun in 1807, effectively countered Napoleon's system. While the French Empire strained to transport goods and raw materials overland to avoid the British blockade, the British successfully developed a lively trade with South America. A second reason for the failure of the system was its internal tariffs. Europe divided into economic camps, at odds with each other as they tried to subsist on what the Continent alone could produce and manufacture. Finally, the system hurt the Continent more than Britain. Stagnant trade in Europe's ports and unemployment in its manufacturing centers eroded public faith in Napoleon's dream of a working European empire.

The Continental System was Napoleon's first serious mistake. His ambition to create a European empire, modeled on Rome and ruled from Paris, was to become a second cause of his decline. The symbols of his empire—reflected in painting, architecture, and the design of furniture and clothing—were deliberately Roman in origin. Where early revolutionaries referred to the Roman Republic for their imagery, Napoleon looked to the more ostentatious style of the Roman emperors. In 1809 he divorced the empress Josephine and ensured himself a successor of royal blood by marrying a Habsburg princess, Marie Louise—the great-niece of Marie-Antionette. Such actions lost Napoleon the support of revolutionaries, former Enlightenment thinkers, and liberals across the Continent.

Over time, the bitter tonic of defeat began to have an effect on Napoleon's enemies, who changed their own approach to waging war. After the Prussian army was humiliated at Jena in 1806 and forced out of the war, a whole generation of younger Prussian officers reformed their military and their state by demanding rigorous practical training for commanders and a genuinely national army made up of patriotic Prussian citizens rather than well-drilled mercenaries.

The myth of Napoleon's invincibility worked against him as well, as he took ever-greater risks with France's military and national fortunes. Russian troops and Austrian artillery inflicted horrendous losses on the French at Wagram in 1809, although these difficulties were forgotten in the glow of victory. Napoleon's allies and supporters shrugged off the British admiral Horatio Nelson's victory at Trafalgar in 1805 as no more than a temporary check to the emperor's ambitions. But Trafalgar broke French naval power in the Mediterranean and led to a rift with Spain, which had been

France's equal partner in the battle and suffered equally in the defeat. In the Caribbean, too, Napoleon was forced to cut growing losses (see page 447).

A crucial moment in Napoleon's undoing came with his invasion of Spain in 1808. Napoleon overthrew the Spanish king, installed his own brother on the throne, and then imposed a series of reforms similar to those he had instituted elsewhere in Europe. Napoleon's blow against the Spanish monarchy weakened its hold on its colonies across the Atlantic, and the Spanish crown never fully regained its grip (see Chapter 20). But in Spain itself, Napoleon reckoned without two factors that led to the ultimate failure of his mission: the presence of British forces and the determined resistance of the Spanish people, who detested Napoleon's interference in the affairs of the church. The Peninsular Wars, as the Spanish conflicts were called, were long and bitter. The smaller British force laid siege to French garrison towns, and the Spanish quickly began to wear down the French invaders through guerrilla warfare. Terrible atrocities were committed by both sides; the French military's torture and execution of Spanish guerrillas and civilians was immortalized by the Spanish artist Francisco Goya (1746–1828) with sickening realism in his prints and paintings. The Spanish campaign was the first indication that Napoleon could be beaten, and it encouraged resistance elsewhere.

The second, and most dramatic stage in Napoleon's downfall began with the disruption of his alliance with Russia. In 1811, Napoleon grew tired of Russia's violations of the Continental System. Tsar Alexander I had turned a blind eye toward trade with Britain because it provided important outlets for Russian grain. To punish Russia, Napoleon collected the largest army ever assembled on the continent: the six-hundred-thousand-strong "Grande Armée." The invasion began in the spring of 1812. The Russians, vastly outmanned, refused to meet Napoleon's army and withdrew deep into the countryside. After an inconsequential victory over Russian forces at Borodino, Napoleon reached Moscow only to find that partisans had burned the Russian capital before departing. Unable to force the tsar to surrender, Napoleon was forced to retreat as the Russian winter set in, with devastating effects on his remaining soldiers. Frostbite, disease, starvation, and almost continuous harrassment by mounted Cossacks reduced Napoleon's army to a few thousand survivors when the emperor arrived in Germany in December, 1812.

After the retreat from Russia, the anti-Napoleonic forces took renewed hope. United by a belief that they might finally succeed in defeating the emperor, Prussia, Russia, Austria, Sweden, and Britain renewed their attack. Citizens of many German states in particular saw this as a war of liberation, and indeed most of the fighting took place in Germany. The climax of the campaign occurred in October 1813 when,

***THE 3RD OF MAY, 1808* BY FRANCISCO GOYA.** This painting of the execution of Spanish rebels by Napoleon's army as it marched through Spain is one of the most memorable depictions of a nation's martyrdom.

at what was thereafter known as the Battle of the Nations, fought near Leipzig, the allies dealt the French a resounding defeat. Meanwhile, allied armies won significant victories in the Low Countries and Spain. By the beginning of 1814, they had crossed the Rhine into France. Left with an army of inexperienced youths, Napoleon retreated to Paris, urging the French people to resist despite constant setbacks at the hands of the larger invading armies. On March 31, Tsar Alexander I of Russia and King Frederick William III of Prussia made their triumphant entry into Paris. Napoleon was forced to abdicate unconditionally and was sent into exile on the island of Elba, off the Italian coast.

Napoleon was back on French soil in less than a year. In the interim the allies had restored the Bourbon dynasty to the throne, in the person of Louis XVIII, brother of Louis XVI. Despite his administrative abilities, Louis could not fill the void left by Napoleon's abdication. It was no surprise that, when the former emperor staged his escape from Elba, his fellow countrymen once more rallied to his side. By the time Napoleon reached Paris, he had generated enough support to cause Louis to flee the country. The allies, meeting in Vienna to conclude peace treaties with the French, were stunned by the news of Napoleon's return. They dispatched a hastily organized army to meet the emperor's characteristically bold offensive push into Belgium. At the battle of Waterloo, fought over three bloody days from June 15 to 18, 1815, Napoleon was stopped by the forces of his two most persistent enemies, Britain and Prussia, and suffered his final defeat. This time the allies took no chances and shipped their prisoner off to the bleak island of St. Helena in the South Atlantic. The once-mighty emperor, now the exile Bonaparte, lived out a dreary existence writing self-serving memoirs until his death in 1821.

Liberty, Politics, and Slavery: The Haitian Revolution

In the French colonies across the Atlantic, the revolution took a different course, with wide-ranging ramifications. The Caribbean islands of Guadeloupe, Martinique, and Saint-Domingue occupied a central role in the eighteenth-century French economy because of the sugar trade. Their planter elites had powerful influence in Paris. The French National Assembly (like its American counterpart) declined to discuss the matter of slavery in the colonies, unwilling to encroach on the property rights of slave owners and fearful of losing the lucrative sugar islands to their British or Spanish rivals should disgruntled slave owners talk of independence from France. (Competition between the European powers for the islands of the Caribbean was intense; that islands would change hands was a real possibility.) French men in the National Assembly also had to consider the question of rights for free men of color, a group that included a significant number of wealthy owners of property (and slaves).

Saint-Domingue had about forty thousand whites of different social classes, thirty thousand free people of color, and five hundred thousand slaves, most of them recently enslaved in West Africa. In 1790, free people of color from Saint-Domingue sent a delegation to Paris, asking to be seated by the assembly, underscoring that they were men of property and, in many cases, of European ancestry. The assembly refused. Their refusal sparked a rebellion among free people of color in Saint-Domingue. The French colonial authorities repressed the movement quickly—and brutally. They captured Vincent Ogé, a member of the delegation to Paris and one of the leaders of the rebellion, and publicly executed him and his allies by breaking on the wheel and decapitation. Radical deputies, in Paris, including Robespierre, expressed outrage but could do little to change the assembly's policy.

In August 1791 the largest slave rebellion in history broke out in Saint-Domingue. How much that rebellion owed to revolutionary propaganda is unclear; like many rebellions during the period, it had its own roots. The British and the Spanish invaded, confident they could crush the rebellion and take the island. In the spring of 1792, the French government, on the verge of collapse and war with Europe, scrambled to win allies in Saint-Domingue by making free men of color citizens. A few months later (after the revolution of August 1792), the new French Republic dispatched commissioners to Saint-Domingue with troops and instructions to hold the island. There they faced a combination of different forces: Spanish and British troops, defiant Saint-Domingue planters, and slaves in rebellion.

TOUSSAINT L'OUVERTURE. A portrait of L'Ouverture, leader of what would become the Haitian Revolution, as a general.

In this context, the local French commissioners reconsidered their commitment to slavery; in 1793 they promised freedom to slaves who would join the French. A year later, the assembly in Paris extended to slaves in all the colonies a liberty that had already been accomplished in Saint-Domingue, by the slave rebellion.

Emancipation and war brought new leaders to the fore, chief among them a former slave, Toussaint Bréda, later Toussaint L'Ouverture (*too-SAN LOO-vehr-tur*), meaning "the one who opened the way." Over the course of the next five years, Toussaint and his soldiers, now allied with the French army, emerged victorious over the French planters, the British (in 1798), and the Spanish (in 1801). Toussaint also broke the power of his rival generals in both the mulatto and former slave armies, becoming the statesman of the revolution. In 1801, Toussaint set up a constitution, swearing allegiance to France but denying France any right to interfere in Saint-Domingue affairs. The constitution abolished slavery, reorganized the military, established Christianity as the state religion (this entailed a rejection of vodou, a blend of Christian and various West and Central African traditions), and made Toussaint governor for life. It was an extraordinary moment in the revolutionary period: the formation of an authoritarian society but also an utterly unexpected symbol of the universal potential of revolutionary ideas.

Toussaint's accomplishments, however, put him on a collision course with the other French general he admired and whose career was remarkably like his own: Napoleon Bonaparte. Saint-Domingue stood at the center of Bonaparte's vision of an expanded empire in the New World, an empire that would recoup North American territories France had lost under the Old Regime and pivot around the lucrative combination of the Mississippi, French Louisiana, and the sugar and slave colonies of the Caribbean. In January 1802, Bonaparte dispatched twenty thousand troops to bring the island under control. Toussaint, captured when he arrived for discussions with the French, was shipped under heavy guard to a prison in the mountains of eastern France, where he died in 1803. Fighting continued in Saint-Domingue, however, with fires now fueled by Bonaparte's decree reestablishing slavery where the convention had abolished it. The war turned into a nightmare for the French. Yellow fever killed thousands of French troops, including Napoleon's brother-in-law, one of his best generals. Armies on both sides committed atrocities. By December 1803 the French army had collapsed. Napoleon scaled back his vision of an American empire and sold the Louisiana territories to Thomas Jefferson. In Saint-Domingue, a general in the army of former slaves, Jean-Jacques Dessalines, declared the independent state of Haiti in 1804.

The Haitian Revolution remained, in significant ways, an anomaly. It was the only successful slave revolution in history and by far the most radical of the revolutions that occurred in this age. It suggested that the emancipatory ideas of the revolution and Enlightenment might apply to non-Europeans and enslaved peoples—a suggestion that residents of Europe attempted to ignore but one that struck home with planter elites in North and South America. Combined with later rebellions in the British colonies, it contributed to the British decision to end slavery in 1838. And it cast a long shadow over nineteenth-century slave societies from the southern United States to Brazil. The Napoleonic episode, then, had wide-ranging effects across the Atlantic: in North America, the Louisiana purchase; in the Caribbean, the Haitian Revolution; in Latin America, the weakening of Spain and Portugal's colonial empires.

CONCLUSION

The tumultuous events in France formed part of a broad pattern of late-eighteenth-century democratic upheaval. The French Revolution was the most violent, protracted,

After You Read This Chapter

Visit StudySpace for quizzes, additional review materials, and multi-media documents. **wwnorton.com/studyspace**

REVIEWING THE OBJECTIVES

- The French Revolution resulted both from an immediate political crisis and long-term social tensions. What was this crisis, and how did it lead to popular revolt against the monarchy?

- The revolutionaries in the National Assembly in 1789 set out to produce a constitution for France. What were their political goals, and what was the reaction of monarchs and peoples elsewhere in Europe?

- After 1792, a more radical group of revolutionaries seized control of the French state. How did they come to power, and how were their political goals different from their predecssors?

- Napoleon's career began during the revolution. What did he owe to the revolution, and what was different about his regime?

- Three major revolutions took place in the Atlantic world at the end of the eighteenth century: the American Revolution, the French Revolution, and the Haitian Revolution. What was similar about these revolutions? What was different?

and contentious of the revolutions of the era; but the dynamics of revolution were much the same everywhere. One of the most important developments of the French Revolution was the emergence of a popular movement, which included political clubs representing people previously excluded from politics, newspapers read by and to the common people, and political leaders who spoke for the sans-culottes. In the French Revolution as in other revolutions, the popular movement challenged the early and moderate revolutionary leadership, pressing for more radical and democratic measures. And as in other revolutions, the popular movement in France was defeated, and authority was reestablished by a quasi-military figure. Likewise, the revolutionary ideas of liberty, equality, and fraternity were not specifically French; their roots lay in the social structures of the eighteenth century and in the ideas and culture of the Enlightenment. Yet French armies brought them, literally, to the doorsteps of many Europeans.

What was the larger impact of the revolution and the Napoleonic era? Its legacy is partly summed up in three key concepts: liberty, equality, and nation. *Liberty* meant individual rights and responsibilities and, more specifically, freedom from arbitrary authority. By *equality*, as we have seen, the revolutionaries meant the abolition of legal distinctions of rank among European men. Though their concept of equality was limited, it became a powerful mobilizing force in the nineteenth century. The most important legacy of the revolution may have been the new term *nation*. Nationhood was a political concept. A nation was formed of citizens, not a king's subjects; it was ruled by law and treated citizens as equal before the law; sovereignty did not lie in dynasties or historic fiefdoms but in the nation of citizens. This new form of nation gained legitimacy when citizen armies repelled attacks against their newly won freedoms; the victories of "citizens in arms" lived on in myth and history and provided the most powerful images of the period. As the war continued, military nationhood began to overshadow its political cousin. By the Napoleonic period, this shift became decisive; a new political body of freely associated citizens was most powerfully embodied in a centralized state, its army, and a kind of citizenship defined by individual commitment to the needs of the nation at war. This understanding of national identity spread throughout Europe in the coming decades.

PEOPLE, IDEAS, AND EVENTS IN CONTEXT

- Why was **LOUIS XVI** forced to convene the **ESTATES GENERAL** in 1789?
- What argument did **ABBÉ SIEYÈS** make about the role of the **THIRD ESTATE**?
- What made the **TENNIS COURT OATH** a revolutionary act?
- What was the role of popular revolt (the attack on the **BASTILLE**, the **GREAT FEAR**, the **OCTOBER DAYS**) in the revolutionary movements of 1789?
- What was the connection between the French Revolution with the **SLAVE REVOLT IN SAINT-DOMINGUE** that began in 1791?
- What was the **DECLARATION OF THE RIGHTS OF MAN AND OF THE CITIZEN**?
- What was the **CIVIL CONSTITUTION OF THE CLERGY**?
- What circumstances led to the abolition of the monarchy in 1792?
- Why did the **JACOBINS** in the **NATIONAL CONVENTION** support a policy of **TERROR**?
- What were **NAPOLEON'S** most significant domestic accomplishments in France? What significance did **NAPOLEON'S MILITARY CAMPAIGNS** have for other parts of Europe and for the French Empire?
- What was the significance of the **HAITIAN REVOLUTION** of 1804?

CONSEQUENCES

- Was the French Revolution a success? Why or why not?
- Who benefited from the French Revolution? Who suffered the most from its consequences?
- In what ways do you think the French Revolution would have an impact on nineteenth-century history?

STORY LINES

- Industrialization put Europe on the path to a new form of economic development, based on the concentration of labor and production in areas with easy access to new sources of energy. This led to rapid growth of new industrial cities and the development of new transportation links to connect industrial centers to growing markets.

- Industrialization created new social groups in society, defined by their place in the new economy. Workers faced new kinds of discipline in the workplace, and women and children entered the industrial workforce in large numbers. A new elite, made up of entrepreneurs, bankers, engineers, and merchants emerged as the primary beneficiaries of industrialization.

- Population growth spurred migration to cities where laborers and the middle classes did not mix socially. They adopted different forms of dress, speech, leisure activities, and had significantly different opportunities when it came to marriage, sex, family life, and the raising of children.

CHRONOLOGY

1780s	Industrialization begins in Britain
1825	First railroad in Britain
1830s	Industrialization begins in France and Belgium
1845–1849	Irish Potato Famine
1850s	Industrialization begins in Prussia and German states of central Europe
1861	Russian tsar emancipates the serfs

Before You Read This Chapter

The Industrial Revolution and Nineteenth-Century Society

CORE OBJECTIVES

- **UNDERSTAND** the circumstances that allowed for industrialization to begin in Great Britain.

- **IDENTIFY** the industries that were the first to adopt new systems for mechanical production and the regions in Europe in which they thrived.

- **DESCRIBE** changes in the nature of work, production, and employment that occurred as a result of the mechanization of industry.

- **EXPLAIN** the effects of industrialization on social life in Europe, especially in the new urban centers associated with industrial development.

- **IDENTIFY** the essential characteristics of the new "middle-classes" in nineteenth-century Europe and their differences from property-owning groups prior to the Industrial Revolution.

The French Revolution transformed the political landscape of Europe suddenly and dramatically. More gradual, but just as consequential for the modern world, was the economic transformation that began in Europe in the 1780s. Following the development of mechanized industry and the emergence of large-scale manufacturing in the British textile trade, industrialization spread to the European Continent and eventually to North America. This "Industrial Revolution" led to the proliferation of more capital-intensive enterprises, new ways of organizing human labor, and the rapid growth of cities. It was accompanied by population growth and made possible by new sources of energy and power, which led to faster forms of mechanized transportation, higher productivity, and the emergence of large consumer markets for manufactured goods. In turn, these interrelated developments triggered social and cultural changes with revolutionary consequences for Europeans and their relationship to the rest of the world.

Of all the changes, perhaps the most revolutionary came at the very root of human endeavor: new forms of energy. Over the space of two or three generations, a society and an economy

451

that had drawn on water, wind, and wood for most of its energy needs came to depend on machines driven by steam engines and coal. In 1800, the world produced ten million tons of coal. In 1900, it produced one billion: a hundred times more. The Industrial Revolution brought the beginning of the fossil-fuel age, altering as it did so the balance of humanity and the environment.

Mechanization made possible enormous gains in productivity in some sectors of the economy, but to focus only on mechanization can be misleading. The new machines were limited to a few sectors of the economy, especially at the outset, and did not always lead to a dramatic break with older techniques. Above all, technology did not dispense with human toil. Historians emphasize that the Industrial Revolution intensified human labor—carrying water on iron rails, digging trenches, harvesting cotton, sewing by hand, or pounding hides—much more often than it eased it. One historian has suggested that we would do better to speak of the "industrious revolution." This revolution did not lie solely in machines but in a new economic system based on mobilizing capital and labor on a much larger scale. The industrious economy redistributed wealth and power, creating new social classes and producing new social tensions.

It also prompted deep-seated cultural shifts. The English critic Raymond Williams has pointed out that in the eighteenth century, *industry* referred to a human quality: a hardworking woman was "industrious," an ambitious clerk showed "industry." By the middle of the nineteenth century, industry had come to mean an economic system, one that followed its own logic and worked on its own—seemingly independent of humans. This is our modern understanding of the term, and it was born in the early nineteenth century. As the Industrial Revolution altered the foundations of the economy, it also changed the very assumptions with which people approached economics and the ways in which they regarded the role of human beings in the economy. These new assumptions could foster a sense of power but also anxieties about powerlessness. The new economy created both opportunity and a new kind of vulnerability for those whose livelihoods were threatened by industrialization. This dynamic ensured that the industrial era would be marked by new forms of social conflict, as well as new forms of wealth.

THE INDUSTRIAL REVOLUTION IN BRITAIN, 1760–1850

Industrialization began in the north of Britain in the late 1700s. In part this was due to a set of fortunate circumstances: Britain was a secure island nation with a robust

ENCLOSED FIELDS IN CENTRAL BRITAIN. The large, uniform, square fields in the background of this photograph are fields that were enclosed from smaller holdings and common lands in the 1830s. They contrast with the smaller and older strip fields in the foreground. The larger enclosed fields were more profitable for their owners, who benefited from legislation that encouraged enclosure, but the process created hardship for the village communities that depended on the use of these lands for their survival. ▪ *What circumstances made enclosure possible?* ▪ *What connection have historians made between enclosure and early industrialization?*

empire, profitable overseas trade networks, and established credit institutions. Perhaps even more important, Britain had ample supplies of coal lying close to the surface, and a well-developed transportation network in its many rivers and canals.

In addition to these advantages, British agriculture was already more thoroughly commercialized than elsewhere. British farming had been transformed by a combination of new techniques and new crops, as well as by the "enclosure" of fields and pastures, which turned small holdings, and in many cases commonly held lands, into large fenced tracts that were privately owned by commercial landlords. The British Parliament encouraged enclosure with a series of bills in the second half of the eighteenth century. Commercialized agriculture was more productive and yielded more food for a growing and increasingly urban population. The concentration of property in fewer hands drove small farmers off the land, sending them to look for work in other sectors of the economy. Finally, commercialized agriculture produced higher profits, wealth that could be invested in industry.

A key precondition for industrialization, therefore, was Britain's growing supply of available capital, in the forms of private wealth and well-developed banking and credit institutions. London had become the leading center for international trade, and the city was a headquarters for the transfer of raw material, capital, and manufactured products throughout the world. This capital was readily available to underwrite new economic enterprises and eased the transfer of money and goods—importing, for instance, silks from the East or Egyptian and North American cottons.

Social and cultural conditions also encouraged investment in enterprises. In Britain far more than on the Continent, the pursuit of wealth was perceived to be a worthy goal. Unlike European nobility, British aristocrats respected commoners with a talent for making money and did not hesitate to invest themselves. Their scramble to enclose their lands reflected a keen interest in commercialization and investment. Outside the aristocracy, an even lower barrier separated merchants from the rural gentry. Many of the entrepreneurs of the early Industrial Revolution came from the small gentry or independent farmer class. Eighteenth-century Britain was not by any means free of social snobbery, but a lord's disdain for a merchant might well be tempered by the fact that his own grandfather had worked in the counting house.

Growing domestic and international markets made eighteenth-century Britain prosperous. The British were voracious consumers. The court elite followed and bought up yearly fashions, and so did most of Britain's landed and professional society. The country's small size and the fact that it was an island encouraged the development of a well-integrated domestic market. Unlike continental Europe, Britain did not have a system of internal tolls and tariffs, so goods could be moved freely to wherever they might fetch the best price. A constantly improving transportation system boosted that freedom of movement. So did a favorable political climate. Some members of Parliament were businessmen themselves; others were investors.

Foreign markets promised even greater returns than domestic ones, though with greater risks. British foreign policy responded to its commercial needs. At the end of every major eighteenth-century war, Britain wrested overseas territories from its enemies. At the same time, Britain penetrated hitherto unexploited territories, such as India and South America. In 1759, over one-third of all British exports went to the colonies; by 1784, if we include the former colonies in North America, that figure had increased to one half. Production for export rose by 80 percent between 1750 and 1770; production for domestic consumption gained just 7 percent over the same period. The British possessed a merchant marine capable of transporting goods around the world and a navy practiced in the art of protecting its commercial fleets. By the 1780s, Britain's markets, together with its fleet and its established position at the center of world commerce, gave its entrepreneurs unrivaled opportunities for trade and profit.

Innovation in the Textile Industries

The Industrial Revolution began with dramatic technological leaps in a few industries, the first of which was cotton textiles. The industry was already long established. British textile manufacturers imported raw materials from India and the American South and borrowed patterns from Indian spinners and weavers. What were the revolutionary breakthroughs?

In 1733, John Kay's invention of the flying shuttle speeded the process of weaving. The spinning jenny, invented by James Hargreaves in 1764, could produce sixteen threads at once. The invention of the water frame by Richard Arkwright, a barber, in 1769, made it possible to produce stronger threads in great quantity. In 1799 Samuel Compton invented the spinning mule, which combined the features of both the jenny and the frame. All of these important technological changes were accomplished by the end of the eighteenth century.

These machines revolutionized production across the textile industry. A jenny could spin from six to twenty-four times more yarn than a hand spinner. By the end of the eighteenth century, a mule could produce two to three hundred times more. The cotton gin, invented by the American Eli Whitney in 1793, mechanized the process of separating cotton seeds from the fiber, thereby speeding up the production of cotton and reducing its price. The supply of cotton fibers could now expand to keep pace with rising demand from cotton cloth manufacturers. This cotton gin had many effects, including, paradoxically, making slavery more profitable in the United States. The cotton-producing slave plantations in the American South became enmeshed in the lucrative trade with manufacturers who produced cotton textiles in the northern United States and England.

The first textile machines were inexpensive enough to be used by spinners in their own cottages. But as machines grew in size and complexity, they were housed instead in workshops or mills located near water that could be used to power the machines. Eventually, the further development of steam-driven equipment allowed manufacturers to build mills wherever they could be used. Frequently, those mills went up in towns and cities in the north of England, away from the older commercial and seafaring centers, but nearer to the coal fields that provided fuel for new machines. From 1780 on, British cotton textiles flooded the world market. In 1760, Britain imported 2.5 million pounds of raw cotton; in 1787, 22 million pounds; in 1837, 366 million pounds. Although the price of manufactured cotton goods fell dramatically, the market expanded so rapidly that profits continued to increase.

The explosive growth of textiles also prompted a debate about the benefits and tyranny of the new industries. By the 1830s, the British House of Commons was holding hearings on employment and working conditions in factories, recording

NED LUDD AND THE LUDDITES. In 1811 and 1812, in northern England, bands of working men who resented the adoption of new mechanical devices in the weaving industries attacked several establishments and destroyed the frames used to weave cloth. The movement took the name Luddites from Ned Ludd, a man who in 1779 had broken the frames belonging to his employer. His mythological presence in the movement is depicted in the illustration at the right. Although their anger was directed at the machines, the real target of their resentment may have been a new pricing scheme imposed on them by the merchants who bought finished work. The debate about prices is a central part of the poster on the left, which offers a reward for information leading to the conviction of frame breakers. The poster is signed by several workers of the establishment, who published the price they received for each piece of clothing and their lack of complaints about their employer. ■ *How might the need to adjust to the price fluctuations of a market economy have been perceived by weavers accustomed to getting fixed prices for their goods?*

century. A series of innovations (coke smelting, rolling, and puddling) enabled the British to substitute coal (which they had in abundance) for wood (which was scarce and inefficient) to heat molten metal and make iron. The new "pig iron" was higher quality and could be used in building an enormous variety of iron products: machines, engines, railway tracks, agricultural implements, and hardware. Those iron products became, literally, the infrastructure of industrialization. Britain found itself able to export both coal and iron to rapidly expanding markets around the industrializing regions of the world. Between 1814 and 1852, exports of British iron doubled, rising to over one million tons of iron, more than half of the world's total production.

Rising demand for coal required mining deeper veins. In 1711, Thomas Newcomen had devised a cumbersome but remarkably effective steam engine for pumping water from mines. Though it was immensely valuable to the coal industry, its usefulness in other industries was limited by the amount of fuel it consumed. In 1763, James Watt improved on Newcomen's machine, and by 1800, Watt and his partner, Matthew Boulton, had sold 289 engines for use in factories and mines.

Steam power was still energy consuming and expensive and so only slowly replaced traditional water power. Even in its early form, however, the steam engine decisively transformed the nineteenth-century world with one application: the steam-driven locomotive. Railroads revolutionized industry, markets, public and private financing, and ordinary people's conceptions of space and time.

testimony about working days that stretched from 3:00 A.M. to 10:00 P.M., the employment of very small children, and workers who lost hair and fingers in the mills' machinery. Women and children counted for roughly two-thirds of the labor force in textiles. The principle of regulating any labor (and emphatically that of adult men), however, was controversial. Only gradually did a series of factory acts prohibit hiring children under age nine and limit the labor of workers under age eighteen to ten hours a day.

Coal and Iron

Meanwhile, decisive changes were transforming the production of iron. As in the textile industry, many important technological changes came during the eighteenth

THE COMING OF RAILWAYS

Transportation had improved during the years before 1830, but moving heavy materials, particularly coal, remained a problem. It is significant that the first modern railway, built in England in 1825, ran from the Durham coal field of Stockton to Darlington, near the coast. The locomotives on the Stockton-Darlington line traveled at fifteen miles

CHILD LABOR IN THE MINES. This engraving of a young worker pulling a coal cart up through the narrow shaft of a mine accompanied a British parliamentary report on child labor. ■ *What attitudes about government and the economy made it difficult for legislatures to regulate working conditions in the new industries?*

per hour, the fastest rate at which machines had yet moved goods overland. Soon they would move people as well, transforming transportation in the process.

Building railways became a massive enterprise and a risky but potentially profitable opportunity for investment. No sooner did the first combined passenger and goods service open in 1830, operating between Liverpool and Manchester, England, than plans were formulated and money pledged to extend rail systems throughout Europe, the Americas, and beyond. In 1830, there were no more than a few dozen miles of railway in the world. By 1840, there were over forty-five hundred miles; by 1850, over twenty-three thousand.

Throughout the world, a veritable army of construction workers built the railways. In Britain, they were called "navvies," derived from *navigator,* a term first used for the construction workers on Britain's eighteenth-century canals. Navvies were a rough lot, living with a few women in temporary encampments as they migrated across the countryside. Often they were immigrant workers and faced local hostility. Later in the century railway building projects in Africa and the Americas were lined with camps of immigrant Indian and Chinese laborers, who became targets of nativist (a term that means "opposed to foreigners") anger.

The magnitude of the navvies' accomplishment was extraordinary. In Britain and in much of the rest of the world, mid-nineteenth-century railways were constructed almost entirely without the aid of machinery. An as-sistant engineer on the London-to-Birmingham line calculated that the labor involved was the equivalent of lifting twenty-five billion cubic feet of earth and stone one foot high. He compared this feat with building the Great Pyramid, which had required over two hundred thousand men and had taken twenty years. The construction of the London-to-Birmingham railway was accomplished by twenty thousand men in less than five years. Railways were produced by toil as much as by technology, by human labor as much as by engineering; they illustrate why some historians prefer to use the term *industrious* revolution.

Steam engines, textile machines, new ways of making iron, and railways— all these were interconnected. Changes in one area endorsed changes in another. Pumps run by steam engines made it possible to mine deeper veins of coal; steam-powered railways made it possible to transport coal. Mechanization fueled the production of iron for machines and the mining of coal to run steam engines. The railway boom multiplied the demand for iron products: rails, locomotives, carriages, signals, and switches. The scale of production expanded and the tempo of economic activity quickened, spurring the search for more coal, the production of more iron, the mobilization of more capital, and the recruitment of more labor. Steam and speed were becoming the foundation of the economy and of a new way of life.

THE INDUSTRIAL REVOLUTION ON THE CONTINENT

Continental Europe followed a different path. Eighteenth-century France, Belgium, and Germany did have manufacturing districts in regions with raw materials, access to markets, and long-standing traditions of craft and skill. Yet for a variety of reasons, changes along the lines seen in Britain did not occur until the 1830s. Britain's transportation system was highly developed; those of France and Germany were not. France was far larger than England: its rivers more difficult to navigate; its seaports, cities, and coal deposits farther apart. Much of central Europe was divided

The Factory System, Science, and Morality: Two Views

> *Reactions to the Industrial Revolution and the factory system it produced ranged from celebration to horror. Dr. Andrew Ure (1778–1857), a Scottish professor of chemistry, was fascinated with these nineteenth-century applications of Enlightenment science. He believed that the new machinery and its products would create a new society of wealth, abundance, and, ultimately, stability through the useful regimentation of production.*
>
> *Friedrich Engels (1820–1895) was one of the many socialists to criticize Dr. Ure as shortsighted and complacent in his outlook. Engels was himself part of a factory-owning family and so was able to examine the new industrial cities at close range. He provides a classic nineteenth-century analysis of industrialization.* The Condition of the Working Class in England *is compellingly written, angry, and revealing about middle-class concerns of the time, including female labor.*

Dr. Andrew Ure (1835)

This island [Britain] is preeminent among civilized nations for the prodigious development of its factory wealth, and has been therefore long viewed with a jealous admiration by foreign powers. This very pre-eminence, however, has been contemplated in a very different light by many influential members of our own community, and has even been denounced by them as the certain origin of innumerable evils to the people, and of revolutionary convulsions to the state. . . .

The blessings which physico-mechanical science has bestowed on society, and the means it has still in store for ameliorating the lot of mankind, has been too little dwelt upon; while, on the other hand, it has been accused of lending itself to the rich capitalists as an instrument for harassing the poor, and of exacting from the operative an accelerated rate of work. It has been said, for example, that the steam-engine now drives the power-looms with such velocity as to urge on their attendant weavers at the same rapid pace; but that the hand-weaver, not being subjected to this restless agent, can throw his shuttle and move his treddles at his convenience. There is, however, this difference in the two cases, that in the factory, every member of the loom is so adjusted, that the driving force leaves the attendant nearly nothing at all to do, certainly no muscular fatigue to sustain, while it produces for him good, unfailing wages, besides a healthy workshop *gratis*: whereas the non-factory weaver, having everything to execute by muscular exertion, finds the labour irksome, makes in consequence innumerable short pauses, separately of little account, but great when added together; earns therefore proportionally low wages, while he loses his health by poor diet and the dampness of his hovel.

Source: Andrew Ure, *The Philosophy of Manufacturers: Or, An Exposition of the Scientific, Moral, and Commercial Economy of the Factory System of Great Britain, 1835,* as cited in J. T. Ward, *The Factory System,* vol. 1 (New York: 1970), pp. 140–41.

---

into small principalities, each with its own tolls and tariffs, which complicated the transportation of goods over any considerable distance. The Continent had fewer raw materials, coal in particular, than Britain. The abundance and cheapness of wood discouraged exploration that might have resulted in new discoveries of coal. It also meant that coal-run steam engines were less economical on the Continent. Capital, too, was less readily available. Early British industrialization was underwritten by private wealth; this was less feasible elsewhere. Different patterns of landholding formed obstacles to the commercialization of agriculture. In the East, serfdom was a powerful disincentive to labor-saving innovations. In the West, especially in France, the large number of small peasants, or farmers, stayed put on the land.

The wars of the French Revolution and Napoleon disrupted economies. During the eighteenth century, the population had grown and mechanization had begun in a few key industries. The ensuing political upheaval and the financial strains of warfare did virtually nothing to help

Friedrich Engels (1844)

Histories of the modern development of the cotton industry, such as those of Ure, Baines, and others, tell on every page of technical innovations. . . . In a well-ordered society such improvements would indeed be welcome, but social war rages unchecked and the benefits derived from these improvements are ruthlessly monopolized by a few persons. . . . Every improvement in machinery leads to unemployment, and the greater the technical improvement the greater the unemployment. Every improvement in machinery affects a number of workers in the same way as a commercial crisis and leads to want, distress, and crime. . . .

Let us examine a little more closely the process whereby machine-labour continually supersedes hand-labour. When spinning or weaving machinery is installed practically all that is left to be done by the hand is the piecing together of broken threads, and the machine does the rest. This task calls for nimble fingers rather than muscular strength. The labour of grown men is not merely unnecessary but actually unsuitable. . . . The greater the degree to which physical labour is displaced by the introduction of machines worked by water- or steampower, the fewer grown men need be employed. In any case women and children will work for lower wages than men and, as has already been observed, they are more skillful at piecing than grown men. Consequently it is women and children who are employed to do this work. . . . When women work in factories, the most important result is the dissolution of family ties. If a woman works for twelve or thirteen hours a day in a factory and her husband is employed either in the same establishment or in some other works, what is the fate of the children? They lack parental care and control. . . . It is not difficult to imagine that they are left to run wild.

Source: Friedrich Engels, *The Condition of the Working Class in England in 1844*, trans. and ed. W. O. Henderson and W. H. Chaloner (New York: 1958), pp. 150–51, 158, 160.

Questions for Analysis

1. According to Andre Ure, why was industrialization good for Britain? How can the blessings of "physico-mechanical science" lead to the improvement of humanity?

2. What criticism did Engels level at Ure and other optimists on industrialization? Why did Engels think conditions for workers were getting worse instead of better?

3. What consequences do these two writers see for society in the wake of technological change? What assumptions do they make about the relationship between economic development and the social order?

economic development. Napoleon's Continental System and British destruction of French merchant shipping hurt commerce badly. Probably the revolutionary change most beneficial to industrial advance in Europe was the removal of previous restraints on the movement of capital and labor—for example, the abolition of craft guilds and the reduction of tariff barriers across the Continent.

After 1815, a number of factors combined to change the economic climate. In those regions with a well-established commercial and industrial base—the northeast of France, Belgium, and swaths of territory across the Rhineland, Saxony, Silesia, and northern Bohemia (see map on page 459)—population growth further boosted economic development. Rising population did not by itself produce industrialization, however: in Ireland, where other necessary factors were absent, more people meant less food.

Transportation improved. The Austrian Empire added over thirty thousand miles of roads between 1830 and 1847; Belgium almost doubled its road network in the same period; France built not only new roads but two thousand miles of canals. These improvements, combined with the construction of railroads in the 1830s and 1840s, opened up new markets and encouraged new methods of manufacturing. In many of the Continent's manufacturing regions, however, industrialists continued to tap large pools of skilled but inexpensive labor. Thus older methods of putting out industry and handwork persisted alongside new-model factories longer than in Britain.

In what other ways was the continental model of industrialization different? Governments played a considerably more direct role in industrialization. France and Prussia granted subsidies to private companies that built railroads. After 1849, the Prussian state took on the task itself, as did Belgium and, later, Russia. In Prussia, the state also operated a large proportion of that country's mines. Governments on the Continent provided incentives for industrialization. Limited-liability laws, to take the most important example, allowed investors to own shares in a corporation or company without becoming liable for the company's debts—and they enabled enterprises to recruit investors to put together the capital for railroads, other forms of industry, and commerce.

Mobilizing capital for industry was one of the challenges of the century. In Great Britain, overseas trade had created well-organized financial markets; on the Continent, capital was dispersed and in short supply. New joint-stock investment banks, unlike private banks, could sell bonds to and take deposits from individuals and smaller companies. They could offer start-up capital in the form of long-term, low-interest commercial loans to aspiring entrepreneurs. The French Crédit Mobilier, for instance, founded in 1852 by the wealthy and well-connected Péreire brothers, assembled enough capital to finance a wide range of infrastructure projects, including a massive railroad-building spree in the 1850s. The Crédit Mobilier collapsed in scandal, but the revolution in banking was well under way.

Finally, continental Europeans actively promoted invention and technological development. They were willing for the state to establish educational systems whose aim, among others, was to produce a well-trained elite capable of assisting in the development of industrial technology. In sum, what Britain had produced almost by chance, the Europeans began to reproduce by design.

Industrialization after 1850

Until 1850 Britain remained the preeminent industrial power. Between 1850 and 1870, however, France, Germany, Belgium, and the United States emerged as challengers to the power of British manufacturers. The British iron industry remained the largest in the world, but it grew more slowly than did its counterparts in France and Germany. Most of continental Europe's gains came as a result of continuing changes in those areas we recognize as important for sustained industrial growth: transport, commerce, and government policy. The spread of railways encouraged the free movement of goods. International monetary unions were established and restrictions removed on international waterways. Free trade went hand in hand with removing guild barriers to entering trades and ending restrictions on practicing business. Guild control over artisanal production was abolished in Austria and most of Germany by the mid-1860s. Laws against usury, most of which had ceased to be enforced, were officially abandoned in Britain, Holland, Belgium, and in many parts of Germany. Investment banks continued to form, encouraged by an increase in the money supply and an easing of credit after the California gold fields opened in 1849.

The first phase of the Industrial Revolution, one economic historian reminds us, was confined to a narrow set of industries and can be summed up rather simply: "cheaper and better clothes (mainly made of cotton), cheaper and better metals (pig iron, wrought iron, and steel) and faster travel (mainly by rail)." The second half of the century brought changes further afield and in areas where Great Britain's early advantages were no longer decisive. Transatlantic cable (starting in 1865) and the telephone (invented in 1876) laid the ground for a revolution in communications. New chemical processes, dyestuffs, and pharmaceuticals emerged. So did new sources of energy: electricity, in which the United States and Germany led both invention and commercial development; and oil, which was being refined in the 1850s and widely used by 1900 (see Chapter 23).

In eastern Europe, the nineteenth century brought different patterns of economic development. Spurred by the ever-growing demand for food and grain, large sections of eastern Europe developed into concentrated, commercialized agriculture regions that played the specific role of exporting food to the West. Many of those large agricultural enterprises were based on serfdom and remained so, in the face of increasing pressure for reform, until 1850. Peasant protest and liberal demands for reform only gradually chipped away at the nobility's determination to hold on to its privilege and system of labor. Serfdom was abolished in most parts of eastern and southern Europe by 1850 and in Poland and Russia in the 1860s.

By 1870, then, the core industrial nations of Europe included Great Britain, France, Germany, Italy, the Netherlands, and Switzerland. Austria stood at the margins. Russia, Spain, Bulgaria, Greece, Hungary, Romania, and

Serbia formed the industrial periphery—and some regions of these nations seemed virtually untouched by the advance of industry. What was more, even in Great Britain, the most fully industrialized nation, agricultural laborers still constituted the single largest occupational category in 1860 (although they formed only 9 percent of the overall population). In Belgium, the Netherlands, Switzerland, Germany, France, Scandinavia, and Ireland, 25 to 50 percent of the population still worked on the land. In Russia, the number was 80 percent. *Industrial*, moreover, did not mean automation or machine production, which long remained confined to a few sectors of the economy. As machines were introduced in some sectors to do specific tasks, they usually intensified the tempo of handwork in other sectors. Thus even in the industrialized regions, much work was still accomplished in tiny workshops—or at home.

Industry and Empire

From an international perspective, nineteenth-century Europe was the most industrial region of the world. Europeans, particularly the British, jealously guarded their international advantages. They preferred to do so through financial leverage. Britain, France, and other European nations gained control of the national debts of China, the Ottoman Empire, Egypt, Brazil, Argentina, and other non-European powers. They also supplied large loans to other states, which bound those nations to their European investors. If the debtor nations expressed discontent, as Egypt did in the 1830s when it attempted to establish its own cotton textile industry, they confronted financial pressure and shows of force. Coercion, however, was not always necessary or even one-sided. Social change in other empires—China, Persia,

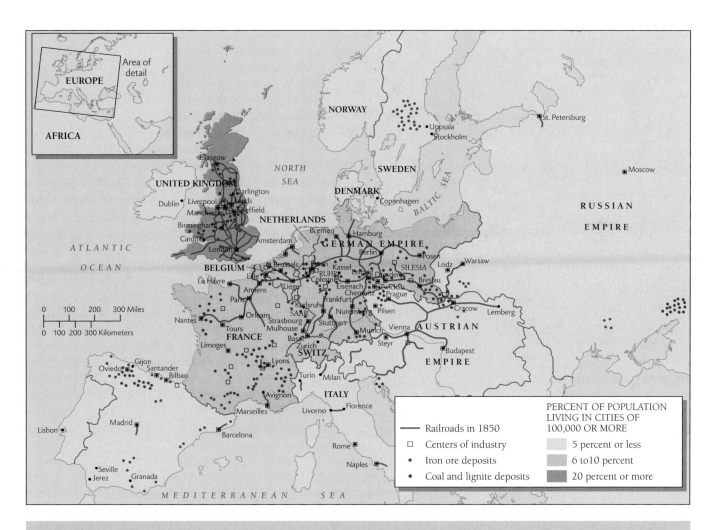

THE INDUSTRIAL REVOLUTION. Rapid industrial growth depended on a circular network of relationships between population, transport, and natural resources. ▪ *How were these elements connected, and how might they have reinforced one another, contributing to rapid growth?* ▪ *Why do you think the percentage of populations living in cities was so much greater in the United Kingdom?*

Interpreting Visual Evidence

Learning to Live in a Global Economy

The commercial networks of the Atlantic world were already well established before the Industrial Revolution, and Europeans were also trading widely with South and East Asia before the end of the eighteenth century. Nevertheless, the advent of an industrial economy in Europe at the beginning of the nineteenth century created such a demand for raw materials and such a need for new markets abroad that it became profitable for manufacturers and merchants to ship much larger amounts of goods over longer distances than ever before. As different industrialized regions in Europe became more and more dependent on overseas markets, people in Europe became aware of the extent to which their own activities were linked to other parts of the world. Awareness of these linkages did not always mean that they possessed complete or accurate information about the people who produced the cotton that they wore, or who purchased the manufactured goods that they made, but the linkages stimulated their imagination and changed their consciousness of their place in the world.

This awareness is well illustrated in the cartoons shown here, which come from the British paper *Punch* in the 1850s and 1860s. The first (image A) depicts John Bull (representing British textile manufacturers) looking on as U.S. cotton suppliers fight one another during the Civil War in the United States. He states, "Oh! If you two like fighting better than business, I shall deal at the other shop." In the background, an Indian cotton merchant is happy to have him as a customer.

The second cartoon (image B) depicts the ways that the increasingly interconnected global economy might

A. John Bull and cotton merchants.

and the Mughal Empire of India, for example—made those empires newly vulnerable and created new opportunities for the European powers and their local partners. Ambitious local elites often reached agreements with Western governments or groups such as the British East India Company. These trade agreements transformed regional economies on terms that sent the greatest profits to Europe after a substantial gratuity to the Europeans' local partners. Where agreements could not be made, force prevailed, and Europe took territory and trade by conquest (see Chapter 22).

Industrialization tightened global links between Europe and the rest of the world, creating new networks of stimulate a new kind of political awareness. Emperor Napoleon III has placed a French worker in irons for participating in a revolutionary movement. The worker compares his situation to an African slave seated next to him, saying, "Courage, my friend! Am I not a man and a brother?" On the wall behind the two men a poster refers to the Portuguese slave trade—Napoleon III himself came to power by overthrowing the Second Republic in France, a government that had abolished the slave trade in French territories.

Questions for Analysis

1. What constellation of private and national interests were at play in the relationships portrayed in image A? What significance might contemporaries have attached to the possibility that the British may have chosen to buy their cotton from an Asian source "over the way" rather than from North America?

2. In image B, what is the message of the cartoon's suggestion that the slave and the worker might discover their equality only in the fact that they are both in chains? What was at stake in comparing a worker to a slave in mid-nineteenth-century Europe? Why does the caption read "Poor Consolation?"

3. How does the racial imagery of these images relate to their intended message?

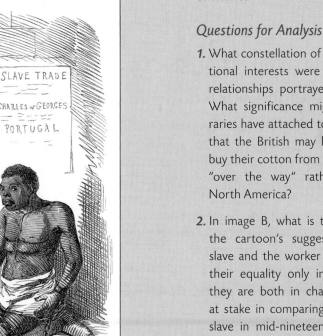

POOR CONSOLATION.

Parisian. "COURAGE, MON AMI; 'AM I NOT A MAN AND A BROTHER?'"

B. Increasing global awarness in France.

trade and interdependence. To a certain extent, the world economy divided between the producers of manufactured goods—Europe itself—and suppliers of the necessary raw materials and buyers of finished goods—everyone else. Cotton growers in the southern United States, sugar growers in the Caribbean, and wheat growers in Ukraine accepted their arrangements with the industrialized West and typically profited by them. If there were disputes, however, those suppliers often found that Europe could look elsewhere for the same goods or dictate the terms of trade down the business end of a bank ledger or a cannon barrel.

In 1811 Britain imported 3 percent of the wheat it consumed. By 1891 that portion had risen to 79 percent. Why? In an increasingly urban society, fewer people lived off the land. The commercialization of agriculture, which began early in Britain, had taken even firmer hold elsewhere, turning new regions—Australia, Argentina, and North America—into centers of grain and wheat production. New forms of transportation, finance, and communication made it easier to shuttle commodities and capital through international networks. Those simple percentages, in other words, dramatize the new interdependence of the nineteenth century; they illustrate as well as any statistics can how ordinary Britons' lives—like their counterparts' in other nations—were embedded in an increasingly global economy.

THE SOCIAL CONSEQUENCES OF INDUSTRIALIZATION

The effects of industrialization in Europe were soon visible in all aspects of social life. Changes in production and the workplace created new centers of employment, unleashing a cascading sequence of population movements that led to the growth of new cities in regions that a short time before had been largely agricultural. The development of these new cities and the sudden growth of older ones strained the infrastructure of Europe's urban centers, creating a demand for new housing, and forcing many to crowd into neighborhoods where newcomers could find short-term rentals as they looked for employment. Growth in these new cities was often uneven, with new and prosperous middle-class neighborhoods developing alongside more densely populated working-class districts. The concentration of new populations in cities that had been built for smaller numbers of people led in turn to environmental degradation, declining air quality, and fears of contagion. Traditional elites watched these developments with some dismay, fearing that the growth of urban populations would be accompanied by increases in crime and disease, or worse, revolution.

Population

By any measure the nineteenth century was a turning point in European demographic history. In 1800 the population of Europe was roughly 205 million. By 1914 the figure had jumped to 480 million. (Over the same span of time, the world population went from about 900 million to 1.6 billion). Britain, with its comparatively high standard of living, saw its population rise from 16 to 27 million. Throughout Europe, increases came in both urban and rural areas. In Russia, which did not begin the process of industrialization until the 1890s, the population rose from 39 million in 1800 to 60 million in 1914.

This population explosion did not occur because people were living longer—declines in mortality were not observable on a large scale until late in the nineteenth century, when improvements in hygiene and medicine had significant impact on the number of people who survived childhood to reach adulthood. Even in 1880, the average male life expectancy at birth in Berlin was no more than thirty years (in rural districts nearby it was forty-three). Population growth in the nineteenth century resulted from increasing fertility—there were simply more babies being born. Men and women married earlier, which raised the average number of children born to each woman and increased the size of families. Peasants tended to set up households at a younger age. The spread of rural manufacturing allowed couples in the countryside to marry and set up households—even before they inherited any land. Not only did the age of marriage fall but more people married. And because population growth increased the proportion of young and fertile people, the process reinforced itself in the next generation, setting the stage for a period of prolonged growth.

Life on the Land: The Peasantry

Even as the West grew more industrial, the majority of people continued to live on the land. Conditions in the countryside were harsh. Peasants still farmed largely by hand. Millions of tiny farms produced, at most, a bare subsistence living. The average daily diet for an entire family in a good year might amount to no more than two or three pounds of bread—a total per family of about three thousand calories daily. By many measures, living conditions for rural inhabitants of many areas in Europe grew worse in the first half of the nineteenth century, a fact of considerable political importance in the 1840s. Rising population put more pressure on the land. Over the course of the century some thirty-seven million people—most of them peasants—left Europe, eloquent testimony to the bleakness of rural life. They settled in the United States, South America, northern Africa, New Zealand, Australia, and Siberia. In many cases, governments encouraged emigration to ease overcrowding.

IRISH POTATO FAMINE, 1845–49. The Irish potato famine was widely held by many in Ireland to have human as well as natural causes. Historians have noted that food exports from Ireland continued and may have even increased for some products during the famine, as merchants sought higher prices abroad. This cartoon depicts armed soldiers keeping starving Irish Catholic families at bay as sacks of potatoes are loaded onto a ship owned by a prosperous Irish Protestant trader.

The most tragic combination of famine, poverty, and population in the nineteenth century came to Ireland in the Great Famine of 1845–49. Potatoes, which had come to Europe from the New World, fundamentally transformed the diets of European peasants, providing much more nutrition for less money than corn and grain. They also grew more densely, an enormous advantage for peasants scraping a living from small plots of land. Nowhere did they become more important than in Ireland, where the climate and soil made growing grain difficult and both overpopulation and poverty were rising. When a fungus hit the potato crop—first in 1845 and again, fatally, in 1846 and 1847—no alternate foods were at hand. At least one million Irish died of starvation; of dysentery from spoiled foods; or of fever, which spread through villages and the overcrowded poorhouses. Before the famine, tens of thousands of Irish were already crossing the Atlantic to North America. In the ten years after 1845, 1.5 million people left Ireland for good. The Irish famine illustrated just how vulnerable the nineteenth-century countryside remained to bad harvests and shortages.

Changes in the land depended partly on particular governments. States sympathetic to commercial agriculture made it easier to transfer land, eliminate small farms, and create larger estates. In Britain, over half the total area of the country, excluding wasteland, was composed of estates of a thousand acres or more. In Russia some of the largest landowners possessed over half a million acres. Until the emancipation of the serfs in the 1860s, landowners claimed the labor of dependent peasant populations for as much as several days per week. But the system of serfdom gave neither landowners nor serfs much incentive to improve farming techniques.

European serfdom, which bound hundreds of thousands of men, women, and children to particular estates for generations, made it difficult to buy and sell land freely and created an obstacle to the commercialization of agriculture. Yet the opposite was also the case. In France, peasant landholders who had benefited from the French Revolution's sale of lands and laws on inheritance stayed in the countryside, continuing to work their small farms. Although French peasants were poor, they could sustain themselves on the land. This had important consequences. France suffered less agricultural distress, even in the 1840s, than did other European countries; migration from country to city was slower than in the other nations; far fewer peasants left France for other countries.

Industrialization came to the countryside in other forms. Improved communication networks not only afforded rural populations a keener sense of events and opportunities elsewhere but also made it possible for governments to intrude into the lives of these men and women to a degree previously impossible. Central bureaucracies now found it easier to collect taxes from the peasantry and to conscript sons of peasant families into armies. Some rural cottage industries faced direct competition from factory-produced goods, which meant less work or lower piece rates and falling incomes for families, especially during winter months. In other sectors of the economy, industry spread out into the countryside, making whole regions producers of shoes, shirts, ribbons, cutlery, and so on in small shops and workers' homes. Changes in the market could usher in prosperity, or they could bring entire regions to the verge of starvation.

Many onlookers considered the nineteenth-century cities dangerous seedbeds of sedition. Yet conditions in the countryside and frequent flareups of rural protest remained the greatest source of trouble for governments. In England in the 1820s, small farmers marched under the banner of the mythical "Captain Swing" to protest the introduction of threshing machines, a symbol of agricultural capitalism. In southwest France, peasants attacked authorities who tried to prevent them from gathering wood in forests. Similar disturbances broke out elsewhere in Europe, and rural politics exploded, as we will see, in the 1840s. Peasants were land poor, deep in debt, and precariously dependent on markets. More important, however, a government's inability to contend with rural misery made it look autocratic, indifferent, or inept—all political failings.

Industrialization and the Urban Landscape

The growth of cities was one of the most important facts of nineteenth-century social history, and one with significant cultural reverberations. Over the course of the nineteenth century, as we have seen, the overall population of Europe doubled. The percentage of that population living in cities tripled—that is, urban populations rose sixfold. Cities like Manchester, Birmingham, and Essen seemed to spring up from nowhere. Between 1750 and 1850, London (Europe's largest city) grew from 676,000 to 2.3 million. The population of Paris went from 560,000 to 1.3 million, and Berlin nearly tripled in size during the first half of the century. Such rapid expansion brought in its wake new social problems.

Almost all nineteenth-century cities were overcrowded and unhealthy, their largely medieval infrastructures strained by the burden of new population and the demands of industry. Construction lagged far behind population growth, and the poorest workers dwelt in wretched basement or attic rooms, often without any light or drainage. Such conditions bred misery and epidemic disease.

Dickens's description of the choking air and polluted water of "Coketown," the fictional city in *Hard Times* (1854) is deservedly well known:

> It was a town of red brick, or of brick that would have been red if the smoke and ashes had allowed it. . . . It was a town of machines and tall chimneys, out of which interminable serpents of smoke trailed themselves forever and ever, and never got uncoiled. It had a black canal in it, and a river that ran purple with ill-smelling dye, and vast piles of building full of windows where there was a rattling and a trembling all day long.

Wood-fired manufacturing and heating for homes had long spewed smoke across the skies, but the new concentration of industrial activity and the transition to coal made the air measurably worse. In London especially, where even homes switched to coal early, smoke from factories, railroads, and domestic chimneys hung heavily over the city; and the last third of the century brought the most intense pollution in its history. Over all of England, air pollution took an enormous toll on health, contributing to the bronchitis and tuberculosis that accounted for 25 percent of British deaths. The coal-rich and industrial regions of North America (especially Pittsburgh) and central Europe were other concentrations of pollution; the Ruhr in particular by the end of the century had the most polluted air in Europe.

Toxic water—produced by industrial pollution and human waste—posed the second critical environmental hazard in urban areas. London and Paris led the way in building municipal sewage systems, though those emptied into the Thames and the Seine. Cholera, typhus, and tuberculosis were natural predators in areas without adequate sewage facilities or fresh water. The Rhine River, which flowed through central Europe's industrial heartland and intersected with the Ruhr, was thick with detritus from coal mining, iron processing, and the chemical industry. Spurred by several epidemics of cholera, in the late nineteenth century the major cities began to purify their water supplies; but conditions in the air, rivers, and land continued to worsen until at least the mid-twentieth century.

Governments gradually adopted measures in an attempt to cure the worst of these ills, if only to prevent the spread of catastrophic epidemics. Yet by 1850, these projects had only just begun. Paris, perhaps better supplied with water than any other European city, had enough for no more than two baths per person per year; in London, human waste remained uncollected in 250,000 domestic cesspools; in Manchester, fewer than one-third of the dwellings were equipped with toilets of any sort.

VIEW OF LONDON WITH SAINT PAUL'S CATHEDRAL IN THE DISTANCE BY WILLIAM HENRY CROME. Despite the smog-filled skies and intense pollution, many entrepreneurs and politicians celebrated the new prosperity of the Industrial Revolution. As W. P. Rend, a Chicago businessman, wrote in 1892, "Smoke is the incense burning on the altars of industry. It is beautiful to me. It shows that men are changing the merely potential forces of nature into articles of comfort for humanity."

The Social Question

Against the backdrop of the French Revolution of 1789 and subsequent revolutions in the nineteenth century (as we will see in the following chapters), the new "shock" cities of the nineteenth century and their swelling multitudes posed urgent questions. Political leaders, social scientists, and public health officials across all of Europe issued thousands of reports—many of them several volumes long—on criminality, water supply, sewers, prostitution, tuberculosis and cholera, alcoholism, wet nursing, wages, and unemployment. Radicals and reformers grouped all these issues under a broad heading known as "the social question." Governments, pressed by reformers and by the omnipresent rumblings of unrest, felt they had to address these issues before complaints swelled into revolution. They did so, in the first social engineering: police forces, public health, sewers and new water supplies, inoculations, elementary schools, Factory Acts (regulating work hours), poor laws (outlining the conditions of receiving relief), and new urban regulation and city planning. Central Paris, for instance, would be almost entirely redesigned in the nineteenth century—the crowded, medieval, and revolutionary poor neighborhoods gutted; markets rebuilt; streets widened and lit (see Chapter 21). From the 1820s on, the social question hung over Europe like a cloud, and it formed part of the backdrop to the revolutions of 1848 (discussed in Chapter 21).

THE MIDDLE CLASSES

Nineteenth-century novelists such as Charles Dickens and William Thackeray in Britain, Victor Hugo and Honoré Balzac in France, and Theodor Fontane in Germany painted a sweeping portrait of middle-class society in the nineteenth century. The plots of these stories explore the ways that older hierarchies of rank, status, and privilege were gradually giving way to a new set of gradations based on wealth and social class. In this new world, money trumped birth, and social mobility was an accepted fact rather than something to be hidden.

Who were the middle classes? The middle class was not one homogeneous unit, in terms of occupation or income. Its ranks included shopkeepers and their households, the families of lawyers, doctors, and other professionals, as well as well-off factory owners who might aspire to marry their daughters to titled aristocrats. At the lower end of the social scale the middle classes included the families of salaried clerks and office workers for whom white-collar employment offered hope of a rise in status.

Movement within middle-class ranks was often possible in the course of one or two generations. Very few, however, moved from the working class into the middle class. Most middle-class success stories began in the middle class itself, with the children of relatively well-off farmers, skilled artisans, or professionals. Upward mobility was almost impossible without education, and education was a rare, though not unattainable, luxury for working-class children. Careers open to talents, that goal achieved by the French Revolution, frequently meant opening jobs to middle-class young men who could pass exams. The examination system was an important path upward within government bureaucracies.

The journey from middle class to aristocratic, landed society was equally difficult. In Britain, mobility of this sort was easier to achieve than on the Continent. Sons from wealthy upper-middle-class families, if they were sent to elite schools and universities and if they left the commercial or industrial world for a career in politics, might actually move up. William Gladstone, son of a Liverpool merchant, attended the exclusive educational preserves of Eton (a private boarding school) and Oxford University, married into the aristocratic Grenville family, and became prime minister of England. Yet Gladstone was an exception to the rule, even in Britain, and most upward mobility was much less spectacular.

Nevertheless, the European middle class helped sustain itself with the belief that it was possible to get ahead by means of intelligence, pluck, and serious devotion to work. The middle classes' claim to political power and cultural influence rested on arguments that they constituted a new and deserving social elite, superior to the common people yet sharply different from the older aristocracy, and the rightful custodians of the nation's future. Thus middle-class respectability, like a code, stood for many values. It meant financial independence, providing responsibly for one's family, avoiding gambling and debt. It suggested merit and character as opposed to aristocratic privilege and hard work as opposed to living off noble estates. Respectable middle-class gentlemen might be wealthy, but they were expected to live modestly and soberly, avoiding conspicuous consumption, lavish dress, womanizing, and other forms of dandyish behavior associated with the aristocracy. Of course, these were aspirations and codes, not social realities. They nonetheless remained key to the middle-class sense of self and understanding of the world.

Private Life and Middle-Class Identity

Family and home played a central role in forming middle-class identity. Few themes were more common in nineteenth-century fiction than men and women pursuing mobility and status by or through marriage. Families

Marriage, Sexuality, and the Facts of Life

In the nineteenth century sexuality became the subject of much anxious debate, largely because it raised other issues: the roles of men and women, morality, and social respectability. Doctors threw themselves into the discussion, offering their expert opinions on the health (including the sexual lives) of the population. Yet doctors did not dictate people's private lives. Nineteenth-century men and women responded to what they experienced as the facts of life more than to expert advice. The first document provides an example of medical knowledge and opinion in 1870. The second offers a glimpse of the daily realities of family life in 1830.

A French Doctor Denounces Contraception

One of the most powerful instincts nature has placed in the heart of man is that which has for its object the perpetuation of the human race. But this instinct, this inclination, so active, which attracts one sex towards the other, is liable to be perverted, to deviate from the path nature has laid out. From this arises a number of fatal aberrations which exercise a deplorable influence upon the individual, upon the family, and upon society. . . .

We hear constantly that marriages are less fruitful, that the increase of population does not follow its former ratio. I believe that this is mainly attributable to genesiac frauds. It might naturally be supposed that these odious calculations of egotism, these shameful refinements of debauchery, are met with almost entirely in large cities, and among the luxurious classes, and that small towns and country places yet preserve that simplicity of manners attributed to primitive society, when the *pater familias* was proud of exhibiting his numerous offspring. Such, however, is not the case, and I shall show that those who have an unlimited confidence in the patriarchal habits of our country people are deeply in error. At the present time frauds are practiced by all classes. . . .

The laboring classes are generally satisfied with the practice of Onan [withdrawal]. . . . They are seldom familiar with the sheath invented by Dr. Condom, and bearing his name.

Among the wealthy, on the other hand, the use of this preservative is generally known. It favors frauds by rendering them easier; but it does not afford complete security. . . .

Case X.—This couple belongs to two respectable families of vintners. They are both pale, emaciated, downcast, sickly. . . .

They have been married for ten years; they first had two children, one immediately after the other, but in order to avoid an increase of family, they have had recourse to conjugal frauds. Being both very amorous, they have found this practice very convenient to satisfy their inclinations. They have employed it to such an extent, that up to a few months ago, when their health began to fail, the husband had intercourse with his wife habitually two and three times in twenty-four hours.

The following is the condition of the woman: She complains of continual pains in the lower part of the abdomen and kidneys. These pains disturb the functions of the stomach and render her nervous. . . . By the touch we find a very intense heat, great sensibility to pressure, and all the signs of a chronic metritis. The patient attributes positively her present state to the too frequent approaches of her husband.

served intensely practical purposes: sons, nephews, and cousins were expected to assume responsibility in family firms when it came their turn; wives managed accounts; and parents-in-law provided business connections, credit, inheritance, and so on. The family's role in middle-class thought, however, did not arise only from these practical considerations; family was part of a larger worldview. A well-governed household offered a counterpoint to the business and confusion of the world, and families offered continuity and tradition in a time of rapid change.

The husband does not attempt to exculpate himself, as he also is in a state of extreme suffering. It is not in the genital organs, however, that we find his disorder, but in the whole general nervous system; his history will find its place in the part of this work relative to general disturbances. . . .

Source: Louis-François-Etienne Bergeret, *The Preventive Obstacle, or Conjugal Onanism*, trans. P. de Marmon (New York: 1870), pp. 3–4, 12, 20–22, 25, 56–57, 100–101, 111–13. Originally published in Paris in 1868.

Death in Childbirth (1830)

rs. Ann B. Pettigrew was taken in Labour after returning from a walk in the garden, at 7 o'clock in the evening of June 30, 1830. At 40 minutes after 11 o'clock, she was delivered of a daughter. A short time after, I was informed that the Placenta was not removed, and, at 10 minutes after 12 was asked into the room. I advanced to my dear wife, and kissing her, asked her how she was, to which she replied, I feel very badly. I went out of the room, and sent for Dr. Warren.

I then returned, and inquired if there was much hemorrhage, and was answered that there was. I then asked the midwife (Mrs. Brickhouse) if she ever used manual exertion to remove the placenta. She said she had more than fifty times. I then, fearing the consequences of hemorrhage, observed, Do, my dear sweet wife, permit Mrs. Brickhouse to remove it: To which she assented. . . .

After the second unsuccessful attempt, I desired the midwife to desist. In these two efforts, my dear Nancy suffered exceedingly and frequently exclaimed: "O Mrs Brickhouse you will kill me," and to me, "O I shall die, send for the Doctor." To which I replied, "I have sent."

After this, my feelings were so agonizing that I had to retire from the room and lay down, or fall. Shortly after which, the midwife came to me and, falling upon her knees, prayed most fervently to God and to me to forgive her for saying that she could do what she could not. . . .

The placenta did not come away, and the hemorrhage continued with unabated violence until five o'clock in the morning, when the dear woman breathed her last 20 minutes before the Doctor arrived.

So agonizing a scene as that from one o'clock, I have no words to describe. O My God, My God! have mercy on me. I am undone forever. . . .

Source: Cited in Erna Olafson Hellerstein, Leslie Parker Hume, and Karen M. Offen, eds., *Victorian Women: A Documentary Account of Women's Lives in Nineteenth-Century England, France, and the United States.* (Stanford, CA: 1981), pp. 193–94, 219–20.

Questions for Analysis

1. The French doctor states that the impulse to have sexual relations is "one of the most powerful instincts" given to humans by nature, while simultaneously claiming that this natural instinct is "liable to be perverted." What does this reveal about his attitude toward "nature"?

2. What does he mean by "genesiac frauds"? Who is being deceived by this fraud? What consequences for individuals and for society as a whole does the doctor fear from this deception?

3. What does the story of Mrs. Pettigrew's death reveal about the dangers of childbirth and the state of obstetric medicine in the nineteenth century?

Gender and the Cult of Domesticity

There was no single type of middle-class family or home. Yet many people held powerful convictions about how a respectable home should be run. According to advice manuals, poetry, and middle-class journals, wives and mothers were supposed to occupy a "separate sphere" of life, in which they lived in subordination to their spouses. These prescriptions were directly applied to young people. Boys were educated in secondary schools; girls at home. This nineteenth-century conception of separate spheres needs to be understood in relation to much-longer-standing traditions of paternal authority, which were codified in law. Throughout Europe, laws subjected women to their husbands' authority. Although unmarried women did enjoy a degree of legal independence in France and Austria, laws generally assigned them to the "protection" of their fathers. Gender relations in the nineteenth century rested on this foundation of legal inequality. Yet the idea or doctrine of separate spheres was meant to underscore that men's and women's spheres complemented each other. Thus, for instance, middle-class writings were full of references to marriages in which the wife was a "companion" and "helpmate."

It is helpful to recall that members of the middle class articulated their values in opposition to aristocratic customs on the one hand and the lives of the common people on the other. They argued, for instance, that middle-class marriages were not arranged to accumulate power and privilege; instead they were to be based on mutual respect and division of responsibilities. A respectable middle-class woman should also be free from the unrelenting toil that was the lot of a woman of the people. Called in Victorian Britain the "angel in the house," the middle-class woman was responsible for the moral education of her children and the management of her household. This "cult of domesticity" was central to middle-class Victorian thinking about women.

As a housewife, a middle-class woman had the task of keeping the household functioning smoothly and harmoniously. She maintained the accounts and directed the activities of the servants. Having at least one servant was a mark of middle-class status. The middle classes included many gradations of wealth, from a well-housed banker with a governess and five servants to a village preacher with one. Moreover, the work of running and maintaining a home was enormous. Linens and clothes had to be made and mended. Only the wealthy had the luxury of running water, and others had to carry and heat water for cooking, laundry, and cleaning. If the "angel in the house" was a cultural ideal, it was partly because she had real economic value.

Outside the home, women had very few respectable options for earning a living. Unmarried women might act as companions or governesses. But nineteenth-century convictions about women's moral nature, combined as they were with middle-class aspirations to political leadership, encouraged middle-class wives to undertake voluntary charitable work or to campaign for social reform. In Britain and the United States, women played an important role in the struggle to abolish the slave trade and slavery in the British Empire. Many of these movements also drew on the energies of religious, especially Protestant, organizations committed to the eradication of social evils and moral improvement. Throughout Europe, a wide range of movements to improve conditions for the poor in schools and hospitals, for temperance, against prostitution, or for legislation on factory hours were often run by women.

Queen Victoria, who came to the British throne in 1837, labored to make her solemn public image reflect contemporary feminine virtues of moral probity and dutiful domesticity. She was a successful queen because she embodied the traits important to the middle class, whose triumph she seemed to epitomize and whose habits of mind we have come to call Victorian. Nineteenth-century ideas about gender had an impact on masculinity as well as femininity. Soon after the revolutionary and Napoleonic period, men began to dress in sober, practical clothing—and to see as effeminate or dandyish the wigs, ruffled collars, and tight breeches that had earlier been the pride of aristocratic masculinity.

"Passionlessness": Gender and Sexuality

Victorian ideas about sexuality are among the most remarked-on features of nineteenth-century culture. They have become virtually synonymous with anxiety, prudishness, and ignorance. An English mother counseling her daughter about her wedding night is said to have told her to "lie back and think of the empire." Many of these anxieties and prohibitions, however, have been caricatured. More recently, historians have tried to disentangle the teachings or prescriptions of etiquette books and marriage manuals from the actual beliefs of men and women. One of the defining aspects of nineteenth-century ideas about men and women is the extent to which they rested on scientific arguments about nature. Codes of morality and methods of science combined to reinforce the certainty that specific characteristics were inherent to each sex. Men and women had different social roles, and those differences were rooted in their bodies. Women were unsuited for higher education because their brains were smaller or because their bodies were fragile. "Fifteen or 20 days of 28 (we may say nearly always) a woman is not only an invalid, but a wounded one. She ceaselessly suffers from love's eternal wound," wrote the well-known French author Jules Michelet about menstruation.

Finally, scientists and doctors considered women's alleged moral superiority to be literally embodied in an absence of sexual feeling, or "passionlessness." Scientists and doctors considered male sexual desire natural, if not admirable—an unruly force that had to be channeled. Many governments legalized and regulated prostitution—which included the compulsory examination of women for venereal disease—precisely because it provided an outlet for male sexual desire. Doctors disagreed about female sexuality, but the British doctor William Acton stood among those who asserted that women functioned differently:

> I have taken pains to obtain and compare abundant evidence on this subject, and the result of my inquiries I may briefly epitomize as follows:— I should say that the majority of women (happily for society) are not very much troubled with sexual feeling of any kind. What men are habitually, women are only exceptionally.

Like other nineteenth-century men and women, Acton also believed that more open expressions of sexuality were disreputable and, also, that working-class women were less "feminine."

Convictions like these reveal a great deal about Victorian science and medicine, but they did not necessarily dictate people's intimate lives. As far as sexuality was concerned, the absence of any reliable contraception mattered more in people's experiences and feelings than sociologists' or doctors' opinions. Abstinence and withdrawal were the only common techniques for preventing pregnancy. Their effectiveness was limited, since until the 1880s doctors continued to believe that a woman was most fertile during and around her menstrual period. Midwives and prostitutes knew of other forms of contraception and abortifacients (all of them dangerous and most ineffective), and surely some middle-class women did as well, but such information was not respectable middle-class fare. Concretely, then, sexual intercourse was directly related to the very real dangers of frequent pregnancies. In England, one in a hundred childbirths ended in the death of the mother; at a time when a woman might become pregnant eight or nine times in her life, this was a sobering prospect. Those dangers varied with social class, but even among wealthy and better-cared-for women, they took a real toll. It is not surprising that middle-class women's diaries and letters are full of their anticipations of childbirth, both joyful and anxious. Queen Victoria, who bore nine children, declared that childbirth was the "shadow side" of marriage—and she was a pioneer in using anesthesia!

Middle-Class Life in Public

As cities grew, they became increasingly segregated. Middle-class people lived far from the unpleasant sights and smells of industrialization. Their homes, usually built out of the path of the prevailing breeze and therefore of industrial pollution, were havens from congestion. Solidly built, heavily decorated, they proclaimed the financial worth and social respectability of those who dwelt within. In provincial cities they were often freestanding villas. In London, Paris, Berlin, and Vienna, they might be in rows of five- or six-story townhouses or large apartments.

The public buildings in the civic center, many constructed during the nineteenth century, were celebrated as signs of development and prosperity. The middle classes increasingly managed their cities' affairs, although members of the aristocracy retained considerable power, especially in central Europe. And it was these new middle-class civic leaders who provided new industrial cities with many of their architectural landmarks: city halls, stock exchanges, museums, opera houses, concert halls, and department stores. One historian has called these buildings the new cathedrals of the industrial age; projects intended to express the community's values and represent public culture, they were monuments to social change.

THE WORKING CLASSES

Like the middle class, the working class was divided into various subgroups and categories, determined in this case by skill, wages, gender, and workplace. Workers' experiences varied, depending on where they worked, where they lived, and, above all, how much they earned. A skilled textile worker lived a life far different from that of a ditch digger, the former able to afford the food, shelter, and clothing necessary for a decent existence, the latter barely able to scrape by.

Some movement from the ranks of the unskilled to the skilled was possible, if children were provided, or provided themselves, with at least a rudimentary education. Yet education was considered by many parents a luxury, especially since children could be put to work at an early age to supplement a family's meager earnings. Downward mobility from skilled to unskilled was also possible, as technological change—the introduction of the power loom, for example—drove highly paid workers into the ranks of the unskilled and destitute.

Working-class housing was unhealthy and unregulated. In older cities, single-family dwellings were broken up into apartments, often of no more than one room per family. In new manufacturing centers, rows of tiny houses, located close by smoking factories, were built back to back, thereby eliminating any cross-ventilation or space for gardens. Crowding was commonplace.

Household routines, demanding in the middle classes, were grinding for the poor. The family remained a survival network, in which everyone played a crucial role. In addition to working for wages, wives were expected to house, feed, and clothe the family on the very little money different members of the family earned. A good wife was able to make ends meet even in bad times. Working women's daily lives involved constant rounds of carrying and boiling water, cleaning, cooking, and doing laundry. Families could not rely on their own gardens to help supply them with food. City markets catered to their needs for cheap foods, but these were regularly stale, nearly rotten, or dangerously adulterated. Formaldehyde was added to milk to prevent spoilage. Pounded rice was mixed into sugar. Fine brown earth was introduced into cocoa.

Working Women in the Industrial Landscape

Few figures raised more public anxiety and outcry in the nineteenth century than the working woman. Contemporaries worried out loud about the "promiscuous mixing of the sexes" in crowded and humid workshops. Nineteenth-century writers, starting in England and France,

CAPITAL AND LABOUR.

CAPITAL AND LABOUR. In its earliest years, the British magazine *Punch*, though primarily a humorous weekly, manifested a strong social conscience. This 1843 cartoon shows the capitalists enjoying the rewards of their investments while the workers shiver in cold and hunger. ▪ *How would a defender of the new industrial order respond to this cartoon?* ▪ *What is the significance of the image on the top right, showing a scene from the British Empire?*

chronicled what they considered to be the economic and moral horrors of female labor: unattended children running in the streets, small children caught in accidents at the mills or the mines, pregnant women hauling coal, or women laboring alongside men in shops.

Women's work was not new, but industrialization made it more visible. Both before and after the Industrial Revolution labor was divided by gender, but as employers implemented new manufacturing processes, ideas about which jobs were appropriate for women shifted. In traditional textile production, for example, women spun and men operated the looms. In industrial textile factories, on the other hand, employers preferred women and children, both because they were considered more docile and less likely to make trouble and because it was believed that their smaller hands were better suited to the intricate job of tying threads on the power looms. Manufacturers sought to recruit women mill hands from neighboring villages, paying good wages by comparison with other jobs open to women. Most began to work at the age of ten or eleven, and when they had children they either put their children out to a wet nurse, brought them to the mills, or continued to work doing piecework at home. This transformation of the gendered structure of work caused intense anxiety in the first half of the nineteenth century and is one of the reasons that the emerging labor movement began to include calls for excluding women from the workplace in their programs.

Most women did not work in factories, however, and continued to labor at home or in small workshops—"sweatshops," as they came to be called—for notoriously low wages paid not by the hour but by the piece for each shirt stitched or each matchbox glued. The greatest number of unmarried working-class women worked less visibly in domestic service, a job that brought low wages and, to judge by the testimony of many women, coercive sexual relationships with male employers or their sons. Domestic service, however, provided room and board. In a time when a single woman simply could not survive on her own wages, a young woman who had just arrived in the city had few choices: marriage, which was unlikely to happen right away; renting a room in a boardinghouse, many of which were often centers of prostitution; domestic service; or living with someone. How women balanced the demands for money and the time for household work varied with the number and age of their children. Mothers were actually more likely to work when their children were very small, for there were more mouths to feed and the children were not yet old enough to earn wages.

Poverty, the absence of privacy, and the particular vulnerabilities of working-class women made working-class sexuality very different from its middle-class counterpart. Illegitimacy rose dramatically between 1750 and 1850. In Frankfurt, Germany, for example, where the illegitimacy rate had been a mere 2 percent in the early 1700s, it reached 25 percent in 1850. In Bordeaux, France, in 1840, one-third of the recorded births were illegitimate. Reasons for this increase are difficult to establish. Greater mobility and urbanization meant weaker family ties, more opportunities for young men and women, and more vulnerabilities. Premarital sex was an accepted practice in preindustrial villages, but because of the social controls that dominated village life, it was almost always followed by marriage. These controls were weaker in the far more anonymous setting of a factory town or commercial city. The economic uncertainties of the early industrial age meant that a young workingman's promise of marriage based on his expectation of a job might frequently be difficult to fulfill. Economic vulnerability drove many single women into temporary relationships that produced children and a continuing cycle of poverty and abandonment. Historians have shown, however, that in the city as in the countryside, many of these temporary relationships became enduring ones: the parents of illegitimate children would marry later. Prostitution flourished in nineteenth-century cities. At mid-century, the number of prostitutes in Vienna was estimated at fifteen thousand; in Paris, where prostitution was a licensed trade, fifty thousand; in London, eighty thousand. London newspaper reports of the 1850s cataloged the elaborate hierarchies of the underworld of prostitutes and their customers. These included entrepreneurs who ran lodging houses, the pimps and "fancy men" who managed the trade of prostitutes on the street; and the relatively few "prima donnas" or courtesans who enjoyed the protection of rich, upper-middle-class lovers, and whose wealth allowed them to entertain lavishly and move on the fringes of more respectable high society.

Yet the vast majority of prostitutes were young women (and some men) who worked long and dangerous hours in port districts of cities or at lodging houses in the overwhelmingly male working-class neighborhoods. Most prostitutes were young women who had just arrived in the city or working women trying to manage during a period of unemployment. Single women in the cities were very vulnerable to sexual exploitation. Many were abandoned by their partners if they became pregnant, others faced the danger of rape by their employers. Such experiences—abandonment and rape—could often lead to prostitution, since women in these circumstances were unlikely to secure "respectable" employment.

Nineteenth-century writers dramatized what they considered the disreputable sexuality of the "dangerous classes" in the cities. Some of them attributed illegitimacy, prostitution, and so on to the moral weakness of working-class people, others to the systematic changes wrought by industrialization. Both sides, however, overstated the collapse of the family and the destruction of traditional morality. Working-class families transmitted expectations about gender roles and sexual behavior: girls should expect to work, daughters were responsible for caring for their younger siblings as well as for earning wages, sexuality was a fact of life, midwives could help desperate pregnant girls, marriage was an avenue to respectability, and so on. The gulf that separated these expectations and codes from those of middle-class women was one of the most important factors in the development of nineteenth-century class identity.

A Life Apart: "Class Consciousness"

The new demands of life in an industrial economy created common experiences and difficulties. The factory system denied skilled workers the pride in craft they had previously enjoyed. Stripped of the protections of guilds and apprenticeships and prevented from organizing by legislation in France, Germany, and Britain in the first half of the nineteenth century, workers felt vulnerable in the face of their socially and politically powerful employers. Factory hours were long—usually twelve to fourteen hours. Textile mills were unventilated, and minute particles of lint lodged in workers' lungs. Machines were unfenced and posed dangers to child workers. British physicians cataloged the toll that long hours tending machines took on children, including spinal curvature and bone malformations. Children were also employed in large numbers in mines—over fifty thousand worked in British mines in 1841.

Factories also imposed new routines and disciplines. Artisans in earlier times worked long hours for little pay, but they set their own schedules and controlled the pace of work, moving from their home workshops to their small garden plots as they wished. In a factory all hands learned the discipline of the clock. To increase production, the factory system encouraged the breaking down of the manufacturing process into specialized steps, each with its own time.

Workers began to see machinery itself as the tyrant that changed their lives and bound them to industrial slavery.

Yet the defining feature of working-class life was vulnerability—to unemployment, sickness, accidents in dangerous jobs, family problems, and spikes in the prices of food. Seasonal unemployment, high in almost all trades, made it impossible to collect regular wages. Markets for manufactured goods were small and unstable, producing cyclical economic depressions; when those came, thousands of workers found themselves laid off with no system of unemployment insurance to sustain them. The early decades of industrialization were also marked by several severe agricultural depressions and economic crises. During the crisis years of the 1840s, half the working population of Britain's industrial cities was unemployed. In Paris, eighty-five thousand went on relief in 1840. Families survived by working several small jobs, pawning their possessions, and getting credit from local wineshops and grocery stores. The chronic insecurity of working-class life helped fuel the creation of workers' self-help societies, fraternal associations, and early socialist organizations. It also meant that economic crises could have explosive consequences (see Chapter 20).

By mid-century, various experiences were beginning to make working people conscious of themselves as different from and in opposition to the middle classes. Changes in the workplace—whether the introduction of machines and factory labor, speedups, subcontracting to cheap labor, or the loss of guild protections—were part of the picture. The social segregation of the rapidly expanding nineteenth-century cities also contributed to the sense that working people lived a life apart. Class differences seemed embedded in a very wide array of everyday experiences and beliefs: work, private life, expectations for children, the roles of men and women, and definitions of respectability. Over the course of the nineteenth century all of these different experiences gave concrete, specific meaning to the word *class*.

CONCLUSION

Why did the Industrial Revolution occur at this moment in human history? Why did it begin in Europe? Why did it not occur in other regions in the world with large populations and advanced technologies, such as China or India? These fundamental questions remain subject to serious debate among historians. One school of explanations focuses on the fact that the mechanization of industry occurred first

After You Read This Chapter

Visit StudySpace for quizzes, additional review materials, and multi-media documents. **wwnorton.com/studyspace**

REVIEWING THE OBJECTIVES

- The Industrial Revolution in Europe began in northern Great Britain. What circumstances made this process of economic development begin there?

- Certain industries were particularly suitable for the kinds of technological developments that encouraged industrialization. What were these industries and where did they exist in Europe?

- Industrial development changed the nature of work and production in significant ways. What were these changes, and how did they change the relations between laborers and their employers, or local producers and wider markets?

- Industrialization had social effects far beyond the factories. What larger changes in European society were associated with the Industrial Revolution?

- A large and diverse group of middle-class people emerged in Europe as a result of the social changes brought on by industrialization. What kinds of people qualified as middle-class during the nineteenth century and how were they different from other social groups?

in northern Europe, and seeks to explain the Industrial Revolution's origins in terms of this region's vibrant towns, its well-developed commercial markets, and the presence of a prosperous land-owning elite that had few prejudices against entrepreneurial activity. These historians have suggested that industrialization is best understood as a process rooted in European culture and history.

More recently, however, historians with a more global approach have argued that it may be incorrect to assert that industrialization developed as it did because of the advantages enjoyed by a central, European, core. Instead, they have explored the possibility that the world's economies constituted a larger interlocking system that had no definitive center until *after* the take-off of European industrialization. Before that period, when it came to agricultural practices, ecological constraints, population densities, urbanization, and technological development, *many* global regions were not so different from the western European model. In the end, suggest these historians, Europe was able to move more quickly to industrial production because its economies were better positioned to mobilize the resources available to them on the periphery of their trading sphere. The access enjoyed by European traders to agricultural products from slave-owning societies in the Americas helped them escape the ecological constraints imposed by their own intensely farmed lands, and made the move to an industrial economy possible. Contingent factors—such as patterns of disease and epidemic or the location of coal fields—may have also played a role.

There is less debate about the consequences of the Industrial Revolution within Europe. New forms of industrial production created a new economy and changed the nature of work for both men and women. Industrialization changed the landscape of Europe and changed the structures of families and the private lives of people in both the cities and the countryside. Industrialization created new forms of wealth along with new kinds of poverty. It also fostered an acute awareness of the disparity between social groups. In the eighteenth century, that disparity would have been described in terms of birth, rank, or privilege. In the nineteenth century, it was increasingly seen in terms of class. Both champions and critics of the new industrial order spoke of a "class society." The identities associated with class were formed in the crowded working-class districts of the new cities, in experiences of work, and in the new conditions of respectability that determined life in middle-class homes. These new identities would be sharpened in the political events to which we now turn.

PEOPLE, IDEAS, AND EVENTS IN CONTEXT

- Why was **ENCLOSURE** an important factor in the Industrial Revolution?
- What was the **FLY SHUTTLE** or the **SPINNING JENNY**? What was the **COTTON GIN**? What effect did these machines have on industrial development?
- What was the significance of **EUROPEAN EMPIRE** and overseas expansion for industrialization?
- How did industrialization affect **POPULATION GROWTH** in Europe? What effects did it have on the **PEASANTRY**? On **URBAN POPULATIONS**?
- What **ENVIRONMENTAL CHANGES** were associated with the use of new sources of fuel such as coal or the construction of large and concentrated centers of industrial manufacture?
- What was the **IRISH POTATO FAMINE** and how was it related to the economic developments of nineteenth-century Europe?

CONSEQUENCES

- What might the changes associated with the Industrial Revolution have done to people's conceptions of time and space? How might they have perceived their lives against what they knew of the experience of their parents' generation or what they anticipated for their children?
- What did the Industrial Revolution do for European nation-states?

STORY LINES

- The conservative regimes that defeated Napoleon in 1815 set out to reestablish the principle of dynastic rule and ensure a balance of forces between European powers. In this they succeeded: for several generations no single country was able to threaten the others as Napoleon had done.

- In spite of their successes, conservative rulers in Europe remained on the defensive against liberalism, nationalism, and socialism, while facing repeated revolutionary challenges, both at home and abroad.

- The conservative political reaction after 1815 found its cultural counterpart in Romanticism. This diverse intellectual, literary, and artistic movement rejected the Enlightenment's rationalism and emphasized instead the power of nature, human emotions, and a freedom of expression unrestrained by social conventions.

CHRONOLOGY

1810–1825	South American revolutions
1814–1815	Congress of Vienna
1821–1827	Greek War of Independence
1823	France restores King Ferdinand of Spain
1825	Decembrist Revolt in Russia
1830	Revolutions in France and Belgium
1832	British Reform Bill
1838	Slavery abolished in British West Indies
1840s	Chartist Movement in Britain
1846	Corn Laws repealed
1848	Karl Marx, *The Communist Manifesto*
1848	Revolutions of 1848 (every major capital in Europe except in Britain, Spain, and Russia)

From Restoration to Revolution, 1815–1848

When the defeated Napoleon left the field of battle at Waterloo on June 18, 1815, headed eventually to exile on the rocky island of St. Helena in the South Atlantic, his victorious opponents hoped the age of revolution had ended. The Austrian foreign minister, Klemens von Metternich, perhaps the most influential conservative diplomat of the early nineteenth century, called revolution a "sickness," "plague," and "cancer," and with his allies set out to inoculate Europe against any outbreak. In their view, revolution produced war and disorder. Peace depended on avoiding political turmoil and reinforcing the power of conservative monarchies in all corners of Europe. Bolstering the legitimacy of such monarchies was Metternich's primary goal in the post-Napoleonic decades.

Within Metternich's lifetime, however, waves of revolution would again sweep across Europe. Conservative efforts to restore the old order succeeded only in part. Why? To begin with, the developments of the eighteenth century proved impossible to reverse. The expansion of an informed public, begun in the Enlightenment, continued. The word *citizen* (and the liberal political ideas contained within it) was controversial in the aftermath

475

of the French Revolution, but it was difficult to banish the term from political debates. Liberalism's fundamental principles—equality before the law, freedom of expression, and the consent of the governed—were still a potent threat to Europe's dynastic rulers, especially when coupled with the emotions stirred up by popular nationalism.

At the same time, the political opposition to the conservative order in Europe began to be infused with new and more radical political ideologies. Whereas some liberals were comfortable living under a constitutional monarch and continued to believe that voting was a privilege that should be extended only to wealthy property owners, republicans called for universal (male) suffrage and an end to monarchy altogether. Socialists disturbed by the inequalities produced in the new market economy went even further and argued that political reform was not enough. To socialists, justice was possible only with a radical reordering of society that redistributed property equitably. Between 1815 and 1848, none of these more radical oppositional movements succeeded in carrying the day, but their ideas circulated widely and occupied the attention of conservative monarchs (and their police spies) throughout Europe.

In culture as well as in politics, imagination and a sense of possibility were among the defining characteristics of the first half of the century. Romanticism broke with what many artists considered the cold Classicism and formality of eighteenth-century art. The Enlightenment had championed reason; the Romantics prized subjectivity, feeling, and spontaneity. Their revolt against eighteenth-century conventions had ramifications far beyond literature and painting. The Romantics had no single political creed: some were fervent revolutionaries and others fervent traditionalists who looked to the past, to religion or history for inspiration. Their sensibility, however, infused politics and culture. And to look ahead, their collective search for new means of expression sent nineteenth-century art off in a new direction.

THE SEARCH FOR ORDER IN EUROPE, 1815–1830

In 1814 the European powers—including the France of the restored king, Louis XVIII—met at the Congress of Vienna to settle pressing questions about the post-Napoleonic political order. An observer of the lavish balls and celebrations that accompanied the Congress's diplomatic negotiations might well have assumed that the calendar had been turned back several decades, to a time when the European nobility had not yet been humiliated and terrorized by violent revolutionaries. But the celebrations of Louis XVIII's return to the throne could not hide the fact that twenty years of war, revolution, and political experimentation had changed Europe in fundamental ways. The task of the Congress of Vienna was to reinforce Europe's monarchical regimes against the powerful social and political forces that had been unleashed in the years since 1789.

The Congress of Vienna and the Restoration

The Russian tsar Alexander I (r. 1801–25) and the Austrian diplomat Klemens von Metternich (1773–1859) dominated the Congress of Vienna. After Napoleon's fall Russia became the most powerful continental state. Alexander I presented himself during the Napoleonic Wars as the "liberator" of Europe, and many feared that he would substitute an all-powerful Russia for an all-powerful France. The French prince Charles Maurice de Talleyrand (1754–1838), a former bishop who served in both the revolutionary and Napoleonic governments, had a surprisingly strong supporting role. Metternich's central concerns at the Congress of Vienna were checking Russian expansionism and preventing political and social change. He favored treating the defeated French with moderation. Nevertheless, he remained an arch-conservative who readily resorted to harsh repressive tactics, including secret police and spying. But the peace he crafted was enormously significant and helped prevent a major European war until 1914.

The Congress sought to restore order and legitimate authority. It recognized Louis XVIII as the sovereign of France and confirmed the restoration of Bourbon rulers in Spain and the two Sicilies. The other monarchs had no interest in undermining the French restoration: Louis XVIII was a bulwark against revolution. But after Napoleon's Hundred Days the allies imposed an indemnity of 700 million francs and an occupying army for five years. France's borders remained the same as in 1789—less than the revolution's "greater France" but not as punitive as they might have been.

The guiding principle of the peace was the balance of power, according to which no country should be powerful enough to destabilize international relations. Metternich's immediate goal, therefore, was to build a barrier against renewed French expansion. The Dutch Republic, conquered by the French in 1795, was restored as the kingdom of the Netherlands, securing France's northern border. The Congress also ceded the left bank of the Rhine to Prussia, and Austria expanded into northern Italy.

THE CONGRESS OF VIENNA. Note how the borders of European nations were established after the final defeat of Napoleon in 1815, and compare these boundaries to Europe in 1713 after the Peace of Utrecht. ▪ *What major changes had occurred in the intervening years in central Europe?* ▪ *Which territorial powers played an active role in determining the balance of power at the Congress of Vienna?* ▪ *What social or political developments might disrupt this balance?*

In central Europe, the allied powers reorganized the German states, reducing them from over three hundred in number to thirty-nine. Prussia and Habsburg Austria joined these German states in a loosely structured German Confederation, with Austria careful to reserve for itself the presidency of this new body, as a check against attempts by the Prussians to increase their regional influence. Eventually, this confederation became the basis for German unification, but this was not the intention in Vienna in 1815. Bavaria, Württemberg, and Saxony remained independent kingdoms. The allies compromised on Poland: a nominally

independent kingdom was placed under the control of Tsar Alexander, with large slices of formerly Polish territory being handed over to Austria and Prussia. Meanwhile, Britain received formerly French territories in South Africa and South America, as well as the island of Ceylon.

The Congress of Vienna also called for a Concert of Europe to secure the peace. Britain, Austria, Prussia, and Russia pledged to cooperate in the suppression of any disturbances—and France officially joined this conservative alliance in 1818. Alexander I pushed for what he called a Holy Alliance, dedicated to justice, Christian charity, and peace. The British foreign minister remained skeptical—calling the Holy Alliance "a piece of sublime mysticism and nonsense"—but agreed that the European powers should defend their conception of authority, centered on legitimacy. A ruler was legitimate if his power was guaranteed not only by claims of divine right but also by international treaties and support by his recognized peers. The Concert of Europe's opposition to liberal notions of political representation and national self-determination could not be more clear.

Revolt against Restoration

Much of the resistance to the Restoration was clandestine. In the Italian peninsula, the Carbonari (the name came from the charcoal they used to blacken their faces) vowed to oppose the government in Vienna and its conservative allies. Their political views varied: some called for constitutions and representative government, and others praised Bonaparte. The Carbonari's influence spread through southern Europe and France in the 1820s, with members meeting in secret and identifying one another with closely guarded rituals. Veterans of Napoleon's armies and military officers were prominent in their ranks.

In Naples and Piedmont and especially in Spain and the Spanish Empire, opposition to Metternich's Concert of Europe turned to revolt when monarchs restored by the Congress of Vienna betrayed their promises of reform. Metternich responded by spurring Austria, Prussia, and Russia to take a strong stand against revolution. In the Troppau Memorandum (1820), the conservative regimes pledged to assist one another in suppressing revolt. Austria dealt firmly with the Italian revolts, while France sent two hundred thousand troops to the Iberian peninsula in 1823, crushing the Spanish revolutionaries and restoring King Ferdinand's authority.

Revolution in Latin America

King Ferdinand's empire in Latin America, however, would not be restored. Napoleon's conquest of Spain (1807) had shaken Spain's once vast empire. Local elites in the colonies who resented Spanish imperial control took advantage of the crown's weakness to push for independence. Rio de la Plata (now Argentina) was the first to succeed, declaring independence in 1816. Soon after, a monarchist general from Rio de la Plata, José de San Martín (1778–1850), led an expedition to liberate Chile and Peru. At the same time, Simón Bolívar (1783–1830), a republican leader, sparked a series of uprisings from Venezuela to Bolivia. Bolívar and San Martín joined forces, though Bolívar's plans were more radical—he envisioned mobilizing free people of color and slaves (who made up roughly a quarter of those fighting the Spanish) as well as Indians to fight against Spanish rule. Bolívar's goal was to create a pan-American republic on the continent, along the lines of the United States. These political revolts unleashed violent social conflicts and, in some cases, civil war. Elites who wanted only to free themselves from Spain opposed groups who wanted land reform and an end to slavery. In the end, the radical movements were suppressed, and the newly independent Latin American nations were dominated by an alliance of conservative landowners and military officers.

Britain and the newly ambitious United States prevented the European powers from intervening in the Latin American revolutions. In 1823, U.S. President James Monroe issued the Monroe Doctrine, declaring that European meddling in the Americas would be seen as a hostile act. Without British support, however, the Monroe doctrine was unenforceable. Britain saw the new South American republics as potential trading partners and used its navy to prevent Spain from intervening. By the 1820s, the once vast Spanish Empire had vanished, ending an age that had begun in 1492. Brazil's independence in 1823 similarly ended the era of Portuguese colonialism in South America. Together, these revolutions demonstrated the circular relationships that bound the Atlantic world together. Encouraged by political movements associated with the French Revolution and Napoleon, the Latin American revolutionaries would in turn inspire nationalists in Europe who sought to overthrow Metternich's conservative Concert of Europe.

Russia: The Decembrists

Revolt also broke out in conservative Russia. In 1825, Tsar Alexander died, and a group of army officers known as the Decembrists led an uprising to push the pace of reform. Many were veterans of the Napoleonic wars, and they feared that Russia could not live up to its promise to be the "liberator of Europe" without abolishing serfdom and ending the tsar's monopoly on power.

The officers failed. The new tsar, Nicholas I (r. 1825–55) sentenced many mutinous soldiers to hard labor and executed the five aristocratic leaders. Fearing they would be seen as martyrs, the tsar had them hung at dawn behind the walls of a fortress in St. Petersburg and buried in secret graves.

Nicholas went on to become Europe's most uncompromising conservative. He created a powerful political police force to prevent further domestic disorder. Still, Russia was not immune to change. Bureaucracy became more centralized, more efficient, and less dependent on the nobility. Russian laws were codified in 1832. Landowners responded to increased demand for Russian grain by reorganizing their estates to increase productivity, and the state began to build railroads to transport the grain to Western markets. Meanwhile, other opponents of the regime, such as the socialist writer Alexander Herzen, carried on the Decembrists unresolved political legacy.

Southeastern Europe: Greece and Serbia

When the Greeks and Serbians revolted against the once powerful Ottoman Empire, the conservative European powers showed themselves to be more tolerant of rebellion. The Greek war for independence (1821–27) drew support from the British government, and sympathy for the Greeks was widespread in Europe. Christians in Europe cast the rebellion as part of an ongoing struggle between Christianity and Islam. From a secular point of view, the Greek's battle could be interpreted as both a crusade for liberty and a struggle to preserve the ancient heritage of the land. Increasingly, Europeans spoke of Greece as the birthplace of the West. "We are all Greeks," wrote Percy Shelley, the Romantic poet. Europeans sought to identify themselves with a Greek heritage, which they contrasted with images of Islamic tyranny. Europeans, in short, saw the struggle through their own lens.

On the ground in Greece, the struggle was brutal and massacres of civilians occurred on both sides. In March 1822, the Greeks invaded the island of Chios and proclaimed its independence. When Ottoman troops arrived to retake the island, the Greek invaders killed their Turkish prisoners and fled. The Turks took revenge by slaughtering thousands of Greeks and selling forty thousand more into slavery. The French Romantic painter Eugène Delacroix memorialized the event in a painting that characteristically depicted only Turkish brutality (see the image at left).

In the end, Greek independence depended on great-power politics. In 1827, British, French, and Russian troops sided against the Turks, who were forced to concede. A similar intervention resulted in Serbian autonomy within the Ottoman Empire in 1828. With Russian aid, Serbia became a semi-independent Orthodox Christian principality (with significant minority populations) under Ottoman rule. Both of these new nations, however, were small and fragile. Only eight hundred thousand Greeks actually lived in the new Greek state, Serbia, whose existence was protected by Russia until 1856. Moreover, neither of the new nations broke their close links with the Ottomans, and Greek and Serbian merchants, bankers, and administrators were still very present in the Ottoman Empire. The region remained a borderland of Europe, a region where peoples alternated between tolerant coexistence and bitter conflict.

THE MASSACRE AT CHIOS BY EUGÈNE DELACROIX (1789–1863). Delacroix was a Romantic painter of dramatic and emotional scenes. Here he put his brush to work for the cause of Greek nationalism, eulogizing the victims of killings on the island Chios during the Greek war of independence against the Ottoman Empire. ■ *How did the choices that Delacroix made in his depiction of the massacre's victims shape the vision of the conflict for his European audience?*

TAKING SIDES: NEW IDEOLOGIES IN POLITICS

These movements for national independence made it clear that ideologies associated with the French Revolution were very much alive. An ideology may be defined as a coherent system of thought regarding the social and political order, one that consciously competes with other views of how the world is or should be. The major political ideologies of modern times—conservatism, liberalism, socialism, and nationalism—were first articulated in this period. Their roots lay in earlier times, but ongoing political battles brought them to the fore. So did the Industrial Revolution (see Chapter 19) and the social changes that accompanied it, which proved a tremendous spur to political and social thought. Would the advance of industry yield progress or misery? What were the "rights of man," and who would enjoy them? Did equality necessarily go hand in hand with liberty? A brief survey of the political horizon will show how different groups formulated their responses to these questions and will dramatize how the ground had shifted since the eighteenth century.

Principles of Conservatism

At the Congress of Vienna and in the Restoration generally, the most important guiding concept was legitimacy. Legitimacy had broad appeal as a general antirevolutionary policy. It might be best understood as a code word for a new political order. Conservatives aimed to make legitimate—and thus to solidify—both the monarchy's authority and a hierarchical social order. The most thoughtful conservatives of the period did not believe that the old order would survive completely intact or that time could be reversed, especially after the events of the 1820s made it clear that the Restoration would be challenged. They did believe, however, that the monarchy guaranteed political stability, that the nobility were the rightful leaders of the nation, and that both needed to play active and effective roles in public life. Edmund Burke, for instance, opposed the French Revolution's talk of natural rights, and counseled deference to tradition and history. He assailed Enlightenment individualism for ignoring the bonds and collective institutions (church and family) that he believed held society together. Conservatives believed that change had to be slow, incremental, and managed so as to strengthen rather than weaken the structures of authority. Conserving the past and cultivating tradition would ensure an orderly future.

Conservatism was not simply the province of intellectuals. A more broadly based revival of religion in the early nineteenth century also expressed a popular reaction against revolution and an emphasis on order, discipline, and tradition. What was more, conservative thinkers also exercised influence well beyond their immediate circle. Their emphasis on history, on the untidy and unpredictable ways in which history unfolded, and their awareness of the past became increasingly central to social thought and artistic visions of the first half of the century.

Liberalism

Liberalism's core was a commitment to individual liberties, or rights. Liberals believed that the most important function of government was to protect liberties and that doing so would benefit all, promoting justice, knowledge, progress, and prosperity. Liberalism had three components. First, liberalism called for equality before the law, which meant ending traditional privileges and the restrictive power of rank and hereditary authority. Second, liberalism held that government needed to be based on political rights and the consent of the governed. Third, in economics liberals believed that individuals should be free to engage in economic activities without interference from the state or their community.

The roots of legal and political liberalism lay in the late seventeenth century, in the work of John Locke, who had defended the English Parliament's rebellion against absolutism and the "inalienable" rights of the British people (see Chapter 15). Liberalism had been developed by the Enlightenment writers of the eighteenth century and, especially, by the founding texts of the American and French Revolutions (the Declaration of Independence and the Declaration of the Rights of Man). Freedom from arbitrary authority, imprisonment, and censorship; freedom of the press; the right to assemble and deliberate: these principles were the starting points for nineteenth-century liberalism. Liberals believed in individual rights, that those rights were inalienable, and that they should be guaranteed in written constitutions. (Conservatives, as we saw earlier, considered constitutions abstract and dangerous.) Most liberals called for constitutional as opposed to hereditary monarchy; all agreed that a monarch who abused power could legitimately be overthrown.

Liberals advocated direct representation in government—at least for those who had the property and public standing to be trusted with the responsibilities of power. Liberalism by no means required democracy. To the contrary, who should have the right to vote was a hotly debated issue. Nineteenth-century liberals, with fresh memories of the French Revolution of 1789, were torn between their belief in rights and their fears of political turmoil. They considered property and education essential prerequisites for participation in politics. Wealthy liberals opposed extending the vote to the common people. To demand universal male suffrage was radical indeed, and to speak of enfranchising women or people of color even more so. As far as slavery was concerned, nineteenth-century liberalism inherited the contradictions of the Enlightenment. Belief in individual liberty collided with vested economic interests, determination to preserve order and property, and increasingly "scientific" theories of racial inequality (see Chapter 19).

Economic liberalism was newer. Its founding text was Adam Smith's *The Wealth of Nations* (1776), which attacked mercantilism (the government practice of regulating manufacturing and trade to raise revenues) in the name of free markets. Smith's argument that the economy should be based on a "system of natural liberty" was reinforced by a second generation of economists and popularized in journals such as the *Economist*, founded in 1838. The economists (or political economists, as they were called) sought to identify basic economic laws: the law of supply and demand, the balance of trade, the law of diminishing returns, and so on. They argued that economic policy had to begin by recognizing these laws, in order to avoid inadvertently distorting what they believed was a naturally self-regulating market system.

For this reason, the political economists believed that economic activity should be unregulated. Labor should be contracted freely, unhampered by guilds or unions. Property should be unencumbered by feudal restrictions. Goods should circulate freely, which meant, concretely, an end to government-granted monopolies and traditional practices of of regulating markets, especially in valuable commodities such as grain, flour, or corn. At the time of the Irish famine, for instance, their writings played a role in hardening opposition to government intervention or relief (see Chapter 19). Government's role was to preserve order and protect property but not to interfere with the natural play of economic forces, a doctrine known as *laissez-faire*, which translates, roughly, as "leave things to go on their own." This strict opposition to government intervention makes nineteenth-century liberalism different from common understandings of "liberalism" in the United States today (see Chapter 29).

In Great Britain, where political freedoms were relatively well established, liberals focused on expanding the franchise, on laissez-faire economics and free trade, and on reforms aimed at creating limited and efficient government. In this respect, one of the most influential British liberals was Jeremy Bentham (1748–1832). Unlike Smith, Bentham did not believe that human interests were naturally harmonious or that a stable social order could emerge naturally from a body of self-interested individuals. Instead he proposed that society adopt the organizing principle of utilitarianism. Social institutions and laws (an electoral system, for instance, or a tariff) should be measured according to their social usefulness—according to whether they produced the "greatest happiness of the greatest number." If a law passed this test, it could remain on the books; if it failed, it should be jettisoned. Utilitarians acknowledged that each individual best understood his or her own inter-

ests and was, therefore, best left free, whenever possible, to pursue those interests as he or she saw fit. Only when an individual's interests conflicted with the interests—the happiness—of the greatest number was individual freedom to be curtailed. The intensely practical spirit of utilitarianism enhanced its influence as a creed for reform.

Radicalism, Republicanism, and Early Socialism

The liberals were flanked on their left by two radical groups: republicans and socialists. Whereas liberals advocated a constitutional monarchy (in the name of stability and keeping power in the hands of men of property), republicans, as their name implies, pressed further, demanding a government by the people, an expanded franchise, and democratic participation in politics. Where liberals called for individualism and laissez-faire, socialists put the accent on equality. To put it in the terms that were used at the time, socialists raised the "social question." How could growing social inequality and the miseries of working people be remedied? Socialists offered varied responses to this question, ranging from new ways of organizing everyday life along cooperative principles to collective ownership of the means of production.

Socialism was a nineteenth-century system of thought and a response in large measure to the visible problems ushered in by industrialization: the intensification of labor, the poverty of working-class neighborhoods in industrial cities, and the widespread perception that a hierarchy based on rank and privilege had been replaced by one based on social class. For the socialists, the problems of industrial society were not incidental; they arose from the core

QUADRILLE DANCING AT LANARK, ROBERT OWEN'S MODEL COMMUNITY. Owen's Scottish experiment with cooperative production and community building, including schooling for infants, was only one of many utopian ventures in early-nineteenth-century Europe and North America.

principles of competition, individualism, and private property. The socialists did not oppose industry and economic development. On the contrary, what they took from the Enlightenment was a commitment to reason and human progress. They believed society could be both industrial and humane.

These radical thinkers were often explicitly utopian. Robert Owen, a wealthy industrialist turned reformer, bought a large cotton factory at New Lanark in Scotland and proceeded to organize the mill and the surrounding town according to the principles of cooperation rather than those of profitability. New Lanark organized good housing and sanitation, good working conditions, child care, free schooling, and a system of social security for the factory's workers. The Frenchman Charles Fourier, too, tried to organize utopian communities based on the abolition of the wage system, the division of work according to people's natural inclinations, the complete equality of the sexes, and collectively organized child care and household labor. The charismatic socialist Flora Tristan (1803–1844) toured France speaking to workers about the principles of cooperation and the equality of men and women. Many people took these utopian visions seriously, a measure of people's unhappiness with early industrialization and of their conviction that society could be organized along radically different lines.

Other socialists proposed simpler, practical reforms. Louis Blanc, a French politician and journalist, campaigned for universal male suffrage with an eye to giving working-class men control of the state, which would then be transformed to offer credit to working people and guarantee employment by establishing producer associations run by workers. Such workshops were established, fleetingly, during the French Revolution of 1848. So were clubs promoting women's rights. Pierre-Joseph Proudhon (1809–1865) also proposed establishing producers' cooperatives that would sell goods at a price workers could afford. Proudhon's "What Is Property?"—to which the famous answer was "property is theft"—became one of the most widely read socialist pamphlets, familiar to artisans, laborers, and middle-class intellectuals, including Karl Marx.

Karl Marx's Socialism

Karl Marx (1818–1883) first became widely known after 1848, when a wave of revolutions and violent confrontation seemed to confirm his distinctive theory of history and make earlier socialists' emphasis on cooperation, setting up experimental communities, and peaceful reorganization of industrial society seem naive.

Marx grew up in Trier, in the western section of Germany. His family was Jewish, but his father had converted to Protestantism to be able to work as a lawyer. Marx studied law briefly at the University of Berlin before turning instead to philosophy and particularly the ideas of a conservative thinker, Georg Wilhelm Friedrich Hegel. In Berlin, Marx associated with the so-called Young Hegelians, a group of rebellious students who chafed under the narrow thinking of a deeply conservative Prussian university system. His radicalism (and atheism, for he repudiated all his family's religious affiliations) made it impossible for him to get a post in the university. He became a journalist, but his criticism of legal privilege and political repression led the Prussian government to send Marx into exile—first in Paris, then Brussels, and eventually London.

While in Paris, Marx studied early socialist theory, economics, and the history of the French Revolution. He also began a lifelong intellectual and political partnership with Friedrich Engels (1820–1895). Engels was the son of a textile manufacturer from the German Rhineland and had been sent to learn business with a merchant firm in Manchester, one of the heartlands of England's Industrial Revolution (see Chapter 19). Engels worked in the family business until 1870, but this did not prevent him from taking up his pen to denounce the miserable working and living conditions in Manchester and what he saw as the systematic inequalities of capitalism (*The Condition of the Working Classes in England,* 1844). Marx and Engels joined a small international group of radical artisans called the League of the Just, in 1847 renamed the Communist League. The league asked Marx to draft a statement of its principles, published in 1848 as the *Communist Manifesto.*

The *Communist Manifesto* laid out Marx's theory of history in short form. World history had passed through three major stages, each characterized by conflict between social groups: master and slave in ancient slavery, lord and serf in feudalism, and bourgeois and proletariat in capitalism. According to Marx's theory, the stage of feudal or aristocratic property relations had ended in 1789, when the French Revolution overthrew the old order, ushering in bourgeois political power and industrial capitalism. In the *Communist Manifesto,* Marx and Engels admired the revolutionary accomplishments of capitalism, saying that the bourgeoisie had "created more impressive and more colossal productive forces than had all preceding generations together." But, they argued, the revolutionary character of capitalism would also undermine the bourgeois economic order. As capital became more concentrated in the hands of the few, a growing army of wage workers would become increasingly aware of its economic and political disenfran-

KARL MARX, 1882. Despite the unusual smile in this portrait, Marx was near the end of his life, attempting to recuperate in Algeria from sickness and the deaths of his wife and daughter.

chisement; struggle between these classes was central to industrial capitalism itself. Eventually, the *Communist Manifesto* predicted, recurring economic crises, caused by capitalism's unending need for new markets and the cyclical instability of overproduction, would bring capitalism to collapse. Workers would seize the state, reorganize the means of production, abolish private property, and eventually create a communist society.

What was distinctive about Marx's version of socialism? It took up the disparity between public proclamations of progress and workers' daily experiences in a systematic, scholarly manner. Marx was an inexhaustible reader and thinker, with an extraordinarily broad range. He took insights where he found them: in British economics, French history, and German philosophy. He wove others' ideas that labor was the source of value and that property was expropriation into a new theory of history that was also a thoroughgoing critique of nineteenth-century liberalism.

Citizenship and Community: Nationalism

Of all the political ideologies of the early nineteenth century, nationalism is most difficult to grasp. What, exactly, counted as a nation? Who demanded a nation, and what did their demand mean? In the early nineteenth century, nationalism was usually aligned with liberalism against the conservative states that dominated Europe after Napoleon's fall. As the century progressed, however, it became increasingly clear that nationalism could be molded to fit any doctrine.

The meaning of *nation* has changed over time. The term comes from the Latin verb *nasci*, "to be born," and suggests "common birth." In sixteenth-century England, the nation designated the aristocracy, or those who shared noble birthright. The French nobility also referred to itself as the nation. Those earlier and unfamiliar usages are important. They highlight the most significant development of the late eighteenth and early nineteenth centuries: the French Revolution redefined nation to mean the people, or the sovereign people. The revolutionaries of 1789 boldly claimed that the nation, and no longer the king, was the sovereign power. *Vive la nation*, or "long live the nation"—a phrase found everywhere, from government decrees to revolutionary festivals, engravings, and memorabilia—celebrated a new political community, not a territory or an ethnicity. Philosophically, the French revolutionaries and the others who developed their views took from Jean-Jacques Rousseau the argument that a regenerated nation, based on the equality of its members (on the limits of that equality, see Chapter 18), was not only more just but also more powerful. On a more concrete level, the revolutionaries built a national state, army, and legal system whose jurisdiction trumped the older regional powers of the nobility, a national system of law, and a national army. In the aftermath of the French Revolution of 1789, the nation became what one historian calls "the collective image of modern citizenry."

In the early nineteenth century, then, *nation* symbolized legal equality, constitutional government, and unity, or an end to feudal privileges and divisions. Conservatives disliked the term. National unity and the creation of national political institutions threatened to erode the local power of aristocratic elites. New nations rested on constitutions, which, as we have seen, conservatives considered dangerous abstractions. Nationalism became an important rallying cry for liberals across Europe in the early nineteenth century precisely because it was associated with political transformation. It celebrated the achievements and political awakening of the common people.

Nationalism also went hand in hand with liberal demands for economic modernity. Economists, such as the influential German Friedrich List (1789–1846), sought to develop national economies and national infrastructures: larger, stronger, better integrated, and more effective systems of banking, trade, transportation, production, and

MAJOR EUROPEAN LANGUAGE GROUPS, c. 1850. Compare the distribution of language groups in Europe with the political boundaries of European nations in 1848. ■ *Do they line up?* ■ *Which political units were forced to deal with a multitude of languages within their borders?* ■ *How might this distribution of language groups be related to the history of European nationalisms?*

It rested on specific nineteenth-century political and economic developments; on rising literacy; on the creation of national institutions such as schools or the military; and on the new importance of national rituals, from voting to holidays, village festivals, and the singing of anthems. Nineteenth-century governments sought to develop national feeling, to link their peoples more closely to their states. State-supported educational systems taught a "national" language, fighting the centrifugal forces of traditional dialects. Italian became the official language of the Italian nation, despite the fact that only 2.5 percent of the population spoke it. In other words, even a minority could define a national culture. Textbooks and self-consciously nationalist theater, poetry, and painting helped elaborate and sometimes "invent" a national heritage.

Political leaders associated the nation with specific causes. But ordinary activities, such as reading a daily newspaper in the morning, helped people imagine and identify with their fellow citizens. As one influential historian puts it, "[A]ll communities larger than primordial villages of face-to-face contact (and perhaps even these) are imagined." The nation is imagined as "limited," "sovereign," and "finally, it is imagined as a community, because regardless of the actual inequality and exploitation that may prevail . . . , the nation is always conceived as a deep, horizontal comradeship." The different meanings of *nationhood*, the various political beliefs it evoked, and the powerful emotions it tapped made nationalism exceptionally unpredictable.

Conservatism, liberalism, republicanism, socialism, and nationalism were the principal political ideologies of the early nineteenth century. They were rooted in the eighteenth century but brought to the forefront by the political turmoil of the early nineteenth century. Some nineteenth-century ideologies were continuations of the French revolutionary trio: liberty (from arbitrary authority), equality (or the end of legal privilege), and fraternity (the creation of new communities of citizens). Others, like conservatism, were reactions against the French Revolution. All could be reinterpreted. All became increasingly common points of reference as the century unfolded.

distribution. List linked ending the territorial fragmentation of the German states and the development of manufacturing to "culture, prosperity, and liberty."

Nationalism, however, could easily undermine other liberal values. When liberals insisted on the value and importance of individual liberties, those committed to building nations replied that their vital task might require the sacrifice of some measure of each citizen's freedom. The Napoleonic army, a particularly powerful symbol of nationhood, appealed to conservative proponents of military strength and authority as well as to liberals who wanted an army of citizens.

Nineteenth-century nationalists wrote as if national feeling were natural, inscribed in the movement of history. They waxed poetic about the sudden awakening of feelings slumbering within the collective consciousness of a "German," an "Italian," a "French," or a "British" people. This is misleading. National identity (like religious, gender, or ethnic identities) developed and changed historically.

CULTURAL REVOLT: ROMANTICISM

Romanticism, the most significant cultural movement in the early nineteenth century, touched all the arts and permeated politics as well. It marked a reaction against the Classicism of the eighteenth century and the Enlightenment. Whereas Classicism aspired to reason, discipline, and harmony, Romanticism stressed emotion, freedom, and imagination. Romantic artists prized intense individual experiences and considered intuition and emotion to be better guides to truth and human happiness than reason and logic.

British Romantic Poetry

Romanticism developed first in England and Germany as a reaction against the Enlightenment. Early Romantics developed ideas originating from some of the Enlightenment's dissenters, such as Jean-Jacque Rousseau (see Chapter 17). The poet William Wordsworth (1770–1834) took up Rousseau's central themes—nature, simplicity, and feeling—in his *Lyrical Ballads* (1798). For Wordsworth, poetry was "the spontaneous overflow of powerful feelings," and like Rousseau, he also emphasized the ties of compassion that bind all humankind, regardless of social class. "We have all of us one

***NEWTON* BY WILLIAM BLAKE, 1795.** Blake was also a brilliant graphic artist. Here he depicts Sir Isaac Newton shrouded in darkness, distracted by his scientific calculations from the higher sphere of the imagination. Blake's image is a Romantic critique of Enlightenment science, for which Newton had become a hero.

human heart," he wrote, "men who do not wear fine cloths can feel deeply." Wordsworth considered nature to be humanity's most trustworthy teacher and the source of true feeling. His poems were inspired by the wild hills and tumbledown cottages of England's Lake District. In "The Ruined Cottage" he quoted from the Scottish Romantic poet Robert Burns:

> Give me a spark of Nature's fire,
> 'Tis the best learning I desire . . .
> My muse, though homely in attire,
> May touch the heart.

Wordsworth's poetry, along with that of his colleague Samuel Taylor Coleridge (1772–1834), offered a key theme of nineteenth-century Romanticism: a view of nature that rejected the abstract mechanism of eighteenth-century Enlightenment thought. Nature was not a system to be dissected by science but the source of a sublime power that nourished the human soul.

The poet William Blake (1757–1827) sounded similar themes in his fierce critique of industrial society and the factories (which he called "dark satanic mills") that blighted the English landscape. Blake championed the individual imagination and poetic vision, seeing both as transcending the limits of the material world. Imagination could awaken human sensibilities and sustain belief in different values, breaking humanity's "mind-forged manacles." Blake's poetry paralleled early socialist efforts to imagine a better world. And like many Romantics, Blake looked back to a past in which he thought society had been more organic and humane.

English Romanticism peaked with the next generation of poets—George Gordon, Lord Byron (1788–1824); Percy Bysshe Shelley (1792–1822); and John Keats (1795–1821). Their lives and loves often appealed as much as their writing. Byron was an aristocrat—rich, handsome, and defiant of convention. Poetry, he wrote, was the "lava of the imagination, whose eruption prevents an earthquake." His love affairs helped give Romantics their reputation as rebels against conformity, but they were hardly carefree. Byron treated his wife cruelly and drove her away after a year. Byron also rebelled against Britain's political leaders, labeling them corrupt and repressive. He defended working-class movements and fought in the war for Greek independence, where he died of tuberculosis, a Romantic hero. Byron's friend Percy Shelley emphasized similar themes of individual audacity in his poem, *Prometheus Unbound* (1820). Prometheus defied Zeus by stealing fire for humanity and was punished by being chained to a rock while an eagle tore out his heart.

Women Writers, Gender, and Romanticism

No romantic work was more popular than Mary Godwin Shelley's *Frankenstein* (1818). Shelley was the daughter of radical celebrities—the philosopher William Godwin and the feminist Mary Wollstonecraft (see Chapter 17), who died as her daughter was born. Mary Godwin met Percy Shelley when she was sixteen, had three children by him before they were married, and published *Frankenstein* at twenty. The novel captured the Romantic critique of science and Enlightenment reason and tells the story of an eccentric doctor determined to find the secret of human life. Conducting his research on corpses and body parts retrieved from charnel houses, Dr. Frankenstein produces life in the form of a monster. The monster has human feel-

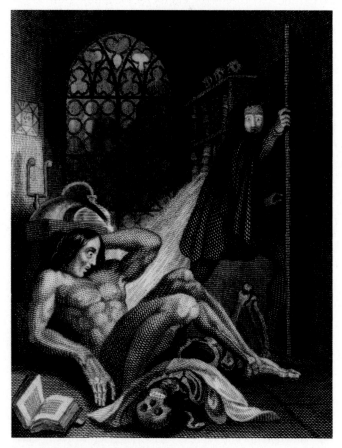

MARY SHELLEY'S *FRANKENSTEIN*. Perhaps the best-known work of Romantic fiction, *Frankenstein* joined the Romantic critique of Enlightenment reason with early-nineteenth-century ambivalence about science to create a striking horror story. Shelley was the daughter of the philosopher William Godwin and the feminist Mary Wollstonecraft; she married the poet Percy Shelley. The engraving, by Theodore Von Holst, is from the first illustrated edition of the work (1831).

ings but is overwhelmed by loneliness and self-hatred when his creator casts him out. Shelley told the story as a twisted creation myth, a study of individual genius gone wrong. The novel remains one of the most memorable characterizations in literature of the limits of reason and the impossibility of controlling nature.

Women played an important role in Romantic writing, and Romanticism stimulated new thinking about gender and creativity. It was common at the time to assert that men were rational and women emotional or intuitive. Many Romantics, like their contemporaries, accepted such gender differences as natural, and some exalted the superior moral virtues of women. Since Romanticism placed such value on the emotions as an essential part of artistic creation, however, some female writers or painters were able to use these ideas to claim a place for themselves in the world of letters and the arts. Germaine de Staël (1766–1817), for example, emigrated from revolutionary France to Germany and played a key part in popularizing German Romanticism in France. Romantics such as Madame de Staël suggested that men too could be emotional and that feelings were a part of a common human nature shared by both sexes. For many literate middle-class people, the language of Romanticism gave them a way to express their own search for individual expression and feeling in writing—and in thinking—about love. In this way, Romanticism reached well beyond small circles of artists and writers into the everyday writing and thoughts of European men and women.

Romantic Painting

Painters carried the Romantic themes of nature and imagination onto their canvases (see **Interpreting Visual Evidence** on page 490). In Great Britain, John Constable (1776–1837) and J. M. W. Turner (1775–1851) developed more emotional and poetic approaches to depicting nature. "It is the soul that sees," wrote Constable, echoing Wordsworth. Constable studied Isaac Newton and the properties of light but aimed to capture the "poetry" of a rainbow. Turner's intensely subjective paintings were even more unconventional. His experiments with brushstroke and color produced remarkable images. Critics assailed the paintings, calling them incomprehensible, but Turner merely responded, "I did not paint it to be understood." In France, Théodore Géricault (1791–1824) and Eugène Delacroix (1799–1863) produced very different paintings from Turner's, but like the English painter they too were preoccupied by subjectivity and the creative process. The poet Charles Baudelaire credited Delacroix with showing him new ways to see: "The whole visible universe is but a storehouse of images and signs. . . . All the faculties of the human soul must be subordinated to the imagination." These Romantic experiments prepared the way for the later development of modernism in the arts.

Romantic Politics: Liberty, History, and Nation

Victor Hugo (1802–1885) wrote that "Romanticism is only . . . liberalism in literature." Hugo's plays, poetry, and historical novels focused sympathetically on the experience of common people, especially *Notre Dame de Paris* (1831) and *Les Misérables* (1862). Delacroix's painting *Liberty Leading the People* gave a revolutionary face to Romanticism, as did the poetry of Shelley and Byron. In works such as these, political life was no longer the preserve of social elites, and the commoners in the street could embrace new freedoms with a violent passion that would have surprised the *philosophes*, with their emphasis on reasoned debate.

Yet Romantics could also be ardently conservative. French conservative François Chateaubriand's *Genius of Christianity* (1802) emphasized the primacy of religious emotions and feeling in his claim that religion was woven into the national past and could not be ignored without threatening the culture as a whole. The period in fact witnessed a broad and popular religious revival and a renewed interest in medieval literature, art, and architecture, all of which drew heavily on religious themes.

Early nineteenth-century nationalism took the Romantic emphasis on individuality and turned it into a faith in the uniqueness of individual cultures. Johann von Herder, among the most influential of nationalist thinkers, argued that civilization sprang from the culture of the common people, not from a learned or cultivated elite, as the *philosophes* had argued in the Enlightenment. Herder extolled the special creative genius of the German people, the *Volk*, and insisted that each nation must be true to its own particular heritage and history.

The Romantics' keen interest in history and the lives of ordinary people led to new kinds of literary and historical works. The brothers Grimm, editors of the famous collection of fairy tales (1812–15), traveled across Germany to study native dialects and folktales. The poet Friedrich Schiller retold the story of William Tell (1804) to promote German national consciousness, but the Italian composer Gioachino Rossini turned Schiller's poem into an opera that promoted Italian nationalism. After 1848 these nation-

alist enthusiasms would overwhelm the political debates that divided conservatives from liberals and socialists in the first half of the nineteenth century (see Chapter 21).

Orientalism

This passion for theories and histories of distinctive cultures also created broad interest in the Orient. Napoleon wrote, "This Europe of ours is a molehill. Only in the East, where 600 million human beings live, is it possible to found great empires and realize great revolutions." The dozens of scholars who accompanied Napoleon on his invasion of Egypt in 1798 collected information on Egyptian history and culture. Among the artifacts the French took from Egypt was the Rosetta stone, with versions of the same text in three different languages: hieroglyphic writing (pictorial script), demotic (an early alphabetic writing), and Greek, which scholars used to decode and translate the first two. The twenty-three volume, lavishly illustrated *Description of Egypt*, published in French between 1809 and 1828, was a major event, heightening the soaring interest in Eastern languages and history. "We are now all Orientalists," wrote

***WOMEN OF ALGIERS* BY EUGÈNE DELACROIX.** This is one of many paintings done during Delacroix's trips through North Africa and a good example of the Romantics' Orientalism.

Victor Hugo in 1829. The political echoes to this cultural fascination with the East could be seen in great power rivalries that surfaced in the British incursion into India, in the Greek war of independence, and in the French invasion of Algeria in 1830.

Nineteenth-century Europeans cast the Orient as a contrasting mirror for their own civilization, a process that did more to create a sense of their own identity as Europeans than it did to promote an accurate understanding of the diversity of cultures that lay beyond Europe's uncertain eastern frontier. During the Greek war for independence, Europeans identified with Greek heritage against Oriental despotism. Romantic painters such as Delacroix depicted the landscapes of the East in bold and sensuous colors and emphasized the sensuality, mystery, and irrationality of Eastern peoples. The fascination with medieval history and religion also bred interest in the medieval crusades in the Holy Land—important subjects for Romantics such as Scott and Chateaubriand. These habits of mind, encouraged by Romantic literature and art, helped to crystallize a sense of what were felt to be essential differences between the East and the West.

Goethe and Beethoven

It is especially difficult to classify two of the most important artists of this period, Johann Wolfgang von Goethe (1749–1832) and Ludwig van Beethoven (1770–1827). Goethe's writing and Beethoven's music bridged the chasm that separated the austere and orderly aesthetic of European classicism from the turbulent and emotional expressions of creativity associated with Romanticism. Goethe's early novel *The Passions of Young Werther* (1774) had an enormous influence on the Romantic movement with its depiction of a young man's failure in love and subsequent suicide. Enthusiastic middle-class readers of *Werther* found in the novel an antidote to the sterility of lives lived in strict conformity with social expectations. Goethe's later masterpiece, *Faust*, finished just before his death in 1832, retold the story of a man who sold his soul to the devil for eternal youth and universal knowledge. Although classical in tone, Goethe's *Faust* still expressed a Romantic concern with spiritual freedom and human daring.

Beethoven's education, meanwhile, began with a rigorous training in the principles of classical music composition, but his insistence that instrumental music without vocal accompaniment could be more expressive of emotion made him a key figure for later Romantic composers. Beethoven began his career in the shadow of Mozart's extraordinary accomplishments but his music acquired new

depth in response to a personal tragedy. He began to lose his hearing at the age of thirty-two and by 1819 was completely deaf. The compositions of his last years expressed his powerfully felt alienation from human society as well as his extraordinary and heroic creativity in the face of debilitating hardship. Like Goethe's works, Beethoven's music searched for new ways to express powerfully felt human longings, and together these two artists took nineteenth-century art in a new direction.

REFORM AND REVOLUTION

In the 1820s, the conservative Restoration faced scattered opposition. The most decisive blow against it came in 1830 in France. There, the Congress of Vienna had returned a Bourbon monarch to the throne. Louis XVIII was the oldest of the former king's surviving brothers. Louis claimed absolute power, but in the name of reconciliation he granted a "charter" and conceded some important rights: legal equality, careers open to talent, and a two-chamber parliamentary government. Voting rights excluded most citizens from government. Louis XVIII's narrow base of support, combined with the sting of military defeat, nostalgia for a glorious Napoleonic past, and memories of the Revolution undermined the Restoration in France.

The 1830 Revolution in France

In 1824, Louis XVIII was succeeded by his far more conservative brother, Charles X (r. 1824–30), who sought to reverse the legacies of Napoleon and the Revolution. Charles pleased the ultra-royalists by pushing the assembly to compensate nobles whose land had been confiscated and sold during the revolution, but the measure antagonized property holders. He restored the Catholic Church to its traditional place in French schools, provoking discontent among French liberals, who began to organize an oppositional movement in parliament. The opposition was bolstered by economic troubles, and in Paris and the provinces worried police reports documented widespread unemployment, hunger, and anger. Confronted with alarming evidence of the regime's unpopularity, Charles called for new elections; when they went against him, he tried to overthrow the parliament with his so-called July Ordinances of 1830: he dissolved the new assembly before it had met, restricted suffrage even further, and announced strict press censorship.

Belgium and Poland in 1830

In 1815, the Congress of Vienna joined Belgium (then called the Austrian Netherlands) to Holland to form a buffer against France. The Belgians had never accepted this arrangement, and the 1830 revolution in France catalyzed the Belgian opposition. The city of Brussels rebelled and forced Dutch troops to withdraw. Unwilling to intervene, the great powers agreed to guarantee Belgian neutrality—a provision that remained in force until 1914.

The years 1830–32 thus became full-fledged crisis for the Concert of Europe. After France and Belgium, revolt also spread to Poland, governed by the Russian tsar's brother, Constantine. Poland had its own parliament (or *diet*), a relatively broad electorate, a constitution, and basic liberties of speech and the press. The Russian head of state increasingly ignored these liberties, however, and news of the French Revolution of 1830 tipped Poland into revolt. The revolutionaries—including aristocrats, students, military officers, and middle-class people—drove Constantine out. Within less than a year, Russian forces retook Warsaw, and the conservative tsar Nicholas crushed the revolt and put Poland under military rule. The movement for Belgian independence succeeded because the great powers declined to act—in Poland, on the other hand, the forcefulness of the Russian response doomed the Polish revolution.

LIBERTY LEADING THE PEOPLE BY EUGÈNE DELACROIX. This painting is among the best-known images of the revolutions of 1830. Delacroix is the same artist who had mourned the extinction of liberty in his painting of the *Massacre at Chios* in Greece (see page 479). The allegorical female figure of liberty leads representatives of the united people: a middle-class man (identified by his top hat), a worker, and a boy of the streets wielding a pistol. Neither middle-class people nor children fought on the barricades, and the image of revolutionary unity was romanticized. ▪ *What made this mix of social classes important for Delacroix's image of the French people in revolt?* ▪ *And why this particular image of liberty, carrying a rifle, with exposed breasts?*

In return, Charles got revolution. Parisian workers, artisans, and students took to the streets in three days of intense street battles. Crucial to the spread of the movement was the press, which defied the censors and quickly spread the news of the initial confrontations between protesters and the forces of order. In the end, the army was unwilling to fire into the crowd, and Charles was forced to abdicate, his support evaporating. Although many revolutionaries who had fought in the streets wanted another republic, the leaders of the movement opted for stability by crowning the former king's cousin, the duke of Orléans, Louis Philippe (r. 1830–48), as a constitutional monarch. The July Monarchy, as it was called, doubled the number of voters, though voting was still based on steep property requirements. The propertied classes benefited most from the revolution of 1830, but it also brought the common people back into politics, revived memories of 1789, and spurred movements elsewhere in Europe. For opponents of the Restoration, 1830 suggested that history was moving in a new direction and that the political landscape had changed since the Congress of Vienna.

Reform in Great Britain

Why was there no revolution in England? One answer is that there almost was. After an era of political conservatism comparable to that of the Continent, however, Britain became one of the most liberal nations in Europe.

The end of the Napoleonic Wars brought a major agricultural depression to Britain. Low wages, unemployment, and bad harvests provoked regular social unrest. In the new industrial towns of the north, radical members of the middle class joined with workers to demand increased representation in Parliament. When sixty thousand people gathered in 1819 to demonstrate for political reform at St. Peter's Field in Manchester, the militia and soldiers on horseback charged the crowd, killing eleven and injuring four hundred. Radicals condemned "Peterloo," a domestic Waterloo, and criticized the nation's army for turning against its own citizens. Parliament quickly passed the Six Acts (1819), outlawing "seditious" literature, increasing the stamp act on newspapers, allowing house searches, and restricting rights of assembly.

Interpreting Visual Evidence

Romantic Painting

Romantic painters shared with Romantic poets a fascination with the power of nature. To convey this vision of nature as both an overwhelming power and source of creative energy, Romantic painters created new and poetic visions of the natural world, where human beings and their activities were reduced in significance, sometimes nearly disappearing altogether. At times these visions also were linked to a backward-looking perspective, as if the dramatic changes associated with industrialization provoked a longing for a premodern past, where Europeans sought and found their sense of place in the world from an awareness of a quasi-divine natural setting invested with powerful mysteries. John Martin's *The Bard* (image A) shows a highly romanticized vision of a medieval subject: a single Welsh bard strides across rocky peaks above a mountain river, after escaping a massacre ordered by the English king Edward I. Across the river, Edward's troops can barely be seen leaving the scene of the crime, which still glows with destructive fires. The emotional qualities of this early expression of Romantic nationalism are reinforced by the forbidding and dynamic sky above, where the clouds merge into the Welsh mountaintops as if they were stirred by the hand of God himself.

Other Romantic painters minimized the significance of human activity in their landscapes, though without reference to history. John Constable's *Weymouth Bay* (image B) contains a tiny, almost imperceptible human figure in the middle ground, a man walking on the beach, near a thin stone wall that snakes up a hill in the background. These passing references to human lives are completely dominated, however, by Constable's sky and the movement of the clouds in particular, which seem to be the real subject of the painting.

Of all the Romantic painters, J. M. W. Turner (image C) may have tackled the tricky subject of the new industrialized landscape in the most novel way. His painting *Rain, Steam, Speed—The Great Western Railway* (1844) boldly places the most modern technology of the period, the steam train on an arched bridge, into a glowing and radiant painting where

A. John Martin, *The Bard*, 1817.

B. John Constable, *Weymouth Bay*, 1816.

C. J. M. W. Turner, *Rain, Steam, Speed—The Great Western Railway*, 1844.

both nature's forces and the tremendous new power unleashed by human activity seem to merge into one continuous burst of energy. To the left of the train, on the river's edge, a fire of indeterminate but evidently industrial origin burns, illuminating several small but ecstatic figures with its light. Most enigmatic of all, an almost invisible rabbit sprints ahead of the train between the rails, highlighting the painting's complex message about nature and human creation. Are they heading in the same direction? Will one overtake the other and destroy it in the process?

Questions for Analysis

1. In Martin's *The Bard*, what vision of the individual emerges from this painting, and how is it different from the rational, rights-bearing individual that political liberalism sought to protect?

2. Is Constable's painting concerned with nature as a source of nourishment for humans or is it presented as a value in itself?

3. How is one to interpret Turner's explicit connection between the power of nature and the new force of industrial societies? Is he suggesting that contemplating the industrial landscape can be just as moving to a human observer as the sight of nature's magnificence?

The conservative Tory party refused to reform representation in the House of Commons. About two-thirds of the members of the House of Commons owed their seats to the patronage of the richest titled landowners in the country. In districts known as "rotten" or "pocket" boroughs, landowners used their power to return members of Parliament who would serve their interests. Defenders of this system argued that the interests of landed property coincided with those of the nation at large.

Liberals in the Whig Party, the new industrial middle class, and radical artisans argued passionately for reform. They were not necessarily democrats—liberals in particular wanted only to enfranchise responsible citizens—but they made common cause with organized middle-class and working-class radicals to push for reform. This agitation peaked in the years 1830–32, leading to fears of social disorder. The Whig party took advantage of this atmosphere and pushed through a reform package that directly challenged the Tories' hold on electoral politics.

The Reform Bill of 1832 eliminated the rotten boroughs and reallocated 143 parliamentary seats, mostly from the rural south, to the industrial north. The bill expanded the franchise, but only one in six men could vote. Landed aristocrats had their influence reduced but not destroyed. This modest reform nevertheless brought British liberals and members of the middle class into a junior partnership with a landed elite that had ruled Britain for centuries.

What changes did this more liberal parliament produce? It abolished slavery in the British colonies in 1838 (see Chapter 21). The most significant example of middle-class power came in the repeal of the Corn Laws in 1846. The Corn Laws (the British term for grain is *corn*) protected British landowners and farmers from foreign competition by establishing tariffs for imports, and they kept bread prices high. The middle-class increasingly saw this as an unfair protection of the aristocracy and pushed for their repeal in the name of free trade. The Anti–Corn Law League held meetings throughout the north of England and lobbied Parliament, eventually resulting in a repeal of the law and a free-trade policy that lasted until the 1920s.

British Radicalism and the Chartist Movement

Reformers disappointed with the narrow gains of 1832 pushed for expanded political reforms. Their attention focused on a petition known as the "People's Charter" which contained six demands: universal white male suffrage, a secret ballot, an end to property qualifications as a condi-

THE GREAT CHARTIST RALLY OF APRIL 10, 1848. The year 1848 brought revolution to continental Europe and militant protest to England. This photo shows the April rally in support of the Chartists' six points, which included expanding the franchise, abolishing property qualifications for representatives, and instituting a secret ballot.

tion of public office, annual parliamentary elections, salaries for members of the House of Commons, and equal electoral districts. The Chartists organized committees across the country and the charter was eventually signed by millions.

Chartism spread in a climate of economic hardship during the 1840s. The movement tapped into local traditions of worker self-help, but the Chartists often disagreed about tactics and goals. Should Irish Catholics be included in the movement or excluded as dangerous competitors? Should women be included in the franchise? The Chartist William Lovett, a cabinetmaker, was a fervent believer in self-improvement and advocated a union of educated workers that could claim its fair share of the nation's increasing industrial wealth. The Chartist Feargus O'Connor appealed to the more impoverished and desperate class of workers by attacking industrialization and the resettlement of the poor on agricultural allotments. Chartist Bronterre O'Brien shocked the crowds by openly expressing his admiration for Robespierre and attacking "the big-bellied, little-brained, numbskull aristocracy." Chartism had many faces, but the movement's common goal was social justice through political democracy.

In spite of the Chartists' efforts to present massive petitions to the parliament in 1839 and 1842, the Parliament rejected them both times. Members of the movement resorted to strikes, trade union demonstrations, and attacks on factories and manufacturers who imposed low wages and long hours or who harassed unionists. The movement peaked in April 1848. Inspired by revolutions in continental Europe, the Chartists' leaders planned a major

Analyzing Primary Sources

Women in the Anti–Corn Law League, 1842

Members of the Anti–Corn Law leagues sought to repeal the protectionist laws that prohibited foreign grain from entering the British market. The laws were seen as an interference with trade that kept bread prices artificially high, benefiting British landowners and grain producers at the expense of the working population. The campaign to repeal the Corn Laws enlisted many middle-class women in its ranks, and some later campaigned for women's suffrage. This article, hostile to the reform, deplored women's participation in the reform movement.

 e find that the council of the Manchester Anti–Corn Law Association had invited the inhabitants to 'an *anti-Corn-law tea-party*, to be held on the 20th of May, 1841—gentlemen's tickets, 2s.; ladies 1s. 6d.' . . . [L]adies were advertised as *stewardesses* of this assembly. So now the names of about 300 Ladies were pompously advertised as the *Patroness* and *Committee* of the *National Bazaar*. We exceedingly wonder and regret that the members of the Association . . . and still more that anybody else, should have chosen to exhibit their wives and daughters in the character of political agitators; and we most regret that so many ladies—modest, excellent, and amiable persons we have no doubt in their domestic circles—should have been persuaded to allow their names to be placarded on such occasions—for be it remembered, this Bazaar and these *Tea-parties* did not even pretend to be for any *charitable* object, but entirely for the purposes of *political agitation*. . . .

We have before us a letter from Mrs. Secretary Woolley to one body of workmen. . . . She 'appeals to them to stand forth and denounce as *unholy*, unjust, and cruel all restrictions on the food of the people'. She acquaints them that 'the ladies are resolved to perform *their* arduous part in the attempt to *destroy a monopoly* which, for *selfishness* and its *deadly* effects, has no parallel in the history of the world'. 'We therefore', she adds, 'ask you for contributions. . . .' Now surely . . . not only should the *poorer classes* have been exempt from such unreasonable solicitations, but whatever subscriptions might be obtainable from the wealthier orders should have been applied, not to *political agitation* throughout England, but to charitable relief at home.

Source: J. Croker, "Anti–Corn Law Legislation," *Quarterly Review* (December, 1842), as cited in Patricia Hollis, ed., *Women in Public: The Women's Movement 1850–1900* (London: 1979), p. 287.

Questions for Analysis

1. Why does the article highlight the participation of women in the Anti–Corn Law Association? What does this argument tell us about attitudes toward women's political activity?

2. Does the article actually mention any of the arguments in favor of repealing the Corn Laws? What alternative to repeal does the article appear to support?

---

demonstration in London. Twenty-five thousand workers carried to Parliament a petition with six million signatures. Confronted with the specter of class conflict, special constables and regular army units were marshaled by the aged duke of Wellington to resist any threat to public order. In the end, only a small delegation presented the petition, and rain and an unwillingness to do battle with the constabulary put an end to the Chartist movement. A relieved liberal observed, "From that day it was a settled matter that England was safe from revolution."

The French Revolution of 1848

Hunger alone cannot cause revolution, but when failed harvests and rising prices drive a people to the edge of desperation, a government's inability to manage the crisis can make it seem illegitimate. Just such a crisis hit Europe in the 1840s, causing famine in Ireland and hunger in Germany and central Europe. As states lost the confidence of their people, a wave of revolution swept across Europe, beginning in France.

Competing Viewpoints

Two Views of the June Days, France, 1848

> These two passages make for an interesting comparison. The socialist Karl Marx reported on the events of 1848 in France as a journalist for a German newspaper. For Marx, the bloodshed of the June Days shattered the "fraternal illusions" of February 1848, when the king had been overthrown and the provisional government established. That bloodshed also symbolized a new stage in history: one of acute class conflict.
>
> The French liberal politician Alexis de Tocqueville also wrote about his impressions of the revolution. (Tocqueville's account, however, is retrospective, for he wrote his memoirs well after 1848.) For Marx, a socialist observer, the June Days represented a turning point: "the working class was knocking on the gates of history." For Tocqueville, a member of the government, the actions of the crowd sparked fear and conservative reaction.

Karl Marx's Journalism

The last official remnant of the February Revolution, the Executive Commission, has melted away, like an apparition, before the seriousness of events. The fireworks of Lamartine [French Romantic poet and member of the provisional government] have turned into the war rockets of Cavaignac [French general in charge of putting down the workers' insurrection]. *Fraternité,* the fraternity of antagonistic classes of which one exploits the other, this *fraternité,* proclaimed in February, on every prison, on every barracks—its true, unadulterated, its prosaic expression is civil war, civil war in its most fearful form, the war of labor and capital. This fraternity flamed in front of all the windows of Paris on the evening of June 25, when the Paris of the bourgeoisie was illuminated, whilst the Paris of the proletariat [Marxist term for the working people] burnt, bled, moaned.... The February Revolution was the beautiful revolution, the revolution of universal sympathy, because the antagonisms, which had flared up in it against the monarchy, slumbered peacefully side by side, still undeveloped, because the social struggle which formed its background had won only a joyous existence, an existence of phrases, of words. The June revolution is the ugly revolution, the repulsive revolution, because things have taken the place of phrases, because the republic uncovered the head of the monster itself, by striking off the crown that shielded and concealed it.— Order! was the battle cry of Guizot ... Order! shouts Cavaignac, the brutal echo of the French National Assembly and of the republican bourgeoisie. Order! thundered his grapeshot, as it ripped up the body of the proletariat. None of the numerous revolutions of the French bourgeoi-

---

The French monarchy after the revolution of 1830 seemed little different from its predecessor. King Louis Philippe gathered around him members of the banking and industrial elite. Confronted with demands to enlarge the franchise, the prime minister quipped that everyone was free to rise into the ranks of the wealthy: "Enrich yourselves!" Building projects, especially the railway, presented ample opportunities for graft. Protest movements, in the form of republican societies, proliferated in French cities. In 1834, the government declared these organizations illegal. Rebellions broke out in Paris and Lyon, bringing a harsh repression that resulted in deaths and arrests. The government's refusal to compromise drove even moderates into opposition. In 1847, the opposition organized a campaign for electoral reform around repeated political "banquets"—an attempt to get around the laws against assembly. When they called for a giant banquet on February 22, 1848, the king responded by banning the meeting. A sudden and surprising popular revolution in the streets caused Louis Philippe to abdicate his throne only days later.

The provisional government of the new republic consisted of liberals, republicans, and—for the first time—socialists. They produced a new constitution, with elections sie since 1789 was an attack on order; for they allowed the rule of the class, they allowed the slavery of the workers, they allowed the bourgeois order to en-

dure, however often the political form of this rule and of this slavery changed. June has attacked this order. Woe to June!"

Source: *Neue Rheinische Zeitung* (New Rhineland Gazette), June 29, 1848; from Karl Marx, *The Class Struggles in France* (New York: 1964), pp. 57–58.

Alexis de Tocqueville Remembers the June Days (1893)

Now at last I have come to that insurrection in June which was the greatest and the strangest that had ever taken place in our history, or perhaps in that of any other nation: the greatest because for four days more than a hundred thousand men took part in it, and there were five generals killed; the strangest, because the insurgents were fighting without a battle cry, leaders, or flag, and yet they showed wonderful powers of coordination and a military expertise that astonished the most experienced officers.

Another point that distinguished it from all other events of the same type during the last sixty years was that its object was not to change the form of government, but to alter the organization of society. In truth it was not a

political struggle (in the sense in which we have used the word "political" up to now), but a class struggle, a sort of "Servile War." . . . One should not see it only as a brutal and a blind, but as a powerful effort of the workers to escape from the necessities of their condition, which had been depicted to them as an illegitimate depression, and by the sword to open up a road towards that imaginary well-being that had been shown to them in the distance as a right. It was this mixture of greedy desires and false theories that engendered the insurrection and made it so formidable. These poor people had been assured that the goods of the wealthy were in some way the result of a theft committed against themselves. They had been assured that inequalities of fortune were

as much opposed to morality and the interests of society as to nature. This obscure and mistaken conception of right, combined with brute force, imparted to it an energy, tenacity and strength it would never have had on its own.

Source: From Alexis de Tocqueville, *Recollections: The French Revolution of 1848*, ed. J. P. Mayer and A. P. Kerr, trans. George Lawrence (New Brunswick, NJ: 1987), pp. 436–37.

Questions for Analysis

1. Was Tocqueville sympathetic to the revolutionaries of June?

2. Did Tocqueville think the events were historically significant?

3. Where did Tocqueville agree and disagree with Marx?

based on universal male suffrage. Yet tensions between propertied republicans and socialists shattered the unity of the coalition that toppled Louis Philippe. Working men and women demanded the "right to work," the right to earn a living wage. The provisional government responded by creating the National Workshops, a program of public works, to give jobs to the unemployed. Initial plans were made to employ ten to twelve thousand workers, but unemployment was so high that one hundred twenty thousand job-seekers had gathered in the city by June 1848.

Popular politics flourished in Paris in 1848. The provisional government lifted restrictions on speech and assem-

bly. One hundred seventy new journals and more than two hundred clubs formed within weeks. Delegations claiming to represent the oppressed of Europe—Chartists, Hungarians, Poles—moved freely about the city. Women's clubs and newspapers appeared, demanding universal suffrage and living wages. Many middle-class Parisians were alarmed, and more conservative rural populations also looked for stern measures to restore order. When elections for parliament were held, the conservative voices won out, and a majority of moderate republicans and monarchists were elected.

A majority in the new assembly believed the National Workshops were a financial drain and a threat to order.

BARRICADE IN THE RUE DE LA MORTELLERIE, JUNE, 1848 BY ERNEST MEISSONIER (1815–1891). Compare this image with Delacroix's image of the revolution of 1830. What made 1848 different from 1830, and how do these images convey that difference?

In May they closed the workshops to new enrollment, excluded recent arrivals to Paris, and sent members between the ages of eighteen and twenty-five into the army. On June 21, they abolished the workshops altogether. In defense of this social program, the workers of Paris—laborers, journeymen, the unemployed—rose in revolt, building barricades across Paris. For four days, June 23–26, they fought a hopeless battle against armed forces recruited from the provinces. The repression shocked many observers. About three thousand were killed and twelve thousand arrested. Many of the prisoners were deported to Algerian labor camps.

In the aftermath, the government moved quickly to restore order. The parliament hoped for a strong leader in the presidential election, and they got their wish: the winner was Louis Napoleon Bonaparte, the nephew of the former emperor, who had spent his life in exile. Buoyed by enthusiastic support from rural voters, the upstart Louis Napoleon polled more than twice as many votes as the other three candidates combined.

Louis Napoleon used his position to consolidate his power. He rallied the Catholics by restoring the Church to its former role in education and by sending an expedition to Rome to rescue the pope from revolutionaries. He banned radical activities, worker's associations, and suspended press freedoms. In 1851 he called for a plebiscite

After You Read This Chapter

REVIEWING THE OBJECTIVES

- The European leaders who met at the Congress of Vienna possessed a conservative vision for post-Napoleonic Europe. What were their goals?
- Resistance to the Congress's restoration of conservative monarchies was expressed throughout Europe and abroad. Where was this resistance to be found, and what were its consequences?
- Postrevolutionary Europe was divided by fierce ideological conflicts. What were the core principles of political liberalism, republicanism, and socialism? How did these three ideologies relate to nationalism?
- Romanticism was a cultural movement defined in opposition to the Enlightenment. Who were the Romantics and what did they believe?
- The conservative order set up in 1815 came to an end with the Revolutions of 1848. What caused these revolutions?

to give him the authority to change the constitution, and one year later another plebiscite allowed him to establish the Second Empire. He assumed the title of Napoleon III (r. 1852–70), emperor of the French.

The dynamics of the French Revolution of 1848 would be repeated elsewhere, especially the pivotal role of the propertied middle classes. Louis Philippe's reign had been proudly bourgeois but alienated many of its supporters. Key groups in the middle class joined the opposition, allying with radicals who could not topple the regime alone. Yet demands for reform soon led to fears of disorder and the desire for a strong state. This dynamic led to the collapse of the republic and to the rule of Napoleon III. The abandonment of the revolution's social goals—most visibly evident in the National Workshops—led to a stark polarization along class lines, with middle-class and working-class people demanding different things from the state. This political conflict would grow even more intense as socialism came into its own as an independent political force.

CONCLUSION

The French Revolution of 1789 polarized Europe. In its aftermath, the Congress of Vienna aimed to establish a new, conservative, international system and to prevent further revolutions. It succeeded in the first aim, but only partially in the second. A combination of new political movements and economic hardship undermined the conservative order. Social grievances and political disappointments created powerful movements for change, first in Latin America and the Balkans, and then in western Europe and Great Britain.

The French Revolution of 1848 (the second since the defeat of Napoleon) became the opening act of a much larger drama. In southern and central Europe, as we will see in the next chapter, the issues were framed differently, around new struggles for national identity. Still, the failure of revolution in France set a pattern that was also observed elsewhere: exhilarating revolutionary successes were followed by a breakdown of revolutionary unity and the emergence of new forms of conservative government. The crisis of 1848 became a turning point for all of Europe. The broad revolutionary alliances that had pushed for revolutionary change since 1789 were broken apart by class politics, and earlier forms of utopian socialism gave way to Marxism. In culture as in politics, Romanticism lost its appeal, its expansive sense of possibility replaced by the more biting viewpoint of realism. Conservatism, liberalism, and socialism adapted to new political conditions. How this happened and the explosive role of nationalism in this process are the subjects of the next chapter.

PEOPLE, IDEAS, AND EVENTS IN CONTEXT

- Who was **KLEMENS VON METTERNICH** and what was the **CONCERT OF EUROPE**?
- How did the **CARBONARI** in Italy, the **DECEMBRISTS** in Russia, and **GREEK NATIONALISTS** in the Balkans in the 1820s disturb the conservative order in Europe after Napoleon's defeat?
- Was **LIBERALISM** or **CONSERVATISM** compatible with **NATIONALISM** during this period?
- What reforms did European **LIBERALS** seek between 1815 and 1848? Where were they successful?
- What was **SOCIALISM**? What made the socialism of **KARL MARX** different from earlier forms of socialism?
- How did the values of **ROMANTICISM** challenge Europeans to reconsider their assumptions about the differences between men and women?
- What beliefs led **ROMANTIC WRITERS** such as **WILLIAM WORDSWORTH, WILLIAM BLAKE**, and **LORD BYRON** to reject the rationalism of the Enlightenment and embrace the emotions and imagination as the most essential and vital aspects of human experience?
- What political changes did movements such as the **CHARTISTS** or the **ANTI–CORN LAW LEAGUES** accomplish in Britain? Why was there no revolution in Britain?

CONSEQUENCES

- How did the French Revolution shape the political debates between conservatives, liberal reformers, and social revolutionaries after 1815?
- What possible connections might be found between Romanticism as a cultural movement and the emergence of new forms of nationalism in Europe before and after 1848?
- How was liberalism linked to nationalism in Europe between 1815 and 1848?

STORY LINES

- In 1848 a wave of liberal revolutions demanded but failed to achieve lasting constitutions and elected parliaments in many European kingdoms. Instead, Europe's conservative monarchs found ways to harness the popular nationalism expressed in the 1848 revolutions to their own ends.

- The emergence of Germany and Italy as unified nation-states upset the European balance of power, as did the increasing weakness of the Ottoman Empire. The resulting wars benefited Germany and diminished the power of Austria-Hungary in central Europe.

- Russia, the United States, and Canada also went through an intense phase of nation building after 1850. Common to all three were the conquest of native peoples, the acquisition of new territories, and economic development. As in Europe, the process of nation building unleashed sectional conflicts and led to fundamental debates about citizenship, slavery (or serfdom, in Russia), and the power of the nation-state.

CHRONOLOGY

1808	Slave trade prohibited by Britain and United States
1833	British Empire abolishes slavery
1834–1871	Unification of Germany
1848	Revolutions of 1848
1848	France and Denmark abolish slavery
1848	Treaty of Guadalupe Hidalgo
1848–1870	Unification of Italy
1853–1856	Crimean War
1861	Emancipation of the serfs in Russia
1861–1865	American Civil War
1871–1888	Brazilian emancipation

Before You Read This Chapter

What Is a Nation? Territories, States, and Citizens, 1848–1871

Eighteen forty-eight was a tumultuous year. From Paris to Berlin, and Budapest to Rome, insurgents rushed to hastily built barricades, forcing kings and princes to beat an equally hasty—though only temporary—retreat. Perhaps the most highly symbolic moment came on March 13, 1848, when Klemens von Metternich, the primary architect of the Concert of Europe, was forced to resign as minister of state, while a revolutionary crowd outside celebrated his departure. Metternich's balanced system of international relations, which had guaranteed stability for over three decades, was swept aside in a wave of enthusiasm for liberal political ideals and popular anger. Metternich himself was forced to flee to England, which less than one month earlier had also welcomed Louis Philippe of France. The French king had also been thrown from power by popular protests in February 1848.

Revolutionary regime change, territorial expansion, economic development, and debates about who deserved citizenship: all of these were issues in 1848, and all were related to the spread of nationalism and nation building in Europe and the Americas. As we saw in the last chapter, the term *nation* had taken on a new meaning at the end of the eighteenth century and had come to mean "a sovereign people." *Nationalism* was a related political ideal, based on the assumption that governments could be legitimate only if they reflected the character, history, and customs of the nation—that is, the common people. This idea, that nations and states should overlap one another, was both powerful and diffuse and was cultivated by intellectuals, revolutionaries, and governments for different purposes.

Between 1789 and 1848, Europeans commonly associated nationalism with liberalism. Liberals saw constitutions, the rule of law, and elected assemblies as necessary expressions of the people's will, and they sought to use popular enthusiasm for liberal forms of nationalism against the conservative monarchs of Europe. The upheavals of 1848 marked the high point of this period of liberal revolution, and their failure marked the end of that age. By the end of the nineteenth century, conservative governments also found ways to mobilize popular support by invoking nationalist themes.

The year 1848 was an important moment in this shift in the connections between nationalism, liberalism, and nation building. In the United States, the treaty of Guadalupe Hidalgo transformed the boundaries of the nation at the end of the Mexican-American War by adding New Mexico and California; equally significant was the American Civil War, which resulted in wrenching political change. The unification of Germany and Italy in the years after 1848 also involved the conquest of territory, but the process could not have been completed without political reforms and new state structures that changed how governments worked and how they related to their citizens. France, Britain, Russia, and Austria were also rebuilt during this period: their bureaucracies overhauled, their electorates expanded; relations among ethnic groups reorganized. As this process of nation building continued, the balance of power shifted in Europe toward the states in northern and western Europe that were the earliest to industrialize and most successful in building strong, centralized states. Older imperial powers such as the Habsburg Empire in Austria-Hungary or the Ottoman Empire found their influence waning. At the heart of this nineteenth-century period of nation building lay changing relations between states and those they governed, and these changes were hastened by reactions to the revolutionary upheavals of 1848.

NATIONALISM AND REVOLUTION IN 1848

In central and eastern Europe, the spring of 1848 brought a dizzying sequence of revolution and repression. The roots of revolution lay in social antagonisms, economic crisis, and political grievances. But these revolutions were also shaped decisively by nationalism. Reformers and revolutionaries in Germany, Italy, Poland, and the Austrian Empire believed that their liberal goals—representative government, an end

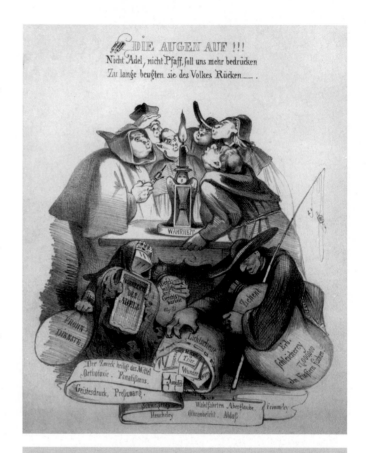

"EYES OPEN!" (c. 1845). This German cartoon from just before the 1848 revolution warns that aristocrats and clergy are conspiring to deny the German people their rights. The caption reads "Eyes Open! Neither the nobility or the clergy shall oppress us any longer. For too long they have broken the backs of the people." Representatives of these groups gather around the table to blow out the flame of truth (*Wahrheit*), while below the table various forms of oppression, including forced labor and religious orthodoxy, are listed.

■ *Did supporters of the revolution consider the aristocracy or the clergy to be legitimate members of the nation? Compare the cartoon with the pamphlet of Abbé Sieyès in the French Revolution (see page 431).*

to privilege, economic development—could only be realized in a vigorous, "modern" nation-state. The fate of the 1848 revolutions in these regions demonstrated nationalism's power to mobilize opponents of the regime but also its potential to splinter revolutionary alliances and to override other allegiances and values entirely.

Who Makes a Nation? Germany in 1848

In 1815, there was no "Germany." The Congress of Vienna had created the German Confederation, a loose organization of thirty-nine states, including Austria and Prussia but not their non-German territories in sections of Poland and Hungary. The confederation was intended to provide only common defense. It had no real executive power. As a practical matter, Prussia and Austria competed with one another to occupy the dominant position in German politics.

Napoleon's defeat of Prussia in 1806 forced the Prussian government to undertake a series of aggressive reforms, beginning with the army. Officers were recruited and promoted on the basis of merit rather than birth, although the large majority continued to come from the Junker (*YUN-kur*, aristocratic) class. Other reforms encouraged the middle class to take a more active role in the civil service. In 1807, serfdom and the estate system were abolished. A year later, in a conscious attempt to increase middle-class Germans' sense of themselves as citizens, cities and towns were allowed to elect their councilmen and handle their own finances. The Prussian reformers expanded facilities for both primary and secondary education and founded the University of Berlin, which numbered among its faculty several ardent nationalists.

Prussia aimed to establish itself as the leading German state and a counter to Austrian power in the region. Prussia's most significant victory in this respect came with the *Zollverein*, or customs union, in 1834, which established free trade among the German states and a uniform protectionist tariff against the rest of the world. By the 1840s, the union included almost all of the German states except German Austria and offered manufacturers a market of almost 34 million people. The spread of the railways after 1835 accelerated exchange within this expanded internal market.

During the 1840s in both Prussia and the smaller German states, political clubs of students and other radicals joined with middle-class groups of lawyers, doctors, and businessmen to press new demands for representative

government and reform. Newspapers multiplied, defying censorship. Liberal reformers attacked the combination of autocracy and bureaucratic authority that stifled political life in Prussia and Austria. German nationhood, they reasoned, would break Austrian or Prussian domination and end the sectional fragmentation that made reform so difficult.

When Frederick William IV (r. 1840–61) succeeded to the Prussian throne in 1840, hopes ran high. The new king did gesture toward liberalizing reforms. When economic troubles hit in the 1840s, however, the regime reverted to authoritarianism. Frederick William sent the army to crush a revolt among the textile weavers of Silesia, who were protesting British imports and, more generally, unemployment, falling wages, and hunger. The brutality of the regime's response shocked many. The king also opposed constitutionalism and any representative participation in issues of legislation and budgets.

As in France, liberals and radicals in Prussia and the German states continued their reform campaigns. And when revolution came to France in the spring of 1848, unrest spread across the Rhine. In the smaller German

"NO PIECE OF PAPER WILL COME BETWEEN MYSELF AND MY PEOPLE" (1848). In this cartoon, Frederick William IV and a military officer refuse to accept the constitution for a new Germany offered to him by the Frankfurt Assembly. Note that the caption refers to a conservative definition of the relationship between a monarch and "his people." Compare this autocratic vision of the nation-state with the liberal nationalist's demand for a government that reflects the people's will. ■ *What contrasting visions of the nation and its relation to the state are contained in this cartoon?*

states, kings and princes yielded surprisingly quickly to revolutionary movements. The governments promised freedom of the press, elections, expanded suffrage, jury trials, and other liberal reforms. In Prussia, Frederick William, shaken by unrest in the countryside and stunned by a showdown in Berlin between the army and revolutionaries in which 250 were killed, finally capitulated.

The Frankfurt Assembly and German Nationhood

A second phase of the 1848 revolution in central Europe began with the election of delegates to an all-German assembly in Frankfurt. Representatives from Austria, Prussia, and the smaller German states met to discuss proposals for unifying the German nation. Many representatives hoped that the Frankfurt Assembly might draft a constitution for a liberal, unified Germany, just as the National Assembly had done for France in 1789. The comparison was not a good one, though, since France was already a unified nation under one government in 1789. The Frankfurt Assembly had no resources, more than one government to please, and no single legal code.

The nationality question was most divisive. Which Germans would join the new state? A majority of the assembly believed that the German nation should include as many Germans as possible from both Prussian and Austrian territory—this became known as the "Great German position." A minority held that a better solution was a "Small Germany" that left out the Habsburg lands, including German Austria, because of the presence of non-German minorities. When the Austrian emperor withdrew his support in the middle of the debate, the assembly retreated to the Small German solution, and offered the crown of a new German nation to Frederick William IV of Prussia.

Frederick William IV refused the offer. The constitution of the new Germany was too liberal, and he found it demeaning to accept a crown from a parliament. The Assembly protested briefly, but was forced by Frederick William's troops to disband. Some disillusioned members emigrated to the United States. Others sought for ways to achieve national unity under Prussian sponsorship.

Elsewhere, the popular revolution took its own course. Peasants ransacked tax offices and workers smashed machines. Newspapers and political clubs multiplied. Some clubs admitted women (for the first time) and newly created women's clubs demanded political rights. Moderate nationalists and disillusioned liberals were uneasy about these popular movements, and they considered demands for universal suffrage too radical. They began to look to the Prussian state to restore order, hoping that national unity might be possible under a sternly enforced rule of law.

Peoples against Empire: The Habsburg Lands

In the sprawling Habsburg (Austrian) Empire, nationalism played a different, centrifugal role. In the nineteenth century the Habsburgs ruled over a wide array of ethnic and language groups: Germans, Czechs, Magyars, Poles, Slovaks, Serbs, and Italians, to name only the most prominent. The Habsburgs found it increasingly difficult to hold their empire together as these groups' varying national demands escalated after 1815.

In the Polish territories of the empire, nationalist sentiment was strongest among aristocrats, who were especially conscious of their historic role as leaders of the Polish nation. Here, the Habsburg Empire successfully set Polish serfs against Polish lords, ensuring that social grievances

HUNGARIAN REVOLUTIONARY LAJOS KOSSUTH, 1851. A leader of the Hungarian nationalist movement who combined aristocratic style with rabble-rousing politics, Kossuth almost succeeded in an attempt to separate Hungary from Austria in 1849.

dampened ethnic nationalism. In the Hungarian region, national claims were likewise advanced by the relatively small Magyar aristocracy. (*Hungarian* is a political term; *Magyar*, which was often used, refers to the Hungarians' non-Slavic language.) Yet they gained an audience under the gifted and influential leadership of Lajos (Louis) Kossuth (*KAW-shut*; 1802–1894). A member of the lower nobility, Kossuth was by turns a lawyer, publicist, newspaper editor, and political leader. He campaigned for independence and a separate Hungarian parliament, but he also (and more influentially) brought politics to the people. Kossuth staged political "banquets" like those in France, at which local and national personalities made speeches in the form of toasts and interested citizens could eat, drink, and participate in politics. The Hungarian political leader combined aristocratic style with rabble-rousing politics: a delicate balancing act but one that, when it worked, catapulted him to the center of Habsburg politics. He was as well known in the Habsburg capital of Vienna as he was in Pressburg and Budapest.

The other major nationalist movement that troubled the Habsburg Empire was pan-Slavism. Slavs included Russians, Poles, Ukrainians, Czechs, Slovaks, Slovenes, Croats, Serbs, Macedonians, and Bulgarians. Before 1848 pan-Slavism was primarily a cultural movement united by a general pro-Slavic sentiment. It was internally divided, however, by the competing claims of different Slavic languages and traditions. The Czech leader František Palacký, the Slovak writer Jan Kollár, and the Polish poet Adam Mickiewicz were all inspired by pan-Slavism.

The fact that Russia and Austria were rivals in eastern Europe made pan-Slavism a volatile and unpredictable political force in the regions of eastern Europe where the two nations vied for power and influence. Tsar Nicholas of Russia sought to use pan-Slavism to his advantage, making arguments about "Slavic" uniqueness part of his "autocracy, orthodoxy, nationality" ideology after 1825. Yet the tsar's Russian-sponsored pan-Slavism alienated Western-oriented Slavs who resented Russia's ambitions. Here, as elsewhere, nationalism created a tangled web of alliances and antagonisms.

Austria and Hungary in 1848

The Habsburg Empire's tensions burst to the surface in 1848. Emboldened by the uprisings in France and Germany, Kossuth stepped up his demands for representative institutions and for autonomy for the Hungarian nation. The Hungarian Diet (parliament) prepared to draft a new con-

stitution. In Vienna, the Habsburg capital, a popular movement of students and artisans built barricades and attacked the imperial palace. The revolutionaries created a militia, the national guard, and a central committee to press demands for reform. Emperor Ferdinand I's regime found itself forced to retreat, while Metternich, whose political system had weathered so many storms, fled to Britain in disguise. The government conceded to radical demands for male suffrage and a single house of representatives and agreed to begin the process of abolishing serfdom. The government also yielded to Czech demands in Bohemia, granting that kindgom a constitution. Meanwhile, Italian liberals and nationalists were in revolt in the Habsburg's southern territories. The Habsburg Empire seemed to be coming apart.

The empire survived the challenge of all these nationalist movements, however, because the many nationalities in the realm could not establish a unified front to confront the government. The paradox of nationalism in central Europe

THE FIRST UNCENSORED NEWSPAPER AFTER THE REVOLUTION IN VIENNA, JANUARY 1848. This watercolor illustrates the power of public information during the 1848 revolution in the Austrian capital. An uncensored newspaper, wall posters, caps with political insignia and slogans, and an armed citizenry all are evidence of a vibrant and impassioned public discussion on the events of the day. Note, too, the modest dress of the woman selling the papers, the top hat and fashionable dress of the middle-class man smoking a pipe, and the presence of military uniforms, all of which illustrate support for the revolution among a broad portion of the population. ▪ *How does this vision of the public sphere in action compare with previous depictions of public debate in the Enlightenment (see page 420) or in the French Revolution (see page 439), or elsewhere in Europe in 1848?*

LANGUAGES OF CENTRAL AND EASTERN EUROPE. Nationalism often served to mobilize movements for liberal revolution in France or Germany. In Habsburg Austria-Hungary ethnic/linguistic boundaries did not conform to political boundaries between states. ▪ *How many different language groups can you count in the Austrian Empire?* ▪ *How does this map illustrate why it was ultimately easier for the German states to unify?* ▪ *How did the diversity of peoples in the Habsburg Empire make a convergence between liberal revolution and nationalism more difficult to achieve?*

liament had prepared new laws to determine the union of Hungary and Austria in the empire, and in the heat of 1848 Ferdinand had accepted them. The Hungarian parliament also abolished serfdom and noble privilege, established freedom of the press and religion, and enfranchised small property holders. Peasants, liberals, and Jews supported these measures, but Croats, Serbs, and Romanians in Hungary opposed the extension of Magyar control. When Kossuth severed all ties between Hungary and Austria on April 14, 1848, the new Austrian emperor, Franz Josef, called on Nicolas I of Russia for support. Three hundred thousand Russian troops came to Franz Josef's aid, and by August 1849 the Hungarian revolt was crushed.

A similar fate awaited the revolution in Vienna. A second uprising, provoked by an economic crisis and high unemployment, gave Franz Josef the excuse he needed. Austrian troops, with Russian support, descended on the capital, and on October 31, 1849, the liberal government surrendered. The regime reestablished press censorship, disbanded the national guard, and executed twenty-five revolutionary leaders. Kossuth went into hiding and lived the rest of his life in exile.

was that no cultural or ethnic majority could declare independence without prompting rebellion from other minority groups in the same area. Czechs and Germans momentarily cooperated to put an end to feudalism in Bohemia, but their alliance soon fractured along national lines. Many Slavs decided that they would rather be ruled by Habsburgs than by Germans or Russians. This bundle of animosities allowed the Austrians to divide and conquer. When workers and students rebelled in Prague in May 1848, Austrian troops entered the city and reasserted control. The regime also sent troops to regain control in the Italian provinces, and quarrels among the Italians helped the Austrians succeed.

The final act of the drama came as nationalists in Hungary confronted their opponents. The Hungarian par-

The Early Stages of Italian Unification in 1848

The Italian peninsula had not been united since the Roman Empire. At the beginning of the nineteenth century it was a patchwork of small states (see map on page 477). Austria occupied the northernmost states of Lombardy and Venetia, and Habsburg dependents also ruled Tuscany, Parma, and Modena. The independent Italian states included the southern kingdom of the Two Sicilies, the Papal States, and most important, Piedmont-Sardinia, ruled by the reform-minded monarch Charles Albert (r. 1831–49). Charles Albert had no particular commitment to creating an Italian national state, but by virtue of Piedmont-Sardinia's economic power, geographical location, and long tradition of opposition to the Habsburgs, Charles Albert's state played a central role in nationalist and anti-Austrian politics.

The leading Italian nationalist in this period was Giuseppe Mazzini (1805–1872) from the city of Genoa, in Piedmont. Mazzini began his political career as a member of the Carbonari (see Chapter 20), an underground society pledged to resisting Austrian control of the region and establishing constitutional rule. In 1831 Mazzini founded his own society, Young Italy, which was anti-Austrian and in favor of constitutional reforms but also dedicated to Italian unification. Charismatic and persuasive, Mazzini spoke of the awakening of the Italian people and of the common people's mission to bring republicanism to the world. Under his leadership Young Italy clubs multiplied. Yet the organization's favored tactics, plotting mutinies and armed rebellions, proved ineffective. In 1834, Mazzini launched an invasion of the kingdom of Sardinia. Without sufficient support, it fizzled, driving Mazzini into exile in England.

Mazzini's republican vision of a united Italy clashed with the goals of his potential allies. Many liberals shared his commitment to creating a single Italian state but not his enthusiasm for the people and popular movements. Mazzini's insistence on a democratic republic committed to social and political transformation struck pragmatic liberals as utopian and well-to-do members of the middle classes as dangerous.

The turmoil that swept across Europe in 1848 raised hopes for political and social change and put Italian unification on the agenda. Popular revolts forced the conservative, independent kingdoms on the peninsula to grant civil liberties and parliamentary government. In the north, the provinces of Venetia and Lombardy rebelled against the Austrian occupation. Charles Albert of Piedmont-Sardinia provided them with military support and took up the banner of Italian nationalism, although many charged that he was primarily interested in expanding his own power. In Rome, a popular uprising challenged the power of the pope and established a republic, with Mazzini as its head. These movements were neither coordinated nor ultimately successful. Within a year, the Austrians had regained the upper hand in the north. French forces under Louis Napoleon intervened in the Papal States; and although they met fierce resistance from the Roman republicans joined by Giuseppe Garibaldi (discussed later in this chapter), they nonetheless restored the pope's power. Like most of the radical movements of 1848, these uprisings failed. Still, they raised the hopes of nationalists who spoke of a *Risorgimento*, or Italian resurgence, that would restore the nation to the position of leadership it had held in Roman times and during the Renaissance.

BUILDING THE NATION-STATE

In the wake of the revolutions of 1848, new nation-states were built—often by former critics of nationalism. Since the French Revolution of 1789, conservative politicians had associated nationhood with liberalism: constitutions, reforms, new political communities. During the second half of the century, however, the political ground shifted dramatically. States and governments took the national initiative. Alarmed by revolutionary ferment, they promoted economic development, pressed social and political reforms, and sought to shore up their base of support. Rather than allow popular nationalist movements to emerge from below, statesmen consolidated their governments' powers and built nations from above.

France under Napoleon III

Napoleon III, like his uncle, believed in personal rule and a centralized state. As emperor, he controlled the nation's finances, the army, and foreign affairs. The assembly, elected by universal male suffrage, could approve only legislation drafted at the emperor's direction. Napoleon's regime aimed to undermine France's traditional elites by expanding the bureaucracy and cultivating a new relationship with the people. "The confidence of our rough peasants can be won by an energetic authority," asserted one of the emperor's representatives.

Napoleon III also took steps to develop the economy. He harbored a near-utopian faith in the power of industrial expansion to bring prosperity, political support, and national glory. His government encouraged credit and new forms of financing, passed new limited-liability laws, and signed a free-trade treaty with Britain in 1860. The government also supported the creation of the Crédit Mobilier, an investment banking institution that sold shares and financed railroads, insurance and gas companies, coal and construction companies, and the building of the Suez Canal (see Chapter 22). Napoleon also reluctantly permitted the existence of trade unions and legalized strikes. By appealing to both workers and the middle class, he sought to gain support for his goal of reestablishing France as a leading world power.

Most emblematic of the emperor's ambition was his transformation of the nation's capital. Paris's medieval infrastructure was buckling under the weight of population growth and industrial development. Cholera epidemics in 1832 and 1849 killed tens of thousands. In 1850, only one house in five had running water. Official concerns about public health were reinforced by political fears of crime and

PARIS REBUILT. Baron Haussmann, prefect of Paris under Napoleon III, presided over the wholesale rebuilding of the city, with effects we still see today. The Arc de Triomphe became the center of an *etoile* (star) pattern, with the wide boulevards named after Napoleon I's famous generals. (Photograph from the 1960s.)

revolutionary militancy in working-class neighborhoods. A massive rebuilding project razed much of the medieval center of the city and erected thirty-four thousand new buildings, including elegant hotels with the first elevators. The construction installed new water pipes and sewer lines, laid out two hundred kilometers of new streets, and rationalized the traffic flow. Wide new boulevards, many named for Napoleon I's most famous generals, radiated from the Arc de Triomphe. The renovation did not benefit everyone. Although the regime built model worker residences, rising rents drove working people from the city's center into increasingly segregated suburbs. Baron Haussman, the prefect of Paris who presided over the project, considered the city a monument to "cleanliness and order." Others called Haussmann an "artist of demolition."

Victorian Britain and the Second Reform Bill (1867)

Less affected by the revolutionary wave of 1848, Great Britain was able to chart a course of significant social and political reform, continuing a process that had begun in 1832 with the First Reform Bill. The government faced mounting demands to extend the franchise beyond the middle classes. Industrial expansion sustained a growing stratum of highly skilled and relatively well-paid workers

(almost exclusively male). These workers, concentrated for the most part within the building, engineering, and textile industries, turned away from the tradition of militant radicalism that had characterized the Hungry Forties. Instead they favored collective self-help through cooperative societies or trade unions, whose major role was to accumulate funds for insurance against old age and unemployment. They saw education as a tool for advancement and patronized the mechanics' institutes and similar institutions founded by them or on their behalf. These prosperous workers created real pressure for electoral reform.

Some argued for the vote in the name of democracy. Others borrowed arguments from earlier middle-class campaigns for electoral reform: they were responsible workers, respectable and upstanding members of society, with strong religious convictions and patriotic feelings. Unquestionably loyal to the state, they deserved the vote and direct representation just as much as the middle class. These workers were joined in their campaign by many middle-class dissenting reformers in the Liberal Party, whose religious beliefs (as dissenters from the Church of England) linked them to the workers' campaigns for reform. Dissenters had long faced discrimination. They were denied posts in the civil service and the military, which liberals felt should be open to talent, and for centuries had been excluded from the nation's premier universities, Oxford and Cambridge, unless they renounced their faith and subscribed to the articles of the Anglican church. Moreover, they resented paying taxes to support the Church of England, which was largely staffed by sons of the gentry and run in the interests of landed society. The fact that the community of dissent crossed class lines was vital to Liberal Party politics and the campaign for reforming the vote.

Working-class leaders and middle-class dissidents joined in a countrywide campaign for a new reform bill and a House of Commons responsive to their interests. They were backed by some shrewd Conservatives, such as Benjamin Disraeli (1804–1881), who argued that political life would be improved, not disrupted, by including the "aristocrats of labor." In actuality, Disraeli was betting that the newly enfranchised demographic would vote Conservative; and in 1867, he steered through Parliament a bill that reached further than anything proposed by his political opponents. The 1867 Reform Bill doubled the franchise by extending the vote to any men who paid poor rates or rent of £10 or more a year in urban areas (this meant, in general, skilled workers) and to rural tenants paying rent of £12 or more. As in 1832, the bill redistributed seats, with large northern cities gaining representation at the expense of the rural south. The responsible working class had been deemed worthy to participate in the affairs of state.

The reform bill was silent on women; but an important minority insisted that liberalism should include women's enfranchisement. These advocates mobilized a woman suffrage movement, building on women's remarkable participation in earlier reform campaigns, especially the Anti–Corn Law League and the movement to abolish slavery. Their cause found a passionate supporter in John Stuart Mill, perhaps the century's most brilliant, committed, and influential defender of personal liberty. Mill's father had worked closely with the Utilitarian philosopher Jeremy Bentham, and the young Mill had been a convinced Utilitarian himself (see Chapter 20). He went on, however, to develop much more expansive notions of human freedom. In 1859 Mill wrote *On Liberty*, which many consider the classic defense of individual freedom in the face of the state and the "tyranny of the majority." During the same period he coauthored—with his lover and eventual wife, Harriet Taylor—essays on women's political rights, the law of marriage, and divorce. His *The Subjection of Women* (1869), published after Harriet died, argued what few could even contemplate: that women had to be considered individuals on the same plane as men and that women's freedom was a measure of social progress. *Subjection* was an international success and with *On Liberty* became one of the defining texts of Western liberalism. Mill's arguments,

however, did not carry the day. Only militant suffrage movements and the crisis of the First World War brought women the vote.

The decade or so following the passage of the Reform Bill of 1867 marked the high point of British liberalism. By opening the doors to political participation, liberalism had accomplished a peaceful restructuring of political institutions and social life. It did so under considerable pressure from below, however; and in Britain as elsewhere, liberal leaders made it clear that these doors were unquestionably not open to everyone. Their opposition to woman suffrage is interesting for what it reveals about their views on male and female nature. They insisted that female individuality (expressed in voting, education, or wage earning) would destabilize family life. Yet their opposition to women's suffrage also reflected their conception of the vote: casting a ballot was a specific privilege granted only to specific social groups in return for their contributions to and vested interest in society. Men of property might champion the rule of law and representative government, but they balked at the prospect of a truly democratic politics and did not shy from heavy-handed, law-and-order politics. Expanding the franchise created new constituencies with new ambitions and paved the way for socialist and labor politics in the last quarter of the century. Tensions within liberalism remained and presaged conflicts in the future.

Italian Unification: Cavour and Garibaldi

After 1848, nationalists in Italy had to choose between two strategies for unification. Giuseppe Mazzini and his follower Giuseppe Garibaldi called for a popular uprising to create an Italian republic. Garibaldi was a guerilla fighter and a democrat who had been sent into exile in Latin America, where he fought alongside movements for national independence. Fearing that Garibaldi was too radical, more conservative Italian nationalists hoped that Italy might be unified as a constitutional monarchy under the new king of Piedmont-Sardinia, Victor Emmanuel II (r. 1849–61). To push for this result, Victor Emmanuel chose as his minister a shrewd Sardinian nobleman, Count Camillo Benso di Cavour (1810–1861), who promoted economic expansion and sought to raise Piedmont-Sardinia's profile in international relations. The choice seemed clear: a radical and democratic movement from below for national unification under Garibaldi's charismatic leadership or a conservative form of unification engineered from above by Cavour.

The main opponent of Italian unification was Austria, which controlled Lombardy and Venetia in the north.

MILL'S LOGIC, OR FRANCHISE FOR FEMALES
" Pray clear the way, there, for these—ah—persons."

JOHN STUART MILL AND SUFFRAGETTES. By 1860, when this cartoon was published, Mill had established a reputation as a liberal political philosopher and a supporter of women's right to vote. Mill argued that women's enfranchisement was essential both from the standpoint of individual liberty and for the good of society as a whole. ■ *What was amusing about Mill's assertion that women be considered persons in their own right?*

GIUSEPPE GARIBALDI. Note the simple uniform Garibaldi wears in this commemorative portrait, with its iconic symbols of his nationalist movement: the red shirt, and the flag of Italy in the background. Compare this with the official portraits of absolutist rulers in previous chapters. ▪ *What was significant about the absence of finery and precious materials in this painting?* ▪ *What does it say about images of masculine leadership in the mid-nineteenth-century nationalist imagination? (Compare this with the drawing of Garibaldi and Victor Emmanuel on the right.)*

"RIGHT LEG IN THE BOOT AT LAST." This image shows Garibaldi helping Victor Emmanuel, former king of Piedmont-Sardinia and the newly crowned king of Italy, get his foot in the Italian boot. What is the significance of their different forms of dress and postures? (Compare this with the portrait of Garibaldi on the left.) ▪ *How does this image portray the outcome of the contest between the conservative nationalism of Cavour and the more romantic and democratic nationalism of Garibaldi?*

Cavour enticed the French to help Piedmont-Sardinia confront the Austrians, in exchange for the territories of Nice and Savoy. France duly provoked a war with Austria in 1859, and Lombardy fell into the hands Piedmont-Sardinia. Napoleon III of France refused to press farther into Venetia, however, because he worried that a growing dispute between Cavour and the pope would alienate French Catholics. The war tipped the balance in Piedmont-Sardinia's favor, however, and the duchies of Parma, Modena, and Tuscany also agreed to join the new state, which had by now doubled in size.

As Cavour consolidated his control over the north, events in the south indicated that he might profitably turn his attention there as well. The unpopular Bourbon king of Two Sicilies, Francis II (r. 1859–60) faced a fast-spreading peasant revolt. Garibaldi seized the opportunity to organize a volunteer army of northerners and southerners, which landed in Sicily in May 1860. Garibaldi's army took Sicily, and joined by large numbers of insurgents, moved on to take Naples as well, toppling the kingdom of Francis II. The next obvious step was Rome, where the pope was guarded by French troops.

Cavour worried that Garibaldi's rising popularity would destabilize his plans for an orderly unification under Piedmont-Sardinian rule. He dispatched Victor Emmanuel to Rome, along with an army, and the king ordered Garibaldi to cede him military authority. Garibaldi obeyed and Victor Emmanuel assumed the title of King of Italy (r. 1861–78). Cavour's vision of Italian nationhood had won the day.

The final steps of Italian unification came indirectly. Venetia remained in Austrian hands until 1866, when Austria's defeat in the Austro-Prussian war led to Venetia's absorption into the Italian kingdom. French troops protected Rome's independence until 1870, when Napoleon III withdrew his soldiers at the outbreak of the Franco-Prussian war. In September 1870, Italian troops occupied Rome, and in July 1871, Rome became the capital of the united Italian kingdom. The pope and his successors refused to recognize

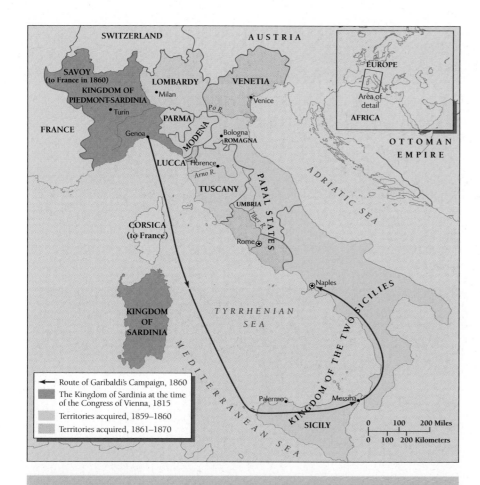

THE UNIFICATION OF ITALY. ▪ *How many phases were involved in Italian unification, according to the map key?* ▪ *Why did it take an extra decade to incorporate Rome and Venetia into the Italian state?* ▪ *Why was Italian unification incomplete until the early twentieth century?*

the new secular government until 1929, when the government and the papacy settled their longstanding dispute.

Nation building in Italy was hardly over, however. A minority of the population spoke Italian, and profound economic and social inequalities divided the north from the south, where the state was weak, banditry common, and insurrections frequent. When the government later sent troops to repress revolts in the south, more people were killed than had died in the wars of unification. Regional differences and deep social tensions made building the Italian nation an ongoing process.

The Unification of Germany: Realpolitik

Hopes for German unity under a liberal constitution had been decisively defeated in 1848. King Frederick William of Prussia nevertheless granted a constitution in 1850 that established a two-house parliament, with the lower house

elected by universal male suffrage. The weight of individual votes depended on the amount of taxes paid by the voter, and a wealthy industrialist or large landowner exercised nearly a hundred times the voting power of a working man. By the late 1850s, however, economic growth and the growing middle class in Germany had produced a liberal intelligentsia, a thoughtful and engaged press, and a civil service dedicated to economic and political modernization.

When William I assumed the throne as prince regent in 1858, therefore, he faced an increasingly confident parliamentary opposition that challenged his policies on liberal grounds, focusing especially on the high levels of military spending. In the face of this challenge, William sought to expand the army and remove the military from parliamentary control. When liberals refused to approve the budget in 1862, William named as his minister-president Otto von Bismarck, a deeply conservative and pragmatic Prussian aristocrat.

Born into the Junker class of Prussian landowning nobility, Bismarck was a fierce opponent of German liberalism. Bismarck believed in the principle of *Realpolitik*—practical, realistic politics—which held that achieving and maintaining power was more important than moral or ideological goals such as justice or freedom. He was not a German nationalist and thought of himself above all as a Prussian. When he maneuvered to bring other German states under Prussian domination, he did so not in pursuit of a grand German design but because he believed that union in some form was inevitable and that Prussia had to seize the initiative.

In Prussia, Bismarck defied the parliamentary opposition. When the liberal majority refused to levy taxes, he dissolved the parliament and collected them anyway. His most decisive actions, however, were in foreign policy. Once opposed to nationalism, he skillfully played the national card to preempt his liberal opponents at home, and gather popular support for expansionist policies abroad. In doing so, he succeeded in associating German nation building solely with Prussian authority, rather than with liberal constitutionalists.

Interpreting Visual Evidence

The New German Nation

In order to silence their critics at home and abroad, nationalists in Germany sought to create a vision of German history that made unification the natural outcome of a deep historical process that had begun hundreds of years before. In image A, the family of a cavalry officer prepares to hang a portrait of King William on the wall, next to portraits of Martin Luther, Frederick the Great, and Field Marshall von Blücher, who commanded the Prussian forces at Waterloo. In the lower left corner, two boys roll up a portrait of the defeated French emperor, Napoleon III. The implication, of course, was that the unification of Germany was the inevitable culmination of generations of German heroes who all worked toward the same goal.

This unity was itself controversial among German people. Image B, a pro-Bismarck cartoon, shows the German minister-president dragging the unwilling liberal members of the Prussian parliament along with him as he pulls a triumphal chariot toward his military confrontation with Austria in 1866. The caption reads: "And in this sense, too, we are in agreement with Count Bismarck, and we have pulled the same rope as him." Image C, on the other hand, expresses reservations about Prussian dominance in the new empire. The title "Germany's Future" and the caption:

A. *Homage to Kaiser Wilhelm I* by Paul Bürde, 1871.

The main obstacle to Bismarck's plan for German union was Austria, which had significant influence over the German confederation. Bismarck skillfully inflamed a long-smoldering dispute with Denmark over Schleswig (*SCHLAYS-vihg*) and Holstein, two provinces peopled by Germans and Danes, and claimed by Prussia and Denmark. When the Danish king attempted to annex the provinces, Bismarck invited the Austrians to help defeat the Danes in a short war. As he hoped, the two allies soon fell into a dispute over the spoils and in 1866 Bismarck declared war on Austria. Prussian victory forced the Austrians to give up all claims to Schleswig and Holstein, cede Venetia to the Italians, and agree to the dissolution of the German Confederation. In its place, Bismarck created a North German Confederation, including all states north of the Main River, and dominated by Prussia.

Both wars generated popular enthusiasm in the German states, and Bismarck's ability to connect his brand of power politics to growing nationalist sentiment further undermined the liberal opposition to the Prussian king in parliament. The liberals surrendered in the disputes over budgets and the military. Meanwhile, Bismarck promoted a

"Will it fit under one hat? I think it will only fit under a [Prussian] Pickelhaube." The *Pickelhaube*—the characteristic pointed helmet of the Prussian army—had already become a much-feared symbol of Prussian military force. Such an image may well have struck a chord with residents of the non-Prussian German states who now paid taxes to the Prussian monarchy and served in an army dominated by Prussian officers.

Questions for Analysis

1. What is the significance of the familial setting in image A? Why was it important for nationalists to emphasize a multigenerational family as the repository of German national spirit?

2. How do images B and C treat the question of Prussia's role within the new German nation? Was German national identity seen as something built from below or defined from above by a strong monarchy?

3. What is the place of the individual citizen in these representations of the German nation?

B. Prussian liberals and Bismarck after Königgrätz (1866).

C. "Germany's Future" (1870).

constitution for the North German Confederation that gave the appearance of a more representative political body, with a two-house legislature, and freedom of the press. In fact, however, the constitution gave decisive political advantages to Prussia and its conservative king.

The final step in completing German unity was the Franco-Prussian War of 1870–71. Bismarck calculated that a war with France would rally the southern German states such as Bavaria and Würtemberg and lead them to join the confederation. His opportunity came when France and Prussia fell into a dispute about whether or not the Prussian ruling family, the Hohenzollerns, could inherit the Spanish throne. When the French asked the Prussians to accept a "perpetual exclusion," Bismarck edited a telegram from William I to make it appear as if the Prussian king had rebuffed the French ambassador. Once the altered telegram reached France, the nation responded with calls for war, and Bismarck rallied the Germans to respond with claims about French plans to take over the Rhineland. Just as Bismarck had hoped, the outbreak of war between France and Prussia brought the southern German states to Prussia's side. The war was quick, and the French defeat

TOWARD THE UNIFICATION OF GERMANY. Note the many elements that made up a unified Germany and the stages that brought them together. ■ *Did this new nation have any resemblance to the unified Germany envisioned by the liberal revolutionaries of the Frankfurt Preparliament in 1848? (See page 502.)* ■ *How many stages were involved in the unification of Germany, and how many years did it take?* ■ *What region filled with German-speaking peoples was not included in the new unified Germany and why?*

total. Napoleon III was captured and his government collapsed, though insurrectionary Parisians held out through the winter of 1870–71.

On January 18, 1871, in the Hall of Mirrors at Versailles, the German Empire was proclaimed, with William I at its head. The new German nation included all the German states of central Europe except Austria. Four months later the French were forced to sign a treaty that ceded the border region of Alsace to the new German state and to pay an indemnity of 5 billion francs. Within the new Germany, Prussia remained intact, with 60 percent of the territory and population, as well as its own monarchy, army, and bureaucracy. This was not the unified Germany imagined by German liberals—it was a revolution from above, not from below, and the authoritarian structure of the Prussian state remained intact.

The State and Nationality: Centrifugal Forces in the Austrian Empire

Germany emerged from the 1860s a stronger, unified nation. The Habsburg Empire faced a very different situation, and emerged a weakened, multiethnic dual monarchy called Austria-Hungary after 1867.

As we have seen, ethnic nationalism was a powerful force in the Habsburg monarchy in 1848. Yet the Habsburg state, with a combination of military repression and tactics that divided its enemies, had proved more powerful. It abolished serfdom but made few other concessions to its opponents. The Hungarians, who had nearly won independence in the spring of 1848, were essentially reconquered. Administrative reforms created a new and more uniform legal system, rationalized taxation, and imposed a single-language policy that favored German. Through the 1850s and 1860s the subject nationalities, as they were often called, bitterly protested against military repression, and cultural disenfranchisement. The Czechs in Bohemia grew increasingly alienated by policies that favored the German minority. In response, they became increasingly insistent on their Slavic identity—a movement welcomed by Russia, which became the sponsor of a broad pan-Slavism. The Hungarians, or Magyars, the most powerful of the subject nationalities, sought to reclaim the autonomy they had glimpsed in 1848.

In this context, Austria's damaging defeats at the hands of Piedmont-Sardinia in 1859 and Prussia in 1866 became especially significant. The 1866 war forced the emperor Francis Joseph to renegotiate the very structure of the empire. To stave off a revolution by the Hungarians, Francis Joseph agreed to a new federal structure in the form of the Dual Monarchy. Austria-Hungary had a common system of taxation, a common army, and made foreign and military policy together. Francis Joseph was emperor of Austria and king of Hungary. But internal and constitutional affairs were separated. The *Ausgleich*, or Settlement, allowed the Hungarians to establish their own constitution; their own legislature; and their own capital, combining the cities of Buda and Pest.

What of the other nationalities? The official policy of the Dual Monarchy stated that they were not to be discriminated against and that they could use their own languages. Official policy was only loosely enforced. More important,

elevating the Hungarians and conferring on them alone the benefits of political nationhood could only worsen relations with other groups. On the Austrian side of the Dual Monarchy, minority nationalities such as the Poles, Czechs, and Slovenes resented their second-class status. On the Hungarian side, the regime embarked on a project of Magyarization, attempting to make the state, the civil service, and the schools more thoroughly Hungarian—an effort that did not sit well with Serbs and Croats.

It was impossible, then, to speak of national unification in the Habsburg lands. The Austrian emperor remained deeply opposed to nationalism, considering it, rightly, a centrifugal force that would destroy his kingdom. Unlike the governments of France, England, Italy, or Germany, the Habsburgs did not seek to build a nation-state based on a common cultural identity. It tried instead to build a state and administrative structure strong enough to keep the pieces from spinning off, playing different minorities off against each other, and conceding autonomy only when essential. As the nineteenth century unfolded, subject nationalities would appeal to other powers—Serbia, Russia, the Ottomans—and this balancing act would become more difficult.

NATION AND STATE BUILDING IN RUSSIA AND THE UNITED STATES

The challenges of nationalism and nation building also occupied Russia, the United States, and Canada. In all three countries, nation building entailed territorial and economic expansion, the incorporation of new peoples, and—in Russia and the United States—contending with the enormous problems of slavery and serfdom.

Territory, the State, and Serfdom: Russia

Serfdom in Russia had already been criticized by the intelligentsia under the reign of Catherine the Great (r. 1762–96). After 1789, and especially after 1848, the abolition of serfdom elsewhere in Europe made the issue more urgent. Abolishing serfdom became part of a larger debate about how Russia might become a modern nation.

Two schools of thought emerged. The "Slavophiles," or Romantic nationalists, sought to preserve Russia's distinctive features. They idealized traditional Russian culture and the peasant commune, rejecting Western secularism, urban commercialism, and bourgeois culture. In contrast, the "westernizers" wished to see Russia adopt European developments in science, technology, and education, which they believed to be the foundation for Western liberalism and the protection of individual rights. Both groups agreed that serfdom must be abolished. The Russian nobility, however, tenaciously opposed emancipation. Tangled debates about how lords would be compensated for the loss of "their" serfs, and how emancipated serfs would survive without full-scale land redistribution, also checked progress on the issue. The Crimean War (discussed later in this chapter) broke the impasse. In its aftermath, Alexander II (r. 1855–81) forced the issue. Worried that the persistence of serfdom had sapped Russian strength and contributed to its defeat in the war, and persuaded that serfdom would only continue to prompt violent conflict, he ended serfdom by decree in 1861.

The emancipation decree of 1861 was a reform of massive scope; but paradoxically, it produced limited change. It granted legal rights to some twenty-two million serfs and authorized their title to a portion of the land they had worked. It also required the state to compensate landowners for the properties they relinquished. Large-scale landowners vastly inflated their compensation claims, however, and managed to retain much of the most profitable acreage for themselves. As a result, the land granted to peasants was often of poor quality and insufficient to sustain themselves and their families. Moreover, the newly liberated serfs had to pay in installments for their land, which was not in fact granted to them individually, but rather to a village commune that collected their payments. As a result, the pattern of rural life in Russia did not change drastically. The system of payment kept peasants in the villages—not as free-standing farmers but as agricultural laborers for their former masters.

While the Russian state undertook reforms, it also expanded its territory. After midcentury, the Russians pressed east and south. They invaded and conquered several independent Islamic kingdoms along the former Silk Road and expanded into Siberia in search of natural resources. Russian diplomacy wrung various commercial concessions from the Chinese that led to the founding of the Siberian city of Vladivostok in 1860. Racial, ethnic, and religious differences made governing a daunting task. In most cases, the Russian state did not try to assimilate the populations of the new territories: an acceptance of ethnic particularity was a pragmatic response to the difficulties of governing such a heterogeneous population. When the state did attempt to impose Russian culture, the results were disastrous. Whether power was wielded by the nineteenth-century tsars or, later, by the Soviet Union, powerful centrifugal forces pulled against genuine unification. Expansion helped Russia create a vast empire that was geographically of one piece, but by no means one nation.

Territory and the Nation: The United States

The American Revolution had bequeathed to the United States a loose union of slave and free states, tied together in part by a commitment to territorial expansion. The so-called Jeffersonian Revolution combined democratic aspirations with a drive to expand the nation's boundaries. Leaders of the movement, at first known as the anti-Federalists because of their mistrust of centralized government, campaigned to add the Bill of Rights to the Constitution and were almost single-handedly responsible for its passage in 1791. Later organized as the Democratic-Republicans under Thomas Jefferson's presidency (1801–09) this movement emphasized the supremacy of the people's representatives and viewed with alarm attempts by the executive and judicial branches to increase their power. They supported a political system based on an aristocracy of "virtue and talent," in which respect for personal liberty would be the guiding principle. They opposed the establishment of a national religion and special privilege, whether of birth or of wealth. Yet the Jeffersonian vision of the republic rested on the independence of yeoman farmers, and the independence and prosperity of those farmers depended on the availability of new lands. This made territorial expansion, as exemplified by the Louisiana Purchase in 1803, central to Jeffersonian America. Expansion brought complications. While it did provide land for many yeoman farmers in the north and south, it also added millions of acres of prime cotton land, thus extending the empire of slavery. The purchase of the port of New Orleans made lands in the south well worth developing but led the American republic forcibly to remove Native Americans from the Old South west of the Mississippi River. This process of expansion and expropriation stretched from Jefferson's administration through the age of Jackson, or the 1840s.

Under Andrew Jackson (president 1829–37) the Democratic-Republicans were transformed again into a more populist movement known simply as the Democrats. They campaigned to extend the suffrage to all white males; they argued that all officeholders should be elected rather than appointed; and they sought the frequent rotation of men in positions of political power—a doctrine that permitted politicians to use patronage to build national political parties. Moreover, the Jacksonian vision of democracy and nationhood carried over into a crusade to incorporate more territories into the republic. It was the United States' "Manifest

Destiny," wrote a New York editor, "to overspread the continent allotted by Providence for the free development of our yearly multiplying millions." Under Jackson's successors in the ensuing decades, that "overspreading" brought Oregon and Washington into the Union through a compromise with the British and brought Arizona, Texas, New Mexico, Utah, Nevada, and California through war with Mexico—all of which led to the wholesale expropriation of Native American lands. Territorial expansion was key to nation building, but it was built on increasingly inevitable conflict over slavery.

The Politics of Slavery in the West

When the age of revolution opened in the 1770s, slavery was legal everywhere in the Americas. By the point we have reached, the close of the age of revolution, slavery remained legal only in the southern United States, Brazil, and Cuba. (It endured, too, in most of Africa and parts of India and the Islamic world.) How and why was slavery, which had been embedded for centuries in economies and culture, abolished elsewhere in the West?

The revolutions of the eighteenth century by no means brought emancipation in their wake. Eighteenth-century Enlightenment thinkers had persuaded many Europeans that slavery contradicted natural law and natural freedom (see Chapter 17). Nevertheless, Virginia planters who helped lead the American Revolution defended plantation slavery while refusing to be "slaves" of the British. The planters' success in throwing off the British king expanded their power and strengthened slavery in the United States. Likewise, the French revolutionaries denounced the tyranny of a king who would "enslave" them but refused to admit free people of color to the revolutionary assembly for fear of alienating the planters in the lucrative colonies of Martinique, Guadelupe, and St. Domingue. Only a slave rebellion in St. Domingue in 1791 forced the French revolutionaries, eventually, to contend with the contradictions of revolutionary policy. Napoleon's failure to repress that rebellion allowed for the emergence of Haiti in 1804 (see Chapter 18). The Haitian revolution sent shock waves through the Americas, alarming slave owners and offering hope to slaves and former slaves. Yet the Haitian revolution had other, contradictory consequences. The "loss" of slave-based sugar production in the former St. Domingue created an opportunity for its expansion elsewhere, in the U.S. South, and in Brazil, where slavery expanded in the production of sugar, gold, and coffee. Finally, slavery remained intact in the French, British, and Spanish colonial islands in the Caribbean, backed by the Congress of Vienna in 1815.

An English abolitionist movement did emerge. The country that ruled the seas was "the world's leading purchaser and transporter of African slaves," and the movement aimed to abolish that trade. From the 1780s on, pamphlets and books detailed the horrors of the slave ships to an increasingly sympathetic audience. Abolitionist leaders like William Wilberforce believed that the slave trade was immoral and hoped that banning it would improve conditions for the enslaved, though like most abolitionists Wilberforce did not want to foment revolt. In 1807 the reform movement compelled Parliament to pass a bill declaring the "African Slave Trade to be contrary to the principles of justice, humanity, and sound policy" and prohibiting British ships from participating in it, effective 1808. The United States joined in the agreement; ten years later the Portuguese agreed to a limited ban on traffic north of the equator. More treaties followed, which slowed but did not stop the trade. Ships carried two and a half million slaves to markets in the Americas in the four decades *after* the abolition of slave trade.

Abolitionists argued that the slave trade and slavery itself represented the arrogance and callousness of wealthy British traders, their planter allies, and the British elite in general. In a culture with high literacy and political traditions of activism, calls for "British liberty" mobilized many. In England, and especially in the United States,

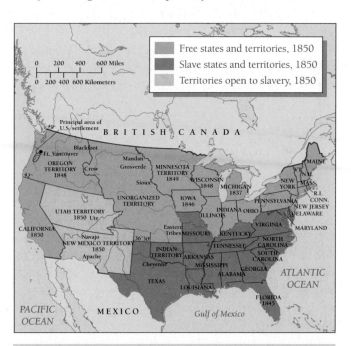

AMERICAN EXPANSION IN THE LATE NINETEENTH CENTURY.
■ *What events enabled the United States to acquire all lands west of the Mississippi River?* ■ *How did the process of westward expansion shape the debate about slavery and citizenship in the United States?*

Competing Viewpoints

The Abolition of Serfdom in Russia

The abolition of serfdom was central to Tsar Alexander II's program of modernization and reform after the Crimean War. Emancipated serfs were now allowed to own their land, ending centuries of bondage. The decree, however, emphasized the tsar's benevolence and the nobility's generosity—not peasant rights. The government did not want emancipation to bring revolution to the countryside; it sought to reinforce the state's authority, the landowners' power, and the peasants' obligations. After spelling out the detailed provisions for emancipation, the decree added the paragraphs reprinted here.

Emancipation did not solve problems in the Russian countryside. On the contrary, it unleashed a torrent of protest, including complaints from peasants that nobles were undermining attempts to reform. These petitions in the second section detail the struggles that came in the wake of emancipation in two villages.

Tsar Alexander II's Decree Emancipating the Serfs, 1861

And We place Our hope in the good sense of Our people.

When word of the Government's plan to abolish the law of bondage [serfdom] reached peasants unprepared for it, there arose a partial misunderstanding. Some [peasants] thought about freedom and forgot about obligations. But the general good sense [of the people] was not disturbed in the conviction that anyone freely enjoying the goods of society correspondingly owes it to the common good to fulfill certain obligations, [a conviction held] both by natural reason and by Christian law, according to which "every soul must be subject to the governing authorities." . . . Rights legally acquired by the landlords cannot be taken from them without a decent return or [their] voluntary concession; and . . . it would be contrary to all justice to make use of the lords' land without bearing the corresponding obligation.

And now We hopefully expect that the bonded people, as a new future opens before them, will understand and accept with gratitude the important sacrifice made by the Well-born Nobility for the improvement of their lives.

Source: James Cracraft, ed., *Major Problems in the History of Imperial Russia* (Lexington, MA: 1994), pp. 340–44.

Emancipation: The View from Below

Petition from Peasants in Podosinovka (Voronezh Province) to Alexander II, May 1863

The most merciful manifesto of Your Imperial Majesty from 19 February 1861, with the published rules, put a limit to the enslavement of the people in blessed Russia. But some former serfowners—who desire not to improve the peasants' lives, but to oppress and ruin them—apportion land contrary to the laws, choose the best land from all the fields for themselves, and give the poor peasants . . . the worst and least usable lands.

To this group of squires must be counted our own, Anna Mikhailovna Raevskaia. . . . Of our fields and resources, she chose the best places from amidst our strips, and, like a cooking ring in a hearth, carved off 300 dessiatines [measures of land] for herself. . . . But our community refused to accept so ruinous an allotment and requested that we be given an allotment in accordance with the local statute. . . . The peace arbitrator . . . and the police chief . . . slandered us before the governor, alleging that we were rioting and that it is impossible for them to enter our village.

The provincial governor believed this lie and sent 1,200 soldiers of the penal command to our village. . . . Without any cause, our village priest Father Peter—rather than give an uplifting pastoral exhortation to stop the spilling of innocent blood—joined these reptiles, with the unanimous incitement of the authorities. . . . They summoned nine township heads and their aides from other townships. . . . In their presence, the provincial governor—without making any investigation and without interrogating a single person—ordered that the birch rods be brought and that the punishment commence, which was carried out with cruelty and mercilessness. They punished up to 200 men and women; 80 people were at four levels (with 500, 400, 300 and 200 blows); some received lesser punishment . . . and when the inhuman punishment of these innocent people had ended, the provincial governor said: "If you find the land unsuitable, I do not forbid you to file petitions wherever you please," and then left. . . .

We dare to implore you, Orthodox emperor and our merciful father, not to reject the petition of a community with 600 souls, including wives and children.

Order with your tsarist word that our community be allotted land . . . as the law dictates without selecting the best sections of fields and meadows, but in straight lines. . . . [Order that] the meadows and haylands along the river Elan be left to our community without any restriction; these will enable us to feed our cattle and smaller livestock, which are necessary for our existence.

Petition from Peasants in Balashov District to Grand Duke Constantin Nikolaevich, January 25, 1862

Your Imperial Excellency! Most gracious sire! Grand Duke Konstantin Nikolaevich! . . .

After being informed of the Imperial manifesto on the emancipation of peasants from serfdom on 1861 . . . we received this [news] with jubilation. . . . But from this moment, our squire ordered that the land be cut off from the entire township. But this is absolutely intolerable for us: it not only denies us profit, but threatens us with a catastrophic future. He began to hold repeated meetings and [tried to] force us to sign that we agreed to accept the above land allotment. But, upon seeing so unexpected a change, and bearing in mind the gracious manifesto, we refused. . . . After assembling the entire township, they tried to force us into making illegal signatures accepting the land cut-offs. But when they saw that this did not succeed, they had a company of soldiers sent in. . . . Then [Colonel] Globbe came from their midst, threatened us with exile to Siberia, and ordered the soldiers to strip the peasants and to punish seven people by flogging in the most inhuman manner. They still have not regained consciousness.

Source: Gregory L. Freeze, ed., *From Supplication to Revolution: A Documentary Social History of Imperial Russia* (New York: 1988), pp. 170–73.

Questions for Analysis

1. What did Tsar Alexander II fear most in liberating the serfs from bondage? What provisions did he make to ensure that the emancipation would not destabilize his regime?

2. What issues mattered most to the peasantry? What is their attitude toward the tsar?

3. Given the immediate danger to social peace, why did the tsar feel that emancipating the serfs was necessary?

religious revivals supplied much of the energy for the abolitionist movement. The moral and religious dimensions of the struggle made it acceptable for women, who would move from antislavery to the Anti–Corn Law League and, later, to woman suffrage. The issue also spoke to working people whose sometimes brutal working conditions and sharply limited political rights we have discussed in the previous chapters. To oppose slavery and to insist that labor should be dignified, honorable, and minimally free resonated broadly in the social classes accustomed to being treated as "servile." Finally, slave rebellions and conspiracies also shook public opinion, especially after the Haitian Revolution (see page 447). The issue, then, cut across material interests and class politics, and antislavery petitions were signed by millions in the 1820s and 1830s.

In Great Britain, the force of abolitionism wore down the defense of slavery. In the aftermath of the Great Reform Bill of 1832, Great Britain emancipated eight hundred thousand slaves in its colonies—effective in 1838, after four years of "apprenticeship." In France, republicans took the strongest antislavery stance, and emancipation came to the French colonies when the revolution of 1848 brought republicans, however briefly, to power.

In Latin America, slavery's fate was determined by demographics, economics, and the politics of breaking away from the Spanish and Portuguese empires. In most of mainland Spanish America (in other words, not Cuba or Brazil), slavery had been of secondary importance, due to the relative ease of escape and the presence of other sources of labor. As the struggles for independence escalated, nationalist leaders recruited slaves and free people of color to fight against the Spanish, promising emancipation in return. Símon de Bolívar's 1817 campaign to liberate Venezuela was fought in part by slaves, ex-slaves, and six thousand troops from Haiti. The new nations in Spanish America passed emancipation measures in stages but had eliminated slavery by the middle of the century.

Cuba was starkly different: with 40 percent of its population enslaved, the Spanish island colony had almost as many slaves as all of mainland Spanish America together. A Cuban independence movement would have detonated a slave revolution, a fact that provided a powerful incentive for Cuba to remain under the Spanish crown. Spain, for its part, needed the immensely profitable sugar industry and could not afford to alienate Cuban planters by pushing for an end to slavery. Only a combination of slave rebellion in Cuba and liberal revolution in Spain brought abolition, beginning in the 1870s. Brazil, too, was 40 percent enslaved and, like Cuba, had a large population of free people of color. Unlike Cuba, Brazil won national independence, breaking away from Portugal with relative ease (1822). Like the American South, Brazil came through the revolution for independence with slavery not only intact but expanding, and slavery endured in Brazil until 1888.

The American Civil War, 1861–65

The politics of slavery, then, were by no means unique to the United States, but in the United States the combination of a growing abolitionist movement, a slave-owning class that feared the economic power of the North, and territorial expansion created deadlock and crisis. As the country expanded west, North and South engaged in a protracted tug of war about whether new states were to be "free" or "slave." In the North, territorial expansion heightened calls for free labor; in the South it deepened whites' commitment to an economy and society based on plantation slavery.

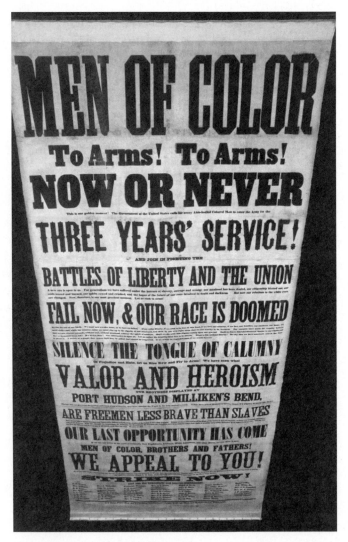

CIVIL WAR RECRUITING POSTER. This poster, created by northern African American abolitionists, exhorts fellow blacks to fight in the American Civil War.

Ultimately, the changes pushed southern political leaders toward secession. The failure of a series of elaborate compromises led to the outbreak of the Civil War in 1861.

The protracted and costly struggle proved a first experience of the horrors of modern war and prefigured the First World War. It also decisively transformed the nation. First, it abolished slavery. Second, it established the preeminence of the national government over states' rights. The Fourteenth Amendment to the Constitution stated specifically that all Americans were citizens of the United States and not of an individual state or territory. In declaring that no citizen was to be deprived of life, liberty, or property without due process of law, it established that "due process" was to be defined by the national, not the state or territorial, government. Third, in the aftermath of the Civil War, the U.S. economy expanded with stunning rapidity. In 1865 there were thirty-five thousand miles of railroad track in the United States; by 1900 there were almost two hundred thousand. Industrial and agricultural production rose, putting the United States in a position to compete with Great Britain. As we will see later on, American industrialists, bankers, and retailers introduced innovations in assembly-line manufacturing, corporate organization, and advertising that startled their European counterparts and gave the United States new power in world politics. These developments were all part of the process of nation building. They did not overcome deep racial, regional, or class divides. Though the war brought the South back into the Union, the rise of northern capitalism magnified the backwardness of the South as an underdeveloped agricultural region whose wealth was extracted by northern industrialists. The railroad corporations, which pieced together the national infrastructure, became the classic foe of labor and agrarian reformers. In these ways, the Civil War laid the foundations for the modern American nation-state.

"EASTERN QUESTIONS": INTERNATIONAL RELATIONS AND THE DECLINE OF OTTOMAN POWER

During the nineteenth century, questions of national identity and international power were inextricable from contests over territory. War and diplomacy drew and redrew boundaries as European nations groped toward a sustainable balance of power. The rise of new powers, principally the German Empire, posed one set of challenges to Continental order. The waning power of older regimes posed another. The Crimean War, which lasted from 1853 to 1856, was a particularly gruesome attempt to cope with the most serious such collapse. As the Ottoman Empire lost its grip on its provinces in southeastern Europe, the "Eastern Question" of who would benefit from Ottoman weakness drew Europe into war. At stake were not only territorial gains but also strategic interests, alliances, and the balance of power in Europe. And though the war occurred before the unification of the German and Italian states, it structured the system of Great Power politics that guided Europe until (and indeed toward) the First World War.

The Crimean War, 1853–56

The root causes of the war lay in the Eastern Question and the decline of the Ottoman Empire. The crisis that provoked it, however, involved religion—namely French and Russian claims to protect religious minorities and the holy places of Jerusalem within the Muslim Ottoman Empire. In 1853 a three-way quarrel among France (on behalf of Roman Catholics), Russia (representing Eastern Orthodox Christians), and Turkey devolved into a Russian confrontation with the Turkish sultan. Confident that Turkey would be unable to resist, concerned that other powers might take advantage of Turkish weakness, and persuaded (mistakenly) that they had British support, the Russians moved troops into the Ottoman-governed territories of Moldavia and Walachia. (See the map on page 520.) In October 1853 Turkey, also persuaded they would be supported by the British, declared war on Russia. The war became a disaster for the Turks, who lost their fleet at the battle of Sinope in November. But Russia's success alarmed the British and the French, who considered Russian expansion a threat to their interests in the Balkans, the eastern Mediterranean, and, for the British, the route to India. Determined to check that expansion, France and Britain each declared war on Russia in March 1854. In September they landed on the Russian peninsula of Crimea and headed for the Russian naval base at Sevastopol, to which they laid siege. France, Britain, and the Ottomans were joined in 1855 by the small but ambitious Italian state of Piedmont-Sardinia, all fighting against the Russians. This was the closest Europe had come to a general war since 1815.

The war was relatively short, but its conduct was devastating. Conditions on the Crimean peninsula were dire, and the disastrous mismanagement of supplies and hygiene by the British and French led to epidemics among the troops. At least as many soldiers died from typhus or cholera as in combat. The fighting was bitter, marked by such notoriously inept strategies as the British "charge of the

THE CRIMEAN WAR. Note the theater of operations and the major assaults of the Crimean War. ■ *Which empires and nations were in a position to take advantage of Ottoman weakness?* ■ *Who benefited from the outcome, and who was most harmed?* ■ *In what ways was the Crimean War the first modern war?*

Light Brigade," in which a British cavalry unit was slaughtered by massed Russian artillery. Vast battles pitted tens of thousands of British and French troops against Russian formations, combat that was often settled with bayonets. Despite the disciplined toughness of the British and French troops, and despite their nations' dominance of the seas around Crimea, the Russians denied them a clear victory. Sevastopol, under siege for nearly a year, did not fall until September 1855. The bitter, unsatisfying conflict was ended by treaty in 1856.

For the French and Sardinians, the bravery of their soldiers bolstered positive national sentiments at home; for the British and Russians, however, the poorly managed war provoked waves of intense criticism. As far as international relations were concerned, the peace settlement dealt a blow to Russia, whose influence in the Balkans was drastically curbed. The provinces of Moldavia and Walachia were united as Romania, which became an independent nation. Austria's refusal to come to the aid of Russia cost her the support of her powerful former ally. The Crimean War embarrassed France and left Russia and Austria considerably weaker, opening an advantage for Bismarck in the 1860s, as we saw earlier.

The Crimean War was important in other ways as well. Though fought largely with the same methods and mentalities employed in the Napoleonic Wars forty years earlier,

After You Read This Chapter

Visit StudySpace for quizzes, additional review material, and multi-media documents. **wwnorton.com/studyspace**

REVIEWING THE OBJECTIVES

- Liberal revolutionaries in Europe demanded more representative political institutions and increased liberties. Why did they fail to achieve these goals?

- Nationalists in both Germany and Italy were divided between those who supported the creation of a new nation from below, through popular movements, and those who preferred nation building from above by heads of state. How did these divisions work themselves out in the process of national unification?

- Creating a modern nation in Russia entailed the end of serfdom, whereas in the United States, political leaders from the North and South debated the place of slavery in the modern nation-state. In what ways were national debates about citizenship in these countries shaped by the widespread practices of bondage in the two economies?

- The three major European wars (the Crimean War, the Austro-Prussian War, and the Franco-Prussian War) of this period were of relatively short duration but they had profound effects on the international balance of power in Europe. Which countries emerged stronger from these conflicts, and which found their interests most damaged?

the war brought innovations that forecast the direction of modern warfare. It saw the first significant use of rifled muskets, underwater mines, and trench warfare, as well as the first tactical use of railroads and telegraphs. Finally, the war was covered by the first modern war correspondents and photojournalists, making it the most public war to date. Reports from the theater of war were sent "live" by telegraph to Britain and France with sobering details about the deplorable conditions British soldiers endured. The care and supply of the troops became national scandals in the popular press, prompting dramatic changes in the military, and making heroes of individual doctors and nurses such as Florence Nightingale.

CONCLUSION

The twenty years between 1850 and 1870 brought intense nation building in the Western world. The unification of Germany and Italy changed the map of Europe, with important consequences for the balance of power. The emergence of the United States as a major power also had international ramifications. For old as well as new nation-states, economic development and political transformation—often on a very large scale—were important means of increasing and securing the state's power. Yet demands for more representative government, the abolition of privilege, and land

reform had to be reckoned with, as did the systems of slavery and serfdom. Trailing the banner of nationhood was an explosive set of questions about how to balance the power and interests of minorities and majorities, of the wealthy and poor, of the powerful and the dispossessed. Nation building not only changed states, it transformed relations between states and their citizens.

These transformations were anything but predictable. Nationalism showed itself to be a volatile, erratic, and malleable force during the mid-nineteenth century. It provided much of the fuel for revolutionary movements in 1848, but it also helped tear their movements apart, undermining revolutionary gains. Those who had linked their democratic goals to the rise of new nation-states were sorely disappointed. In the aftermath of the defeated revolutions, most nation building took a conservative tack. Nationalism came to serve the needs of statesmen and bureaucrats who did not seek an "awakening of peoples" and who had serious reservations about popular sovereignty. For them, nations simply represented modern, organized, and stronger states.

The upshot of this fit of nation building was a period of remarkable stability on the Continent, which ushered in an era of unprecedented capitalist and imperial expansion. The antagonisms unleashed by German unification and the crumbling of the Ottoman Empire would reemerge, however, in the Great Power politics that precipitated the First World War.

PEOPLE, IDEAS, AND EVENTS IN CONTEXT

- What role did the **ZOLLVEREIN** and the **FRANKFURT PARLIAMENT** play in the creation of a unified Germany?
- How and why did **OTTO VON BISMARCK** aim for a policy of German national unification during his time in office?
- How did **GIUSEPPE GARIBALDI** and **CAMILLO DI CAVOUR** initially see the process of Italian unification? Whose vision came closest to reality?
- Who was **NAPOLEON III** and how did his policies contribute to nation building in France?
- What was the contribution of **JOHN STUART MILL** to debates about citizenship in Britain?
- Why were nationalist movements such as **PAN-SLAVISM** or **MAGYAR NATIONALISM** such a danger to the Austro-Hungarian Empire?
- Why did **TSAR ALEXANDER II** decide to **EMANCIPATE THE SERFS**?
- What made the **CRIMEAN WAR** different from previous conflicts and more like the wars of the twentieth century?

CONSEQUENCES

- How can one account for the fact that nationalism was simultaneously a unifying force and a force for division in nineteenth-century Europe?
- What accounts for the success of movements to abolish slavery in Europe and the Americas?
- What were the long-term consequences of the strong forms of national identity that took root in Europe in the nineteenth century? Do they lead straight to the First World War?

Before You Read This Chapter

Imperialism and Colonialism, 1870–1914

CORE OBJECTIVES

- **DEFINE** *imperialism* and locate the major colonies established by European powers in Africa and Asia in the nineteenth century.

- **UNDERSTAND** the major reasons for European colonial expansion in the nineteenth century.

- **DESCRIBE** the choices faced by colonized peoples in the face of European power and culture.

- **EXPLAIN** how imperialism shaped the culture of European nations at home.

- **UNDERSTAND** the nature of the crisis faced by European imperial powers at the end of the nineteenth century.

In 1869, the Suez Canal opened with a grand celebration. The imperial yacht *Eagle,* with Empress Eugénie of France on board, entered the canal on November 17, followed by sixty-eight steamships carrying the emperor of Austria, the crown prince of Prussia, the grand duke of Russia, and scores of other dignitaries. Flowery speeches flowed freely, as did the champagne. The ceremony cost a staggering £1.3 million (about $121 million today). Even so, the size of the celebration paled in comparison to the canal itself. The largest project of its kind, the canal sliced through a hundred miles of Egyptian desert to link the Mediterranean and Red seas, cutting the trip from London to Bombay in half. The canal dramatically showcased the abilities of Western power and technology to transform the globe, but the human cost was high: thirty thousand Egyptians worked on the canal as forced laborers, and thousands died during cholera epidemics in the work camps.

The building of the canal was the result of decades of European involvement in Egypt. French troops under Napoleon led the way, but Britain's bankers soon followed. European financial interests developed a close relationship with those who governed Egypt as a semi-independent state inside the Ottoman Empire. By 1875 the British controlled the canal, after purchasing 44 percent of the canal's shares from the Egyptian khedive (viceroy) when he was threatened with bankruptcy. By the late 1870s, these economic and political relationships had produced debt and instability in Egypt. In a bid for national independence, a group of Egyptian army officers led by 'Urabi Pasha took control of Egypt's government in 1882.

The British government, determined to protect their investments, decided to intervene. The Royal Navy shelled Egyptian forts along the canal into rubble, and a British task force landed near 'Urabi Pasha's central base, overwhelming the Egyptian lines. This striking success rallied popular support at home, and the political consequences lasted for seventy years. Britain took effective control of Egypt. A British lord, Evelyn Baring, assumed the role of proconsul in a power-sharing relationship with Egyptian authorities, but real power rested with Britain. Britain demanded the repayment of loans and regulated the trade in Egyptian cotton that helped supply Britain's textile mills. Most important, the intervention secured the route to India and the markets of the East.

The Suez Canal and the conquest of Egypt was made possible by the convergence of technology, money, politics, and a global strategy of imperial control. A similar interplay between economics and colonialism produced the stunning expansion of European empires in the late nineteenth century. The years 1870 to 1914 brought both rapid industrialization throughout the West and an intense push to expand the power and influence of Western power abroad. The "new imperialism" of the late nineteenth century was distinguished by its scope, intensity, and long-range consequences. It transformed cultures and states in Europe, Africa, and Asia. Projects such as the Suez Canal changed—literally—the landscape and map of the world. They also represented an ideology: the belief in technology and Western superiority. In the minds of imperialists, the elimination of geographic barriers had opened the entire world, its lands and its peoples, to the administrative power of the West.

The new imperialism, however, was not a one-way street. Europeans could not simply conquer vast territories and dictate their terms to the rest of the world. The new political and economic relationships between colonies and dependent states on the one hand and the "metropole" (the colonizing power) on the other ran both ways, bringing changes to both parties. Fierce competition among nations upset the balance of power. The new imperialism was an expression of European strength, but it was also profoundly destabilizing.

THE INAUGURATION OF THE SUEZ CANAL. This allegory illustrates the union of the Mediterranean and Red Seas attended by Ismail Pasha, the khedive of Egypt, Abdul Aziz, sultan of the Ottoman Empire, Ferdinand de Lesseps, president of the Suez Canal Company, Empress Eugénie of France, and several mermaids. It also represents the nineteenth-century vision of imperialism as a bearer of global progress, promoting technological advance and breaking down barriers between the Orient and the West. ▪ *Who was the audience for this image?*

IMPERIALISM

Imperialism is the process of extending one state's control over another—a process that takes many forms. Sometimes this control was exercised by *direct rule,* by which the colonizing nation annexed territories outright and subjugated the peoples who lived there. At times colonialism worked through *indirect rule,* by which conquering European nations reached agreements with local leaders and governed through them. Finally, *informal imperialism* could be a less visible exercise of state power, where stronger states allowed weaker states to maintain their independence while reducing their sovereignty. Informal imperialism took the form of carving out zones of European influence and privilege, such as treaty ports, within other states. There was no single technique of colonial control; as we will see, resistance forced colonial powers to shift strategies frequently.

Both formal and informal imperialism expanded dramatically in the nineteenth century. The "scramble for Africa" was the most startling case of formal imperialism: from 1875 to 1902 Europeans seized up to 90 percent of the continent. The overall picture is no less remarkable:

EUROPEAN EMPIRES IN 1900. ■ *Where were Britain's major imperial interests, and what trade routes did they have most incentive to protect?* ■ *Where were France's most important imperial holdings and who was their major competitor?* ■ *How substantial were German, Dutch, Portuguese, or U.S. colonies in comparison to British and French holdings?*

between 1870 and 1900, a small group of states (France, Britain, Germany, the Netherlands, Russia, and the United States) colonized about one quarter of the world's land surface. In addition, these same states extended informal empire in China and Turkey, across South and East Asia, and into Central and South America. So striking was this expansion of European power that contemporaries spoke of the "new imperialism." Nevertheless, imperialism was not new. It is more helpful to think of these nineteenth-century developments as a new stage of European empire building, after the collapse of Europe's early modern empires in North and South America at the end of the eighteenth century.

The nineteenth-century empires rose against the backdrop of industrialization, liberal revolution, and the rise of nation-states. Industrialization produced greater demand for raw materials from distant locations. At the same time, many Europeans became convinced in the nineteenth century that their economic development, science, and technology would inevitably bring progress to the rest of the world. Finally, especially in Britain and France, nineteenth-century imperial powers were in principle democratic nations, where government authority relied on consent and on notions of civic equality. This made conquest difficult to justify and raised thorny questions about the status of colonized peoples. Earlier European conquerors had claimed a missionary zeal to convert people to Christianity as a justification for their actions.

Nineteenth-century imperialists justified their projects by saying that their investment in infrastructure—railroads, harbors, and roads—and their social reforms would fulfill Europe's secular mission to bring civilization to the rest of the world. This vision of the "white man's burden"—the phrase is Rudyard Kipling's—became a powerful argument in favor of imperial expansion throughout Europe (see page 542).

In spite of these ambitious goals, the resistance of colonized peoples did as much to shape the history of colonialism as did the ambitious plans of the colonizers. The Haitian revolution of 1804 compelled the British and the French to end the slave trade and slavery in their colonies in the 1830s and the 1840s, though new systems of forced labor cropped up to take their places. The American Revolution encouraged the British to grant self-government to white settler states in Canada (1867), Australia (1901), and New Zealand (1912). Rebellion in India in 1857 caused the British to place the colony under the direct control of the crown, rather than the East India Company. In general, nineteenth-century imperialism involved less independent entrepreneurial activity by merchants and traders and more "settlement and discipline." This required legal distinctions made on racial or religious grounds in order to organize relationships between Europeans and different indigenous groups, and an administration to enforce such distinctions. (The apartheid system in South Africa developed out of such practices.) Defending such empires thus

IMAGES OF WOMEN IN THE COLONIES. Photographs and engravings of women in Africa and Asia circulated widely in Europe during the nineteenth century, and these images shaped attitudes toward colonization. Many images—some openly pornographic—portrayed African or Asian women as attractive, exotic, and in postures that invited European fantasies of domination. "Reclining Jewess" (left) is a typical example of such imagery, from French Algeria. Other images portrayed colonial women as victims of barbaric customs, as in the depiction of *sati*, a Hindu practice in which a widow would immolate herself on her husband's funeral pyre (right). This image, which first appeared in a work by a missionary who had been to Calcutta, was widely reproduced later as an illustration of the need for British intervention in Indian culture, to bring "civilization" to India. ■ *Could these images have the same impact without the emphasis on the gender of the subject?*

became a vast project, involving legions of government officials, schoolteachers, and engineers. Nineteenth-century imperialism produced new forms of government and management in the colonies, and as it did so, it forged new interactions between Europeans and indigenous peoples.

IMPERIALISM IN SOUTH ASIA

India was the center of the British Empire, the jewel of the British crown, secured well before the period of the new imperialism. The conquest of most of the subcontinent began in the 1750s and quickened during the age of revolution. Conquering India helped compensate for "losing" North America. By the mid-nineteenth century, India was the focal point of Britain's newly expanded global power, which reached from southern Africa across South Asia and to Australia. Keeping this region involved changing tactics and forms of rule.

Until the mid-nineteenth century, British territories in India were under the control of the British East India Company. The company had its own military, divided into European and (far larger) Indian divisions. The company held the right to collect taxes on land from Indian peasants. Until the early nineteenth century, the company had legal monopolies over trade in all goods, including indigo, textiles, salt, minerals, and—most lucrative of all—opium. Unlike North America, India never became a settler state. In the 1830s Europeans were a tiny minority, numbering 45,000 in an Indian population of 150 million. The company's rule was repressive and enforced by the military. Soldiers collected taxes; civil servants wore military uniforms; British troops brashly commandeered peasants' oxen and carts for their own purposes. Typically, though, the company could not enforce its rule uniformly. It governed some areas directly, others through making alliances with local leaders, and still others by simply controlling goods and money. Indirect rule, here as in other empires, meant finding indigenous collaborators and maintaining their good will. They offered economic privileges, state offices, or military posts to groups or nations that agreed to ally with the British against others.

British policy shifted between two poles: one group wanted to "Westernize" India, another believed it safer, and more practical, to defer to local culture. Christian missionaries, whose numbers rose as occupation expanded, were determined to replace "blind superstition" with the "genial influence of Christian light and truth." Indignant at such practices as child marriage and *sati* (in which a widow im-

molated herself on her husband's funeral pyre), missionaries sought support in England for a wide-ranging assault on Hindu culture. Secular reformers, many of them liberal, considered "Hindoos" and "Mahommedans" susceptible to forms of despotism—both in the family and in the state. They turned their reforming zeal to legal and political change. But other British administrators warned their countrymen not to meddle with Indian institutions. Indirect rule, they argued, would work only with the cooperation of local powers. Conflicts such as these meant that the British never agreed on any single cultural policy.

From Mutiny to Rebellion

The East India Company's rule often met resistance and protest. In 1857–58, it was badly shaken by a revolt of Indian soldiers in the British army, now known in India as the Great Mutiny of 1857. The uprising began near Delhi, when the military disciplined a regiment of *sepoys* (the traditional term for Indian soldiers employed by the British) for refusing to use rifle cartridges greased with pork fat—unacceptable to either Hindus or Muslims. The causes of the mutiny were deeper, however, and involved social, economic, and political grievances. Indian peasants attacked law courts and burned tax rolls, protesting debt and corruption. In areas that had recently been annexed, rebels defended their traditional leaders, who had been ousted by the British. The mutiny spread through large areas of northwest India. European troops, which counted for fewer than one fifth of those in arms, found themselves losing control. Religious leaders, both Hindu and Muslim, seized the occasion to denounce Christian missionaries sent in by the British and their assault on local traditions.

At first the British were faced with a desperate situation, with areas under British control cut off from one another and pro-British cities under siege. Loyal Indian troops were brought south from the frontiers, and British troops, fresh from the Crimean War, were shipped directly from Britain to suppress the rebellion. The fighting lasted more than a year, and the British matched the rebels' early massacres with a systematic campaign of repression. Whole rebel units were killed rather than being allowed to surrender, or they were tried on the spot and executed. Towns and villages that supported the rebels were burned, just as the rebels had burned European homes and outposts. Yet the defeat of the rebellion caught the British public's imagination. After the bloody, inconclusive mess of the Crimean War, the terrifying threat to British India and the heroic rescue of European hostages and British territory by British troops were electrifying news. At a political level, British leaders were stunned

THE EXECUTION OF INDIANS WHO PARTICIPATED IN THE REBELLION OF 1857. The British were determined to make an example of rebel Indian soldiers after the Great Mutiny. The engraving on the left shows executions in which the condemned were blown apart by cannons. The cartoon on the right, "The Execution of 'John Company,'" shows the same cannons destroying the British East India Company, which was abolished by the British government as a result of the rebellion. ▪ *What do these images tell us about public awareness of the rebellion's violence and its suppression?*

by how close the revolt had brought them to disaster and were determined never to repeat the same mistakes.

After the mutiny, the British were compelled to reorganize their Indian empire, developing new strategies of rule. The East India Company was abolished, replaced by the British crown. The British *raj* (or rule) was governed directly, though the British also sought out collaborators and cooperative interest groups. Princely India was left to the local princes, who were subject to British advisers. The British also reorganized the military and tried to change relations among soldiers. Indigenous troops were separated from each other to avoid the kind of fraternization that proved subversive. Even more than before, the British sought to rule through the Indian upper classes rather than in opposition to them. Civil-service reform opened new positions to members of the Indian upper classes. The British had to reconsider their relationship to Indian cultures. Missionary activity was no longer encouraged, and the British channeled their reforming impulses into the more secular projects of economic development, railways, roads, irrigation, and so on. Still, consensus on effective colonial strategies was lacking. Some administrators counseled more reform; others sought to support the princes.

The British tried both policies, in fits and starts, until the end of British rule in 1947.

What did India do for Great Britain? By the eve of the First World War, India was Britain's largest export market. One tenth of all the British Empire's trade passed through India's port cities of Madras, Bombay, and Calcutta. India mattered enormously to Britain's balance of payments; surpluses earned there compensated for deficits with Europe and the United States. Equally important to Great Britain were the human resources of India. Indian laborers worked on tea plantations in Assam, near Burma, and they built railways and dams in southern Africa and Egypt. Over a million indentured Indian servants left their country in the second half of the century to work elsewhere in the empire. India also provided the British Empire with highly trained engineers, land surveyors, clerks, bureaucrats, schoolteachers, and merchants. The nationalist leader Mohandas Gandhi, for instance, first came into the public eye as a young lawyer in Pretoria, South Africa, where he worked for an Indian law firm. The British deployed Indian troops across the empire. (They would later call up roughly 1.2 million troops in the First World War.) Many British leaders found it impossible to imagine their empire, or even their nation, without India.

How did the British raj shape Indian society? The British practice of indirect rule sought to create an Indian elite that would serve British interests, a group "who may be the interpreters between us and the millions whom we govern—a class of persons Indian in colour and blood, but English in tastes, in opinion, in morals, and in intellect," as one British writer put it. Eventually, this practice created a class of British-educated Indian civil servants and businessmen, well trained for government and skeptical about British claims that the Empire brought progress to the subcontinent. This group provided the leadership for the nationalist movement that challenged British rule in India. At the same time, this group became increasingly distant from the rest of the nation. The overwhelming majority of Indians remained desperately poor peasants struggling to subsist on diminishing plots of land and, in many cases, in debt to British landlords.

IMPERIALISM IN CHINA

In China, too, European imperialism began early, well before the period of the new imperialism. Yet there it took a different form. Europeans did not conquer and annex whole regions. Instead, they forced favorable trade agreements at gunpoint, set up treaty ports where Europeans lived and worked under their own jurisdiction, and established outposts of European missionary activity.

Since the seventeenth century, European trade with China focused on coveted luxuries such as silk, porcelain, art objects, and tea. The Chinese government, however, was determined to keep foreign traders, and foreign influence in general, at bay. By the early nineteenth century Britain's global ambitions and rising power were setting the stage for a confrontation. Freed from the task of fighting Napoleon, the British set their sights on improving the terms of the China trade, demanding the rights to come into open harbors and to have special trading privileges. The other source of constant friction involved the harsh treatment of British subjects by Chinese law courts—including the summary execution of several Britons convicted of crimes. By the 1830s, these diplomatic conflicts had been intensified by the opium trade.

The Opium Trade

Opium provided a direct link among Britain, British India, and China. Since the sixteenth century, the drug had been produced in India and carried by Dutch and, later, British traders. In fact, opium (derived from the poppy plant) was one of the very few commodities that Europeans could sell in China. For this reason it became crucial to the balance of East-West trade. When the British conquered northeast India, they also annexed one of the world's richest opium-growing areas and became deeply involved in the trade—so much so that historians have called the East India Company's rule a "narco-military empire." British agencies designated specific poppy-growing regions and gave cash advances to Indian peasants who cultivated the crop. Producing opium was a labor-intensive process: in the opium-producing areas northwest of Calcutta, "factories" employed as many as a thousand Indian workers.

From India, the East India Company sold the opium to "country traders"—small fleets of British, Dutch, and Chinese shippers who carried the drug to Southeast Asia and China. The East India Company used the silver it earned from the sale of opium to buy Chinese goods for the European market. The trade, therefore, was not only profitable, it was key to a triangular European-Indian-Chinese economic relationship. Production and export rose dramatically in the early nineteenth century, in spite of the Chinese emperor's attempts to discourage the trade. By the 1830s, when the British-Chinese confrontation was taking shape, opium provided British India with more revenue than any other source except taxes on land.

People all over the world consumed opium, for medicinal reasons as well as for pleasure. The Chinese market was especially lucrative. Eighteenth-century China witnessed

AN OPIUM FACTORY IN PATNA, INDIA, c. 1851. Balls of opium dry in a huge warehouse before being shipped to Calcutta for export to China and elsewhere.

a craze for tobacco smoking that taught users how to smoke opium. A large, wealthy Chinese elite of merchants and government officials provided much of the market, but opium smoking also became popular among soldiers, students, and Chinese laborers. In the nineteenth century opium imports followed Chinese labor all over the world—to Southeast Asia and San Francisco. In 1799, in an effort to control the problem, the Chinese government banned opium imports, prohibited domestic production, criminalized smoking, and in the 1830s began a full-scale campaign to purge the drug from China. That campaign set the Chinese emperor on a collision course with British opium traders. In one confrontation the Chinese drug commissioner Lin confiscated three million pounds of raw opium from the British and washed it out to sea. In another the Chinese authorities blockaded British ships in port, and local citizens demonstrated angrily in front of British residences.

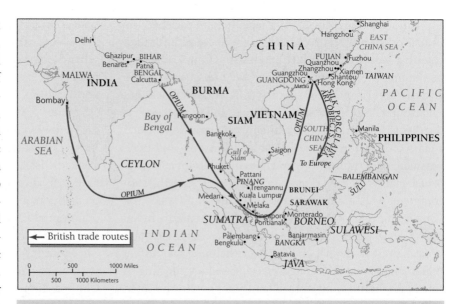

BRITISH OPIUM TRADE. Note the way that the British trade in opium linked the economies of India, China, and Europe. ▪ *What were the major products involved in trade between East Asia, South Asia, and Europe during this period?* ▪ *In what ways did the opium trade destabilize East Asia?* ▪ *What efforts did the Chinese government make to restrict the sale of opium?* ▪ *What was the response of European nations involved in this trade?*

THE OPIUM WARS

In 1839, these simmering conflicts broke into what was called the first Opium War. Drugs were not the core of the matter. The dispute over the drug trade highlighted larger issues of sovereignty and economic status. The Europeans claimed the right to trade with whomever they pleased, bypassing Chinese monopolies. They wished to set up zones of European residence in defiance of Chinese sovereignty and to proselytize and open schools. The Chinese government could not accept these challenges to its authority, and war flared up several times over the course of the century. After the first war of 1839–42, in which British steam vessels and guns overpowered the Chinese fleet, the Treaty of Nanking (1842) compelled the Chinese to give the British trading privileges, the right to reside in five cities, and the port of Hong Kong "in perpetuity." After a second war, the British secured yet more treaty ports and privileges, including the right to send in missionaries. In the aftermath of those agreements between the Chinese and the British, other countries demanded similar rights and economic opportunities. By the end of the nineteenth century the French, Germans, and Russians had claimed mining rights and permission to build railroads, to begin manufacturing with cheap Chinese labor, and to arm and police European communities in Chinese cities. The United States, not wanting to be shouldered aside, demanded its own Open Door Policy. Japan was an equally active imperialist power in the Pacific, and the Sino-Japanese War of 1894–95 was a decisive moment in the history of the region. The Japanese victory forced China to concede trading privileges, the independence of Korea, and the Liaotung Peninsula in Manchuria. It opened a scramble for spheres of influence and for mining and railway concessions.

Surrendering privileges to Europeans and the Japanese seriously undermined the authority of the Chinese Qing (Ching) emperor at home and heightened popular hostility to foreign intruders. Authority at the imperial center had been eroding for more than a century by 1900, hastened by the Opium Wars and by the vast Taiping Rebellion (1852–64), an enormous, bitter, and deadly conflict in which radical Christian rebels in south-central China challenged the authority of the emperors. On the defensive against the rebels, the dynasty hired foreign generals, including the British commander Charles Gordon, to lead its forces. The war devastated China's agricultural heartland; and the death toll, never confirmed, may have reached twenty million. This ruinous disorder and the increasing inability of the emperor to keep order and collect the taxes necessary to repay foreign loans led European countries to take more and more direct control of the China trade.

IMPERIALISM IN SOUTH AND EAST ASIA, c. 1914. ▪ *Which imperial powers were most present in Asia and where were their primary zones of control and influence?* ▪ *Why were European nations and the United States interested in establishing treaty ports in China?* ▪ *How were the Chinese treaty ports different from the territorial conquest pursued by the British, French, and Dutch in their respective Asian colonies?*

The Boxer Rebellion

From a Western perspective, the most important of the nineteenth-century rebellions against the corruptions of foreign rule was the Boxer Rebellion of 1900. The Boxers were a secret society of young men trained in Chinese martial arts and believed to have spiritual powers. Antiforeign and antimissionary, they provided the spark for a loosely organized but widespread uprising in northern China. Bands of Boxers attacked foreign engineers, tore up railway lines, and in the spring of 1900 marched on Beijing. They laid siege to the foreign legations in the city, home to several thousand Western diplomats and merchants and their families. The legations' small garrison defended their walled compound with little more than rifles, bayonets, and improvised artillery; but they withstood the siege for fifty-five days until a large relief column arrived. The rebellion, particularly the siege at Beijing, mobilized a global response. Europe's Great Powers, rivals everywhere else in the world, drew together in response to this crisis to tear China apart. An expedition numbering twenty thousand troops—combining the forces of Britain, France, the United States, Germany, Italy, Japan, and Russia—ferociously repressed the Boxer movement. The outside powers then demanded indemnities, new trading concessions, and reassurances from the Chinese government.

The Boxer Rebellion was one of several anti-imperialist movements at the end of the nineteenth century. The rebellion testified to the vulnerability of Europeans' imperial power. It dramatized the resources Europeans would have to devote to maintaining their far-flung influence. In the process of repression, the Europeans became committed to propping up corrupt and fragile governments to protect their agreements and interests, and they were drawn into putting down popular uprisings against local inequalities and foreign rule.

In China the age of the new imperialism capped a century of conflict and expansion. By 1900, virtually all of Asia had been divided up among the European powers. Japan, an active imperial power in its own right, maintained its independence. British rule extended from India across Burma,

Malaya, Australia, and New Zealand. The Dutch, Britain's longstanding trade rivals, secured Indonesia. Thailand remained independent. During the 1880s, the French moved into Indochina. Imperial rivalries (among Britain, France, and Russia, China and Japan, Russia and Japan) drove European powers to press for influence and economic advantage in Asia; that struggle, in turn, encouraged the development of nationalist feeling among local populations. Imperial expansion was showing its destabilizing effects.

Russian Imperialism

Russia championed a policy of annexation—by conquest, treaty, or both—of lands bordering on the existing Russian state throughout the nineteenth century. Beginning in 1801, with the acquisition of Georgia after a war with Persia, the tsars continued to pursue their expansionist dream. Bessarabia and Turkestan (taken from the Turks) and

Armenia (from the Persians) vastly increased the empire's size. This southward colonization brought large Muslim populations in central Asia into the Russian Empire. It also brought the Russians close to war with the British twice: first in 1881, when Russian troops occupied territories in the trans-Caspian region, and again in 1884–87, when the tsar's forces advanced to the frontier of Afghanistan. In both cases the British feared incursions into areas they deemed within their sphere of influence in the Middle East. They were concerned, as well, about a possible threat to India. The maneuvering, spying, and support of friendly puppet governments by Russia and Britain became known as the "Great Game" and foreshadowed Western countries' jockeying for the region's oil resources in the twentieth century.

Russian expansion also moved east. In 1875, the Japanese traded the southern half of Sakhalin Island for the previously Russian Kurile Islands. The tsars' eastward advance was finally halted in 1904, when Russian expansion in Mongolia and Manchuria came up against Japanese

BUILDING THE RUSSIAN EMPIRE. ▪ *In what directions did the Russian Empire primarily expand after 1795?* ▪ *What drove Russian expansion?* ▪ *Which areas were most contentious and why?*

expansion. In the Russo-Japanese War of 1904, Russia's huge imperial army more than met its match. Russia's navy was sent halfway around the world to reinforce the beleaguered Russian troops but was ambushed and sunk by the better-trained and -equipped Japanese fleet. This national humiliation helped provoke a revolt in Russia and led to an American-brokered peace treaty in 1905 (see Chapter 23). The defeat shook the already unsteady regime of the tsar and proved that European nations were not the only ones who could play the imperial game successfully.

THE FRENCH EMPIRE AND THE CIVILIZING MISSION

Like British expansion into India, French colonialism in northern Africa began before the new imperialism of the late nineteenth century. France invaded Algeria in 1830, and the conquest took nearly two decades. From the outset the Algerian conquest was different from most other colonial ventures: Algeria became a settler state, one of the few apart from South Africa. The settlers were by no means all French; they included Italian, Spanish, and Maltese merchants and shopkeepers of modest means, laborers, and peasants. By the 1870s, in several of the coastal cities, this new creole community outnumbered indigenous Algerians, and within it, other Europeans outnumbered the French. With the French military's help, the settlers appropriated land, and French business concerns took cork forests and established mining in copper, lead, and iron. Economic activity was for European benefit. The first railroads, for instance, did not even carry passengers; they took iron ore to the coast for export to France, where it would be smelted and sold.

The settlers and the French government did not necessarily pursue common goals. In the 1870s, the new and still fragile Third Republic (founded after Napoleon III was defeated in 1870; see Chapter 21), in an effort to ensure the settlers' loyalty, made the colony a department of France. This gave the French settlers the full rights of republican citizenship. It also gave them the power to pass laws in Algeria that consolidated their privileges and community (naturalizing all Europeans, for instance) and further disenfranchised indigenous Muslim populations, who had no voting rights at all. France's divide and rule strategy, which treated European settlers, Arabs, Berbers, and Jews very differently, illustrates the contradictions of "the civilizing mission" in action.

Before the 1870s, colonial activities aroused relatively little interest among the French at home. But after the humiliating defeat in the Franco-Prussian War (1870–71) and the establishment of the Third Republic, colonial lobby groups and politicians became increasingly adamant about the benefits of colonialism. These benefits were not simply economic. Taking on the "civilizing mission" would reinforce the international influence of the French republic and the prestige of the French people. Jules Ferry, a republican leader, argued that "the superior races have a right vis-à-vis the inferior races . . . they have a right to civilize them."

Under Ferry, the French acquired Tunisia (1881), northern and central Vietnam (Tonkin and Annam; 1883), and Laos and Cambodia (1893). They also carried this civilizing mission into their colonies in West Africa. European and Atlantic trade with the west coast of Africa—in slaves, gold, and ivory—had been well established for centuries. In the late nineteenth century, trade gave way to formal administration. The year 1895 saw the establishment of a Federation of French West Africa, a loosely organized administration to govern an area nine times the size of France, including Guinea, Senegal, the Ivory Coast, and vast stretches of the western Sahara. Even with reforms and centralization in 1902, French control remained uneven. Despite military campaigns of pacification, resistance remained. The French dealt gingerly with tribal leaders, at times deferring to their authority and at others trying to break their power. They established French courts and law only in cities, leaving Islamic or tribal courts to run other areas. The federation aimed to rationalize the economic exploitation of the area and to replace "booty capitalism" with a more careful management and development of resources. They embarked on ambitious public works projects including the construction of railroads, harbors, and sanitation systems. The French called this "enhancing the value" of the region, which was part of the civilizing mission of the modern republic.

Such programs plainly served French interests. "Officially this process is called civilizing, and after all, the term is apt, since the undertaking serves to increase the degree of prosperity of our civilization," remarked one Frenchman who opposed the colonial enterprise. None of these measures aimed to give indigenous peoples political rights. As one historian puts it, "the French Government General was in the business not of making citizens, but of civilizing its subjects." More telling, however, the French project was not often successful. The French government did not have the resources to carry out its plans, which proved much more expensive and complicated than anyone imagined. Transportation costs ran very high. Labor posed the largest problems. Here as elsewhere, Europeans faced massive resistance from the African peasants, whom they

SLAVES IN CHAINS, 1896. In Africa, native labor was exploited by Europeans and by other Africans, as here.

wanted to do everything from building railroads to working mines and carrying rubber. The Europeans resorted to forced labor, signing agreements with local tribal leaders to deliver workers, and they turned a blind eye to the continuing use of slave labor in the interior. For all of these reasons, the colonial project did not produce the profits some expected.

THE "SCRAMBLE FOR AFRICA" AND THE CONGO

French expansion into West Africa was only one instance of Europe's voracity on the African continent. The scope and speed with which the major European powers conquered and asserted formal control was astonishing. The effects were profound. In 1875, 11 percent of the continent was in European hands. By 1902, the figure was 90 percent. European powers mastered logistical problems of transport and communication; they learned how to keep diseases at bay. They also had new weapons. The Maxim gun, adopted by the British army in 1889 and first used by British colonial troops, pelted out as many as five hundred rounds a minute; it turned encounters with indigenous forces into bloodbaths and made armed resistance virtually impossible.

The Congo Free State

In the 1870s, the British had formed new imperial relationships in the north and west of Africa and along the southern and eastern coasts. A new phase of European involvement

struck right at the heart of the continent. Until the latter part of the nineteenth century this territory had been out of bounds for Europeans. The rapids downstream on such strategic rivers as the Congo and the Zambezi made it difficult to move inland, and tropical diseases were lethal to most European explorers. But during the 1870s, a new drive into central Africa produced results. The target was the fertile valleys around the river Congo, and the European colonizers were a privately financed group of Belgians paid by their king, Leopold II (r. 1865–1909). They followed in the footsteps of Henry Morton Stanley, an American newspaperman and explorer who later became a British subject and a knight of the realm. Stanley hacked his way through thick canopy jungle into territory where no European had previously set foot. His "scientific" journeys inspired the creation of a society of researchers and students of African culture in Brussels, in reality a front organization for the commercial company set up by Leopold. The ambitiously named International Association for the Exploration and Civilization of the Congo was set up in 1876 and soon set about signing treaties with local elites, which opened the whole Congo River basin to commercial exploitation. The vast resources of palm oil and natural rubber and the promise of minerals (including diamonds) were now within Europeans' reach.

The strongest resistance that Leopold's company faced came from other colonial powers, particularly Portugal, which objected to this new drive for occupation. In 1884, a conference was called in Berlin to settle the matter of control over the Congo River basin. It was chaired by the master of European power politics, German chancellor Otto von Bismarck, and attended by all the leading colonial nations as well as by the United States. The conference established ground rules for a new phase of European economic and political expansion. Europe's two great overseas empires, Britain and France, and the strongest emerging power inside Europe, Germany, joined forces in a settlement that seemed to be perfectly in line with nineteenth-century liberalism. The Congo valleys would be open to free trade and commerce; a slave trade still run by some of the Islamic kingdoms in the region would be suppressed in favor of free labor; and a Congo Free State would be set up, denying the region to the formal control of any single European country.

In reality the Congo Free State was run by Leopold's private company, and the region was opened up to unrestricted exploitation by a series of large European corporations. The older slave trade was suppressed, but the European companies took the "free" African labor guaranteed in Berlin and placed workers in equally bad conditions. Huge tracts of land, larger than whole European countries,

Atrocities in the Congo

George Washington Williams (1849–1891), an African American pastor, journalist, and historian, was among a handful of international observers who went to the Congo in the 1890s to explore and report back on conditions. He wrote several reports: one for the U.S. government, another that he presented at an international antislavery conference, several newspaper columns, and an open letter to King Leopold, from which the following is excerpted.

ood and Great Friend,

I have the honour to submit for your Majesty's consideration some reflections respecting the Independent State of Congo, based upon a careful study and inspection of the country and character of the personal Government you have established upon the African Continent. . . .

I was led to regard your enterprise as the rising of the Star of Hope for the Dark Continent, so long the habitation of cruelties. . . . When I arrived in the Congo, I naturally sought for the results of the brilliant programme:—*"fostering care," "benevolent enterprise,"* an *"honest and practical effort"* to increase the knowledge of the natives *"and secure their welfare."* . . .

I was doomed to bitter disappointment. Instead of the natives of the Congo "adopting the fostering care" of your Majesty's Government, they everywhere complain that their land has been taken from them by force; that the Government is cruel and arbitrary, and declare that they neither love nor respect the Government and its flag. Your Majesty's

Government has sequestered their land, burned their towns, stolen their property, enslaved their women and children, and committed other crimes too numerous to mention in detail. It is natural that they everywhere shrink from *"the fostering care"* your Majesty's Government so eagerly proffers them.

There has been, to my absolute knowledge, no *"honest and practical effort made to increase their knowledge and secure their welfare."* Your Majesty's Government has never spent one franc for educational purposes, nor instituted any practical system of industrialism. Indeed the most unpractical measures have been adopted *against* the natives in nearly every respect; and in the capital of your Majesty's Government at Boma there is not a native employed. The labour system is radically unpractical. . . . [R]ecruits are transported under circumstances more cruel than cattle in European countries. They eat their rice twice a day by the use of their fingers; they often thirst for water when the season is dry; they are exposed to the heat and rain, and sleep upon the damp and filthy decks of the vessels often so closely

crowded as to lie in human ordure. And, of course, many die. . . .

All the crimes perpetrated in the Congo have been done in *your* name, and *you* must answer at the bar of Public Sentiment for the misgovernment of a people, whose lives and fortunes were entrusted to you by the august Conference of Berlin, 1884–1885. . . .

Source: George Washington Williams, "An Open Letter to His Serene Majesty Leopold II, King of the Belgians, and Sovereign of the Independent State of Congo, July 1890," in *George Washington Williams: A Biography*, ed. John Hope Franklin (Chicago: 1985), pp. 243–54.

Questions for Analysis

1. What expectations did Williams have on arriving in the Congo and how did he think of Africa in relation to Europe?

2. What promises had the Belgian monarch made as justification for their expansion into the Congo?

3. What evidence did Williams look for to evaluate the reality of these commitments?

became diamond mines or plantations for the extraction of palm oil, rubber, or cocoa. African workers labored in appalling conditions, with no real medicine or sanitation, too little food, and according to production schedules that made European factory labor look mild by comparison.

Hundreds of thousands of African workers died from disease and overwork. Because European managers did not comprehend or respect the different cycle of seasons in central Africa, whole crop years were lost, leading to famines. Laborers working in the heat of the dry season often carried on their backs individual loads that would have been handled by heavy machinery in a European factory. Thousands of Africans were pressed into work harvesting goods Europe wanted. They did so for little or no pay, under the threat of beatings and mutilation for dozens of petty offenses against the plantation companies, who made the laws of the Free State. Eventually the scandal of the Congo became too great to go on unchallenged. A whole generation of authors and journalists, most famously Joseph Conrad in his *Heart of Darkness,* publicized the arbitrary brutality and the vast scale of suffering. In 1908 Belgium was forced to take direct control of the Congo, turning it into a Belgian colony. A few restrictions at least were imposed on the activities of the great plantation companies that had brought a vast new store of raw materials to European industry by using slavery in all but name.

The Partition of Africa

The occupation of the Congo, and its promise of great material wealth, pressured other colonial powers into expanding their holdings. By the 1880s, the "scramble for Africa" was well under way. The guarantees made at the 1884 Berlin conference allowed the Europeans to take further steps. The French and Portugese increased their holdings. Italy moved into territories along the Red Sea, beside British-held land and the independent kingdom of Ethiopia.

Germany came relatively late to empire overseas. Bismarck was reluctant to engage in an enterprise that he believed would yield few economic or political advantages. Yet he did not want either Britain or France to dominate Africa, and Germany seized colonies in Cameroon and Tanzania. Though the Germans were not the most enthusiastic colonialists, they were fascinated by the imperial adventure and jealous of their territories. When the Herero people of German Southwest Africa (now Namibia) rebelled in the early 1900s, the Germans responded with a vicious campaign of village burning and ethnic killing that nearly annihilated the Herero.

Great Britain and France had their own ambitions. The French aimed to move west to east across the continent, an important reason for the French expedition to Fashoda (in the Sudan) in 1898 (discussed later). Britain's part in the scramble took place largely in southern and eastern Africa and was encapsulated in the dreams and career of one man: the diamond tycoon, colonial politician, and imperial visionary Cecil Rhodes. Rhodes, who made a fortune from the South African diamond mines in the 1870s and 1880s and founded the diamond-mining company DeBeers, became prime minister of Britain's Cape Colony in 1890.

(He left part of this fortune for the creation of the Rhodes Scholarships to educate future leaders of the empire at Oxford.) In an uneasy alliance with the Boer settlers in their independent southern African republics and with varying levels of support from London, Rhodes pursued two great personal and imperial goals. The personal goal was to build a southern African empire that was founded on diamonds. "Rhodesia" would fly the Union Jack out of pride but send its profits into Rhodes's own companies. Through bribery, double dealing, careful coalition politics with the British and Boer settlers, warfare, and outright theft, Rhodes helped carve out territories occupying the modern nations of Zambia, Zimbabwe, Malawi, and Botswana—most of the savannah of southern Africa. Rhodes's second goal was a British presence along the whole of eastern Africa, symbolized by the goal of a Cape-to-Cairo railway. He believed that the empire should make Britain self-sufficient, with British industry able to run on the goods and raw materials shipped in from its colonies, then exporting many finished products back to those lands. Once the territories of Zambeziland and Rhodesia were taken, Rhodes found himself turning against the Boer settlers in the region, a conflict that led to the Boer war in 1899 (discussed later in this chapter).

As each European power sought its "place in the sun," in the famous phrase of the German kaiser William II, they brought more and more of Africa under direct colonial control. African peoples thus faced a combination of direct European control and indirect rule, which allowed local elites friendly to European interests to lord over those who resisted. The partition of Africa was the most striking instance of the new imperialism, with broad consequences for the subject peoples of European colonies and for the international order as a whole.

IMPERIAL CULTURE

Imperialism was thoroughly anchored in the culture of late-nineteenth-century Europe and the United States. Images of empire were everywhere. Not just in the propagandist literature of colonialism's supporters, but on tins of tea and boxes of cocoa, as background themes in posters advertising everything from dance halls to sewing machines. Museums and world's fairs displayed the products of empire and introduced spectators to "exotic peoples." Music halls rang to the sound of imperialist songs. Empire was present in novels of the period, sometimes appearing as a faraway setting for fantasy, adventure, or stories of self-discovery. The popular literature of empire showed a particular fascination with sexual practices in faraway places—photos and postcards of North African harems and unveiled Arab women were common in European pornography, as were colonial memoirs that chronicled the sexual adventures of their authors.

Empire thus played an important part in establishing European identity during these years. In France, the "civilizing mission" demonstrated to French citizens the grandeur of their nation. Building railroads and "bringing progress to other lands" illustrated the vigor of the French republic. Many British writers spoke in similar tones. One author wrote, "The British race may safely be called a missionary race. The command to go and teach all nations is one that the British people have, whether rightly or wrongly, regarded as specially laid upon themselves."

This sense of high moral purpose was not restricted to male writers or to figures of authority. In England, the United States, Germany, and France, the speeches and projects of women's reform movements were full of references to empire and the civilizing mission. Britain's woman suffrage movement, for example, was fiercely critical of the government but was also nationalist and imperialist. For these militants, women's participation in politics also meant the right to participate in imperial projects. British women reformers wrote about the oppression of Indian women by child marriage and sati, and saw themselves shouldering the "white women's burden" of reform. In France, suffragist Hubertine Auclert criticized the colonial government in Algeria for their indifference to the condition of Muslim women in their domains. She used an image of women suffering in polygamous marriages abroad to dramatize the need for reform. Arguments such as these enabled European women in their home countries to see themselves as bearers of progress, as participants in a superior civilization. Similarly, John Stuart Mill often used Hindu or Muslim culture as a foil when he wanted to make a point of freedom of speech and religion. This contrast between colonial backwardness and European civility and cultural superiority shaped Western culture and political debate about liberal ideas in particular.

THE WHITE MAN'S BURDEN AND PEARS' SOAP. The presence of imperial themes in advertising is well illustrated by this advertisement, which appeared in 1899 in the American magazine *McClure's*. The ad connects the theme of cleanliness and personal hygiene to racial superiority and the necessity of bringing civilization to "the dark corners of the earth." The goal of the ad, of course, was to sell soap—but the fact that such themes could work for advertisers reveals the extent to which such ideas were widespread within the culture.

Imperialism and Racial Thought

Imperial culture gave new prominence to racial thinking. Count Arthur de Gobineau (*GOH-bih-noh*, 1816–1882) wrote a massive work, *The Inequality of the Races*, in the 1850s, but it sparked little interest until the period of the new imperialism, when it was translated into English and widely discussed. For Gobineau, race offered the "master key" for understanding human societies in the modern world. Gobineau's work followed from Enlightenment investigations of different cultures in the world, but unlike Enlightenment authors who attributed these differences largely to environmental factors, Gobineau argued that "blood" was the determining factor in human history. Gobineau claimed that humans were originally divided into three races, "black," "white," and "yellow," and that the peoples of the present day were variously mixed from these original components. The white race, he argued, had preserved purer blood lines, and was therefore superior. The others suffered "adulteration" and were therefore degenerate and no longer capable of civilization. Gobineau's

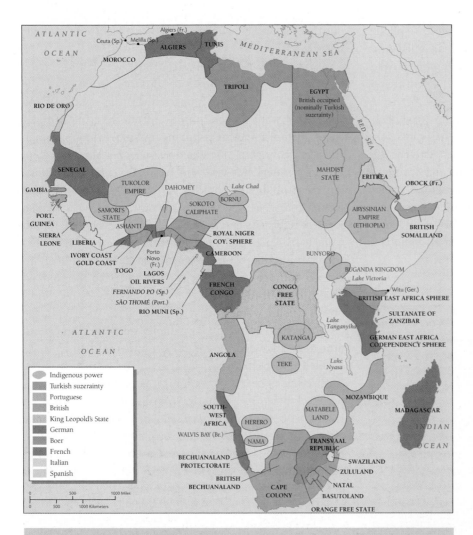

Indigenous power
Turkish suzerainty
Portuguese
British
King Leopold's State
German
Boer
French
Italian
Spanish

AFRICA, c. 1886. ▪ *What is the single biggest difference in terms of rulership between the two maps?* ▪ *Who were the winners and losers in the scramble for Africa before the First World War?* ▪ *What does the result of the scramble for Africa suggest about how European powers regarded each other?*

the evolution of social groups, suggesting that inequalities of wealth or ability could also be explained as the result of a process of "natural selection." Racial theorists and followers of Gobineau such as Houston Stewart Chamberlain (1855–1927) wasted little time in harnessing such scientific arguments to the claim that human "races" evolved over time. Chamberlain's books sold tens of thousands of copies in England and Germany.

Francis Galton (1822–1911), a half-cousin of Charles Darwin and a scientist who studied evolution, went so far as to advocate improving the population's racial characteristics by selective breeding of "superior types." Galton and others feared that improvements in health care and hygiene might allow individuals with inferior traits to survive to reproductive age, and his system of racial management, which he called *eugenics*, would save European populations from a decline in their vitality and biological fitness. Theories such as Galton's or Gobineau's did not cause imperialism, and they were closely linked with other developments in European culture, in particular renewed anxieties about social class and a fresh wave of European anti-Semitism. Yet the increasingly scientific racism of late-nineteenth-century Europe made it easier for many to reconcile the rhetoric of progress, individual freedom, and the civilizing mission with contempt for other peoples.

readers included some defenders of the confederacy during the American Civil War and Adolf Hitler in the twentieth century.

Followers of Gobineau's racial thinking looked increasingly to science to legitimate their theories. The natural scientist Charles Darwin, no racist himself, attracted wide attention with a theory of evolution that sought to explain the variety of species observable in the natural world. Darwin suggested that only the most "fit" individuals in a species survived to bear viable offspring, and that this process of "natural selection" explained how species diverged from one another: variations that made certain individuals better able to find food and mates were likely to be passed on to future generations. Social scientists such as Herbert Spencer sought to use a similar logic of competition among individuals for scarce resources to explain

Opposition to Imperialism

Support for imperialism was not unanimous. Hobson and Lenin condemned the entire enterprise for being rooted in greed and arrogance. Polish-born Joseph Conrad, a British novelist, shared much of the racial attitudes of his contemporaries, but he nevertheless believed that imperialism was an expression of deeply rooted pathologies in European culture. Other anti-imperialists were men and women from the colonies themselves who brought their case to the metropole. The British Committee of the Indian National Congress gathered together many members of London's

Indian community to educate British public opinion about the exploitation of Indian peoples and resources.

Perhaps the most defiant anti-imperialist action was the London Pan-African conference of 1900, staged at the height of the scramble for Africa and during the Boer War (discussed on page 541). The conference grew out of an international tradition of African American, British, and American antislavery movements and brought the rhetoric used earlier to abolish slavery to bear on the tactics of European imperialism. They protested forced labor in the mining compounds of South Africa as akin to slavery and asked in very moderate tones for some autonomy and representation for African peoples. The Pan-African Conference of 1900 was small, but it drew delegates from the Caribbean, West Africa, and North America, including the thirty-two-year-old Harvard Ph.D. and leading African American intellectual, W. E. B. Du Bois (1868–1963). The conference issued a proclamation "To the Nations of the World," with a famous introduction written by Du Bois. "The Problem of the twentieth century is the problem of the color line. . . . In the metropolis of the modern world, in this closing year of the nineteenth century," the proclamation read, "there has been assembled a congress of men and women of African blood, to deliberate solemnly the present situation and outlook of the darker races of mankind." The British government ignored the conference, but Pan-Africanism, like Indian nationalism, grew rapidly after the First World War.

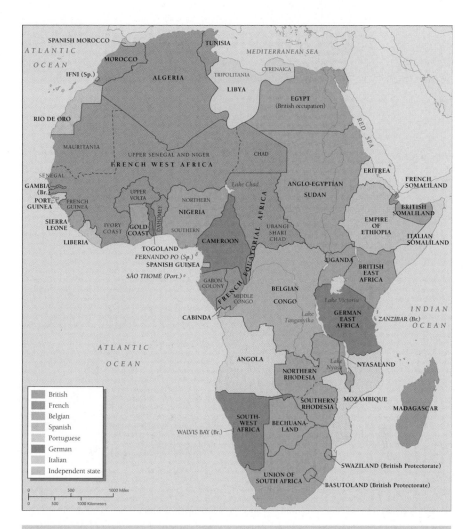

AFRICA, c. 1914.

Colonial Cultures

Imperialism also created new colonial cultures in other parts of the world. Cities such as Bombay, Calcutta, and Shanghai boomed, more than tripling in size. Treaty ports like Hong Kong were transformed as Europeans built banks, shipping enterprises, schools, and religious missions. As Europeans and indigenous peoples encountered one another and transformed one another, new hybrid cultures emerged. Elsewhere, new social instabilities were produced as European demands for labor brought men out of their villages, away from their families, and crowded them into shantytowns bordering sprawling new cities. Hopes that European rule would create a well-disciplined labor force were quickly dashed.

People on both sides of the colonial divide worried about preserving national traditions and identity in the face of these hybrid and changing colonial cultures. In Africa and the Middle East, Islamic scholars debated the proper response to European control. In China and India, suggestions that local populations adopt European models of education set off fierce controversies. Chinese elites, already divided over such customs as footbinding and concubinage (the legal practice of maintaining formal sexual partners for men outside their marriage), found their dilemmas heightened as imperialism became a more powerful force. Should they defend such practices as integral to their culture? Should they argue for a Chinese path to reform? Proponents of change in China or India thus had to sort through their stance toward Western culture and traditional popular culture.

Displays of Imperial Culture: The Paris Exposition of 1889

The French colonies were very visible during the celebration of the centenary of the French Revolution in 1889. In that year, the French government organized a "Universal Exposition" in the capital that attracted over six million visitors to a broad esplanade covered with exhibitions of French industry and culture, including the newly constructed Eiffel Tower, a symbol of modern French engineering.

At the base of the Eiffel Tower (image A), a colonial pavilion placed objects from France's overseas empire on display, and a collection of temporary architectural exhibits placed reproductions of buildings from French colonies in Asia and Africa as well as samples of architecture from other parts of the world. The photographs here show a reproduction of a Cairo Street (image B); the Pagoda of Angkor, modeled after a Khmer temple

A. The Eiffel Tower in 1889.

in Cambodia, a French protectorate (image C); and examples of West African dwellings (image D). The Cairo Street was the second most popular tourist destination at the fair, after the Eiffel Tower. It contained twenty-five shops

and restaurants, and employed dozens of Egyptian servers, shopkeepers, and artisans who had been brought to Paris to add authenticity to the exhibit. Other people on display in the colonial pavilion included Senegalese villagers and a Vietnamese theater troupe.

Questions for Analysis

1. What vision of history and social progress is celebrated in this linkage between France's colonial holdings and the industrial power on display in the Eiffel Tower?

2. What might account for the popularity of the Cairo Street exhibit among the public?

3. Why was it so important for the exposition to place people from European colonies on display for a French audience?

B. Reproduction of a Cairo Street at the Paris World's Fair, 1889.

C. Pagoda of Angkor at the Paris World's Fair, 1889.

D. West African houses at the Paris World's Fair, 1889.

For their part, British, French, and Dutch authorities fretted that too much familiarity between colonized and colonizer would weaken European prestige and authority. In Phnom Penh, Cambodia (part of French Indochina), French citizens lived separated from the rest of the city by a moat, and authorities required "dressing appropriately and keeping a distance from the natives." Sexual relations provoked the most anxiety and the most contradictory responses. "In this hot climate, passions run higher," wrote a French administrator in Algeria. "French soldiers seek out Arab women due to their strangeness and newness." "It was common practice for unmarried Englishmen resident in China to keep a Chinese girl, and I did as the others did," reported a British man stationed in Shanghai. He married an Englishwoman, however, and sent his Chinese mistress and their three children to England to avoid awkwardness. European administrators fitfully tried to prohibit liaisons between European men and local women, labeling such affairs as "corrupting." Such prohibitions only drove these relations underground, increasing the gap between the public facade of colonial rule and the private reality of colonial lives.

CRISES OF EMPIRE AT THE TURN OF THE TWENTIETH CENTURY

The turn of the twentieth century brought a series of crises to the Western empires. Those crises did not end European rule. They did, however, create sharp tensions among Western nations. The crises also drove imperial nations to expand their economic and military commitments in territories overseas. They shook Western confidence. In all of these ways, they became central to Western culture in the years before the First World War.

Fashoda

In the fall of 1898, British and French armies nearly went to war at Fashoda, in the Egyptian Sudan. The crisis had complex causes: in the early 1880s the British had used a local uprising in the Sudan as an excuse to move southward from Egypt in an attempt to control the headwaters of the Nile River. This project began with grandiose dreams of connecting Cairo to the Cape of Good Hope, but it ran into catastrophe when an army led by Britain's most flamboyant general, Charles Gordon, was massacred in Khartoum in 1885 by the forces of the Mahdi, a Sufi religious leader who

claimed to be the successor to the prophet Muhammad. Avenging Gordon's death preoccupied the British for more than a decade, and in 1898 a second large-scale rebellion gave them the opportunity. An Anglo-Egyptian army commanded by General Horatio Kitchener attacked Khartoum and defeated the Mahdi's army using modern machine guns and artillery.

The victory brought complications, however. France, which held territories in central Africa adjacent to the Sudan, saw the British victory as a threat. A French expedition was sent to the Sudanese town of Fashoda (now Kodok) to challenge British claims in the area. The French faced off with troops from Kitchener's army, and for a few weeks in September 1898 the situation teetered on the brink of war. The matter was resolved diplomatically, however, and France ceded the southern Sudan to Britain in exchange for a stop to further expansion. The incident was a sobering reminder of the extent to which imperial competition could lead to international tensions between European powers.

Ethiopia

During the 1880s and 1890s Italy had been developing a small empire on the shores of the Red Sea. Italy annexed Eritrea and parts of Somalia, and shortly after the death of Gordon at Khartoum, the Italians defeated an invasion of their territories by the Mahdi's forces. Bolstered by this success, the Italians set out to conquer Ethiopia in 1896. Ethiopia was the last major independent African kingdom, ruled by a shrewd and capable emperor, Menelik II. His largely Christian subjects engaged in profitable trade on the east African coast, and revenues from this trade allowed Menelik to invest in the latest European artillery. When the Italian army—mostly Somali conscripts and a few thousand Italian troops—arrived, Menelik allowed them to penetrate into the mountain passes of Ethiopia. To keep to the roads, the Italians were forced to divide their forces into separate columns. Meanwhile, the Ethiopians moved over the mountains themselves, and at Adowa, in March 1896, Menelik's army attacked, destroyed the Italian armies completely, and killed six thousand. Adowa was a national humiliation for Italy and an important symbol for African political radicals during the early twentieth century.

South Africa: The Boer War

In the late 1800s, competition between Dutch settlers in South Africa—known as Afrikaners or Boers—and the British led to a shooting war between Europeans. The Boers

Competing Viewpoints

Rudyard Kipling and His Critics

Rudyard Kipling (1865–1936) remains one of the most famous propagandists of empire. His novels, short stories, and poetry about the British imperial experience in India were defining texts for the cause in which he believed. Kipling's poem, was—and continues to be—widely read, analyzed, attacked, and praised. Some scholars have asserted that this poem was intended to influence American public opinion during the Spanish-American War, and that it should be read as a celebration of the moral and religious values of European imperialism in general. Others read the poem as a subtle satire of the colonial project and claim that it should be read as irony.

The White Man's Burden

Take up the White Man's burden—
　　Send forth the best ye breed—
Go, bind your sons to exile
　　To serve your captives' need;
To wait, in heavy harness,
　　On fluttered folk and wild—
Your new-caught sullen peoples,
　　Half devil and half child.

Take up the White Man's burden—
　　In patience to abide,
To veil the threat of terror
　　And check the show of pride;
By open speech and simple,
　　An hundred times made plain,
To seek another's profit
　　And work another's gain.

Take up the White Man's burden—
　　The savage wars of peace—
Fill full the mouth of Famine,
　　And bid the sickness cease;

And when your goal is nearest
　　(The end for others sought)
Watch sloth and heathen folly
　　Bring all your hope to nought.

Take up the White Man's burden—
　　No iron rule of kings,
But toil of serf and sweeper—
　　The tale of common things.
The ports ye shall not enter,
　　The roads ye shall not tread,
Go, make them with your living
　　And mark them with your dead.

Take up the White Man's burden,
　　And reap his old reward—
The blame of those ye better
　　The hate of those ye guard—
The cry of hosts ye humour
　　(Ah, slowly!) toward the light:—
"Why brought ye us from bondage,
　　Our loved Egyptian night?"

Take up the White Man's burden—
　　Ye dare not stoop to less—
Nor call too loud on Freedom
　　To cloak your weariness.
By all ye will or whisper,
　　By all ye leave or do,
The silent sullen peoples
　　Shall weigh your God and you.

Take up the White Man's burden!
　　Have done with childish days—
The lightly-proffered laurel,
　　The easy ungrudged praise:
Comes now, to search your manhood
　　Through all the thankless years,
Cold, edged with dear-bought wisdom,
　　The judgment of your peers.

Source: Rudyard Kipling, "The White Man's Burden," *McClure's Magazine* 12 (Feb. 1899).

To the Editor of *The Nation*

Sir: The cable informs us that "Kipling's stirring verses, the 'Call to America,' have created a ... profound impression" on your side. What that impression may be, we can only conjecture. There is something almost sickening in this "imperial" talk of assuming and bearing burdens for the good of others. They are never assumed or held where they are not found to be of material advantage or ministering to honor or glory. Wherever empire (I speak of the United Kingdom) is extended, and the climate suits the white man, the aborigines are, for the benefit of the white man, cleared off or held in degradation for his benefit. . . .

Taking India as a test, no one moves a foot in her government that is not well paid and pensioned at her cost. No appointments are more eagerly contended for than those in the Indian service. A young man is made for life when he secures one. The tone of that service is by no means one "bound to exile," "to serve . . . captives' need," "to wait in heavy harness," or in any degree as expressed in Mr. Kipling's highfalutin lines. It is entirely the contrary: "You are requested not to beat the servants" is a not uncommon notice in Indian hotels. . . . So anxious are we, where good pay is concerned, to save Indians the heavy burden of enjoying them, that, while our sons can study and pass at home for Indian appointments, her sons must study and pass in England; and even in India itself whites are afforded chances closed to natives. . . .

There never was a fostered trade and revenue in more disastrous consequences to humanity than the opium trade and revenue. There never was a more grinding and debilitating tax than that on salt. . . .

Source: Alfred Webb, "Mr. Kipling's Call to America," *The Nation* 68 (Feb. 23, 1899).

Questions for Analysis

1. What benefits did Kipling think imperialism brought, and to whom?

2. What, exactly, was the "burden"? Are there any indications that Kipling's language is meant to be read as satire?

3. What were Webb's arguments against Kipling? Why did he think that imperial talk was "almost sickening"? Did Europeans really suffer in their colonial outposts? In British India, with its well-established civil service, Webb thought not. Why did he mention the opium trade and the salt tax?

(an appropriation of the Dutch word for farmer) arrived in South Africa in the mid-seventeenth century and had long had a troubled relationship with their British neighbors in the colony. In the 1830s the Boers trekked inland from the cape, setting up two republics away from British influence: the Transvaal, and the Orange Free State. Gold reserves were found in the Transvaal in the 1880s, and Cecil Rhodes, the diamond magnate, tried to provoke war between Britain and the Boers in order to gain control of the Afrikaners' diamond mines. The war finally broke out in 1899, but the British were unprepared for the ferocity of Boer resistance. British columns were shot to pieces by Afrikaner forces who knew the territory, and the British towns of Ladysmith and Mafeking were besieged. Angered by these early failures, the British replaced their commanders and began to fight in deadly earnest, using the railroads built to service the diamond mines to bring in modern military hardware.

The Afrikaners responded by taking to the hills, fighting a costly guerrilla war that lasted another three years. The British tactics became more brutal as the campaign went on, setting up concentration camps—the first use of the term—where Afrikaner civilians were rounded up and forced to live in appalling conditions so that they would not be able to help the guerrillas. Nearly twenty thousand civilians died in the camps due to disease and poor sanitation over the course of two years. Black Africans, despised by both sides, also suffered the effects of famine and disease as the war destroyed valuable farmland.

Meanwhile, the concentration camps aroused opposition in Britain and internationally, and protesters campaigned against these violations of "European" rights, without saying anything about the fate of Africans in the conflict. In the end, the Afrikaners ceded control of their republics to a new British Union of South Africa that gave them a share of political power. In the aftermath of the war, both British and Afrikaners preserved their high standards of living by relying on cheap African labor and, eventually, a system of racial segregation known as apartheid.

U.S. Imperialism: The Spanish-American War of 1898

Imperialism also brought Spain and the United States to war in 1898. American imperialism in the nineteenth century was closely bound up with nation building, the conquest of new territories, and the defeat of the North American Indians (see Chapter 21). In the 1840s, the United States provoked Mexico into war over Texas and California after unsuccessfully trying to purchase the territories. Mexico's defeat, and the treaty of Guadalupe Hidalgo that followed in 1848, gave the American southwest to the United States, an enormous territorial gain that made the question of slavery more acute in the years before the American Civil War.

The conflict with Spain followed a similar pattern. In the 1880s and 1890s, Spain was considerably weakened as an imperial power, and they faced rebellion in their colonies in the Caribbean and the Pacific. American economic interests had considerable investments in Cuba, and when an American battleship accidentally exploded while at anchor in Havana, advocates of empire and the press in general clamored for revenge. President William McKinley gave in to political necessity, in spite of his misgivings, and the United States declared war on Spain in 1898, determined to protect its economic interests in the Americas and the Pacific. The United States swiftly won.

In Spain, the Spanish-American War provoked an entire generation of writers, politicians, and intellectuals to national soul searching. The defeat undermined the Spanish monarchy, which fell in 1912. The ensuing political tensions resurfaced in the Spanish Civil War of the 1930s, an important episode in the origins of the Second World War.

In the United States, this "splendid little war" was followed by the annexation of Puerto Rico, the establishment of a protectorate over Cuba, and a short but brutal war against Philippine rebels who liked American colonialism no better than the Spanish variety. In the Americas, the United States intervened in a rebellion in Panama in 1903, quickly backing the rebels and helping establish a republic while building the Panama Canal on land leased from the new government. The Panama Canal opened in 1914, and like Britain's canal at Suez, it cemented U.S. dominance of the seas

After You Read
This Chapter

Visit StudySpace for quizzes, additional review materials, and multi-media documents. **wwnorton.com/studyspace**

REVIEWING THE OBJECTIVES

- European imperialism in the nineteenth century differed from earlier phases of colonial expansion. How was it different, and which parts of the globe were singled out for special attention by European imperial powers?

- European nations justified the cost and effort of their colonial policies in many ways. What were the major reasons for colonial expansion in the nineteenth century?

- The subjugated peoples of European colonies faced a choice between resistance and accommodation, though these choices were rarely exclusive of one another. What examples of resistance to colonialism can you identify? Of accommodation?

- Imperialism also shaped cultural developments within Europe in the nineteenth century. How did imperialism change the lives of Europeans and their sense of their place in the world?

- Imperialism unleashed destabilizing competitive forces that drove European colonial powers into conflict with one another by the end of the nineteenth century. Where were the flashpoints of these conflicts?

in the Western Hemisphere and the eastern Pacific. Later interventions in Hawaii and Santo Domingo gave further evidence of U.S. imperial power, and committed the former colony to a broad role in its new and greater sphere of influence.

CONCLUSION

In the last quarter of the nineteenth century, the long-standing relationship between Western nations and the rest of the world entered a new stage. That stage was distinguished by the stunningly rapid extension of formal Western control, by new forms of economic exploitation, and by new patterns of social discipline and settlement. It was driven by the rising economic needs of the industrial West; by territorial conflict; and by nationalism, which by the late nineteenth century linked nationhood to empire. Among its immediate results was the creation of a self-consciously imperial culture in the West. At the same time, however, it plainly created unease and contributed powerfully to the sense of crisis that swept through the late-nineteenth-century West.

For all its force, this Western expansion was never unchallenged. Imperialism provoked resistance and required constantly changing strategies of rule. During the First World War, mobilizing the resources of empire would become crucial to victory. In the aftermath, reimposing the conditions of the late nineteenth century would become nearly impossible. And over the longer term, the political structures, economic developments, and racial ideologies established in this period would be contested throughout the twentieth century.

PEOPLE, IDEAS, AND EVENTS IN CONTEXT

- What was the **EAST INDIA COMPANY**? How did the British reorganize their rule in India after the **SEPOY MUTINY**?
- What did the French mean when they justified colonial expansion in the name of the **CIVILIZING MISSION**?
- How did the **OPIUM WARS** change the economic and political relationships between Europe and China?
- How did the **BERLIN CONFERENCE** of 1884 shape the subsequent colonization of Africa?
- What limits to the exercise of colonial power were revealed by the **BOXER REBELLION**, the failed **ITALIAN INVASION OF ETHIOPIA**, or the **RUSSO-JAPANESE WAR**?
- What expressions of anti-imperialism emerged from the **LONDON PAN-AFRICAN CONFERENCE**?
- How did the **BOER WAR** and the **FASHODA INCIDENT** contribute to a sense of crisis among European colonial powers?
- What effects did the **SPANISH-AMERICAN WAR** have on attitudes toward imperialism in the United States, itself a former European colony?

CONSEQUENCES

- What links do you see between the idea of civilization and imperialism?
- How was the history of industrialization connected to the history of colonialism?
- By what logic could so many Europeans support liberal or democratic principles at home and colonialism abroad?

Before You Read This Chapter

Modern Industry and Mass Politics, 1870–1914

CORE OBJECTIVES

- **UNDERSTAND** the origins and consequences of the second industrial revolution.

- **DEFINE** *mass politics* and explain how the expansion of voting rights in European nations led to the development of organized political parties that sought the support of the working classes.

- **UNDERSTAND** the arguments both for and against women's suffrage during this period.

- **IDENTIFY** the ways that European liberalism and conservatism evolved as new social and political tensions emerged with the advent of mass politics and intensifying industrial development.

- **EXPLAIN** the contributions of scientists and other cultural figures who came to prominence in the final decades of the nineteenth century, and their contributions to debates about human nature, modern society, and the natural world.

e are on the extreme promontory of ages!" decreed the Italian poet and literary editor F. T. Marinetti in 1909. In a bombastic manifesto—a self-described "inflammatory declaration" printed on the front page of a Paris newspaper—Marinetti introduced Europe to an aggressive art movement called *futurism*. Revolting against what he considered the tired and impotent conservatism of Italian culture, Marinetti called for a radical renewal of civilization through "courage, audacity, and revolt." Enamored with the raw power of modern machinery, with the dynamic bustle of urban life, he trumpeted "a new form of beauty, the beauty of speed." Most notably, Marinetti celebrated the heroic violence of warfare and disparaged the moral and cultural traditions that formed the bedrock of nineteenth-century liberalism.

Few Europeans embraced the modern era with the unflinching abandon of the futurists, but many would have agreed with Marinetti in his claim that modern life was characterized above all by flux, movement, and an accelerating rate of change. In the last decades of the nineteenth century, a second

547

industrial revolution produced new techniques for manufacturing and new sources of power, including electricity and petroleum-based fuels. These developments transformed the infrastructure of European towns and cities, and immediately people felt the effects of these changes in their daily lives.

At the same time, European nation-states faced new political realities as their electorates expanded and new blocs of voters began participating directly in shaping parliamentary bodies and their legislative agendas. New mass-based political parties brought new demands to the political arena, and national governments struggled to maintain order and legitimacy in the face of these challenges. Socialists mobilized growing numbers of industrial workers, while suffragists demanded the franchise for women. The ability of traditional elites to control political life was sorely tested, even in nations that continued to be governed by hereditary monarchs.

In the arts and sciences new theories challenged older notions of nature, society, truth, and beauty. Since the eighteenth century at least, science had been a frequent ally of political liberalism, as both liberals and scientists shared a common faith in human reason and an openness to rational inquiry into the laws of society and nature. In the late nineteenth century, however, this common agenda was strained by scientific investigations in new fields such as biology and psychology that challenged liberal assumptions about human nature. Meanwhile, in the arts, a new generation of artists and writers embraced innovation and rejected the established conventions in painting, sculpture, poetry, and literature. A period of intense experimentation in the arts followed, leading artists and writers to develop radically new forms of expression.

The nineteenth century, then, ended in a burst of energy as many Europeans embraced a vision of their society racing headlong into what they hoped was a more promising and better future. Behind this self-confidence, however, lay significant uncertainty about the eventual destination. What aspects of the European past would continue to be relevant in the modern age? In politics and social life and in the culture as a whole, such questions produced more conflict than consensus.

NEW TECHNOLOGIES AND GLOBAL TRANSFORMATIONS

In the last third of the nineteenth century, new technologies transformed the face of manufacturing in Europe, leading to new levels of economic growth and complex realignments among industry, labor, and national governments. This second industrial revolution relied on innovation in three key areas: steel, electricity, and chemicals.

Steel had long been prized as a construction material. But until the mid-nineteenth century, producing steel cheaply and in large quantities was impossible. Between the 1850s and 1870s, different processes for mass-producing alloy steel revolutionized the metallurgical industry. Britain's shipbuilders switched to steel construction and thus kept their lead in the industry. Germany and America dominated the rest of the steel industry. By 1901 Germany was producing almost half again as much steel as Britain, allowing Germany to build a massive national and industrial infrastructure.

Electricity was made available for commercial and domestic use in the 1880s, after the development of alternators and transformers capable of producing high-voltage alternating current. By century's end, large power stations, which often used cheap water power, could send electric current over vast distances. In 1879 Thomas Edison and his associates invented

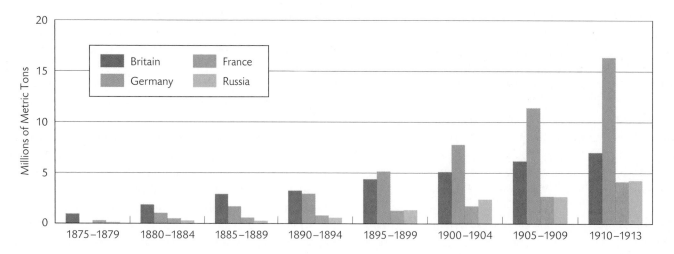

FIGURE 23.1 ANNUAL OUTPUT OF STEEL (IN MILLIONS OF METRIC TONS).
Source: Carlo Cipolla, *The Fontana Economic History of Europe*, vol. 3(2) (London: 1976), p. 775.

the light bulb and changed electricity into light. The demand for electricity skyrocketed, and soon entire metropolitan areas were electrified. Electrification powered subways, tramways, and, eventually, long-distance railroads; it made possible new techniques in the chemical and metallurgical industries, and dramatically altered living habits in ordinary households.

Advances in the chemical industry transformed the manufacture of such consumer goods as paper, soaps, textiles, and fertilizer. Britain and particularly Germany became leaders in the field. Heightened concerns for household hygiene and new techniques in mass marketing enabled the British entrepreneur Harold Lever to market his soaps and cleansers around the world. German production, on the other hand, focused on industrial uses, such as developing synthetic dyes and methods for refining petroleum, and came to control roughly 90 percent of the world's chemical market.

Other innovations contributed to the second industrial revolution. The growing demand for efficient power spurred the invention of the liquid-fuel internal combustion engine. By 1914 most navies had converted from coal to oil, as had domestic steamship companies. The new engines' dependence on crude petroleum and distilled gasoline at first threatened their general application, but the discovery of oil fields in Russia, Borneo, Persia, and Texas around 1900 allayed fears. Protecting these oil reserves thus became a vital state prerogative. The adoption of oil-powered machinery had another important consequence: industrialists who had previously depended on nearby rivers or coal mines for power were free to take their enterprises to regions bereft of natural resources. The potential for worldwide industrialization was in place.

Changes in Scope and Scale

These technological changes were part of a much larger process—impressive increases in the scope and scale of industry. At the end of the nineteenth century, size mattered. The rise of heavy industry and mass marketing had factories and cities growing hand in hand, while advances in media and mobility spurred the creation of national mass cultures. For the first time, ordinary people followed the news on national and global levels. They watched as European powers divided the globe, enlarging their empires with prodigious feats of engineering mastery; railroads, dams, canals, and harbors grew to monumental proportions. Such projects embodied the ideals of modern European industry. They also generated enormous income for builders, investors, bankers, entrepreneurs, and, of course, makers of steel and concrete. Canals in central Europe, railroads in the Andes, and telegraph cables spanning the ocean floors: these "tentacles of empire," as one historian dubs them, stretched across the globe.

THE SECOND INDUSTRIAL REVOLUTION. A German electrical engineering works illustrates the scale of production during the second industrial revolution. ■ *What changes in business practices and labor management made factories of this size possible?*

Industrialization was also accompanied by broader social changes. The population grew constantly, particularly in central and eastern Europe. Russia's population increased by nearly a quarter and Germany's by half in the space of a generation. Britain's population, too, grew by nearly one-third between 1881 and 1911. Thanks to improvements in both crop yields and shipping, food shortages declined, which rendered entire populations less susceptible to illness and high infant mortality. Advances in medicine, nutrition, and personal hygiene diminished the prevalence of dangerous diseases such as cholera and typhus, and improved conditions in housing and public sanitation helped relieve the pressure on Europe's growing cities.

Credit and Consumerism

Changes in scope and scale not only transformed production but also altered consumption. The era in which economists would worry about consumer confidence and experts could systematically track the public's buying habits did not begin until the middle of the twentieth century, but developments pointed toward that horizon. Department stores offering both practical and luxury goods to the middle class were one mark of the times—of urbanization, economic expansion, and the new importance attached to merchandising. Advertising took off as well. Even more significant, by the 1880s new stores sought to attract working-class people by introducing the all-important innovation of credit payment. In earlier times, working-class families pawned watches, mattresses, or furniture to borrow money; now they began to buy on credit, a change that would eventually have seismic effects on both households and national economies.

THE INDUSTRIAL REGIONS OF EUROPE. This map shows the distribution of mineral resources, rail lines, and industrial activity. ▪ *What nations enjoyed advantages in the development of industry and why?* ▪ *What resources were most important for industrial growth in the second half of the nineteenth century?* ▪ *What resources in England became dominant as a result of industrialization?*

These new, late-nineteenth-century patterns of consumption, however, were largely urban. In the countryside, peasants continued to save money under mattresses and to make, launder, and mend their own clothes and linens. Only slowly did retailers whittle away at these traditional habits. Mass consumption remained difficult to imagine in what was still a deeply stratified society.

The Rise of the Corporation

Economic growth and the demands of mass consumption spurred the reorganization, consolidation, and regulation of capitalist institutions. Businesses had sold shares to investors

in joint-stock companies since the sixteenth century, but it was during the late nineteenth century that the modern corporation came into its own. To provide protection for investors, most European countries enacted or improved their limited-liability laws, which ensured that stockholders could lose only the value of their shares in the event of bankruptcy. Prior to such laws, investors could be held liable for company debts. Insured in this way, many thousands of middle-class men and women now considered corporate investment a promising venture. After 1870, stock markets ceased to be primarily a clearinghouse for state paper and railroad bonds, and instead attracted new commercial and industrial ventures.

Limited liability was one part of a larger trend of incorporation. Whereas most firms had been small or middle size,

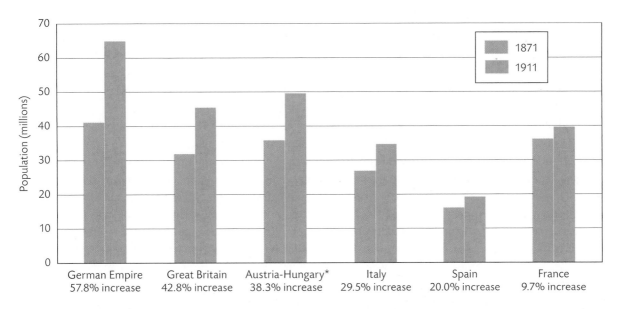

FIGURE 23.2 POPULATION GROWTH IN MAJOR STATES BETWEEN 1871 AND 1911 (POPULATION IN MILLIONS).
*Not including Bosnia-Herzegovina.
Source: Colin Dyer, *Population and Society in Twentieth-Century France* (New York: 1978), p. 5.

companies now incorporated to attain the necessary size for survival. In doing so, they tended to shift control from company founders and local directors to distant bankers and financiers whose concern for the bottom line encouraged a more impersonal style of financial management.

Equally important, the second industrial revolution created a strong demand for technical expertise, which undercut traditional forms of family management. University degrees in engineering and chemistry became more valuable than on-the-job apprenticeships. The emergence of a white-collar class (middle-level salaried managers who were neither owners nor laborers) marked a significant change in work life and for society's evolving class structure.

The drive toward larger business enterprises was encouraged by a belief that consolidation protected society against the hazards of boom-and-bust economic fluctuations. Some industries combined vertically, attempting to control every step of production, from the acquisition of raw materials to the distribution of finished products. A second form of corporate self-protection was horizontal alignment. Organizing into cartels, companies in the same industry would band together to fix prices and control competition, if not eliminate it outright. Coal, oil, and steel companies were especially suited to the organization of cartels, since only a few major players could afford the huge expense of building, equipping, and running mines, refineries, and foundries. Cartels were particularly strong in Germany and America but less so in Britain, where dedication to free-trade policies made price fixing difficult, and in France, where family firms and laborers alike opposed cartels and where there was also less heavy industry.

Though governments sometimes tried to stem the burgeoning power of cartels, the dominant trend of this period was increased cooperation between governments and industry. Contrary to the laissez-faire mentality of early capitalism, corporations developed close relationships with the states in the West—most noticeably in colonial industrial projects, such as the construction of railroads, harbors, and seafaring steamships. These efforts were so costly, or so unprofitable, that private enterprise would not have undertaken them alone. But because they served larger political and strategic interests, governments funded them willingly.

Global Economics

From the 1870s on, the rapid spread of industrialization heightened competition among nations. The search for markets, goods, and influence fueled much of the imperial expansion and, consequently, often put countries at odds with each other. Trade barriers arose again to protect home markets. All nations except Britain raised tariffs, arguing that the needs of the nation-state trumped laissez-faire doctrine. Yet changes in international economics fueled the continuing growth of an interlocking, worldwide system of manufacturing, trade, and finance. For example, the near universal adoption of the gold standard in currency exchange greatly facilitated world trade. Pegging the value of currencies, particularly Britain's powerful pound sterling, against the value of gold meant that currencies could be readily exchanged. The common standard also allowed nations to use a third country to mediate trade and exchange to mitigate trade imbalances—a common problem for the industrializing West. Almost all European countries, dependent on vast supplies of raw materials to sustain their rate of industrial production, imported more than they exported. To avoid the mounting deficits that this practice would otherwise incur, European economies relied on "invisible" exports: shipping, insurance, and banking services. The extent of Britain's exports in these areas was far greater than that of any other country. London was the money market of the world, to which would-be borrowers looked for assistance before turning elsewhere.

During this period the relationship between European manufacturing nations and the overseas sources of their materials—whether colonies or not—was transformed, as detailed in the last chapter. Those changes, in turn, reshaped economies and cultures on both sides of the imperial divide. Europeans came to expect certain foods on their tables; whole regions of Africa, Latin America, and Asia geared toward producing for the European market. This international push toward mass manufacturing and commodity production necessarily involved changes in deep-seated patterns in consumption and in production. It altered the landscape and habits of India as well as those of Britain. It brought new rhythms of life to women working in clothing factories in Germany, to porters carrying supplies to build railways in Senegal, to workers dredging the harbor of Dakar.

LABOR POLITICS, MASS MOVEMENTS

The rapid expansion of late-nineteenth-century industry brought a parallel growth in the size, cohesion, and activism of Europe's working classes. The men and women who worked as wage laborers resented corporate power—resentment fostered not only by the exploitation and inequalities they experienced on the job but also by living "a life apart" in Europe's expanding cities (see Chapter 19). Corporations had devised new methods of protecting and promoting their interests, and workers did the same. Labor unions, which were traditionally limited to skilled male workers in small-scale enterprises, grew during the late nineteenth century into mass, centralized, nationwide organizations. This "new unionism" emphasized organization across entire industries and, for the first time, brought unskilled workers into the ranks, increasing their power to negotiate wages and job conditions. More important, though, the creation of national unions provided a framework for a new type of political movement: the socialist mass party.

Why did socialism find increased support in Europe after 1870? Changing national political structures provide part of the answer. Parliamentary constitutional governments opened the political process to new participants, including socialists. Now part of the legislative process, socialists in Parliament led efforts to expand voting rights in the 1860s and 1870s. Their success created new constituencies of working-class men. At the same time, traditional struggles between labor and management moved up to the national level; governments aligned with business interests, and legislators countered working-class agitation with antilabor and antisocialist laws. To radical leaders, the organization of national mass political movements seemed the only effective way to counter industrialists' political strength. Thus, during this period, socialist movements abandoned their earlier revolutionary traditions (exemplified by the romantic image of barricaded streets) in favor of legal, public competition within Europe's parliamentary systems.

The Spread of Socialist Parties— and Alternatives

The emergence of labor movements in Europe owed as much to ideas as to social changes. The most influential radical thinker was Karl Marx, whose early career was discussed in Chapter 20. Since the 1840s, Marx and his collaborator Friedrich Engels had been intellectuals and activists, participating in the organization of fledgling socialist movements. Marx's three-volume study, *Capital,* attacked capitalism using the tools of economic analysis, allowing Marx to claim a scientific validity for his work. Marx's work claimed to offer a systematic analysis of how capitalism forced workers to exchange their labor for subsistence wages while enabling their employers to amass both wealth and power. Followers of Marx called for workers everywhere to ally with one another to create an independent political force, and few other groups pushed so strongly to secure civil liberties, expand conceptions of citizenship, or build a welfare state. Marxists also made powerful claims for gender equality, though in practice women's suffrage took a backseat to class politics.

Not all working-class movements were Marxist, however. Differences among various left-wing groups remained strong, and the most divisive issues were the role of violence and whether socialists should cooperate with liberal governments—and if so, to what end. Some "gradualists" were willing to work with liberals for piecemeal reform, while anarchists and syndicalists rejected parliamentary politics altogether. When European labor leaders met in 1864 at the first meeting of the International Working Men's Association, Marx argued strongly in favor of political mass movements, which would prepare the working classes for revolution. He was strongly opposed by the anarchist Mikhail Bakunin, who rejected any form of state or party organization, and called instead for terror and violence to destabilize society.

Between 1875 and 1905, Marxist socialists founded political parties in Germany, Belgium, France, Austria, and Russia. These parties were disciplined workers' organizations that aimed to seize control of the state to make revolutionary changes in the social order. The most successful was the German Social Democratic Party (SPD). Initially intending to work for political change within the parliamentary political system, the SPD became more radical in the face of Bismarck's oppressive antisocialist laws. By the outbreak of the First World War, the German Social Democrats were the largest, best-organized workers' party in the world. Rapid and extensive industrialization, a large urban working class, and a national government hostile to organized labor, made German workers particularly receptive to the goals and ideals of social democracy.

In Britain—the world's first and most industrialized economy—the socialist presence was much smaller and more moderate. Why? The answer lies in the fact that much of the socialist agenda was advanced by radical liberals in Britain, which forestalled the growth of an independent socialist party. Even when a separate Labour Party was formed in 1901, it remained moderate, committed to reforming capitalism with measures such as support for public housing or welfare benefits, rather than a complete overhaul of the economy. For the Labour Party, and for Britain's many trade unions, Parliament remained a legitimate vehicle for achieving social change, limiting the appeal of revolutionary Marxism.

Militant workers seeking to organize themselves for political action found alternatives to Marxism in the ideas of anarchists and syndicalists. Anarchists were opposed to centrally organized economies and to the very existence of the state. They aimed to establish small-scale, localized, and self-sufficient democratic communities that could guarantee a maximum of individual sovereignty. Renouncing any form of modern mass organization, the anarchists fell back on the tradition of conspiratorial violence, which Marx had denounced. Anarchists assassinated Tsar Alexander II in 1881 and five other heads of state in the following years, believing that such "exemplary terror" would spark a popular revolt. Syndicalists, on the other hand, embraced a strategy of strikes and sabotage by workers. Their hope was that a general strike of all workers would bring down the capitalist state and replace it with workers' syndicates or trade associations. Anarchism's opposition to any form of organization kept it from making substantial gains as a

SOCIALIST PARTY PAMPHLET, c. 1895. Socialism emerged as a powerful political force throughout Europe in the late nineteenth century, although appearing in different forms depending on the region. This German pamphlet quotes from Marx's *Communist Manifesto* of 1848, calling for workers of the world to unite under the banners of equality and brotherhood. ▪ *Were nationalism and socialism compatible with one another?*

movement. Likewise, the syndicalists' refusal to participate in politics limited their ability to command wide influence.

By 1895, popular socialist movements had made impressive gains in Europe: seven socialist parties had captured between a quarter and third of the votes in their countries. But just as socialists gained a permanent foothold in national politics, they were also straining under limitations and internal conflicts. Working-class movements, in fact, had never gained full worker support. Some workers remained loyal to older liberal traditions or to religious parties, and many others were excluded from socialist politics by its narrow definition of who constituted the working class—male industrial workers.

Furthermore, some committed socialists began to question Marx's core assumptions about the inevitability of workers' impoverishment and the collapse of the capitalist order. A German group of so-called revisionists, led by Eduard Bernstein, challenged Marxist doctrine and called for a shift to moderate and gradual reform, accomplished through electoral politics. Radical supporters of direct action were incensed at Bernstein's betrayal of Marxist theory of revolution, because they feared that the official reforms that favored workers might make the working class more accepting of the status quo. The radicals within the labor movement called for mass strikes, hoping to ignite a widespread proletarian revolution.

Conflicts over strategy peaked just before the First World War. On the eve of the war, governments discreetly consulted with labor leaders about workers' willingness to enlist and fight. Having built impressive organizational and political strength since the 1870s, working-class parties now affected the ability of nation-states to wage war. Much to the disappointment of socialist leaders, however, European laborers—many of whom had voted for socialist candidates in previous elections—nevertheless donned the uniforms of their respective nations and marched off to war in 1914, proving that national identities and class identities were not necessarily incompatible with one another.

DEMANDING EQUALITY: SUFFRAGE AND THE WOMEN'S MOVEMENT

After the 1860s, working-class activism and liberal constitutionalism expanded male suffrage rights across Europe, and by 1884 most men could vote in Germany, France, and Britain. But nowhere could women vote. Excluded from parliamentary politics, women pressed their interests through independent organizations and direct action. This new women's movement won some crucial legal reforms, as British, French, and German women gained access to education and won the rights to control their own property and to initiate divorce. The next step was the vote.

To the suffragists, the enfranchisement of women meant not merely political progress but economic, spiritual, and moral advancement as well. Throughout western Europe, middle-class women founded clubs, published journals, organized petitions, and sponsored assemblies to press for the vote. To the left of middle-class movements were movements of feminist socialists, women such as Clara Zetkin and Lily Braun who believed that only a socialist revolution would free women from economic as well as political exploitation. Meanwhile, the French celebrity journalist and novelist Gyp (the pseudonym of Sibylle de Riguetti de Mirabeau) carved out a name for herself on the nationalist and anti-Semitic right with her acerbic commentary on current events.

In Britain, campaigns for women's suffrage exploded in violence. Millicent Fawcett brought together sixteen different organizations into the National Union of Women's Suffrage Societies in 1897, a group that was committed to peaceful reform. When the major political parties rejected their proposals, however, many members became exasperated and in 1903 Emmeline Pankhurst founded a new group, the Women's Social and Political Union (WSPU), which adopted militant tactics and civil disobedience. WSPU women chained themselves to the visitors' gallery in Parliament, slashed paintings in museums, burned politicians' houses and smashed department-store windows. The government countered with repression. When arrested women went on hunger strikes in prisons, they were tied down and force-fed through tubes inserted in their throats. The intensity of the suffragists' moral claims was embodied by the 1913 martyrdom of Emily Wilding Davison, who, wearing a "Votes for Women" sash, threw herself in front of the king's horse on Derby day and was trampled to death.

Redefining Womanhood

The campaign for women's suffrage was perhaps the most visible and inflammatory aspect of a larger cultural shift in which traditional Victorian gender roles were redefined. In the last third of the nineteenth century, economic, political, and social changes were undermining the view that men and women should occupy distinctly different spheres. Women became increasingly visible in the workforce as growing numbers of them took up a greater variety of jobs. Many working-class women joined the new factories and workshops in an effort to stave off their families' poverty, in spite of many working-class men's insistence that stable families required women at home. In addition, the expansion of government as well as business, health care, and education brought middle-class women to the workforce as social workers, clerks, nurses, and teachers. A shortage of male workers and a need to fill so many new jobs as cheaply as possible made women a logical choice. Thus women, who had campaigned vigorously for access to education, began to see doors opening to them. These changes in women's employment began to deflate the myth of female domesticity.

Women became more active in politics—an area previously termed off limits. This is not to say that female political activity was unprecedented; reform movements of the early nineteenth century depended on women and raised women's standing in public. First with charity work in religious associations and later with hundreds of secular associations, women throughout Europe directed their energies toward poor relief, prison reform, Sunday school, temperance, ending slavery and prostitution, and expanding educational opportunities for women. Reform groups brought in the process. For some onlookers, women's newfound independence amounted to shirking domestic responsibilities, and they attacked women who defied convention as ugly "half-men," unfit and unable to marry. For supporters, though, these new women symbolized a welcome era of social emancipation.

Opposition to these changes was intense, sometimes violent, and not exclusively male. Men scorned the women who threatened their elite preserves in universities, clubs, and public offices; but a wide array of female antisuffragists also denounced the movement. Conservatives such as Mrs. Humphrey Ward maintained that bringing women into the political arena would sap the virility of the British Empire. Christian commentators criticized suffragists for bringing moral decay through selfish individualism. Still others believed feminism would dissolve the family, a theme that fed into a larger discussion on the decline of the West amid a growing sense of cultural crisis. Indeed, the struggle for women's rights provided a flashpoint for an array of European anxieties over labor, politics, gender, and biology—all of which suggested that an orderly political consensus, so ardently desired by middle-class society, was slipping from reach.

LIBERALISM AND ITS DISCONTENTS: NATIONAL POLITICS AT THE TURN OF THE CENTURY

Having championed doctrines of individual rights throughout the nineteenth century, middle-class liberals found themselves on the defensive after 1870. Previously, political power had rested on a balance between middle-class interests and traditional elites. The landed aristocracy shared power with industrial magnates; monarchical rule coexisted with constitutional freedoms. During the late nineteenth century, the rise of mass politics upset this balance. An expanding franchise and rising expectations brought newcomers to the political stage. As we have seen, trade unions, socialists, and feminists all challenged Europe's governing classes by demanding that political participation be open to all. Governments responded in turn, with a mix of conciliatory and repressive measures. As the twentieth century approached, political struggles became increasingly fierce, and by the First World War, the foundation of traditional parliamentary politics was crumbling. For both the left and the right, for both insiders and outsiders, negotiating this unfamiliar terrain required the creation of new and distinctly modern forms of mass politics.

women together outside the home, encouraging them to speak their minds as free thinking equals and to pursue political goals—a right denied them as individual females.

These changes in women's roles were paralleled by the emergence of a new social type, dubbed the "new woman." A new woman demanded education and a job; she refused to be escorted by chaperones when she went out; she rejected the restrictive corsets of mid-century fashion. In other words, she claimed the right to a physically and intellectually active life and refused to conform to the norms that defined nineteenth-century womanhood. The new woman was an image—in part the creation of artists and journalists, who filled newspapers, magazines, and advertising billboards with pictures of women riding bicycles, smoking cigarettes, and enjoying other emblems of consumption. Very few women actually fit this image: among other things, most were too poor. Still, middle- and working-class women demanded more social freedom and redefined gender norms

France: The Third Republic and the Paris Commune

The Franco-Prussian War of 1870 resulted in a bruising defeat for France. The Second Empire collapsed and a republic, France's third, was declared in its wake. Profound divisions between political leaders and between social classes meant that the early years of the republic were extremely volatile.

Even before its first year was complete, the republic faced a revolutionary challenge from militants in Paris. During the war of 1870, the city had appointed its own municipal government, the Commune, which broke with the politicians who negotiated the armistice with Germany, and refused to surrender to the German troops who besieged the city. In March 1871 the national government sent troops into Paris to disarm the Commune and its working-class supporters. The Communards responded by declaring a revolutionary socialist movement in the city, and the struggle quickly took on aspects of a violent class war. After holding out for over fifty days, the Commune was finally defeated in a week of bloody street fighting in which over twenty thousand Parisians were killed and much of the city burned. Thousands of Commune supporters were deported to penal colonies in the South Pacific. Paris's working-class populations did not forget the repression of the Commune, and socialist leaders such as Karl Marx argued that it showed the futility of the older insurrectionary tradition. Instead, Marx argued in favor of organizing mass-based democratic movements founded on the principle of working-class unity.

The Dreyfus Affair and Anti-Semitism as Politics

On the other side of the French political spectrum, new forms of radical right-wing politics emerged that would foreshadow developments elsewhere. As the age-old foundations of conservative politics, the Catholic Church and the landed nobility, slipped, more radical right-wing politics took shape. Stung by the defeat of 1870 and critical of the republic and its premises, the new right was nationalist, antiparliamentary, and antiliberal (in the sense of commitment to individual liberties). During the first half of the nineteenth century, nationalism had been associated with the left (see Chapter 20). Now it was more often invoked by the right and linked to xenophobia (fear of foreigners) in general and anti-Semitism in particular.

The power of popular anti-Semitism in France was made clear by a public controversy that erupted in the 1890s known as the Dreyfus Affair. In 1894 a group of monarchist officers in the army accused Alfred Dreyfus, a Jewish captain on the general staff, of selling military secrets to Germany. Dreyfus was convicted and deported for life to Devil's Island, a ghastly South American prison colony in French Guiana. Two years later, an intelligence officer named Georges Picquart discovered that the documents used to convict Dreyfus were forgeries. The War Department refused to grant Dreyfus a new trial, and the case became an enormous public scandal, fanned on both sides by the involvement of prominent intellectual figures. Republicans, some socialists, liberals, and intellectuals such as the writer Émile Zola backed Dreyfus, claiming that the case was about individual rights and the legitimacy of the republic and its laws. Nationalists, prominent Catholics, and other socialists who believed that the case was a distraction from economic issues, opposed Dreyfus and refused to question the military's judgment. One Catholic newspaper insisted that the question was not whether Dreyfus was guilty or innocent but whether Jews and unbelievers were not the "secret masters of France."

The anti-Semitism of the anti-Dreyfus camp was a combination of three strands of anti-Jewish thinking in Europe: (1) long-standing currents of anti-Semitism within Christianity, which damned the Jewish people as Christ-killers; (2) economic anti-Semitism, which insisted that the wealthy banking family of Rothschild was representative of all Jews; and (3) late-nineteenth-century racial thinking, which opposed a so-called Aryan (Indo-European) race to an inferior Semitic race. Anti-Dreyfus propagandists whipped these ideas into a potent form of propaganda in anti-Semitic newspapers such as Edouard Drumont's *La Libre Parole* (Free Speech), a French daily that claimed a circulation of two hundred thousand during the height of the Dreyfus affair.

In 1899, Dreyfus was pardoned and freed by executive order. In 1906 the French Supreme Court declared him free of all guilt, and he was reinstated in the army as a major. A major consequence of the controversy was passage of laws between 1901 and 1905 that separated church and state in France. Convinced that the church and the army were hostile to the republic, the republican legislature passed new laws that prohibited any religious orders in France that were not authorized by the state and forbade clerics to teach in public schools.

The French Republic withstood the attacks of radical anti-Semites in the first decade of the twentieth century, but the same right-wing and nationalist forces made their voices known elsewhere in Europe. The mayor of Vienna in 1897 was elected on an anti-Semitic platform. The Russian secret police forged and published a book called *The Protocols of the Learned Elders of Zion* (1903 and 1905), which imagined

Analyzing Primary Sources

Anti-Semitism in Late-Nineteenth-Century France

Over the course of the nineteenth century, European (though not Russian) Jewish people slowly gained more legal and political rights: access to occupations from which they had been barred, the right to vote and hold political office, the right to marry non-Jews, and so on. France, the land of the Revolution of 1789, appeared to many European Jews the beacon of liberty. But in the late nineteenth century, France also proved the birthplace of new forms of anti-Semitism. This excerpt from Édouard Drumont's best-selling Jewish France *(1885) illustrates some themes of that ideology: the effort to displace economic grievances; conservative hatred of the republic and parliamentary government; the legacy of 1789; and conservative nationalism.*

he only one who has benefitted from the Revolution [of 1789] is the Jew. Everything comes from the Jew; everything returns to the Jew.

We have here a veritable conquest, an entire nation returned to serfdom by a minute but cohesive minority, just as the Saxons were forced into serfdom by William the Conqueror's 60,000 Normans.

The methods are different, the result is the same. One can recognize all the characteristics of a conquest: an entire population working for another population, which appropriates, through a vast system of financial exploitation, all of the profits of the other. Immense Jewish fortunes, castles, Jewish townhouses, are not the fruit of any actual labor, of any production: they are the booty taken from an enslaved race by a dominant race.

It is certain, for example, that the Rothschild family, whose French branch alone possesses a declared fortune of three billion [francs], did not have that money when it arrived in France; it has invented nothing, it has discovered no mine, it has tilled no ground. It has therefore appropriated these three billion francs from the French without giving them anything in exchange. . . .

Thanks to the Jews' cunning exploitation of the principles of '89, France was collapsing into dissolution. Jews had monopolized all of the public wealth, had invaded everything, except the army. The representatives of the old [French] families, whether noble or bourgeois . . . gave themselves up to pleasure, and were corrupted by the Jewish prostitutes they had taken as mistresses or were ruined by the horse-sellers and money-lenders, also Jews, who aided the prostitutes. . . .

The *fatherland*, in the sense that we attach to that word, has no meaning for the Semite. The Jew . . . is characterized by an *inexorable universalism*.

I can see no reason for reproaching the Jews for thinking this way. What does the word "Fatherland" mean? Land of the fathers. One's feelings for the Fatherland are engraved in one's heart in the same way that a name carved in a tree is driven deeper into the bark with each passing year, so that the tree and the name eventually become one. You can't become a patriot through improvization; you are a patriot in your blood, in your marrow.

Can the Semite, a perpetual nomad, ever experience such enduring impressions? . . .

Source: Édouard Drumont, *La France juive. Essai d'histoire contemporaine* (Paris: 1885), excerpt trans. Cat Nilan, 1997.

Questions for Analysis

1. What historical changes does Drumont blame on the Jews over the course of the nineteenth century? Why?

2. Drumont tries to elicit several anxieties. What does he think his readers should fear, and why? What does he mean by "inexorable universalism"?

3. In what ways was anti-Semitism an ideology?

a Jewish plot to dominate the world and held Jews responsible for the French Revolution and the dislocating effects of industrialization. Political anti-Semitism remained popular among a substantial number of Europeans who accepted its insistence that social and political problems could be understood in racial terms.

Zionism

Among the many people who watched with alarm as the Dreyfus Affair unfolded was Theodor Herzl (1860–1904), a Hungarian-born journalist working in Paris. The rise of virulent anti-Semitism in the land of the French Revolution troubled Herzl deeply. He considered the Dreyfus Affair "only the dramatic expression of a much more fundamental malaise." Despite Jewish emancipation, or the granting of civil rights, Herzl came to believe Jewish people might never be assimilated into Western culture and that staking the Jewish community's hopes on acceptance and tolerance was dangerous folly. Herzl endorsed the different strategy of Zionism, the building of a separate Jewish homeland outside of Europe (though not necessarily in Palestine). A small movement of Jewish settlers, mainly refugees from Russia, had already begun to establish settlements outside of Europe. Herzl was not the first to voice these goals, but he was the most effective advocate of political Zionism. He argued that Zionism should be recognized as a modern nationalist movement, capable of negotiating with other states. Although Herzl's writings met with much skepticism, they received an enthusiastic reception among Jews who lived in areas of eastern Europe where anti-Semitism was especially violent. During the turmoil of the First World War, specific wartime needs prompted the British to become involved in the issue, embroiling Zionism in international diplomacy (see Chapter 24).

Germany's Search for Imperial Unity

Through deft foreign policy, three short wars, and a groundswell of national sentiment, Otto von Bismarck united Germany under the banner of Prussian conservatism during the years 1864 to 1871. In constructing a federal political system, Bismarck sought to create the centralizing institutions of a modern nation-state while safeguarding the privileges of Germany's traditional elites, including a dominant role for Prussia. Bismarck's constitution gave the Emperor full control of foreign and military affairs, and the power of the parliament's lower house was checked by a conservative upper house whose members were appointed by the Emperor.

Under a government that was neither genuinely federal nor democratic, building a nation with a sense of common purpose was no easy task. Three fault lines in Germany's political landscape especially threatened to crack the national framework: the divide between Catholics and Protestants; the growing Social Democratic Party; and the potentially divisive economic interests of agriculture and industry.

Between 1871 and 1878, Bismarck governed principally with liberal factions interested in promoting free trade and economic growth. To strengthen ties with these liberal coalitions, Bismarck unleashed an anti-Catholic campaign in Prussia. In what is known as the *Kulturkampf,* or "cultural struggle," Bismarck passed laws that imprisoned priests for political sermons, banned Jesuits from Prussia, and curbed the church's control over education and marriage. The campaign backfired, however, and public sympathy for the persecuted clergy helped the Catholic Center party win fully one-quarter of the seats in the Reichstag in 1874.

Bismarck responded by fashioning a new coalition that would bring socially conservative Catholics into an alliance with agricultural and industrial interests. This alliance passed protectionist legislation (tariffs on grain, iron, and steel) that satisfied German producers but alienated free-trade liberals and the social democrats whose constituents faced higher prices as a result of the tariffs. Bismarck responded by declaring that the Social Democrats were enemies of the empire, and he passed laws that prevented them from meeting or distributing their literature. The Social Democrats became a clandestine party, and many of its members increasingly viewed socialism as the sole answer to their political persecution.

To woo the working classes away from their militant leadership, Bismarck offered a package of social reforms: old-age pensions, health and accident insurance, factory inspections, limited working hours for women and children, and a maximum workday for men. By 1890, Germany's social legislation was unrivaled in Europe and it became a prototype for the majority of Western nations in the decades to come. The reforms failed to win workers' loyalty, however, and by 1912 the Social Democrats were the largest bloc in the German parliament. The standoff between the German government and its increasingly well-organized working-class population remained unresolved until the outbreak of the First World War in 1914.

Britain: From Moderation to Militance

The Second Reform Bill of 1867 in Britain extended the vote to more than a third of the nation's adult males, and in 1884 further legislation gave the vote to more than three-fourths of adult men. The two major political parties, Liberals and Conservatives, competed to win the support of this growing electorate, and Parliament passed legislation that recognized the legality of trade unions, provided education for all children, commissioned large projects of urban rebuilding, and ended discrimination against religious dissenters at the universities of Oxford and Cambridge.

Given this record of orderly reform, many in Britain felt that their system of government was more stable than others on the European continent. The leader of the Conservative party, Benjamin Disraeli, may have disagreed vehemently in Parliament with the Liberal leader William Gladstone, but the members of both parties were drawn

Anti-Semitism and the Popular Press in France

The Dreyfus Affair lasted twelve years, from 1894, when Captain Alfred Dreyfus was first arrested and convicted of treason by a military court, to 1906, when he was finally absolved of all guilt and reinstated in the army. During the affair, most people in France followed the events of the case through the popular press, which had undergone rapid expansion as public schooling became more general and literacy spread through the population. The newspapers milked every episode of the case for all of its sensational drama, and editors openly took sides in order to increase their circulation and profits. The illustrated press was particularly popular, and the images associated with expressions of anti-Semitism became ubiquitous in both the respectable and the more sensationalist press. Image A shows Jakob Rothschild, a French Jewish banker, stretching his demonic hands around the globe. Edouard Drumont, the anti-Semitic editor of *La Libre Parole* (Free Speech) used the scandal to launch his own political career. His celebrity status is evident in a caricature of himself that appeared in a competing paper, *Le Rire* (image B). Even illustrations that did not aim at caricature could carry a powerful message about the intensity of popular anti-Semitism in France during the affair, as in image C, which depicts young people burning Alfred Dreyfus's brother Mathieu in effigy during a demonstration.

Questions for Analysis

1. What fears about the economy are exploited in image A? (Compare this with the image on page 553 of socialists circling the globe, hand in hand.)

2. Is *Le Rire*'s portrait of Edouard Drumont (image B) an anti-Semitic image or is it critical of Drumont's anti-Semitism?

3. Taken together, what do these images tell us about the connections among anti-Semitism, the popular press, and the definitions of national identity that were current in France during the affair?

A. Anti-Semitic French cartoon with caricature of Jakob Rothschild, 1898.

B. "The Ogre's Meal," caricature of Edouard Drumont, editor of *La Libre Parole*, from *Le Rire*, 1896.

0124016 PARIS: DREYFUS AFFAIR, 1898.
Credit: Rue des Archives / The Granger Collection, New York

C. "Anti-Semitic Agitation in Paris: Mathieu Dreyfus burned in effigy in Montmartre (Paris)."

from the same social strata—the upper middle class and the landed gentry—and both parties offered moderate programs that appealed to the voting population.

Even Britain's working-class movements were notably moderate before 1900. A more strident tone was first heard in 1901, when the Independent Labour Party was founded from a coalition of trade unions and middle-class socialist societies. The Labour Party pressured the Liberal government to enact sickness, accident, old-age, and unemployment insurance, which the government paid for through progressive income and inheritance taxes. The House of Lords strenuously opposed these innovations, and ended up losing not only the debate about taxation, but also their ability to veto legislation passed by the House of Commons. The acrimony of this debate pointed to an increasing bitterness in British politics.

Outside of Parliament, militants began to challenge the moderate pace of reform. Coal and rail workers launched nationwide strikes against laboring conditions, and city workers shut down transport networks in London and Dublin. It was in this atmosphere that women agitating for the vote adopted violent forms of direct action (discussed earlier). Meanwhile, in Ireland, disagreements over Irish self-government threatened to produce armed confrontations between Irish nationalists and Irish Protestants opposed to home rule.

The British Parliament had ruled Ireland directly since 1800, and previous efforts to re-establish Irish sovereignty had failed. After the 1880s a modern nationalist party began to exert some political influence, but more radical organizers who disdained the party as out of touch and ineffectual increasingly eclipsed its agenda. Newer groups began to promote an interest in Irish history and culture and to provide support to militant organizations such as Sinn Féin and the Irish Republican Brotherhood. Firmly opposed to the nationalists was the Protestant Ulster Volunteer force, determined to resist home rule by violence if necessary. In 1913, as the Liberal government once more discussed home rule, Ireland seemed on the verge of civil war—a prospect delayed only by the outbreak of the First World War in Europe.

Russia: The Road to Revolution

The industrial and social changes that swept Europe proved especially unsettling in Russia. An autocratic political system was ill equipped to handle conflict and the pressures of modern society. Western industrialization challenged Russia's military might, and Western political doctrines—liberalism, democracy, socialism—threatened its internal political stability. Like other nations, tsarist Russia negotiated these challenges with a combination of repression and reform.

In the 1880s and 1890s, Russia launched a program of industrialization that made it the world's fifth largest economy by the early twentieth century. The state largely directed this industrial development, for despite the creation of a mobile workforce after the emancipation of the serfs in 1861, no independent middle class capable of raising capital and stewarding industrial enterprises emerged.

Rapid industrialization heightened social tensions. The transition from country to city life was sudden and harsh. Men and women left agriculture for factory work, straining the fabric of village life and rural culture. In the industrial areas, workers lived in large barracks and were marched, military style, to and from the factories, where working conditions were among the worst in Europe. They coped by leaving their villages only temporarily and returning to their farms for planting or the harvest. Social change strained Russia's legal system, which did not recognize trade unions or employers' associations. Laws still distinguished among nobles, peasants, clergy, and town dwellers, categories that did not correspond to an industrializing society. Outdated banking and financial laws failed to serve the needs of a modern economy.

Real legal reform, however, would threaten the regime's stability. When Alexander II (r. 1855–81), the liberator of the serfs, was killed by a radical assassin in 1881, his successor, Alexander III (r. 1881–94), steered the country sharply to the right. Russia had nothing in common with western Europe, Alexander III claimed; his people had been nurtured on mystical piety for centuries and would be utterly lost without a strong autocratic system. This principle guided stern repression. The regime curtailed all powers of local assemblies, increased the authority of the secret police, and subjected villages to the governmental authority of nobles appointed by the state. The press and schools remained under strict censorship.

Nicholas II (r. 1894–17) continued these counterreforms. Like his father, he ardently advocated Russification, or government programs to extend the language, religion, and culture of greater Russia over the empire's non-Russian subjects. Russification amounted to coercion, expropriation, and physical oppression: Finns lost their constitution, Poles studied their own literature in Russian translation, and Jews perished in pogroms. (*Pogrom* is a Russian term for violent attacks on civilians, which in the late nineteenth century were usually aimed at Jewish communities.) The Russian government did not organize pogroms, but it was openly anti-Semitic and made a point of looking the other way when villagers massacred Jews and destroyed their homes, businesses, and synagogues. Other groups whose repression by the state led to long-lasting undercurrents of anti-Russian nationalism included the Georgians, Armenians, and Azerbaijanis of the Caucasus Mountains.

The most important radical political group in late-nineteenth-century Russia was a large, loosely knit group of men and women who called themselves populists. Populists believed that Russia needed to modernize on its own terms, not the West's. They envisioned an egalitarian Russia based on the ancient institution of the village commune (*mir*). Advocates of populism sprang primarily from the middle class; many of its adherents were young students, and women made up about 15 percent—a significantly large proportion for the period. They formed secret bands, plotting the overthrow of tsarism through anarchy and insurrection. They dedicated their lives to "the people," attempting wherever possible to live among common laborers so as to understand and express the popular will. Populism's emphasis on peasant socialism influenced the Social Revolutionary party, formed in 1901, which also concentrated on increasing the political power of the peasant and building a socialist society based on the agrarian communalism of the mir.

The emergence of industrial capitalism and a new, desperately poor working class created Russian Marxism. Organized as the Social Democratic Party, Russian Marxists concentrated their efforts on behalf of urban workers and saw themselves as part of the international working-class movement. They made little headway in a peasant-dominated Russia before the First World War, but they provided disaffected urban factory workers and intellectuals alike with a powerful ideology that stressed the necessity of overthrowing the tsarist regime and the inevitability of a better future. Autocracy would give way to capitalism and capitalism to an egalitarian, classless society. Russian Marxism blended radical, activist opposition with a rational, scientific approach to history, furnishing revolutionaries with a set of concepts with which to understand the upheavals of the young twentieth century.

In 1903 the leadership of the Social Democratic Party split over an important disagreement on revolutionary strategy. One group, temporarily in the majority and quick to name itself the Bolsheviks (majority group), believed that the Russian situation called for a strongly centralized party of active revolutionaries. The Bolsheviks also insisted that the rapid industrialization of Russia meant that they did not have to follow Marx's model for the West. Instead of working for liberal capitalist reforms, Russian revolutionaries could skip a stage and immediately begin to build a socialist state. The Mensheviks (which means minority) were more cautious or "gradualist," seeking slow changes and reluctant to depart from Marxist orthodoxy. When

the Mensheviks regained control of the Social Democratic Party, the Bolsheviks formed a splinter party under the leadership of the dedicated young revolutionary Vladimir Ilyich Ulyanov, who lived in political exile in western Europe between 1900 and 1917. He wrote under the pseudonym of Lenin, from the Lena River in Siberia, where he had been exiled earlier.

Lenin's theoretical abilities and organizational energy commanded respect, enabling him to remain the leader of the Bolsheviks even while living abroad. From exile Lenin preached unrelenting class struggle; the need for a coordinated revolutionary socialist movement throughout Europe; and, most important, the belief that Russia was passing into an economic stage that made it ripe for revolution. It was the Bolsheviks' responsibility to organize a revolutionary party on behalf of workers, for without the party's discipline, workers could not effect change. Lenin's treatise *What Is to Be Done?* (1902) set out his vision of Russia's special destiny: revolution was the only answer to Russia's problems, and organizing for revolution needed to be done, soon, by vanguard agents of the party acting in the name of the working class.

THE FIRST RUSSIAN REVOLUTION

The revolution that came in 1905, however, took all of these radical movements by surprise. Its unexpected occurrence resulted from Russia's resounding defeat in the Russo-Japanese War of 1904–5. But the revolution had deeper roots. Rapid industrialization had transformed Russia unevenly; certain regions were heavily industrial, while others were less integrated into the market economy. The economic boom of the 1880s and 1890s turned to bust in the early 1900s, as demand for goods tapered off, prices plummeted, and the nascent working class suffered high levels of unemployment. At the same time, low grain prices resulted in a series of peasant uprisings, which, combined with students' energetic radical organizing, became overtly political.

As dispatches reported the defeats of the tsar's army and navy, the Russian people grasped the full extent of the regime's inefficiency. Hitherto apolitical middle-class subjects clamored for change, and radical workers organized strikes and held demonstrations in every important city. Trust in the benevolence of the tsar was severely shaken on January 22, 1905—"Bloody Sunday"—when a mass of 200,000 workers and their families, led by a priest, Father Gapon, went to demonstrate their grievances at the tsar's winter palace in St. Petersburg. When government troops killed 130 demonstrators and wounded several hundred, the government seemed not only ineffective but arbitrary and brutal.

Lenin's View of a Revolutionary Party

At the turn of the century, Russian revolutionaries debated political strategy. How could Russian autocracy be defeated? Should revolutionaries follow the programs of their counterparts in the West? Or did the Russian situation require different tactics? In What Is to Be Done? *(1902) Lenin (Vladimir Ilyich Ulyanov, 1870–1924) argued that Russian socialists needed to revise the traditional Marxist view, according to which a large and politically conscious working class would make revolution. In Russia, Lenin argued, revolution required a small but dedicated group of revolutionaries to lead the working class. Lenin's vision was important, for it shaped the tactics and strategies of the Bolsheviks in 1917 and beyond.*

he national tasks of Russian Social-Democracy are such as have never confronted any other socialist party in the world. We shall have occasion further on to deal with the political and organisational duties which the task of emancipating the whole people from the yoke of autocracy imposed upon us. At this point, we wish to state only that the *role of vanguard fighter can be fulfilled only by a party that is guided by the most advanced theory.* . . .

I assert: (1) that no revolutionary movement can endure without a stable organisation of leaders maintaining continuity; (2) that the broader the popular mass drawn spontaneously into the struggle, which forms the basis of the movement and participates in it, the more urgent the need for such an organisation, and the more solid this organisation must be (for it is much easier for all sorts of demagogues to side-track the more backward sections of the masses); (3) that such an organisation must consist chiefly of people professionally engaged in revolutionary activity; (4) that in an autocratic state, the more we *confine* the membership of such an organisation to people who are professionally engaged in revolutionary activity and who have been professionally trained in the art of combating the political police, the more difficult will it be to unearth the organisation; and (5) the *greater* will be the number of people from the working class and from the other social classes who will be able to join the movement and perform active work in it. . . .

Social-Democracy leads the struggle of the working class, not only for better terms for the sale of labour-power, but for the abolition of the social system that compels the propertyless to sell themselves to the rich. Social-Democracy represents the working class, not in its relation to a given group of employers alone, but in its relation to all classes of modern society and to the state as an organised political force. Hence, it follows that not only must Social-Democrats not confine themselves exclusively to the economic struggle. . . . We must take up actively the political education of the working class and the development of its political consciousness.

Source: Vladimir Lenin, *What Is to Be Done?* in *Collected Works of V. I. Lenin,* vol. 5 (Moscow: 1964), pp. 369–70, 373, 375.

Questions for Analysis

1. What were the key features of Lenin's thought?

2. Here Lenin more or less set down the rules for the revolutionary vanguard. What historical experiences and political theories shaped his thinking? In what ways was the Russian experience unique?

Over the course of 1905 general protest grew. Merchants closed their stores, factory owners shut down their plants, lawyers refused to plead cases in court. The autocracy lost control of entire rural towns and regions as local authorities were ejected and often killed by enraged peasants. Forced to yield, Tsar Nicholas II issued the October Manifesto, pledging guarantees of individual liberties, a moderately liberal franchise for the election of a Duma, and genuine legislative veto powers for the Duma. Although the 1905 revolution brought the tsarist system perilously close to collapse, it failed to convince the tsar that fundamental political change was necessary. Between 1905 and 1907 Nicholas revoked most of the promises made in the October Manifesto. Above all, he deprived the Duma of its principal powers and decreed that it be elected indirectly on a class basis, which ensured a legislative body of obedient followers.

Nonetheless, the revolt of 1905 persuaded the tsar's more perceptive advisers that reform was urgent. The agrarian programs sponsored by the government's leading minister, Peter Stolypin, were especially significant. Between 1906 and 1911 the Stolypin reforms provided for the sale of 5 million acres of royal land to peasants, granted permission to peasants to withdraw from village cooperatives and form independent farms, and canceled peasant property debts. Further decrees legalized labor unions, reduced the working day (to ten hours in most cases), and established sickness and accident insurance. Liberals could reasonably hope that Russia was on the way to becoming a progressive nation on the Western model, yet the tsar remained stubbornly autocratic. Russian agriculture remained suspended between an emerging capitalist system and the traditional peasant commune; Russian industry, though powerful enough to allow Russia to maintain its status as a world power, had hardly created a modern, industrial society capable of withstanding the enormous strains that Russia would face during the First World War.

Nationalism and Imperial Politics: The Balkans

In southeastern Europe in the last decades of the nineteenth century, nationalism continued to divide the disintegrating Ottoman Empire. Russia intervened on behalf of uprisings in Bosnia, Herzegovina, and Bulgaria in 1875–76, and in the ensuing Russo-Turkish War (1877–78), won a smashing victory. The Ottoman sultan surrendered nearly all of his European territory, except for a remnant around Constantinople. In 1878 a congress of great powers in Berlin divided the spoils: Bessarabia went to Russia, Thessaly to Greece, and Bosnia and Herzegovina fell under the control of the Austrian Empire. Montenegro, Serbia, and Romania became independent states, launching the modern era of Balkan nationalism. This trend continued in 1908, when the Bulgars succeeded in wresting independence for Bulgaria from the Ottomans—a move that drove the Austrians to annex Bosnia and Herzegovina outright. The power vacuum in the Orient significantly strained Europe's imperial balance of power.

A nationalist movement also emerged in the Ottoman Empire itself. Educated Turks had grown impatient with the sultan's weakness, and some began to call for national rejuvenation through the introduction of Western science and democratic reforms. These reformers called themselves "Young Turks," and in 1908 they successfully forced the sultan to establish a constitutional government. In the fol-

lowing year they deposed Sultan Abdul Hamid II (r. 1876–1909) and placed his brother, Mohammed V (r. 1909–18), on the throne. The powers of government were entrusted to a grand vizier and ministers responsible to an elected parliament. Non-Turkish inhabitants of the empire were not given the vote, however; and the Young Turks launched a vigorous effort to "Ottomanize" all their imperial subjects, trying to bring both Christian and Muslim communities under centralized, Turkish, control. That effort, intended to compensate for the loss of territories in Europe, undercut the popularity of the new reformist regime.

THE SCIENCE AND SOUL OF THE MODERN AGE

Nineteenth-century liberals believed in individualism, progress, and science. Not only did science deliver technological and material rewards but it also confirmed liberals' faith in the power of human reason to uncover and command the laws of nature. Toward the end of the century, however, scientific developments defied these expectations. Darwin's theory of evolution, psychology, and social science all introduced visions of humanity that were sharply at odds with conventional wisdom. At the same time, artists and intellectuals mounted their own revolt against nineteenth-century conventions. Morals, manners, institutions, traditions: all established values and assumptions were under question, as a generation of self-consciously avant-garde artists called for a radical break with the past. These upheavals in the world of ideas unsettled older conceptions of individuality, culture, and consciousness. The modern individual no longer seemed the free and rational agent of Enlightenment thought, but rather the product of irrational inner drives and uncontrollable external circumstances.

Darwin's Revolutionary Theory

If Marx changed conceptions of society, Charles Darwin did him one better, perhaps, for his theory of organic evolution by natural selection transformed conceptions of nature itself. As both a scientific explanation and an imaginative metaphor for political and social change, Darwin's theory of evolution introduced an unsettling new picture of human biology, behavior, and society.

Theories of evolution did not originate with Darwin, but none of the earlier theories had gained widespread scientific or popular currency. Geologists in the nineteenth

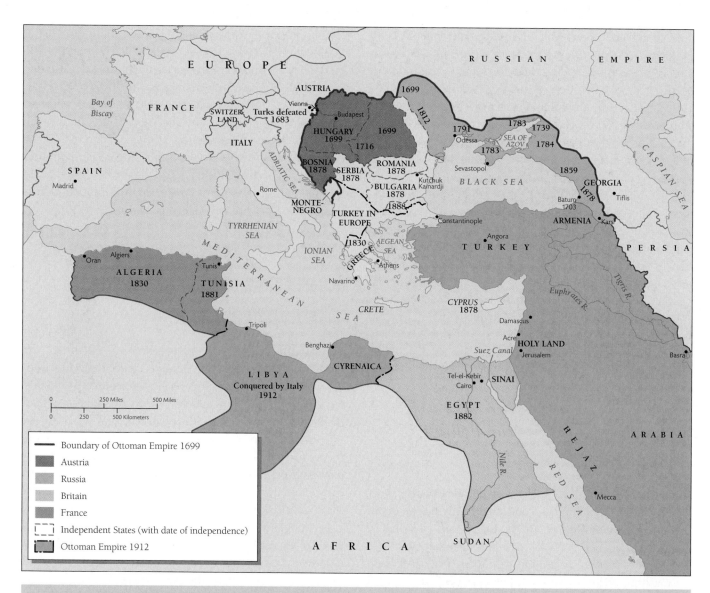

THE DECLINE OF THE OTTOMAN EMPIRE, 1699–1912. ▪ *What were the farthest points that the Ottoman Empire reached into Europe and Africa?* ▪ *How do you explain the slow decline of Ottoman power in relationship to Europe and the emerging global economy?* ▪ *The decline of Ottoman power had enormous significance for relations among European nations themselves. Why?*

century had challenged the biblical account of creation with evidence that the world was formed by natural processes over millions of years, but no one had found a satisfactory explanation for the existence of different species. One important attempt at an answer was proposed in the early nineteenth century by the French biologist Jean Lamarck, who argued that behavioral changes could alter an animal's physical characteristics within a single generation and that these new traits would be passed on to offspring. Over time, Lamarck suggested, the inheritance of acquired characteristics produced new species of animals.

A more convincing hypothesis of organic evolution appeared in 1859, however, with the publication of *On*

the Origin of Species by British naturalist Charles Darwin. Darwin traveled for five years as a naturalist on the HMS *Beagle*, a ship that had been chartered for scientific exploration on a trip around the world. He observed the diversity of species in different lands and wondered about their origins. From a familiarity with pigeon breeding, Darwin knew that particular traits could be selected through controlled breeding. Was a similar process of selection at work in nature?

His answer was yes. He theorized that variations within a population (such as longer beaks or protective coloring) made certain individual organisms better equipped for survival, increasing their chances of reproducing and passing their advantageous traits to the next generation. His theory drew on the work of Thomas Malthus, a political economist who argued that human populations grow faster than the available food supply, leading to a fatal competition for scarce resources. In Darwin's explanation, this Malthusian competition was a general rule of nature, where the strong survived and the weak perished. Competition with other individuals and struggle with the environment produced a "natural selection" of some traits over others, leading to a gradual evolution of different species over time. Eventually, Darwin applied this theory of evolution not only to plant and animal species but also to humans. In his view, the human race had evolved from an apelike ancestor, long since extinct but probably a common precursor of the existing anthropoid apes and humans.

DARWINIAN THEORY AND RELIGION

The implications of Darwin's writings went far beyond the domain of the evolutionary sciences. Most notably, they challenged the basis of deeply held religious beliefs, sparking a public discussion on the existence and knowability of God. Although popular critics denounced Darwin for contradicting literal interpretations of the Bible, those contradictions were not what made religious middle-class readers uncomfortable. The work of prominent theologians such as David Friedrich Strauss had already helped Christians adapt their faith to biblical inaccuracies and inconsistencies. They did not need to abandon either Christianity or faith simply because Darwin showed (or argued) that the world and its life forms had developed over millions of years rather than six days. What religious readers in the nineteenth century found difficult to accept was Darwin's challenge to their belief in a benevolent God and a morally guided universe. By Darwin's account, the world was governed not by order, harmony, and divine will, but by random chance and constant, undirected struggle. Moreover, the Darwinian worldview seemed to redefine notions of good and bad only in terms of an ability to survive, thus robbing humanity of critical moral certainties. Darwin himself was able to reconcile his theory with a belief in God, but others latched onto his work in order to fiercely attack Christian orthodoxy. One such figure was the philosopher Thomas Henry Huxley, who earned himself the nickname "Darwin's bulldog" by inveighing against Christians who were appalled by the implications of Darwinian theory. Opposed to all forms of dogma, Huxley argued that the thinking person should simply follow reason "as far as it can take you" and recognize that the ultimate character of the universe lay beyond his or her grasp.

Social Darwinism

The theory of natural selection also influenced the social sciences, which were just developing at the end of the nineteenth century. New disciplines such as sociology, psychology, anthropology, and economics aimed to apply scientific methods to the analysis of society and introduced new ways of quantifying, measuring, and interpreting human experience. Under the authoritative banner of "science," these disciplines exerted a powerful influence on society, oftentimes to improve the health and well-being of European men and women. But, as we will see with the impact of Social Darwinism, the social sciences could also provide justification for forms of economic, imperial, and racial discrimination.

The so-called Social Darwinists, whose most famous proponent was the English philosopher Herbert Spencer (1820–1903), adapted Darwinian thought in a way that would have shocked Darwin himself, by applying his concept of individual competition and survival to relationships among classes, races, and nations. Spencer, who coined the phrase *survival of the fittest*, used evolutionary theory to expound the virtues of free competition and attack state welfare programs. As a champion of individualism, Spencer condemned all forms of collectivism as primitive and counterproductive, relics of an earlier stage of social evolution. Government attempts to relieve economic and social hardships—or to place constraints on big business—were, in Spencer's view, hindrances to the vigorous advancement of civilization, which could occur only through individual adaptation and competition. Particularly in America, such claims earned Spencer high praise from some wealthy industrialists, who were no doubt glad to be counted among the fittest.

Unlike the science of biological evolution, a popularized Social Darwinism was easy to comprehend, and its concepts (centering on a struggle for survival) were soon integrated into the political vocabulary of the day. Proponents of laissez-faire capitalism and opponents of socialism used Darwinist rhetoric to justify marketplace competition and the "natural order" of rich and poor. Nationalists embraced Social Darwinism to rationalize imperialist expansion and warfare. Spencer's doctrine also became closely tied to theories of racial hierarchy and white superiority, which claimed that the white race had reached the height of evolutionary development and had thus earned the right to dominate and rule other races (see Chapter 25). Ironically, some progressive middle-class reformers relied on a similar set of racial assumptions: their campaigns to improve the health and welfare of society played to fears that Europe, though dominant, could move down the evolutionary ladder. Despite its unsettling potential, Darwinism was used to advance a range of political objectives and to shore up an array of ingrained prejudices.

Darwin and His Readers

> *Charles Darwin's* On the Origin of Species *(1859) and his theory of natural selection transformed Western knowledge of natural history. The impact of Darwin's work, however, extended well beyond scientific circles. It assumed a cultural importance that exceeded even Darwin's scholarly contribution. How Darwinism was popularized is a complex question, for writers and readers could mold Darwin's ideas to fit a variety of political and cultural purposes. The first excerpt comes from the conclusion to* On the Origin of Species *itself, and it sets out the different laws that Darwin thought governed the natural world. The second excerpt comes from the autobiography of Nicholas Osterroth (1875–1933), a clay miner from western Germany. Osterroth was ambitious and self-educated. The passage recounts his reaction to hearing about Darwin and conveys his enthusiasm for late-nineteenth-century science.*

On the Origin of Species

The natural system is a genealogical arrangement, in which we have to discover the lines of descent by the most permanent characters, however slight their vital importance may be.

The framework of bones being the same in the hand of a man, wing of a bat, fin of the porpoise, and leg of the horse,—the same number of vertebrae forming the neck of the giraffe and of the elephant,—and innumerable other such facts, at once explain themselves on the theory of descent with slow and slight successive modifications. The similarity of pattern in the wing and leg of a bat, though used for such different purposes,—in the jaws and legs of a crab,—in the petals, stamens, and pistils of a flower, is likewise intelligible on the view of the gradual modification of parts or organs, which were alike in the early progenitor of each class. . . .

It is interesting to contemplate an entangled bank, clothed with many plants of many kinds, with birds singing on the bushes, with various insects flitting about, and with worms crawling through the damp earth, and to reflect that these elaborately constructed forms, so different from each other, and dependent on each other in so complex a manner, have all been produced by laws acting around us. These laws, taken in the largest sense, being Growth with Reproduction; Inheritance which is almost implied by reproduction; Variability from the indirect and direct action of the external conditions of life, and from use and disuse; a Ratio of Increase so high as to lead to a Struggle for Life, and as a consequence to Natural Selection, entailing Divergence of Character and the Extinction of less-improved forms. Thus, from the war of nature, from famine and death, the most exalted object which we are capable of conceiving, namely, the production of the higher animals, directly follows. There is grandeur in this view of life, with its several powers, having been originally breathed into a few forms or into one; and that, whilst this planet has gone cycling on according to the fixed law of gravity, from so simple a beginning endless forms most beautiful and most wonderful have been, and are being, evolved.

Source: Charles Darwin, *On the Origin of Species* (Harmondsworth: 1968), pp. 450–51, 458–60.

Challenges to Rationality: Pavlov, Freud, and Nietzsche

Although the new social scientists self-consciously relied on the use of rational, scientific principles, their findings often stressed the opposite: the irrational, even animalistic nature of human experience. Darwin had already called into question the notion that humanity was fundamentally superior to the rest of the animal kingdom, and similarly discomfitting conclusions came from the new field of psychology. The Russian physician Ivan Pavlov (1849–1936) asserted that animal behavior could be understood as a series of trained responses to physical stimuli. Pavlov's famous experiment showed that if dogs were fed after they heard the ringing of a bell, the animals would eventually salivate at the sound of

Nicholas Osterroth: A Miner's Reaction

The book was called *Moses or Darwin?* . . . Written in a very popular style, it compared the Mosaic story of creation with the natural evolutionary history, illuminated the contradictions of the biblical story, and gave a concise description of the evolution of organic and inorganic nature, interwoven with plenty of striking proofs.

What particularly impressed me was a fact that now became clear to me: that evolutionary natural history was monopolized by the institutions of higher learning; that Newton, Laplace, Kant, Darwin, and Haeckel brought enlightenment only to the students of the upper social classes; and that for the common people in the grammar school the old Moses with his six-day creation of the world still was the authoritative worldview. For the upper classes there was evolution, for us creation; for them productive liberating knowledge, for us rigid faith; bread for those favored by fate, stones for those who hungered for truth!

Why do the people need science? Why do they need a so-called *Weltanschauung* [worldview]? The people must keep Moses, must keep religion; religion is the poor man's philosophy. Where would we

end up if every miner and every farmhand had the opportunity to stick his nose into astronomy, geology, biology, and anatomy? Does it serve any purpose for the divine world order of the possessing and privileged classes to tell the worker that the Ptolemaic heavens have long since collapsed; that out there in the universe there is an eternal process of creation and destruction; that in the universe at large, as on our tiny earth, everything is in the grip of eternal evolution; that this evolution takes place according to inalterable natural laws that defy even the omnipotence of the old Mosaic Jehovah? . . . Why tell the dumb people that Copernicus and his followers have overturned the old Mosaic creator, and that Darwin and modern science have dug the very ground out from under his feet of clay?

That would be suicide! Yes, the old religion is so convenient for the divine world order of the ruling class! As long as the worker hopes faithfully for the beyond, he won't think of plucking the blooming roses in this world. . . .

The possessing classes of all civilized nations need servants to make possible their godlike existence. So they cannot

allow the servant to eat from the tree of knowledge.

Source: Alfred Kelly, ed., *The German Worker: Working-Class Autobiographies from the Age of Industrialization* (Berkeley, CA: 1987), pp. 185–86.

Questions for Analysis

1. Was the theory of evolution revolutionary? If so, how? Would it be fair to say that Darwin did for the nineteenth century what Newton did for the seventeenth and eighteenth centuries?

2. Why did people think the natural world was governed by laws? Was this a religious belief or a scientific fact?

3. What aspects of Darwin appealed to Osterroth and why?

---

the bell alone, exactly as if they had smelled and seen food. Moreover, Pavlov insisted that such conditioning constituted a significant part of human behavior as well. Known as "behaviorism," this type of physiological psychology avoided vague concepts such as mind and consciousness, concentrating instead on the reaction of muscles, nerves, glands, and visceral organs. Rather than being governed by reason, human activity was recast by behaviorists as a bundle of physiological responses to stimuli in the environment.

Like behaviorism, a second major school of psychology also suggested that human behavior was largely motivated by unconscious and irrational forces. Founded by the Austrian physician Sigmund Freud (1856–1939), the discipline of psychoanalysis posited a new, dynamic, and unsettling theory of the mind, in which a variety of unconscious drives and desires conflict with a rational and moral conscience. Developed over many years of treating patients with nervous ailments, Freud's model of the psyche contained three elements: (1) the id, or undisciplined desires for pleasure, sexual gratification, aggression, and so on; (2) the superego, or conscience, which registers the prohibitions of morality and culture; and (3) the ego, the arena in which the conflict between id and superego works itself out. Freud believed that most cases of mental disorder result from an irreconcilable tension between natural drives and the restraints placed on individuals. Freud believed that by studying such disorders, as well as dreams and slips of the tongue, scientists could glimpse the submerged areas of consciousness and thus understand seemingly irrational behavior. Freud's search for an all-encompassing theory of the mind was deeply grounded in the tenets of nineteenth-century science. By stressing the irrational, however, Freud's theories fed a growing anxiety about the value and limits of human reason. Likewise, they brought to the fore a powerful critique of the constraints imposed by the moral and social codes of Western civilization.

No one provided a more sweeping or more influential assault on Western values of rationality than the German philosopher Friedrich Nietzsche (*NEE-chuh*, 1844–1900). Like Freud, Nietzsche had observed a middle-class culture that he believed to be dominated by illusions and self-deceptions, and he sought to unmask them. He argued that bourgeois faith in such concepts as science, progress, democracy, and religion represented a futile, and reprehensible, search for security and truth. He famously ridiculed Judeo-Christian morality for instilling a repressive conformity that drained civilization of its vitality. Nietzsche's philosophy resounded with themes of personal liberation, especially freedom from the stranglehold of history and tradition. Indeed, Nietzsche's ideal individual, or "superman," was one who abandoned the burdens of cultural conformity and created an independent set of values based on artistic vision and strength of character. Only through individual struggle against the chaotic universe did Nietzsche foresee salvation for Western civilization.

Religion and Its Critics

Faced with these various scientific and philosophical challenges, the institutions responsible for the maintenance of traditional faith found themselves on the defensive. The Roman Catholic Church responded to the encroachments of secular society by appealing to its dogma and venerated traditions. In 1864 Pope Pius IX issued a Syllabus of Errors, condemning what he regarded as the principal religious and philosophical errors of the time. Among them were material-

ism, free thought, and indifferentism (the idea that one religion is as good as another). The pope also convoked the first Church council since the Catholic Reformation, which in 1871 pronounced the dogma of papal infallibility. This meant that in his capacity "as pastor and doctor of all Christians," the pope was infallible in regard to all matters of faith and morals. Though generally accepted by pious Catholics, the claim of papal infallibility provoked a storm of protest and was denounced by the governments of several Catholic countries, including France, Spain, and Italy. The death of Pius IX in 1878 and the accession of Pope Leo XIII, however, brought a more accommodating climate to the Church. The new pope acknowledged that there was good as well as evil in modern civilization. He added a scientific staff to the Vatican and opened archives and observatories, but made no further concessions to liberalism in the political sphere.

Protestants were also compelled to respond to a modernizing world. Since they were taught to understand God with the aid of little more than the Bible and a willing conscience, Protestants, unlike Catholics, had little in the way of doctrine to help them defend their faith. Some fundamentalists chose to ignore the implications of scientific and philosophical inquiry altogether and continued to believe in the literal truth of the Bible. Others were willing to agree with the school of American philosophers known as pragmatists (principally Charles S. Peirce and William James), who taught that "truth" was whatever produced useful, practical results; by their logic, if belief in God provided mental peace

***BLACK LINES* BY WASSILY KANDINSKY, 1913.** Kandinsky broke from the traditional representational approach of nineteenth-century painting with his abstractions and was one of a generation of turn-of-the-century artists who reexamined and experimented with their art forms.

or spiritual satisfaction, then the belief was true. Other Protestants sought solace from religious doubt in founding missions, laboring among the poor, and other good works. Many adherents to this social gospel were also modernists who accepted the ethical teachings of Christianity but discarded beliefs in miracles and original sin.

New Readers and the Popular Press

The effect of various scientific and philosophical challenges on the men and women who lived at the end of the nineteenth century cannot be measured precisely. Millions undoubtedly went about the business of life untroubled by the implications of evolutionary theory, content to believe as they had believed before. Yet the changes we have been discussing eventually had a profound impact. Darwin's theory was not too complicated to be popularized. If educated men and women had neither the time nor inclination to read *On the Origin of Species*, they read magazines and newspapers that summarized (not always correctly) its implications. They encountered some of its central concepts in other places, from political speeches to novels and crime reports.

The diffusion of these new ideas was facilitated by rising literacy rates and by new forms of printed mass culture. Between 1750 and 1870, readership had expanded from the aristocracy to include middle-class circles and, thereafter, to an increasingly literate general population. In 1850 approximately half the population of Europe was literate. In subsequent decades, country after country introduced state-financed elementary and secondary education to provide opportunities for social advancement, to diffuse technical and scientific knowledge, and to inculcate civic and national pride. By 1900, approximately 85 percent of the population in Britain, France, Belgium, the Netherlands, Scandinavia, and Germany could read.

In those countries where literacy rates were highest, commercial publishers such as Alfred Harmsworth in Britain and William Randolph Hearst in the United States hastened to serve the new reading public. New newspapers appealed to the newly literate by means of sensational journalism and spicy, easy-to-read serials. Advertisements drastically lowered the costs of the mass-market newspapers, enabling even workers to purchase one or two newspapers a day. The yellow journalism of the penny presses merged entertainment and sensationalism with the news, aiming to increase circulation and thus secure more lucrative advertising sales. The era of mass readership had arrived, and artists, activists, and—above all—governments would increasingly focus their message on this mass audience.

The First Moderns: Innovations in Art

The widely shared sense in late nineteenth-century Europe that the culture had launched itself headlong into a period of profound and unpredictable changes had its effects in the world of artistic production. Rather than accept the classical forms of artistic expression taught in the academies and subsidized by wealthy patrons, a new generation of artists began to think of themselves as cultural revolutionaries, and they cast a critical eye on the values of European society. In so doing, they pioneered a style known as "modernism" which came to dominate the art world of the twentieth century.

Modernism spanned the entire range of artistic creation—from painting, sculpture, literature, and architecture to theatre, dance, and musical composition. The modernists shared a common conviction that change should be embraced, and that experimental forms of expression were essential to unleash the creativity of the human spirit. Some modernists, such as the Russian painter Wassily Kandinsky, remained interested in purely aesthetic questions: his abstract paintings were shaped by his belief that color and form had emotional resonance for the viewer. Other modernists boldly sought to use their art to change the world, and they saw their work as part of the revolutionary or antiliberal movements of the extreme left or right.

SELF-PORTRAIT, STUDY FOR *ERMITEN* BY EGON SCHIELE, 1912. The Viennese artist Schiele represents another side of early modernism that, instead of moving toward abstraction, sought to portray raw psychological expression.

PORTRAIT OF AMBROISE VOLLARD BY PABLO PICASSO, 1909.
In the early twentieth century, Picasso and George Braque radically transformed painting with their cubist constructions, breaking the depiction of reality into fragmented planes. Vollard, an important art dealer of the period, loses recognizable form as his figure descends. ▪ *Compare this portrait with Schiele's self-portrait. What do these paintings say about the task of the artist?* ▪ *What makes them "modern"?*

THE REVOLT ON CANVAS

The first significant breaks with traditional representational art came with the French impressionists in the 1870s. The impressionists were realists, but they were more interested in the science of perception than they were with questions of accurate reproduction of objects in the world. Their paintings focused on the transitory play of light on surfaces, giving their paintings a shimmering quality that differed sharply from older forms of realism. By developing new techniques without reference to past styles, impressionists such as Claude Monet (*moh-NAY*, 1840–1926) and Pierre-Auguste Renoir (1841–1919), encouraged experimentation among the younger generation of artists. When their works were rejected by the conservative French Academy, the impressionists simply organized their own exhibitions, and their prestige was only enhanced by their outsider status.

Frenchman Paul Cezanne (1839–1906) and the Dutch painter Vincent Van Gogh (1853–1890) picked up where the impressionists left off, insisting on the expressive capacity of paintings in vivid works that refused conventional techniques of perspective and composition. After the turn of the century, painters such as these had avant-garde followers across Europe. In Germany and Scandinavia, expressionists such as Emile Nolde (1867–1956) and Edvard Munch (1863–1944) turned to acid colors and

After You Read This Chapter

Visit StudySpace for quizzes, additional review materials, and multi-media documents. **wwnorton.com/studyspace**

REVIEWING THE OBJECTIVES

▪ The second industrial revolution was made possible by technological innovations that stimulated the production of steel and new energy sources. What were the consequences of this era of rapid growth for the economy and for European society?

▪ Expanded electorates meant that more people were participating in politics, especially among the working classes. What parties and movements emerged to represent European workers and what were their goals?

▪ At the end of the nineteenth century, militant agitation in favor of women's suffrage increased. What obstacles faced women who demanded the vote?

▪ Liberalism and nationalism were changed by the advent of mass politics. How did the expansion of the electorate change political life across Europe?

▪ Technological innovations and scientific ideas about human nature and modern society changed the way that people thought about their place in the world, stimulating artists and writers to new and revolutionary forms of creative expression. What were these scientific ideas and why were they so controversial at the end of the nineteenth century?

violent distortions to illustrate the inner depths of the human mind. Egon Schiele (1890–1918) explored sexuality and the body with graphic imagery. Henri Matisse (1869–1954) and Pablo Picasso (1881–1973) pursued groundbreaking experiments in bohemian Paris, eventually becoming celebrities of the twentieth-century art world by the end of their long careers.

Some modernists—including Picasso—looked to the art of non-Western cultures for inspiration. Others embraced the hard-edged, aggressive, and angular aesthetic of the machine age, at times justifying this faith in modernity with the kind of hypermasculine and violent visual rhetoric that later emerged as a hallmark of fascism. In the twentieth century, the line between political revolution and aesthetic revolution blurred, and artists were quick to take their place on the barricades.

CONCLUSION

Many Europeans who had grown up in the period from 1870 to 1914, but lived through the hardships of the First World War, looked back on the prewar period as a golden age of European civilization. In one sense this retrospective view is apt. After all, the continental powers had successfully avoided major wars, enabling a second phase of industrialization to provide better living standards for the growing populations of mass society. An overall spirit of confidence and purpose fueled Europe's perceived mission to exercise political, economic, and cultural dominion in the far reaches of the world. Yet European politics and culture also registered the presence of powerful—and destabilizing—forces of change. Industrial expansion, relative abundance, and rising literacy produced a political climate of rising expectations. As the age of mass politics arrived, democrats, socialists, and feminists clamored for access to political life, threatening violence, strikes, and revolution. Marxist socialism especially changed radical politics, redefining the terms of debate for the next century. Western science, literature, and the arts explored new perspectives on the individual, undermining some of the cherished beliefs of nineteenth-century liberals. The competition and violence central to Darwin's theory of evolution, the subconscious urges that Freud found in human behavior, and the rebellion against representation in the arts all pointed in new and baffling directions. These experiments, hypotheses, and nagging questions accompanied Europe into the Great War of 1914. They would help shape Europeans' responses to the devastation of that war. After the war, the political changes and cultural unease of the period from 1870 to 1914 would reemerge in the form of mass movements and artistic developments that would define the twentieth century.

PEOPLE, IDEAS, AND EVENTS IN CONTEXT

- Why was the **BRITISH LABOUR PARTY** more moderate in its goals than the **GERMAN SOCIAL DEMOCRATS**?
- What disagreements about political strategy divided **ANARCHISTS** and **SYNDICALISTS** from **MARXISTS** in European labor movements?
- What legal reforms were successfully achieved by **WOMEN'S ASSOCIATIONS** in late-nineteenth-century western European nations?
- What was the **DREYFUS AFFAIR** and how was it related to the spread of popular **ANTI-SEMITISM** and the emergence of **ZIONISM** in European Jewish communities?
- What were the goals of the **BOLSHEVIKS** and the **MENSHEVIKS** in the **RUSSIAN REVOLUTION OF 1905**?
- Who were the **YOUNG TURKS**?
- What was **CHARLES DARWIN'S THEORY OF EVOLUTION** and why did it stimulate so much debate between religious and secular thinkers?
- Why was the **PSYCHOLOGY OF SIGMUND FREUD** so troubling for liberals in Europe?
- What common ideas did the artists and writers who came to be known as **MODERNISTS** share?

CONSEQUENCES

- Did the emergence of mass politics mean that ordinary people in Europe had more control over their lives and their governments?
- Why did the nineteenth century, which had witnessed so much successful economic and technological development, end with so much disagreement about the benefits of these changes?

STORY LINES

- In 1914, the balance of power in Europe collapsed in a total war that mobilized the full resources of modern industrialized nations, their global empires, and their populations.

- The war transformed the relationship between state and society. Governments conscripted an entire generation of young men, encouraged women to work in industry, and took control of the economy to produce goods and material for the military.

- The war provoked the first successful socialist revolution in modern history when the Russian Empire collapsed and the Bolsheviks seized power in October 1917. The Russian Revolution set the stage for the major ideological confrontations of the twentieth century.

CHRONOLOGY

1879	The Dual Alliance (Germany and Austria-Hungary)
1904	The Triple Entente (France, Russia, and Britain)
June 1914	Assassination of Franz Ferdinand in Sarajevo
September 1914	Battle of the Marne
April 1915	Gallipoli campaign begins
May 1915	Italy enters the war against Austria-Hungary
February 1916	Battle of Verdun begins
July 1916	British offensive on the Somme begins
January 1917	Germany begins unrestricted submarine warfare
April 1917	United States enters the war
November 1917	Bolshevik "October" Revolution
March 1918	Treaty of Brest-Litovsk
November 1918	Armistice
June 1919	Treaty of Versailles signed

Before You Read This Chapter

The First
World War

CORE OBJECTIVES

- **EXPLAIN** the origins of the First World War.

- **UNDERSTAND** the circumstances that led to trench warfare on the Western Front, and the consequences of the offensive strategy pursued by all sides.

- **IDENTIFY** the major effects of the war on civilian life.

- **EXPLAIN** the war's effects on territories beyond Europe's borders—in the Middle East, in Africa, and in Asia.

- **UNDERSTAND** the origins and goals of the Bolshevik movement in Russia and the circumstances that allowed them to seize power in 1917.

- **IDENTIFY** the people responsible for the final terms of the Versailles Peace Treaty, and understand its goals.

T he battle of the Somme began on June 24, 1916, with a fearsome British artillery barrage against German trenches along a twenty-five-mile front. Hour after hour, day and night, the British guns swept across the barbed wire and fortifications that faced their own lines, firing 1.5 million rounds over seven days. Mixing gas with explosive rounds, the gunners pulverized the landscape and poisoned the atmosphere. Deep in underground bunkers on the other side, the German defenders huddled in their masks. When the big guns went silent, tens of thousands of British soldiers rose up out of their trenches, each bearing sixty pounds of equipment, and made their way into the cratered No Man's Land that separated the two armies. They had been told that wire-cutting explosives would destroy the labyrinth of barbed wire between the trenches during the barrage, leaving them free to charge across and occupy the front trench before the stunned Germans could recover. To their horror, they found the barbed wire intact. Instead of taking the German trench, they found themselves caught in the open when the German machine-gunners manned the defensive parapets. The result proved all too eloquently the efficiency of the First World

573

War's mechanized methods of killing. Twenty-one thousand British soldiers were killed on the first day of the battle of the Somme. A further thirty thousand were wounded. Because some British units allowed volunteers to serve with their friends—the "Pals Battalions"—there were neighborhoods and villages in Britain in which every married woman became a widow in the space of a few minutes. The British commanders pressed the offensive for nearly five more months, and the combined casualties climbed over a million. The German line never broke.

This contest between artillery and machine gun was a war that was possible only in an industrialized world. Before beginning the assault, the British had stockpiled 2.9 million artillery shells—Napoleon had only 20,000 at Waterloo. Although European armies marched off to war in 1914 with a confidence and ambition bred by their imperial conquests, they soon confronted the ugly face of industrial warfare and the grim capacities of the modern world. In a catastrophic combination of old mentalities and new technologies, the war left nine million dead soldiers in its wake.

Soldiers were not the only casualties. Four years of fighting destroyed many of the institutions and assumptions of the previous century, from monarchies and empires to European economic dominance. It disillusioned many, even the citizens of the victorious nations. As the British writer Virginia Woolf put it, "It was a shock—to see the faces of our rulers in the light of shell-fire." The war led European states to take over their national economies, as they set quotas for production and consumption and took responsibility for sustaining the civilian population during the crisis. By toppling the Prussian and Austrian monarchies, the war banished older forms of authoritarianism, and by provoking the Russian Revolution of 1917, the war ushered in new ones that bore the distinctive mark of the twentieth century. Finally, the war proved nearly impossible to settle; antagonisms bred in battle only intensified in the war's aftermath and would eventually lead to the Second World War. Postwar Europe faced more problems than peace could manage.

THE JULY CRISIS

In the decades before 1914, Europe had built a seemingly stable peace around two systems of alliance: the Triple Entente (later the Allied Powers) of Britain, France, and Russia faced the Triple Alliance (later the Central Powers) of Germany, Austria-Hungary, and Italy. Within this balance of power, the nations of Europe challenged one another for economic, military, and imperial advantage. The scramble for colonies abroad accompanied a fierce arms race at home, where military leaders on all sides assumed that superior technology and larger armies would result in a quick victory in a European war. Nobody expected that the Balkan crisis of July 1914 would touch off a general war that would engulf all of Europe.

The Balkan peninsula was a satellite of the Ottoman Empire. As Ottoman power became weaker throughout the nineteenth century, Austria-Hungary and Russia competed to replace the Ottomans as the dominant force in the region. Meanwhile, Slavic nationalist movements in Serbia and Bulgaria pushed for independence and expansion in the same region. Russia, with its own Slavic traditions, encouraged these nationalist movements while Austria-Hungary was deeply threatened by the challenge that Slavic nationalists posed to its own multi-ethnic empire.

In 1912 and 1913 two wars pitted the Ottoman Empire against the independent Balkan states of Serbia, Greece, Bulgaria, and Montenegro. During these crises, the Great Powers (Britain, France, Germany, Austria, and Russia) preserved a general peace by remaining neutral. If any of the Great Powers intervened, the network of defensive alliances that tied Russia to France and Great Britain, and Austria-Hungary to Germany, would lead directly to a wider war in Europe.

This is precisely what happened in the summer of 1914. The spark came in the Austrian province of Bosnia, a multi-ethnic region of Serbs, Croats, and Bosnian Muslims. Bosnian Serbs longed to secede from Austria and join the independent state of Serbia, and on June 28, 1914, a group of Bosnian Serbs assassinated the heir to the Austro-Hungarian throne, Franz Ferdinand (1889–1914) as he paraded through the Bosnian capital, Sarajevo.

FRANZ FERDINAND AND HIS WIFE, SOPHIE. The Austrian archduke and archduchess, in Sarajevo on June 28, 1914, approaching their car before they were assassinated. ▪ *What made their deaths the spark that unleashed a general war in Europe?*

EUROPEAN ALLIANCES ON THE EVE OF THE FIRST WORLD WAR. ▪ *What major countries were part of the Triple Alliance?* ▪ *Of the Triple Entente?* ▪ *Why would Germany have declared war on France so quickly once Russia began to mobilize?* ▪ *Why were the Balkan countries such a volatile region?*

The shocked Austrians treated the assassination as an attack by the Serbian government. They sent an ultimatum to Serbia, demanding that they allow the Austrian government to prosecute Serbian officials whom they believed to be responsible for the assassination. The demands were designed to be rejected: the Austrians wanted war to crush Serbia. After agreeing to all but the most important demands, Serbia mobilized its army, and Austria responded with its own mobilization order on July 28, 1914. Shaken from their summer distractions, Europeans suddenly realized that their treaty system threatened to involve Austria and Germany in a war against Serbia, Russia, and by extension, Russia's ally, France.

Diplomats tried and failed to prevent the outbreak of wider war. When Russia announced a "partial mobilization" to defend Serbia against Austria, the German ministers telegraphed the French to find out if they intended to honor France's defensive treaty with Russia. The French responded that France would "act in accordance with her interests"—meaning that they would immediately mobilize against Germany. Facing the dual threat from both sides that they had long feared, Germany mobilized on August 1 and declared war on Russia—and two days later, on France. The next day, the German army invaded Belgium on its way to take Paris.

The invasion of neutral Belgium gave Britain the reason it needed to honor its treaty with France and enter the war against Germany. Other nations were quickly drawn into the struggle. On August 7 the Montenegrins joined the Serbs against Austria. Two weeks later the Japanese declared war on Germany, mainly to attack German possessions in the Far East. On August 1 Turkey allied with Germany, and in October began the bombardment of Russian ports on the Black Sea. Italy had been allied with Germany and Austria before the war, but at the outbreak of hostilities, the Italians declared neutrality, insisting that since Germany had invaded neutral Belgium, they owed Germany no protection.

The diplomatic maneuvers during the five weeks that followed the assassination at Sarajevo have been called a "tragedy of miscalculation." Austria's determination to punish Serbia, Germany's unwillingness to restrain their Austrian allies, and Russia's desire to use Serbia as an excuse to extend their influence in the Balkans all played a part in making the war more likely. Diplomats were further constrained by the strategic thinking and rigid timetables set by military leaders, and all sides clearly felt that it was important to make a show of force during the period of negotiation that preceded the outbreak of war. It is clear, however, that powerful German officials were arguing that war was inevitable. They insisted that Germany should fight before Russia recovered from their 1905 loss to Japan and before the French army could benefit from its new three-year conscription law, which would put more men in uniform. This sense of urgency characterized the strategies of all combatant countries. The lure of a bold, successful strike against one's enemies, and the fear that too much was at stake to risk losing the advantage, created a rolling tide of military mobilization that carried Europe into battle.

THE MARNE AND ITS CONSEQUENCES

Declarations of war were met with a mix of public fanfare and private concern. Nationalists hoped the war would bring glory and spiritual renewal, while others recognized that a general war put decades of prosperity at risk. Bankers

Competing Viewpoints

Toward the First World War: Diplomacy in the Summer of 1914

The assassination of Franz Ferdinand in Sarajevo on June 28, 1914, set off an increasingly desperate round of diplomatic negotiations. As the following exchanges show, diplomats and political leaders on both sides swung from trying to provoke war to attempting to avert or, at least, contain it. A week after his nephew, the heir to the throne, was shot, Franz Joseph set out his interpretation of the long-standing conflict with Serbia and its larger implications—reprinted here.

The second selection comes from an account of a meeting of the Council of Ministers of the Austro-Hungarian Empire on July 7, 1914. The ministers disagreed sharply about diplomatic strategies and about how crucial decisions should be made.

The British foreign secretary Sir Edward Grey, for one, was shocked by Austria's demands, especially its insistence that Austrian officials would participate in Serbian judicial proceedings. The Serbian government's response was more conciliatory than most diplomats expected, but diplomatic efforts to avert war still failed. The Austrians' ultimatum to Serbia included the following demands given in the final extract here.

Emperor Franz Joseph of Austria-Hungary to Kaiser William II of Germany, July 5, 1914

The plot against my poor nephew was the direct result of an agitation carried on by the Russian and Serb Pan-Slavs, an agitation whose sole object is the weakening of the Triple Alliance and the destruction of my realm.

So far, all investigations have shown that the Sarajevo murder was not perpetrated by one individual, but grew out of a well-organized conspiracy, the threads of which can be traced to Belgrade. Even though it will probably be impossible to prove the complicity of the Serb government, there can be no doubt that its policy, aiming as it does at the unification of all Southern Slavs under the Serb banner, encourages such crimes, and that the continuation of such conditions constitutes a permanent threat to my dynasty and my lands....

This will only be possible if Serbia, which is at present the pivot of Pan-Slav policies, is put out of action as a factor of political power in the Balkans.

You too are [surely] convinced after the recent frightful occurrence in Bosnia that it is no longer possible to contemplate a reconciliation of the antagonism between us and Serbia and that the [efforts] of all European monarchs to pursue policies that preserve the peace will be threatened if the nest of criminal activity in Belgrade remains unpunished.

Austro-Hungarian Disagreements over Strategy

Count Leopold Berchtold, foreign minister of Austria-Hungary] ... both Emperor Wilhelm and [Chancellor] Bethmann Hollweg had assured us emphatically of Germany's unconditional support in the event of military complications with Serbia.... It was clear to him that a military conflict with Serbia might bring about war with Russia....

[Count Istvan Tisza, prime minister of Hungary] ... We should decide what our demands on Serbia will be [but] should only present an ultimatum if Serbia rejected them. These demands must be hard but not so that they cannot be complied with. If Serbia accepted them, we could register a noteworthy diplomatic success and our prestige in the Balkans would be enhanced. If Serbia rejected our demands, then he too would favor military action. But he would already now go on record that we could aim at the downsizing but not the complete annihilation of Serbia because, first, this would provoke Russia to fight to the death and, second, he—as Hungarian premier—could never consent to the monarchy's annexation of a part of Serbia. Whether or not we ought to go to war with Serbia was not a matter for Germany to decide....

[Count Berchtold] remarked that the history of the past years showed that diplomatic successes against Serbia might enhance the prestige of the monarchy temporarily, but that in reality the tension in our relations with Serbia had only increased.

[Count Karl Stürgkh, prime minister of Austria] . . . agreed with the Royal Hungarian Prime Minister that we and not the German government had to determine whether a war was necessary or not . . . [but] Count Tisza should take into account that in pursuing a hesitant and weak policy, we run the risk of not being so sure of Germany's unconditional support. . . .

[Leo von Bilinsky, Austro-Hungarian finance minister] . . . The Serb understands only force, a diplomatic success would make no impression at all in Bosnia and would be harmful rather than beneficial. . . .

Austro-Hungary's Ultimatum to Serbia

The Royal Serb Government will publish the following declaration on the first page of its official *journal* of 26/13 July:

"The Royal Serb Government condemns the propaganda directed against Austria-Hungary, and regrets sincerely the horrible consequences of these criminal ambitions.

"The Royal Serb Government regrets that Serb officers and officials have taken part in the propaganda above-mentioned and thereby imperiled friendly and neighbourly relations.

"The Royal Government . . . considers it a duty to warn officers, officials, and indeed all the inhabitants of the kingdom [of Serbia], that it will in future use great severity against such persons who may be guilty of similar doings.

The Royal Serb Government will moreover pledge itself to the following.

1. to suppress every publication likely to inspire hatred and contempt against the Monarchy;

2. to begin immediately dissolving the society called *Narodna Odbrana*,* to seize all its means of propaganda and to act in the same way against all the societies and associations in Serbia, which are busy with the propaganda against Austria-Hungary;

3. to eliminate without delay from public instruction everything that serves or might serve the propaganda against Austria-Hungary, both where teachers or books are concerned;

4. to remove from military service and from the administration all officers and officials who are guilty of having taken part in the propaganda against Austria-Hungary, whose names and proof of whose guilt the I. and R. Government [Imperial and Royal, that is, the Austro-Hungarian Empire] will communicate to the Royal Government;

5. to consent to the cooperation of I. and R. officials in Serbia in suppressing the subversive movement directed against the territorial integrity of the Monarchy;

6. to open a judicial inquest [*enquête judiciaire*] against all those who took part in the plot of 28 June, if they are to be found on Serbian territory; the I. and R. Government will delegate officials who will take an active part in these and associated inquiries;

The I. and R. Government expects the answer of the Royal government to reach it not later than Saturday, the 25th, at six in the afternoon. . . .

*Narodna Odbrana, or National Defense, was pro-Serbian and anti-Austrian but nonviolent. The Society of the Black Hand, to which Franz Ferdinand's assassin belonged, considered Narodna Odbrana too moderate.

Source (for all three excerpts): Ralph Menning, *The Art of the Possible: Documents on Great Power Diplomacy, 1814–1914* (New York: 1996), pp. 400, 402–3, and 414–15.

Questions for Analysis

1. Emperor Franz Joseph's letter to Kaiser Wilhelm II tells of the Austrian investigation into the assassination of Archduke Franz Ferdinand. What did Franz seek from his German ally? What did the emperors understand by the phrase, "if Serbia . . . is put out of action as a factor of political power in the Balkans"? Why might the Germans support a war against Serb-sponsored terrorism?

2. Could the Serbians have accepted the Austrian ultimatum without total loss of face and sacrifice of their independence? British and Russian foreign ministers were shocked by the demands on Serbia. Others thought the Austrians were justified, and that Britain would act similarly if threatened by terrorism. If, as Leo von Bilinsky said, "The Serb understands only force," why didn't Austria declare war without an ultimatum?

and financiers were among those most opposed to war, correctly predicting that the conflict would create financial crisis. Many young men, however, enlisted with excitement, swelling Europe's conscript armies with volunteers (Britain did not introduce conscription until 1916). Like the military commanders, these volunteers thought they would be finished by Christmas—the general consensus was that modern weaponry made protracted war impossible.

The German high command had long foreseen the danger of a two-front war against France and Russia. Their offensive strategy, developed earlier by General Alfred von Schlieffen, was to attack France first, in the hopes that a quick victory would allow them to turn and face the slower Russian army in turn. Schlieffen's plan almost worked—the German army swept through Belgium and northern France and nearly attained its goal, the city of Paris. Early attempts by the French to counterattack failed, but at the crucial moment the French commander, Jules Joffre, drew the German attackers into a trap on the very outskirts of Paris. The French counterattack on the Marne river in September stopped the German advance for good. The Germans retreated to the Aisne river, both sides dug deeper in their trenches, and what remained of the Schlieffen plan was dead.

The Marne was the most strategically important battle of the entire war, and it dashed the hopes of those who hoped for a rapid end to the fighting. The war of movement was stopped in its tracks, and the western front moved little between 1914 and 1918. Politicians and military commanders sought for ways to break the stalemate in the trenches by seeking new allies, new theaters of conflict, and new weapons. They also remained committed to offensive tactics, and in a combination of stubbornness, callousness, and desperation, military leaders continued to order their troops to go "over the top."

Allied sucess at the Marne resulted in part from an unexpectedly strong Russian assault in eastern Prussia, which pulled some German units away from the attack on the west. But Russia's initial gains were obliterated at the battle of Tannenberg, August 26–30. Plagued with an array of problems, the Russian army was tired and half-starved; the Germans devastated it, taking nearly one hundred thousand prisoners and virtually destroying the Russian Second Army. The Russian general killed himself on the battlefield. Two weeks later, the Germans won another decisive victory at the battle of the Masurian Lakes, forcing the Russians to retreat from German territory. Despite this, Russian forces were able to defeat Austrian attacks to their south, inflicting terrible losses and thereby forcing the Germans to commit more troops to Russia. Through 1915 and 1916, the Eastern Front remained bloody and indecisive, with neither side able to capitalize on its gains.

STALEMATE, 1915

In the search for new points of attack, both the Allies and the Central Powers added new partners. The Ottoman Empire (Turkey) joined Germany and Austria at the end of 1914. In May 1915, Italy joined the Allies, lured by promises of financial reparations, parts of Austrian territory, and pieces of Germany's African colonies. Bulgaria joined the war on the side of the Central Powers a few months later. The entry of these new belligerents introduced the possibility of breaking the stalemate in the west by waging offensives on other fronts.

Gallipoli and Naval Warfare

Turkey's involvement, in particular, altered the dynamics of the war, for it threatened Russia's supply lines and endangered Britain's control of the Suez Canal. To defeat Turkey quickly—and in hopes of bypassing the Western Front—the British first lord of the admiralty, Winston Churchill (1911–15), argued for a naval offensive in the Dardanelles, the narrow strait separating Europe and Asia Minor. Under particularly incompetent leadership, however, the Royal Navy lacked adequate planning, supply lines, and maps to mount a successful campaign, and quickly lost six ships. The Allies then attempted a land invasion of the Gallipoli peninsula, in April 1915, with a combined force of French, British, Australian, and New Zealand troops. The Turks defended the narrow coast from positions high on fortified cliffs, and the shores were covered with nearly impenetrable barbed wire. During the disastrous landing, a British officer recalled, "the sea behind was absolutely crimson, and you could hear the groans through the rattle of musketry." The battle became entrenched on the beaches at Gallipoli, and the casualties mounted for seven months before the Allied commanders admitted defeat and ordered a withdrawal in December. The Gallipoli campaign—the first large-scale amphibious attack in history—brought death into London's neighborhoods and the cities of Britain's industrial north. Casualties were particularly devastating to the "white dominions"—practically every town and hamlet in Australia, New Zealand, and Canada lost young men, sometimes all the sons of a single family. The defeat cost the Allies two hundred thousand soldiers and did little to shift the war's focus away from the deadlocked Western Front.

By 1915 both sides realized that fighting this prolonged war of attrition would require countries to mobilize all of their resources. Accordingly, the Allies started to wage war on the economic front. Germany was vulnerable, dependent as it was on imports for at least one-third of its food supply. The Allies' naval blockade against all of central Europe aimed to slowly drain their opponents of food and raw materials. Germany responded with a submarine blockade, threatening to attack any vessel in the seas around Great Britain. On May 7, 1915, the German submarine *U-20*, without warning, torpedoed the passenger liner *Lusitania*, which was secretly carrying war supplies. The attack killed 1,198 people, including 128 Americans. The attack provoked the animosity of the United States, and Germany was forced to promise that it would no longer fire without warning. (This promise proved only temporary: in 1917 Germany would again declare unrestricted submarine warfare, drawing America into the war.) Although the German blockade against Britain destroyed more tonnage, the blockade against Germany was more devastating in the long run, as the continued war effort placed unsustainable demands on the national economy.

WAR: OLD AND NEW. Chlorine gas entered the war at the first battle of Ypres in 1915; mustard gas, which burned eyes and skin, came soon after. Gas did not tilt the military balance, but it was frightening, and pictures like this added to the surreal image of the First World War.

Trench Warfare

While the war escalated economically and politically, life in the trenches—the "lousy scratch holes," as a soldier called them—remained largely the same: a cramped and miserable existence of daily routines and continual killing. Some twenty-five thousand miles of trenches snaked along the Western Front. Behind the front lay a maze of connecting trenches and lines, leading to a complex of ammunition dumps, telephone exchanges, water points, field hospitals, and command posts. These logistical centers were supposed to allow an army to project its power forward, but just as often, they acted as a tether, making it difficult to advance.

The common assertion that railroads, the central symbol of an industrial age, made war more mobile, is misleading. Trains might take men to the front, but mobility ended there. Machine guns and barbed wire gave well-supplied and entrenched defenders an enormous advantage even against a larger attacking force, and logistics stymied generals' efforts to regain a war of movement.

The British and French trenches were wet, cold, and filthy. Rain turned the dusty corridors into squalid mud pits and flooded the floors up to waist level. Soldiers lived with lice and large black rats, which fed on the dead soldiers and horses that cast their stench over everything. Cadavers could go unburied for months and were often just embedded in the trench walls. Meanwhile the threat of enemy fire was constant: seven thousand British men were killed or wounded daily. This "wastage," as it was called, was part of the routine, along with the inspections, rotations, and mundane duties of life on the Western Front.

As the war progressed, new weapons added to the frightening dimensions of daily warfare. Besides artillery, machine guns, and barbed wire, the instruments of war now included exploding bullets, liquid fire, and poison gas. Gas, in particular, brought visible change to the battlefront. First used effectively by the Germans in April 1915 at the second battle of Ypres, poison gas was not only physically devastating—especially in its later forms—but also psychologically unnerving. The deadly cloud frequently hung over the trenches, although the quick appearance of gas masks limited its effectiveness. Like other new weapons, poison gas solidified the lines and took more lives but could not end the stalemate. The war dragged through its second year, bloody and stagnant.

SLAUGHTER IN THE TRENCHES: THE GREAT BATTLES, 1916–1917

The bloodiest battles of all—those that epitomize the First World War—occurred in 1916–1917, when first the Germans and later the British and French launched major offensives in attempts to end the stalemate. Massive campaigns in the war of attrition, these assaults produced hundreds of thousands of casualties and only minor territorial gains. These battles encapsulated the military tragedy of the war: a strategy of soldiers in cloth uniforms marching against machine guns.

Interpreting Visual Evidence

War Propaganda

Poster art was a leading form of propaganda used by all belligerents in the First World War to enlist men, sell war bonds, and sustain morale on the home front. Posters also demonized the enemy and glorified the sacrifices of soldiers in order to better rationalize the unprecedented loss of life and national wealth. The posters shown here, from a wide range of combatant nations during the war, share a common desire to link the war effort to a set of assumptions about the different roles assigned to men and women in the national struggle.

A. British Poster: "Women of Britain say 'Go!'"

B. Russian Poster: "Women Workers! Take up the Rifle!"

Questions for Analysis

1. Why would nationalists resort to such gendered images in a time of crisis?

2. What do these images tell us about the way that feelings of national belonging are created and sustained in times of urgency?

3. How might the changes that the war brought about—an increase in the number of women working in industry or outside the home, increased autonomy for women in regard to their wages or management of their household affairs—have affected the way that individuals responded to such images?

C. German Poster: "Collect women's hair that has been combed out. Our industry needs it for drive belts."

D. American Poster: "Destroy This Mad Brute. Enlist." The mad beast, meant to represent Germany, with *militarism* on his helmet, threatens American civilization with a club of *Kultur* (culture).

Verdun

The first of these major battles began with a German attack on the French stronghold of Verdun, near France's eastern border, in February 1916. Verdun had little strategic importance, but it quickly became a symbol of France's strength and was defended at all costs. Germany's goal was not necessarily to take the city but rather to break French morale. As the German general Erich von Falkenhayn (1914–16) said, the offensive would "compel the French to throw in every man they have. If they do so the forces of France will bleed to death." One million shells were fired on the first day of battle, inaugurating a ten-month struggle of back-and-forth fighting—offensives and counteroffensives of intense ferocity at enormous cost and zero gain. Led by General Henri Pétain (1914–18), the French pounded the Germans with artillery and received heavy bombardment in return. The Germans relied on large teams of horses, seven thousand of which were killed in a single day, to drag their guns through the muddy, cratered terrain. The French moved supplies and troops into Verdun continually. Approximately twelve thousand delivery trucks were employed for service. So were 259 out of the 330 regiments of the French army. Neither side could gain a real advantage—one small village on the front changed hands thirteen times in one month alone—but both sides incurred devastating losses of life. By the end of June, over four hundred thousand French and German soldiers were dead. In the end, the advantage fell to the French, who survived and who bled the Germans as badly as they suffered themselves.

The Somme

Meanwhile, the British opened their own offensive against Germany farther west, beginning the battle of the Somme on June 24, 1916. The Allied attack began with a fierce bombardment, blasting the German lines with fourteen hundred guns. The blasts could be heard all the way across the English Channel. The British assumed that this preliminary attack would break the mesh of German wire, destroy Germany's trenches, and clear the way for Allied troops to advance forward. They were tragically wrong. On the first day of battle alone, a stunning twenty thousand British soldiers died, and another forty thousand were wounded. The carnage continued from July until mid-November, resulting in massive casualties on both sides: five hundred thousand German, four hundred thousand British, and two hundred thousand French. The losses were unimaginable, and the outcome was equally hard to fathom: for all their sacrifices, neither side made any real gains. The futility of offensive

THE LINES OF BATTLE ON THE WESTERN FRONT. A British reconnaissance photo showing three lines of German trenches (right), No Man's Land (the black strip in the center), and the British trenches (partially visible to the left). The upper right hand quadrant of the photo shows communications trenches linking the front to the safe area. ▪ *What technologies gave these defenses such decisive advantages?*

war was not lost on the soldiers, yet morale remained surprisingly strong. Mutinies and desertions were rare before 1917; and surrenders became an important factor only in the final months of the war.

With willing armies and fresh recruits, military commanders maintained their strategy and pushed for victories on the Western Front again in 1917. The French general Robert Nivelle (1914–17) promised to break through the German lines with overwhelming manpower, but the "Nivelle Offensive" (April–May 1917) failed immediately, with first-day casualties like those at the Somme. The British also reprised the Somme at the third battle of Ypres (July–October 1917), in which a half million casualties earned Great Britain only insignificant gains—and no breakthrough. The one weapon with the potential to break the stalemate, the tank, was finally introduced into battle in 1916, but with such reluctance by tradition-bound commanders that its half-hearted employment made almost no difference. Other innovations were equally indecisive. Airplanes were used almost exclusively for reconnaissance, though occasional "dogfights" did occur between German and Allied pilots. And though the Germans sent airships to raid London, they did little significant damage.

Off the Western Front, fighting produced further stalemate. The Austrians continued to fend off attacks in Italy and Macedonia, while the Russians mounted a successful

THE GREAT WAR, 1917–1918. ▪ *What were the key events of 1917, and how did they change the course of the war?* ▪ *Consider the map of 1918. Why might many German people have believed they nearly won the war?* ▪ *Why were developments in the Middle East significant in the war's aftermath?*

offensive against them on the Eastern Front. The initial Russian success brought Romania into the war on Russia's side, but the Central Powers quickly retaliated and knocked the Romanians out of the war within a few months.

The war at sea was equally indecisive, with neither side willing to risk the loss of enormously expensive battleships. The British and German navies fought only one major naval battle early in 1916, which ended in stalemate. Afterward they used their fleets primarily in the economic war of blockades.

As a year of great bloodshed and growing disillusionment, 1916 showed that not even the superbly organized Germans had the mobility or fast-paced communications to win the western ground war. Increasingly, warfare would be turned against entire nations, including civilian populations on the home front and in the far reaches of the European empires.

WAR OF EMPIRES

Coming as it did at the height of European imperialism, the Great War quickly became a war of empires, with far-reaching repercussions. As the demands of warfare rose, Europe's colonies provided soldiers and material support. Britain, in particular, benefited from its vast network of colonial dominions and dependencies, bringing in soldiers from Canada, Australia, New Zealand, India, and South Africa. Nearly 1.5 million Indian troops served as British forces, some on the Western Front and many more in the Middle East. The French Empire, especially North and West Africa, sent 607,000 soldiers to fight with the Allies; 31,000 of them died in Europe. Colonial recruits from China, Vietnam, Egypt, India, the West Indies, and Madagascar were also employed in industry.

As the war stalled in Europe, colonial areas also became strategically important theaters for armed engagement. In 1916 Allied forces won a series of battles in the Middle East, pushing the Turks out of Egypt and eventually capturing Baghdad, Jerusalem, Beirut, and other cities. The British sought and gained the support of different Arab peoples who sought independence from the Turks, resulting in a successful revolt of Bedouin tribes (nomadic peoples of the Arabian Peninsula) that split the Ottoman Empire. When one of the senior Bedouin aristocrats, the emir Abdullah, captured the strategic port of Aqaba in July 1917, a British officer, T. E. Lawrence (1914–18), took credit and entered popular mythology as "Lawrence of Arabia."

Britain encouraged Arab nationalism for its own strategic purposes, offering a qualified acknowledgment of Arab political aspirations. At the same time, for similar but conflicting strategic reasons, the British declared their support of "the establishment in Palestine of a national home for the Jewish people." Britain's foreign secretary, Arthur Balfour, made the pledge. European Zionists, who were seeking a Jewish homeland, took the Balfour Declaration very seriously. The conflicting pledges to Bedouin leaders and Zionists sowed the seeds of the future Arab-Israeli conflict. First the war and then the promise of oil drew Europe more deeply into the Middle East, where conflicting dependencies and commitments created numerous postwar problems.

Irish Revolt

The Ottoman Empire was vulnerable; so was the British. The demands of war strained precarious bonds to the breaking point. Before the war, long-standing tensions between Irish Catholics and the Protestant British government had reached fever pitch, and some feared civil war. The Sinn Féin (We Ourselves) Party had formed in 1900 to fight for Irish independence, and a home rule bill had passed Parliament in 1912. But with the outbreak of war in 1914, the "Irish question" was tabled, and two hundred thousand Irishmen volunteered for the British army. The problem festered, however; and on Easter Sunday 1916, a group of nationalists revolted in Dublin. The insurgents' plan to smuggle in arms from Germany failed, and they had few delusions of achieving victory. The British army arrived with artillery and machine guns; they shelled parts of Dublin and crushed the uprising within a week.

The revolt was a military disaster but a striking political success. Britain shocked the Irish public by executing the rebel leaders. Even the British prime minister David Lloyd George (1916–22) thought the military governor in Dublin exceeded his authority with these executions. The martyrdom of the "Easter Rebels" seriously damaged Britain's relationship with its Irish Catholic subjects. The deaths galvanized the cause of Irish nationalism and touched off guerrilla violence that kept Ireland in turmoil for years. Finally, a new home rule bill was enacted in 1920, establishing separate parliaments for the Catholic south of Ireland and for Ulster, the northeastern counties where the majority population was Protestant. The leaders of the so-called Dáil Éireann (Irish Assembly), which had proclaimed an Irish Republic in 1918 and therefore been outlawed by Britain, rejected the bill but accepted a treaty that granted dominion status to Catholic Ireland in 1921. Dominion was followed almost immediately by civil war between those who abided by the treaty and those who wanted to absorb Ulster, but the conflict ended in

BRITISH REPRESSION OF EASTER REBELLION, DUBLIN, 1916. British troops line up behind a moveable barricade made up of household furniture during their repression of the Irish revolt. The military action did not prevent further conflict.

an uneasy compromise. The Irish Free State was established, and British sovereignty was partially abolished in 1937. Full status as a republic came, with some American pressure and Britain's exhausted acquiescence, in 1945.

THE HOME FRONT

When the war of attrition began in 1915, the belligerent governments were unprepared for the strains of sustained warfare. The costs of war—in both money and manpower—were staggering. In 1914 the war cost Germany 36 million marks per day (five times the cost of the war of 1870), and by 1918 the cost had skyrocketed to 146 million marks per day. Great Britain had estimated it would need a hundred thousand soldiers but ended up mobilizing three million. The enormous task of feeding, clothing, and equipping the army became as much of a challenge as breaking through enemy lines; civilian populations were increasingly asked—or forced—to support these efforts. Bureaucrats and industrialists led the effort to mobilize the home front, focusing all parts of society on the single goal of military victory. The term *total war* was introduced to describe this intense mobilization of society. Goverment propagandists insisted that civilians were as important to the war effort as soldiers, and in many ways they were. As workers, taxpayers, and consumers, civilians were vital parts of the war economy. They produced munitions; purchased war bonds; and shouldered the burden of tax hikes, inflation, and material privations.

The demands of industrial warfare led first to a transition from general industrial manufacturing to munitions production and then to increased state control of all aspects of production and distribution. The governments of Britain and France managed to direct the economy without serious detriment to the standard of living in their countries. Germany, meanwhile, put its economy in the hands of army and industry; under the Hindenburg Plan, named for Paul von Hindenburg, the chief of the imperial staff of the German army (1916–19), pricing and profit margins were set by individual industrialists.

Largely because of the immediate postwar collapse of the German economy, historians have characterized Germany's wartime economy as a chaotic, ultimately disastrous system governed by personal interest. New research, however, suggests that this was not the case: Germany's systems of war finance and commodity distribution, however flawed, were not decisively worse than those of Britain or France.

Women in the War

As Europe's adult men left farms and factories to become soldiers, the composition of the workforce changed: thousands of women were recruited into fields that had previously excluded them. Young people, foreigners, and unskilled workers were also pressed into newly important tasks; in the case of colonial workers, their experiences had equally critical repercussions. But because they were more visible, it was women who became symbolic of many of the changes brought by the Great War. In Germany, one-third of the labor force in heavy industry was female by the end of the war; and in France, 684,000 women worked in the munitions industry alone. In England the "munitionettes," as they were dubbed, numbered nearly a million. Women also entered the clerical and service sectors. In the villages of France, England, and Germany, women became mayors, school principals, and mail carriers. Hundreds of thousands of women worked with the army as nurses and ambulance drivers, jobs that brought them very close to the front lines. With minimal supplies and under squalid conditions, they worked to save lives and patch bodies together.

In some cases, war offered new opportunities. Middle-class women often said that the war broke down the restrictions on their lives; those in nursing learned to drive and acquired rudimentary medical knowledge. At home they could now ride the train, walk the street, or go out to dinner without an older woman present to chaperone them. In terms of gender roles, an enormous gulf sometimes seemed to separate the wartime world from nineteenth-century Victorian society. In one of the most famous autobiographies of the war, *Testament of Youth*, author Vera Brittain (1896–1970) recorded the dramatic new social norms that she and others forged during the rapid changes of wartime.

"As a generation of women we were now sophisticated to an extent which was revolutionary when compared with the romantic ignorance of 1914. Where we had once spoken with polite evasion of 'a certain condition,' or 'a certain profession,' we now unblushingly used the words 'pregnancy' and 'prostitution.'" For every Vera Brittain who celebrated the changes, however, journalists, novelists, and other observers grumbled that women were now smoking, refusing to wear the corsets that gave Victorian dresses their hourglass shape, or cutting their hair into the fashionable new bobs. The "new woman" became a symbol of profound and disconcerting cultural transformation.

How long lasting were these changes? In the aftermath of the war, governments and employers scurried to send women workers home, in part to give jobs to veterans, in part to deal with male workers' complaints that women were undercutting their wages. Efforts to demobilize women faced real barriers. Many women wage earners—widowed, charged with caring for relatives, or faced with inflation and soaring costs—needed their earnings more than ever. It was also difficult to persuade women workers who had grown accustomed to the relatively higher wages in heavy industry to return to their poorly paid traditional sectors of employment: the textile and garment industries and domestic service. The demobilization of women after the war, in other words, created as many dilemmas as had their mobilization. Governments passed "natalist" policies to encourage

WOMEN AT WORK. The all-out war effort combined with a manpower shortage at home brought women into factories across Europe in unparalleled numbers. In this photo men and women work side by side in a British shell factory. ▪ *How might the increased participation of women in the industrial workforce have changed attitudes toward women's labor?* ▪ *What tensions might this participation have created within families or between male and female workers?*

women to go home, marry, and—most important—have children. These policies did make maternity benefits—time off, medical care, and some allowances for the poor—available to women for the first time. Nonetheless, birth rates had been falling across Europe by the early twentieth century, and they continued to do so after the war. One upshot of the war was the increased availability of birth control—Marie Stopes (1880–1958) opened a birth-control clinic in London in 1921—and a combination of economic hardship, increased knowledge, and the demand for freedom made men and women more likely to use it. Universal suffrage, and the vote for all adult men and women, and for women in particular, had been one of the most controversial issues in European politics before the war. At the end of the fighting it came in a legislative rush. Britain was first off the mark, granting the vote to all men and women over thirty with the Representation of the People Act in 1918; the United States gave women the vote with the Nineteenth Amendment the following year. Germany's new republic and the Soviet Union did likewise. France was much slower to offer woman suffrage (1945) because the persistent antifeminism of conservatives was reinforced by fears among anticlerical republicans that women would vote for candidates close to the Catholic church.

Mobilizing Resources

Along with mobilizing the labor front, the wartime governments had to mobilize men and money. All the belligerent countries except for Great Britain had conscription laws before the war. Military service was seen as a duty, not an option. Bolstered by widespread public support for the war, this belief brought millions of young Europeans into recruitment offices in 1914. The French began the war with about 4.5 million trained soldiers, but by the end of 1914—just four months into the war—300,000 were dead and 600,000 injured. Conscripting citizens and mustering colonial troops became increasingly important. Eventually, France called up eight million citizens: almost two-thirds of Frenchmen aged eighteen to forty. In 1916, the British finally introduced conscription, dealing a serious blow to civilian morale; by the summer of 1918, half its army was under the age of nineteen.

Government propaganda, while part of a larger effort to sustain both military and civilian morale, was also important to the recruitment effort. From the outset, the war had been sold to the people on both sides of the conflict as a moral and righteous crusade. In 1914, the French president Raymond Poincaré (1913–20) assured his fellow citizens that France had no other purpose than to stand "before the universe for Liberty, Justice, and Reason." Germans were presented with the task of defending their superior *Kultur* (culture) against the wicked encirclement policy of the Allied nations. By the middle of the war, massive propaganda campaigns were under way. Film, posters, postcards, newspapers—all forms of media proclaimed the strength of the cause, the evil of the enemy, and the absolute necessity of total victory. The success of these campaigns is difficult to determine, but it is clear that they had at least one painful effect—they made it more difficult for any country to accept a fair, nonpunitive peace settlement.

Financing the war was another heavy obstacle. Military spending accounted for 3 to 5 percent of government expenditure in the combatant countries before 1914 but soared to perhaps half of each nation's budget during the war. Governments had to borrow money or print more of it. The Allied nations borrowed heavily from the British, who borrowed even more from the United States. American capital flowed across the Atlantic long before the United States entered the war. And though economic aid from the United States was a decisive factor in the Allies' victory, it left Britain with a $4.2 billion debt and hobbled the United Kingdom as a financial power after the war. The situation was far worse for Germany, which faced a total blockade of money and goods. In an effort to get around this predicament, and lacking an outside source of cash, the German government funded its war effort largely by increasing the money supply. The amount of paper money in circulation increased by over 1,000 percent during the war, triggering a dramatic rise in inflation. During the war, prices in Germany rose about 400 percent, double the inflation in Britain and France. For middle-class people living on pensions or fixed incomes, these price hikes were a push into poverty.

The Strains of War, 1917

The demands of total war worsened as the conflict dragged into 1917. After the debacle of the Nivelle Offensive, the French army recorded acts of mutiny in two-thirds of its divisions; similar resistance arose in nearly all major armies in 1917. Military leaders portrayed the mutineers as part of a dangerous pacifist movement, but most were nonpolitical. Resistance within the German army was never organized or widespread but existed in subtler forms. Self-mutilation rescued some soldiers from the horror of the trenches; many more were released because of various emotional disorders.

The war's toll also mounted for civilians, who often suffered from the same shortages of basic supplies that afflicted the men at the front. In 1916–17, the lack of clothing, food, and fuel was aggravated in central Europe by abnormally cold, wet weather. These strains provoked rising discontent on the home front. Although governments attempted to solve the problem with tighter controls on the economy, their policies often provoked further hostility from civilians.

In urban areas, where undernourishment was worst, people stood in lines for hours to get food and fuel rations that scarcely met their most basic needs. The price of bread and potatoes—still the central staples of working-class meals—soared. Prices were even higher in the thriving black market that emerged in cities. Consumers worried aloud that speculators were hoarding supplies and creating artificial shortages, selling tainted goods, and profiting from others' miseries. Governments, meanwhile, concentrated on the war effort and faced difficult decisions about who needed supplies the most—soldiers at the front, workers in the munitions industry, or hungry and cold families.

Like other nations, Germany moved from encouraging citizens to restrain themselves—"those who stuff themselves full, those who push out their paunches in all directions, are traitors to the Fatherland"—to direct control, issuing ration cards in 1915. Britain was the last to institute control, rationing bread only in 1917 when Germany's submarines sank an average of 630,000 tons per month and brought British food reserves within two weeks of starvation level. But rations indicated only what was allowed, not what was available. Hunger continued despite mass

DESPERATION ON THE GERMAN HOME FRONT, 1918. A German photograph of women digging through garbage in search of food. The last year of the war brought starvation to cities in Germany and Austria-Hungary, sending many people into the countryside to forage for provisions. Such foraging was often illegal, a violation of rationing rules. ■ *How might the need to break the law in this way have affected support for the war effort and the state?*

bureaucratic control. Governments regulated not only food but also working hours and wages; and unhappy workers directed their anger at the state, adding a political dimension to labor disputes and household needs. The bread lines, filled mainly by women, were flash points of political dissent, petty violence, even large-scale riots. Likewise, the class conflicts of prewar Europe had been briefly muffled by the outbreak of war and mobilization along patriotic lines, but as the war ground on, political tensions reemerged with new intensity. Thousands of strikes erupted throughout Europe, involving millions of frustrated workers. In April 1917, three hundred thousand in Berlin went on strike to protest ration cuts. In May, a strike of Parisian seamstresses touched off a massive work stoppage that included even white-collar employees and munitions workers. Shipbuilders and steelworkers in Glasgow went on strike as well, and the British government replied by sending armored cars to "Red Glasgow." Stagnation had given way to crisis on both sides. The strains of total war and the resulting social upheavals threatened political regimes throughout Europe. The Russian Revolution, which resulted in the overthrow of the tsar and the rise of Bolshevism, was only the most dramatic response to widespread social problems.

Total War

As early as 1915 contemporaries were speaking of "the Great War"; the transformations were there for all to see. This was modern, industrialized warfare, first glimpsed in the American Civil War but now more advanced and on a much larger scale. It still deployed cloth-uniformed men, heartbreakingly unprotected against the newly destructive weapons. And it still required human intelligence, speed, brute force—or courage—on a massive scale. The statistics and what they imply still strain the imagination: seventy-four million soldiers were mobilized on both sides; six thousand people were killed each day for more than fifteen hundred days.

The warring nations, Europe's new industrial powerhouses, were also empires, and this "world" war consumed resources and soldiers from all over the globe. Mobilization also reached more deeply into civilian society. Economies bent to military priorities. Propaganda escalated to sustain the effort, fanning old hatreds and creating new ones. Atrocities against civilians came in its wake. Europe had known brutal wars against civilians before, and guerilla war during the time of Napoleon, but the First World War vastly magnified the violence and multiplied the streams of refugees. Minorities who lived in the crumbling Russian, Austro-Hungarian, or Ottoman empires were especially vulnerable. Jewish populations in Russia had lived in fear of pogroms before 1914; now they were attacked by Russian soldiers who accused them of encouraging the enemy. Austria-Hungary, likewise, summarily executed minorities suspected of Russian sympathies. The worst atrocities came against the Armenian community in Turkey. Attacked by the Allies at Gallipoli and at war with the Russians to the north, the Turkish government turned on its Armenian subjects, labeling them a security risk. Orders came down for "relocation," and relocation became genocide. Armenian leaders were arrested; Armenian men were shot; and entire Armenian villages were forcibly marched to the south, robbed, and beaten to death along the way. Over the course of the war, a million Armenians died.

All of these developments—military, economic, and psychological mobilization; a war that tested the powers of a state and its economy; violence against civilians—were the component parts of total war and foreshadowed the conflict to be unleashed in 1939.

THE RUSSIAN REVOLUTIONS OF 1917

The first country to break under the strain of total war was tsarist Russia. The outbreak of war temporarily united Russian society against a common enemy, but Russia's military effort quickly turned sour. All levels of Russian society became disillusioned with Tsar Nicholas II, who was unable to provide effective leadership but was nonetheless unwilling to open government to those who could. The political and social strains of war brought two revolutions in 1917. The first, in February, overthrew the tsar and established a transitional government. The second, in October, was a communist revolution that marked the emergence of the Soviet Union.

The First World War and the February Revolution

Like the other participants in the First World War, Russia entered the war with the assumption that it would be over quickly. Autocratic Russia, plagued by internal difficulties before 1914 (see Chapter 23), could not sustain the political strains of extended warfare. Tsar Nicholas II's political authority had been shaky since the October Revolution of 1905 and corruption in the royal court further tarnished the tsar's image. Once war broke out the tsar insisted on personally commanding Russian troops, leaving the government in the hands of his court, especially his wife, Alexandra, and her eccentric spiritual mentor and faith healer, Grigorii Rasputin (1869–1916). Rasputin won the tsarina's sympathy by treating her hemophiliac son, and he used his influence to operate corrupt and self-aggrandizing schemes. His presence only added to the image of a court mired in decadence, incompetent to face the modern world.

In 1914 and 1915 Russia suffered terrible defeats. All of Poland and substantial territory in the Baltics fell to the Germans at the cost of a million Russian casualties. Although the Russian army was the largest in Europe, it was poorly trained and, at the beginning of the war, under-supplied and inadequately equipped. In the first battles of 1914, generals sent soldiers to the front without rifles or shoes, instructing them to scavenge supplies from fallen comrades. By 1915, to the surprise of many, Russia was producing enough food, clothing, and ammunition, but political problems blocked the supply effort. Another major offensive in the summer of 1916 brought hope for success but turned into a humiliating retreat. When word came that the government was requisitioning grain from the countryside to feed the cities, peasants in the army began to desert en masse, returning to their farms to guard their families' holdings. By the end of 1916, a combination of political ineptitude and military defeat brought the Russian state to the verge of collapse.

The same problems that hampered the Russian war effort also crippled the tsar's ability to override domestic discontent and resistance. As the war dragged on, the government faced not only liberal opposition in the Duma, soldiers unwilling to fight, and an increasingly militant labor movement, but also a rebellious urban population. City dwellers were impatient with inflation and shortages of food and fuel. In February 1917, these forces came together in Petrograd (now St. Petersburg). The revolt began on International Women's Day, February 23, an occasion for a loosely organized march of women—workers, mothers, wives, and consumers—demanding food, fuel, and political reform. The march was the latest in a wave of demonstrations and strikes that had swept through the country during the winter months. This time, within a few days the unrest spiraled into a mass strike of three hundred thousand people. Nicholas II sent in police and military forces to quell the disorder. When nearly sixty thousand troops in Petrograd mutinied and joined the revolt, what was left of the tsar's power evaporated. Nicholas II abdicated the throne on March 2. This abrupt decision brought a century-long struggle over Russian autocracy to a sudden end.

After the collapse of the monarchy, two parallel centers of power emerged. Each had its own objectives and policies. The first was the provisional government, organized by

leaders in the Duma and composed mainly of middle-class liberals. The new government hoped to establish a democratic system under constitutional rule. Its main task was to set up a national election for a constituent assembly, and it also acted to grant and secure civil liberties, release political prisoners, and redirect power into the hands of local officials. The other center of power lay with the *soviets*, a Russian term for local councils elected by workers and soldiers. Since 1905, socialists had been active in organizing these councils, which claimed to be the true democratic representatives of the people. A soviet, organized during the 1905 revolution and led by the well-known socialist Leon Trotsky, reemerged after February 1917 and asserted its claim to be the legitimate political power in Russia. The increasingly powerful soviets pressed for social reform, the redistribution of land, and a negotiated settlement with Germany and Austria. Yet the provisional government refused to concede military defeat. Continuing the war effort made domestic reform impossible and cost valuable popular support. More fighting during 1917 was just as disastrous as before, and this time the provisional government paid the price. By autumn desertion in the army was rampant, administering the country was nearly impossible, and Russian politics teetered on the edge of chaos.

The Bolsheviks and the October Revolution

The Bolsheviks, a branch of the Russian socialist movement, had little to do with the events of February 1917. Over the course of the next seven months, however, they became enough of a force to overthrow the provisional government. The chain of events leading to the October Revolution surprised most contemporary observers, including the Bolsheviks themselves. Marxism had been quite weak in late-nineteenth-century Russia, although it made small but rapid inroads during the 1880s and 1890s. In 1903 the leadership of the Russian Social Democrats split over revolutionary strategy and the steps to socialism. One group, which won a temporary majority (and chose to call itself the Bolsheviks, or "members of the majority"), favored a centralized party of active revolutionaries. They believed that revolution alone would lead directly to a socialist regime. The Mensheviks (members of the minority), like most European socialists, wanted to move toward socialism gradually, supporting bourgeois or liberal revolution in the short term. Because peasants constituted 80 to 85 percent of the population, the Mensheviks also reasoned that a proletarian revolution was premature and that Russia needed to complete its capitalist development first. The Mensheviks

Analyzing Primary Sources

Toward the October Revolution: Lenin to the Bolsheviks

In the fall of 1917, Lenin was virtually the only Bolshevik leader who believed that an insurrection should be launched immediately. As the provisional government faltered, he attempted to convince his fellow Bolsheviks that the time for revolution had arrived.

aving obtained a majority in the Soviets of Workers' and Soldiers' Deputies of both capitals, the Bolsheviks can and *must* take power into their hands.

They can do so because the active majority of the revolutionary elements of the people of both capitals is sufficient to attract the masses, to overcome the resistance of the adversary, to vanquish him, to conquer power and to retain it. For, in offering immediately a democratic peace, in giving the land immediately to the peasants, in re-establishing the democratic institutions and liberties which have been mangled and crushed by Kerensky [leader of the provisional government], the Bolsheviks will form a government which *nobody* will overthrow....

The majority of the people is *with* us.... [T]he majority in the Soviets of the capitals is the *result* of the people's progress *to our side.* The vacillation of the Socialist-Revolutionaries and Mensheviks ... is proof of the same thing....

To "wait" for the Constituent Assembly would be wrong.... Only our party, having assumed power, can secure the convocation of the Constituent Assembly, and, after assuming power, it could blame the other parties for delaying it and could substantiate its accusations....

It would be naive to wait for a "formal" majority on the side of the Bolsheviks, no revolution ever waits for *this.* . . . History will not forgive us if we do not assume power now.

No apparatus? There is an apparatus: the Soviets and democratic organisations. The international situation *just now*, on the *eve* of a separate peace between the English and the Germans, is *in our favour.* It is precisely now that to offer peace to the peoples means to *win.*

Assume power *at once* in Moscow and in Petrograd ...; we will win *absolutely and unquestionably.*

Source: Vladimir Ilyich Lenin, *Bol'sheviki dolzhny vzyat'vlast'* (*The Bolsheviks must seize power*), cited in Richard Sakwa, *The Rise and Fall of the Soviet Union, 1917–1991* (New York and London: 1999), p. 45.

Questions for Analysis

1. Lenin was surprised by the sudden collapse of the tsarist regime in the February revolution of 1917. Why did he think the Bolsheviks could seize power? What were the key elements of his strategy for winning the necessary popular support?

2. Convinced he was right, Lenin returned to Petrograd in disguise and personally presented his arguments for an armed takeover to the Bolshevik Central Committee. What did he mean by saying that "it would be naive to wait for a 'formal' majority on the side of the Bolsheviks; no revolution ever waits for *this*"?

---

regained control of the party, but the Bolshevik splinter party survived under the leadership of the young, dedicated revolutionary Vladimir Ilyich Ulyanov, who adopted the pseudonym Lenin.

Lenin was a member of the middle class; his father had been an inspector of schools and a minor political functionary. Lenin himself had been expelled from university for engaging in radical activity after his elder brother was executed for involvement in a plot to assassinate Tsar Alexander III. Lenin spent three years as a political prisoner in Siberia. After that, from 1900 until 1917, he lived and wrote as an exile in western Europe.

Lenin believed that the development of Russian capitalism made socialist revolution possible. To bring revolution, he argued, the Bolsheviks needed to organize on behalf of the new class of industrial workers. Without the party's disciplined leadership, Russia's factory workers could not accomplish change on the necessary scale. Lenin's Bolsheviks remained a minority among Social Democrats well into 1917, and industrial workers were a small part of the population. But the Bolsheviks' dedication to the singular goal of revolution and their tight, almost conspiratorial organization gave them tactical advantages over larger and more loosely organized opposition parties. The Bolsheviks merged a peculiarly Russian tradition of revolutionary zeal with western European Marxism, creating a party capable of seizing the moment when the tsar left the scene.

Throughout 1917 the Bolsheviks consistently demanded an end to the war, improvement in working and living conditions for workers, and redistribution of aristocratic land to the peasantry. While the provisional government struggled to hold together the Russian war effort, Lenin led the Bolsheviks on a bolder course, shunning any collaboration with the "bourgeois" government and condemning its imperialist war policies. Even most Bolsheviks considered Lenin's approach too radical. Yet as conditions in Russia deteriorated, his uncompromising calls for "Peace, Land, and Bread, Now" and "All Power to the Soviets" won the Bolsheviks support from workers, soldiers, and peasants. As many ordinary people saw it, the other parties could not govern, win the war, or achieve an honorable peace. While unemployment continued to climb and starvation and chaos reigned in the cities, the Bolsheviks' power and credibility were rising fast.

In October 1917, Lenin convinced his party to act. He goaded Trotsky, who was better known among workers, into organizing a Bolshevik attack on the provisional government on October 24–25, 1917. On October 25, Lenin appeared from hiding to announce to a stunned meeting of soviet representatives that "all power had passed to the Soviets." The head of the provisional government fled to rally support at the front lines, and the Bolsheviks took over the Winter Palace, the seat of the provisional government. The initial stage of the revolution was quick and relatively bloodless. In fact, many observers believed they had seen nothing more than a coup d'état, one that might quickly be reversed. Life in Petrograd went on as normal.

The Bolsheviks took the opportunity to rapidly consolidate their position. First, they moved against all political competition, beginning with the soviets. They immediately expelled parties that disagreed with their actions, creating a new government in the soviets composed entirely of Bolsheviks. The Bolsheviks did follow through on the provisional government's promise to elect a Constituent Assembly. But when they did not win a majority in the elections, they refused to let the assembly reconvene. From that point on, Lenin's Bolsheviks ruled socialist Russia, and later the Soviet Union, as a one-party dictatorship.

In the countryside, the new Bolshevik regime did little more than ratify a revolution that had been going on since the summer of 1917. When peasant soldiers at the front heard that a revolution had occurred, they streamed home to take land they had worked for generations and believed was rightfully theirs. The provisional government had set up commissions to deal methodically with the legal

VLADIMIR ILYICH LENIN. Lenin speaking in Moscow in 1918, at the first anniversary of the October Revolution. A forceful speaker and personality, Lenin was the single most powerful politician in Russia between October 1917 and his death in 1924.

issues surrounding the redistribution of land, a process that threatened to become as complex as the emancipation of the serfs in 1861. The Bolsheviks simply approved the spontaneous redistribution of the nobles' land to peasants without compensation to former owners. They nationalized banks and gave workers control of factories.

Most important, the new government sought to take Russia out of the war. It eventually negotiated a separate treaty with Germany, signed at Brest-Litovsk in March 1918. The Bolsheviks surrendered vast Russian territories: the rich agricultural region of Ukraine, Georgia, Finland, Russia's Polish territories, the Baltic states, and more. However humiliating, the treaty ended Russia's role in the fighting and saved the fledgling communist regime from almost certain military defeat at the hands of the Germans. The treaty enraged Lenin's political enemies, both moderates and reactionaries, who were still a force to be reckoned with—and who were prepared to wage a civil war rather than accept the revolution. Withdrawing from Europe's war only plunged the country into a vicious civil conflict (see Chapter 28).

THE ROAD TO GERMAN DEFEAT, 1918

Russia's withdrawal dealt an immediate strategic and psychological blow to the Allies. Germany could soothe domestic discontent by claiming victory on the Eastern Front, and it could now concentrate its entire army in the west. The Allies feared that Germany would win the war before the United States, which entered the conflict in April 1917, could make a difference. It almost happened. With striking results,

Germany shifted its offensive strategy to infiltration by small groups under flexible command. On March 21, 1918, Germany initiated a major assault on the west and quickly broke through the Allied lines. The British were hit hardest. Some units, surrounded, fought to the death with bayonets and grenades, but most recognized their plight and surrendered, putting tens of thousands of prisoners in German hands. The British were in retreat everywhere and their commander, Sir Douglas Haig, issued a famous order warning that British troops "now fight with our backs to the wall." The Germans advanced to within fifty miles of Paris by early April. Yet the British—and especially troops from the overseas empire—did just as they were asked and stemmed the tide. As German forces turned southeast instead, the French, who had refused to participate in the foolish attacks over the top, showed stubborn courage on the defensive, where they bogged down in heat, mud, and casualties. It had been a last great try by the well-organized German army; exhausted, it now waited for the Allies to mount their own attack.

The final turning point of the war was the entry of the United States in April 1917. Although America had supported the Allies financially throughout the war, its official intervention undeniably tipped the scales. The United States created a fast and efficient wartime bureaucracy, instituting conscription in May 1917. About ten million men were registered, and by the next year, three hundred thousand soldiers a month were being shipped "over there." Large amounts of food and supplies also crossed the Atlantic, under the armed protection of the U.S. Navy. This system of convoys effectively neutralized the threat of German submarines to Allied merchant ships: the number of ships sunk fell from 25 to 4 percent. America's entry—though not immediately decisive—gave a quick, colossal boost to British and French morale, while severely undermining Germany's.

When it came in July and August, the Allied counterattack was devastating and quickly gathered steam. New offensive techniques had finally materialized. The Allies improved their use of tanks and the "creeping barrage," in which infantry marched close behind a rolling wall of shells to overwhelm their targets. In another of the war's ironies these new tactics were pioneered by the conservative British, who launched a crushing counterattack in July, relying on the survivors of the armies of the Somme reinforced by troops from Australia, Canada, and India. The French made use of American troops, whose generals attacked the Germans with the same harrowing indifference to casualties shown in 1914. Despite their lack of experience, the American troops were tough and resilient. When combined with more experienced French and Australian forces, they punched several large holes through German lines, crossing into the "lost provinces" of Alsace

and Lorraine by October. At the beginning of November, the sweeping British offensive had joined up with the small Belgian army and was pressing toward Brussels.

The Allies finally brought their material advantage to bear on the Germans, who were suffering acutely by the spring of 1918. This was not only because of the continued effectiveness of the Allied blockade but also because of growing domestic conflict over war aims. On the front lines, German soldiers were exhausted. Following the lead of their distraught generals, the troops let morale sink, and many surrendered. Facing one shattering blow after another, the German army was pushed deep into Belgium. Popular discontent mounted, and the government, which was now largely in the hands of the military, seemed unable either to win the war or to meet basic household needs.

Germany's network of allies was also coming undone. By the end of September, the Central Powers were headed for defeat. In the Middle East, the British army, which combined Bedouin guerrillas, Indian sepoys, Scottish highlanders, and Australian light cavalry, decisively defeated Ottoman forces in Syria and Iraq. In the Balkans, the French brought Greece into the war on the side of the Allies and knocked Bulgaria out of the war in September 1918. Meanwhile Austria-Hungary faced disaster on all sides, collapsing in Italy as well as the Balkans. Czech and Polish representatives in the Austrian government began pressing for self-government. Croat and Serb politicians proposed a "kingdom of Southern Slavs" (soon known as Yugoslavia). When Hungary joined the chorus for independence, the emperor, Karl I, accepted reality and sued for peace. The empire that had started the conflict surrendered on November 3, 1918, and disintegrated soon after.

Germany was now left with the impossible task of carrying on the struggle alone. By the fall of 1918, the country was starving and on the verge of civil war. When German sailors

CASUALTY OF WAR. A German soldier killed during the Allies' October 1917 offensive.

mutinied in early November, the Kaiser's government collapsed. On November 8 a republic was proclaimed in Bavaria, and the next day nearly all of Germany was in the throes of revolution. The kaiser's abdication was announced in Berlin on November 9; he fled to Holland early the next morning. Control of the German government fell to a provisional council headed by Friedrich Ebert (1912–23), the socialist leader in the Reichstag. Ebert and his colleagues immediately took steps to negotiate an armistice. The Germans could do nothing but accept the Allies' terms, so at five o'clock in the morning of November 11, 1918, two German delegates met with the Allied army commander in the Compiègne forest and signed papers officially ending the war. Six hours later the order for cease fire was given across the Western Front. That night thousands of people danced through the streets of London, Paris, and Rome, engulfed in a different delirium from that four years before, a joyous burst of exhausted relief.

The Peace Settlement

The Paris Peace Conference, which opened in January 1919, was an extraordinary moment, one that dramatized just how much the world had been transformed by the war and the decades that preceded it. Gone were the Russian, Austro-Hungarian, and German empires. That the American president Woodrow Wilson played such a prominent role marked the emergence of the United States as a world power. The United States' new status was rooted in the economic development of the second industrial revolution during the nineteenth century. In mass production and technological innovation, it had rivaled the largest European powers (England and Germany) before the war. During the war, American intervention (although it came late) had decisively broken the military-economic deadlock. And in the war's aftermath American industrial culture, engineering, and financial networks loomed very large on the European continent. Wilson and his entourage spent several months in Paris at the conference—a first for an American president while in office and European leaders' first extended encounter with an American head of state.

American prominence was far from the only sign of global change. Some thirty nations sent delegates to the peace conference, a reflection of three factors: the scope of the war, heightened national sentiments and aspirations, and the tightening of international communication and economic ties in the latter part of the nineteenth century. The world in 1900 was vastly more globalized than it had been fifty years earlier. Many more countries had political, economic, and human investments in the war and its settlement. A belief that peace would secure and be secured by free peoples in

"LONG LIVE WILSON!" Paris crowds greet President Wilson after the war. Despite public demonstrations of this sort, Wilson's attempt to shape the peace was a failure.

sovereign nations represented the full flowering of nineteenth-century liberal nationalism. Delegates came to work for Irish home rule, for a Jewish state in Palestine and for nations in Poland, Ukraine, and Yugoslavia. Europe's colonies, which had been key to the war effort and were increasingly impatient with their status, sent delegates to negotiate for self-determination. They discovered, however, that the western European leaders' commitment to the principle of national self-determination was hedged by their imperial assumptions. Non-state actors—in other words, international groups asking for women's suffrage, civil rights, minimum wages, or maximum hours—came to the Paris Peace Conference as well, for these were now seen as international issues. Last, reporters from all over the world wired news home from Paris, a sign of vastly improved communications, transatlantic cables, and the mushrooming of the mass press.

Although many attended, the conference was largely controlled by the so-called Big Four: the U.S. president Woodrow Wilson, the British prime minister David Lloyd George (1916–22), the French premier Georges Clemenceau (1917–20), and the Italian premier Vittorio Orlando (1917–19). The debates among these four personalities were fierce, as they all had conflicting ambitions and interests. In total, five separate treaties were signed, one with each of the defeated nations: Germany, Austria, Hungary, Turkey, and Bulgaria. The settlement with Germany was called the Treaty of Versailles, after the France town in which it was signed.

Wilson's widely publicized Fourteen Points represented the spirit of idealism. Wilson had proposed the Fourteen Points before the war ended, as the foundation of a permanent peace. Based on the principle of "open covenants of peace, openly arrived at," they called for an end to secret diplomacy, freedom of the seas, removal of international tariffs, and reduction of national armaments "to the lowest point consistent with safety." They also called for the "self-determination of peoples" and for the establishment of a League of Nations to settle international conflicts. Thousands of copies of the Fourteen Points had been scattered by Allied planes over the German trenches and behind the lines in an attempt to convince both soldiers and civilians that the Allied nations were striving for a just and durable peace. Wilson's Fourteen Points thus shaped the expectations that Germans brought to the peace talks. When Wilson said, "The day of conquest and aggrandizement is gone by," many Germans expected that the treaty would not single Germany out for punishment.

Idealism, however, was undermined by other imperatives. Throughout the war, Allied propaganda led soldiers and civilians to believe that their sacrifices to the war effort would be compensated by payments extracted from the enemy. Total war demanded total victory. Lloyd George had campaigned during the British election of 1918 on the slogan "Hang the Kaiser!" Clemenceau had twice in his long lifetime seen France invaded and its existence imperiled. With the tables turned, he believed that the French should take full advantage of their opportunity to place Germany under strict control. The devastation of the war and the fiction that Germany could be made to pay for it made compromise impossible. The settlement with Germany was shaped more by this desire for punishment than by Wilson's idealism.

The Versailles treaty required Germany to surrender the "lost provinces" of Alsace and Lorraine to France and to give up other territories to Denmark and the new state of Poland. Germany's province of East Prussia was cut off from the rest of its territory. The port of Danzig, where the majority of the population was German, was put under the administrative control of the League of Nations and the economic domination of Poland. The treaty disarmed Germany, forbade a German air force, and reduced its navy to a token force to match an army capped at a hundred thousand volunteers. To protect France and Belgium, all German soldiers and fortifications were to be removed from the Rhine Valley.

The most important part of the Versailles treaty, and one of the parts at odds with Wilson's original plan, was the "war-guilt" provision in Article 231. Versailles held Germany and its allies responsible for the loss and damage suffered by the Allied governments and their citizens "as a consequence of the war imposed upon them by the aggression of Germany and her allies." Germany would be forced to pay massive reparations. The exact amount was left to a Reparations Commission, which set the total at $33 billion in 1921. The Germans deeply resented these harsh demands, but others outside of Germany also warned of the dangers of punitive reparations. In *The Economic Consequences of the Peace*, the noted British economist John Maynard Keynes (1883–1946) argued that reparations would undermine Europe's most important task: repairing the world economy.

The other treaties at the Paris Peace Conference were based partly on the Allies' strategic interests, partly on the principle of national self-determination. The experience of the prewar years convinced leaders that they should draw nations' boundaries to conform to the ethnic, linguistic, and historical traditions of the people they were to contain. Wilson's idealism about freedom and equal representation confirmed these aims. Thus representatives of Yugoslavia were granted a state. Czechoslovakia was created, Poland reestablished, Hungary separated from Austria, and the Baltic states made independent (see the map on page 595). These national boundaries did not, indeed in most cases could not, follow ethnic divisions; they were created according to facts on the ground, hasty compromises, and political dictates—such as insulating western Europe from the communist threat of the Soviet Union. The peacemakers carved new nations from older, multiethnic empires, especially the Austro-Hungarian Empire, whose fragility had helped spark the war and whose structure had collapsed with the conflict. Creating nations, however, almost invariably created new minorities within those nations. The architects of the new Europe wrestled, briefly, with the problem of minorities, but did not resolve it. The issue would return to undermine European stability in the 1930s.

The Ottoman Empire ended as well, with two results: the creation of the modern Turkish state and a new structure for British and French colonial rule. As territories were taken from the Ottomans, Greece chose to seize some by force. The effort was successful at first, but the Turks counterattacked, driving out Greek forces by 1923 and creating the modern state of Turkey under the charismatic leadership of General Mustafa Kemal Attaturk (1923–38). Ottoman territories placed under French and British control became part of the colonial "mandate system," which legitimized Europe's dominance over territories in the Middle East, Africa, and the Pacific. Territories were divided into groups on the basis of their location and their "level of development," or how far, in European eyes, they would have to travel to earn self-government. Choice pieces of land became mandates held, in principle, by the League of Nations but administered by Britain (Transjordan, Iraq, and Palestine) and France (Lebanon and Syria). The British and French empires, then, expanded after the war, although those territories held trouble ahead—the British faced revolt in Iraq and escalating tensions in Palestine, where they tried to juggle promises made to Zionist settlers and claims of indigenous Arab communities. Arab leaders, accompanied by their advocate T. E. Lawrence, attended the Versailles conference and listened as their hopes for independence were strictly circumscribed.

The peoples of the Allies' existing colonies were also disappointed. Ho Chi Minh, a young student from French Indochina attending a Parisian university, was one of many colonial activists who attended the conference to protest conditions in the colonies and to ask that the rights of nations be extended to their homelands. Well-organized delegations from French West Africa and from the Congress Party of India, which favored dominion status in return for the wartime efforts of millions of Indian soldiers who had fought for the British Empire, were also snubbed. The peacemakers' belief in democracy and self-determination collided with their baseline assumptions—inherited from the nineteenth century—about Western superiority; those assumptions justified imperial rule. Although the European powers spoke about reforming colonialism, little was done. Many nationalists in the colonies who had favored moderate legislative change decided that active struggle might be the only answer to the injustices of colonialism.

Each of the five peace treaties incorporated the Covenant of the League of Nations, an organization envisioned as the arbiter of world peace, but it never achieved the idealistic aims of its founders. The League was handicapped from the start by a number of changes to its original design. The arms-reduction requirement was watered down, and the League's power to enforce it was rendered almost nonexistent. Japan would not join unless it was allowed to keep former German concessions in China. France demanded that both Germany and Russia be excluded

TERRITORIAL CHANGES IN EUROPE AND THE NEAR EAST AFTER THE FIRST WORLD WAR. Note the changes in geography as a result of the First World War. ▪ *What areas were most affected by the changes within Europe, and why?* ▪ *Can you see any obvious difficulties created by the redrawing of the map of Europe?* ▪ *What historical circumstances and/or new threats guided the victors to create such geopolitical anomalies?*

from the League. This contradicted Wilson's goals but had already been legitimized in Paris, where neither Soviet Russia nor the defeated Central Powers were allowed at the talks. The League received an even more debilitating blow when the U.S. Congress, citing the long-standing national preference for isolation, refused to approve U.S. membership in the League. Hobbled from the start, the international organization had little potential to avert conflicts.

The League began as a utopian response to global conflict and registered the urgency of reorganizing world governance. Its history, however, reflected the larger problems of power politics that emerged after the war.

CONCLUSION

Europe fought the First World War on every front possible—military, political, social, and economic. Consequently, the war's effects extended far beyond the devastated landscapes of the Western Front. Statistics can only hint at the enormous loss of human life: of the seventy million men who were mobilized, nearly nine million were killed. Russia, Germany, France, and Hungary recorded the highest number of deaths, but the smaller countries of southeast Europe had the highest percentages of soldiers killed. Almost

40 percent of Serbia's soldiers died in battle. With the addition of war-related deaths caused by privation and disease, Serbia lost 15 percent of its population. In comparison, Britain, France, and Germany lost only 2 to 3 percent of their populations. But the percentages are much more telling if we focus on the young men of the war generation. Germany lost one-third of men aged nineteen to twenty-two in 1914. France and Britain sustained similar losses, with mortality among young men reaching eight to ten times the normal rate. This was the "lost generation."

The breakdown of the prewar treaty system and the scale of the diplomatic failure that produced the war discredited the political classes in many countries. Meanwhile, the war itself planted seeds of political and social discontent around the globe. Relations between Russia and western Europe grew sour and suspicious. The Allies had attempted to overthrow the Bolsheviks during the war and had excluded them from the negotiations afterward; these actions instilled in the Soviets a mistrust of the West that lasted for generations. The Allied nations feared that Russia would dominate the new states of eastern Europe, building a "Red Bridge" across the continent. Elsewhere, the conflicting demands of colonialism and nationalism struck only a temporary balance, while the redrawn maps left ethnic and linguistic minorities in every country. The fires of discontent raged most fiercely in Germany, where

After You Read This Chapter

Ⓢ Visit StudySpace for quizzes, additional review materials, and multi-media documents. **wwnorton.com/studyspace**

REVIEWING THE OBJECTIVES

- The First World War broke out as a result of conflicts in the Balkans. Why?
- The Western Front was seen by all sides as a crucial theater of the conflict. What measures did the French, British, and Germans take to break the stalemate, and why did they fail?
- European governments intervened in extraordinary ways in the economy to ensure the production of material for the war effort and to remedy the social crisis caused by mobilization. How did governments intervene in the economy?
- The war led European nations to mobilize people and resources from their colonies. How did colonial subjects participate in the war effort, and what did many of them expect in return?
- Russia was devastated by the war, and the population lost confidence in the tsar's government. What circumstances allowed the Bolsheviks to seize power in 1917 and what were their goals?
- The Versailles Peace Treaty blamed the Germans for the war. Who were the most important participants in the peace conference, and who shaped the terms of the treaty the most?

the Treaty of Versailles was decried as outrageously unjust. Nearly all national governments agreed that it would eventually have to be revised. Neither war nor peace had ended the rivalries that caused the Great War.

The war also had powerful and permanent economic consequences. Beset by inflation, debt, and the difficult task of industrial rebuilding, Europe found itself displaced from the center of the world economy. The war had accelerated the decentralization of money and markets. Many Asian, African, and South American nations benefited financially as their economies became less dependent on Europe, and they were better able to profit from Europe's need for their natural resources. The United States and Japan reaped the biggest gains and emerged as leaders in the new world economy.

The war's most powerful cultural legacy was disillusionment. A generation of men had been sacrificed to no apparent end. Surviving soldiers—many of them permanently injured, both physically and psychologically—were sickened by their participation in such useless slaughter. Women and other civilians had also made extraordinary sacrifices on the home front, for little apparent gain. Both veterans and civilians were disgusted by the greedy abandonment of principles by the politicians at Versailles. In the postwar period many younger men and women mistrusted the "old men" who had dragged the world into the war. These feelings of loss and alienation were voiced in the vastly popular genre of war literature—memoirs and fiction that commemorated the experience of soldiers on the front lines. The German writer and ex-soldier Erich Maria Remarque captured the disillusion of a generation in his novel *All Quiet on the Western Front*: "Through the years our business has been killing;—it was our first calling in life. Our knowledge of life is limited to death. What will happen afterwards? And what shall come out of us?"

That was the main question facing postwar Europe. The German novelist Thomas Mann recognized that 1918 had brought "an end of an epoch, revolution and the dawn of a new age," and that he and his fellow Germans were "living in a new and unfamiliar world." The struggle to define this new world would increasingly be conceived in terms of rival ideologies—democracy, communism, and fascism—competing for the future of Europe. The eastern autocracies had fallen with the war, but liberal democracy was soon on the decline as well. While militarism and nationalism remained strong, calls for major social reforms gained force during worldwide depression. Entire populations had been mobilized during the war, and they would remain so afterward—active participants in the age of mass politics. Europe was about to embark on two turbulent decades of rejecting and reinventing its social and political institutions. As Tomas Masaryk, the first president of newly formed Czechoslovakia, described it, postwar Europe was "a laboratory atop a graveyard."

PEOPLE, IDEAS, AND EVENTS IN CONTEXT

- Why was **FRANZ FERDINAND** assassinated and how did his death contribute to the outbreak of the war?
- What was the **SCHLIEFFEN PLAN** and how was it related to the outbreak of the war?
- What was the significance of the first **BATTLE OF THE MARNE** in 1914?
- Why did the British attempt to attack the Ottoman Empire at **GALLIPOLI**?
- What was the goal of the attacking forces at **VERDUN** and the **SOMME** in 1916? What was accomplished?
- Why did many people in Russia, and especially soldiers in the Russian army, lose faith in **NICHOLAS II** of Russia?
- Who were the **BOLSHEVIKS** and the **MENSHEVIKS** and what were their disagreements?
- How did **LENIN** make use of the **SOVIETS** in challenging the **PROVISIONAL GOVERNMENT** in Russia after the fall of the tsar?
- What policies did the **BOLSHEVIKS** follow after seizing power in Russia?
- What were **WOODROW WILSON'S GOALS** at the negotiations for the Versailles Treaty?
- What treatment did Germany receive under the terms of the **TREATY OF VERSAILLES**?

CONSEQUENCES

- How did the First World War change the relationship between state and society in different European nations? Which combatant nation-states emerged relatively unscathed? Which were transformed the most?
- Did enthusiasm for the national cause mean that tensions between different social groups disappeared in the European nations that fought in the First World War? What kinds of tensions persisted, in spite of the war effort?
- What changes did the First World War bring for European women?
- What changes did the First World War bring for Europe's colonial subjects?

STORY LINES

- With the exception of Bolshevik Russia, European states attempted to find stability in the traumatic aftermath of the First World War by reinforcing democratic institutions and focusing on an orderly transition from wartime production to a peacetime economy.

- The Bolsheviks won the civil war that followed the Russian Revolution in 1917, and by the late 1920s Joseph Stalin embarked on an unprecedented revolution from above, industrializing the nation and transforming rural life through the collectivization of agriculture. The human costs were enormous, as millions died of hunger and millions more were arrested and deported to labor camps in the east.

- The Great Depression undermined political support for Europe's democracies in the 1930s, and the decade saw the consolidation of fascist regimes in Italy and Germany and an anti-capitalist communist regime in the Soviet Union.

CHRONOLOGY

1918	The November Revolution establishes the Weimar Republic
1918–1920	Russian Civil War
1920	National Socialist Worker's party founded in Germany
1922	Mussolini comes to power in Italy
1923	Hitler's Beer Hall Putsch in Munich
1928	First Soviet Five-Year Plan
1928–1929	Stalin gains power in Russia
1929–1933	Collectivization and famine in Soviet Union
1933	Hitler becomes chancellor of Germany
1937–1938	The Great Terror in Soviet Union

Before
You
Read
This
Chapter

Turmoil between the Wars

Käthe Kollwitz, a Berlin painter and sculptor, understood as well as anybody in Europe the terrible costs and futility of the First World War. Her youngest son, Peter, was killed on October 22, 1914, in Germany's failed attack on France. Her diary recorded the last moments she spent with him, an evening walk from the barracks on October 12, the day before his departure for the front: "It was dark, and we went arm in arm through the wood. He pointed out constellations to me, as he had done so often before." Her entry for October 30 was more succinct, a quotation from the postcard she had received from his commanding officer: "Your son has fallen." Kollwitz's pain at this loss found expression in her later work, which explored in naked terms the grief and powerlessness that she and her family had felt during the war years. Her suffering found expression, too, in a commitment to socialism, a political ideology that provided her with an antidote to the nationalism that pervaded German society during the war years and after. Kollwitz's socialism drew her to the attention of the Gestapo (state police) after the Nazis came to power in 1933, and she was fired from her position at the Academy of Art. She put up with house searches and harrassment, but refused invitations from friends abroad to go into exile. She died in Germany in 1945, having survived long enough to see her cherished grandson, also named Peter, killed in a second war while fighting as a German soldier on the Eastern Front in Russia in 1942.

The story of Käthe Kollwitz and her family between 1914 and 1945 is only unusual for the fact that she was a well-known artist. The suffering was all too familiar to others, as was the search for new political ideologies that might save Europeans from their past. The Great War left nine million dead in its wake, and shattered the confidence that had been such a characteristic of nineteenth-century European culture. It led tragically to another world war, even more horrific than the first. Many in the interwar years shared Kollwitz's hope for a socialist or communist future, and many others turned to extremisms of the right. The result was a near collapse of democracy. By the late 1930s, few Western democracies remained. Even in those that did, most notably Britain, France, and the United States, regimes were frayed by the same pressures and strains that wrecked democratic governments elsewhere.

The foremost cause of democracy's decline in this period was a series of continuing disruptions in the world economy, caused first by the First World War and later, by the Great Depression of 1929–1933. A second source of crisis lay in increased social conflict, exacerbated by the war. Although many hoped that these conflicts would be resolved by the peace and a renewed commitment to democratic institutions, the opposite occurred. Broad swaths of the electorate rallied to extremist political parties that promised radical transformations of nations and their cultures. Nationalism, sharpened by the war, proved a key source of discontent in its aftermath, and in Italy and Germany, frustrated nationalist sentiment turned against their governments.

The most dramatic instance of democracy's decline came with the rise of new authoritarian dictatorships, especially in the Soviet Union, Italy, and Germany. The experiences of these three nations differed significantly as a result of varying historical circumstances and personalities. In each case, however, many citizens allowed themselves to be persuaded that only drastic measures could bring order from chaos. Those measures, including the elimination of parliamentary government, strict restrictions on political freedom, and increasingly virulent repression of "enemies" of the state, were implemented with a combination of violence, intimidation, and propaganda. That so many citizens seemed willing to sacrifice their freedoms—or those of others—was a measure of their alienation, impatience, or desperation.

***WIDOWS AND ORPHANS* BY KÄTHE KOLLWITZ, 1919.** Kollwitz (1867–1945), a German artist and socialist active in Berlin, lost a son in the First World War and a grandson in the Second World War. Her work poignantly displayed the effects of poverty and war on the lives of ordinary people.

THE SOVIET UNION UNDER LENIN AND STALIN

The Russian Civil War

The Bolsheviks seized power in October 1917. They signed a separate peace with Germany in March 1918 (the Treaty of Brest-Litovsk), but Russia collapsed into civil war soon after. Fury at the terms of Brest-Litovsk mobilized the Bolsheviks' enemies. Known collectively as "Whites," the Bolsheviks' opponents included supporters of the old regime, the former nobility, and liberal supporters of the provisional government. They were joined by anti-Bolshevik dissident groups and peasant bands who opposed all central state power. The Bolsheviks, or "Reds," also faced insurrections from strong nationalist movements in the Ukraine, Georgia, and the north Caucasus. Finally, several foreign powers, including the United States, Great Britain, and Japan, landed troops on the periphery of the old empire. These interventions were only a minor threat, but they heightened Bolshevik mistrust of the capitalist world which, in the Marxists' view, would naturally oppose the existence of the world's first "socialist" state.

The Bolsheviks eventually won the civil war because they gained greater support—or at least tacit acceptance—from the majority of the population and because they were better organized for the war effort itself. Leon Trotsky, the revolutionary hero of 1905 and 1917, became the new commissar of war and created a hierarchical, disciplined military machine that grew to some five million men by 1920. Trotsky's Red Army triumphed over the White armies by the end of 1920, although fighting continued into 1922. The Bolsheviks also invaded Poland and nearly reached Warsaw before being thrown back.

The costs of the civil war were even greater than Russia's losses in the First World War: one million combat casualties, several million deaths from famine caused by the war, and one to three hundred thousand executions of noncombatants as part of Red and White terror. The barbarism of the war engendered lasting hatreds within the emerging Soviet nation, especially among ethnic minorities, and it brutalized the fledgling society that came into existence under the new Bolshevik regime.

The civil war also shaped the Bolsheviks' approach to the economy. On taking power in 1917, Lenin expected to create, for the short term at least, a state-capitalist system that resembled the successful European wartime economies. The new government took control of large-scale industry, banking, and all other major capitalist concerns while allowing small-scale private economic activity, including agriculture, to continue. The civil war pushed the new government toward a more radical economic stance known as "war communism." The Bolsheviks began to requisition grain from the peasantry, and they outlawed private trade in consumer goods as "speculation," militarized production facilities, and abolished money. Many believed that war communism would replace the capitalist system that had collapsed in 1917.

Such hopes were largely unfounded. War communism sustained the Bolshevik military effort, but further disrupted the already war-ravaged economy. The civil war devastated Russian industry and emptied major cities. The population of Moscow fell by 50 percent between 1917 and 1920. The masses of urban workers, who had strongly supported the Bolshevik revolution, melted back into the countryside; and industrial output in 1920–21 fell to only 20 percent of prewar levels. Most devastating were the effects of war communism on agriculture. The peasants had initially benefited from the revolution when they spontaneously seized and redistributed lands held by the former nobility. Nonetheless, the agricultural system was severely disrupted by the civil war, by the grain requisitioning of war communism, and by the outlawing of all private trade in grain. Large-scale famine resulted in 1921 and claimed some five million lives.

As the civil war came to a close, urban workers and soldiers became increasingly impatient with the Bolshevik

LENIN AND STALIN. Under Stalin this picture was used to show his close relationship with Lenin. In fact, the photograph has been doctored. ▪ *What opportunities for propaganda and manipulation were offered by new technologies of photography and film?*

regime, which had promised socialism and workers' control but had delivered something more akin to a military dictatorship. Large-scale strikes and protests broke out in late 1920, but the Bolsheviks moved swiftly and effectively to subdue the "popular revolts." In crushing dissent, the Bolshevik regime that emerged from the civil war made a clear statement that public opposition would not be tolerated.

The NEP Period

In response to these political and economic difficulties, the Bolsheviks abandoned war communism and in March 1921 embarked on a radically different course known as the New Economic Policy (NEP). The state continued to own all major industry and financial concerns, while individuals were allowed to own private property, trade freely within limits, and—most important—farm their land for their own benefit. Fixed taxes on the peasantry replaced grain requisitioning; what peasants grew beyond the tax requirements was theirs to do with as they saw fit. The Bolshevik most identified with the NEP was Nikolai Bukharin (1888–1938), who argued that the Bolsheviks could best industrialize the Soviet Union by taxing private peasant economic activity.

The NEP was undeniably successful in allowing Soviet agriculture to recover from the civil war; by 1924 agricultural harvests had returned to prewar levels. Peasants were largely left alone to do as they pleased, and they responded by producing enough grain to feed the country, though they continued to use very primitive farming methods to do so. The NEP was less successful, however, in encouraging peasants to participate in markets to benefit urban areas. The result was a series of shortages in grain deliveries to cities, a situation that prompted many Bolsheviks to call for revival of the radical economic practices of war communism. The fate of these radical proposals, however, was tied to the fate of the man who would, contrary to all expectations, replace Lenin as the leader of the USSR and become one of the most notorious dictators of all time: Joseph Stalin.

Stalin and the "Revolution from Above"

Stalin's rise was swift and unpredicted. His political success was rooted in intraparty conflicts in the 1920s, but it was also closely tied to the abrupt end of the NEP period in the late 1920s and to the beginning of a massive program of social and economic modernization. This "revolution from above" was the most rapid social and economic transformation any nation has seen in modern history. It was carried out, however, at unprecedented human cost.

Stalin (1879–1953), the son of a poor shoemaker, was a Bolshevik from the Caucasus nation of Georgia. His real name was Iosep Jughashvili. Receiving his early education in an Orthodox seminary, he participated in revolutionary activity in the Caucasus and spent many years in Siberian exile before the revolution. He was an important member of the Bolshevik party during the Russian Revolution, but he was not one of the central figures and was certainly not a front runner for party leadership. After Lenin's death in 1924, the civil war hero Leon Trotsky was widely assumed to be the best candidate to succeed him.

Stalin shrewdly played the game of internal party politics after Lenin's death. He sidelined his opponents within the Bolshevik party by isolating and expelling each of them successively. Trotsky was the first to go, driven out by a coalition of Stalin and others who feared Trotsky's desire to take control of the party himself. Stalin then turned on his former allies and removed them in turn, culminating in the removal of Bukharin from the Politburo (short for political bureau, which governed the Communist party and state) in 1928–29.

Stalin's campaign against Bukharin was connected to his desire to discard the NEP system and to launch an all-out industrialization drive. By the late 1920s, Stalin

WINTER DEPORTATIONS, 1929–30. Ukrainian families charged with being kulaks were deported from their homes because of their refusal to join Stalin's collective farming plan. Many of the evicted families were shipped north by train to the Arctic, where they perished due to the lack of adequate food and shelter.

believed that the Soviet Union could not hope to industrialize by relying on taxes generated from small-scale peasant agriculture. He began to push for an increase in the tempo of industrialization as early as 1927, prompted by fears of falling behind the West and by the perceived threat of another world war. Almost all of the Bolshevik leaders supported Stalin's plan to step up the tempo of industrialization. But hardly anybody supported what happened next: an abrupt turn toward forced industrialization and collectivization of agriculture.

COLLECTIVIZATION

In late 1929 Stalin embarked on collectivization of agriculture by force. Peasants would either pool their resources and join collective farms or work on state farms as paid laborers. Within a few months, the Politburo began to issue orders to use force against peasants who resisted collectivization. The process that ensued was brutal and chaotic. Local party and police officials forced peasants to give up their private land, farming implements, and livestock and to join collective farms. Peasants resisted, often violently. There were some sixteen hundred large-scale rebellions in the Soviet Union between 1929 and 1933; some involved several thousand people, and quelling them required military intervention, including the use of artillery. By 1935 collectivization of agriculture was complete in most areas of the Soviet Union.

To facilitate collectivization, Stalin also launched an all-out attack on peasants designated as *kulaks* (a derogatory term for well-to-do farmers, literally meaning "tight-fisted ones"). Most kulaks, though, were not any better off than their neighbors, and the word became one of many terms for peasants hostile to collectivization. Between 1929 and 1933, some one and a half million peasants were uprooted, dispossessed of their property, and resettled from their farmlands to either inhospitable reaches of the Soviet east and north or to poor farmland closer to their original homes. The liquidation of kulaks as a class magnified the disruptive effects of agricultural collectivization, and the two together produced one of the most devastating famines in modern European history. Peasants who were forced into collective farms had little incentive to produce extra food, and exiling many of the most productive peasants not surprisingly weakened the agricultural system. In 1932–33, famine spread across the southern region of the Soviet Union. This was the most productive agricultural area in the country, and the famine that struck there was thus particularly senseless. The 1933 famine cost some three to five million lives. During the famine, the Bolsheviks maintained substantial grain reserves in other parts of the country, enough to save many hundreds of thousands of lives at a minimum, but they refused to send this grain to the affected areas, preferring instead to seal off famine-stricken regions and allow people to starve. Grain reserves were instead sold overseas for hard currency and stockpiled in case of war. After 1935 there would never again be any large-scale resistance to Soviet power in the countryside.

The Five-Year Plans

In Stalin's view, collectivization provided the resources for the other major aspect of his revolution from above: a rapid campaign of forced industrialization. The road map for this industrialization process was the first Five-Year Plan (1928–32), an ambitious set of goals that Stalin and his cohorts drew up in 1927. The results rank as one of the most stunning periods of economic growth the modern world has ever seen. Soviet statistics boasted of annual growth rates of 20 percent a year. Even the more cautious Western estimates of 14 percent annual growth were remarkable, given the worldwide depression elsewhere. The Bolsheviks built entirely new industries in entirely new cities. In 1926, only one fifth of the population lived in towns. Fifteen years later, in 1939, roughly a third did. The urban population had grown from 26 million to 56 million in under fifteen years. The Soviet Union was well on its way to becoming an urban, industrial society.

This rapid industrialization came, however, at enormous human cost. Many large-scale projects were carried out with prison labor, especially in the timber and mining

industries. The labor camp system, known as the *gulag*, became a central part of the Stalinist economic system. People were arrested and sent to camps on a bewildering array of charges, ranging from petty criminal infractions to contact with foreigners to having the ill fortune to be born of bourgeois or kulak parents. The camp system spread throughout the Soviet Union in the 1930s: by the end of the decade, roughly 3.6 million people were incarcerated by the regime. This army of prisoners was used to complete the most arduous and dangerous industrialization tasks.

The economic system created during this revolution from above was also fraught with structural problems that would plague the Soviet Union for its entire history. The command economy, with each year's production levels entirely planned in advance in Moscow, never functioned in a rational way. Heavy industry was always favored over light industry, and the emphasis on quantity made quality practically meaningless. A factory that was charged with producing a certain number of pairs of shoes, for example, could cut costs by producing all one style and size. The consumer would be left with useless goods, but the producer would fulfill the plan. Stalin's industrialization drive did

"IMPERIALISTS CANNOT STOP THE SUCCESS OF THE FIVE-YEAR PLAN!" ▪ *Did propaganda like this also appeal to Russian nationalist pride?*

Stalin's Industrialization of the Soviet Union

How did the Soviet people experience Stalin's industrialization drive? New archives have helped historians glimpse what the common people lived through and how they responded. The first excerpt is a speech Stalin gave at a Conference of Managers of Socialist Industry in 1931. In his usual style, he invoked fears of Soviet backwardness and Russian nationalism while summoning all to take up the task of industrial production.

The letters in the second selection come from several hundred that workers and peasants sent to Soviet newspapers and authorities recounting their experiences and offering their opinions. Both of the ones printed here were sent to the Soviet newspaper Pravda.

"The Tasks of Business Executives"

It is sometimes asked whether it is not possible to slow down the tempo somewhat, to put a check on the movement. No, comrades, it is not possible! The tempo must not be reduced! On the contrary, we must increase it as much as is within our powers and possibilities. This is dictated to us by our obligations to the workers and peasants of the USSR. This is dictated to us by our obligations to the working class of the whole world.

To slacken the tempo would mean falling behind. And those who fall behind get beaten. But we do not want to be beaten. No, we refuse to be beaten. One feature of the history of old Russia was the continual beatings she suffered because of her backwardness. She was beaten by the Mongol khans. She was beaten by the Turkish beys. . . . She was beaten by the British and French capitalists. She was beaten by the Japanese barons. All beat her—for her backwardness: for military backwardness, for cultural backwardness, for political backwardness, for industrial backwardness, for agricultural backwardness. . . .

We are fifty or a hundred years behind the advanced countries. We must make good this distance in ten years. Either we do it, or we shall be crushed. . . .

In ten years at most we must make good the distance which separates us from the advanced capitalist countries. We have all the 'objective' possibilities for this. The only thing lacking is the ability to take proper advantage of these possibilities. And that depends on us. *Only* on us! . . . It is time to put an end to the rotten policy of non-interference in production. It is time to adopt a new policy, a policy adapted to the present times—the policy of interfering in everything. If you are a factory manager, then interfere in all the affairs of the factory, look into everything, let nothing escape you, learn and learn again. Bolsheviks must master technique. It is time Bolsheviks themselves became experts. . . .

transform the country from an agrarian nation to a world industrial power in the space of a few short years, but in the longer run, the system would become an economic disaster.

The Stalin revolution also produced fundamental cultural and economic changes. The revolution from above altered the face of Soviet cities and the working class populating them. New cities were largely made up of first-generation peasants who brought their rural traditions to the cities with them, changing the fragile urban culture that had existed during the 1920s. Women, too, entered the urban workforce in increasing numbers in the 1930s—women went from 20 percent to almost 40 percent of the workforce in one decade, and in light industry they made up two-thirds of the labor force by 1940.

At the same time, Stalin promoted a sharply conservative shift in all areas of culture and society. In art, the radical modernism of the 1920s was crushed by socialist realism, a deadening aesthetic that celebrated the drive toward socialism and left no room for experimentation. Family policy and gender roles underwent a similar reversal. Early Bolshevik activists had promoted a utopian attempt to rebuild one of the basic structures of prerevolutionary society—the family—and to create a genuinely new proletarian social structure. The Bolsheviks in the 1920s legalized divorce,

There are no fortresses which Bolsheviks cannot capture. We have assumed power. We have built up a huge socialist industry. We have swung the middle peasants to the path of social-ism. . . . What remains to be done is not so much: to study technique, to master science. And when we have done that we will develop a tempo of which we dare not even dream at present.

Source: Joseph Stalin, "The Tasks of Business Executives" [speech given at the First All-Union Conference of Managers of Socialist Industry, February 4, 1931], as cited in Richard Sakwa, *The Rise and Fall of the Soviet Union, 1917–1991* (New York: 1999), pp. 187–88.

Stalin's Industrial Development: The View from Below

It should not be forgotten that many millions of workers are participating in the building of socialism. A horse with its own strength can drag seventy-five poods,* but its owner has loaded it with a hundred poods, and in addition he's fed it poorly. No matter how much he uses the whip, it still won't be able to move the cart.

This is also true for the working class. They've loaded it with socialist competition, shock work, over-fulfilling the industrial and financial plan, and so forth. A worker toils seven hours, not ever leaving his post, and this is not all he does. Afterward he sits in meetings or else attends classes for an hour and a half or two in order to increase his skill level, and if he doesn't do these things, then he's doing things at home. And what does he live on? One hundred fifty grams of salted mutton, he will make soup without any of the usual additives, neither carrots, beets, flour, nor salt pork. What kind of soup do you get from this? Mere "dishwater."

—B. N. Kniazev, Tula, Sept. 1930

Comrade Editor, Please give me an answer. Do the local authorities have the right to forcibly take away the only cow of industrial and office workers? What is more, they demand a receipt showing that the cow was handed over voluntarily and they threaten you by saying if you don't do this, they will put you in prison for failure to fulfill the meat procurement. How can you live when the cooperative distributes only black bread, and at the market goods have the prices of 1919 and 1920? Lice have eaten us to death, and soap is given only to railroad workers. From hunger and filth we have a massive outbreak of spotted fever.

—Anonymous, from Aktybinsk, Kazakhstan

*A pood is a Russian unit of weight, equal to 36.11 pounds.

Source: Lewis Siegelbaum and Andrei Sokolov, *Stalinism as a Way of Life: A Narrative in Documents* (New Haven, CT: 2000), pp. 39–41.

Questions for Analysis

1. What are Stalin's priorities?

2. What images does Stalin use to capture his audience's attention?

3. How did the Soviet people experience Stalin's industrialization drive?

---

expelled the Orthodox Church from marriage ceremonies, and legalized abortion. Stalin abandoned these ideas of communist familial relations in favor of efforts to strengthen traditional family ties: divorce became more difficult, abortion was outlawed in 1936 except in cases that threatened the life of the mother, and homosexuality was declared a criminal offense. State subsidies and support for mothers, which were progressive for the time, could not change the reality that Soviet women were increasingly forced to carry the double burden of familial and wage labor to support Stalin's version of Soviet society. All areas of Soviet cultural and social policy experienced similar reversals.

The Great Terror

The "Great Terror" of 1937–38 left nearly a million people dead and as many as one and a half million more in labor camps. As Stalin consolidated his personal dictatorship over the country, he eliminated enemies—real and imagined—along with individuals and groups he considered superfluous to the new Soviet society.

The Terror was aimed at various categories of internal "enemies," from the top to the very bottom of Soviet society. The top level of the Bolshevik party itself was purged almost completely; some one hundred thousand party members were removed, most facing prison sentences or execution. The purge also struck—with particular ferocity—nonparty elites, industrial managers, and intellectuals. In 1937 and 1938 Stalin purged the military, arresting some forty thousand officers and shooting at least ten thousand. These purges disrupted the government and the economy but allowed Stalin to promote a new, young cadre of officials who owed their careers, if not their lives, to Stalin personally. Whole ethnic groups were viewed with suspicion, including Poles, Ukrainians, Lithuanians, Latvians, Koreans, and others. From the bottom, some two to three hundred thousand "dekulakized" peasants, petty criminals, and other social misfits were arrested, and many shot.

The Great Terror remains one of the most puzzling aspects of Stalin's path to dictatorial power. The Terror succeeded, with a certain paranoid logic, in solidifying Stalin's personal control over all aspects of social and political life in the Soviet Union, but it did so by destroying the most talented elements in Soviet society.

The results of the Stalin revolution were profound. No other regime in the history of Europe had ever attempted to reorder completely the politics, economy, and society of a major nation. The Soviets had done so in a mere ten years. By 1939 private manufacturing and trade had been almost entirely abolished. Factories, mines, railroads, and public utilities were exclusively owned by the state. Stores were either government enterprises or cooperatives in which consumers owned shares. Agriculture had been almost completely socialized. The society that emerged from this terrible decade was industrial, more urban than rural, and more modern than traditional. But the USSR that emerged from this tumultuous period would barely be able to withstand the immense strains placed on it when the Germans struck less than three years after the end of the Terror.

THE EMERGENCE OF FASCISM IN ITALY

Like many European nations, Italy emerged from the First World War as a democracy in distress. Italy was on the winning side but the war had cost nearly 700,000 Italian lives and over $15 billion. Moreover, Italy had received secret promises of specific territorial gains during the war, only to find those promises withdrawn when they conflicted with principles of self-determination. Italian claims to the west coast of the Adriatic, for instance, were denied by Yugoslavia. At first the nationalists blamed the "mutilated victory" on President Wilson, but after a short time they turned on their own rulers and what they considered the weaknesses of parliamentary democracy.

Italy had long-standing problems that were made worse by the war. Since unification, the Italian nation had been rent by an unhealthy economic split—divided into a prosperous industrialized north and a poor agrarian south. Social conflict over land, wages, and local power caused friction in the countryside as well as in urban centers. Governments were often seen as corrupt, indecisive, and defeatist. This was the background for the more immediate problems that Italy faced after the war.

Inflation and unemployment were perhaps the most destructive effects of the war. Inflation produced high prices, speculation, and profiteering. And though normally wages would have risen also, the postwar labor market was glutted by returning soldiers. Furthermore, business elites were shaken by strikes, which became increasingly large and frequent, and by the closing of foreign markets. The parliamentary government that was set up after the war failed to ease these dire conditions, and Italians wanted radical reforms. For the working class, this meant socialism. The movement grew increasingly radical: in 1920, the socialist and anarchist workers seized scores of factories, most in the metallurgy sector, and tried to run them for the benefit of the workers themselves. In some rural areas, so-called Red Leagues tried to break up large estates and force landlords to reduce their rents. In all these actions, the model of the Russian Revolution, although it was only vaguely understood, encouraged the development of local radicalism.

The rising radical tide, especially seen against the backdrop of the Bolshevik revolution, worried other social groups. Industrialists and landowners feared for their property. Small shopkeepers and white-collar workers—social groups that did not think the working-class movement supported their interests—found themselves alienated by business elites on the one hand and by apparently revolutionary radicals on the other. The threat from the left provoked a strong surge to the right. Fascism appeared in the form of vigilante groups breaking up strikes, fighting with workers in the streets, or ousting the Red Leagues from lands occupied in the countryside.

The Rise of Mussolini

"I am fascism," said Benito Mussolini, and indeed, the success of the Italian fascist movement depended heavily on his leadership. Mussolini (1883–1945) was the son of a socialist blacksmith and a schoolteacher. He studied to become a teacher, but settled on journalism as a career, writing for socialist newspapers. After a brief period in Switzerland he was expelled from the country for fomenting strikes. He returned to Italy, where he became the editor of *Avanti,* the leading socialist daily.

When war broke out in August 1914, Mussolini broke with the socialists and became an ardent nationalist, urging Italy to join the Allies. Deprived of his position as the editor of *Avanti,* he founded a new paper, *Il Popolo d'Italia,* and dedicated its columns to arousing enthusiasm for war.

As early as October 1914, Mussolini had organized groups, called *fasci,* to help drum up support for the war. Members of the fasci were young idealists, fanatical nationalists. After the war, these groups formed the base of Mussolini's fascist movement. (The word *fascism* derives from the Latin *fasces:* an ax surrounded by a bundle of sticks that represented the authority of the Roman state. The Italian *fascio* means "group" or "band.") In 1919 Mussolini drafted the original platform of the Fascist party. It had several surprising elements, including universal suffrage (including woman), an eight-hour workday, and a tax on inheritances. A new platform, adopted in 1920, abandoned all references to economic reforms. Neither platform earned the fascists many followers.

EUROPE IN 1923. ▪ *Which countries and empires lost territories after the First World War, and with what consequences?* ▪ *How did the Russian Revolution change European politics?* ▪ *What problems arose in the central and eastern European nations created after the First World War?*

What the fascists lacked in political support, they made up for in aggressive determination. They gained the respect of the middle class and landowners, and intimidated many others, by forcefully repressing radical movements of industrial workers and peasants. They attacked socialists, often physically, and succeeded in taking over some local governments. As the national regime weakened, Mussolini's coercive politics made him look like a solution to the absence of leadership, and the number of his supporters grew. In September 1922, he began to negotiate with other parties and the king for fascist participation in government. On October 28 an army of about fifty thousand fascist militiamen, in black-shirted uniforms, marched into Rome and occupied the capital. The premier resigned, and the following day the king, Victor Emmanuel III, reluctantly invited Mussolini to form a cabinet. Without firing a shot the Black Shirts had gained control of the Italian government. The explanation of their success is to be found less in the strength of the fascist movement itself than in the Italian disappointments after the war and the weakness of the older governing classes.

The parliamentary system had folded under pressure. And though Mussolini had "legally" been granted his power, he immediately began to establish a one-party dictatorship. The doctrines of Italian fascism had three components. The first was statism. The state was declared to incorporate every interest and every loyalty of its members. There was to be "nothing above the state, nothing outside the state, nothing against the state." The second was nationalism. Nationhood was the highest form of society, with a life and a soul of its own, transcending the individuals who composed it. The third was militarism. Nations that did not expand would eventually wither and die. Fascists believed that war ennobled man and regenerated sluggish and decadent peoples.

Mussolini began to rebuild Italy in accordance with these principles. The first step was to change electoral laws so they granted his party solid parliamentary majorities and to intimidate the opposition. He then moved to close down parliamentary government and other parties entirely. He abolished the cabinet system and all but extinguished the powers of the parliament. He made the Fascist party an integral part of the Italian constitution. Mussolini assumed the dual position of prime minister and party leader (*duce*), and he used the party's militia to eliminate his enemies by intimidation and violence. Mussolini's government also controlled the police, muzzled the press, and censored academic activity.

Meanwhile, Mussolini preached the end of class conflict and its replacement by national unity. He began to reorganize the economy and labor, taking away the power of the country's labor movement. The Italian economy was placed under the management of twenty-two corporations,

each responsible for a major industrial enterprise. In each corporation were representatives of trade unions, whose members were organized by the Fascist party, the employers, and the government. Together, the members of these corporations were given the task of determining working conditions, wages, and prices. It is not surprising, however, that the decisions of these bodies were closely supervised by the government and favored the position of management. Indeed, the government quickly aligned with big business, creating more of a corrupt bureaucracy than a revolutionary economy.

Mussolini secured some working-class assent with state-sponsored programs, including massive public-works projects, library building, paid vacations for workers, and social security. In 1929, he settled Italy's sixty-year-old conflict with the Roman Catholic Church. He signed a treaty that granted independence to the papal residence in the Vatican City and established Roman Catholicism as the official religion of the state. The treaty also guaranteed religious education in the nation's schools and made religious marriage ceremonies mandatory.

In fact, Mussolini's regime did much to maintain the status quo. Party officers exercised some political supervision over bureaucrats, yet did not infiltrate the bureaucracy in significant numbers. Moreover, Mussolini remained on friendly terms with the elites who had assisted his rise to power. Whatever he proclaimed about the distinctions between fascism and capitalism, the economy of Italy remained dependent on private enterprise. Fascism, however, did little to lessen Italy's plight during the worldwide depression of the 1930s.

Like Nazism later, fascism had contradictory elements. It sought to restore traditional authority and, at the same time, mobilize all of Italian society for economic and nationalist purposes—a process that inevitably undercut older authorities. It created new authoritarian organizations and activities that comported with these goals: exercise programs to make the young fit and mobilized, youth camps, awards to mothers of large families, political rallies, and parades in small towns in the countryside. Activities like these offered people a feeling of political involvement though they no longer enjoyed political rights. This mobilized but essentially passive citizenship was a hallmark of fascism.

WEIMAR GERMANY

On November 9, 1918—two days before the armistice ending the First World War—a massive and largely unexpected uprising in Berlin resulted in the kaiser's abdication and the birth of a new German republic. The leader of the new government was Friedrich Ebert, a member of the Social Democratic party (SPD) in the Reichstag. The revolution spread quickly. By the end of the month, councils of workers and soldiers controlled hundreds of German cities. The "November Revolution" was fast and far reaching, though not as revolutionary as many middle- and upper-class conservatives feared. The majority of socialists steered a cautious, democratic course: they wanted reforms but were willing to leave much of the existing imperial bureaucracy intact. Above all, they wanted a popularly elected national assembly to draft a constitution for the new republic.

Two months passed, however, before elections could be held—a period of crisis that verged on civil war. The revolutionary movement that had brought the SPD to power now threatened it. Independent socialists and a nascent Communist party wanted radical reforms, and in December 1918 and January 1919, they staged armed uprisings in the streets of Berlin. Fearful of a Bolshevik-style revolution, the Social Democratic government turned against its former allies and sent militant bands of workers and volunteers to crush the uprisings. During the conflict, the government's fighters murdered Rosa Luxemburg and Karl Liebknecht—two German communist leaders who became instant martyrs. Violence continued into 1920, creating a lasting bitterness among groups on the left.

More important, the revolutionary aftermath of the war gave rise to bands of militant counterrevolutionaries. Veterans and other young nationalists joined so-called *Freikorps* (free corps). Such groups developed throughout the country, drawing as many as several hundred thousand members. Former army officers who led these militias continued their war experience by fighting against Bolsheviks, Poles, and communists. The politics of the Freikorps were fiercely right wing. Anti-Marxist, anti-Semitic, and antiliberal, they openly opposed the new German republic and its parliamentary democracy. Many of the early Nazi leaders had fought in the First World War and participated in Freikorps units.

Germany's new government—known as the Weimar Republic (*VY-mahr*) for the city in which its constitution was drafted—rested on a coalition of socialists, Catholic centrists, and liberal democrats, a necessary compromise since no single party won a majority of the votes in the January 1919 election. The Weimar constitution was based on the values of parliamentary liberalism and set up an open, pluralistic framework for German democracy. Through a series of compromises, the constitution established universal suffrage (for both women and men) and a bill of rights that guaranteed not only civil liberties but also a range of social entitlements. On paper, at least, the revolutionary movement had succeeded.

Yet the Weimar government lasted just over a decade. By 1930 it was in crisis, and in 1933 it collapsed. What happened? Many of Weimar's problems were born from Germany's defeat in the First World War, which was not only devastating but also humiliating. Many Germans soon latched onto rumors that the army hadn't actually been defeated in battle but instead had been stabbed in the back by socialists and Jewish leaders in the German government. Army officers cultivated this story even before the war was over; and though untrue, it helped salve the wounded pride of German patriots. In the next decade, those in search of a scapegoat also blamed the republican regime, which had signed the Versailles treaty. What was needed, many critics argued, was authoritative leadership to guide the nation and regain the world's respect.

The Treaty of Versailles magnified Germany's sense of dishonor. Germany was forced to cede a tenth of its territory, accept responsibility for the war, and slash the size of its army to a mere hundred thousand men—a punishment that riled the politically powerful corps of officers. Most important, the treaty saddled Germany with $33 billion in punitive reparations. Some opponents of the reparations settlement urged the government not to pay, arguing that the enormous sum would doom Germany's economy. In 1924 Germany accepted a new schedule of reparations designed by an international committee headed by the American financier Charles G. Dawes. At the same time, the German chancellor Gustav Stresemann moved Germany toward a foreign policy of cooperation and rapprochement that lasted throughout the 1920s. Many German people, however, continued to resent the reparations, Versailles, and the government that refused to repudiate the treaty.

Major economic crises also played a central role in Weimar's collapse. The republic's attempt to fund postwar demobilization programs while meeting French demands for reparation payments led to a period of extraordinary hyperinflation that peaked in 1923 with a currency so lacking in value that a pound of beef cost almost 2 trillion marks. Millions of Germans saw their savings wiped out, and those on fixed incomes became destitute. Government borrowing from the United States succeeded in establishing an atmosphere of normalcy after 1925, but the dangers of this dependent relationship were revealed in 1929 when the U.S. stock market crashed, throwing the world's economy into depression. Capital flow to Germany virtually stopped.

The Great Depression pushed Weimar's political system to the breaking point. In 1929, there were two million unemployed; in 1932, six million. In those three years production dropped by 44 percent. Artisans and small shopkeepers lost both status and income. Farmers

HITLER AND THE NATIONAL SOCIALISTS

HYPERINFLATION. German children use stacks of money as toys. In July 1922, the American dollar was worth 670 German marks; in November 1923 it was worth 4,210,500,000,000.
■ *How might hyperinflation have affected attitudes in Germany toward the Weimar Republic's government?*

National Socialism drew its support from many sources—bitterness at defeat in the First World War, fears of communism, and strong feelings of anti-Semitism. Nevertheless, Adolf Hitler's political party did not gain mass support until the economic crisis caused by the Great Depression in 1929. The combination of unprecedented unemployment and a lack of faith in traditional parties to meet the crisis led many in Germany to voice support for Hitler's aggressive nationalism and his violent targeting of internal and external enemies.

Adolf Hitler was born in 1889 in Austria, the son of a petty customs official. He dropped out of school to become an artist in 1909, but was rejected by the academy and lived a hand-to-mouth existence on the street, doing manual labor. During this time he listened closely to Austrian politicians preaching anti-Semitism, anti-Marxism, and pan-Germanism. He joined the German army in 1914, and later claimed that the experience gave his life meaning for the first time. After the war, he joined the newly formed German Workers' Party, which soon changed its name to the National Socialist Workers' Party (abbreviated in popular usage to Nazi).

Hitler quickly became a leader of this small group of nationalist militants who refused to accept Germany's defeat, which they blamed on socialists and Jews. In 1923, the group made a failed attempt to seize power in Bavaria—the so-called Beer Hall Putsch—and Hitler spent seven months in prison, where he wrote his autobiography, *Mein Kampf* (*Myn KAHMPF*—"My Struggle") in 1924, arguing that communists and Jews had weakened Germany and that the Weimar Republic was incapable of leading the nation. Hitler concluded, however, that the putsch had been a mistake and that the Nazis' only hope of seizing power lay in the ballot box.

Between 1924 and 1933, the Nazis persisted in their attempts to win seats in the German parliament through elections. At first this strategy brought meager results—after a high of 6.6 percent of the vote in the "inflation election" of 1924, the Nazis made little progress as the economy stabilized. After 1928, however, political polarization in the Weimar Republic worked to Hitler's advantage, and the unemployment crisis brought about by the beginning of the depression proved to be the decisive factor. Hitler stopped in his attempts to attract votes from workers (who tended to vote on the left) and switched instead to a campaign designed to win support from rural voters and members of the middle classes.

fared even worse, having never recovered from the crisis of the early 1920s. Peasants staged mass demonstrations against the government's agricultural policies even before the depression hit. For white-collar and civil service employees, the depression meant lower salaries, poor working conditions, and a constant threat of unemployment. Burdened with plummeting tax revenues and spiraling numbers of Germans in need of relief, the government repeatedly cut welfare benefits, which further demoralized the electorate. Finally, the crisis created an opportunity for Weimar's opponents. Many leading industrialists supported a return to authoritarian government, and they were allied with equally conservative landowners, united by a desire for protective economic policies to stimulate the sale of domestic goods and foodstuffs. Those conservative forces wielded considerable power in Germany, beyond the control of the government. So too did the army and the civil service, which were staffed with opponents of the republic—men who rejected the principles of parliamentary democracy and international cooperation that Weimar represented.

The Nazi electoral campaigns focused on a few themes: the dangers of communism, the "degenerate" and "decadent" culture of the postwar years, the weakness of parliamentary government, and the influence of "cosmopolitan" (a code word for Jewish or insufficiently nationalist) movies such as *All Quiet on the Western Front*. In 1930 the Nazis received 18.3 percent of the vote and won 107 of 577 seats in the parliament, second only to the Social Democrats. Hitler ran for president in 1932 and lost, but the results showed Hitler drawing support across class lines, among all age groups, and in all regions of Germany. Later that year, the Nazis polled 37.4 percent of the vote in parliamentary elections, a significant plurality.

In January 1933, therefore, President Hindenburg invited Hitler to be chancellor of Germany, hoping to create a conservative coalition that would bring the Nazis into line with less radical parties. Once legally installed in power, however, Hitler made the most of it. When a Dutch anarchist with links to the Communist party set fire to the Reichstag on the night of Feburary 27, Hitler seized the opportunity to suspend civil rights "as a defensive measure against communist acts of violence." He convinced Hindenburg to dissolve the Reichstag and to order a new election on March 5, 1933. Under Hitler's sway, the new parliament granted him unlimited powers for the next four years. Hitler proclaimed his government the "Third Reich"—the first was the realm of Charlemagne in the Middle Ages, and the second was the German Empire of 1870–1918.

Nazi Germany

By the fall of 1933, Germany had become a one-party state. The socialist and communist left was crushed by the new regime. Almost all non-Nazi organizations had been either abolished or forced to become part of the Nazi system. Party propaganda sought to impress citizens with the regime's "monolithic efficiency." But in fact, the Nazi government was a tangled bureaucratic maze, with both agencies and individuals vying fiercely for Hitler's favor.

Ironically, at the end of the party's first year in power, the most serious challenges to Hitler came from within the party. Hitler's paramilitary Nazi storm troopers (the SA) had been formed to maintain discipline within the party and impose order in society. SA membership soared after 1933, and many in the SA hailed Hitler's appointment as the beginning of a genuinely Nazi revolution. Such radicalism was alarming to the more traditional conservative groups that had helped make Hitler chancellor. If Hitler was to maintain power, then, he needed to tame the SA. On the night of June 30, 1934, more than a thousand high-ranking SA officials, in-

cluding several of Hitler's oldest associates, were executed in a bloody purge known as the Night of Long Knives.

The purge was accomplished by a second paramilitary organization, the *Schutzstaffel* ("bodyguard"), or SS. Headed by the fanatical Heinrich Himmler, the SS became the most dreaded arm of Nazi terror. As Himmler saw it, the mission of the SS was to fight political and racial enemies of the regime, which included building the system of concentration camps. The first camp, at Dachau, opened in March 1933. The secret state police, known as the Gestapo, were responsible for the arrest, incarceration in camps, and murder of thousands of Germans. But the police force was generally understaffed and deluged with paperwork—as one historian has shown, the Gestapo was not "omniscient, omnipotent, and omnipresent." In fact, the majority of arrests was based on voluntary denunciations made by ordinary citizens against each other, often as petty personal attacks. It was not lost on the Gestapo leadership that these denunciations created a level of control that the Gestapo itself could never achieve.

Hitler and the Nazis enjoyed a sizable degree of popular support. Many Germans approved of Hitler's use of violence against the left. The Nazis could play on deep-seated fears of communism, and they spoke a language of intense national pride and unity that had broad appeal. Many Germans saw Hitler as a symbol of a strong, revitalized Germany. Propagandists fostered a Führer cult, depicting Hitler as a charismatic leader endowed with magnetic energy. Hitler's appeal also rested on his ability to give the German people what they wanted: jobs for workers, a productive economy for industrialists, a bulwark against communism for those who feared the wave of revolution. His appeal lay not so much in the programs he championed, many of which were ill-conceived or contradictory, but in his revolt against politics as they had been practiced in Germany. Finally, he promised to lead Germany back to national greatness and to "overthrow" the Versailles settlement.

Hitler's plans for national recovery called for full-scale rearmament and economic self-sufficiency. With policies similar to those of other Western nations, the Nazis made massive public investments, set strict market controls to stop inflation and stabilize the currency, and sealed Germany off from the world economy. The regime launched state-financed construction projects—highways, public housing, reforestation. Late in the decade, as the Nazis rebuilt the entire German military complex, unemployment dropped from over six million to under two hundred thousand. The German economy looked better than any other in Europe. Hitler claimed this as his "economic miracle." Such improvements were significant, especially in the eyes of Germans who had lived through the continual turmoil of war, inflation, political instability, and economic crisis.

Nazi Propaganda

The Nazis promised many things to many people. As the document by Goebbels shows, anti-Semitism allowed them to blend their racial nationalism, vaguely defined (and anti-Marxist) socialism, and disgust with the state of German culture and politics. Joseph Goebbels, one of the early members of the party, became director of propaganda for the party in 1928. Later Hitler appointed him head of the National Ministry for Public Enlightenment and Propaganda. The Nazis worked hard to win the rural vote, as evidenced by the Nazi campaign pamphlet reprinted in the second excerpt. The Nazis tried to appeal to farmers' economic grievances, their fears of socialism on the one hand and big business on the other, and their more general hostility to urban life and culture.

Joseph Goebbels, "Why Are We Enemies of the Jews?"

 We are NATIONALISTS because we see in the NATION the only possibility for the protection and the furtherance of our existence.

The NATION is the organic bond of a people for the protection and defense of their lives. He is nationally minded who understands this IN WORD AND IN DEED. . . .

Young nationalism has its unconditional demands, BELIEF IN THE NATION is a matter of all the people, not for individuals of rank, a class, or an industrial clique. The eternal must be separated from the contemporary. The maintenance of a rotten industrial system has nothing to do with nationalism. I can love Germany and hate capitalism; not only CAN I do it, I also MUST do it. The germ of the rebirth of our people LIES ONLY IN THE DESTRUCTION OF THE SYSTEM OF PLUNDERING THE HEALTHY POWER OF THE PEOPLE.

WE ARE NATIONALISTS BECAUSE WE, AS GERMANS, LOVE GERMANY. And because we love Germany, we demand the protection of its national spirit and we battle against its destroyers.

WHY ARE WE SOCIALISTS?

We are SOCIALISTS because we see in SOCIALISM the only possibility for maintaining our racial existence and through it the reconquest of our political freedom and the rebirth of the German state. SOCIALISM has its peculiar form first of all through its comradeship in arms with the forward-driving energy of a newly awakened nationalism. Without nationalism it is nothing, a phantom, a theory, a vision of air, a book. With it, it is everything, THE FUTURE, FREEDOM, FATHERLAND! . . .

WHY DO WE OPPOSE THE JEWS?

We are ENEMIES OF THE JEWS, because we are fighters for the freedom of the German people. THE JEW IS THE CAUSE AND THE BENEFICIARY OF OUR MISERY. He has used the social difficulties of the broad masses of our people to deepen the unholy split between Right and Left among our people. He has made two halves of Germany. He is the real cause for our loss of the Great War.

The Jew has no interest in the solution of Germany's fateful problems. He CANNOT have any. FOR HE LIVES ON THE FACT THAT THERE HAS BEEN NO SOLUTION. If we would make the German people a unified community and give them freedom before the world, then the Jew can have no place among us. He has the best trumps in his hands when a people lives in inner and outer slavery. THE JEW IS RESPONSIBLE FOR OUR MISERY AND HE LIVES ON IT.

That is the reason why we, AS NATIONALISTS and AS SOCIALISTS, oppose the Jew. HE HAS CORRUPTED OUR RACE, FOULED OUR MORALS, UNDERMINED OUR CUSTOMS, AND BROKEN OUR POWER.

Like Mussolini, Hitler moved to abolish class conflict by stripping working-class institutions of their power. He outlawed trade unions and strikes, froze wages, and organized workers and employers into a National Labor Front. At the same time, the Nazis increased workers' welfare benefits, generally in line with those of the other Western nations. Class distinctions were somewhat blurred by the regime's attempts to infuse a new national "spirit" into the entire society. Popular organizations cut across class lines, especially among the youth. The Hitler Youth, a club modeled on the Boy Scouts, was highly successful at teaching children the values of Hitler's Reich; the National Labor Service drafted students for a term to work on state-sponsored building and reclamation projects.

National Socialist Campaign Pamphlet, 1932

 ERMAN FARMER YOU BELONG TO HITLER! WHY?

The German farmer stands between two great dangers today:

The one danger is the American economic system—Big capitalism!

it means "world economic crisis"

it means "eternal interest slavery" . . .

it means that the world is nothing more than a bag of booty for Jewish finance in Wall Street, New York, and Paris

it enslaves man under the slogans of progress, technology, rationalization, standardization, etc.

it knows only profit and dividends

it wants to make the world into a giant trust

it puts the machine over man

it annihilates the independent, earth-rooted farmer, and its final aim is the world dictatorship of Jewry [. . .]

it achieves this in the political sphere through parliament and the swindle of democracy. In the economic sphere, through the control of credit, the mortgaging of land, the stock exchange and the market principle [. . .]

The farmer's leagues, the Landvolk and the Bavarian Farmers' League all pay homage to this system.

The other danger is the Marxist economic system of bolshevism:

it knows only the state economy

it knows only one class, the proletariat

it brings in the controlled economy

it doesn't just annihilate the self-sufficient farmer economically—it roots him out [. . .]

it brings the rule of the tractor

it nationalizes the land and creates mammoth factory-farms

it uproots and destroys man's soul, making him the powerless tool of the communist idea—or kills him

it destroys the family, belief, and customs [. . .]

it is anti-Christ, it desecrates the churches [. . .]

its final aim is the world dictatorship of the proletariat, that means ultimately the world dictatorship of Jewry, for the Jew controls this powerless proletariat and uses it for his dark plans

Big capitalism and bolshevism work hand in hand; they are born of Jewish thought and serve the master plan of world Jewry.

Who alone can rescue the farmer from these dangers?

NATIONAL SOCIALISM!

Source (for both documents): Anton Kaes, Matin Jay, and Edward Dimendberg, *The Weimar Republic Sourcebook* (Los Angeles: 1994), pp. 137–38, 142.

Questions for Analysis

1. How did Goebbels use metaphors of illness and health, growth and decay? Do the metaphors suggest what the Nazis would try to do to cure the ills of Germany if they took power?

2. How does Goebbels's anti-Semitism differ from the nineteenth-century French anti-Semitism documented on page 559?

3. The Nazi campaign pamphlet of 1932 targeted German farmers. How did the pamphlet play on their fears of market manipulation by American big business and Bolshevik demands for collectivization and seizure of private land? How did the Nazis identify themselves with Christianity and traditional values, sincerely or not?

4. How, specifically, does the party propose to deal with the "two great dangers of today"?

Government policy encouraged women to withdraw from the labor force, both to ease unemployment and to conform to Nazi notions of a woman's proper role. "Can woman," one propagandist asked, "conceive of anything more beautiful than to sit with her husband in her cozy home and listen inwardly to the loom of time weaving the weft and warp of motherhood?"

NAZI RACISM

At the core of Nazi ideology lay a particularly virulent racism. Much of this racism was not new. Hitler and the Nazis drew on a revived and especially violent form of nineteenth-century social Darwinism, according to which nations and people struggled for survival, with the superior peoples strengthening themselves in the process. By the early twentieth century, the rise of the social sciences had taken nineteenth-century prejudices and racial thinking into new terrain. Just as medical science had cured bodily ills, doctors, criminologists, and social workers sought ways to cure social ills. Across the West, scientists and intellectuals worked to purify the body politic, improve the human race, and eliminate the "unfit." Even progressive-minded individuals sometimes subscribed to eugenics, a program of racial engineering to improve either personal or public fitness. Eugenic policies in the Third Reich began with a 1933 law for the compulsory sterilization of "innumerable inferior and hereditarily tainted" people. This "social-hygienic racism" later became the systematic murder of mentally and physically ill patients. Social policy was governed by a basic division between those who possessed "value" and those who did not, with the aim of creating a racial utopia.

The centerpiece of Nazi racism was anti-Semitism. This centuries-old phenomenon had been part of Christian society from the Middle Ages on. By the nineteenth century, traditional Christian anti-Semitism was joined by a current of nationalist anti-Jewish theory. A great many of the theorists of European nationalism saw the Jewish people as permanent outsiders who could only be assimilated and become citizens if they denied their Jewish identity. At the end of the nineteenth century, during the Dreyfus affair in France (see Chapter 23), French and other European anti-Semites launched a barrage of propaganda against Jews—scores of books, pamphlets, and magazines blamed Jews for all the troubles of modernity, from socialism to international banks and mass culture. The late nineteenth century also brought a wave of pogroms—violent assaults on Jewish communities—especially in Russia. Racial anti-Semitism drew the line between Jews and non-Jews on the basis of erroneous biology. Religious conversion, which traditional Christian anti-Semites encouraged, would not change biology. Nor would assimilation, which was counseled by more-secular nationalist thinkers.

Anti-Semitism in these different forms was a well-established and open political force in most of the West. By attacking Jews, anti-Semites attacked modern institutions—from socialist parties and the mass press to international banking—as part of an "international Jewish conspiracy" to undermine traditional authority and nationality. Conservative party leaders told shopkeepers and workers that "Jewish capitalists" were responsible for the demise of small businesses, for the rise of giant department stores, and for precarious economic swings that threatened their livelihoods. In Vienna, middle-class voters supported the openly anti-Semitic Christian Democrats. In Germany, in 1893, sixteen avowed anti-Semites were elected to the

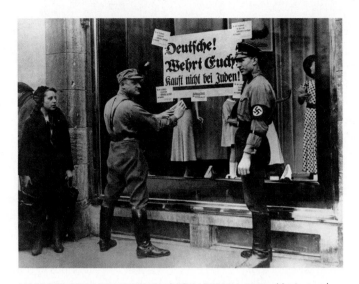

NAZI BOYCOTT OF JEWISH SHOPS IN BERLIN, 1933. Nazis stand in front of a Jewish-owned clothing store. "Germans! Buy nothing from the Jews!"

Reichstag, and the Conservative party made anti-Semitism part of its official program. Hitler gave this anti-Semitism an especially murderous twist by tying it to doctrines of war and biological racism.

To what extent was the Nazis' virulent anti-Semitism shared? Although the "Jewish Question" was clearly Hitler's primary obsession during the early 1920s, he made the theme less central in campaign appearances as the Nazi movement entered mainstream politics, shifting instead to attacks on Marxism and the Weimar democracy. Moreover, anti-Semitic beliefs would not have distinguished the Nazi from any other party on the political right; it was likely of only secondary importance to people's opinions of the Nazis. Soon after Hitler came to power, though, German Jews faced discrimination, exclusion from rights as citizens, and violence. Racial laws excluded Jews from public office as early as April 1933. The Nazis encouraged a boycott of Jewish merchants, while the SA created a constant threat of random violence. In 1935, the Nuremberg Decrees deprived Jews (defined by bloodline) of their German citizenship and prohibited marriage between Jews and other Germans. Violence escalated. In November 1938, the SA attacked some seventy-five hundred Jewish stores, burned nearly two hundred synagogues, killed ninety-one Jews, and beat up thousands more in a campaign of terror known as *Kristallnacht*, "the Night of Broken Glass." Violence like this did raise some opposition from ordinary Germans. Legal persecution, however, met only silent acquiescence. And from the perspective of Jewish people, *Kristallnacht* made it plain that there was no safe place for them in Germany. Unfortunately, only one year remained before the outbreak of war made it impossible for Jews to escape.

What did national socialism and fascism have in common? Both arose in the interwar period as responses to the First World War and the Russian Revolution. Both were violently antisocialist and anticommunist, determined to "rescue" their nations from the threat of Bolshevism. Both were intensely nationalistic; they believed that national solidarity came before all other allegiances and superseded all other rights. Both opposed parliamentary government and democracy as cumbersome and divisive. Both found their power in mass-based authoritarian politics. Similar movements existed in all the countries of the West, but only in a few cases did they actually form regimes. Nazism, however, distinguished itself by making a racially pure state central to its vision, a vision that would lead to global struggle and mass murder.

THE GREAT DEPRESSION IN THE DEMOCRACIES

The histories of the three major Western democracies—Great Britain, France, and the United States—run roughly parallel during the years after the First World War. In all three countries governments put their trust in prewar policies and assumptions until the Great Depression forced them to make major social and economic reforms, reforms that would lay the foundations of the modern welfare state. These nations weathered the upheavals of the interwar years, but they did not do so easily.

Both France and Britain sought to keep the price of manufactured goods low in the 1920s, in order to stimulate demand in the world markets. This policy of deflation kept businessmen happy but placed a great burden on French and British workers, whose wages and living standards remained low. In both countries, class conflict boiled just below the surface, as successive governments refused to raise taxes to pay for social reforms. Workers' resentment in Britain helped elect the first Labour Party government in 1924 and another in 1929. A general strike in Britain in 1926 succeeded only in increasing middle-class antipathy toward workers. In France a period of strikes immediately after the war subsided and was followed by a period where employers refused to bargain with labor unions. When the French government passed a modified social insurance program in 1930—insuring against sickness, old age, and death—French workers remained unsatisfied.

Among the democracies, the United States was a bastion of conservatism. Presidents Warren G. Harding, Calvin Coolidge, and Herbert Hoover held a social philosophy formulated by the barons of big business in the nineteenth century. The Supreme Court used its power of judicial review to nullify progressive legislation enacted by state governments and occasionally by Congress.

The conservative economic and social policies of the prewar period were dealt their deathblow by the Great Depression of 1929. This worldwide depression peaked during the years 1929–33, but its effects lasted a decade. For those who went through it, the depression was perhaps the formative experience of their lives and the decisive crisis of the interwar period. In Germany, the depression was an important factor in the rise of Nazism; but in fact, it forced every country to forge new economic policies and to deal with unprecedented economic turmoil.

The Origins of the Great Depression

What caused the Great Depression? Its deepest roots lay in the instability of national currencies, and in the interdependence of national economies. Throughout the 1920s, Europeans had seen a sluggish growth rate. A major drop in world agricultural prices hurt the countries of southern and eastern Europe, where agriculture was small in scale and high in cost. Unable to make a profit on the international market, these agricultural countries bought fewer manufactured goods from the more industrial sectors of northern Europe, causing a widespread drop in industrial productivity. Restrictions on free trade crippled the economy even more. Although debtor nations needed open markets to sell their goods, most nations were raising high trade barriers to protect domestic manufacturers from foreign competition.

Then in October of 1929, prices on the New York Stock Exchange collapsed. On October 24, "Black Thursday," twelve million shares were traded amid unprecedented chaos. Even more surprising, the market kept falling. Black Thursday was followed by Black Monday and then Black Tuesday: falling prices, combined with an enormously high number of trades, made for the worst day in the history of the stock exchange to that point. The rise of the United States as an international creditor during the Great War meant that the crash had immediate, disastrous consequences in Europe. When the value of stocks dropped, banks found themselves short of capital and then, when not rescued by the government, forced to close. The financial effects of bank closures rippled through the economy: firms closed their factories, workers lost their jobs—indeed, manufacturers laid off virtually entire workforces. In 1930, four million Americans were unemployed, in 1933, thirteen million—nearly a third of the workforce. By then, per capita income in the United States had fallen 48 percent. In Germany, too, the drop was brutal. In 1929, two million were unemployed; in 1932, six million.

Interpreting Visual Evidence

The Fascist Spectacle of Mass Participation

Like other revolutionary movements, fascism in Italy and national socialism in Germany needed to project an image of popular support for their political programs. As far back as the French Revolution of 1789, representations of "the people" as political actors took on special significance in revolutionary propaganda (see *Interpreting Visual Evidence*, Chapter 18, page 440), and both Hitler and Mussolini understood how to use such images to create the impression of an organic and seamless connection between the party's leadership and the rank and file who made up the movement.

A. Benito Mussolini visits a youth camp where recruits to his Black Shirts were in training, 1935.

B. Still image from Leni Riefenstahl, *Triumph of the Will* (1935), a film about a Nazi party rally in Nuremberg, Germany, 1934.

The governments of the West initially responded to the depression with monetary measures. In 1931 Great Britain abandoned the gold standard; the United States followed suit in 1933. By no longer pegging their currencies to the price of gold, these countries hoped to make money cheaper and thus more available for economic recovery programs. This action was the forerunner of a broad program of currency management, which became an important element in a general policy of economic nationalism. In another important move, Great Britain abandoned its time-honored policy of free trade in 1932, raising protective tariffs as high as 100 percent. But monetary policy alone could not end the hardships of ordinary families. Governments were increasingly forced to address their concerns with a wide range of social reforms.

Britain was the most cautious in its relief efforts. A national government composed of Conservative, Liberal, and Labour party members came to power in 1931. To underwrite effective programs of public assistance, however, the government would have to spend beyond its income—something it was reluctant to do. France, on the other hand, adopted the most advanced set of policies to combat the effects of the depression. In 1936, responding to a threat from ultraconservatives to overthrow the republic, a Popular Front government under the leadership of the socialist Léon Blum was formed by the Radical, Socialist, and Communist parties, and lasted for two years. The Popular Front nationalized the munitions industry and reorganized the Bank of France to break the largest stockholders' monopolistic control over credit. The government also de-

C. I. M. Swire (right), a leading figure in the women's section of the British Union of Fascists wearing the organization's female blackshirt uniform (1933).

Representations of the people in nineteenth-century liberal revolutionary movements emphasized an activist definition of political participation, as citizens came together to constitute a national body that reflected their will. Both Italian fascism and German national socialism defined themselves in opposition to democratic or parliamentary regimes, and they explicitly rejected the individualism that was the basis for liberal citizenship. In their orchestration of public celebrations for their program, both fascists and national socialists emphasized images of obedience and subordination to the leader (image A), or to the national movement (image B). Though the pageantry of fascism and national socialism typically emphasized an aggressively masculine image of enthusiastic devotion, most fascist movements also organized special female sections. In these groups, women could clothe themselves in uniforms like their male counterparts and express their own allegiance to the spirit of self-sacrifice that was at the heart of such collective movements (image C).

Questions for Analysis

1. Each of these images was carefully staged and orchestrated to project a specific message. What are the messages contained in each of these images? What details are important?

2. What do these images tell us about the place of the individual in fascist society?

3. What sense of belonging do you think these images are designed to produce? What made such images so attractive to so many people?

creed a forty-hour week for all urban workers and initiated a program of public works. For the benefit of the farmers it established a wheat office to fix the price and regulate the distribution of grain. Although the Popular Front temporarily quelled the threat from the political right, conservatives were generally uncooperative and unimpressed by the attempts to aid the French working class. Both a socialist and Jewish, Blum faced fierce anti-Semitism in France. Fearing that Blum was the forerunner of a French Lenin, conservatives declared, "Better Hitler than Blum." They got their wish before the decade was out.

The most dramatic response to the depression came in the United States, where its effects were most severe. In 1933, Franklin D. Roosevelt succeeded Herbert Hoover as president and announced the New Deal, a program of reform and reconstruction to rescue the country. The New Deal aimed to get the country back on its feet without destroying the capitalist system. The government would manage the economy, sponsor relief programs, and fund public-works projects to increase mass purchasing power. These policies were shaped by the theories of the British economist John Maynard Keynes, who had already proved influential during the 1919 treaty meetings at Paris. Keynes argued that capitalism could create a just and efficient society if governments played a part in its management. First, Keynes abandoned the sacred cow of balanced budgets. Without advocating continuous deficit financing, he would have the government deliberately operate in the red whenever private investments weren't enough. Keynes also favored the creation of large amounts of venture capital—money for high-risk, high-reward investments—

which he saw as the only socially productive form of capital. Finally, he recommended monetary control to promote prosperity and full employment.

Along with Social Security and other programs, the United States adopted a Keynesian program of "currency management," regulating the value of the dollar according to the needs of the economy. The New Deal helped both individuals and the country recover, but it left the crucial problem of unemployment unsolved. In 1939, after six years of the New Deal, the United States still had more than nine million jobless workers—a figure that exceeded the combined unemployment of the rest of the world. Only with the outbreak of a new world war—which required millions of soldiers and armament workers—did the United States reach the full recovery that the New Deal had failed to deliver.

ARCHITECTURAL STYLE IN GERMANY BETWEEN THE WARS. The Bauhaus, by Walter Gropius (1883–1969). This school in Dessau, Germany, is a starkly functional prototype of the interwar "international style."

INTERWAR CULTURE

The interwar period also brought dramatic upheavals in the arts and sciences. Artists, writers, architects, and composers brought the revolutionary artistic forms of the turn of the century into the mainstream as they rejected traditional aesthetic values and experimented with new forms of expression. Scientists and psychologists challenged deeply held beliefs about the universe and human nature. Finally, radio, movies, and advertising created a new kind of mass culture that fed off the atmosphere of crisis in politics and the arts, and contributed to the anxieties of the age.

Interwar Artists and Intellectuals

Europe's intellectuals—writers, artists, philosophers, and cultural critics—were disillusioned by World War I. The mood of frustration and disenchantment was captured by the early work of the American writer Ernest Hemingway, whose novel *The Sun Also Rises* (1926) portrayed a "lost generation" whose experiences in the war produced a profound loss of faith. Others felt that the mechanized age had at its heart a spiritual emptiness that fostered only cynicism: Bertolt Brecht's plays described the corruption of Germany's elites, and T. S. Eliot's poetry explored the intense boredom and hollowness of modern life. Some writers sought new forms of expression to capture this particularly modern sensibility: the Irish writer James Joyce, the French author Marcel Proust, and the British novelist Virginia Woolf all experimented with a technique that became known as "stream of consciousness," an attempt to capture in words the disjointed flow of the mind in real time.

Meanwhile, the visual arts responded to the rapid transformations of twentieth-century society. Pablo Picasso continued to challenge the codes of artistic representation with his "cubist" experiments, while the "expressionists" sought an unflinching portrayal of human reality in all its emotional complexity. The "dadaists" went further, rebelling against any and all aesthetic principles. They pulled their name at random from a dictionary and preferred random combinations, including cutouts and collages, to formal compositions.

Architects also rejected tradition. Charles Edouard Jeanneret (Le Corbusier) in France, Otto Wagner in Austria, and Frank Lloyd Wright in the United States pioneered a new "functionalist" style that minimized decorative elements and explored the use of new materials—chrome, glass, steel, and concrete. In 1919 the German functionalist Walter Gropius established a school—the Bauhaus—to serve as a center of what became known as the international style, literally creating the blueprints for what became the familiar twentieth-century urban landscape, from New York to Brazil to Tokyo.

Scientists in the interwar period also contributed to this sense of bewildering rejection of past assumptions. In 1915, German physicist Albert Einstein proposed his general theory of relativity, a new way of thinking about space, matter, time, and gravity. Einstein's theories, based on the understanding that mass and energy could be converted into one another, paved the way for the splitting of the atom by German physicists in 1939, and led to an arms race during the Second World War, as both Germany and the United States competed to produce an atomic weapon. Einstein himself devoted his life to pacifism and social justice, but the weapons that emerged from interwar physics were the most destructive ever created by humans.

Mass Culture and Its Possibilities

Cultural change, however, extended far beyond circles of artistic and intellectual elites. The explosive rise of mass media in the interwar years transformed popular culture and the lives of ordinary people. New mass media—especially radio and films—reached audiences of unprecedented size. Political life incorporated many of these new media, setting off worries that the common people, increasingly referred to as the "masses," could be manipulated by demagogues and propaganda. In 1918, mass politics was rapidly becoming a fact of life: that meant nearly universal suffrage (varying by country), well-organized political parties reaching out to voters, and in general, more participation in political life. Mass politics was accompanied by the rise of mass culture: books, newspapers, films, and fashions were produced in large numbers and standardized formats, which were less expensive and more accessible, appealing not only to more people but to more kinds of people. Older forms of popular culture were often local and class specific; mass culture, at least in principle, cut across lines of class and ethnic-

VOICE OF THE PEOPLE, VOICE OF GOD BY GEORGE GROSZ (1920). Industrialization, the First World War, and political change combined to make early-twentieth-century Berlin a center of mass culture and communication. In this drawing, the radical artist and social critic George Grosz deplores the newspapers' power over public opinion. That public opinion could be manipulated was a common theme for many who wrote about early-twentieth-century democracy. ■ *How does this cynicism about the public sphere compare with earlier defenders of free speech, such as John Stuart Mill?*

ity, and even nationality. The term, however, can easily become misleading. The world of culture did not suddenly become homogenous. No more than half the population read newspapers regularly. Not everyone listened to the radio, and those who did certainly did not believe everything they heard. The pace of cultural change, however, did quicken perceptibly. And in the interwar years, mass culture showed that it held both democratic and authoritarian potential.

The expansion of mass culture rested on widespread applications of existing technologies. Wireless communication, for instance, was invented before the turn of the twentieth century and saw limited use in the First World War. With major financial investment in the 1920s, though, the radio industry boomed. Three out of four British families had a radio by the end of the 1930s, and in Germany the ratio was even higher. In every European country, broadcasting rights were controlled by the government; in the United States, radio was managed by corporations. The radio broadcast soon became the national soapbox for politicians, and it played no small role in creating new kinds of political language. President Franklin Roosevelt's reassuring "fireside chats" took advantage of the way that radio bridged the public world of politics with the private world of the home. Hitler cultivated a different kind of radio personality, barking his fierce invectives; he made some fifty addresses in 1933 alone. In Germany, Nazi propagandists beamed their messages into homes or blared them through loudspeakers in town squares, constant and repetitive. Broadcasting created new rituals of political life—and new means of communication and persuasion.

So did advertising. Advertising was not new, but it was newly prominent. Businesses spent vastly more on advertising than they had before. Hard-hitting visual images replaced older ads that simply announced products, prices, and brand names. Many observers considered advertising the most "modern" of art forms. Why? It was efficient communication, streamlined and standardized, producing images that would appeal to all. It was scientific, drawing on modern psychology; advertising agencies claimed to have created a science of selling to people. In a world remade by mass politics, and at a moment when the purchasing power of the common people was beginning to rise, however slowly, the high stakes in advertising (as in much of mass culture) were apparent to many.

The most dramatic changes came on movie screens. The technology of moving pictures had come earlier; the 1890s were the era of nickelodeons and short action pictures. And in that period, France and Italy had strong film industries. Further popularized by news shorts during the war, film boomed in the war's aftermath throughout Europe. When sound was added to movies in 1927, costs

FRITZ LANG'S M. In this film Peter Lorre, a Jewish actor, played the role of a child murderer who maintains that he should not be punished for his crimes. Lorre's speech at the end of the film was used in the Nazi propaganda film *The Eternal Jew* as proof that Jews were innate criminals who showed no remorse for their actions.

soared, competition intensified, and audiences grew rapidly. By the 1930s, an estimated 40 percent of British adults went to the movies once a week, a strikingly high figure. Many went more often than that.

Many found the new mass culture disturbing. As they perceived it, the threat came straight from the United States, which deluged Europe with cultural exports after the war. Hollywood westerns, cheap dime novels, and jazz music—which became increasingly popular in the 1920s—introduced Europe to new ways of life. Advertising, comedies, and romances disseminated new and often disconcerting images of femininity. With bobbed haircuts and short dresses, "new women" seemed assertive, flirtatious, capricious, and materialistic. The Wild West genre was popular with teenage boys, much to the dismay of their parents and teachers, who saw westerns as an inappropriate, lower-class form of entertainment. In Europe, the cross-class appeal of American popular culture grated against long-standing social hierarchies. Conservative critics abhorred the fact that "the parson's wife sat nearby his maid at Sunday matinees, equally rapt in the gaze of Hollywood stars."

Authoritarian governments, in particular, decried these developments as decadent threats to national culture. Fascist, communist, and Nazi governments alike tried to control not only popular culture but also high culture and modernism, which were typically out of line with the designs of the dictators. Stalin much preferred

After You Read This Chapter

Visit StudySpace for quizzes, additional review materials, and multi-media documents. **wwnorton.com/studyspace**

REVIEWING THE OBJECTIVES

- After 1917 the Bolsheviks in Russia debated how fast they should move to reorganize society along the lines demanded by their revolutionary ideology. What circumstances determined the outcome of this debate and what were the consequences of Stalin's revolution from above in the 1930s?

- Mussolini's Fascist party offered an alternative to Italian voters disappointed with their government in the aftermath of the First World War. What was fascism and how did Mussolini come to power?

- The Weimar Republic failed in its attempt to establish a stable democracy in Germany, while other democracies in France, Britain, and the United States underwent severe strain. What challenges did democratic regimes face during the interwar period?

- Hitler came to power legally in 1933 through the German electoral system. What did he stand for and why did so many Germans support his cause?

- Artists, writers, and other intellectuals in the interwar period could not help but reflect the atmosphere of social and political crisis in their work. How did artists and writers react to the crisis of the interwar period?

socialist realism to the new Soviet avant-garde. Mussolini had a penchant for classical kitsch, though he was far more accepting of modern art than Hitler, who despised its decadence. Nazism had its own cultural aesthetic, promoting "Aryan" art and architecture and rejecting the modern, international style they associated with the "international Jewish conspiracy." This led them to condemn jazz, modern art, and the new architecture, and to encourage the development of artistic movements that celebrated the accomplishments of "Aryan" culture.

The Nazis, like other authoritarian governments, used mass media as efficient means of indoctrination and control. Movies became part of the Nazis' pioneering use of "spectacular politics." Media campaigns, mass rallies, parades and ceremonies: all were designed to display the strength and glory of the Reich and to impress and intimidate spectators. In 1934 Hitler commissioned the filmmaker Leni Riefenstahl to record a political rally staged by herself and Albert Speer in Nuremberg. The film, titled *Triumph of the Will*, was a visual hymn to the Nordic race and the Nazi regime. Everything in the film was on a huge scale: masses of bodies stood in parade formation, flags rose and fell in unison; the film invited viewers to surrender to the power of grand ritual and symbolism. The comedian Charlie Chaplin riposted in his celebrated lampoon *The Great Dictator* (1940), an enormously successful parody of Nazi pomposities.

CONCLUSION

The strains of the First World War created a world that few recognized—transformed by revolution, mass mobilization, and loss. In retrospect, it is hard not to see the period that followed as a succession of failures. Capitalism foundered in the Great Depression, democracies collapsed in the face of authoritarianism, and the Treaty of Versailles proved hollow. Stalin's Soviet Union paid a terrible price for the creation of a modern industrial economy in the years of famine, political repression, and state terror. Hitler's Germany and Mussolini's Italy offered a vision of the future that held no comfort for those committed to basic human freedoms and equality under the law. Yet we better understand the experiences and outlooks of ordinary people if we do not treat the failures of the interwar period as inevitable. By the late 1920s, many were cautiously optimistic that the Great War's legacy could be overcome and that problems were being solved. The Great Depression wrecked these hopes, bringing economic chaos and political paralysis. Paralysis and chaos, in turn, created new audiences for political leaders offering authoritarian solutions and brought more voters to their political parties. Finally, economic troubles and political turmoil made contending with rising international tensions, to which we now turn, vastly more difficult. By the 1930s, even cautious optimism about international relations had given way to apprehension and dread.

PEOPLE, IDEAS, AND EVENTS IN CONTEXT

- What is the difference between the Bolshevik policies of **WAR COMMUNISM** and the **NEW ECONOMIC POLICY (NEP)**?
- What were **JOSEPH STALIN**'s goals in implementing his catastrophic plan for **COLLECTIVIZATION** of agriculture, and what did he hope to accomplish with his purging of an entire generation of Bolshevik leaders, along with millions of other Soviet citizens, in the **GREAT TERROR**?
- What was the basis of **BENITO MUSSOLINI**'s rejection of liberal democracy? What kinds of changes in Italian society followed from the adoption of **FASCISM** as the official state ideology?
- How important was **ANTI-SEMITISM** to **ADOLF HITLER**'s political career? What do events like *KRISTALLNACHT* tell us about the depth of German anti-Semitism?
- What effects did the **GREAT DEPRESSION** have on the European economy and how did this economic crisis affect the political developments of the 1930s?
- How did the **NEW DEAL** attempt to deal with the economic crisis in the United States?

CONSEQUENCES

- Did Soviet communism, national socialism in Germany, and Italian fascism amount to the same thing in terms of their effects on the population? What makes them different?
- What accounts for the weakness of democratic regimes in the interwar period?
- The global financial crisis of 2008, like the Great Depression of the 1930s, is often described as a "crisis of capitalism." Are the two events comparable? Have they had similar political consequences?

Before You Read This Chapter

The Second World War

CORE OBJECTIVES

- **IDENTIFY** the broader political and economic causes of the Second World War.

- **EXPLAIN** the reasons for the British and French policy of "appeasement" when they were faced with Hitler's violations of international law.

- **UNDERSTAND** the consequences of German conquest and occupation for European nations and their populations, and the challenges facing those who chose to resist.

- **DESCRIBE** how the Holocaust became possible after the German conquest of territory in eastern Europe during the invasion of the Soviet Union.

- **UNDERSTAND** the military operations that led to the defeat of the Nazi regime and its allies in Europe.

- **EXPLAIN** the main areas of conflict in Asia and the Pacific, and the circumstances that led to Japanese surrender in 1945.

n September 1939, Europe was consumed by another world war. Like the First World War, the Second World War was triggered by threats to the European balance of power. Yet even more than the Great War, the Second World War was a conflict among nations, whole peoples, and fiercely opposing ideals. Adolf Hitler and his supporters in Germany and abroad cast the conflict as a racial war against the twin enemies of national socialism: the democracies in western Europe and the United States, on the one hand, and the communist order of the Soviet Union, on the other. Hitler's opponents in the West and the East believed just as fervently that they were defending a way of life and a vision of justice that was bigger than narrow definitions of national interest.

Belief that the world was now characterized by ideologies and worldviews that were necessarily in mortal combat with one another meant that the scale of the killing overtook even that of the First World War. In 1914, military firepower outmatched mobility, resulting in four years of static, mud-sodden slaughter. In 1939, mobility was joined to firepower on a massive scale, with terrifying results. On the battlefield, the tactics of high-speed armored warfare (*Blitzkrieg*), aircraft carriers sinking

623

ships far beyond the horizon, and submarines used in vast numbers to dominate shipping lanes all changed the scope and the pace of fighting. This was not a war of trenches and barbed wire but a war of motion, dramatic conquests, and terrible destructive power. The devastation of 1914–18 paled in comparison to this new, global conflict.

The other great change involved not tactics, but targets. Much of the unprecedented killing power now available was aimed directly at civilians. Cities were laid waste by artillery and aerial bombing. Whole regions were put to the torch, while towns and villages were systematically cordoned off and leveled. Whole populations were targeted as well, in ways that continue to appall. The Nazi regime's systematic murder of gypsies, homosexuals, and other "deviants," along with its effort to exterminate the Jewish people completely, made the Second World War a horrifyingly unique event. So did the United States' use of a weapon whose existence would dominate politics and society for the next fifty years: the atomic bomb. The naive enthusiasm that had marked the outbreak of war in 1914 was absent from the start. Terrible memories of the First World War lingered. Yet those who fought against the Axis Powers (and many of those who fought for them) found that their determination to fight and win grew as the war went on. Unlike the seemingly meaningless killing of the Great War, the Second World War was cast as a war of absolutes, of good and evil, of national and global survival. Nevertheless, the scale of destruction brought with it a profound weariness. It also provoked deep-seated questions about the value of Western "civilization" and the terms on which the West, and the rest of the world, might live peaceably in the future.

THE CAUSES OF THE WAR: UNSETTLED QUARRELS, ECONOMIC FALLOUT, AND NATIONALISM

Historians have isolated four main causes for the Second World War: the punishing terms of the Versailles peace settlement, the failure to create international guarantees for peace and security after 1918, the successive economic crises of the interwar years, and the violent forms of nationalism that emerged in Europe in the 1930s.

The peace settlement of 1919–20 created as many problems as it solved. The Versailles treaty created new nations out of the ruins of the eastern European empires and proclaimed the principle of self-determination for the peoples of eastern and southern Europe. In doing so, the peacemakers sowed fresh bitterness and conflict. The treaty created new states that crossed ethnic boundaries, and it created new minorities without protecting them. Many of these boundaries would be redrawn by force in the 1930s. The Allied powers also imposed harsh terms in the treaty, saddling the German economy with a heavy bill for reparations and forcing the Weimar Republic to accept a humiliating reduction in the size of the German military. Most galling to the German public was the Versailles treaty's "war guilt" clause, which blamed the Germans for starting the war. Since the Allied powers refused to lift the naval blockade of Germany until the treaty was signed, the new German government had no choice but to accept the terms. As a consequence, many Germans saw the treaty as illegitimate and unjust. The fact that the victors used the peace settlement to lay claim to German colonies reinforced their impression that the peace was fundamentally an alliance of the victors against the vanquished.

Another cause of the outbreak of another world war was the victors' failure to create binding standards for peace and security. Some diplomats put their faith in the legal and moral authority of the League of Nations. Others pursued disarmament as a means of securing peace. In 1928, the Kellogg-Briand Pact declared war an international crime, but such measures carried little weight. The League of Nations was hampered by the absence of key players. Germany and the Soviet Union were excluded for most of the interwar period and the United States never joined.

Economic conditions were a third cause of the Second World War. The reparations imposed on Germany and France's occupation of Germany's industrial heartland slowed Germany's recovery. Disagreements about the reparations led to the German hyperinflation of the early 1920s, making German money nearly worthless. The stability and credibility of the fragile new German republic were damaged almost beyond repair. The German economy had barely emerged from this catastrophe when the world economy collapsed in 1929.

The Great Depression of the 1930s contributed to the outbreak of war by weakening Europe's democracies at a moment when they were under siege by political extremists on the left and the right. The depression intensified economic nationalism and inflamed tensions between labor and management. The collapse of the economy caused mass unemployment and business failure throughout Europe, and this crisis was the last blow to the Weimar Republic. In 1933, with unemployment peaking at nearly 6 million (roughly one out of every three workers), power passed to the Nazis.

Despite the misgivings of many inside the governments of Britain and France, Germany was allowed to ignore the terms of the peace treaties and rearm. Armaments expansion on a large scale first began in Germany in 1935, with the result that unemployment was reduced and the effects of the depression eased. Other nations followed the German example, not simply as a way to boost their economies but in response to growing Nazi military power.

While Hitler was rearming Germany, other nations were also pushing against the League of Nations and the international order set up after World War I. In the Pacific, Japan's military regime had embarked on a program of imperial expansion aimed at China. They began in 1931 with the invasion of Manchuria. Meanwhile, in Italy, Mussolini tried to distract his public with overseas conquests, culminating in the invasion of Ethiopia in 1935.

In sum, the tremendous economic hardship of the depression, a contested peace treaty, and political weakness all undermined international stability. But the decisive factor in the crises of the 1930s and the trigger for another world war lay in a blend of violent nationalism and modern ideologies that glorified the nation and national destiny. This blend, particularly in the forms of fascism and militarism, appeared around the world in many countries. By the middle of the 1930s, recognizing common interests, fascist Italy and Nazi Germany formed an Axis, an alliance binding their goals of national glory and international power. They were later joined by Japan's military regime. In the 1930s these regimes tested the resolve of their opponents. The Japanese invaded Manchuria in 1931, and Nazi Germany and fascist Italy supported the nationalists in the Spanish Civil War (1936–39). After 1939 the Axis embarked on a much more ambitious set of conquests, initiating a second global war even more destructive than the first.

ANTIFASCIST PROPAGANDA, SPANISH CIVIL WAR. This poster, produced by a left-wing labor organization affiliated with the international anarchist movement, shows a worker about to deliver a killing blow to a fascist snake.

THE 1930s: CHALLENGES TO THE PEACE

The 1930s brought the tensions and failures caused by the treaties of 1919–20 to a head, creating a global crisis. Fascist and nationalist governments flouted the League of Nations by launching new conquests and other aggressive efforts at national expansion. With the memories of 1914–18 still fresh, these new crises created an atmosphere of deepening fear and apprehension. Each new conflict seemed to warn that another, much wider war would follow unless it could somehow be averted. Ordinary people, particularly in Britain, France, and the United States, were divided. Some saw the actions of the aggressors as a direct challenge to civilization, one that had to be met with force if necessary. Others hoped to avoid premature or unnec-

essary conflict. Their governments tried instead at several points to negotiate with the fascists and keep a tenuous peace. Writers, intellectuals, and politicians on the left vilified these efforts. Many saw the period as a series of missed opportunities to prevent renewed warfare.

Most controversial was the policy of "appeasement" pursued by Western governments in the face of German, Italian, and Japanese aggression. Appeasement was neither simple power politics nor pure cowardice. It was grounded in three deeply held assumptions. The first was that doing anything to provoke another war was unthinkable. With the memory of the slaughter of 1914–18 fresh in their minds, many in the West embraced pacifism, or did not want to deal with the uncompromising aggression of the fascist governments, especially Nazi Germany. Second, many in Britain and the United States argued that Germany had been mistreated by the Versailles treaty and harbored legitimate grievances that should be acknowledged and resolved. Finally, many appeasers were staunch anticommunists. They believed that the fascist states in Germany and Italy were an essential bulwark against the advance of Soviet communism and that division among the major European states only played into the hands of the USSR. It took most of the 1930s for the debate among appeasers to come to a head. Meanwhile, the League of Nations faced more immediate and pressing challenges.

The 1930s brought three crucial tests for the League: crises in China, Ethiopia, and Spain. In China, the Japanese invasion of Manchuria in 1931 turned into an invasion of the whole country. Chinese forces were driven before the Japanese advance, and the Japanese deliberately targeted civilians in order to break the Chinese will to fight. In 1937 the Japanese laid siege to the strategic city of Nanjing. More than two hundred thousand Chinese citizens were slaughtered in what came to be known as the "Rape of Nanjing." The League voiced shock and disapproval but did nothing. In 1935 Mussolini began his efforts to make the Mediterranean an Italian empire by returning to Ethiopia to avenge the defeat of 1896. This time the Italians came with tanks, bombers, and poison gas. The Ethiopians fought bravely but hopelessly, and this imperial massacre aroused world opinion. The League attempted to impose sanctions on Italy and condemned Japan. But for two reasons, no enforcement followed. The first was British and French fear of communism and their hope that Italy and Japan would act as counterweights to the Soviets. The second reason was practical. Enforcing sanctions would involve challenging Japan's powerful fleet or Mussolini's newly built battleships. Britain and France were unwilling, and dangerously close to unable, to use their navies to achieve those ends.

The Spanish Civil War

The third challenge came closer to home. In 1936 civil war broke out in Spain. A series of weak republican governments, committed to large-scale social reforms, could not overcome opposition to those measures and political polarization. War broke out as extreme right-wing military officers rebelled. Hitler and Mussolini both sent troops and equipment to assist the rebel commander, Francisco Franco (1892–1975). The Soviet Union countered with aid to communist troops serving under the banner of the Spanish Republic. Again Britain and France failed to act decisively. Thousands of volunteers from England, France, and the United States—including many working-class socialists and writers such as George Orwell and Ernest Hemingway—took up arms as private soldiers for

GUERNICA BY PABLO PICASSO (1937). One of Picasso's most influential works, *Guernica* was painted as a mural for the Spanish republican government as it fought for survival in the Spanish Civil War. The Basque town of Guernica had been bombed by German fighters just a few months earlier, in April 1937. Near the center a horse writhes in agony; to the left a distraught woman holds her dead child. Compare Picasso's image to the antifascist propaganda poster reproduced on page 625. ▪ *What is different about the way that the two images deliver their political messages?* ▪ *Does Picasso's rejection of realism diminish the power of his political message?* ▪ *Does the antifascist poster seek any outcome other than the annihilation of the enemy?*

the Republican government. Their governments were much more hesitant. For the British, Franco was anticommunist at least, just like Mussolini and the Japanese. French prime minister Léon Blum, a committed antifascist, stood at the head of a Popular Front government—an alliance of socialists, communists, and republicans. The Popular Front had been elected on a program of social reform and opposition to Hitler abroad and to fascism in France. Yet Blum's margin of support was limited. He feared that intervening in Spain would further polarize his country, bring down his government, and make it impossible to follow through on any commitment to helping resolve the conflict. In Spain, despite some heroic fighting, the Republican camp degenerated into a hornet's nest of competing factions: republican, socialist, communist, and anarchist.

The Spanish Civil War was brutal. Both the German and the Soviet "advisers" saw Spain as a "dress rehearsal" for a later war between the two powers. They each brought in their newest weapons and practiced their skills in destroying civilian targets from the air. In April 1937, a raid by German dive bombers utterly destroyed the town of Guernica in northern Spain in an effort to cut off Republican supply lines and terrorize civilians. It shocked public opinion and was commemorated by Pablo Picasso in one of the most famous paintings of the twentieth century. Both sides committed atrocities. The Spanish Civil War lasted three years, ending with a complete victory for Franco in 1939. In the aftermath, Britain and France proved reluctant to admit Spanish Republicans as refugees, even though Republicans faced recriminations from Franco's regime. Franco sent one million of his Republican enemies to prison or concentration camps.

Hitler drew two lessons from Spain. The first was that if Britain, France, and

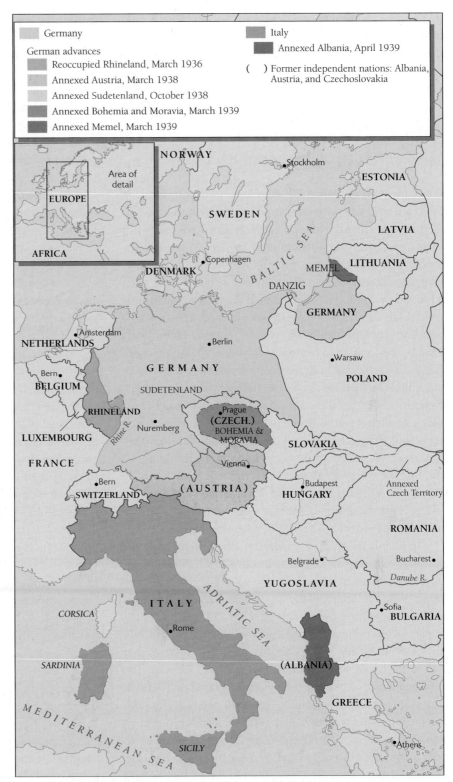

GERMAN AND ITALIAN EXPANSION, 1936–39. ▪ *What were Hitler's first steps to unify all the ethnic Germans in Europe?* ▪ *How did he use these initial gains to annex territory from the Czechs?* ▪ *What were the official reactions from Britain, France, and the Soviet Union?*

the Soviet Union ever tried to contain fascism, they would have a hard time coordinating their efforts. The second was that Britain and France were deeply averse to fighting another European war. This meant that the Nazis could use almost any means to achieve their goals.

German Rearmament and the Politics of Appeasement

Hitler took advantage of this combination of international tolerance and war weariness to advance his ambitions. As Germany rearmed, Hitler played on Germans' sense of shame and betrayal, proclaiming their right to regain their former power in the world. In 1933 he removed Germany from the League of Nations, to which it had finally been admitted in 1926. In 1935 he defied the disarmament provisions of the Treaty of Versailles and revived conscription and universal military training. Hitler's stated goals were the restoration of Germany's power and dignity inside Europe and the unification of all ethnic Germans inside his Third German Reich. As the first step in this process, Germany reoccupied the Rhineland in 1936. It was a risky move, chancing war with the much more powerful French army. But France and Britain did not mount a military response. In retrospect, this was an important turning point; the balance of power tipped in Germany's favor. Only as long as the Rhineland remained demilitarized and German industry in the Ruhr valley was unprotected, did France hold the upper hand. After 1936, it no longer did so.

In March 1938 Hitler annexed Austria, reaffirming his intention to bring all Germans into his Reich. Once more, no official reaction came from the West. The Nazis' next target was the Sudetenland in Czechoslovakia, a region with a large ethnic German population. With Austria now a part of Germany, Czechoslovakia was almost entirely surrounded by its hostile neighbor. Hitler declared that the Sudetenland was a natural part of the Reich and that he intended to occupy it. Many in the French and Polish governments were willing to come to the Czechs' aid. According to plans already being laid for a wider European war, Germany would not be ready for another three to four years. But Hitler gambled, and British prime minister Neville Chamberlain (1937–40) obliged him. Chamberlain decided to take charge of international talks about the Sudetenland and agreed to Hitler's terms. Chamberlain's logic was that this dispute was about the balance of power in Europe. If Hitler were allowed to unify all Germans in one state, he reasoned, then German ambitions would be satisfied. Chamberlain also believed that his country could not commit to a sustained war. Finally, defending eastern European boundaries against Germany ranked low on Great Britain's list of priorities, at least in comparison to ensuring free trade in western Europe and protecting the strategic centers of the British Empire.

On September 29, 1938, Hitler met with Chamberlain, French premier Édouard Daladier (1938–40), and Mussolini in a four-power conference in Munich. The result was another capitulation by France and Britain. The four negotiators bargained away a major slice of Czechoslovakia, while Czech representatives were left to await their fate outside the conference room. Chamberlain returned to London proclaiming "peace in our time." Hitler soon proved that boast hollow. In March 1939 Germany invaded what was left of Czechoslovakia, annexed Bohemia and Moravia, and established a puppet regime in Slovakia. This was Germany's first conquest of non-German territory, and it sent shock waves across Europe. It convinced public and political opinion outside Germany of the futility of appeasement. Chamberlain was forced to shift his policies completely. British and French rearmament sped up dramatically. Together with France, Britain guaranteed the sovereignty of the two states now directly in Hitler's path, Poland and Romania.

Meanwhile, the politics of appeasement had fueled Stalin's fears that the Western democracies might strike a deal with Germany at Soviet expense, thus diverting Nazi expansion eastward. The Soviet Union had not been invited to the Munich conference, and, suspicious that Britain and France were unreliable allies, Stalin became convinced that he should look elsewhere for security. Tempted by the traditional Russian desire for territory in Poland, Stalin was promised a share of Poland, Finland, the Baltic states, and Bessarabia by Hitler's representatives. In a reversal of their anti-Nazi proclamations that stunned many, the Soviets signed a nonaggression pact with the Nazis in August 1939. By going to Munich, Britain and France had put their interests first; the Soviet Union would now look after its own.

THE OUTBREAK OF HOSTILITIES AND THE FALL OF FRANCE

After his success in Czechoslovakia, Hitler turned his attention to Poland. With the Soviets now in his camp, he expected that the Western allies would back down again. On September 1, 1939, German troops crossed the Polish border. Britain and France sent a joint warning to Germany to withdraw. There was no reply. On September 3, Britain and France declared war.

The conquest of Poland was shockingly quick. It demanded great resources—Germany committed nearly all of its combat troops and planes to the invasion—but the results were remarkable. Well-coordinated attacks by German panzers (tanks) and armored vehicles, supported by devastating air power, cut the large but slow-moving Polish army to pieces. The Poles fought doggedly but were so stunned and disorganized that they had little hope of mounting an effective defense. The "lightning war" (*Blitzkrieg, blitz-KREEG*) for which the German officer corps had trained so long was a complete success. Poland, a large country with a large army, was dismembered in four weeks.

In accordance with its agreement with Nazi Germany, the Soviet Union also invaded Poland from the east, taking their share of Polish territory and using Stalin's signature methods to deal with the enemy: rounding up millions to be deported, imprisoned, or executed. Shortly after the invasion of Poland, the Soviets also attacked Finland, in an attempt to secure their Northern border. Despite the Soviets' overwhelming superiority in numbers and material, the Finns fought back tenaciously. The Soviets faced a very difficult campaign—an alarming demonstration of the damaging effects of Stalin's terror on the Soviet military. Although the Soviet Union concluded the undeclared four-month Winter War with a precarious victory in March 1940, Hitler and the rest of the world had made note of Stalin's weaknesses.

The fighting in Poland was followed by a winter of anxious nonactivity in Western Europe, known as the "phony war." In the spring of 1940 that calm was broken by a terrible storm. The Germans struck first in Scandinavia, taking Denmark in a day and invading Norway. On May 10, German forces swarmed through Belgium and the Netherlands on their way to France. The two nations were conquered in short order. When the Dutch succeeded in flooding canals that protected their major cities and defended that line with hard-fighting marines, Hitler ordered his air force to bomb the city of Rotterdam. More than eight hundred Dutch civilians died, and the Netherlands surrendered the next day. The Belgians' stubborn and effective defense of their nation was cut short when King Albert suddenly surrendered after two weeks of fighting, fearing similar destruction. Albert stayed on as a figurehead for the Nazis, reviled by Belgians who found other ways to carry on the fight against Germany.

The large French army was carved up by the *Blitzkrieg*. Its divisions were isolated, outflanked, and overwhelmed by German aircraft and armored columns working according to an exacting plan. The French army and French artillery (much of it better built than its German equivalent) were poorly organized and rendered useless in the face of rapid German maneuvers. The defeat turned quickly into a rout. Hundreds of thousands of civilians, each carrying a few precious possessions loaded onto carts, fled south. They were joined by thousands of Allied soldiers without weapons, and these columns of refugees were attacked constantly by German dive bombers. The disorganized British made a desperate retreat to the port of Dunkirk on the English Channel, where many of Britain's best troops were sacrificed holding off the panzers. At the beginning of June 1940, despite heavy German air attacks, Britain's Royal Navy evacuated more than three hundred thousand British and French troops, with the help of commercial and pleasure boats that had been pressed into emergency service.

After Dunkirk, the conflict was bitter but the outcome inevitable. French reservists fought, as their commanders asked, "to the last cartridge," killing thousands of Germans. The Germans nevertheless swept through the northwest and the heart of the country, reaching Paris in mid-June 1940. The political will of France's government collapsed along with its armies, and the French surrendered on June 22. The armistice cut the country in two. The Germans occupied all of northern France, including Paris and the Channel ports. The south, and French territories in North Africa, lay under the jurisdiction of a deeply conservative government formed at the spa town of Vichy (*VIH-shee*) under the leadership of an elderly First World War hero, Marshal Henri Philippe Pétain. France had fallen. One of Germany's historic enemies, the victor of the previous war, an imperial power and nation of almost sixty million citizens, was reduced to chaos and enemy occupation in forty days.

The penalties exacted on France did not end with defeat. Many liberals within France, and most of the Free French movement quickly established in London, soon felt they had two enemies to fight: Germany and Pétain's regime. The Vichy government proposed to collaborate with the Germans in return for retaining a small measure of sovereignty, or so it believed. The regime also instituted its own National Revolution, which came very close to fascism. Vichy repudiated the republic, accusing it of sapping France's strength. The state proceeded to reorganize French life and political institutions, strengthening the authority of the Catholic Church and the family and helping the Germans crush any resistance. "Work, Family, and Country"—this was Vichy's call to order.

NOT ALONE: THE BATTLE OF BRITAIN AND THE BEGINNINGS OF A GLOBAL WAR

Before launching an invasion across the Channel, the Nazis attempted to establish superiority in the air. From July 1940 to June 1941, in the Battle of Britain, thousands of German planes dropped millions of tons of bombs on British targets: first aircraft and airfields and then, as the focus shifted to breaking Britain's will, civilian targets such as London. More than forty thousand British civilians died. Yet the British stood firm. This was possible in part because of a German mistake. After a daring British bombing raid on Berlin, Hitler angrily told his generals to concentrate on civilian targets. This spared the Royal Air Force, whose bases had been steadily devastated up to that point. Given the chance to keep fighting, the R.A.F. forced a costly stalemate in the air. Hitler scrapped the invasion plans, turning his attention east toward Russia.

Another important reason for the determined British resistance was a change of political leadership. In May 1940 Chamberlain's catalog of failures finished his career. He was toppled by a coalition government that brought together Conservative, Liberal, and Labour politicians under Winston Churchill (1940–45, 1951–55). Churchill was a political maverick who had changed parties more than once. He was extremely talented, but also arrogant. He had a sharp temper and sometimes seemed unstable, and before 1939 his political career was judged to be over. As prime minister he was not much of an administrator, constantly proposing wild schemes, but he had two genuine strengths. The first was a gift for language. Churchill spoke extraordinary words of courage and defiance just when the British public wanted and needed to hear them. He was utterly committed to winning the war. "You ask what is our policy," Churchill said in his first speech as prime minister in May of 1940, before the Battle of Britain began. "I will say, it is

to wage war with all our might, with all the strength that God can give us, to wage war against a monstrous tyranny never surpassed in the dark, lamentable catalogue of human crime."

Churchill's other strength was personal diplomacy. He convinced the American president, Franklin Roosevelt (1933–45), who supported the Allies, to break with American neutrality and send massive amounts of aid and weapons to Britain free of charge, under a program called Lend-Lease. Churchill also allowed the new government coalition to work to best effect. The ablest Conservative ministers stayed, but Labour politicians were also allowed to take positions of genuine power. Most of the Labour representatives turned out to be excellent administrators and were directly in touch with Britain's huge working class, which now felt fully included in the war effort.

With Britain's survival, the war moved into different theaters: the Atlantic (a battle over sea lanes and supplies), North Africa (strategically important for the Suez Canal and access to oil), the Pacific (the war with Japan), and the Soviet Union (where Hitler's determination to annihilate Stalin merged with his murderous campaign against the Jewish populations of Europe).

The Atlantic and North Africa

German submarines in the Atlantic Ocean were a dire threat to the Allies, with Britain's supply of weapons, raw materials, and food hanging in the balance. The British devoted a huge naval effort to saving their convoys, developing modern sonar and new systems of aerial reconnaissance. They also broke the German code for communicating with the submarine "wolf packs" roving the shipping lanes. When the United States entered the war in December 1941, the British shared their technology and experience, and many more U-boats (German submarines) were sunk. By late 1942 the threat receded.

The British defense of the Suez Canal made North Africa an important area of conflict, but the stakes soon grew as both the Germans and the Italians sought to end British dominance in this region and the Middle East. The Soviets and the British invaded Iran to keep that country's oil from falling in the hands of the Germans, and in Egypt a small British army humiliated a much larger Italian force. The British nearly succeeded in taking Libya from the Italians in 1941, but Hitler responded by sending his most daring tank commander, Erwin Rommel, at the head of an invasion force. Rommel's Afrika Korps gradually drove the British back, but when the German commander tried to

LONDON DURING THE BATTLE OF BRITAIN. German air raids that lasted from August 1940 to June 1941 wrought destruction but did not achieve Hitler's goal of breaking the British. The Holland House Library in London lost its roof but managed to engage in business as usual.

THE SECOND WORLD WAR IN EUROPE. ▪ *What parts of the European theater were controlled by the Allies?* ▪ *The Axis?* ▪ *What countries were neutral in 1941?* ▪ *In what parts of the European theater did the major Axis and Allied campaigns occur?* ▪ *What was Germany's greatest geographical challenge during the Second World War?*

follow up by invading Egypt in the autumn of 1942, his army was stopped near the town of El Alamein. Meanwhile, the United States intervened in November 1942, landing in the French territories of Morocco and Algeria. The Vichy French commanders surrendered peacefully, and the combined Allied forces finally broke through Rommel's line in March 1943, ending the fighting in Africa.

The Allies and Japan in the Pacific

The war became truly global when Japan struck the American naval base at Pearl Harbor, Hawaii, on the morning of December 7, 1941. To establish a Japanese empire in Asia, they would have to destroy America's Pacific fleet and seize the colonies of the British, Dutch, and French

"A DATE WHICH WILL LIVE IN INFAMY"—DECEMBER 7, 1941. The USS *West Virginia* was one of eight battleships sunk during the Japanese surprise attack targeting Battleship Row at the American naval base at Pearl Harbor. More than two thousand people were killed, but most of the American fleet, en route to or from other locations in the Pacific, was spared.

empires. The attack on Pearl Harbor was a brilliant act of surprise that devastated the American fleet and shocked the American public. It was not, however, the success that the Japanese wanted. Eight U.S. battleships were sunk and more than two thousand lives lost; but much of the American fleet was safely at sea on the day of the strike. The unprovoked attack galvanized American public opinion in a way the war in Europe had not. When Germany rashly declared war on the United States as well, America declared itself ready to take on all comers and joined the Allies.

Despite the mixed results at Pearl Harbor the Japanese enjoyed other stunning successes. Japanese troops swept through the British protectorate of Malaya in weeks, sinking the Pacific squadrons of both the British and Dutch navies in the swift attacks. Britain's fortified island port at Singapore, the keystone of British defenses in the Pacific, fell at the end of December 1941. Thousands of British and Australian troops were captured and sent off to four years of torture, forced labor, and starvation in Japanese prison camps. The Japanese also invaded the Philippines in December; and while American soldiers and marines held out on the island of Corregidor for some time, they too were forced to surrender. Some took to the hills to fight as guerrillas; the rest were forced on a death march to Japanese labor camps. The Dutch East Indies fell next, and it seemed there would be no stopping Japanese ships and soldiers before they reached Australia.

Reeling from Japan's blows, the Allies finally reorganized during 1942. After taking Singapore, Japanese troops pressed on into Burma, threatening India. Their defense of Burma failed, but the British were able to regroup, and a joint force of British and Indian troops defeated an attempted Japanese invasion of India at the border near the end of 1942. After that, with an army drawn from around the world, the British began to push the Japanese back.

At sea, America's navy benefited from a rapidly increased production schedule that turned out enough new ships and planes to outnumber the Japanese. In 1942 the United States won crucial victories in the Coral Sea and at Midway, battles fought by aircraft flown from each side's carriers. American marines landed on the island of Guadalcanal in early 1942 and captured this strategic Japanese base after months of bitter fighting. Their success began a campaign of island hopping as the marines destroyed Japan's network of island bases throughout the Pacific. This was brutal warfare, often settled with grenades and bayonets. Each side considered the other racially inferior. The Japanese often refused to surrender; the Americans and Australians were able to take few prisoners. By 1943 the Japanese advance had been halted, the Japanese navy had lost most of its capital ships, and the Allies began a slow march to Singapore and the Philippines.

THE RISE AND RUIN OF NATIONS: GERMANY'S WAR IN THE EAST AND THE OCCUPATION OF EUROPE

While battles ebbed and flowed in the Atlantic and the North African desert, Germany moved southeast into the Balkans. In 1941 Germany took over Yugoslavia almost without a fight. The Germans split Yugoslavia's ethnic patchwork by establishing a Croatian puppet state, pitting Croats against their Serb neighbors, who were ruled directly by the Nazis. Romania, Hungary, and Bulgaria joined the Nazis' cause as allies. The Greeks, who had dealt a crushing defeat to an Italian invasion, were suddenly confronted with a massive German force that overran the country. The Greeks stubbornly refused to surrender. An unexpected combination of Greek, British, and New Zealand troops nearly defeated the German paratroopers sent to capture the island of Crete in June of 1941. Many Greeks also took to the mountains as guerrillas, but in the end the country fell. By the summer of 1941, the whole European continent, with the exceptions of Spain, Portugal, Sweden, and

Switzerland, was either allied with the Nazis or subject to their rule. These victories, and the economy of plunder that enriched Germany with forced labor and other nations' wealth, won Hitler considerable popularity at home. But these were only the first steps in a larger plan.

Hitler's ultimate goals, and his conception of Germany's national destiny, lay to the east. Hitler had always seen the nonaggression pact with the Soviet Union as an act of convenience, to last only until Germany was prepared for this final conflict. By the summer of 1941, it seemed Germany was ready. On June 22, 1941, Hitler began Operation Barbarossa, the invasion of the Soviet Union. The elite of the German army led the way, defeating all the forces the Russians could put in front of them. Stalin's purges of the 1930s had exiled or executed many of his most capable army officers, and the effects showed in Russian disorganization and disaffection in the face of the panzers. Hundreds of thousands of prisoners were taken as German forces pressed deep into Byelorussia (modern Belarus), the Baltic states, and Ukraine. Like Napoleon, the Germans led a multinational army; it included Italians, Hungarians, most of the Romanian army,

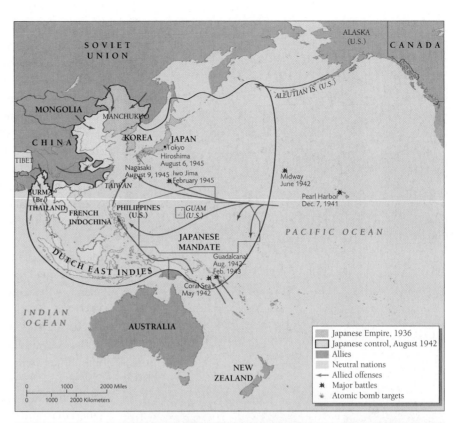

WORLD WAR II IN THE PACIFIC. ▪ *What areas did the Japanese and Allies each control in the Pacific theater during the Second World War?* ▪ *Based on tracing the route of the Allied offense of the map, what did the main Allied strategy appear to be?* ▪ *What factors led the Americans to decide that the dropping of atomic bombs on Hiroshima and Nagasaki was the most expedious way to end the war, rather than invading Japan?*

and freelance soldiers from the Baltics and Ukraine who bore grudges against Stalin's authoritarian regime. During the fall of 1941 the Nazis destroyed much of the Red Army's fighting strength and vigorously pursued their two goals: the destruction of communism and racial purification.

The war against the Soviets was a war of ideologies and of racial hatred. The advancing Nazi forces left burning fields and towns in their wake and methodically wiped the occupied territories clean of "undesirable elements." When Russian guerrillas counterattacked with sniping and sabotage, German forces shot or hanged hundreds of innocent hostages at a time in reprisal, often torturing their victims first. The Russian guerrillas quickly chose to deliver the same punishment to any captured Germans. By the end of 1941 it was clear that the war in the East was a war of destruction and that both sides believed that only one side would be allowed to survive. In 1941, it seemed the victors would be German: their forces were on the march toward the capital at Moscow. On orders from Berlin, however,

some of the German forces pushing toward Moscow were diverted southward to attack Russia's industrial heartland in an effort to destroy the Soviets' ability to resist before the Russian winter set in. Moscow was never taken, and the Russian population, its leaders, and its armies, began to organize a much more determined resistance.

Hitler nonetheless managed to piece together an empire that stretched across the entire continent of Europe. "We come as the heralds of a New Order and a new justice," his regime announced. Hitler specifically compared his rule to a "new Indian empire," and claimed to have studied British imperial techniques. Much of the "New Order" was improvised and rested on a patchwork of provisional regimes: military government in Poland and Ukraine, collaborators in France, allied fascists in Hungary, and so on. The clearest principle was German supremacy. The empire was meant to feed German citizens and maintain their morale and support for the war, which would prevent the "stab in the back" that Hitler believed had thwarted

"CULTURAL TERROR," 1944. Produced in Nazi-occupied Holland, this cultural Frankenstein's monster warns of the looming destruction of European identity with the advance of American troops who will bring American culture with them. The terror of this culture is embodied in a long list of references: aerial bombardment, the violence of lynching and the Ku Klux Klan, African American jazz, Jewish racial threats, sexual license, common criminality, and financial manipulation. ▪ *What image of European culture was this image designed to defend?*

out acts of sabotage. In Denmark, the population was much more united against their German occupiers, engaging in regular acts of passive resistance that infuriated German administrators. They also banded together as private citizens to smuggle most of the country's Jewish population out to safety in neutral Sweden.

Elsewhere the relationship between collaboration, resistance, and self-interested neutrality was more complex. In France, collaboration ranged from simple survival tactics under occupation to active support for Nazi ideals and goals. The worst example of this was the Vichy regime's active anti-Semitism and the aid given by French authorities in isolating and criminalizing French Jews and deporting them to the concentration camps. Living with the German conquerors forced citizens in France (and elsewhere) to make choices. Many chose to protect their own interests by sacrificing those of others, particularly such "undesirables" as Jews and communists. At the same time, communist activists, some members of the defeated French military, and ordinary citizens—such as the people of France's central mountains, who had a long tradition of smuggling and resisting government—became active guerrillas and saboteurs. They established links with the Free French movement in London, led by the charismatic, stiff-necked general Charles de Gaulle, and supplied important intelligence to the Allies. In eastern Europe, resistance movements provoked both open warfare against the fascists and civil war within their own countries. The Germans' system of occupation in Yugoslavia pitted a fascist Croat regime against most Serbs; the Croatian fascist guard, the Ustasha, massacred hundreds of thousands of Orthodox Christian Serbs. Josip Broz (Tito), born in Croatia to a Croatian father and a Slovene mother, emerged as the leader of the most powerful Yugoslavian resistance movement—militarily the most significant resistance in the war. Tito's troops were communists and strong enough to form a guerrilla army. They fought Germans, Italians, and Croat fascists, gaining support and supplies from the Allies.

Perhaps the most important moral issue facing citizens of occupied Europe was not their national allegiance but rather their personal attitude to the fate of the Nazis' sworn enemies: Jews, communists, gypsies, homosexuals, and political "undesirables." Some French Jews along the Riviera found the Italian Catholic army officers who occupied the area more willing to save them from deportation than their fellow Frenchmen. This deeply personal choice—whether to risk family, friends, and careers to aid the deportees or simply to look the other way and allow mass murder—was one of the most powerful dilemmas of the war.

a German victory in 1914–18. Occupied countries paid inflated "occupation costs" in taxes, food, industrial production, and manpower. More than 2 million foreign workers were brought into Germany in 1942–43 from France, Belgium, Holland, and the Soviet Union.

The demands of enemy occupation, and the political and moral questions of collaboration and resistance, were issues across occupied Europe. The Nazis set up puppet regimes in a number of occupied territories. Both Norway and the Netherlands were deeply divided by the occupation. In each country a relatively small but dedicated party of Nazis governed in the name of the Germans, while at the same time well-organized and determined resistance movements gathered information for the Allies and carried

RACIAL WAR, ETHNIC CLEANSING, AND THE HOLOCAUST

From the beginning, the Nazis had seen the conflict as a racial war. In *Mein Kampf* Hitler had already outlined his view that war against the *Untermenschen*, or "subhuman" Jews, Gypsies, and Slavs, was natural and necessary. Not only would it purify the German people, but it would also conquer territory for their expansion. Thus as soon as the war broke out, the Nazis began to implement the Reich's ambitious plans for redrawing the racial map—what is now called ethnic cleansing. In the fall of 1939, with Poland conquered, Heinrich Himmler directed the SS to begin massive population transfers. Ethnic Germans were moved from elsewhere into the borders of the Reich, while Poles and Jews were deported to specially designated areas in the east. Over two hundred thousand ethnic Germans from the Baltic states were resettled in Western Prussia. Welcoming these ethnic Germans went hand in hand with a brutal campaign of terror against the Poles, especially Polish Jews. The Nazis sought to root out all sources of potential resistance. Professors at the University of Cracow, considered dangerous intellectuals, were deported to concentration camps, where they died. The SS shot "undesirables," such as the inmates of Polish mental asylums, partly to allow SS troops to occupy the asylums' barracks. Poles were deported to forced labor camps. The Nazis began to transport Jews by the thousands to the region of Lublin, south of Warsaw. Special death squads also began to shoot Jews in the streets and in front of synagogues. These Polish campaigns took one hundred thousand Jewish lives in 1940.

The elimination of European Jewry stood at the center of the Nazis' *Rassenkampf*, or "racial struggle." We have seen the role of anti-Semitism in Hitler's rise to power and the escalating campaign of terror against the Jewish community inside Germany in the 1930s, including the Night of Broken Glass (see Chapter 25). Most historians now agree that although Hitler and other Nazis verbally announced "war" against the Jews early on, such a policy was not possible until the conquest of territory in the east after 1941 suddenly brought millions of Jews under Nazi control. Until the organized pogroms of 1938 the Nazis' anti-Jewish policy aimed not at extermination but at emigration, and until 1941 the Nazi leadership continued to consider plans to deport Europe's Jews to Madagascar, a French colony off the eastern coast of Africa. These schemes took shape against the background of daily terror and frequent massacres, especially in Poland. The invasion of the Soviet Union turned these atrocities into something much more deadly.

Operation Barbarossa was animated by the Nazis' intense ideological and racial hatreds, directed against Slavs, Jews, and Marxists. The campaign's initial success also created pressing practical problems for the German army in the newly conquered territories as officials debated how to control the millions of people, including military prisoners, Eastern European Jews, and other civilians, who had now fallen into Nazi hands. Although Hitler had certainly prepared the way for what followed in his long-nurtured campaigns against Jews, historians now believe that much of the driving force for the Holocaust came from rivalries within the Nazi bureaucracy that led to a radicalization of persecution and murder on a scale few could have imagined.

As the Nazi army swept into the Soviet Union in 1941, captured communist officials, political agitators, and any hostile civilians were imprisoned, tortured, or shot. About 5.5 million military prisoners were taken and marched to camps. Over half of them died of starvation or were executed. Poles from regions that had been under Soviet rule, Jews, and Russians were deported to Germany to work as slave labor in German factories. On the heels of the army came special battalions of *Einsatzgruppen*—special operations troops working as death squads. Joined by eleven thousand extra SS troops, they stormed through Jewish villages and towns with Russian or Polish populations identified as "difficult." The men of the villages were shot; the women and children either deported to labor camps or massacred along with the men. By September 1941, the *Einsatzgruppen* reported that in their efforts at pacification they had killed 85,000 people, most of them Jews. By April 1942, the number was 500,000. This killing began before the gas chambers had gone into operation and continued through the campaigns on the Eastern Front. As of 1943, the death squads had killed roughly 2.2 million Jews.

As Operation Barbarossa progressed, German administrations of occupied areas herded local Jewish populations even more tightly into the ghettos some Jewish communities had occupied for centuries; Warsaw and Lodz in Poland were the largest. There, Nazi administrators, accusing Jewish people in the ghettos of hoarding supplies, refused to allow food to go in. The ghettos became centers of starvation and disease. Those who left the ghetto were shot rather than returned. A German doctor summarized the regime's logic about killing this way: "One must, I can say it quite openly in this circle, be clear about it. There are only two ways. We sentence the Jews in the ghetto to death by hunger or we shoot them. Even if the end result is the same, the latter is more intimidating." In other words, the point was not simply death, but terror.

OPENING THE CONCENTRATION CAMPS. Many Allied soldiers documented the liberation of the concentration camps at the end of the war, recording in photographs and films the appalling scenes they encountered. In many cases, German civilians were brought into the camps and compelled to witness the countless bodies of camp prisoners that remained unburied, before being conscripted to help with the disposal of the corpses in order to prevent the spread of disease. In this photograph, local residents view the victims of Nazi crimes at Landesburg camp near Dachau in 1945. ▪ *What complications faced the Allies in the task of assigning responsibility for these crimes?*

Through the late summer and fall of 1941, Nazi officials formulated plans for mass killings in death camps. The ghettos had already been sealed; now orders came down that no Jews were to leave any occupied areas. That summer the Nazis had experimented with vans equipped with poison gas, which could kill thirty to fifty people at a time. Those experiments and the gas chambers were designed with the help of scientists from the T-4 euthanasia program, which had already killed eighty thousand racially, mentally, or physically "unfit" individuals in Germany. By October 1941, the SS was building camps with gas chambers and deporting people to them. Auschwitz-Birkenau *(OWSH-vihts BIHR-kuh-now),* which had been built to hold Polish prisoners, was expanded to be the largest of the camps. Auschwitz eventually held many different types of prisoners—"undesirables" like Jehovah's Witnesses and homosexuals, Poles, Russians, and even some British POWs—but Jews and gypsies were the ones systematically annihilated there. Between the spring of 1942 and the fall of 1944 over one million people were killed at Auschwitz-Birkenau alone. The creation of the death camps set off the greatest wave of slaughter from 1942 to 1943. Freight cars were used to haul Jewish people to the camps, first from the ghettos of Poland, then from France, Holland, Belgium, Austria, the Balkans, and later from Hungary and Greece. Bodies were buried in pits dug by prisoners or burned in crematoria.

The death camps have come to symbolize the horrors of Nazism as a system of modern mass murder. Yet it is worth emphasizing that the slaughter was not all anonymous, industrialized, or routine and that much of it took place in face-to-face encounters outside the camps. Jews and other victims were not simply killed. They were tortured, beaten, and executed publicly while soldiers and other onlookers recorded the executions with cameras—and sent photos home to their families. During the last phases of the war, inmates still in the concentration camps were taken on death marches whose sole purpose was suffering and death. Nor was the killing done by the specially indoctrinated troops of the SS and *Einsatzgruppen.* The Nazi regime called up groups of conscripts, such as Reserve Police Battalion 101, from duty in its home city of Hamburg and sent it into

"JEWISH COUPLE IN BUDAPEST," EVGENY KHALDEI (1945). Khaldei, a Soviet photographer and journalist who traveled with the Red Army, left a remarkable and moving account of his encounter with this woman and man. "There was a Jewish couple wearing Stars of David. They were afraid of me. There was still fighting going on in the city, and they thought I might be an SS soldier. So I said *Sholem Aleichem* [hello] to them, and the woman began to cry. After I'd taken the picture, I pulled their stars off and said, 'The fascists are beaten. It's terrible to be marked like that.'"

for a different task. In one Polish town, occupied first by the Soviets and then retaken by the Nazis, the Polish villagers themselves, with minimal guidance or help from German soldiers, turned on their Jewish neighbors and killed hundreds in a day.

How many people knew of the extent of the Holocaust? No operation of this scale could be carried out without the cooperation or knowledge of many: the Nazi hierarchy; architects who helped build the camps; engineers who designed the gas chambers and crematoria; municipal officials of cities from which people were deported; train drivers; residents of villages near the camps, who reported the smell of bodies burning; and so on. It is not surprising that most who suspected the worst were terrified and powerless. It is also not surprising that many people did not want to know and did their best to ignore evidence and carry on with their lives. Many who continued to support the Nazis did so for other reasons, out of personal opportunism or because they opposed communism and wanted order restored. Yet mere popular indifference does not provide a satisfactory explanation for the Nazis' ability to accomplish the murder of so many people. Many Europeans—German, French, Dutch, Polish, Swiss, and Russian—had come to believe that there was a "Jewish problem" that had to be "solved." The Nazis tried to conceal the death camps. Yet they knew they could count on vocal support for requiring Jews to be specially identified, for restrictions on marriage and property ownership, and for other kinds of discrimination. For reasons that had to do with both traditional Christian anti-Semitism and modern, racialized nationalism, many Europeans had come to see Jewish Europeans as "foreign," no longer members of their national communities.

What of other governments? Their level of collaboration with the Nazis' plans varied. The French Vichy regime, on its own initiative, passed laws that required Jews to wear identifying stars and strictly limited their movements and activities. When the German government demanded roundups and deportations of Jews, Vichy cooperated. On the other hand, Italy, though a fascist country, participated less actively. Not until the Germans occupied the north of Italy in 1943 were drastic anti-Semitic measures implemented. The Hungarian government, also fascist and allied with the Nazis, persecuted Jews but dragged its heels about deportations. Thus the Hungarian Jewish community survived—until March 1944, when Germans, disgusted with their Hungarian collaborators, took direct control and immediately began mass deportations. So determined were the Nazis to carry out their "final solution" that they killed up to twelve thousand Hungarian Jews a day at Auschwitz in May 1944, contributing to a total death toll of six hundred thousand Jews from Hungary.

occupied territories. Once there, the unit of middle-aged policemen received and obeyed orders to kill, in one day, fifteen hundred Jewish men, women, and children in one village. The commander offered to excuse men who did not feel they could carry out this assignment; only a few asked

Interpreting Visual Evidence

The Architecture of Mass Murder

The camp at Auschwitz-Birkenau was the largest of the German concentration camps whose central purpose was the murder of Europe's Jews. Almost 1.1 million people, of whom 1 million were Jews, were murdered in Auschwitz.

Auschwitz-Birkenau was in fact a complex of three camps: an extermination center, a prisoner-of-war camp, and a labor camp built with the cooperation of German industrial firms such as IG Farben. Forty other smaller installations and work camps in the surrounding area were also run by the camp's administration. The

construction of the Auschwitz-Birkenau complex occupied thousands of workers and continued throughout the war. When the Soviet Army arrived in January 1945, they found that the Germans had burned the camp archives before fleeing, but they had not burned the construction archive, which was kept separately. Hun-

A. Blueprint for Crematorium II, Birkenau, dated November 1941. The five shaded squares in the lower drawing are the gas ovens in the structure's underground level, and the area to the right is labeled "Corpses Room."

In the face of this Nazi determination, little resistance was possible. The concentration camps were designed to numb and incapacitate their inmates, making them acquiesce in their own slow deaths even if they were not killed right away. In his famous account, the survivor Primo Levi, an Italian Jew, writes: "Our language lacks words to express this offence, the demolition of a man. . . . It is not possible to sink lower than this; no human condition is more miserable than this, nor could it conceivably be so. Nothing belongs to us anymore; they have taken away our clothes, our shoes, even our hair; if we speak, they will not listen to us, and if they listen, they will not understand." A few rebellions in Auschwitz and Treblinka were repressed with savage efficiency. In the villages of Poland, Ukraine, and elsewhere, people rounded up to be deported or shot had to make split-second decisions to escape. Saving oneself nearly always meant abandoning one's children or parents, which very few could—or would—do. The countryside ofdreds of technical drawings were found in this archive, and after the collapse of the Soviet Union in 1991, these drawings became accessible to historians. A further cache of such documents was discovered in an abandoned building in Berlin in 2008. They are now held by Yad Vashem, the Holocaust archive in Jerusalem, Israel.

The discovery of these drawings did not add substantially to what was already known about the murder of Jews and other prisoners at Auschwitz, but they provide an arresting example of the bureaucratic apparatus—and the chilling coldness of the planning—that went into the Nazi extermination policy.

Questions for Analysis

1. Who would have seen these plans and been made aware of their purpose?

2. What do these images tell us about the nature of the effort that went into the Nazi extermination policy?

3. Is there a way to understand the relationship between the careful renderings, the precise measurements, the rectilinear lines, and the ultimate purpose of the buildings depicted?

B. Blueprint for the "Delousing Facility" at Auschwitz-Birkenau, showing a room of 11.6 meters by 11.2 meters marked "*Gaskammer*" (gas chamber).

fered no shelter; local populations were usually either hostile or too terrified to help. Reprisals horrified all. Families of Jews and gypsies were ordinary people whose lives could not have prepared them for the kind of violence that rolled over them.

The largest Jewish resistance came in the Warsaw ghetto, in the spring of 1943. The previous summer, the Nazis had deported 80 percent of the ghetto's residents to the camps, making it clear that those left behind had little

hope of survival. Those in the ghetto had virtually no resources, yet, when deportations started again, a small Jewish underground movement—a thousand fighters, perhaps, in a community of seventy thousand—took on the Nazis with a tiny arsenal of gasoline bombs, pistols, and ten rifles. The Nazis responded by burning the ghetto to the ground and executing and deporting to the camps nearly everyone who was left. Some fifty-six thousand Jews died. "The Warsaw Ghetto is no more," reported the SS commander at the end.

Word of the uprising did spread, but the repression made it clear that the targets of Nazi extermination could choose only between death in the streets or death in the camps. Sustained resistance, as one person remarked, would have required "the prospect of victory."

The Holocaust claimed between 4.1 and 5.7 million Jewish lives. Even those numbers do not register the nearly total destruction of some cultures. In the Baltic states (Latvia, Estonia, and Lithuania), Germany, Czechoslovakia, Yugoslavia, and Poland, well over 80 percent of the long-established Jewish communities were annihilated. Elsewhere, the figures were closer to 50 percent. The Holocaust was part of a racial war and of an even longer period of ethnically motivated mass murder. Through both world wars and afterward ethnic and religious groups—Jews, Armenians, Poles, Serbian Orthodox, ethnic Germans—were hunted, massacred, and legally deported en masse. Hitler's government had planned to build a "new Europe," safe for ethnic Germans and their allies and secure against communism, on the graveyards of whole cultures.

TOTAL WAR: HOME FRONTS, THE WAR OF PRODUCTION, BOMBING, AND THE BOMB

The Second World War was a "total war." Even more than the First World War, it involved the combined efforts of whole populations, massive resources, and a mobilization of entire economies within combatant nations. In the lands occupied by Germany or Japan, economies of forced extraction robbed local areas of resources, workers, and even food. In East Asia deprivations caused rising resentment of the Japanese, who had been seen initially as liberators ending the rule of the old colonial powers. Everywhere work schedules were grueling. Women and the elderly, pressed back into wage work or working for the first time, put in long shifts before returning home to cook, clean, and care for families and neighbors also affected by enemy bombing and wartime shortages. Diets changed. Though Germany lived comfortably off the farmlands of Europe for several years and the United States could lean on its huge agricultural base, food, gasoline, and basic household goods were still rationed. In occupied Europe and the Soviet Union rations were just above starvation level and sometimes fell below in areas near the fighting.

Production—the industrial ability to churn out more tanks, tents, planes, bombs, and uniforms than the other side—was essential to winning the war. Britain, the Soviet Union, and America each launched comprehensive, well-designed propaganda campaigns that encouraged the production of war equipment on an unmatched scale. Appeals to patriotism, to communal interests, and to a common stake in winning the war struck a chord. The Allied societies proved willing to regulate themselves and commit to the effort. Despite strikes and disputes with government officials, the Allied powers devoted more of their economies to war production, more efficiently, than any nations in history. They built tanks, ships, and planes capable of competing with advanced German and Japanese designs by the tens of thousands, swamping the enemy with constant resupply and superior firepower. Japan nearly reached comparable levels of production but then slowly declined, as Allied advances on land and American submarines cut off overseas sources of vital supplies. Germany, despite its reputation for efficiency and its access to vast supplies of slave labor, was less efficient in its use of workers and materials than the Allied nations.

Because industry was essential to winning the war, centers of industry became vital military targets. The Allies began bombing German ports and factories almost as soon as the Germans started their own campaigns. Over time, American and British planners became as ruthless as the Germans on an even larger scale. Both of these Allied nations made a major commitment to strategic bombing, developing new planes and technology that allowed them to put thousands of bombers in the air both night and day over occupied Europe. As the war wore on and Germany kept fighting, the Allies expanded their campaign. They moved from pinpoint bombing of the military and industry in Germany to striking such targets across all of occupied Europe and bombing Germany's civilian population in earnest. For the British, despite a public debate about the morality of bombing, it was a war of retribution; for the Americans, it was an effort to grind the Germans down without sacrificing too many Allied lives. The Allies killed tens of thousands of German civilians as they struck Berlin, ports such as Hamburg, and the industrial cities of the Ruhr, but German war production persisted. At the same time German fighter planes shot down hundreds of Allied bombers, causing heavy losses. After the Allied invasion of Europe, bombing expanded well beyond targets of military value. The German city of Dresden, a center of culture and education that lacked heavy industry, was firebombed with a horrifying death toll. This gave Allied generals and politicians pause, but strategic bombing continued. German industry was slowly degraded, but the German will to keep fighting, like Britain's or the Soviet Union's, remained intact.

The Race to Build the Bomb

Allied scientists in the United States also developed the world's first nuclear weapon during the war years, a bomb that worked by splitting the atom, creating a chain reaction that could release tremendous energy in an explosion. Physicists in Britain and Germany first suggested that such a weapon might be possible, but only the United States had the resources to build such a bomb before the end of the war. Fearful that the Germans would develop a bomb of their own, the U.S. government built a laboratory at Los Alamos, New Mexico, and charged a group of scientists to build an atomic bomb. Physicist J. Robert Oppenheimer directed the top-secret plan, known to the researchers as the Manhattan Project. The idea was to perfect a bomb that could be dropped by plane and detonated above the target. The physicists successfully tested a device on July 16, 1945, in New Mexico, vaporizing the test tower in a wave of heat and fire that rose in a mushroom-shaped cloud overhead. The United States now possessed the most destructive weapon ever devised.

"RAISING THE RED FLAG OVER THE REICHSTAG," EVGENY KHALDEI, MAY 1, 1945. Khaldei was one of several Soviet Jewish photographers to document Nazi atrocities and (in this case) Soviet heroism on the Eastern Front. In this photograph, which became the best-known image of Soviet victory, a Soviet soldier raises a flag over the Reichstag in Berlin. ■ *How was the Soviet occupation of the German capital seen from the perspective of the other Allied governments?*

THE ALLIED COUNTERATTACK

Hitler had invaded the Soviet Union in June 1941. Within two years the war in the East had become his undoing; within four years it brought about his destruction.

The early successes of the German-led invasion were crippling. Nearly 90 percent of the Soviets' tanks, most of their aircraft, and huge stores of supplies were destroyed or captured. Nazi forces penetrated deep into European Russia. The Soviets fought regardless. By late 1941 German and Finnish forces had cut off and besieged Leningrad (St. Petersburg). Yet the city held out for 844 days—through three winters, massive destruction by artillery and aircraft, and periods of starvation—until a large relief force broke the siege. Russian partisans stepped up their campaigns of ambush and terrorism, and many of the Germans' former allies in Ukraine and elsewhere turned against them in reaction to Nazi pacification efforts.

The Eastern Front

In the East, the character of the war changed as Russians rallied to defend the *rodina*—the Russian motherland. Stalin's efforts were aided by the weather: successive winters took a heavy toll in German lives. At the same time, Soviet industry made an astonishing recovery during the war years. Whole industries were rebuilt behind the safety of the Ural mountains and entire urban populations were sent to work in them, turning out tanks, fighter planes, machine guns, and ammunition. Finally, the Germans were the victims of their own success with their *Blitzkrieg* tactics, as their lines extended deep into Russian territory, spreading their forces more thinly and opening them up to attack from unexpected angles.

The turning point came in 1942–43, when the Germans attempted to take Stalingrad in an effort to break the back of Soviet industry. The Russians drew the invading army into the city, where they were bogged down in house-to-house fighting that neutralized the German tanks and gave the outnumbered Soviet forces greater chances of success, despite their lack of equipment. The Germans found their supplies running low as winter set in, and in November 1942 large Russian armies encircled the city and besieged the invaders in a battle that continued through a cruel winter. At the end of January 1943, the German commander defied his orders and surrendered. More than half a million German, Italian, and Romanian soldiers had been killed; Russian casualties were over a million, including a hundred thousand civilians.

After Stalingrad, a series of Soviet attacks drove the Germans back toward the frontier and beyond. In what may have been the largest land battle ever fought, Soviet

STORMING "FORTRESS EUROPE." American troops landing on Omaha Beach in Normandy, France on June 6, 1944. In the three months that followed, the Allies poured more than two million men, almost half a million vehicles, and four million tons of supplies onto the Continent—a measure of how firmly the Germans were established.

The most important Western European front was opened on June 6, 1944, with the massive Allied landings in Normandy. Casualties were high, but careful planning and deception allowed the Allied invasion to gain a foothold in northern Europe, eventually leading to breakthrough of the German lines. A second landing in southern France also succeeded, aided by the resistance. By August, these Allied armies had liberated Paris and pushed into Belgium. In the fall, the Germans managed to defeat a British airborne invasion in the Netherlands and an American thrust into the Rhineland forests before mounting a devastating attack in December 1944, in the Battle of the Bulge. The Allied lines nearly broke, but the American forces held long enough for a crushing counterattack. In April 1945 the Allies crossed the Rhine into Germany, and the last defenders of the German Reich were swiftly overwhelmed. This military success was helped by the fact that most Germans preferred to surrender to Americans or Britons than face the Russians to the east.

Those Soviet troops were approaching fast. The Russian Army took Prague and Vienna, and by late April they reached the suburbs of Berlin. In the savage ten-day battle to take the German capital more than a hundred thousand Russians and Germans died. Adolf Hitler killed himself in a bunker beneath the Chancellery on April 30. On May 2 the heart of the city was captured, and the Soviets' red banner flew from the Brandenburg Gate. On May 7 the German high command signed a document of unconditional surrender. The war in Europe was over.

armies destroyed a German force at Kursk in the summer of 1943—the battle involved over six thousand tanks and two million men. Following this victory, the Russians launched a major offensive into Ukraine, and by the spring of 1944 Ukraine was back in Soviet hands. Meanwhile, Leningrad was liberated and Romania forced to capitulate. Soviet armies entered the Balkans, where they met up with Tito's partisans in Yugoslavia. In Poland, successive German armies collapsed, and the Soviets, joined by communist partisans from eastern Europe, retook large parts of Czechoslovakia. Hitler's ambitious goal of conquest in the East had brought the downfall of the Nazi regime and death to another generation of German soldiers.

The Western Front

When the Nazis invaded Russia, Stalin called on the Allies to open a second front in the West. In response, the Americans led an attack on Italy in 1943, beginning with an invasion of Sicily in July. Italy's government deposed Mussolini and surrendered in the summer of 1943, while the nation collapsed into civil war. Italian partisans, especially the communists, sided with the Americans, while dedicated fascists fought on. The Germans occupied Italy with more than a dozen elite divisions, and the hard-fought and bitter campaign with American and British forces lasted eighteen months.

The War in the Pacific

The war in the Pacific ended four months later. The British pushed the Japanese out of Burma while the Germans were surrendering in the West, and soon afterwards Australian forces recaptured the Dutch East Indies. In the fall of 1944, the U.S. Navy had destroyed most of Japan's surface ships in the gulfs of the Philippine Islands, and American troops took Manila house by house in bloody fighting. The remaining battles—amphibious assaults on a series of islands running toward the Japanese mainland—were just as brutal. Japanese pilots mounted suicide attacks on American ships, while American marines and Japanese soldiers fought over every inch of the shell-blasted rocks in the Pacific. The Japanese island of Okinawa fell to the Americans after eighty-two days of desperate fighting, giving the United States a foothold less than five hundred miles from the Japanese home islands. At the same time, the Soviet Union

THE ATOM BOMB. A mushroom cloud hovers over Nagasaki after the city was bombed on August 9, 1945. Hiroshima had been bombed three days earlier.

marched an army into Manchuria and the Japanese colonial territory of Korea. The government in Tokyo called on its citizens to defend the nation against an invasion.

On July 26, the U.S., British, and Chinese governments jointly called on Japan to surrender or be destroyed. The United States had already been using long-range B-29 bombers in systematic attacks on Japanese cities, killing hundreds of thousands of Japanese civilians in firestorms produced by incendiary bombs. When the Japanese government refused to surrender, the United States decided to use their atomic bomb.

Many senior military and naval officers argued that the use of the bomb was not necessary, on the assumption that Japan was already beaten. Some of the scientists involved, who had done their part to defeat the Nazis, believed that using the bomb would set a deadly precedent. Harry Truman, who became president when Roosevelt died in April 1945, decided otherwise. On August 6 a single American plane dropped an atomic bomb on Hiroshima, obliterating 60 percent of the city. Three days later, the United States dropped

a second bomb on Nagasaki. On August 14 Japan surrendered unconditionally.

The decision to use the bomb was extraordinary. It did not greatly alter the American plans for the destruction of Japan—in fact many more Japanese died in the earlier fire bombings than in the two atomic blasts. Yet the bomb was an entirely new kind of weapon, revealing a new and terrifying relationship between science and political power. The nearly instantaneous, total devastation of the blasts, and the lingering effects of cancerous radiation that could claim victims decades later, was something terribly new. The world now had a weapon that could destroy not just cities and peoples, but humanity itself.

CONCLUSION

After the First World War, many Europeans awoke to find a world they no longer recognized. In 1945 many Europeans came out from shelters or began the long trips back to their homes, faced with a world that hardly existed at all. The products of industry—tanks, submarines, strategic bombing—had destroyed the structures of industrial society—factories, ports, and railroads. The tools of mass culture—fascist and communist appeals, patriotism proclaimed via radios and movie screens, mobilization of mass armies and industry—had been put to full use. In the aftermath, much of Europe lay destroyed and, as we will see, vulnerable to the rivalry of the postwar superpowers: the United States and the Soviet Union.

The two world wars profoundly affected Western empires. Nineteenth-century imperialism had made twentieth-century war a global matter. In both conflicts the warring nations had used the resources of empire to their fullest. Key campaigns, in North Africa, Burma, Ethiopia, and the Pacific, were fought in and over colonial territories. Hundreds of thousands of colonial troops—sepoys and Gurkhas from India and Nepal, Britain's King's African Rifles, French from Algeria and West Africa—served in armies during the conflict. After two massive mobilizations, many anticolonial leaders found renewed confidence in their own peoples' courage and resourcefulness, and they seized the opportunity of European weakness to press for independence. In many areas that had been under European or Japanese imperial control, from sections of China, to Korea, Indochina, Indonesia, and Palestine—the end of the Second World War only paved the way for a new round of conflict. This time, the issue was when imperial control would be ended, and by whom.

Competing Viewpoints

The Atomic Bomb and Its Implications

> In July 1945, scientists associated with the Manhattan Project became involved in debates about how the atomic bomb could be deployed. Members of the Scientific Panel of the secretary of war's Interim Advisory Committee agreed that a bomb could be used militarily but disagreed about whether it could be used without prior warning and demonstration. Other groups of scientists secretly began to circulate petitions, such as the one reprinted here, in which they set out their views. The petitions never reached the president, but they raised issues that did emerge in the postwar period.
>
> In the section of his memoirs reprinted here, President Harry S. Truman sets out the views of other scientists on the secretary of war's advisory committee. He explains the logic of his decision to use the atomic bomb against Hiroshima (August 6, 1945) and Nagasaki (August 9, 1945) and the events as they unfolded.

A Petition to the President of the United States

July 17, 1945

A PETITION TO THE PRESIDENT OF THE UNITED STATES

We, the undersigned scientists, have been working in the field of atomic power. Until recently we have had to fear that the United States might be attacked by atomic bombs during this war and that her only defense might lie in a counterattack by the same means. Today, with the defeat of Germany, this danger is averted and we feel impelled to say what follows:

The war has to be brought speedily to a successful conclusion and attacks by atomic bombs may very well be an effective method of warfare. We feel, however, that such attacks on Japan could not be justified, at least not unless the terms which will be imposed after the war on Japan were made public in detail and Japan were given an opportunity to surrender. . . .

[I]f Japan still refused to surrender our nation might then, in certain circumstances, find itself forced to resort to the use of atomic bombs. Such a step, however, ought not to be made at any time without seriously consider-

ing the moral responsibilities which are involved.

The development of atomic power will provide the nations with new means of destruction. The atomic bombs at our disposal represent only the first step in this direction, and there is almost no limit to the destructive power which will become available in the course of their future development. Thus a nation which sets the precedent of using these newly liberated forces of nature for purposes of destruction may have to bear the responsibility of opening the door to an era of devastation on an unimaginable scale.

If after this war a situation is allowed to develop in the world which permits rival powers to be in uncontrolled possession of these new means of destruction, the cities of the United States as well as the cities of other nations will be in continuous danger of sudden annihilation. . . .

The added material strength which this lead [in the field of atomic power] gives to the United States brings with it the obligation of restraint and if we were to violate this obligation our moral posi-

tion would be weakened in the eyes of the world and in our own eyes. It would then be more difficult for us to live up to our responsibility of bringing the unloosened forces of destruction under control.

In view of the foregoing, we, the undersigned, respectfully petition: first, that you exercise your power as Commander-in-Chief, to rule that the United States shall not resort to the use of atomic bombs in this war unless the terms which will be imposed upon Japan have been made public in detail and Japan knowing these terms has refused to surrender; second, that in such an event the question of whether or not to use atomic bombs be decided by you in the light of the considerations presented in this petition as well as all the other moral responsibilities which are involved.

Source: Michael B. Stoff, Jonathan F. Fanton, and R. Hal Williams, eds., *The Manhattan Project: A Documentary Introduction to the Atomic Age* (New York: 2000), p. 173.

President Truman's Memoirs

I had realized, of course, that an atomic bomb explosion would inflict damage and casualties beyond imagination. On the other hand, the scientific advisers of the committee reported, "We can propose no technical demonstration likely to bring an end to the war; we see no acceptable alternative to direct military use." It was their conclusion that no technical demonstration they might propose, such as over a deserted island, would be likely to bring the war to an end. It had to be used against an enemy target.

The final decision of where and when to use the atomic bomb was up to me. Let there be no mistake about it. I regarded the bomb as a military weapon and never had any doubt that it should be used. The top military advisers to the President recommended its use, and when I talked to Churchill he unhesitatingly told me that he favored the use of the atomic bomb if it might aid to end the war.

In deciding to use this bomb I wanted to make sure that it would be used as a weapon of war in the manner prescribed by the laws of war. That meant that I wanted it dropped on a military target. I had told Stimson that the bomb should be dropped as nearly as possibly upon a war production center of prime military importance.

Stimson's staff had prepared a list of cities in Japan that might serve as targets. Kyoto, though favored by General Arnold as a center of military activity, was eliminated when Secretary Stimson pointed out that it was a cultural and religious shrine of the Japanese.

Four cities were finally recommended as targets: Hiroshima, Kokura, Niigata, and Nagasaki. They were listed in that order as targets for the first attack. The order of selection was in accordance with the military importance of these cities, but allowance would be given for weather conditions at the time of the bombing. Before the selected targets were approved as proper for military purposes, I personally went over them in detail with Stimson, Marshall, and Arnold, and we discussed the matter of timing and the final choice of the first target. . . .

On August 6, the fourth day of the journey home from Potsdam, came the historic news that shook the world. I was eating lunch with members of the *Augusta's* crew when Captain Frank Graham, White House Map Room watch officer, handed me the following message:

To the President from the Secretary of War

Big bomb dropped on Hiroshima August 5 at 7:15 P.M. Washington time. First reports indicate complete success which was even more conspicuous than earlier test.

I was greatly moved. I telephoned Byrnes aboard ship to give him the news and then said to the group of sailors around me, "This is the greatest thing in history. It's time for us to get home."

Source: Harry S. Truman, *Memoirs*, Vol. 1 (Garden City, NY: 1955), pp. 419–21.

Questions for Analysis

1. To express their fears about how the atomic bomb would be used, scientists circulated petitions. Look at the outcomes the scientists proposed. Which came closest to subsequent events? Which was the most prudent? The most honest?

2. Is it appropriate for scientists to propose how new weapons should be used? Are they overreaching in trying to give advice in foreign affairs and military strategy? Or are they obligated to voice moral qualms?

The Second World War also carried on the Great War's legacy of massive killing. Historians estimate that nearly 50 million people died. The killing fields of the east took the highest tolls: 25 million Soviet lives (8.5 million in the military, and the rest civilians); 20 percent of the Polish population and nearly 90 percent of the Polish Jewish community; 1 million Yugoslavs, including militias of all sides; 4 million German soldiers and 500,000 German civilians, not including the hundreds of thousands of ethnic Germans who died while being deported west at the end of the war in one of the many acts of ethnic cleansing that ran through the period. Even the United States, shielded from the full horrors of total war by two vast oceans, lost 292,000 soldiers in battle and more to accidents or disease.

Why was the war so murderous? The advanced technology of modern industrial warfare and the openly genocidal ambitions of the Nazis offer part of the answer. The global reach of the conflict offers another. Finally, the Second World War overlapped with, and eventually devolved into, a series of smaller, no less bitter conflicts: a

After You Read This Chapter

Visit StudySpace for quizzes, additional review materials, and multi-media documents. **wwnorton.com/studyspace**

REVIEWING THE OBJECTIVES

- The causes of the Second World War can be found in the political and economic crises of the 1930s. What caused the war?

- British and French leaders in the 1930s hoped to avoid another war in Europe through diplomatic negotiation with Hitler. What were the consequences of these negotiations?

- The populations of nations occupied by the Germans faced a difficult set of choices. What were the consequences of occupation for European nations and what possibilities existed for resistance?

- The mass murder of European Jews, homosexuals, and gypsies reached a climax during the invasion of the Soviet Union, though the victims came from every corner of Europe. What efforts did this enormous project entail and how did it come about?

- The Nazi regime and its allies eventually collapsed after costly defeats in both eastern and western Europe. Where and when did the major defeats take place and what was their human cost?

- The Japanese government surrendered in August 1945 after the United States dropped two atomic bombs, on Hiroshima and Nagasaki. What events led to the decision to drop these bombs and what were their consequences?

civil war in Greece; conflicts between Orthodox, Catholics, and Muslims in Yugoslavia; and political battles for control of the French resistance. Even when those struggles claimed fewer lives, they left deep political scars and traumatic memories. Hitler's empire could not have lasted as long as it did without active collaboration or passive acquiescence from many, a fact that produced bitterness and recrimination for years.

In this and many other ways, the war haunted the second half of the century. Fifty years after the battle of Stalingrad, the journalist Timothy Rybeck discovered that hundreds of skeletons still lay in open fields outside the city. Many bodies had never been buried. Others had been left in shallow mass graves. As wind and water eroded the soil, farmers plowed the fields, and teenagers dug for medals and helmets to sell as curiosities, more bones kept rising to the surface. One of the supervisors charged with finding permanent graves and building memorials to the fallen contemplated the task with more than simple weariness. "This job of reburying the dead," he said, "will never be done."

PEOPLE, IDEAS, AND EVENTS IN CONTEXT

- What was Hitler asking for at the **MUNICH CONFERENCE** of 1938, and what made many people in Europe think that **APPEASEMENT** was their best option?
- What was the **HITLER-STALIN PACT** of 1939?
- What was *BLITZKRIEG* and what effect did it have on those who faced Hitler's invasions?
- What was the **HOLOCAUST**?
- What were Hitler's goals in **OPERATION BARBAROSSA**, the invasion of the Soviet Union in 1941? What were the consequences of the German defeat at **STALINGRAD**?
- What made the Second World War a **GLOBAL WAR**? Where were the main consequences of the war felt most keenly outside of Europe?
- What was the **MANHATTAN PROJECT** and how did it affect the outcome of the Second World War?

CONSEQUENCES

- In what ways can one see the Second World War as being linked to the First World War, and in what ways was the Second World War different from the First?
- Why did so many people in Germany support Hitler's war aims for so long?
- What was the situation in Europe in 1945? What challenges faced those who sought to rebuild after the war's destruction?

Before
You
Read
This
Chapter

The Cold War World: Global Politics, Economic Recovery, and Cultural Change

CORE OBJECTIVES

- **UNDERSTAND** the origins of the Cold War and the ways that the United States and the Soviet Union sought to influence the political and economic restructuring of Europe in the postwar period.

- **IDENTIFY** the policies that led to the economic integration of Western European nations in the postwar decades and the reasons for the rapid economic growth that accompanied this integration.

- **DESCRIBE** the process of decolonization that brought the colonial era in Africa and Asia to an end.

- **EXPLAIN** developments in European postwar culture, as intellectuals, writers, and artists reacted to the loss of European influence in the world and the ideological conflicts of the Cold War.

T he war ended the way a passage through a tunnel ends," wrote Heda Kovály, a Czech woman who had survived the concentration camps. "From far away you could see the light ahead, a gleam that kept growing, and its brilliance seemed ever more dazzling to you huddled there in the dark the longer it took to reach it. But when at last the train burst out into the glorious sunshine, all you saw was a wasteland." The war left Europe a land of wreckage and confusion. Millions of refugees trekked hundreds or thousands of miles on foot to return to their homes while others were forcibly displaced from their lands. In some areas housing was practically nonexistent, with no available means to build anew. Food remained in dangerously short supply; a year after the war, roughly a hundred million people in Europe still lived on less than fifteen hundred calories per day. Families scraped vegetables from their gardens or traded smuggled goods on the black market. Governments continued to ration food, and without rationing a large portion of the Continent's population would have starved. During the winter of 1945–46, many regions had little or no fuel for heat. What coal there was—less than half the prewar supply—could not be transported to the areas that needed it most. The brutality of international war, civil war, and occupation had divided countries against themselves, shredding relations among ethnic groups and fellow citizens. Ordinary people's intense relief at liberation often went hand in hand with recriminations over their neighbors' wartime betrayal, collaboration, or simple opportunism.

How does a nation, a region, or a civilization recover from a catastrophe on the scale of the Second World War? Nations had to do much more than deliver food and rebuild economic infrastructures. They had to restore—or create—government authority, functioning bureaucracies, and legitimate legal systems. They had to rebuild bonds of trust and civility between citizens, steering a course between demands for justice on the one hand and the overwhelming desire to bury memories of the past on the other. Rebuilding entailed a commitment to renewing democracy—to creating democratic institutions that could withstand threats such as those the West had experienced in the 1930s. Some aspects of this process were extraordinarily successful, more so than even the most optimistic forecaster might have thought possible in 1945. Others failed or were deferred until later in the century.

The war's devastating effects brought two dramatic changes in the international balance of power. The first change was the emergence of the so-called superpowers, the United States and the Soviet Union, and the swift development of a "Cold War" between them. The Cold War

THE REMAINS OF DRESDEN, 1947. Dresden was devastated by a controversial Allied bombing in February, 1945. Kurt Vonnegut dramatically portrayed its destruction and the aftermath in his novel *Slaughterhouse-Five*. ▪ *How did the war's new strategies of aerial bombardment—culminating in the use of atomic weapons—change the customary division between combatants and noncombatant civilians?*

divided Europe, with Eastern Europe occupied by Soviet troops, and Western Europe dominated by the military and economic presence of the United States. In both Western and Eastern Europe, the Cold War led to increased political and economic integration, resulting in the emergence of the European Common Market in the West and a socialist bloc dominated by the Soviet Union in the East. The second great change came with the dismantling of the European empires that had once stretched worldwide. The collapse of empires and the creation of newly emancipated nations raised the stakes in the Cold War and brought superpower rivalry to far-flung sections of the globe. Those events, which shaped the postwar recovery and necessarily created a new understanding of what "the West" meant, are the subject of this chapter.

THE COLD WAR AND A DIVIDED CONTINENT

No peace treaty ended the Second World War. Instead, as the war drew to a close, relations between the Allied powers began to fray over issues of power and influence in Central and Eastern Europe. After the war, they descended from mistrust to open conflict. The United States and Soviet Union rapidly formed the centers of two imperial blocs. Their rivalry, which came to be known as the Cold War, pitted against each other two military powers, two sets of state interests, and two ideologies: capitalism and communism.

The Iron Curtain

As the war drew to a close, the Soviet Union insisted that it had a legitimate claim to control Eastern Europe, a claim that some Western leaders accepted as the price of defeating Hitler. Stalin's siege mentality pervaded his authoritarian regime and cast nearly everyone at home or abroad as a potential threat or enemy of the state. Yet Soviet policy did not rest on one man's personal paranoia alone. The country's catastrophic wartime losses made the Soviets determined to maintain political, economic, and military control of the lands they had liberated from Nazi rule. When their former allies resisted their demands, the Soviets became suspicious, defensive, and aggressive.

In Eastern Europe, the Soviet Union used a combination of diplomatic pressure, political infiltration, and military power to create "people's republics" sympathetic to Moscow. In country after country, the same process unfolded: first, states set up coalition governments that excluded former

TERRITORIAL CHANGES IN EUROPE AFTER THE SECOND WORLD WAR. At the end of the Second World War, the Soviet Union annexed territory in Eastern Europe to create a buffer between itself and Western Europe. At the same time, the United States established a series of military alliances in Western Europe to stifle the spread of communism in Europe. ▪ *What Eastern European countries fell under Russian control?* ▪ *Where is Berlin located, and why did its location and control cause so much tension?* ▪ *How did these new territorial boundaries aggravate the tensions between the Soviet Union and the United States?*

Nazi sympathizers; next came coalitions dominated by communists; finally, the communist party took hold of all the key positions of power. This was the process that prompted Winston Churchill, speaking at a college graduation in Fulton, Missouri, in 1946, to say that "an Iron Curtain" had "descended across Europe." In 1948, the Soviets crushed a Czechoslovakian coalition government—a break with Yalta's guarantee of democratic elections that shocked many. By that year, governments dependent on Moscow had also been established in Poland, Hungary, Romania, and Bulgaria. Together these states were referred to as the Eastern bloc.

Exceptionally, the Yugoslavian communist and resistance leader Marshal Tito (Josip Broz, 1892–1980) fought

to keep his government independent of Moscow. Unlike most Eastern European communist leaders, Tito came to power on his own during the war. He drew on support from Serbs, Croats, and Muslims in Yugoslavia—thanks to his wartime record, which gave him political authority rooted in his own country. Moscow charged that Yugoslavia had "taken the road to nationalism," or become a "colony of the imperialist nations," and expelled the country from the communist countries' economic and military pacts. Determined to reassert control elsewhere, the Soviets demanded purges in the parties and administrations of various satellite governments. These began in the Balkans and extended through Czechoslovakia, East Germany, and Poland. The fact that democratic institutions had been shattered before the war made it easier to establish dictatorships in its aftermath. The purges succeeded by playing on fears and festering hatreds; in several areas those purging the governments attacked their opponents as Jewish. Anti-Semitism, far from being crushed, remained a potent political force—it became common to blame Jews for bringing the horrors of war.

The end of war did not mean peace. In Greece, as in Yugoslavia and through much of the Balkans, war's end brought a local communist-led resistance to the verge of seizing power. The British and the Americans, however, were determined to keep Greece in their sphere of influence, as per informal agreements with the Soviets. Only large infusions of aid to the anticommunist monarchy allowed them to do so. The bloody civil war that lasted until 1949 took a higher toll than the wartime occupation. Greece's bloodletting became one of the first crises of the Cold War and a touchstone for the United States' escalating fear of communist expansion.

Defeated Germany lay at the heart of these two polarizing power blocs and soon became the front line of their conflict. The Allies had divided Germany into four zones of occupation. Although the city of Berlin was deep in Soviet territory, it too was divided. The occupation zones were intended to be temporary, pending an official peace settlement, but quarrels between the occupying powers were frequent. The quickening Cold War put those

Interpreting Visual Evidence

The End of the Second World War and the Onset of the Cold War

The need to defeat Nazi Germany brought the United States and the Soviet Union together in a common struggle, in spite of their contrasting political systems. Both nations emerged from the Second World War with a renewed sense of purpose, and both tried to use the victory against fascism to promote their claims for legitimacy and leadership in Europe. These circumstances placed a special burden on European nations and their postwar governments, as they were forced to take sides in this global confrontation at a moment of weakness and uncertainty.

The images here, all from May 1945 in Czechoslovakia, display several different possibilities for representing the German defeat in this Eastern European country. Image A shows a Czech civilian rending the Nazi flag, with the Prague skyline in the background and the flags

of the major Allied powers and Czechoslovakia overhead. Image B depicts a triumphant Czech laborer wielding a rifle and socialist red flag standing over the body of a dead German soldier. Image C depicts portraits of Stalin and the

A. Czech propaganda poster celebrating German defeat, May 1945.

B. Czech propaganda poster celebrating German defeat, May 1945.

arguments on hold, and in 1948 the three Western allies began to create a single government for their territories. They passed reforms to ease the economic crisis and introduced a new currency—a powerful symbol of economic unity. The Soviets retaliated by cutting all road, train, and river access from the western zone to West Berlin, but the Western allies refused to cede control over the capital. For eleven months they airlifted supplies over Soviet territory to the besieged western zone of Berlin, a total of twelve thousand tons of supplies carried by hundreds of flights every day. The Berlin blockade lasted nearly a year, from June 1948 to May 1949. It ended with the creation of two Germanies: the Federal Republic in the west and the German Democratic Republic in the former Soviet zone. Within a few short years both countries looked strikingly like armed camps.

The Marshall Plan

The United States countered the expansion of Soviet power and locally based communist movements with massive programs of economic and military aid to Western Europe. In a 1947 speech to Congress arguing for military assistance to anticommunists in Greece, President Harry Truman set out what would come to be called the Truman Doctrine, a pledge to support the resistance of "free peoples" to communism. The Truman Doctrine, however, also tied the contest for political power to economics. A few months later, Secretary of State George Marshall outlined an ambitious plan of economic aid to Europe including, initially, the Eastern European states: the European Recovery Program. The Marshall Plan provided $13 billion of aid over four years (beginning in

Czech president, Edvard Benes, above two columns of Soviet and Czech soldiers marching together under their respective flags. Benes, who had been president of Czechoslovakia before the war, was returned to office in October 1945, only to be forced to resign in 1948 after a successful coup by the Soviet-backed Communist party.

Questions for Analysis

1. How do these three images portray the victory over the Germans?

2. How do these images deal with the question of Czechoslovakian nationalism?

3. Which of the three images most coincides with the Soviet view of the Czech situation?

C. Czech propaganda card, May 1945.

1948), focused on industrial redevelopment. Unlike a relief plan, however, the Marshall Plan encouraged the participating states to diagnose their own economic problems and to develop their own solutions. With a series of other economic agreements, the Marshall Plan became one of the building blocks of European economic unity. The American program, however, required measures such as decontrol of prices, restraints on wages, and balanced budgets. The Americans encouraged opposition to left-leaning politicians and movements that might be sympathetic to communism.

The United States also hastened to shore up military defenses. In April 1949, Canada, the United States, and representatives of Western European states signed an agreement establishing the North Atlantic Treaty Organization (NATO). Greece, Turkey, and West Germany were later added as members. An armed attack against any one of the NATO members would now be regarded as an attack against all and would bring a united military response. NATO's ground forces included a dozen divisions from the young state of West Germany. Among the most striking aspects of the Second World War's aftermath was how rapidly Germany was reintegrated into Europe. In the new Cold War world, *the West* quickly came to mean anticommunism. Potentially reliable allies, whatever their past, were not to be punished or excluded.

NATO's preparations for another European war depended heavily on air power, a new generation of jet bombers that would field the ultimate weapon of the age, the atomic bomb. Thus any conflict that broke out along the new German frontier threatened to dwarf the slaughter that had so recently passed.

Two Worlds and the Race for the Bomb

The Soviets viewed NATO, the Marshall Plan, and especially the United States' surprising involvement in Europe's affairs with mounting alarm. Rejecting an initial offer of Marshall Plan aid, they established an Eastern European version of the plan, the Council for Mutual Economic Assistance, or Comecon. In 1947 the Soviets organized an international political arm, the Cominform (Communist Information Bureau), responsible for coordinating worldwide communist policy and programs. They responded to NATO with the establishment of their own military alliances, confirmed by the Warsaw Pact of 1955. This agreement set up a joint command among the states of Albania, Bulgaria, Czechoslovakia, Hungary, Poland, Romania, and East Germany, and guaranteed the continued presence of Soviet troops in all those countries.

All these conflicts were darkened by the shadow of the nuclear arms race. In 1949, the Soviet Union surprised American intelligence by testing its first atomic bomb (modeled on the plutonium bomb that Americans had tested in 1945). In 1953 both superpowers demonstrated a new weapon, the hydrogen or "super" bomb, which was a thousand times more powerful than the bomb dropped on Hiroshima. Within a few years both countries developed intercontinental missiles that could deliver first one and then several nuclear warheads, fired from land or from a new generation of atomic-powered submarines that roamed the seas at all times, ready to act. These developments caused some to wonder if the West's faith in science was misplaced. Beyond the grim warnings that nuclear war would wipe out human civilization, the bomb had more specific strategic consequences. The nuclearization of warfare fed into the polarizing effect of the Cold War, for countries without nuclear arms found it difficult to avoid joining either the Soviet or American pact. Over the long term, it encouraged a disparity between two groups of nations: on the one hand, the superpowers, with their enormous military budgets, and on the other nations that came to rely on agreements and international law. It changed the nature of face-to-face warfare as well, encouraging "proxy wars" between clients of the superpowers and raising fears that local conflicts might trigger general war.

Was the Cold War inevitable? Could the Americans and the Soviets have negotiated their disagreements? On the Soviet side, Stalin's personal suspiciousness, ruthlessness, and autocratic ambitions combined with genuine security concerns to fuel the Cold War mentality. The United States, too, was unwilling to give up the military, economic, and political power it had acquired during the war. As it turned away from its traditional isolationism, the U.S. thus articu-

THE ARMS RACE: A SOVIET VIEW. *Nyet!* (No!) An arm raised in protest and fear against the backdrop of a bomb exploding.

lated new strategic interests with global consequences, including access to European industry and far-flung military bases. These interests played into Soviet fears. In this context, trust became all but impossible.

A new international balance of power quickly produced new international policies. In 1946 George Kennan argued that the United States needed to make containing the Soviet threat a priority. The Soviets had not embarked on world revolution, Kennan said. Thus the United States needed to respond, not with "histrionics: with threats or blustering or superfluous gestures of outward toughness" but rather "by the adroit and vigilant application of counterforce at a series of constantly shifting geographical and political points." Containment became the principal goal of U.S. foreign policy for the next forty years.

At its height, the Cold War had a chilling effect on domestic politics in both countries. In the Soviet Union writers and artists were attacked for deviation from the party line. The party disciplined economists for suggesting that Western European industry might recover from the damage it had sustained. The radio blared news that Czech or Hungarian leaders had been exposed as traitors. In the United States, congressional committees launched campaigns to root out "communists" everywhere. On both sides of the Iron Curtain, the Cold War intensified everyday anxiety, bringing air-raid drills, spy trials, warnings that a way of life was at stake, and appeals to defend family and home against the menacing "other."

Khrushchev and the Thaw

Stalin died in 1953. Nikita Khrushchev's slow accession to power, not secure until 1956, signaled a change of direction. Khrushchev possessed a kind of earthy directness that, despite his hostility to the West, helped for a time to ease tensions. On a visit to the United States in 1959, he traded quips with Iowa farmers and was entertained at Disneyland. Showing his desire to reduce international conflict, Khrushchev soon agreed to a summit meeting with the leaders of Britain, France, and the United States. This summit led to a series of understandings that eased the frictions in heavily armed Europe and produced a ban on testing nuclear weapons above ground in the early 1960s.

Khrushchev's other change of direction came with his famous "secret speech" of 1956, in which he acknowledged (behind the closed doors of the Twentieth Party Congress) the excesses of Stalin's era. Though the speech was secret, Krushchev's accusations were widely discussed. The harshness of Stalin's regime had generated popular discontent and demands for a shift from the production of heavy machinery and armaments to the manufacture of consumer goods, for a measure of freedom in the arts, and for an end to police repression. How, under these circumstances, could the regime keep de-Stalinization within safe limits? The thaw did unleash forces that proved difficult to control. Between 1956 and 1958 the Soviet prison camps released thousands of prisoners. Soviet citizens besieged the regime with requests to rehabilitate relatives who had been executed or imprisoned under Stalin, partly to make themselves again eligible for certain privileges of citizenship, such as housing.

The thaw provided a brief window of opportunity for some of the Soviet Union's most important writers. In 1957 Boris Pasternak's novel *Doctor Zhivago* could not be published in the Soviet Union, and in 1958 Pasternak was barred from receiving the Nobel Prize in Literature. That Aleksandr Solzhenitsyn's (*suhl-zhih-NYEE-tsihn*) first novel, *One Day in the Life of Ivan Denisovich*, could be published in 1962 marked the relative cultural freedom of the thaw. *Ivan Denisovich* was based on Solzhenitsyn's own experiences in

NIKITA KHRUSHCHEV. Premier (1958–64) and first secretary of the Communist party (1953–64) of the Soviet Union, Khrushchev visited the United States in 1959. Here he is shown joking with an Iowa farmer. ▪ *Why was it important for Khrushchev to engage a foreign audience in this way?*

the labor camps, where he had spent eight years for criticizing Stalin in a letter, and was a powerful literary testimony to the repression Khrushchev had acknowledged. By 1964, however, Khrushchev had fallen and the thaw ended, driving criticism and writers such as Solzhenitsyn underground. Solzhenitsyn kept working on what would become *The Gulag Archipelago*, the first massive historical and literary study of the Stalinist camps (gulags).

Repression in Eastern Europe

Stalin's death in 1953 coincided with mounting tensions in Eastern Europe. The East German government, burdened by reparations payments to the Soviet Union, faced an economic crisis. The illegal exodus of East German citizens to the West rose sharply: fifty-eight thousand left in March 1953 alone. In June, when the government demanded hefty increases in industrial productivity, strikes broke out in East Berlin. Unrest spread throughout the country. The Soviet army put down the uprising, and hundreds were executed in the subsequent purge. In the aftermath, the East German government, under the leadership of Walter Ulbricht, used fears of disorder to solidify one-party rule.

In 1956, emboldened by Khrushchev's de-Stalinization, Poland and Hungary rebelled, demanding more independence

The Cold War: Soviet and American Views

> The first excerpt is from a speech titled "The Sinews of Peace" that was delivered by Winston Churchill at Westminster College in Fulton, Missouri, in early 1946. In it, he coined the phrase Iron Curtain, warning of the rising power of the Soviet Union in Eastern Europe.
>
> The next excerpt is from an address by Nikita Khrushchev, who became first secretary of the Communist party in 1953. Three years later, his power secure, he began publicly to repudiate the crimes of Joseph Stalin. Khrushchev presided over a short-lived thaw in Soviet–American relations. Yet, as can be seen in his address, Khrushchev shared Churchill's conception of the world divided into two mutually antagonistic camps.

Winston Churchill's "Iron Curtain" Speech

A shadow has fallen upon the scenes so lately lighted by the Allied victory. Nobody knows what Soviet Russia and its Communist international organization intend to do in the immediate future, or what are the limits, if any, to their expansive and proselytizing tendencies. I have a strong admiration and regard for the valiant Russian people and for my wartime comrade, Marshal Stalin. There is deep sympathy and goodwill in Britain . . . towards the people of all the Russias and a resolve to persevere through many differences and rebuffs in establishing lasting friendships. We understand the Russian need to be secure on her western frontiers by the removal of all possibility of German aggression. We welcome Russia to her rightful place among the leading nations of the world. We welcome her flag upon the seas. Above all, we welcome constant, frequent and growing contacts between the Russian people and our own people on both sides of the Atlantic. It is my duty however . . . to place before you certain facts about the present position in Europe.

From Stettin in the Baltic to Trieste in the Adriatic, an iron curtain has descended across the Continent. Behind that line lie all the capitals of the ancient states of Central and Eastern Europe. Warsaw, Berlin, Prague, Vienna, Budapest, Belgrade, Bucharest and Sofia, all these famous cities and the populations around them lie in what I must call the Soviet sphere, and all are subject in one form or another, not only to Soviet influence but to a very high and, in many cases, increasing measure of control from Moscow. . . .

From what I have seen of our Russian friends and Allies during the war, I am convinced that there is nothing they admire so much as strength, and there is nothing for which they have less respect than for weakness, especially military weakness. For that reason the old doctrine of a balance of power is unsound. We cannot afford, if we can help it, to work on narrow margins, offering temptations to a triad of strength. If the Western Democracies stand together in strict adherence to the principles of the United Nations Charter, their influences for furthering those principles

in the management of their domestic affairs. Striking workers led the opposition in Poland. The government wavered, responding first with military repression and then with a promise of liberalization. Eventually the anti-Stalinist Polish leader Wladyslaw Gomulka won Soviet permission for his country to pursue its own "ways of Socialist development" by pledging Poland's loyalty to the terms of the Warsaw Pact.

Events in Hungary turned out very differently. The charismatic leader of Hungary's communist government, Imre Nagy, was as much a Hungarian nationalist as a communist. Under his government, protests against Moscow's policies developed into a much broader anticommunist struggle and, even more important, attempted secession from the Warsaw Pact. Khrushchev might contemplate looser ties between Eastern Europe and Moscow, but he would not tolerate an end to the pact. On November 4, 1956, Soviet troops occupied Budapest, arresting and executing leaders of the Hungarian rebellion. The Hungarians took up arms, and street fighting continued for several weeks. The Hungarians will be immense and no one is likely to molest them. If however they become divided or falter in their duty and if these all-important years are allowed to slip away then indeed catastrophe may overwhelm us all.

Source: Winston Churchill, *Winston S. Churchill: His Complete Speeches, 1897–1963*, vol. 7, 1943–1949, ed. Robert Rhodes James (New York: 1983), pp. 7290–91.

Nikita Khrushchev, "Report to the Communist Party Congress" (1961)

Comrades! The competition of the two world social systems, the socialist and the capitalist, has been the chief content of the period since the 20th party Congress. It has become the pivot, the foundation of world development at the present historical stage. Two lines, two historical trends, have manifested themselves more and more clearly in social development. One is the line of social progress, peace, and constructive activity. The other is the line of reaction, oppression, and war.

In the course of the peaceful competition of the two systems capitalism has suffered a profound moral defeat in the eyes of all peoples. The common people are daily convinced that capitalism is incapable of solving a single one of the urgent problems confronting mankind. It becomes more and more obvious that only on the paths to socialism can a solution to these problems be found. Faith in the capitalist system and the capitalist path of development is dwindling. Monopoly capital, losing its influence, resorts more and more to intimidating and suppressing the masses of the people, to methods of open dictatorship in carrying out its domestic policy, and to aggressive acts against other countries. But the masses of the people offer increasing resistance to reaction's acts.

It is no secret to anyone that the methods of intimidation and threat are not a sign of strength but evidence of the weakening of capitalism, the deepening of its general crisis. As the saying goes, if you can't hang on by the mane, you won't hang on by the tail! Reaction is still capable of dissolving parliaments in some countries in violation of their constitutions, of casting the best representatives of the people into prison, of sending cruisers and marines to subdue the "unruly." All this can put off for a time the approach of the fatal hour for the rule of capitalism. The imperialists are sawing away at the branch on which they sit. There is no force in the world capable of stopping man's advance along the road of progress.

Source: *Current Soviet Policies IV*, ed. Charlotte Saikowski and Leo Gruliow, from trans. *Current Digest of the Soviet Press*, Joint Committee on Slavic Studies (1962) pp. 42–45.

Questions for Analysis

1. Whom did Churchill blame for building the Iron Curtain between the Soviet sphere and the Western sphere?

2. Was the Soviet Union actively trying to create international communism? Was the United States trying to spread the Western way of life on a global scale?

---

had hoped for Western aid, but Dwight Eisenhower, newly elected to a second term as U.S. president, steered clear of giving support. Soviet forces installed a new government under the staunchly communist Janos Kadar, the repression continued, and tens of thousands of Hungarian refugees fled for the West. Khrushchev's efforts at presenting a gentler, more conciliatory Soviet Union to the West had been shattered by revolt and repression.

What was more, East Germans continued to flee the country via West Berlin. Between 1949 and 1961, 2.7 million East Germans left, blunt evidence of the unpopularity of the regime. Attempting to stem the tide, Khrushchev demanded that the West recognize the permanent division of Germany with a free city in Berlin. When that demand was refused, in 1961 the East German government built a ten-foot wall separating the two sectors of the city. For almost thirty years, until 1989, the Berlin Wall remained a monument to how the hot war had gone cold, and mirrored, darkly, the division of Germany and Europe as a whole.

THE BERLIN WALL, 1961. Thirteen years after the blockade, the East German government built a wall between East and West Berlin to stop the flow of escapees to the West. This manifestation of the Iron Curtain was dismantled in 1989.

ECONOMIC RENAISSANCE

Despite the ongoing tensions of a global superpower rivalry, the postwar period brought a remarkable recovery in Western Europe: the economic "miracle." The war encouraged a variety of technological innovations that could be applied in peacetime: improved communications (the invention of radar, for example), the development of synthetic materials, the increasing use of aluminum and alloy steels, and advances in the techniques of prefabrication. Wartime manufacturing had added significantly to nations' productive capacity. The Marshall Plan seems to have been less central than many claimed at the time, but it solved immediate problems having to do with the balance of payments and a shortage of American dollars to buy American goods. The boom was fueled by high consumer demand and, consequently, very high levels of employment throughout the 1950s and 1960s. Brisk domestic and foreign consumption encouraged expansion, continued capital investment, and technological innovation. Rising demand for Europe's goods hastened agreements that encouraged the free flow of international trade and currencies (discussed later).

It was now assumed that states would do much more economic management—directing investment, making decisions about what to modernize, coordinating policies between industries and countries—than before. This, too, was a legacy of wartime. As one British official observed, "We are all planners now." The result was a series of "mixed" economies combining public and private ownership. In France, where public ownership was already well advanced

in the 1930s, railways, electricity and gas, banking, radio and television, and a large segment of the automobile industry were brought under state management. In Britain, the list was equally long: coal and utilities; road, railroad, and air transport; and banking. Though nationalization was less common in West Germany, the railway system (state owned since the late nineteenth century); some electrical, chemical, and metallurgical concerns; and the Volkswagen company—the remnant of Hitler's attempt to produce a "people's car"—were all in state hands, though the latter was largely returned to the private sector in 1963.

These government policies and programs contributed to astonishing growth rates. Between 1945 and 1963 the average yearly growth of West Germany's gross domestic product (gross national product [GNP] minus income received from abroad) was 7.6 percent; in Austria, 5.8 percent; in Italy, 6 percent; in the Netherlands, 4.7 percent; and so on. Not only did the economies recover from the war but they reversed prewar economic patterns of slack demand, overproduction, and insufficient investment. Production facilities were hard pressed to keep up with soaring demand.

West Germany's recovery was particularly spectacular, and particularly important to the rest of Europe. Production increased sixfold between 1948 and 1964. Unemployment fell to record lows, reaching 0.4 percent in 1965, when there were six unfilled jobs for every unemployed person. The contrast with the catastrophic unemployment of the Great Depression heightened the impression of a miracle. In the 1950s, the state and private industry built half a million new housing units each year to accommodate citizens whose homes had been destroyed, new resident refugees from East Germany and Eastern Europe, and transient workers from Italy, Spain, Greece, and elsewhere drawn by West Germany's high demand for labor.

European nations with little in common in terms of political traditions or industrial patterns all shared in the general prosperity. Economic growth, however, did not level the differences among and within states. In southern Italy, illiteracy remained high and land continued to be held by a few rich families; the per capita GNP in Sweden was almost ten times that of Turkey. Britain remained a special case. British growth was respectable when compared with past performance. Yet the British economy remained sluggish. The country was burdened with obsolete factories and methods, the legacy of its early industrialization, and by an unwillingness to adopt new techniques in old industries or invest in more successful new ones. It was plagued as well by a series of balance-of-payments crises precipitated by an inability to sell more goods abroad than it imported.

European Economic Integration

The Western European renaissance was a collective effort. From the Marshall Plan on, a series of international economic organizations began to bind the Western European countries together. The first of these was the European Coal and Steel Community (ECSC), founded in 1951 to coordinate trade in, and the management of, Europe's most crucial resources. Coal was still king in mid-twentieth-century Europe; it fueled everything from steel manufacturing and trains to household heating, and counted for 82 percent of Europe's primary energy consumption. It was also key to relations between West Germany, with abundant coal mines, and France, with its coal-hungry steel mills. The ECSC was soon followed by a broader agreement. In 1957, the Treaty of Rome transformed France, West Germany, Italy, Belgium, Holland, and Luxembourg into the European Economic Community (EEC), or Common Market. The EEC aimed to abolish trade barriers among its members. Moreover, the organization pledged itself to common external tariffs, to the free movement of labor and capital among the member nations, and to building uniform wage structures and social security systems to create similar working conditions throughout the Common Market.

Integration did not proceed smoothly. Great Britain stayed away, fearing the effects of the ECSC on its declining coal industry and on its long-time trading relationship with Australia, New Zealand, and Canada. Britain did not share France's need for raw materials and the others' need for markets; it continued to rely on its economic relations with the Empire and Commonwealth. One of the few victors in the Second World War, Britain assumed that it could hold its global economic position in the postwar world.

The European Economic Community was a remarkable success. By 1963, it had become the world's largest importer. Its steel production was second only to that of the United States, and total industrial production was over 70 percent higher than it had been in 1950. It also established a new long-term political trend: individual countries sought to Europeanize solutions to their problems.

European integration was also shaped by crucial agreements reached in Bretton Woods, New Hampshire, in July 1944 aimed to coordinate the movements of the global economy and to internationalize solutions to economic crises, avoiding catastrophes such as those that plagued the 1930s. Bretton Woods created the International Monetary Fund and the World Bank, both designed to establish predictable and stable exchange rates, prevent speculation, and enable currencies—and consequently trade—to move freely. All other currencies were pegged to the dollar, which both reflected and enhanced the United States' role as the foremost financial power. The new international system was formed with the American–European sphere in mind, but these organizations soon began to play a role in economic development in what came to be known as the Third World. The postwar period, then, quickened global economic integration, largely on American terms.

Economic Development in the East

Although economic development in Eastern Europe was not nearly so dramatic as that in the West, significant advances occurred there as well. National incomes rose and output increased. Poland and Hungary, in particular, strengthened their economic connections with the West, primarily with France and West Germany. By the late 1970s, about 30 percent of Eastern Europe's trade was conducted outside the Soviet bloc. Nevertheless, the Soviet Union required its satellites to design their economic policies to serve more than their own national interests. Regulations governing Comecon, the Eastern European equivalent of the Common Market, ensured that the Soviet Union could sell its exports at prices well above the world level and compelled other members to trade with the Soviet Union to their disadvantage. Emphasis initially was on heavy industry and collectivized agriculture, though political tension in countries such as Hungary and Poland forced the Soviets eventually to moderate their policies so as to permit the manufacture of more consumer goods and the development of a modest trade with the West.

The Welfare State

Economic growth became one of the watchwords of the postwar era. Social welfare was another. The roots of the new legislation extended back to the insurance plans for old age, sickness, and disability introduced by Bismarck in Germany in the late 1880s. But economic expansion allowed postwar European states to fund more comprehensive social programs, and commitments to putting democracy on a stronger footing provided the political motivation. Clement Atlee, a socialist and the leader of the British Labour party, coined the term *welfare state*; his government, in power until 1951, led the way in enacting legislation that provided free medical care to all through the National Health Service, as well as assistance to families and guaranteed secondary education of some kind. The welfare state also rested on the assumption that governments could and should try to support popular purchasing power, generate demand, and provide either employment or unemployment insurance, assumptions spelled out earlier by John Maynard Keynes (*General Theory*, 1936) or William Beveridge's important 1943 report

EUROPE DURING THE COLD WAR. Examine the membership of NATO and the Warsaw Pact, respectively. ▪ *What were the member states in NATO?* ▪ *Why do you think some countries did not join NATO?* ▪ *Why did the membership of each alliance stay relatively stable for nearly half a century?*

on full employment. Although the British Labour party and continental socialist parties pressed these measures, welfare was a consensus issue, backed by the moderate coalitions that governed most postwar Western European states. Understood in this way, welfare was not poor relief, but an entitlement. Thus it marked a break with centuries-old ways of thinking about poverty and citizenship.

European Politics

Postwar political leaders were overwhelmingly pragmatic. Konrad Adenauer, the West German chancellor from 1949 to 1963, despised German militarism and blamed that

tradition for Hitler's rise to power. Still, he was apprehensive about German parliamentary democracy and governed in a paternalistic, sometimes authoritarian, manner. His determination to end the centuries-old hostility between France and Germany contributed significantly to the movement toward economic union. Alcide De Gasperi, the Italian premier from 1948 to 1953, was also centrist. Among postwar French leaders, the most colorful was the Resistance hero General Charles de Gaulle. De Gaulle had retired from politics in 1946 when French voters refused to accept his proposals for strengthening the executive branch of the government. In 1958, faced with civil turmoil caused by the Algerian war (see page 667) and an abortive coup attempt by a group of right-wing army officers, France's government collapsed and de Gaulle was invited to return. De Gaulle accepted but insisted on a new constitution. That constitution, which created the Fifth Republic in 1958, strengthened the executive branch of the government in an effort to avoid the parliamentary deadlocks that had weakened the country earlier. De Gaulle used his new authority to restore France's power and prestige. Resisting U.S. influence in Europe, he pulled French forces out of NATO in 1966. He cultivated better relations with the Soviet Union and with West Germany, and presided over the decolonization of Algeria. Finally, he accelerated French economic and industrial expansion by building a modern military establishment, complete with atomic weapons. Like his counterparts, de Gaulle was not, by nature, a democrat. He steered a centrist course, working hard to produce practical solutions to political problems and thereby undermine radicalism in any form. Most other Western European nations did the same.

REVOLUTION, ANTICOLONIALISM, AND THE COLD WAR

In the colonial world as in Europe, the end of war unleashed new conflicts. Those conflicts became closely bound up with Europe's political and economic recovery, they had an enormous if delayed effect on Western culture, and they complicated the Cold War. The Cold War, as we have seen, created two powerful centers of gravity for world politics. But the wave of anticolonial independence movements that swept through postwar Asia and Africa created a new group of nations that would attempt to avoid aligning with one or the other bloc, and would call itself the "Third World."

The Chinese Revolution

The Chinese Revolution was the single most radical change in the developing world after the Second World War. A civil war had raged in China since 1926, with Mao Zedong's (*mow zeh-DOONG*, 1893–1976) communist insurgents in the north in revolt against the Nationalist forces of Jiang Jeishi (Chiang Kai-shek, 1887–1975). Though they agreed on a truce to face the Japanese during the war years, the civil war resumed after the Japanese defeat, and in 1949, Mao's insurgents took control of the Chinese government and drove the Nationalists into exile.

The Chinese Revolution was above all a peasant revolution, even more so than the Russian Revolution. Mao adapted Marxism to conditions very different from those imagined by Marx himself, emphasizing radical reform in the coun-

tryside (reducing rents, providing health care and education, and reforming marriage) and autonomy from Western colonial powers. The leaders of the revolution set about turning China into a modern industrial nation within a generation, at huge human cost and with very mixed results.

To anticolonial activists in many parts of the world, the Chinese Revolution stood as a model. To colonial powers, it represented the dangers inherent in decolonization. The "loss of China" provoked fear and consternation in the West, particularly in the United States. Although Mao and Stalin distrusted each other and relations between the two regimes were extremely difficult, the United States considered both nations a communist bloc until the early 1970s, and the Chinese Revolution intensified Western military and diplomatic anxiety about governments in Asia.

The Korean War

Anxiety about China turned Korea into a hot spot in the Cold War. Korea, a former Japanese colony, was divided into two states after World War II: communist North Korea, run by the Soviet client Kim Il Sung, and South Korea, led by the anticommunist autocrat Syngman Rhee, who was backed by the United States. When communist North Korean troops attacked the South in 1950, the United Nations Security Council gave permission for the U.S. to defend South Korea.

U.S. General Douglas MacArthur, a Second World War hero, drove the Korean communists to the Chinese border, but was relieved of his command by President Harry Truman (1945–53) after calling for attacks on Chinese territory. More than a million Chinese troops flooded across the border in support of the North Koreans, forcing the international troops into a bloody retreat. The war became a stalemate, pitting Chinese and North Korean troops against UN forces—made up largely of American and South Korean forces but also containing contingents from Britain, Australia, Ethiopia, the Netherlands, Turkey, and elsewhere. Two years later, the war ended inconclusively, with Korea divided roughly along the original line. South Korea had not been "lost," but with over fifty-three thousand Americans and over one million Koreans and Chinese dead, neither side could claim a decisive victory. As in Germany, the inability of major powers to achieve their goals resulted in a divided nation.

Decolonization

The Chinese Revolution proved the start of a larger wave. Between 1947 and 1960 the sprawling European empires built during the nineteenth century disintegrated. Opposition to colonial rule had stiffened after the First World War, forcing war-weakened European states to renegotiate the terms of empire. After the Second World War, older forms of empire quickly became untenable. In some regions, European states simply sought to cut their losses and withdraw. In others, well-organized and tenacious nationalist movements successfully demanded new constitutional arrangements and independence. In a third set of cases, European powers were drawn into complicated, multifaceted, and extremely violent struggles between different movements of indigenous peoples and European settler communities—conflicts the European states had helped create.

The British Empire Unravels

India was the first and largest of the colonies to win self-government after the war. As we have seen, rebellions such as the Sepoy Mutiny challenged the representatives of Britain in India throughout the nineteenth century (see Chapter 25). During the early stages of the Second World War, the Indian National Congress (founded in 1885), the umbrella party for the independence movement, called on Britain to "quit India." The extraordinary Indian nationalist Mohandas K. (Mahatma) Gandhi (1869–1948) had been at work in India since the 1920s and had pioneered anticolonial ideas and tactics that echoed the world over. In the face of colonial domination, Gandhi advocated not violence but *swaraj*, or self-rule, urging Indians individually and collectively to develop their own resources and to withdraw from the imperial economy—by going on strike, refusing to pay taxes, or boycotting imported textiles and wearing homespun. By 1947 Gandhi and his fellow nationalist Jawaharlal Nehru (1889–1964, prime minister 1947–64), the leader of the pro-independence Congress party, had gained such widespread support that the British found it impossible to continue in power. The Labour party government elected in Britain in 1945 had always favored Indian independence. Now that independence became a British political necessity.

While talks established the procedures for independence, however, India was torn by ethnic and religious conflict. A Muslim League, led by Mohammed Ali Jinnah (1876–1948), wanted autonomy in largely Muslim areas and feared the predominantly Hindu Congress party's authority in a single united state. Cycles of rioting broke out between the two religious communities. In June 1947, British India was partitioned into the nations of India (majority Hindu) and Pakistan (majority Muslim). The process of partition brought brutal religious and ethnic warfare. More than one million Hindus and Muslims died, and an estimated twelve million became refugees, evicted from their lands

or fleeing the fighting. Throughout the chaos Gandhi, now eighty, continued to protest violence and to focus attention on overcoming the legacy of colonialism. He argued that "real freedom will come when we free ourselves of the dominance of western education, western culture, and western way of living which have been ingrained in us." In January 1948, he was assassinated by a Hindu zealot. Conflict continued between the independent states of India and Pakistan. Nehru, who became first prime minister of India, embarked on a program of industrialization and modernization—not at all what Gandhi would have counseled. Nehru proved particularly adept at maneuvering in the Cold War world, steering a course of nonalignment with either of the blocs, getting aid for industry from the Soviet Union and food imports from the United States.

PALESTINE

The year 1948 brought more crises for the British Empire, including an end to the British mandate in Palestine. During the First World War, British diplomats had encouraged Arab nationalist revolts against the Ottoman Empire. With the 1917 Balfour Declaration, they had also promised a "Jewish homeland" in Palestine for European Zionists. Contradictory promises and the flight of European Jews from Nazi Germany contributed to rising conflict between Jewish settlers and Arabs in Palestine during the 1930s and provoked an Arab revolt bloodily suppressed by the British. At the same time, the newly important oil concessions in the Middle East were multiplying Britain's strategic interests in the Suez Canal, Egypt, and the Arab nations generally. Mediating local conflicts and balancing their own interests proved an impossible task. In 1939, in the name of regional stability, the British strictly limited further Jewish immigration. They tried to maintain that limit after the war, but now they faced pressure from tens of thousands of Jewish refugees from Europe. The conflict quickly became a three-way war: among Palestinian Arabs fighting for what they considered their land and their independence, Jewish settlers and Zionist militants determined to defy British restrictions, and British administrators with divided sympathies, embarrassed and shocked by the plight of Jewish refugees and committed to maintaining good Anglo-Arab relations. The British responded militarily. By 1947, there was one British soldier for every eighteen inhabitants of the Mandate. The years of fighting, however, with terrorist tactics on all sides, persuaded the British to leave. The United Nations voted (by a narrow margin) to partition the territory into two states. Neither Jewish settlers nor Palestinian Arabs found the partition satisfactory and both began to fight for territory even before British troops withdrew. No sooner did Israel declare its independence in

Mohandas Gandhi and Nonviolent Anticolonialism

After leading a campaign for Indian rights in South Africa between 1894 and 1914, Mohandas K. Gandhi (1869–1948), known as Mahatma ("great-souled") Gandhi, became a leader in the long battle for home rule in India. This battle was finally won in 1947 and brought with it the partition of India and the creation of Pakistan. Gandhi's insistence on the power of nonviolent noncooperation brought him to the forefront of Indian politics and provided a model for many later liberation struggles, including the American civil rights movement. Gandhi argued that only nonviolent resistance, which dramatized the injustice of colonial rule and colonial law, had the spiritual force to unite a community and end colonialism.

assive resistance is a method of securing rights by personal suffering; it is the reverse of resistance by arms. When I refuse to do a thing that is repugnant to my conscience, I use soul-force. For instance, the Government of the day has passed a law which is applicable to me. I do not like it. If by using violence I force the Government to repeal the law, I am employing what may be termed body-force. If I do not obey the law and accept the penalty for its breach, I use soul-force. It involves sacrifice of self.

Everybody admits that sacrifice of self is infinitely superior to sacrifice of others. Moreover, if this kind of force is used in a cause that is unjust, only the person using it suffers. He does not make others suffer for his mistakes. Men have before now done many things which were subsequently found to have been wrong. . . . It is therefore meet that he should not do that which he knows to be wrong, and suffer the consequence whatever it may be. This is the key to the use of soul-force. . . .

It is contrary to our manhood if we obey laws repugnant to our conscience. Such teaching is opposed to religion and means slavery. If the Government were to ask us to go about without any clothing, should we do so? If I were a passive resister, I would say to them that I would have nothing to do with their law. But we have so forgotten ourselves and become so compliant that we do not mind any degrading law.

A man who has realized his manhood, who fears only God, will fear no one else. Man-made laws are not necessarily binding on him. Even the Government does not expect any such thing from us. They do not say: "You must do such and such a thing." But they say: "If you do not do it, we will punish you." We are sunk so low that we fancy that it is our duty and our religion to do what the law lays down. If man will only realize that it is unmanly to obey laws that are unjust, no man's tyranny will enslave him. This is the key to self-rule or home-rule.

Source: M. K. Gandhi, "Indian Home Rule (1909)," in *The Gandhi Reader: A Source Book of His Life and Writings*, ed. Homer A. Jack (Bloomington, IN: 1956), pp. 104–21.

Questions for Analysis

1. Why did Gandhi believe that "sacrifice of self" was superior to "sacrifice of others"?

2. What did Gandhi mean when he said that "it is contrary to our manhood if we obey laws repugnant to our conscience"?

May 1948 than five neighboring states invaded. The new but well-organized Israeli nation survived the war and extended its boundaries. On the losing side, a million Palestinian Arabs who fled or were expelled found themselves clustered in refugee camps in the Gaza Strip and on the West Bank of the Jordan River, which the armistice granted to an enlarged state of Jordan. It is remarkable that the conflict did not become a Cold War confrontation at the start. For their own reasons, both Soviets and Americans recognized Israel. The new nation, however, marked a permanent change to the culture and balance of power in the region.

AFRICA

A number of West African colonies established assertive independence movements before and during the 1950s, and the British government moved hesitantly to meet their demands. By the middle of the 1950s, Britain agreed to a variety of terms for independence in these territories, leaving them with written constitutions and a British legal system but little else in terms of modern infrastructure or economic support. Defenders of British colonialism claimed that these formal institutions would give advantages to the independent states, but without other resources, even the most promising

DECOLONIZATION IN ASIA. ▪ *Among colonial powers, who were the biggest losers post–World War II?* ▪ *What was the single most important geopolitical change in Asia during this period?* ▪ *What role did the Soviet Union and the United States play in Asia during this period?*

killing civilians. Internment camps set up by colonial security forces became sites of atrocities that drew public investigations and condemnation by even the most conservative British politicians and army officers. In 1963, a decade after the rebellion began, the British conceded Kenyan independence.

In the late 1950s, the British prime minister Harold Macmillan endorsed independence for a number of Britain's African colonies as a response to powerful winds of change. In southern Africa, the exceptionally large and wealthy population of European settlers set their sails against those winds, a resistance that continued for decades. These settlers, a mixture of English migrants and the Franco-Dutch Afrikaners who traced their arrival to the eighteenth century, controlled huge tracts of fertile farmland along with some of the most lucrative gold and diamond mines on earth. This was especially true in South Africa. There, during the late 1940s, Britain's Labour government set aside its deep dislike of Afrikaner racism in a fateful political bargain. In return for guarantees that South African gold would be used carefully to support Britain's

foundered. Ghana, known formerly as the Gold Coast and the first of these colonies to gain independence, was seen in the early 1960s as a model for free African nations. Its politics soon degenerated, however, and its president, Kwame Nkrumah, became the first of several African leaders driven from office for corruption and autocratic behavior.

Belgium and France also withdrew from their holdings. By 1965 virtually all of the former African colonies had become independent, and virtually none of them possessed the means to redress losses from colonialism to make that independence work. As Belgian authorities raced out of the Congo in 1960, they left crumbling railways and fewer than two dozen indigenous people with college educations.

The process of decolonization was relatively peaceful—except where large populations of European settlers complicated European withdrawal. In the north, settler resistance made the French exit from Algeria wrenching and complex (discussed later). In the east, in Kenya, the majority Kikuyu population revolted against British rule and against a small group of settlers. The uprising, which came to be known as the Mau Mau rebellion, soon turned bloody. British troops fired freely at targets in rebel-occupied areas, sometimes

global financial power, Britain tolerated the introduction of the apartheid system in South Africa. Even by other standards of segregation, apartheid was especially harsh. Under its terms, Africans, Indians, and colored persons of mixed descent lost all political rights. All the institutions of social life, including marriage and schools, were segregated. What was more, the government tried to block the dramatic social consequences of the expansion of mining and industrialization in general, especially African migration to cities and a new wave of labor militancy in the mines. Apartheid required Africans to live in designated "homelands," forbade them to travel without specific permits, and created elaborate government bureaus to manage the labor essential to the economy. The government also banned any political protest. These measures made Western powers uncomfortable with the segregationist regime, but white South Africans held on to American support by presenting themselves as a bulwark against communism.

To the north, in the territories of Rhodesia, the British government encouraged a large federation, controlled by white settlers but with the opportunity for majority rule in the future. By the early 1960s, however, the federation was

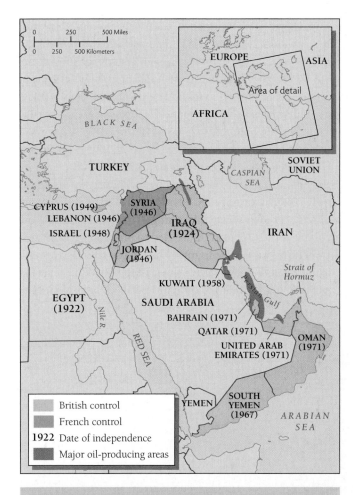

DECOLONIZATION IN THE MIDDLE EAST. ■ *What were the colonial possessions of the British and French in the Middle East?* ■ *What were the three stages of decolonization in the Middle East?* ■ *Why did the British hold on to the small states bordering the Persian Gulf and Arabian Sea until 1971?*

on the verge of collapse; the majority-rule state of Malawi was allowed to exit the federation in 1964, and Rhodesia split on northern and southern lines. In the north, the premier relented and accepted majority government under the black populist Kenneth Kaunda. In the south, angry Afrikaners backed by two hundred thousand right-wing English migrants who had arrived since 1945 refused to accept majority rule. When the British government attempted to force their hand, the settlers unilaterally declared independence in 1965 and began a bloody civil war against southern Rhodesia's black population that lasted half a generation.

CRISIS IN SUEZ AND THE END OF AN ERA

For postwar Britain, empire was not only politically complicated but too costly. Britain began to withdraw from naval and air bases around the world because they had become too expensive to maintain. Still, the Labour government did

try to maintain British power and prestige in the postwar world. In Malaya, British forces repressed a revolt by ethnic Chinese communists and then helped support the independent states of Singapore and Malaysia, maintaining British companies' and banks' ties with Malaysia's lucrative rubber and oil reserves. Labour also launched carefully targeted efforts at "colonial development" to tap local natural resources that Britain hoped to sell on world markets. "Development," however, was underfunded and largely disregarded in favor of fulfilling Cold War commitments elsewhere. In the Middle East, the British government protected several oil-rich states with its military and helped overthrow a nationalist government in Iran to ensure that the oil states invested their money in British financial markets.

In Egypt, however, the British refused to yield a traditional point of imperial pride. In 1951 nationalists compelled the British to agree to withdraw their troops from Egyptian territory within three years. In 1952 a group of nationalist army officers deposed Egypt's King Farouk, who had close ties to Britain, and proclaimed a republic. Shortly after the final British withdrawal an Egyptian colonel, Gamal Abdel Nasser (1918–1970), became president of the country (1956–70). His first major public act as president was to nationalize the Suez Canal Company. So doing would help finance the construction of the Aswan Dam on the Nile, and both the dam and nationalizing the canal represented economic independence and Egyptian national pride. Nasser also helped develop the anticolonial ideology of pan-Arabism, proposing that Arab nationalists throughout the Islamic world should create an alliance of modern nations, no longer beholden to the West. Finally, Nasser was also willing to take aid and support from the Soviets to achieve that goal, which made the canal a Cold War issue.

Three nations found Nasser and his pan-Arab ideals threatening. Israel, surrounded on all sides by unfriendly neighbors, was looking for an opportunity to seize the strategic Sinai Peninsula and create a buffer between itself and Egypt. France, already fighting a war against Algerian nationalists, hoped to destroy what it considered the Egyptian source of Arab nationalism. Britain depended on the canal as a route to its strategic bases and was stung by this blow to imperial dignity. Though the British were reluctant to intervene, they were urged on by their prime minister, Sir Anthony Eden, who had developed a deep personal hatred of Nasser. In the autumn of 1956, the three nations colluded in an attack on Egypt. Israel occupied the Sinai while British and French jets destroyed Egypt's air force on the ground. The former colonial powers landed troops at the mouth of the canal but lacked the resources to push on in strength toward Cairo. As a result, the war left Nasser in power and made him a hero to the Egyptian public for holding the imperialists at bay. The attack was condemned around the world. The United States angrily called its allies' bluff, inflicting severe financial penalties on Britain and France. Both countries were forced to withdraw their expeditions. For policy makers in Great Britain and France, the failure at Suez marked the end of an era.

French Decolonization

In two particular cases, France's experience of decolonization was bloodier, more difficult, and more damaging to French prestige and domestic politics than any in Britain's experience, with the possible exception of Northern Ireland. The first was Indochina, where French efforts to restore imperial authority after losing it in the Second World War only resulted in military defeat and further humiliation. The second case, Algeria, became not only a violent colonial war but also a struggle with serious political ramifications at home.

THE FIRST VIETNAM WAR, 1946–1954

Indochina was one of France's last major imperial acquisitions in the nineteenth century. Here, as elsewhere, the two world wars had helped galvanize first nationalist and then, also, communist independence movements. In Indonesia, nationalist forces rebelled against Dutch efforts to restore colonialism, and the country became independent in 1949. In Indochina, the communist resistance became particularly effective under the leadership of Ho Chi Minh who campaigned for Vietnamese independence. Ho was French educated and, his expectations raised by the Wilsonian principles of self-determination, had hoped Vietnam might win independence at Versailles in 1919 (see Chapter 24). He read Marx and Lenin and absorbed the Chinese communists' lessons about organizing peasants around social and agrarian as well as national issues. During the Second World War, Ho's movement fought first the Vichy government of the colony and later Japanese

occupiers, and also provided intelligence reports for the Allies. In 1945, however, the United States and Britain repudiated their relationship with Ho's independence movement and allowed the French to reclaim their colonies throughout Southeast Asia. The Vietnamese communists, who were fierce nationalists as well as Marxists, renewed their guerrilla war against the French.

The fighting was protracted and bloody; France saw in it a chance to redeem its national pride. After one of France's most capable generals, Jean de Lattre de Tassigny, finally achieved a military advantage against the rebels in 1951, the French government might have decolonized on favorable terms. Instead, it decided to press on for total victory, sending troops deep into Vietnamese territory to root out the rebels. One major base was established in a valley bordering modern Laos, at a hamlet called Dien Bien Phu.

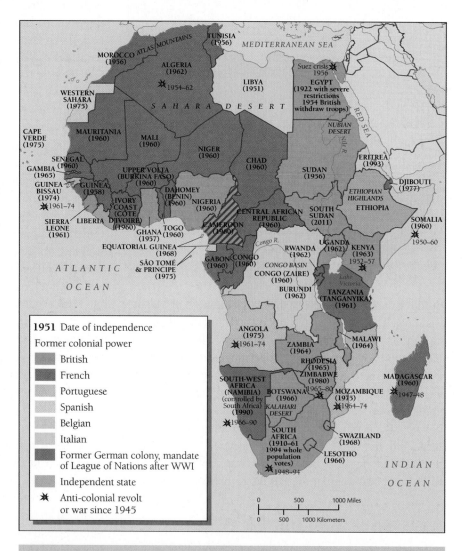

1951 Date of independence

Former colonial power

- British
- French
- Portuguese
- Spanish
- Belgian
- Italian
- Former German colony, mandate of League of Nations after WWI
- Independent state
- ✳ Anti-colonial revolt or war since 1945

DECOLONIZATION OF AFRICA. ▪ *Who were the biggest imperial losers in the decolonization of Africa?* ▪ *By what decade had most African countries achieved their independence?* ▪ *What were the forces behind decolonization in Africa?*

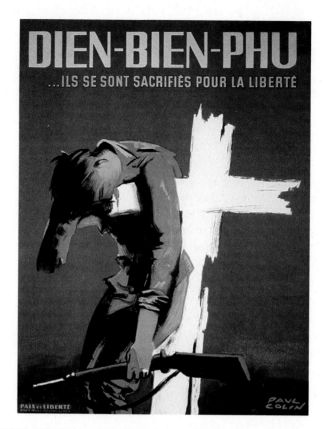

"DIEN-BIEN-PHU: ... THEY SACRIFICED THEMSELVES FOR LIBERTY." The sentiments expressed in this poster, which was intended to commemorate the French soldiers who died at Dien Bien Phu in May 1954, helped to deepen French commitments to colonial control in Algeria.

Ringed by high mountains, this vulnerable spot became a base for thousands of elite French paratroopers and colonial soldiers from Algeria and West Africa—the best of France's troops. The rebels besieged the base. Tens of thousands of Vietnamese nationalist fighters hauled heavy artillery by hand up the mountainsides and bombarded the network of forts set up by the French. The siege lasted for months, becoming a protracted national crisis in France.

When Dien Bien Phu fell in May 1954, the French government began peace talks in Geneva. The Geneva Accords, drawn up by the French, Vietnamese politicians including the communists, the British, and the Americans, divided Indochina into three countries: Laos, Cambodia, and Vietnam, which was partitioned into two states. North Vietnam was taken over by Ho Chi Minh's party; South Vietnam by a succession of Vietnamese leaders with Western support. Corruption, repression, and instability in the south, coupled with Ho Chi Minh's nationalist desire to unite Vietnam, guaranteed that the war would continue. The U.S. government, which had provided military and financial aid to the French, began to send aid to the South Vietnamese regime. The Americans saw the conflict through the prism of the Cold War: their project was not to restore colonialism

but to contain communism and prevent it from spreading through Southeast Asia. The limits of this policy would not become clear until the mid-1960s.

ALGERIA

The French faced a complex colonial problem closer to home—in Algeria, the North African colony that they had first conquered in the 1830s. By the 1950s, there were close to one million European settlers in Algeria, and their representatives dominated both the political establishment and the economy of the colony. The rest of the diverse population consisted of Berbers and Arabs who had few political rights and scarce opportunities for education or economic advancement.

At the end of the Second World War, Algerian nationalists called for the Allies to recognize Algerian independence. Public demonstrations turned violent, and when settlers were attacked in the town of Sétif in May 1945, the French responded with a harsh repression that killed thousands of Algerians. These events convinced a younger generation of nationalists that independence could only be achieved by force. On November 1, 1954, the Algerian National Liberation Front (FLN) announced their rebellion with a series of attacks on military and police targets.

The war in Algeria was fought on several fronts. The struggle between the French and the Algerian nationalists was fought first as a guerrilla war between the French army and the FLN in the countryside. In 1956, the FLN launched an urban campaign of terror bombings against the settler population, and the French army responded with the systematic use of torture against thousands of suspected FLN members. At the same time, however, the war also had elements of civil conflict on both sides. In both France and Algeria, rival groups of Algerian nationalists fought with one another, and as the strains of the war dragged on, increasingly bitter splits opened up within the French side as well, as radical elements in the settler population turned violently against French politicians who were seen to be too moderate in their defense of French Algeria.

The Algerian crisis brought Charles de Gaulle back to power in France in 1958, and although the settlers in Algeria saw his return favorably, he disappointed them by engaging in negotiations that led to a referendum on independence in July 1962. The FLN entered the capital in triumph, and nearly a million settlers and thousands of Algerians who had fought on the French side fled into exile in France.

The war cut deep divides through French society and left much of Algeria scarred and in ruins. Withdrawing from Algeria meant recasting French views of what it meant to be a modern power. In France and other imperial powers, the

Anticolonialism and Violence

Born in the French Caribbean colony of Martinique, Frantz Fanon (1925–1961) studied psychiatry in France before moving on to work in Algeria in the early 1950s. Fanon became a member of the Algerian revolutionary National Liberation Front (FLN) and an ardent advocate of decolonization. Black Skin, White Masks, published in 1952 with a preface by Jean-Paul Sartre, was a study of the psychological effects of colonialism and racism on black culture and individuals. The Wretched of the Earth (1961) was a revolutionary manifesto, one of the most influential of the period. Fanon attacked nationalist leaders for their ambition and corruption. He believed that revolutionary change could come only from poor peasants, those who "have found no bone to gnaw in the colonial system." Diagnosed with leukemia, Fanon sought treatment in the Soviet Union and then in Washington, D.C., where he died.

In decolonization, there is therefore the need of a complete calling in question of the colonial situation. If we wish to describe it precisely, we might find it in the well-known words: "The last shall be first and the first last." Decolonization is the putting into practice of this sentence. . . .

The naked truth of decolonization evokes for us the searing bullets and bloodstained knives which emanate from it. For if the last shall be first, this will only come to pass after a murderous and decisive struggle between the two protagonists. That affirmed intention to place the last at the head of things, and to make them climb at a pace (too quickly, some say) the well-known steps which characterize an organized society, can only triumph if we use all means to turn the scale, including, of course, that of violence.

You do not turn any society, however primitive it may be, upside down with such a program if you have not decided from the very beginning, that is to say from the actual formation of that program, to overcome all the obstacles that you will come across in so doing. The native who decides to put the program into practice, and to become its moving force, is ready for violence at all times. From birth it is clear to him that this narrow world, strewn with prohibitions, can only be called in question by absolute violence.

Source: Frantz Fanon, *The Wretched of the Earth*, trans. Constance Farrington (New York: 1963), pp. 35–37.

Questions for Analysis

1. Why did Fanon believe that violence lay at the heart of both the colonial relationship and anticolonial movements?

2. What arguments would he offer to counter Gandhi?

---

conclusions seemed clear. Traditional forms of colonial rule could not withstand the demands of postwar politics and culture; the leading European nations, once distinguished by their empires, would have to look for new forms of influence.

POSTWAR CULTURE AND THOUGHT

The devastation of the Second World War, followed by the looming confrontation between superpowers armed with nuclear weapons, set the stage for a remarkable burst of cultural production in the postwar decades. Writers and artists did not hesitate to tackle the big issues: freedom, civilization, and the human condition. The process of decolonization meanwhile ensured that these issues could not be seen as the property of Europeans alone.

Black Voices

A generation of intellectuals from European colonies achieved new prominence in the late 1940s. Writers Aimé Césaire (1913–2008) of Martinique and Léopold Senghor from Senegal were elected to the French National Assembly and were prominent voices associated with the *Négritude* movement, which asserted that people of African descent could and should retain a sense of black identity (a rough translation of *Négritude*), even as they sought to participate in the civic life of European nations. Both asserted that colonialism damaged the colonizers as much as the colonized peoples of Africa and Asia.

Frantz Fanon, a student of Césaire's who was also from Martinique, went further, arguing that the promotion of *Négritude* was not an effective response to racism. People of color, he argued, needed a theory of radical social change. Fanon's manifesto, *The Wretched of the Earth* (1961) bluntly rejected Gandhi's prescriptions for change, arguing that colonialism was inherently violent, and had to be met with force to be overcome. Fanon worked in Algeria as a psychiatrist, and eventually joined the National Liberation Front.

The provocative arguments of these writers complicated efforts by European intellectuals to promote humanism and democratic values after the atrocities of the Second World War, since the European powers who were victorious over the Nazis proved to be capable of brutality themselves in defending their colonial empires. Their work pointed to the ironies of Europe's civilizing mission and forced Europeans to reevaluate the universal claims of their culture.

THE COLD WAR IN EVERYDAY LIFE. A Soviet matchbook label, 1960, depicts a Soviet fist destroying a U.S. plane. Soviet nationalism had been a potent force since the Second World War. ■ *Could the Soviet leadership sustain this nationalist sentiment without an external threat?*

Existentialism, Amnesia, and the Aftermath of War

Existentialism was a postwar intellectual movement in Europe that posed challenging questions about the possibility of individual choice and moral commitment—questions that seemed especially urgent in this period of intense ideological competition. The existentialist writers, most prominently Jean-Paul Sartre (SAHR-truh, 1905–1980) and Albert Camus (KAM-oo, 1913–1960) shared a common pessimism about European "civilization." Most radically, they declared that human lives had no meaning that could be learned or understood through the study of traditional morality, religion, or science. Instead, they argued that "existence precedes essence," by which they meant that there was no predetermined meaning for human lives. Humans exist—and they create their own meanings by making choices and accepting responsibility for what follows. To deny this freedom to choose was to live in "bad faith." It is no accident that this vision of human ethics emerged from writers who had lived through the moral ambiguities of the German occupation of France, when even the quiet pursuit of a "normal" life could be seen as accepting or abetting a great evil.

Existentialist insights opened other doors. Black writers of African descent, such as Frantz Fanon, used existentialist claims about the absence of predetermined "essences" to insist that skin color had no significance, and that identity could only emerge from a lived experi-

ence. Simone de Beauvoir (*duh bohv-WAHR*, 1908–1986) made a similar claim about gender, arguing that "One is not born a woman, one becomes one." In *The Second Sex* (1949), de Beauvoir questioned the tendency of women to accept a secondary status in society, insisting that they should become the authors of their own lives, rather than accept unquestioningly the roles of wife or mother that society had prepared for them.

The theme of individual helplessness in the face of state power and empty moral teachings pervaded the literature of the period. George Orwell's *Animal Farm* (1946) explored the fearsome capacities of the Stalinist state in a barnyard allegory, while his novel *1984* (1949) imagined a future in which the state—"Big Brother"—was omnipresent and all-powerful. Hannah Arendt (1906–1975) was the first to propose that both Nazism and Stalinism should be understood as forms of a novel twentieth-century form of government: totalitarianism (*The Origins of Totalitarianism*, 1951). Unlike earlier forms of tyranny, totalitarianism worked by mobilizing mass support and using terror to crush resistance. In such a world, a collective response was impossible—social and political institutions were broken down, the public realm disappeared, and individuals were reduced to powerlessness, becoming atomized beings with no meaningful connection to one another.

Discussions of the war itself were limited. Few memoirs received wide attention in the immediate aftermath, though an exception was Anne Frank's *Diary of a Young Girl* (1947), a posthumously published diary by a child who had died at Auschwitz. The main current in postwar culture ran more toward forgetting than exploring the painful memories of the war years. Postwar governments did not purge all those implicated in war crimes. In France, the courts sentenced 2,640 to death and executed 791; in Austria, 13,000 were convicted of war crimes and 30 executed. Many who called for justice grew demoralized and cynical, as it was also clear that Cold War politics favored forgetting rather than punishing the guilty. The eagerness of the United States, Britain, and France to embrace West Germany as an ally, the preoccupation with economic rebuilding, and anticommunism all worked to discourage the difficult task of investigating who in Germany had actively supported the Nazi regime and who had been responsible for their murderous policies.

THE CUBAN MISSILE CRISIS

One of the last serious and most dramatic confrontations of the Cold War came in 1962, in Cuba. A revolution in 1958 had brought the charismatic communist Fidel Castro to power. Immediately after, the United States began to work with exiled Cubans, supporting among other ventures a bungled attempt to invade via the Bay of Pigs in 1961. Castro not only aligned himself with the Soviets but invited them to base nuclear missiles on Cuban soil, just a few minutes' flying time from Florida. When American spy planes identified the missiles and related military equipment in 1962, Kennedy confronted Khrushchev. After deliberating about the repercussions of an air strike, Kennedy ordered a naval blockade of Cuba. On October 22, he appeared on television, visibly tired and without makeup, announced the grave situation to the public, and challenged Khrushchev to withdraw the weapons and "move the world back from the abyss of destruction." Terrified of the looming threat of nuclear war, Americans fled urban areas, prepared for a cramped and uncomfortable existence in fallout shelters, and bought firearms. After three nerve-wracking weeks, the Soviets agreed to withdraw and to remove the bombers and missiles already on Cuban soil. But citizens of both countries spent many anxious hours in their bomb shelters, and onlookers the world over wrestled with their rising fears that a nuclear Armageddon was upon them.

CONCLUSION

The Cold War reached deep into postwar culture and dominated postwar politics. It decisively shaped the development of both the Soviet and American states. Fearful of losing

After You Read This Chapter

Visit StudySpace for quizzes, additional review materials, and multi-media documents. **wwnorton.com/studyspace**

REVIEWING THE OBJECTIVES

- The Cold War between the United States and the Soviet Union began as the Second World War ended. How did these two nations seek to influence the postwar political order in Europe?

- Postwar economic growth was accompanied by greater economic integration among Western European nations. What were the goals of those who sought to create the unified European market, and which nations played key roles in its development?

- Between the late 1940s and the mid-1960s, almost all the European colonies in Asia and Africa demanded and received their independence, either peacefully or through armed conflict. What combination of events made Europeans less able to defend their colonial empires against the claims of nationalists who sought independence from Europe?

- Decolonization and the Cold War reinforced a sense that Europe's place in the world needed to be rethought. How did intellectuals, writers, and artists react to the loss of European influence in the world?

control of territory they had conquered at such cost in the Second World War, the Soviets intervened repeatedly in the politics of their Eastern European allies in the 1940s and 1950s, ensuring the creation of hard-line governments in East Germany, Czechoslovakia, Poland, Hungary, and elsewhere in the Eastern bloc. In the United States, anti-communism became a powerful political force, shaping foreign policy and preparations for military confrontation with the Soviet Union to such an extent that President Eisenhower warned in his farewell address that a "military-industrial complex" had taken shape in the U.S. and that its "total influence—economic, political, even spiritual—is felt in every city, every statehouse, every office of the federal government."

In Western Europe, rebuilding the economy and creating a new political order in the aftermath of the Second World War meant accepting the new power and influence of the United States, but Europeans also searched for ways to create and express a European identity that would retain some independence and freedom of action. Led by the efforts of France and Germany, Western Europeans eventually found elements of this freedom in increasing integration and economic cooperation. In Eastern Europe, on the other hand, the political leadership found fewer opportunities for independent action, and the threat of military intervention by the Soviet Union made any innovations or experimentation difficult or impossible.

The sense that Europeans were no longer in a position to act independently or to exert their influence in other parts of the world was compounded by the loss of colonies abroad. Former European colonies in Africa and Asia became independent nations, and this loss of influence may have further encouraged the former European imperial powers in their attempts to lay the groundwork for a more integrated Europe. The consensus in the West about the new role that the state should take in economic planning, education, and social welfare helped lay the groundwork for a Europe that was dedicated to ensuring equal opportunities to its citizens. These commitments were driven by the search for stable forms of democratic government—the memories of the violent ideological conflicts of the 1920s and 1930s were still fresh, and the achievement of an integrated Western Europe (under U.S. sponsorship) on the hinge of Franco-German cooperation must be seen as one of the major victories of the postwar decades. The hard-won stability of this period was to be temporary, however, and beginning in the 1960s a new series of political conflicts and economic crises would test the limits of consensus in Cold War Europe.

PEOPLE, IDEAS, AND EVENTS IN CONTEXT

- When Allied leaders met to discuss the postwar order at **YALTA** in 1945, what were the major issues they discussed?
- What were the goals of the U.S. **MARSHALL PLAN**? How did **STALIN** react to its implementation?
- What was the **TRUMAN DOCTRINE** and how was it related to the creation of **NATO**?
- How did the Soviet Union's successful explosion of an **ATOMIC BOMB** in 1949 change the dynamic of the **COLD WAR**?
- How did the political climate in the Soviet Union and Eastern Europe change under **NIKITA KHRUSHCHEV** during the so-called **THAW** that followed Stalin's death?
- What nations were key to the plans for the **EUROPEAN COMMON MARKET**?
- Why was the **DECOLONIZATION** of settler colonies in Africa such as Algeria, Kenya, and Rhodesia more violent than in other colonies on the continent?
- What was **APARTHEID** and why was it adopted by the settler government in South Africa?

CONSEQUENCES

- Could European integration have happened without the Cold War?
- Could decolonization have happened without the Second World War?
- What effects of the Cold War do we still see today?

STORY LINES

- The postwar economy in Western Europe saw record growth that lasted until the 1970s. Labor shortages led many nations to recruit workers from abroad, causing tensions when unemployment rates went up as the postwar boom came to an end.

- Radio, television, and film combined to create a new kind of global mass culture that contributed to a spirit of novelty and rebellion among young people. More open discussion of sexual matters and an end to restrictions on contraception led some to speak of a "sexual revolution."

- Movements for national independence found an echo in the Civil Rights Movement in the United States and in student protests in Europe and the Americas in the 1960s. These protest movements peaked in 1968, provoking a conservative backlash in the 1970s and 1980s.

- Support for the Soviet Union waned in the 1980s as its economy stagnated and its political system failed to adapt. The Eastern bloc collapsed suddenly in 1989, ending the Cold War.

CHRONOLOGY

1957	Treaty of Rome forms European Common Market
1961	Berlin Wall built
1963	Betty Friedan, *The Feminine Mystique*
1964–1975	Vietnam War
mid-1960s	Birth control pill becomes available
1968	Czech revolt, Prague spring
1968	Student protests in Europe and the Americas
1970s	Détente between Soviet Union and Western powers
1973–1980s	Rising oil prices and worldwide recession
1980	Polish Solidarity workers movement
1989	Berlin Wall falls
1990	Reunification of Germany
1991–1995	Yugoslavian civil wars
1992	Soviet Union dissolved
1993	European Union

Before
You
Read
This
Chapter

Red Flags and Velvet Revolutions: The End of the Cold War, 1960s–1990s

CORE OBJECTIVES

- **DESCRIBE** postwar changes in employment and consumption, and their effects on daily life and mass culture in Europe.

- **UNDERSTAND** the shift in attitudes toward sexuality, reproduction, and conceptions of male and female social roles that took place in the postwar decades, and the consequences of this shift for women in Europe.

- **IDENTIFY** the motives and goals of the social and political movements that climaxed in 1968 in both Western and Eastern Europe.

- **EXPLAIN** the reasons for the economic downturn that began in the 1970s and its consequences for governments and populations in Europe.

- **UNDERSTAND** the events that led to the collapse of the Soviet bloc in 1989.

- **EXPLAIN** the reasons for the uncertainty and violence that followed the conclusion of the Cold War in Europe in the 1990s.

I n 1964, a photograph of a Portuguese laborer named Armando Rodriguez appeared on the cover of the German newsmagazine *Der Spiegel*. Rodriguez had been met at the border by an official delegation and celebrated as the one millionth "guest worker" to arrive in Germany. As a prize, he received the gift of a motorcycle. The moment reflected the confidence of the West German government that their postwar economic recovery would continue, and that material prosperity would bring a new stability to Europe. In fact, the early 1960s seemed golden and full of promise for many in Western Europe. Despite nearly constant international tension, everyday life seemed to be improving. Full employment drove increases in living standards, the mass availability of consumer items and modern appliances transformed daily life, and a life of relative prosperity and ample leisure now seemed accessible to many. Television, radio, and film promoted images of American middle-class life, and Europeans looked across the Atlantic and saw their own aspirations reflected back at them. Even amid the uncertainties of the Cold War, a new spirit of cooperation animated European governments, party divisions had given way to a broad consensus in favor of an expanded welfare state, and the future looked good.

By the 1990s, however, most of that confidence was gone, and the European landscape had been dramatically transformed. Western Europeans could no longer be so certain of their prosperity or of their leaders' ability to provide the sort of life they took for granted. Already in the late 1960s, the economic boom had come to an end, and movements of social protest, especially among young people, shattered the postwar consensus. The material comforts of a consumer society proved less satisfying than they had once seemed, and environmentalists, feminists, and other cultural critics criticized the assumptions of the older generation. These problems were compounded after 1975 by a continuing economic crisis that threatened the security that the postwar generation had labored so hard to achieve. European societies began to fragment in unexpected ways, well before the epochal transformations that accompanied the end of the Cold War.

The challenges of these decades proved even more fundamental in the Soviet sphere. Economic decay combined with political and social stagnation to produce another wave of revolt. The year 1989 marked the beginning of an extraordinarily rapid and surprising series of events. Communist rule collapsed in Eastern Europe. Hopes for peace were soon replaced by fears of conflict from unexpected quarters. Immigrants were no longer celebrated in Germany and elsewhere—instead they became targets of suspicion or even violence. Shortly after the reunification of Germany in 1991, a wave of attacks against immigrants and refugees in Eastern Germany by right-wing extremists took the lives of seventeen foreigners in Germany, including two Turkish women and a Turkish girl who died in an arson attack by neo-Nazi skinheads in Schleswig-Holstein. Similar attacks took place in France, Britain, Italy, and elsewhere. When postsocialist Yugoslavia collapsed into a brutal civil war in the early 1990s, Europeans faced once again the spectacle of mass political movements motivated by hatred and fear, leading to ethnic violence and mass murder in a European land.

The startlingly sudden dissolution of the Soviet bloc brought an end to the postwar era of superpower confrontation, and observers of European society were forced to confront the uncomfortable fact that the Cold War had provided its own form of stability. Seen from the early 1990s, the future looked much less certain. Could the emerging institutions of an integrated Europe absorb *all* the peoples of the former Soviet sphere? What would such a Europe look like, and who would determine its larger boundaries? What these changes meant for the future of democracy, the stability of the European economy, and definitions of European identity, remained an open question.

SOCIAL CHANGE AND CULTURAL DYNAMISM, 1945–1968

The "boom" of the 1950s, made especially striking by contrast with the bleak years immediately after the Second World War, had profound and far-reaching effects on social life. Both West Germany and France found it necessary to import workers to sustain their production booms. Most came from the south, particularly from the agrarian areas of southern Italy, where unemployment remained high. Workers from former colonies emigrated to Britain, often to take low-paid, menial jobs and encounter pervasive discrimination at work and in the community. Migrations of this sort, in addition to the vast movement of political and ethnic refugees that occurred during and immediately after the war, contributed to the breakdown of national barriers that was accelerated by the creation of the Common Market.

The most dramatic changes were encapsulated in the transformation of the land and agriculture. Agricultural productivity had barely changed over the first half of the century. After mid-century it soared. Common Market policy, state-sponsored programs of modernization, new agricultural machinery, and new kinds of fertilizer, seed, and animal feed helped produce the transformation. In Poland and the Eastern bloc, socialist regimes replaced small peasant holdings with large-scale agriculture. The effects reached across the economic and social landscape. Abundance meant lower food prices. Families spent a smaller proportion of their budgets on food, freeing up money for other forms of consumption and fueling economic growth. Peasants with large holdings or valuable specialized crops (dairy products or wine), who could withstand debt, adjusted. Others lost ground. Many farmers resorted to protest movements in an attempt to protect their standard of living.

Change also came in the workplace. Many commentators noted the striking growth in the number of middle-class, white-collar employees—the result, in part, of the dramatic bureaucratic expansion of the state. By 1964, the total number of men and women employed in government service in most European states exceeded 40 percent of the labor force, significantly higher than the number in the 1920s and 1930s. In business and industry, the number of middle-management employees grew as well. And industrial labor meant something far different from what it had meant in the nineteenth century. Skills were more specialized, based on technological expertise rather than custom and routine. *Skill* meant the ability to monitor automatic controls; to interpret abstract signals; and to make precise, mathematically calculated adjustments. More women entered the workforce, meeting less resistance than they had in the past, and their jobs were less starkly differentiated from men's.

Nineteenth-century society had been marked by clearly defined class cultures. In 1900, no one would have mistaken a peasant for a worker, and middle-class people had their own schools, recreations, and stores. But economic changes after 1950 chipped away at those distinctive cultures. Trade unions remained powerful institutions and workers still identified themselves as such, but class had a less rigidly defined meaning.

The expansion of education helped shift social hierarchies. All Western nations passed laws providing for the extension of compulsory secondary education. New legislation combined with rising birthrates to boost school populations dramatically. Education did not automatically produce social mobility, but when combined with economic prosperity, new structures of labor, and the consumerist boom, it began to lay the foundation for what would be called "postindustrial" society.

How did patterns differ in the Eastern bloc? Soviet workers were not noted for their specialized skills—in fact, a major factor in the slowdown of the Soviet economy was its failure to innovate. Factory workers in the "workers' state" commonly enjoyed higher wages than people in middle-class positions (with the exception of managers), but they had far less status. Their relatively high wages owed little to independent trade unions, which had been effectively abolished under Stalin; they were the product of persistent labor shortages and the accompanying fear of labor unrest. As far as the middle classes were concerned, two

MORNING CALISTHENICS AT RUSSIAN FACTORY, 1961. The growing number of industrial workers and of women in the workforce in the latter half of the twentieth century was reflected in this Soviet factory. The workers' state still bestowed little status on its workers, however—a factor that contributed to weakening the Russian economy.

wars and state socialism devastated traditional, insular bourgeois culture throughout Eastern Europe, though the regimes also created new ways of gaining privilege and status. Commentators spoke of a new class of bureaucrats and party members. Soviet education also aimed to unify a nation that remained culturally and ethnically heterogeneous. Afraid that the pull of ethnic nationality might tear at the none-too-solid fabric of the Soviet "union" increased the government's desire to impose one unifying culture by means of education, though not always with success.

Mass Consumption

Rising employment, higher earnings, and lower agricultural prices combined to give households and individuals more purchasing power. Household appliances and cars were the most striking emblems of what was virtually a new world of everyday objects. In 1956, 8 percent of British households had refrigerators. By 1979 that figure had skyrocketed to 69 percent. Vacuum cleaners, washing machines, and telephones all became common features of everyday life. They did not simply save labor or create free time, for household appliances came packaged with more demanding standards of housekeeping and new investments in domesticity—"more work for mother," in the words of one historian.

In 1948, five million Western Europeans had cars; in 1965, forty million did. Cars captured imaginations throughout the world; in magazines, advertisements, and countless films, the car was central to new images of romance, movement, freedom, and vacation. Of course, automobiles alone did not allow workers to take inexpensive holidays; reducing the workweek from forty-eight hours to about forty-two was more important, as was the institution of annual vacations—in most countries workers received over thirty days of paid vacation per year.

These changes marked a new culture of mass consumption. They were boosted by new industries devoted to marketing, advertising, and credit payment. They also entailed shifts in values. In the nineteenth century, a responsible middle-class family did not go into debt; discipline and thrift were hallmarks of respectability. By the second half of the twentieth century, banks and retailers, in the name of mass consumption and economic growth, were persuading middle- and working-class people alike not to be ashamed of debt. *Abundance, credit, consumer spending,* and *standards of living*—all these terms became part of the vocabulary of everyday economic life. This new vocabulary gradually came to reshape how citizens thought about their needs, desires, and entitlements. Standards of living, for instance, created a yardstick for measuring—and protesting—glaring social inequalities.

In Eastern Europe and the Soviet Union, consumption was organized differently. Governments rather than markets determined how consumer goods would be distributed. Economic policy channeled resources into heavy industry at the expense of consumer durables. This resulted in general scarcity, erratic shortages of even basic necessities, and often poor-quality goods. Women in particular often waited for hours in store lines after finishing a full day of wage work. Though numbers of household appliances increased dramatically in the Soviet Union and in Eastern Europe, the inefficiencies of the Soviet Union's consumer economy meant that women's double burden of work and housework remained especially heavy. Citizens' growing unhappiness with scarcities and seemingly irrational policies posed serious problems. As one historian puts it, the failure of policies on consumption was "one of the major dead ends of communism," and it contributed to the downfall of communist regimes.

Mass Culture

New patterns of consumption spurred wide-ranging changes in mass culture. The origins of "mass" culture lay in the 1890s, in the expansion of the popular press, music halls, organized sports, and "nickelodeons," all of which started the long process of displacing traditional, class-based forms of entertainment: village dances, boulevard theater, middle-class concerts, and so on. Mass culture quickened in the 1920s, its importance heightened by mass politics (see Chapter 25). The social transformations of the 1950s, which we have traced above, meant that families had both more spending money and more leisure time. The combination created a golden opportunity for the growing culture industry. The postwar desire to break with the past created further impetus for change. The result can fairly be called a cultural revolution: a transformation of culture, of its role in the lives of ordinary men and women, and of the power wielded by the media.

MUSIC AND YOUTH CULTURE

Much of the new mass culture of the 1960s depended on the spending habits and desires of the new generation. That new generation stayed in school longer, prolonging their adolescent years. Young people had more distance from their parents and the workforce and more time to be with each other. In the countryside especially, schooling began to break down the barriers that had separated the activities

MUSIC MEETS TELEVISION. The Beatles' Paul McCartney instructs popular variety show host Ed Sullivan on the electric bass, 1964.

of boys and girls, creating one factor in the "sexual revolution" (discussed later). From the late 1950s on, music became *the* cultural expression of this new generation. The transistor radio came out at the time of the Berlin airlift; by the mid-1950s these portable radios began to sell in the United States and Europe. Radio sets gave birth to new radio programs and, later, to new magazines reporting on popular singers and movie stars. All of these helped create new communities of interest. As one historian puts it, these radio programs were the "capillaries of youth culture." Social changes also affected the content of music: its themes and lyrics aimed to reach the young. Technological changes made records more than twice as long-playing as the old 78s and less expensive. The price of record players fell, multiplying the number of potential buyers. Combined, these developments changed how music was produced, distributed, and consumed. It was no longer confined to the concert hall or café but instead reverberated through people's homes or cars and teenagers' rooms—providing a soundtrack for everyday life.

Postwar youth culture owed much to the hybrid musical style known as rock and roll. During the 1930s and 1940s, the synthesis of music produced by whites and African Americans in the American South found its way into northern cities. After the Second World War, black rhythm and blues musicians and white Southern rockabilly performers found much wider audiences through the use of new technology—electric guitars, better equipment for studio recording, and wide-band radio stations in large cities. The blend of styles and sounds and the cultural daring of white teenagers who listened to what recording studios at the time called "race music" came together to create rock and roll. The music was exciting, sometimes aggressive, and full of energy.

MASS CULTURE IN A MEDIA AGE. When John Lennon declared the Beatles were "more popular than Jesus," he raised a storm of protest. Here an American teenager tosses *Meet the Beatles* into a bonfire. ■ *What was different about this kind of celebrity when compared with earlier generations of popular entertainers?*

In Europe, rock and roll found its way into working-class neighborhoods, particularly in Britain and Ireland. There, local youths took American sounds, echoed the inflections of poverty and defiance, and added touches of music-hall showmanship to produce successful artists and bands, who went on to dominate the U.S. charts in what became known as the "British invasion." As the music's popularity spread, music culture came loose from its national moorings. The Beatles managed to get their own music on the hit lists in France, Germany, and the United States. By the time a half a million young people gathered near Woodstock, New York, for "Three Days of Peace and Music," youth music culture was international. Rock became the sound of worldwide youth culture, providing a bridge across the Cold War divide. Despite Eastern bloc limits on importing "capitalist" music, pirated songs circulated—sometimes on X-ray plates salvaged from hospitals. Recording studios latched onto the earning potential of the music and became corporations as powerful as car manufacturers or steel companies.

Art and Painting

The cultural revolution we have been tracing changed high as well as popular art. Record companies' influence reached well beyond rock. New recording techniques made it possible to reissue favorites in classical music, and companies marketed them more aggressively. Record companies buoyed the careers of internationally acclaimed stars, such as the soprano Maria Callas and (much later) the tenor Luciano Pavarotti, staging concerts, using their influence on orchestras, and offering new recordings of their art.

Painting and other visual arts, too, were changed by the rise of mass and consumer culture. The art market boomed. The power of the dollar was one factor in the rise of New York as a center of modern art, one of the most striking developments of the period. Immigration was another: a slow stream of immigrants from Europe nourished American art as well as social and political thought (see Chapter 27), and New York proved hospitable to European artists. The creative work of the school of abstract expressionism sealed New York's postwar reputation. The abstract expressionists—William de Kooning (from the Netherlands), Mark Rothko (from Russia), Franz Kline, Jackson Pollock, Helen Frankenthaler, and Robert Motherwell—followed trends established by the cubists and surrealists, experimenting with color, texture, and technique to find new forms of expression. Many of them emphasized the physical aspects of paint and the act of painting. Pollock is a good example: he poured and even threw paint on the canvas, creating powerful images of personal and physical expressiveness that some dubbed "action painting." Critics called the drip paintings "unpredictable, undisciplined, and explosive" and saw in them the youthful exuberance of postwar American culture.

But abstract expressionism also produced its opposite, sometimes called pop art. Pop artists distanced themselves from the moody and elusive meditations of abstract

ACTION PAINTING. Photographer Martha Holmes reveals the dynamic technique of abstract expressionist Jackson Pollock as he paints, 1950.

expressionism. They refused to distinguish between avant garde and popular art, or between the artistic and the commercial. They lavished attention on commonplace, instantly recognizable, often commercial images; they borrowed techniques from graphic design; they were interested in the immediacy of everyday art and ordinary people's visual experience. Jasper Johns's paintings of the American flag formed part of this trend. So did the work of Andy Warhol and Roy Lichtenstein, who took objects such as soup cans and images of comic-strip heroes as their subjects. Treating popular culture with this tongue-in-cheek seriousness became one of the central themes of 1960s art.

Film

Mass culture made its most powerful impact in the visual world, especially through film. Film flourished after the Second World War, developing along several different lines. The Italian neorealists of the late 1940s and 1950s, antifascists and socialists, set out to capture authenticity, or "life as it was lived," by which they usually meant working-class existence. They dealt with the same themes that marked the literature of the period: loneliness, war, and corruption. They shot on location, using natural light and little-known actors, deliberately steering away from the artifice and high production values they associated with the tainted cinema of fascist and wartime Europe. Not strictly realists, they played with nonlinear plots as well as unpredictable characters and motivations. Roberto Rossellini's *Rome: Open City* (1945) was a loving portrait of Rome under Nazi occupation. Vittorio de Sica's *Bicycle Thief* (1948) tells a story of a man struggling against unemployment and poverty, who desperately needs his bicycle to keep his job as a poster hanger. Federico Fellini came out of the neorealist school and began his career writing for Rossellini. Fellini's breakout film *La Dolce Vita* (1959, starring Marcello Mastroianni) took Italian film to screens throughout Europe and the United States, and it also marked Fellini's transition to his signature surrealist and carnivalesque style, developed further in *8½* (1963).

The French directors of the new wave continued to develop this unsentimental, naturalistic, and enigmatic social vision. New wave directors worked closely with each other, casting each other (and their wives and lovers) in their films, encouraging improvisation, and experimenting with disjointed narrative. François Truffaut's (1932–1984) *The 400 Blows* (1959) and *The Wild Child* (1969), and Jean-Luc Godard's (1930–) *Breathless* (1959) and *Contempt* (1963, with Brigitte Bardot), are leading examples. *Closely Watched Trains* (1966) was the Czech director Jiří Menzel's (1938–)

contribution to the new wave. The new wave raised the status of the director, insisting that the film's camera work and vision (rather than the writing) constituted the real art—part, again, of the new value accorded to the visual. France made other contributions to international film by sponsoring the Cannes Film Festival. The first Cannes Festival was held before the Second World War, but the city opened its gates again in 1946 under the banner of artistic internationalism. Placing itself at the center of an international film industry became part of France's ongoing recovery from the war, and Cannes became one of the world's largest marketplaces for film.

HOLLYWOOD AND THE AMERICANIZATION OF CULTURE

The American film industry, however, had considerable advantages, and the devastating aftereffects of the Second World War in Europe allowed Hollywood to consolidate its earlier gains (see Chapter 27). The United States' huge domestic market gave Hollywood its biggest advantage. By the 1950s Hollywood was making five hundred films a year and accounted for between 40 and 75 percent of films shown in Europe. The same period brought important innovations in filmmaking: the conversion to color and new optical formats, including widescreen.

The Cold War also weighed heavily on the film industry in the United States. Between 1947 and 1951, the House Un-American Activities Committee called before it hundreds of actors, directors, and writers in their investigation of Hollywood's political allegiances. The major studios blacklisted many, fearing their associations with communism or left-wing political activity. Paradoxically, this occurred as the American censorship system was breaking down. Since the 1930s, the Motion Picture Production Code had refused to approve "scenes of passion" (including married couples sharing a bed), immorality, realistic violence, and profanity. In the mid-1950s, popular films such as *Rebel without a Cause* (1955) challenged these standards, dealing frankly with teenage rebellion, sexual themes, or other previously taboo subjects. By the 1960s the Production Code had been scuttled—the extremely graphic violence at the end of Arthur Penn's *Bonnie and Clyde* (1967) marked the scope of the transformation.

Gender Roles and Sexual Revolution

What some called the sexual revolution of the 1960s had several aspects. The first was less censorship, which we have already seen in film, and fewer taboos regarding discussion of sexuality in public. In the United States, the notorious Kinsey Reports on male and female sexuality (in 1948 and 1953, respectively) made morality and sexual behavior front-page news. Alfred Kinsey was a zoologist turned social scientist, and the way in which he applied science and statistics to sex attracted considerable attention. Kinsey showed that moral codes and private behaviors did not line up neatly. For instance, 80 to 90 percent of the women he interviewed disapproved of premarital sex, but 50 percent of the women he interviewed had had it. *Time* magazine warned that publicizing disparities between beliefs and behavior might prove subversive—that women and men would decide there was "morality in numbers."

Was the family crumbling? Transformations in agriculture and life in the countryside did mean that the peasant family was no longer the institution that governed birth, work, courtship, marriage, and death. Yet the family became newly important as the center of consumption, spending, and leisure time, for television took people (usually men) out of bars, cafés, and music halls. It became the focus of government attention in the form of family allowances, health care, and Cold War appeals to family values. People brought higher expectations to marriage, which raised rates of divorce, and they paid more attention to children, which brought smaller families. Despite a postwar spike in the birthrate that produced the "baby boom," over the long term, fertility declined, even in countries that outlawed contraception. The family assumed new meanings as its traditional structures of authority—namely paternal control over wives and children—eroded under the pressure of social change.

A second aspect of the revolution was the growing centrality of sex and eroticism to mass consumer culture. Magazines, which flourished in this period, offered advice on how to succeed in love and how to be attractive. Cultivating one's looks, including sexiness, fit with the new accent on consumption; indeed health and personal hygiene was the fastest rising category of family spending. Advertising, advice columns, TV, and film blurred boundaries between buying consumer goods, seeking personal fulfillment, and sexual desire. There was nothing new about appeals to eroticism. But the fact that sexuality was now widely considered a form of self-expression—perhaps even the core of one's self—was new to the twentieth century. These developments helped propel change, and they also made the sexual revolution prominent in the politics of the time.

The third aspect of the revolution came with legal and medical or scientific changes in contraception. Oral contraceptives, first approved for development in 1959, became mainstream in the next decade. "The Pill" did not have rev-

olutionary effects on birthrates, which were already falling. It marked dramatic change, however, because it was simple (though expensive) and could be used by women themselves. By 1975, two-thirds of British women between fifteen and forty-four said they were taking the Pill. Numbers like these marked a long, drawn-out end to centuries-old views that to discuss birth control was pornographic, an affront to religion, and an invitation to indulgence and promiscuity. By and large, Western countries legalized contraception in the 1960s and abortion in the 1970s. In 1965, for instance, the U.S. Supreme Court struck down laws banning the use of contraception, though selling contraceptives remained illegal in Massachusetts until 1972. The Soviet Union legalized abortion in 1950, after banning it during most of Stalin's regime. Throughout Eastern Europe, abortion rates were extremely high. Why? Contraceptives proved as difficult to obtain as other consumer goods; men often refused to use them; and women—doubly burdened with long hours of work and housework, and facing, in addition, chronic housing shortages—had little choice but to resort to abortion.

Legal changes would not have occurred without the women's movements of the time. For nineteenth-century feminists, winning the right to vote was the most difficult practical and symbolic struggle (see Chapter 23). For the revived feminism of the 1960s and 1970s, the family, work, and sexuality—all put on the agenda by the social changes of the period—were central. Since the Second World War the assumption that middle-class women belonged in the home had been challenged by the steadily rising demand for workers, especially in education and the service sector. Thus many more married women and many more mothers were part of the labor force. Moreover, across the West young middle-class women, like men, were part of the rising number of university students. But in the United States, to take just one example, only 37 percent of women who enrolled in college in the 1950s finished their degrees, believing they should marry instead. As one of them explained, "We married what we wanted to be": doctor, professor, manager, and so on. Women found it difficult to get nonsecretarial jobs; they received less pay for the same work; and, even when employed, they had to rely on their husbands to establish credit.

The tension between rising expectations that stemmed, on the one hand, from abundance, growth, and the emphasis on self-expression, and, on the other, the reality of narrow horizons, created quiet waves of discontent. Betty Friedan's *The Feminine Mystique* (1963) brought much of this discontent into the open, contrasting the cultural myths of the fulfilled and happy housewife with the realities of economic inequality, hard work, and narrowed horizons. In 1949, Simone de Beauvoir had asked how Western culture (myth, literature, and psychology) had created an image of woman as the second and lesser sex; Friedan, using a more journalistic style and writing at a time when social change had made readers more receptive to her ideas, showed how the media, the social sciences, and advertising at once exalted femininity and also lowered women's expectations and possibilities. Friedan founded NOW (the National Organization of Women) in the United States in 1966; smaller and often more radical women's movements multiplied across Europe in the following decades. For this generation of feminists, reproductive freedom was both a private matter and a basic right—a key to women's control over their lives. Outlawing contraception and abortion made women alone bear responsibility for the consequences of sweeping changes in Western sexual life. Such measures were ineffective as well as unjust, they argued. Mass consumption, mass culture, and startlingly rapid transformations in public and private life were all intimately related.

SOCIAL MOVEMENTS DURING THE 1960s

The social unrest of the 1960s was international. Its roots lay in the political struggles and social transformations of the postwar period. Of these, the most important were anticolonial and civil rights movements. The successful anticolonial movements (see Chapter 27) reflected a growing racial consciousness and also helped encourage that consciousness. Newly independent African and Caribbean nations remained wary about revivals of colonialism and the continuing economic hegemony of Western Europe and

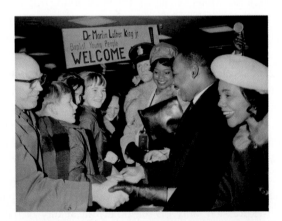

MARTIN LUTHER KING JR., 1964. The African American civil rights leader is welcomed in Oslo, Norway, on a trip to accept the Nobel Peace Prize. He would be assassinated four years later. ▪ *How might Europeans have viewed King's campaign?* ▪ *Would it affect their vision of the United States?*

America. Black and Asian immigration into those nations produced tension and frequent violence. In the West, particularly in the United States, people of color identified with these social and economic grievances.

The Civil Rights Movement in the United States Seen from Europe

Increasingly vocal demands by African Americans for equal rights and an end to segregation in the United States paralleled the emergence of new black nations in Africa and the Caribbean following decolonization. The American Civil Rights Movement had its origins in local organizing by prewar organizations such as the National Association for the Advancement of Colored People (NAACP). By 1960 a new generation of civil rights activists, led by the Congress of Racial Equality (CORE) sought a more confrontational approach to end segregation, organizing boycotts and demonstrations against private businesses and public services that discriminated against blacks in the South.

Martin Luther King (1929–1968), a Baptist minister who embraced the philosophy of non-violence promoted by the Indian social and political activist Mohandas K. Gandhi, emerged as the most visible and effective leader of the movement until his assassination in 1968. Other African American leaders, such as Malcolm X (1925–1965), rejected King's goal of integration and called instead for African Americans to develop a nationalist consciousness of their own, emphasizing their own heritage and rejecting white domination. Although the Civil Rights Movement in the United States could point to real success—voting rights and school desegregation among them—the visible and violent resistance to civil rights organizers in the South and persistent racism in housing and job opportunities hurt the image of the United States in Europe.

Many Europeans watched the U.S. Civil Rights Movement—and the vocal resistance it faced from American defenders of segregation—with real discomfort. American troops had been stationed in Western European nations since the Second World War as part of their Cold War defense system, and for many people in Europe, the persistence of racial discrimination in the United States undermined American claims to be the defenders of liberty in Europe. At the same time, the U.S. civil rights campaign served as a reminder of the injustices of European colonial empires. West Indian, Indian, and Pakistani immigrants faced racial discrimination in Britain, as did Algerian immigrants in France and Turkish "guest workers" in Germany.

The root causes of these enduring problems lay in the long and different histories of American slavery and

European imperial expansion, but whatever the cause, the question of racial equality proved challenging to democracies on both sides of the Atlantic in the postwar decades and after. In Western Europe, as in the United States, struggles for racial and ethnic integration became central to the postcolonial world.

The Antiwar Movement

By the late 1960s the United States' escalating war in Vietnam had become a lightning rod for discontent. In 1961, President John F. Kennedy (1961–63) had promised to "bear any burden" necessary to fight communism and to ensure the victory of American models of representative government and free-market economics in the developing nations. Kennedy's plan entailed massive increases in foreign aid, much of it in weapons. It provided the impetus for humanitarian institutions such as the Peace Corps, intended to improve local conditions and show Americans' benevolence and good intentions. Bearing burdens, however, also meant fighting guerrillas who turned to the Soviets for aid. This involved covert interventions in Latin America, the Congo, and, most important, Vietnam.

By the time of Kennedy's death in 1963, nearly fifteen thousand American "advisers" were on the ground alongside South Vietnamese troops. Kennedy's successor, Lyndon Johnson, began the strategic bombing of North Vietnam and rapidly drew hundreds of thousands of American troops into combat in South Vietnam. The rebels in the south, known as the Viet Cong, were solidly entrenched, highly experienced guerrilla fighters, and were backed by the professional, well-equipped North Vietnamese army under Ho Chi Minh, who also received support from the Soviet Union. The South Vietnamese government resisted efforts at reform, losing popular support. Massive efforts by the United States produced only stalemate, mounting American casualties, and rising discontent.

Opposition to the Vietnam War helped to galvanize a broad protest movement in the United States and in other countries. In the United States, protesters focused on the military draft, which, when combined with deferments for educational purposes, ended up conscripting a disproportionate number of African Americans. The failure to achieve military victory in spite of escalating numbers of troops discredited the U.S. government's policy, and by the late 1960s the Vietnam War was seen by many people in the world as a tragedy and a folly: the wealthiest, most powerful nation in the world seemed intent on destroying a land of poor peasants in the name of anticommunism, democracy, and freedom. This tarnished

image of Western values stood at the center of the 1960s protest movements in the United States and Western Europe.

The Student Movement

The student movement itself can be seen as a consequence of postwar developments: a rapidly growing cohort of young people with more time and wealth than in the past; generational consciousness heightened, in part, by the marketing of mass youth culture; and educational institutions unable to deal with rising numbers and expectations. By 1969, universities and high schools in Western Europe had five times as many students as in 1949. Lecture halls were packed, university bureaucracies did not respond to requests, and thousands of students took exams at the same time. More philosophically, students raised questions about the role and meaning of elite education in a democratic society and about relations between universities, state-funded scientific research, and the Cold War military intervention in Vietnam. In addition, student demands for fewer restrictions on personal life—for instance, permission to have a member of the opposite sex in a dormitory room—provoked authoritarian reactions from university officials. Waves of student protest were not confined to the United States and Western Europe. They also swept across Poland and Czechoslovakia, where students protested one-party bureaucratic rule, stifling intellectual life, and authoritarianism, and helped sustain networks of dissidents. By the mid-1960s, simmering anger in Eastern Europe had once again reached a dangerous point.

1968

Nineteen sixty-eight was an extraordinary year, quite similar to 1848 with its wave of revolution (see Chapter 20). International youth culture fostered a sense of collective identity. The new media relayed images of civil rights protests in the United States to Europe, and broadcast news footage of the Vietnam War on television screens from West Virginia to West Germany. The wave of unrest shook both the Eastern and Western blocs.

PARIS

The most serious outbreak of student unrest in Europe came in Paris in the spring of 1968. The French Republic had been shaken by conflicts over the Algerian war in the early 1960s. Even more important, the economic boom had undermined the foundations of the regime and de Gaulle's traditional style of rule. French students at the University of Paris

Competing Viewpoints

The "Woman Question" on Both Sides of the Atlantic

How did Western culture define femininity, and how did women internalize those definitions? These questions were central to postwar feminist thought, and they were sharply posed in two classic texts: Simone de Beauvoir's The Second Sex (1949) and Betty Friedan's The Feminine Mystique (1963). Beauvoir (1908–1986) started from the existentialist premise that humans were "condemned to be free" and to give their own lives meaning. Why, then, did women accept the limitations imposed on them and, in Beauvoir's words, "dream the dreams of men"? Although dense and philosophical, The Second Sex was read throughout the world. Betty Friedan's equally influential bestseller drew heavily on Beauvoir. Friedan sought the origins of the "feminine mystique," her term for the model of femininity promoted by experts, advertised in women's magazines, and seemingly embraced by middle-class housewives in the postwar United States. As Friedan points out in the excerpt here, the new postwar mystique was in many ways more conservative than prewar ideals had been, despite continuing social change, a greater range of careers opening up to women, the expansion of women's education, and so on. Friedan (1921–2006) co-founded the National Organization for Women in 1966 and served as its president until 1970.

Simone de Beauvoir, *The Second Sex* (1949)

But first, what is a woman?... Everyone agrees there are females in the human species; today, as in the past, they make up about half of humanity; and yet we are told that "femininity is in jeopardy;" we are urged. "Be women, stay women, become women."... Although some women zealously strive to embody it, the model has never been patented. It is typically described in vague and shimmering terms borrowed from a clairvoyant's vocabulary....

If the female function is not enough to define woman, and if we also reject the explanation of the "eternal feminine," but if we accept, even temporarily, that there are women on the earth, we then have to ask: what is a woman?

Merely stating the problem suggests an immediate answer to me. It is significant that I pose it. It would never occur to a man to write a book on the singular situation of males in humanity. If I want to define myself, I first have to say, "I am a woman;" all other assertions will arise from this basic truth. A man never begins by positing himself as an individual of a certain sex: that he is a man is obvious. The categories "masculine" and "feminine" appear as symmetrical in a formal way on town hall records or identification papers. The relation of the two sexes is not that of two electrical poles: the man represents both the positive and the neuter.... Woman is the negative, to such a point that any determination is imputed to her as a limitation, without reciprocity.... [A] man is in his right by virtue of being man; it is the woman who is in the wrong.... Woman has ovaries and a uterus; such are the particular conditions that lock her in her subjectivity; some even say she thinks with her hormones. Man vainly forgets that his anatomy also includes hormones and testicles. He grasps his body as a direct and normal link with the world that he believes he apprehends in all objectivity whereas he considers woman's body an obstacle, a prison, burdened by everything that particularises it. "The female is female by virtue of a certain *lack* of qualities," Aristotle said. "We should regard women's nature as suffering from natural defectiveness." And St. Thomas in his turn decreed that woman was an "incomplete man," an "incidental" being. This is what the Genesis story symbolises, where Eve appears as if drawn from Adam's "supernumerary" bone, in Bossuet's words. Humanity is male, and man defines woman, not in herself, but in relation to himself; she is not considered an autonomous being.... And she is nothing other than what man decides; she is thus called "the sex," meaning that the male sees her essentially as a sexed being; for him she is sex, so she is it in the absolute. She determines and differentiates herself in relation to man, and he does not in relation to her; she is the inessential in front of the essential. He is the Subject, he is the Absolute. She is the Other.

Source: Simone de Beauvoir, *The Second Sex*, trans. Constance Borde and Sheila Malovany-Chevallier (London: 2009), pp. 3–6.

Betty Friedan, *The Feminine Mystique* (1963)

In 1939, the heroines of women's magazine stories were not always young, but in a certain sense they were younger than their fictional counterparts today. They were young in the same way that the American hero has always been young: they were New Women, creating with a gay determined spirit a new identity for women—a life of their own. There was an aura about them of becoming, of moving into a future that was going to be different from the past. . . .

These stories may not have been great literature. But the identity of their heroines seemed to say something about the housewives who, then as now, read the women's magazines. These magazines were not written for career women. The New Woman heroines were the ideal of yesterday's housewives; they reflected the dreams, mirrored the yearning for identity and the sense of possibility that existed for women then. . . .

In 1949 . . . the feminine mystique began to spread through the land. . . .

The feminine mystique says that the highest value and the only commitment for women is the fulfillment of their own femininity. It says that the great mistake of Western culture, through most of its history, has been the undervaluation of this femininity. . . . The mistake, says the mystique, the root of women's troubles in the past, is that women envied men, women tried to be like men, instead of accepting their own nature, which can find fulfillment only in sexual passivity, male domination, and nurturing maternal love.

But the new image this mystique gives to American women is the old image: "Occupation: housewife." The new mystique makes the housewife-mothers, who never had a chance to be anything else, the model for all women; it presupposes that history has reached a final and glorious end in the here and now, as far as women are concerned. . . .

It is more than a strange paradox that as all professions are finally open to women in America, "career woman" has become a dirty word; that as higher edu-

cation becomes available to any woman with the capacity for it, education for women has become so suspect that more and more drop out of high school and college to marry and have babies; that as so many roles in modern society become theirs for the taking, women so insistently confine themselves to one role. Why . . . should she accept this new image which insists she is not a person but a "woman," by definition barred from the freedom of human existence and a voice in human destiny?

Source: Betty Friedan, *The Feminine Mystique* (New York: 2001), pp. 38, 40, 42–43, 67–68.

Questions for Analysis

1. Why does Beauvoir ask, "What is a woman?"

2. Why does Friedan think that a "feminine mystique" emerged after the Second World War?

---

demanded reforms that would modernize their university. In the face of growing disorder, the entire University of Paris shut down—sending students into the streets and into uglier confrontations with the police. The police reacted with repression and violence, which startled onlookers and television audiences and backfired on the regime. Sympathy with the students' cause expanded rapidly, bringing in other opponents of President de Gaulle's regime. Massive trade-union strikes broke out. Workers in the automobile industry, technical workers, and public-sector employees—from gas and electricity utilities to the mail system to radio and television—went on strike. By mid-May, an astonishing ten million French workers had walked off their jobs. At one point, it looked as if the government would fall. The regime, however, was able to satisfy the strikers with wage increases and to appeal to public demand for order. Isolated, the student movements gradually petered out and students agreed to resume university life. The regime did recover, but the events of 1968 helped weaken de Gaulle's position as president and contributed to his retirement from office the following year.

Paris was not the only city to explode in 1968. Student protest broke out in West Berlin, targeting the government's close ties to the autocratic shah of Iran and the power of media corporations. Clashes with the police turned violent. In Italian cities, undergraduates staged several demonstrations to draw attention to university overcrowding. Twenty-six universities were closed. The London School of Economics was nearly shut down by protest. In the United States, antiwar demonstrations and student rebellions spread across the country after the North Vietnamese and Viet Cong launched the Tet offensive. President Johnson, battered by the effects of Tet and already worn down by the war, chose not to run for reelection. The year 1968 also saw damage and trauma for the country's political future because of the assassinations of Martin Luther King Jr. (April 4) and presidential candidate Robert F. Kennedy (June 5). King's assassination was followed by a wave of rioting in more than fifty cities across the United States, followed in late summer by street battles between police and student protesters at the 1968 Democratic National Convention in Chicago. Some saw the flowering of protest as another "springtime of peoples." Others saw it as a long nightmare.

"PRAGUE SPRING"

The student movement in the United States and Western Europe also took inspiration from one of the most significant challenges to Soviet authority since the Hungarian revolt of 1956 (see Chapter 27): the "Prague spring" of 1968. The events began with the emergence of a liberal communist government in Czechoslovakia, led by the Slovak Alexander Dubček (*DOOB-chehk*). Dubček had outmaneuvered the more traditional, authoritarian party leaders. He advocated "socialism with a human face," encouraging debate within the party, academic and artistic freedom, and less censorship. As was often the case, party members were divided between proponents of reform and those fearful that reform would unleash revolution. The reformers, however, also gained support from outside the party, from student organizations, the press, and networks of dissidents. As in Western Europe and the United States, the protest movement overflowed the bounds of traditional party politics.

In the Soviet Union, Khrushchev had fallen in 1964, and the reins of Soviet power passed to Leonid Brezhnev as secretary of the Communist party. Brezhnev was more conservative than Khrushchev, less inclined to bargain with the West, and prone to defensive actions to safeguard the Soviet sphere of influence. Initially, the Soviets tolerated Dubček as a political eccentric. The events of 1968 raised their fears. Most Eastern European communist leaders denounced Czech reformism, but student demonstrations of

A RUSSIAN TANK ATTACKED FOLLOWING THE PRAGUE SPRING, 1968.

support broke out in Poland and Yugoslavia, calling for an end to one-party rule, less censorship, and reform of the judicial system. In addition, Josip Broz Tito of Yugoslavia and Nicolae Ceausescu (*chow-SHEHS-koo*) of Romania—two of the more stubbornly independent communists in Eastern Europe—visited Dubček. To Soviet eyes these activities looked as if they were directed against the Warsaw Pact and Soviet security; they also saw American intervention in Vietnam as evidence of heightened anticommunist activities around the world. When Dubček attempted to democratize the Communist party and did not attend a meeting of members of the Warsaw Pact, the Soviets sent tanks and troops into Prague in August 1968. Again the world watched as streams of Czech refugees left the country and a repressive government, picked by Soviet security forces, took charge. Dubček and his allies were subjected to imprisonment or "internal exile." Twenty percent of the members of the Czech Communist party were expelled in a series of purges. After the destruction of the Prague spring, Soviet diplomats consolidated their position according to the new Brezhnev Doctrine. The doctrine stated that no socialist state could adopt policies endangering the interests of international socialism, and that the Soviet Union could intervene in the domestic affairs of any Soviet bloc nation if communist rule was threatened. In other words, the repressive rules applied to Hungary in 1956 would not change.

What were the effects of 1968? De Gaulle's government recovered. The Republican Richard M. Nixon won the U.S. presidential election of 1968. From 1972 to 1975 the United States withdrew from Vietnam; in the wake of that war came a refugee crisis and a new series of horrific regional conflicts. In Prague, Warsaw Pact tanks put down the uprising, and in the Brezhnev Doctrine the Soviet regime reasserted its right to control its satellites. Serious Cold War confrontations rippled along Czechoslovakia's western border as refugees fled west,

Ludvík Vaculík, "Two Thousand Words" (1968)

During the Prague spring of 1968, a group of Czech intellectuals published a document titled "Two Thousand Words That Belong to Workers, Farmers, Officials, Scientists, Artists, and Everybody" that has become known simply as the "Two Thousand Words." This manifesto called for further reform, including increased freedom of the press. Seen as a direct affront by Moscow, the manifesto heightened Soviet-Czech tensions. In August 1968, Warsaw Pact tanks rolled into Prague, overthrowing the reformist government of Alexander Dubček.

 ost of the nation welcomed the socialist program with high hopes. But it fell into the hands of the wrong people. It would not have mattered so much that they lacked adequate experience in affairs of state, factual knowledge, or philosophical education, if only they had enough common prudence and decency to listen to the opinion of others and agree to being gradually replaced by more able people....

The chief sin and deception of these rulers was to have explained their own whims as the "will of the workers." Were we to accept this pretense, we would have to blame the workers today for the decline of our economy, for crimes committed against the innocent, and for the introduction of censorship to prevent anyone writing about these things. The workers would be to blame for misconceived investments, for losses suffered in foreign trade, and for the housing shortage. Obviously no sensible person will hold the working class responsible for such things. We all know, and every worker knows especially, that they had virtually no say in deciding anything....

Since the beginning of this year we have been experiencing a regenerative process of democratization....

Let us demand the departure of people who abused their power, damaged public property, and acted dishonorably or brutally. Ways must be found to compel them to resign. To mention a few: public criticism, resolutions, demonstrations, demonstrative work brigades, collections to buy presents for them on their retirement, strikes, and picketing at their front doors. But we should reject any illegal, indecent, or boorish methods.... Let us convert the district and local newspapers, which have mostly degenerated to the level of official mouthpieces, into a platform for all the forward-looking elements in politics; let us demand that editorial boards be formed of National Front representatives, or else let us start new papers. Let us form committees for the defense of free speech....

There has been great alarm recently over the possibility that foreign forces will intervene in our development. Whatever superior forces may face us, all we can do is stick to our own positions, behave decently, and initiate nothing ourselves. We can show our government that we will stand by it, with weapons if need be, if it will do what we give it a mandate to do....

The spring is over and will never return. By winter we will know all.

Source: Jaromir Navratil, *The Prague Spring 1968*, trans. Mark Kramer, Joy Moss, and Ruth Tosek (Budapest: 1998), pp. 177–81.

Questions for Analysis

1. Where, according to the authors of this document, did socialism go wrong?

2. What specific reforms do they demand?

---

and in the Korean peninsula after North Korea's seizure of a U.S. Navy eavesdropping ship. Over the long term, however, the protesters' and dissidents' demands proved more difficult to contain. In Eastern Europe and the Soviet Union, dissent was defeated but not eliminated. The crushing of the Czech rebellion proved thoroughly disillusioning, and in important respects the events of 1968 prefigured the collapse of Soviet control in 1989. In Western Europe and the United States, the student movement subsided but its issues and the kinds of politics that it pioneered proved more enduring. Feminism (or, more accurately, second-wave feminism) really came into its own after 1968, its numbers expanded by women a generation younger than Simone de Beauvoir and Betty Friedan. Finally, the environmental movement took hold—concerned not only with pollution and the world's dwindling resources but also with mushrooming urbanization and the kind of unrestrained economic growth that had characterized the 1960s. Over the long term, in both Europe and the United States, voters' loyalties to traditional political parties became less reliable and smaller parties multiplied; in this way, new social movements eventually became part of a very different political landscape.

ECONOMIC STAGNATION: THE PRICE OF SUCCESS

Economic as well as social problems plagued Europe during the 1970s and 1980s, but these problems had begun earlier. By the middle of the 1960s, for example, the postwar economic boom had slowed. Demand for manufactured goods fell, and unemployment crept up. Though new industries continued to prosper, the basic industries—coal, steel, and railways—began to run up deficits. The Common Market—expanded in 1973 to include Britain, Ireland, and Denmark, and again in the early 1980s to admit Greece, Spain, and Portugal—struggled to overcome problems stemming from the conflict between the domestic economic regulations characteristic of many European states and the free-market policies that prevailed within what would become the European Economic Community (EEC) countries.

Oil prices spiked for the first time in the early 1970s, compounding these difficulties. In 1973, the Arab-dominated Organization of the Petroleum Exporting Countries (OPEC) instituted an oil embargo against the Western powers. In 1973, a barrel of oil cost $1.73; in 1975, it cost $10.46; by the early 1980s, the price had risen to over $30. This increase produced an inflationary spiral; interest rates rose and with them the price of almost everything else Western consumers were used to buying. Rising costs at a time of economic slowdown produced wage demands and strikes. The calm industrial relations of the 1950s and early 1960s were a thing of the past. At the same time, European manufacturers encountered serious competition, not only from such highly developed countries as Japan but also from the increasingly active economies of Asia and Africa, in which the West had eagerly invested capital in the previous decades. By 1980 Japan had captured 10 percent of the automobile market in West Germany and 25 percent in Belgium. In 1984 unemployment in Western Europe reached about 19 million. The lean years had arrived.

Economies in the Soviet bloc also stalled. The expansion of heavy industry had helped recovery in the postwar period, but by the 1970s, those sectors no longer provided growth or innovation. The Soviet Communist party proclaimed in 1961 that by 1970 the USSR would exceed the United States in per capita production. By the end of the 1970s, however, Soviet per capita production was not much higher than in the less industrialized countries of southern Europe. The Soviets were also overcommitted to military defense industries that had become inefficient, though lucrative for the party members who ran them. The Soviet economy did get a boost from the OPEC oil price hikes of 1973 and 1979. (OPEC was founded in 1961; the Soviet Union did not belong, but as the world's largest producer of oil, it benefited from rising prices.) Without this boost, the situation would have been far grimmer.

Western governments struggled for effective reactions to the abrupt change in their economic circumstances. The new leader of the British Conservative party, Margaret Thatcher, was elected prime minister in 1979—and reelected in 1983 and 1987—on a program of curbing trade-union power, cutting taxes to stimulate the economy, and privatizing publicly owned enterprises. The economy remained weak, with close to 15 percent of the workforce unemployed by 1986. In West Germany, a series of Social Democratic governments attempted to combat economic recession with job-training programs and tax incentives, both financed by higher taxes. These programs did little to assist economic recovery, and the country shifted to the right.

The fact that governments of right and left were unable to recreate Europe's unprecedented postwar prosperity suggests the degree to which economic forces remained outside the control of individual states. The continuing economic malaise renewed efforts to Europeanize common problems. By the end of the 1980s, the EEC embarked on an ambitious program of integration. Long-term goals, agreed on when the EU (European Union) was formed in 1991, included a monetary union—with a central European bank and a single currency—and unified social policies to reduce poverty and unemployment.

Solidarity in Poland

In 1980, unrest again peaked in Eastern Europe, this time with the Polish labor movement Solidarity. Polish workers organized strikes that brought the government of the country to a standstill. The workers objected to laboring conditions, high prices, and especially shortages, all of which had roots in government policy. Above all, though, the Polish workers in Solidarity demanded truly independent labor unions instead of labor organizations sponsored by the government. Their belief that society had the right to organize itself and, by implication, to create its own government, stood at the core of the movement. The strikers were led by an electrician from the Gdansk shipyards, Lech Walesa, whose charismatic personality appealed not only to the Polish citizenry but to sympathizers in the West. Again, however, the Soviets assisted a military regime in reimposing authoritarian rule. The Polish president, General Wojciech Jaruzelski, had learned from Hungary and Czechoslovakia and played a delicate game of diplomacy to maintain the Polish government's freedom of action while repressing Solidarity itself. But the implied Soviet threat remained.

EUROPE RECAST: THE COLLAPSE OF COMMUNISM AND THE END OF THE SOVIET UNION

The sudden collapse of the Eastern European communist regimes in 1989 led to the dramatic end of the Cold War and the subsequent disintegration of the once-powerful Soviet Union.

Gorbachev and Soviet Reform

This collapse flowed, unintended, from a new wave of reform begun in the mid-1980s. In 1985 a new generation of officials began taking charge of the Soviet Communist party, a change heralded by Mikhail Gorbachev's appointment to the party leadership. In his mid-fifties, Gorbachev was significantly younger than his immediate predecessors and less subject to the habits of mind that had shaped Soviet domestic and foreign affairs. He was frankly critical of the repressive aspects of communist society as well as its sluggish economy, and he did not hesitate to voice those criticisms openly. His twin policies of *glasnost* (intellectual openness) and *perestroika* (economic restructuring) held out hope for a freer, more prosperous Soviet Union.

The policies of glasnost took aim at the privileges of the political elite and the immobility of the state bureaucracy by allowing greater freedom of speech, instituting competitive elections to official positions, and limiting terms of office. Gorbachev's program of perestroika called for a shift from the centrally planned economy instituted by Stalin to a mixed economy combining state planning with the operation of market forces. In agriculture, perestroika accelerated the move away from cooperative production and instituted incentives for the achievement of production targets. Gorbachev planned to integrate the Soviet Union into the international economy by participating in organizations such as the International Monetary Fund.

GORBACHEV IN POLAND AT THE HEIGHT OF HIS POWER IN 1986. His policy of perestroika undermined the privileges of the political elite and would eventually lead to his own fall from power.

Even these dramatic reforms, however, were too little too late. Ethnic unrest, a legacy of Russia's nineteenth-century imperialism, threatened to split the Soviet Union apart, while secession movements gathered steam in the Baltic republics and elsewhere. From 1988 onward, fighting between Armenians and Azerbaijanis over an ethnically Azerbaijani region located inside Armenia threatened to escalate into a border dispute with Iran. Only Soviet troops patrolling the border and Gorbachev's willingness to suppress a separatist revolt in Azerbaijan by force temporarily quelled the conflict.

Spurred on by these events in the Soviet Union, the countries of Eastern Europe began to agitate for independence from Moscow. Gorbachev encouraged open discussion—glasnost—not only in his own country but also in the satellite nations. He revoked the Brezhnev Doctrine's insistence on single-party socialist governments and made frequent and inspiring trips to the capitals of neighboring satellites.

Glasnost rekindled the flame of opposition in Poland, where Solidarity had been defeated but not destroyed by the government in 1981. In 1988 the union launched a new series of strikes. These disturbances culminated in an agreement between the government and Solidarity that legalized the union and promised open elections. The results, in June 1989, astonished the world: virtually all of the government's candidates lost; the Citizen's Committee, affiliated with Solidarity, won a sizable majority in the Polish parliament.

In Hungary and Czechoslovakia, events followed a similar course during 1988 and 1989. Janos Kadar, the Hungarian leader since the Soviet crackdown of 1956, resigned in the face of continuing demonstrations in May 1988 and was replaced by the reformist government of the Hungarian Socialist Workers' party. By the spring of 1989 the Hungarian regime had been purged of Communist party supporters. The government also began to dismantle its security fences along the Austrian border.

The Czechs, too, staged demonstrations against Soviet domination in late 1988. Brutal beatings of student demonstrators by the police in 1989 radicalized the nation's workers and provoked mass demonstrations. Civic Forum, an opposition coalition, called for the installation of a coalition government to include noncommunists, for free elections, and for the resignation of the country's communist leadership. It reinforced its demands with continuing mass demonstrations and threats of a general strike that resulted in the toppling of the old regime and the election of the playwright and Civic Forum leader Václav Havel as president.

Fall of the Berlin Wall

The most significant political change in Eastern Europe during the late 1980s was the collapse of communism in East Germany and the unification of East and West Germany. Although long considered the most prosperous of the Soviet satellite countries, East Germany suffered from severe economic stagnation and environmental degradation. Waves of East Germans registered their discontent with worsening conditions by massive illegal emigration to the West. This exodus combined with evidence of widespread official corruption to force the resignation of East Germany's long-time, hard-line premier, Erich Honecker. His successor, Egon Krenz, promised reforms, but he was nevertheless faced with continuing protests and continuing mass emigration.

On November 4, 1989, in a move that acknowledged its powerlessness to hold its citizens captive, the government opened its border with Czechoslovakia. This move effectively freed East Germans to travel to the West. In a matter of days, the Berlin Wall—the embodiment of the Cold War, the Iron Curtain, and the division of East from West—was demolished, first by groups of ordinary citizens and later by the East German government. Jubilant throngs from both sides walked through the gaping holes that now permitted men, women, and children to take the few steps that symbolized the return to freedom and a chance for national unity. Free elections were held throughout Germany in March 1990, resulting in a victory for the Alliance for Germany, a coalition allied with the West German chancellor Helmut Kohl's Christian Democratic Union. With heavy

U.S. PRESIDENT RONALD REAGAN AT BERLIN'S BRANDENBURG GATE, JUNE 12, 1987.

emigration continuing, reunification talks quickly culminated in the formal proclamation of a united Germany on October 3, 1990.

The public mood, in Eastern Europe and perhaps worldwide, was swept up with the jubilation of these peaceful "velvet revolutions" during the autumn of 1989. Yet the end of one-party rule in Eastern Europe was not accomplished without violence. The single most repressive government in the old Eastern bloc, Nicolae Ceaucescu's outright dictatorship in Romania, came apart with much more bloodshed. By December, faced with the wave of popular revolts in surrounding countries and riots by the ethnic Hungarian minority in Transylvania, a number of party officials and army officers in Romania tried to hold on to their own positions by deposing Ceaucescu. His extensive secret police, however, organized resistance to the coup; the result was nearly two weeks of bloody street fighting in the capital Bucharest. Ceaucescu himself and his wife were seized by populist army units and executed; images of their bloodstained bodies flashed worldwide by satellite television.

Throughout the rest of Eastern Europe, single-party governments in the countries behind what was left of the tattered Iron Curtain—Albania, Bulgaria, and Yugoslavia—collapsed in the face of democratic pressure for change. Meanwhile, in the Soviet Union itself, inspired by events in Eastern Europe, the Baltic republics of Lithuania and Latvia strained to free themselves from Soviet rule. In 1990 they unilaterally proclaimed their independence from the Soviet Union, throwing into sharp relief the tension between "union" and "republics." Gorbachev reacted with an uncertain mixture of armed intervention and promises of greater local autonomy. In the fall of 1991 Lithuania and Latvia, along with the third Baltic state of Estonia, won international recognition as independent republics.

The Collapse of the Soviet Union

While Soviet influence eroded in Eastern Europe, at home the unproductive Soviet economy continued to fuel widespread ire. With the failure of perestroika—largely the result of a lack of resources and an inability to increase production—came the rise of a powerful political rival to Gorbachev, his erstwhile ally Boris Yeltsin. The reforming mayor of Moscow, Yeltsin was elected president of the Russian Federation—the largest Soviet republic—on an anti-Gorbachev platform in 1990. Pressure from the Yeltsin camp weakened Gorbachev's ability to maneuver independent of reactionary factions in the Politburo and the military, undermining his reform program and his ability to remain in power.

The Soviet Union's increasingly severe domestic problems led to mounting protests in 1991, when Gorbachev's policies failed to improve—and indeed diminished—the living standards of the Soviet people. Demands increased that the bloated government bureaucracy respond with a dramatic cure for the country's continuing economic stagnation. Gorbachev appeared to lose his political nerve, having first ordered and then canceled a radical "five-hundred-day" economic reform plan, at the same time agreeing to negotiations with the increasingly disaffected republics within the union, now clamoring for independence. Sensing their political lives to be in jeopardy, a group of highly placed hard-line Communist party officials staged an abortive coup in August 1991. They made Gorbachev and his wife prisoners in their summer villa, then declared a return to party-line orthodoxy in an effort to salvage what remained of the Soviet Union's global leverage and the Communist party's domestic power. The Soviet citizenry, especially in large cities like Moscow and Leningrad, defied their self-proclaimed saviors. Led by Boris Yeltsin, who at one point mounted a tank in a Moscow street to rally the people, they gathered support among the Soviet republics and the military and successfully called the plotters' bluff. Within two weeks, Gorbachev was back in power and the coup leaders were in prison.

Ironically, this people's counterrevolution returned Gorbachev to office while destroying the power of the Soviet state he led. Throughout the fall of 1991, as Gorbachev struggled to hold the union together, Yeltsin joined the presidents of the other large republics to capitalize on the discontent. On December 8, 1991, the presidents of the republics of Russia, Ukraine, and Byelorussia (now called Belarus) declared that the Soviet Union was no more: "The USSR as a subject of international law and geopolitical reality is ceasing to exist." Though the prose was flat, the message was momentous. The once-mighty Soviet Union, founded seventy-five years before in a burst of revolutionary fervor and violence, had evaporated nearly overnight, leaving in its wake a collection of eleven far from powerful nations loosely joined together as the Commonwealth of Independent States. On December 25, 1991, Gorbachev resigned and left political life, not pushed from office in the usual way but made irrelevant as other actors dismantled the state. The Soviet flag—the hammer and sickle symbolizing the nation that for fifty years had kept half of Europe in thrall—was lowered for the last time over the Kremlin.

The dramatic collapse of the Soviet Union left enormous problems in its wake. Boris Yeltsin pleaded for and received economic assistance from the West, but the Russian economy was soon in severe crisis. The sudden establishment of a market economy caused a dramatic increase in unemployment and created opportunities for profiteering and corruption as state assets were sold off to a new class of oligarchs, many with ties to the former leadership. Conservative politicians allied with military officers attempted a coup against Yeltsin in September 1993, claiming that the reforms had gone too quickly. Yeltsin's administration shelled the rebel-held parliament building in response. The government's show of force succeeded, but Yeltsin faced discontented voters in the elections that followed. Meanwhile, ethnic and religious conflict plagued the former Soviet republics, with war breaking out in Georgia, Armenia, Azerbaijan, and Chechnya. The worst of these conflicts, in Chechnya, dragged on into the new century, a brutal war that overshadowed the optimism that many in Russia and the West had felt at the downfall of the Soviet regime.

The Iron Curtain had established one of the most rigid borders in European history. The collapse of the Soviet Union opened up both Russia and its former imperial dominions, bringing the Cold War to an end. It also created a host of unforeseen problems throughout Eastern Europe and the advanced industrial world: ethnic conflict, diplomatic uncertainty about both the new Russian government and single-superpower domination, sometimes called American unilateralism. Within the Russian and several of the other former Soviet republics there emerged a new era that some called the Russian "Wild West." Capitalist market relations began to develop without clearly defined property relations or a stable legal framework. Former government officials profited from their positions of power to take over whole sectors of the economy. Corruption ran rampant. Organized crime controlled entire industries, stock exchanges, a thriving trade in illegal drugs, and even some local governments. Even the most energetic central governments in the large republics such as Russia, Ukraine, and Kazakhstan found themselves faced with enormous problems. Post-Soviet openness could lay the groundwork for a new democratic Russia; it could also set in motion the resurgence of older forms of tyranny.

EASTERN EUROPE IN 1989. ■ *What political changes in the Soviet Union allowed for the spread of demonstrations throughout Eastern Europe?* ■ *Why did the first political upheavals of 1989 occur in Poland and East Germany?* ■ *In what countries were demonstrations the most widespread and why?*

Postrevolutionary Troubles: Eastern Europe after 1989

The velvet revolutions of Central and Eastern Europe raised high hopes: local hopes that an end to authoritarian government would produce economic prosperity and cultural pluralism, and Western hopes that these countries would join them as capitalist partners in an enlarged European Community. The reality has been slower and harder than the optimists of 1989 foresaw. The reunification of Germany

produced new and unexpected political challenges. The euphoria of reunification masked uncertainty even among Germans themselves. The foundering East German economy has remained a problem. Piled onto other economic difficulties in the former West Germany during the 1990s, it has produced much resentment of the need to "rescue" the east. What the writer Günter Grass described as the "wall in the mind" continued to divide the country after reunification.

Adapting to change has been difficult throughout Eastern Europe. Attempts to create free-market economies have brought inflation, unemployment, and—in their wake—anticapitalist demonstrations. Inefficient industries, a workforce resistant to change, energy shortages, lack of venture capital, and a severely polluted environment have combined to hinder progress and dash hopes. In addition, racial and ethnic conflicts have continued to divide newly liberated democracies, recalling the divisions that led to the First World War and that have plagued Eastern Europe throughout its history.

Czechoslovakia's Velvet Revolution collapsed into a velvet divorce, as Slovakia declared itself independent from the Czechs, forcing Havel's resignation and slowing down the promising cultural and economic reforms begun in 1989. Poland enjoyed an upswing in its economy during the 1990s, after many years of hardship, but most of the rest of Eastern Europe continues to find transformation rough going. These difficulties have been accompanied by revived ethnic tensions formerly suppressed by centralized communist governments. There has been violence against non-European immigrants throughout Eastern Europe, against gypsies (Romani) in the Czech Republic and Hungary, and against ethnic Hungarians in Romania.

The most extreme example of these conflicts came with the implosion of the state of Yugoslavia. After the death of Tito in 1980, the government that had held Yugoslavia's federalist ethnic patchwork together came undone. A number of Serb politicians, most notably Slobodan Milosevic, who became the president of Yugoslavia's Serbian Republic

RUSSIA AND EASTERN EUROPE AFTER THE COLD WAR. Examine closely the geography of southeastern and central Europe. ■ *How were political boundaries reorganized?* ■ *How did the collapse of the Soviet Union and the end of the Cold War allow for the reemergence of certain forces in the political landscape of Europe?* ■ *How were the boundaries of the Soviet Union reorganized after 1991?*

in 1989, began to redirect Serbs' frustration with economic hardship toward subjects of national pride and sovereignty.

Nationalism, particularly Serb and Croat nationalism, had long dogged Yugoslavia's firmly federal political system. Feelings ran especially deep among Serbs. Serbian national myths reach back to the Middle Ages, and the country also has more recent traditions of political separatism on ethnic grounds. Milosevic and the Serb nationalists who gathered around him ignited those political sensibilities in ways that capitalized on the fears and frustrations of his times. More important for Milosevic, Serbian nationalism catapulted him into crucial positions of authority in which he alienated officials from the non-Serb republics. Inspired by the peaceful transformations of 1989, representatives of the small province of Slovenia declared they had been denied adequate representation and economic support inside the republic. In 1991, on a tide of Slovenian nationalism and reform, the Slovenes seceded from Yugoslavia. After a brief attempt to hold the union together by force, the Yugoslav government relented and let Slovenia claim its independence. Ethnic nationalists in the other republics followed suit. A much deeper, bloodier process of disintegration had begun.

The large republic of Croatia, once part of the Habsburg Empire and briefly an independent state allied with the Nazis during the Second World War, cited injustices by Serb officials in the Yugoslav government and declared indepen-

dence as a free, capitalist state. War broke out between federal Yugoslav forces and the well-armed militias of independent Croatia, a conflict that ended in arbitration by the United Nations.

The next conflict came in the same place that in 1914 had sparked a much larger war: the province of Bosnia-Herzegovina. Bosnia was the most ethnically diverse republic in Yugoslavia with a large population of Muslims, a legacy of the Ottoman Empire. Its capital, Sarajevo, was home to several major ethnic groups and had often been praised as an example of peaceful coexistence. When Bosnia seceded from Yugoslavia in 1992, ethnic coexistence came apart. Bosnia began the war with no formal army: armed bands equipped by the governments of Serbian Yugoslavia, Croatia, and Bosnia battled each other throughout the new country. The Serbs and Croats, both of whom disliked the Muslim Bosnians, were especially well equipped and organized. All sides committed atrocities. The Serbs, however, orchestrated and carried out the worst crimes, including what came to be called ethnic cleansing. This involved sending irregular troops on campaigns of murder and terror through Muslim or Croat territories to encourage much larger populations to flee the area. During the first eighteen months of the fighting as many as a hundred thousand people were

MASS FUNERAL IN KOSOVO, 1999. Ethnic Albanians bury victims of a Serbian massacre toward the end of Yugoslavia's ten years of fighting. ■ *Although the nature of war has changed radically in the last hundred years, "ethnic cleansing" has remained remarkably constant and frequent in the modern period. What prevents states from taking effective action to prevent it?*

Representing the People in Eastern Europe, 1989

The enthusiasm of the mass demonstrations that preceded the revolutionary changes in Eastern Europe in 1989 gave the events a sense of immediate drama, and images of Eastern Europeans massed together in protest, crossing boundaries that had been closed to them, and celebrating the downfall of their repressive governments spread quickly around the world. The symbolism of these images was stark and resonated with a triumphant story about the progress of democratic ideals in an increasingly unified and integrated Europe. In the East, the people's desire to join with the West, long denied, had finally been realized.

The unity of these early days nevertheless obscured a basic uncertainty about the aspirations of the populations of the newly independent nations in Eastern Europe. Many East Germans expressed reservations about the rapid pace of German reunification, and people from the West and the East continued to talk about "the wall in the mind" long after the Berlin wall had been torn down. The unity of Czechoslovakia's peaceful Velvet Revolution in 1989 led quickly to the "velvet divorce" that produced the

dissolution of Czechoslovakia into the Czech Republic and Slovakia in 1993. Throughout the region, many commentators continued to speak of a persistent *Ostalgia*—a nostalgia for an alternative Eastern European past that had been lost in the abrupt transition.

We have seen in earlier chapters how representations of the people served to give meaning to moments of rapid social and political change in the French Revolution or in the unification of Germany (see **Interpreting Visual Evidence** in Chapter 18, page 440 and Chapter 21, page 510). The images here, from media coverage of the events of 1989, also serve to frame the interpretations that contemporaries gave to the unfolding events. Image A shows a crowd in Prague waving the Czechoslovakian flag in November 1989. Image B shows a line of East Berliners forming in front of a West Berlin grocery store in the days after the fall of the Berlin Wall. Image C shows the last of the Leipzig Monday demonstrations on March 12, 1990—the caption reads, "Also after the last demon-

A. Crowd during Czechoslovakia's Velvet Revolution.

killed, including eighty thousand civilians, mostly Bosnian Muslims. Although the campaigns appalled Western governments, those countries worried that intervention would result only in another Vietnam or Afghanistan, with no clear resolution of the horrific ethnic slaughter itself. The outside forces, mostly European troops in United Nations blue helmets, concentrated on humanitarian relief, separating combatants, and creating safe areas for persecuted ethnic populations from all parties.

The crisis came to a head in the autumn of 1995. Sarajevo had been under siege for three years, but a series of mortar attacks on public marketplaces in Sarajevo produced fresh Western outrage and moved the United States to act. Already Croat forces and the Bosnian army

B. East Berliners line up to shop in West Berlin, November 12, 1989.

C. "We are the people. We are one people."

stration: We are the People. *We are one people.*" "We are the people" was the slogan of the weekly demonstrations in Leipzig in 1989 that did so much to discredit the government in the months before the wall fell. "We are one people" became the slogan of Helmut Kohl's government as it pushed for rapid reunification of the two Germanies.

Questions for Analysis

1. In image A, how should one interpret the wave of nationalist enthusiasm that engulfed Czechoslovakia in 1989, in light of what we know of the subsequent failure to keep Czechoslovakia together as a unified nation?

2. Photographs such as image B were extremely common in the media in 1989, showing East Berliners shopping in Western stores. What do such images suggest about how the East's previous isolation was interpreted in the West, and what does it say about how both sides may have viewed the consequences of their newfound freedom?

3. What is the difference between "We are the people" and "We are one people" as political slogans?

had turned the war on the ground against the Serb militias, and now they were supported by a rolling wave of American air strikes. The American bombing, combined with a Croat-Bosnian offensive, forced the Bosnian Serbs to negotiate. Elite French troops supported by British artillery broke the siege of Sarajevo. Peace talks were held at Dayton, Ohio. The agreement divided Bosnia, with the majority of land in the hands of Muslims and Croats, and a small, autonomous "Serb Republic" in areas that included land ethnically cleansed in 1992. Stability was restored, but three years of war had killed over two hundred thousand people.

The legacy of Bosnia flared into conflict again regarding Kosovo, the medieval homeland of the Orthodox Christian

Serbs, now occupied by a largely Albanian, Muslim population. Milosevic accused the Albanians of plotting secession and of challenging the Serb presence in Kosovo. In the name of a "greater Serbia," Serb soldiers fought Albanian separatists rallying under the banner of "greater Albania." Both sides used terrorist tactics. Western nations were anxious lest the conflict might spread to the strategic, ethnically divided country of Macedonia and touch off a general Balkan conflict. Western political opinion was outraged, however, as Serbian forces used many of the same murderous tactics in Kosovo that they had employed earlier in Bosnia.

Finally, Serb-dominated Yugoslavia, worn by ten years of war and economic sanctions, turned against Milosevic's regime. Wars and corruption had destroyed Milosevic's credentials as a nationalist and populist. After he attempted to reject the results of a democratic election in 2000, his government fell to popular protests. He died in 2006, while being tried by a UN tribunal for war crimes.

As we gain perspective on the twentieth century, it is clear that the Yugoslavian wars of the 1990s were not an isolated instance of Balkan violence. The issues are thoroughly Western. The Balkans form one of the West's borderlands, where cultures influenced by Roman Catholicism, Eastern Orthodoxy, and Islam meet, overlap, and contend for political domination and influence. Since the nineteenth century, this region of enormous religious, cultural, and ethnic diversity has struggled with the implications of nationalism. We have seen how conflicts over the creation of new national states drawn mostly on ethnic lines were worked out in Central Europe, with many instances of tragic violence. The Yugoslav wars fit into some of the same patterns.

CONCLUSION

The protest movements of the 1960s and 1970s revealed that postwar hopes for stability in Western Europe through economic development alone were shortsighted, and in any case, the astounding rates of growth from 1945 to 1968 could not be sustained forever. The great success of these first postwar decades was the establishment of the European Common Market and the spirit of cooperation

After You Read This Chapter

Ⓢ Visit StudySpace for quizzes, additional review materials, and multi-media documents. **wwnorton.com/studyspace**

REVIEWING THE OBJECTIVES

- The success of economic rebuilding after the Second World War produced a new prosperity in Western Europe. What contributed to this success, and what were its effects on daily life and mass culture in Europe?

- The postwar decades witnessed an important shift in attitudes about women and their place in society. What caused this shift and what were its consequences for European women?

- In Europe and the United States, significant movements of social and political protest emerged in the 1960s. What were the goals of these movements and what did they accomplish?

- The postwar economic boom ended in the 1970s, leading to a prolonged period of economic contraction. What were the consequences of this recession for governments and populations in Europe?

- In the 1980s Mikhail Gorbachev proposed reforms for the Soviet Union that failed to prevent the collapse of the Soviet bloc in Eastern Europe. What combination of events led to this collapse?

- The first post-Soviet decade in Europe was marked by political uncertainty, economic dislocation, and violence, with war in Yugoslavia and Chechnya. What circumstances made these years so difficult for Europeans?

between Western European nations that had only a few years before had been locked in deadly conflict.

The Eastern European revolutions of 1989 and the subsequent collapse of the Soviet Union were a revolutionary turning point, however, and posed challenging questions to those who sought to guarantee stability by continuing down the path of further integration between European nations. Like the French Revolution of 1789, the 1989 revolutions brought down not only a regime but also an empire. Like the French Revolution, they gave way to violence, and like the French Revolution, they provided no easy consensus for the peoples who were left to reconstruct some form of political and social stability in their wake. In the former Yugoslavia, in Slovakia, and in Russia itself, the uncertainty of the post-1989 years gave fresh impetus to energetic nationalist movements. Although militant nationalism might be a useful short-term political strategy for certain politicians, such nationalism is unlikely to create stability in Europe, however, because the broad population movements of the postwar years—from east to west and from south to north—have continued unabated, and there is no part of Europe that possesses the ethnic or cultural homogeneity demanded by hard-line nationalists. Europe's long history is one of heterogeneity, and there is no reason to think that the future will be different in this respect.

Profound differences in wealth and economic capacity between Western and Eastern Europe were the most challenging hurdle to a stable integration of the newly independent nations of the post-Soviet empire. In the 1980s it was possible to imagine that a relatively wealthy country like the Netherlands or Belgium might be willing to subsidize the integration of a less wealthy small country like Portugal into Europe. It has proved quite another task to convince the Dutch, the Belgians, or the Danes to help shoulder the burden for bringing large countries like Ukraine or Turkey into the European fold. Given this difficulty, can one say with confidence where Europe's outermost borders now lie? In the broader context of the global conflicts that emerged in the aftermath of the Cold War, Europe's boundaries and future remain both uncertain and linked to developments elsewhere in the world. This broader context and these global linkages are the subject of the last chapter of this book.

PEOPLE, IDEAS, AND EVENTS IN CONTEXT

- How did the wide availability of the **BIRTH CONTROL PILL** change public attitudes toward sex and sexuality in the 1960s?

- What made the **MASS CULTURE** of the postwar decades different from popular culture in previous historical eras?

- How did the struggles of the **CIVIL RIGHTS MOVEMENT** in the United States affect American efforts to promote democracy in Europe during the Cold War?

- What circumstances made **UNIVERSITIES** in particular the center of international protest movements in **1968**? How did the **STUDENTS' REVOLT** in Western Europe or the United States become connected to larger movements for political change?

- What were the goals of **ALEXANDER DUBČEK'S** government in Czechoslovakia during the **PRAGUE SPRING**?

- How did the **1973 OPEC OIL EMBARGO** affect the economies of Eastern and Western Europe?

- How did **LECH WALESA** challenge the Polish government in the early 1980s?

- How did **MIKHAIL GORBACHEV** envision reforming the Soviet Union? What did he mean by **PERESTROIKA** and **GLASNOST**?

- What were the **VELVET REVOLUTIONS** of Central and Eastern Europe in 1989?

- What made **NATIONALISM** such a powerful force in Yugoslavia in the early 1990s, and what role did **SLOBODAN MILOSEVIC** play in the breakup of the Yugoslavian federation?

CONSEQUENCES

- How did the relatively prosperous decades after the Second World War in Europe give way so suddenly to protest and political alienation in the 1960s and 1970s?

- Did the Cold War contribute to stability in Europe between 1945 and 1989?

- Why did some parts of Eastern Europe collapse into violence after 1989, while others managed to make the transition to the post–Cold War world more peacefully?

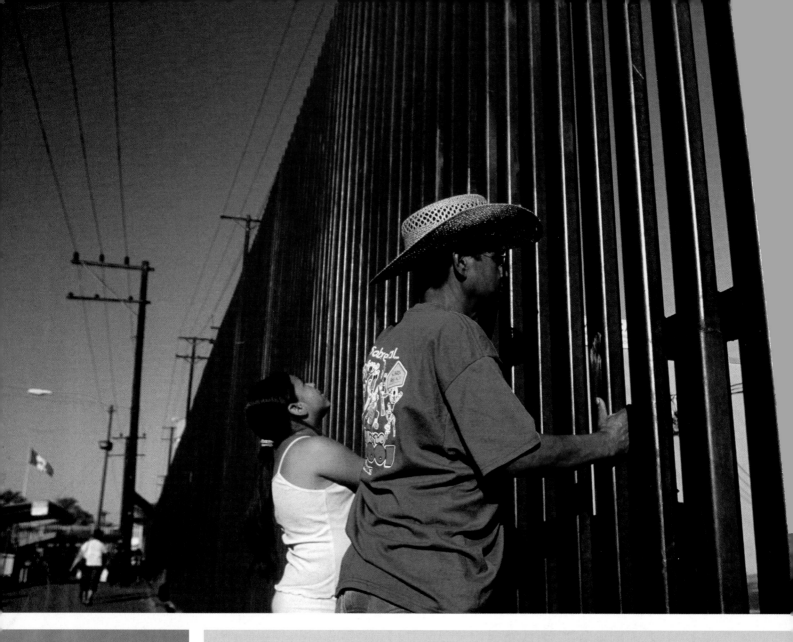

STORY LINES

- After 1989, the trend toward globalization in the twentieth century became more visible. Improved communications and flows of money and products from one part of the world to another offered many opportunities for economic growth, but also reinforced existing inequalities between the world's different regions.

- The legacy of colonialism weighed heavily on former colonies, and some became the arena for conflicts related to the Cold War, such as the end of apartheid in South Africa, civil war and ethnic conflict in Rwanda and Zaire, and postwar economic development in Japan and South Korea.

- In the second half of the twentieth century, events in the Middle East took on global significance. The Arab-Israeli conflict, bitterness against foreign interventions in Muslim countries, and frustration with the first generation of nationalist governments in the region led to the development of modern forms of Islamic radicalism aiming at revolutionary change in the Middle East and confrontation with the West.

CHRONOLOGY

1948	State of Israel formed
1948–1949	First Arab-Israeli War
1960	Formation of OPEC
1967	Six-Day War, Israel occupies West Bank
1973	Second Arab-Israeli War
1973	Arab members of OPEC announce oil embargo
1978	Camp David Peace Accords
1979	Soviet invasion of Afghanistan
1979	Islamic revolution in Iran
1980–1988	Iran-Iraq War
1991	Persian Gulf War
1994	Genocide against Tutsis in Rwanda
1997	China reclaims Hong Kong
2001	9/11 terrorist attacks
2001	U.S. action against al Qaeda and Taliban in Afghanistan
2003	U.S. invasion of Iraq

Before
You
Read
This
Chapter

A World without Walls: Globalization and the West

CORE OBJECTIVES

- **DEFINE** *globalization* and understand what is new about current patterns of interconnection in the world as well as the continuities that can be seen with earlier periods of global interconnection.

- **EXPLAIN** the continued relevance of the colonial past in shaping the politics, economies, and societies of independent states in Asia and Africa, and the nature of their ongoing relationships to the societies and states of Europe and North America.

- **UNDERSTAND** the global connections that link societies in other parts of the world to the events and persistent conflicts in the Middle East.

n the twenty-first century, the world has reentered a period in which basic assumptions about the role of nation-states, the roots of prosperity, and the boundaries of cultures are changing fast. The Industrial Revolution of the nineteenth century is an example of an earlier period that also witnessed comparable changes in the relations between global regions. Globalization is not new, therefore, but the speed with which these changes have taken place since the end of the Cold War has contributed to a sense that we have entered a new era of global transformation.

We know, intuitively, what globalization means: the Internet, protests against the World Trade Organization (WTO), outsourcing of jobs and services, Walmart in Mexico, the dismantling of the Berlin wall. All of these are powerful images of larger and enormously significant developments. The Internet represents the stunning transformation of global communication, the media, and forms of knowledge. The Berlin wall once stood for a divided Cold War world; its fall marked a dramatic reconfiguration of international relations, an end to the ideological battle over communism, the creation of new alliances, markets, and communities. The attack on the World

Trade Center in 2001 gave the term *globalization* a new and frightening meaning as well. It shattered many Americans' sense of relative isolation and security. Globalization, then, conjures up new possibilities but also new vulnerabilities.

What, precisely, does the term mean? What causes or drives globalization, and what are its effects? To begin simply, globalization means integration. It is the process of creating a rising number of networks—political, social, economic, and cultural—that span larger sections of the globe. Information, ideas, goods, and people now move rapidly and easily across national boundaries. Yet *globalization* is not synonymous with *internationalization*, and the distinction is important. International relations are established between nation-states. Global exchange can be quite independent of national control: today trade, politics, and cultural exchange often happen "underneath the radar of the nation-state," in the words of one historian.

Globalization has radically altered the distribution of industry and patterns of trade around the world. Supranational economic institutions such as the International Monetary Fund are examples of globalization and also work to quicken its pace. Likewise, the International Criminal Court represents an important trend in law: the globalization of judicial power. New, rapid, and surprisingly intimate forms of mass communication (blogs, social media sites, Internet-based political campaigns, and so on) have spawned new forms of politics. Perhaps most interesting, the sovereignty of nation-states and the clear boundaries of national communities seem to be eroded by many globalizing trends.

All these developments seem to be characteristic of our time. But are they new? For centuries, religion, empire, commerce, and industry have had globalizing impulses and effects. The East India Companies (Dutch and English), for instance, were to the seventeenth century what Microsoft is to the early twenty-first: the premier global enterprises of the time. The economic development of Europe in general was thoroughly enmeshed in global networks that supplied raw materials, markets, and labor. It has always been hard to strip the "West" of its global dimensions.

For another striking example, consider migration and immigration. We think of the contemporary world as fluid, characterized by vast movements of people. Mass, long-distance migration and immigration, however, peaked during the nineteenth century. Between 1846 (when the first reliable statistics were kept) and 1940, fifty-five to fifty-eight million people left Europe for the Americas, especially for the United States, Canada, Argentina, and Brazil. During that same period, forty-eight to fifty-two million Indians and southern Chinese migrated to Southeast Asia, the Southern Pacific, and the areas surrounding the Indian Ocean (many of the Indian migrants going to other parts of the British Empire). Roughly another fifty million people left northeastern Asia and Russia for Manchuria, Siberia, central Asia, and Japan. Faster long-distance transportation (railways and steamships) made these long journeys possible; the industrialization of the receiving regions provided the economic dynamics. The demographic, social, economic, and cultural effects of these migrations were transformative. After the First World War, governments set out to close their gates; from the 1920s on, laborers (and refugees) found it much harder to move. If migration is a measure of globalization, our world is less "globalized" than it was a century ago.

What is more, to equate globalization with integration may be misleading. Globalizing trends do not necessarily produce peace, equality, or homogeneity. Their effects are hard to predict. During the early 1900s many Europeans firmly believed that the world, at least the part of the world dominated by Western empires, would become harmonious, that Western culture would be exported, and that Western standards would become universal. History defied those expectations. Some scholars argue that the term *globalization* should be jettisoned because it suggests a uniform, leveling process, one that operates similarly everywhere. Globalization has very different and very disparate effects, effects shaped by vast asymmetries of power and wealth among nations or regions. In the last several decades, worldwide inequality has increased. Global processes encounter obstacles and resistance; they sow division as well as unity.

In this chapter we explore three subjects crucial to our early efforts to understand globalization, especially as it relates to the post–Cold War world of the twenty-first century. The first subject is the set of global changes that have accelerated the free flow of money, people, products, and ideas. The second subject is what we have come to call postcolonial politics—the varied trajectories that mark the contemporary experience of former colonies. Finally, we will consider in greater depth the complex and important role of Middle Eastern politics in contemporary global affairs. Throughout, we hope to suggest ways in which recent developments relate to familiar historical issues we have already examined in other contexts.

LIQUID MODERNITY? THE FLOW OF MONEY, IDEAS, AND PEOPLES

A key feature of late-twentieth-century globalization has been the transformation of the world economy, highlighted by the rapid integration of markets since 1970. In a series of historic changes, the international agreements that had regulated the movement of people, goods, and money since the Second World War were overturned. To begin with, the postwar eco-

"CHECKERBOARD OF POVERTY AND AFFLUENCE." Scenes of slums confronting towering skylines, such as this one from Argentina in 2000, are visible around the world as one of the side effects of development.

nomic arrangements sealed at Bretton Woods (see Chapter 27) steadily eroded in the late 1960s, as Western industrial nations faced a double burden of inflation and economic stagnation. A crucial shift in monetary policy occurred in 1971, when the United States abandoned the postwar gold standard and allowed the dollar—the keystone of the system—to range freely. As a result, formal regulations on currencies, international banking, and lending among states faded away. They were replaced with an informal network of arrangements managed autonomously by large private lenders, their political friends in leading Western states, and independent financial agencies such as the International Monetary Fund and the World Bank. The economists and administrators who dominated these new networks steered away from the interventionist policies that shaped postwar planning and recovery. Instead they relied on a broad range of market-driven models dubbed "neoliberalism." In a variation on classic liberal economics, neoliberal economists stressed the value of free markets, profit incentives, and sharp restraints on both budget deficits and social welfare programs, whether run by governments or corporations. The new systems of lending they backed had mixed results, funding breakneck growth in some cases and bringing catastrophic debt in others. Industrial development in the globalized economy has created jarring juxtapositions of development and deterioration across entire continents and even within single cities—a phenomenon described as a "checkerboard of poverty and affluence."

At the same time, the world's local, national, and regional economies became far more connected and interdependent. Export trade flourished and, with the technological advances of the 1960s and 1980s, came to include an increasing proportion of high-technology goods. The boom in export commerce was tied to important changes in the division of labor worldwide. More industrial jobs were created in the postcolonial world, not just among the Asian "tigers" but also in India, Latin America, and else-

where. Although such steady, skilled manual employment started to disappear in Western nations—often replaced by lower-paying menial work—financial and service sector employment leaped ahead. The exchange and use of goods became much more complex. Goods were designed by companies in one country, manufactured in another, and tied into a broader interchange of cultures. Taken together, these global economic changes had deep political effects, forcing painful debates about the nature of citizenship and entitlement inside national borders, about the power and accountability of transnational corporations, and about the human and environmental costs of global capitalism.

Another crucial change involved not only the widespread flow of information but also the new commercial and cultural importance attached to information itself. Electronic systems and devices designed to create, store, and share information multiplied, becoming staggeringly more powerful and accessible—none with so great an impact on the everyday lives of men and women around the world as the personal computer. By the early 1990s increasingly sophisticated computers brought people into instant communication with each other across continents, not only by new means but also in new cultural and political settings. Electronic communications over the Internet gave a compelling new meaning to the term *global village,* Marshall McLuhan's term for the new global audience for mass media in the 1960s. The Internet revolution shared features of earlier print revolutions. It was pioneered by entrepreneurs with utopian ambitions and driven by the new network's ability to deliver personal or commercial messages as well as culturally illicit and politically scandalous material that could be published easily and informally. It offered new possibilities to social and political groups, constituting new "publics." And it attracted large, established corporate interests, eager to cash in on new channels of culture and business.

However common their use seems, the Internet and similar technologies have had wide-ranging effects on political struggles around the globe. Embattled ethnic minorities have found worldwide audiences through online campaign sites. Satellite television arguably sped the sequence of popular revolts in Eastern Europe in 1989. That same year, fax machines brought Chinese demonstrators at Tiananmen Square news of international support for their efforts. More recently, Facebook and Twitter allowed Egyptians to express their unhappiness with Hosni Mubarak in early 2011, ultimately leading to his resignation as the president of Egypt. Meanwhile, leaps forward in electronic technologies provided new worldwide platforms for commercial interests. Companies such as Sony and RCA produced entertainment content, including music, motion pictures, and television shows, as well as the electronic equipment to play that content. Bill Gates's

AN AFGHAN GIRL WEEDS A POPPY FIELD, 2004. Though Afghanistan was historically a center for the silk trade, opium (derived from poppies) is its most important cash crop today.
■ *How is this development related to globalization?*

Microsoft emerged as the world's major producer of computer software—with corporate profits that surpassed Spain's gross domestic product. At the level of production, marketing, and management, information industries are global, spread widely across the United States, India, Western Europe, and parts of the developing world. Their corporate headquarters, however, typically remain in the West and support neoliberal politics. The international media, news, and entertainment conglomerates run by the Australian Rupert Murdoch or by Time Warner, for example, are firmly allied to U.S. institutions and worldviews, edging aside state-run companies.

Like the movement of money, goods, and ideas, the flow of labor has become a central aspect of globalization. Since 1945, the widespread migration of peoples, particularly between former colonies and imperial powers, has changed everyday life around the world. Groups of immigrant workers have filled the lower rungs of expanding economies not only in Europe but also in oil-rich Arab states that have attracted Asian and Filipino laborers and in the United States, where both permanent and seasonal migrations from Mexico and other Latin American nations have spread across the continent. This fusion of peoples and cultures has produced striking new blends of music, food, language, and other forms of popular culture and sociability. It has also raised tensions over the definition of citizenship and the boundaries of political and cultural communities—familiar themes from modern history. As a result, cycles of violent xenophobic backlash, bigotry, and political extremism have appeared in host countries and regions, but so too have new conceptions of civil rights and cultural belonging.

As suggested earlier, sharp divides exist between the most successful global players and the poorer, disadvan-taged, sometimes embattled states and cultures. In one particular area of manufacture, however, poorer postcolonial regions have been able to respond to a steady and immensely profitable market in the West. The production of illegal drugs such as opium, heroin, and cocaine is a thriving industry in countries such as Colombia, Myanmar (formerly Burma), and Malaysia. Though the trade in such substances is banned, the fragile economies of the countries where they are produced have encouraged public and private powers to turn a blind eye to their production—or even to intervene for their own profit. Other, similar forms of illegal commerce have also grown far beyond the old label of "organized crime" in their structure and political importance. Trafficking in illegal immigrants, the management of corrupt financial dealings, trade in illicit animal products, and "conflict" diamonds from several brutal postcolonial civil wars are all indicative of this trend. The organizations behind these criminal trades grew out of the political violence and economic breakdown of failing postcolonial states or from the human and commercial traffic between these parts of the world and leading Western economic powers. They have exploited cracks, loopholes, and unsupervised opportunities in the less regulated system of global trade and carved out centers of power not directly subject to the laws of any single state.

Demographics and Global Health

The developments of globalization are tied in complex ways to the evolving size and health of the world's population. Between 1800 and the middle of the twentieth century, the worldwide population roughly tripled, rising from one to three billion. Between 1960 and 2010, however, the growth rate soared and population more than doubled again, to almost seven billion. Huge, if uneven, improvements in basic standards of health, particularly for young children and childbearing women, contributed to the increase—as did local efforts to improve the urban-industrial environment. Asia's population as a whole has increased nearly fourfold since 1900. Such growth has strained underdeveloped social services, public-health facilities, and urban infrastructures, increasing the potential for epidemic disease as well as for cycles of ethnic and ideological violence nursed by poverty and dislocation.

A different type of demographic crisis confronts parts of the West, where steadily shrinking populations erode social welfare systems. Longer life spans, broadened welfare programs, and rising health-care costs have contributed to the challenge. Populations in the United States and Great Britain have been stable or have been slowly expanded by immigration; in Italy, Scandinavia, and, recently, Russia, sharp drops in the birthrate have led to population decline. Declining

GOVERNMENT EFFORTS TO CURTAIL THE SPREAD OF SEVERE ACUTE RESPIRATORY SYNDROME (SARS). In May 2003, migrant workers at a Beijing railway station line up to have their temperatures checked before boarding the trains.

AFTER EMPIRE: POSTCOLONIAL POLITICS IN THE GLOBAL ERA

Even after the superpower rivalry of the Cold War collapsed, another legacy of the postwar era continued to shape international relations into the twenty-first century. The so-called postcolonial relationships between former colonies and Western powers emerged from the decolonization struggles detailed in Chapter 27. Former colonies, as well as other nations that had fallen under the political and economic sway of imperial powers, gained formal independence at the least, along with new kinds of cultural and political authority. In other respects, however, very little changed for people in the former colonies. In some cases the former colonizers or their local allies retained so much power that formal independence actually meant very little, leading some to speak of a "neo-colonialism." In others, bloody independence struggles poisoned the political culture. The emergence of new states and new kinds of politics was sometimes propelled by economic goals, sometimes by the revival of cultural identities that preceded colonization, and in other cases by ethnic conflict. The results ranged from breakneck industrial success to ethnic slaughter, from democratization to new local models of absolutism. During the Cold War, these postcolonial regions were often the turf on which the superpower struggle was waged. They benefited from superpower patronage but also became the staging ground for proxy wars funded by the West in the fight against communism. Their various trajectories since 1989 point to the complex legacy of the imperial past in the post–Cold War world of globalization.

Emancipation and Ethnic Conflict in Africa

The legacies of colonialism have weighed heavily on sub-Saharan Africa. Most of the continent's former colonies came into their independence after the Second World War with their basic infrastructures deteriorating after decades of imperial negligence (see map on page 666 in Chapter 27). The Cold War decades brought scant improvement, as governments across the continent were plagued by both homegrown and externally imposed corruption, poverty, and civil war. In sub-Saharan Africa, two very different trends began to emerge around 1989, each shaped by a combination of the end of the Cold War and volatile local conditions.

The first trend can be seen in South Africa, where politics had revolved for decades around the brutal racial

birthrates have been accompanied by growing populations of older adults, whose health and vitality resulted from decades of improved medical standards and state-run entitlement programs. Maintaining the long-term solvency of such programs poses difficult choices for European countries in particular, as they struggle to balance guarantees of social well-being with fiscal and political realities.

Globalization has also changed public health and medicine, creating dangerous new threats as well as promising new treatments. Better and more comprehensive health care has generally accompanied other kinds of prosperity and has thus been more accessible in the West. In Africa, Latin America, and elsewhere, political chaos, imbalances of trade, and the practices of some large pharmaceutical companies have often resulted in shortages of medicine and a rickety medical infrastructure, making it difficult to combat deadly new waves of disease. Indeed, the worldwide risk of exposure to epidemic diseases is a new reality of globalization—a product of increased cultural interaction, exposure of new ecosystems to human development, and the speed of intercontinental transportation. By the 1970s the acceleration of airplane travel led to fears that an epidemic would leapfrog the globe much faster than the pandemics of the Middle Ages. Such fears were confirmed by the worldwide spread of infection by the human immunodeficiency virus (HIV), whose final stage is acquired immunodeficiency syndrome (AIDS), which first appeared at the end of the 1970s. As HIV-AIDS became a global health crisis—particularly in Africa, where the disease spread catastrophically—international organizations recognized the need for an early, swift, and comprehensive response to future outbreaks of disease, as evidenced by the successful global containment of severe acute respiratory syndrome (SARS) in 2003.

NELSON MANDELA VOTES IN SOUTH AFRICA'S FIRST FULLY DEMO-CRATIC ELECTIONS, 1994. He would be elected the country's president.

policies of apartheid, sponsored by the white minority government. The most prominent opponent of apartheid, Nelson Mandela, who led the African National Congress (ANC), had been imprisoned since 1962. Intense repression and violent conflict continued into the 1980s and reached a dangerous impasse by the end of the decade. Then the South African government chose a daring new tack: in early 1990 it released Mandela from prison. He resumed active leadership of the ANC and turned the party toward a combination of renewed public demonstrations and plans for negotiation. Politics changed within the Afrikaner-dominated white regime as well when F. W. de Klerk succeeded P. W. Botha as prime minister. A pragmatist who feared civil war and national collapse over apartheid, de Klerk was well matched to Mandela. In March 1992 the two men began direct talks to establish majority rule. Legal and constitutional reforms followed, and in May 1994, during elections in which all South Africans took part, Nelson Mandela was chosen the country's first black president. Although many of his government's efforts to reform housing, the economy, and public health foundered, Mandela defused the climate of organized racial violence. He also gained and kept tremendous personal popularity among black and white South Africans alike as a living symbol of a new political culture. Mandela's popularity extended abroad, within sub-Saharan Africa and worldwide. In a number of smaller postcolonial states such as Benin, Malawi, and Mozambique, the early 1990s brought political reforms that ended one-party or one-man rule in favor of parliamentary democracy and economic reform.

The other major trend ran in a different, less encouraging direction. Even as some former autocracies gave way to calls for pluralism, other states across the continent collapsed into ruthless ethnic conflict. In Rwanda, a former Belgian colony, conflicts between the Hutu and Tutsi populations erupted into a highly organized campaign of genocide against the Tutsi after the country's president was assassinated. Carried out by ordinary Hutus of all backgrounds, the ethnic slaughter left over eight hundred thousand Tutsi dead in a matter of weeks. International pressure eventually turned local Rwandan politics against the perpetrators. Many of them fled to neighboring Zaire and became hired mercenaries in the many-sided civil war that followed the overthrow of Mobutu Sese Seko, the country's long-time dictator, infamous for diverting billions of dollars in foreign aid into his personal bank accounts. A number of ambitious neighboring countries intervened in Zaire, hoping not only to secure its valuable resources but also to settle conflicts with their own ethnic minorities that spilled over the border. Fighting continued through the late 1990s into the new century, dubbed "Africa's world war" by many observers. Public services, normal trade, even basic health and safety inside Zaire—renamed the Democratic Republic of Congo by an ineffective government in Kinshasa—collapsed. With a death toll that reached into the millions from combat, massacre, and disease, the fighting remained unresolved in the next decade.

Economic Power on the Pacific Rim

By the end of the twentieth century, East Asia had become a center of industrial and manufacturing production. China, whose communist government began to establish commercial ties with the West in the 1970s, had become the world's leading heavy industrial producer by the year 2000. Its state-owned companies acquired contracts from Western firms to produce products cheaply and in bulk, for sale back to home markets in the United States and Europe. In a deliberate reversal of Europe's nineteenth-century intrusions on the China trade, Beijing established semicapitalist commercial zones around major port cities like Shanghai, a policy whose centerpiece was the transfer of sovereignty over Hong Kong from Britain to China in 1997. The commercial zones were intended to encourage massive foreign investment on terms that left China a favorable balance of trade for its huge volume of cheap exports.

Other Asian nations emerged as global commercial powers as well. Industry flourished in a string of countries, starting with Japan and extending along Asia's Pacific coastline into Southeast Asia and Oceania, during the decades after the Second World War. By the 1980s their robust industrial expansion and their apparent staying power earned them the collective nickname of "the Asian tigers," taken from the ambitious, forward-looking tiger in Chinese mythology. These Pacific Rim states collectively formed the most important industrial region in the world outside the United States and Europe. Among them, Japan not only led the way but also became the most influential model of success, with a postwar revival that eventually surpassed West Germany's economic miracle (see Chapter 28). Other East Asian nations, newer or less stable than Japan, tried to mimic its success. Some, such as South Korea and the Chinese Nationalist stronghold of Taiwan, treated the creation of prosperity as a fundamental patriotic duty. In postcolonial nations such as Malaysia and Indonesia, governments parlayed their natural resources and expansive local labor pools (which had made them attractive to imperial powers in earlier times) into investment for industrialization. As in China, the factories that emerged were either run as subsidiaries of Western companies or operated on their behalf in new multinational versions of the putting-out system of early industrialization.

The Pacific Rim's boom, however, also contained the makings of a first postwar "bust." During the 1990s a confluence of factors resulted in an enormous slowdown of growth and the near collapse of several currencies. Japan experienced rising production costs, overvalued stocks, rampant speculation on its high-priced real estate market, and the customary kickbacks that rewarded staunch corporate loyalty. Responses to the economic downturn varied widely. In South Korea, an older generation that remembered economic catastrophe after the Korean War responded to national calls for sacrifice, frequently by investing their own savings to prop up ailing companies. Japan launched programs of monetary austerity to cope with its first serious spike in unemployment in two generations. In Indonesia, inflation and unemployment reignited sharp ethnic conflicts that prosperity and violent state repression had dampened in earlier times. This predominantly Muslim country, with a long tradition of tolerance and pluralism inside the faith, also saw outbursts of violent religious fundamentalism popularly associated with another region—the Middle East.

A NEW CENTER OF GRAVITY: ISRAEL, OIL, AND POLITICAL ISLAM IN THE MIDDLE EAST

Perhaps no other region has drawn more of the West's attention in the age of globalization than the Middle East, where a volatile combination of Western military, political, and economic interests converged with deep-seated regional conflicts and transnational Islamic politics. The results of this ongoing confrontation promise to shape the twenty-first century. Here we consider three of the most important aspects of recent history in the region. First is the unfolding of the Arab-Israeli conflict. Second is the region's development as the vital global center of oil production. The third emerges from inside the Arab world, largely as a reaction against the region's recent relations with the West. This is the development of a specific, modern brand of Islamic radicalism that challenges the legacies of imperialism and promises revolutionary and sometimes apocalyptic change in postcolonial nations, and whose most violent elements generate a cycle of fear, anger, and ultimately direct conflict with Western governments.

The Arab-Israeli Conflict

As we saw in Chapter 27, Israel's existence has been fraught from the start. The national aspirations of Jewish immigrants from Europe fleeing the Holocaust and violent postwar anti-Semitism clashed with the motives of pan-Arabists—secular, anticolonial nationalists who urged Arab pride and self-reliance against European domination. By the late 1970s, in the aftermath of two Arab-Israeli wars, it appeared that a generation of fighting might come to an end. American mediators began sponsoring talks to prevent further, sudden outbursts of conflict, while Soviet leaders remained neutral but did not discourage peace efforts. Most notably, the Egyptian president Anwar Sadat, who authorized and directed the 1973 war against Israel, decided that coexistence rather than the destruction of Israel was the long-term answer to regional conflict. Aided by the American president, Jimmy Carter, Sadat brokered a peace between Egypt and Israel's staunchly conservative leader, Menachem Begin, in 1978. Leaders on both sides of the conflict believed the potential rewards were greater than the obvious risks.

Hopes for a lasting peace were soon dashed. Hostilities escalated between Israel and the Palestinian Arabs displaced by Arab-Israeli warfare, a confrontation that increasingly polarized a much larger group of people. On each side of the Israeli-Palestinian conflict, a potent blend of ethnic and religious nationalism began to control both debate and action. Conservatives in Israel played to a public sentiment that put security ahead of other priorities, particularly among the most recent Jewish immigrants, many from the former Soviet Union. On the other side, younger Palestinians, angered by their elders' failures to provoke revolution, turned against the secular radicalism of the Palestinian Liberation Organization (PLO) and toward radical Islam.

In this combustible political environment, the Palestinians living on the West Bank and in the desperately

Interpreting Visual Evidence

Media Representations of Globalization

Because the set of historical developments collectively known as *globalization* are so complex and because the local effects of these developments have often been felt as disruptions of well-entrenched habits or ways of life, debates about globalization are particularly open to manipulation through the presentation of charged imagery. Since the end of the Cold War, provocative images that capture certain aspects of the world's new interconnectedness—and the accompanying need for new kinds of boundaries—have become ubiquitous in the media. The movement of peoples and goods are variously defined as necessary to maintaining standards of living or as a threat to local jobs and local production. Globalization is defended as good for the economy, good for the consumer, and good for competition—but is also blamed for hurting workers, destroying local cultures, and eroding long-standing definitions of national identity.

The images here all illustrate essential aspects of globalization. Image A shows ships waiting for loading and unloading at one of the largest container terminals in the world, in Hong Kong. Most of the shipping from China comes through this terminal. Image B shows family members separated by the border fence between the United States and Mexico in Mexicali, Mexico. In the twentieth century, Mexicali grew to be a city of 1.5 million people, in large part

A. Cargo ships in Kowloon Bay, 2002.

overcrowded Gaza Strip revolted in an outburst of street rioting in 1987. This rebellion—called the *intifada* (literally, a "throwing off" or uprising)—continued for years in daily battles between stone-throwing Palestinian youths and armed Israeli security forces. The street fights escalated into cycles of Palestinian terrorism, particularly suicide bombings of civilian targets, and reprisals from the Israeli military. International efforts to broker a peace produced some results, including the official autonomy of a Palestinian authority led by the PLO chief, Yasser Arafat. Yet the peace was always fragile at best—suffering perhaps fatal damage from the assassination of Israel's reformist prime minister Yitzhak Rabin in 1995 by a reactionary Israeli, and from continued attacks

by Islamist terrorists. By the turn of the twenty-first century the cycle of violence flared again, with a "second intifada" launched by Palestinians in late 2000. Thus continued the war of riots and bombings fought by next-door neighbors.

Oil, Power, and Economics

The struggles between the state of Israel and its neighbors have been important in their own right. Yet one of the most compelling reasons that this conflict mattered to outside powers was material: oil. The global demand for oil skyrocketed during the postwar era and has accelerated since. Starting

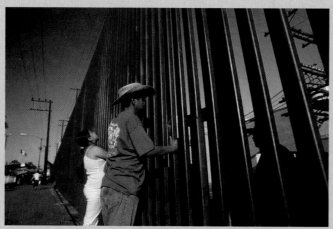

B. Mexican family members talk through border fence, 2003.

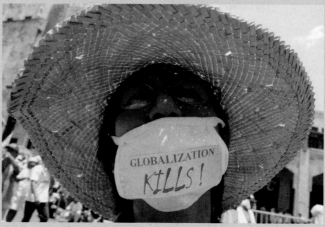

C. Filipino protester on Labor Day, 2003.

on the prosperity generated by sending field workers across the border to the United States. Image C shows a Labor Day protester in Manila, Philippines, at a demonstration in which globalization was blamed for amendments to the labor code favorable to employers, a ban on strikes, and antiterrorist measures that were perceived to be an infringement of personal liberties. The medical mask is a reference to the SARS epidemic.

Questions for Analysis

1. Image A is typical of images that emphasize the economic consequences of globalization. Does globalization appear to be a force subject to human control in this image? How do such images shape perceptions of China's place in the global economy?

2. Compare images A and B. Is there a connection between the accelerating flows of money and goods between different parts of the world and restrictions on the movements of people?

3. In image C, the woman's medical mask names globalization as the enemy of Filipino workers. Who is being targeted by this protest? What does this say about the local contest over the conditions of labor in the Philippines?

with the consumer boom in the Cold War West, ordinary citizens bought cars and other petroleum-powered consumer durable goods, while industrial plastics made from petroleum by-products were used to manufacture a wealth of basic household items. Those needs, and the desires for profit and power that went with them, drew Western corporations and governments steadily toward the oil-rich states of the Middle East, whose vast reserves were discovered in the 1930s and 1940s. Large corporations conducted joint diplomacy with Middle Eastern states and their own home governments to design concessions for drilling, refining, and shipping the oil. Pipelines were laid by contractors based around the world, from California to Rome to Russia.

The enormous long-term economic value of the Middle Eastern oil reserves made oil a fundamental tool in new struggles over political power. Many producer states sought to turn their resources into leverage with the West's former imperial powers. In 1960, the leading Middle Eastern, African, and Latin American producers banded together in a cartel to take advantage of this vital resource, forming the Organization of the Petroleum Exporting Countries (OPEC) to regulate the production and pricing of crude oil. During the 1970s, OPEC played a leading role in the global economy. Its policies reflected not only the desire to draw maximum profits out of bottlenecks in oil production but also the militant politics of some OPEC leaders who wanted

THE ARAB-ISRAELI WARS OF 1967 AND 1973. ▪ *What were the major changes in the political geography of the Middle East as a result of the Arab-Israeli conflict of 1967?* ▪ *Why did the Israelis wish to occupy the Sinai and West Bank regions at the end of the 1967 war?* ▪ *What problems did this create, and how might it have led to the conflict in 1973?*

The Rise of Political Islam

In North Africa and the Middle East, processes of modernization and globalization produced tremendous discontents. The new nations that emerged from decolonization often shared the characteristics of the "kleptocracies" south of the Sahara: corrupt state agencies, cronyism based on ethnic or family kinship, decaying public services, rapid increases in population, and constant state repression of dissent. Disappointment with these conditions ran deep, perhaps nowhere more so than in the seat of pan-Arabism, Nasser's Egypt. During the 1960s, Egyptian academics and cultural critics leveled charges against Nasser's regime that became the core of a powerful new political movement. Their critique offered modern interpretations of certain legal and political currents in Islamic thought, ideas linked loosely across centuries by their association with revolt against foreign interference and official corruption. They denounced Egypt's nationalist government as greedy, brutal, and corrupt.

to use oil as a weapon against the West in the Arab-Israeli conflict. After the 1973 Arab-Israeli war, an embargo inspired by the hard-liners sparked spiraling inflation and economic troubles in Western nations, triggering a cycle of dangerous recession that lasted nearly a decade.

In response, Western governments treated the Middle Eastern oil regions as a vital strategic center of gravity, the subject of constant Great Power diplomacy. If conflict directly threatened the stability of oil production or friendly governments, Western powers were prepared to intervene by force, as demonstrated in 1991 when the United States went to war against Iraq after the latter nation had invaded Kuwait, a small but important oil producer. By the 1990s another new front of competition and potential conflict emerged as the energy demands of other nations also grew. In particular, the new industrial giants China and India eyed the Middle Eastern oil reserves with the same nervousness as the West. The oil boom also generated violent conflict inside Middle Eastern producer states as oil revenue produced uneven economic development. The huge gaps between or inside Middle Eastern societies that divided oil's haves and have-nots caused deep resentments, official corruption, and a new wave of radical politics. With the pan-Arab nationalists fading from the scene, the rising revolutionary force gathered instead around modern readings of Islamic fundamentalism, now tied to postcolonial politics.

There was a twist to their claims, however: that the roots of the Arab world's moral failure lay in centuries of colonial contact with the West. The most influential of these Islamist critics, Sayyid Qutb (*KUH-tub*, 1906–1966), presented these ideas in a series of essays for which he was arrested several times by Egyptian authorities and ultimately executed. His argument ran as follows. As a result of corrupting outside influences, the ruling elites of the new Arab states pursued policies that frayed local and family bonds, deepening economic divides while abandoning the government's responsibility for charity and stability. What was more, the nation's elites were morally bankrupt—their lives defied codes of morality, self-discipline, and communal responsibility rooted in Islamic faith. To maintain power, the elites lived in the pockets of Western imperial and corporate powers. From Qutb's point of view, this collaboration not only caused cultural impurity but also eroded authentic Muslim faith. This dire judgment of Arab societies—that they were poisoned from without and within—required an equally drastic solution. Arab societies should reject not only oppressive postcolonial governments but also all the political and cultural ideas that traveled with them, especially those that could be labeled "Western." After popular revolts, the Arab autocracies would be replaced by an idealized form of conservative Islamic government—a system in which a rigid form of Islam would link law, government, and culture.

GAMAL ABDEL NASSER AND SOVIET MINISTER ALEKSEY KOSYGIN, 1966. As the most prominent spokesman for secular pan-Arabism, Nasser became a target for Islamist critics, such as Sayyid Qutb and the Muslim Brotherhood, angered by the Western-influenced policies of his regime.

In a formula familiar to historians of European politics throughout the nineteenth and twentieth centuries, this particular brand of Islamist politics combined popular anger, intellectual opposition to "foreign" influences, and a highly idealized vision of the past. By the 1970s it began to express itself openly in regional politics. Qutb's ideas were put into practice by Egypt's Muslim Brotherhood, a secretive but widespread society rooted in anticolonial politics, local charity, and violently fundamentalist Islam. Similar ideas spread among similar organizations in other urbanized Arab countries and leading Islamic universities, which were historically centers of debate about political theory and religious law. These forms of political Islam emerged as a driving force in criticism and defiance of autocratic Arab regimes. Secular critics and more-liberal Islamists, who called for open elections and a free press, were more fragmented and thus easier to silence, whereas the new wave of fundamentalists gained concessions that allowed them to preach and publish in public so long as they did not launch actual revolts. In Egypt, where an Islamic militant assassinated President Anwar Sadat in 1981, the Muslim Brotherhood eventually renounced violence. Meanwhile, political Islam's defining moment came in an unexpected place: Iran.

IRAN'S ISLAMIC REVOLUTION

Iran offered one of the most dramatic examples of modernization gone sour in the Middle East. Despite tremendous economic growth in the 1960s and 1970s, Iranians labored with legacies of foreign intervention and corrupt rule at the hands of the shah, Reza Pahlavi, a Western-friendly leader installed during a 1953 military coup supported by Britain and the United States. In exchange for the shah's role as a friend to the West during the Cold War and for providing a steady source of reasonably priced oil, the Iranian government received vast sums in oil contracts, weapons, and development aid. Thousands of Westerners, especially Americans, came to Iran, introducing foreign influences that not only challenged traditional values but also offered economic and political alternatives. The shah, however, kept these alternatives out of reach, consistently denying democratic representation to Westernizing middle-class Iranian workers and deeply religious university students alike. He governed through a small aristocracy divided by constant infighting. His army and secret police conducted regular and brutal campaigns of repression. Despite all this, and the public protests it spurred in the West, governments such as the conservative Nixon administration embraced the shah as a strategically vital ally: a key to anti-Soviet alliances and a safe source of oil.

Twenty-five years after the 1953 coup, the shah's autocratic route to an industrial state ended. After a lengthy economic downturn, public unrest, and personal illness, the shah realized he could not continue in power. He retired from public life under popular pressure in February 1979. Eight months of uncertainty followed, most Westerners fled the country, and the provisional government appointed by the shah collapsed. The strongest political coalition among Iran's revolutionaries surged into the vacuum—a broad-based Islamic movement centered on the ayatollah Ruhollah Khomeini (1902–1989), Iran's senior cleric and theologian, returned from exile in France. Other senior clerics and the country's large population of unemployed, deeply religious university students provided the movement's energy. Disenfranchised secular protesters joined the radical Islamists in condemning decades of Western indifference and the shah's oppression. Under the new regime, some limited economic and political populism combined with strict constructions of Islamic law, restrictions on women's public life, and the prohibition of many ideas or activities linked to Western influence.

The new Iranian government also defined itself against its enemies: against the Sunni religious establishment of neighboring states, against "atheistic" Soviet communism, but especially against Israel and the United States. Iranians feared the United States would try to overthrow Khomeini as it had other leaders. Violence in the streets of Tehran reached a peak when militant students stormed the American embassy in November 1979 and seized fifty-two hostages. The act quickly became an international crisis that heralded a new kind of confrontation between Western powers and postcolonial Islamic radicals. Democratic

The Place of Islam in Modern Societies

The end of the colonial era and the impact of postcolonial migrations provided the backdrop for a renewed discussion in Europe and the Middle East about the presence of Muslim peoples in European nations and the relationship of religion to politics in traditionally Muslim societies. Among Muslim scholars and clerics, a wide range of opinions has been expressed about the place of Islam in the modern world, and the two figures here represent two distinct voices within this discussion.

Born into a family of Shi'ite Muslim religious leaders, Ruhollah Khomeini (c. 1900–1989) was recognized as the leading Iranian religious authority in the 1950s. He represented a highly conservative Islamic fundamentalism intended to unite Iranian Muslims in violent opposition to the Western-supported government of the shah of Iran, and he continues to have a powerful influence on Muslims seeking an alternative to Western cultural, political, and economic domination.

Tariq Ramadan (born in 1962 in Geneva, Switzerland) is a professor of religion and philosophy, and a leading voice speaking for the increasingly large number of Muslims who live in Europe and North America—members of a religious minority in non-Muslim societies. He has taught at the University of Fribourg, the College de Saussure in Geneva, and St. Antony's College, Oxford. In 2004 he was forced to decline an offer to become a professor at the University of Notre Dame in the United States when the State Department denied him a visa. Ramadan argues that Muslims can and should be productive and active citizens in Western societies while remaining true to their religious beliefs.

Ruhollah Khomeini, Islamic Government (1979)

The Islamic government is not similar to the well-known systems of government. It is not a despotic government in which the head of state dictates his opinion and tampers with the lives and property of the people. The prophet, may God's prayers be upon him, and 'Ali, the amir of the faithful, and the other imams had no power to tamper with people's property or with their lives.[1] The Islamic government is not despotic but constitutional. However, it is not constitutional in the well-known sense of the word, which is represented in the parliamentary system or in the people's councils. It is constitutional in the sense that those in charge of affairs observe a number of conditions and rules underlined in the Koran and in the Sunna and represented in the necessity of observing the system and of applying the dictates and laws of Islam.[2] This is why the Islamic government is the government of the divine law. The difference between the Islamic government and the constitutional governments, both monarchic and republican, lies in the fact that the people's representatives or the king's representatives are the ones who codify and legis-

late, whereas the power of legislation is confined to God, may He be praised, and nobody else has the right to legislate and nobody may rule by that which has not been given power by God. . . .

The government of Islam is not monarchic, . . . and not an empire, because Islam is above squandering and unjustly undermining the lives and property of people. This is why the government of Islam does not have the many big palaces, the servants, the royal courts, the crown prince courts, and other trivial requirements that consume half or most of the country's resources and that the sultans and the emperors have. The life of the great prophet was a life of utter simplicity, even though the prophet was the head of the state, who ran and ruled it by himself. . . . Had this course continued until the present, people would have known the taste of happiness and the country's treasury would not have been plundered to be spent on fornication, abomination, and the court's costs and expenditures. You know that most of the corrupt aspects of our society are due to the corruption of the ruling dynasty and the royal family. What is the legitimacy

of these rulers who build houses of entertainment, corruption, fornication, and abomination and who destroy houses which God ordered be raised and in which His name is mentioned? Were it not for what the court wastes and what it embezzles, the country's budget would not experience any deficit that forces the state to borrow from America and England, with all the humiliation and insult that accompany such borrowing. Has our oil decreased or have our minerals that are stored under this good earth run out? We possess everything and we would not need the help of America or of others if it were not for the costs of the court and for its wasteful use of the people's money.

[1] "The prophet" refers to Muhammed; 'Ali was Muhammed's son-in-law and, according to the Shi'ite tradition, his legitimate heir; an amir is a high military official; and an imam, in the Shi'ite tradition, is an important spiritual leader with sole power to make decisions about doctrine.

[2] The Koran (Qu'ran) is the book of the holy scriptures of Islam; the Sunna is the body of customary Islamic law second only to the Koran in authority.

Source: Ruhollah Khomeini, *Islamic Government*, trans. Joint Publications Research Service (New York: 1979).

Tariq Ramadan, Western Muslims and the Future of Islam (2002)

... [W]ith the emergence of the young Muslim generation ... it has been deemed necessary to reanalyze the main Islamic sources (Qu'ran and Sunnah) when it comes to interpreting legal issues (*fiqh*) in the European context. Many of these young people intend to stay permanently in a European country, and a large number have already received their citizenship. New forms of interpretation (known as *ijtihad*) have made it possible for the younger generation to practice their faith in a coherent manner in a new context. It is important to note that this has been a very recent phenomenon. Only within the past few years have Muslim scholars and intellectuals felt obliged to take a closer look at the European laws, and at the same time, to think about the changes that have been taking place within the diverse Muslim communities * * * [F]ive main points * * * have been agreed upon by those working on the basis of the Islamic sources and by the great majority of Muslims living in Europe:

1. Muslims who are residents or citizens of a non-Islamic state should understand that they are under a moral and social contract with the country in which they reside. In other words, they should respect the laws of the country.

2. Both the spirit and the letter of the secular model permit Muslims to practice their faith without requiring a complete assimilation into the new culture and, thereby, partial disconnection from their Muslim identity.

3. The ancient division of the world into denominations of *dar al-harb* (abode of war) and *dar al-Islam* (abode of Islam), used by the jurists during a specific geopolitical context, namely the ninth-century Muslim world, is invalid and does not take into account the realities of modern life. Other concepts have been identified as exemplifying more positively the presence of Muslims in Europe.

4. Muslims should consider themselves full citizens of the nations in which they reside and can participate with conscience in the organizational, economic, and political affairs of the country without compromising their own values.

5. With regard to the possibilities offered by European legislation, nothing stops Muslims, like any other citizens, from making choices that respond to the requirements of their own consciences and faith. If any obligations should be in contradiction to the Islamic principles (a situation that is quite rare), the specific case must be studied in order to identify the priorities and the possibility of adaptation (which should be developed at the national level). . . .

For some Muslims, the idea of an "Islamic culture," similar to the concepts of identity and community, connotes the necessity of Muslim isolation from and rejection of European culture. Such an understanding suggests that Muslims are not genuine in their desire to integrate into the society in which they live. They play the citizenship card, while trying to maintain such cultural particularities as dress code, management of space when it comes to men and women, concern about music, and other issues. For them, real integration means becoming European in every aspect of one's character and behavior. This is, in fact, a very narrow vision of integration, almost resembling the notion of assimilation. One admits theoretically that Muslims have the right to practice their religion but revokes these rights when expression of faith becomes too *visible*.

In actuality, the future of Muslim presence in Europe must entail a truly "European Islamic culture" disengaged from the cultures of North Africa, Turkey, and Indo-Pakistan, while naturally referring to them for inspiration. This new culture is just in the process of being born and molded. By giving careful consideration to everything from appropriate dress to the artistic and creative expression of Islam, Muslims are mobilizing a whole new culture. The formation of such a culture is a pioneering endeavor, making use of European energy while taking into account various national customs and simultaneously respecting Islamic values and guidelines.

Source: Tariq Ramadan, "Islam and Muslims in Europe: A Silent Revolution toward Rediscovery," in *Muslims in the West: From Sojourners to Citizens*, ed. Yvonne Yazbeck Haddad (New York: 2002), pp. 160–63.

Questions for Analysis

1. What prevents Islamic government from being despotic, according to Khomeini? Why is there no legislative branch in an Islamic government, in his view?

2. What criticism does Ramadan make of those Muslims who seek to isolate themselves from European culture while living in Europe? What does he mean by "European Islamic culture"?

3. In what ways do these two Muslim thinkers show an engagement with European traditions of political thought?

president Jimmy Carter's administration ultimately gained the hostages' release, but not before the catalog of earlier failures led to the election of the Republican Ronald Reagan.

Iran, Iraq, and Unintended Consequences of the Cold War

Iran's victory in the hostage crisis was fleeting. During the later part of 1980, Iran's Arab neighbor and traditional rival Iraq invaded, hoping to seize Iran's southern oil fields during the revolutionary confusion. Iran counterattacked. The result was a murderous eight-year conflict marked by the use of chemical weapons and human waves of young Iranian radicals fighting the Soviet-armed Iraqis. The war ended in stalemate with Iran's theocratic regime intact. In the short term, their long defense of Iranian nationalism left the clerics more entrenched at home, while abroad they used oil revenues to back grass-roots radicals in Lebanon and elsewhere who engaged in anti-Western terrorism. The strongest threats to the Iranian regime ultimately came from within, from a new generation of young students and disenfranchised service workers who found their prospects for prosperity and active citizenship had not changed much since the days of the shah.

The Iran-Iraq conflict created another problem for Western interests and the governments of leading OPEC states: Iraq. Various governments—including an unlikely alliance of France, Saudi Arabia, the Soviet Union, and the United States—supported Iraq during the war in an effort to bring down Iran's clerics. Their patronage went to one of the most violent governments in the region, Saddam Hussein's dictatorship. Iraq exhausted itself in the war, politically and economically. To shore up his regime and restore Iraq's influence, Hussein looked elsewhere in the region. In 1990 Iraq invaded its small, oil-rich neighbor Kuwait. With the Cold War on the wane, Iraq's Soviet supporters would not condone Iraqi aggression. A coalition of nations led by the United States reacted forcefully. Within months Iraq faced the full weight of the United States military—trained intensively since Vietnam to face much more capable Soviet-armed forces than Iraq's—along with forces from several OPEC states, French troops, and armored divisions from Britain, Egypt, and Syria. This coalition pummeled Iraqi troops from the air for six weeks, then routed them and retook Kuwait in a brief, well-executed ground campaign. This changed the tenor of relations between the United States and Arab oil producers, encouraging not only closeness between governments but also the anti-Americanism of radicals angry at a new Western presence. It was also the beginning rather than the end of Western confrontation with Iraq in response to Hussein's efforts to develop nuclear and biological weapons.

Elsewhere in the region, the proxy conflicts of the Cold War snared both superpowers in the new and growing networks of Islamic radicalism. In 1979 the socialist government of Afghanistan turned against its Soviet patrons. Fearing a result like Iran, with a spread of fundamentalism into the Muslim regions of Soviet Central Asia, Moscow responded by overthrowing the Afghan president and installing a pro-Soviet faction. The new government, backed by more than a hundred thousand Soviet troops, found itself immediately at war with fighters who combined local conservatism with militant Islam and who attracted volunteers from radical Islamic movements in Egypt, Lebanon, Saudi Arabia, and elsewhere. These fighters, who called themselves *mujahidin*—Arabic for "holy warriors." The mujahidin benefited from advanced weapons and training, supplied by Western powers led by the United States. Those who provided the aid saw the conflict in Cold War terms, as a chance to sap Soviet resources in a fruitless imperial war. On those terms the aid worked; the war dragged on for nearly ten years, taking thousands of Russian lives and damaging the Soviet government's credibility at home. Soviet troops withdrew in 1989. After five years of clan warfare, hard-line Islamic factions tied to the foreign elements in the mujahidin took over the country. Their experiment in theocracy would make Iran's seem mild by comparison.

VIOLENCE BEYOND BOUNDS: WAR AND TERRORISM IN THE TWENTY-FIRST CENTURY

The global networks of communication, finance, and mobility discussed at the beginning of this chapter gave radical political violence a disturbing new character at the end of the twentieth century. In the 1960s, organized, sectarian terrorist tactics had become an important part of political conflict in the Middle East, Europe, and Latin America. Most of these early terrorist organizations (including the Irish Republican Army, the Italian Red Brigades, and the different Palestinian revolutionary organizations) had specific goals, such as ethnic separatism or the establishment of revolutionary governments. By the 1980s and increasingly during the 1990s, such groups were complemented and then supplanted by a different brand of terrorist organization, one that ranged freely across territory and local legal systems. These newer, apocalyptic terrorist groups called for decisive conflict to eliminate their enemies and grant themselves martyrdom. Some such groups emerged from the social dislocations of the postwar boom, others were linked directly to brands of radical religion. They often divorced themselves from the local crises that first spurred their anger, roaming widely among countries in search of recruits to their cause.

A leading example of such groups, and soon the most famous, was the radical Islamist umbrella organization al Qaeda. It was created by leaders of the foreign mujahidin who had fought against the Soviet Union in Afghanistan. Its official leader and financial supporter was the Saudi-born multimillionaire Osama bin Laden. Among its operational chiefs was the famous Egyptian radical Ayman al-Zawahiri, whose political career linked him directly to Sayyid Qutb and other founding thinkers in modern revolutionary Islam. These leaders organized broad networks of largely self-contained terrorist cells around the world, from the Islamic regions of Southeast Asia to Europe, East Africa, and the United States, funded by myriad private accounts, front companies, illegal trades, and corporate kickbacks throughout the global economy. Their organization defied borders, and so did their goals. They did not seek to negotiate for territory, or to change the government of a specific state. Instead, they spoke of the destruction of the state of Israel and American, European, and other non-Islamic systems of government worldwide and called for a united, apocalyptic revolt by fundamentalist Muslims to create an Islamic community bounded only by faith. During the 1990s they involved themselves in a variety of local terrorist campaigns in Islamic countries and organized large-scale suicide attacks against American targets, notably the American embassies in Kenya and Tanzania in 1998.

At the beginning of the twenty-first century, al Qaeda's organizers struck again at their most obvious political enemy, the symbolic seat of globalization: the United States. Small teams of suicidal radicals, aided by al Qaeda's organization, planned to hijack airliners and use them as flying bombs to strike the most strategically important symbols of America's global power. On September 11, 2001, they carried out this mission in the deadliest series of terrorist attacks ever to occur on American soil. In the space of an hour, hijacked planes struck the Pentagon, the headquarters of the U.S. military, and the World Trade Center towers in New York City. A fourth plane, possibly aimed at the U.S. Capitol, crashed in open farmland in Pennsylvania, its attack thwarted when the passengers fought back against their captors. The World Trade Center towers, among the tallest buildings in the world, crumbled into ash and wreckage in front of hundreds of millions of viewers on satellite television and the Internet. In these several simultaneous attacks more than three thousand people died.

The attacks were at once a new brand of terror, deeply indebted to globalization in both its outlook and its method, and something older: the extreme, opportunistic violence of marginal groups against national cultures during a period of general dislocation and uncertainty. The immediate

TWENTY-FIRST CENTURY TERRORISM. New York's World Trade Center Towers under attack on September 11, 2001.

American response was action against al Qaeda's central haven in Afghanistan, a state in near collapse after the warfare of the previous thirty years. The United States' versatile professional soldiers and unmatched equipment, along with armed Afghan militias angry at the country's disarray quickly routed al Qaeda's Taliban sponsors and scattered the terrorists. That effort, however, failed to pinpoint and eliminate the hidden networks of leadership, finance, and information that propel apocalyptic terrorism. The rebuilding and rehabilitation of Afghanistan, a necessary consequence of American and European action, began from almost nothing in terms of administration and infrastructure. Pressing crises elsewhere and the changeable nature of Western popular concerns made a recovery difficult. Meanwhile, fears that Iraq's government might transfer chemical or nuclear weapons to apocalyptic terrorists provided the rationale for an American-led invasion of Iraq in 2003. No immediate evidence of recent, active weapons development programs was found, however; and in the process, the United States inherited the complex reconstruction of a broken state, fractured by guerrilla violence and anti-Western terrorism.

TRANSFORMATIONS: HUMAN RIGHTS

Some of the same globalizing processes have dramatically expanded our conception of citizenship, rights, and law. High school halls and college walkways are crammed with

The United Nations, Report of the Fourth World Conference on Women (1995)

In September 1995, women representing 185 of the world's nations gathered in Beijing to attend the UN's Fourth World Conference on Women. Delegates to the conference adopted a platform for action that outlined the problems confronting women in the world, including poverty, violence, armed conflict, human rights violations, pollution, and differing access to medical treatment, education, economic advancement, and political power. The passage excerpted here highlights the particular burdens that poverty places on women in many societies throughout the world.

47. More than 1 billion people in the world today, the great majority of whom are women, live in unacceptable conditions of poverty, mostly in the developing countries. . . .

48. In the past decade the number of women living in poverty has increased disproportionately to the number of men, particularly in the developing countries. The feminization of poverty has also recently become a significant problem in the countries with economies in transition as a short-term consequence of the process of political, economic, and social transformation. In addition to economic factors, the rigidity of socially ascribed gender roles and women's limited access to power, education, training, and productive resources as well as other emerging factors that may lead to insecurity for families are also responsible. The failure to adequately mainstream a gender perspective in all economic analysis and planning and to address the structural causes of poverty is also a contributing factor.

49. Women contribute to the economy and to combating poverty through both remunerated and unremunerated work at home, in the community, and in the workplace. The empowerment of women is a critical factor in the eradication of poverty.

50. While poverty affects households as a whole, because of the gender division of labour and responsibilities for household welfare, women bear a disproportionate burden, attempting to manage household consumption and production under conditions of increasing scarcity. Poverty is particularly acute for women living in rural households.

51. Women's poverty is directly related to the absence of economic opportunities and autonomy, lack of access to economic resources, including credit, land ownership and inheritance, lack of access to education and support services, and their minimal participation in the decision-making process. Poverty can also force

the tables of international organizations, such as Amnesty International, that promote universal human rights. How has this notion of human rights become so familiar? What older traditions has it built on or replaced?

The contemporary language of human rights is anchored in a tradition of political thought that reaches back to at least the seventeenth century. It took its present form in response to the atrocities of the First World War and, especially, the Second World War. Atrocities and people's shocked responses to them, however, did not create either a new concern with human rights or the institutions dedicated to upholding them. Enforcing *universal* human rights challenges the sovereignty of nation-states and an individual nation-state's power over its citizens. International courts and human rights organizations thus require and hasten what political thinkers call the globalization of judicial power.

Human rights are part of the Western political tradition. So is opposition to them. The belief that rights were embedded in "nature," natural order, or "natural law" formed a powerful strain of early modern political thought. John Locke argued that absolutist monarchies violated "natural laws," and the natural rights of man became a rallying cry for opponents of Europe's dynastic regimes in the seventeenth and eighteenth centuries (see Chapter 15). In point of fact, of course, those bold declarations of rights were not universal: women, slaves, people of color, and people of different religions were excluded, wholly or partially, and many nineteenth-century political theorists and scientists dedicated women into situations in which they are vulnerable to sexual exploitation.

52. In too many countries, social welfare systems do not take sufficient account of the specific conditions of women living in poverty, and there is a tendency to scale back the services provided by such systems. The risk of falling into poverty is greater for women than for men, particularly in old age, where social security systems are based on the principle of continuous remunerated employment. In some cases, women do not fulfil this requirement because of interruptions in their work, due to the unbalanced distribution of remunerated and unremunerated work. Moreover, older women also face greater obstacles to labour-market re-entry.

53. In many developed countries, where the level of general education and professional training of women and men are similar and where systems of protection against discrimination are available, in some sectors the economic transformations of the past decade have strongly increased either the unemployment of women or the precarious nature of their employment. The proportion of women among the poor has consequently increased. In countries with a high level of school enrolment of girls, those who leave the educational system the earliest, without any qualification, are among the most vulnerable in the labour market. . . .

55. Particularly in developing countries, the productive capacity of women should be increased through access to capital, resources, credit, land, technology, information, technical assistance, and training so as to raise their income and improve nutrition, education, health care, and status within the household. The release of women's productive potential is pivotal to breaking the cycle of poverty so that women can share fully in the benefits of development and in the products of their own labour.

56. Sustainable development and economic growth that is both sustained and sustainable are possible only through improving the economic, social, political, legal, and cultural status of women. Equitable social development that recognizes empowering the poor, particularly women, to utilize environmental resources sustainably is a necessary foundation for sustainable development.

Source: United Nations, *Report of the Fourth World Conference on Women, Beijing*, September 4–15, 1995 (www.un.org/womenwatch/daw/beijing/platform, accessed June 2010).

Questions for Analysis

1. According to the UN report, why are women more likely to be poor than men?

2. What are the special challenges faced by women in developing countries?

3. What are the differing challenges faced by women residing in more developed nations?

countless volumes to the proposition that these groups were *not* created equal. Which human beings might receive the "rights of man," then, was bitterly contested for the better part of the nineteenth and twentieth centuries, and only slowly did a more inclusive conception of human rights displace a narrower historical tradition of the rights of man.

Even the rights of man, relatively limited by present-day standards, met with opposition and skepticism. The distinguished conservative Edmund Burke (1730–1797) denounced the French Declaration of the Rights of Man as dangerous metaphysical nonsense, which rested on "paltry blurred shreds of paper" rather than on well-grounded institutions and customs (see Chapter 18). The equally distinguished radical Karl Marx (1818–1883) considered the French and American declarations illusory because the political rights they promised were eviscerated by social and economic inequality.

As far as the history of human rights is concerned, perhaps the most important development of the nineteenth century was the rise of nationalism and nation-states. Rights, and political movements claiming them, became increasingly inseparable from nationhood. "What is a country . . . but the place in which our demands for individual rights are most secure?" asked the Italian nationalist Giuseppe Mazzini. For nineteenth-century Italians, Germans, Serbs, and Poles and for twentieth-century Indians, Vietnamese, and Algerians—to name just a few—fighting for national independence was the way to secure the rights of citizens. National sovereignty, once achieved, was tightly woven into the fabric of politics and international relations and would not be easily relinquished.

The world wars marked a turning point. The First World War, an unprecedented global conflict, almost inevitably fostered dreams of global peace under the auspices of international organizations. The Peace of Paris aimed for more than a territorial settlement: with the League of Nations it tried, tentatively, to establish an organization that would transcend the power of individual nations and uphold the (ill-defined) principles of "civilization." (Despite this commitment, the League bowed to British and American objections to a statement condemning racial discrimination.) The experiment failed: the fragile League was swept aside by the surge of extreme nationalism and aggression in the 1930s. The shock and revulsion at the atrocities of the war that followed, however, brought forth more decisive efforts. The Second World War's aftermath saw the establishment of the United Nations, an International Court of Justice at the Hague (Netherlands), and the UN's High Commission on Human Rights. Unlike anything attempted after the First World War, the Commission on Human Rights set out to establish the rights of individuals—against the nation-state.

This Universal Declaration of Human Rights, published by the High Commission in 1948, became the touchstone of our modern notion of human rights. It was very much a product of its time. Its authors included Eleanor Roosevelt and the French jurist René Cassin, who had been wounded in the First World War (and held his intestines together during a nearly four-hundred-mile train ride to medical treatment), lost his family in the Holocaust, and had seen his nation collaborate with the Nazis. The High Commission argued that the war and the "barbarous acts which have outraged the conscience of mankind" showed that no state should have absolute power over its citizens. The Universal Declaration prohibited torture, cruel punishment, and slavery. A separate convention, also passed in 1948, dealt with the newly defined crime of genocide. The Universal Declaration of 1948 built on earlier declarations that universalized the rights to legal equality, freedom of religion and speech, and the right to participate in government. Finally, it reflected the postwar period's effort to put democracy on a more solid footing by establishing *social* rights—to education, work, a "just and favorable remuneration," a "standard of living," and social security, among others.

Few nations were willing to ratify the Universal Declaration of Human Rights. For decades after the war, its idealistic principles could not be reconciled with British and French colonialism, American racial segregation, or Soviet dictatorship. For as long as wars to end colonialism continued, declarations of universal principles rang hollow.

(Mahatma Gandhi, asked to comment on Western civilization, replied that he thought it "would be a good idea.") For as long as the Cold War persisted, human rights seemed only a thinly veiled weapon in the sparring between the superpowers. Thus decolonization and, later, the end of the Cold War began to enhance the legitimacy and luster of human rights. International institutions set up after the Second World War matured, gaining expertise and stature. Global communications and media dramatically expanded the membership and influence of organizations that, like Amnesty International (founded in 1961), operated outside the economic or political boundaries of the nation-state. Memories of the Second World War, distorted or buried by the Cold War, continue to return, and the force of those memories helped drive the creation of International Criminal Tribunals for Yugoslavia and Rwanda in 1993. Finally, as one historian points out, at a time when many feel vulnerable to the forces of globalization, human rights offers a way of talking about rights, goods, and protections (environmental, for example) that the nation-state cannot—or can no longer—provide. The language of human rights, then, captures both the aspirations and some of the precariousness of globalization.

EUROPE AND THE UNITED STATES IN THE TWENTY-FIRST CENTURY

As the first decade of the twenty-first century drew to a close, the initial confidence that Europeans felt in the aftermath of the revolutions of 1989 seemed badly shaken. The process of European integration, which had contributed so much to the political stability of Europe in the decades after the Second World War, seemed to have reached its limits in the East. Although a few independent nations that were formerly a part of the Soviet Union, such as Ukraine, might be interested in joining the European Union, it is unlikely that Russia would be comfortable with this realignment toward the West. Even the future membership of Turkey, an official candidate for entry into the EU since 1999 and an associate member of the European Union since 1963, remains uncertain because of growing discomfort in many European nations about admitting a historically Muslim nation into Europe. Turkey is a modern industrial nation that has been governed by a secular government since the 1920s, participated in the Marshall Plan after the Second World War, was a member of the Council of Europe in 1949, and became a member of NATO in 1952. A 2010 poll carried out in five European countries nevertheless found that 52 percent of respondents were opposed to Turkish membership in the European Union, and only 41 percent in favor.

In the economic realm, the global financial crisis of 2007–10 caused many in Europe and North America to rethink the central assumptions of late-twentieth-century neoliberalism, especially the belief that markets were by definition self-regulating. The crisis had its origins in a classic bubble in global housing prices, which encouraged banks to make ever-riskier bets in the real estate market, while also experimenting with the sale of complicated securities whose risk became difficult to gauge with accuracy. When housing prices fell, many key banks in different parts of the world found themselves unable to state clearly the value of their plummeting investments tied to real estate. Since nobody knew how much money the largest financial institutions had, banks simply stopped lending money to one another, and in the resulting liquidity crisis many businesses failed and trillions of dollars of consumer savings were wiped out. Massive government bailouts of the largest banks with taxpayer money were required to stabilize the global financial system, and popular resentment against the financial industry stimulated many nations to consider widespread reform and government regulation of banks as a result.

Contemporary debates about political integration in Europe or the benefits of free-market capitalism are closely connected with the developments that followed the end of the Cold War in the early 1990s and the period of economic globalization that followed, but they can also be seen as a continuation of debates within the traditions of political and economic liberalism that go back to the eighteenth century. In its classic formulation as put forth by liberal theorists such as Adam Smith, political and economic liberties were best defended in a nation that possessed a small and limited government. The closely related traditions of social democracy that developed in Europe in the nineteenth and twentieth century, on the other hand, arose out of a concern that limited governments in the classic liberal mold could not do enough to remedy the inequalities that emerged from modern industrial societies, and the result was the creation of welfare state institutions that aimed to use the power of the state to maintain a base level of social and economic equality. This tension between the goals of liberty and equality is a constant one within the liberal tradition, and the different trajectories of Europe and the United States in the twentieth century reflect the respective priorities of successive governments in both places.

Many Europeans, therefore, watched the election of Barack Obama to the presidency of the United States in 2008 with great interest. Since the election of Ronald Reagan in 1980, the divergences between governments in the United States and Europe in their attitudes toward the role that the state might play in remedying social problems

had become even wider. With few exceptions, European governments were much more willing to use the power of the state to assist the unemployed or the aged, to support families, and to provide subsidies for education, public transportation, and national programs for health care. As we have seen, this consensus emerged in part because of a belief that the economic dislocations of the 1920s and 1930s had led directly to the emergence of destabilizing and antidemocratic extremist political movements. In the United States, on the other hand, widespread discontent with attempts by the Johnson administration in the 1960s to use the power of the federal government to end racial segregation and address broad problems such as urban poverty and environmental pollution contributed to a conservative backlash in the 1980s and 1990s. Throughout those years, conservatives in the United States called for an end to welfare programs, repeal of environmental regulations, and less government oversight in the marketplace.

Obama's election in 2008, following on the heels of the financial meltdown earlier the same year, seemed to mark a turning point of sorts in American politics, as his pragmatic campaign was predicated on a claim that government itself was not the problem facing industrial democracies at the outset of the twenty-first century. The Obama administration's ambitious plan to overhaul the health care system faced stiff opposition from many quarters, but a compromise package succeeded in passing the Congress and was signed into law in 2010. Although the eventual outcome of Barack Obama's health care plan remains uncertain at this writing, it is safe to say that the Obama administration's rhetoric about the power of the state to address social problems is one that is recognizable to many of the mainstream parties in Europe. The fierceness of the health care debate—which revolved around questions about the power of the state, the responsibilities of elected governments, the nature of the public good, and the balance between liberty and equality—should not obscure the fact that partisans on both sides of these controversies are using a vocabulary and a set of references that are part of the same liberal democratic political traditions that emerged in Europe and North America in the previous two centuries.

On the international front, the Obama administration in its first months in office showed more continuity than rupture with the president's immediate predecessor from the Republican party. Obama pursued essentially the same policy as George W. Bush in the ongoing war against the Taliban in Afghanistan, alienating many of his supporters in the United States and abroad who expected a different approach. As the U.S. government pursues its military goals in defense of its national interests abroad, debates about the use of American military power in other parts of the world and the form that this power should take have become pressing domestic concerns, and again, the issues turn on questions that have been a central part of the liberal democratic political tradition since it emerged in opposition to monarchist forms of government in the seventeenth century. How should a nation determine the balance between individual freedoms and national security? What forms of force or violence can the state legitimately use against its enemies at home and abroad? What kinds of information about its citizenry should a government be allowed to keep? Are the terrorist threats and emergencies that Western democracies routinely face today so serious that they justify the suspension of internationally recognized human rights? No easy answers to these questions exist—but the answers that governments and societies in Europe and the United States give to them will shape how people everywhere will perceive the legitimacy of the democratic political traditions that they claim to represent.

CONCLUSION

Globalization—defined loosely as the process by which the economies, societies, and cultures of different parts of the world become increasingly interconnected—has been hailed as a solution to old problems even as it has been criticized as a source of new ones. Although some thought that the end of the Cold War in 1989 meant that economic liberalism—that is, a global free-market capitalist system unfettered by government regulations—had triumphed for good in the world, continued political instability in many parts of the globe and the global economic crisis of 2008 have called into question such optimistic interpretations of world events. In the economic realm, national states have looked for ways to reassert their control over the flow of currencies and goods and protect their populations against decisions made elsewhere by financial speculators and investors. Meanwhile, the danger of radical forms of terrorism, both foreign and domestic, has caused even strongly democratic governments in the West to create new and pervasive surveillance bureaucracies, demonstrating that global threats can have real and seemingly permanent local effects on definitions of citizenship, the permeability of borders, and extensions of state power.

In such uncertain times, it is difficult to remain consistent or to determine national priorities: is the threat of terrorism greater than the threat of a loss of liberty stemming from extensions in government power? Is it fair of the International Monetary Fund to ask developing nations to adhere to austere

After You Read This Chapter

Visit StudySpace for quizzes, additional review materials, and multi-media documents. **wwnorton.com/studyspace**

REVIEWING THE OBJECTIVES

- Globalization in the second half of the twentieth century was not new. What does *globalization* mean, and what was similar or different about the most recent phase of globalization in human history?

- The burden of the colonial past continued to weigh heavily on many former colonies after the 1960s. What accounts for the success of some former colonies in the global economy and the continued social and political challenges facing others?

- Since the end of the Second World War, conflicts and events in the Middle East have taken on a global significance far beyond the region's borders. What are the crucial conflicts that occupied the attention of other nations, and what events have proved to be crucial turning points in the emergence of the Middle East as a region that drives developments elsewhere?

cuts to their social welfare spending when wealthy private investment banks receive billion-dollar bailouts for making bad bets in the financial markets because they are "too big to fail"? The complexity of the world's interconnections makes it difficult to determine definitive answers to such questions, and even if one could, any ensuing policy decisions would create winners and losers, ensuring that the political struggles implicit in such questions will endure. Globalization, therefore, is not a final destination—it is the new complex reality of human existence, the context for future struggles about the goals of political association, the meanings of liberty or equality, and the possibility of shared values.

The loss of familiar moorings makes fundamental questions about human behavior and political community difficult to answer. History offers no quick solutions. Historians are reluctant to offer what historian Peter Novick calls "pithy lessons that fit on a bumper sticker." As Novick puts it:

If there is, to use a pretentious word, any wisdom to be acquired from contemplating an historical event, I would think it would derive from confronting it in all its complexity and its contradictions; the ways in which it resembles other events to which it might be compared as well as the way it differs from them. . . . If there are lessons to be extracted from encountering the past, that encounter has to be with the past in all its messiness; they're not likely to come from an encounter with a past that's been shaped so that inspiring lessons will emerge.

The untidy and contradictory evidence that historians discover in the archives rarely yields unblemished heroes or irredeemable villains. Good history reveals the complex processes and dynamics of change over time. It helps us understand the many layers of the past that have formed and constrain us in our present world. At the same time, it shows again and again that these constraints do not preordain what happens next or how we can make the history of the future.

PEOPLE, IDEAS, AND EVENTS IN CONTEXT

- What were the policy goals of **NEOLIBERALISM** after the 1970s, as exemplified by the activities of institutions such as the **INTERNATIONAL MONETARY FUND** and the **WORLD BANK**?
- How do the **HIV EPIDEMIC** of the 1980s or the **SARS EPIDEMIC** of 2003 illustrate the new realities of public health in a globalized world?
- What was the significance of **NELSON MANDELA**'s election as president of South Africa in 1994?
- How was the **1973 OIL EMBARGO** related to the **ARAB-ISRAELI CONFLICT** and what were its effects on the global economy?
- What did radical critics dislike about secular forms of **ARAB NATIONALISM** such as that represented by **GAMAL ABDEL NASSER** in Egypt?
- What led the United States and Britain to support the regime of **REZA PAHLAVI** in Iran, and what events brought **RUHOLLAH KHOMEINI** to power in Iran in 1979?
- What circumstances link the Soviet invasion of Afghanistan in 1979, at the height of the Cold War, with the origins of **AL QAEDA?**
- What made it difficult for European and North American governments to sign the **UN'S UNIVERSAL DECLARATION OF HUMAN RIGHTS** in 1948? What events have occurred since 1948 that indicate that at least some nations might agree to international treaties guaranteeing human rights throughout the world?

CONSEQUENCES

- What successes can the supporters of economic globalization point to? Do the successes of globalization at the end of the twentieth century mean that the goals of economic liberalism have largely been realized?
- Do the anticolonial nationalist movements active in Africa or Asia during the period of decolonization share any common goals with the radical forms of political Islam that emerged after the 1960s in the Middle East?
- What is the relationship between individual liberties as outlined in documents like the American Declaration of Independence and more recent definitions of universal human rights?
- Do contemporary governments have any choice but to continue down the path of globalization, even as they struggle to contain the conflicts produced by the process?

Rulers of Principal States

THE CAROLINGIAN DYNASTY

Pepin of Heristal, Mayor of the Palace, 687–714
Charles Martel, Mayor of the Palace, 715–741
Pepin III, Mayor of the Palace, 741–751; King, 751–768
Charlemagne, King, 768–814; Emperor, 800–814
Louis the Pious, Emperor, 814–840

West Francia

Charles the Bald, King, 840–877; Emperor, 875–877
Louis II, King, 877–879
Louis III, King, 879–882
Carloman, King, 879–884

Middle Kingdoms

Lothair, Emperor, 840–855
Louis (Italy), Emperor, 855–875
Charles (Provence), King, 855–863
Lothair II (Lorraine), King, 855–869

East Francia

Ludwig, King, 840–876
Carloman, King, 876–880
Ludwig, King, 876–882
Charles the Fat, Emperor, 876–887

HOLY ROMAN EMPERORS

Saxon Dynasty

Otto I, 962–973
Otto II, 973–983
Otto III, 983–1002
Henry II, 1002–1024

Franconian Dynasty

Conrad II, 1024–1039
Henry III, 1039–1056
Henry IV, 1056–1106
HenryV, 1106–1125
Lothair II (Saxony), 1125–1137

Hohenstaufen Dynasty

Conrad III, 1138–1152
Frederick I (Barbarossa), 1152–1190
Henry VI, 1190–1197
Philip of Swabia, 1198–1208 } Rivals
Otto IV (Welf), 1198–1215

Frederick II, 1220–1250
Conrad IV, 1250–1254

Interregnum, 1254–1273

Emperors from Various Dynasties

Rudolf I (Habsburg), 1273–1291
Adolf (Nassau), 1292–1298
Albert I (Habsburg), 1298–1308
Henry VII (Luxemburg), 1308–1313
Ludwig IV (Wittelsbach), 1314–1347
Charles IV (Luxemburg), 1347–1378
Wenceslas (Luxemburg), 1378–1400
Rupert (Wittelsbach), 1400–1410
Sigismund (Luxemburg), 1410–1437

Habsburg Dynasty

Albert II, 1438–1439
Frederick III, 1440–1493

Maximilian I, 1493–1519
Charles V, 1519–1556
Ferdinand I, 1556–1564
Maximilian II, 1564–1576
Rudolf II, 1576–1612
Matthias, 1612–1619
Ferdinand II, 1619–1637
Ferdinand III, 1637–1657

Leopold I, 1658–1705
Joseph I, 1705–1711
Charles VI, 1711–1740
Charles VII (not a Habsburg), 1742–1745
Francis I, 1745–1765
Joseph II, 1765–1790
Leopold II, 1790–1792
Francis II, 1792–1806

RULERS OF FRANCE FROM HUGH CAPET

Capetian Dynasty

Hugh Capet, 987–996
Robert II, 996–1031
Henry I, 1031–1060
Philip I, 1060–1108
Louis VI, 1108–1137
Louis VII, 1137–1180
Philip II (Augustus), 1180–1223
Louis VIII, 1223–1226
Louis IX (St. Louis), 1226–1270
Philip III, 1270–1285
Philip IV, 1285–1314
Louis X, 1314–1316
Philip V, 1316–1322
Charles IV, 1322–1328

Valois Dynasty

Philip VI, 1328–1350
John, 1350–1364
Charles V, 1364–1380
Charles VI, 1380–1422
Charles VII, 1422–1461
Louis XI, 1461–1483
Charles VIII, 1483–1498
Louis XII, 1498–1515
Francis I, 1515–1547

Henry II, 1547–1559
Francis II, 1559–1560
Charles IX, 1560–1574
Henry III, 1574–1589

Bourbon Dynasty

Henry IV, 1589–1610
Louis XIII, 1610–1643
Louis XIV, 1643–1715
Louis XV, 1715–1774
Louis XVI, 1774–1792

After 1792

First Republic, 1792–1799
Napoleon Bonaparte, First Consul, 1799–1804
Napoleon I, Emperor, 1804–1814
Louis XVIII (Bourbon dynasty), 1814–1824
Charles X (Bourbon dynasty), 1824–1830
Louis Philippe, 1830–1848
Second Republic, 1848–1852
Napoleon III, Emperor, 1852–1870
Third Republic, 1870–1940
Pétain regime, 1940–1944
Provisional government, 1944–1946
Fourth Republic, 1946–1958
Fifth Republic, 1958–

RULERS OF ENGLAND

Anglo-Saxon Dynasty

Alfred the Great, 871–899
Edward the Elder, 899–924
Ethelstan, 924–939
Edmund I, 939–946
Edred, 946–955
Edwy, 955–959
Edgar, 959–975

Edward the Martyr, 975–978
Ethelred the Unready, 978–1016
Canute, 1016–1035 (Danish Nationality)
Harold I, 1035–1040
Hardicanute, 1040–1042
Edward the Confessor, 1042–1066
Harold II, 1066

House of Normandy

William I (the Conqueror), 1066–1087
William II, 1087–1100
Henry I, 1100–1135
Stephen, 1135–1154

House of Plantagenet

Henry II, 1154–1189
Richard I, 1189–1199
John, 1199–1216
Henry III, 1216–1272
Edward I, 1272–1307
Edward II, 1307–1327
Edward III, 1327–1377
Richard II, 1377–1399

House of Lancaster

Henry IV, 1399–1413
Henry V, 1413–1422
Henry VI, 1422–1461

House of York

Edward IV, 1461–1483
Edward V, 1483
Richard III, 1483–1485

House of Tudor

Henry VII, 1485–1509
Henry VIII, 1509–1547
Edward VI, 1547–1553
Mary, 1553–1558
Elizabeth I, 1558–1603

House of Stuart

James I, 1603–1625
Charles I, 1625–1649

Commonwealth and Protectorate, 1649–1659

House of Stuart Restored

Charles II, 1660–1685
James II, 1685–1688
William III and Mary II, 1689–1694
William III alone, 1694–1702
Anne, 1702–1714

House of Hanover

George I, 1714–1727
George II, 1727–1760
George III, 1760–1820
George IV, 1820–1830
William IV, 1830–1837
Victoria, 1837–1901

House of Saxe-Coburg-Gotha

Edward VII, 1901–1910
George V, 1910–1917

House of Windsor

George V, 1917–1936
Edward VIII, 1936
George VI, 1936–1952
Elizabeth II, 1952–

RULERS OF AUSTRIA AND AUSTRIA-HUNGARY

*Maximilian I (Archduke), 1493–1519
*Charles V, 1519–1556
*Ferdinand I, 1556–1564
*Maximilian II, 1564–1576
*Rudolf II, 1576–1612
*Matthias, 1612–1619
*Ferdinand II, 1619–1637
*Ferdinand III, 1637–1657
*Leopold I, 1658–1705
*Joseph I, 1705–1711
*Charles VI, 1711–1740
Maria Theresa, 1740–1780

*Joseph II, 1780–1790
*Leopold II, 1790–1792
*Francis II, 1792–1835 (Emperor of Austria as Francis I after 1804)
Ferdinand I, 1835–1848
Francis Joseph, 1848–1916 (after 1867 Emperor of Austria and King of Hungary)
Charles I, 1916–1918 (Emperor of Austria and King of Hungary)
Republic of Austria, 1918–1938 (dictatorship after 1934)
Republic restored, under Allied occupation, 1945–1956
Free Republic, 1956–

*also bore title of Holy Roman Emperor

RULERS OF PRUSSIA AND GERMANY

*Frederick I, 1701–1713
*Frederick William I, 1713–1740
*Frederick II (the Great), 1740–1786
*Frederick William II, 1786–1797
*Frederick William III,1797–1840
*Frederick William IV, 1840–1861
*William I, 1861–1888 (German Emperor after 1871)
Frederick III, 1888

*Kings of Prussia

*William II, 1888–1918
Weimar Republic, 1918–1933
Third Reich (Nazi Dictatorship), 1933–1945
Allied occupation, 1945–1952
Division into Federal Republic of Germany in west and
    German Democratic Republic in east, 1949–1991
Federal Republic of Germany (united), 1991–

RULERS OF RUSSIA

Ivan III, 1462–1505
Vasily III, 1505–1533
Ivan IV, 1533–1584
Theodore I, 1534–1598
Boris Godunov, 1598–1605
Theodore II,1605
Vasily IV, 1606–1610
Michael, 1613–1645
Alexius, 1645–1676
Theodore III, 1676–1682
Ivan V and Peter I, 1682–1689
Peter I (the Great), 1689–1725
Catherine I, 1725–1727
Peter II, 1727–1730

Anna, 1730–1740
Ivan VI, 1740–1741
ElIzabeth, 1741–1762
Peter III, 1762
Catherine II (the Great), 1762–1796
Paul, 1796–1801
Alexander I,1801–1825
Nicholas I, 1825–1855
Alexander II,1855–1881
Alexander III, 1881–1894
Nicholas II, 1894–1917
Soviet Republic, 1917–1991
Russian Federation, 1991–

RULERS OF UNIFIED SPAIN

Ferdinand
{ and Isabella, 1479–1504
{ and Philip I, 1504–1506
{ and Charles I, 1506–1516

Charles I (Holy Roman Emperor Charles V), 1516–1556
Philip II, 1556–1598
Philip III, 1598–1621
Philip IV, 1621–1665
Charles II, 1665–1700
Philip V, 1700–1746
Ferdinand VI, 1746–1759
Charles III, 1759–1788
Charles IV, 1788–1808

Ferdinand VII, 1808
Joseph Bonaparte, 1808–1813
Ferdinand VII (restored), 1814–1833
Isabella II, 1833–1868
Republic, 1868–1870
Amadeo, 1870–1873
Republic, 1873–1874
Alfonso XII, 1874–1885
Alfonso XIII, 1886–1931
Republic, 1931–1939
Fascist Dictatorship, 1939–1975
Juan Carlos I, 1975–

RULERS OF ITALY

Victor Emmanuel II, 1861–1878
Humbert I, 1878–1900
Victor Emmanuel III, 1900–1946

Fascist Dictatorship, 1922-1943 (maintained in northern
  Italy until 1945)
Humbert II, May 9–June 13, 1946
Republic, 1946–

PROMINENT POPES

Silvester I, 314–335
Leo I, 440–461
Gelasius I, 492–496
Gregory I, 590–604
Nicholas I, 858–867
Silvester II, 999–1003
Leo IX, 1049–1054
Nicholas II, 1058–1061
Gregory VII, 1073–1085
Urban II, 1088–1099
Paschal II, 1099–1118
Alexander III, 1159–1181
Innocent III, 1198–1216
Gregory IX, 1227–1241
Innocent IV, 1243–1254
Boniface VIII, 1294–1303
John XXII, 1316–1334
Nicholas V, 1447–1455
Pius II, 1458–1464

Alexander VI, 1492–1503
Julius II, 1503–1513
Leo X, 1513–1521
Paul III, 1534–1549
Paul IV, 1555–1559
Sixtus V, 1585–1590
Urban VIII, 1623–1644
Gregory XVI, 1831–1846
Pius IX, 1846–1878
Leo XIII, 1878–1903
Pius X, 1903–1914
Benedict XV, 1914–1922
Pius XI, 1922–1939
Pius XII, 1939–1958
John XXIII, 1958–1963
Paul VI, 1963–1978
John Paul I, 1978
John Paul II, 1978–2005
Benedict XVI 2005–

CHAPTER 1

Aldred, Cyril. *The Egyptians*. 3d ed. London, 1998. An indispensable, lively overview of Egyptian culture and history by one of the great masters of Egyptology.

Baines, J., and J. Málek. *Atlas of Ancient Egypt*. Rev. ed. New York, 2000. A reliable, well-illustrated survey, with excellent maps.

Bottéro, Jean. *Everyday Life in Ancient Mesopotamia*. Trans. Antonia Nevill. Baltimore, MD, 2001. A wide-ranging, interdisciplinary account.

Bottéro, Jean. *Religion in Ancient Mesopotamia*. Chicago, 2001. An accessible, engaging survey.

George, Andrew, trans. *The Epic of Gilgamesh: A New Translation. The Babylonian Epic Poem and Other Texts in Akkadian and Sumerian*. New York and London, 1999. The newest and most reliable translation, which carefully distinguishes the chronological "layers" of this famous text; also includes many related texts.

Hodder, Ian. *The Leopard's Tale:Revealing the Mysteries of Çatalhöyük*. London and New York, 2006. The most up-to-date account of this fascinating archaeological site, written for general readers by the director of the excavation.

Hornung, Erik. *History of Ancient Egypt: An Introduction*. Ithaca, NY, 1999. Concise and authoritative.

Kemp, Barry J. *Ancient Egypt: Anatomy of a Civilization*. London, 1989. An imaginative examination of Egyptian social and intellectual history.

Leick, Gwendolyn. *The Babylonians: An Introduction*. London and New York, 2002. A wide-ranging survey of Babylonian civilization across the centuries.

Lichteim, Miriam. *Ancient Egyptian Literature: A Book of Readings*. 3 vols. Berkeley, CA, 1973–1980. A compilation used by students and scholars alike.

McDowell, A. G. *Village Life in Ancient Egypt: Laundry Lists and Love Songs*. Oxford, 1999. A fascinating collection of translated texts recovered from an Egyptian peasant village, dating from 1539 to 1075 B.C.E.

Mertz, Barbara. *Red Land, Black Land: Daily Life in Ancient Egypt*. Rev. ed. New York, 1990. Emphasizes the role of the Nile and the forbidding natural environment of Egypt.

Pollock, Susan. *Ancient Mesopotamia*. Cambridge, 1999. An advanced textbook that draws on theoretical anthropology to interpret Mesopotamian civilization up to 2100 B.C.E.

Redford, Donald B., ed. *The Oxford Encyclopedia of Ancient Egypt*. 3 vols. New York, 2001. An indispensible reference work, intended for both specialists and beginners.

Roaf, Michael. *Cultural Atlas of Mesopotamia and the Ancient Near East*. New York, 1990. An informative, authoritative, and lavishly illustrated guide, with excellent maps.

Robins, Gay. *The Art of Ancient Egypt*. London, 1997. An excellent survey, now the standard account.

Shafer, Byron E., ed. *Religion in Ancient Egypt: Gods, Myths, and Personal Practice*. London, 1991. A scholarly examination of Egyptian belief and ritual, with contributions from leading authorities.

Shaw, Ian, ed. *The Oxford History of Ancient Egypt*. Oxford, 2000. An outstanding collaborative survey of Egyptian history from the Stone Age to c. 300 C.E., with excellent bibliographical essays.

Smail, Daniel Lord. *On Deep History and the Brain*. Berkeley, 2008. A pioneering introduction to the historical uses of neuroscience and evolutionary biology.

Snell, Daniel C., ed. *A Companion to the Ancient Near East*. Oxford, 2005. A topical survey of recent scholarly work, particularly strong on society, economy, and culture.

Wengrow, David. *The Archaeology of Early Egypt: Social Transformations in North-East Africa, 10,000 to 2650 B.C*. Cambridge, 2006. An authoritative account of archeological evidence and its interpretation.

CHAPTER 2

Aubet, Maria Eugenia. *Phoenicia and the West: Politics, Colonies, and Trade*. Trans. Mary Turton. Cambridge, 1993. An intelligent and thought-provoking examination of Phoenician civilization and its influence.

Boardman, John. *Assyrian and Babylonian Empires and Other States of the Near East from the Eighth to the Sixth Centuries B.C.* New York, 1991. Scholarly and authoritative.

Boardman, John. *Persia and the West*. London, 2000. A great book by a distinguished scholar, with a particular focus on art and architecture as projections of Persian imperial ideologies.

Boyce, Mary. *Textual Sources for the Study of Zoroastrianism*. Totowa, NJ, 1984. An invaluable collection of documents.

Bryce, Trevor. *The Kingdom of the Hittites*. Oxford, 1998. And *Life and Society in the Hittite World*. Oxford, 2002. An extraordinary synthesis, now the standard account of Hittite political, military, and daily life.

Curtis, John. *Ancient Persia*. Cambridge, MA, 1990. Concise, solid, reliable.

Dever, William. *Who Were the Early Israelites and Where Did They Come From?* Grand Rapids, MI, 2003. A balanced, fair-minded account with excellent bibliographical guidance to recent work.

Dickinson, O. T. P. K. *The Aegean Bronze Age*. Cambridge, 1994. An excellent summary of archaeological evidence and scholarly argument concerning Minoan, Mycenaean, and other cultures of the Bronze Age Aegean basin.

Dothan, Trude, and Moshe Dothan. *Peoples of the Sea: The Search for the Philistines*. New York, 1992. The essential starting point for understanding Philistine culture and its links to the Aegean basin.

Drews, Robert. *The End of the Bronze Age: Changes in Warfare and the Catastrophe ca. 1200 B.C.* Princeton, NJ, 1993. A stimulating analysis and survey, with excellent bibliographies.

Finkelstein, Israel, and Nadav Na'aman, eds. *From Nomadism to Monarchy: Archaeological and Historical Aspects of Early Israel*. Jerusalem, 1994. Scholarly articles on the Hebrews' transformation from pastoralists to a sedentary society focused on the worship of Yahweh.

Fitton, J. Lesley. *Minoans: Peoples of the Past* (British Museum Publications). London, 2002. A careful, reliable debunking of myths about the Minoans, written for nonspecialists.

Kamm, Antony. *The Israelites: An Introduction*. New York, 1999. A short, accessible history of the land and people of Israel up to 135 C.E., aimed at students and general readers.

Kuhrt, Amélie. *The Ancient Near East, c. 3000–330 B.C.* 2 vols. London and New York, 1995. An outstanding survey, written for students, that includes Egypt and Israel as well as Mesopotamia, Babylonia, Assyria, and Persia.

Luckenbill, Daniel David, ed. and trans. *Ancient Records of Assyria and Babylonia*. 2 vols. Chicago, 1926–27. Still one of the best and most readily accessible collections of primary sources on Assyrian attitudes and policies in war, religion, and politics.

Metzger, Bruce M., and Michael D. Coogan, eds. *The Oxford Companion to the Bible*. New York, 1993. An outstanding reference work, with contributions by leading authorities.

Niditch, Susan. *Ancient Israelite Religion*. New York, 1997. A short introduction designed for students, emphasizing the diversity of Hebrew religious practices.

Redford, Donald B. *Egypt, Canaan, and Israel in Ancient Times*. Princeton, NJ, 1992. An overview of the interactions between these peoples from about 1200 B.C.E. to the beginning of the Common Era.

Renfrew, Colin. *Archaeology and Language: The Puzzle of Indo-European Origins*. Cambridge, 1987. A masterful but controversial work by one of the most creative archaeologists of the twentieth century.

Saggs, H. W. F. *The Might That Was Assyria*. London, 1984. A lively narrative history of the Assyrian Empire, with analysis of the institutions that underlay its strength.

Sandars, Nancy K. *The Sea Peoples: Warriors of the Ancient Mediterranean*. Rev. ed. London, 1985. An introductory account for students and scholars.

Tubb, Jonathan N., and Rupert L. Chapman. *Archaeology and the Bible*. London, 1990. A good starting point for students that clearly illustrates the difficulties in linking archeological evidence to biblical accounts of early Hebrew history and society.

Wood, Michael. *In Search of the Trojan War*. New York, 1985. Aimed at a general audience, this carefully researched and engagingly written book is an excellent introduction to the late–Bronze Age context of the Trojan War.

CHAPTER 3

Penguin Classics and the Loeb Classical Library both offer reliable translations of Greek literary, philosophical, and historical texts.

Beard, Mary. *The Parthenon*. Cambridge, MA, 2003. A book that traces the successive stages of this monument's construction, deconstruction, reconstruction, and restoration.

Boardman, John, Jaspar Griffin, and Oswyn Murray, eds. *Greece and the Hellenistic World*. Oxford, 1988. A reprint of the Greek and Hellenistic chapters from *The Oxford History of the Classical World,* originally published in 1986. Excellent, stimulating surveys, accessible to a general audience.

Brunschwig, Jacques, and Geoffrey E. R. Lloyd. *Greek Thought: A Guide to Classical Knowledge*. Translated by Catherine Porter. Cambridge, MA, 2000. An outstanding work of reference.

Buckley, Terry, ed. *Aspects of Greek History, 750–323 B.C.: A Source-Based Approach*. London, 1999. An outstanding collection of source materials.

Cartledge, Paul A. *The Spartans: An Epic History*. New York, 2003. A lively and authoritative history of Sparta from its origins to the Roman conquest.

Dover, Kenneth J. *Greek Homosexuality*. Cambridge, MA, 1978. The standard account of an important subject.

Fantham, Elaine, Helene Foley, Natalie Kampen, Sarah B. Pomeroy, and H. A. Shapiro. *Women in the Classical World: Image and Text*. Oxford, 1994. Wide-ranging analysis drawing on both visual and written sources, covering both the Greek and the Roman periods.

Fornara, Charles W., and Loren J. Samons II. *Athens from Cleisthenes to Pericles*. Berkeley, 1991. An excellent narrative history of Athenian politics during the first half of the fifth century B.C.E.

Freeman, Charles. *The Greek Achievement: The Foundation of the Western World*. New York, 1999. An admiring survey written for a general audience.

Garlan, Yvon. *Slavery in Ancient Greece*. Ithaca, NY, 1988. Now the standard account.

Hanson, Victor Davis. *The Other Greeks: The Family Farm and the Agrarian Roots of Western Civilization*. New York, 1995. Polemical and idiosyncratic, but convincing in its emphasis on smallholding farmers as the backbone of Greek urban society.

Havelock, Eric A. *The Literate Revolution in Greece and Its Cultural Consequences*. Princeton, 1982. A now-classic account of the wide-ranging effects of writing on Greek society.

Jones, Nicholas F. *Ancient Greece: State and Society*. Upper Saddle River, NJ, 1997. A concise survey from the Minoans up to the end of the Classical Period that emphasizes the connections between the social order and politics.

Lefkowitz, Mary, and Maureen Fant. *Women's Life in Greece and Rome: A Source Book in Translation*. 3rd ed. Baltimore, MD, 2005. A remarkably wide-ranging collection, topically arranged, invaluable to students.

Levi, Peter. *Atlas of the Greek World*. New York, 1984. Excellent maps and illustrations supplement an outstanding text.

Morris, Ian, and Barry Powell, eds. *A New Companion to Homer*. Leiden, 1997. A collection of thirty specialized but accessible scholarly articles, encompassing the most recent research on Homer and Dark Age Greece.

Pomeroy, Sarah B., Stanley M. Burstein, Walter Donlan, and Jennifer Tolbert Roberts. *Ancient Greece: A Political, Social, and Cultural History*. Oxford, 1999. An outstanding textbook; clear and lively.

Price, Simon. *Religions of the Ancient Greeks*. Cambridge, 1999. Concise and authoritative, this survey extends from the Archaic Period up to the fifth century C.E.

Seaford, Richard. *Money and the Greek Mind: Homer, Philosophy, Tragedy*. Cambridge, 2004. A provocative study of portable wealth and its far-reaching effects.

Strassler, Robert B., ed. *The Landmark Thucydides*. New York, 1996. Reprints the classic Richard Crawley translation with maps, commentary, notes, and appendices by leading scholars.

Thomas, Carol G., and Craig Conant. *Citadel to City-State: The Transformation of Greece, 1200–700 B.C.E.* Bloomington, IN, 1999. A lucid and accessible study that examines developments at a number of different Dark Age sites.

Thomas, Rosalind. *Oral Tradition and Written Record in Classical Athens*. Cambridge, 1989. A fascinating look at how oral epic, lyric, and drama were transmitted over time.

CHAPTER 4

Penguin Classics and the Loeb Classical Library both offer reliable translations of scores of literary and historical texts from this period. Particularly important are historical works by Arrian (*Anabasis of Alexander*), Plutarch (*Life of Alexander*), and Polybius (*The Histories*).

Adcock, F. E. *The Greek and Macedonian Art of War*. Berkeley, 1957. Still a valuable introduction to the guiding principles and assumptions of warfare in the fourth century.

Austin, M. M. *The Hellenistic World from Alexander to the Roman Conquest: A Selection of Ancient Sources in Translation*. Cambridge, 1981. A good collection of primary documents.

Bagnall, R. S., and P. Derow. *Greek Historical Documents: The Hellenistic Period*. Chico, CA, 1981. Another useful collection.

Borza, Eugene N. *In the Shadow of Olympus: The Emergence of Macedon*. Princeton, NJ, 1990. The standard account of the rise of Macedon up to the accession of Philip II.

Bosworth, A. B. *Conquest and Empire: The Reign of Alexander the Great*. Cambridge, 1988. A political and military analysis of Alexander's career that strips away the romance, maintaining a clear vision of the ruthlessness and human cost of his conquests.

Bosworth, A. B. *The Legacy of Alexander: Politics, Warfare, and Propaganda under the Successors*. Oxford, 2002. The most recent survey of the half century following Alexander's death and of the people who created the Hellenistic kingdoms of Egypt, Persia, and Macedon.

Burstein, Stanley M., ed. and trans. *The Hellenistic Age from the Battle of Ipsos to the Death of Kleopatra VII*. Cambridge, 1985. An excellent collection, with sources not found elsewhere.

Cartledge, Paul. *Agesilaus and the Crisis of Sparta*. Baltimore, MD, 1987. A thorough but readable analysis of the social and political challenges besetting Sparta in the fourth century B.C.E.

Cartledge, Paul. *Alexander the Great: The Hunt for a New Past*. Woodstock, NY, 2004. A compelling account of Alexander's life, times, and influences.

Green, Peter. *Alexander to Actium: The Historical Evolution of the Hellenistic Age*. Berkeley, CA. 1990. An outstanding, comprehensive, and wide-ranging history of the period.

Green, Peter. *Alexander of Macedon, 356–323 B.C.* Berkeley, CA, 1991. Revised edition of the author's earlier biography; entertainingly written, rich in detail and insight.

———. *The Hellenistic Age: A Short History*. New York, 2007. An authoritative synthesis that carries the history of Greek influence into the fourth century C.E.

Nicholas, G. L. *The Genius of Alexander the Great*. Chapel Hill, NC, 1998. A clear, authoritative, admiring account, distilling a lifetime of research on the subject.

Hansen, Mogens H. *The Athenian Democracy in the Age of Demosthenes*. Oxford, 1991. An examination of the political institutions of Athens in the fourth century B.C.E.

Lloyd, Geoffrey, and Nathan Sivin. *The Way and the Word: Science and Medicine in Early China and Greece*. New Haven, CT, 2002. An extraordinary comparative study.

Ober, Josiah. *Mass and Elite in Democratic Athens: Rhetoric, Ideology, and the Power of the People*. Princeton, NJ, 1989. An excellent study of the ideology of democracy in Athens that borrows from the insights of modern social science.

Pollitt, Jerome J. *Art in the Hellenistic Age*. New York, 1986. The standard account, blending cultural history with art history.

Sherwin-White, Susan, and Amélie Kuhrt. *From Samarkhand to Sardis: A New Approach to the Seleucid Empire*. London, 1993. A stimulating examination of the relationship between rulers and ruled in the vast expanses of the Seleucid Empire.

Shipley, Graham. *The Greek World after Alexander, 323–30 B.C.* New York and London, 2000. A study of the social, intellectual, and artistic changes in the Hellenistic era.

Thomas, Carol G. *Alexander the Great in His World*. Oxford and Malden, MA, 2007. A study of the contexts—familial, political, and social—that shaped Alexander's career.

Tripolitis, Antonia. *Religions of the Hellenistic-Roman Age*. Grand Rapids, MI, 2002. Survey of the variety of religious experience, ritual, and belief in the centuries before the emergence of Christianity.

Tritle, Lawrence A., ed. *The Greek World in the Fourth Century: From the Fall of the Athenian Empire to the Successors of Alexander*. New York, 1997. A wide-ranging collection of scholarly essays.

Worthington, Ian. *Alexander the Great: A Reader*. London and New York, 2002. A collection of influential interpretations of Alexander by modern historians.

CHAPTER 5

Translations of Roman authors are available in both the Penguin Classics series and in the Loeb Classical Library.

Barker, Graeme, and Tom Rasmussen. *The Etruscans.* Oxford and Malden, MA, 1998. A fine survey, from the Blackwell *Peoples of Europe* series.

Beard, Mary. *Pompeii: The Life of a Roman Town.* A fascinating, cutting-edge study of daily life.

Boardman, John, Jasper Griffin, and Oswyn Murray. *The Oxford History of the Roman World.* Oxford, 1990. Reprint of relevant portions of the excellent *Oxford History of the Classical World* (1986). Stimulating, accessible topical chapters by British specialists.

Cornell, T. J. *The Beginnings of Rome: Italy and Rome from the Bronze Age to the Punic Wars (c. 1000–264 B.C.).* London, 1995. An ambitious survey of the archaeological and historical evidence for early Rome.

Crawford, Michael. *The Roman Republic,* 2d ed. Cambridge, MA, 1993. A lively, fast-paced survey of republican Rome. An excellent place to start.

Fantham, Elaine, Helene Peet Foley, Natalie Boymel Kampen, Sarah B. Pomeroy, and H. Alan Shapiro. *Women in the Classical World.* Oxford, 1994. An expert survey of both Greece and Rome.

Garnsey, Peter, and Richard Saller. *The Roman Empire: Economy, Society, and Culture.* Berkeley, CA, 1987. A straightforward short survey.

Gruen, Erich S. *The Hellenistic World and the Coming of Rome.* 2 vols. Berkeley, CA, 1984. A massive survey, focused on the unpredictable rise of Rome to a position of dominance within the Mediterranean world.

Harris, William V. *War and Imperialism in Republican Rome, 327–70 B.C.* Oxford, 1979. A challenging study arguing that Rome's need for military conquest and expansion was deeply embedded in the fabric of Roman life.

Lancel, Serge. *Carthage: A History.* Trans. Antonia Nevill. Oxford, 1995. An account of Rome's great rival for control of the Mediterranean world.

Lewis, Naphtali, and M. Reinhold. *Roman Civilization: Selected Readings.* 2 vols. New York, 1951–55. The standard collection, especially for political and economic subjects. Vol. 1 covers the republic; vol. 2, the empire.

Millar, Fergus G. B. *The Emperor in the Roman World, 31 B.C.–A.D. 337.* London, 1977. A classic work that showed (among much else) the importance of emperor worship to the religious outlook of the Roman Empire.

———. *The Crowd in Rome in the Late Republic.* Ann Arbor, MI, 1999. A revisionist account that emphasizes the reality of Roman democracy in the late republic, against those who would see the period's politics as entirely under the control of aristocratic families.

Ward, Allen M., Fritz Heichelheim, and Cedric A. Yeo. *A History of the Roman People,* 3d ed. Upper Saddle River, NJ, 1999. An informative, well-organized textbook covering Roman history from its beginnings to the end of the sixth century C.E.

Watkin, David. *The Roman Forum.* London, 2009. A history of the successive buildings and archeological excavations of this central Roman space.

Wells, Colin. *The Roman Empire,* 2d ed. Cambridge, MA, 1992. An easily readable survey from the reign of Augustus to the mid-third century C.E., particularly useful for its treatment of the relationship between the Roman central government and its Italian provinces.

Wiseman, T. P. *Remembering the Roman People.* Oxford, 2009. A collection of studies devoted to popular politics in the late republic.

Woolf, Greg. *Becoming Roman: The Origins of Provincial Civilization in Gaul.* Cambridge, 1998. An exemplary study of how provincial elites made themselves "Roman."

CHAPTER 6

Augustine. *The City of God.* Trans. Henry Bettenson. Baltimore, MD, 1972.

———. *Confessions.* Trans. Henry M. Chadwick. Oxford, 1991.

———. *On Christian Doctrine.* Trans. D. W. Robertson Jr. New York, 1958.

Boethius. *The Consolation of Philosophy.* Trans. R. Green. Indianapolis, IN, 1962.

Bowersock, G. W., Peter Brown, and Oleg Grabar. *Late Antiquity: A Guide to the Postclassical World.* Cambridge, MA, 1999. An authoritative compilation. The first half is devoted to essays on the cultural features of the period; the second half is organized as an encyclopedia.

Brown, Peter. *Augustine of Hippo.* Berkeley, CA, 1967. A great biography by the great scholar of late antiquity.

———. *The Body and Society: Men, Women and Sexual Renunciation in Early Christianity.* New York, 1988. A revealing study of the fundamental transformations wrought by Christianity in the late antique world.

———. *Power and Persuasion in Late Antiquity: Toward a Christian Empire.* Madison, WI, 1992. An important account of Christianity's effects on the political culture of the later Roman Empire.

———. *The Rise of Western Christendom: Triumph and Diversity, 200–1000,* 2d ed. Oxford, 2002. An evocative picture of Christianity's spread eastward and northward from the Mediterranean world.

Brown, Peter. *The World of Late Antiquity.* New York, 1971. Still the best short survey of the period, with excellent illustrations.

Cameron, Averil. *The Later Roman Empire, A.D. 284–430.* London, 1993. Now the standard account of its period, with an emphasis on imperial politics.

———. *The Mediterranean World in Late Antiquity, A.D. 395–600.* London, 1993. Masterful, with excellent, succinct bibliographical essays.

Cassiodorus. *An Introduction to Divine and Human Readings.* Trans. L. W. Jones. New York, 1946.

Chadwick, Henry M. *Augustine.* Oxford, 1986. A short introduction to Augustine's thought.

———. *Boethius*. Oxford, 1981. An intellectual biography of this important thinker.

Clark, Gillian. *Christianity and Roman Society*. Cambridge, 2004. A short, stimulating survey that places early Christianity firmly in its Roman social context.

Clark, Gillian. *Women in Late Antiquity*. Oxford, 1993. A clear, compact account of an important subject.

Coogan, Michael, ed. *The Oxford History of the Biblical World*. Oxford, 1998. A reliable but rather traditional account of the historical events recounted in the Hebrew Bible and the New Testament.

Ehrman, Bart D. *The New Testament: A Historical Introduction to the Early Christian Writings,* 4th ed. Oxford, 2008. The standard textbook by a leading authority.

Eusebius. *The History of the Church*. Trans. G. A. Williamson. Baltimore, MD, 1965. A contemporary account of Constantine's reign, written by one of his courtier-bishops.

———. *Eusebius' Life of Constantine*. Trans. Averil Cameron and Stuart Hall. Oxford, 1999. An admiring biography that reflects Constantine's own vision of his religious authority.

Hopkins, Keith. *A World Full of Gods: The Strange Triumph of Christianity*. Penguin, 1999. An imaginative study of religious pluralism in the Roman world and the context in which Christianity emerged.

Kulikowski, Michael. *Rome's Gothic Wars: From the Third Century to Alaric*. Cambridge, 2007. An authoritative and critical account.

Lane Fox, Robin. *Pagans and Christians*. New York, 1987. A subtle, perceptive, and highly readable exploration of the pagan world within which Christianity grew up.

Lawrence, Clifford Hugh. *Medieval Monasticism*, 3d ed. London, 2000. Concise, perceptive survey of monasticism from its beginnings to the end of the Middle Ages.

Markus, R. A. *The End of Ancient Christianity*. New York, 1990. An expert synthetic study of Christianity in the western Roman Empire between 350 and 600 C.E.

Pagels, Elaine. *The Gnostic Gospels*. New York, 1979. A pathbreaking study of the noncanonical gospels and the history of their exclusion from the Bible.

Pelikan, Jaroslav. *The Christian Tradition*. Vol. 1, *The Emergence of the Catholic Tradition*. Chicago, 1971. A history of Christian doctrine that is one of the tours-de-force of twentieth-century scholarship.

Potter, David. *The Roman Empire at Bay, A.D. 180–395*. London and New York, 2004. The most up-to-date account of the empire's reorganization and transformation in this era.

Sanders, E. P. *The Historical Figure of Jesus*. London and New York, 1993. A fine study of Jesus in his first-century Jewish context.

Shanks, Hershel, ed. *Christianity and Rabbinic Judaism: A Parallel History of Their Origins and Early Development*. Washington, DC, 1992. Accessible chapters written by top authorities, describing both Jewish and Christian developments from the first to the sixth centuries C.E.

Sherwin-White, A. N. *Roman Society and Roman Law in the New Testament*. Oxford, 1963. A fascinating reading of the New Testament in its historical context.

Wallace-Hadrill, John Michael. *The Barbarian West*, 3d ed. London, 1966. A classic analysis of the hybrid culture of the late Roman West.

Whittaker, C. R. *Frontiers of the Roman Empire: A Social and Economic Study*. Baltimore, MD, 1994. A convincing picture of the frontiers of the Roman Empire as zones of intensive cultural interaction.

Williams, Stephen. *Diocletian and the Roman Recovery*. New York, 1997. Thorough and authoritative.

CHAPTER 7

Bede. *A History of the English Church and People*. Trans. Leo Sherley-Price. Baltimore, MD., 1955. The fundamental source for early Anglo-Saxon history.

Bloom, Jonathan M. *Paper Before Print: The Impact and History of Paper in the Islamic World*. New Haven, CT, 2001. A fascinating account, with beautiful illustrations.

Boniface. *Letters of Saint Boniface*. Trans. Ephraim Emerton. New York, 1972.

Campbell, James, ed. *The Anglo-Saxons*. Oxford, 1982. An authoritative and splendidly illustrated volume.

Collins, Roger. *Early Medieval Europe, 300–1000*. 2d ed. New York, 1999. Dry and detailed, but a useful textbook nonetheless.

Donner, Fred. *The Early Islamic Conquests*. Princeton, NJ, 1981. A scholarly but readable narrative and analysis.

Einhard and Notker the Stammerer. *Two Lives of Charlemagne*. Trans. Lewis Thorpe. Baltimore, MD, 1969. Lively and entertaining works of contemporary biography.

Fletcher, Richard A. *The Barbarian Conversion: From Paganism to Christianity*. Berkeley, CA, 1999. Slow paced but informative and perceptive.

———. *Moorish Spain*. Berkeley, CA, 1993. The best short survey in English.

Geanakoplos, Deno John, ed. *Byzantium: Church, Society and Civilization Seen through Contemporary Eyes*. Chicago, 1984. An outstanding source book.

Gregory, Timothy E. *A History of Byzantium*. Malden, MA, and Oxford, 2005. The most accessible of the recent textbooks on Byzantium. An excellent place to start.

Herrin, Judith. *The Formation of Christendom*. Princeton, NJ, 1987. A synthetic history of the Christian civilizations of Byzantium and western Europe from 500 to 800, written by a prominent historian.

Hodges, Richard, and David Whitehouse. *Mohammed, Charlemagne and the Origins of Europe*. London, 1983. A critical analysis of the "Pirenne thesis," reexaming the relationship between the Mediterranean world and northern Europe.

Hourani, Albert. *A History of the Arab Peoples*. New York, 1992. A sympathetic and clear survey written for nonspecialists.

Kazhdan, Alexander P., ed. *The Oxford Dictionary of Byzantium*. 3 vols. Oxford, 1991. An authoritative reference work.

Kennedy, Hugh. *The Prophet and the Age of the Caliphates*. 2d ed. Harlow, UK, 2004. A lucid introduction to the political history of the Islamic world from the sixth through the eleventh centuries.

Krautheimer, Richard. *Early Christian and Byzantine Architecture*. 4th ed. New York, 1986. A classic work by one of the greatest Byzantine art historians of the twentieth century.

Mango, Cyril, ed. *The Oxford History of Byzantium*. Oxford and New York, 2002. Full of sharp judgments and attractively illustrated.

McCormick, Michael. *The Origins of the European Economy: Communications and Commerce A.D. 300–900*. Cambridge, 2002. An astonishing reinterpretation of the evidence for the myriad contacts between Christian Europe and Islam.

McKitterick, Rosamond. *Charlemagne: The Formation of a European Identity*. Cambridge, 2008. A history of Charlemagne's career and its lasting impact by an eminent scholar of the Carolingian world.

———, ed. *The Uses of Literacy in Early Medieval Europe*. New York, 1990. A superb collection of essays.

McNamara, Jo Ann, and John E. Halborg, eds. *Sainted Women of the Dark Ages*. Durham, NC, 1992. Translated saints' lives from Merovingian and Carolingian Europe.

Murray, A. C., ed. *From Roman to Merovingian Gaul: A Reader*. Toronto, 2000. An excellent collection of sources.

Pelikan, Jaroslav. *The Christian Tradition*. Vol. II, *The Spirit of Eastern Christendom*. Chicago, 1974. An outstanding synthetic treatment of the doctrines of Byzantine Christianity.

Procopius. *The Secret History*. Trans. G. A. Williamson. Baltimore, MD, 1966. An "unauthorized" account of Justinian's reign, written by the emperor's offical historian.

Reuter, Timothy. *Germany in the Early Middle Ages, 800–1056*. New York, 1991. The best survey in English.

Sawyer, Peter, ed. *The Oxford Illustrated History of the Vikings*. Oxford, 1997. The best one-volume account, lavishly illustrated.

Todd, Malcolm. *The Early Germans*. Oxford, 1992. A reliable survey, particularly strong in its use of archaeological evidence.

Treadgold, Warren. *A History of the Byzantine State and Society*. Stanford, CA, 1997. A massive, encyclopedic narrative of the political, economic, and military history of Byzantium from 284 until 1461.

Wallace-Hadrill, John Michael. *Early Germanic Kingship in England and on the Continent*. Oxford, 1971. A classic analysis of changing ideas about kingship in early medieval Europe, emphasizing the links between Anglo-Saxon and Carolingian cultures.

———. *The Frankish Church*. Oxford, 1983. A masterful account that links the Merovingian and Carolingian churches.

Watt, W. Montgomery. *Islamic Philosophy and Theology*, 2d ed. Edinburgh, UK, 1985. The standard English account.

Wemple, Suzanne Fonay. *Women in Frankish Society: Marriage and the Cloister, 500–900*. Philadelphia, PA, 1981. An influential account of changing attitudes toward marriage among the early Franks.

Whittow, Mark. *The Making of Orthodox Byzantium, 600–1025*. London, 1996. Emphasizes the centrality of orthodoxy in shaping Byzantine history. Particularly good on Byzantine relations with the peoples outside the empire.

Wickham, Chris. *Framing the Middle Ages: Europe and the Mediterranean, 400–800*. Oxford, 2007. An eye-opening history that spans the transitional periods of late antiquity and the early Middle Ages, paying careful attention to regional differences.

Wood, Ian. *The Merovingian Kingdoms, 450–751*. New York, 1994. A detailed study, but difficult for beginners.

CHAPTER 8

Amt, Emily, ed. *Women's Lives in Medieval Europe: A Sourcebook*. New York, 1993. An excellent collection of primary texts.

The Song of Roland. Trans. Robert Harrison. Penguin, 1970. A lively translation.

Arnold, Benjamin. *Princes and Territories in Medieval Germany*. Cambridge and New York, 1991. The best such survey in English.

Blumenthal, Uta-Renate. *The Investiture Controversy*. Philadelphia, 1988. A clear review of a complicated subject.

Burman, Thomas E. *Reading the Qur'ān in Latin Christendom, 1140–1560*. Philadelphia, 2007. A fascinating account of the Qu'ran's reception in medieval Europe.

Dunbabin, Jean. *France in the Making, 843–1180*, 2d ed. Oxford and New York, 2000. An authoritative survey of the disparate territories that came to make up the medieval French kingdom.

Dyer, Christopher. *Making a Living in the Middle Ages: The People of Britain 850–1520*. New Haven, 2002. A splendid new synthesis that combines social, economic, and archaeological evidence.

Fuhrmann, Horst. *Germany in the High Middle Ages, c. 1050–1200*. Cambridge, 1986. A useful, short history of twelfth-century Germany.

Hicks, Carola. *The Bayeux Tapestry: The Life Story of Masterpiece*. London, 2006. An art historian's engrossing account of the making, reception, and interpretation of this amazing artifact.

Jones, P. J. *The Italian City-State: From Commune to Signoria*. Oxford and New York, 1997. A fundamental reinterpretation of the evidence.

Kaeuper, Richard W. *Chivalry and Violence in Medieval Europe*. Oxford and New York, 1999. A darker view of chivalry than Keen's.

Keen, Maurice. *Chivalry*. New Haven, CT, 1984. A comprehensive treatment of chivalry from its origins to the sixteenth century.

Leyser, Henrietta. *Medieval Women: A Social History of Women in England, 440–1500*. New York, 1995. Although limited to one country, this is the best of the recent surveys treating medieval women.

Leyser, Karl. *Rule and Conflict in an Early Medieval Society: Ottonian Saxony*. Oxford, 1979. A concise, challenging account of the dynamics of rule in tenth-century Saxony, paying special attention to the importance of royal women.

Lopez, Robert S., and Irving W. Raymond, eds. *Medieval Trade in the Mediterranean World*. New York, 1990. A pathbreaking collection of source material.

Miller, Maureen C. *Power and the Holy in the Age of the Investiture Conflict. A Brief History with Documents*. Boston, 2005. A stimulating approach to the eleventh-century conflicts over temporal and spiritual power, with many newly translated sources.

Moore, Robert I. *The First European Revolution, c. 970–1215*. Oxford and Cambridge, MA, 2000. A remarkable description of the ways in which European society was fundamentally reshaped during the eleventh and twelfth centuries.

Peters, F. E. *Aristotle and the Arabs*. New York, 1968. Well written and engaging.

Reilly, Bernard F. *The Medieval Spains.* New York, 1993. A succinct account that covers the entire Iberian peninsula from 500 to 1500.

Reynolds, Susan. *Fiefs and Vassals: The Medieval Evidence Reinterpreted.* Oxford and New York, 1994. A detailed revisionist history of "feudalism."

Sheingorn, Pamela, trans. *The Book of Sainte Foy.* Philadelphia, 1995.

Southern, Richard W. *The Making of the Middle Ages.* New Haven, CT, 1992. A classic work, first published in 1951 but still fresh and exciting.

Stillman, Norman A. *The Jews of Arab Lands: A History and Source Book.* Philadelphia, PA, 1979. An essential resource.

Stow, Kenneth R. *Alienated Minority: The Jews of Medieval Latin Europe.* Cambridge, MA, 1992. An excellent survey.

Tierney, Brian. *The Crisis of Church and State, 1050–1300.* Toronto, 1988. An indispensable collection for both teachers and students.

CHAPTER 9

Abelard and Heloise. *The Letters and Other Writings.* Trans. William Levitan. Indianapolis, 2007. A beautiful and accurate translation of the correspondence and related documents, with a full introduction and notes.

Abulafia, David. *Frederick II: A Medieval Emperor.* London and New York, 1988. A reliable biography that strips away much of the legend that has hitherto surrounded this monarch.

Abulafia, David, ed. *The New Cambridge Medieval History. Volume 5: c. 1198–c. 1300.* Cambridge, 1999. Contributions by more than thirty specialists. Excellent bibliographies.

Baldwin, John W. *The Government of Philip Augustus.* Berkeley and Los Angeles, CA, 1986. A landmark scholarly account.

Bartlett, Robert. *The Making of Europe: Conquest, Colonization and Cultural Change, 950–1350.* Princeton, NJ, 1993. A wide-ranging examination of the economic, social, and religious expansion of Europe, full of stimulating insights.

Bisson, Thomas N. *The Crisis of the Twelfth Century: Power, Lordship, and the Origins of European Government.* Princeton, NJ, 2009. A new interpretation of the evidence.

Boswell, John E. *Christianity, Social Tolerance, and Homosexuality: Gay People in Western Europe from the Beginning of the Christian Era to the Fourteenth Century.* Chicago, 1980. A pioneering account, hotly debated but highly respected.

Camille, Michael. *Gothic Art: Glorious Visions.* New York, 1996. A succinct and beautifully illustrated introduction.

Chrétien de Troyes. *Arthurian Romances.* Trans. W. W. Kibler. New York, 1991.

Clanchy, Michael T. *Abelard: A Medieval Life.* Oxford and Cambridge, MA, 1997. A great biography.

———. *From Memory to Written Record: England, 1066–1307.* Oxford, 1992. A fascinating and hugely influential account of this revolutionary shift.

Cobban, Alan B. *The Medieval Universities.* London, 1975. The best short treatment in English.

Colish, Marcia. *Medieval Foundations of the Western Intellectual Tradition, 400–1400.* New Haven, CT, 1997. An encyclopedic work, best used as a reference.

Dante Alighieri. *The Divine Comedy.* Trans. Mark Musa. 3 vols. Baltimore, MD, 1984–86.

Dronke, Peter. *Women Writers of the Middle Ages.* New York, 1984. A rich literary study.

Fassler, Margot. *Gothic Song: Victorine Seqeunces and Augustinian Reform in Twelfth-Century Paris.* Cambridge, UK, 1993. The emergence of new musical genres and their cultural context.

Gillingham, John. *The Angevin Empire,* 2d ed. Oxford and New York, 2001. The best treatment by far of its subject, brief but full of ideas.

Gottfried von Strassburg. *Tristan.* Trans. A. T. Hatto. Baltimore, MD, 1960.

Hallam, Elizabeth, and Judith Everard. *Capetian France, 987–1328,* 2d ed. New York, 2001. A clear and well-organized account.

Haskins, Charles Homer. *The Renaissance of the Twelfth Century.* Cambridge, MA, 1927. A classic and influential study.

Jordan, William C. *Europe in the High Middle Ages: The Penguin History of Europe.* Vol. III. New York and London, 2003. An outstanding new survey.

Knowles, David. *The Evolution of Medieval Thought,* 2d ed. London, 1988. An authoritative survey, thoroughly revised in the second edition.

Lambert, Malcolm. *Medieval Heresy,* 3d ed. Oxford and Cambridge, 2002. The standard synthesis; deeply learned and fully annotated.

Lawrence, Clifford Hugh. *The Friars: The Impact of the Early Mendicant Movement on Western Society.* London and New York, 1994. The best short introduction to the early history of the Franciscans and the Dominicans.

Leclerq, Jean. *The Love of Learning and the Desire for God,* 3d ed. New York, 1982. A beautiful interpretation of twelfth-century monastic culture and the influence of Bernard of Clairvaux.

Little, Lester. *Religious Poverty and Profit Economy in Medieval Europe.* Ithaca, 1978. A fascinating study of the relationship between religious practice and economic reality.

Marie de France. *Lais.* Trans. Glyn S. Burgess and Keith Busby. Harmondsworth, UK, 1999. A compelling and entertaining prose translation.

Moore, R. I. *The Formation of a Persecuting Society: Authority and Deviance in Western Europe, 950–1250.* 2d ed. Malden, MA, 2007. This new edition responds to some of the debates generated by the publication of the first in 1987.

Morris, Colin. *The Papal Monarchy: The Western Church from 1050 to 1250.* Oxford, 1989. An excellent scholarly survey; part of the Oxford History of the Christian Church series.

Newman, Barbara, ed. *Voice of the Living Light: Hildegard of Bingen and Her World.* Berkeley and Los Angeles, CA, 1998. An introduction to Hildegard's life and work.

Otto, Bishop of Freising. *The Deeds of Frederick Barbarossa.* Trans. C. C. Mierow. New York, 1953. A contemporary chronicle interesting enough to read from start to finish.

Smalley, Beryl. *The Study of the Bible in the Middle Ages,* 3d ed. Oxford, 1983. The standard work, gracefully written and illuminating.

Southern, Richard W. *Western Society and the Church in the Middle Ages.* Baltimore, MD, 1970. An insightful interpretation of the interplay between society and religion by one of the greatest historians of the twentieth century.

Strayer, Joseph R. *On the Medieval Origins of the Modern State.* With new forewords by Charles Tilly and William Chester Jordan. Princeton, 2005. This new edition of Strayer's series of lectures places them in their scholarly context.

Swanson, R. N. *The Twelfth-Century Renaissance.* Manchester, UK, 1999. An updated survey of the intellectual developments of the twelfth century.

Symes, Carol. *A Common Stage: Theater and Public Life in Medieval Arras.* Ithaca, NY, 2007. A study of a vibrant cultural hub.

Wakefield, Walter, and Austin P. Evans, eds. and trans. *Heresies of the High Middle Ages.* New York, 1969, 1991. A comprehensive collection of sources.

Wilhelm, James J., ed. and trans. *Medieval Song: An Anthology of Hymns and Lyrics.* New York, 1971. An excellent collection of sacred and secular poetry that illustrates the connections between them.

Wolfram von Eschenbach. *Parzival.* Trans. H. M. Mustard and C. E. Passage. New York, 1961.

CHAPTER 10

Allmand, Christopher T., ed. *Society at War: The Experience of England and France During the Hundred Years' War.* Edinburgh, 1973. An outstanding collection of documents.

———. *The Hundred Years' War: England and France at War, c. 1300–c. 1450.* Cambridge and New York, 1988. Still the best analytic account of the war; after a short narrative, the book is organized topically.

Boccaccio, Giovanni. *The Decameron.* Trans. Mark Musa and P. E. Bondanella. New York, 1977.

Bynum, Caroline Walker. *Holy Feast and Holy Fast: The Religious Significance of Food to Medieval Women.* Berkeley and Los Angeles, 1988. One of the most influential and important works of scholarship published in the late twentieth century.

Chaucer, Geoffrey. *The Canterbury Tales.* Trans. Nevill Coghill. New York, 1951. A modern English verse translation, lightly annotated.

Cohn, Samuel K., Jr. *Lust for Liberty: The Politics of Social Revolt in Medieval Europe, 1200–1425. Italy, France, and Flanders.* Cambridge, MA, 2006. An important new study.

Cole, Bruce. *Giotto and Florentine Painting, 1280–1375.* New York, 1976. A clear and stimulating introduction.

Crummey, Robert O. *The Formation of Muscovy, 1304–1613.* New York, 1987. The standard account.

Dobson, R. Barrie. *The Peasants' Revolt of 1381,* 2d ed. London, 1983. A comprehensive source collection, with excellent introductions to the documents.

Dyer, Christopher. *Standards of Living in the Later Middle Ages: Social Change in England, c. 1200–1520.* Cambridge and New York, 1989. Detailed but highly rewarding.

Froissart, Jean. *Chronicles.* Trans. Geoffrey Brereton. Baltimore, MD, 1968. A selection from the most famous contemporary account of the Hundred Years' War to about 1400.

Hobbins, Daniel, ed. and trans. *The Trial of Joan of Arc.* Cambridge, MA, 2007. A new and excellent translation of the transcripts of Joan's trial.

Horrox, Rosemary, ed. *The Black Death.* New York, 1994. A fine collection of documents reflecting the impact of the Black Death, especially in England.

John Hus at the Council of Constance. Trans. M. Spinka, New York, 1965. The translation of a Czech chronicle with an expert introduction and appended documents.

Jordan, William Chester. *The Great Famine: Northern Europe in the Early Fourteenth Century.* Princeton, NJ, 1996. An outstanding social and economic study.

Keen, Maurice, ed. *Medieval Warfare: A History.* Oxford and New York, 1999. The most attractive introduction to this important subject. Lively and well illustrated.

Kempe, Margery. *The Book of Margery Kempe.* Trans. Barry Windeatt. New York, 1985. A fascinating personal narrative by an early-fifteenth-century Englishwoman who hoped she might be a saint.

Lerner, Robert E. *The Heresy of the Free Spirit in the Later Middle Ages,* 2d ed. Notre Dame, IN, 1991. A revealing study of a heretical movement that hardly existed at all.

Lewis, Peter S. *Later Medieval France: The Polity.* London, 1968. Still fresh and suggestive after forty years. A masterwork.

Memoirs of a Renaissance Pope: The Commentaries of Pius II. Abridged ed. Trans. F. A. Gragg, New York, 1959. Remarkable insights into the mind of a particularly well-educated mid-fifteenth-century pope.

Nicholas, David. *The Transformation of Europe, 1300–1600.* Oxford and New York, 1999. The best textbook presently available.

Oakley, Francis C. *The Western Church in the Later Middle Ages.* Ithaca, NY, 1979. The best book by far on the history of conciliarism, the late medieval papacy, Hussitism, and the efforts at institutional reform during this period. On popular piety, see Swanson.

Shirley, Janet, trans. *A Parisian Journal, 1405–1449.* Oxford, 1968. A marvelous panorama of Parisian life recorded by an eyewitness.

Sumption, Jonathan. *The Hundred Years' War.* Vol. 1: *Trial by Battle.* Vol. 2: *Trial by Fire.* Philadelphia, 1999. The first two volumes of a massive narrative history of the war, carrying the story up to 1369.

Swanson, R. N. *Religion and Devotion in Europe, c. 1215–c. 1515.* Cambridge and New York, 1995. An excellent study of late-medieval popular piety; an excellent complement to Oakley.

Vaughan, Richard. *Valois Burgundy.* London, 1975. A summation of the author's four-volume study of the Burgundian dukes.

Ziegler, Philip. *The Black Death.* New York, 1969. A popular account, but reliable and engrossing.

CHAPTER 11

Abu-Lughod, Janet L. *Before European Hegemony: The World System A.D. 1250–1350.* Oxford and New York, 1989. A study of the trading links among Europe, the Middle East, India, and China, with special attention to the role of the Mongol Empire; extensive bibliography.

Allsen, Thomas T. *Culture and Conquest in Mongol Eurasia.* Cambridge and New York, 2001. A synthesis of the author's earlier studies, emphasizing Mongol involvement in the cultural and commercial exchanges that linked China, Central Asia, and Europe.

Amitai-Preiss, Reuven, and David O. Morgan, eds. *The Mongol Empire and Its Legacy*. Leiden, 1999. A collection of essays that represents some of the new trends in Mongol studies.

Christian, David. *A History of Russia, Central Asia and Mongolia*. Vol. 1, *Inner Eurasia from Prehistory to the Mongol Empire*. Oxford, 1998. The authoritative English-language work on the subject.

Coles, Paul. *The Ottoman Impact on Europe*. London, 1968. An excellent introductory text, still valuable despite its age.

Fernández-Armesto, Felipe. *Before Columbus: Exploration and Colonisation from the Mediterranean to the Atlantic, 1229–1492*. London, 1987. An indispensible study of the medieval background to the sixteenth-century European colonial empires.

———. *Columbus*. Oxford and New York, 1991. An excellent biography that stresses the millenarian ideas that underlay Columbus's thinking.

Flint, Valerie I. J. *The Imaginative Landscape of Christopher Columbus*. Princeton, NJ, 1992. A short, suggestive analysis of the intellectual influences that shaped Columbus's geographical ideas.

Goffman, Daniel. *The Ottoman Empire and Early Modern Europe*. Cambridge and New York, 2002. A revisionist account that presents the Ottoman Empire as a European state.

The History and the Life of Chinggis Khan: The Secret History of the Mongols. Trans. Urgunge Onon. Leiden, 1997. A newer version of *The Secret History*, now the standard English version of this important Mongol source.

Inalcik, Halil. *The Ottoman Empire: The Classical Age, 1300–1600*. London, 1973. The standard history by the dean of Turkish historians.

———, ed. *An Economic and Social History of the Ottoman Empire, 1300–1914*. Cambridge, 1994. An important collection of essays, spanning the full range of Ottoman history.

Jackson, Peter. *The Mongols and the West, 1221–1410*. Harlow, UK, 2005. A well-written survey that emphasizes the interactions among the Mongol, Latin Christian, and Muslim worlds.

Kafadar, Cemal. *Between Two Worlds: The Construction of the Ottoman State*. Berkeley and Los Angeles, 1995. An important study of Ottoman origins in the border regions between Byzantium, the Seljuk Turks, and the Mongols.

Larner, John. *Marco Polo and the Discovery of the World*. New Haven, CT, 1999. A study of the influence of Marco Polo's *Travels* on Europeans.

Morgan, David. *The Mongols*. 2d ed. Oxford, 2007. An accessible introduction to Mongol history and its sources, written by a noted expert on medieval Persia.

Parker, Geoffrey. *The Military Revolution: Military Innovation and the Rise of the West (1500–1800)*. 2d ed. Cambridge and New York, 1996. A work of fundamental importance for understanding the global dominance achieved by early modern Europeans.

Phillips, J. R. S. *The Medieval Expansion of Europe*. 2d ed. Oxford, 1998. An outstanding study of the thirteenth- and fourteenth-century background to the fifteenth-century expansion of Europe. Important synthetic treatment of European relations with the Mongols, China, Africa, and North America. The second edition includes a new introduction and a bibliographical essay; the text is the same as in the first edition (1988).

Phillips, William D., Jr., and Carla R. Phillips. *The Worlds of Christopher Columbus*. Cambridge and New York, 1991. The first book to read on Columbus: accessible, engaging, and scholarly. Then read Fernández-Armesto's biography.

Ratchnevsky, Paul. *Genghis Khan: His Life and Legacy*. Trans. Thomas Nivison Haining. Oxford, 1991. An English translation and abridgment of a book first published in German in 1983. The author was one of the greatest Mongol historians of his generation.

Rossabi, M. *Khubilai Khan: His Life and Times*. Berkeley, CA, 1988. The standard English biography.

Russell, Peter. *Prince Henry "The Navigator": A Life*. New Haven, CT, 2000. A masterly biography by a great historian who has spent a lifetime on the subject. The only book one now needs to read on Prince Henry.

Saunders, J. J. *The History of the Mongol Conquests*. London, 1971. Still the standard English-language introduction; somewhat more positive about the Mongols' accomplishments than is Morgan.

Scammell, Geoffrey V. *The First Imperial Age: European Overseas Expansion, 1400–1715*. London, 1989. A useful introductory survey, with a particular focus on English and French colonization.

The Book of Prophecies, Edited by Christopher Columbus. Trans. Blair Sullivan, ed. Roberto Rusconi. Berkeley and Los Angeles, 1996. After his third voyage, from which Columbus was returned to Spain in chains, he compiled a book of quotations from various sources selected to emphasize the millenarian implications of his discoveries; a fascinating insight into the mind of the explorer.

The Four Voyages: Christopher Columbus. Trans. J. M. Cohen. New York, 1992. Columbus's own self-serving account of his four voyages to the Indies.

Mandeville's Travels. Ed. M. C. Seymour. Oxford, 1968. An edition of the *Book of Marvels* based on the Middle English version popular in the fifteenth century.

The Secret History of the Mongols. Trans. F. W. Cleaves. Cambridge, MA, 1982.

The Secret History of the Mongols and Other Pieces. Trans. Arthur Waley. London, 1963. The later Chinese abridgment of the Mongol original.

The Travels of Marco Polo, trans. R. E. Latham. Baltimore, MD, 1958. The most accessible edition of this remarkably interesting work.

CHAPTER 12

Alberti, Leon Battista. *The Family in Renaissance Florence (Della Famiglia)*. Trans. Renée Neu Watkins. Columbia, SC, 1969.

Baxandall, Michael. *Painting and Experience in Fifteenth-Century Italy*. Oxford, 1972. A classic study of the perceptual world of the Renaissance.

Brucker, Gene. *Florence, the Golden Age, 1138–1737*. Berkeley and Los Angeles, CA, 1998. The standard account.

Bruni, Leonardo. *The Humanism of Leonardo Bruni: Selected Texts.* Trans. Gordon Griffiths, James Hankins, and David Thompson. Binghamton, NY, 1987. Excellent translations, with introductions, to the Latin works of a key Renaissance humanist.

Burke, Peter. *The Renaissance.* New York, 1997. A brief introduction by an influential modern historian.

Burkhardt, Jacob. *The Civilization of the Renaissance in Italy.* Many editions. The nineteenth-century work that first crystallized an image of the Italian Renaissance, and with which scholars have been wrestling ever since.

Cassirer, Ernst, et al., eds. *The Renaissance Philosophy of Man.* Chicago, 1948. Important original works by Petrarch, Ficino, and Pico della Mirandola, among others.

Castiglione, Baldassare. *The Book of the Courtier.* Many editions. The translations by C. S. Singleton (New York, 1959) and by George Bull (New York, 1967) are both excellent.

Cellini, Benvenuto. *Autobiography.* Trans. George Bull. Baltimore, MD, 1956. This Florentine goldsmith (1500–1571) is the source for many of the most famous stories about the artists of the Florentine Renaissance.

Cochrane, Eric, and Julius Kirshner, eds. *The Renaissance.* Chicago, 1986. An outstanding collection, from the University of Chicago Readings in Western Civilization series.

Erasmus, Desiderius. *The Praise of Folly.* Trans. J. Wilson. Ann Arbor, MI, 1958.

Fox, Alistair. *Thomas More: History and Providence.* Oxford, 1982. A balanced account of a man too easily idealized.

Grafton, Anthony, and Lisa Jardine. *From Humanism to the Humanities: Education and the Liberal Arts in Fifteenth- and Sixteenth-Century Europe.* London, 1986. An account that presents Renaissance humanism as the elitist cultural program of a self-interested group of pedagogues.

Grendler, Paul, ed. *Encyclopedia of the Renaissance.* New York, 1999. A valuable reference work.

Hale, John R. *The Civilization of Europe in the Renaissance.* New York, 1993. A synthetic volume summarizing the life's work of a major Renaissance historian.

Hankins, James. *Plato in the Italian Renaissance.* Leiden and New York, 1990. A definitive study of the reception and influence of Plato on Renaissance intellectuals.

———, ed. *Renaissance Civic Humanism: Reappraisals and Reflections.* Cambridge and New York, 2000. An excellent collection of scholarly essays reassessing republicanism in the Renaissance.

Jardine, Lisa. *Worldly Goods.* London, 1996. A revisionist account that emphasizes the acquisitive materialism of Italian Renaissance society and culture.

Kanter, Laurence, Hilliard T. Goldfarb, and James Hankins. *Botticelli's Witness: Changing Style in a Changing Florence.* Boston, 1997. This catalog for an exhibition of Botticelli's works, at the Gardner Museum in Boston, offers an excellent introduction to the painter and his world.

King, Margaret L. *Women of the Renaissance.* Chicago, 1991. Deals with women in all walks of life and in a variety of roles.

Kristeller, Paul O. *Eight Philosophers of the Italian Renaissance.* Stanford, 1964. An admirably clear and accurate account that fully appreciates the connections between medieval and Renaissance thought.

———. *Renaissance Thought: The Classic, Scholastic, and Humanistic Strains.* New York, 1961. Very helpful in defining the main trends of Renaissance thought.

Lane, Frederic C. *Venice: A Maritime Republic.* Baltimore, MD, 1973. An authoritative account.

Machiavelli, Niccolò. *The Discourses* and *The Prince.* Many editions. These two books must be read together if one is to understand Machiavelli's political ideas properly.

Martines, Lauro. *Power and Imagination: City-States in Renaissance Italy.* New York, 1979. Insightful account of the connections among politics, society, culture, and art.

More, Thomas. *Utopia.* Many editions.

Murray, Linda. *High Renaissance and Mannerism.* London, 1985. The place to begin a study of fifteenth- and sixteenth-century Italian art.

Olson, Roberta, *Italian Renaissance Sculpture.* New York, 1992. The most accessible introduction to the subject.

Perkins, Leeman L. *Music in the Age of the Renaissance.* New York, 1999. A massive new study that needs to be read in conjunction with Reese.

Rabelais, François. *Gargantua and Pantagruel.* Trans. J. M. Cohen. Baltimore, MD, 1955. A robust modern translation.

Reese, Gustave. *Music in the Renaissance,* rev. ed. New York, 1959. A great book; still authoritative, despite the more recent work by Perkins, which supplements but does not replace it.

Rice, Eugene F., Jr., and Anthony Grafton. *The Foundations of Early Modern Europe, 1460–1559,* 2d ed. New York, 1994. The best textbook account of its period.

Rowland, Ingrid D. *The Culture of the High Renaissance: Ancients and Moderns in Sixteenth-Century Rome.* Cambridge and New York, 2000. Beautifully written examination of the social, intellectual, and economic foundations of the Renaissance in Rome.

CHAPTER 13

Bainton, Roland. *Erasmus of Christendom.* New York, 1969. Still the best biography in English of the Dutch reformer and intellectual.

———. *Here I Stand: A Life of Martin Luther.* Nashville, TN, 1950. Although old and obviously biased in Luther's favor, this remains an absorbing and dramatic introduction to Luther's life and thought.

Benedict, Philip. *Christ's Churches Purely Reformed: A Social History of Calvinism.* New Haven, CT, 2002. A wide-ranging recent survey of Calvinism in both western and eastern Europe.

Bossy, John. *Christianity in the West, 1400–1700.* Oxford and New York, 1985. A brilliant, challenging picture of the changes that took place in Christian piety and practice as a result of the sixteenth-century reformations.

Bouwsma, William J. *John Calvin: A Sixteenth-Century Portrait.* Oxford and New York, 1988. The best biography of the magisterial reformer.

Collinson, Patrick. *The Religion of Protestants: The Church in English Society, 1559–1625.* Oxford, 1982. A great book by a noted historian of early English Protestantism.

Dixon, C. Scott, ed. *The German Reformation: The Essential Readings.* Oxford, 1999. A collection of important recent articles.

Duffy, Eamon. *The Stripping of the Altars: Traditional Religion in England, c. 1400–c. 1550.* A brilliant study of religious exchange at the parish level.

Hillerbrand, Hans J., ed. *The Protestant Reformation.* New York, 1967. Source selections are particularly good for illuminating the political consequences of Reformation theological ideas.

John Calvin: Selections from His Writings, ed. John Dillenberger. Garden City, NY, 1971. A judicious selection, drawn mainly from Calvin's *Institutes*.

Loyola, Ignatius. *Personal Writings.* Trans. by Joseph A. Munitiz and Philip Endean. London and New York, 1996. An excellent collection that includes Loyola's autobiography, his spiritual diary, and some of his letters, as well as his *Spiritual Exercises*.

Luebke, David, ed. *The Counter-Reformation: The Essential Readings.* Oxford, 1999. A collection of nine important recent essays.

MacCulloch, Diarmaid. *Reformation: Europe's House Divided, 1490–1700.* London and New York, 2003. A definitive new survey; the best single-volume history of its subject in a generation.

Martin Luther: Selections from His Writings, ed. John Dillenberger. Garden City, NY, 1961. The standard selection, especially good on Luther's theological ideas.

McGrath, Alister E. *Reformation Thought: An Introduction.* Oxford, 1993. A useful explanation, accessible to non-Christians, of the theological ideas of the major Protestant reformers.

Mullett, Michael A. *The Catholic Reformation.* London, 2000. A sympathetic survey of Catholicism from the mid-sixteenth to the eighteenth century that presents the mid-sixteenth-century Council of Trent as a continuation of earlier reform efforts.

Oberman, Heiko A. *Luther: Man between God and the Devil.* Trans. by Eileen Walliser-Schwarzbart. New Haven, CT, 1989. A biography stressing Luther's preoccupations with sin, death, and the devil.

O'Malley, John W. *The First Jesuits.* Cambridge, MA, 1993. A scholarly account of the origins and early years of the Society of Jesus.

———. *Trent and All That: Renaming Catholicism in the Early Modern Era.* Cambridge, MA, 2000. Short, lively, and with a full bibliography.

Pettegree, Andrew, ed. *The Reformation World.* New York, 2000. An exhaustive multi-author work representing the most recent thinking about the Reformation.

Pelikan, Jaroslav. *Reformation of Church and Dogma, 1300–1700.* Vol. 4 of *A History of Christian Dogma.* Chicago, 1984. A masterful synthesis of Reformation theology in its late-medieval context.

Roper, Lyndal. *The Holy Household: Women and Morals in Reformation Augsburg.* Oxford, 1989. A pathbreaking study of Protestantism's effects on a single town, with special attention to its impact on attitudes toward women, the family, and marriage.

Shagan, Ethan H. *Popular Politics and the English Reformation.* Cambridge, 2002. Argues that the English Reformation reflects an ongoing process of negotiation, resistance, and response.

Tracy, James D. *Europe's Reformations, 1450–1650.* 2d ed. Lanham, MD, 2006. An outstanding survey, especially strong on Dutch and Swiss developments, but excellent throughout.

Williams, George H. *The Radical Reformation.* 3d ed. Kirksville, MO, 1992. Originally published in 1962, this is still the best book on Anabaptism and its offshoots.

CHAPTER 14

Bonney, Richard. *The European Dynastic States, 1494–1660.* Oxford and New York, 1991. An excellent survey of continental Europe during the "long" sixteenth century.

Briggs, Robin. *Early Modern France, 1560–1715,* 2d ed. Oxford and New York, 1997. Updated and authoritative, with new bibliographies.

———. *Witches and Neighbors: The Social and Cultural Context of European Witchcraft.* New York, 1996. An influential recent account of Continental witchcraft.

Cervantes, Miguel de. *Don Quixote.* Trans. Edith Grossman. New York, 2003. A splendid new translation.

Clarke, Stuart. *Thinking with Demons: The Idea of Witchcraft in Early Modern Europe.* Oxford and New York, 1999. By placing demonology into the context of sixteenth- and seventeenth-century intellectual history, Clarke makes sense of it in new and exciting ways.

Cochrane, Eric, Charles M. Gray, and Mark A. Kishlansky. *Early Modern Europe: Crisis of Authority.* Chicago, 1987. An outstanding source collection from the University of Chicago Readings in Western Civilization series.

Held, Julius S., and Donald Posner. *Seventeenth- and Eighteenth-Century Art: Baroque Painting, Sculpture, Architecture.* New York, 1971. The most complete and best-organized introductory review of the subject in English.

Hibbard, Howard. *Bernini.* Baltimore, MD, 1965. The basic study in English of this central figure of Baroque artistic activity.

Hirst, Derek. *England in Conflict, 1603–1660: Kingdom, Community, Commonwealth.* Oxford and New York, 1999. A complete revision of the author's *Authority and Conflict* (1986), this is an up-to-date and balanced account of a period that has been a historical battleground over the past twenty years.

Hobbes, Thomas. *Leviathan.* Ed. Richard Tuck. 2d ed. Cambridge and New York, 1996. The most recent edition, containing the entirety of *Leviathan*, not just the first two parts.

Holt, Mack P. *The French Wars of Religion, 1562–1629.* Cambridge and New York, 1995. A clear account of a confusing time.

Kors, Alan Charles, and Edward Peters. *Witchcraft in Europe, 400–1700: A Documentary History,* 2d ed. Philadelphia, 2000. A superb collection of documents, significantly expanded in the second edition, with up-to-date commentary.

Kingdon, Robert. *Myths about the St. Bartholomew's Day Massacres, 1572–1576.* Cambridge, MA, 1988. A detailed account of this pivotal moment in the history of France.

Levack, Brian P. *The Witch-Hunt in Early Modern Europe,* 2d ed. London and New York, 1995. The best account of the persecution of suspected witches; coverage extends from Europe in 1450 to America in 1750.

Levin, Carole. *The Heart and Stomach of a King: Elizabeth I and the Politics of Sex and Power.* Philadelphia, 1994. A provocative argument for the importance of Elizabeth's gender for understanding her reign.

Limm, Peter, ed. *The Thirty Years' War*. London, 1984. An outstanding short survey, followed by a selection of primary-source documents.

Lynch, John. *Spain, 1516–1598: From Nation-State to World Empire*. Oxford and Cambridge, MA, 1991. The best book in English on Spain at the pinnacle of its sixteenth-century power.

MacCaffrey, Wallace. *Elizabeth I*. New York, 1993. An outstanding traditional biography by an excellent scholar.

Martin, Colin, and Geoffrey Parker. *The Spanish Armada*. London, 1988. Incorporates recent discoveries from undersea archaeology with more traditional historical sources.

Martin, John Rupert. *Baroque*. New York, 1977. A thought-provoking, thematic treatment, less a survey than an essay on the painting, sculpture, and architecture of the period.

Mattingly, Garrett. *The Armada*. Boston, 1959. A great narrative history that reads like a novel; for more recent work, however, see Martin and Parker.

Parker, Geoffrey. *The Dutch Revolt*, 2d ed. Ithaca, NY, 1989. The standard survey in English on the revolt of the Netherlands.

———. *Philip II*. Boston, 1978. A fine biography by an expert in both the Spanish and the Dutch sources.

———, ed. *The Thirty Years' War*, rev. ed. London and New York, 1987. A wide-ranging collection of essays by scholarly experts.

Pascal, Blaise. *Pensées* (French-English edition). Ed. H. F. Stewart. London, 1950.

Quint, David. *Montaigne and the Quality of Mercy: Ethical and Political Themes in the "Essais."* Princeton, NJ, 1999. A fine treatment that presents Montaigne's thought as a response to the French wars of religion.

Roberts, Michael. *Gustavus Adolphus and the Rise of Sweden*. London, 1973. Still the authoritative English-language account.

Russell, Conrad. *The Causes of the English Civil War*. Oxford, 1990. A penetrating and provocative analysis by one of the leading "revisionist" historians of the period.

Tracy, James D. *Holland under Habsburg Rule, 1506–1566: The Formation of a Body Politic*. Berkeley and Los Angeles, CA, 1990. A political history and analysis of the formative years of the Dutch state.

Van Gelderen, Martin. *Political Theory of the Dutch Revolt*. Cambridge, 1995. A fine book on a subject whose importance is too easily overlooked.

CHAPTER 15

Beik, William. *Louis XIV and Absolutism*. New York, 2000. A helpful short examination of the French king, the theory of absolutism, and the social consequences of absolutist rule. Supplemented by translated documents from the period.

Jones, Colin. *The Great Nation: France From Louis XV to Napoleon*. New York, 2002. An excellent and readable scholarly account that argues that the France of Louis XV in the eighteenth century was even more dominant than the kingdom of Louis XIV in the preceding century.

Kishlansky, Mark A. *A Monarchy Transformed: Britain, 1603–1714*. London, 1996. An excellent survey that takes seriously its claims to be a "British" rather than merely an "English" history.

Klein, Herbert S. *The Atlantic Slave Trade*. Cambridge and New York, 1999. An accessible survey by a leading quantitative historian.

Koch, H. W. *A History of Prussia*. London, 1978. Still the best account of its subject.

Lewis, William Roger, gen. ed. *The Oxford History of the British Empire*. Vol. I: *The Origins of Empire: British Overseas Enterprise to the Close of the Seventeenth Century*, ed. Nicholas Canny. Vol. II: *The Eighteenth Century*, ed. Peter J. Marshall. Oxford and New York, 1998. A definitive, multiauthor account.

Locke, John. *Two Treatises of Government*. Ed. Peter Laslett. Rev. ed. Cambridge and New York, 1963. Laslett has revolutionized our understanding of the historical and ideological context of Locke's political writings.

Miller, John, ed. *Absolutism in Seventeenth-Century Europe*. London, 1990. An excellent, multiauthor survey, organized by country.

Monod, Paul K. *The Power of Kings: Monarchy and Religion in Europe, 1589–1715*. New Haven, Conn. 1999. A study of the seventeenth century's declining confidence in the divinity of kings.

Quataert, Donald. *The Ottoman Empire, 1700–1822*. Cambridge and New York, 2000. Well balanced and intended to be read by students.

Riasanovsky, Nicholas V., and Steinberg, Mark D. *A History of Russia*. 7th ed. Oxford and New York, 2005. Far and away the best single-volume textbook on Russian history: balanced, comprehensive, intelligent, and with full bibliographies.

Saint-Simon, Louis. *Historical Memoirs*. Many editions. The classic source for life at Louis XIV's Versailles.

Thomas, Hugh. *The Slave Trade: The History of the Atlantic Slave Trade, 1440–1870*. London and New York, 1997. A survey notable for its breadth and depth of coverage and for its attractive prose style.

Tracy, James D. *The Rise of Merchant Empires: Long-Distance Trade in the Early Modern World, 1350–1750*. Cambridge and New York, 1990. Important collection of essays by leading authorities.

White, Richard. *It's Your Misfortune and None of My Own: A History of the American West*. Norman, Okla., 1991. An outstanding textbook with excellent introductory chapters on European colonialism in the Americas.

CHAPTER 16

Biagioli, Mario. *Galileo, Courtier*. Chicago, 1993. Emphasizes the importance of patronage and court politics in Galileo's science and career.

Cohen, I. B. *The Birth of a New Physics*. New York, 1985. Emphasizes the mathematical nature of the revolution; unmatched at making the mathematics understandable.

Dear, Peter. *Revolutionizing the Sciences: European Knowledge and Its Ambitions, 1500–1700*. Princeton, N.J., 2001. Among the best short histories.

Drake, Stillman. *Discoveries and Opinions of Galileo*. Garden City, N.Y., 1957. The classic translation of Galileo's most important papers by his most admiring modern biographer.

Feingold, Mardechai, *The Newtonian Moment: Isaac Newton and the Making of Modern Culture*. New York, 2004. An engaging essay on the dissemination of Newton's thought, with excellent visual material.

Gaukroger, Stephen. *Descartes: An Intellectual Biography.* Oxford, 1995. Detailed and sympathetic study of the philosopher.

Gleick, James. *Isaac Newton.* New York, 2003. A vivid and well-documented brief biography.

Grafton, Anthony. *New Worlds, Ancient Texts: The Power of Tradition and the Shock of Discovery.* Cambridge, Mass., 1992. Accessible essay by one of the leading scholars of early modern European thought.

Hall, A. R. *The Revolution in Science, 1500–1750.* New York, 1983. Revised version of a 1954 classic.

Jones, Richard Foster. *Ancients and Moderns: A Study of the Rise of the Scientific Movement in Early Modern England.* Berkeley, Calif., 1961. Still a persuasive study of the scientific revolutionaries' attempts to situate their work in relation to that of the Greeks.

Koestler, Arthur. *The Sleepwalkers: A History of Man's Changing Vision of the Universe.* London, 1958. A readable classic.

Kuhn, Thomas. *The Structure of Scientific Revolutions.* Chicago, 1962. A classic and much-debated study of how scientific thought changes.

Pagden, Anthony, *European Encounters with the New World.* New Haven, Conn., and London, 1993. Subtle and detailed on how European intellectuals thought about the lands they saw for the first time.

Scheibinger, Londa. *The Mind Has No Sex? Women in the Origins of Modern Science.* Cambridge, Mass., 1989. A lively and important recovery of the lost role played by women mathematicians and experimenters.

Shapin, Steven. *The Scientific Revolution.* Chicago, 1996. Engaging, accessible, and brief—organized thematically.

———, and Simon Schaffer. *Leviathan and the Air Pump.* Princeton, N.J., 1985. A modern classic, on one of the most famous philosophical conflicts in seventeenth-century science.

Stephenson, Bruce. *The Music of the Heavens: Kepler's Harmonic Astronomy.* Princeton, N.J., 1994. An engaging and important explanation of Kepler's otherworldly perspective.

Thoren, Victor. *The Lord of Uraniborg: A Biography of Tycho Brahe.* Cambridge, 1990. A vivid reconstruction of the scientific revolution's most flamboyant astronomer.

Westfall, Richard. *The Construction of Modern Science.* Cambridge, 1977.

Westfall, Richard. *Never at Rest: A Biography of Isaac Newton.* Cambridge, 1980. The standard work.

Wilson, Catherine. *The Invisible World: Early Modern Philosophy and the Invention of the Microscope.* Princeton, N.J., 1995. An important study of how the "microcosmic" world revealed by technology reshaped scientific philosophy and practice.

Zinsser, Judith P. *La Dame d'Esprit: A Biography of the Marquise Du Châtelet.* New York, 2006. An excellent cultural history. To be issued in paper as *Emilie du Châtelet: Daring Genius of the Enlightenment* (2007).

CHAPTER 17

Baker, Keith. *Condorcet: From Natural Philosophy to Social Mathematics.* Chicago, 1975. An important reinterpretation of Condorcet as a social scientist.

Bell, Susan, and Karen Offen, eds. *Women, the Family, and Freedom: The Debate in Documents.* Vol. 1, *1750–1880.* Stanford, Calif., 1983. An excellent introduction to Enlightenment debates about gender and women.

Blum, Carol. *Rousseau and the Republic of Virtue: The Language of Politics in the French Revolution.* Ithaca and London, 1986. Fascinating account of how eighteenth-century readers interpreted Rousseau.

Buchan, James. *The Authentic Adam Smith: His Life and Ideas.* New York, 2006.

Calhoun, Craig, ed. *Habermas and the Public Sphere.* Cambridge, Mass., 1992. Calhoun's introduction is a good starting point for Habermas's argument.

Cassirer, E. *The Philosophy of the Enlightenment.* Princeton, N.J., 1951.

Chartier, Roger. *The Cultural Origins of the French Revolution.* Durham, N.C., 1991. Looks at topics from religion to violence in everyday life and culture.

Darnton, Robert. *The Business of Enlightenment: A Publishing History of the* Encyclopédie, *1775–1800.* Cambridge, Mass., 1979. Darnton's work on the Enlightenment offers a fascinating blend of intellectual, social, and economic history. See his other books as well: *The Literary Underground of the Old Regime* (Cambridge, Mass., 1982); *The Great Cat Massacre and Other Episodes in French Cultural History* (New York, 1984); and *The Forbidden Best Sellers of Revolutionary France* (New York and London, 1996).

Davis, David Brion. *The Problem of Slavery in Western Culture.* New York, 1988. A Pulitzer Prize–winning examination of a central issue as well as a brilliant analysis of different strands of Enlightenment thought.

Gay, Peter. *The Enlightenment: An Interpretation.* Vol. 1, *The Rise of Modern Paganism.* Vol. 2, *The Science of Freedom.* New York, 1966–1969. Combines an overview with an interpretation. Emphasizes the *philosophes'* sense of identification with the classical world and takes a generally positive view of their accomplishments. Includes extensive annotated bibliographies.

Gray, Peter. *Mozart.* New York, 1999. Brilliant short study.

Goodman, Dena. *The Republic of Letters: A Cultural History of the French Enlightenment.* Ithaca, N.Y., 1994. Important in its attention to the role of literary women.

Hazard, Paul. *The European Mind: The Critical Years (1680–1715).* New Haven, Conn., 1953. A basic and indispensable account of the changing climate of opinion that preceded the Enlightenment.

Hildesheimer, Wolfgang. *Mozart.* New York, 1982. An exceptionally literate and thought-provoking biography.

Israel, Jonathan Irvine. *Radical Enlightenment: Philosophy and the Making of Modernity, 1650–1750.* New York, 2001. Massive and erudite, a fresh look at the international movement of ideas.

Israel, Jonathan Irvine. *Enlightenment Contested: Philosophy, Modernity, and the Emancipation of Man, 1670–1752.* New York, 2006. Massive and erudite, a fresh look at the international movement of ideas.

Munck, Thomas. *The Enlightenment: A Comparative Social History 1721–1794.* London, 2000. An excellent recent survey, especially good on social history.

Outram, Dorinda. *The Enlightenment.* Cambridge, 1995. An excellent short introduction and a good example of new historical approaches.

Porter, Roy. *The Creation of the Modern World: The Untold Story of the British Enlightenment.* New York, 2000.

Rendall, Jane. *The Origins of Modern Feminism: Women in Britain, France and the United States, 1780–1860.* New York, 1984. A very basic survey.

Sapiro, Virginia. *A Vindication of Political Virtue: The Political Theory of Mary Wollstonecraft.* Chicago, 1992. A subtle and intelligent analysis for more advanced readers.

Shklar, Judith. *Men and Citizens: A Study of Rousseau's Social Theory.* London, 1969.

Shklar, Judith. *Montesquieu.* Oxford, 1987. Shklar's studies are brilliant and accessible.

Taylor, Barbara. *Mary Wollstonecraft and the Feminist Imagination.* Cambridge and New York, 2003. Fascinating study that sets Wollstonecraft in the radical circles of eighteenth-century England.

Venturi, Franco. *The End of the Old Regime in Europe, 1768–1776: The First Crisis.* Trans. R. Burr Litchfield. Princeton, N.J., 1989.

Venturi, Franco. *The End of the Old Regime in Europe, 1776–1789.* Princeton, N.J. 1991. Both detailed and wide-ranging, particularly important on international developments.

Watt, Ian P. *The Rise of the Novel.* London, 1957. The basic work on the innovative qualities of the novel in eighteenth-century England.

CHAPTER 18

Applewhite, Harriet B., and Darline G. Levy, eds. *Women and Politics in the Age of the Democratic Revolution.* Ann Arbor, Mich., 1990. Essays on France, Britain, the Netherlands, and the United States.

Bell, David A. *The First Total War: Napoleon's Europe and the Birth of Warfare as We Know It.* Boston and New York, 2007. Lively and concise study of the "cataclysmic intensification" of warfare.

Blackburn, Robin. *The Overthrow of Colonial Slavery.* London and New York, 1988. A longer view of slavery and its abolition.

Blanning, T. C. W. *The French Revolutionary Wars, 1787–1802.* Oxford, 1996. On the revolution and war.

Blum, Carol. *Rousseau and the Republic of Virtue: The Language of Politics in the French Revolution.* Ithaca, N.Y., 1986. Excellent on how Rousseau was read by the revolutionaries.

Cobb, Richard. *The People's Armies.* New Haven, Conn., 1987. Brilliant and detailed analysis of the popular militias.

Cole, Juan. *Napoleon's Egypt: Invading the Middle East.* New York, 2007. Readable history by a scholar familiar with sources in Arabic as well as European languages.

Connelly, Owen. *The French Revolution and Napoleonic Era.* 3rd ed. New York, 2000. Accessible, lively, one-volume survey.

Darnton, Robert, *The Forbidden Best-Sellers of Pre-Revolutionary France.* New York, 1995. One of Darnton's many imaginative studies of subversive opinion and books on the eve of the revolution.

Doyle, William. *Origins of the French Revolution.* New York, 1988. A revisionist historian surveys recent research on the political and social origins of the revolution and identifies a new consensus.

———. *Oxford History of the French Revolution.* New York, 1989.

Dubois, Laurent. *Avengers of the New World. The Story of the Haitian Revolution.* Cambridge, Mass., 2004. Now the best and most accessible study.

———, and John D. Garrigus. *Slave Revolution in the Caribbean, 1789–1804: A Brief History with Documents.* New York, 2006. A particularly good collection.

Englund, Steven. *Napoleon, A Political Life.* Cambridge, Mass., 2004. Prize-winning biography, both dramatic and insightful.

Forrest, Alan. *The French Revolution and the Poor.* New York, 1981. A moving and detailed social history of the poor, who fared little better under revolutionary governments than under the Old Regime.

Furet, Francois. *Revolutionary France, 1770–1880.* Trans. Antonia Nerill. Cambridge, Mass., 1992. Overview by the leading revisionist.

Geyl, Pieter. *Napoleon: For and Against.* Rev. ed. New Haven, Conn., 1964. The ways in which Napoleon was interpreted by French historians and political figures.

Hunt, Lynn. *The French Revolution and Human Rights.* Boston, 1996. A collection of documents.

———. *Politics, Culture, and Class in the French Revolution.* Berkeley, Calif., 1984. An analysis of the new culture of democracy and republicanism.

Hunt, Lynn, and Jack R. Censer. *Liberty, Equality, Fraternity: Exploring the French Revolution.* University Park, Pa., 2001. Two leading historians of the revolution have written a lively, accessible study, with excellent documents and visual material.

Landes, Joan B. *Women and the Public Sphere in the Age of the French Revolution.* Ithaca, N.Y., 1988. On gender and politics.

Lefebvre, Georges. *The Coming of the French Revolution.* Princeton, N.J., 1947. The classic Marxist analysis.

Lewis, G., and C. Lucas. *Beyond the Terror: Essays in French Regional and Social History, 1794–1815.* New York, 1983. Shifts focus to the understudied period after the Terror.

O'Brien, Connor Cruise. *The Great Melody: A Thematic Biography of Edmund Burke.* Chicago, 1992. Passionate, partisan, and brilliant study of Burke's thoughts about Ireland, India, America, and France.

Palmer, R. R. *The Age of the Democratic Revolution: A Political History of Europe and America, 1760–1800.* 2 vols. Princeton, N.J., 1964. Impressive for its scope; places the French Revolution in the larger context of a worldwide revolutionary movement.

———, and Isser Woloch. *Twelve Who Ruled: The Year of the Terror in the French Revolution.* Princeton, N.J. 2005. The terrific collective biography of the Committee of Public Safety, now updated.

Schama, Simon. *Citizens: A Chronicle of the French Revolution.* New York, 1989. Particularly good on art, culture, and politics.

Soboul, Albert. *The Sans-Culottes: The Popular Movement and Revolutionary Government, 1793–1794.* Garden City, N.Y., 1972. Dated, but a classic.

Sutherland, D. M. G. *France, 1789–1815: Revolution and Counterrevolution.* Oxford, 1986. An important synthesis of work on the revolution, especially in social history.

Thompson, J. M. *Robespierre and the French Revolution.* London, 1953. An excellent short biography.

Tocqueville, Alexis de. *The Old Regime and the French Revolution.* Garden City, N.Y., 1955. Originally written in 1856, this remains a provocative analysis of the revolution's legacy.

Trouillot, Michel Rolph. *Silencing the Past.* Boston, 1995. Essays on the Haitian revolution.

Woloch, Isser. *The New Regime: Transformations of the French Civic Order, 1789–1820.* New York, 1994. The fate of revolutionary civic reform.

Woolf, Stuart. *Napoleon's Integration of Europe.* New York, 1991. Technical but very thorough.

CHAPTER 19

Berg, Maxine. *The Age of Manufactures: Industry, Innovation, and Work in Britain, 1700–1820.* Oxford, 1985. Good on new scholarship and on women.

Bridenthal, Renate, Claudia Koonz, and Susan Stuard, eds. *Becoming Visible: Women in European History.* 2d ed. Boston, 1987. Excellent, wide-ranging introduction.

Briggs, Asa. *Victorian Cities.* New York, 1963. A survey of British cities, stressing middle-class attitudes toward the new urban environment.

Cameron, R. E. *France and the Industrial Development of Europe.* Princeton, 1968. Valuable material on the Industrial Revolution outside Britain.

Chevalier, Louis. *Laboring Classes and Dangerous Classes during the First Half of the Nineteenth Century.* New York, 1973. An important, though controversial, account of crime, class, and middle-class perceptions of life in Paris.

Cipolla, Carlo M., ed. *The Industrial Revolution, 1700–1914.* New York, 1976. A collection of essays that emphasizes the wide range of industrializing experiences in Europe.

Cott, Nancy. *The Bonds of Womanhood: "Woman's Sphere" in New England, 1780–1935.* New Haven, Conn., and London, 1977. One of the most influential studies of the paradoxes of domesticity.

Davidoff, Leonore, and Catherine Hall. *Family Fortunes: Men and Women of the English Middle Class, 1780–1850.* Chicago, 1985. A brilliant and detailed study of the lives and ambitions of several English families.

Ferguson, Niall. *The Cash Nexus: Money and Power in the Modern World, 1700–2000* (New York, 2001). A very stimulating and fresh overview of the period.

———. "The European Economy, 1815–1914." In *The Nineteenth Century*, ed. T. C. W. Blanning. Oxford and New York, 2000. A very useful short essay.

Gay, Peter. *The Bourgeois Experience: Victoria to Freud.* New York, 1984. A multivolume, path-breaking study of middle-class life in all its dimensions.

———. *Schnitzler's Century: The Making of Middle-Class Culture, 1815–1914.* New York and London, 2002. A synthesis of some of the arguments presented in *The Bourgeois Experience.*

Hellerstein, Erna, Leslie Hume, and Karen Offen, eds. *Victorian Women: A Documentary Account.* Stanford, Calif., 1981. Good collection of documents, with excellent introductory essays.

Hobsbawm, Eric J. *The Age of Capital, 1848–1875.* London, 1975. Among the best introductions.

———. *The Age of Revolution, 1789–1848.* London, 1962.

———, and George Rudé. *Captain Swing: A Social History of the Great English Agricultural Uprising of 1830.* New York, 1975. Analyzes rural protest and politics.

Horn, Jeff. *The Path Not Taken: French Industrialization in the Age of Revolution, 1750–1830.* Cambridge, 2006. Argues that industrialization in France succeeded in ways that other historians have not appreciated, and was much more than a failed attempt to imitate the British model.

Jones, Eric. *The European Miracle: Environments, Economies and Geopolitics in the History of Europe and Asia.* Cambridge, 2003. Argues that the Industrial Revolution is best understood as a European phenomenon.

Kemp, Tom. *Industrialization in Nineteenth-Century Europe.* London, 1985. Good general study.

Kindelberger, Charles. *A Financial History of Western Europe.* London, 1984. Emphasis on finance.

Landes, David S. *The Unbound Prometheus: Technological Change and Industrial Development in Western Europe from 1750 to the Present.* London, 1969. Excellent and thorough on technological change and its social and economic context.

Langer, William L. *Political and Social Upheaval, 1832–1852.* New York, 1969. Comprehensive and detailed survey.

McNeill, J. R. *Something New under the Sun: An Environmental History of the Twentieth-Century World.* New York and London, 2000. Short section on the nineteenth century.

Mokyr, Joel. *The Lever of Riches: Technological Creativity and Economic Progress.* New York, 1992. A world history, from antiquity through the nineteenth century

O'Gráda, Cormac. *Black '47 and Beyond: The Great Irish Famine.* Princeton, N.J., 1999.

———. *The Great Irish Famine.* Cambridge, 1989. A fascinating and recent assessment of scholarship on the famine.

Kenneth Pomeranz. *The Great Divergence: China, Europe, and the Making of the Modern World Economy.* Princeton, N.J., 2000. Path-breaking global history of the Industrial Revolution that argues that Europe was not as different from other parts of the world as scholars have previously thought.

Rendall, Jane. *The Origins of Modern Feminism: Women in Britain, France and the United States, 1780–1860.* New York, 1984. Helpful overview.

Rose, Sonya O. *Limited Livelihoods: Gender and Class in Nineteenth-Century England.* Berkeley, Calif., 1992. On the intersection of culture and economics.

Sabean, David Warren. *Property, Production, and Family Neckarhausen, 1700–1870.* New York, 1990. Brilliant and very detailed study of gender roles and family.

Sabel, Charles, and Jonathan Zeitlin. "Historical Alternatives to Mass Production." *Past and Present* 108 (August 1985): 133–176. On the many forms of modern industry.

Schivelbusch, Wolfgang. *Disenchanted Night: The Instrialization of Light in the Nineteenth Century.* Berkeley, Calif., 1988.

———. *The Railway Journey.* Berkeley, 1986. Schivelbusch's imaginative studies are among the best ways to understand how the transformations of the nineteenth century changed daily experiences.

Thompson, E. P. *The Making of the English Working Class*. London, 1963. Shows how the French and Industrial Revolutions fostered the growth of working-class consciousness. A brilliant and important work.

Tilly, Louise, and Joan Scott. *Women, Work and the Family*. New York, 1978. Now the classic study.

Valenze, Deborah. *The First Industrial Woman*. New York, 1995. Excellent and readable on industrialization and economic change in general.

Williams, Raymond. *Keywords: A Vocabulary of Culture and Society*. New York, 1976. Brilliant and indispensable for students of culture, and now updated as *New Keywords: A Revised Vocabulary of Culture and Society* (2005), by Lawrence Grossberg and Meaghan Morris.

Zeldin, Theodore. France, 1848–1945, 2 vols. Oxford, 1973–1977. Eclectic and wide-ranging social history.

CHAPTER 20

Agulhon, Maurice. *The Republican Experiment, 1848–1852*. New York, 1983. A full treatment of the revolution in France.

Anderson, Benedict. *Imagined Communities: Reflections on the Origin and Spread of Nationalism*. London, 1983. The most influential recent study of the subject, highly recommended for further reading.

Barzun, Jacques. *Classic, Romantic, and Modern*. Chicago, 1943. An enduring and penetrating mid-twentieth-century defense of the Romantic sensibility by a humane and influential cultural historian.

Briggs, Asa. *The Age of Improvement, 1783–1867*. New York, 1979. A survey of England from 1780 to 1870, particularly strong on Victorian attitudes.

Colley, Linda. *Britons: Forging the Nation, 1707–1837*. New Haven, Conn., 1992. An important analysis of Britain's emerging national consciousness in the eighteenth and early nineteenth centuries.

Furet, François. *Revolutionary France, 1770–1880*. New York, 1970. An excellent and fresh overview by one of the preeminent historians of the revolution of 1789.

Gilbert, Sandra M., and Susan Gubar. *The Madwoman in the Attic: The Woman Writer and the Nineteenth-Century Literary Imagination*. New Haven, Conn., and London, 1970. A study of the history of women writers and on examination of women writers as historians of their time.

Hobsbawm, Eric. *The Age of Revolution: Europe 1789 to 1848*. New York, 1970. A classic, and still very useful, account of the period.

Kramer, Lloyd. *Nationalism: Political Cultures in Europe and America, 1775–1865*. London, 1998. Excellent recent overview.

Langer, William. *Political and Social Upheaval, 1832–1851*. New York, 1969. Long the standard and still the most comprehensive survey.

Laven, David, and Lucy Riall. *Napoleon's Legacy: Problems of Government in Restoration Europe*. London, 2002. A recent collection of essays.

Levinger, Matthew. *Enlightened Nationalism: The Transformation of Prussian Political Culture 1806–1848*. New York, 2000. A recent and nuanced study of Prussian conservatism, with implications for the rest of Europe.

Macfie, A. L. *Orientalism*. London, 2002. Introductory but very clear.

Merriman, John M., ed. *1830 in France*. New York, 1975. Emphasizes the nature of revolution and examines events outside Paris.

Pinkney, David. *The French Revolution of 1830*. Princeton, N.J., 1972. A reinterpretation, now the best history of the revolution.

Porter, Roy, and Mikulas Teich, eds. *Romanticism in National Context*. Cambridge, 1988.

Raeff, Marc. *The Decembrist Movement*. New York, 1966. A study of the Russian uprising with documents.

Sahlins, Peter. *Forest Rites: The War of the Demoiselles in Nineteenth-Century France*. Cambridge, Mass., 1994. A fascinating study of relations among peasant communities, the forests, and the state.

Said, Edward W. *Orientalism*. New York, 1979. A brilliant and biting study of the imaginative hold of the Orient on European intellectuals.

Saville, John. *1848: The British State and the Chartist Movement*. New York, 1987. A detailed account of the movement's limited successes and ultimate failure.

Schroeder, Paul. *The Transformation of European Politics, 1763–1848*. Oxford and New York, 1994. For those interested in international relations and diplomacy; massively researched and a fresh look at the period. Especially good on the Congress of Vienna.

Sewell, William H. *Work and Revolution in France: The Language of Labor from the Old Regime to 1848*. Cambridge, 1980. A very influential study of French radicalism and its larger implications.

Smith, Bonnie. *The Gender of History: Men, Women, and Historical Practice*. Cambridge, Mass., 1998. On Romanticism and the historical imagination.

Wordsworth, Jonathan, Michael C. Jaye, and Robert Woof. *William Wordsworth and the Age of English Romanticism*. New Brunswick, N.J., 1987. Wide ranging and beautifully illustrated, a good picture of the age.

CHAPTER 21

Beales, Derek. *The Risorgimento and the Unification of Italy*. New York, 1971. Objective, concise survey of Italian unification.

Blackbourn, David. *The Long Nineteenth Century: A History of Germany, 1780–1918*. New York, 1998. Recent and excellent.

Blackburn, Robin. *The Overthrow of Colonial Slavery*. London, 1988. Brilliant and detailed overview of the social history of slavery and antislavery movements.

Brophy, James M. *Capitalism, Politics, and Railroads in Prussia, 1830–1870*. Columbus, Ohio, 1998. Important, clear, and helpful.

Coppa, Frank. *The Origins of the Italian Wars of Independence*. London, 1992. Lively narrative.

Craig, Gordon. *Germany, 1866–1945*. New York, 1978. An excellent and thorough synthesis.

Davis, David Brian. *Inhuman Bondage: The Rise and Fall of Slavery in the New World*. New York, 2006. As one reviewer aptly puts it, "A gracefully fashioned masterpiece."

Deak, Istvan. *The Lawful Revolution: Louis Kossuth and the Hungarians, 1848–1849.* New York, 1979. The best on the subject.

Eyck, Erich. *Bismarck and the German Empire.* 3d ed. London, 1968. The best one-volume study of Bismarck.

Hamerow, Theodore S. *The Birth of a New Europe: State and Society in the Nineteenth Century.* Chapel Hill, N.C., 1983. A discussion of political and social change, and their relationship to industrialization and the increase in state power.

————. *The Social Foundations of German Unification, 1858–1871.* 2 vols. Princeton, N.J., 1969–1972. Concentrates on economic factors that determined the solution to the unification question. An impressive synthesis.

Higonnet, Patrice. *Paris: Capital of the World.* London, 2002. Fascinating and imaginative study of Paris as "capital of the nineteenth century."

Hobsbawm, Eric J. *Nations and Nationalism since 1870: Programme, Myth, Reality.* 2d ed. Cambridge, 1992. A clear, concise analysis of the historical and cultural manifestations of nationalism.

Howard, Michael. *The Franco-Prussian War.* New York, 1981. The war's effect on society.

Hutchinson, John, and Anthony Smith, eds. *Nationalism.* New York, 1994. A collection of articles, not particularly historical, but with the merit of discussing non-European nationalisms.

Johnson, Susan. *Roaring Camp.* New York, 2000. A history of one mining camp in California and a micro-history of the larger forces changing the West and the world.

Kolchin, Peter. *Unfree Labor: American Slavery and Russian Serfdom.* Cambridge, Mass., 1987. Pioneering comparative study.

Mack Smith, Denis. *Cavour and Garibaldi.* New York, 1968.

————. *The Making of Italy, 1796–1870.* New York, 1968. A narrative with documents.

McPherson, James. *Battle Cry of Freedom: The Civil War Era.* New York, 1988. Universally acclaimed and prize-winning book on the politics of slavery and the conflicts entailed in nation building in mid-nineteenth-century United States.

Pflanze, Otto. *Bismarck and the Development of Germany.* 2d ed. 3 vols. Princeton, N.J., 1990. Extremely detailed analysis of Bismarck's aims and policies.

Pinkney, David. *Napoleon III and the Rebuilding of Paris.* Princeton, N.J., 1972. An interesting account of the creation of modern Paris during the Second Empire.

Robertson, Priscilla. *Revolutions of 1848: A Social History.* Princeton, N.J., 1952. Old-fashioned narrative, but very readable.

Sammons, Jeffrey L. *Heinrich Heine: A Modern Biography.* Princeton, N.J., 1979. An excellent historical biography as well as a study of culture and politics.

Scott, Rebecca J. *Degrees of Freedom: Louisiana and Cuba after Slavery.* Cambridge, Mass., 2008. Brings the lives of slaves and their owners to life during the era of emancipation in a comparative history that places the southern United States in the context of the Atlantic world.

Sheehan, James J. *German Liberalism in the Nineteenth Century.* Chicago, 1978. Fresh and important synthesis.

Sperber, Jonathan. *The European Revolutions, 1848–1851.* New York, 1994. Now the best single volume on the period, with bibliography.

————. *Rhineland Radicals: The Democratic Movement and the Revolution of 1848–1849.* Princeton, N.J., 1993. A detailed study of Germany, by the author of an overview of the revolutions of 1848.

Stearns, Peter N. *1848: The Revolutionary Tide in Europe.* New York, 1974. Stresses the social background of the revolutions.

Zeldin, Theodore. *The Political System of Napoleon III.* New York, 1958. Compact and readable, by one of the major scholars of the period.

CHAPTER 22

Achebe, Chinua. *Things Fall Apart.* Expanded edition with notes. Portsmouth, N.H., 1996. An annotated edition of the now classic novel about colonial Africa.

Adas, Michael. *Machines as the Measure of Man: Science, Technology, and Ideologies of Western Dominance.* Ithaca, N.Y., and London, 1989. An important study of Europeans' changing perceptions of themselves and others during the period of industrialization.

Bayly, C. A. *Indian Society and the Making of the British Empire.* Cambridge, 1988. A good introduction, and one that bridges eighteenth- and nineteenth-century imperialisms.

Burbank, Jane, and Frederick Cooper. *Empires in World History: Power and the Politics of Difference.* Princeton, NJ, 2010. Powerful synthesis that sets European empires in the broader context of world history.

Burton, Antoinette. *Burdens of History: British Feminists, Indian Women, and Imperial Culture, 1865–1915.* Chapel Hill, N.C., 1994. On the ways in which women and feminists came to support British imperialism.

Cain, P. J., and A. G. Hopkins. *British Imperialism, 1688–2000.* London, 2002. One of the most influential studies. Excellent overview and exceptionally good on economics.

Clancy Smith, Julia, and Frances Gouda. *Domesticating the Empire: Race, Gender, and Family Life in French and Dutch Colonialism.* Charlottesville, Va., and London, 1998. A particularly good collection of essays that both breaks new historical ground and is accessible to nonspecialists. Essays cover daily life and private life in new colonial cultures.

Conklin, Alice. *A Mission to Civilize: The Republican idea of Empire in France and West Africa, 1895–1930.* Stanford, Calif., 1997. One of the best studies of how the French reconciled imperialism with their vision of the Republic.

Cooper, Frederick, and Ann Laura Stoler. *Tensions of Empire: Colonial Cultures in a Bourgeois World.* Berkeley, Calif., 1997. New approaches, combining anthropology and history, with an excellent bibliography.

Darwin, John. *The Empire Project: The Rise and Fall of the British World System.* Cambridge, 2009.

Headrick, Daniel R. *The Tools of Empire: Technology and European Imperialism in the Nineteenth Century.* Oxford, 1981. A study of the relationship between technological innovation and imperialism.

Hobsbawm, Eric. *The Age of Empire, 1875–1914.* New York, 1987. Surveys the European scene at a time of apparent stability and real decline.

Hochschild, Adam. *King Leopold's Ghost: A Story of Greed, Terror, and Heroism in Colonial Africa.* Boston, 1998. Reads like a great novel.

Lorcin, Patricia. *Imperial Identities: Stereotyping, Prejudice and Race in Colonial Algeria.* New York, 1999.

Louis, William Roger. *The Oxford History of the British Empire.* 5 vols. Oxford, 1998. Excellent and wide-ranging collection of the latest research.

Metcalf, Thomas. *Ideologies of the Raj.* Cambridge, 1995.

Pakenham, Thomas. *The Scramble for Africa, 1876–1912.* London, 1991. A well-written narrative of the European scramble for Africa in the late nineteenth century.

Prochaska, David. *Making Algeria French: Colonialism in Bône, 1870–1920.* Cambridge, 1990. One of the few social histories of European settlement in Algeria in English.

Robinson, Ronald, and J. Gallagher. *Africa and the Victorians: The Official Mind of Imperialism.* London, 1961. A classic.

Said, Edward. *Culture and Imperialism.* New York, 1993. A collection of brilliant, sometimes controversial, essays.

Sangari, Kumkum, and Sudesh Vaid. *Recasting Women: Essays in Colonial History.* New Delhi, 1989. A collection of essays on women in India.

Schneer, Jonathan. *London 1900: The Imperial Metropolis.* New Haven, Conn., 1999. Excellent study of the empire—and opposition to empire—in the metropole.

Spence, Jonathan. *The Search for Modern China.* New York, 1990. An excellent and readable introduction to modern Chinese history.

CHAPTER 23

Berlanstein, Lenard. *The Working People of Paris, 1871–1914.* Baltimore, Md. 1984. A social history of the workplace and its impact on working men and women.

Berlin, Isaiah. *Karl Marx: His Life and Environment.* 4th ed. New York, 1996. An excellent short account.

Blackbourn, David. *The Long Nineteenth Century: A History of Germany, 1780–1918.* New York, 1998. Among the best surveys of German society and politics.

Bowler, Peter J. *Evolution: The History of an Idea.* Berkeley, Calif., 1984. One of the author's several excellent studies of evolution of Darwinism.

Bredin, Jean-Denis. *The Affair: The Case of Alfred Dreyfus.* New York, 1986. Detailed and readable.

Burns, Michael. *Dreyfus: A Family Affair.* New York, 1992. Follows the story Dreyfus through the next generations.

Chipp, Herschel B. *Theories of Modern Art: A Source Book by Artists and Critics.* Berkeley, Calif., 1968.

Clark, T. J. *The Painting of Modern Life: Paris in the Art of Manet and His Followers.* New York, 1985. Argues for seeing impressionism as a critique of French society.

Eley, Geoff. *Forging Democracy.* Oxford, 2002. Wide-ranging and multinational account of European radicalism from 1848 to the present.

Frank, Stephen. *Crime, Cultural Conflict, and Justice in Rural Russia, 1856–1914.* Berkeley, Calif., 1999. A revealing study of social relations from the ground up.

Gay, Peter. *The Bourgeois Experience: Victoria to Freud,* 5 vols. New York, 1984–2000. Imaginative and brilliant study of private life and middle class culture.

———. *Freud: A Life of Our Time.* New York, 1988. Beautifully written and lucid about difficult concepts; now the best biography.

Herbert, Robert L. *Impressionism: Art, Leisure, and Parisian Society.* New Haven, 1988. An accessible and important study of the impressionists and the world they painted.

Hughes, H. Stuart. *Consciousness and Society.* New York, 1958. A classic study on late-nineteenth-century European thought.

Jelavich, Peter. *Munich and Theatrical Modernism: Politics, Playwriting, and Performance, 1890–1914.* Cambridge, Mass., 1985. On modernism as a revolt against nineteenth-century conventions.

Jones, Gareth Stedman. *Outcast London.* Oxford, 1971. Studies the breakdown in class relationships during the second half of the nineteenth century.

Joyce, Patrick. *Visions of the People: Industrial England and the Question of Class, 1848–1914.* New York, 1991. A social history of the workplace.

Kelly, Alfred. *The German Worker: Autobiographies from the Age of Industrialization.* Berkeley, Calif., 1987. Excerpts from workers' autobiographies provide fresh perspective on labor history.

Kern, Stephen. *The Culture of Time and Space.* Cambridge, Mass., 1983. A cultural history of the late nineteenth century.

Landes, David. *The Unbound Prometheus: Technological Change and Industrial Development in Western Europe from 1750 to the Present.* New York, 1969. Includes a first-rate analysis of the second industrial revolution.

Lidtke, Vernon. *The Alternative Culture: Socialist Labor in Imperial Germany.* New York, 1985. A probing study of working-class culture.

Marrus, Michael Robert. *The Politics of Assimilation: A Study of the French Jewish Community at the Time of the Dreyfus Affair.* Oxford, 1971. Excellent social history.

Micale, Mark S. *Approaching Hysteria: Disease and Its Interpretations.* Princeton, N.J., 1995. Important study of the history of psychiatry before Freud.

Rupp, Leila J. *Worlds of Women: The Making of an International Women's Movement.* Princeton, N.J., 1997.

Schivelbusch, Wolfgang. *Disenchanted Night: The Industrialization of Light in the Nineteenth Century.* Berkeley, Calif., 1995. Imaginative study of how electricity transformed everyday life.

Showalter, Elaine. *The Female Malady: Women, Madness, and English Culture, 1890–1980.* New York, 1985. Brilliant and readable on Darwin, Freud, gender, and the First World War.

Silverman, Deborah L. *Art Nouveau in Fin-de-Siècle France: Politics, Psychology, and Style.* Berkeley, Calif., 1989. A study of the relationship between psychological and artistic change.

Smith, Bonnie. *Changing Lives: Women in European History since 1700.* New York, 1988. A useful overview of European women's history.

Tickner, Lisa. *The Spectacle of Women: Imagery of the Suffrage Campaign, 1907–14.* Chicago, 1988. A very engaging study of British suffragism.

Verner, Andrew. *The Crisis of Russian Autocracy: Nicholas II and the 1905 Revolution.* Princeton, N.J., 1990. A detailed study of this important event.

Vital, David. *A People Apart: A Political History of the Jews in Europe, 1789-1939.* Oxford and New York, 1999. Comprehensive and extremely helpful.

Weber, Eugen. *Peasants into Frenchmen: The Modernization of Rural France, 1870–1914.* Stanford, Calif., 1976. A study of how France's peasantry was assimilated into the Third Republic.

CHAPTER 24

Chickering, Roger. *Imperial Germany and the Great War, 1914–1918.* New York, 1998. An excellent synthesis.

Eksteins, Modris. *Rites of Spring: The Great War and the Birth of the Modern Age.* New York, 1989. Fascinating, though impressionistic, on war, art, and culture.

Ferguson, Niall. *The Pity of War.* London, 1998. A fresh look at the war, including strategic issues, international relations, and economics.

Ferro, Marc. *The Great War, 1914–1918.* London, 1973. Very concise overview.

Figes, Orlando. *A People's Tragedy: A History of the Russian Revolution.* New York, 1997. Excellent, detailed narrative.

Fischer, Fritz. *War of Illusions.* New York, 1975. Deals with Germany within the context of internal social and economic trends.

Fitzpatrick, Sheila. *The Russian Revolution, 1917–1932.* New York and Oxford, 1982. Concise overview.

Fussell, Paul. *The Great War and Modern Memory.* New York, 1975. A brilliant examination of British intellectuals' attitudes toward the war.

Higonnet, Margaret Randolph, et al., eds. *Behind the Lines: Gender and the Two World Wars.* New Haven, Conn., 1987. A collection of essays.

Hynes, Samuel. *A War Imagined: The First World War and English Culture.* New York, 1991. The war as perceived on the home front.

Jelavich, Barbara. *History of the Balkans: Twentieth Century.* New York, 1983. Useful for an understanding of the continuing conflict in eastern Europe.

Joll, James. *The Origins of the First World War.* London, 1984. Comprehensive and very useful.

Keegan, John. *The First World War.* London, 1998. The best overall military history.

Macmillan, Margaret, and Richard Holbrooke. *Paris 1919: Six Months That Changed the World.* New York, 2003. Fascinating fresh look at the peace conference.

Mazower, Mark. *Dark Continent: Europe's Twentieth Century.* New York, 1999. An excellent survey, particularly good on nations and minorities in the Balkans and eastern Europe.

Rabinowitch, Alexander. *The Bolsheviks Come to Power.* New York, 1976. A well-researched and carefully documented account.

Roberts, Mary Louise. *Civilization without Sexes: Reconstructing Gender in Postwar France, 1917–1927.* Chicago, 1994. A prize-winning study of the issues raised by the "new woman."

Schivelbusch, Wolfgang. *The Culture of Defeat: On National Trauma, Mourning, and Recovery.* New York, 2001. Fascinating if impressionistic comparative study.

Smith, Leonard. *Between Mutiny and Obedience: The Case of the French Fifth Infantry Division during World War I.* Princeton, N.J., 1994. An account of mutiny and the reasons behind it.

Stevenson, David. *Cataclysm: The First World War as Political Tragedy.* New York, 2003. Detailed and comprehensive, now one of the best single-volume studies.

Stites, Richard. *Revolutionary Dreams: Utopian Visions and Experimental Life in the Russian Revolution.* New York, 1989. The influence of utopian thinking on the revolution.

Williams, John. *The Home Fronts: Britain, France and Germany, 1914–1918.* London, 1972. A survey of life away from the battlefield and the impact of the war on domestic life.

Winter, J. M. *The Experience of World War I.* New York, 1989. Comprehensive illustrated history viewing the war from different perspectives.

CHAPTER 25

Carr, E. H. *The Bolshevik Revolution, 1917–1923.* London and New York, 1950–1953. One of the classics.

Cohen, Stephen F. *Bukharin and the Bolshevik Revolution: A Political Biography, 1888–1938.* New York, 1973. Excellent study of one of the early Bolshevik leaders and of the significance of the revolution as a whole.

Conquest, Robert. *The Great Terror: A Reassessment.* New York, 1990. One of the first histories of the Terror, should be read in conjunction with others in this list.

Crew, David F., ed. *Nazism and German Society, 1933–1945.* New York, 1994. An excellent and accessible collection of essays.

Degrazia, Victoria. *Irresistible Empire: America's Advance through 20th-Century Europe.* Cambridge, Mass., 2005. Brilliant analysis of "Americanization" in many forms, including business practices, movie studios, and models of gender relations.

Figes, Orlando. *Peasant Russia Civil War: The Volga Countryside in Revolution, 1917–1921.* Oxford, 1989. Detailed and sophisticated but readable. Study of the region from the eve of the revolution through the civil war.

Fitzpatrick, Shelia. *Everyday Stalinism: Ordinary Life in Extraordinary Times: Soviet Russia in the 1930s.* Oxford and New York, 1999. Gripping on how ordinary people dealt with famine, repression, and chaos.

Friedlander, Saul. *Nazi Germany and the Jews: The Years of Persecution. 1933–1939.* Rev. ed. New York, 2007. Excellent; the first of a two-volume study.

Gay, Peter. *Weimar Culture.* New York, 1968. Concise and elegant overview.

Getty, J. Arch, and Oleg V. Naumov. *The Road to Terror: Stalin and the Self-Destruction of the Bolsheviks, 1932–1939.* New Haven, Conn., 1999. Combines analysis with documents made public for the first time.

Goldman, Wendy Z. *Women, the State, and Revolution: Soviet Family Policy and Social Life, 1917–1936.* New York, 1993. On the Bolshevik attempts to transform gender and family.

Kershaw, Ian. *Hitler.* 2 vols: *1889–1936 Hubris,* New York, 1999; *1936–1945: Nemesis,* New York, 2001. The best biography: insightful about politics, culture, and society as well as the man.

———. *The Hitler Myth: Image and Reality in the Third Reich.* New York, 1987. Brilliant study of how Nazi propagandists sold the myth of the Fuhrer and why many Germans bought it.

Klemperer, Victor. *I Will Bear Witness: A Diary of the Nazi Years, 1933–1941.* New York, 1999. *I Will Bear Witness: A Diary of the Nazi Years, 1942–1945.* New York, 2001. Certain to be a classic.

Lewin, Moshe. *The Making of the Soviet System: Essays in the Social History of Interwar Russia.* New York, 1985. One of the best to offer a view from below.

McDermott, Kevin. *Stalin: Revolutionary in an Era of War.* Basingstoke, UK, and New York, 2006. Useful, short, and recent.

Montefior, Simon Sebag. *Stalin: The Court of the Red Tsar.* London, 2004. On the relations among the top Bolsheviks, an interesting personal portrait. Takes you inside the inner circle.

Orwell, George. *The Road to Wigan Pier.* London, 1937. On unemployment and life in the coal mining districts of England, by one of the great British writers of the twentieth century.

———. *Homage to Catalonia.* London, 1938. A firsthand account of the Spanish Civil War.

Rentschler, Eric. *The Ministry of Illusion: Nazi Cinema and Its Afterlife.* Cambridge, Mass., 1996. For the more advanced student.

Service, Robert. *Stalin: A Biography.* London, 2004. Updates Tucker.

Suny, Ronald Grigor. *The Revenge of the Past: Nationalism, Revolution, and the Collapse of the Soviet Union.* Stanford, Calif., 1993. Pathbreaking study of the issues of nationalism and ethnicity form the revolution to the end of the Soviet Union.

Tucker, Robert C. *Stalin as Revolutionary, 1879–1929.* New York, 1973.

———. *Stalin in Power: The Revolution from Above, 1928–1941.* New York, 1990. With *Stalin as Revolutionary* emphasizes Stalin's purpose and method and sets him in the tradition of Russian dictators.

CHAPTER 26

The U.S. Holocaust Memorial Museum has an extraordinary collection of articles, photographs, and maps. See www.ushmm.org.

Bartov, Omer. *Hitler's Army: Soldiers, Nazis, and War in the Third Reich.* New York, 1991. A Study of the radicalization of the German army on the Russian front.

Braithwaite, Rodric. *Moscow. 1941: A City and Its People at War.* London, 2006. Readable account of one of the turning points of the war.

Browning, Christopher R. *The Path to Genocide: Essays on Launching the Final Solution.* Cambridge, 1992. Discusses changing interpretations and case studies. See also the author's *Ordinary Men: Reserve Police Battalion 101 and the Final Solution in Poland.*

Burrin, Philippe. *France under the Germans: Collaboration and Compromise.* New York, 1996. Comprehensive on occupation and collaboration.

Carr, Raymond. *The Spanish Tragedy: The Civil War in Perspective.* London, 1977. A thoughtful introduction to the Spanish Civil War and the evolution of Franco's Spain.

Dawidowicz, Lucy S. *The War against the Jews, 1933–1945.* New York, 1975. A full account of the Holocaust.

Divine, Robert A. *Roosevelt and World War II.* Baltimore, Md., 1969. A diplomatic history.

Djilas, Milovan. *Wartime.* New York, 1977. An insider's account of the partisans' fighting in Yugoslavia and a good example of civil war within the war.

Gellately, Robert, and Ben Kiernan, eds. *The Specter of Genocide: Mass Murder in Historical Perspective.* New York, 2003. A particularly thoughtful collection of essays.

Gilbert, Martin. *The Appeasers.* Boston, 1963. Excellent study of British pro-German sentiment in the 1930s.

Graham, Helen. *The Spanish Civil War: A Very Short Introduction.* Oxford and New York, 2005. Excellent and very concise, based on the author's new interpretation in the more detailed *The Spanish Republic at War, 1936–1939.* Cambridge, 2002.

Hilberg, Raul. *The Destruction of the European Jews.* 2nd ed. 3 vols. New York, 1985. An excellent treatment of the Holocaust, its origins, and its consequences.

Kedward, Roderick. *In Search of the Maquis: Rural Resistance in Southern France, 1942–1944.* Oxford, 1993. An engaging study of French guerilla resistance.

Keegan, John. *The Second World War.* New York, 1990. By one of the great military historians of our time.

Mann, Michael. *The Dark Side of Democracy: Explaining Ethnic Cleansing.* New York, 2005. Brilliant and theoretical as well as historical.

Marrus, Michael R. *The Holocaust in History.* Hanover, N.H., 1987. Thoughtful analysis of central issues.

Mawdsley, Evan. *Thunder in the East: The Nazi-Soviet War, 1941–1945.* New York, 2005.

Megargee, Geoffrey. *War of Annihilation: Combat and Genocide on the Eastern War, 1941.* Lanham, Md., 2006. Represents some of the new historical work on the eastern front.

Merridale, Catherine. *Ivan's War: Life and Death in the Red Army, 1939–1945.* New York, 2006. Raised many questions and insights.

Michel, Henri. *The Shadow War: The European Resistance, 1939–1945.* New York, 1972. Compelling reading.

Milward, Alan S. *War, Economy, and Society, 1939–1945.* Berkeley, Calif., 1977. On the economic impact of the war and the strategic impact of the economy.

Noakes, Jeremy, and Geoffrey Pridham. *Nazism: A History in Documents and Eyewitness Accounts, 1919–1945.* New York, 1975. An excellent combination of analysis and documentation.

Overy, Richard. *Russia's War.* New York, 1998. A very readable account that accompanies the PBS series by the same title.

———. *Why the Allies Won.* New York, 1995. Excellent analysis; succint.

Paxton, Robert O. *Vichy France: Old Guard and New Order, 1940–1944.* New York, 1982. Brilliant on collaboration and Vichy's National Revolution.

Snyder, Timothy. *Bloodlands: Europe between Hitler and Stalin.* New York, 2010. Thorough and penetrating account of the methods and motives of Hitler's and Stalin's regimes.

Stoff, Michael B. *The Manhattan Project: A Documentary Introduction to the Atomic Age.* New York, 1991. Political, scientific, and historical; excellent documents and commentary.

Weinberg, Gerhard L. *A Global History of World War II*. New York, 1995. Now the most comprehensive history.

Wilkinson, James D. *The Intellectual Resistance in Europe*. Cambridge, Mass., 1981. A comparative study of the movement throughout Europe.

CHAPTER 27

Aron, Raymond. *The Imperial Republic: The United States and the World, 1945–1973*. Lanham, Md., 1974. An early analysis by a leading French political theorist.

Carter, Erica. *How German Is She? Postwar West German Reconstruction and the Consuming Woman*. Ann Arbor, Mich., 1997. A thoughtful examination of gender and the reconstruction of the family in West Germany during the 1950s.

Clayton, Anthony. *The Wars of French Decolonization*. London, 1994. Good survey.

Connelly, Matthew. *A Diplomatic Revolution: Algeria's Fight for Independence and the Origins of the Post–Cold War Era*. New York and Oxford, 2003. An international history.

Cooper, Frederick, and Ann Laura Stoler, eds. *Tensions of Empire: Colonial Cultures in a Bourgeois World*. Berkeley, Calif., 1997. Collection of new essays, among the best.

Darwin, John. *Britain and Decolonization: The Retreat from Empire in the Postwar World*. New York, 1988. Best overall survey.

Deák, István, Jan T. Gross, and Tony Judt, eds. *The Politics of Retribution in Europe: World War II and Its Aftermath*. Princeton, N.J., 2000. Collection focusing on the attempt to come to terms with the Second World War in Eastern and Western Europe.

Farmer, Sarah. *Martyred Village: Commemorating the 1944 Massacre at Oradour-sur-Glane*. Berkeley, Calif., 1999. Gripping story of French attempts to come to terms with collaboration and complicity in atrocities.

Holland, R. F. *European Decolonization 1918–1981: An Introductory Survey*. New York, 1985. Sprightly narrative and analysis.

Jarausch, Konrad Hugo, ed. *Dictatorship as Experience: Towards a Socio-Cultural History of the GDR*. Trans. Eve Duffy. New York, 1999. Surveys recent research on the former East Germany.

Judt, Tony. *The Burden of Responsibility: Blum, Camus, and the French Twentieth Century*. Chicago and London, 1998. Also on French intellectuals.

———. *A Grand Illusion? An Essay on Europe*. New York, 1996. Short and brilliant.

———. *Past Imperfect: French Intellectuals, 1944–1956*. Berkeley, Calif., 1992. Very readable, on French intellectuals, who loomed large during this period.

———. *Postwar. A History of Europe Since 1945*. London, 2005. Detailed, comprehensive, and ground breaking, this single volume surpasses any other account of the entire postwar period.

Koven, Seth, and Sonya Michel. *Mothers of a New World: Maternalist Politics and the Origins of Welfare States*. New York, 1993. Excellent essays on the long history of welfare politics.

LaFeber, Walter. *America, Russia, and the Cold War*. New York, 1967. A classic, now in its ninth edition.

Large, David Clay. *Berlin*. New York, 2000. Accessible and engaging.

Leffler, Melvyn P. *A Preponderance of Power: National Security, the Truman Administration, and the Cold War*. Stanford, Calif., 1992. Solid political study.

Louis, William Roger. *The Ends of British Imperialism: The Scramble for Empire, Suez, and Decolonization*. London, 2006. Comprehensive and wide ranging.

Macey, David. *Frantz Fanon*. New York, 2000. Comprehensive recent biography.

Medvedev, Roy. *Khrushchev*. New York, 1983. A perceptive biography of the Soviet leader by a Soviet historian.

Milward, Alan S. *The Reconstruction of Western Europe, 1945–1951*. Berkeley, Calif., 1984. A good discussion of the "economic miracle."

Moeller, Robert G. *War Stories: The Search for a Usable Past in the Federal Republic of Germany*. Berkeley, Calif., 2001. Revealing analyses of postwar culture and politics.

Reynolds, David. *One World Divisible: A Global History Since 1945*. New York, 2000. Fresh approach, comprehensive, and very readable survey.

Rousso, Henri. *The Vichy Syndrome: History and Memory in France since 1944*. Cambridge, Mass., 1991. First in a series of books by one of the preeminent French historians.

Schissler, Hanna, ed. *The Miracle Years: A Cultural History of West Germany, 1949–1968*. Princeton, N.J., 2001. The cultural effects of the economic miracle.

Schneider, Peter. *The Wall Jumper: A Berlin Story*. Chicago, 1998. A fascinating novel about life in divided Berlin.

Shepard, Todd. *The Invention of Decolonization: The Algerian War and the Remaking of France*. Ithaca, N.Y., 2006. Excellent and original: a study of the deeply wrenching war's many ramifications.

Shipway, Martin. *Decolonization and Its Impact: A Comparative Approach to the End of the Colonial Empires*. Malden, Mass., 2008. Accessible account emphasizing the unintended consequences of decolonization.

Trachtenberg, Mark. *A Constructed Peace: The Making of the European Settlement, 1945–1963*. Princeton, N.J., 1999. A detailed study of international relations that moves beyond the Cold War framework.

Tessler, Mark. *A History of the Israeli-Palestinian Conflict*. 2nd ed. Bloomington, Ind., 2009. Updated edition of the definitive account from the 1990s.

Westad, Odd Arne. *The Global Cold War*. New York, 2005. An international history that sees the roots of the world's present conflict in the history of the Cold War.

Wilder, Gary. *The French Imperial Nation-State: Negritude and Colonial Humanism between the Two World Wars*. Chicago, 2005. Fascinating new study of the Negritude thinkers in their context.

Yergin, Daniel. *Shattered Peace: The Origins of the Cold War*. New York, 1977. Rev. ed. 1990. Dramatic and readable.

Young, Marilyn B. *The Vietnam Wars, 1945–1990*. New York, 1991. Excellent account of the different stages of the war and its repercussions.

CHAPTER 28

Bailey, Beth. *From Front Porch to Back Seat: Courtship in Twentieth-Century America.* Baltimore, Md., 1988. Good historical perspective on the sexual revolution.

Beschloss, Michael, and Strobe Talbott. *At the Highest Levels: The Inside Story of the End of the Cold War.* Boston, 1993. An analysis of the relationship between presidents Gorbachev and George H. W. Bush and their determination to ignore hard-liners.

Brown, Archie. *The Gorbachev Factor.* Oxford and New York, 1996. One of the first serious studies of Gorbachev, by an Oxford scholar of politics.

Caute, David. *The Year of the Barricades: A Journey through 1968.* New York, 1988. A well-written global history of 1968.

Charney, Leo, and Vanessa R. Schwartz, eds. *Cinema and the Invention of Modern Life.* Berkeley, Calif., 1995. Collection of essays.

Dallin, Alexander, and Gail Lapidus. *The Soviet System: From Crisis to Collapse.* Boulder, Colo., 1995.

Echols, Alice. *Daring to Be Bad: Radical Feminism in America, 1967–1975.* Minneapolis, Minn., 1989. Good narrative and analysis.

Eley, Geoff. *Forging Democracy: The History of the Left in Europe, 1850–2000.* Oxford and New York, 2002. Among its other qualities, one of the best historical perspectives on the 1960s.

Fink, Carole, Phillipp Gassert, and Detlef Junker, eds. *1968: The World Transformed.* Cambridge, 1998. A transatlantic history of 1968.

Fulbrook, Mary, ed. *Europe since 1945* (The Short Oxford History of Europe). Oxford, 2001. Particularly good articles on economics and political economy. Structural analysis.

Garton Ash, Timothy. *In Europe's Name: Germany and the Divided Continent.* New York, 1993. An analysis of the effect of German reunification on the future of Europe.

Glenny, Misha. *The Balkans, 1804–1999: Nationalism, War and the Great Powers.* London, 1999. Good account by a journalist who covered the fighting.

Victoria de Grazia, *Irresistible Empire: America's Advance through Twentieth-Century Europe.* Cambridge, Mass., 2006. Thorough exploration of the history of consumer culture in Europe and its links to relations with the United States.

Horowitz, Daniel. *Betty Friedan and the Making of the Feminine Mystique: The American Left, the Cold War, and Modern Feminism.* Amherst, Mass., 1998. A reconsideration.

Hosking, Geoffrey. *The Awakening of the Soviet Union.* Cambridge, Mass., 1990. The factors that led to the end of the Soviet era.

Hughes, H. Stuart. *Sophisticated Rebels: The Political Culture of European Dissent, 1968–1987.* Cambridge, Mass., 1990. The nature of dissent on both sides of the disintegrating Iron Curtain in the years 1988–1989.

Hulsberg, Werner. *The German Greens: A Social and Political Profile.* New York, 1988. The origins, politics, and impact of environmental politics.

Jarausch, Konrad. *The Rush to German Unity.* New York, 1994. The problems of reunification analyzed.

Judah, Tim. *The Serbs: History, Myth, and the Destruction of Yugoslavia.* New Haven, Conn., 1997. Overview of Serbian history by journalist who covered the war.

Judt, Tony. *Postwar.* London, 2005. The most thorough and sophisticated account.

Kaplan, Robert D. *Balkan Ghosts: A Journey through History.* New York, 1993. More a political travelogue than a history, but very readable.

Kotkin, Stephen. *Armegeddon Averted: The Soviet Collapse, 1970–2000.* Oxford, 2001. Excellent short account.

Kurlansky, Mark. *1968: The Year that Rocked the World.* New York, 2005. An accessible introduction for nonspecialists.

Lewin, Moshe. *The Gorbachev Phenomenon.* Expanded ed. Berkeley, Calif., 1991. Written as a firsthand account, tracing the roots of Gorbachev's successes and failures.

Lieven, Anatol. *Chechnya, Tomb of Russia Power.* New Haven, Conn., and London, 1998. Longer view of the region, by a journalist.

Maier, Charles S. *Dissolution: The Crisis of Communism and the End of East Germany.* Princeton, N.J., 1997. Detailed and sophisticated.

Mann, Michael. *The Dark Side of Democracy: Explaining Ethnic Cleansing.* New York, 2005. Brilliant essay on different episodes from Armenia to Rwanda.

Marwick, Arthur. *The Sixties.* Oxford and New York, 1998. An international history.

Pells, Richard. *Not Like Us: How Europeans Have Loved, Hated, and Transformed American Culture since World War II.* New York, 1997. From the point of view of an American historian.

Poiger, Uta G. *Jazz, Rock, and Rebels: Cold War Politics and American Culture in a Divided Germany.* Berkeley, Calif., 2000. Pioneering cultural history.

Sheehan, Neil. *A Bright Shining Lie: John Paul Vann and America in Vietnam.* New York, 1988. A study of the war and its escalation through one of the U.S. Army's field advisers.

Strayer, Robert. *Why Did the Soviet Union Collapse? Understanding Historical Change.* Armonk, N.Y., and London, 1998. A good introduction, with bibliography.

Suri, Jeremi. *Power and Protest.* New ed. Cambridge, Mass., 2005. One of the best of the new global histories of the 1960s, looking at relations between social movements and international relations.

Wright, Patrick. *On Living in an Old Country: The National Past in Contemporary Britain.* New York, 1986. The culture of Britain in the 1980s.

CHAPTER 29

Cmiel, Kenneth, "The Recent History of Human Rights." *American Historical Review.* (February 2004). One of the first scholars to treat human rights historically.

Coetzee, J. M. *Waiting for the Barbarians.* London, 1980. A searing critique of apartheid-era South Africa by a leading Afrikaner novelist.

Cooper, Frederick. *Colonialism in Question: Theory, Knowledge, History.* Los Angeles and Berkeley, Calif., 2005. Excellent collection of essays and valuable critical analysis of the term globalization.

Epstein, Helen. *The Invisible Cure: Africa, the West, and the Fight Against AIDS*. New York, 2007. One of the best recent studies.

Frieden, Jeffrey H. *Global Capitalism: Its Rise and Fall in the Twentieth Century*. New York, 2007. Broad-ranging history for the advanced student.

Geyer, Michael, and Charles Bright. "World History in a Global Age." *American Historical Review* (October 1995). An excellent short discussion.

Glendon, Mary Ann. *A World Made New: Eleanor Roosevelt and the Universal Declaration of Human Rights*. New York, 2001. A fascinating study of the High Commission in its time by a legal scholar.

Harvey, David. *A Brief History of Neoliberalism*. New York, 2007, A critical account of the history of neoliberalism that encompasses the U.S., Europe, and Asia.

Held, David, et al. *Global Transformations: Politics, Economics, and Culture*. Stanford, Calif., 1999. Major survey of the globalization of culture, finance, criminality, and politics.

Hopkins, A. G., ed. *Globalization in World History*. New York, 2002. Excellent introduction, written by one of the first historians to engage the issue.

Hunt, Lynn. *Inventing Human Rights: A History*. New York, 2007. A short study of the continuities and paradoxes in the West's human rights tradition, by one of the foremost historians of the French Revolution. On 1776, 1789, and 1948.

Keddie, Nikki. *Modern Iran: Roots and Results of Revolution*. New Haven, Conn., 2003. A revised edition of her major study of Iran's 1979 revolution, with added perspective on Iran's Islamic government.

Lacqueur, Walter. *The Age of Terrorism*. Boston, 1987. An important study of the first wave of post-1960s terrorism.

Landes, David. *The Wealth and Poverty of Nations: Why Some Are So Rich and Some So Poor*. New York, 1998. Leading economic historian's account of globalization's effects on the international economy.

Lewis, Bernard. *The Crisis of Islam: Holy War and Unholy Terror*. New York, 2003. Conservative scholar of the Arab world discussing the political crises that fueled terrorism.

Mckeown, Adam. "Global Migration, 1846–1940." *Journal of World History* 15.2 (2004). Includes references to more work on the subject.

McNeill, J. R. *Something New under the Sun: An Environmental History of the Twentieth-Century World*. New York and London, 2000. Fascinating new approach to environmental history.

Novick, Peter. *The Holocaust in American Life*. Boston, 1999.

Power, Samantha. *The Problem from Hell: America in the Age of Genocide*. A prize-winning survey of the entire twentieth century, its genocides, and the different human rights movements that responded to them.

Reynolds, David. *One World Divisible: A Global History since 1945*. New York and London, 2000. Excellent study of the different dimensions of globalization.

Shilts, Randy. *And the Band Played On: Politics, People, and the AIDS Epidemic*. New York, 1987. An impassioned attack on the individuals and governments that failed to come to grips with the early spread of the disease.

Shlaim, Avi. *The Iron Wall: Israel and the Arab World*. New York, 2000. Leading Israeli historian on the evolution of Israel's defensive foreign policy.

Stiglitz, Joseph E. *Globalization and Its Discontents*. New York, 2002. A recent and important consideration of contemporary globalization's character and the conflicts it creates, particularly over commerce and culture.

Turkle, Sherry. *Life on the Screen: Identity in the Age of the Internet*. New York, 1995. An important early study of Web culture and the fluid possibilities of electronic communication.

Winter, Jay. *Dreams of Peace and Freedom: Utopian Moments in the Twentieth Century*. New Haven, Conn., 2006. One of the leading historians of war and atrocity turns here to twentieth-century hopes for peace and human rights.

1973 OPEC oil embargo Some leaders in the Arab-dominated Organization of the Petroleum Exporting Countries (OPEC) wanted to use oil as a weapon against the West in the Arab-Israeli conflict. After the 1972 Arab-Israeli war, OPEC instituted an oil embargo against Western powers. The embargo increased the price of oil and sparked spiraling inflation and economic troubles in Western nations, triggering in turn a cycle of dangerous recession that lasted nearly a decade. In response, Western governments began viewing the Middle Eastern oil regions as areas of strategic importance.

Abbasid Caliphate (750–930) The Abbasid family claimed to be descendants of Muhammad, and in 750 they successfully led a rebellion against the Umayyads, seizing control of Muslim territories in Arabia, Persia, North Africa, and the Near East. The Abbasids modeled their behavior and administration on that of the Persian princes and their rule on that of the Persian Empire, establishing a new capital at Baghdad.

Peter Abelard (1079–1142) Highly influential philosopher, theologian, and teacher, often considered the founder of the University of Paris.

absolutism Form of government in which one body, usually the monarch, controls the right to make war, tax, judge, and coin money. The term was often used to refer to the state monarchies in seventeenth- and eighteenth-century Europe. In other countries the end of feudalism is often associated with the legal abolition of serfdom, as in Russia in 1861.

abstract expressionism The mid-twentieth-century school of art based in New York that included Jackson Pollock, Willem de Kooning, and Franz Kline. It emphasized form, color, gesture, and feeling instead of figurative subjects.

Academy of Sciences This French institute of scientific inquiry was founded in 1666 by Louis XIV. France's statesmen exerted control over the academy and sought to share in the rewards of any discoveries its members made.

Aeneas Mythical founder of Rome, Aeneas was a refugee from the city of Troy whose adventures were described by the poet Virgil in the *Aeneid,* which mimicked the oral epics of Homer.

Aetolian and Achaean Leagues These two alliances among Greek poleis formed during the Hellenistic period in opposition to the Antigonids of Macedonia. Unlike the earlier defensive alliances of the classic period, each league represented a real attempt to form a political federation.

African National Congress (ANC) Multiracial organization founded in 1912 whose goal was to end racial discrimination in South Africa.

Afrikaners Descendants of the original Dutch settlers of South Africa; formerly referred to as Boers.

agricultural revolution Numerous agricultural revolutions have occurred in the history of western civilizations. One of the most significant began in the tenth century C.E., and increased the amount of land under cultivation as well as the productivity of the land. This revolution was made possible through the use of new technology, an increase in global temperatures, and more efficient methods of cultivation.

AIDS Acquired Immunodeficiency Syndrome. AIDS first appeared in the 1970s and has developed into a global health catastrophe; it is spreading most quickly in developing nations in Africa and Asia.

Akhenaten (r. 1352–1336) Pharaoh whose attempt to promote the worship of the sun god, Aten, ultimately weakened his dynasty's position in Egypt.

Alexander the Great (356–323 B.C.E.) The Macedonian king whose conquests of the Persian Empire and Egypt created a new Hellenistic world.

Tsar Alexander II (1818–1881) After the Crimean War, Tsar Alexander embarked on a program of reform and modernization, which included the emancipation of the serfs. A radical assassin killed him in 1881.

Alexius Comnenus (1057–1118) This Byzantine emperor requested Pope Urban II's help in raising an army to recapture Anatolia from the Seljuq Turks. Instead, Pope Urban II called for knights to go to the Holy Land and liberate it from its Muslim captors, which launched the First Crusade.

Algerian War (1954–1962) The war between France and Algerians seeking independence. Led by the National Liberation Front (FLN), guerrillas fought the French army in the mountains and desert of Algeria. The FLN also initiated a campaign of bombing and terrorism in Algerian cities that led French soldiers to torture many Algerians, attracting world attention and international scandal.

Allied Powers The First World War coalition of Great Britain, Ireland, Belgium, France, Italy, Russia, Portugal, Greece, Serbia, Montenegro, Albania, and Romania.

al Qaeda The radical Islamic organization founded in the late 1980s by former *mujahidin* who had fought against the Soviet Union in Afghanistan. Al Qaeda carried out the 9/11 terrorist attacks and is responsible as well for attacks in Africa, southeast Asia, Europe, and the Middle East.

Americanization The fear of many Europeans, since the 1920s, that U.S. cultural products, such as film, television, and music,

A29

exerted too much influence. Many of the criticisms centered on America's emphasis on mass production and organization. The fears about Americanization were not limited to culture. They extended to corporations, business techniques, global trade, and marketing.

Americas The name given to the two great land masses of the New World, derived from the name of the Italian geographer Amerigo Vespucci. In 1492, Christopher Columbus reached the Bahamas and the island of Hispaniola, which began an era of Spanish conquest in North and South America. Originally, the Spanish sought a route to Asia. Instead they discovered two continents whose wealth they decided to exploit. They were especially interested in gold and silver, which they either stole from indigenous peoples or mined using indigenous peoples as labor. Silver became Spain's most lucrative export from the New World.

Ambrose (c. 340–397) One of the early "fathers" of the Church, he helped to define the relationship between the sacred authority of bishops and other Church leaders and the secular authority of worldly rulers. He believed that secular rulers were a part of the Church, and therefore subject to it.

Amnesty International Nongovernmental organization formed in 1961 to defend "prisoners of conscience"—those detained for their beliefs, color, sex, ethnic origin, language, or religion.

Anabaptists Protestant movement that emerged in Switzerland in 1521; its adherents insisted that only adults could be baptized Christians.

anarchists In the nineteenth century, they were a political movement with the aim of establishing small-scale, localized, and self-sufficient democratic communities that could guarantee a maximum of individual sovereignty. Renouncing parties, unions and any form of modern mass organization, the anarchists fell back on the tradition of conspiratorial violence.

Anti–Corn Law League This organization successfully lobbied Parliament to repeal Britain's Corn Laws in 1846. The Corn Laws of 1815 had protected British landowners and farmers from foreign competition by establishing high tariffs, which kept bread prices artificially high for British consumers. The League saw these laws as unfair protection of the aristocracy and pushed for their repeal in the name of free trade.

anti-Semitism Anti-Semitism refers to hostility toward Jewish people. Religious forms of anti-Semitism have a long history in Europe, but in the nineteenth century anti-Semitism emerged as a potent ideology for mobilizing new constituencies in the era of mass politics. Playing on popular conspiracy theories about alleged Jewish influence in society, anti-Semites effectively rallied large bodies of supporters in France during the Dreyfus Affair, and then again during the rise of National Socialism in Germany after the First World War. The Holocaust would not have been possible without the acquiescence or cooperation of many thousands of people who shared anti-Semitic views.

apartheid The racial segregation policy of the Afrikaner-dominated South African government. Legislated in 1948 by the Afrikaner National Party, it existed in South Africa for many years.

appeasement The policy pursued by Western governments in the face of German, Italian, and Japanese aggression leading up to the Second World War. The policy, which attempted to accommodate and negotiate peace with the aggressive nations, was based on the belief that another global war like the First World War was unimaginable, a belief that Germany and its allies had been mistreated by the terms of the Treaty of Versailles, and a fear that fascist Germany and its allies protected the West from the spread of Soviet communism.

Thomas Aquinas (1225–1274) Dominican friar and theologian whose systematic approach to Christian doctrine was influenced by Aristotle.

Arab-Israeli conflict Between the founding of the state of Israel in 1948 and the present, a series of wars has been fought between Israel and neighboring Arab nations: the war of 1948 when Israel defeated attempts by Egypt, Jordon, Iraq, Syria, and Lebanon to prevent the creation of the new state; the 1956 war between Israel and Egypt over the Sinai peninsula; the 1967 war, when Israel gained control of additional land in the Golan Heights, the West Bank, the Gaza strip, and in the Sinai; and the Yom Kippur War of 1973, when Israel once again fought with forces from Egypt and Syria. A particularly difficult issue in all of these conflicts has been the situation of the 950,000 Palestinian refugees made homeless by the first war in 1948, and the movement of Israeli settlers into the occupied territories (outside of Israel's original borders). In the late 1970s, peace talks between Israel and Egypt inspired some hope of peace, but an on-going cycle of violence between Palestinians and the Israeli military have made a final settlement elusive.

Arab nationalism During the period of decolonization, secular forms of Arab nationalism, or pan-Arabism, found a wide following in many countries of the Middle East, especially in Egypt, Syria, and Iraq.

Arianism A variety of Christianity condemned as a heresy by the Roman Church, it derives from the teaching of a fourth-century priest called Arius, who rejected the idea that Jesus could be the divine equal of God.

aristocracy From the Greek word meaning "rule of the best." By 1000 B.C.E., the accumulated wealth of successful traders in Greece had created a new type of social class, which was based on wealth rather than warfare or birth. These men saw their wealth as a reflection of their superior qualities and aspired to emulate the heroes of old.

Aristotle (384–322 B.C.E.) A student of Plato, his philosophy was based on the rational analysis of the material world. In contrast to his teacher, he stressed the rigorous investigation of real phenomena, rather than the development of universal ethics. He was, in turn, the teacher of Alexander the Great.

Asiatic Society A cultural organization founded in 1784 by British Orientalists who lauded native culture but believed in colonial rule.

Assyrians A Semitic-speaking people that moved into northern Mesopotamia around 2400 B.C.E.

Athens Athens emerged as the Greek polis with the most markedly democratic form of government through a series of political struggles during the sixth century B.C.E. After its key role in the defeat of two invading Persian forces, Athens became the preeminent naval power of ancient Greece and the exemplar of Greek culture. But it antagonized many other poleis, and became embroiled in a war with Sparta and her allies in 431 B.C.E. Called the Peloponnesian War, this bloody conflict lasted until Athens was defeated in 404 B.C.E.

atomic bomb In 1945, the United States dropped atomic bombs on Hiroshima and Nagasaki in Japan, ending the Second World War. In 1949, the Soviet Union tested their first atomic bomb, and in 1953 both superpowers demonstrated their new hydrogen bombs. Strategically, the nuclearization of warfare polarized the world. Countries without nuclear weapons found it difficult to avoid joining either the Soviet or American military pacts. Over time countries split into two groups: the superpowers with enormous military budgets and those countries that relied on agreements and international law. The nuclearization of warfare also encouraged "proxy wars" between clients of superpowers. Culturally, the hydrogen bomb came to symbolize the age and both humanity's power and vulnerability.

Augustine of Hippo (c. 354–397) One of the most influential theologians of all time, Augustine described his conversion to Christianity in his autobiographical *Confessions* and articulated a new Christian worldview in *The City of God*, among other works.

Augustus (63 B.C.E.–14 C.E.) Born Gaius Octavius, this grandnephew and adopted son of Julius Caesar came to power in 27 B.C.E. His reign signals the end of the Roman Republic and the beginning of the Principate, the period when Rome was dominated by autocratic emperors.

Auschwitz-Birkenau The Nazi concentration camp in Poland that was designed to systematically murder Jews and gypsies. Between 1942 and 1944 over one million people were killed in Auschwitz-Birkenau.

Austro-Hungarian Empire The dual monarchy established by the Habsburg family in 1867; it collapsed at the end of the First World War.

authoritarianism A centralized and dictatorial form of government, proclaimed by its adherents to be superior to parliamentary democracy. Authoritarian governments claim to be above the law, do not respect individual rights, and do not tolerate political opposition. Authoritarian regimes that have developed a central ideology such as fascism or communism are sometimes termed "totalitarian."

Avignon A city in southeastern France that became the seat of the papacy between 1305 and 1377, a period known as the "Babylonian Captivity" of the Roman Church.

Aztecs An indigenous people of central Mexico; their empire was conquered by Spanish conquistadors in the sixteenth century.

baby boom (1950s) The post–Second World War upswing in U.S. birth rates; it reversed a century of decline.

Babylon An ancient city between the Tigris and Euphrates rivers, which became the capital of Hammurabi's empire in the eighteenth century B.C.E. and continued to be an important administrative and commercial capital under many subsequent imperial powers, including the Neo-Assyrians, Chaldeans, Persians, and Romans. It was here that Alexander the Great died in 323 B.C.E.

Francis Bacon (1561–1626) British philosopher and scientist who pioneered the scientific method and inductive reasoning. In other words, he argued that thinkers should amass many observations and then draw general conclusions or propose theories on the basis of this data.

Balfour Declaration A letter dated November 2, 1917, by Lord Arthur J. Balfour, British Foreign Secretary, that promised a homeland for the Jews in Palestine.

Laura Bassi (1711–1778) She was accepted into the Academy of Science in Bologna for her work in mathematics, which made her one of the few women to be accepted into a scientific academy in the seventeenth century.

Bastille The Bastille was a royal fortress and prison in Paris. In June of 1789, a revolutionary crowd attacked the Bastille to show support for the newly created National Assembly. The fall of the Bastille was the first instance of the people's role in revolutionary change in France.

Bay of Pigs (1961) The unsuccessful invasion of Cuba by Cuban exiles, supported by the U.S. government. The rebels intended to incite an insurrection in Cuba and overthrow the communist regime of Fidel Castro.

Cesare Beccaria (1738–1794) An influential writer during the Enlightenment who advocated for legal reforms. He believed that the only legitimate rationale for punishments was to maintain social order and to prevent other crimes. He argued for the greatest possible leniency compatible with deterrence and opposed torture and the death penalty.

Beer Hall Putsch (1923) An early attempt by the Nazi party to seize power in Munich; Adolf Hitler was imprisoned for a year after the incident.

Benedict of Nursia (c. 480–c. 547) Benedict's rule for monks formed the basis of western monasticism and is still observed in monasteries all over the world.

Benedictine Monasticism This form of monasticism was developed by Benedict of Nursia. Its followers adhere to a defined cycle of daily prayers, lessons, communal worship, and manual labor.

Berlin airlift (1948) The transport of vital supplies to West Berlin by air, primarily under U.S. auspices, in response to a blockade of the city that had been instituted by the Soviet Union to force the Allies to abandon West Berlin.

Berlin Conference (1884) At this conference, the leading colonial powers met and established ground rules for the partition of Africa by European nations. By 1914, 90 percent of African territory was under European control. The Berlin Conference ceded control of the Congo region to a private company run by King Leopold II of Belgium. They agreed to make the Congo valleys open to free trade and commerce, to end the slave trade in the region, and to establish a Congo Free State. In reality, King Leopold II's company established a regime that was so brutal in its treatment of local populations that an international scandal forced the Belgian state to take over the colony in 1908.

Berlin wall The wall built in 1961 by East German Communists to prevent citizens of East Germany from fleeing to West Germany; it was torn down in 1989.

birth control pill This oral contraceptive became widely available in the mid-1960s. For the first time, women had a simple method of birth control that they could take themselves.

Otto von Bismarck (1815–1898) The prime minister of Prussia and later the first chancellor of a unified Germany, Bismarck was the architect of German unification and helped to consolidate the new nation's economic and military power.

Black Death The epidemic of bubonic plague that ravaged Europe, Asia, and North Africa in the fourteenth century, killing one third to one half of the population.

Black Jacobins A nickname for the rebels in Saint Domingue, including Toussaint L'Ouverture, a former slave who in 1791 led the slaves of this French colony in the largest and most successful slave insurrection.

Black Panthers A radical African American group that came together in the 1960s; the Black Panthers advocated black separatism and pan-Africanism.

Blackshirts The troops of Mussolini's fascist regime; the squads received money from Italian landowners to attack socialist leaders.

Black Tuesday (October 29, 1929) The day on which the U.S. stock market crashed, plunging U.S. and international trading systems into crisis and leading the world into the "Great Depression."

William Blake (1757–1827) Romantic writer who criticized industrial society and factories. He championed the imagination and poetic vision, seeing both as transcending the limits of the material world.

Blitzkrieg The German "lightning war" strategy used during the Second World War; the Germans invaded Poland, France, Russia, and other countries with fast-moving and well-coordinated attacks using aircraft, tanks and other armored vehicles, followed by infantry.

Bloody Sunday On January 22, 1905, the Russian tsar's guards killed 130 demonstrators who were protesting the tsar's mistreatment of workers and the middle class.

Jean Bodin (1530–1596) A French political philosopher whose *Six Books of the Commonwealth* advanced a theory of absolute sovereignty, on the grounds that the state's paramount duty is to maintain order and that monarchs should therefore exercise unlimited power.

Boer War (1898–1902) Conflict between British and ethnically European Afrikaners in South Africa, with terrible casualties on both sides.

Boethius (c. 480–524) Member of a prominent Roman family, he sought to preserve aspects of ancient learning by compiling a series of handbooks and anthologies appropriate for Christian readers. His translations of Greek philosophy provided a crucial link between classical Greek thought and the early intellectual culture of Christianity.

Simon de Bolivar (1783–1830) Venezuelan-born general called "The Liberator" for his assistance in helping Bolivia, Panama, Colombia, Ecuador, Peru, and Venezuela win independence from Spain.

Bolsheviks Former members of the Russian Social Democratic Party who advocated the destruction of capitalist political and economic institutions and started the Russian Revolution. In 1918 the Bolsheviks changed their name to the Russian Communist Party. Prominent Bolsheviks included Vladimir Lenin and Josef Stalin. Leon Trotsky joined the Bolsheviks late but became a prominent leader in the early years of the Russian Revolution.

Napoleon Bonaparte (1769–1821) Corsican-born French general who seized power and ruled as dictator from 1799 to 1814. After the successful conquest of much of Europe, he was defeated by Russian and Prussian forces and died in exile.

Sandro Botticelli (1445–1510) An Italian painter devoted to the blending of classical and Christian motifs by using ideas associated with the pagan past to illuminate sacred stories.

bourgeoisie Term for the middle class, derived from the French word for a town-dweller, *bourgeois*.

Boxer Rebellion (1899–1900) Chinese peasant movement that opposed foreign influence, especially that of Christian missionaries; it was finally put down after the Boxers were defeated by a foreign army composed mostly of Japanese, Russian, British, French, and American soldiers.

Tycho Brahe (1546–1601) Danish astronomer who believed that the careful study of the heavens would unlock the secrets of the universe. For over twenty years, he charted the movements of significant objects in the night sky, compiling the finest set of astronomical data in Europe.

British Commonwealth of Nations Formed in 1926, the Commonwealth conferred "dominion status" on Britain's white settler colonies in Canada, Australia, and New Zealand.

Bronze Age (3200–1200 B.C.E.) The name given to the era characterized by the discovery of techniques for smelting bronze (an alloy of copper and tin), which was then the strongest known metal.

Brownshirts Troops of young German men who dedicated themselves to the Nazi cause in the early 1930s by holding street marches, mass rallies, and confrontations. They engaged in beatings of Jews and anyone who opposed the Nazis.

Lord Byron (1788–1824) Writer and poet whose life helped give the Romantics their reputation as rebels against conformity. He was known for his love affairs, his defense of working-class movements, and his passionate engagement in politics, which led to his death in the war for Greek independence.

Byzantium The name of a small settlement located at the mouth of the Black Sea and at the crossroads between Europe and Asia, it was chosen by Constantine as the site for his new imperial capital of Constantinople in 324 C.E. Modern historians use this name to refer to the eastern Roman Empire that persisted in this region until 1453, but the inhabitants of that empire referred to themselves as Romans.

Julius Caesar (100–44 B.C.E.) The Roman general who conquered the Gauls, invaded Britain, and expanded Rome's territory in Asia Minor. He became the dictator of Rome in 46 B.C.E. His assassination led to the rise of his grandnephew and adopted son, Gaius Octavius Caesar, who ruled the Roman Empire as Caesar Augustus.

caliphs Islamic rulers who claim descent from the prophet Muhammad.

John Calvin (1509–1564) French-born theologian and reformer whose radical form of Protestantism was adopted in many Swiss cities, notably Geneva.

Canary Islands Islands off the western coast of Africa that were colonized by Portugal and Spain in the mid-fifteenth century, after which they became bases for further expeditions around the African coast and across the Atlantic.

Carbonari An underground organization that opposed the Concert of Europe's restoration of monarchies. They held influence in southern Europe during the 1820s, especially in Italy.

Carolingian Derived from the Latin name Carolus (Charles), this term refers to the Frankish dynasty that began with the rise to power of Charlemagne's grandfather, Charles Martel (688–741). At its height under Charlemagne (Charles the Great), the dynasty controlled what is now France, Germany, northern Italy, Catalonia and portions of central Europe. The Carolingian Empire collapsed under the combined weight of Viking raids, economic disintegration, and the growing power of local lords.

Carolingian Renaissance A cultural and intellectual flowering that took place around the court of Charlemagne in the late eighth and early ninth centuries.

Carthage The great maritime empire that grew out of Phoenician trading colonies in North Africa and rivaled the power of Rome. Its wars with Rome, collectively known as the Punic Wars, ended in its destruction in 146 B.C.E.

Cassidorus (c. 490–c. 583) Member of an old senatorial family, he was largely responsible for introducing classical learning into the monastic curriculum and for turning monasteries into centers for the collection, preservation, and transmission of knowledge. His *Institutes*, an influential handbook of classical literature for Christian readers, was intended as a preface to more intensive study of theology and the Bible.

Catholic Church The "universal" (catholic) church based in Rome, which was redefined in the sixteenth century, when the Counter-Reformation resulted in the rebirth of the Catholic faith at the Council of Trent.

Margaret Cavendish (1623–1673) English natural philosopher who developed her own speculative natural philosophy. She used this philosophy to critique those who excluded her from scientific debate.

Camillo Benso di Cavour (1810–1861) Prime minister of Piedmont-Sardinia and founder of the Italian Liberal Party; he played a key role in the movement for Italian unification under the Piedmontese king, Victor Emmanuel II.

Central Powers The First World War alliance between Germany, Austria-Hungary, Bulgaria, and Turkey.

Charlemagne (742–814) As king of the Franks (767–813), Charles "the Great" consolidated much of western Europe under his rule. In 800 he was crowned emperor by the pope in Rome, establishing a problematic precedent that would have wide-ranging consequences for western Europe's relationship with the eastern Roman Empire in Byzantium and for the relationship between the papacy and secular rulers.

Charles I (1625–1649) The second Stuart king of England, Charles attempted to rule without the support of Parliament, sparking a controversy that erupted into civil war in 1642. The king's forces were ultimately defeated and Charles himself was executed by act of Parliament, the first time in history that a reigning king was legally deposed and executed by his own government.

Chartists A working-class movement in Britain which called for reform of the political system in Britain during the 1840s. They were supporters of the "People's Charter," which had six demands: universal white male suffrage, secret ballots, an end to property qualifications as a condition of public office, annual parliamentary elections, salaries for members of the House of Commons, and equal electoral districts.

Chernobyl (1986) Site of the world's worst nuclear power accident; in Ukraine, formerly part of the Soviet Union.

Christine de Pisan (c. 1364–c. 1431) Born in Italy, Christine spent her adult life attached to the French court and, after her husband's death, became the first lay woman to earn her living by writing. She is the author of treatises in warfare and chivalry, as well as of books and pamphlets that challenge longstanding misogynistic claims.

Church of England Founded by Henry VIII in the 1530s, as a consequence of his break with the authority of the Roman pope.

Winston Churchill (1874–1965) British prime minister who led the country during the Second World War. He also coined the phrase "Iron Curtain" in a speech at Westminster College in 1946.

Cicero (106–43 B.C.E.) Influential Roman senator, orator, Stoic philosopher, and prose stylist. His published writings still form the basis of the instruction in classical Latin grammar and usage.

Cincinnatus (519–c. 430 B.C.E.) A legendary citizen-farmer of Rome who reluctantly accepted an appointment as dictator. After defeating Rome's enemies, he allegedly left his political office and returned to his farm.

Civil Constitution of the Clergy Issued by the French National Assembly in 1790, the Civil Constitution of the Clergy decreed that all bishops and priests should be subject to the authority of the state. Their salaries were to be paid out of the public treasury, and they were required to swear allegiance to the new state, making it clear they served France rather than Rome. The Assembly's aim was to make the Catholic Church of France a truly national and civil institution.

civilizing mission An argument made by Europeans to justify colonial expansion in the nineteenth century. Supporters of this idea believed that Europeans had a duty to impose western ideas of economic and political progress on the indigenous peoples they ruled over in their colonies. In practice, the colonial powers often found that ambitious plans to impose European practices on colonial subjects led to unrest that threatened the stability of colonial rule, and by the early twentieth century most colonial powers were more cautious in their plans for political or cultural transformation.

Civil Rights Movement The Second World War increased African American migration from the American South to northern cities, intensifying a drive for rights, dignity, and independence. By 1960, civil rights groups had started organizing boycotts and demonstrations directed at discrimination against blacks in the South. During the 1960s, civil rights laws passed under President Lyndon B. Johnson did bring African Americans some equality with regard to voting rights and, to a much lesser degree, school desegregation. However, racism continued in areas such as housing, job opportunities, and the economic development of African American communities.

Civil War (1861–1865) Conflict between the northern and southern states of America that cost over 600,000 lives; this struggle led to the abolition of slavery in the United States.

Classical learning The study of ancient Greek and Latin texts. After Christianity became the only legal religion of the Roman Empire, scholars needed to find a way to make classical learning applicable to a Christian way of life. Christian monks played a significant role in resolving this problem by reinterpreting the classics for a Christian audience.

Cluny A powerful Benedictine monastery founded in 910 whose enormous wealth and prestige would derive from its independence from secular authorities, as well as from its wide network of daughter houses (priories).

Cold War (1945–1991) Ideological, political, and economic conflict in which the USSR and Eastern Europe opposed the United States and Western Europe in the decades after the Second World War. The Cold War's origins lay in the breakup of the wartime alliance between the United States and the Soviet Union in 1945, and resulted in a division of Europe into two spheres: the West, commited to market capitalism, and the East, which sought to build Socialist republics in areas under Soviet Control. The Cold War ended with the collapse of the Soviet Union in 1991.

collectivization Stalin's plan for nationalizing agricultural production, begun in 1929. 25 million peasants were forced to give up their land and join 250,000 large collective farms. Many who resisted were deported to labor camps in the Far East, and Stalin's government cut off food rations to those areas most marked by resistance to collectivization. In the ensuing man-made famines, millions of people starved to death.

Christopher Columbus (1451–1506) A Genoese sailor who persuaded King Ferdinand and Queen Isabella of Spain to fund his expedition across the Atlantic, with the purpose of discovering a new trade route to Asia. His miscalculations landed him in the Bahamas and the island of Hispaniola in 1492.

Committee of Public Safety Political body during the French Revolution that was controlled by the Jacobins, who defended the revolution by executing thousands during the Reign of Terror (September 1793–July 1794).

commune A community of individuals who have banded together in a sworn association, with the aim of establishing their independence and setting up their own form of representative government. Many medieval towns originally founded by lords or monasteries gained their independence through such methods.

The Communist Manifesto Radical pamphlet by Karl Marx (1818–1883) that predicted the downfall of the capitalist system and its replacement by a classless egalitarian society. Marx believed that this revolution would be accomplished by workers (the proletariat).

Compromise of 1867 Agreement between the Habsburgs and the peoples living in Hungarian parts of the empire that the Habsburg state would be officially known as the Austro-Hungarian Empire.

Concert of Europe (1814–1815) The body of diplomatic agreements designed primarily by Austrian minister Klemens von Metternich between 1814 and 1848, and supported by other European powers until 1914. Its goal was to maintain a balance of power on the Continent and to prevent destabilizing social and political change in Europe.

Congress of Vienna (1814–1815) **and Restoration** International conference to reorganize Europe after the downfall of Napoleon and the French Revolution. European monarchies restored the Bourbon family to the French throne, agreed to respect each other's borders and to cooperate in guarding against future revolutions and war.

conquistador Spanish term for "conqueror," applied to the mercenaries and adventurers who campaigned against indigenous peoples in central and southern America.

Conservatism In the nineteenth century, conservatives aimed to legitimize and solidify the monarchy's authority and the hierarchical social order. They believed that change had to be slow, incremental, and managed so that the structures of authority were strengthened and not weakened.

Constantine (275–337) The first emperor of Rome to convert to Christianity, Constantine came to power in 312. In 324, he founded a new imperial capital, Constantinople, on the site of a maritime settlement known as Byzantium.

Constantinople Founded by the emperor Constantine on the site of a village called Byzantium, Constantinople became the new capital of the Roman Empire in 324 and continued to be the seat of imperial power after its capture by the Ottoman Turks in 1453. It is now known as Istanbul.

Nicholas Copernicus (1473–1543) Polish astronomer who advanced the idea that the earth moved around the sun.

cosmopolitanism Stemming from the Greek word meaning "universal city," the culture characteristic of the Hellenistic world challenged and transformed the more narrow worldview of the Greek polis.

cotton gin Invented by Eli Whitney in 1793, this device mechanized the process of separating cotton seeds from the cotton fiber, which sped up the production of cotton and reduced its price. This change made slavery profitable in the United States.

Council of Constance (1417–1420) A meeting of clergy and theologians in an effort to resolve the Great Schism within the Roman Church. The council deposed all rival papal candidates and elected a new pope, Martin V, but it also adopted the doctrine of conciliarism, which holds that the supreme authority within the Church rests with a representative general council and not with the pope. However, Martin V himself was an opponent of this doctrine, and refused to be bound by it.

Council of Trent The name given to a series of meetings held in the Italian city of Trent (Trento) between 1545 and 1563, when leaders of the Roman Church reaffirmed Catholic doctrine and instituted internal reforms.

Counter-Reformation The movement to counter the Protestant Reformation, initiated by the Catholic Church at the Council of Trent in 1545.

coup d'état French term for the overthrow of an established government by a group of conspirators, usually with military support.

Crimean War (1854–1856) War waged by Russia against Great Britain and France. Spurred by Russia's encroachment on Ottoman territories, the conflict revealed Russia's military weakness when Russian forces fell to British and French troops.

Cuban missile crisis (1962) Diplomatic standoff between the United States and the Soviet Union that was provoked by the Soviet Union's attempt to base nuclear missiles in Cuba; it brought the world closer to nuclear war than ever before or since.

Cuius regio, eius religio A Latin phrase meaning "as the ruler, so the religion." Adopted as a part of the settlement of the Peace of Augsburg in 1555, it meant that those principalities ruled by Lutherans would have Lutheranism as their official religion and those ruled by Catholics must practice Catholicism.

cult of domesticity Concept associated with Victorian England that idealized women as nurturing wives and mothers.

cult of the Virgin The beliefs and practices associated with the veneration of Mary the mother of Jesus, which became increasingly popular in the twelfth century.

cuneiform An early writing system that began to develop in Mesopotamia in the fourth millennium B.C.E. By 3100 B.C.E., its distinctive markings were impressed on clay tablets using a wedge-shaped stylus.

Cyrus the Great (c. 585–529 B.C.E.) As architect of the Persian Empire, Cyrus extended his dominion over a vast territory stretching from the Persian Gulf to the Mediterranean and incorporating the ancient civilizations of Mesopotamia. His successors ruled this Persian Empire as "Great Kings."

Darius (521–486 B.C.E.) The Persian emperor whose conflict with Aristagoras, the Greek ruler of Miletus, ignited the Persian Wars. In 490 B.C.E., Darius sent a large army to punish the Athenians for their intervention in Persian imperial affairs, but this force was defeated by Athenian hoplites on the plain of Marathon.

Charles Darwin (1809–1882) British naturalist who wrote *On the Origin of Species* and developed the theory of natural selection to explain the evolution of organisms.

D-Day (June 6, 1944) Date of the Allied invasion of Normandy, under General Dwight Eisenhower, to liberate Western Europe from German occupation.

Decembrists Russian army officers who were influenced by events in France and formed secret societies that espoused liberal governance. They were put down by Nicholas I in December 1825.

Declaration of Independence (1776) Historic document stating the principles of government on which the United States was founded.

Declaration of the Rights of Man and of the Citizen (1789) French charter of liberties formulated by the National Assembly during the French Revolution. The seventeen articles later became the preamble to the new constitution, which the Assembly finished in 1791.

democracy In ancient Greece, this form of government allowed a class of propertied male citizens to participate in the governance of their polis; but excluded women, slaves, and citizens without property from the political process. As a result, the ruling class amounted to only a small percentage of the entire population.

René Descartes (1596–1650) French philosopher and mathematician who emphasized the use of deductive reasoning.

Denis Diderot (1713–1784) French *philosophe* and author who was the guiding force behind the publication of the first encyclopedia. The encyclopedia showed how reason could be applied to nearly all realms of thought, and aimed to be a compendium of all human knowledge.

Dien Bien Phu (1954) Defining battle in the war between French colonialists and the Viet Minh that secured North Vietnam for Ho Chi Minh and his army and left the south to form its own government, to be supported by France and the United States.

Diet of Worms The select council of the Church that convened in the German city of Worms and condemned Martin Luther on a charge of heresy in 1521.

Diocletian (245–316) As emperor of Rome from 284 to 305, Diocletian recognized that the empire could not be governed by one man in one place. His solution was to divide the empire into four parts, each with its own imperial ruler, but he himself remained the dominant ruler of the resulting tetrarchy (rule of four). He also initiated the Great Persecution, a time when many Christians became martyrs to their faith.

Directory (1795–1799) Executive committee that governed after the fall of Robespierre and held control until the coup of Napoleon Bonaparte.

Discourse on Method Philosophical treatise by René Descartes (1596–1650) proposing that the path to knowledge was through logical deduction, beginning with one's own self: "I think, therefore I am."

Dominican Order Also called the Order of Preachers, it was founded by Dominic of Osma (1170–1221), a Castilian preacher and theologian, and approved by Innocent III in 1216. The order was dedicated to the rooting out of heresy and the conversion of Jews and Muslims. Many of its members held teaching positions in European universities and contributed to the development of medieval philosophy and theology. Others became the leading administrators of the Inquisition.

Dominion in the British Commonwealth Canadian promise to maintain their fealty to the British crown, even after their independence in 1867. Later applied to Australia and New Zealand.

Dreyfus Affair The 1894 French scandal surrounding accusations that a Jewish captain, Alfred Dreyfus, sold military secrets to the Germans. Convicted, Dreyfus was sentenced to solitary confinement for life. However, after public outcry, it was revealed that the trial documents were forgeries, and Dreyfus was pardoned after a second trial in 1899. In 1906 he was fully exonerated and reinstated in the army. The affair revealed the depths of popular anti-Semitism in France.

Alexander Dubček (1921–1992) Communist leader of the Czechoslovakian government who advocated for "socialism with a human face." He encouraged debate within the party, academic and artistic freedom, and less censorship, which led to the "Prague spring" of 1968. People in other parts of Eastern Europe began to demonstrate in support of Dubček and demand their own reforms. When Dubček tried to democratize the Communist party and did not attend a meeting of the

Warsaw Pact, the Soviets sent tanks and troops into Prague and ousted Dubček and his allies.

Duma The Russian parliament, created in response to the revolution of 1905.

Dunkirk The French port on the English Channel where the British and French forces retreated after sustaining heavy losses against the German military. Between May 27 and June 4, 1940, the Royal Navy evacuated over three hundred thousand troops using commercial and pleasure boats.

Earth Summit (1992) Meeting in Rio de Janeiro between many of the world's governments in an effort to address international environmental problems.

Eastern Front Battlefront between Berlin and Moscow during the First and Second World Wars..

East India Company (1600–1858) British charter company created to outperform Portuguese and Spanish traders in the Far East; in the eighteenth century the company became, in effect, the ruler of a large part of India. There was also a Dutch East India Company.

Edict of Nantes (1598) Issued by Henry IV of France in an effort to end religious violence. The edict declared France to be a Catholic country, but tolerated some forms of Protestant worship.

Eleanor of Aquitaine (1122–1204) Ruler of the wealthy province of Aquitaine and wife of Louis VII of France, Eleanor had her marriage annulled in order to marry the young count of Anjou, Henry Plantagenet, who became King Henry of England a year later. Mother of two future kings of England, she was an important patron of the arts.

Elizabeth I (1533–1603) Protestant daughter of Henry VIII and his second wife, Anne Boleyn, Elizabeth succeeded her sister Mary as the second queen regnant of England (1558–1603).

emancipation of the serfs (1861) The abolition of serfdom was central to Tsar Alexander II's program of modernization and reform, but it produced a limited amount of change. Former serfs now had legal rights. However, farm land was granted to the village communes instead of to individuals. The land was of poor quality and the former serfs had to pay for it in installments to the village commune.

emperor Originally the term for any conquering commander of the Roman army whose victories merited celebration in an official triumph. After Augustus seized power in 27 B.C.E., it was the title born by the sole ruler of the Roman Empire.

empire A centralized political entity consolidated through the conquest and colonization of other nations or peoples in order to benefit the ruler and/or his homeland.

Enabling Act (1933) Emergency act passed by the Reichstag (German parliament) that helped transform Hitler from Germany's chancellor, or prime minister, into a dictator, following the suspicious burning of the Reichstag building and a suspension of civil liberties.

enclosure Long process of privatizing what had been public agricultural land in eighteenth-century Britain; it helped to stimulate the development of commercial agriculture and forced many people in rural areas to seek work in cities during the early stages of industrialization.

The Encyclopedia Joint venture of French *philosophe* writers, led by Denis Diderot (1713–1784), which proposed to summarize all modern knowledge in a multivolume illustrated work with over 70,000 articles.

Friedrich Engels (1820–1895) German social and political philosopher who collaborated with Karl Marx on many publications.

English Civil War (1642–1649) Conflicts between the English Parliament and King Charles I erupted into civil war, which ended in the defeat of the royalists and the execution of Charles on charges of treason against the crown. A short time later, Parliament's hereditary House of Lords was abolished and England was declared a Commonwealth.

English Navigation Act of 1651 Act stipulating that only English ships could carry goods between the mother country and its colonies.

Enlightenment Intellectual movement in eighteenth-century Europe, that believed in human betterment through the application of reason to solve social, economic, and political problems.

Epicureanism A philosophical position articulated by Epicurus of Athens (c. 342–270 B.C.E.), who rejected the idea of an ordered universe governed by divine forces; instead, he emphasized individual agency and proposed that the highest good is the pursuit of pleasure.

Desiderius Erasmus (c. 1469–1536) Dutch-born scholar, social commentator, and Catholic humanist whose new translation of the Bible influenced the theology of Martin Luther.

Estates-General The representative body of the three estates in France. In 1789, King Louis XVI summoned the Estates-General to meet for the first time since 1614 because it seemed to be the only solution to France's worsening economic crisis and financial chaos.

Etruscans Settlers of the Italian peninsula who dominated the region from the late Bronze Age until the rise of the Roman Republic in the sixth century B.C.E.

Euclid Hellenistic mathematician whose *Elements of Geometry* forms the basis of modern geometry.

eugenics A Greek term, meaning "good birth," referring to the project of "breeding" a superior human race. It was popularly championed by scientists, politicians, and social critics in the late nineteenth and early twentieth centuries.

European Common Market (1957) The Treaty of Rome created the European Economic Community (EEC) or Common Market. The original members were France, West Germany, Italy, Belgium, Holland, and Luxembourg. The EEC sought to abolish trade barriers between its members and it pledged itself to common external tariffs, the free movement of labor and capital among the member nations, and uniform wage structures and social security systems to create similar working conditions in all member countries.

European Union (EU) Successor organization to the European Economic Community or European Common Market, formed by the Maastricht Treaty, which took effect in 1993. Currently 27 member states compose the EU, which has a governing council, an international court, and a parliament. Over time, member states of the EU have relinquished some of their sovereignty, and cooperation has evolved into a community with a single currency, the euro.

Exclusion Act of 1882 U.S. congressional act prohibiting nearly all immigration from China to the United States; fueled by animosity toward Chinese workers in the American West.

existentialism Philosophical movement that arose out of the Second World War and emphasized the absurdity of human condition. Led by Jean-Paul Sartre and Albert Camus, existentialists encouraged humans to take responsibility for their own decisions and dilemmas.

fascism The doctrine founded by Benito Mussolini, which emphasized three main ideas: statism ("nothing above the state, nothing outside the state, nothing against the state"), nationalism, and militarism. Its name derives from the Latin *fasces*, a symbol of Roman imperial power adopted by Mussolini.

Fashoda Incident (1898) Disagreements between the French and the British over land claims in North Africa led to a standoff between armies of the two nations at the Sudanese town of Fashoda. The crisis was solved diplomatically. France ceded southern Sudan to Britain in exchange for a stop to further expansion by the British.

The Feminine Mystique Groundbreaking book by feminist Betty Friedan (b. 1921), which tried to define "femininity" and explored how women internalized those definitions.

Franz Ferdinand (1863–1914) Archduke of Austria and heir to the Austro-Hungarian Empire; his assassination led to the beginning of the First World War.

Ferdinand (1452–1516) **and Isabella** (1451–1504) In 1469, Ferdinand of Aragon married the heiress to Castile, Isabella. Their union allowed them to pursue several ambitious policies, including the conquest of Granada, the last Muslim principality in Spain, and the expulsion of Spain's large Jewish community. In 1492, Isabella granted three ships to Christopher Columbus of Genoa (Italy), who went on to claim portions of the New World for Spain.

Fertile Crescent An area of fertile land in what is now Syria, Israel, Turkey, eastern Iraq, and western Iran that was able to sustain settlements due to its wetter climate and abundant natural food resources. Some of the earliest known civilizations emerged there between 9000 and 4500 B.C.E.

feudalism A problematic modern term that attempts to explain the diffusion of power in medieval Europe, and the many different kinds of political, social, and economic relationships that were forged through the giving and receiving of fiefs (*feoda*). But because it is anachronistic and inadequate, this term has been rejected by most historians of the medieval period.

First Crusade (1095–1099) Launched by Pope Urban II in response to a request from the Byzantine emperor Alexius Comnenus, who had asked for a small contingent of knights to assist him in fighting Turkish forces in Anatolia; Urban instead directed the crusaders' energies toward the Holy Land and the recapture of Jerusalem, promising those who took the cross (*crux*) that they would merit eternal salvation if they died in the attempt. This crusade prompted attacks against Jews throughout Europe

and resulted in six subsequent—and unsuccessful—military campaigns.

First World War A total war from August 1914 to November 1918, involving the armies of Britain, France, and Russia (the Allies) against Germany, Austria-Hungary, and the Ottoman Empire (the Central Powers). Italy joined the Allies in 1915, and the United States joined them in 1917, helping to tip the balance in favor of the Allies, who also drew upon the populations and raw materials of their colonial possessions. Also known as the Great War.

Five Pillars of Islam The Muslim teaching that salvation is only assured through observance of five basic precepts: submission to God's will as described in the teachings of Muhammad, frequent prayer, ritual fasting, the giving of alms, and an annual pilgrimage to Mecca (the Hajj).

Five-Year Plan Soviet effort launched under Stalin in 1928 to replace the market with a state-owned and state-managed economy in order to promote rapid economic development over a five-year period and thereby "catch and overtake" the leading capitalist countries. The First Five-Year Plan was followed by the Second Five-Year Plan (1933–1937) and so on, until the collapse of the Soviet Union in 1991.

fly shuttle Invented by John Kay in 1733, this device sped up the process of weaving.

Fourteen Points President Woodrow Wilson proposed these points as the foundation on which to build peace in the world after the First World War. They called for an end to secret treaties, "open covenants, openly arrived at," freedom of the seas, the removal of international tariffs, the reduction of arms, the "self-determination of peoples," and the establishment of a League of Nations to settle international conflicts.

Franciscan Order Also known as the Order of the Friars Minor. The earliest Franciscans were followers of Francis of Assisi (1182–1226) and strove, like him, to imitate the life and example of Jesus. The order was formally established by Pope Innocent III in 1209. Its special mission was the care and instruction of the urban poor.

Frankfurt Parliament (1848–1849) Failed attempt to create a unified Germany under constitutional principles. In 1849, the assembly offered the crown of the new German nation to Frederick William IV of Prussia, but he refused the offer and suppressed a brief protest. The delegates went home disillusioned.

Frederick the Great (1712–1786) Prussian ruler (1740–1786) who engaged the nobility in maintaining a strong military and bureaucracy, and led Prussian armies to notable military victories. He also encouraged Enlightenment rationalism and artistic endeavors.

French Revolution of 1789 In 1788, a severe financial crisis forced the French monarchy to convene an assembly known as the Estates General, representing the three estates of the realm: the clergy, the nobility, and the commons (known as the Third Estate). When the Estates General met in 1789, representatives of the Third Estate demanded major constitutional changes, and when the King and his government proved uncooperative, the Third Estate broke with the other two estates and renamed themselves the National Assembly, demanding a written constitution. The position of the National Assembly was confirmed by a popular uprising in Paris and the King was forced to accept the transformation of France into a constitutional monarchy. This constitutional phase of the revolution lasted until 1972, when the pressures of foreign invasion and the emergence of a more radical revolutionary movement caused the collapse of the monarchy and the establishment of a Republic in France.

French Revolution of 1830 The French popular revolt against Charles X's July Ordinances of 1830, which dissolved the French Chamber of Deputies and restricted suffrage to exclude almost everyone except the nobility. After several days of violence, Charles abdicated the throne and was replaced by a constitutional monarch, Louis Philippe.

French Revolution of 1848 Revolution overthrowing Louis Philippe in February, 1848, leading to the formation of the Second Republic (1848–1852). Initially enjoying broad support from both the middle classes and laborers in Paris, the new government became more conservative after elections in which the French peasantry participated for the first time. A workers' revolt was violently repressed in June, 1848, and in December 1848, Napoleon Bonaparte's nephew, Louis-Napoleon Bonaparte, was elected president. In 1852, Louis-Napoleon declared himself emperor and abolished the republic.

Sigmund Freud (1856–1939) The Austrian physician who founded the discipline of psychoanalysis and suggested that human behavior was largely motivated by unconscious and irrational forces.

Galileo Galilei (1564–1642) Italian physicist and inventor; the implications of his ideas raised the ire of the Catholic Church, and he was forced to retract most of his findings.

Gallipoli (1915) In the First World War, a combined force of French, British, Australian and New Zealand troops tried to invade the Gallipoli peninsula, in the first large-scale amphibious attack in history, and seize it from the Turks. After seven months of fighting, the Allies had lost 200,000 soldiers. Defeated, they withdrew.

Mohandas K. (Mahatma) Gandhi (1869–1948) The Indian leader who advocated nonviolent noncooperation to protest colonial rule and helped win home rule for India in 1947.

Giuseppe Garibaldi (1807–1882) Italian revolutionary leader who led the fight to free Sicily and Naples from the Habsburg Empire; the lands were then peaceably annexed by Sardinia to produce a unified Italy.

Gaul The region of the Roman Empire that was home to the Celtic people of that name, comprising modern France, Belgium, and western Germany.

Geneva Peace Conference (1954) International conference to restore peace in Korea and Indochina. The chief participants were the United States, the Soviet Union, Great Britain, France, the People's Republic of China, North Korea, South Korea, Vietnam, the Viet Minh party, Laos, and Cambodia. The conference resulted in the division of North and South Vietnam.

Genoese Inhabitants of the maritime city on Italy's northwestern coast, the Genoese were active in trading ventures along the Silk Road and in the establishment of trading colonies in the Mediterranean. They were also involved in the world of finance and backed the commercial ventures of other powers, especially Spain's.

German Democratic Republic Nation founded from the Soviet zone of occupation of Germany after the Second World War; also known as East Germany.

German Social Democratic Party Founded in 1875, it was the most powerful socialist party in Europe before 1917.

Gilgamesh Sumerian ruler of the city of Uruk around 2700 B.C.E., Gilgamesh became the hero of one of the world's oldest epics, which circulated orally for nearly a millennium before being written down.

globalization The term used to describe political, social, and economic networks that span the globe. These global exchanges are not limited by nation-states and in recent decades are associated with new technologies, such as the Internet. Globalization is not new, however, as human cultures and economies have been in contact with one another for centuries.

Gold Coast Name that European mariners and merchants gave to that part of West Equatorial Africa from which gold and slaves were exported. Originally controlled by the Portuguese, this area later became the British colony of the Gold Coast.

Mikhail Gorbachev (1931–) Soviet leader who attempted to reform the Soviet Union through his programs of *glasnost* and *perestroika* in the late 1980s. He encouraged open discussions in other countries in the Soviet bloc, which helped inspire the velvet revolutions throughout Eastern Europe. Eventually the political, social, and economic upheaval he had unleashed would lead to the breakup of the Soviet Union.

Gothic style A type of graceful architecture emerging in twelfth- and thirteenth-century England and France. The style is characterized by pointed arches, delicate decoration, and large windows.

Olympe de Gouges (1748–1793) French political radical and feminist whose *Declaration of the Rights of Woman* demanded an equal place for women in France.

Great Depression Global economic crisis following the U.S. stock market crash on October 29, 1929, and ending with the onset of the Second World War.

Great Fear (1789) Following the outbreak of revolution in Paris, fear spread throughout the French countryside, as rumors circulated that armies of brigands or royal troops were coming. The peasants and villagers organized into militias, while others attacked and burned the manor houses in order to destroy the records of manorial dues.

Great Schism (1378–1417) Also known as the Great Western Schism, to distinguish it from the longstanding rupture between the Greek East and Latin West. During the schism, the Roman Church was divided between two (and, ultimately, three) competing popes. Each pope claimed to be legitimate and each denounced the heresy of the others.

Great Terror (1936–1938) The systematic murder of nearly a million people and the deportation of another million and a half to labor camps by Stalin's regime in an attempt to consolidate power and remove perceived enemies.

Greek East After the founding of Constantinople, the eastern Greek-speaking half of the Roman Empire grew more populous, prosperous and central to imperial policy. Its inhabitants considered themselves to be the true heirs of Rome, and their own Orthodox Church to be the true manifestation of Jesus' ministry.

Greek Independence Nationalists in Greece revolted against the Ottoman Empire and fought a war that ended in Greek independence in 1827. They received crucial help from British, French, and Russian troops as well as widespread sympathy throughout Europe.

Pope Gregory I (r. 590–604) Also known as Gregory the Great, he was the first bishop of Rome to successfully negotiate a more universal role for the papacy. His political and theological agenda widened the rift between the western Latin (Catholic) Church and the eastern Greek (Orthodox) Church in Byzantium. He also articulated the Church's official position on the status of Jews, promoted affective approaches to religious worship, encouraged the Benedictine monastic movement, and sponsored missionary expeditions.

Guernica The Basque town bombed by German planes in April 1937 during the Spanish Civil War. It is also the subject of Pablo Picasso's famous painting from the same year.

guilds Professional organizations in commercial towns that regulated business and safeguarded the privileges of those practicing a particular craft. Often identical to confraternities ("brotherhoods").

Gulag The vast system of forced labor camps under the Soviet regime; it originated in 1919 in a small monastery near the Arctic Circle and spread throughout the Soviet Union. Penal labor was required of both ordinary criminals and those accused of political crimes. Tens of millions of people were sent to the camps between 1928 and 1953; the exact figure is unknown.

Gulf War (1991) Armed conflict between Iraq and a coalition of thirty-two nations, including the United States, Britain, Egypt, France, and Saudi Arabia. The seeds of the war were planted with Iraq's invasion of Kuwait on August 2, 1990.

Habsburg Empire Ruling house of Austria, which once ruled the Netherlands, Spain, and central Europe but came to settle in lands along the Danube River. It played a prominent role in European affairs for many centuries. In 1867, the Habsburg Empire was reorganized into the Austro-Hungarian Dual Monarchy, and in 1918 it collapsed.

Hagia Sophia The enormous church dedicated to "Holy Wisdom," built in Constantinople at the behest of the emperor Justinian in the sixth century C.E. When Constantinople fell to Ottoman forces in 1453, it became an important mosque.

Haitian Revolution (1802–1804) In 1802, Napoleon sought to reassert French control of Saint-Domingue, but stiff resistance and yellow fever crushed the French army. In 1804, Jean-Jacques Dessalines, a general in the army of former slaves, declared the independent state of Haiti. (See **slave revolt in Saint-Domingue**)

Hajj The annual pilgrimage to Mecca; an obligation for Muslims.

Hammurabi Ruler of Babylon from 1792 to 1750 B.C.E., Hammurabi issued a collection of laws that were greatly influential in the Near East and which constitute the world's oldest surviving law code.

Harlem Renaissance Cultural movement in the 1920s that was based in Harlem, a part of New York City with a large African American population. The movement gave voice to black novelists, poets, painters, and musicians, many of whom used their art to protest racial subordination.

Hatshepsut (1479–1458 C.E.) As a pharaoh during the New Kingdom, she launched several successful military campaigns and extended trade and diplomacy. She was an ambitious builder who probably constructed the first tomb in the Valley of the Kings. Though she never pretended to be a man, she was routinely portrayed with a masculine figure and a ceremonial beard.

Hebrews Originally a pastoral people divided among several tribes, they were briefly united under the rule of David and his son, Solomon, who promoted the worship of a single god, Yahweh, and constructed the first temple at the new capital city of Jerusalem. After Solomon's death, the Hebrew tribes were divided between the two kingdoms of Israel and Judah, which were eventually conquered by the Neo-Assyrian and Chaldean empires. It was in captivity that the Hebrews came to define themselves through worship of Yahweh, and to develop a religion, Judaism, that could exist outside of Judea. They were liberated by the Persian king Cyrus the Great in 539 B.C.E.

Hellenistic art The art of the Hellenistic period bridged the tastes, ideals, and customs of classical Greece and those that would be more characteristic of Rome. The Romans strove to emulate Hellenistic city planning and civic culture, and thereby exported Hellenistic culture to their own far-flung colonies in western Europe.

Hellenistic culture The "Greek-like" culture that dominated the ancient world in the wake of Alexander's conquests.

Hellenistic kingdoms Following the death of Alexander the Great, his vast empire was divided into three separate states: Ptolemaic Egypt (under the rule of the general Ptolemy and his successors), Seleucid Asia (ruled by the general Seleucus and his heirs) and Antigonid Greece (governed by Antigonus of Macedonia). Each state maintained its independence, but the shared characteristics of Greco-Macedonian rule and a shared Greek culture and heritage bound them together in a united cosmopolitan world.

Hellenistic world The various western civilizations of antiquity that were loosely united by shared Greek language and culture, especially around the eastern Mediterranean.

Heloise (c. 1090–1164) One of the foremost scholars of her time, she became the pupil and the wife of the philosopher and teacher Peter Abelard. In later life, she was the founder of a new religious order for women.

Henry VIII (1491–1547) King of England from 1509 until his death, Henry rejected the authority of the Roman Church in 1534 when the pope refused to annul his marriage to his queen, Catherine of Aragon; he became the founder of the Church of England.

Henry of Navarre (1553–1610) Crowned King Henry IV of France, he renounced his Protestantism but granted limited toleration for Huguenots (French Protestants) by the Edict of Nantes in 1598.

Prince Henry the Navigator (1394–1460) A member of the Portuguese royal family, Henry encouraged the exploration and conquest of western Africa and the trade in gold and slaves.

hieroglyphs The writing system of ancient Egypt, based on a complicated series of pictorial symbols. It fell out of use when Egypt was absorbed into the Roman Empire, and was only deciphered after the discovery of the Rosetta Stone in the early nineteenth century.

Hildegard of Bingen (1098–1179) A powerful abbess, theologian, scientist, musician, and visionary who claimed to receive regular revelations from God. Although highly influential in her own day, she was never officially canonized by the Church, in part because her strong personality no longer matched the changing ideal of female piety.

Hiroshima Japanese port devastated by an atomic bomb on August 6, 1945.

Adolf Hitler (1889–1945) The author of *Mein Kampf* and leader of the Nazis who became chancellor of Germany in 1933. Hitler and his Nazi regime started the Second World War and orchestrated the systematic murder of over five million Jews.

Hitler-Stalin Pact (1939) Treaty between Stalin and Hitler, which promised Stalin a share of Poland, Finland, the Baltic States, and Bessarabia in the event of a German invasion of Poland, which began shortly thereafter, on September 1, 1939.

HIV epidemic The first cases of HIV-AIDS appeared in the late 1970s. As HIV-AIDS became a global crisis, international organizations recognized the need for an early, swift, and comprehensive response to future outbreaks of disease.

Thomas Hobbes (1588–1679) English political philosopher whose *Leviathan* argued that any form of government capable of protecting its subjects' lives and property might act as an all-powerful sovereign. This government should be allowed to trample over both liberty and property for the sake of its own survival and that of his subjects. For in his natural state, Hobbes argued, man was like "a wolf" toward other men.

Holy Roman Empire The loosely allied collection of lands in central and western Europe ruled by the kings of Germany (and later Austria) from the twelfth century until 1806. Its origins are usually identified with the empire of Charlemagne, the Frankish king who was crowned emperor of Rome by the pope in 800.

homage A ceremony in which an individual becomes the "man" (French: *homme*) of a lord.

Homer (fl. 8ᵗʰ c. B.C.E.) A Greek rhapsode ("weaver" of stories) credited with merging centuries of poetic tradition in the epics known as the *Iliad* and the *Odyssey*.

hoplite A Greek foot-soldier armed with a spear or short sword and protected by a large round shield (*hoplon*). In battle, hoplites stood shoulder to shoulder in a close formation called a phalanx.

Huguenots French Protestants who endured severe persecution in the sixteenth and seventeenth centuries.

humanism A program of study associated with the movement known as the Renaissance, humanism aimed to replace the scholastic emphasis on logic and philosophy with the study of ancient languages, literature, history, and ethics.

human rights The belief that all people have the right to legal equality, freedom of religion and speech, and the right to participate in government. Human rights laws prohibit torture, cruel punishment, and slavery.

David Hume (1711–1776) Scottish writer who applied Newton's method of scientific inquiry and skepticism to the study of morality, the mind, and government.

Hundred Years' War (1337–1453) A series of wars between England and France, fought mostly on French soil and prompted by the territorial and political claims of English monarchs.

Jan Hus (c. 1373–1415) A Czech reformer who adopted many of the teachings of the English theolojan John Wyclif, and who also demanded that the laity be allowed to receive both the consecrated bread and wine of the Eucharist. The Council of Constance burned him at the stake for heresy. In response, his supporters, the Hussites, revolted against the Church.

Saddam Hussein (1937–2006) The former dictator of Iraq who invaded Iran in 1980 and started the eight-year-long Iran-Iraq War; invaded Kuwait in 1990, which led to the Gulf War of 1991; and was overthrown when the United States invaded Iraq in 2003. Involved in Iraqi politics since the mid-1960s, Hussein became the official head of state in 1979.

Iconoclast Controversy (717–787) A serious and often violent theological debate that raged in Byzantium after Emperor Leo III ordered the destruction of religious art on the grounds that any image representing a divine or holy personage is prone to promote idol worship and blasphemy. Iconoclast means "breaker of icons." Those who supported the veneration of icons were called "iconodules," "adherents of icons."

Il-khanate Mongol-founded dynasty in thirteenth-century Persia.

Indian National Congress Formed in 1885, this Indian political party worked to achieve Indian independence from British colonial control. The Congress was led by Ghandi in the 1920s and 1930s.

Indian Rebellion of 1857 The uprising began near Delhi, when the military disciplined a regiment of Indian soldiers employed by the British for refusing to use rifle cartridges greased with pork fat—unacceptable to either Hindus or Muslims. Rebels attacked law courts and burned tax rolls, protesting debt and corruption. The mutiny spread through large areas of northwest India before being violently suppressed by British troops.

Indo-Europeans A group of people speaking variations of the same language who moved into the Near East and Mediterranean region shortly after 2000 B.C.E.

indulgences Grants exempting Catholic Christians from the performance of penance, either in life or after death. The abusive trade in indulgences was a major catalyst of the Protestant Reformation.

Inkas The highly centralized South American empire that was toppled by the Spanish conquistador Francisco Pizarro in 1533.

Innocent III (1160/61–1216) As pope, he wanted to unify all of Christendom under papal hegemony. He furthered this goal at the Fourth Lateran Council of 1215, which defined one of the Church's dogmas as the acknowledgement of papal supremacy. The council also took an unprecedented interest in the religious education and habits of every Christian.

Inquisition Tribunal of the Roman Church that aims to enforce religious orthodoxy and conformity.

International Monetary Fund (IMF) Established in 1945 to ensure international cooperation regarding currency exchange and monetary policy, the IMF is a specialized agency of the United Nations.

Investiture Conflict The name given to a series of debates over the limitations of spiritual and secular power in Europe during the eleventh and early twelfth century, it came to a head when Pope Gregory VII and Emperor Henry IV of Germany both claimed the right to appoint and invest bishops with the regalia of office. After years of diplomatic and military hostility, it was partially settled by the Concordat of Worms in 1122.

Irish potato famine Period of agricultural blight from 1845 to 1849 whose devastating results produced widespread starvation and led to mass emigration to America.

Iron Curtain Term coined by Winston Churchill in 1946 to refer to the borders of Eastern European nations that lay within the zone of Soviet control.

Italian invasion of Ethiopia (1896) Italy invaded Ethiopia, which was the last major independent African kingdom. Menelik II, the Ethiopian emperor, soundly defeated them.

Ivan the Great (1440–1505) Russian ruler who annexed neighboring territories and consolidated his empire's position as a European power.

Jacobins Radical French political group during the French Revolution that took power after 1792, executed the French king, and sought to remake French culture.

Jacquerie Violent 1358 peasant uprising in northern France, incited by disease, war, and taxes.

James I (1566–1625) Monarch who ruled Scotland as James VI, and who succeeded Elizabeth I as king of England in 1603. He oversaw the English vernacular translation of the Bible known by his name.

Janissaries Corps of enslaved soldiers recruited as children from the Christian provinces of the Ottoman Empire and brought up to display intense personal loyalty to the Ottoman sultan, who used these forces to curb local autonomy and as his personal bodyguards.

Jerome (c. 340–420) One of the early "fathers" of the Church, he translated the Bible from Hebrew and Greek into a popular form of Latin—hence the name by which this translation is known: the Vulgate, or "vulgar" (popular), Bible.

Jesuits The religious order formally known as the Society of Jesus, founded in 1540 by Ignatius Loyola to combat the spread of Protestantism. The Jesuits would become active in politics, education, and missionary work.

Jesus (c. 4 B.C.E.–c. 30 C.E.) A Jewish preacher and teacher in the rural areas of Galilee and Judea who was arrested for seditious political activity, tried, and crucified by the Romans. After his execution, his followers claimed that he had been resurrected from the dead and taken up into heaven. They began to teach that Jesus had been the divine representative of God, the Messiah foretold by ancient Hebrew prophets, and that he had suffered for the sins of humanity and would return to judge all the world's inhabitants at the end of time.

Joan of Arc (c. 1412–1431) A peasant girl from the province of Lorraine who claimed to have been commanded by God to lead French forces against the English occupying army during the Hundred Years' War. Successful in her efforts, she was betrayed by the French king and handed over to the English, who condemned her to death for heresy. Her reputation underwent a process of rehabilitation, but she was not officially canonized as a saint until 1920.

Judaism The religion of the Hebrews as it developed in the centuries after the establishment of the Hebrew kingdoms under David and Solomon, especially during the period of Babylonian Captivity.

Justinian (527–565) Emperor of Rome who unsuccessfully attempted to reunite the eastern and western portions of the empire. Also known for his important codification of Roman law, in the *Corpus Juris Civilis*.

Justinian's Code of Roman Law Formally known as the *Corpus Juris Civilis* or "body of civil law," this compendium consisted of a systematic compilation of imperial statutes, the writings of Rome's great legal authorities, a textbook of legal principles, and the legislation of Justinian and his immediate successors. As the most authoritative collection of Roman law, it formed the basis of canon law (the legal system of the Roman Church) and became essential to the developing legal traditions of every European state, as well as of many countries around the world.

Das Kapital (Capital) The 1867 book by Karl Marx that outlined the theory behind historical materialism and attacked the socioeconomic inequities of capitalism.

Johannes Kepler (1571–1630) Mathematician and astronomer who elaborated on and corrected Copernicus's theory and is chiefly remembered for his discovery of the three laws of planetary motion that bear his name.

Keynesian Revolution Post-depression economic ideas developed by the British economist John Maynard Keynes, wherein the state took a greater role in managing the economy, stimulating it by increasing the money supply and creating jobs.

KGB Soviet political police and spy agency, first formed as the Cheka not long after the Bolshevik coup in October 1917. It grew to more than 750,000 operatives with military rank by the 1980s.

Chingiz Khan (c. 1167–1227) "Oceanic Ruler," the title adopted by the Mongol chieftain Temujin, founder of a dynasty that conquered much of southern Asia.

Khanate The major political unit of the vast Mongol Empire. There were four Khanates, including the Yuan Empire in China, forged by Chingiz Khan's grandson Kubilai in the thirteenth century.

Ruhollah Khomeini (1902–1989) Iranian Shi'ite religious leader who led the revolution in Iran after the abdication of the Shah in 1979. His government allowed some limited economic and political populism combined with strict constructions of Islamic law, restrictions on women's public life, and the prohibition of ideas or activities linked to Western influence.

Nikita Khrushchev (1894–1971) Leader of the Soviet Union during the Cuban missile crisis, Khrushchev came to power after Stalin's death in 1953. His reforms and criticisms of the excesses of the Stalin regime led to his fall from power in 1964.

Kremlin Once synonymous with the Soviet government, it refers to Moscow's walled city center and the palace originally built by Ivan the Great.

Kristallnacht Organized attack by Nazis and their supporters on the Jews of Germany following the assassination of a German embassy official by a Jewish man in Paris. Throughout Germany, thousands of stores, schools, cemeteries and synagogues were attacked on November 9, 1938. Dozens of people were killed, and tens of thousands of Jews were arrested and held in camps, where many were tortured and killed in the ensuing months.

Labour party Founded in Britain in 1900, this party represented workers and was based on socialist principles.

Latin West After the founding of Constantinople, the western Latin-speaking half of the Roman Empire became poorer and more peripheral, but it also fostered the emergence of new barbarian kingdoms. At the same time, the Roman pope claimed to have inherited both the authority of Jesus and the essential elements of Roman imperial authority.

League of Nations International organization founded after the First World War to solve international disputes through arbitration; it was dissolved in 1946 and its assets were transferred to the United Nations.

Vladimir Lenin (1870–1924) Leader of the Bolshevik Revolution in Russia (1917) and the first leader of the Soviet Union.

Leviathan A book by Thomas Hobbes (1588–1679) that recommended a ruler have unrestricted power.

liberalism Political and social theory that judges the effectiveness of a government in terms of its ability to protect individual rights. Liberals support representative forms of government, free trade, and freedom of speech and religion. In the economic realm, liberals believe that individuals should be free to engage in commercial or business activities without interference from the state or their community.

lithograph Art form that involves putting writing or design on stone and producing printed impressions.

John Locke (1632–1704) English philosopher and political theorist known for his contributions to liberalism. Locke had great faith in human reason, and believed that just societies were those which infringed the least on the natural rights and freedoms of individuals. This led him to assert that a government's legitimacy depended on the consent of the governed, a view that had a profound effect on the authors of the United States' Declaration of Independence.

Louis XIV (1638–1715) Called the "Sun King," he was known for his success at strengthening the institutions of the French absolutist state.

Louis XVI (1754–1793) Well-meaning but ineffectual king of France, finally deposed and executed during the French Revolution.

Ignatius Loyola (1491–1556) Founder of the Society of Jesus (commonly known as the Jesuits), whose members vowed to serve God through poverty, chastity, and missionary work. He abandoned his first career as a mercenary after reading an account of Christ's life written in his native Spanish.

Lucretia According to Roman legend, Lucretia was a virtuous Roman wife who was raped by the son of Rome's last king and who virtuously committed suicide in order to avoid bringing shame on her family.

Luftwaffe Literally "air weapon," this is the name of the German air force, which was founded during the First World War, disbanded in 1945, and reestablished when West Germany joined NATO in 1950.

Lusitania The British passenger liner that was sunk by a German U-boat (submarine) on May 7, 1915. Public outrage over the sinking contibuted to the U.S. decision to enter the First World War.

Martin Luther (1483–1546) A German monk and professor of theology whose critique of the papacy launched the Protestant Reformation.

ma'at The Egyptian term for the serene order of the universe, with which the individual soul (*ka*) must remain in harmony. The power of the pharaoh was linked to ma'at, insofar as it ensured the prosperity of the kingdom. After the upheavals of the First Intermediate Period, the perception of the pharaoh's relationship with ma'at was revealed to be conditional, something that had to be earned.

Niccolo Machiavelli (1469–1527) As the author of *The Prince* and the *Discourses on Livy*, he looked to the Roman past for paradigms of greatness, while at the same time hoping to win the patronage of contemporary rulers who would restore Italy's political independence.

Magna Carta The "Great Charter" of 1215, enacted during the reign of King John of England and designed to limit his powers. Regarded now as a landmark in the development of constitutional government. In its own time, its purpose was to restore the power of great lords.

Magyar nationalism Lajos Kossuth led this national movement in the Hungarian region of the Habsburg Empire, calling for national independence for Hungary in 1848. With the support of Russia, the Habsburg army crushed the movement and all other revolutionary activities in the empire. Kossuth fled into exile.

Moses Maimonides (c. 1137–1204) Jewish scholar, physician, and scriptural commentator whose *Mishneh Torah* is a fundamental exposition of Jewish law.

Thomas Malthus (1766–1834) British political economist who believed that populations inevitably grew faster than the available food supply. Societies that could not control their population growth would be checked only by famine, disease, poverty, and infant malnutrition. He argued that governments could not alleviate poverty. Instead, the poor had to exercise "moral restraint," postpone marriage, and have fewer children.

Nelson Mandela (b. 1918) The South African opponent of apartheid who led the African National Congress and was imprisoned from 1962 until 1990. After his release from prison, he worked with Prime Minister Frederik Willem De Klerk to establish majority rule. Mandela became the first black president of South Africa in 1994.

Manhattan Project The secret U.S. government research project to develop the first nuclear bomb. The vast project involved dozens of sites across the United States, including New Mexico, Tennessee, Illinois, California, Utah, and Washington. The first test of a nuclear bomb was near Alamogordo, New Mexico on July 16, 1945.

manors Common farmland worked collectively by the inhabitants of entire villages, sometimes on their own initiative, sometimes at the behest of a lord.

Mao Zedong (1893–1976) The leader of the Chinese Revolution who defeated the Nationalists in 1949 and established the Communist regime in China.

Marne A major battle of the First World War in September 1914, which halted the German invasion of France and led to protracted trench warfare on the Western Front.

Marshall Plan Economic aid package given to Europe by the United States after the Second World War to promote reconstruction and economic development and to secure the countries from a feared communist takeover.

Karl Marx (1818–1883) German philosopher and economist who believed that a revolution of the working classes would overthrow the capitalist order and create a classless society. Author of *Das Kapital* and *The Communist Manifesto.*

Marxists Followers of the socialist political economist Karl Marx who called for workers everywhere to unite and create an independent political force. Marxists believed that industrialization produced an inevitable struggle between laborers and the class of capitalist property owners, and that this struggle would culminate in a revolution that would abolish private property and establish a society committed to social equality.

Mary; see **cult of the Virgin.**

Mary I (1516–1558) Catholic daughter of Henry VIII and his first wife, Catherine of Aragon, Mary Tudor was the first queen regnant of England. Her attempts to reinstitute Catholicism in England met with limited success, and after her early death she was labeled "Bloody Mary" by the Protestant supporters of her half sister and successor, Elizabeth I.

mass culture The spread of literacy and public education in the nineteenth century created a new audience for print entertainment and a new class of entrepreneurs in the media to cater to this audience. The invention of radio, film, and television in the twentieth century carried this development to another level, as millions of consumers were now accessible to the producers of news, information, and entertainment. The rise of this "mass culture" has been celebrated as an expression of popular tastes but also criticized as a vehicle for the manipulation of populations through clever and seductive propaganda.

Mayans Native American peoples whose culturally and politically sophisticated empire encompassed lands in present-day Mexico and Guatemala.

Giuseppe Mazzini (1805–1872) Founder of Young Italy and an ideological leader of the Italian nationalist movement.

Mecca Center of an important commercial network of the Arabian Peninsula and birthplace of the prophet Muhammad. It is now considered the holiest site in the Islamic world.

Medici A powerful dynasty of Florentine bankers and politicians whose ancestors were originally apothecaries ("medics").

Meiji Empire Empire created under the leadership of Mutsuhito, emperor of Japan from 1868 until 1912. During the Meiji period Japan became a world industrial and naval power.

Mensheviks Within the Russian Social Democratic Party, the Mensheviks advocated slow changes and a gradual move toward socialism, in contrast with the Bolsheviks, who wanted to push for a proletarian revolution. Mensheviks believed that a proletarian revolution in Russia was premature and that the country needed to complete its capitalist development first.

mercantilism A theory and policy for directing the economy of monarchical states between 1600 and 1800 based on the assumption that wealth and power depended on a favorable balance of trade (more exports and fewer imports) and the accumulation of precious metals. Mercantilists advocated forms of economic protectionism to promote domestic production.

Maria Sybilla Merian (1647–1717) A scientific illustrator and an important early entomologist. She conducted research on two continents and published the well-received *Metamorphosis of the Insects of Surinam.*

Merovingian A Frankish dynasty that claimed descent from a legendary ancestor called Merovic, the Merovingians were the only powerful family to establish a lasting kingdom in western Europe during the fifth and sixth centuries.

Mesopotamia The "land between the Tigris and the Euphrates rivers," Tigris and Euphrates where the civilization of Sumer, the first urban society, flourished.

Klemens von Metternich (1773–1859) Austrian foreign minister whose primary goals were to bolster the legitimacy of monarchies and, after the defeat of Napoleon, to prevent another large-scale war in Europe. At the Congress of Vienna, he opposed social and political change and wanted to check Russian and French expansion.

Michelangelo Buonarroti (1475–1564) A virtuoso Florentine sculptor, painter, and poet who spent much of his career in the service of the papacy. He is best known for the decoration of the Sistine Chapel and for his monumental sculptures.

Middle Kingdom of Egypt (2055–1650 B.C.E.) The period following the First Intermediate Period of dynastic warfare, which ended with the reassertion of pharonic rule under Mentuhotep II.

Miletus A Greek polis and Persian colony on the Ionian coast of Asia Minor. Influenced by the cultures of Mesopotamia, Egypt, and Lydia, it produced several of the ancient world's first scientists and sophists. Thereafter, a political conflict between the ruler of Miletus, Aristagoras, and the Persian Emperor, Darius, sparked the Persian Wars with Greece.

John Stuart Mill (1806–1873) English liberal philosopher whose faith in human reason led him to support a broad variety of civic and political freedoms for men and women, including the right to vote and the right to free speech.

Slobodan Milosevic (1941–2006) The Serbian nationalist politician who became president of Serbia and whose policies during the Balkan wars of the early 1990s led to the deaths of thousands of Croatians, Bosnian Muslims, Albanians, and Kosovars. After leaving office in 2000 he was arrested and tried for war crimes at the International Court in The Hague. The trial ended before a verdict with his death in 2006.

Minoan Crete A sea empire based at Knossos on the Greek island of Crete and named for the legendary King Minos. The Minoans dominated the Aegean for much of the second millennium B.C.E.

Modernism There were several different modernist movements in art and literature, but they shared three key characteristics. First, they had a sense that the world had radically changed and that this change should be embraced. Second, they believed that traditional aesthetic values and assumptions about creativity were ill-suited to the present. Third, they developed a new conception of what art could do that emphasized expression over representation and insisted on the value of novelty, experimentation, and creative freedom.

Mongols A nomadic people from the steppes of Central Asia who were united under the ruler Chingiz Khan. His conquest of China was continued by his grandson Kubilai and his great-grandson son Ogedei, whose army also seized southern Russia and then moved through Hungary and through Poland toward eastern Germany. The Mongol armies withdrew from Eastern Europe after the death of Ogedei, but his descendents continued to rule his vast empire for another half century.

Michel de Montaigne (1533–1592) French philosopher and social commentator, best known for his *Essays*.

Montesquieu (1689–1755) An Enlightenment *philosophe* whose most influential work was *The Spirit of Laws*. In this work he analyzed the structures that shaped law and categorized governments into three types: republics, monarchies, and despotisms. His ideas about the separation of powers between the executive, the legislative, and the judicial branches of government influenced the authors of the United States Constitution.

Thomas More (1478–1535) Christian humanist, English statesman, and author of *Utopia*. In 1529, he was appointed Lord Chancellor of England but resigned because he opposed King Henry VIII's plans to establish a national church under royal control. He was eventually executed for refusing to take an oath acknowledging Henry to be the head of the Church of England, and has since been canonized by the Catholic Church.

mos maiorum Literally translated as "the code of the elders" or "the custom of ancestors." This unwritten code governed the lives of Romans under the Republic and stressed the importance of showing reverence to ancestral tradition. It was sacrosanct and essential to Roman identity, and an important influence on Roman culture, law, and religion.

Wolfgang Amadeus Mozart (1756–1791) Austrian composer, famous at a young age as a concert musician and later celebrated as a prolific composer of instrumental music and operas that are seen as the apogee of the Classical style in music.

Muhammad (570–632 c.e.) The founder of Islam, regarded as God's last and greatest prophet by his followers.

Munich Conference (1938) Hitler met with the leaders of Britain, France, and Italy and negotiated an agreement that gave Germany a major slice of Czechoslovakia. British prime minister Chamberlain believed that the agreement would bring peace to Europe. Instead, Germany invaded and seized the rest of Czechoslovakia.

Muscovy The duchy centered on Moscow whose dukes saw themselves as heirs to the Roman Empire. In the early fourteenth century, Moscow was under the control of the Mongol Khanate. After the collapse of the Khanate, the Muscovite grand duke, Ivan III, conquered all the Russian principalities between Moscow and the border of Poland-Lithuania, and then Lithuania itself. By the time of his death, Ivan had established Muscovy as a dominant power.

Muslim learning and culture The Crusades brought the Latin West in contact with the Islamic world, which impacted European culture in myriad ways. Europeans adapted Arabic numerals and mathematical concepts as well as Arabic and Persian words. Through Arabic translations, western scholars gained access to Greek learning, which had a profound influence on Christian theology. European scholars also learned from the Islamic world's accomplishments in medicine and science.

Benito Mussolini (1883–1945) The Italian founder of the Fascist party who came to power in Italy in 1922 and allied himself with Hitler and the Nazis during the Second World War.

Mycenaean Greece (1600–1200 b.c.e.) The term used to describe the civilization of Greece in the late Bronze Age, when territorial kingdoms like Mycenae formed around a king, a warrior caste, and a palace bureaucracy.

Nagasaki Second Japanese city on which the United States dropped an atomic bomb. The attack took place on August 9, 1945; the Japanese surrendered shortly thereafter, ending the Second World War.

Napoleon III (1808–1873) Nephew of Napoleon Bonaparte, Napoleon III was elected president of the French Second Republic in 1848 and made himself emperor of France in 1852. During his reign (1852–70), he rebuilt the French capital of Paris. Defeated in the France-Prussian War of 1870, he went into exile.

Napoleonic Code Legal code drafted by Napoleon in 1804 and based on Justinian's *Corpus Iuris Civilis*. It distilled different legal traditions to create one uniform law. The code confirmed the abolition of feudal privileges of all kinds and set the conditions for exercising property rights.

Napoleon's military campaigns In 1805, the Russians, Prussians, Austrians, Swedes, and British attempted to contain Napoleon, but he defeated them. Out of his victories, Napoleon created a new empire and affiliated states. In 1808, he invaded Spain, but fierce resistance prevented Napoleon from achieving a complete victory. In 1812, Napoleon invaded Russia, and his army was decimated as it retreated from Moscow during the winter. After the Russian campaign, the united European powers defeated Napoleon and forced him into exile. He escaped and reassumed command of his army, but the European powers defeated him for the final time at the Battle of Waterloo.

Gamal Abdel Nasser (1918–1970) Former president of Egypt and the most prominent spokesman for secular pan-Arabism. He became a target for Islamist critics, such as Sayyid Qutb and the Muslim Brotherhood, angered by the Western-influenced policies of his regime.

National Assembly of France Governing body of France that succeeded the Estates-General in 1789 during the French Revolution. It was composed of, and defined by, the delegates of the Third Estate.

National Association for the Advancement of Colored People (NAACP) Founded in 1910, this U.S. civil rights organization was dedicated to ending inequality and segregation for black Americans.

National Convention The governing body of France from September 1792 to October 1795. It declared France a republic and then tried and executed the French king. The Convention also confiscated the property of the enemies of the revolution, instituted a policy of de-Christianization, changed marriage and inheritance laws, abolished slavery in its colonies, placed a cap on the price of necessities, and ended the compensation of nobles for their lost privileges.

nationalism Movement to unify a country under one government based on perceptions of the population's common history, customs, and social traditions.

nationalism in Yugoslavia In the 1990s, Slobodan Milosevic and his allies reignited Serbian nationalism in the former Yugoslavia, which led non-Serb republics in Croatia and Slovenia to seek independence. The country erupted into war, with the worst violence taking place in Bosnia, a multi-ethnic region with Serb, Croatian and Bosnian Muslim populations. European diplomats proved powerless to stop attempts by Croatian and Serbian military and paramilitary forces to claim territory through ethnic cleansing and violent intimidation. Atrocities were committed on all sides, but pro-Serb forces were responsible for the most deaths.

NATO The North Atlantic Treaty Organization, a 1949 military agreement between the United States, Canada, Great Britain, and eight Western European nations, which declared that an armed attack against any one of the members would be regarded as an attack against all. Created during the Cold War in the face of the Soviet Union's control of Eastern Europe, NATO continues to exist today and the membership of twenty-eight states includes former members of the Warsaw Pact as well as Albania and Turkey.

Nazi party Founded in the early 1920s, the National Socialist German Workers' Party (NSDAP) gained control over Germany under the leadership of Adolf Hitler in 1933 and continued in power until Germany was defeated in 1945.

Nazism The political movement in Germany led by Adolf Hitler, which advocated a violent anti-Semitic, anti-Marxist, pan-German ideology.

Neo-Assyrian Empire (883–859 B.C.E.–612–605 B.C.E.) Assurnasirpal II laid the foundations of the Neo-Assyrian Empire through military campaigns against neighboring peoples. Eventually, the empire stretched from the Mediterranean Sea to Western Iran. A military dictatorship governed the empire through its army, which it used to frighten and oppress both its subjects and its enemies. The empire's ideology was based on waging holy war in the name of its principal god, Assur, and the exaction of tribute through terror.

Neoliberalism Neoliberals believe that free markets, profit incentives, and restraints on both budget deficits and social welfare programs are the best guarantee of individual liberties. Beginning in the 1980s, neoliberal theory was used to structure the policy of financial institutions like the International Monetary Fund and the World Bank, which turned away from interventionist policies in favor of market-driven models of economic development.

Neolithic Revolution The "New" Stone Age, which began around 11,000 B.C.E., saw new technological and social developments, including managed food production, the beginnings of permanent settlements, and the rapid intensification of trade.

Neoplatonism A school of thought based on the teachings of Plato and prevalent in the Roman Empire, which had a profound effect on the formation of Christian theology. Neoplatonists argued that nature is a book written by its creator to reveal the ways of God to humanity. Convinced that God's perfection must be reflected in nature, neoplatonists searched for the ideal and perfect structures that they believed must lie behind the "shadows" of the everyday world.

New Deal President Franklin Delano Roosevelt's package of government reforms that were enacted during the depression of the 1930s to provide jobs for the unemployed, social welfare programs for the poor, and security to the financial markets.

New Economic Policy In 1921, the Bolsheviks abandoned war communism in favor of the New Economic Policy (NEP). Under NEP, the state still controlled all major industry and financial concerns, while individuals could own private property, trade freely within limits, and farm their own land for their own benefit. Fixed taxes replaced grain requisition. The policy successfully helped Soviet agriculture recover from the civil war, but was later abandoned in favor of collectivization.

Isaac Newton (1642–1727) One of the foremost scientists of all time, Newton was an English mathematician and physicist; he is noted for his development of calculus, work on the properties of light, and theory of gravitation.

Tsar Nicholas II (1868–1918) The last Russian tsar, who abdicated the throne in 1917. He and his family were executed by the Bolsheviks on July 17, 1918.

Friedrich Nietzsche (1844–1900) The German philosopher who denied the possibility of knowing absolute "truth" or "reality," since all knowledge comes filtered through linguistic, scientific, or artistic systems of representation. He also criticized Judeo-Christian morality for instilling a repressive conformity that drained civilization of its vitality.

nongovernmental organizations (NGOs) Private organizations like the Red Cross that play a large role in international affairs.

North American Free Trade Agreement (NAFTA) Treaty negotiated in the early 1990s to promote free trade among Canada, the United States, and Mexico.

Novum Organum Work by English statesman and scientist Francis Bacon (1561–1626) that advanced a philosophy of study through observation.

October Days (1789) The high price of bread and the rumor that the king was unwilling to cooperate with the assembly caused the women who worked in Paris's large central market to march to Versailles along with their supporters to address the king. Not satisfied with their initial reception, they broke through the palace gates and called for the king to return to Paris from Versailles, which he did the following day.

Old Kingdom of Egypt (c. 2686–2160 B.C.E.) During this time, the pharaohs controlled a powerful and centralized bureaucratic state whose vast human and material resources are exemplified by the pyramids of Giza. This period came to an end as the pharaoh's authority collapsed, leading to a period of dynastic warfare and localized rule.

OPEC (Organization of the Petroleum Exporting Countries) Organization created in 1960 by oil-producing countries in the Middle East, South America, and Africa to regulate the production and pricing of crude oil.

Operation Barbarossa The codename for Hitler's invasion of the Soviet Union in 1941.

Opium Wars (1839–1842) War fought between the British and Qing China to protect British trade in opium; resulted in the ceding of Hong Kong to the British.

Oracle at Delphi The most important shrine in ancient Greece. The priestess of Apollo who attended the shrine was believed to have the power to predict the future.

Ottoman Empire (c.1300–1923) During the thirteenth century, the Ottoman dynasty established itself as leader of the Turks. From the fourteenth to sixteenth centuries, they conquered Anatolia, Armenia, Syria, and North Africa as well as parts of southeastern Europe, the Crimea, and areas along the Red Sea. Portions of the Ottoman Empire persisted up to the time of the First World War, but it was dismantled in the years following it.

Reza Pahlavi (1919–1980) The Western-friendly Shah of Iran who was installed during a 1953 coup supported by Britain and the United States. After a lengthy economic downturn, public unrest, and personal illness, he retired from public life under popular pressure in 1979.

Pan-African Conference 1900 assembly in London that sought to draw attention to the sovereignty of African people and their mistreatment by colonial powers.

Panhellenism The "all Greek" culture that allowed ancient Greek colonies to maintain a connection to their homeland and to each other through their shared language and heritage. These colonies also exported their culture into new areas and created new Greek-speaking enclaves, which permanently changed the cultural geography of the Mediterranean world.

pan-Slavism Cultural movement that sought to unite native Slavic peoples within the Russian and Habsburg empires under Russian leadership.

Partition of India (1947) At independence, British India was partitioned into the nations of India and Pakistan. The majority of the population in India was Hindu and the majority of the population in Pakistan was Muslim. The process of partition brought brutal religious and ethnic warfare. More than one million Hindus and Muslims died and twelve million became refugees.

Blaise Pascal (1623–1662) A Catholic philosopher who wanted to establish the truth of Christianity by appealing simultaneously to intellect and emotion. In his *Pensées*, he argued that faith alone can resolve the world's contradictions and that his own awe in the face of evil and uncertainty must be evidence of God's existence.

Paul of Tarsus Originally known as Saul, Paul was a Greek-speaking Jew and Roman citizen who underwent a miraculous conversion experience and became the most important proponent of Christianity in the 50s and 60s C.E.

Pax Romana (27 B.C.E.–180 C.E.) Literally translated as "the Roman Peace." During this time, the Roman world enjoyed an unprecedented period of peace and political stability.

Peace of Augsburg A settlement negotiated in 1555 among factions within the Holy Roman Empire, it formulated the principle *cuius regio, eius religio,* "he who rules, his religion": meaning that the inhabitants of any given territory should follow the religion of its ruler, whether Catholic or Protestant.

Peace of Paris The 1919 Paris Peace Conference established the terms to end the First World War. Great Britain, France, Italy, and the United States signed five treaties with each of the defeated nations: Germany, Austria, Hungary, Turkey, and Bulgaria. The settlement is notable for the territory that Germany had to give up, including large parts of Prussia to the new state of Poland, and Alsace and Lorraine to France; the disarming of Germany; and the "war guilt" provision, which required Germany and its allies to pay massive reparations to the victors.

Peace of Westphalia (1648) An agreement reached at the end of the Thirty Years' War that altered the political map of Europe. France emerged as the predominant power on the Continent, while the Austrian Habsburgs had to surrender all the territories they had gained and could no longer use the office of the Holy Roman Emperor to dominate central Europe. Spain was marginalized and Germany became a volatile combination of Protestant and Catholic principalities.

Pearl Harbor The American naval base in Hawaii that was bombed by the Japanese on December 7, 1941, bringing the United States into the Second World War.

peasantry Term used in continental Europe to refer to rural populations that lived from agriculture. Some peasants were free, and could own land. Serfs were peasants who were legally bound to the land, and subject to the authority of the local lord.

Peloponnesian War The name given to the series of wars fought between Sparta (on the Greek Peloponnesus) and Athens from 431 B.C.E. to 404 B.C.E., and which ended in the defeat of Athens and the loss of her imperial power.

perestroika Introduced by Soviet leader Mikhail Gorbachev in June 1987, perestroika was the name given to economic and political reforms begun earlier in his tenure. It restructured the state bureaucracy, reduced the privileges of the political elite, and instituted a shift from the centrally planned economy to a mixed economy, combining planning with the operation of market forces.

Periclean Athens Following his election as *strategos* in 461 B.C.E., Pericles pushed through political reforms in Athens, which gave poorer citizens greater influence in politics. He promoted Athenians' sense of superiority through ambitious public works projects and lavish festivals to honor the gods, thus ensuring his continual reelection. But eventually, Athens' growing arrogance and aggression alienated it from the rest of the Greek world.

Pericles (c. 495–429) Athenian politician who occupied the office of strategos for thirty years and who presided over a series of civic reforms, building campaigns, and imperialist initiatives.

Persian Empire Consolidated by Cyrus the Great in 559, this empire eventually stretched from the Persian Gulf to the Mediterranean, and also encompassed Egypt. Persian rulers were able to hold this empire together through a policy of tolerance and a mixture of local and centralized governance. This imperial model of government would be adopted by many future empires.

Persian Wars (490–479 B.C.E.) In 501 B.C.E., a political conflict between the Greek ruler of Miletus, Aristagoras, and the Persian Emperor, Darius, sparked the first of the Persian Wars when Darius sent an army to punish Athens for its intervention on the side of the Greeks. Despite being heavily outnumbered, Athenian hoplites defeated the Persian army at the plain of Marathon. In 480 B.C.E., Darius' son Xerxes invaded Greece but was defeated at sea and on land by combined Greek forces under the leadership of Athens and Sparta.

Peter the Great (1672–1725) Energetic tsar who transformed Russia into a leading European country by centralizing government, modernizing the army, creating a navy, and reforming education and the economy.

Francesco Petrarca (Petrarch) (1304–1374) Italian scholar who revived interest in classical writing styles and was famed for his vernacular love sonnets.

pharaoh A term meaning "household" which became the title borne by the rulers of ancient Egypt. The pharaoh was regarded as the divine representative of the gods and the embodiment of Egypt itself. The powerful and centralized bureaucratic state ruled by the pharaohs was more stable and long-lived than any another civilization in world history, lasting (with few interruptions) for approximately three thousand years.

Pharisees A group of Jewish teachers and preachers that emerged in the third century B.C.E. They insisted that all of Yahweh's (God's) commandments were binding on all Jews.

Philip II (382–336 B.C.E.) King of Macedonia and father of Alexander, he consolidated the southern Balkans and the Greek city-states under Macedonian domination.

Philip II Augustus (1165–1223) The first French ruler to use the title "king of France" rather than "king of the French." After he captured Normandy and its adjacent territories from the English, he built an effective system of local administration, which recognized regional diversity while promoting centralized royal control. This administrative pattern would characterize French government until the French Revolution.

Philistines Descendants of the Sea Peoples who fled to the region that now bears their name, Palestine, after their defeat at the hands of the pharaoh Ramses III. They dominated their neighbors, the Hebrews, who used writing as an effective means of discrediting them (the Philistines themselves did not leave a written record to contest the Hebrews' views).

philosophe During the Enlightenment, this word referred to a person whose reflections were unhampered by the constraints of religion or dogma.

Phoenicians A Semitic people known for their trade in exotic purple dyes and other luxury goods, they originally settled in present-day Lebanon around 1200 B.C.E. and from there established commercial colonies throughout the Mediterranean, notably Carthage.

Plato (429–349 B.C.E.) A student of Socrates, Plato dedicated his life to transmitting his teacher's legacy through the writing of dialogues on philosophical subjects, in which Socrates himself plays the major role. The longest and most famous of these, known as the *Republic*, describes an idealized polis governed by a superior group of individuals chosen for their natural attributes of intelligence and character, who rule as "philosopher-kings."

Plotinus (204–270 C.E.) A Neoplatonist philosopher who taught that everything in existence has its ultimate source in the divine, and that the highest goal of life should be the mystic reunion of the soul with this divine source, something that can be achieved through contemplation and asceticism. This outlook blended with that of early Christianity and was instrumental in the spread of that religion within the Roman Empire.

poleis One of the major political innovations of the ancient Greeks was the *polis*, or city-state (plural *poleis*). These independent social and political entities began to emerge in the ninth century B.C.E., organized around an urban center and fostering markets, meeting places, and religious worship; frequently, poleis also controlled some surrounding territory.

Marco Polo (1254–1324) Venetian merchant who traveled through Asia for twenty years and published his observations in a widely read memoir.

population growth In the nineteenth century, Europe experienced a dramatic population growth. During this period, the spread of rural manufacturing allowed men and women to begin marrying younger and raising families earlier, which increased the size of the average family. As the population grew, the portion of young and fertile people also increased, which reinforced the population growth. By 1900, population growth was strongest in Britain and Germany, and slower in France.

Potsdam (1945) At this conference, Truman, Churchill and Stalin met to discuss their options at the conclusion of the Second World War, including making territorial changes to Germany and its allies and the question of war reparations.

Prague spring A period of political liberalization in Czechoslovakia between January and August 1968 that was initiated by Alexander Dubček, the Czech leader. This period of expanding freedom and openness in this Eastern bloc nation ended on August 20, when the USSR and Warsaw Pact countries invaded with 200,000 troops and 5,000 tanks.

pre-Socratics A group of philosophers in the Greek city of Miletus, who raised questions about humans' relationship with the natural world and the gods, and who formulated rational theories to explain the physical universe they observed. Their name reflects the fact that they flourished prior to the lifetime of Socrates.

Price Revolution An unprecedented inflation in prices in the latter half of the sixteenth century, resulting in part from the enormous influx of silver bullion from Spanish America.

Principate Modern term for the centuries of autocratic rule by the successors of Augustus, who seized power in 27 B.C.E. and styled himself *princeps* or Rome's "first man." See **Roman Republic**.

Protestantism The name given to the many dissenting varieties of Christianity that emerged during the Reformation in sixteenth-century western Europe. While Protestant beliefs and practices differed widely, all were united in their rejection of papal authority and the dogmas of the Roman Catholic Church.

Provisional Government After the collapse of the Russian monarchy, leaders in the Duma organized this government and hoped to establish a democratic system under constitutional rule. They also refused to concede military defeat, and it was impossible to institute domestic reforms and fight a war at the same time. As conditions worsened, the Bolsheviks gained support. In October 1917, they attacked the provisional government and seized control.

Claudius Ptolomeus, called Ptolemy (c. 85–165 C.E.) A Greek-speaking geographer and astronomer active in Roman Alexandria, he rejected the findings of previous Hellenistic scientists in favor of the erroneous theories of Aristotle, publishing highly influential treatises that promulgated these errors and suppressed (for example) the accurate findings of Aristarchus (who had discovered the Heliocentric universe) and Erathosthenes (who had calculated the circumference of the earth).

Ptolemaic system Ptolemy of Alexandria promoted Aristotle's understanding of cosmology. In this system, the heavens orbit the earth in an organized hierarchy of spheres, and the earth and the heavens are made of different matter and subject to different laws of motion. A prime mover produces the motion of the celestial bodies.

Ptolemy (c. 367–c. 284 B.C.E.) One of Alexander the Great's trusted generals (and possibly his half brother), he became pharaoh of Egypt and founded a new dynasty that lasted until that kingdom's absorption into the Roman Empire in 30 B.C.E.

Punic Wars (264–146 B.C.E.) Three periods of warfare between Rome and Carthage, two maritime empires who struggled for dominance of the Mediterranean. Rome emerged as the victor, destroyed the city of Carthage and took control of Sicily, North Africa and Hispania (Spain).

pyramid Constructed during the third millennium B.C.E., these structures were monuments to the power and divinity of the pharaohs entombed inside them.

Qu'ran (often Koran) Islam's holy scriptures, comprised of the prophecies revealed to Muhammad and redacted during and after his death.

Raphael (Raffaelo Sarazio) (1483–1520) Italian painter active in Rome, his works include *The School of Athens.*

realism Artistic and literary style which sought to portray common situations as they would appear in reality.

Realpolitik Political strategy based on advancing power for its own sake.

reason The human capacity to solve problems and discover truth in ways that can be verified intellectually. Philosophers distinguish the knowledge gained from reason from the teachings of instinct, imagination, and faith, which are verified according to different criteria.

Reformation Religious and political movement in sixteenth-century Europe that led to a break between dissenting forms of

Christianity and the Roman Catholic Church; notable figures include Martin Luther and John Calvin.

Reich A term for the German state. The First Reich corresponded to the Holy Roman Empire (9th c.–1806), the Second Reich was from 1871 to 1919, and the Third Reich lasted from 1933 through May 1945.

Renaissance From the French word "rebirth," this term came to be used in the nineteenth century to describe the artistic, intellectual, and cultural movement that emerged in Italy after 1300, and which sought to recover and emulate the heritage of the classical past.

Restoration period (1815–1848) European movement after the defeat of Napoleon to restore Europe to its pre–French Revolution status and to prevent the spread of revolutionary or liberal political movements.

Cardinal Richelieu (1585–1642) First minister to King Louis XIII, he is considered by many to have ruled France in all but name, centralizing political power and suppressing dissent.

Roman army Under the Republic, the Roman army was made up of citizen-soldiers who were required to serve in wartime. As Rome's empire grew, the need for more fighting men led to the extension of citizenship rights and, eventually, to the development of a vast, professional, standing army that numbered as many as 300,000 by the middle of the third century B.C.E. By that time, however, citizens were not themselves required to serve, and many legions were made up of paid conscripts and foreign mercenaries.

Roman citizenship The rights and responsibilities of Rome's citizens were gradually extended to the free (male) inhabitants of other Italian provinces and later to most provinces in the Roman world. In contrast to slaves and non-Romans, Romans had the right to be tried in an imperial court and could not be legally subjected to torture.

Roman Republic The Romans traced the founding of their republic to the overthrow of their last king and the establishment of a unique form of constitutional government, in which the power of the aristocracy (embodied by the Senate) was checked by the executive rule of two elected consuls and the collective will of the people. For hundreds of years, this balance of power provided the Republic with a measure of political stability and prevented any single individual or clique from gaining too much power.

Romanticism Beginning in Germany and England in the late eighteenth century and continuing up to the end of the nineteenth century, Romanticism was a movement in art, music, and literature that countered the rationalism of the Enlightenment by placing greater value on human emotions and the power of nature to stimulate creativity.

Jean-Jacques Rousseau (1712–1778) Philosopher and radical political theorist whose *Social Contract* attacked privilege and inequality. One of the primary principles of Rousseau's political philosophy is that politics and morality should not be separated.

Royal Society This British society's goal was to pursue collective research. Members would conduct experiments, record the results, and share them with their peers, who would study the methods, reproduce the experiment, and assess the results.

The arrangement gave English scientists a sense of common purpose as well as a system to reach a consensus on facts.

Russian Revolution of 1905 After Russia's defeat in the Russo-Japanese War, Russians began clamoring for political reforms. Protests grew over the course of 1905, and the autocracy lost control of entire towns and regions as workers went on strike, soldiers mutinied, and peasants revolted. Forced to yield, Tsar Nicholas II issued the October Manifesto, which pledged individual liberties and provided for the election of a parliament (called the Duma). The most radical of the revolutionary groups were put down with force, and the pace of political change remained very slow in the aftermath of the revolution.

Russo-Japanese War (1904–1905) Japanese and Russian expansion collided in Mongolia and Manchuria. Russia was humiliated after the Japanese navy sunk its fleet, which helped provoke a revolt in Russia and led to an American-brokered peace treaty.

Saint Bartholomew's Day Massacre The mass murder of French Protestants (Huguenots) instigated by Queen Catherine de' Medici of France and carried out by Catholics. It began in Paris on 24 August 1572 and spread to other parts of France, continuing into October of that year. More than 70,000 people were killed.

salons Informal gatherings of intellectuals and aristocrats that allowed discourse about Enlightenment ideas.

Sappho (c. 620–c. 550 B.C.E.) One of the most celebrated Greek poets, she was revered as "the Tenth Muse" and emulated by many male poets. Ironically, though, only two of her poems survive intact, and the rest must be pieced together from fragments quoted by later poets.

Sargon the Great (r. 2334–2279 B.C.E.) The Akkadian ruler who consolidated power in Mesopotamia.

SARS epidemic (2003) The successful containment of severe acute respiratory syndrome (SARS) is an example of how international health organizations can effectively work together to recognize and respond to a disease outbreak. The disease itself, however, is a reminder of the dangers that exist in a globalized economy with a high degree of mobility in both populations and goods.

Schlieffen Plan Devised by German general Alfred von Schlieffen in 1905 to avoid the dilemma of a two-front war against France and Russia. The Schlieffen Plan required that Germany attack France first through Belgium and secure a quick victory before wheeling to the east to meet the slower armies of the Russians on the Eastern Front. The Schlieffen Plan was put into operation on August 2, 1914, at the outset of the First World War.

Scientific Revolution of Antiquity The Hellenistic period was the most brilliant age in the history of science before the seventeenth century C.E. Aristarchus of Samos posited the existence of a heliocentric universe. Eratosthenes of Alexandria accurately calculated the circumference of the earth. Archimedes turned physics into its own branch of experimental science. Hellenistic anatomists became the first to practice human dissection, which improved their understanding of human physiology. Ironically, most of these discoveries were suppressed by pseudo-scientists who flourished under the Roman Empire during the second century C.E., notably Claudus Ptolomeus Ptolemy) and Aelius Galenus (Galen).

second industrial revolution The technological developments in the last third of the nineteenth century, which included new techniques for refining and producing steel; increased availability of electricity for industrial, commercial, and domestic use; advances in chemical manufacturing; and the creation of the internal combustion engine.

Second World War Worldwide war that began in September 1939 in Europe, and even earlier in Asia (the Japanese invasion of Manchuria began in 1931), pitting Britain, the United States, and the Soviet Union (the Allies) against Nazi Germany, Italy, and Japan (the Axis). The war ended in 1945 with Germany and Japan's defeat.

Seleucus (d. 280 B.C.E.) The Macedonian general who ruled the Persian heartland of Alexander the Great's empire.

Semitic The Semitic language family has the longest recorded history of any linguistic group and is the root for most languages of the Middle and Near East. Ancient Semitic languages include those of the ancient Babylonians and Assyrians, Phoenician, the classical form of Hebrew, early dialects of Aramaic, and the classical Arabic of the Qu'ran.

Sepoy Mutiny of 1857 See **Indian Rebellion of 1857**.

serf An unfree peasant laborer. Unlike slaves, serfs are "attached" to the land they work, and are not supposed to be sold apart from that land.

William Shakespeare (1564–1616) An English playwright who flourished during the reigns of Elizabeth I and James I, Shakespeare received a basic education in his hometown of Stratford-upon-Avon and worked in London as an actor before achieving success as a dramatist and poet.

Shi'ites An often-persecuted minority within Islam, Shi'ites believe that only descendants of Muhammad's successor Ali and his wife Fatimah (Muhammad's daughter) can have any authority over the Muslim community. Today, Shi'ites constitute the ruling party in Iran and are numerous in Iraq, but otherwise comprise only 10 percent of Muslims worldwide.

Abbé Sieyès (1748–1836) In 1789, he wrote the pamphlet "What is the Third Estate?" in which he posed fundamental questions about the rights of the Third Estate and helped provoke its secession from the Estates-General. He was a leader at the Tennis Court Oath, but he later helped Napoleon seize power.

Sinn Féin The Irish revolutionary organization that formed in 1900 to fight for Irish independence.

Sino-Japanese War (1894–1895) Conflict over the control of Korea in which China was forced to cede the province of Taiwan to Japan.

slave revolt in Saint-Domingue (1791–1804) In September of 1791, the largest slave rebellion in history broke out in Saint-Domingue, an important French colony in the Caribbean. In 1794, the revolutionary government in France abolished slavery in the colonies, though this act was essentially only recognizing the liberty that the slaves had seized by their own actions. Napoleon reestablished slavery in the French Caribbean in 1802, but failed in his attempt to reconquer Saint-Domingue. Armies commanded by former slaves succeeded in winning independence for a new nation, Haiti, in 1804, making the revolt in Saint-Domingue the first successful slave revolt in history.

slavery The practice of subjugating people to a life of bondage, and of selling or trading these unfree people. For most of human history, slavery had no racial or ethnic basis, and was widely practiced by all cultures and civilizations. Anyone could become a slave, for example, by being captured in war or by being sold for the payment of a debt. It was only in the fifteenth century, with the growth of the African slave trade, that slavery came to be associated with particular races and peoples.

Adam Smith (1723–1790) Scottish economist and liberal philosopher who proposed that competition between self-interested individuals led naturally to a healthy economy. He became famous for his influential book, *The Wealth of Nations* (1776).

Social Darwinism Belief that Charles Darwin's theory of natural selection (evolution) was applicable to human societies and justified the right of the ruling classes or countries to dominate the weak.

social democracy The belief that democracy and social welfare go hand in hand, and that diminishing the sharp inequalities of class society is crucial to fortifying democratic culture.

socialism Political ideology that calls for a classless society with collective ownership of all property.

Society of Jesus; see **Jesuits**.

Socrates (469–399 B.C.E.) The Athenian philosopher and teacher who promoted the careful examination of all inherited opinions and assumptions on the grounds that "the unexamined life is not worth living." A veteran of the Peloponnesian War, he was tried and condemned by his fellow citizens for engaging in allegedly seditious activities, and was executed in 399 B.C.E. His most influential pupils were the philosopher Plato and the historian and social commentator Xenophon.

Solon (d. 559 B.C.E.) Elected archon in 594 B.C.E., this Athenian aristocrat enacted a series of political and economic reforms that formed the basis of Athenian democracy.

Somme (1916) During this battle of the First World War, Allied forces attempted to take entrenched German positions from July to mid-November of 1916. Neither side was able to make any real gains despite massive casualties: 500,000 Germans, 400,000 British, and 200,000 French.

Soviet bloc International alliance that included the East European countries of the Warsaw Pact as well as the Soviet Union; it also came to include Cuba.

soviets Local councils elected by workers and soldiers in Russia. Socialists started organizing these councils in 1905, and the Petrograd soviet in the capital emerged as one of the centers of power after the Russian monarchy collapsed in 1917 in the midst of World War I. The soviets became increasingly powerful and pressed for social reform, the redistribution of land, and called for Russian withdrawal from the war effort.

Spanish-American War (1898) War between the United States and Spain in Cuba, Puerto Rico, and the Philippines. It ended with a treaty in which the United States took over the Philippines, Guam, and Puerto Rico; Cuba won partial independence.

Spanish Armada Supposedly invincible fleet of warships sent against England by Philip II of Spain in 1588 but vanquished by the English fleet and bad weather in the English Channel.

Sparta Around 650 B.C.E., after the suppression of a slave revolt, Spartan rulers militarized their society in order to prevent future rebellions and to protect Sparta's superior position in Greece, orienting their society toward the maintenance of their army. Sparta briefly joined forces with Athens and other poleis in the second war with Persia in 480–479 B.C.E., but these two rivals ultimately fell out again in 431 B.C.E., when Sparta and her Peloponnesian allies went to war against Athens and her allies. This bloody conflict lasted until Athens was defeated in 404 B.C.E., after Sparta received military aid from the Persians.

Spartiate A full citizen of Sparta, hence a professional soldier of the hoplite phalanx.

spinning jenny Invention of James Hargreaves (c. 1720–1774) that revolutionized the British textile industry by allowing a worker to spin much more thread than was possible on a hand spinner.

SS (Schutzstaffel) Formed in 1925 to serve as Hitler's personal security force and to guard Nazi party (NSDAP) meetings, the SS grew into a large militarized organization that became notorious for their participation in carrying out Nazi policies.

Joseph Stalin (1879–1953) The Bolshevik leader who succeeded Lenin as the leader of the Soviet Union and ruled until his death in 1953.

Stalingrad (1942–1943) The turning point on the Eastern Front during the Second World War came when the German army tried to take the city of Stalingrad in an effort to break the back of Soviet industry. The German and Soviet armies fought a bitter battle, in which more than half a million German, Italian, and Romanian soldiers were killed and the Soviets suffered over a million casualties. The German army surrendered after over five months of fighting. After Stalingrad, the Soviet army launched a series of attacks that pushed the Germans back.

Stoicism An ancient philosophy derived from the teachings of Zeno of Athens (fl. c. 300) and widely influential within the Roman Empire; it also impacted the development of Christianity. Stoics believe in the essential orderliness of the cosmos, and that everything that occurs happens for the best. Since everything is determined in accordance with rational purpose, no individual is master of his or her fate, and the only agency that human beings have consists in their responses to good fortune or adversity.

Sumerians The ancient inhabitants of southern Mesopotamia (modern Iraq and Kuwait) whose sophisticated civilization emerged around 4000 B.C.E.

Sunnis Proponents of Islam's customary religious practices (*sunna*) as they developed under the first two caliphs to succeed Muhammad, his father-in-law Abu-Bakr and his disciple Umar. Sunni orthodoxy is dominant within Islam, but is opposed by the Shi'ites (from the Arabic word *shi'a*, "faction").

Syndicalists A nineteenth century political movement that embraced a strategy of strikes and sabotage by workers. Their hope was that a general strike of all workers would bring down the capitalist state and replace it with workers' syndicates or trade associations. Their refusal to participate in politics limited their ability to command a wide influence.

tabula rasa Term used by John Locke (1632–1704) to describe man's mind before he acquired ideas as a result of experience; Latin for "clean slate."

Tennis Court Oath (1789) Oath taken by representatives of the Third Estate in June, 1789, in which they pledged to form a National Assembly and write a constitution limiting the powers of the king.

Reign of Terror (1793–1794) Campaign at the height of the French Revolution in which violence, including systematic executions of opponents of the revolution, was used to purge France of its "enemies" and to extend the revolution beyond its borders; radicals executed as many as 40,000 persons who were judged enemies of the state.

Tetrarchy The result of Diocletian's political reforms of the late third century C.E., which divided the Roman Empire into four quadrants.

Theban Hegemony The term describing the period when the polis of Thebes dominated the Greek mainland, which reached its height after 371 B.C.E., under leadership of the Theban general Epaminondas. It was in Thebes that the future King Philip II of Macedon spent his youth, and it was the defeat of Thebes and Athens at the hands of Philip and Alexander—at the Battle of Chaeronea in 338—that Macedonian hegemony was forcefully asserted.

theory of evolution Darwin's theory that linked biology to history. Darwin believed that competition between different organisms and struggle with the environment were fundamental and unavoidable facts of life. In this struggle, those individuals who were better adapted to their environment survived, while the weak perished. This produced a "natural selection," or favoring of certain adaptive traits over time, leading to a gradual evolution of different species.

Third Estate The population of France under the Old Regime was divided into three estates, corporate bodies that determined an individual's rights or obligations under royal law. The nobility constituted the First Estate, the clergy the Second, and the commoners (the vast bulk of the population) made up the Third Estate.

Third Reich The German state from 1933 to 1945 under Adolf Hitler and the Nazi party.

Third World Nations—mostly in Asia, Latin America, and Africa—that are not highly industrialized.

Thirty Years' War (1618–1648) Beginning as a conflict between Protestants and Catholics in Germany, this series of skirmishes escalated into a general European war fought on German soil by armies from Sweden, France, and the Holy Roman Empire.

Timur the Lame (1336–1405) Also known as Tamerlane, he was the last ruler of the Mongol Khans' Asian empire.

Marshal Tito (1892–1980) The Yugoslavian communist and resistance leader who became the leader of Yugoslavia and fought to keep his government independent of the Soviet Union. In response, the Soviet Union expelled Yugoslavia from the communist countries' economic and military pacts.

towns Centers for markets and administration. Towns existed in a symbiotic relationship with the countryside. They provided markets for surplus food from outlying farms as well as producing manufactured goods. In the Middle Ages, towns tended to grow up around a castle or monastery which afforded protection.

Treaty of Brest-Litovsk (1918) Separate peace between imperial Germany and the new Bolshevik regime in Russia. The treaty acknowledged the German victory on the Eastern Front and withdrew Russia from the war.

Treaty of Utrecht (1713) Resolution to the War of Spanish Succession that reestablished a balance of power in Europe, to the benefit of Britain and in ways that disadvantaged Spain, Holland, and France.

Treaty of Versailles Signed on June 28, 1919, this peace settlement ended the First World War and required Germany to surrender a large part of its most valuable territories and to pay huge reparations to the Allies.

trench warfare Weapons such as barbed wire and the machine gun gave tremendous advantage to defensive positions in World War I, leading to prolonged battles between entrenched armies in fixed positions. The trenches eventually consisted of twenty-five thousand miles of holes and ditches that stretched across the Western Front in northern France, from the Atlantic cost to the Swiss border during the First World War, On the eastern front, the large expanse of territories made trench warfare less significant.

triangular trade The eighteenth-century commercial Atlantic shipping pattern that took rum from New England to Africa, traded it for slaves taken to the West Indies, and brought sugar back to New England to be processed into rum.

Triple Entente Alliance developed before the First World War that eventually included Britain, France, and Russia.

Truman Doctrine (1947) Declaration promising U.S. economic and military intervention to counter any attempt by the Soviet Union to expand its influence. Often cited as a key moment in the origins of the Cold War.

tsar Russian word for "emperor," derived from the Latin *caesar* and similar to the German *kaiser,* it was the title claimed by the rulers of medieval Muscovy and of the later Russian Empire.

Ubaid culture An early civilization that flourished in Mesopotamia between 5500 and 4000 B.C.E., it was characterized by large village settlements and temple complexes: a precursor to the more urban civilization of the Sumerians.

Umayyad Caliphate (661–930) The Umayyad family resisted the authority of the first two caliphs who succeeded Muhammad, but eventually placed a member of their own family in that position of power. The Umayyad Caliphate ruled the Islamic world from 661 to 750, modeling their administration on that of the Roman Empire. But after a rebellion led by the rival Abbasid family, the power of the Umayyad Caliphate was confined to their territories in al-Andalus (Spain).

Universal Declaration of Human Rights (1948) United Nations declaration that laid out the rights to which all human beings were entitled.

University of Paris The reputation of Peter Abelard and his students attracted many intellectuals to Paris in the twelfth century, some of whom began offering instruction to aspiring scholars. By 1200, this loose association of teachers had formed themselves into a UNIVERSITAS, or corporation. They began collaborating in the higher academic study of the liberal arts with a special emphasis on theology.

Pope Urban II (1042?–1099) Instigator of the First Crusade (1096–1099), who promised that anyone who fought or died in the service of the Church would receive absolution from sin.

urban populations During the nineteenth century, urban populations in Europe increased six fold. For the most part, urban areas had medieval infrastructures, which new populations and industries overwhelmed. As a result, many European cities became overcrowded and unhealthy.

Utopia Title of a semi-satirical social critique by the English statesman Sir Thomas More (1478–1535); the word derives from the Greek "best place" or "no place."

Lorenzo Valla (1407–1457) One of the first practitioners of scientific philology (the historical study of language), Valla's analysis of the so-called Donation of Constantine showed that the document could not possibly have been written in the fourth century C.E., but must have been forged centuries later.

vassal A person who pledges to be loyal and subservient to a lord in exchange for land, income, or protection.

velvet revolutions The peaceful political revolutions throughout Eastern Europe in 1989.

Verdun (1916) This battle between German and French forces lasted for ten months during the First World War. The Germans saw the battle as a chance to break French morale through a war of attrition, and the French believed the battle to be a symbol of France's strength. In the end, over 400,000 lives were lost and the German offensive failed.

Versailles Conference (1919) Peace conference between the victors of the First World War; resulted in the Treaty of Versailles, which forced Germany to pay reparations and to give up its colonies to the victors.

Queen Victoria (1819–1901) Influential monarch who reigned from 1837 until her death; she presided over the expansion of the British Empire as well as the evolution of English politics and social and economic reforms.

Viet Cong Vietnamese communist group formed in 1954; committed to overthrowing the government of South Vietnam and reunifying North and South Vietnam.

Vikings (800–1000) The collapse of the Abbasid Caliphate disrupted Scandinavian commercial networks and turned traders into raiders (the word "viking" describes the activity of raiding). These raids often escalated into invasions that contributed to the collapse of the Carolingian Empire, resulted in the devastation of settled territories, and ended with the establishment of Viking colonies. By the tenth century, Vikings controlled areas of eastern England, Scotland, the islands of Ireland, Iceland, Greenland, and parts of northern France. They had also established the beginnings of the kingdom that became Russia and made exploratory voyages to North America, founding a settlement at Newfoundland (Canada).

Leonardo da Vinci (1452–1519) Florentine inventor, sculptor, architect, and painter whose breadth of interests typifies the ideal of "the Renaissance man."

*A **Vindication of the Rights of Woman*** Noted work of Mary Wollstonecraft (1759–1797), English republican who applied Enlightenment political ideas to issues of gender.

Virgil (70–19 B.C.E.) An influential Roman poet who wrote under the patronage of the emperor Augustus. His *Aeneid* mimicked the ancient Greek epics of Homer, and told the mythical tale of Rome's founding by the Trojan refugee Aeneas.

Visigoths The tribes of "west" Goths who sacked Rome in 410 C.E. and later established a kingdom in the Roman province of Hispania (Spain).

Voltaire Pseudonym of French philosopher and satirist Francois Marie Arouet (1694–1778), who championed the cause of human dignity against state and church oppression. Noted deist and author of *Candide*.

Lech Walsea (1943–) Leader of the Polish labor movement Solidarity, which organized a series of strikes across Poland in 1980. They protested working conditions, shortages, and high prices. Above all, they demanded an independent labor union. Solidarity's leaders were imprisoned and the union banned, but they launched a new series of strikes in 1988, which led to the legalization of Solidarity and open elections.

war communism The Russian civil war forced the Bolsheviks to take a more radical economic stance. They requisitioned grain from the peasantry and outlawed private trade in consumer goods as "speculation." They also militarized production facilities and abolished money.

Wars of the Roses Fifteenth-century civil conflict between the English dynastic houses of Lancaster and York, each of which was symbolized by the heraldic device of a rose (red and white, respectively). It was ultimately resolved by the accession of the Lancastrian king Henry VII, who married Elizabeth of York.

Warsaw Pact (1955–1991) Military alliance between the USSR and other communist states that was established as a response to the creation of the NATO alliance.

*The **Wealth of Nations*** 1776 treatise by Adam Smith, whose laissez-faire ideas predicted the economic boom of the Industrial Revolution.

Weimar Republic The government of Germany between 1919 and the rise of Hitler and the Nazi party.

Western Front Military front that stretched from the English Channel through Belgium and France to the Alps during the First World War.

Whites Refers to the "counterrevolutionaries" of the Bolshevik Revolution (1918–1921) who fought the Bolsheviks (the "Reds"); included former supporters of the tsar, Social Democrats, and large independent peasant armies.

William the Conqueror (1027–1087) Duke of Normandy who laid claim to the throne of England in 1066, defeating the Anglo-Saxon King Harold at the Battle of Hastings. He and his Norman followers imposed imperial rule in England through a brutal campaign of military conquest, surveillance, and the suppression of the indigenous Anglo-Saxon language.

William of Ockham (d. 1349) An English philosopher and Franciscan friar, he denied that human reason could prove fundamental theological truths, such as the existence of God: he argued that there is no necessary connection between the observable laws of nature and the unknowable essence of divinity. His theories, derived from the work of earlier scholastics, form the basis of the scientific method.

Woodrow Wilson (1856–1924) U.S. president who requested and received a declaration of war from Congress so that America could enter the First World War. After the war, his prominent role in the Paris Peace Conference signaled the rise of the United States as a world power. He also proposed the Fourteen Points, which influenced the peace negotiations.

Maria Winkelmann (1670–1720) German astronomer who worked with her husband in his observatory. Despite discovering a comet and preparing calendars for the Berlin Academy of Sciences, the academy would not let her take her husband's place within the body after he died.

Witch craze The rash of persecutions that took place in both Catholic and Protestant countries of early modern Europe and her colonies, facilitated by secular governments and religious authorities.

women's associations Because European women were excluded from the workings of parliamentary and mass politics, some women formed organizations to press for political and civil rights. Some groups focused on establishing educational opportunities for women, while others campaigned energetically for the vote.

William Wordsworth (1770–1850) Romantic writer whose central themes were nature, simplicity, and feeling. He considered nature to be man's most trustworthy teacher and source of sublime power that nourished the human soul.

World Bank International agency established in 1944 to provide economic assistance to war-torn nations and countries in need of economic development.

John Wyclif (c. 1330–1384) A professor of theology at the University of Oxford, Wyclif urged the English king to confiscate ecclesiastical wealth and to replace corrupt priests and bishops with men who would live according to the apostolic standards of poverty and piety. He advocated direct access to the Scriptures and promoted an English translation of the Bible. His teachings played an important role in the Peasants' Revolt of 1381 and inspired the still more radical initiatives of a group known as Lollards.

Xerxes (519?–465 B.C.E.) Xerxes succeeded his father, Darius, as Great King of Persia. Seeking to avenge his father's shame and eradicate any future threats to Persian hegemony, he launched his own invasion of Greece in 480 B.C.E. An allied Greek army defeated his forces in 479 B.C.E.

Yalta Accords Meeting between President Franklin D. Roosevelt, Prime Minister Winston Churchill, and Premier Joseph Stalin that occurred in the Crimea in 1945 shortly before the end of the Second World War to plan for the postwar order.

Young Turks The 1908 Turkish reformist movement that aimed to modernize the Ottoman Empire, restore parliamentary rule, and depose Sultan Abdul Hamid II.

ziggurats Temples constructed under the Dynasty of Ur in what is now Iraq, beginning around 2100 B.C.E.

Zionism A political movement dating to the end of the nineteenth century holding that the Jewish people constitute a nation and are entitled to a national homeland. Zionists rejected a policy of Jewish assimilation, and advocated the reestablishment of a Jewish homeland in Palestine.

Zollverein In 1834, Prussia started a customs union, which established free trade among the German states and a uniform tariff against the rest of the world. By the 1840s, the union included almost all of the German states except German Austria. It is considered an important precedent for the political unification of Germany, which was completed in 1870 under Prussian leadership.

Zoroastrianism One of the three major universal faiths of the ancient world, alongside Judaism and Christianity, it was derived from the teachings of the Persian Zoroaster around 600 B.C.E. Zoroaster redefined religion as an ethical practice common to all, rather than as a set of rituals and superstitions that cause divisions among people. Zoroastrianism teaches that there is one supreme god in the universe, Ahura-Mazda (Wise Lord), but that his goodness will be constantly assailed by the forces of evil until the arrival of a final "judgment day." Proponents of this faith should therefore help good to triumph over evil by leading a good life, and by performing acts of compassion and charity. Zoroastrianism exercised a profound influence over many early Christians, including Augustine.

Ulrich Zwingli (1484–1531) A former priest from the Swiss city of Zurich, Zwingli joined Luther and Calvin in attacking the authority of the Roman Catholic Church.

Chapter 1: p. 2–3: The Louve, Paris. Giraudon/Art Resource, NY; **p. 5**: The Bridgeman Art Library; **p. 7**: Nick Wheeler; **p. 8 left**: Ashmolean Museum, University of Oxford, UK/The Bridgeman Art Library; **p. 8 right**: British Museum/Art Resource, NY; **p. 13**: Bettmann/Corbis; **p. 14**: Hirmer Fotoarchiv; **p. 17**: Art Resource, NY; **p. 20 a, b** :Scala/Art Resource, NY; **p. 21**: Eric Lessing/Art Resource, NY; **p. 22**: Roger Wood/Corbis

Chapter 2: p. 28–29: Erich Lessing/Art Resource, NY; **p. 33**: Wikimedia Commons; **p. 34 left**: PCL/Alamy; **p. 34 right**: Ian M Butterfield (P)/Alamy; **p. 35 left**: Sebastian Bergmann/Flickr/Creative Commons; **p. 35 right**: Jim Henderson/Alamy; **p. 37**: Erich Lessing/Art Resource, NY; **p. 38**: Gianni Dagli Orti/Corbis; **p. 45**: British Museum, London, Great Britain, photo: Erich Lessing/Art Resource, NY; **p. 50**: The Art Gallery Collection/Alamy; **p. 51**: Courtesy of Zev Radovan; **p. 52**: Bildarchiv Preussischer Kulturbesitz/Art Resource, NY

Chapter 3: p. 56–57: Erich Lessing/Art Resource, NY; **p. 58**: Nagelestock.com/Alamy; **p. 62**: Wikimedia Commons; **p. 63**: Hirmer Fotoarchiv; **p. 69** Paul Lipke/Trireme Trust, Montague, MA; **p. 71**: National Museums of Scotland/Bridgeman Art Library; **p. 72 right**: Vanni/Art Resource, NY; **p. 73 center**: Photo © RMN Paris; **p. 73 left**: Hartwig Koppermann; **p. 73 right**: Wikimedia Commons; **p. 77**: Erich Lessing/Art Resource, NY

Chapter 4: p. 82–83: Erich Lessing/Art Resource, NY; **p. 86**: Scala/Art Resource, NY; **p. 87 left**: Marie-Lan Nguyen/Ludovisi Collection/Wikimedia; **p. 87 right**: Vanni/Art Resource, NY; **p. 88**: Gianni Dagli Orti/Corbis; **p. 89**: Erin Babnik/Alamy; **p. 92**: Erich Lessing/Art Resource, NY; **p. 95 left**: The Trustees of the British Museum; **p. 95 right**: Bildarchiv Preussischer Kulturbesitz/Art Resource, NY; **p. 101**: INTERFOTO/Alamy; **p. 102**: Scala/Art Resource, NY; **p. 103 left**: Marie-Lan Nguyen/Wikimedia Commons; **p. 103 right**: Scala/Art Resource, NY

Chapter 5: p. 106–07: Scala/Art Resource, NY; **p. 109**: Italic, Etruscan, Late Classical or Early Hellenistic Period, about 330–300 BC; Findspot and Place of Manufacture: Italy, Lazio, Vulci; Marble, 93.3cm high x 117.4 cm width x 213.8 cm length; Museum of Fine Arts, Boston, Gift of Mrs. Gardner Brewer, 86.145a–b. Photograph © 2004 Museum of Fine Arts, Boston; **p. 112**: Scala/Art Resource, NY; **p. 119 left**: Sandro Vannini/Corbis; **p. 119 right**: Wikimedia Commons; **p. 120**: The Granger Collection, New York; **p. 124**: Courtesy of Carol Symes; **p. 125**: Silver Stock/Alamy; **p. 127 top**: Vanni/Art Resource, NY; **p. 127 bottom**: Scala/Art Resource, NY

Chapter 6: p. 132–33: Alinari/Art Resource, NY; **p. 139**: AKG-images/Pirozzi; **p. 145 left**: Wikipedia Commons; **p. 145 right**: Wikipedia Commons; **p. 147**: The Louvre, Paris. Photo: Herve Lewandowski, Reunion des Musees Nationaux/Art Resource, NY; **p. 153**: Biblioteca Medicea Laurenziana, Florence

Chapter 7: p. 156–157: AKG-images; **p. 159 left**: Scala/Art Resource, NY; **p. 159 right**: Scala/Art Resource, NY; **p. 161**: Wikipedia Commons; **p. 168**: Bildarchiv Preussischer Kulturbesitz/Art Resource, NY; **p. 171**: The Granger Collection, New York; **p. 172 left**: Birmingham Museums & Art Gallery; **p. 172 right**: The Trustees of the British Museum/Art Resource, NY; **p. 173 top**: The Trustees of the British Museum; **p. 173 bottom**: The Trustees of the British Museum; **p. 177**: Bibliotheque Nationale, Paris, France/The Bridgeman Art Library;

Chapter 8: p. 182–183: The Granger Collection, New York; **p. 186 left**: Wikimedia Commons; **p. 186 right**: Bildarchiv Preussischer Kulturbesitz/Art Resource, NY; **p. 190**: Wikimedia Commons; **p. 192 top**: French School/The Bridgeman Art Library/Getty Images; **p. 192 bottom**: French School/The Bridgeman Art Library/Getty Images; **p. 193**: The Granger Collection, New York; **p. 194**: Treasury, Abbey Ste. Foy, Conques, France. Photo: Giraudon/Art Resource, NY; **p. 199**: HIP/Art Resource, NY; **p. 205 top**: Giraudon/Art Resource, NY; **p. 205 bottom**: The Metropolitan Museum of Art/Art Resource, NY

Chapter 9: p. 208–09: The Granger Collection, New York; **p. 210**: Giraudon/Art Resource, NY; **p. 211**: The Walters Art Gallery, Baltimore; **p. 216 right**: The Granger Collection, New York; **p. 216 left**: The Art Archive/Archivo de la Corona de Aragon Barcelona/Laurie Platt Winfrey; **p. 217**: Bibliotheque Sainte-Genevieve, Paris, France/Archives Charmet/The Bridgeman Art Library; **p. 219**: Copyright Otto Muller Verlag, Salzburg, Austria; **p. 220**: The Metropolitan Museum of Art/Art Resource, NY; **p. 221**: Sueddeutsche Zeitung Photo/The Image Works; **p. 224**: Bayerische Staatsbibliothek, München; **p. 225**: Erich Lessing/Art Resource, NY; **p. 230**: AKG-images; **p. 233 left**: Richard List/Corbis; **p. 233 right**: Richard List/Corbis

Chapter 10: p. 236–237: Réunion des Musées Nationaux/Art Resource, NY; **p. 238**: HIP/Art Resource, NY; **p. 243**: Réunion des Musées Nationaux/Art Resource, NY; **p. 246**: Réunion des Musées Nationaux/Art Resource, NY; **p. 247**: Museo del Prado, Madrid/Art Archive; **p. 250**: Chris Hellier/Corbis; **p. 254**: The Art Archive; **p. 255**: The Art Archive/British Library; **p. 256**: British Library/Art Resource, NY; **p. 257**: Cameraphoto Arte, Venice/Art Resource, NY;

p. 259: Bibliothèque Royale Albert I, Brussels; **p. 260 left**: Bildarchiv Preussischer Kulturbesitz/Art Resource, NY; **p. 260 right**: Scala/Art Resource, NY

Chapter 11: p. 264–265: The Art Archive/Topkapi Museum Istanbul/Gianni Dagli Orti; **p. 267**: John Massey Stewart Picture Library; **p. 270**: Bibliotheque Nationale, Paris, France/The Bridgeman Art Library; **p. 271**: Werner Forman Archive/Topkapi Palace Library, Istanbul/Art Resource, NY; **p. 274**: Mansell/TimePix; **p. 275**: Myriam Thyes/Wikimedia commons; **p. 276**: Wikimedia Commons; **p. 280**: AKG-images; **p. 281**: Bibliotheque Nationale, Paris, France/Giraudon/The Bridgeman Art Library; **p. 282**: Wikimedia Commons

Chapter 12: p. 286–287: Erich Lessing/Art Resource, NY; **p. 289**: Erich Lessing/Art Resource, NY; **p. 294**: Erich Lessing/Art Resource, NY; **p. 295**: Galleria degli Uffizi, Florence, Italy/The Bridgeman Art Library; **p. 298 top**: Erich Lessing/Art Resource, NY; **p. 298 bottom**: Réunion des Musées Nationaux/Art Resource, NY; **p. 299**: Scala/Art Resource, NY; **p. 300 top**: Vatican Museums and Galleries, Vatican City, Italy/Alinari/The Bridgeman Art Library; **p. 300 bottom**: Scala/Art Resource, NY; **p. 301 left**: Nimatallah/Art Resource, NY; **p. 301 center**: Scala/Art Resource, NY; **p. 301 right**: Erich Lessing/Art Resource, NY; **p. 303**: Bildarchiv Preussischer Kulturbesitz/Art Resource, NY; **p. 304**: Louvre, Paris, France/Giraudon/The Bridgeman Art Library; **p. 305 top**: National Portrait Gallery, London, UK/The Bridgeman Art Library; **p. 305 bottom**: Bildarchiv Preussischer Kulturbesitz/Art Resource, NY

Chapter 13: p. 308–309: The Art Archive/Nationalmuseet Copenhagen Denmark/Alfredo Dagli Orti; **p. 310**: Scala/Art Resource, NY; **p. 311**: Bildarchiv Preussischer Kulturbesitz/Art Resource, NY; **p. 312**: Sandro Vannini/Corbis; **p. 313**: Bayerische taatsgemäldesammlungen/Alte Pinakothek, Munich; **p. 314 left**: Staatsbibliothek, Bern; **p. 314 right**: Staatsbibliothek, Bern; **p. 315 left**: By permission of the British Library/Art Resource, NY; **p. 315 right**: Staatliche Museen zu Berlin-Preußischer Kulturbesitz, Kupferstichkabinett; **p. 323**: National Trust/Art Resource, NY; **p. 324 left**: Scala/Art Resource, NY; **p. 324 right**: Scala/Art Resource, NY; **p. 326**: Kunsthistorisches Museum, Vienna

Chapter 14: p. 330–331: Woburn Abbey, Bedfordshire, UK/The Bridgeman Art Library International; **p. 337**: Wikimedia Commons; **p. 341**: Wikimedia Commons; **p. 344**: Wikimedia Commons; **p. 345**: Interfoto/Alamy; **p. 349**: Scala/Art Resource, NY; **p. 350 top**: Image copyright © The Metropolitan Museum of Art/Art Resource, NY; **p. 350 bottom**: Museo del Prado, Madrid; **p. 351 top L**: Erich Lessing/Art Resource, NY; **p. 351 top R**: Nimatallah/Art Resrouce, NY; **p. 351 bottom L**: © English Heritage Photo Library; **p. 351 bottom R**: Gift of Mr. and Mrs. Robert Woods Bliss, © 1997 Board of Trustees, National Gallery of Art, Washington, D.C.

Chapter 15: p. 354–355: The Royal Collection © 2010 Her Majesty Queen Elizabeth II; **p. 360 left**: Erich Lessing/Art Resource, NY; **p.360 right**: Réunion des Musées Nationaux/Art Resource, NY; **p.361 bottom**: Giraudon/Art Resource, NY; **p.361 top**: With kind permission of the University of Edinburgh/The Bridgeman Art Library International; **p. 362**: The Royal Collection © 2010 Her Majesty Queen Elizabeth II; **p. 363**: Snark/Art Resource, NY; **p. 366**: Scala/Art Resource, NY; **p.367**: Bildarchiv Preussischer Kulturbesitz/Art Resource, NY; **p. 368**: Courtesy Dr. Alexander Boguslawski, Professor of Russian Studies, Rollins College; **p. 369**: Giraudon/Art Resource, NY; **p. 372**: Ali Meyer/Corbis; **p. 373**: Corbis; **p. 377**: Wikimedia Commons

Chapter 16: p. 382–383: Cellarius, Andreas/The Bridgeman Art Library; **p. 385**: Jeffery Coolidge/Getty Images; **p. 386**: Erich Lessing/Art Resource, NY; **p. 388 left**: The Granger Collection, New York; **p. 388 right**: wikimedia commons; **p. 389 left**: Image Select/Art Resource, NY; **p. 389 right**: Royal Astronomical Society/Photo Researchers, Inc.; **p. 393**: Rene Descartes, L'homme de René Descartes, et la formation du foetus, Paris: Compagnie des Libraires, 1729/"Courtesy of Historical Collections & Services, Claude Moore Health Sciences Library, University of Virginia."; **p. 396**: Bodleian Library; **p. 397**: The Natural History Museum, London/The Image Works; **p. 399**: Giraudon/Art Resource, NY

Chapter 17: p. 402–403: Bridgeman Art Library; **p. 407 left**: Historisches Museum der Stadt Wien; **p. 407 right**: Historisches Museum der Stadt Wien; **p. 408**: Moritz Daniel Oppenheim, "Lavater and Lessing Visit Moses Mendelssohn." In the permanent collections, Judah L. Magnes Museum. Photo: Ben Ailes; **p. 412 left**: Sir Joshua Reynolds/Omai of the Friendly Isles/National Library of Australia; right: Wikimedia Commons; **p. 413** Francesco Bartolozzi/A view of the inside of a house in the island of Ulietea, with the representation of a dance to the music of the country/National Library of Australia; **p. 415**: © Tate Gallery, London/Art Resource, NY; **p. 417**: Louvre (Cabinet de dessins), Paris, France/Bridgeman Art Library; **p. 420**: Bettmann/Corbis

Chapter 18: p. 425–426: Erich Lessing/Art Resource, NY; **p. 428**: The Art Archive/Musée Carnavalet Paris/Marc Charmet; **p. 429**: Giraudon/The Bridgeman Art Library; **p. 430 bottom**: Musee de la Ville de Paris, Musee Carnavalet, Paris, France/Giraudon/The Bridgeman Art Library; **p. 430 top**: Chateau de Versailles, France/The Bridgeman Art Library; **p. 435**: Bibliotheque Nationale, Paris, France/The Bridgeman Art Library; **p. 438**: Giraudon/Art Resource, NY; **p. 439**: Giraudon/Art Resource, NY: Musée de la Ville de Paris, Musée Carnavalet, Paris, France; **p. 440 left**: Risma Archivo/Alamy; **p. 440 right**: The Art Archive; **p. 441 left**: Musee de la Ville de Paris, Musee Carnavalet, Paris, France/Lauros/Giraudon/The Bridgeman Art Library; **p. 441 right**: Courtesy of the Warden and Scholars of New College, Oxford/The Bridgeman Art Library; **p. 444**: The Gallery Collection/Corbis; **p. 446**: Museo del Prado, Madrid; **p. 447**: Gianni Dagli Orti/Corbis

Chapter 19: p. 450–451: National Gallery, London/Art Resource, NY; **p. 452**: Peak District National Park; **p. 454 left**: The National Archives of the UK; **p. 454 right**: The Granger Collection, New York; **p. 455**: The Hulton Deutsch Collection; **p. 460**: HIP-Archive/Topham/The Image Works; **p. 461**: HIP-Archive/Topham/The Image Works; **p. 463**: Fotomas/Topham/The Image Works; **p. 464**: Geoffrey Clements/Corbis; **p. 470**: The Granger Collection, NY

Chapter 20: p. 474–475: Erich Lessing/Art Resource, NY; **p. 479**: RMN, Paris/Art Resource, NY; **p. 481**: The Stapleton Collection/

Index

ARCTIC OCEAN

GREENLAND

NORTH AMERICA

NORTH PACIFIC OCEAN

NORTH ATLANTIC OCEAN

TROPIC OF CANCER

Hawaii

EQUATOR

CENTRAL AMERICA

SOUTH AMERICA

MID ATLANTIC RIDGE

SOUTH PACIFIC OCEAN

TROPIC OF CAPRICORN

SOUTH ATLANTIC OCEAN

ANTARCTIC CIRCLE

ANTARCTIC PENINSULA

WEDDELL SEA

ANTAR

GLOBAL SATELLITE MOSAIC

The beauty and complexity of Earth's landscapes, both above and below the sea, is revealed with the Global Satellite Mosaic. The mosaic was produced for the National Geographic Society by NASA's Jet Propulsion Laboratory, Administration. This cloud-free image, show Earth in its natural colors as it would be seen from space. One can easily identify the world's major glaciers, deserts, mountain ranges, and rain forests. For example, follow the green ribbon of lush vegetation of the Nile into the dark, dry Sahara. The mountain ranges seem to rise off the map due to digital elevation databases from the Department of Defense. The deepest areas of the ocean realm are colored dark blue in contrast to the light blue areas highlighting continental shelves, submarine ridges, and underwater mountains.

BIOSPHERE

Thousands of satellite images combined to show a picture of life's productivity. In the oceans, red, yellow, green indicate waters rich in phytoplankton; green areas show high potential plant productivity; browns suffer from productivity limitations due to aridity and temperature.

THE W

SATEL